Ivosic

Man
Nature
and
Society

To Professor John A. Moore,
a distinguished scientist,
my teacher and friend,
this book is affectionately
dedicated.

Second Edition

E. Peter Volpe
Tulane University

Man
Nature
and
Society
An Introduction to Biology

wcb

Wm. C. Brown Company Publishers
Dubuque, Iowa 52001

wcb **Wm. C. Brown,** Chairman of the Board
Larry W. Brown, President, WCB Group

Book Team

Harry C. Benson, Editor
Marilyn A. Phelps, Designer
Marla Schafer, Design Layout
Assistant
Patricia L.A. Hendricks, Production Editor
Mary Heller, Visual Research
Editor

Wm. C. Brown Company Publishers, College Division

Lawrence E. Cremer, President
Richard C. Crews, Publisher
Robert Nash, Executive Editor
Raymond C. Deveaux, Director of Sales and Marketing
David Wm. Smith, National Marketing Manager
James Farrell, Director of Marketing Research
David A. Corona, Director of Production Development and Design
Ruth Richard, Production Editorial Manager
Marilyn A. Phelps, Manager of Design

Contents

Preface
to the Second Edition

The favorable response accorded the first edition of *Man, Nature, and Society* reinforces my conviction that scientists must communicate, without sensationalism and in language intelligible to the uninitiated, the extraordinary advances made in the biological and medical sciences during this century. The remarkable advances have raised a whole spectrum of serious ethical, social, and legal problems, such as those associated with birth control, genetic engineering, organ transplantation, prolongation of life, and *in vitro* fertilization. These problems—and many others—present acute challenges to existing moral codes and conventional wisdom.

It is much easier to live in a society with fixed values or a single moral standard than to live in a society that is constantly changing. There can be little doubt that we have witnessed recently the emergence of a pluralistic society and the disruption of many traditional values. Some now contend that a person should have the freedom to act as he or she believes right and that each individual should establish his or her own morality. The quality of being "good" or "bad" becomes simply the dictate of individual conscience. It would be ideal if each of us could pursue his or her own ends without thwarting other peoples' pursuits, however, the actions of one person do affect, sometimes adversely, other people.

The antithesis of total freedom is total coercion or mandatory action, which is repugnant to most of the people who make up society today. Between the two extremes of uninhibited freedom and overt coercion there is a middle ground. This middle ground represents the thinking and convictions of a majority of society. To express communal convictions, society must have technological and scientific knowledge so its determinations will be as reasoned as possible.

Our hope, then, can only lie in education—in a public informed about the meanings, findings, and limits of science and enlightened in its use of technology. This new edition of *Man, Nature, and Society* seeks to provide you with a maximal understanding of modern biological phenomena and to help you assess your prevailing beliefs and practices. Throughout the book, problems with an ethical impact are highlighted in framed "boxes." Struggle with these ethical dilemmas associated with real situations—in the myriad of knotty problems presented, no clearcut answers will be found. We may not all agree when life begins; we may never reach unanimity about "mercy killing"; and we may change our opinions numerous times about consent for artificial insemination or the wisdom of heart transplantation. It is important, however, that all judgments are based on a thorough, educated understanding of all the problem's facets.

Hopefully, this new edition will serve to emphasize that the consideration of ethical questions with biological underpinnings is not restricted to scientists. Ethical problems are issues of society, of which the scientist is but a member. Moreover, moral principles or values generally cannot be deduced directly from scientific facts. Morality is that which a person believes to be good or bad. Just because something is a scientific fact does not mean necessarily that it is good or bad. Nevertheless, it would be desirable to employ the strategy of using scientific knowledge as a means of weighing our values. We can aim for the rejection of those values whose consequences contradict scientific accounts of human nature and reality.

As in the first edition, the revised text examines all biological aspects of man: his reproductive behavior, embryological development, structure and function, inherited potentialities, evolutionary history, relationship to the environment, and behavior. This second edition is augmented by new chapters on the body's various functions—digestion, circulation, gas exchange, excretion, nervous coordination, and endocrine mechanisms. These bodily functions are presented from the viewpoint of "homeostasis," the important state in which the varied, seemingly unrelated activities of the body are integrated to ensure the stable conditions required for life or survival.

This second edition continues to take special note of man's social behavior. Throughout life man remains a social creature, and many of his needs and aspirations must be understood in a social context. The scope of social behavior has been broadened, particularly with the addition of material on mother-infant interactions and the behavior of play. The new concluding chapter of the book (chapter 49) launches the reader into "sociobiology," the most recent, but controversial, field of modern biology.

This book remains more concerned with basic principles than with details that would interest only a specialist. I am again grateful to the intellectually curious students, both kind and unkind, who have suggested ways of improving the presentation and organization. Many of the new illustrations that illuminate the text owe their origin to the students' vivid insight. The drawings were prepared by my wife Carolyn, who showed remarkable patience and care in transposing my crude sketches into artistic illustrations.

E. Peter Volpe

Preface
to the First Edition

Man, Nature, and Society has been prepared for the beginning college student seeking a liberal education. Events of the comparatively recent past have made students more eager than ever to know the broad principles, fundamental ideas, and new discoveries in biology that so significantly affect their present and future existence. The primary emphasis throughout the book is on man. However, other forms of life are not neglected, since only by considering them can we place man in proper perspective in the whole realm of life. The text is not the traditional survey of the anatomy and physiology of man, but rather an exposition of biological concepts and findings that affect man's life, values, and culture. Issues such as overpopulation, pollution, aggression, malnutrition, birth control, abortion, and euthanasia all directly or tangentially relate to biology. My purpose in writing this book will have been achieved if the presentation enables the student to relate the knowledge of biology intelligently to the pressing social and cultural issues of our day.

I have endeavored to explain, as fully and interestingly as possible, the implications of modern biological findings for the individual and society. There have been some extremely provocative social and ethical consequences of the spectacular surge of biological discoveries. If the meteoric output of new knowledge disturbs one's serenity, it is because scientific advances have occurred much more rapidly than man can accommodate himself to live with them. There is absolutely no doubt that we live in an era of profound change. Whether we choose to be optimistic or cynical, the fact remains that man faces the necessity of accepting change and the challenges and hazards that necessarily accompany change. It appears to me that we can cope with the changing scene realistically if we rely on our intellect rather than on emotions founded on ignorance and prejudice. Accordingly, this book has as its high hope the development of increasing rationality in human affairs.

The search for knowledge affords a special satisfaction, and scientists, like artists and humanists, derive untold pleasure from their work. Rarely, however, does the student sense the fervor in scientific inquiry, nor does he take more than a fleeting interest in how scientific investigations are conducted. A truly distinguished piece of research is little understood and less appreciated by most persons. Another purpose in preparing this book has been to foster an appreciation of man's intellectual effort by presenting the spirit of biology as an investigative technique. Man distinguishes himself from other animals by his ability to observe phenomena, form ideas out of the observations, and transform the ideas in his mind into hypotheses and experimental procedures. Out of patient investigations, man accumulates knowledge about himself and of the universe in which he lives. This in itself is thoroughly praiseworthy. It may sound trite to state, but it is nevertheless true, that human beings enrich their lives through learning. When man loses his thirst for knowledge and understanding, he loses the power to improve.

The book has been written for students who have had little or no training in the biological sciences. Although it is intended primarily for students who take biology as part of their general education, it can be used with profit in introductory courses designed for prospective majors in biology. Since the book shows how biological knowledge relates to the issues of the day, the potential major would benefit from being introduced to the relevance of his chosen field. The textbook can serve the needs of either a one- or a two-semester course. It can be adapted to the shorter one-semester or one-quarter courses by omitting selected chapters or portions of chapters. The organization is sufficiently flexible that each teacher can rearrange the chapters according to his conceptual approach to the subject.

The book is divided into four general parts, or units, as follows:

1. Man: Life Processes
2. Man: Patterns of Heredity
3. Man: Origin and Evolution
4. Man: Environment and Behavior

The text begins with the twin themes of human sexual reproduction and human development. The embryo is presented not merely as a human being in the making, but also as a marvelously integrated living individual with all the physiological activities of other living organisms. An examination of the many factors regulating the development of the cells, tissues, and organs of the embryo reveals the complexities of the living organism, particularly at the cellular and molecular levels.

Genetic concepts are presented in part 2. Here the full force of the unprecedented advances in unraveling the nature of the gene is applied to many sensitive problems that the student will have to contend with in society. It has been said that man is on the threshold of a new era in which he will be able to control or design his genetic future. This statement has been examined carefully by evaluating the current facts and expected developments in genetics.

How man came into existence is the subject of part 3. Man is both part and product of nature. If there is any one main idea, or concept, of biology that unifies the field, it is organic evolution. Insight into the past evolutionary history of other organisms, and into man's descent from an apelike creature, is crucially important for the understanding of man by man. In man's emergence, he discarded the arboreal, defensive, and herbivorous habits of his ape relatives and became a terrestrial, weapon-making, carnivorous predator. Man became endowed with genetic attributes that enabled him to be successful as a predatory hunter. Indeed, the hunting way of life dominated man's existence for well over 600,000 years. It is highly probable that many inherent adaptive characteristics of the hunting era have continued to persist in present-day man.

The last section (part 4) concerns itself with how man interacts with his environment on various levels, continually altering it and in turn being affected by the changes he creates. Man's power to manipulate and exploit his world has tended to obscure his comprehension of the damage he inflicts on the environment. Despite man's proven ingenuity in tapping and expanding the natural resources of the earth, the resources are not unlimited but finite. The profound changes in the environment wrought by man's activities call to mind a macabre sign displayed at a local drugstore, "Prescriptions dispensed with deadly accuracy."

The text is simplified by numerous illustrations. The drawings, most of them original, are the accomplished work of my wife, Carolyn. The illustrations do not merely adorn the pages; all are important in supporting the writing. Selected references accompany each chapter in the hope that the student will want to extend his knowledge beyond the material presented.

The book could not have been prepared without the knowledge derived from my past teachers and students. The students, unknowingly, have been my teachers also. If simplicity and clarity of presentation of the subject matter have been achieved in this book, it is in greatest measure owing to the long-suffering freshman college students in my introductory general biology classes over some twenty years. I appreciate the helpful suggestions and advice from several biologists, particularly Daryl Sweeney of the University of Illinois at Urbana, W. Brian O'Connor of the University of Massachusetts, D. II. Kenyon of San Francisco State University, Gil Desha of Tarrant County Junior College, and Brian Myres of Cypress College. The presentation has benefited from the editorial suggestions of my colleague at Tulane University, Claudia deGruy, who intently read the entire manuscript. The painstaking, indepth editing of the entire manuscript was undertaken by Janet B. Wright of West Newton, Massachusetts. Mary Eastin and Helen Mequet cheerfully typed the manuscript in its various forms. I am indebted to the authors and publishers who have generously granted permission to use figures and tables from their books. Individual acknowledgments are made where the figures and charts appear in the text. My greatest debt is to my wife for help and encouragement in more ways than I can enumerate.

E. Peter Volpe

Prologue

Modern man has a dual heritage. He is a product of both biological and cultural evolution. Biologically, the human species is the outcome of the same natural evolutionary forces that have shaped other forms of animal life. Man is a recent arrival on the earth, representing the latest adaptive advance in the animal kingdom. Although man occupies a lofty position in the living world, he is clearly part of the fabric of nature and has many ancestral ties with other animals. In the biologist's scheme of "who's who" in the animal world, man is classified as a *vertebrate,* a *placental mammal,* and a *primate.* In possessing a backbone or vertebral column, man has structural features in common with other vertebrate animals—fishes, amphibians, reptiles, birds, and mammals. He is said to be a placental mammal by virtue of such important evolutionary novelties as a placenta to nourish the fetus and mammary glands to suckle the young. As a primate, man shares, along with the kindred monkeys and apes, great visual acuity and unusual dexterity of the hands. He is, however, a unique primate. Man alone has a fully upright posture and gait, the power of speech, and a highly distinctive brain, which enables him to reflect on his impressions of the external world.

As a consequence of his higher mental faculties, man has been able, through cultural endowments, to supplement and transcend his purely biological inheritance. Human culture has emerged out of man's exercise of reason and his ability to communicate rational thoughts. The child is born uncivilized, and acquires customs, beliefs, and values by instruction and imitation. Each new generation can draw on the rich store of past accumulated knowledge and ideas.

Through a capacity to absorb, transmit, and modify the body of learned tradition known as culture, man has been able to reach beyond himself. In contrast to other, humbler animals, he can imagine and plan. He is the only animal who can write a book, and he is the only animal who can assemble in conferences to discuss his goals and achievements. Each new success serves only to bring to light new areas of difficulty. Considering these facts, it seems inevitable that man is uncertain about his capacities and limitations, and hence sets his goals either too high or too low. His ambivalence concerning his goals forever plagues him.

Man has gained a large measure of control over his environment. He is no longer completely at nature's mercy. He produces food for himself, and makes his clothing and shelter. His success in defending himself against his natural enemies is largely a measure of his ingenuity. But it is clear that man is only part master of the world in which he lives. While knowledge and the advances of science have broadened his command over nature, he still is unable to govern either himself or his environment. He remains dependent on his fellowmen and their benevolent concern for his survival, as well as on the impersonal forces of nature that are outside his control.

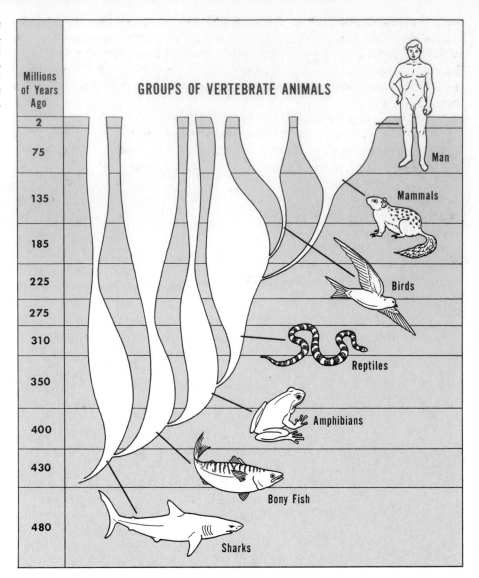

GROUPS OF VERTEBRATE ANIMALS

Millions of Years Ago
2
75
135
185
225
275
310
350
400
430
480

Man

Mammals

Birds

Reptiles

Amphibians

Bony Fish

Sharks

Man lives today in a drastically changed environment. The growing concern about environmental despoliation arises from the fact that man has failed to value his natural surroundings. Nature can exist without man, but man cannot exist without nature. Man is progressively creating for himself an almost totally man-made environment. Several species of organisms already have been exterminated by man's plundering efforts, and many others are likely to become prematurely extinct. Man is covering the face of the earth with steel, concrete, and asphalt. Few animals and plants, if any, have the capacity to adjust to a sterile, mechanical environment.

Man has not learned to manage his numbers. He has admirably reduced his mortality rate and has prolonged his life span, but he has yet voluntarily to restrict his explosive birth rate. Man today is multiplying in great numbers. Some 180,000 persons are added daily in the world, and most can anticipate a longer life span than ever before. The current heavy demands on the food supply and the extravagant use of resources of energy, notably fossil fuels, are endangering or depressing the existing levels of living. Some writers believe that man's ingenuity and technological sophistication will make it possible to obtain nutrients and energy materials from sources that cannot now be exploited economically, so that the food and energy requirements of an expanding population will be met. Many others, however, contend that, despite technological progress, basic resources must inevitably come into short supply under heavy population pressure.

Clearly, the human species is now facing the most crucial period in its entire history. The new and dangerous environment that man has created for himself provides an unprecedented challenge. Man has the potentiality for regulating his numbers, living in harmony with his environment, and controlling his very destiny. Although many aspects of human behavior remain an enigma, an exploration of man's biological and cultural heritage may enable us to predict or judge the extent to which man can guide his own future course. The more complete our knowledge, the greater our ability for both judicious judgment and effective action. It is this penchant for learning and the capacity for integrating knowledge that largely distinguishes man from the lower animals.

Reviewers

Dr. Paul F. Biersuck
Department of Biology
Nassau Community College
Professor Lonnie Eiland
Natural Sciences Department
Michigan State University
Professor Joseph L. Hindman
Chairperson - Department of
    Biology
Washington State University
Professor Joseph G. Kunkel
Zoology Department
University of Massachusetts
Professor Rodney C. Mowbray
Biology Department
University of Wisconsin-
    LaCrosse

Professor Eugene C. Bovee
Division of Biological Sciences
University of Kansas
Dr. Craig L. Himes
Biology Department
Bloomsburg State College
Professor Kenneth E. Hutton
Department of Biology
San Jose State College
Professor Francis E. McKay
Department of Biology
SUNY at Stony Brook
Professor Robert L. Packard
Department of Biological
    Sciences
Texas Technical University

Part

1

Man
Life
Processes

Seeds of Life 1

It is not generally known that the distinguished 17th century British scientist William Harvey—the surgeon who provided the first genuine understanding of the circulation of human blood—spent many fruitful years observing vertebrate (backboned) embryos, particularly those of the chicken and the deer. Harvey's careful observations, made with simple lenses, are recorded in his monumental treatise published in 1651, *Exercitationes de generatione animalium.* The frontispiece to his book shows an ornamental figure of the Greek deity Zeus—the supreme chief of the Olympian gods—opening an egg from which various animals, including man, are springing forth (fig. 1.1). Upon the egg is imprinted the phrase *ex ovo omnia,* which, in abbreviated form, conveys the universal truth that the egg is the starting point of all organisms.

Before the microscope was perfected, ideas concerning development of the egg were largely speculative. It was formerly thought by the school of *ovists* in the 17th and 18th centuries that the egg contained a miniature replica of the new individual. In other words, the preexisting parts of the new individual were contained, or *preformed,* within the egg. Harvey, an ovist, denied that the sperm participated in the formation of the embryo, but did attribute to the sperm some vague salutary influence to account for the resemblance of offspring to the father. Other scientists of the day, popularly known as *spermatists,* contended that the preformed individual resided rather in the sperm cell. A leading proponent of this view was Niklaas Hartsoeker, who in 1694 portrayed the tiny body of a human individual—*homunculus,* or "little man"—encased within the head of the sperm cell (fig. 1.2). The function of the woman's womb was simply to protect and nourish the diminutive human being until it unfolded into the adult form. Hartsoeker was one of the first scientists to view the sperm cell under the microscope, and in his later writings (1708) he acknowledged that he was never able to discern microscopically his imaginary "little man."

An extreme form of the preformation idea was advocated by the Swiss scientist Charles Bonnet in the late 1700s. He argued that each female harbored within her body the eggs of all her descendants encapsulated one generation within the other like boxes or cases, as in a series of Chinese puzzle boxes. Bonnet's extraordinary concept became known as *emboîtement,* or "encasement." The concept was pushed to an absurd extreme. The first female on earth, presumably Eve, was said to have possessed the complete supply of eggs, successively encased, for all subsequent generations of mankind.

There is in the egg no hint of the form that is eventually to emerge. One does not see the preformed parts of the new individual within the

Figure 1.1 Copy of an engraving in William Harvey's treatise (1651) on development, *Exercitationes de generatione animalium,* which shows the deity Zeus opening an egg from which various animals, including man, are emerging.

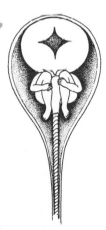

Figure 1.2 Homunculus, or "little man." A miniature human being was imagined by some 17th century scientists to be encased in the sperm cell.

3

egg or, for that matter, within the sperm. The egg does contain a highly complex chemical organization capable of producing a new individual through gradual development. The intricate process of development of the egg is typically initiated by entry of the sperm cell. Thus, the sperm cell imparts the stimulus that triggers development. The union of sperm and egg also ensures that the offspring inherits characteristics from both parental lines. Only rarely can an egg develop without the necessity of the sperm cell. A striking instance is the egg of the honeybee, which, unassisted by the sperm, has the capacity to develop into a drone, or male bee.

EGG CELLS OF VERTEBRATES

The eggs of vertebrates differ impressively in size, amount of nutritive material (yolk), and outer protective coverings. The ostrich egg, enclosed in a hard shell, is immense compared with the egg of a frog, while the frog's egg is inordinately large compared with the microscopic egg of a mammal, such as the human, cow, or sow (fig. 1.3). The eggs of amphibians, such as frogs and salamanders, are extruded into the water and are protected from mechanical injury by thick layers of jelly. Reptiles and birds produce eggs that contain a generous supply of stored nutritive yolk. The egg proper, from which the embryo develops, is merely a small crescent-shaped fleck on the surface of the yellowish yolk. These yolk-

Figure 1.3 Relative sizes of different kinds of vertebrate eggs, and enlarged views of the hen's egg, the frog's egg, and the human egg.

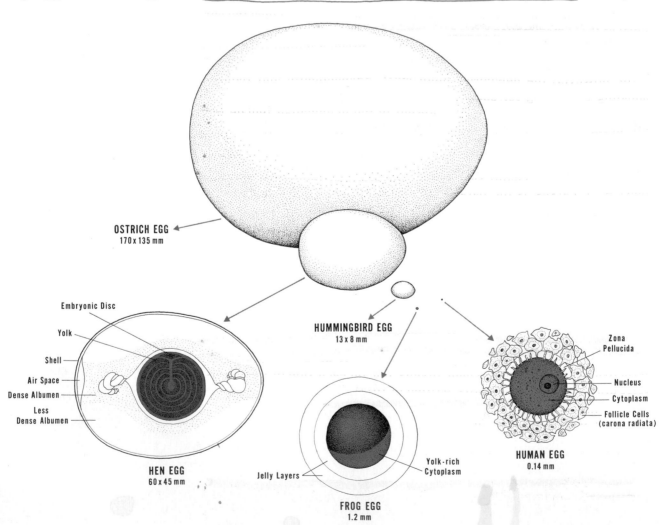

OSTRICH EGG
170 x 135 mm

HUMMINGBIRD EGG
13 x 8 mm

Embryonic Disc
Yolk
Shell
Air Space
Dense Albumen
Less Dense Albumen

HEN EGG
60 x 45 mm

Jelly Layers
Yolk-rich Cytoplasm

FROG EGG
1.2 mm

Zona Pellucida
Nucleus
Cytoplasm
Follicle Cells (carona radiata)

HUMAN EGG
0.14 mm

laden eggs are invested by albumen (the white of a hen's egg) and an outer protective shell.

With few exceptions, the eggs of mammals are microscopic and are practically devoid of stored nourishment. Only the duckbill platypus and the spiny anteater, both primitive mammals (monotremes) inhabiting the Australian region, possess exceptionally large and yolky eggs. The monotreme egg, encased as it is in a tough shell, is much like the reptilian egg. Aside from these unique monotremes, mammals rarely have eggs that exceed 0.2 mm in diameter. The human egg is 0.14 mm ($\frac{1}{175}$ inch) in diameter and weighs 4 millionths of a gram (0.000004 g). It is about the size of the period at the end of this sentence. Although the human egg is exceedingly small, it is nevertheless 50,000 times larger in volume than a single sperm cell.

There is a tendency in nature for fewer eggs to be produced as the chance of survival for the offspring increases. The number of eggs shed from the ovary appears to be correlated with the amount of care given to the young. In most fishes and amphibians, the eggs are untended and left to the hazards of the open environment. The codfish, for example, produces several million eggs during a single breeding season, but only a small percentage of the unprotected eggs survive. In contrast to the extravagance of fish, usually only a single egg is released at a time in the cow, horse, elephant, and human. Such reproductive economy is possible since prenatal protection and postnatal care combine to enhance the survival of these mammalian young.

The mammalian embryo is retained and nourished within the mother until a relatively advanced stage of development and growth. Even at birth, however, the newborn cannot exist independently and requires suckling or nursing for some time. It is not surprising, therefore, that highly specialized structures are present in the mammalian female that are designed exclusively for bearing and rearing the young. With increased complexity of the mammalian reproductive system comes also an increased likelihood of malfunctioning of the intricate system at some point. Here then, as expressed by the University of Cambridge physiologist A. S. Parkes, is the paradox confronting modern man—he simultaneously attempts "to remedy the infertility of the infertile and to limit the fertility of the fertile."

THE FEMALE REPRODUCTIVE SYSTEM

One of the earliest scientists to study the embryos of a mammal was the 17th century Dutch anatomist Regnier de Graaf. He is credited with disproving the then common belief that the lining of the uterus secreted the egg. The eggs of mammals, de Graaf concluded from his observations on pregnant rabbits, were produced by organs near the uterus, which had earlier been termed *female testicles*. Regnier de Graaf applied the term *ovaries* to the paired female organs, one on each side of the uterus. Here are de Graaf's own words, written in 1672:

> Thus, the general function of the female testicles is to generate the ova, to nourish them, and to bring them to maturity so that they serve the same purpose in women as the ovaries of birds. Hence, they should rather be called ovaries than testes because they show no similarity, either in form or contents, with the male testes properly so called.

The developing egg with its associated nurse cells (follicle cells) is called the *Graafian follicle*, so named after its discoverer. Once every

28 days or so in the human female, after the onset of puberty, a Graafian follicle at the surface of the ovary ruptures. The liberation of the egg from the ruptured follicle comprises *ovulation*. As figure 1.4 shows, the open end of each *oviduct* is funnel-shaped and bears fingerlike processes, or *fimbriae* (Latin, meaning "fringe"). The fringed projections embrace the ovary and sweep over its surface at the time of ovulation. The discharged egg thus passes almost directly into the oviduct. The oviduct is frequently called the *Fallopian tube*, in honor of the 16th century Italian anatomist Gabriele Falloppio. It is of peculiar interest that Falloppio envisioned the tubes as "tubular chimneys" to permit the egress of "sooty fluids" from the uterus.

The ovulated egg is swept into the oviduct by the action of hairlike cilia and muscular contractions in the oviducal walls. In rare instances, the egg fails to pass into the oviduct and remains in the abdominal cavity. It is scarcely imaginable that fertilization could occur within the abdominal cavity. However, motile sperm have been recovered in the abdominal cavity and a fertilized egg can invade and become implanted in the abdominal wall. The fertilized egg of a rabbit can even be transferred to the anterior chamber of the eye, where it grows without difficulty and actually forms a placenta in the iris. In humans, an abdominal pregnancy may proceed normally, and the baby is delivered by Caesarean section. In most cases, however, an *ectopic pregnancy*—that is, implantation of the embryo elsewhere than in the uterus—terminates unsuccessfully.

An egg cannot move by its own effort. Moreover, an egg does not survive long if fertilization does not take place. Fertilization almost invariably takes place in the upper reaches of the oviduct, and the human egg probably remains fertile for only 10 to 15 hours after ovulation. In other mammals, the eggs of guinea pigs are known to degenerate as early as 8 hours after ovulation, and rabbit eggs do not survive for more than

Figure 1.4 Human ovary and its associated genital tract. The frilled, or fringed, end of the oviduct embraces the ovary and sweeps over its surface at the time of ovulation.

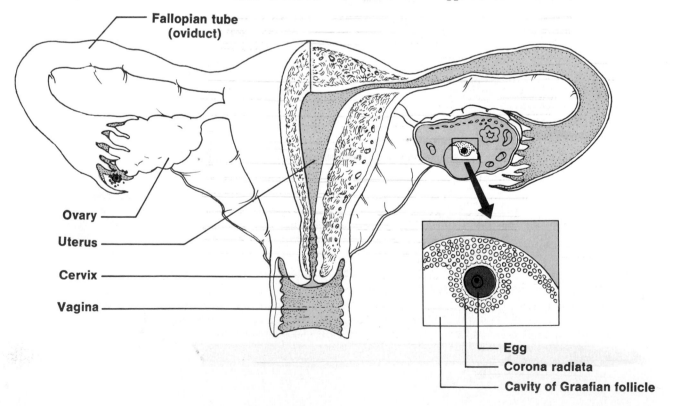

Fallopian tube (oviduct)

Ovary

Uterus

Cervix

Vagina

Egg

Corona radiata

Cavity of Graafian follicle

6 hours. Abnormal development frequently results when eggs are fertilized at the close of their life span. Such eggs are said to be "aged," or "overripe." By experimentally delaying the time of insemination of rabbit eggs, the British biologist C. R. Austin established that at least 50 percent of the overripe eggs met early death before they even became implanted in the uterus. In guinea pigs and cattle, aging of eggs is associated with a high incidence of abortion and stillbirths. Apparently, for best chances of fertilization as well as better chances of normal development, sperm should lie in wait for the egg so that the meeting of the two takes place soon after ovulation.

The hollow, pear-shaped *uterus* (womb) occupies a central position in the pelvic cavity (fig. 1.5). Early Greek philosophers speculated that the *hystera* (Greek word for the uterus) was the seat of emotional excitability (hysteria) and the cause of mental derangements. No such views, of course, are held today. The internal wall of the uterus has a special kind of spongy, blood-rich lining, termed the *endometrium*. Approximately every 28 days in the sexually mature human female, the greater part of the endometrium breaks down and is discharged into the cavity of the uterus. The raw surface of the uterus bleeds for about four days. The mixture of blood and disrupted endometrium delivered into the cavity of the uterus and passed out through the cervical canal and vagina constitutes the menstrual flow (Latin, *mensis*, meaning "month"). Following menstruation, the endometrium repairs itself. Menstruation does not coincide with ovulation, but rather occurs about halfway between the times of ovulation. Among mammals, the phenomenon of menstruation is peculiar to humans and their primate relatives (monkeys and

Figure 1.5 Internal and external genitalia of the human female.

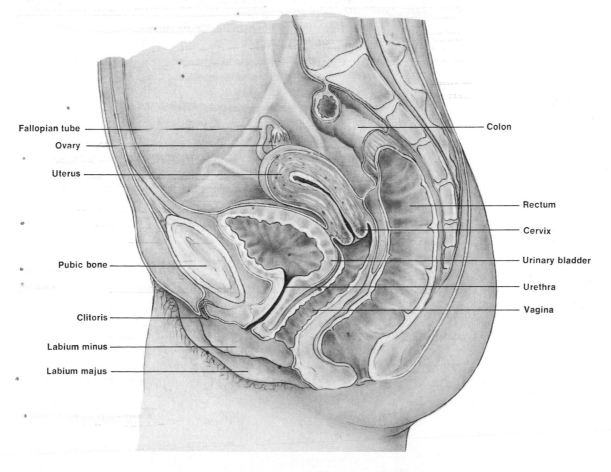

Fallopian tube

Ovary

Uterus

Colon

Rectum

Cervix

Urinary bladder

Urethra

Vagina

Pubic bone

Clitoris

Labium minus

Labium majus

Figure 1.6 The external genitalia of the human female.

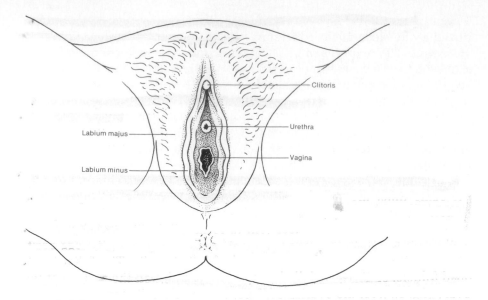

apes). The periodic blood-stained discharge from the genital openings of female domestic mammals, such as the mare and cow, is not associated with menstruation, but is a manifestation of ovulation. In the human, save for a possible slight abdominal pain, most women are unaware that they have ovulated.

The uterus terminates in the cervix (fig. 1.5), which projects into the upper part of the vagina. The inner lining of the cervix secretes a viscid material, or *mucus*, that varies in consistency at different occasions. At the time of ovulation, the cervical mucus is relatively thin and readily penetrable by sperm. During pregnancy, the cervical opening is sealed with a thick plug of mucus, which prevents bacteria and other harmful agents from entering the uterus. The *vagina* (Latin, meaning "sheath") lies almost at right angles to the uterus. The *hymen*, a vascularized thin membrane that stretches across the vaginal opening, is often torn before the first intercourse. Although the hymen has no known biological function, it has been the subject culturally of a number of fanciful legends.

The vagina opens into a cleft, or *vestibule*, bounded by two delicate folds of skin, the *labia minora* (fig. 1.6). Near the anterior end of the vestibule between the labia minora is a small body of erectile tissue, the *clitoris*. This erogenous structure corresponds to the penis of the male. Between the opening of the vagina and the clitoris is the opening of the *urethra*, the passageway for urine from the bladder. Two additional fleshy folds of skin, known as the *labia majora*, enclose the vagina (fig. 1.6). These prominent external folds of skin are derived from the same embryonic structures that give rise to the scrotum of the male. The external sexual organs of the female are referred to collectively as the *vulva*.

THE HUMAN OVARY

Women are endowed with far more eggs than they will ever need in their reproductive life. The paired, compact ovaries at puberty (ages 11 to 14) contain an estimated 500,000 potential eggs, of which about 400 mature and are released during a woman's fertile years. Those remaining degenerate at various intervals, so that scarcely any eggs are present by the time the woman reaches menopause (ages 45 to 50). All the potential eggs for the human female are found in her ovaries when she is born; there is not a continual renewal of eggs throughout the reproductive years. Hence, an ovulated egg of a 40-year-old woman has been dormant for 40 years. There is suggestive evidence that the maturation of the egg is impaired with advancing age. The incidence of hydrocephaly (abnormally large head) and Down's syndrome (mongolism) among newborn infants increases markedly with advancing age of the mother.

Figure 1.7 illustrates the development of a single egg in the ovary. At an early stage, the potential egg lies near the surface of the ovary, surrounded by a single layer of follicle cells. The combination of egg and follicle cells is referred to as a *primary follicle.* The egg enlarges and, at the same time, the follicle cells multiply to form several layers. The follicle layers then separate and a clear fluid accumulates in the spaces between the layers. The spaces join to form a fluid-filled cavity known as the *antrum.* With the further expansion of the antrum, the egg occupies a position at one side in a mound of follicle cells. The fully developed follicle, or *Graafian follicle,* appears as a bulge on the surface of the ovary (fig. 1.7). At the ovarian surface, the follicle cells form a very thin and translucent wall. It is at this thin site—which resembles a blister—that the rounded and turgid follicle eventually ruptures. The extruded egg is covered by a thick protective capsule, the *zona pellucida,* external to which are irregularly arranged follicle cells, collectively called the *corona radiata* (fig. 1.3).

Normally, each month, several primary follicles begin to enlarge simultaneously, but usually only one reaches maturity and ruptures to release an egg. The spurious development and degeneration of a follicle is termed *atresia* (fig. 1.7). Occasionally, however, two or more follicles

Figure 1.7 Cyclic changes that occur in the human ovary. The events are shown here in successive stages, although they occur in one place in an ovary. (Modified after B. M. Patten, *Human embryology,* 3rd ed., 1968, The Blakiston Co.)

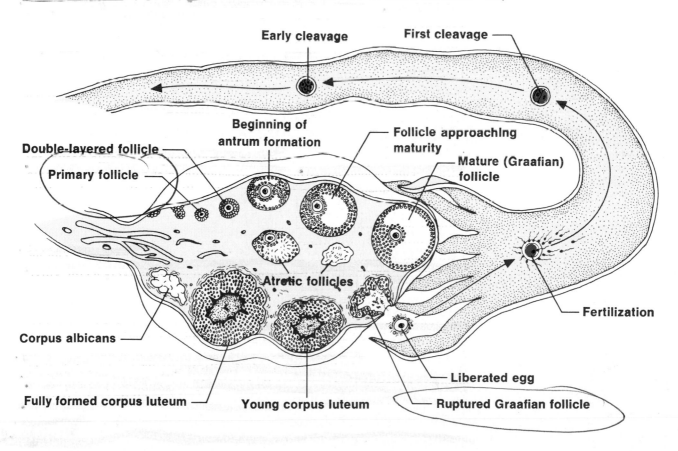

Early cleavage

First cleavage

Beginning of antrum formation

Follicle approaching maturity

Double-layered follicle

Primary follicle

Mature (Graafian) follicle

Atretic follicles

Fertilization

Corpus albicans

Liberated egg

Fully formed corpus luteum

Young corpus luteum

Ruptured Graafian follicle

mature, and more than one egg is released. Successful fertilization of the multiple eggs may lead to multiple births; in such an event, the sibling offspring are fraternal (nonidentical). In recent years, infertile women suffering hormonal dysfunction have been treated with synthetic compounds, particularly clomiphene, that stimulate follicular development. The response to clomiphene is largely unpredictable, and several follicles may be stimulated to mature simultaneously. There have been an unusually large number of cases of twins and other multiple births in women who have had clomiphene administered to them.

FORMATION OF CORPUS LUTEUM

After the discharge of the egg, the follicle collapses. The cells lining the collapsed follicle increase in size, and blood vessels grow inward to form a new glandlike structure, the *corpus luteum* (fig. 1.7). The corpus luteum is invariably associated with the recently extruded egg. Its fate depends on whether or not fertilization ensues. If fertilization does not occur, the corpus luteum degenerates to form a scarlike whitish streak, called a *corpus albicans*. If fertilization does occur, the corpus luteum continues to grow and exerts an important influence on the lining of the uterus.

The persistence of the corpus luteum following fertilization of the egg suggests that it has some relation to implantation of the embryo. Indeed, the German embryologist Guenther Born theorized in 1880 that the removal of the corpus luteum should interfere with, or interrupt, pregnancy. Born died before testing his hypothesis but passed the idea on to one of his students, Ludwig Fraenkel, who soon substantiated Born's thesis. Experiments that Fraenkel performed in 1903 showed for the first time that the mammalian ovary had another function besides producing eggs. He found that removing the corpus luteum in the rabbit during the first few days of pregnancy invariably ended pregnancy. The corpus luteum was obviously indispensable for continuation of pregnancy. The hypothesis first set forth by Born was fully substantiated.

In 1910, two French investigators, Paul Ancel and Pol Bouin, provided an explanation of Fraenkel's results by showing that the rabbit's uterus, while under the influence of the corpus luteum, undergoes very remarkable changes. The uterus becomes greatly enlarged and highly glandular; this specialized state was interpreted as being necessary for implantation of the fertilized egg. Hence, the uterus must be properly prepared for receiving the fertilized egg. The preparation of the uterus is under the influence of hormones, which are blood-borne chemical messengers of the body. A given hormone typically exerts a specific effect on one particular organ, which is usually called the target organ for that hormone. Numerous investigators in many years of patient work have enlarged our understanding of how these hormones act in reproduction. Virtually all aspects of reproduction depend on the presence of appropriate hormones at specific times.

THE MENSTRUAL CYCLE

The typical menstrual cycle covers 28 days and is illustrated in figure 1.8. There can be unpredictable variations in the length of the individual menstrual cycle. The cycle, which begins on the first day of menstruation, is set into motion by the pituitary gland. This gland, about the size of an acorn, is embedded in the bones of the skull just below the brain. The pituitary produces many different hormones that are secreted into the bloodstream and carried to various parts of the body. Those hormones that stimulate and control gonadal activity are known as *gonado-*

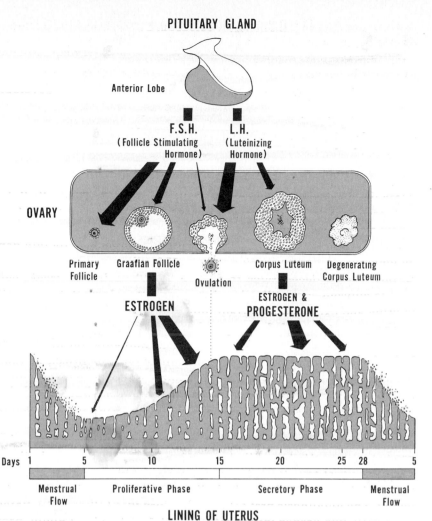

PITUITARY GLAND

Anterior Lobe

F.S.H.
(Follicle Stimulating
Hormone)

L.H.
(Luteinizing
Hormone)

OVARY

Primary Follicle   Graafian Follicle   Ovulation   Corpus Luteum   Degenerating Corpus Luteum

ESTROGEN

ESTROGEN & PROGESTERONE

Days 1   5   10   15   20   25 28   5

Menstrual Flow   Proliferative Phase   Secretory Phase   Menstrual Flow

LINING OF UTERUS

Figure 1.8 Menstrual cycle showing the relative concentrations of hormones (by different widths of arrows), ovarian events, and changes in the uterine wall (endometrium).

tropins. Specifically, the anterior lobe of the pituitary gland secretes two important gonadotropins, the *follicle-stimulating hormone* (FSH) and the *luteinizing hormone* (LH), each having different effects (fig. 1.8).

The follicle-stimulating hormone acts on the primary follicle and promotes its growth. The growing follicle produces a class of hormones known as *estrogen*. Several chemically different, although closely related, estrogens have been identified, including estradiol, estrone, and estriol. Of these, estradiol is the most potent and the principal estrogen secreted by the ovaries. Estrogens are produced in small amounts by the adrenal glands and also the testes.

Estrogen has manifold effects in the female. The rising level of estrogen has the effect of curtailing the production of the follicle-stimulating hormone by the pituitary gland. Hence, by inhibiting the flow of FSH, estrogen serves to prevent development of other follicles in the ovary. Estrogen also initiates the special changes in the endometrium that prepare the uterus for implantation of a fertilized egg. The first half of the cycle, characterized by a thickening of the uterine endometrium under the influence of estrogen, is often called the *proliferative phase* (fig. 1.8). Another effect of estrogen is to stimulate development of the milk-producing glands of the breasts. Estrogen is also responsible for the development of the female secondary sexual characteristics at puberty —the mature genitalia, breasts, bodily hair, and feminine contours, in-

cluding broadening of the pelvis and fat deposition in the hips and abdomen.

Toward the end of the two-week proliferative phase, the concentration of estrogen in the bloodstream reaches its peak. The high level of estrogen inhibits the production of FSH and promotes the release of LH by the pituitary gland. The presence of large quantities of LH is essential for ovulation. A sudden great outpouring of LH, around the 14th day, triggers the release of the egg from the mature follicle (fig. 1.8).

Once the follicle has ruptured and transforms into the corpus luteum, its function changes. The corpus luteum continues to produce estrogen and begins to manufacture another important hormone, *progesterone*. Progesterone inhibits the production of LH and completes the preparation of the wall of the uterus for the implantation of the fertilized egg. In conjunction with estrogen, progesterone causes the uterine wall to grow thicker and become gorged with the large supply of blood that is required during the early stages of pregnancy. This period is known as the *secretory phase*, which begins at the time of ovulation and extends to the beginning of the next menstruation.

Thus, on or shortly after the 14th day of the cycle, all the events necessary for conception have been consummated. The egg is discharged into the Fallopian tube to await the sperm and the uterine wall is generously endowed with blood vessels. If pregnancy occurs, the menstrual cycle is interrupted and the high levels of estrogen and progesterone prevent the development of a new Graafian follicle in the ovary. Accordingly, ovulation is inhibited during the gestation period.

If the egg is not fertilized, the corpus luteum diminishes both in size and in hormonal activity. As the corpus luteum degenerates, the flow of estrogen and progesterone drops markedly. The thickened endometrium of the uterus, no longer stimulated by these hormones, commences to break down about the 28th day (fig. 1.8). Menstrual bleeding occurs from the disintegrating blood vessels of the endometrium. With the marked decrease of estrogen and progesterone, the pituitary gland is then able to secrete FSH. As the concentration of FSH rises, the growth of a primary follicle is initiated and the cycle begins anew.

The fluctuations in the gonadotropic and ovarian hormones during one complete cycle are graphically represented in figure 1.9. Ovulation is brought about by a sharp surge of LH around the 14th day. The exact nature of the signal for the LH ovulatory peak is currently the focus of extensive investigations. It seems likely that high levels of estrogen just prior to ovulation trigger the strong, sudden release of LH at midcycle. Recent studies show that FSH also peaks at midcycle, coincident with the LH peak (fig. 1.9). This is a curious finding since FSH secretion tends to be inhibited by rising levels of estrogen. The midcycle surge of FSH may be a defensive, or safety, measure to guard against the failure of LH to cause ovulation.

The combination of high concentrations of estrogen and progesterone during the secretory phase prevents the development of a new egg follicle. Oral contraceptives work by maintaining the estrogen and progesterone levels through the secretory phase of the cycle. The essential ingredients of "the pill" are estrogen and progesterone in synthetic form. The pill duplicates the hormonal state that normally occurs during pregnancy. The small daily dose of estrogen and progesterone ensures that ovulation is inhibited, just as ovulation is blocked throughout normal pregnancy.

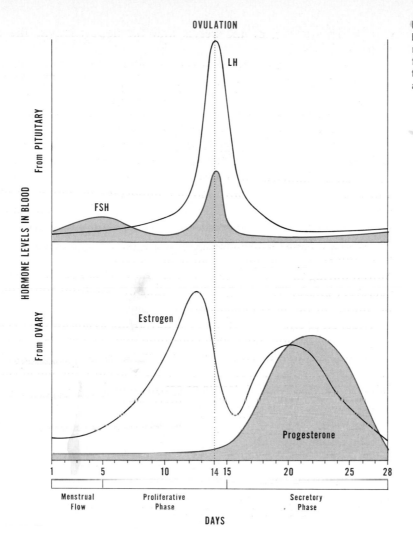

Figure 1.9 The fluctuations in blood-borne hormones during the menstrual cycle of the human female. Note the elevation of FSH that accompanies the surge of LH at ovulation.

A woman's fertile life ceases at menopause because her ovaries lose the capacity to respond to the gonadotropic hormones secreted by the pituitary. Some of the discomforting symptoms experienced by the menopausal woman result from an overabundance of FSH, the production of which is no longer held in check by the ovarian estrogen. Estrogen has been administered to women in menopause to alleviate the unpleasant symptoms, which include hot flashes, sleeplessness, anxiety, and depression. There is, however, continuing controversy as to the safety of estrogen therapy. The sharp rise in recent years of uterine cancer among older women has been linked to the increasing use of estrogen to relieve menopausal discomfort.

HYPOTHALAMUS

Over the past several years, especially since 1964, the realization has been growing that the pituitary gland receives its instructions from a higher authority in the brain. It is well known that psychological stress from unsettling conditions can play havoc with the normal 28-day cycle. This psychological stress involves the brain, and in particular, a part termed the *hypothalamus*, which is visible on the undersurface of the brain as a small band of gray matter from which the pituitary gland is suspended (fig. 1.10). The pituitary gland is under the command of the hypothalamus (fig. 1.10). A network of blood vessels from the hypothala-

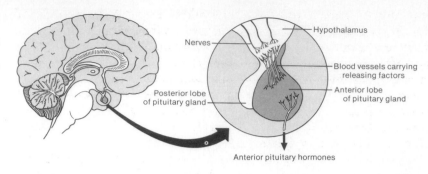

Figure 1.10 Interrelations between the pituitary gland and the hypothalamus of the human brain. Blood vessels carry the releasing factors from the hypothalamus to the pituitary gland. This pathway enables the brain to participate in the control of production of anterior pituitary hormones.

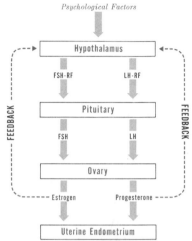

Figure 1.11 The principle of *feedback inhibition* between the pituitary and the ovary, incorporating the role of the hypothalamus and its chemical releasing factors (RF). Estrogen curtails the secretion of follicle-stimulating hormone (FSH) by inhibiting the production of FSH-RF in the hypothalamus. Progesterone curtails the secretion of luteinizing hormone (LH) by suppressing the production of LH-RF in the hypothalamus. Psychological factors can affect the release of FSH-RF and LH-RF, thereby disturbing the normal cycle.

mus carries chemical agents, now known as *releasing factors,* which act to stimulate production of the appropriate hormone in the pituitary gland. Thus, the brain is intimately involved in hormonal regulation.

The hormones of the menstrual cycle are produced and regulated by a mechanism that involves the principle of *negative feedback* (or *feedback inhibition*). This principle is illustrated by such mechanical devices as a room air-conditioning unit equipped with thermostatic control. If the room temperature falls below the desired level, the thermostat causes the cooling compressor to be cut off. Should the temperature rise, the thermostat switches the compressor on again and cooling continues until the desired temperature is reached again. With reference to the human menstrual cycle, the feedback mechanism operates between the ovary and the pituitary via the hypothalamus. The hypothalamus serves essentially as a thermostat, exerting a very fine control over the secretions of gonadotropic and gonadal hormones. The pituitary gland is stimulated to produce FSH and LH only under the influence of releasing factors (RF)—namely, FSH-RF and LH-RF, respectively—from the hypothalamus (fig. 1.11). After ovulation, the cells of the corpus luteum secrete estrogen and progesterone, the large quantities of which "feed back" to the hypothalamus and inhibit the production of the releasing factors. Accordingly, the secretions of FSH and LH by the pituitary are curtailed. If fertilization does not occur, the levels of estrogen and progesterone decline, thus permitting the releasing factors to be produced again. Although feedback inhibition is the general rule, there are instances of *positive feedback*. The triggering of high levels of LH at ovulation by high levels of estrogen is an example of positive feedback.

ESTRUS

With the notable exception of humans, the female of mammalian species becomes sexually aroused only at certain seasons. At specific times the female comes into heat, or *estrus* (Greek, *oistros,* meaning "frenzy"), and only during these restricted periods is the female receptive to the male. Some mammals, such as the goat and mare, have several estrous periods annually; others come into heat only once or twice a year. The female dog, for example, has two estrous periods per year, about four to six months apart, in the spring and fall.

In most female mammals, the onset of heat is synchronized with the release of the ripe egg. In other words, in mammals such as the cow, pig, horse, and sheep, ovulation occurs automatically or spontaneously at the time of estrus, irrespective of mating. On the other hand, in the domestic cat and the rabbit, sexual receptivity occurs preceding maturation of the follicle. The female rabbit (doe) remains in continuous heat until she mates. The stimulus for release of the egg is copulation. Since ovulation is

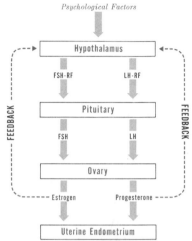 *(Psychological Factors — Hypothalamus — FSH-RF / LH-RF — Pituitary — FSH / LH — Ovary — Estrogen / Progesterone — Uterine Endometrium — FEEDBACK)*

triggered only by copulation, the female rabbit is said to be an induced ovulator. Pregnancy is almost always assured, as the sperm lie in wait for the egg, which is released shortly after copulation. It is not unusual for a doe to be both pregnant and lactating through most of the breeding season.

It is a curious finding that ovulation still occurs when the female rabbit is mated with a sterile male. Ovulation thus does not depend on the presence of sperm cells, but rather on the nervous stimuli that arise during copulation and pass to the brain. In turn, the pituitary gland is stimulated to release large quantities of luteinizing hormone. There also follows a period of false pregnancy (pseudopregnancy), during which the corpus luteum secretes progesterone and the doe behaves as if she were pregnant. Eventually the corpus luteum degenerates, pseudopregnancy is terminated, and the doe enters a period of relative quiescence until the next estrus.

Except for the human species, the females of all primates, at least those who live in the wild, experience estrus. Interestingly, rhesus monkeys in captivity may breed throughout the year, just like humans. Evidently, the estrous cycle is subject to appreciable change when monkeys are taken from the wild and held in confinement. Several authors have pointed out that the loss of the phenomenon of estrus in human evolution was an event of great importance. The constancy in sexual receptivity of the human female has apparently fostered permanent male-female relations, and has favored integration of the male into family life. In the vast majority of mammalian species, the primary role of the male is insemination, and rarely does he participate actively in the care of the young.

Although an estrous period is not evident in the human female, she apparently experiences emotional or personality changes during the menstrual cycle. Several studies, particularly those by the American psychologist Therese F. Benedek, suggest that high levels of estrogen are correlated with high levels of a positive sexual mood. With heightened concentrations of estrogen at or near the time of ovulation, the emotions of the woman are said to be outward and heterosexual. The time of ovulation is accompanied by a feeling of well-being; thus, at ovulation, the woman is both biologically and emotionally prepared for conception. In contrast, the low-estrogen, premenstrual period is generally associated with feelings of anxiety, irritability, and depression. Surveys by A. C. Kinsey, on the other hand, indicate that the peak of sexual receptivity or response among women is just prior to menstruation, and not during ovulation. In interpreting Kinsey's findings, psychologist Judith Bardwick suggests that many women have low feelings of self-esteem during premenstrual days and emotionally desire male contact. It may be, then, that there is no direct causal or predictable relation between estrogen levels and emotional shifts in the human female.

HUMAN SPERM

The highly motile spermatozoon, or sperm cell, bears little resemblance to the ordinary, or typical, cell (fig. 1.12). Indeed, spermatozoa were first described in 1677 by the Dutchman Anton van Leeuwenhoek as animalcules, or "little animals." The motility of the sperm is accomplished by a long, thin tail; the source of energy for the sperm's movements resides in the spiral middle piece. Within the head of the sperm is the nucleus, which contains the blueprints for heredity. A caplike structure, called the acrosome, fits over the anterior part of the head. The sperm measures

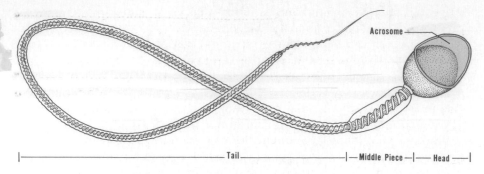

Figure 1.12 Mature human sperm cell, consisting of a distinct head, an intricate middle piece, and a long filamentous tail. A conelike structure, the acrosome, caps the head.

Acrosome

|————————————— Tail ——————————————|— Middle Piece —|— Head —|

Figure 1.13 Internal and external genitalia of the human male.

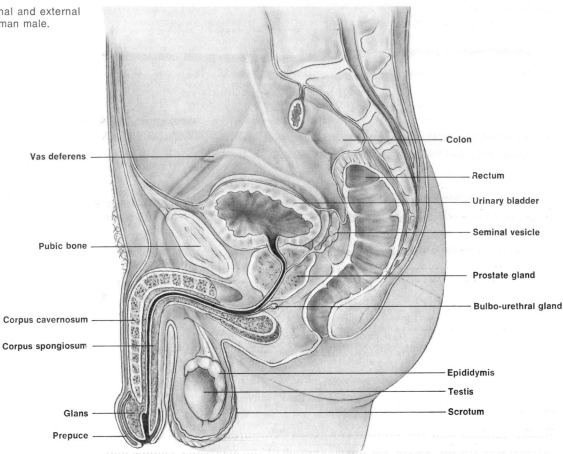

Vas deferens

Pubic bone

Corpus cavernosum

Corpus spongiosum

Glans

Prepuce

Colon

Rectum

Urinary bladder

Seminal vesicle

Prostate gland

Bulbo-urethral gland

Epididymis

Testis

Scrotum

about $\frac{1}{500}$ inch overall, with the tail comprising the greater part of the length. The sperm are produced in two ovoid testes, which in mammals are normally located in a thin-walled external sac, the scrotum (fig. 1.13). The scrotum has two compartments, one for each testis. The word *testis* is the Latin expression for "witness." In former days, individuals testifying under oath placed their hands on this reproductive organ.

The interior of each testis contains a network of thin *seminiferous tubules,* within which sperm are produced (fig. 1.14). The spaces between the seminiferous tubules are filled with hormone-producing cells called *interstitial cells,* or *cells of Leydig.* The male sex hormones are a group of chemicals collectively known as *androgens.* The principal androgen in the human male is *testosterone.* The chemical composition of testosterone is remarkably similar to the chemical structure of estradiol. In fact, all normal adult males produce some estradiol, and testosterone circulates in detectable amounts in the blood of adult females.

Two hormones of the pituitary gland regulate sperm production and testosterone secretion. The follicle-stimulating hormone (FSH) acts on the seminiferous tubules to promote sperm production, and luteinizing hormone (LH) acts on the interstitial cells to stimulate hormone secretion. In the male, LH is more often referred to as the *interstitial-cell-stimulating hormone* (ICSH). This is merely a difference in terminology, inasmuch as the molecular structure of LH (or ICSH) is precisely the same in both sexes. As in the female, the secretions of these pituitary hormones are regulated by the hypothalamus of the brain. However, in contrast to the female mechanism, release of both FSH and ICSH in the male is at a fixed, continuous rate, rather than intermittently or cyclically.

Testosterone is necessary for normal sperm production, and for development of all the obvious masculine secondary sexual characteristics. Although sexual activity wanes in their fifties and sixties, many men can maintain sexual vigor throughout life. In other words, for males there is usually no termination of gamete production comparable to menopause. Testosterone secretion does decline steadily with age, but the level of secretion remains sufficiently high to permit continuous fertility. Moreover, although the formation of sperm depends on testosterone, the production of testosterone does not depend on sperm formation. Hence, male sexual behavior and appearance is not affected in any way when the function of the seminiferous tubules is impaired or curtailed. Vasectomy, or the surgical removal of a portion of the sperm-carrying duct, does not alter the secretion of testosterone.

From the seminiferous tubules the sperm pass into a long, narrow tube that is so highly coiled, or wound on itself, that it forms a compact body, the *epididymis*. The crescent-shaped epididymis is located along one border of each testis (fig. 1.13). Sperm are stored in the epididymis prior to ejaculation. The epididymis emerges from the testis to join a thicker walled and relatively straight tube, the *vas deferens*. The vas deferens, together with blood vessels and nerves, traverses an opening (the inguinal canal) in the anterior abdominal wall. The vas deferens passes through the abdominal cavity and pursues a course around the urinary bladder. It then passes through the substance of the prostate gland and finally empties into the urethra (fig. 1.13). The urethra is the common passageway for the sperm, for the secretions of the accessory glands, and for the excretion of urine. Three accessory glands—the bilobed *seminal vesicles*, the median *prostate*, and the paired *bulbo-urethral glands* (or *Cowper's glands*)—produce a mucous fluid. This fluid medium, together with the suspended sperm, comprises the *semen*. The milky appearance of ejaculated semen is due primarily to the secretions of the prostate gland. Prostatic fluid is alkaline, and thereby neutralizes the acidic vaginal secretions.

Much of the substance of the penis consists of erectile tissue, disposed in three long cylindrical columns—two side by side, known as the *corpora cavernosa*, and one medially situated, known as the *corpus spongiosum* (fig. 1.13). The erectile tissue is a spongelike system of vascular spaces, or blood chambers. Normally the chambers are collapsed and contain very little blood; the penis is accordingly soft and flaccid.

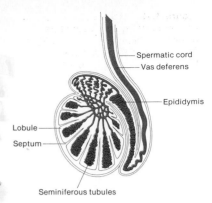

Figure 1.14 The internal architecture of a testis of the human male.

Spermatic cord
Vas deferens
Epididymis
Lobule
Septum
Seminiferous tubules

During sexual excitement, the chambers become filled with blood under high pressure. The penis enlarges and becomes rigid; the erected state permits entry into the vagina. The skin covering the surface of the penis terminates in a loose-fitting hood, the *prepuce,* or *foreskin.* The foreskin surrounds the enlarged, acorn-shaped tip, or *glans*. In many societies it has been the practice to remove the foreskin surgically in an operation called *circumcision.*

The average volume of semen ejaculated is 4 ml, containing as many as 350 million sperm. A minimum of 80 million motile sperm per ejaculate is considered necessary for fertility. Not all sperm cells produced are exactly alike in structure; indeed, ejaculates typically contain a variety of sperm types, of which only one kind is normal. When the percentage of abnormal types in an ejaculate exceeds 25 percent, the male is sterile. An inadequate sperm count and poor sperm morphology may be responsible for as many as 4 out of every 10 infertile marriages.

Sperm have a limited life span in the female genital tract. Their capability for swimming may last up to 3 or 4 days, but their fertilizing ability is probably lost within 24 hours. The fertile life span of sperm in most mammals is typically short, as brief as 6 hours in the mouse. A notable exception is the bat, whose sperm, deposited in the fall, can actually winter in the female tract until eggs are ovulated in the spring.

Sperm can reach the Fallopian tubes within 15 minutes of ejaculation. Such rapidity of transport cannot be ascribed solely to the swimming capacity of the sperm. Sperm actually swim aimlessly in wide circles. It is now generally conceded that muscular contractions of the uterus and oviducts provide the main impetus for sperm transport. Strange as it may seem, freshly ejaculated sperm cannot fertilize an egg. They require a period of residence, or maturation, in the female genital tract. The subtle physiological changes by which the sperm cell acquires the ability to penetrate an egg has been termed *capacitation.*

Capacitation appears to be related to changes in the terminal cap, or acrosome, of the sperm. Concepts of the acrosome's function have changed perceptibly since the structure was first described in 1887. The acrosome was originally thought to act simply as a mechanical device, enabling the sperm to bore or cut its way into the egg. The more recent concept that the substance of the acrosome has lytic (dissolving) properties has been borne out by experimentation. The acrosome can release its lytic agent, *hyaluronidase,* only after capacitation has occurred. The follicle cells (corona radiata) surrounding the egg are dispersed by the action of hyaluronidase, and the sperm can then penetrate the zona pellucida.

Although hundreds of millions of sperm are deposited in the vagina, comparatively few reach the site of fertilization in the Fallopian tube. Most meet death or entrapment as they pass from the vagina through the uterus and into the Fallopian tubes. Of the few hundred that reach the site of fertilization, only one sperm successfully penetrates the egg. The entry of one sperm causes an immediate chemical change in the zona pellucida that makes the egg impenetrable to other sperm. Microscopic studies show that several sperm invade the zona pellucida and that the excess ones remain trapped within the thick zona. Once the one successful sperm is inside the egg, the head of the sperm detaches from the tail, and the nucleus of the sperm head unites with the nucleus of the egg. The union of the two nuclei completes the process of fertilization.

GENETIC BLUEPRINTS

Although the egg is many times greater in volume than the sperm, the two have equal potentialities as far as inheritance is concerned. The blueprints for traits are carried in the nucleus of each gamete (the mature sex cell—egg or sperm). The genetic characteristics of the future child are established at the time the sperm nucleus unites with the egg nucleus.

Knowledge of the internal organization of the nucleus came slowly to science. Its advance depended primarily on perfection of the microscope and development of techniques of staining the cell with various dyes. The most significant visible components of the nucleus are threadlike strands, termed *chromosomes* (Greek, meaning "colored bodies"), so named because of their affinity for certain dyes. Every form of life has a definite and characteristic number of chromosomes. The fruit fly has 8 in every body cell, the frog has 26, and man has 46. The chromosomes occur in pairs in each body cell; man has therefore 23 pairs. One member of each pair comes from the mother and the other from the father. Stated another way, each of the gametes has only half the number of chromosomes of the parents. Fertilization restores the original number: in man, a full complement of 46 chromosomes (fig. 1.15). The 46 chromosomes of the fertilized egg are passed on to all the cells during development, so that all body cells of the adult have the same number.

It is now well documented that the actual entities responsible for determination of traits are submicroscopic molecules, the *genes*, which are arranged in a linear sequence in the chromosomes. Genes are not pure abstractions but portions, or units, of a complex molecule—*deoxyribonucleic acid*, or DNA. This giant molecule carries a coded blueprint in its molecular structure. It has been estimated that the amount of DNA present in each human cell carries coded information corresponding to 2 million genes. The fertilized egg carries two representatives of each kind of gene, one from each parent. This knowledge is one of the cornerstones in the foundation of the science of genetics.

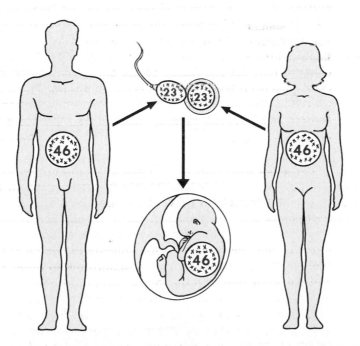

Figure 1.15 The newborn contains 46 chromosomes, having received 23 chromosomes from the mother and 23 from the father.

SUMMARY

Individuals die only to be replaced by others. The continuity of life is assured by reproduction, the process by which an organism leaves descendants. The essential feature of sexual reproduction is that each parent contributes to its offspring only a single specialized sex cell, either an egg or a sperm cell. These two minute sex cells, or gametes, are the only physical bridge between the parents and offspring. The offspring begins its existence the moment the sperm nucleus unites with the egg nucleus. The new individual is endowed with a unique package of inherited units, or genes, which directs its development and growth in a specific way.

Mammals have evolved an economical reproductive system. Rather than produce large numbers of eggs, many of which would perish, mammals have relatively few offspring, which enjoy high survival. The chances of survival are improved by the retention and nourishment of the fertilized egg within the mother, as well as by the parental care afforded the young after birth. Many of the complex anatomical and physiological features of the mammalian female relate to the dual aspects of prenatal nourishment and postnatal care.

Ethical Probe 1
Defining Human Life

Of great importance is the question whether human life exists in the womb, and if so, when it begins. The traits of an individual are largely determined by the genetic composition of the individual. A specific genetic code is locked into each cell of an individual at the very moment of the union of the sperm and egg nuclei. Genetically speaking, an egg cell by itself or a sperm cell by itself is merely a half-cell. Only the fertilized egg—the zygote—contains the full complement of genes and hence a specific program for development. The genetic code for each species of organism deals with all the characteristics of that species, and the code for each individual deals with all the traits the individual will show. Indeed, the genetic code for every human zygote is unique. Except for possible mutational changes, the code established in the zygote is the same 30 years later and, in fact, until whenever the individual dies. Viewed in this manner, human life traces back to the fertilized egg when this new cell acquires a unique genetic package.

The aforementioned view is not necessarily conclusive. Some contend that a fertilized egg is scarcely more than the blueprints for a human being. Stated another way, the genetic code of a zygote is not actually a human being, just as a set of blueprints is not really a house. Others have asserted that the fertilized egg may not be a "person" since the egg may subsequently divide to form identical twins. (The formation of identical twins also raises searching questions by theologians as to when the soul enters the body, since the soul cannot split.)

Does human life begin at fertilization? If not, how do you decide whether 1 day, 1 week, 12 weeks, or 17 weeks constitutes the beginning of human life? Is the decision arbitrary, or is there a sharp line of demarcation at which the developing embryo becomes a human being?

Control of Fertility

2

Birth control is not a new undertaking of contemporary man. Societies throughout history have made use of various contraceptive techniques and devices to prevent pregnancy. In a papyrus written about 1550 B.C., the Egyptians prescribed a recipe for a medicated tampon. Lint was moistened with honey and mixed with a powder ground from the tips of *Acacia* shrubs. This mixture was inserted into the vagina. This is a surprisingly advanced recipe, since the *Acacia* shrub contains gum arabic, which is mildly acidic and capable of immobilizing sperm cells.

In the second century, the Greek gynecologist Soranus prepared, in his *Gynaecia,* a comprehensive compendium of contraceptive techniques. His writings contained a mixture of rational and mystical techniques, the latter ranging from prayer to varied ceremonial acts. Women were advised to wear a magic charm made from the womb of a lioness, or the liver of a cat, or the tooth of a child. Some of these customs, in modified form, survived into the Victorian era, and some exist even in the present. At one time, the women of Japan ate dead bees, and the women of North Africa stoically swallowed froth from a camel's mouth. In parts of medieval Europe, women were calmly instructed to spit three times into the mouth of a frog. To this day, women of Australasian tribes hold themselves perfectly rigid during intercourse in the mistaken belief that an orgasm causes the release of the egg.

The Italian anatomist Gabriele Falloppio introduced, in 1564, the forerunner of the modern condom. He devised a linen sheath to cover the penis as a guard against syphilis. In 1929, the Berlin gynecologist Ernst Gräfenberg fashioned a ring of surgical silk or silver that was inserted into the uterus. This was the predecessor of the modern IUD (intrauterine device). The principle of the IUD dates back to the ancient practice of Arabian and Turkish camel drivers, who put smooth, round pebbles into the womb of a camel at the start of a long trip to avoid the problem of a pregnant animal en route.

Because of the more liberal climate of recent years, we tend to forget that public acceptance of contraception was initially slow and turbulent. Prominent in organizing an active birth control movement in the early 1900s were Marie Stopes in England and Margaret Sanger in America. Sanger's relentless cause was "to give every woman control over her own body" by offering her the means to prevent pregnancy. Sanger crusaded so vigorously that she was once imprisoned for 30 days in New York as a "public nuisance." She had been convicted for being too vocal in encouraging women not to be burdened with unwanted children. She zealously sought for women freedom from fear of an unwanted pregnancy.

Convinced that a trouble-free female technique of birth control could be developed, Sanger offered a small research fund ($2,100) in 1950 to Gregory Pincus, a biologist at the Worcester Institute for Experimental Biology in Massachusetts. Within one year, in 1951, Pincus and his associate Min-Chueh Chang had found that the oral intake of a synthetic progesterone (progestin) in female rabbits and rats inhibited ovulation. In collaboration with gynecologist John Rock of Harvard University, clinical tests were undertaken on human subjects in 1956 in several American cities. The synthetic progesterone proved an effective contraceptive, but abnormal and irregular menstrual bleeding was encountered. Additional tests revealed that the combination of progesterone and estrogen gave excellent control of both ovulation and menstrual flow. The first oral contraceptive, G. D. Searle's Enovid, was approved for public use in 1960, and the modern contraceptive era had been launched.

There is at present no ideal contraceptive; no method is as yet entirely free of complicating or disquieting features. We will examine the varied contraceptive techniques practiced today, although some are of very limited effectiveness.

COITUS INTERRUPTUS

One of the oldest methods of contraception is *coitus interruptus*, in which the male withdraws the penis from the vagina just prior to ejaculation. It is commonly called "withdrawal," and often "being careful." This practice is forbidden by the Roman Catholic Church, since the technique is "unnatural" and therefore sinful to use. On the grounds that sex itself is sinful unless procreation in intended, the Old Testament also prohibits withdrawal for those of the Jewish faith. Nevertheless, the sociological reality is that coitus interruptus remains as one of the more commonly used contraceptive techniques in European cultures.

The failure rate of withdrawal is high, as table 2.1 shows, because many men experience difficulty in terminating intercourse abruptly. Aside from creating tension in the sexual relation, the method is unsatisfactory because a drop of semen may issue from the penis even before ejaculation. The first drops of semen expelled usually contain high concentrations of sperm. The advantages of the method are its availability to all, lack of need for appliances or prior preparation, and lack of cost. It can be practiced without apparent physical harm, but the risks are high.

THE CONDOM

The most prevalent contraceptive device is the condom, a term derived from the Latin *condus*, meaning "receptacle." This cylinderlike receptacle, worn tightly over the erect penis, was originally designed as a prophylactic against venereal infection. Condoms were initially prepared from the intestine of sheep and other animals; later they were manufactured from rubber, and more recently from thin plastics that are inert and able to be stored indefinitely. The condom is inexpensive, easily obtainable, and simple to use. When properly used, condoms rank relatively high in effectiveness (table 2.1).

The most popular condoms are prelubricated, but the lubricant (glycerine or silicone) is only mildly spermicidal. Medical specialists advocate the addition of a spermicidal cream or jelly for maximum safety. The condom often contains a dome-shaped tip, or reservoir, at the end to hold the ejaculate. The condom is without clinical side effects, although it tends to dull sensation during intercourse. High standards of manufacture ensure that condoms are virtually free of structural defects; most failures

Table 2.1
Effectiveness of Contraceptive Methods

	PREGNANCIES PER 100 WOMEN PER YEAR[a]	
Method	*High*[b]	*Low*
No contraceptive[c]	80	40
Coitus interruptus	23	15
Condom[d]	17	8
Douche	61	34
Chemicals (spermicides)[e]	40	9
Diaphragm and jelly	28	11
Rhythm[f]	58	14
Pill	2	0.03
IUD	8	3
Sterilization	0.003	0

[a] Data describe the number of women per 100 who will become pregnant in a one-year period while using a given method.

[b] High and low values represent best and worst estimates from various demographic and clinical studies.

[c] In the complete absence of contraceptive practice, 8 out of 10 women can expect to become pregnant within one year.

[d] Effectiveness increases if spermicidal jelly or cream is used in addition.

[e] Aerosol foam is considered to be the best of the chemical barriers.

[f] Use of a clinical thermometer to record daily temperatures increases effectiveness.

of the condom are attributable to faulty use. In particular, care must be taken to prevent leakage of semen into or near the vagina when the condom is removed following the male orgasm.

DOUCHING AND SPERMICIDES

Douching solutions, typically prepared from household substances such as vinegar, lemon juice, or soap chips, have been used to flush the vagina immediately after intercourse. Vinegar was first used in Greek and Roman times. The intent is to remove sperm from the vagina before they migrate through the cervix. Not only is it virtually impossible to wash away all sperm, but sperm can reach the cervical opening within 90 seconds of the male's ejaculation. The method is of limited effectiveness (table 2.1), and is rapidly giving way to more efficient, modern contraceptive choices. Douching was once popular in European countries, particularly where a standard bathroom fixture is the bidet, a low sink in which the woman bathes in a sitting posture.

Chemical preparations or spermicides—creams and jellies, foaming tablets, and suppositories—act by immobilizing the sperm that are deposited in the vagina. Placing suppositories in the vagina before coitus dates back 3,000 years to the practice in Egypt. At that time, the suppository was made of crocodile dung. The modern equivalent consists of an oil base (gelatine or cocoa butter) to which an artificial chemical spermicide (hexylresorcinol or quinine, for example) has been added. An aerosol foam has been developed that is essentially a spermicidal cream in compressed form in an aerosol-type container. Presumably the thick efferves-

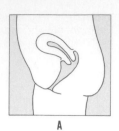

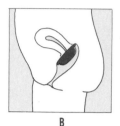

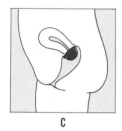

Figure 2.1 Position of the uterus in relation to the vagina *(A),* and the manner in which the diaphragm *(B)* and cervical cap *(C)* occlude the entrance to the cervix.

cent foam coats the walls of the vagina with a protective film that prevents sperm penetration. The aerosol foam is considered the best of the chemical barriers.

The varied chemical preparations are easy to apply, do not require a physician's prescription, and have no harmful side effects. However, the overriding consideration is the relatively high failure rate of spermicides (table 2.1). Spermicides are superior to douching or the rhythm method, but are less effective than the condom or diaphragm. The contraceptive creams and jellies are best employed in conjunction with the diaphragm or cervical cap.

DIAPHRAGM AND CERVICAL CAP

An important method of contraception is the use of a mechanical barrier that covers the cervix. Until the oral contraceptive appeared on the scene, the dome-shaped diaphragm and the thimble-shaped cap were the basic devices that many birth control clinics advocated. A study in 1959 revealed that one in three American couples used the diaphragm. The diaphragm, a shallow rubber cup with a semirigid rim, must be correctly fitted for size by a physician (fig. 2.1). A spermicidal cream is customarily spread around the rim and squeezed into the cup itself. Rubber cervical caps are tight-fitting and are partly held in place by suction.

A correctly positioned diaphragm cannot be felt by the woman or her sexual partner and does not lessen sexual sensations. This device is suitable for the woman who conscientiously uses it on every occasion she has or expects to have intercourse. Many women routinely insert the diaphragm each night. Since sperm retain the capacity to fertilize an egg for several hours, the diaphragm should be left in place for at least six hours after intercourse.

The diaphragm is reasonably effective when properly inserted. It can be used over and over, and has no harmful medical side effects. The failure rate (table 2.1) reflects improper fit of the diaphragm or its displacement during intercourse. Refitting of the diaphragm is essential after the birth of a child.

THE RHYTHM METHOD

Rhythm means abstaining from intercourse during the fertile days of the month. The rhythm method requires no equipment but a calendar; however, no amount of calendar watching can provide assurance that a particular time in the month is absolutely safe in the sense that conception will not occur. The efficiency of the rhythm method depends entirely on calculating the time of ovulation, or rather on estimating it. Needless to say, the precise date of this event cannot be accurately predicted. This method of birth control is quite unreliable (table 2.1), but it is the only one, other than abstinence, that is cautiously condoned by the Roman Catholic Church. Aside from the unreliability of this method, great self-discipline is required to confine intercourse to a limited number of days in the month.

The high rate of failure of the rhythm method is largely due to irregularities of the menstrual cycles of women. Ideally, in a perfect 28-day cycle, ovulation occurs on the 14th day after the 1st day of the preceding menstrual period (fig. 2.2). This is, in reality, subject to a variation of two days in either direction; thus, days 12 to 16 are possible times for the release of the egg. Two days are allowed for freshly deposited sperm to perish; hence, days 10 and 11 are viewed as unsafe (conception may

THE THEORY OF RHYTHM

28 DAY CYCLE

1 MENSTRUATION BEGINS	**2**	**3**	**4**	**5**	**6**	**7**
8	**9**	**10** | **11** INTERCOURSE ON THESE DAYS LEAVES LIVE SPERM TO FERTILIZE EGG		**12** | **13** | **14** RIPE EGG MAY BE RELEASED ON ANY OF THESE DAYS		
15 | **16** RIPE EGG MAY ALSO BE RELEASED ON THESE DAYS		**17** EGG MAY STILL BE PRESENT	**18**	**19**	**20**	**21**
22	**23**	**24**	**25**	**26**	**27**	**28**
1 MENSTRUATION BEGINS AGAIN						

BLACK NUMBERS - "SAFE DAYS"

COLORED NUMBERS - "UNSAFE DAYS"

occur) since intercourse on these days may leave live sperm to fertilize the egg. One additional day (day 17) after ovulation is provided for the unfertilized egg itself to perish. Thus, eight days (10–17) constitute the period of maximum fertility, when it is unsafe to have intercourse.

Very few women show an absolutely regular 28-day cycle. Typically the menstrual period varies at different times. A woman can keep a record of her menstrual cycles for a year, counting the day on which menstruation begins as the first day of each period. Knowing the number of days in her shortest and longest cycles, she can calculate from a standard chart (table 2.2) her first and last unsafe days. Thus, in the case of a woman whose cycles ranged from 26 days (shortest period) to 30 days (longest period), the unsafe periods would extend from the 8th day through and including the 19th day (table 2.2). For women who have cycles of less than 20 days or cycles varying by more than 10 days, the rhythm method is wholly unsuitable. The cycles of these women are virtually unpredictable; it is estimated that one-sixth of all women in the population are irregular. Moreover, the rhythm method is quite unsuitable for several months following childbirth, during which time the woman's menstrual cycle is being reorganized and even rearranged. In menopausal women with highly irregular cycles, the rhythm method would be ill-fated and ill-advised.

A ready solution to the problem of accurately determining the exact time of ovulation has thus far been elusive. A slight shift in body temperature sometimes occurs following the rupture of the follicle. As seen in figure 2.3, the body temperature drops about 0.3 degree on the Fahrenheit scale at the time of ovulation, and rises about 0.6°F immediately following ovulation. The relatively high body temperature (98.4°F) of the postovulatory phase of the menstrual cycle is associated with the increased levels of progesterone in the bloodstream. With a basal thermometer, a woman may keep a daily record of her normal resting body temperature. This means that the temperature must be taken upon waking

Table 2.2
The Rhythm Method: Calculation of Safe and Unsafe Days

Length of Shortest Menstrual Cycle (in Days)	First Unsafe Day after Start of Any Menstrual Period	Length of Longest Menstrual Cycle (in Days)	Last Unsafe Day after Start of Any Menstrual Period
20	2nd	20	9th
21	3rd	21	10th
22	4th	22	11th
23	5th	23	12th
24	6th	24	13th
25	7th	25	14th
26	8th	26	15th
27	9th	27	16th
28	10th	28	17th
29	11th	29	18th
30	12th	30	19th
31	13th	31	20th
32	14th	32	21st
33	15th	33	22nd
34	16th	34	23rd
35	17th	35	24th
36	18th	36	25th
37	19th	37	26th
38	20th	38	27th
39	21st	39	28th
40	22nd	40	29th

Note: Safe means that conception probably will not occur. *Unsafe* means that conception probably will occur.

To use this table, define shortest and longest menstrual cycles over a year. Extent of probable unsafe period is from first to last unsafe day, judged from length of shortest cycle and longest cycle during the year.

Figure 2.3 Temperature curve showing the slight rise in temperature (less than 1°F) *after* ovulation has occurred on day 14 of an absolutely regular 28-day menstrual cycle. (From J. Peel and M. Potts, *Textbook of contraceptive practice,* 1969, Cambridge University Press.)

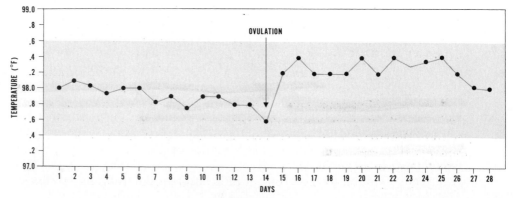

each morning—after having rested for at least one hour, and without smoking or drinking before taking the temperature. Even then, the temperature chart is subject to misinterpretation, since minor illness and mild emotional problems can affect the body temperature. This procedure has not been enthusiastically received by women.

Another attempt to pinpoint ovulation depends on the observation that the consistency of the cervical mucus varies with the time of the month. This mucus has its thinnest consistency at the time of ovulation, and forms an interesting fernlike pattern after being dried on a glass slide (fig. 2.4). The cyclic variations in the pattern, however, are not sufficiently sensitive to establish the time of ovulation with any degree of accuracy.

The rhythm method seems to be a failure in another important respect. There is suggestive evidence that sexual activity on the so-called safe 18th day, which typically is heightened following several days of abstinence, may be associated with a higher-than-expected incidence of fertilization of aging, or aged, eggs. Two birth abnormalities in humans—anencephaly (absence of brain) and spina bifida (split spinal cord)—occur with such relatively high frequencies as to suggest that factors in addition to inheritance are operating. According to hospital records in Boston, Massachusetts, the newborn of Catholic parents have the highest incidence of both malformations, a combined rate of 2.8 per 1,000 births. Two per 1,000 offspring of Protestant parents are afflicted, whereas only 0.7 per 1,000 offspring of Jewish parents are affected with both abnormalities. The British scientist Raymond G. Cross has attributed the high incidence of the two birth abnormalities among Catholics to the rhythm method. This interpretation is enhanced by the low rate of birth abnormalities among Orthodox Jews, who observe the rule of Niddah—complete abstinence from intercourse for seven days after menstruation. In Orthodox Jewish marriages, therefore, intercourse commences at, or close to, the expected date of ovulation (the 13th day).

ORAL CONTRACEPTIVES

The oral contraceptive ("the pill") has modified the lives of many modern women. The pill is widely used by women in many countries and of every social stratum. It is a method of contraception that is aesthetically acceptable to women and almost completely effective. The failure rate of oral contraceptives is very low, less than 1 pregnancy among 100 women in the course of a year (table 2.1).

The action of the pill is suppression of ovulation. There are at least 20 different kinds of pills, but all fall essentially into two general categories: the *combined* type and the *sequential* type. Combined tablets contain an estrogen derivative (typically mestranol) together with a synthetic progesterone (such as norethynodrel). The combined tablet is taken on 20 successive days, starting on the fifth day of the cycle (that is, the fifth day after menstruation starts). After 20 days, the dose is discontinued to permit withdrawal bleeding, which is similar to normal menstruation. Uterine bleeding follows about 3 days after the dose is discontinued. The 20-day regime of tablets then starts again 5 days after the onset of menstruation. Menstrual flow is generally reduced, which is an additional benefit for women who normally have heavy and uncomfortable periods. Moreover, there is general agreement that the pill alleviates premenstrual tension.

With the sequential type of pill, estrogen is administered alone for the first 15 days, followed by a mixture of estrogen and progesterone for 5

PREOVULATION
(Day 9)

OVULATION
(Day 14)

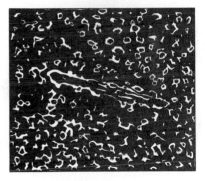

POSTOVULATION
(Day 17)

Figure 2.4 The varied appearances microscopically of the cervical mucus of the human female at different times of the menstrual cycle. When a drop of cervical mucus is placed on a glass slide, crystal patterns are seen under the microscope as the mucus dries. The patterns are most pronounced (fernlike) at ovulation, when the mucus is thin, watery, and readily penetrated by sperm.

days. The sequential pill is said to be more natural than the combined type, since the sequence of administered hormones more nearly parallels the hormonal changes that occur during the normal menstrual cycle. However, the sequential pill has been claimed to be slightly less effective than the combined pill. It has been suggested that the sequential preparation produces less alteration of the endometrium. Stated another way, the combined preparation apparently has a more drastic effect on the uterine lining, and hence causes the endometrium to be completely unsuitable for receiving the fertilized egg even if ovulation and fertilization were to take place. Hence, occasional ovulation or occasional pregnancy breakthroughs, or both, are less likely to occur with the combined preparation.

However, accompanying the reduced risk of pregnancy with the combined type is the hazard that the combined pill has a more severe effect than the sequential pill on the release of hormones by the pituitary gland. The vast majority of women using the combined preparation resume normal ovulation within six months after stopping the medication. It has been estimated that 10 percent require up to a year to return to normal, and that 1 to 2 percent require a longer period, or even drug therapy (for example, with clomiphene), to overcome the apparently strong suppression of the pituitary.

The mechanism of action of either the combined or the sequential pill is complex and not all aspects are as yet understood. The known effects on LH and FSH are shown in Figure 2.5. Both LH and FSH production are suppressed by the combination type of pill, and their levels

Figure 2.5 Fluctuations in FSH and LH during a normal menstrual cycle (A), and during fertility control with a combined type of pill (B) and a sequential type of pill (C). (From W. D. Odell and D. L. Moyer, *Physiology of reproduction,* 1971, The C. V. Mosby Co.)

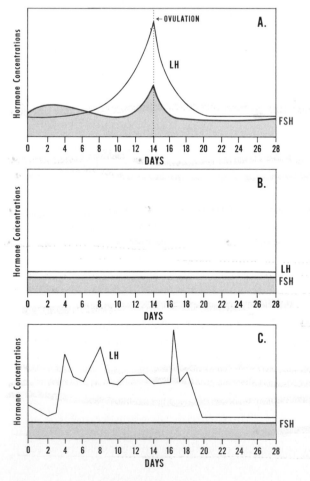

remain remarkably low and constant throughout the cycle. There is no early rise in FSH secretion and no midcycle peak in LH secretion (fig. 2.5B). In the absence of the normal ovulatory LH surge, the egg cannot be released. In the sequential type, the estrogen treatment appears to stimulate production of LH, but not of FSH. The blood concentration of LH increases repeatedly in unusual multiple peaks (fig. 2.5C). When progesterone is added, one or more surges of LH secretion occur. It appears, then, that ovulation is inhibited primarily by influencing the output of FSH. By abolishing the normally early rise of FSH, the initiation of follicle growth is impeded.

Women have now taken the pill for well over 10 years, and the side effects are generally minimal. There may be initially a period of nausea and dizziness, a tendency to put on weight, some discomforting tenderness of the breasts, and occasional dark pigmentation under the eyes, but these effects are not usually serious and are often temporary. Only in exceptional cases are these problems sufficiently severe for discontinuation of the medication to be prescribed.

One real caution must be observed in prescribing the pill for women who are overweight for their height, and for women past 35 years of age. Such women are prone to *thromboembolism*, the formation of obstructive clots within blood vessels. Several studies have confirmed that thromboembolism is a potential complication of oral contraception. The mortality directly owing to oral contraceptives has been calculated at 1.3 per 100,000 women in the 20 to 34 age group, and 3.4 per 100,000 in the 35 to 44 age group.

Unfavorable publicity in 1968–70 dampened the popularity of the pill, but only temporarily. While evidence does indicate that the pill occasionally causes thromboembolism, the danger has finally been placed in its proper perspective. Thromboembolism also occurs as an unwelcome by-product of pregnancy. Specifically, the chances of developing thromboembolic disease as a complication of pregnancy are about 3 times greater than the risk of this disease as a consequence of taking the pill. Viewed in this manner, pregnancy is the more hazardous affair.

The tendency of oral contraceptives to cause obstructive blood clots is attributable to the presence of high estrogen levels. It appears, then, that preparations with low estrogen dosage are less detrimental in relation to thromboembolism. The risks would be negligible if progesterone alone could be made into an acceptable oral contraceptive. As stated earlier, progesterone alone causes menstrual disturbances, particularly bleeding at irregular, unexpected times.

There are provocative findings in the medical literature that the sequential type of pill, which is highly estrogenic in both dosage and activity, is associated with malignant changes in the breast and uterine endometrium. There is, at present, no absolute proof that the prolonged use of the pill induces, or increases the risk of, cancer of the breast and of the reproductive organs. Reported cases of malignancy may have been due to excessive estrogenic stimulation or some other unknown carcinogenic agent. It is exceedingly difficult to prove in humans that a specific substance or agent causes cancer. Certain cancerous growths appear to be associated with imbalances of circulating hormones, but the data are inconclusive and incomplete. The causes of cancer are not now known, and the situation is further complicated by the long latent period before cancer expresses itself. In essence, no definitive statements can now be made about possible long-term harmful effects of the pill.

Certain investigators have offered yet another possible hazard of the use of the pill: the risks of birth defects may be increased in babies born to women who become pregnant soon after discontinuing the pill. Women are advised to change to a different type of birth control after going off the pill and await the time when the regular menstrual cycle is reestablished before planning to become pregnant.

THE INTRAUTERINE DEVICE

In the 1920s, the German physician Ernst Gräfenberg attempted to popularize the *intrauterine device, or IUD,* a pliable coil of silver placed in the uterus after dilation of the cervix. His silver ring fell into disfavor because of unwelcome side effects, which included uterine irritation and perforation (that is, migration through the uterine wall into the body cavity). About two decades ago, less reactive plastic (polyethylene) devices were introduced, and these inert IUDs were found to have minimal side effects and a high degree of effectiveness. Some IUDs are made of copper or stainless steel with a plastic coating.

The IUD still carries a risk of pregnancy, but the failure rate is lower than any other contraceptive method except the pill (table 2.1). Unlike the pill, however, the IUD requires no daily motivation, forethought, or planned program. Once inserted, the IUD requires no continued effort; it is not subject to carelessness or memory failure. The IUD is inserted by a physician, usually during menstruation when the cervical canal is dilated. Unfortunately, IUDs tend to be expelled spontaneously from the uterus; between 4 and 30 percent are expelled in the first year of insertion. Women may initially experience uterine cramps and heavy bleeding, but the IUD is later tolerated well by most women despite heavier menstruation.

There are a variety of IUD designs (fig. 2.6). John Lippes of the University of Buffalo designed a double-S polyethylene loop. The Lippes loop has a nylon thread projecting into the vagina, by which the presence of

Figure 2.6 Variety of intrauterine devices.

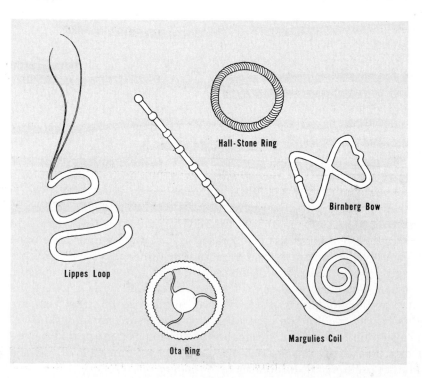

the loop can be continually checked. Other kinds of IUDs include the Margulies spiral, the Birnberg bow in the shape of an hourglass, the Hall-Stone ring, and the Ota ring (used extensively in Japan). The shape apparently affects efficiency; the spiral and the loop appear to be most effective in preventing pregnancy, but these are the ones that are most likely to be expelled from the uterus. On the other hand, the bow is less safe but the least likely to be expelled. The highest incidence of uterine perforation occurs with the bow. A new IUD design called the Dalkon shield ("crab") was introduced in 1970 and hailed as eminently suitable for women who have never been pregnant. The shield is no longer prescribed because of complaints of pain and irregular bleeding, and a relatively high rate of pregnancy breakthroughs.

The mode of action of the IUD is still not fully understood. It was once believed that the device inhibited the movement of sperm through the uterus, but sperm have been found in the Fallopian tubes of women wearing IUDs. Another early suggestion, subsequently shown to be false, was that the IUD hastened the movement of the egg down the Fallopian tube. Hence, it was incorrectly held that the egg either entered the uterus before the uterine wall was prepared to receive the egg or was expelled prematurely before fertilization could take place. Current studies show increased quantities of white blood cells in the uterine lining with the use of the IUD. The response of the uterine wall to the foreign object is inflammation, but not of the infectious type. The increased numbers of white blood cells, or their products, thus appear to affect the endometrium of the uterus by rendering it unsuitable for implantation or survival of the embryo. In a large sense, the IUD erases the distinction between contraception and abortion. The IUD is generally dispensed as a contraceptive, but it acts as an aborticide in preventing the implantation of the embryo in the uterine wall.

Since the modern versions of the IUDs have been used for only about a decade, the possible long-term effects are not yet recognizable. One favorable aspect is that IUDs do not interfere with the hormonal cycle of the woman. There is no evidence that IUDs are carcinogenic.

STERILIZATION

The ultimate method of suppressing conception is sterilization. This is an effective method of fertility control. In the male, the vas deferens on each side is ligated and a small piece excised (fig. 2.7). This procedure, known as vasectomy, blocks the pathway of the sperm from the testes, and the sperm are resorbed in the vasa deferentia. The procedure is almost wholly successful; it is also nearly always irreversible, for there is only a slight possibility of the spontaneous reunion of the severed vasa deferentia. Vasectomy is a simple surgical procedure that requires only local anesthesia and can be completed in 10 minutes. A man's sexual life can continue unchanged following the operation.

Vasectomy is not entirely free of medical consequences. Inflammation of the walls of veins and blood clotting are at least two of the complications that may occur following vasectomy. Clots in blood vessels have occurred within one or two years after the operation. The unexpected complications have raised reasonable doubt concerning the assumed complete safety of vasectomy.

Sterilization of the woman is usually carried out by *tubal ligation*. In the conventional operation, the Fallopian tubes are cut on each side and tied (fig. 2.7). A new surgical procedure, called *laparoscopic sterilization*,

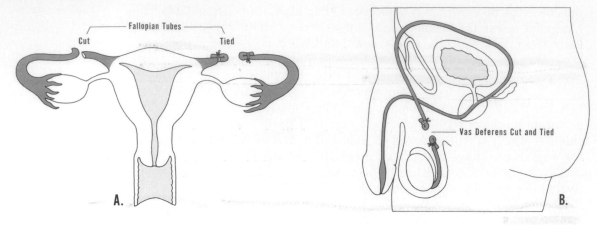

Figure 2.7 Sterilization operations: Tubal ligation in the female *(A)* and vasectomy in the male *(B)*.

involves introducing a specialized instrument through a very small abdominal incision and severing the Fallopian tubes with a weak electric current. The cut ends eventually become sealed with scar tissue. The eggs cannot reach the uterus, nor can sperm reach the site of fertilization. Blockage of the Fallopian tubes is permanent; reversal of the surgical procedure is theoretically possible but practically difficult.

ABORTION

The unpredictability of human sexual practices, the uncontrolled variations in the female menstrual cycle, and the imperfect nature of contraceptives all contribute to making unwanted pregnancy inevitable. While one may deplore the idea of deliberate abortion, one has to come to terms with abortion as a means of ending unwanted pregnancies. Irrespective of whether a fetus is incomplete and expendable, or whether a fetus is human and inviolable, the problem is unwanted pregnancy and how to treat it. The way to deal with the problem, many contend, is on terms that permit the individual, guided by conscience and intelligence, to make a decision unhampered by social, religious, and legal sanctions. But social, religious, and legal restraints do exist.

Abortion is illegal in many countries, and is condemned on religious and moral grounds. Only very recently and gradually have some of the sanctions been lifted. On January 22, 1973, the United States Supreme Court, in a landmark decision entitled *Roe v. Wade,* granted American women the constitutionally protected right to seek termination of a pregnancy under suitable medical safeguards. The Court's decision placed great emphasis on the right of the woman to decide what to do with her own body. The states cannot interfere with the decision of a woman to have an abortion during the first three months of pregnancy. After the end of this first trimester of pregnancy, a state may regulate abortion procedures to an extent reasonably related to the preservation and protection of the mother's health.

Almost immediately after the Court's decision, several state legislatures attempted to undermine the right of the woman to terminate a pregnancy. The legal maze remains extraordinary. Hospital policy boards continue to debate the issue sharply. Some still-existing state laws stipulate that a threat to the life of the pregnant woman is the sole legal ground on which interruption of pregnancy may be based. Abortion policies are substantially more liberal in such countries as Sweden and Denmark than in the United States. In Japan, interruption of pregnancy is permissible for economic as well as medical reasons, with the result that abortion is available without restriction.

Hospital abortions are usually quite safe, especially during the first trimester of pregnancy. Until the 12th week of pregnancy, a technique that was once standard is *dilatation and curettage*, or D & C. The cervical opening is gently enlarged using graduated instruments (*dilators*), and the lining of the uterus is scraped with a small, scoop-shaped device called a *curette*. The entire procedure, done under either general or local anesthesia, can take as little as 15 minutes. A newer method, also performed only through the 12th week of pregnancy, is known as *vacuum aspiration*, or *suction curettage*. The operation consists of dilating the cervix, inserting a metal tube attached to a small vacuum pump, and drawing off the conceptus. Vacuum aspiration involves less loss of blood and leads to fewer complications than dilatation and curettage. In more advanced pregnancies (after three months), abortion can be induced by injecting a salt solution into the amniotic sac, thus starting labor contractions that expel the fetus (within about 20 hours).

According to Roman Catholic moral theology, the right to life of a human being derives not from the parents or from society, but directly from God. The Catholic Church's stand is that abortion is forbidden, even to save a woman's life, because the fetus is equally sacred. Modern Catholic clerics, adopting the knowledge of the recently discovered DNA code, have urged that a newly fertilized egg is a human being because it contains a unique genetic code that characterizes that individual throughout life. As they see it, the conceptus is a living continuum from the moment of fertilization. If humanness is established at fertilization, then birth control methods that prevent implantation of the conceptus, such as the intrauterine device, would be considered methods of abortion rather than of contraception. In the final analysis, there is no convincing retort to those who have the firm conviction that abortion takes the life of a real human being. Certainly those who adhere to this position will themselves avoid abortion and will continue to condemn those who condone abortion.

In contrast to Roman Catholic doctrine, most other Western religions view the mother's life as primary. Many Jews (particularly those of the Reform wing) accept abortion because they regard a fetus, until birth, as an organic part of the mother and not as a living soul. The National Council of Churches has approved performing of hospital abortions "when the health or life of the mother is at stake," and many clergymen broadly define health to mean social as well as physical well-being.

It should be clear that no woman subjects herself to an abortion unless she *has* to. Most women who have an abortion do not regard it as "just another" surgical treatment. Abortion remains, at best, an unpleasant experience.

FUTURE DEVELOPMENTS

Today's contraceptive methods are likely to be superseded by better methods. On the horizon are procedures that may give permanent, but reversible, protection from conception. Tests are being made of long-acting injections of hormones. A plastic capsule containing a synthetic progesterone, used either alone or combined with estrogen, can be implanted under the skin. The hormones would be released very slowly over many months, and possibly several years. When pregnancy is desired, the subcutaneous capsule can be removed.

There is widespread interest in the development of a postcoital, or "morning-after," pill. Initially, small-scale trials involving the oral intake of a synthetic estrogen (diethylstilbestrol, or DES) for five days after intercourse proved encouraging. However, the large daily doses of DES typically cause severe adverse reactions, including nausea, vomiting, and excessive bleeding. Moreover, DES has been implicated in the occurrence of a rare form of vaginal cancer in the daughters of women who took DES during pregnancy to prevent miscarriages. In the United States, the Food and Drug Administration approved the use of DES in postcoital pills only in cases of "rape, incest, or other emergencies so deemed by the physician."

Circulating in high concentration in the blood of pregnant women at or near labor are hormonelike substances called *prostaglandins*. They are important in starting labor contractions at term. They also can induce menstruation. The prostaglandins have already been used clinically to induce abortion, and they show promise of being effective precautionary "month-after" contraceptive agents. To minimize the controversy that is bound to arise from the abortifacient aspect of these chemicals, a woman can use these substances (in the form of intravaginal tablets) a day or so *before* her normal mensis. Thus, it would not be known whether the bleeding that ensues constitutes an abortion or simply normal menstrual flow.

Satisfactory methods for controlling fertility in the male do not now exist, although attempts to interfere chemically with sperm production or sperm maturation are being undertaken. Any chemical agent that suppresses the pituitary secretions (FSH and LH) will produce antifertility effects. Estrogen and progesterone are as effective in inhibiting sperm production as in suppressing ovulation. But estrogen and progesterone also inhibit the secretions of testosterone by the testes, thereby reducing sexual drive and promoting feminizing effects (such as enlargement of the breasts). The use of estrogen as an antifertility agent in the male may not have much chance for enthusiastic acceptance.

Methods using inoculation, as in producing immunity to disease, could be highly acceptable for controlling fertility in some circumstances. Some men are naturally sterile because they produce antibodies that cause their own sperm to collect in clumps. When experimental animals (for example, guinea pigs) are injected with testicular cells, they produce an antisperm substance that severely impairs formation of sperm in their own testes. Conceivably then, antibodies that clump or inactivate sperm can be produced experimentally. The development of a long-acting antisperm agent that offers reversibility without affecting libido remains a distinct possibility.

UNPLANNED PREGNANCIES

The extensive research on how to control fertility suggests that a perfect, or nearly perfect, contraceptive device will soon be developed. Exhaustive studies are imperative, since it can be demonstrated that the available methods are grossly inadequate for maintaining a desired family size. The number of unplanned pregnancies in the course of couples' lives is astonishingly high, notwithstanding the good reliability of such current devices as the pill and IUD.

In the Western world, women usually marry in their early twenties, plan two or three children, and complete their desired child-bearing by their late twenties or early thirties. They then face a long postmaternity risk period during which they use the available methods of contraception to avoid additional pregnancies. Analyses in 1969 by J. F. Hulka of the

Family Size	Percentage of Couples Using Diaphragm or Condom[a]	Percentage of Couples Using Pill or IUD[b]
Four children (one unplanned)	33	26
Five children (two unplanned)	30	4
Six or more children (three or more unplanned)	21	1
Total percentage of families over planning goal	84%	31%
Three children (desired size)	16	69
	100%	100%

Source: Based on analyses by J. F. Hulka (1969).

[a] A contraceptive effectiveness of 95 percent is assumed.

[b] A contraceptive effectiveness of 99 percent is assumed.

University of North Carolina showed that among young couples who rely on the pill or IUD after reaching a desired family size of three children, about 3 out of every 10 can expect to have additional (unplanned) children during the remaining 12 to 18 years of their fertile marriage (table 2.3). If a less effective contraceptive is used (such as the diaphragm or condom), the expectation is that 8 of 10 couples would finally have more children than planned (table 2.3).

Until better contraceptive methods are developed, Hulka's calculations present a formidable argument favoring voluntary sterilization after the last planned delivery, unless one wishes to accept induced abortion as a means of regulating family size.

SUMMARY

The once fatalistic acceptance of recurring pregnancies by many women is being replaced in recent years by a general realization that family size can be controlled. The ideal contraceptive has yet to be devised. Present methods of contraception act on differing principles. Some are mechanical barriers that keep the sperm from the presence of the egg; some are chemical in their action and cause a hostile environment for the sperm. Other methods are behavioral in that they rely on the time or mode of intercourse. The search has ever been directed toward a safe, inexpensive, simple, and individually acceptable means for limiting fertility. This search has so far culminated in the oral contraceptive, "the pill," which approaches meeting these requirements but whose action and long-term effects are still incompletely understood. The intrauterine device (IUD) has an excellent record of effectiveness, but an unsolved problem is the high rate of spontaneous expulsion from the uterus. Sterilization is the ultimate contraception method, but it has the drawback of irreversibility. Unwanted pregnancies raise the issue of abortion, but problems of legality, morality, and conscience are prevalent. Many avenues of investigation in the control of fertility remain open, and the male has not escaped attention in such research. A variety of chemical agents are known that inhibit sperm production, but unwanted effects such as the suppression of the hormonal activity of the testes have yet to be overcome.

Ethical Probe 2
Rights of the Father

The primary issue in the Supreme Court's 1973 decision in *Roe v. Wade* was whether a state has the constitutional power to interfere with the decision of a woman to have an abortion performed. The Court relegated the problem of abortion to the status of an issue in private morality. The decision to terminate a pregnancy, at least during the first trimester, was left essentially to the conscience of the pregnant woman. The interests and rights of the fetus were not directly in issue. Moreover, the Supreme Court left unanswered the question of the father's rights with respect to an abortion decision.

To many women, the right of abortion is simply the absolute right of a woman to control her own reproductive life. The compelling argument is that a woman is entitled to become pregnant (or terminate her pregnancy) at whatever time, in whatever way, and for whatever reason she alone chooses. Nevertheless, the man contributes to the fetus a comparable number of chromosomes as does the woman. Specifically, the human fetus contains 46 hereditary-bearing chromosomes— 23 from the mother and 23 from the father. Should the woman consult her partner if she wishes to terminate the pregnancy? Should the woman be required to obtain the consent of her partner prior to the abortion operation? Would such a requirement be tantamount to granting the man the right to veto the decision to abort the fetus? Such veto power would give the man the right to compel his partner to be pregnant! From a strictly legal point of view, such compulsion would undoubtedly be challenged as unconstitutional, infringing upon the right of privacy of the woman.

Does or should the man have any valid interests or rights in contributing to the woman's decision concerning abortion?

Development, Implantation, and Placentation

It takes the fertilized human egg nearly a week to find its way into the wall of the uterus (fig. 3.1). Three or four days are spent journeying through the Fallopian tube, during which time the egg has divided several times. The successive divisions of the egg are referred to as *cleavages*. After several cleavages, the embryo (no longer an egg) consists of a solid ball of cells resembling a mulberry—hence its name, *morula* (fig. 3.2). The embryo floats free in the uterine cavity for three or four days before invading and burrowing into the uterine wall. Prior to implantation, fluid-filled spaces appear between the inner cells of the morula; these spaces subsequently combine into one large cavity, or *blastocoel*. At the time of implantation, the zona pellucida disintegrates and the embryo resembles a hollow sphere, the *blastocyst*, containing approximately 100 cells.

The structure of the blastocyst is shown in figure 3.2. It bears at one pole an aggregation of cells called the *inner cell mass*, which is destined

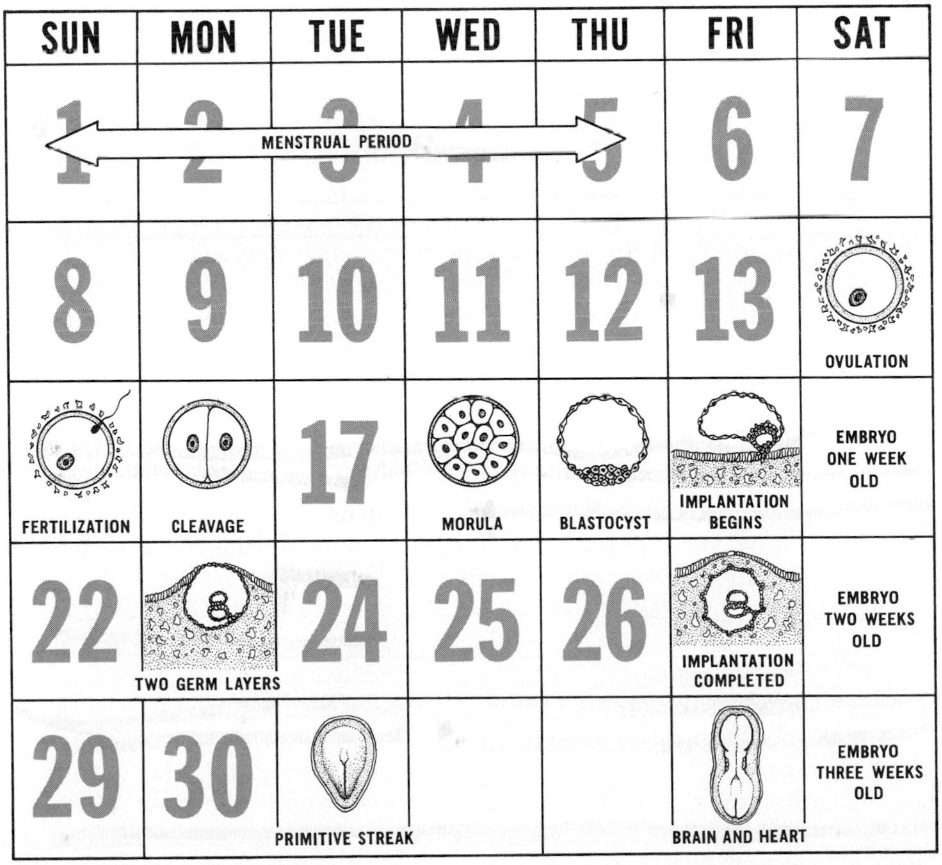

Figure 3.1 Timing of events in the development of the fertilized egg, assuming ovulation on the 14th day.

Figure 3.2 Early development of the human zygote to the blastocyst stage. A series of cleavage divisions results in a rapid increase in the number of cells. The formation of the polar bodies and the intricate chromosomal events during the division of a cell are reserved for detailed discussion later (chapter 15).

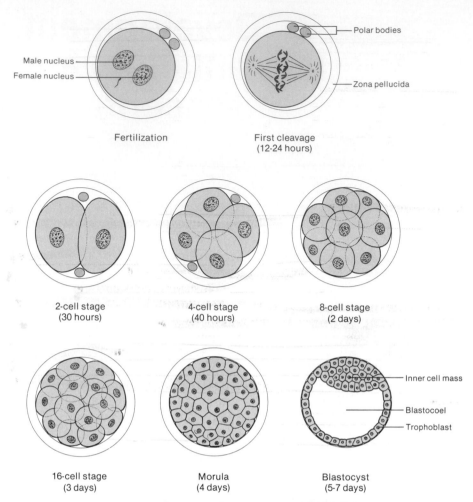

Male nucleus

Female nucleus

Fertilization

Polar bodies

Zona pellucida

First cleavage
(12-24 hours)

2-cell stage
(30 hours)

4-cell stage
(40 hours)

8-cell stage
(2 days)

16-cell stage
(3 days)

Morula
(4 days)

Inner cell mass

Blastocoel

Trophoblast

Blastocyst
(5-7 days)

to form the fetus itself. The outer rim of cells has developed into a specialized layer, known as the *trophoblast*. The highly invasive, sticky trophoblast cells attach to the endometrial surface of the uterus and secrete enzymes that break down and liquefy the endometrial tissue (fig. 3.3). The embryo thus actively digests its way into the wall of the uterus and becomes completely embedded within the rich environment of the endometrium. The nutrients that are released from the endometrial cells by the erosive action of the trophoblast are used by the developing embryo. The expanding trophoblast layer erodes the maternal blood vessels to form a system of lacunae (spaces) filled with maternal blood (fig. 3.3). During this early period, the embryo depends wholly for its nourishment and growth on the disintegrating maternal tissue that is engulfed by the trophoblastic cells. This means of obtaining nutrient material is, however, primitive and adequate only during the first few weeks. Eventually an elaborate and efficient *placenta* is formed.

The basic feature of the placenta is the intimate apposition of fetal blood vessels with the maternal circulation. But at no time during pregnancy is there an actual mingling of the blood of the mother and fetus. The placenta performs for the growing fetus the functions of gas exchange, food absorption, and excretion. To the placenta the maternal circulation carries food and oxygen, while conversely the fetal vessels convey carbon dioxide and nitrogenous wastes from its body activities. The mother disposes of the fetal wastes through her lungs and kidneys.

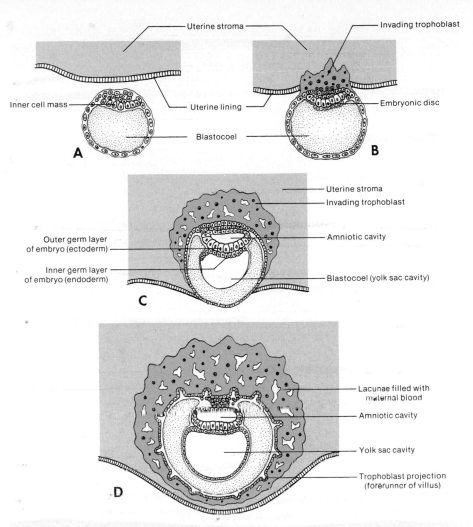

Figure 3.3 Implantation of human blastocyst. *(A)* Blastocyst in its free state in the uterine cavity. *(B)* Invasive mass of trophoblast cells spreads into the uterine tissue or stroma. *(C)* Blastocyst deeply embedded in uterine wall. The splitting apart of the trophoblast from the embryonic disc creates the amniotic cavity. *(D)* Blastocyst entirely enclosed in maternal tissue. Lacunae in the trophoblast later form the basis of the maternal circulation in the placenta (see fig. 3.6). When the endodermal layer of the embryonic disc completely lines the inside of the blastocyst, it forms an inner closed space called the *yolk sac* although it contains no yolk. (From *Reproduction in mammals*, vol. 2, eds. C. R. Austin and R. V. Short, 1972, Cambridge University Press.)

The placenta also produces several hormones that are essential for maintaining pregnancy.

Other structures besides the placenta, such as the amnion, are important to the fetus. The formation of the placenta and allied structures in the human is complex, and we can best understand these structures by comparing them with their simpler counterparts in reptiles and birds.

EXTRAEMBRYONIC MEMBRANES

Reptiles and birds, in contrast to mammals, have eggs that contain large yolk masses. Moreover, development of the embryo of these lower animals takes place entirely within a thick shell. These circumstances make necessary some special provision whereby food derived from the yolk, and oxygen obtained from an external source, can be made accessible to all parts of the developing embryo. The embryo itself constructs a complex system of membranes, known as *extraembryonic membranes*, which serve for protection, nutrition, and respiration. These are the amnion, chorion, yolk sac, and allantois. The extraembryonic membranes found in the chick embryo may be taken as an illustrative type.

Early in the development of the chick, as shown in figure 3.4, the outer layer of the embryo throws up a system of folds that arch over and ultimately enclose the whole of the definitive embryo—much as if an animal should enwrap itself in a highly exaggerated fold of its own skin. By this means, two investing, or enveloping, membranes, known as the *amnion* and the *chorion*, are formed. The amnion is derived from the inner layer of the fold whereas the chorion is derived from the outer layer. The chorion becomes abundantly supplied with blood vessels. The chick embryo depends, in part, on this outermost, vascularized enveloping membrane for carrying on gaseous exchange with the outer air through the porous shell.

When fully developed, the amnion is a thin membrane loosely enclosing the embryo. It does not fit the embryo snugly. The space between the amnion and the embryo, or *amniotic cavity*, is filled with a watery fluid, the *amniotic fluid*. The fluid is a cushion that protects the embryo from mechanical pressures and impacts and, at the same time, allows it freedom of movement. The chemical composition of the amniotic fluid resembles the chemical makeup of blood. Thus the embryo during its development is bathed by a fluid that is compatible in its chemical nature with the embryo's blood. An interesting fact is that for the chick embryo, as well as for the human fetus, the amniotic fluid resembles seawater in chemical composition, in terms of elements (ions) such as sodium, potassium, calcium, and magnesium. After approximately 400 million years of evolution on land, vertebrates still carry essentially the chemical composition of seawater in their fluids—amniotic fluid, blood, and other body fluids. This has been interpreted as indicating that life originated in the sea, and that the balance of salts in various body fluids did not change very much in subsequent evolution. University of Michigan embryologist Bradley Patten picturesquely characterized the amnion as a sort of private aquarium in which the embryos of land-living vertebrates recapitulate the water-living mode of existence of their remote ancestors.

In reexamining figure 3.4, we can see that the enormous mass of yolk has been enclosed by an internal circular membrane, the *yolk sac*. This membrane, which has formed by growing over the yolk, is attached to the embryonic body by a narrow stalk. The yolk sac is highly vascular, its many blood vessels communicating with the blood channels of the embryo proper. The blood circulating through the vessels of the yolk sac

Figure 3.4 Stages in the formation of the extraembryonic membranes of the chick—the amnion, allantois, chorion, and yolk sac. Color highlights the distribution of the intermediate germ layer, or mesoderm. (From L. B. Arey, *Developmental anatomy*, 7th rev. ed., 1960, W. B. Saunders Co.)

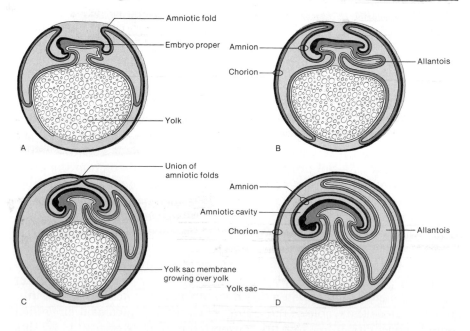

carries dissolved yolk materials to all parts of the embryo, thus making the yolk available for chemical activities and growth in all regions.

From the hind region of the embryonic body, a sac bulges out on the underside and pushes its way between the yolk sac and chorion. This sac is the *allantois* (fig. 3.4). The allantois grows rapidly and eventually enlarges so that the greater part of its outer surface occupies an extensive area just inside the shell. An appreciable part of the blood of the embryo is diverted into the allantois, where a rich system of blood vessels lies close to the inner surface of the shell. The porous shell permits the ready exchange of respiratory gases between the external air and the internal blood. The allantoic sac serves also as a receptacle for urinary wastes. Waste fluids excreted by the embryonic kidneys pass into the cavity of the allantois. The allantois thus has both respiratory and excretory functions.

HUMAN EXTRAEMBRYONIC MEMBRANES

The amnion, chorion, allantois, and yolk sac in the human embryo are essentially similar to these structures developed in the reptiles and birds. The method of origin of the membranes, particularly the amnion, differs in the human embryo, which largely reflects the dearth of yolk in the human egg. The human amnion does not form in a leisurely manner by a folding process, but arises precociously in a unique manner. As seen in figure 3.3, the amniotic cavity arises when the trophoblast simply splits apart from the embryonic disc. The yolk sac also forms very early as a layer of cells that spreads around the inside of the hollow blastocyst (fig. 3.3). Nevertheless, once the membranes are established, the composition of the membranes, their relations to the embryonic body, and also their relations to each other reveal the basic similarities of the extraembryonic membranes of man and the other land-living vertebrates. This may be seen by examining figure 3.5 and comparing the illustration with figure 3.4.

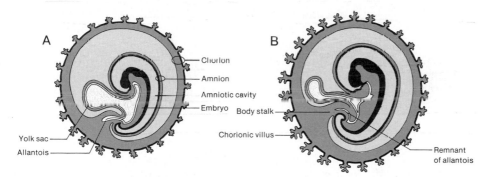

Figure 3.5 Stages in the formation of the extraembryonic membranes of the human—the amnion, allantois, chorion, and yolk sac. Color highlights the distribution of the intermediate germ layer, or mesoderm. (Compare with figure 3.4.)

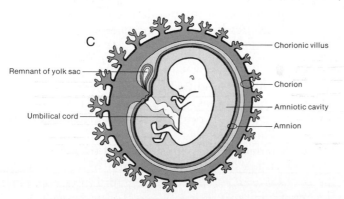

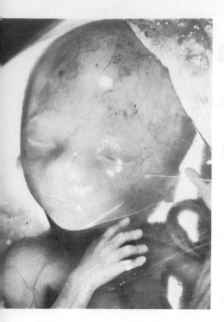

Figure 3.6 The thin amniotic sac, or "bag," typically ruptures during birth, liberating the "waters." Occasionally the head of a child is born with an unbroken amnion still surrounding it like a veil, a condition that has long been superstitiously considered an omen of good luck.

During early development, the embryonic cells become rearranged into three *germ layers*, called the *ectoderm* (outer layer), *endoderm* (inner layer), and *mesoderm* (intermediate layer). These germ layers comprise the material out of which the embryo and all its parts will differentiate. As a generalization, the ectoderm gives rise to the skin and nervous system (brain, spinal cord, and nerves); the endoderm gives rise to the digestive organs (stomach, intestine, liver, and pancreas) and respiratory organs (trachea, bronchi, and lungs); and the mesoderm provides the muscles, connective tissues, blood, heart, and skeletal components. Although the germ layers will be discussed in detail in a subsequent chapter, brief knowledge of them is useful at this point for descriptive and comparative purposes. The germ layers are involved in the establishment of the extraembryonic membranes. In both the chick and the human embryos, the amnion and the chorion are double-layered membranes, made up of ectoderm and mesoderm (figs. 3.4 and 3.5). As in the chick, water diffuses from the developing human embryo into the amniotic cavity to form the cushiony amniotic fluid. The thin, tough human amniotic sac is popularly called the "bag of waters" (fig. 3.6).

The germ layer composition of the yolk sac is also the same in chick and human embryos. The yolk sac is an endodermal derivative of the primitive digestive cavity that becomes lined with mesoderm. There are, accordingly, striking similarities in the composition of the extraembryonic membranes of birds and man. Curiously, the yolk sac does develop in the human embryo in spite of the absence of any appreciable amount of yolk (fig. 3.5). The human yolk sac, however, remains small and functionless.

There is no elaborate development of the allantois in the human embryo. The allantoic sac never becomes more than a rudimentary tube of minute size. The allantoic blood vessels, however, become vastly important since in humans they not only carry off waste products from the embryo, as in reptiles and birds, but also assume the function of conveying nutrients from the mother to the embryo. In assuming this new function they are no longer concerned with the allantoic sac proper but enter into a new relation with the chorion.

The yolk sac and allantoic sac bear the same anatomical relation to the embryonic body as they do in the yolk-laden embryos of reptiles and birds. The appearance of the yolk sac and allantois in the human embryo is one of the strongest pieces of evidence documenting the evolutionary relationships between the widely different kinds of vertebrates. To the student of evolution this means that the mammals, including man, are descended from animals that reproduced by means of externally laid eggs rich in yolk. As a matter of fact, the most primitive mammals, the monotremes, possess large eggs with abundant yolk. These eggs are deposited by the female, are developed in a parchmentlike shell, and are carried about in a brood pouch.

HUMAN PLACENTA

The chorion is the most highly modified and specialized of all the mammalian extraembryonic membranes. The chorion represents the outermost investing membrane, and its origin in humans is traceable back to the trophoblast of the blastocyst stage. The original trophoblastic capsule, when it becomes underlaid with mesoderm, is transformed into the chorion. The chorion enters into the composition of the placenta. The basic step in the formation of the human placenta is the appearance of *villi* (Latin, *villus*, meaning "tuft of hair"). As seen in figure 3.7, villi are

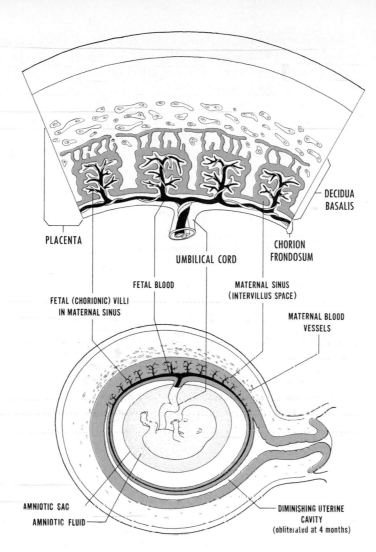

Figure 3.7 Structure of the human placenta, revealing that the blood of the fetus and the blood of the mother circulate independently in totally separate channels.

DECIDUA
BASALIS

PLACENTA

CHORION
FRONDOSUM

UMBILICAL CORD

FETAL BLOOD

MATERNAL SINUS
(INTERVILLUS SPACE)

FETAL (CHORIONIC) VILLI
IN MATERNAL SINUS

MATERNAL BLOOD
VESSELS

AMNIOTIC SAC

AMNIOTIC FLUID

DIMINISHING UTERINE
CAVITY
(obliterated at 4 months)

slender, fingerlike extensions of the chorion that penetrate deeply into the uterine tissue. The villi enlarge and branch extensively until they form a very dense growth of treelike structures. The villi become highly vascular, fetal blood circulating in them under the drive of the fetal heart. The villi are bathed by maternal blood that is continually replaced, but there is no open communication between the blood vessels of the villi and the sinuses (intervillous spaces) through which maternal blood flows. However, the fetal and maternal vessels are so close together that materials have the opportunity to be readily interchanged.

At first, the whole surface of the chorion is covered with villi. However, those villi on the surface toward the uterine cavity gradually thin out and degenerate, leaving the surface smooth. This smooth side is known as the *chorion laeve.* As the fetus grows, the chorion laeve eventually crowds against the opposite wall of the uterus, virtually obliterating the cavity of the uterus (fig. 3.7). The side bearing the persisting villi is called the *chorion frondosum;* this constitutes the fetal part of the definitive human placenta. Within the villi are small blood vessels (capillaries) branching from the larger umbilical vessels, which run through the umbilical cord. Two umbilical arteries and one umbilical vein carry blood between the fetus and the chorion frondosum. These umbilical vessels are the counterpart of the allantoic blood vessels in reptiles and birds.

That portion of the uterus wall that houses the chorionic villi is referred to as the *decidua basalis;* this makes up the maternal portion of the placenta. Structurally, then, the placenta has two components: (1) fetal (chorion frondosum) and (2) maternal (decidua basalis). Functionally, the circulation of the placenta is also twofold, involving distinct parts: (1) the fetal blood vessels in the chorionic villi and (2) the maternal blood in the intervillous spaces. When fully developed, the disc-shaped human placenta is about the size of a small soup plate (*placenta* means "flat cake"), approximately 15–20 cm in diameter and 3 cm in thickness, and weighing 500 g (a little more than 1 pound). It is about one-sixth the weight of the average newborn baby. The average infant at term weighs 3,200 g (7 pounds), males being roughly 100 g (3 ounces) heavier than females.

HORMONAL CHANGES DURING PREGNANCY

It was indicated earlier (chapter 1) that persistence of the corpus luteum is essential for continued secretion of estrogen and progesterone to maintain the uterine lining and to prevent menstruation during pregnancy. The corpus luteum produces estrogen and progesterone under the influence of the luteinizing hormone (LH). In a reverse action, however, a rising progesterone level has the effect of inhibiting LH production. Since LH production is inhibited, some factor must replace LH to promote the secretion of estrogen and progesterone by the corpus luteum.

Shortly after the blastocyst becomes implanted in the uterine wall, the trophoblast cells secrete a hormone called *chorionic gonadotropin* (CG) into the maternal blood. Although chemically different from LH, CG has very similar properties. Thus, chorionic gonadotropin replaces LH in stimulating the appropriate secretions by the corpus luteum. The concentration of CG in the maternal blood rises rapidly and reaches a peak by the seventh week of pregnancy (fig. 3.8). The concentration of CG during early pregnancy is so high that this hormone is excreted in the urine of pregnant women. The urine of a woman late in the first month of pregnancy already contains sufficient CG to form the basis for pregnancy testing. A small amount of pregnancy urine injected into a mature rabbit will induce ovulation in the rabbit within less than one day. This response constitutes the Friedman test for pregnancy. Similarly, the Ascheim-Zondek test makes use of the ability of CG in the pregnancy urine to induce rapid maturation of the ovaries of immature mice. Still other tests are based on the stimulation by CG of the release of sperm by the common male frog. All these tests, although highly accurate, are now being replaced by a quick and highly sensitive direct chemical determination of CG in the maternal urine or blood.

It should be noted (fig. 3.8) that the concentration of CG falls off rapidly and has largely subsided by the end of the third month. Associated with this abrupt decrease of CG secretion, the corpus luteum becomes reduced in size. However, the degenerative changes in the corpus luteum are now inconsequential, since the placenta itself begins to produce large quantities of estrogen and progesterone. In fact, the placental secretions account for nearly all the estrogen and progesterone circulating in the maternal blood during the last six months of pregnancy. In essence, the placenta becomes specialized as a hormone-producing organ, and takes over the function of the corpus luteum. Accordingly, pregnancy would proceed unimpeded if the ovaries were to be removed

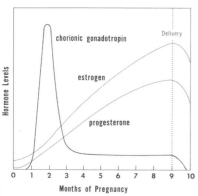

Figure 3.8 Concentrations of chorionic gonadotropin, estrogen, and progesterone in the blood of a pregnant woman.

during the last six months of pregnancy. It should be clear, however, that earlier removal of the ovaries (prior to three months) would result in the loss of the fetus.

EMBRYONIC AND FETAL STAGES

We may survey briefly the changes in general shape and general body plan of the human embryo during development. The embryonic body as seen externally at the fourth week is illustrated in figure 3.9A. The four-week-old embryo bears no resemblance to a human being. The embryo is so markedly bent or curled that the head almost touches the tail. The head is vaguely defined, but it bears a primitive three-lobed brain. A prominent bulge in the trunk region signifies the early beginnings of the heart. The simple-looped heart is functional, pumping blood through vessels within the embryo and through the umbilical arteries to the placenta. Vague, rounded elevations on the surface of the head foreshadow development of the eyes. Oral and anal openings appear at this time, although they are functionless. At the end of the fourth week, the embryo is only one-quarter of an inch long.

A characteristic feature of the four-week-old embryo (fig. 3.9A) is the alternating series of ridges and furrows on the sides of the head, known as *branchial (gill) arches* and *branchial (gill) grooves*, respectively. Five pairs of branchial arches form in the same manner as the gill arches in fishes. The branchial grooves correspond to the gill slits of fishes. However, the grooves in humans are not normally perforated nor do they ever function in breathing. The branchial arches of the human embryo contribute ultimately to several important structures in the facial region; the first arch, for example, is involved in the formation of the upper and lower jaws. Once again, in the embryonic system of branchial arches and grooves, the student of evolution finds evidence that the backboned animals, or vertebrates, had a common ancestor.

The rudiments of the arms and legs appear about the middle of the fifth week. They arise as two pairs of flattened elevations, known as *limb buds* (fig. 3.9B). The upper limb buds appear first and develop more rapidly. Behind the hind limb bud may be seen a small tail rudiment, which does not ever grow into a full-fledged tail. Although muscles develop in the tail, they remain functionless. The head is now appreciably larger than the trunk; the brain has become the prominent feature of the embryo. Nerve cells have become aggregated into nerves, which pervade the body. By the end of the fifth week, the embryo has the foundations of the main systems: nervous, muscular, circulatory, excretory, reproductive, digestive, and skeletal. Paired gonads have formed, but they are not yet recognizable as either ovaries or testes.

In the sixth week, the head is disproportionately large, the abdomen bulges because of the great size of the liver, and digits are evident in the paddle-shaped hands and feet (fig. 3.9C and Plate 1). In development, the hands are always a little ahead of the feet. This is an expression of the general rule that anterior structures develop more rapidly than posterior structures. Rapid growth and development has occurred in the facial region. The eyes and external ears are well defined, the upper lip has formed, and the nose has definition.

In the eighth week (fig. 3.9D), the head is recognizably human: eyes, ears, nose, and mouth are relatively well formed. The tail of earlier stages has regressed, and the umbilical cord is prominent. The arms have grown extensively, and the embryo can now touch its face. The embryo is

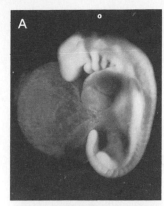

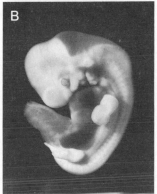

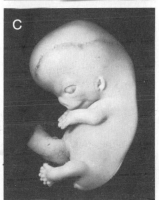

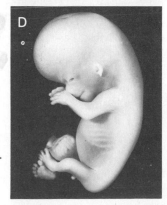

Figure 3.9 Human embryo at various stages of development: fourth week *(A)*, fifth week *(B)*, sixth week *(C)*, and eighth week *(D)*. (Courtesy of the Carnegie Institution of Washington, Baltimore, Maryland.)

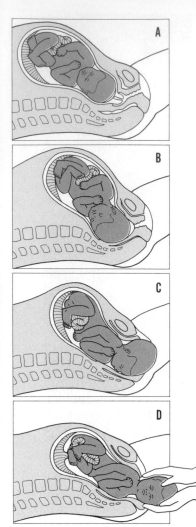

Figure 3.10 Process of birth (parturition). The first stage in labor is the dilation, or opening, of the cervix (A). The period of actual birth begins when the cervix is fully dilated (B). The baby descends through the vaginal canal in a head-down position, with the back of the baby's head toward the front of the mother (C). The baby's head passes through the vaginal chamber, and the rest of the body follows readily (D). The moment that the baby's head (or "crown") becomes visible is often referred to as "crowning."

capable of moving its body, but the movements are too slight for the mother to detect them.

By the end of the eighth week, all the organs of the body are well established (Plate 2). The embryo is remarkably complex, even though it is only one inch long. The developing individual has a form that is unmistakably human; thenceforth until birth, seven months later, it is known as a *fetus*. The fetal period is one primarily of growth and refinement of structures formed during the first eight weeks (Plates 3–6).

The gross structural changes that take place during the early weeks of embryonic life reflect equally profound alterations in the cells that make up the embryo. In the eight-week embryo, liver cells are clearly distinguishable from cells of the heart. Muscle cells cannot substitute for blood cells, and bone cells cannot function as brain cells. Yet all these cells contain genes that are exactly alike. Except for the sperm and the egg, every cell in the body has a full complement of hereditary material. Accordingly, each cell is potentially capable of performing the functions of any other kind of cell. As the embryo develops, however, the cells begin to specialize, or *differentiate,* along specific lines. We shall go further into the intricate process of differentiation of cells in other sections of the book.

It bears emphasizing that the unborn child is almost fully formed by the time it completes its eighth week of development. This fact alone is sufficient to reveal the absurdity of the popular and long-persisting belief in maternal impressions or old wives' tales. A five-month fetus is no more likely to develop a strawberry-shaped birthmark from a mother's yearning for strawberries than the mother herself is. Nor can the infant develop a clawlike deformity of the hands because the mother was frightened in her sixth month of pregnancy by the sight of live lobsters.

PARTURITION

Parturition, or childbirth, occurs on the average about 40 weeks (280 days) after the last menstrual period. Although childbirth is a continuous process, three stages are recognized for descriptive purposes. In the first stage, the cervix of the uterus dilates (fig. 3.10A) as the woman experiences rhythmic contractions of the uterine muscles (commonly referred to as *labor*). At the onset of labor, the muscular contractions of the uterus are coordinated at approximately 10- to 15-minute intervals. The uterine contractions increase in intensity and frequency as the cervix continues to stretch gradually to accommodate the width of the baby's head. The cervical opening, which normally has a diameter of 0.5 centimeters, widens to 10 centimeters ("five fingers") in diameter (fig. 3.10B). This first stage, encompassing the dilation of the cervix, may last as long as 20 hours for the firstborn; it tends to be much shorter in subsequent births (3 to 8 hours).

The second stage, or period of actual birth, commences when the cervix is completely dilated. The uterine contractions occur every 2 or 3 minutes, and have a duration of about 30 seconds. The amniotic sac ruptures expelling its fluid ("waters") and the fetus is extruded (delivered) through the fully dilated cervix and vagina (birth canal). In the majority of human births, the baby rotates and descends in the head-down position (fig. 3.10C). As the baby's head stretches the birth canal maximally, the obstetrician is able to grip the head ("crown") and assist in the emergence of the baby (fig. 3.10D). The delivery stage may last from 20 minutes to 2 hours. Shortly after delivery, the umbilical vessels collapse and the

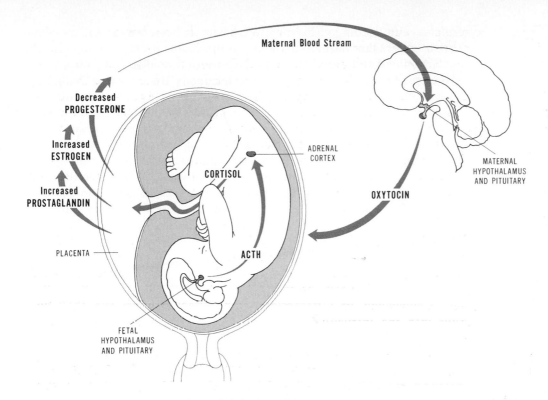

Maternal Blood Stream

Decreased **PROGESTERONE**

Increased **ESTROGEN**

Increased **PROSTAGLANDIN**

PLACENTA

CORTISOL

ADRENAL CORTEX

ACTH

OXYTOCIN

MATERNAL HYPOTHALAMUS AND PITUITARY

FETAL HYPOTHALAMUS AND PITUITARY

umbilical cord is tied and severed. Mucus is removed from the baby's throat and the newborn takes its first breath.

Within 10 to 15 minutes after delivery, forceful uterine contractions expel the placenta ("afterbirth"). The expulsion of the placenta constitutes the third stage of parturition; it may last for a few minutes to a half hour. There is hemorrhage from the maternal blood vessels, but the bleeding is held in check by the firmly contracted state of the uterine muscles. Less than 500 milliliters of blood are discharged from the uterine wall. The condition of the uterine lining at parturition has been described as an exaggeration of its condition at the end of menstruation.

The precise mechanisms that trigger the onset of parturition are currently the subject of extensive investigations. At one time, it was believed that only the release from the mother's pituitary gland of the hormone *oxytocin* (from Greek, meaning "swift birth") was instrumental in initiating labor. Later, it was found that the sensitivity of the uterine muscles was enhanced by estrogen and depressed by progesterone. High levels of estrogen circulate in the maternal blood during the last 7 to 10 days before parturition, whereas the concentration of progesterone falls sharply immediately before the onset of labor. Additional studies then showed that, at parturition, the placenta contains very high concentrations of prostaglandin, a potent stimulator of uterine muscles. The subsequent discovery that the placental prostaglandin is synthesized under the direction of the fetal adrenal gland ushered in the astonishing hypothesis that the fetus influences, if not actually controls, its own process of birth.

These recent findings can be unified in an elaborate scheme shown in figure 3.11. The chain of events leading to parturition begins in the hypothalamus of the fetus. The hypothalamus activates the fetal pituitary gland to release *adrenocorticotropin* (ACTH), which in turn stimulates the adrenal gland of the fetus to secrete *cortisol*, a steroid hormone. Fetal cortisol is now recognized as an indispensable link in the series of hor-

Figure 3.11 Diagrammatic representation of recent findings which indicate that the fetus, not the mother, controls the process of birth. The chain of events leading to parturition begins in the fetal hypothalamus. See text for details.

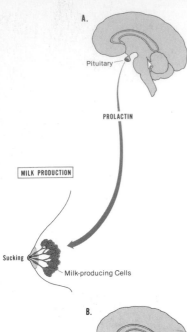

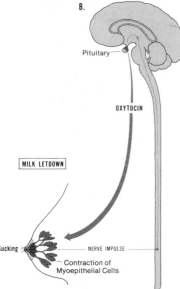

Figure 3.12 The events associated with milk production (*A*) and the passage of milk into the ducts of the mammary glands—the so-called "milk letdown" (*B*).

monal events leading to parturition. There is persuasive evidence that cortisol directs or stimulates the synthesis of prostaglandins in the placenta. Prostaglandins may influence uterine contractility by a direct action on the muscles of the uterus or indirectly by elevating the release of oxytocin from the maternal pituitary gland. The prostaglandins are currently thought to play a role of great importance in inducing labor.

The foregoing scheme is supported by experimental observations, particularly in sheep. The surgical removal of the pituitary gland or the suppression of ACTH secretion in fetal lambs results in the prolongation of pregnancy—that is, the continuation of pregnancy for several weeks beyond term. Contrarily, the infusion of synthetic ACTH into the fetal lamb results in premature delivery. Although there are many questions still to be answered, it does appear that the fetus determines the length of gestation and the timing of parturition.

LACTATION

During pregnancy, milk production (*lactation*) by the mammary glands (breasts) is inhibited by the high levels of estrogen and progesterone secreted by the placenta. With the delivery of the child and the expulsion of the placenta, the concentrations of estrogen and progesterone decline in the bloodstream of the mother. This decline removes the inhibitory effects on lactation, and the pituitary hormone *prolactin* stimulates milk secretion. Milk is secreted by numerous glandular cells that are arranged in grapelike clusters around minute ducts in the breasts. The milk-producing cells and ducts are surrounded by musclelike, or contractile, cells called *myoepithelial cells.*

The production of milk ceases soon after the mother stops nursing her infant. The major factor that ensures the release of prolactin is suckling, or tactile stimulation of the breasts (fig. 3.12). In the absence of suckling, prolactin fails to be secreted and lactation is suppressed.

One other pathway is essential for nursing (fig. 3.12). Milk is unaccessible to the infant if the milk is unable to flow, or be "let down," from the glandular cells to the ducts. The passage of milk into the ducts is technically called *milk letdown,* and is accomplished by the contraction of the myoepithelial cells surrounding the milk-producing cells. The ejection of milk into the ducts is under the control of oxytocin, a pituitary hormone that is released by suckling, just like prolactin. The pathway is not only hormonal but also nervous. The act of suckling triggers nerve impulses from sensitive receptors in the nipple of the breast. The nerve impulses travel to the spinal cord and then to the hypothalamus. The nervous portion of the pathway can be conditioned; many lactating mothers actually leak milk in anticipation of nursing or when the baby cries.

Breast-feeding tends to inhibit the production of FSH and LH by the pituitary. Theoretically, then, ovulation should be suppressed during nursing. For reasons not completely understood, the inhibiting influences on ovulation are weak. Accordingly, many women do ovulate despite continued nursing, and pregnancy can occur in the lactating woman.

CONTROL OF HUMAN DEVELOPMENT

An awe-inspiring accomplishment in recent years has been the successful fertilization of the human egg by sperm in laboratory glassware, or technically, *in vitro* (Latin, *vitrum,* meaning "glass"). In the late 1960s, the developmental physiologist Robert Edwards, at the University of Cambridge in England, sought the means of obtaining a mature egg directly from the ovarian follicle just prior to ovulation. At the suggestion of his clinician colleague, Dr. Patrick Steptoe, a surgical technique called *laparoscopy* was modified to extract the preovulatory egg. A clear view of the ovary is obtained with a slender illuminated telescope, or laparoscope, which is inserted through a small incision made in the abdominal wall (fig. 3.13). A specially designed hypodermic needle is then passed through a second slit in the abdomen, and the contents of the thin-walled, bulging Graafian follicle are aspirated.

In a suitable culture medium, the extracted egg can be fertilized with the husband's sperm. In September 1970, Edwards and his co-workers announced that several *in vitro* fertilized human eggs divided, or cleaved, normally as far as the 16-cell stage of development. This was followed by a published report in January 1971 stating that the human embryo can be cultured to the blastocyst stage, the stage at which implantation in the uterus normally occurs. After several unproductive implantations of laboratory-grown embryos in the uteri of women, a successful full-term pregnancy was finally achieved. On July 26, 1978, the world's first "test-tube" baby was delivered in healthy condition to a 30-year-old woman in Oldham, England.

Concern has been voiced that the implantation of a test-tube embryo involves far too great a risk. One cannot assess or predict whether or not the resulting infant— if it should survive—would be deformed because of the experimental manipulations. However, it may be argued that all new medical technologies are risky. In any new and dramatic technological procedure, the searching questions that invariably arise are: *Can man, will man,* and *should* man? Edwards believes that we should attempt artificial implantation in a human recipient. The techniques of *in vitro* fertilization and artificial implantation provide a means of overcoming a form of female infertility in which the Fallopian tubes are occluded or blocked. Blocked or abnormal oviducts account for approximately 20 percent of the causes of infertility in women. These techniques could also be helpful to those women who fail to conceive because the chemical fluids in the cervical canal have harmful effects on the sperm. Additionally, some men suffer from low sperm counts, and the *in vitro* fertilization procedure requires fewer sperm cells compared with the massive numbers normally needed.

Since the egg and sperm are furnished by the wife and husband, society may come to accept the idea of artificial implantation. A more thorny problem arises when one contemplates the use of either egg or sperm, or both, from strange donors. It is of particular interest that society today sanctions the adoption of postnatal children and the adoptive parents rarely have knowledge of the true, or biological, mother and father of the adopted child. Tracy Sonneborn, the geneticist at Indiana University, has cogently commented that essentially only one new feature is introduced by the new medical technologies—the earlier age of the child to be adopted. With the situation viewed in this manner, a couple, rather than adopt a grown child, could choose to accept an early blastocyst that could grow in the woman's womb.

Figure 3.13 Laparoscopy, a technique for performing various abdominal operations, including the extraction of a preovulatory egg from a woman's ovary. (From *Reproduction in mammals,* vol. 5, eds. C. R. Austin and R. V. Short, 1972, Cambridge University Press.)

SUMMARY

During the embryonic life of reptiles, birds, and mammals, important structures external to the embryo arise that serve for protection, nutrition, respiration, and excretion. These are the so-called extraembryonic membranes, represented by the amnion, chorion, yolk sac, and allantois. In the human embryo, the yolk sac is small and functionless, and the allantois is rudimentary. The appearance of the yolk sac and allantois in human development, despite the loss of their original functions, is indicative of the strong evolutionary affinities of the widely different kinds of vertebrates. Additionally, knowledge of the anatomical relations of the extraembryonic membranes in reptiles and birds contributes greatly to an understanding of the formation of the placenta in advanced mammals, including man. The fetal component of the mammalian placenta is essentially an elaborate modification of the chorion of birds and reptiles. The placenta is a combination of interlocking fetal and maternal tissues that serves for the exchange of nutritive and gaseous products between the mother and fetus. At no time during pregnancy is there an actual mingling of the blood of the mother and fetus.

The human embryo is remarkably complex by the end of the eighth week of development. Although the eight-week embryo is only about one inch long, virtually all the organs of the body are well established. Modern investigators have been able to culture human eggs in a completely artificial environment from fertilization to the blastocyst stage. Recent attempts to culture the artificially grown human blastocysts to more advanced developmental stages raise difficult questions about purposes and ends.

Ethical Probe 3
Animal Husbandry for Mankind?

In the 1950s, several fertilized eggs of a sheep were inserted into the oviduct of a rabbit in Cambridge, England, and the rabbit was flown to South Africa. There the embryos were removed and transferred into a recipient ewe of a different breed. The embryos survived to term and hardy lambs were born. The successful embryo transfers, coupled with the favorable export of embryos, were hailed as valuable and challenging new tools for improving livestock production in different countries.

Two decades later, once again in the vicinity of Cambridge, the technique of embryo transfer helped produce a "test-tube" baby. On July 25, 1978, a woman delivered a child who was conceived in a culture dish. The birth was acclaimed as a major medical breakthrough for women who are infertile because of irreparable defects in their Fallopian tubes. The dual procedures of artificial fertilization and embryo transfer are humanely intended to allow some infertile couples the profound satisfaction of procreation. This medical innovation has also been viewed as another dehumanizing step toward subverting a sense of reverence for life.

In rabbits and mice, the total probability of success in withdrawing an egg from an ovarian follicle, carrying out **in vitro** fertilization, and obtaining a live offspring after embryo transfer is only 10 percent. To enhance the probability of success in humans, it is likely that several pre-ovulatory eggs will be taken from the prospective mother for **in vitro** fertilization. When only one of several artificially fertilized eggs is implanted, who decides what is to be done with the surplus embryos? If life begins at fertilization, who is responsible for the lives of the surplus specimens? Will mothers delegate embryos to surrogate mothers?

The ethical questions can only become more urgent as the technical capabilities provide new alternatives. Prior to implantation, small cellular fragments of the blastocyst can be excised and diagnosed for the identification of sex, chromosomal abnormalities, and biochemical defects. Would you condone the use of the technique for selecting the offspring's sex? Would you sanction the elimination of a male embryo carrying the gene for a serious sex-linked disease, such as hemophilia or the Duchenne type of muscular dystrophy? Is there a way of developing a standard for decision-making?

Molecules of Life and Placental Transfer

Every living system, whether it be the smallest primitive cell or the largest complex organism, is in a state of continuous and intense chemical activity. All cells and organisms take certain chemicals from their surroundings. These chemicals, called *nutrients*, or "foods," are transformed in various ways by the cell. Some of the nutrients are changed into more complicated substances that become part of the structure or machinery of the cell, while others are oxidized, or burned, to provide energy. The living system has superficial resemblances to an internal combustion engine. The cell obtains its energy from the oxidation, or combustion, of certain nutrients; it differs strikingly, however, from the ordinary gasoline engine in that the combustion occurs at an exceedingly low temperature. Moreover, not only does the cell oxidize the "fuel" nutrients for energy, but unlike the gasoline engine, it can produce or synthesize elaborate (organic) substances from relatively simple molecules.

Although the emphasis here is primarily on the nutritional requirements of the human fetus, the principles illustrated apply to many diverse kinds of animals. There is practically a universal demand for carbohydrates, proteins, and fats. As we see from table 4.1, the human newborn is composed principally of these substances, and also water, which makes up almost two-thirds of the infant's weight. Of critical importance to the developing fetus is the means by which the essential nutrients are transferred across the placenta. An analysis of placental transfer will reveal some of the fundamental principles involved in the traffic of molecules between cells.

ORGANIC CONSTITUENTS OF CELLS

All organic compounds contain carbon (see Appendix A). The three principal classes of organic compounds in living cells are carbohydrates, proteins, and fats. Carbohydrates are the primary source of energy for organisms, supplying about one-half the total energy requirements. The basic units in carbohydrates are composed of carbon (C), hydrogen (H), and oxygen (O), with the hydrogen and oxygen atoms always occurring in the ratio 2:1 (as in water). The simplest carbohydrates are *simple sugars*, or *monosaccharides*, of which glucose is an example. A glucose molecule contains six carbon atoms, and is represented by the formula $C_6H_{12}O_6$. Glucose is readily oxidized and is easily transportable. Indeed, it is the blood sugar of humans. Another readily oxidized simple sugar is fructose, which has the same molecular formula as glucose ($C_6H_{12}O_6$) but is structurally different in terms of the three-dimensional arrangement of its atoms (fig. 4.1). Glucose and fructose are found in many fruits, seeds, and roots of plants.

Table 4.1
Chemical Composition of a Newborn Infant

Component	Percentage
Water	66.0%
Proteins	16.0
Fats	12.5
Carbohydrates	0.5
Minerals[a]	5.0

Note: Based on total body weight of 3,500 g.

[a] The largest mineral constituents are calcium and phosphorus, the main components of bone.

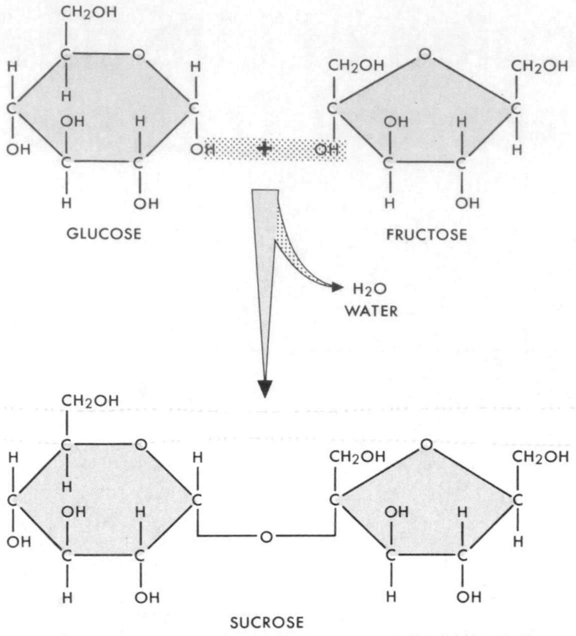

Figure 4.1 Molecular configurations of the two monosaccharides, glucose and fructose, and the synthesis of the disaccharide, sucrose, through the removal of a molecule of water between the two monosaccharides.

Two simple sugars may, with the loss of a molecule of water, combine to form a *double sugar*, or *disaccharide* (fig. 4.1). Thus, glucose may be linked to fructose to form cane sugar, or sucrose ($C_{12}H_{22}O_{11}$). In advanced plants, but not in animals, sucrose is easily transported (in sap). Sucrose occurs abundantly in sugar cane and sugar beet, and is the familiar sugar of the dining table.

Large molecules, or *polysaccharides*, result when the simple sugars are linked in long chains. That is to say, each of several hundred molecules of a monosaccharide loses one molecule of water in uniting with each other to form one large polysaccharide with the general formula $(C_6H_{10}O_5)_n$. Starch and glycogen, both of which are composed of many glucose units, are the storage form of energy, the former typically in plants and the latter typically in animals. In plants, the surplus sugar is converted into starch, and plant starch is the main external source of carbohydrates for animals. Starch is insoluble; hence, before it can be used in the animal body, it must be reconverted to simple, soluble monosaccharides (glucose). This conversion or breakdown is known as *digestion*. Since the conversion involves the addition or reinsertion of water molecules to the individual glucose units, the digestive process is called *hydrolysis*.

In animals, the counterpart of starch is glycogen, which is a much larger molecule than starch. In humans, the principal storage centers of glycogen are the liver and the muscles. The liver of the human fetus has an exceptionally large store of glycogen, which is made available for use immediately after birth. Liver glycogen is essential to the newborn for the maintenance of body temperature and for the breathing movements that are initiated at birth.

Humans also rely on another energy reserve, *fats,* deposited in various areas of the body. Fats, like carbohydrates, are composed of carbon, hydrogen, and oxygen atoms, but molecules of fat typically contain much higher proportions of hydrogen. For example, the composition of a common fat, stearin, is expressed by the formula $C_{57}H_{110}O_6$. A given amount of fat can liberate appreciably more energy—in fact, slightly more than twice as many calories—than the same weight of carbohydrate. This relatively large energy production is one of the important roles of fats in the human body.

A molecule of fat is formed by linking a three-carbon *glycerol* with three molecules of straight-chained *fatty acids*. A fat molecule is often referred to as a *triglyceride* because the fatty acids are attached to the three sites available in the backbone of the glycerol molecule. Since the three fatty acid residues linked to glycerol need not be identical, a great variety of fat molecules can be formed with varied permutations of different fatty acid chains. Just as carbohydrates can be hydrolyzed by the insertion of water, fats can be broken down into their constituent subunits (fatty acids and glycerol) by hydrolysis (digestion). Depending on the kind of fatty acid present, fats may be largely saturated (butter fat or milk fat, for example) or mainly unsaturated (olive oil, soybean oil, or cottonseed oil, for example). In recent years, investigators have linked the high incidence of coronary diseases in man to diets rich in saturated fats (usually animal oils).

There are only a few fatty acids that must be taken in with the diet. Most of the fatty acids in the human body can be manufactured in the body itself from the breakdown products of chemical processes involving carbohydrates. Thus, when excess sugar occurs in the body, fat is synthesized in the liver and transported by the blood to various tissues for storage. Fats belong to a class of water-insoluble compounds called *lipids*; other major lipids in organisms are the *phospholipids* and *steroids*. The phospholipids are similar in structure to the triglycerides, except that a phosphate-containing group is substituted for one of the three fatty acids. As will be discussed in detail later (chapter 5), phospholipids form one of the major structural components of cell membranes. Steroids are structurally quite different from other kinds of lipids; the basic pattern is a system of four interconnected carbon rings. Important steroid molecules in the body are *cholesterol* and a variety of hormones, including progesterone, testosterone, estrogen, and cortisol.

Proteins (Greek, *proteios*, "of the first rank") are the most important substances in the living cell, being present in the greatest quantity, except for water. Proteins are vitally important in a variety of activities of the cell. A special protein, myosin, forms the fibers responsible for the contraction of muscles. Another protein, hemoglobin, is instrumental in the uptake of oxygen in the circulating red blood cells. Still another protein, collagen, is an important constituent of tendons and bones. The skin protein, keratin, provides protection for the internal soft tissues. All antibodies and certain hormones are also protein in nature. Probably the most important of the proteins are enzymes, which promote the vast number of chemical reactions in the body. The diversity of functions is matched by a corresponding diversity of chemical structure. It is estimated that the human body contains as many as 100,000 different kinds of proteins.

Proteins are large molecules of high molecular weight that are made principally of carbon, hydrogen, oxygen, and nitrogen. Small amounts of sulphur are usually found and phosphorus may sometimes be present. A typical protein, lactoglobulin, vividly demonstrates the complexity and large size of most proteins. This protein is found in milk and has the approximate formula $C_{1864}H_{3012}O_{576}N_{468}S_{21}$ and a molecular weight of 42,000 (meaning 42,000 times as heavy as a hydrogen atom). Hemoglobin has a molecular weight of 68,000 and fibrinogen has a weight of 400,000.

Table 4.2
Major Amino Acids

Name	Abbreviation	Structure of R—
Alanine	Ala	CH_3-
Arginine	Arg	$\begin{array}{c} NH \\ \| \| \\ C-NH-CH_2-CH_2-CH_2- \\ \| \\ NH_2 \end{array}$
Aspartic acid	Asp	$COOH-CH_2-$
Asparagine	Asp (NH_2)	$CONH_2-CH_2-$
Cysteine	Cys	$SH-CH_2-$
Glutamic acid	Glu	$COOH-CH_2-CH_2-$
Glutamine	Glu (NH_2)	$CONH_2-CH_2-CH_2-$
Glycine	Gly	$H-$
Histidine	His	$\begin{array}{c} HC = C - CH_2- \\ \| \qquad \| \\ HN \qquad NH \\ \diagdown \ \diagup \\ C \\ \| \\ H \end{array}$

Given such awesome complexity, it is almost incredulous that the structural formula of any protein could be accurately established. Yet the exact sequence of the basic units of the protein *insulin* was worked out, after 10 years of painstaking studies, by the British biochemist Frederick Sanger and his colleagues at the University of Cambridge. Their elaborate report of the insulin molecule, $C_{257}H_{380}N_{64}O_{76}S_6$, published in 1955, has encouraged others to undertake similar analyses of other proteins.

The first clue to the structural composition of protein comes from the hydrolysis of protein. Here too, as in the breakdown of carbohydrate and fat, hydrolysis involves the insertion of water to re-form the basic units of which the molecule is composed. The basic building blocks in proteins are *amino acids*; proteins, therefore, are essentially long chains of amino acids linked together. The simplest amino acid isolated from hydrolysis of protein was glycine; the French chemist Henri Braconnot accomplished this in 1820. Today, there are 20 important amino acids that have been obtained from natural proteins.

All amino acids have in common both a nitrogen-containing subunit, known as an *amino* group (—NH_2), and an acid subunit, known as a *carboxyl* group (—COOH). The general structure is as follows:

$$\begin{array}{c} H \\ \| \\ R-C-COOH \\ \| \\ NH_2 \end{array}$$

The side group, designated *R*, is different for each kind of amino acid and thus imparts a distinctive character to each of the individual amino

Name	Abbreviation	Structure of R—
Isoleucine	Ileu	CH₃—CH₂—CH— │ CH₃
Leucine	Leu	CH₃—CH—CH₂— │ CH₃
Lysine	Lys	NH₂—CH₂—CH₂—CH₂—CH₂
Methionine	Met	CH₃—S—CH₂—CH₂—
Phenylalanine	Phe	⬡—CH₂—
Serine	Ser	CH₂OH—
Threonine	Thr	CH₃CHOH—
Tryptophan	Try	⬡—CH₂— N │ H
Tyrosine	Tyr	HO—⬡—CH₂—
Valine	Val	CH₃—CH— │ CH₃

acids. As seen in table 4.2, the R group may consist solely of a hydrogen atom, as in glycine, or may be relatively complex, as in histidine. A peptide bond forms when the carboxyl group of one amino acid is linked, or joined, to the amino group of another (—CO—NH—). As shown in figure 4.2, the union is accomplished by the elimination of the elements of water from the molecules that unite (see Appendix A). It is this peptide bond that is broken when water is reintroduced during digestion (hydrolysis). A chain of several amino acids is referred to as a polypeptide; when the chain exceeds 70 amino acid units, it is generally thought of as a protein. The 20 different kinds of amino acids can be combined in an extraordinarily large number of ways, just as the 26 letters of the English alphabet can be arranged into potentially millions of words. Each of the different kinds of cells in the body has certain proteins that are unique to that cell.

The specific order of different amino acids in a polypeptide chain is termed its primary structure (first degree, or 1°). To produce a biologically active molecule, the polypeptide chain becomes folded or coiled, typically in the form of a helix. This secondary structure (2°) undergoes further modification; the helix folds and bends to form a tertiary (3°) level of structural organization (fig. 4.3). Finally, since a polypeptide chain, for some reason not completely understood, does not generally exceed 500 amino acids, two or more polypeptide chains become associated with each other to form superproteins. The so-called quaternary structure (4°) of the hemoglobin molecule is shown in figure 4.3. Hemoglobin consists of four chains, two alpha and two beta, closely packed together. Only in this quaternary form is the hemoglobin biologically active.

Figure 4.2 Synthesis of a polypeptide chain. The union of three amino acids to form a polypeptide (in this case, a tripeptide) involves the loss of a molecule of water between each subunit. The peptide bond links the carboxyl group of one amino to the amino group of the next amino acid. (See Appendix A.)

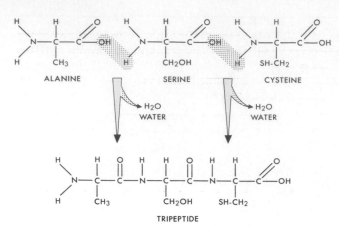

ALANINE   SERINE   CYSTEINE

H₂O WATER   H₂O WATER

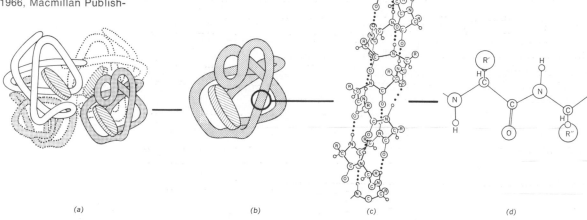

TRIPEPTIDE

Figure 4.3 Levels of structural organization in the hemoglobin molecule: *(A) quaternary,* showing aggregation of two alpha and two beta chains; *(B) tertiary,* showing folding of a beta chain helix; *(C) secondary,* showing composition of a helical structure; and *(D) primary,* showing formation of a peptide bond. (From T. M. Bennett and E. Frieden, *Modern topics in biochemistry,* 1966, Macmillan Publishing Co.)

(a)   (b)   (c)   (d)

Figure 4.4 Structural components of a chorionic villus.

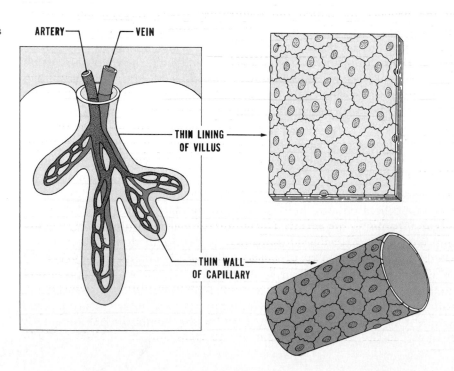

ARTERY   VEIN

THIN LINING OF VILLUS

THIN WALL OF CAPILLARY

FINE STRUCTURE OF THE VILLUS

An adequate transfer of nutrients from the mother to the fetus is essential for normal development of the fetus. The transfer of soluble nutritive substances from the mother's bloodstream occurs through the walls of the innumerable branches of the chorionic villi. The villi are admirably constructed for this purpose. As seen in figure 4.4, the external wall of a villus is sufficiently thin to permit gases (oxygen and carbon dioxide) and dissolved food substances (glucose, amino acids, and fatty acids) to pass through the wall to reach the small vessels (capillaries) in the inner core of the villus. Likewise, it may be noted that the capillaries within the villi are also composed of a pavement of thin, flat compartments, or *cells*, that fit tightly together. Indeed, the common denominator of all systems of the body is the cell.

The maternal blood pool (in the intervillous spaces) surrounds the highly branched villi. This is an efficient arrangement that permits material to be taken out of the maternal blood or put into the maternal blood without the blood either entering or leaving the villi. It is the exceptionally thin covering at the surface of each cell—the *cell* (or *plasma*) *membrane*—that actually controls or regulates the interchange of material. The cell membrane is so thin that its structure can be defined only through the powerful tool of electron microscopy. The membrane is typically only about 10 millionths of a millimeter thick. The plasma membranes of the cells of the villi, and also the membranes of the flat cells lining the fetal capillaries, serve as *selectively permeable* membranes. The surface membrane is also often said to be *differentially permeable*. Cell membranes are so delicately fashioned or fine that large molecules such as proteins are held back, whereas substances of small molecular size are able to pass through them with relative ease. All cell membranes are selectively permeable systems that permit the passage of certain materials while excluding others.

A cardinal problem is the mechanism of movement of various substances across the membrane system of the placenta. We shall consider first the process by which the respiratory gases, oxygen and carbon dioxide, are exchanged between mother and fetus.

SIMPLE DIFFUSION AND OXYGEN TRANSFER

Substances dissolved in a solution are referred to as *solutes*, and the medium in which they are dissolved is the *solvent*. Solute particles tend to distribute themselves evenly throughout a solvent (fig. 4.5). By random movements, the solute molecules will disperse from an area of high concentration to an area of lower concentration. This process of *diffusion* ultimately results in a uniform distribution of the solute molecules within the solvent.

The same principles that govern diffusion in an open system are in effect when a concentration difference occurs across a membrane that is freely permeable to the solute. The solute diffuses unhindered across the membrane to equalize the concentration on both sides of the cell membrane (fig. 4.6). This type of passive transport of solute involves no expenditure of energy by the cell. When an equal concentration of solute is attained on each side of the membrane, a state of *diffusion equilibrium* is reached. This steady-state does not mean that the diffusion process has come to a standstill. Rather, at equilibrium, for every solute particle that moves across the membrane from left to right, another solute particle

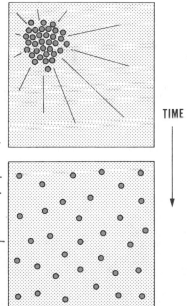

TIME

Figure 4.5 Simple diffusion. Through random movements, solute molecules (large colored dots) become uniformly distributed throughout solvent (water) molecules (small black dots).

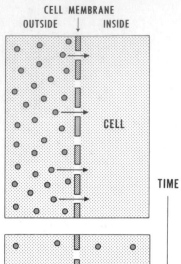

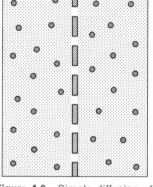

CELL MEMBRANE
OUTSIDE | INSIDE

CELL

TIME

Figure 4.6 Simple diffusion of solute molecules (colored dots) through pores of the cell membrane from a region of higher concentration of the solute to an area of lower concentration.

moves from right to left. In essence, the *net* transfer of the solute particle is zero.

The dissolved oxygen molecules in the blood of the maternal pool pass through the membranes of the villi and subsequently through the thin fetal capillaries by simple diffusion. The concentration of oxygen is greater on the maternal side of the villi membranes than on the fetal side. There are, however, certain problems associated with supplying oxygen to the fetus. Oxygen is an essential element for fetal life and its transfer from the mother to the fetus should be maintained at rapid, continuous rates. Yet, the fetus lives in a uterine environment in which the concentration of oxygen is relatively low. Stated another way, the diffusion gradient across the membranes of the villi is small compared with the diffusion gradient, for example, across the adult lungs. We may then wonder how it is possible for the fetus to obtain sufficient oxygen.

Here we encounter an important property of the biological system—the capacity of the organism for making certain physiological adjustments to maintain proper, or constant, conditions in its internal environment when the organism is subjected to temporary or fluctuating changes in its external environment. This has been termed *homeostasis*. There are several interesting homeostatic mechanisms that ensure relatively stable oxygen transfer and consumption despite a narrow oxygen gradient in the uterine environment. In the first place, the lining of the fetal capillaries, although initially thin, may thin even more (by stretching) to increase efficiency of diffusion. Secondly, the hemoglobin molecule of the fetus, appropriately called *fetal hemoglobin*, has a higher affinity for oxygen than adult hemoglobin does. This fetal hemoglobin carries as much as 30 percent more oxygen at low tensions than adult hemoglobin can. Another adaptation to oxygen deficiency is that the hemoglobin concentration of the fetus is about 50 percent greater than the hemoglobin concentration of the mother. This allows an increased amount of oxygen to be transported to the fetal tissues. Finally, the fetal tissues can build up an "oxygen debt," whereby they perform their functions, at least temporarily, without oxygen present. This involves the breakdown of glucose to obtain energy in the absence of oxygen, a process known as *glycolysis*. The oxygen debt must be repaid quickly; the 3-month fetus, for example, cannot withstand a deficiency of oxygen for more than 20 minutes. With prolonged oxygen insufficiency, the store of glycogen in the liver is dissipated, lactic acid (a toxic substance) accumulates in the blood and tissues, and blood circulation gradually fails.

Notwithstanding all the favorable adaptive mechanisms, the fetus still is at a risk when the oxygen levels in the uterine environment fall precipitously. Recent evidence indicates that insufficient oxygen may be responsible for a third of the deaths of stillborn infants.

FACILITATED DIFFUSION AND GLUCOSE TRANSPORT

Glucose is made readily available to the fetus in virtually unlimited quantities from the maternal bloodstream. The glucose level in the maternal blood is approximately 25 percent higher than the glucose level in the fetal blood. Accordingly, one would suspect that glucose is transported across the placental barrier by simple diffusion. However, the fetal requirements for glucose are great; it has been established that the rate of transfer of glucose to the fetal blood is in excess of that expected from only simple diffusion. It appears probable that glucose transport is facilitated by a carrier molecule. A carrier molecule specific for glucose picks up glucose on one side of the membrane, moves across the membrane, unloads the glucose, and then moves back across the membrane to its original place so that it can pick up another molecule of glucose for transport (fig. 4.7). This process is known as *facilitated diffusion*. It is the process by which glucose has been shown to cross the membrane of a red blood cell, and most likely is the mechanism by which glucose is transported across the membranes of the villi. Thus, this represents another homeostatic mechanism to ensure that the fetus fulfills its immense requirements for glucose. The rules of diffusion are followed since transport occurs from a region of high concentration to a region of lower concentration, but the transport is augmented by a carrier system. The carrier system may be compared to a hotel shuttle bus that conveys its registrants from the hotel to the airport. The shuttle bus, after depositing its passengers at the airline terminal, returns to the hotel for additional passengers. The analogy extends even further: although the bus has a limited capacity (just as carrier molecules may be at a premium), the capacity of the airport is relatively unlimited (just as a cell can receive large quantities of glucose).

Although the level of blood glucose is always lower in the fetus than in the mother, it bears a direct relation to the level of maternal blood glucose. Thus, the amount of fetal blood glucose rises with increasing levels of maternal blood glucose. The rate at which glucose is used by the growing tissues, or stored as glycogen or fat, is regulated by insulin that the fetal pancreas secretes. Excessive fetal blood glucose is diverted into fat synthesis. About 1 in 1,000 of all pregnancies involves a diabetic woman, who typically has an elevated blood glucose level. The newborn of a diabetic mother is characteristically heavier than normal (often over 10 pounds), is round-faced and edematous (puffy), and has thick subcutaneous fat deposits. The infant is large because it was supplied in fetal life with an excessive amount of glucose, to which it reacted by producing excessive amounts of insulin. This, in turn, led to increased growth and fat storage.

ACTIVE TRANSPORT AND AMINO ACID PASSAGE

High-molecular-weight proteins do not generally pass through the placenta as such. The fetus rebuilds its own proteins from the smaller molecules of amino acids abstracted from the blood. It would be advantageous to the rapidly growing fetus to have high blood levels of amino acids to facilitate the rapid synthesis of body proteins. Indeed, it is now well documented that the fetus amasses large amounts of amino acids. In fact, the concentration of amino acids is higher in the fetal blood than in the maternal blood. Thus, amino acids cannot be transferred from mother to fetus by simple diffusion.

There is evidence that amino acids and certain elements, like sodium and potassium, are "actively transported" across the membrane of the villus. In this process appropriately called *active transport*, the transfer of molecules occurs against the concentration gradient ("uphill") and accordingly in a direction opposite to what would occur by diffusion alone (fig. 4.8). Details of the mechanism of active transport are as yet poorly understood, but it is clear that the cell must expend energy to accomplish the movement of a diffusible substance from a region of low to a region of high concentration. Stated another way, the cell must work against the forces of passive transport. In active transport, as in facilitated diffusion, the molecule being transported combines temporarily with a carrier (fig. 4.8).

As previously mentioned, phospholipids are a major component of

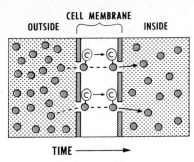

Figure 4.7 Process of catalyzed diffusion. A carrier molecule *(C)* mediates the transfer of a solute molecule, such as glucose (large colored dots), from a region of higher concentration to one of lower. The carrier molecule augments the transport without energy expenditure.

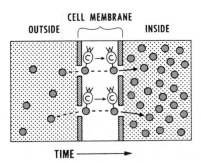

Figure 4.8 Process of active transport. Solute molecules, such as amino acids (large colored dots), are transferred against the concentration gradient with the aid of carrier molecules *(C)*. The process requires the expenditure of energy (symbolized by *W*).

cell membranes. The more readily a molecule dissolves in the membrane lipids, the more easily it can pass through the membrane. Although fat-soluble substances penetrate membranes easily, large fat molecules as such do not cross the placenta. However, the precursors of fats (that is, small droplets of fatty acids) readily cross the wall of the villus by dissolving in the membrane. The fetus then synthesizes its own fats from the smaller precursor molecules. The fetus rarely uses its synthesized fats as a source of energy.

Lipid-soluble compounds, such as vitamin A, D, and E, should cross the placenta with relative ease. Yet, vitamin A crosses the villi membranes as smaller molecules (carotens), which are then reconstructed into vitamin A by the fetus.

PINOCYTOSIS AND GAMMA GLOBULIN TRANSPORT

There is a mechanism for the passage of large molecules whose size precludes their transfer by any other process. The mechanism was given the name *pinocytosis*, which means "cell drinking." As seen in figure 4.9, the cell engulfs a solute by folding inward, or invaginating, a portion of the cell membrane. The resulting vesicle that encloses the substance being transferred is called a *pinocytotic vesicle*, or *pinosome*. The process is like the phagocytotic activity of an amoeba in ingesting small microorganisms or the scavenger activity of a white blood cell in engulfing infectious bacteria.

It is possible, although not proved, that important antibody-producing proteins—specifically, the gamma globulins—are relocated across the villus membrane by pinocytosis. The gamma globulins have a molecular weight of 160,000 and it scarcely seems possible that such high-molecular-weight substances can diffuse through a membrane. Yet admittedly, molecular weight is not the sole determinant of the ease, or difficulty, with which a substance enters a cell. It is clear that the gamma globulins do traverse the villi; however, the albumin molecule, with a molecular weight (70,000) appreciably less than that of gamma globulin, passes from maternal to fetal circulation with considerably less ease than gamma globulins.

The maternal gamma globulins are important to the fetus since they protect the fetus against bacterial, viral, and protozoan infections. Some of the varied antibodies associated with the gamma globulins are as follows: antityphoid, antidiphtheria, antitetanus, antimeasles, antipolio, and antimumps. Not all antibodies traverse the placenta. The precise mechanism responsible for this remarkable selectivity remains an unsolved and perplexing problem. For example, the antibodies against measles readily traverse the placenta and provide excellent protection to the newborn (for at least four months), whereas the antibodies against intestinal bacteria (colon bacilli) do not and therefore the newborn is highly susceptible to bacterial infection of the intestinal tract. Moreover, some of the maternal antibodies are potentially harmful to the fetus. Maternal Rh antibodies provide the basis for a very disquieting disease of the newborn infant—*erythroblastosis fetalis*—which we shall consider in a subsequent section (chapter 21).

Intact fetal red blood cells, by virtue of their size, would seem to be precluded from entering the maternal circulation. Yet, numerous observers have reported the passage of fetal blood cells into the maternal circulation. The passage of intact cells probably takes place through microscopic breaks in the thin membranes of the villi. The transfer of

CELL MEMBRANE
OUTSIDE | INSIDE

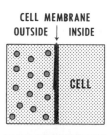

CELL

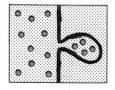

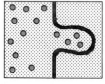

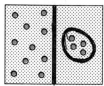

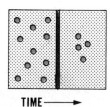

TIME ⟶

Figure 4.9 *Pinocytosis.* Large solute molecules, such as protein molecules (large colored dots), are drawn into the cell interior by being enclosed in a small channel or vesicle (pinosome) formed by an infolding of the cell membrane. The solute molecules then leave the vesicle within the cell and distribute themselves throughout the cytoplasm.

blood cells usually occurs in the latter part of pregnancy and seems to be wholly in the direction of fetus to mother. The one-way traffic of blood cells explains why the blood of a fetus of a leukemic mother does not contain leukemic cells.

THE PRENATAL ENVIRONMENT

We have seen that a variety of substances, though more or less complex transfer mechanisms, find their way across the placenta. For many decades, the prevailing belief was that the fetus, sheltered in the interior of its mother, was well protected from chemical or physiological disturbances in the mother. Only in recent years has it become clear that any alteration in the maternal chemical milieu is likely to affect the fetus. Maternal diseases such as diabetes, syphilis, tuberculosis, German measles (rubella), and other viral infections represent potential danger to the developing fetus.

Pregnant women who contract German measles during early pregnancy may give birth to infants who are blind. The infants are afflicted with cataract, a condition in which the lenses are opaque, obstructing the passage of light. The risk of damage to the fetus from the virus causing German measles is almost wholly during the first three months of pregnancy. The earlier in pregnancy the occurrence of the infection, the greater the chances of injury to the infant. A study has shown that approximately 50 percent of the newborn babies are abnormal if their mothers acquire the disease during the first month of pregnancy. The incidence of fetal defects decreases to 22 percent when maternal German measles occurs in the second month, and to 7 percent in the third month. After the third month of pregnancy, the risk of fetal malformations from maternal German measles is negligible.

Improper diet, obesity, excessive smoking, alcoholism, and the use or abuse of drugs (such as tranquilizers, antidepressants, and sleeping pills) may interfere with proper development or delivery of the fetus. Excessive maternal weight before and during pregnancy is associated with a greater incidence of premature births, prolonged labor, and Caesarean sections. At the other extreme, maternal malnutrition contributes to low-birth-weight infants and poor performance in lactation.

Cigarette smoking during pregnancy has been shown to affect the well-being of the fetus. The concentration of carbon monoxide is abnormally high in the fetuses of mothers who smoke, which may lead to a rapid and irregular fetal heartbeat. The incidence of premature births is approximately twice as high among mothers who smoke during pregnancy as among nonsmokers. Some 4,500 stillbirths each year in the United States have been attributed to the smoking habits of pregnant women. Additionally, hospital records reveal that mothers who smoke tend to have smaller babies; the babies weigh 5 to 8 ounces less than babies born to mothers who abstain from smoking during pregnancy.

Drugs may have little or no detrimental effect on the mother and yet may prove harmful to the fetus. Numerous drugs have been suspected of acting as potent *teratogens*—that is, substances capable of causing marked developmental deviations. Current knowledge of the potential teratogenic hazards of many drugs is limited. Nevertheless, fetal malformations have been associated with tranquilizing drugs taken by the pregnant mother, such as chlorpromazine, meprobramate, and reserpine. All commonly used sulfonamides (sulfanilamide and sulfathiazole) readily cross the placenta to the fetal circulation and may have toxic

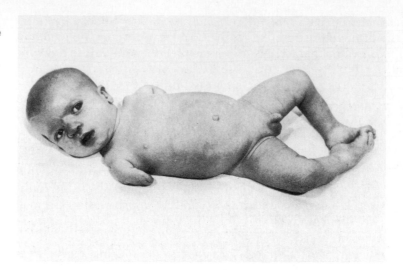

effects. Barbiturates (such as sodium barbital and pentobarbital) and certain antibiotics (streptomycin, terramycin, and chloromycetin) are possible hazards to the fetus. The behavioral traits of the offspring may be affected by the intake of certain drugs during pregnancy. In laboratory experiments, it has been shown that the administration of the tranquilizer, meprobramate, to pregnant rats seriously interferes with the learning capacity of the offspring. In the human, adverse behavioral effects, such as speech disorders and reading difficulties in children, have been associated with maternal complications such as eclampsia (convulsions), vaginal bleeding, and premature delivery.

An estimated 10,000 infants born with rudimentary stumps instead of normal limbs provided grim evidence of the placental transmission of the drug *thalidomide,* the main ingredient of a supposedly harmless sleeping pill. As seen in figure 4.10, the arms of the afflicted infant are absent or reduced to tiny, flipperlike stumps. Dr. Widukind Lenz of the Hamburg Clinic showed that damage to the developing arms resulted when the drug had been taken by the mother during the first month of pregnancy. Several of the women had taken the drug during the period when they were unaware that they were pregnant. It has been shown that only one or two tablets (a single dose of 100 mg) are enough to cause the limb abnormality.

Pregnant women, despite the thalidomide scare, are still consuming large quantities of drugs in the early part of their pregnancy. The pregnant mother today in the United States consumes an average of four drugs. It should be emphasized that the unborn child has little control over the chemical environment furnished it by the mother. Restraint on the part of the pregnant woman in using drugs would appear to be an exemplary virtue.

SPONTANEOUS TWINNING IN HUMANS

The simultaneous birth of two infants is most commonly due to the development of two different eggs that are released from separate follicles at approximately the same time. The two eggs are fertilized by different sperm and become implanted in separate sites in the uterus. Each fetus possesses its own amnion, umbilical cord, and placenta. Such *dizygotic* twins are generally spoken of as fraternal twins. The two members may or may not be of the same sex, and may be as unalike in traits as their brothers and sisters. In a strict sense, fraternal members are litter mates rather than twins. Whereas plural births are the rule in lower mammals, multiple births in humans are exceptional.

The factors that predispose a woman to dizygotic twinning are incompletely known. Certain families exhibit a high recurrence of multiple births, which suggests that genetic factors play a role. The likelihood of twin pregnancies increases steadily with advancing maternal age. A 30-year-old woman has twice as much chance of giving birth to fraternal twins as her counterpart 10 years younger. Additionally, hormones of the pituitary gland affect the rate of multiple ovulation. The use of pituitary gonadotropin for treating infertility has resulted in an unusually high incidence of dizygotic twinning. Multiple pregnancies also appear to be associated with cessation of use of the oral contraceptive pill. There is no truth to the ancient belief that a twin birth can be prevented by the amputation of one of the male testicles.

From an embryological point of view, the greater interest is the origin of identical (or *monozygotic*) twins, derived from a single fertilized egg. Monozygotic twins occur in 4 per 1,000 births, and this figure is remarkably constant for different populations of the world. The frequency of monozygotic twinning appears to be independent of maternal age and ethnic groups. In contrast, the incidence of dizygotic twinning is as high as 40 per 1,000 deliveries among Nigerian Negroes, and as low as 2 per 1,000 deliveries among the Japanese. There are no satisfactory explanations for the startling differences.

An early hypothesis held that the spontaneous separation of the first two cleavage cells (or blastomeres) would produce identical twins. However, a complicating feature in humans is that the cleavage cells are tightly enclosed within a thick, tough zona pellucida until the blastocyst stage of development. Modern investigators believe that the zona pellucida would prevent the blastomeres from coming apart. This is not to say, however, that the mammalian blastomeres are incapable individually of developing into whole, complete embryos. It has been demonstrated that the blastomeres of the two-cell stage of the rat embryo, when separated by experimental means, do give rise to two complete embryos, after each has been implanted in the female genital tract.

Current evidence indicates that, in man, the twinning process is delayed until the blastocyst is formed (fig. 4.11). The inner cell mass of the young blastocyst is considered to be *equipotent* (also termed *totipotent*). In other words, the inner cell mass has the potentialities of forming a single, a dual, or even a multiple embryonic disc. If the inner cell mass should become separated into two nearly equal halves, two embryos would arise from the totipotent primordial cluster of cells. Each embryo would be provided with its own amnion and yolk sac, but would have a single chorion (fig. 4.11*A*). A single chorion (placenta) is one of the criteria for establishing derivation of twins from a single egg. In some cases, the twin embryos are contained in a single amnion. This condition arises when the embryonic disc becomes fissioned in two equal parts, after implantation of the blastocyst (fig. 4.11*B*). Occasionally the embryonic disc divides unequally, with the result that one twin is smaller than its mate. The diminutive twin member usually does not survive after birth.

As seen in figure 4.11*C*, the embryonic disc may be incompletely fissioned; that is, the two new embryonic axes fail to separate in their en-

Figure 4.11 Twinning process in humans. Identical twins may arise by the separation of the inner cell mass into two equal halves *(A)* or by the separation of the embryonic disc *(B)*. Conjoined twins may result when the embryonic disc is incompletely separated *(C)*.

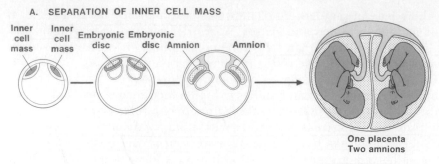

A. SEPARATION OF INNER CELL MASS

One placenta
Two amnions

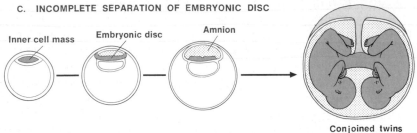

B. SEPARATION OF EMBRYONIC DISC

One placenta
One amnion

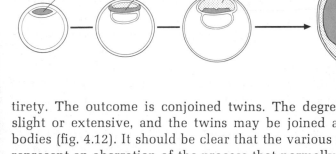

C. INCOMPLETE SEPARATION OF EMBRYONIC DISC

Conjoined twins

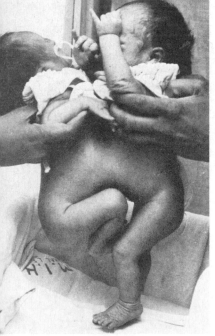

Figure 4.12 Conjoined twins, delivered in a New Delhi hospital on January 14, 1969. The two girls were diagnosed as having separate hearts and intestines, but shared a common liver. (Courtesy of Wide World Photos).

tirety. The outcome is conjoined twins. The degree of union may be slight or extensive, and the twins may be joined at any part of their bodies (fig. 4.12). It should be clear that the various forms of conjoining represent an aberration of the process that normally leads to the formation of identical twins. It is incorrect to suppose that conjoined twins originate from dizygotic twins that began to develop separately and later became fused. Most conjoined twins do not survive after birth. Notable exceptions are the famous Siamese twins, Eng and Chang Bunker, who lived for 63 years, and the Bohemian twins, Rosa and Josepha Blazek, who survived for 43 years. The majority of conjoined twins (7 out of 10) are females.

SUMMARY

The human embryo, like all living organisms, requires nutrients for its development and growth. It obtains energy for its internal chemical activities from carbon-containing carbohydrates, and owes much of its structure and functioning to a vast assortment of proteins. Glucose, a simple carbohydrate, is the primary source of energy for the living system. Proteins, which have many functional roles, are composed of long chains of amino acids. Fats, a third class of organic compounds, form important structural components of the cell membrane. The cell membrane, a selective barrier at the surface of each cell, is the key unit in the ability of the fetus to receive raw materials from the mother and to

Plate 1 Six-week old human embryo. (Photo by Martin Rotker/Taurus Photos.)

Plate 2 Human fetus at eight weeks. (Photo by Donald Yeager.)

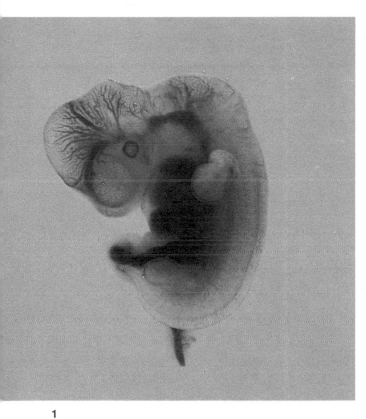

1

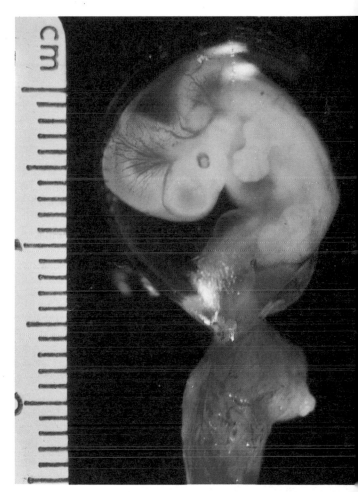

2

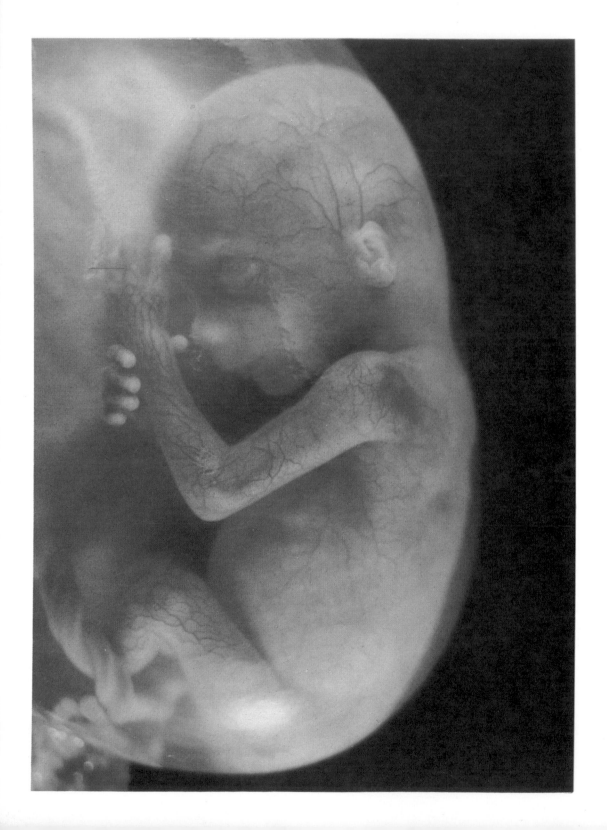

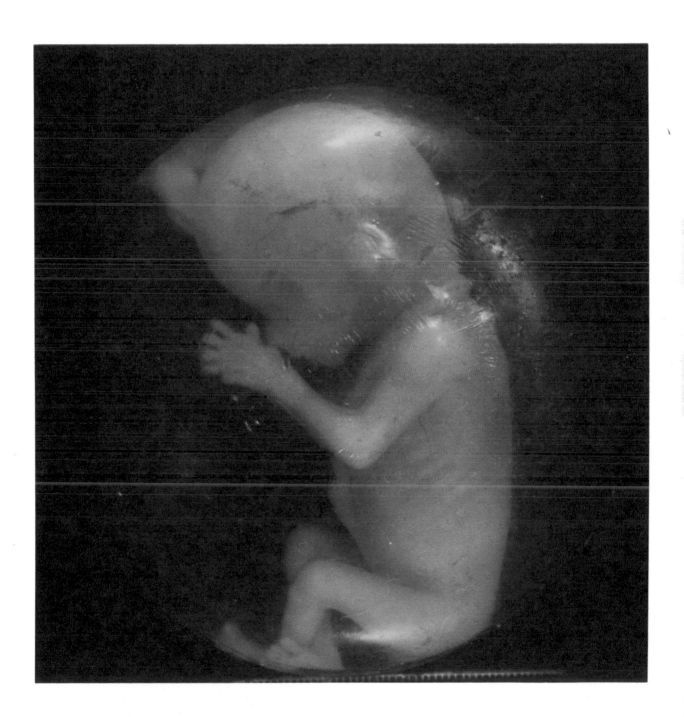

Plate 5 The vein network is readily apparent in this closeup of a human fetus. (Photo by Donald Yeager.)

Plate 6 Human fetus in amniotic sac. (Photo by Donald Yeager.)

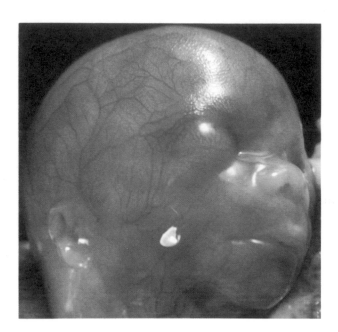

5

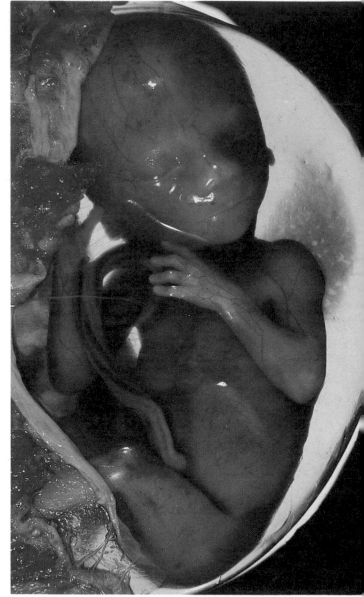

6

release products. Cell membranes are selectively permeable in that they allow some substances to pass through and restrain others. Large molecules generally are unable to penetrate the cell membrane; smaller molecules can move readily across the membrane by simple diffusion.

The cell is not entirely passive in the movement of diffusible substances into and out of it. There are "carrier" systems for specific molecules such as glucose and amino acids. The rate of transport of glucose across cell membranes by the carrier system far exceeds the passage of glucose by the forces of simple diffusion. Some carrier systems require energy and are able to transport materials against the concentration gradient. In particular, amino acids are transferred across membranes in a direction opposite to what would occur by diffusion alone. In general, cells take an active role to ensure that the organism maintains a constant internal chemical environment. The human fetus shares with other biological systems the property of homeostasis—the capacity for making certain functional adjustments to maintain proper conditions in its internal environment in the face of transient fluctuations or alterations of conditions in its external environment.

In humans, the crucial period of development precedes the eighth week of pregnancy, before any visible sign of the trait itself. The vast majority of deformities originate at an early stage of development, even before the mother may suspect that she is pregnant.

Ethical Probe 4
The Human Fetus as Research Material

Investigators have been quick to notice that the pattern of developmental abnormalities induced by altered environmental conditions or adverse agents (teratogens) may be quite different in different species of animals. Thus, when pregnant rats are fed on a diet deficient in vitamin A, the offspring are typically hydrocephalic (enlarged head). On the other hand, mice maintained on diets deficient in vitamin A during pregnancy produce offspring with ocular and kidney defects. The sleeping pill, made of the drug thalidomide, when taken by a pregnant woman, can lead to a gross deformity in the newborn—the baby's arms are absent or reduced to tiny, flipperlike stumps. Yet, on testing with a wide variety of laboratory animals, thalidomide has proved to be relatively innocuous. The wide variability of response of different species prompted one medical scientist to remark that "the only test for teratogenicity in man is man himself."

In essence, while indispensible information can and should be obtained from research on other animals, the effects of drugs, viruses, and other agents on embryonic tissues are often specific to man. Human fetuses would be obtained from women who spontaneously abort them, and the informed consent of these women would be obtained for the experimental use of the abortuses.

Do you support the use in research of human embryonic and fetal tissues in the hope of obtaining meaningful information on the causes of human genetic and developmental abnormalities?

5 Biological Membranes and the Architecture of Cells

There are very few structures in the living cell that are not fabricated of membranes. The entire surface of the cell is covered continuously by a thin membrane, which separates the cell contents from the surrounding medium. The surface membrane is called the *plasma membrane,* or simply the *cell membrane.* Membranes also enclose the nucleus and fill the interior of the cell with a network of elaborate channels of communication between the nucleus and cell exterior (fig. 5.1). Such channels are indispensable for the transport of the diverse products of the cell. Indeed, the internal membrane system may be thought of as the circulatory system of the cell.

As late as 1950, the living membrane was thought to be a static mechanical barrier comparable to a rigid cooking strainer with fixed openings or pores. Currently, the cell membrane is viewed as an exceedingly pliable lining in which the pores are not literally holes but adjustable portals. This new view was profoundly shaped by the advent in the 1950s of the electron microscope and its extraordinary resolving capabilities. At the same time, much of the uncertainty about the molecular organization of the membrane has been removed by increasing refinements of biochemical and biophysical techniques.

There is growing awareness that the living membrane plays a vital role in virtually all cellular phenomena. The surface membrane regulates the chemical composition of the interior of the cell by excluding some substances and permitting the penetration of others. Membranes inside the cell serve as sites for energy-generating reactions (such as, the breakdown of glucose) and the synthesis of cell components (such as, proteins). Membranes are also instrumental in bringing together, or assembling, specific cells to form organized tissues. During development, cells of similar types, such as liver cells or heart cells, sort themselves into discrete aggregations of liver tissue or heart tissue. The incredible capacity

Figure 5.1 A generalized cell showing extensive connections between all the membranous components. A controversial issue at present is the degree of continuity of mitochondria with other membranous elements of the cell.

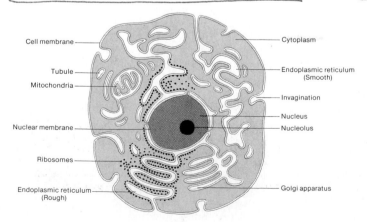

Cell membrane — Cytoplasm

Tubule

Mitochondria

Endoplasmic reticulum (Smooth)

Invagination

Nucleus

Nuclear membrane — Nucleolus

Ribosomes

Endoplasmic reticulum (Rough) — Golgi apparatus

of like cells to recognize one another and adhere together is due to unique recognition sites on the surface membranes.

MEMBRANE ORGANIZATION

Cellular membranes are composed almost entirely of protein and lipid molecules, the latter mainly present as phospholipids. The phospholipid molecule merits attention because there exist, within the same molecule, two regions that behave chemically in contradictory fashions. One region (the so-called head end) is polar or *hydrophilic* (literally, "water-loving"), while another portion (the tail end) is nonpolar or *hydrophobic* ("water-fearing"). Thus, when phospholipid molecules are mixed with water, they associate in a regular pattern: the polar heads, with their affinity for water, are oriented toward the water molecules, whereas the nonpolar tails, with their aversion for water, are extended toward each other, or away from the water (fig. 5.2A). In 1935, James F. Danielli, then at Princeton University, and Hugh Davson, at the University College in London, proposed that the phospholipids in the cell membrane are organized in the same bilayer manner as in phospholipid-water mixtures. In other words, the cell membrane contains a double layer of phospholipid molecules with the nonpolar tails pointing inwardly and the polar heads facing outwardly (fig. 5.2B). Danielli and Davson also envisioned the polar ends of the lipid molecules as being associated with a monolayer of protein molecules. Films of unfolded protein coat the two outer surfaces of the lipid bilayer, much like thin spreads of butter over the faces of a piece of bread. The Danielli-Davson scheme became widely known as the *bimolecular leaflet model*.

Viewed with the electron microscope, the cell membrane appears as "railroad tracks"—two parallel dark lines separated by a light central zone (fig. 5.3). The heavily stained lines are created by deposits of heavy metals (such as osmium tetroxide), which are used as electron-dense stains in electron microscopy. The deposition of heavy metals is most pronounced in the regions occupied by the protein coats and the polar lipid heads. The central unstained area has been identified with the non-polar lipid tails, which do not react or combine with the heavy metals. In the 1950s, J. David Robertson applied the term *unit membrane* to the three-layered (trilaminer) configuration. Robertson also generalized that the unit membrane represents the basic organizational pattern present at all cell surfaces and in all internal membranous systems.

The Danielli-Davson model of the membrane, although reasonable and

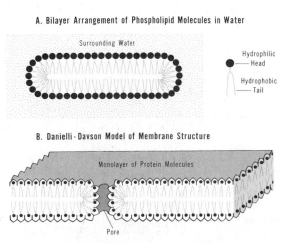

A. Bilayer Arrangement of Phospholipid Molecules in Water

Surrounding Water

Hydrophilic — Head

Hydrophobic — Tail

B. Danielli-Davson Model of Membrane Structure

Monolayer of Protein Molecules

Pore

Figure 5.2 The pattern of arrangement of phospholipid molecules in water (*A*), and the bilayer organization of phospholipid molecules in a cell membrane, as envisioned by J. F. Danielli and H. A. Davson (*B*).

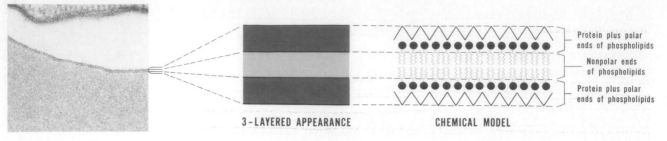

3-LAYERED APPEARANCE   CHEMICAL MODEL

Protein plus polar
ends of phospholipids

Nonpolar ends
of phospholipids

Protein plus polar
ends of phospholipids

ELECTRON MICROSCOPE IMAGE

Figure 5.3 Cell membrane of a mammalian red blood cell as viewed under the electron microscope, and a model of the triple-layered structure of the cell membrane. (Electron micrograph by courtesy of Dr. Richard Lumsden, Tulane University.)

widely accepted at one time, has been shown recently to have inherent flaws. There is now evidence that argues persuasively against the notion of a continuous unfolded layer of protein. As demonstrated by high-resolution electron microscopy, the protein molecules are folded into compact globules. In 1966, S. J. Singer, at the University of California in San Diego, compared the structure of the membrane to that of icebergs (globular proteins) floating in a sea of lipids (fig. 5.4). The globular proteins are inserted at random intervals in the membrane rather than being spread thinly and uniformly over the entire surface of the lipid bilayer. Some of the protein molecules extend completely through the membrane, stretching from one surface to the other. These are classified as *integral* proteins. Others, known as *peripheral* proteins, are located on only the outer surface or the inner surface.

The protein "icebergs" are free to move laterally, a finding which indicates that the lipid region is in a liquid or semiliquid state. The mobility of the globular proteins in the lipid matrix of the membrane has been demonstrated dramatically by fusing human and mouse cells. Immediately after fusion, the distinctly human proteins and the characteristic mouse proteins are identifiable and segregated in the two halves of the fused membrane. Within an hour, however, the human and mouse protein globules are able to migrate unimpeded within the membrane. Comparable studies have shown that the nonpolar tails of the lipid molecules are not held rigidly perpendicular to the membrane surface, but are in constant motion. The Singer model of membrane structure has been aptly called the *fluid-mosaic* model.

To account for the passage of simple substances across the membrane, Danielli postulated the existence of small pores that are coated with protein and extend through the lipid bilayer (fig. 5.2B). Singer has suggested,

Figure 5.4 The fluid-mosaic model of membrane structure proposed by S. J. Singer, in which globular proteins ("icebergs") are embedded in the lipid matrix at varied intervals.

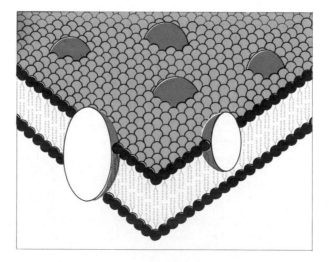

however, that the channels for the transport of low-molecular substances are formed by groupings of four or more subunits of proteins, as schematized in figure 5.5.

OSMOSIS

In an earlier section (chapter 4), we learned that the living cell membrane is remarkably precise in its selectivity: it allows only certain solutes to pass through while restricting the penetration of others. With respect to water molecules, natural membranes are freely permeable. The movement of water across a barrier (membrane) as a result of a difference in water concentration when the barrier restricts the passage of solute is called osmosis.

Figure 5.6 shows two fluid compartments separated by a membrane. The left-hand compartment (A) initially contains only water molecules (pure water). In the right-hand compartment (B), an impermeable solute (sucrose) is added to the water. Although sucrose cannot move across the membrane, it does occupy space. In other words, the addition of solute decreases the concentration of water molecules in solution B. Accordingly, water will flow in the direction of the concentration gradient—from a region of high water concentration (A) to a region of lower water concentration (B). Theoretically, the diffusion of water should continue until the concentration of water molecules in each compartment becomes equal. Actually, however, such equalization is unattainable. As the fluid level in compartment B rises (fig. 5.6), a new force arises that counteracts the inflow of water into compartment B. This force is the *hydrostatic pressure* exerted by the weight of the water in compartment B. The increasing hydrostatic pressure pushes against the water so as to drive water molecules back into compartment A. Ultimately, this backward driving force will exert a pressure just equal to the tendency of water molecules to enter compartment B. At this point, water flows in both directions at the same rate. The hydrostatic pressure that builds up as a consequence of the flow of water in the presence of a concentration gradient is called the *osmotic pressure*.

A living cell exhibits osmotic properties. If a given solute cannot pass through the surface membrane of the cell, any change in the concentration of the solute results in a water concentration gradient across the membrane. Compartment B in figure 5.6 may be thought of as a living cell, with

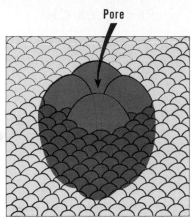

Figure 5.5 A channel, or pore, for the transport of substances through the membrane may be formed by groupings of four (or more) subunits of protein.

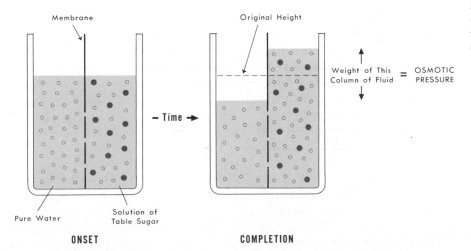

- ○ Permeable Water Molecule
- ● Impermeable Sugar Molecule

Membrane

Original Height

Weight of This Column of Fluid = OSMOTIC PRESSURE

— Time →

Pure Water

Solution of Table Sugar

ONSET

COMPLETION

Figure 5.6 The movement of water (osmosis) across a selectively permeable membrane in response to the concentration difference in water when the membrane restricts the passage of solute (impermeable sugar molecules).

Red Blood Cell

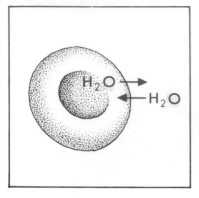

ISOSMOTIC
(Blood Plasma)

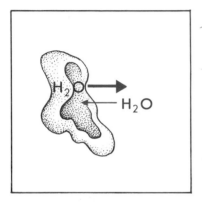

HYPEROSMOTIC
(Sea H$_2$O)

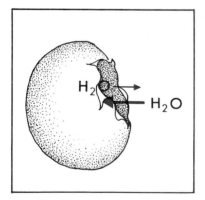

HYPOSMOTIC
(Distilled H$_2$O)

Figure 5.7 The stable volume of a red blood cell in an isosmotic medium, and the volume change (shrinkage or swelling) that occurs when the cell is placed in a hyper-somatic medium (such as sea water) or a hypersomotic medium (such as distilled water).

the important provision that a cell has an expansible, although finite, volume. The movement of water into a cell creates a pressure in the cell, just as pumping air into a basketball gives rise to a pressure exerted against the sides of the ball. As water enters the cell (or air enters the ball), the pressure grows until it is sufficient to oppose the force propelling the water (or air) inward. At this moment, the *net* movement of water into the cell ceases. Thus, an equilibrium is reached when the driving force of water entering the cell is exactly opposed by the pressure that has built up within the cell interior to prevent the further inflow of water. This latter pressure, which exerts a force on the cell membrane, is the osmotic pressure of the cell contents.

When the solute concentration of a solution surrounding a cell is higher than the solute concentration within the cell, more water will diffuse out of the cell than will enter the cell. In such a *hyperosmotic* solution, the cell will shrink since the net effect will be a loss of water from the cell (fig. 5.7). When the bathing solution is *hyposmotic*—that is, the solute concentration of the solution is less than that within the cell—the cell will swell in volume because the net flow of water will be into the cell.

It is common knowledge that human red cells become disrupted when pure (distilled) water is injected into a blood vessel. The red cells swell until they burst. The cell is capable of much stretching, but there is a limit to the expansion in volume. In distilled water, the red cells can never retain their integrity because there are no solute molecules in pure water and water molecules flow continuously into the cell. Accordingly, if a solution is to be injected into the bloodstream, the solution should have the same number of impermeable solute molecules as the red cell. Such a solution is said to be *isosmotic* to the cell (fig. 5.7).

Most cells in the human body maintain a relatively stable volume. This would indicate that the body fluids bathing the cells maintain a relatively constant water concentration. As we shall learn later, the kidneys, by regulating the elimination of water and solutes in the urine, are primarily responsible for the chemical constancy of the extracellular fluids.

SELECTIVE AFFINITY OF CELLS

Virtually all cell membranes are more or less "sugar-coated"—that is, they contain small amounts of carbohydrates. The carbohydrates may be linked to the surface proteins (as glycoproteins) or may be attached to the lipids (as glycolipids). The membrane-bound sugars, particularly the glycoproteins, have been implicated in the recognition and adhesion of cells.

The developing embryo is an assembly of innumerable cells. Although cells continually shift positions during development, they eventually assort themselves into specific tissues and organs. A key problem in development is how cells recognize and interact with one another to form discrete tissues. One approach to the problem involves isolating, or dissociating, cells from their normal relationships and then observing the manner in which the varied cells reassemble. An unusual experiment of this kind was performed in 1907 by Henry Wilson of the University of North Carolina. He gently pressed a whole sponge through fine bolting silk, and obtained a suspension of free, or individual, cells. Within a few hours, Wilson observed that the isolated individual cells came into contact with one another and clumped together to form progressively larger clusters. The clusters of cells ultimately aggregated into a complete functional sponge, in which each cell type had reassumed its proper position in the whole organism.

The same phenomenon of mutual rearrangement of cells was demonstrated in early amphibian embryos by Johannes Holtfreter of the University of Rochester in the 1940s. At an early stage of development, only three germ layers—ectoderm, mesoderm, and endoderm—are present. The frog embryo can be dissociated into suspensions of isolated cells and the cells can be separated according to germ layer. Ectodermal, mesodermal, and endodermal cells can then be recombined in various combinations. When, for example, isolated ectodermal cells (normally external) and mesodermal cells (normally internal) are mixed together, one can actually observe the lightly pigmented mesoderm cells move inwardly into the depths of the mass and the darkly pigmented ectoderm cells move to the periphery of the mass. Within 36 hours, two concentric layers of cells become evident—an external layer of ectoderm and an internal layer of mesoderm (fig. 5.8). Each cell type reconstitutes the precise germ layer from which each originated.

The recognition and selective adhesion of cells depends on the presence of certain proteins on the cell surface. These membrane proteins are specific for each type of cell, causing the adhesion only of cells of the same type. The cell-to-cell interactions involve the reactions of protein molecules (glycoproteins) at the cellular interfaces in a "lock and key" manner analogous to the familiar antigen-antibody reaction (see chapter 14).

The cell membranes are also of special interest in defending the body against invading organisms. Certain blood cells (specifically, lymphocytes) contain glycoprotein receptors on their surfaces that can detect foreign bacteria and viruses and thereby set the cells' defense mechanisms into action. Other surface glycoprotein molecules serve as transplantation antigens, which are instrumental in the acceptance or rejection of transplants of tissues and organs between different individuals. The transplantation antigens are unique for each person. The familiar ABO blood groups of individuals are also due to sharp differences in the membrane proteins.

Recent studies on cancer have drawn attention to the proteins of the cell membrane. The cell-to-cell adhesions are markedly reduced among cancerous cells, which suggests some failure in surface interactions. Moreover, the membranes of cancerous cells possess molecules that are

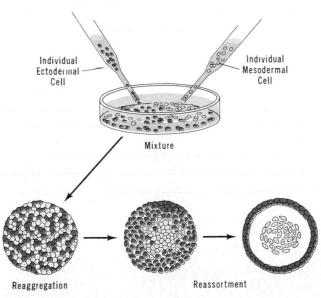

Individual Ectodermal Cell

Individual Mesodermal Cell

Mixture

Reaggregation

Reassortment

Figure 5.8 Isolated cells of similar type recognize one another and recombine with each other when mixed together.

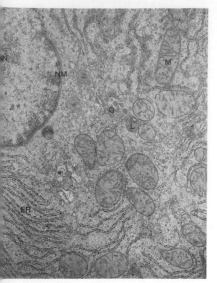

Figure 5.9 Electron micrograph of a thin section through a liver cell of a mouse (*N*, nucleus; *NM*, nuclear membrane; *M*, mitochondrion; *G*, Golgi apparatus; *ER*, endoplasmic reticulum; *L*, lysosome). A single liver cell has several hundred mitochondria. (Courtesy of Dr. Richard Lumsden, Tulane University.)

Figure 5.10 Tubelike appearance of the endoplasmic reticulum (ER) when viewed under the electron microscope *(left)* and a three-dimensional representation of the ER *(right)*. Particles (ribosomes) attached to the membranes impart a roughened appearance. (Electron micrograph by courtesy of Dr. Richard Lumsden, Tulane University.)

not present in normal cells. These foreign surface molecules may be involved in the characteristic ability of malignant cells to break away from surrounding cells and invade distant normal tissues. One goal of modern biomedical research is the early detection of cancerous growth through an early recognition of foreign membrane molecules.

INTERNAL MEMBRANES

Plate 6 shows an idealized, or typical, animal cell. An electron micrograph of a thin section of a liver cell is shown in figure 5.9. An impressive feature of both illustrations is the countless numbers of *organelles* of varied sizes and intricate shapes that densely fill the cytoplasm. Once thought to be small particulate bodies of little consequence, the organelles are now recognized as internal structures of great importance to the manifold chemical activities of the cell. Many of the organelles seen in cells are membranous structures, comprising varied themes on the unit membrane pattern.

The bulk of the internal membranous system takes the form of a delicate fabric of flattened membranes that ramify throughout the cytoplasm. This branching system, first described in 1945 by Keith Porter in tissue culture cells, has been called the *endoplasmic reticulum* (literally, "lace-like network inside the plasma"). Biologists typically connote the endoplasmic reticulum by the abbreviated symbols ER. When seen under the electron microscope, thin sections of ER membranes look like long parallel tubes or flattened sacs (fig. 5.10 and Plate 8). Their actual structure, however, in three-dimensional view, is that of a network of interconnected membranous sheets with channels between the sheets. These membrane-lined channels, or *cisternae,* are continuous with pores in the nuclear envelope and open onto the surface membrane of the cell. The channels thus furnish a means of communication between the nucleus and cytoplasm and between the cytoplasm and cell surface.

In cells that are actively synthesizing protein, the outer surfaces of the ER membranes are studded with small, dense particles called *ribosomes* (fig. 5.10). These particles are rich in ribonucleic acid (RNA), and play a dominant role in protein synthesis. The ribosomes represent the sites where specific amino acids join to form particular proteins. Because of the attachment of ribosomes to its outer surface, the endoplasmic reticulum is said to be *rough* (or *granular*). Rough ER is prominently in-

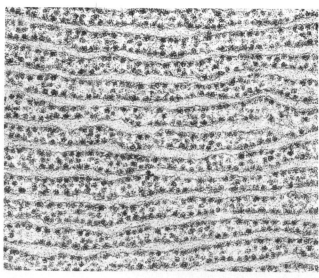

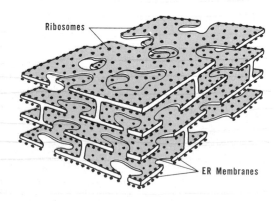

Ribosomes

ER Membranes

volved in the transport of protein. The proteins synthesized on the surface of the ribosomes are released in the channels of the reticulum and stored there for eventual export. Cells with exceptionally large amounts of rough ER are those that synthesize proteins to be secreted to the outside. Examples of protein-secreting cells are plasma cells, which produce soluble antibodies; fibroblasts, which produce collagen; and pancreatic cells, which produce digestive enzymes.

Not all ER membranes have ribosomes attached to their surfaces; these are called *smooth* (or *agranular*) endoplasmic reticulum. The membranes of smooth ER appear to contain several enzymes involved in fat metabolism and the synthesis of nonprotein steroid hormones. The hormone-secreting cells of the cortex of the adrenal glands, for example, have relatively few membrane-bound ribosomes.

GOLGI APPARATUS AND LYSOSOMES

Located near the cell nucleus are stacks, or parallel arrays, of flattened sacs, which have been called the *Golgi apparatus*, after its discoverer, the Italian microscopist Camillo Golgi (fig. 5.11 and Plate 9). When the Golgi apparatus (also called the Golgi body) was first observed in nerve cells in 1898, it was presumed to have a role in the secretory process—that is, the passage of materials out of the cell. Current evidence indicates that, in a manner of speaking, the Golgi apparatus collects and packages proteins for export.

Cell biologists, in a masterly accomplishment, have woven together the relations among protein synthesis, the ER, the Golgi apparatus, and protein secretion (fig. 5.12). The sequence commences with the synthesis of proteins in the rough-surfaced endoplasmic reticulum and the subsequent accumulation, or temporary storage, of the proteins in the channels of the reticulum. Small portions of the endoplasmic reticulum then break away to form membrane-enclosed vesicles containing the accumulated proteins. These vesicles migrate to the Golgi apparatus, which serves as a packaging depot for the proteins. The packaging is more than the mere application of a wrapping. Through the removal of water, the protein solution becomes concentrated, and by the addition of carbohydrate groups, certain proteins are modified into glycoproteins. The final products, now concentrated and modified, leave the Golgi apparatus as *secretory granules.* These granules migrate to the cell membrane, where the concentrated contents are released.

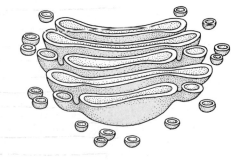

Figure 5.11 Electron micrograph of the Golgi apparatus *(left)* and a three-dimensional representation *(right).* The pattern of parallel, double-membraned sacs resembles a flattened stack of pancakes. Numerous small vesicles are typically associated with the flattened sacs. (Electron micrograph by courtesy of Dr. Richard Lumsden, Tulane University.)

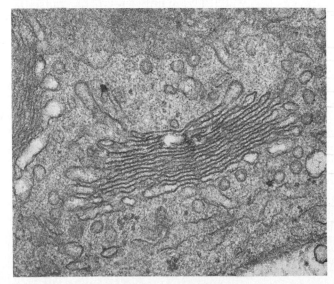

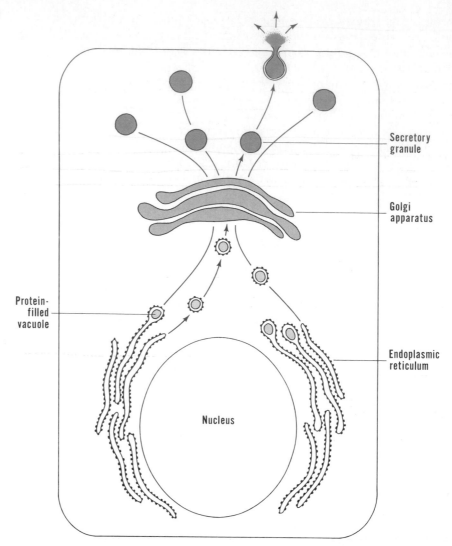

Secretory granule

Golgi apparatus

Protein-filled vacuole

Endoplasmic reticulum

Nucleus

There is evidence that the Golgi apparatus can take hydrolytic (or digestive) enzymes formed in the endoplasmic reticulum and release them within the cytoplasm as membrane-enclosed bodies known as lysosomes. As the name indicates ("lytic bodies"), these are bodies that can lyse, or digest, substances in the cell. The membrane of the lysosome segregates these lytic enzymes from the rest of the cell, so that the cell normally is unattacked by its own enzymes. In abnormal situations, the enzymes in this organelle may leak out, particularly if the membrane ruptures, and digest the cell itself. The abnormal release of lytic enzymes may be involved in carcinogenesis (the changing of normal cells to cancerous cells) and the aging process. The discoverer of the lysosome, Christian de Duve of the Catholic University of Louvain, has nicknamed this organelle the "suicide sac."

The normal activity of a lysosome is to digest large complex molecules without causing damage to the cell. Lysosomes are particularly numerous in certain white blood cells, such as phagocytic macrophages, which engulf invading microorganisms (bacteria). Lysosome action is shown in figure 5.13. The white blood cell engulfs the microbe by invaginating its membrane and forming an internal pouch or *phagocytic vesicle*. The lysosome, filled with a variety of hydrolytic enzymes, makes contact and merges with the phagocytic vesicle. The fused product be-

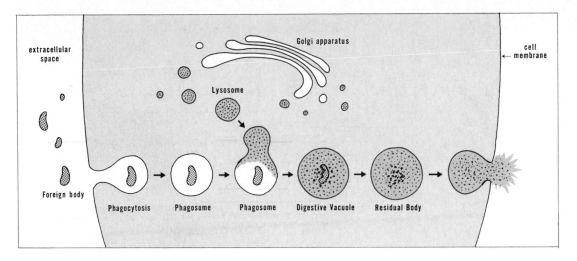

Inside the figure:

extracellular
space

Golgi apparatus

cell
← membrane

Lysosome

Foreign body

Phagocytosis Phagosome Phagosome Digestive Vacuole Residual Body

comes a *digestive vacuole*. The hydrolytic enzymes destroy the micro-organisms and release the products of digestion into the cytoplasm. The cell can actually use the digested products of low molecular weight for its own metabolic processes. Finally, the indigestible material is ejected from the cell.

Lysosomes have been found in a wide variety of cells, and all classes of large complex molecules, such as proteins, nucleic acids, and poly-saccharides, have been shown to be susceptible to degradation by the enzymes contained in these particles. Accordingly, high-molecular-weight nutrients that cannot be absorbed by the cell membrane are taken in by the process of *pinocytosis* (previously described in chapter 4) and are broken down by the lysosomes. The lysosomes make up essentially a miniature digestive system of the cell.

Figure 5.13 Activities of a lysosome. (*Phagosome* is another expression for *phagocytic vesicle*.)

NUCLEUS

The nucleus, which contains the hereditary material, is the control center for the cell. The nucleus has a strong affinity for basic dyes, which indicates that it contains a strongly acidic substance. In fact, this acid material is *deoxyribonucleic acid* (DNA), the macromolecule in which the hereditary information is encoded. The long, threadlike DNA molecules form a loose network of thin filaments, which impart a granular appearance to the resting nucleus. Granules and flakes of different densities may be seen in an electron micrograph of a nucleus (fig. 5.14). The areas of varied density reflect different degrees of coiling of the DNA threads. In earlier days, the granular network was called *chromatin*. This ineffectual term simply means "color," but it has been retained in the modern literature for descriptive purposes. During the division of the cell, the DNA filaments become highly coiled and condense to form recognizable, rodlike bodies, the *chromosomes* (see chapter 17). The nucleus is enclosed by a double membrane, which, at intervals, is traversed by several pores. Through these pores the nucleus is in direct communication with the cytoplasm.

A conspicuous structural feature of the nucleus is the dense, spherical body known as the *nucleolus* (literally, "small nucleus"). As revealed by the electron microscope (fig. 5.14), the nucleolus is packed with small granules similar to the ribosomes of the cytoplasm. The nucleolus is the site at which molecules of *ribonucleic acid* (RNA) are synthesized specifically for the ribosomes of the cytoplasm. The ribosomes, as earlier mentioned, are involved in the cellular production of proteins. Cells that

Figure 5.14 Electron micrograph of the nucleus in the skin cell of a frog (N, nucleolus; C, chromatin granules). The double membrane of the nuclear envelope is conspicuous. (Courtesy of Dr. Richard Lumsden, Tulane University.)

Figure 5.15 Electron micrograph of a mitochondrion *(left)* and a three-dimensional, cut-away representation of the mitochondrion *(right)*. (Electron micrograph by courtesy of Dr. Richard Lumsden, Tulane University.)

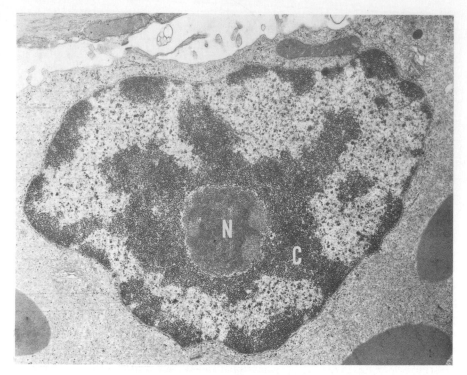

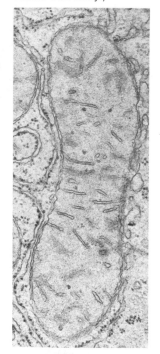

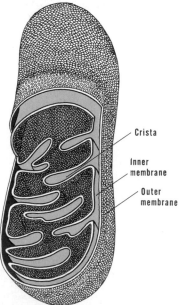

Crista

Inner membrane

Outer membrane

are very active in protein synthesis, with a concomitant great requirement for ribosomes, have a large nucleolus or even several nucleoli. Certain exceptional cells that have relatively short lifespans and synthesize little protein (such as sperm cells) have been shown to lack nucleoli.

MITOCHONDRIA

Under the light microscope, mitochondria are barely visible as thread-like granules in the cytoplasm; they were named as such by early cytologists (Greek, *mitos,* "thread," and *chondros,* "granule"). Using improved methods of high-speed differential centrifugation, Albert Claude of the Rockefeller Institute in New York in the 1940s isolated mitochondria from liver cells of the rat. Electron microscopy carried on at the Rockefeller Institute in the 1950s by George Palade and Keith Porter revealed that mitochondria have a complex anatomy. They are typically cylinder-shaped bodies bounded by a double-walled membrane (fig. 5.15 and Plate 10). The outer membrane serves as a limiting wall for the entire organelle, while the inner membrane is extended into numerous finger-like folds or projections, known as *cristae* (Latin, meaning "ridges"). The central space of a mitochondrion is occupied by extremely fine particles, collectively referred to as the *matrix.* Electron micrographs of a mitochondrion typically show several dense granules distributed throughout the matrix, which are thought to be deposits of calcium phosphate (fig. 5.16).

Mitochondria can now be defined biochemically. Many of the enzymes that preside over the breakdown of glucose for the purpose of obtaining energy have been localized in the mitochondria. The numerous cristae effectively increase the surface area for the attachment of enzyme molecules. The inner surface of the cristae is coated with an assembly of rounded protrusions that resemble lollipops (fig. 5.17). These stalked spheres, or *elementary particles,* have been demonstrated to contain enzymes involved specifically in the formation of the high-energy compound

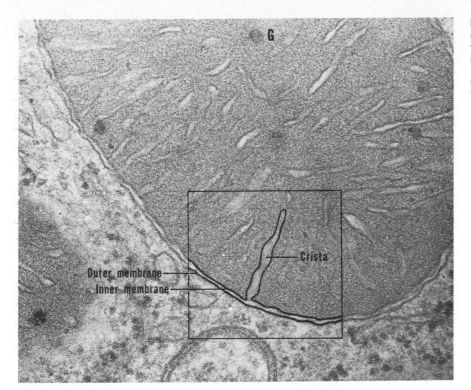

Figure 5.16 Electron micrograph of a mitochondrion showing to advantage the double-walled membrane, the cristae, and scattered calcium granules (labeled G). (Courtesy of Dr. Richard Lumsden, Tulane University.)

G

Crista

Outer membrane

Inner membrane

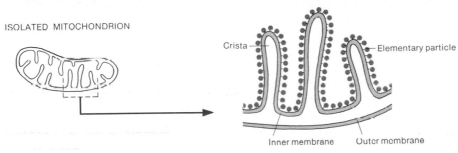

ISOLATED MITOCHONDRION

Crista

Elementary particle

Inner membrane

Outer membrane

Figure 5.17 The assembly of stalked spheres ("lollipops") on the inner membrane of a mitochondrion.

adenosine triphosphate, or ATP (see chapter 6). Since most of the cell's ATP is packaged in the mitochondria, this organelle has been aptly called the "powerhouse" of the cell. A cell engaged in energy-consuming work, such as a heart muscle cell, contains as many as 1,000 mitochondria. The destruction of mitochondria by potent poisons, such as cyanide, leads to instantaneous death of the cell.

Mitochondria are often thought of as semi-autonomous cellular inclusions. New mitochondria can arise in a cell by a division of pre-existing ones. Interestingly, mitochondrial duplication is not necessarily synchronized with the division of the cell. Mitochondria also possess small quantities of DNA by which they can synthesize some of their own proteins.

CHLOROPLASTS

Green plant cells have *chloroplasts* (Plate 11), which are membranous organelles that contain the light-absorbing pigments (particularly *chlorophyll*) and the varied enzymes involved in the photosynthetic production of sugar. The disc-shaped chloroplasts are bounded by two concentric membranes that enclose an inner region called the *stroma*. The stroma contains numerous dotlike ribosomes and a rich network of thin, parallel membranes known as *lamellae*. In many plants, the normally flattened lamellae are organized at intervals into disclike sacs, individually called a *thylakoid*. Often the thylakoids are arranged in parallel arrays that resemble a pile of coins. Each miniature coinlike stack is referred to as a *granum*. The grana contain high concentrations of chlorophyll molecules.

Chloroplasts have many features in common with mitochondria. They can grow and divide, and they possess their own DNA and associated mechanism for protein synthesis. Additionally, the division of chloroplasts is not always in harmony with the division of the cell.

ORGANELLES AND EVOLUTION

Some of the simplest cells in nature include bacteria and blue-green algae, which have been classified as *procaryotic cells*. These cells have no nuclear membrane by which the hereditary materials (DNA) are set apart from the cytoplasm and lack specialized cytoplasmic bodies (organelles) such as mitochondria and chloroplasts. In a bacterial cell, the DNA forms a simple closed loop that is attached to the inside of the cell's membrane. In contrast, the cells of higher plants and animals, or *eucaryotic cells*, have a distinct nuclear membrane (that encloses strands of DNA) as well as an elaborate system of membrane-bound cytoplasmic organelles.

J. David Robertson has suggested that very primitive cells may have consisted solely of protoplasm bounded by a surface membrane and devoid of organelles. The internal membranous compartments of eucaryotic cells may have evolved by the invagination, or drawing inward, of the primitive surface membrane. The invaginated structures may then have differentiated into the specialized organelles characteristic of present-day eucaryotes. In support of this idea, it is of interest that bacteria have no mitochondria; their enzymes for the breakdown of glucose are incorporated in the structure of the cell surface membrane. Figure 5.18 shows the postulated mechanism for the origin of mitochondria from the cell surface membrane.

Not all authorities agree that the membrane-bound organelles of eucaryotes were derived by modifications from the surface membrane. In particular, mitochondria have a number of interesting properties that suggest that they were once free-living, bacterialike organisms. Mitochondria have small amounts of their own DNA; this DNA exists as a loop-shaped molecule like the DNA of bacteria. Also, mitochondria are able to actively transport substances across their membranes, and they possess the genetic capacity to incorporate amino acids into proteins. These properties that the mitochondria exhibit have led to the hypothesis that mitochondria may have been derived from primitive aerobic bacteria that were engulfed by predatory eucaryotes about a billion years ago. Since then, the eucaryotic cells have become completely dependent on their enslaved mitochondria, and the latter, in turn, have become de-

Figure 5.18 Hypothetical scheme of the development of the mitochrondrion from the surface membrane. (Based on hypothesis of J. D. Robertson.)

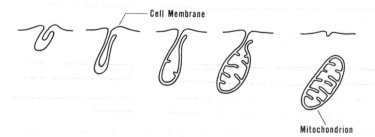

Cell Membrane

Mitochondrion

pendent on their hosts. In essence, the mitochondria became permanent residents within the eucaryotic hosts. This view, however, remains in the realm of conjecture.

SUMMARY

One of the notable highlights of our recent knowledge of living systems has been the realization of the ubiquity of membranes. A cell may be considered a collection of membrane-lined chemical compartments. The membrane at the surface of the cell serves as a selective barrier that regulates the passage of substances into and out of the cell. Cellular membranes are rich in proteins and lipids, particularly phospholipids. Several molecular models of membrane structure have been proposed, of which the *fluid-mosaic* model presently enjoys wide appeal.

Most of the organelles within cells are membranous structures. The sheetlike endoplasmic reticulum (ER) is a membranous system that pervades the cytoplasm and is important in the production, storage, and transport of proteins. The Golgi apparatus, stacks of flattened sacs, is involved in the secretion of protein from the cell. Another cytoplasmic organelle bounded by a membrane is the lysosome, which contains enzymes capable of breaking down large molecules. Almost all of the chemical energy (ATP) required by the cell comes from reactions that take place within the cylinder-shaped mitochondria. The evolutionary origin of organelles, mitochondria in particular, has attracted speculation. In the distant past, mitochondria may have been primitive, bacterialike organisms that became engulfed by predatory advanced cells and became, with time, permanent residents.

Ethical Probe 5
Screening for Breast Cancer

Women are highly susceptible to cancer of the breast. More women succumb to breast cancer than any other form of malignancy. The National Cancer Institute has advocated that women be screened routinely in the hope of detecting malignant growth in its earliest stages. However, medical scientists continue to debate the issues of which screening techniques are effective and safe and the age at which routine screening should commence. Mammography, or the use of X rays to detect early breast tumors, is very effective, especially when employed in association with palpation, or the manual exploration of the breasts for cancerous lumps. Nevertheless, concern has been voiced that cumulative exposures to X rays may actually trigger or promote breast cancer. Unfortunately, thermography, or the use of heat rather than X rays, has not proven to be a particularly effective diagnostic procedure. The crucial question, then, is whether the benefits of early detection by mammography outweigh the potential risks of radiation-induced breast cancer.

Since breast cancer is more likely to occur in women older than the age of 50, it has been suggested that screening by mammography be undertaken on women past the age of 50. Moreover, women between the ages of 40 and 49 should be screened only if they have a family history of breast cancer. Since women below 40 have a relatively long life ahead of them, routine screening by mammography would entail too great a risk of being exposed to potentially large doses of X rays.

Evaluate the benefit-versus-risk ratio for women younger than 40. Would you advise that women below 40 *not* be screened by mammography? Would it be advisable to use routinely the less dangerous, but less effective, detection technique of thermography?

6 Cellular Metabolism

The living cell is in a state of ceaseless chemical activity. Organic molecules, notably carbohydrates, are continually degraded to release the energy stored in their chemical bonds. At the same time, new molecules are synthesized that enable the cell to maintain its structural integrity. All the chemical reactions occurring within the cell are known collectively as *metabolism*. Metabolism embraces both *catabolism*, the destructive or degradative reactions that provide energy, and *anabolism*, the constructive or synthetic processes that create new structural molecules. By a balance between the rates of catabolic and anabolic processes, life is maintained. Any disturbance of the balance between catabolism and anabolism can lead to cell destruction.

The turnover of molecules in the cell, or in the organism, takes place in an astonishingly short period of time. Julian Huxley likened an organism to the famous falls of the Niagara River. At one point, the river plunges 500,000 tons of water a minute into a steep-walled gorge. At no two moments of time does the falls contain the same body of water. Yet the integrity of the falls remains, and to an observer the falls looks the same from day to day. Similarly, the chemical components of an organism are in a dynamic state of flux. Molecules are replaced every few seconds, and no organism in a chemical sense is exactly the same from moment to moment. Yet the organism maintains a continuous individuality.

The living cell can extract energy from a sugar molecule without losing most of the energy in the form of wasted heat. This is remarkable when one considers that all the energy from the breakdown of sugar in a test tube is lost in the form of heat. An organism has the extraordinary capacity to degrade an organic molecule in a way that the energy is largely released in a form that is useful or usable to the cell.

ENERGY AND THE ROLE OF ATP

All organisms require a continuous supply of energy to perform various kinds of work. In adults, energy is required for such diverse activities as the contraction of muscles, the movement of blood cells in the vessels, and the active transport of molecules across the cell membrane. In the embryo, energy is necessary for the movements and rearrangements of cells during the formation of bodily structures.

We define energy simply as the capacity to bring about specific changes. In this respect, figure 6.1 may prove helpful. A physical object, such as a boulder, has *potential energy* associated with its position or internal structure (fig. 6.1A). A portion of this potential energy is converted into *kinetic energy* of motion when the boulder rolls downhill. Some of the potential energy becomes dissipated as *heat energy* and is unavailable to promote motion. Accordingly, the potential energy, when released, ap-

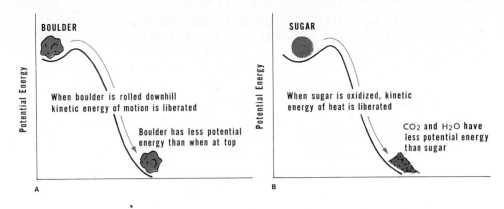

Figure 6.1 Potential and kinetic energies of a boulder *(A)* and a sugar molecule *(B, C)*. (© 1971 by Harcourt Brace Jovanovich, Inc. and reprinted with their permission from *Human design* by W. S. Beck.)

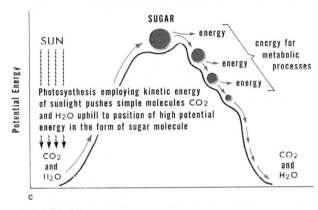

pears as motion and heat. Although heat represents unusable energy, the total energy content of the system remains constant. In other words, energy can be transformed from one of its form to another, as from mechanical energy to heat energy, without any net gain or loss in the total energy of the system. This is known as the *first law of thermodynamics* or, more generally, as the *law of the conservation of energy.*

The type of energy that is most important in the life of a cell is *chemical energy.* Whereas a boulder represents stored mechanical energy, an organic molecule has chemical energy locked within the structure of the molecule. When the chemical bonds in a molecule are broken, the chemical energy is liberated as useful energy (such as the energy of motion in muscles) and heat energy. In any transaction converting energy from one form to another, some energy is always wasted as heat. In the breakdown of sugar (fig. 6.1B), the process is inefficient and results in nonusable waste heat. This inefficiency is an expression of the *second law of thermodynamics:* any system tends spontaneously toward increasing disorder, or randomness. The term *entropy* is used as a measure of the degree of disorder. Stated simply, entropy is a measure of the amount of energy that becomes unavailable for useful work. All systems tend spontaneously toward a state of increasing entropy or disorder. Familiar examples of the tendency toward increasing entropy are the uncontrolled formation of weeds in a garden, the eventual collapse of a brick wall, the customary disarray of a dormitory room, and the inevitable breakdown of an automobile. To reverse the process of disorganization and provide for a decrease in the entropy of a system, work must be accomplished or energy expended.

A sugar molecule is in a more highly organized state (or possesses less entropy) than carbon dioxide or water. The degradation of sugar is an energy-yielding reaction. As seen in figure 5.1C, the reconstruction of chemical bonds, as in the formation of a sugar molecule from carbon dioxide and water, requires that energy be added. The ultimate source of all energy is the radiant energy of sunlight, which is trapped by green plants. The process of *photosynthesis* enables the green plant to store the energy of sunlight within organic compounds (fig. 6.1C). Specifically, the energy is transformed into the carbon-hydrogen bonds of glucose.

The amount of heat released in a system is measured in units of *calories*. A calorie is technically defined as the amount of heat energy required to raise the temperature of one gram of water one degree Celsius. Since chemical reactions generally release large quantities of heat, the unit more often employed is the *kilocalorie* (1 Kcal = 1,000 calories). By burning one mole of glucose (180 grams) in the laboratory, it can be shown that glucose breaks down into six molecules of water and six molecules of carbon dioxide, with the liberation of 686 Kcal of energy. In the test tube, all the energy is lost as heat, whereas the living cell is able to capture about 40 percent (277 Kcal) of the released energy to effect the changes necessary to sustain the integrity of the cell. The remaining 60 percent is dissipated as heat (which is used in birds and mammals to maintain constant body temperatures). The rate of recovery of utilizable energy by the living cell is extremely favorable; by comparison, an internal combustion engine has an efficiency no greater than 25 percent. The customary automobile engine converts less than 10 percent of the heat of combustion into useful mechanical energy.

A living cell transfers chemical potential energy from one molecule to the chemical structure of another molecule so as not to lose all energy as wasted heat. The cell transfers useful energy to a special, highly reactive molecule called *adenosine triphosphate* (ATP). This molecule consists of three components: a nitrogen-containing unit called *adenine*; the five-carbon sugar *ribose*; and three *phosphate* radicals linked in series to the sugar (fig. 6.2). The two terminal phosphate groups are joined to the remainder of the ATP molecule by *high-energy bonds*, designated by a wavy line (~) instead of the usual straight line. Each of these two high-energy phosphates, when split off, liberates 7,300 calories of usable energy (7.3 Kcal/mole). After the ATP molecule loses one energy-rich phosphate group, it becomes *adenosine diphosphate* (ADP); the loss of the second phosphate group results in *adenosine monophosphate* (AMP).

Figure 6.2 Chemical structure of the energy-rich adenosine triphosphate (ATP), and the portions that comprise ADP and AMP.

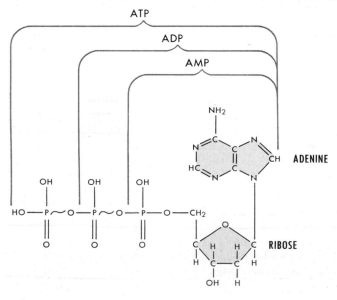

A reaction involving phosphate, particularly the formation of ATP from ADP, is called *phosphorylation.*

Adenosine triphosphate is the cell's carrier of chemical energy and the cell's immediate source of energy for all reactions. When glucose is oxidized, the energy released from the carbon-hydrogen bonds of glucose is trapped to form ATP. When energy is required for cellular processes, it is obtained directly from the energy stored in ATP. Accordingly, ATP is involved in both the energy-yielding and the energy-demanding reactions of the cell. This important molecule has been appropriately termed the "energy currency" of the cell. It is noteworthy that ATP is universal; all living organisms use the same energy currency.

ENZYMES

The combustion, or oxidation, of glucose in a test tube requires high temperatures. The breakdown of organic molecules (as well as their synthesis) can occur in the living cell without the necessity of high temperatures. The cell contains protein catalysts, or enzymes, which enable the cell to perform reactions at relatively low temperatures. Enzymes were first discovered in the 1890s in cell-free extracts of yeast; the word, in fact, means "in yeast." The enzymes in yeast cells are responsible for accelerating conversion (or fermentation) of the sugar in grape juice into alcohol and carbon dioxide. The yeast enzymes, like all enzymes, affect only the rates of the reactions; they are not consumed or chemically altered in the reactions that they promote.

A chemical reaction represents essentially a rearrangement of the atoms of molecules; that is, old bonds between atoms are broken and are replaced by new bonds. Most reactions must be supplied initially with energy in order to proceed. For example, some form of energy (such as a spark) is required to promote the collision of gaseous molecules of hydrogen and oxygen to form water. The collisions weaken the bonds between the atoms of hydrogen (H—H) as well as the bonds linking oxygen atoms (O—O), and increase the probability of the formation of water bonds (O—H). Once a few molecules of hydrogen and oxygen interact, the heat released sets into motion other molecules and the reaction can proceed on its own. As seen in figure 6.3A, the amount of energy input that is required to promote contact (hence, a reaction) between molecules is called the *activation energy.* It may be likened to the invest-

Figure 6.3 Energy barrier in chemical reactions. Enzyme lowers the energy barrier, permitting the hydrogen and oxygen molecules to react without the necessity for a strong initial expenditure of energy (high temperature, in particular).

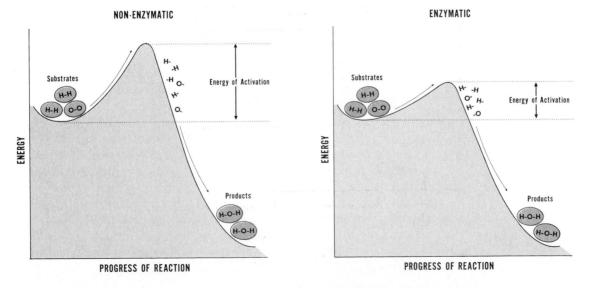

NON-ENZYMATIC

Substrates · Energy of Activation · Products · ENERGY · PROGRESS OF REACTION

ENZYMATIC

Substrates · Energy of Activation · Products · ENERGY · PROGRESS OF REACTION

Figure 6.4 Specificity of an enzyme for a particular substrate. When the products of the reaction are released, the enzyme is then free to engage in further reactions with additional substrate molecules.

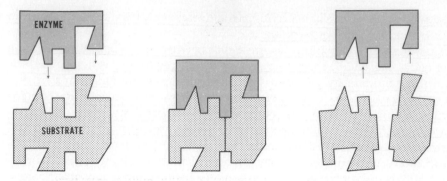

ment of effort necessary to pull a hand sled to the top of a hill. Once this hurdle is surmounted, the sled can spontaneously roll downhill, generating its own energy.

Enzymes are important because they largely do away with the need for the strong expenditure of energy (for example, high temperature) to initiate a reaction (fig. 6.3B). An enzyme lowers the activation energy so as to permit the reactant molecules to surmount the energy barrier with relative ease. This requires that the enzyme come into contact with the reactant molecules, or technically, the *substrate* molecules. Presumably the enzyme lowers the energy barrier by placing a stress on the chemical bonds of the substrate molecules. With their bonds weakened, the substrate molecules become more reactive.

The union between enzyme and substrate may be written as follows:

$$
\begin{array}{cccccc}
\text{S} & + & \text{E} & \longrightarrow \text{ES} \longrightarrow & \text{P} & + & \text{E} \\
\text{substrate} & & \text{enzyme} & \text{enzyme-substrate} & \text{product} & & \text{enzyme} \\
& & & \text{complex} & & &
\end{array}
$$

The enzyme-substrate complex is only temporary. When the products of the reaction are released, the enzyme is then free to engage in further reactions with additional substrate molecules. Innumerable reactions occur within a cell, and almost all are catalyzed by different enzymes. The explanation for the high degree of specificity of an enzyme is the "lock-and-key" concept advanced by the 19th-century chemists Emil Fischer and Paul Ehrlich. The surface configuration of a given enzyme (the lock) is specific only to a substrate with a complementary shape (the key). The particular area of the enzyme molecule that accommodates the substrate molecule is known as its *active site* (fig. 6.4).

ROLE OF COENZYMES

Several enzymes are inactive unless associated with trace amounts of organic substances known as *coenzymes*. Most vitamins taken into the body are converted into coenzymes. For example, the essential ingredient in the coenzyme *nicotinamide adenine dinucleotide* (NAD) is derived from the vitamin *niacin,* one of the several B vitamins. Since coenzymes are necessary to maintain the activity of certain enzymes, they are, as first asserted in 1912 by the Polish biochemist Funk, essential for life (Latin, *vita,* meaning "life"). Coenzymes, like enzymes, are recycled and only minute amounts are required in the diet to replace those eventually broken down or excreted. Large quantities of vitamins do not enhance the effectiveness of enzymes; accordingly, an increase in the required dietary level of vitamins has no measurable benefit.

Coenzymes typically function in the transfer of small molecules or atoms (such as the hydrogen atom) from one substrate to another. The aforementioned NAD acts as a temporary carrier of hydrogen. As an example, the reaction from lactic acid to pyruvic acid is catalyzed by the enzyme lactic dehydrogenase. As this enzyme binds to the substrate molecule, NAD associates with the enzyme and picks up two atoms of hydrogen from the lactic acid molecule. The NAD then dissociates from the enzyme. The reaction can be written as follows:

$$\text{lactic acid} + \text{NAD} \xrightarrow{\substack{\text{lactic} \\ \text{dehydrogenase}}} \text{pyruvic acid} + \text{NADH}_2$$

An important consideration is that $NADH_2$ can be converted back to NAD through a second reaction, in which it delivers its two hydrogen atoms to another molecule. This other molecule may be oxygen, as follows:

$$O_2 + 2NADH_2 \longrightarrow 2H_2O + 2NAD$$

Hence, the NAD has served as an intermediary carrier of hydrogen atoms as they are transferred from one molecule to another. To stress the fact that NAD is not consumed in any of the reactions, biochemists often denote the role of NAD as an acceptor-donor of hydrogen in the following way:

The AH_2 represents a substrate (such as lactic acid) that transfers two hydrogen atoms to NAD to form $NADH_2$. In turn, $NADH_2$ reconstitutes NAD by passing its hydrogen atoms to substrate B (such as oxygen) to form BH_2 (water). This coenzyme plays a key role in several reactions involved in the metabolism of glucose.

CARBOHYDRATE METABOLISM

Slightly less than two dozen reactions are involved in the breakdown of glucose into carbon dioxide and water, each catalyzed by a specific enzyme. The primary objective in degrading glucose is to trap the chemical energy in the form of ATP. The overall, or total, reaction may be depicted as follows, where ~ⓅＰ denotes the high-energy phosphate radical:

$$C_6H_{12}O_6 + 6O_2 + 38ADP + 38 \sim Ⓟ$$
$$\longrightarrow 6CO_2 + 6H_2O + 38ATP$$

The 38 ATPs are not released all at once in any one reaction, but in an orderly fashion in a carefully integrated series of reactions. Each of the stepwise reactions is enzyme-mediated, which means that each reaction has a low energy of activation. Accordingly, the glucose molecule is degraded with a minimum expenditure of energy by the cell and a maximum realization of energy.

Many of the chemical reactions in the breakdown of glucose involve the removal of hydrogen atoms from various intermediate products. In biological systems, the removal of hydrogen atoms from organic molecules represents a highly efficient way of transferring chemical energy. As previously mentioned, the hydrogen atoms are passed on to coenzymes, notably NAD, which serve as hydrogen carriers. Only in the very terminal steps of glucose degradation is the stored energy in the hydrogen carriers finally funneled into ATP.

For purposes of discussion, the many individual reactions may be grouped into four stages. These stages may be characterized as follows: (1) glycolysis, (2) pyruvate conversion, (3) Krebs cycle, and (4) the respiratory chain.

GLYCOLYSIS (STAGE 1)

The initial stage is *glycolysis*, which can proceed under anaerobic conditions (that is, in the absence of oxygen). The glycolytic pathway results in the transformation of each 6-carbon glucose molecule into 2 molecules of a 3-carbon compound, pyruvic acid (or pyruvate). The series of intermediate, stepwise reactions are shown in figure 6.5. To initiate the breakdown of glucose, a certain amount of high-energy phosphate is expended. Although the process begins with an energy deficit as 2 molecules of ATP are used up in the early stages of glycolysis, 4 molecules of ATP are ultimately generated. There is thus a net gain by the cell of 2 ATP molecules.

Despite the many chemical reactions in the glycolytic series, very little energy is conserved in ATP—only about 2 percent of the utilizable energy in a glucose molecule. However, the chemical reactions in the

Figure 6.5 Glycolytic pathway by which a molecule of glucose (or glycogen) is converted into two molecules of pyruvic acid.

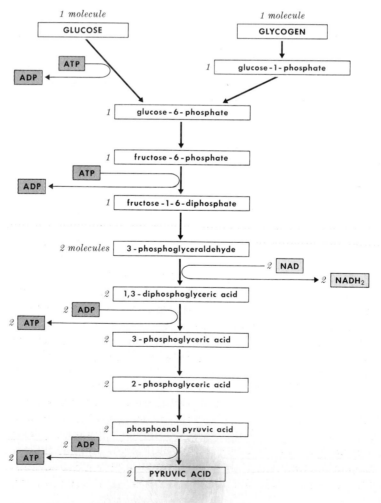

glycolytic breakdown of glucose to pyruvic acid require no oxygen; hence, under conditions of insufficient oxygen supply, a small amount of energy can still be made available to the cell. When the supply of oxygen to the cell is inadequate, lactic acid is formed instead of pyruvic acid. There are circumstances in which certain cells function anaerobically. In man and other vertebrates, a need for immediate energy may arise at the onset of strong muscular exertion, when the bloodstream cannot supply an adequate amount of oxygen. Under these conditions, the muscle cells are obliged to function anaerobically, and lactic acid accumulates. When the concentration of lactic acid rises too high, muscle fatigue results. Typically, however, prior to muscle fatigue, the oxygen supply becomes sufficient, and the lactic acid is reconverted to pyruvic acid.

In essence, at the completion of glycolysis, no carbon dioxide (CO_2) is produced, no oxygen (O_2) is utilized, and 4 hydrogen atoms are released for eventual union with oxygen. The hydrogen atoms are not released in the form of free hydrogen. Rather, they are delivered to NAD (nicotinamide adenine dinucleotide) molecules, which serve as hydrogen carriers. The hydrogen is thus held until it can be transferred ultimately to gaseous oxygen. The attachment of the 4 atoms of hydrogen to NAD is symbolized as $2NADH_2$, or simply, 2 carrier-H_2. The glycolytic pathway to pyruvic acid may then be summarized as follows:

Stage 1 $C_6H_{12}O_6 + 2ADP + 2\sim$ⓅP
$\longrightarrow$ 2 pyruvic acid + 2ATP + 2 carrier-H_2

Another aspect of the glycolytic pathway should be underscored. There are organisms—yeast and many other microorganisms—that are capable of living in the total absence of oxygen. They carry on glycolysis as far as pyruvic acid, and then convert the pyruvic acid to ethyl alcohol and carbon dioxide. The production of ethyl alcohol under anaerobic conditions is termed *alcoholic fermentation*. The terminal reaction may be written as follows:

$$2C_3H_4O_3 + 2H_2 \longrightarrow 2C_2H_5OH + 2CO_2$$
pyruvic acid   ethyl alcohol

It should be noted that the hydrogen atoms released during glycolysis are transferred to pyruvic acid. In other words, pyruvic acid substitutes for oxygen as a final hydrogen acceptor. Anaerobic organisms are thus obliged to forgo the greater part of the chemical energy bound up in the glucose molecule. The fermentative metabolic scheme is characteristic only of very small, primitive organisms (for example, certain species of bacteria and yeast). The limited evolutionary potential of these one-celled organisms reflects, in part, the fact that most of the energy of the glucose molecule remains untapped in fermentation. At a net gain of 2 ATP per mole of glucose broken down, anaerobic organisms extract only 2 percent of the usable energy available in the glucose molecule.

PYRUVATE CONVERSION (STAGE 2)

We may now consider the fate of pyruvic acid—the second stage in the metabolism of glucose (fig. 6.6). Each of the two pyruvic acid molecules combines with coenzyme A to form a formidable compound, acetyl coenzyme A, or acetyl CoA. It is in this reaction (fig. 6.6) that the first molecule of carbon dioxide (CO_2) is produced, derived from the carboxyl group (—COOH) of the pyruvic acid. It should be noted that, in metabolic

Figure 6.6 Conversion of pyruvic acid into acetyl coenzyme A.

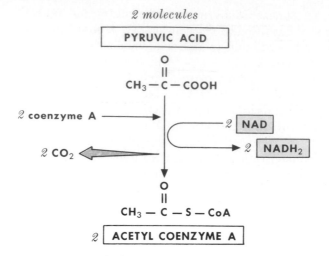

reactions, CO_2 is typically formed by the removal of the carboxyl group from organic acids.

The remaining fragment of pyruvic acid (the acetate or CH_3—CO— portion) is transferred to coenzyme A to form the acetyl coenzyme A. The coenzyme A molecule acts as a carrier for the acetate fragment of pyruvic acid, just as NAD is a carrier for hydrogen. Like most coenzymes, CoA is a derivative of a vitamin (in this instance, pantothenic acid, one of the B vitamins). The final outcome is the removal of 2 CO_2 molecules from the 2 pyruvic acid molecules and the release of 4 hydrogen atoms, which are delivered to NAD carriers. Again, no oxygen is utilized. The major events may be represented in highly abbreviated form as follows:

Stage 2   2 pyruvic acid + 2CoA $\longrightarrow$
2 acetyl CoA + 2CO_2 + 2 carrier-H_2

KREBS CYCLE (STAGE 3)

The two molecules of acetyl CoA enter into a complex metabolic cycle, representing the third stage (fig. 6.7). The 2-carbon acetyl CoA attaches to a 4-carbon molecule, oxaloacetic acid, to form a new 6-carbon compound, citric acid. In the process, coenzyme A is released, and is free to combine with another pyruvic acid molecule. Once formed, the 6-carbon citric acid is systematically broken down in a series of reactions, first to a 5-carbon molecule (α-ketoglutaric acid) and then eventually a 4-carbon molecule, oxaloacetic acid. The oxaloacetic acid produced in the last step turns immediately around to react with a fresh molecule of acetyl CoA, thus forming a new molecule of citric acid. The cycle is accordingly renewed. Because the initial compound formed is citric acid, the series of reactions is called the *citric acid cycle*. It is also known as the *Krebs cycle*, in honor of Sir Hans Krebs, who pioneered in its elucidation in the 1930s and received the Nobel prize in 1952 for this work.

For every 2 molecules of acetyl coenzyme A entering the Krebs cycle, 4 molecules of CO_2 are released. We saw earlier (fig. 6.6) that 2 molecules of CO_2 are liberated in the breakdown of pyruvic acid. These events fully account for the 6 molecules of CO_2 formed from a single glucose molecule as expressed in the generalized equation. Stated differently, the original 6 carbon atoms of glucose are now in the form of CO_2. These carbon dioxide molecules are eventually expired through our lungs.

At three separate points in the Krebs cycle (fig. 6.7), pairs of hydrogen atoms are transferred to NAD. In one instance, *flavin adenosine dinu-*

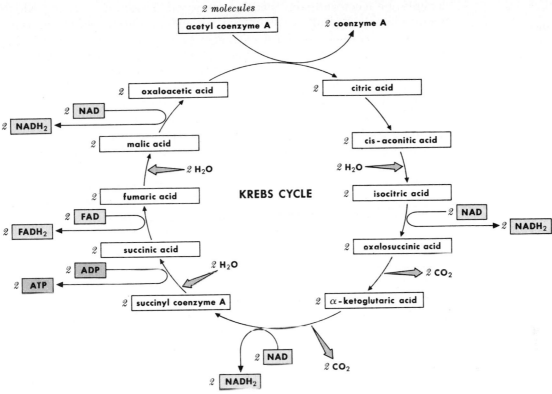

Figure 6.7 Reactions of the Krebs cycle.

cleotide (FAD) serves as a carrier of hydrogen atoms. Although functionally similar to NAD, FAD is derived from the vitamin *riboflavin* rather than from niacin. Thus far, no oxygen has been used. Nevertheless, 8 pairs of hydrogen atoms have been made available for eventual attachment to oxygen. The reactions of the Krebs cycle may be summarized as follows:

Stage 3   2 acetyl CoA + 6H$_2$O + 2ADP + 2~Ⓟ
     $\longrightarrow$ 4CO$_2$ + 2ATP + 2CoA + 8 carrier-H$_2$

RESPIRATORY CHAIN (STAGE 4)

The net result of the Krebs cycle is the formation of only 2 energy-rich ATP molecules. However, most of the chemical energy has been transferred to hydrogen carriers, and the potential for ATP production from these hydrogen carriers is great. Indeed, the fourth, or final, stage is especially designed for the generation of large quantities of ATP. In this terminal stage, hydrogen is passed successively through a complex series of coenzymes, an event associated with the release of energy to synthesize ATP (fig. 6.8). In fact, the series of transfers result in the synthesis of 34 molecules of ATP, the greatest quantity of energy trapped in the entire metabolic scheme. The chain of coenzymes, appropriately termed the *respiratory chain*, includes NAD, FAD, and a variety of different iron-containing compounds called *cytochromes*. A complicating feature is that, whereas NAD and FAD can carry hydrogen atoms, the cytochromes carry only electrons. For this reason, the system is often referred to as the *electron transport system.*

Each hydrogen atom consists of one negative *electron* (e$^-$) and a hydrogen *ion* (H$^+$). The removal of either an electron or H$^+$ from a compound results in the compound becoming *oxidized*. The compound that

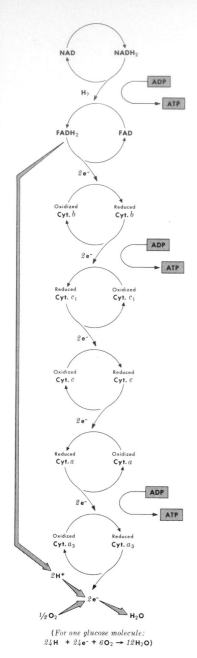

(For one glucose molecule:
$24H + 24e^- + 6O_2 \rightarrow 12H_2O$)

Figure 6.8 Respiratory chain involving the transport of hydrogen ions (H+) and electrons (e−), and the synthesis of ATP.

accepts the electron or H+ becomes *reduced*. These two events, which occur virtually simultaneously, are termed *oxidation-reduction reactions*. In the respiratory chain, each coenzyme, beginning with NAD, becomes reduced and then oxidized as it picks up and then transfers hydrogen atoms (in the case of NAD and FAD) or electrons (in the case of the cytochromes) to the next member of the chain.

When the hydrogen atoms ionize to contribute their electrons to the cytochrome sequence, the hydrogen ions (H+) are released to the surrounding medium. However, the hydrogen ions cannot remain free in solution but must combine with another molecule. When the electrons finally come off the terminal cytochrome, the molecule that accepts the electrons and the hydrogen ions (H+) is oxygen, resulting in the formation of water. This step, in which oxygen serves as the final electron and hydrogen acceptor, is properly termed *respiration*. It should be evident that the oxygen we breathe ends up in the form of water. It should also be appreciated that most organisms require oxygen to survive because this element is used as the final hydrogen acceptor in the electron transport system.

During the passage of hydrogen atoms and electrons along the respiratory chain, a high level of energy is liberated from the system and converted to the bond energy of ATP. For every NADH₂ introduced into the respiratory chain at the level of NAD, there is a generation of 3 ATP molecules. Each FADH₂ shuttled in at a lower level (the level of flavoprotein) can generate only 2 ATP molecules. The formation of ATP molecules in association with the respiratory chain is called *oxidative phosphorylation*. The fourth stage may be generalized as follows:

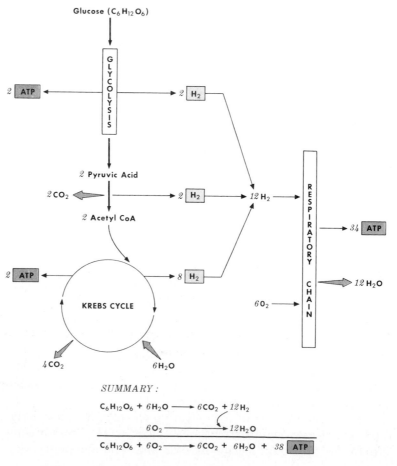

SUMMARY:

$$C_6H_{12}O_6 + 6H_2O \longrightarrow 6CO_2 + 12H_2$$

$$6O_2 \longrightarrow 12H_2O$$

$$\overline{C_6H_{12}O_6 + 6O_2 \longrightarrow 6CO_2 + 6H_2O + 38\ \boxed{ATP}}$$

Figure 6.9 Summary of major events during the aerobic breakdown of glucose to carbon dioxide and water.

Table 6.1
Energy Harnessed in ATP during
Oxidation of Glucose

Reaction	Number and Type of Hydrogen Carrier	Loss (−) or Gain (+) of ATP
Phosphorylation of glucose (glucose to glucose-6-phosphate)		−1
Phosphorylation of fructose-6-phosphate (fructose-6-phosphate to fructose-1,6-diphosphate)		−1
Conversion of 3-phosphoglyceraldehyde to 1,3-diphosphoglyceric acid	2 NADH$_2$	+6[a]
Transfer of energy-rich phosphate from 1,3-diphosphoglyceric acid to 3-phosphoglyceric acid		+2
Transfer of energy-rich phosphate from phosphoenol pyruvic acid to pyruvic acid		+2
Conversion of pyruvic acid to acetyl CoA	2 NADH$_2$	+6
Conversion of isocitric acid to oxalosuccinic acid	2 NADH$_2$	+6
Conversion of $\propto$-ketoglutaric acid to succinyl CoA	2 NADH$_2$	+6
Conversion of succinyl CoA to succinic acid		+2[b]
Conversion of succinic acid to fumeric acid	2 FADH$_2$	+4[c]
Conversion of malic acid to oxaloacetic acid	2 NADH$_2$	+6
TOTAL	12 Hydrogen Carriers	+38 ATP[d]

[a] This NADH$_2$ is produced in the cytoplasm during glycolysis. Current evidence suggests that cytoplasmically produced NADH$_2$ generates 2 ATPs per molecule rather than the 3 ATPs characteristic of mitochondrial-produced NADH$_2$.

[b] The high-energy molecule produced is not ATP but actually guanosine triphosphate (GTP). This molecule is structurally much like ATP and readily interconverted into ATP.

[c] Each pair of electrons passing from FADH$_2$ down the respiratory chain generates 2 ATPs instead of the customary 3 ATPs.

[d] If we accept the recent finding that cytoplasmically produced NADH$_2$ generates only 2 ATPs per molecule, then the total number of ATPs derived from the complete oxidation of glucose is 36 rather than 38.

Stage 4 $12 \text{ carrier-H}_2 + 6O_2 + 34ADP + 34 \sim \text{P}$
$\longrightarrow 12H_2O + 34ATP$

The stage-four total of 34 molecules of ATP *plus* the 4 molecules of ATP produced outside the cytochrome system (stages one and three) amount to a grand total of 38 molecules of ATP for each mole of glucose. If one were to add up the equations describing the changes in the four stages of glucose metabolism, the net result would be the overall equation presented in the introduction of this section, namely.

$$C_6H_{12}O_6 + 6O_2 + 38ADP + 38 \sim \text{P}$$
$$\longrightarrow 6CO_2 + 6H_2O + 38ATP$$

Figure 6.9 summarizes the formation of ATP during the aerobic breakdown of glucose to carbon dioxide and water. Additional details, with certain complicating features, are presented in table 6.1.

METABOLIC INTEGRATION

The metabolic pathway for glucose degradation serves as the common denominator for the breakdown of the other two principal classes of dietary organic molecules—fats and proteins. The initial step in the metabolism of fat involves the separation of the fatty acid molecules from the glycerol component (fig. 6.10). The glycerol and fatty acids then proceed through different pathways. Glycerol enters the glycolytic pathway as 3-phosphoglyceraldehyde, whereas the fatty acids are transformed into acetyl CoA. Acetyl CoA is also formed from pyruvic acid, and directly enters into the reactions of the Krebs cycle. The quantity of acetyl CoA produced by a single molecule of fat is considerably greater than the quantity produced by a glucose molecule. Thus, the amount of ATP ultimately synthesized from the breakdown of fat is correspondingly greater—at least 3 times as much ATP is derived from fat as from glucose, on a gram-for-gram basis.

Amino acids, the products of protein breakdown, enter the pathways of glucose metabolism at various places after their nitrogen groups have been removed (fig. 6.10). One of the end products of protein metabolism is the nitrogen-containing ammonia (NH_3), which is highly toxic to cells in large quantities. The ammonia is converted rapidly into an innocuous molecule, *urea*, which is excreted from the body in the urine.

Not only can the three classes of dietary organic molecules serve as a potential source of energy for the synthesis of ATP, but each class, to a large extent, can provide the raw materials for the synthesis of one another. Glucose, in excess, is converted into fat or into amino acids. Thus, persons on high-carbohydrate diets are able to synthesize sufficient proteins. When carbohydrate sources are insufficient, amino acids

Figure 6.10 Interrelations between the metabolism of carbohydrates, fats, and proteins.

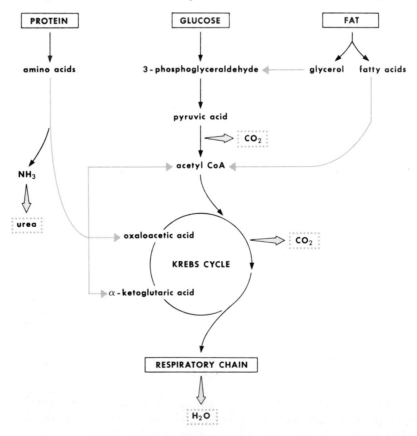

and glycerol can be transformed to glucose. Similarly, amino acids can be converted into fats through certain intermediate steps. Evidently, the metabolic processes are highly integrated.

INTERRELATIONS OF STRUCTURE AND FUNCTION

During the 1940s, techniques were devised for isolating the various components of the cell and studying their relation to the manifold chemical activities of the cell. The disruption of cells is carried out using the procedures illustrated in figure 6.11. The cells are broken by grinding them with a pestle in a glass homogenizer or subjecting the cells to the shearing forces of a blender. The resulting homogenate consists of a suspension of small particulate bodies, or organelles, plus all the cytoplasmic components, such as soluble enzymes, that are not bound to the organelles. The fractions can be separated more thoroughly by high-speed centrifugation. Large, dense particles settle to the bottom of the centrifuge tube as a result of the centrifugal force, whereas the smaller particles sediment as layers on top of the denser particles. The nonorganelle components, made up of soluble molecules, can be found in the liquid, or supernatant, fraction.

The first stage in the breakdown of glucose—that is, glycolysis—always takes place outside the mitochondria in the cytoplasm, since the glycolytic enzymes are soluble molecules that are not bound to any particular cell organelles. The enzymes associated with the Krebs cycle as well as those of the electron transport system are localized in the mitochondria. The enzymes of the Krebs cycle are dissolved in the matrix within the mitochondria, whereas the electron transport molecules are associated with the cristae of the inner membrane. Specifically, the electron transport molecules are tightly adherent in close physical proximity in the knob-like spheres (elementary particles). Each elementary particle contains a complete set of respiratory enzymes arranged in a precise spatial pattern. With the NAD, FAD, and cytochromes arranged in an order appropriate to their functioning in the respiratory chain, the transfer of electrons is accomplished rapidly and efficiently. The final transfer of energy to ATP thus proceeds in a very controlled manner. A cell engaged in energy-consuming work, such as a heart muscle cell, contains as many as 15,000 respiratory chains in the cristae of a single mitochondrion.

Figure 6.11 Separation and isolation of cellular components by homogenization and centrifugation. The liquid, or supernatant, fraction (level *a*) contains the glycolytic enzymes. Other fractions contain membraneous structures, such as the endoplasmic reticulum (level *b*), mitochondria (level *c*), and nuclei (level *d*). (See chapter 5 for descriptions of organelles of the cell.)

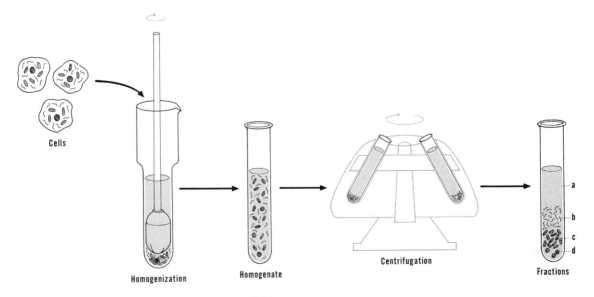

Cells

Homogenization

Homogenate

Centrifugation

Fractions

a
b
c
d

SUMMARY

All cells require energy to carry on life activities. Energy is obtained from the continual breakdown of organic molecules, particularly glucose; the breakdown releases the energy locked within the glucose molecule. The release of the stored energy of glucose involves a carefully integrated series of enzymatic reactions. The stepwise, enzyme-mediated reactions ensure that glucose is degraded with a minimum expenditure of energy and a maximum release of energy made available to the cell. The early pathways, called *glycolysis*, involve the breakdown of glucose to pyruvic acid (which need not involve oxygen); subsequent numerous reactions are concerned with the conversion of pyruvic acid to carbon dioxide and water in the presence of oxygen. An important metabolic pathway in the aerobic transformation of pyruvic acid is the Krebs cycle.

The energy originally present in the glucose molecule is trapped in a highly reactive molecule that is present in all cells—adenosine triphosphate (ATP). Adenosine triphosphate is the cell's carrier of chemical energy and the cell's ready source of energy for immediate work. The chemical energy of the glucose molecule is transferred to hydrogen atoms before its incorporation into ATP. Large quantities of energy are released to form ATP when hydrogen atoms are oxidized in an elaborate electron transport system (respiratory chain). The oxidized hydrogen is then available to unite with oxygen to form water. Respiration, properly defined, is the process in which ATP is produced from the energy made available when oxygen interacts with hydrogen to form water.

Cellular Differentiation 7

Like an individual, a cell undergoes changes from the moment it arises to its final dissolution. An early embryonic cell is spherical in form and so generalized in appearance that its actual destiny is not at all apparent. As the embryo develops, however, a given cell takes on a particular functional role. Such specialization of function is attended by a corresponding structural specialization. Thus, the flat, tilelike cells composing the thin walls of capillaries are admirably designed to facilitate the exchange of dissolved nutrients. The human red blood cell is not a sphere but a concave disc; this shape renders it more efficient in absorbing and releasing gases. Examples can be multiplied endlessly. As seen in figure 7.1, a muscle cell is drawn out into a long, threadlike structure (a fiber) to enhance contractility, and a nerve cell has numerous branching processes for the more effective transmission of impulses. The gross morphology of these cells clearly shows that structure and function are interrelated; the cell is specifically adapted in shape and form to perform a given function.

The transition of a cell from an embryonic to a specialized state is called *differentiation*. The differentiation of a cell to its mature state is, for the most part, irreversible. A nerve cell, for example, is so extensively modified that it cannot perform any other function than that to which it has become committed. Moreover, many cells, after having attained specialization, lose the capacity to replace themselves. After varying periods of usefulness to the body, highly differentiated cells wear out without leaving successors.

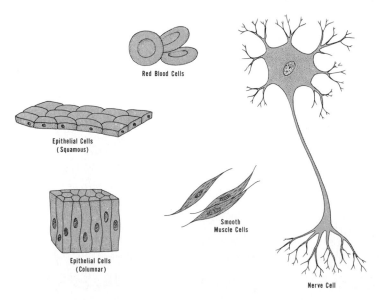

Figure 7.1 Variety of shapes of human cells, each structurally adapted for a particular function.

Red Blood Cells

Epithelial Cells
(Squamous)

Epithelial Cells
(Columnar)

Smooth
Muscle Cells

Nerve Cell

The human body has well over 100 different types of specialized cells, yet all are derived from embryonic cells of equal genetic potentialities. Most embryonic cells have more than one developmental potentiality. The full range of developmental possibilities of an early embryonic cell far exceeds the actual destiny of that cell in normal development. Biologists continue to search for the causative factors that promote a given cell to adhere to only one of the many possible fates that the cell might attain. Some clues to the process of differentiation have come from intriguing studies on the embryos of salamanders and frogs.

NORMAL DEVELOPMENT OF THE FROG EGG

The early developmental history of the frog (specifically, the common leopard frog, *Rana pipiens*) is shown in figure 7.2. The cells of the top, or *animal,* half (or hemisphere) of the egg are black-pigmented, whereas the cells of the bottom, or *vegetal,* hemisphere are creamish-white. The vegetal half is heavily laden with yolk, which affects the division of the egg.

The fertilized egg first increases its surface by dividing into small cells. Numerous cells are thus made available for the initiation of different developmental enterprises. The early divisions of the fertilized egg are known as *cleavage.* As figure 7.2 shows, the first cleavage furrow is longitudinal (meridional); the second is also longitudinal, but at right angles to the first. The third division is unequally latitudinal (equatorial), cutting off four smaller, upper animal hemisphere cells and four larger vegetal

Figure 7.2 Early stages in the development of the embryo of the common meadow frog, *Rana pipiens.*

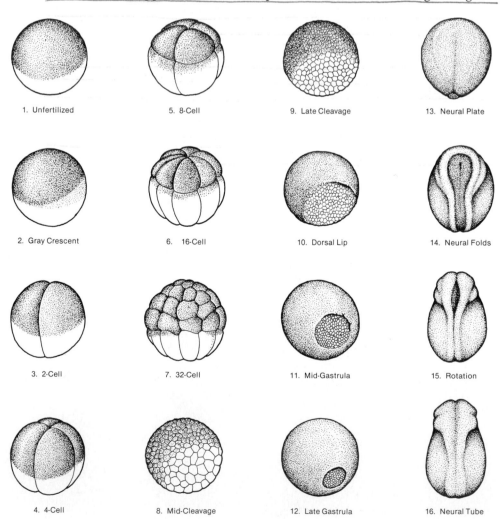

1. Unfertilized
5. 8-Cell
9. Late Cleavage
13. Neural Plate

2. Gray Crescent
6. 16-Cell
10. Dorsal Lip
14. Neural Folds

3. 2-Cell
7. 32-Cell
11. Mid-Gastrula
15. Rotation

4. 4-Cell
8. Mid-Cleavage
12. Late Gastrula
16. Neural Tube

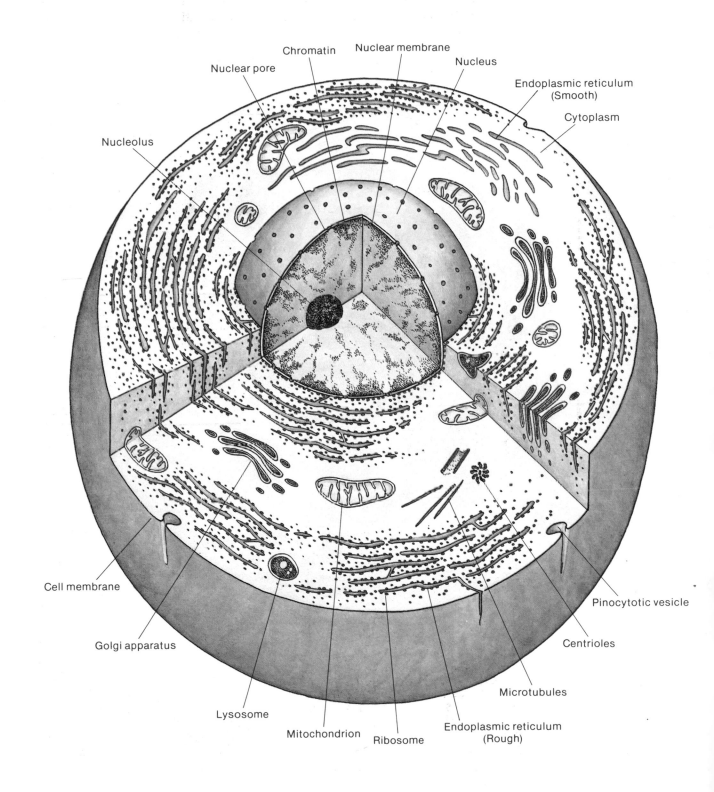

Plate 7 A contemporary cell, based on modern electron microscopy. (Artwork by Carolyn Volpe.)

Chromatin

Nuclear membrane

Nucleus

Nuclear pore

Endoplasmic reticulum (Smooth)

Cytoplasm

Nucleolus

Cell membrane

Golgi apparatus

Pinocytotic vesicle

Centrioles

Lysosome

Microtubules

Mitochondrion

Ribosome

Endoplasmic reticulum (Rough)

Plate 8 Three-dimensional represen-
tation of the endoplasmic reticulum
(ER) of a cell. (Artwork by Carolyn
Volpe.)

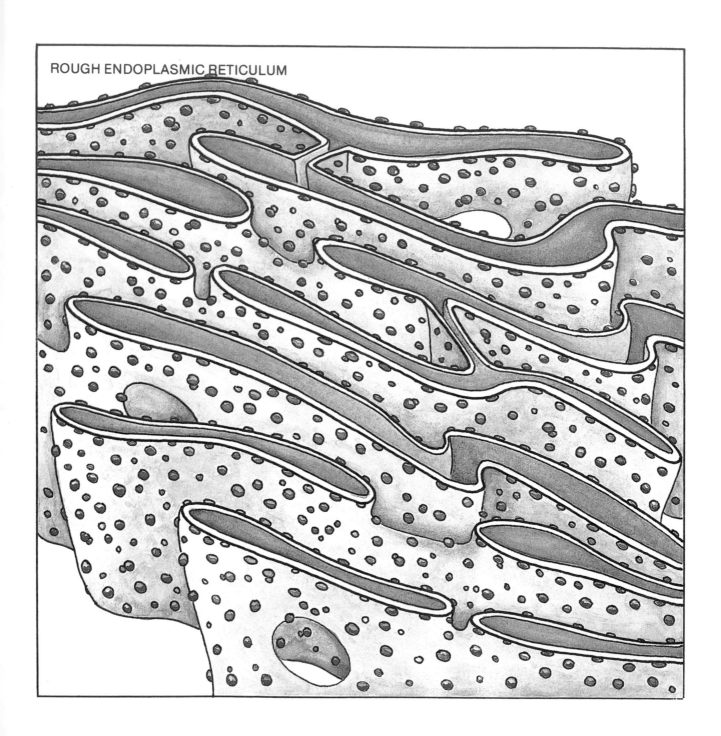

ROUGH ENDOPLASMIC RETICULUM

Plate 9 Three-dimensional representation of the Golgi apparatus of a cell. (Artwork by Carolyn Volpe.)

Plate 10 Three-dimensional representation of a mitochondrion of a cell. (Artwork by Carolyn Volpe.)

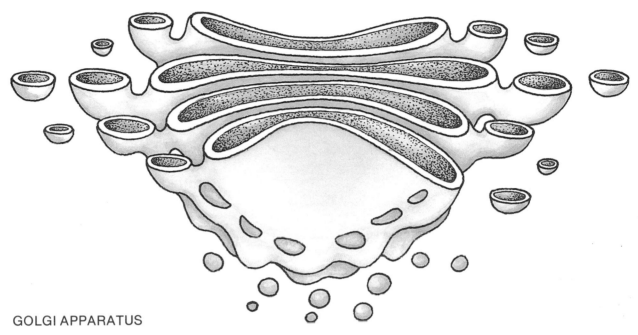

GOLGI APPARATUS

MITOCHONDRION

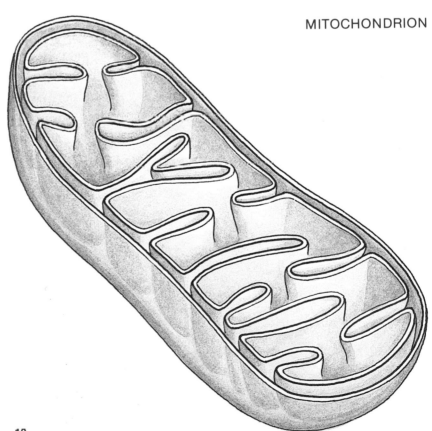

Plate 11 Three-dimensional representation of a chloroplast of a plant cell.
(Artwork by Carolyn Volpe.)

CHLOROPLAST

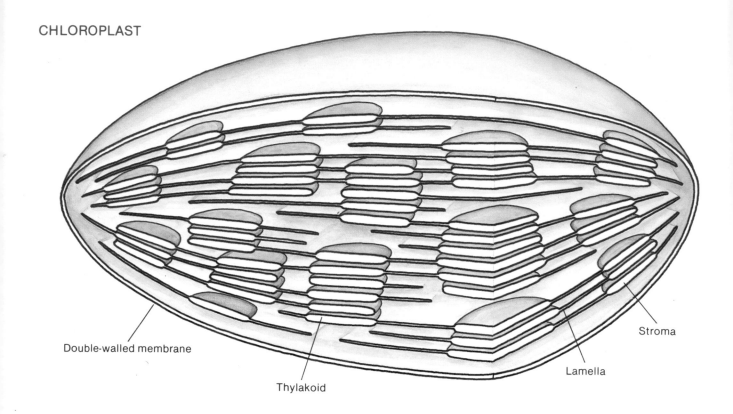

Double-walled membrane

Thylakoid

Lamella

Stroma

hemisphere cells. After the first few divisions, the cleavage pattern becomes irregular. That is to say, the divisions of the cells in the vegetal hemisphere lag behind divisions of the animal hemisphere cells, which are relatively free of yolk. Consequently, the yolky hemisphere cells remain larger than the animal pole cells.

As cleavage ensues, the embryo comes to consist of many cells, or blastomeres, which enclose a hemispherical cavity. This eccentrically located cavity, which lies wholly in the animal hemisphere, is the *blastocoel*, and the embryo is now known as the *blastula* (fig. 7.3). The blastocoel does not arise abruptly; in fact, it may be detected as a small space among the blastomeres as early as the 8-cell stage. The cavity enlarges primarily by the absorption of water from the external medium.

The blastula stage is succeeded by the *gastrula* stage. The events during the formation of the gastrula, or *gastrulation*, are concerned essentially with disposing the cells in the form of germ layers. There are basically three germ layers: the outer, or *ectoderm;* the inner, or *endoderm,* and the *mesoderm,* which is interpolated between the outer and inner layers. As a generalization, the outer ectodermal layer is protective and sensory; the inner endodermal layer is nutritive. The process of gastrulation in the frog embryo is intricate because the endodermal region is composed of the large mass of inert yolky cells. The yolky endodermal cells cannot move actively to the inside of the embryo. The eventual interior position of

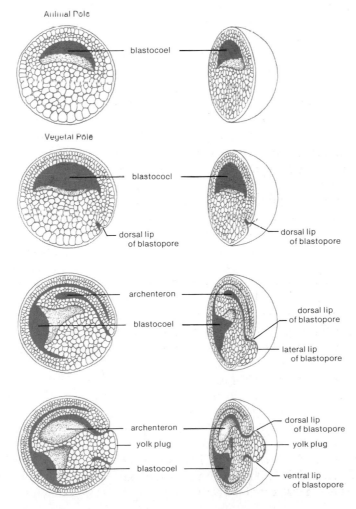

Figure 7.3 Process of gastrulation in the frog embryo.

the endoderm is accomplished by an overgrowing activity of the surface (ectodermal) cells. In other words, the endoderm in the frog embryo is literally placed inside by virtue of having been covered over by the animal hemisphere cells.

Figure 7.3 illustrates the process of gastrulation in the frog. The illustrations on the left represent the developing embryo cut in the median plane; on the right are stereodiagrams of the same embryos. The onset of gastrulation is heralded by the appearance of a deeply pigmented, pitlike depression. The depression itself is known as the *blastopore* and the rim of the depression as the *dorsal lip of the blastopore*. The animal hemisphere cells, which have been actively dividing and have actually extended downward below the equator, roll around the lip of the blastopore into the interior. Laterally, to the right and left of the dorsal lip, animal hemisphere cells roll, or tuck, in to establish the lateral lips of the blastopore. Accordingly, the blastopore becomes crescent-shaped. As animal hemisphere cells become folded under the ventral lip of the blastopore, the blastopore becomes ring-shaped and filled with a mass of yolk cells known as the *yolk plug*. The blastocoel has become reduced to a small space in the gastrula, and will eventually become entirely obliterated. The ingrowth of cells has led to the formation of a new cavity, the primitive gut or *archenteron*.

The embryo as viewed externally shows only a small fraction of the events occurring internally. If we reexamine figure 7.2, we observe only that the lips of the blastopore pass through a succession of shapes—quarter moon (stage 10 in fig. 7.2), half moon (stage 11), and full moon (stage 12). At stage 12, only a small area of the vegetal pole cells is visible. This remaining visible yolk area is the yolk plug.

SIGNIFICANCE OF GASTRULATION

Gastrulation involves two main types of movements of cells. The overgrowth of cells, or the downward growth of animal hemisphere cells to envelop the yolk-laden cells of the vegetal hemisphere, is known as *epiboly*. The ingrowth of cells, or the inward movement of cells at the blastopore lips, is referred to as *involution*. There is thus a considerable streaming of surface cells into the interior of the embryo.

The movements of surface cells can be followed by staining localized regions of the late blastula or early gastrula. Using Nile blue as a vital dye, the German embryologist W. Vogt in the 1920s marked the surface of the early gastrula stage of the egg of a salamander. The marking experiments revealed that the animal hemisphere cells actually stretch down over the yolk. The movement and fate of cells during gastrulation are shown in figure 7.4. The cells just in front of the dorsal lip of the blastopore turn in to become the *notochord* (a dorsal, supporting rod), while the cells to the right and left become the *mesoderm* (presomite mesoderm). Hence, the animal hemisphere cells that roll inward are said to form the *chordamesoderm*. The yolk cells form the floor and sides of the *archenteron*, or primitive gut. Later, the sides grow up beneath the chordamesoderm sheet to form the roof of the archenteron. The chordamesoderm thus comes to lie between the endodermal roof of the archenteron and the outer layer of the embryo, which constitutes the ectoderm of the embryo. The close of gastrulation is thus marked by the formation of the third germ layer, the mesoderm (or chordamesoderm).

It should be noted (fig. 7.4) that considerable shifting of the yolk mass occurs, with a concomitant displacement of the center of gravity. The

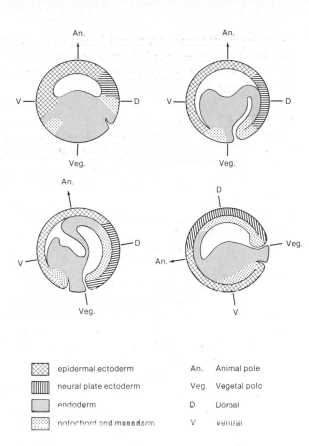

An.

An.

V — D

V — D

Veg.

Veg.

An.

D

V — D

— Veg.

An. —

Veg.

V

▨ epidermal ectoderm	An.	Animal pole
▥ neural plate ectoderm	Veg.	Vegetal pole
▨ endoderm	D	Dorsal
▨ notochord and mesoderm	V	Ventral

Figure 7.4 Allocation of the presumptive regions to their definitive locations during gastrulation of the frog embryo.

original animal pole of the egg becomes the anterior side of the future embryo, while the blastopore marks the posterior end of the future embryo. With the exception of the yolk plug, the outer surface of the egg is now covered with a layer of cells, the presumptive ectoderm. Two regions of this ectodermal surface are distinguishable: the *epidermal ectoderm* (the precursor of skin ectoderm) and the *neural plate ectoderm* (the precursor of the spinal cord). This distinction in the ectodermal surface is important for our future discussions.

As a result of Vogt's experimentation, an idealized *fate map* can be constructed showing the location of the presumptive regions of a given part of the early gastrula (fig. 7.5). The orderly migration of cells during gastrulation brings the presumptive regions into their definitive positions in the embryo. Thus, the significance of gastrulation is the allocation of the presumptive regions to their definitive locations.

Once the presumptive regions have migrated to their definitive locations, the major organ systems proceed to differentiate. Prominent among these organs is the primitive *neural tube,* the forerunner of the adult spinal cord. As seen in figure 7.6, the neural tube has its origin as a thickened plate of ectodermal cells (the *neural plate*) along the dorsal surface of the embryo. The lateral edges of the neural plate subsequently become elevated as *neural folds.* Finally, the neural folds curve inward and converge toward the midline to form the neural tube.

The central portion of the chordamesoderm differentiates as a solid rod of cells, the *notochord,* which serves to support the embryo dorsally. In later development of the amphibian embryo, the notochord becomes replaced by the vertebral column, or backbone. The mesodermal component spreads laterally and ventrally around the endodermal lining of the archenteron. The mesodermal bands on either side of the neural tube and notochord, called the *dorsal mesoderm*, become divided transversely into components known as *somites*. The somites ultimately develop into the segmental muscles of the body.

The mesodermal portion distal to the somites constitutes the *lateral mesoderm*. Each lateral mesodermal sheet splits into an outer *somatic layer*, adjacent to the ectoderm, and an inner *splanchnic layer*, next to the ectoderm. The new cavity thus formed, which lies wholly within the mesoderm, is the *coelom*, or body cavity.

Figure 7.5 A map of the presumptive fate of groups of cells found on the surface of the early gastrula of the frog, based on Vogt's experiments with vital dyes.

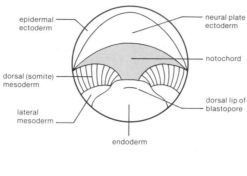

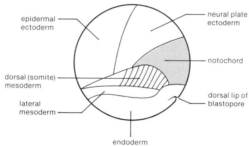

Figure 7.6 Formation of the neural tube in the frog embryo.

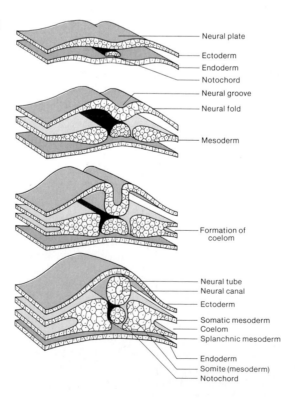

TRANSPLANTATION EXPERIMENTS

In the very early gastrula, the fates of most regions are not irrevocably fixed, or *determined*. This was demonstrated in 1918 by Hans Spemann, an embryologist at the University of Würzburg in Germany. Spemann experimentally interchanged portions of the presumptive epidermal ectoderm and the presumptive neural ectoderm. As seen in figure 7.7, Spemann used two different species of salamanders, *Triton taeniatus*, whose eggs are darkly pigmented, and *Triton cristatus*, whose eggs are lightly pigmented, almost pigmentless. The distinctive differences in pigmentation provided a convenient, visible means of following the progress of the transplants. From the early gastrula of *T. cristatus*, Spemann cut a microscopic piece from the presumptive epidermal ectoderm that normally develops into external skin. From the early gastrula of *T. taeniatus*, he sliced a fragment of equal size from the presumptive neural plate ectoderm that normally forms part of the brain. He then exchanged the excised pieces between the two gastrulae. In later development, the transplanted presumptive neural plate ectoderm did not form nervous tissue, but rather became ordinary ectoderm like that surrounding it in its new location. The implant of presumptive epidermis in the future neural tube area differentiated into nervous tissue. Thus, the regions removed from their normal sites developed in harmony with their new surroundings, regardless of their origin and former surroundings.

However, in 1924, Spemann and one of his pupils, Hilde Mangold, demonstrated that the fate of one region of the early gastrula is fixed or determined. This is the region of the dorsal lip of the blastopore, which is destined to form the chordamesoderm (notochord and mesoderm). A piece of dorsal lip of one gastrula was transplanted to another gastrula in a position opposite to the host's dorsal lip (fig. 7.8). The transplanted cells actually rolled in through a secondary blastopore and produced a small archenteron. A small, secondary embryo formed,

Figure 7.7 Spemann's classic experiments revealing that the fates of regions of the early gastrula are not irrevocably determined. In experiment *A*, a piece of presumptive epidermal ectoderm was transplanted to a region destined to become neural plate tissue. Conversely, in experiment *B*, a piece of presumptive neural plate ectoderm was placed into the appropriate region of the presumptive epidermal ectoderm. In each case, the development of the transplant was conditioned by the new surrounding region.

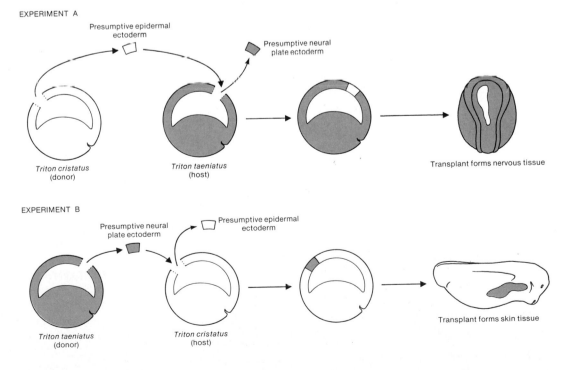

EXPERIMENT A

Presumptive epidermal ectoderm

Presumptive neural plate ectoderm

Triton cristatus (donor)

Triton taeniatus (host)

Transplant forms nervous tissue

EXPERIMENT B

Presumptive neural plate ectoderm

Presumptive epidermal ectoderm

Triton taeniatus (donor)

Triton cristatus (host)

Transplant forms skin tissue

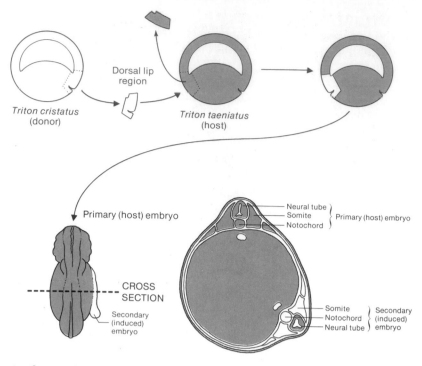

Figure 7.8 Dorsal lip transplantation experiment of Spemann and Mangold. Under the influence of an additional dorsal lip (chordamesoderm), a secondary embryo is formed. The transplanted chordamesoderm (highly pigmented) directed the formation of a neural tube (darkly pigmented) from host cells.

Triton cristatus (donor)

Dorsal lip region

Triton taeniatus (host)

Primary (host) embryo

Neural tube
Somite
Notochord
} Primary (host) embryo

CROSS SECTION

Secondary (induced) embryo

Somite
Notochord
Neural tube
} Secondary (induced) embryo

similar to the primary (host) embryo in virtually all features. In the secondary embryo, the material of the dorsal lip self-differentiated into notochord and mesodermal elements. Hence, the transplanted chordamesoderm had a fixed fate. Moreover, the transplanted dorsal lip material caused, or stimulated, the overlying ectoderm with which it was in contact to form neural plate tissue (and subsequently a neural tube). In other words, the dorsal lip of the blastopore has the capacity to *induce* other tissue to differentiate in certain directions. Thus, another significant feature of gastrulation in the amphibian embryo is revealed: The dorsal lip of the blastopore is essential for the future formation of the neural tube. Because of its property of organizing the ectoderm into nervous tissue, the region above the dorsal lip (or chordamesoderm) is termed the *organizer*. For his discovery of the organizer effect in embryonic development, Spemann was later (1935) to become the recipient of the Nobel prize in physiology and medicine.

The action of the dorsal lip in causing the overlying ectoderm cells to respond by forming a specific tissue (neural tissue) is known as *induction*. It may be recalled that prior to gastrulation (that is, prior to the involution of the chordamesoderm), the presumptive neural plate ectoderm was *not* determined with respect to its capacity to form a neural tube. However, after the chordamesoderm has made contact with the presumptive neural plate ectoderm, the latter is no longer plastic in regard to its final fate, but has been induced to differentiate solely as nervous tissue. Stated in the parlance of the embryologist, the prospective potency of the neural plate ectoderm no longer exceeds its presumptive fate, but is restricted or committed to only one pathway.

The dorsal lip organizer is more properly called the *primary organizer* of the amphibian egg. One should not suppose that the organizer controls the whole process of development. A succession of organizers comes into play, one taking up where the other leaves off, each having a specific role in the progressive development of the embryo. A striking

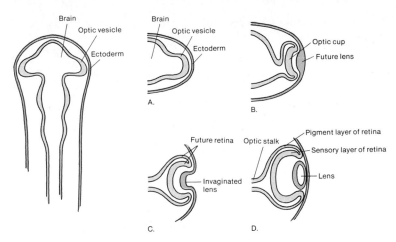

example of an organizer effect in later development is the induction of the lens of the eye by the optic cups. As seen in figure 7.9, the vertebrate eye begins to develop as lateral outgrowths of the brain. The optic vesicle on each side will take the form of a cup, whose inner layer will differentiate into the retina and outer layer into the pigmented coat of the eye. The optic cup grows outward until it comes into contact with the ectoderm. This ectoderm thickens and forms the lens of the eye. The intimate association of the optic cup and the future lens suggests a causal connection between the two. Indeed, experiments have clearly shown that the lens owes its origin to some specific action by the optic cup.

When the primordium of the eye vesicle is surgically removed and the surface ectoderm heals over the wound, this overlying ectoderm fails to develop a lens. The failure of the ectoderm to develop a lens may be ascribed to the elimination of the eye vesicle. Now, one can transplant the extirpated eye vesicle to an unusual ectoderm region, such as the flank region of the embryo, which, of course, does not normally form a lens. Under the influence of the eye cup, the strange ectoderm readily furnishes a lens. The eye cup thus induces the formation of the lens. Just as the chordamesoderm in early development induces the overlying ectoderm to form a neural tube, so the optic cup induces the overlying ectoderm to form a lens. The overall picture of development is of a series of progressive changes so related that each step in differentiation causes further differentiation. This is like a chain reaction, in which each reaction sets off another.

IDENTITY OF THE PRIMARY ORGANIZER

How the primary organizer (the dorsal lip of the blastopore) of the amphibian embryo operates as an inducer is still a puzzle. Tests were performed in which the dorsal lip tissue was subjected to crushing, freezing, heating, and other injuries, and then implanted into a gastrula, in much the same manner as Spemann had implanted an intact secondary dorsal lip. Ironically, the dissociated organizer tissue induced the emergence of a neural tube in the same way that undamaged organizer tissue had done. The conclusion was that induction must be a chemical effect, and an intensive search began for the potent chemical or chemicals released by the organizer cells.

Johannes Holtfreter, who studied under Spemann, found that even after the dorsal lip tissue was killed in alcohol it was able to induce neural development. The same discovery was made by C. H. Wadding-ton at the University of Cambridge. Holtfreter then tested both living and dead tissues—boiled mouse heart, pieces of calf liver, fragments of worms, and extracts from chick embryos. Each induced the embryo to form a neural tube. The situation became rather involved when it was found that many unrelated chemical substances—steroids, higher fatty acids, nucleoproteins, and proteins—will stimulate the formation of a neural tube. With this medley of different chemical substances, there is no way of deciding which, if any, represents the naturally occurring organizer. The situation became even more clouded when investigators discovered the astonishing fact that even the synthetic dye methylene blue, a substance that cannot by any stretch of the imagination be sup-posed to exist in the normal embryo, induced formation of nervous tissue when injected into an early gastrula.

The current idea is that some substance, as yet unidentifiable, diffuses out from the chordamesoderm and activates the overlying ectoderm. More specifically, the diffusible substance triggers ectodermal cells that have been *repressed*. A repressed cell is one in which the expression of certain genes has been blocked. The inducer apparently removes or re-leases the block. This scheme fits well with our current knowledge of gene action. Our model of gene action leads us to believe that the inducer acts by activating, or derepressing, certain genes in the reacting ecto-derm cell. The proper genes are stimulated, or "turned on," to produce the action necessary for converting the cell into a nerve cell.

ORGAN FIELDS AND MALFORMATIONS

After gastrulation is completed and a neural tube begins to form, one can construct a map of the various organ fields of the embryo, in much the same manner as the fate map of the gastrula was prepared. As seen in figure 7.10, the future organ-forming areas can be localized, although there are no visible signs of each structure. If a disc of tissue is removed from the eye field and transferred to the flank of another embryo, it will give rise only to an eye. In this classic experiment, the eye disc forms a functional eye in its new and abnormal environment, complete with pig-ment layer, retinal layer, lens, and transparent cornea. The parts of the field become determined by induction, as demonstrated by the organiz-ing action of the eye vesicle on the lens.

It is important to remember that establishment of a localized field antedates the actual appearance of the given organ. The sensitivity of the embryo to external, or environmental, disturbances is greatest im-mediately preceding or during the differentiation of a given organ field.

Figure 7.10 Future organ-forming regions localized in a frog embryo.

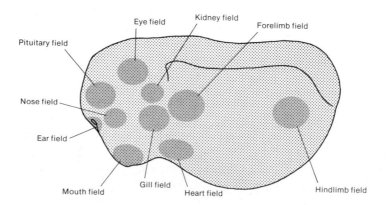

In the human embryo, the limb buds are seen about the middle of the fifth week, but the limb field can be delineated much earlier—approximately the third to fourth week of embryonic life. It is at this earlier time that the human embryo is extremely sensitive to toxic agents, as vividly evidenced by the detrimental action of the thalidomide drug (see chapter 4).

CELL DIFFERENTIATION

As the embryo develops, its cells become specialized and give rise to the various *tissues* that constitute the adult body. A tissue is an intimate association of cells that perform a specific task. Combinations of different tissues give rise to the varied *organs* of the body and, in turn, organs make up the bodily *systems*.

Although the human body is highly complex, it is constructed of only four basic types of tissues: *epithelial, connective, muscular,* and *nervous*. These four tissues, representing radically different types of specializations, resemble one another to the extent that each is composed of cells and intercellular material. The amounts of intercellular material vary greatly from tissue to tissue.

One of the primary functions of epithelial tissue is protection. In its protective role, the epithelium exists in the form of sheets of cells that clothe the external surfaces of the body and line various internal cavities, including the blood vessels. The epithelial tissues are composed of one or more layers of cells lying so close to one another that there is a minimum amount of intercellular material. Epithelial cells may assume one of three shapes: flat (technically, *squamous*), cubelike (*cuboidal*), or rectangular (*columnar*). When the epithelial sheet consists of only a single layer of cells, it is said to be a *simple epithelium*. When two or more layers are involved, the epithelium is *stratified*. Examples of the different categories of epithelium are shown in figure 7.11.

One of the more interesting arrangements of epithelial cells occurs in certain organs and ducts, such as the urinary bladder and the ureter, which are subject to special stresses. The inner wall of the bladder is lined with *transitional epithelium*, which is capable of extraordinary changes in shape under tension (fig. 7.12). When the bladder is relaxed, the epithelium resembles the stratified cuboidal type, with rounded sur-

Figure 7.11 The variety of epithelial tissues.

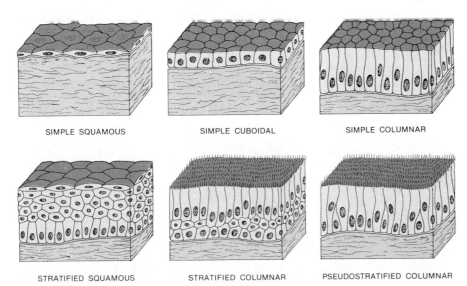

SIMPLE SQUAMOUS

SIMPLE CUBOIDAL

SIMPLE COLUMNAR

STRATIFIED SQUAMOUS

STRATIFIED COLUMNAR

PSEUDOSTRATIFIED COLUMNAR

Figure 7.12 Transitional epithelium, the pliable tissue lining the urinary bladder.

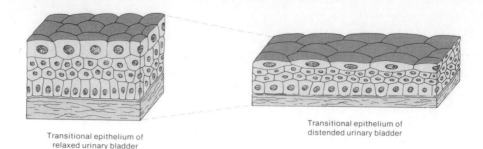

Transitional epithelium of relaxed urinary bladder

Transitional epithelium of distended urinary bladder

face cells that bulge into the lumen. When the bladder is full, the epithelial lining stretches thinly and its surface cells become greatly flattened. When the tension is released, the cells assume their original shape so that the thickness and marked stratification of the relaxed membrane is once again apparent.

The cells of some epithelial linings are absorptive in that they are primarily concerned with passing materials through them. The cells that line the small intestine are responsible for absorbing nutrients into the body. Although protection and absorption are the major tasks of epithelial cells, there are still other epithelial types that are concerned primarily with the process of secretion. In epithelial cells active in secretion, small secretory granules accumulate in the cytoplasm. Groups of actively secreting epithelial cells are called *glands*. There are numerous kinds of glands in the human body, including digestive glands, sebaceous (oil) glands, sweat glands, and endocrine glands.

CONNECTIVE TISSUES

Connective tissues serve as supporting elements for almost all structures within the body. The cells of connective tissues do not form layers, as do epithelial tissues, but are separated from each other by various types of intercellular material. The intercellular substance in which the cells are embedded are generally secreted by the cells themselves. The intercellular deposits can be rigid, like mortar between bricks, as exemplified by the hard matrix of bone. The intercellular material may be flexible, as in cartilage. It may also take the form of delicate fibers, which provide a meshlike support to many of the softer internal organs, like the liver and spleen.

One of the most important intercellular materials is the fluid substance,

Figure 7.13 Areolar tissue, a loose, filmy form of subcutaneous connective tissue.

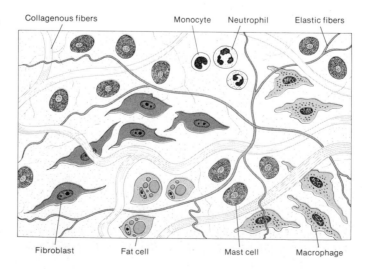

Collagenous fibers Monocyte Neutrophil Elastic fibers

Fibroblast Fat cell Mast cell Macrophage

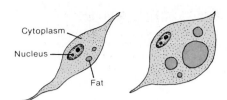
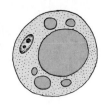
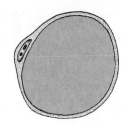

Cytoplasm

Nucleus

Fat

Figure 7.14 The transformation of a thin fibroblast into a bulky fat cell.

the *tissue fluid,* which occurs in variable amounts in all tissues of the body. Tissue fluid is vitally important in the transfer of metabolic products to and from cells. This fluid is readily seen in the moist, whitish tissue that is exposed when skin is removed from the underlying muscle. The fibers of this filmy subcutaneous tissue are loosely woven together, as demonstrated in figure 7.13. This tissue is called *areolar* (or "loose connective tissue") because open spaces (ordinarily filled with tissue fluid) are seen among the fibers when the tissue is spread out on a microscopic slide. The prominent fibers are *collagenous* fibers, which are grouped into large parallel bundles to provide tensile strength, and rubberlike *elastic* fibers, which are capable of stretching under tension. The resident cells of areolar tissue are the spindle-shaped *fibroblasts,* the phagocytic *macrophages,* and the pharmacologically important *mast cells.* The macrophages ingest many pathogenic microorganisms, and the mast cells participate in conditions such as asthma, hay fever, sensitization to drugs, and anaphylactic shock. As part of the inflammatory reaction to tissue injury, certain immigrant blood cells (notably *neutrophils* and *monocytes*) pass in large numbers from the blood vessels into the surrounding connective tissues (fig. 7.13).

A fibroblast (or fibroblastlike cell) can accumulate droplets of fat within its cytoplasm. A fat-laden cell is characterized by one large lipid inclusion, with the nucleus and the thin layer of cytoplasm pushed to the periphery (fig. 7.14). An abundant accumulation of fat cells comprises *adipose* tissue. Roughly 15–20 percent of the body weight of a normal human adult is adipose tissue.

Blood is considered a special type of connective tissue in which the intercellular material, the *plasma,* is a fluid that conveys a variety of free cells. Both the fluid and the cellular elements circulate through the body in epithelial-lined vessels. Blood plays an indispensable role in regulating the activities of the other tissues through the nutrients it carries, as well as the hormones that it conveys. The properties of blood are considered in detail in a subsequent section (chapter 9).

MUSCULAR AND NERVOUS TISSUE

The capacity of movement in animals depends upon the contraction of specialized cells called *muscle cells.* Because the muscle cells are elongated to permit an effective contraction of their protoplasm, the cells themselves are often called *muscle fibers.* Three types of muscle tissues are distinguishable in the vertebrate body: *smooth, skeletal,* and *cardiac* (fig. 7.15).

Smooth muscle, which consists of narrow, tapering cells, occurs in the walls of the digestive tract and in blood vessels (arteries and veins). Skeletal muscle is associated, as the name implies, with skeletal parts of the body. Skeletal muscle consists principally of unbranched, long bundles of parallel cells (or fibers). In longitudinal section, the fibers are

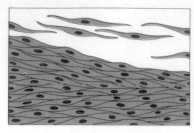  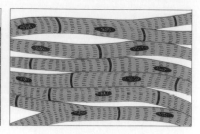

SMOOTH MUSCLE   STRIATED (SKELETAL) MUSCLE   CARDIAC MUSCLE

Figure 7.15   The types of muscular tissues.

conspicuously marked by transverse striations. For this reason, skeletal muscle is frequently called *striated muscle*. The internal organization of skeletal muscle and the ultrastructural basis of contraction are reserved for later discussion (chapter 11). Cardiac muscle is a highly specialized form of striated muscle found only in the heart. Unlike striated muscle, the fibers of cardiac muscle are branched (fig. 7.15).

Nervous tissue is highly specialized with respect to irritability and conductivity. A nerve cell, or *neuron,* can receive various kinds of stimuli and transform them into impulses that can be conducted over long distances. To effectively receive stimuli and efficiently conduct impulses, parts of the cytoplasm of the nerve cell are drawn into long processes called *nerve fibers* (fig. 7.1). The functional aspects of nerve cells and their fibers are treated in chapter 11.

SUMMARY

Development consists of the progressive restriction of the wide potentialities of embryonic regions. In very early development, the fates of most regions of the embryo are not indelibly fixed or unalterable. This has been shown by transplantation experiments on salamander embryos, which involve the transfer, or grafting, of one part of an embryo to another area of the same or different embryo. A transplanted region develops according to the new surroundings in which it has been artificially placed, without regard to its former surroundings. The process of gastrulation is critical, since at this time the various regions of the embryo lose their original plasticity and become committed to specific developmental pathways.

One region of the early salamander embryo has a definite developmental assignment. This is the region of the dorsal lip of the blastopore, which has been termed the *organizer.* The organizer has the property of directing or determining the fate of the region with which it comes in contact. In particular, the dorsal lip of the blastopore stimulates or instructs adjacent ectoderm tissue to form nervous tissue. In later development, a succession of different organizers comes into play, each having a specific role in the progressive development of the embryo.

Differentiated cells become organized into groups of highly specialized tissues, of which there are four basic types. Epithelial tissue covers the surfaces of the body; connective tissue supports and binds parts of the body; muscular tissue is specialized for contractility; and nervous tissue has the capacity for irritability and conductivity.

Digestion and Absorption 8

Man cannot escape his ancestral heritage. He has inherited the meat-eating dentition of his carnivorous relatives and the lengthy, twisting digestive tract of the herbivores. Today man is omnivorous, eating about everything and finding suitable food almost everywhere. Man's energy needs are met through the breakdown of energy-rich carbon compounds, notably carbohydrates and fats.

Carbohydrates constitute the most prevalent energy source. The average daily intake of carbohydrates in the American diet is 500 grams per day, mostly in the form of starch. All of the dietary carbohydrates are derived from plant sources. Wheat, rice, maize (commonly called corn), potatoes, and sugar cane are the dominant plant staples, accounting for at least 60 percent of the food-energy intake of mankind. Wheat is the leading starchy staple in economically advanced countries, whereas the mainstay of diets in most Asiatic countries is rice. In many Central and South American nations, maize is the important source of carbohydrates.

The amino acid units of proteins are required for tissue repair and the construction of new tissues. An intake of at least 50 grams per day meets the amino acid requirements of adult tissues. Plants contain proteins, but the consumption of plant food alone may not furnish all the necessary amino acids in adequate amounts to achieve good health. There are eight amino acids—the so-called *essential amino acids*—that cannot be synthesized by the body and therefore must be provided by the diet. Livestock products and fish generally contain all of the essential amino acids in substantial quantities. The eight essential amino acids have been identified as lysine, tryptophan, phenylalanine, threonine, valine, methionine, leucine, and isoleucine.

A well-balanced diet contains approximately 20 vitamins and a comparable number of inorganic minerals in small quantities. Vitamins are not used up in the process of participating in various metabolic reactions. This suggests that only minute amounts of vitamins are required to sustain good health. Some nutritionists contend that the prescribed minimal daily intakes of several vitamins are grossly insufficient for optimum health. The contentions, as yet unproven, are that the customary small daily amounts of vitamins are adequate only to avoid deficiency diseases and that larger doses are definitely necessary to promote ideal health and vigor.

HUMAN DIGESTIVE SYSTEM

The principal nutrients—carbohydrates, fats, and proteins—are useful to the body only after they have been reduced to molecules small enough to be taken in by the individual cells. The elaborate digestive system of man is concerned with the chemical breakdown of large complex food molecules into small, diffusible molecules that can penetrate the membranes of the intestinal cells. The polysaccharides (starch) are degraded into the simpler monosaccharides (glucose), proteins are broken down into their constituent amino acids, and fats (triglycerides) are reduced to fatty acid and glycerol (monoglyceride) molecules. The passage of small molecules from the intestinal cells to the circulatory fluids is called *absorption*. Once in the bloodstream, the energy-rich molecules ultimately find their way into all cells of the body.

The human digestive, or gastrointestinal tract, is essentially a continuous canal, approximately 28 feet in length, coursing through the body from mouth to anus (fig. 8.1). Digestion begins in the *oral cavity*, where food is masticated to a size convenient for swallowing. Man and his primate relatives have two dentitions: the temporary (or deciduous) teeth, composed of two chisel-shaped incisors, one pointed canine, and two broad-crowned molars for each lateral half of each jaw; and the permanent teeth, composed of two incisors, one canine, two premolars (bicus-

Figure 8.1 Anatomy of the digestive system of man.

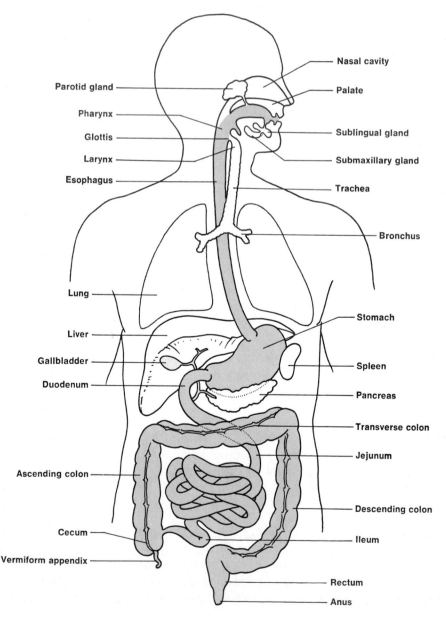

pids), and three molars for each lateral half of each jaw. The temporary teeth erupt from about the sixth month (central incisors) to the 24th month (second molars). These are gradually replaced by the permanent teeth starting about the fifth year and continuing into young adulthood (fig. 8.2). The molars of the adult can exert a crushing force of 160 pounds, which is more than sufficient to crack a hazelnut.

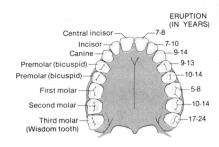

ERUPTION (IN YEARS)

Central incisor — 7-8
Incisor — 7-10
Canine — 9-14
Premolar (bicuspid) — 9-13
Premolar (bicuspid) — 10-14
First molar — 5-8
Second molar — 10-14
Third molar (Wisdom tooth) — 17-24

Figure 8.2 The permanent human dentition, composed of two incisors, one canine, two premolars (bicuspids), and three molars for each lateral half of each jaw.

The food particles are moistened by saliva. Saliva is produced by three pairs of glands, the *parotid,* the *submaxillary,* and the *sublingual.* Almost three pints of saliva (one liter) are secreted by an adult during the course of one day. The lubrication of food particles by saliva is indispensable since an absolutely dry food mass can scarcely be swallowed. Moreover, the sensation of taste depends on the moistening of the food particles. Taste buds, which are housed mainly in the tongue, are sensitive only to substances in solution. An enzyme, *salivary amylase* (earlier named *ptyalin*), initiates the process of digestion by catalyzing the breakdown of polysaccharides (starch) into disaccharides (maltose). Salivary secretions do not chemically affect proteins and fats.

Mumps is a viral disease affecting the salivary glands, chiefly the parotids. One or both of these glands may swell up as the tissue responds to the virus with the accumulation of fluid and white blood cells. Other glands may be involved, especially the pancreas and the testes. If the inflammation is particularly intense in the testes, the adult male may become sterile.

SWALLOWING

In the act of swallowing, the moistened food passes through the short *pharynx* and is propelled rapidly (in about 5 seconds) down the long *esophagus* by successive waves of contractions of the muscle layers. Such repetitive muscle constrictions, known as *peristalsis,* allow food contents to move towards the stomach of a person, even though he or she may be standing on his or her head. Water gulped by a horse at a stream is a good example of material moved against gravity by peristalsis.

The pharynx may be short, but it is important, both functionally and from an evolutionary point of view. Among fishes and amphibians, the pharynx is the region of the gills, and in land animals, it is the point of origin of the lungs. Indeed, as figure 8.1 shows, the pharynx in man acts as a common passageway for both the digestive and the respiratory systems. Thus, we cannot swallow and breathe simultaneously. This anatomical "defect" has some serviceable aspects—for instance, a person whose nasal passages are obstructed can breathe through the mouth. Moreover, if a person's mouth happens to be immobilized after surgery, the individual can be fed with a tube through the nose. It should also be mentioned that an individual can breathe and chew at the same time. This is because of the distinctly mammalian structure—the *palate,* which separates the mouth cavity from the respiratory passages.

Normally, food does not enter the respiratory passages to either the nose or the lungs (fig. 8.3). As food moves into the pharynx, the soft palate is raised and seals off the nasal cavity. Food is prevented from entering the trachea (the passageway to the lungs) by the closure of the *glottis,* which is the opening between the vocal cords. The approximation of the vocal cords to close the glottis is accomplished by the elevation of the *larynx*—the familiar "bobbing of the Adam's apple." At the same time, a cartilaginous flap, the *epiglottis,* tilts down to cover the closed glottis. The epiglottis is not as essential as once thought; its surgical removal has no

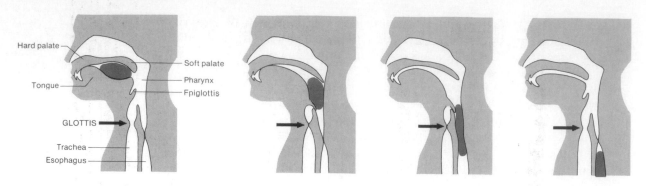

Figure 8.3 Passage of a food particle through the pharynx and esophagus during swallowing.

adverse effects on the swallowing movements. Air, of course, is swallowed during a meal, lodges in the esophagus, and is generally expelled by belching.

STOMACH

When the stomach is empty, it is tubular and not as saclike as conventional drawings show. It can, however, become appreciably distended because its walls have great elasticity. In fact, the volume of the cavity increases to adapt to the amount of food entering it. A ring of muscle regulates the opening into the thick-walled muscular stomach; it relaxes only when food particles enter the stomach. Occasionally, the acid contents of the stomach empty back into the esophagus and irritate the walls of the esophagus. This irritation (muscular spasm) is experienced as a burning sensation and is popularly called "heartburn," since the pain appears to emanate from the heart region.

The lining of the stomach wall contains numerous microscopic glands (gastric glands) that secrete *gastric juice,* a clear, colorless, strongly acid fluid. The food mass is churned in the stomach for 3 to 4 hours and is transformed by the mixing movements of the stomach and chemical treatment into a soft, semifluid state called *chyme.* The chemical changes are due to the activity of gastric juice. The important constituents of gastric juice are mucus (essentially a lubricant), hydrochloric acid (HCl), and two enzymes, *pepsin* and *rennin* (table 8.1).

Protein digestion begins in the stomach; pepsin splits the bonds between certain amino acids in protein molecules and thus creates shorter chains of amino acids (that is, polypeptides). Rennin is the enzyme that curdles milk; it causes the protein *casein* to precipitate out of milk as a fine, flocculent mass, or *curd.* Rennin is particularly important in infants because its curdling action slows down the passage of milk through the stomach, and thus permits the casein to be thoroughly acted on by pepsin. In general, proteins are associated with rapid passage through the stomach, whereas fats inhibit gastric emptying. A meal with a high fat content may stay in the stomach as long as six hours. A person may drink milk before a cocktail party or eat high-fat appetizers to inhibit the rate of gastric emptying and, accordingly, to delay the absorption of alcohol in the small intestine. Nevertheless, some of the alcohol, because of its highly diffusible character, is absorbed directly across the walls of the stomach into the bloodstream. Acetylsalicylic acid (aspirin) also readily penetrates the stomach lining.

About two liters of HCl assist the digestive processes by providing an acid medium for the action of pepsin. Hydrochloric acid also helps to destroy bacteria that unavoidably enter with the food. The thick, alkaline

Place of Action	Source (Secretion)	Enzymes	Substrates	Products
Oral cavity	Salivary glands (Saliva)	Salivary amylase (Ptyalin)	Starches (Polysaccharides)	Disaccharides (Maltose)
Stomach	Gastric glands (Gastric juice)	Pepsin	Proteins	Polypeptides
		Rennin	Milk protein (Casein)	Curd (Clotted casein)
Small intestine	Pancreas (Pancreatic juice)	Trypsin	Protein and long-chain peptides	Short-chain peptides
		Chymotrypsin	Protein and long-chain peptides	Short-chain peptides
		Carboxypeptidase	Short-chain peptides	Amino acids
		Pancreatic amylase (Amylopsin)	Starches	Disaccharides (Maltose)
		Lipase (Steapsin)	Fats	Fatty acids and glycerol
Small intestine	Intestinal glands (Intestinal juice)	Aminopeptidase	Short-chain peptides	Amino acids
		Tripeptidase	Tripeptides	Amino acids
		Dipeptidase	Dipeptides	Amino acids
		Glucosaccharase (Sucrase)	Sucrose	Glucose and fructose
		α-glucosidase (Maltase)	Maltose	Glucose
		β-galactosidase (Lactase)	Lactose	Glucose and galactose

Table 8.1
Digestive Enzymes and Their Activities

mucus that coats the lining of the stomach forms a protective barrier against the potentially corrosive action of either HCl or pepsin. In 1 out of 10 persons, however, this protection fails and erosions (*peptic ulcers*) of the lining occur. Peptic ulcers occur more frequently in the intestinal region adjacent to the stomach (the duodenum) than in the stomach itself. Bleeding into the lumen occurs when the ulcer damages blood vessels in the tissues of the wall. Although no one has yet discovered how peptic ulceration is caused, prolonged emotional stress and persistent nervous tension have been incriminated as contributory factors.

SMALL INTESTINE

From the stomach the liquefied chyme passes into the small intestine through an opening that is controlled by a muscular band, the *pyloric sphincter*. The highly coiled small intestine is about 23 feet in length; its first portion, the *duodenum,* is approximately 10 to 12 inches long (fig. 8.1). The two other segments are the *jejunum* (8 feet long) and the terminal ileum (14 feet long). In the small intestine, the digestion of every type of food is completed and the final products of digestion are absorbed. Since most of the absorption occurs in the upper regions (duodenum and jejunum), more than half the length of the small intestine can be surgically removed without seriously disrupting the digestive and absorptive processes (fig. 8.4).

Three important secretions act on the chyme in the intestine—namely, *pancreatic juice* secreted by the pancreas, *intestinal juice* produced by intestinal glands, and *bile* elaborated by the liver. The pancreatic secretion contains a high concentration of sodium bicarbonate, an alkaline salt that tends to neutralize the acidic chyme. Despite the high alkalinity of

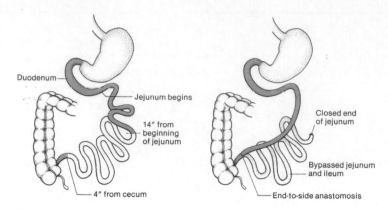

Figure 8.4 The surgical removal of a major portion of the small intestine. This type of "bypass" operation is a last-effort therapy in cases of gross obesity.

Duodenum

Jejunum begins

14" from beginning of jejunum

4" from cecum

Closed end of jejunum

Bypassed jejunum and ileum

End-to-side anastomosis

pancreatic juice, the intestinal contents are not entirely neutralized and remain acidic. This condition prevails even though the enzymes in the intestinal lumen are thought to function best in an alkaline medium. Molecules of starch that escaped the action of salivary amylase are broken down to maltose by a *pancreatic amylase.* Then, maltose and other disaccharides are split into monosaccharides such as glucose, fructose, and galactose by specific enzymes in the intestinal juice (table 8.1). Since these monosaccharides are highly diffusible, carbohydrate digestion is completed.

Some human infants suffer from an inherited disorder that prevents them from synthesizing *lactase,* the enzyme that breaks down lactose, or milk sugar. Such newborn infants react to milk with abdominal pains and severe diarrhea. The indigestible milk sugar is attacked by bacteria in the large intestine; the excessive acids produced by bacterial action irritate the intestinal wall and cause frequent bowel movements. The disturbing symptoms disappear when milk is omitted from the diet. Ironically, even normal children in later life may not be able to digest milk sugar. Although most normal children have high lactase activity immediately after birth, the capacity to synthesize this enzyme declines during the first year. In fact, the ability to produce lactase is completely lost within 3 to 4 years in most children. Thus, the majority of adults in the human population cannot digest the sugar in milk!

To further the digestion of protein, there are proteolytic enzymes in both the pancreatic and intestinal juices; these enzymes supplement and extend the action of pepsin secreted by the stomach. The enzymes *trypsin* and *chymotrypsin* in the pancreatic juice cleave peptide bonds to yield peptides of short lengths. Amino acids are split off one at a time from the ends of peptide chains through the actions of *carboxypeptidase* in the pancreatic juice and various peptidases in the intestinal juice, notably *aminopeptidase* (table 8.1). As noted earlier, amino acids constitute the final products of protein digestion.

ROLE OF BILE

Bile, which the liver produces, enters the gallbladder, where it becomes concentrated (through the loss of water) and stored until needed (fig. 8.5). If there is too much concentration, one of bile's ingredients, *cholesterol,* precipitates out of solution as crystalline gallstones. The gallstones may block the flow of bile into the duodenum and impair the intestine's ability to digest fat. Nevertheless, a person can function effectively without a gallbladder; indeed, some mammals (the horse and rat, for example) do not even possess gallbladders.

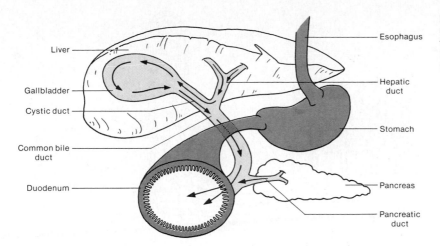

Figure 8.5 Pathway of bile produced in the liver and released from the gallbladder into the duodenum. Pancreatic secretion also enters the duodenum.

Labels: Liver, Gallbladder, Cystic duct, Common bile duct, Duodenum, Esophagus, Hepatic duct, Stomach, Pancreas, Pancreatic duct

The yellow-brown bile does not contain digestive enzymes, but the *bile salts* are important in breaking down (emulsifying) large globules of fat into very fine droplets. The small fat droplets are hydrolyzed into fatty acids and glycerol under the influence of pancreatic *lipase*. This lipase is the only active fat-hydrolyzing enzyme in the entire alimentary canal. Under conditions of pancreatic insufficiency, large amounts of undigested fat appear in the feces. In such cases, fat digestion can be moderately restored by the oral intake of pancreatic enzymes.

Bile salts also prepare the products of fat digestion for absorption. After being liberated by pancreatic lipase, the fatty acids and glycerol are dissolved in water through the action of the bile salts. The resulting water-soluble aggregate is called a *micelle*. These micelles facilitate the absorption of fatty acids and glycerol through the intestinal lining. In the absence of micelles, fat absorption would take place very slowly.

The body carefully conserves the bile salts. Most of the bile salts (80–90 percent) entering the duodenum are reabsorbed in the lower part of the intestine and returned to the liver. The salts are again secreted in the bile. If the bile duct is blocked, the bile pigments accumulate in the blood and body tissues, imparting to the skin a yellowish or *jaundiced* tint.

INTESTINAL VILLI AND ABSORPTION

The complex nutrients that have been hydrolyzed into simpler molecules pass from the cavity of the small intestine into the bloodstream for distribution to all parts of the body. The diffusible end products are first absorbed into the epithelial cells that line the inner surface of the small intestine, particularly the duodenum. Not only is the inner surface of the small intestine highly folded, but its circular folds are studded with numerous (as many as 5 million) microscopic, fingerlike projections known as *villi*, which are very much like the chorionic villi of the placenta. In addition, the epithelial cells themselves contain submicroscopic projections known as *microvilli*, which greatly augment the absorptive capacity of the individual cells. Taken all together, the circular intestinal folds, the dense forest of villi, and the innumerable microvilli offer a great amount of surface to the digested products. Compared with a flat-surfaced tube of similar length and diameter, the small intestine has a 600-fold greater total surface area.

The structure of the thimble-like villus is illustrated in figure 8.6. A thin-walled capillary network extends through the core of the villus.

Figure 8.6 Intestinal villi *(left)* and the microscopic structure of a villus *(right).*

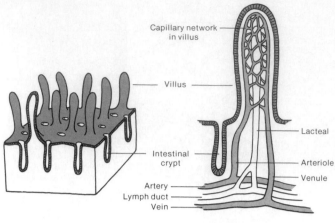

Capillary network in villus

Villus

Lacteal

Intestinal crypt

Arteriole

Venule

Artery

Lymph duct

Vein

Figure 8.7 The transport of glucose across the intestinal lining is dependent on sodium ions.

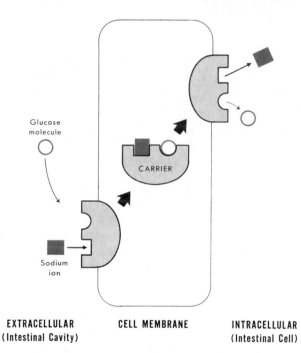

Glucose molecule

CARRIER

Sodium ion

EXTRACELLULAR
(Intestinal Cavity)

CELL MEMBRANE

INTRACELLULAR
(Intestinal Cell)

Dissolved nutritive substances, which have already been absorbed through the epithelial cells, pass into the capillaries. As previously described (chapter 4), amino acids are actively transported across the epithelium of the villus into the capillaries. The products of fat digestion do not pass into the blood capillaries, but instead enter a central, blind-ending vessel called a *lacteal* (fig. 8.6). Lacteals are part of the lymphatic system of the body (see chapter 9). The absorbed fat droplets are transported to adipose tissue, where they are stored.

Recent studies indicate that the membrane of an intestinal cell contains a specific carrier for the glucose molecule. This carrier can transport the glucose molecule across the intestinal lining, but only if it can simultaneously transport a sodium ion. Thus, current concepts link the absorption of glucose with the transport of sodium. The mechanism is shown in figure 8.7. The extracellular fluid in the intestinal cavity contains a high concentration of sodium ions. When the carrier molecule interacts with a sodium ion, the carrier attracts a glucose molecule. The loaded carrier then moves across the membrane into the intestinal cell, where it releases the sodium ion (since the sodium level is low within the cell). Without the sodium ion, the carrier has a low affinity for glucose and releases the glucose molecule as well. The empty carrier then moves back to the external surface of the cell membrane, where the process repeats itself. As the cell accumulates glucose, it might be anticipated that glucose molecules would recombine with the carriers inside the cell and move back out of the cell. However, this reverse event is unlikely because glucose is not attracted to a carrier that is devoid of sodium. In turn, some mechanism must be operative to maintain a low sodium level inside the cell to ensure that sodium ions do not load the internal carriers. This is accomplished by "ejecting" the sodium ions into the intestinal cavity. The cell actively transports sodium ions out of the cell by a different carrier system, which involves the expenditure of energy. By the active "pumping" of sodium out of the cells, the extracellular fluid in the intestinal cavity normally has a concentration of sodium ions that is 10 times greater than the concentration inside the intestinal cell.

ROLE OF THE LIVER
The typically large quantities of absorbed glucose and other dissolved nutrients from the intestinal lumen are not immediately distributed by the circulatory system to all parts of the body. Rather, the glucose-rich blood from the intestinal region passes to the liver. In the liver cells, surplus glucose is removed from the bloodstream and stored as glycogen. During intervals when glucose is not being absorbed from the intestinal tract, the liver provides from storage a steady supply of glucose for distribution to the body tissues. The liver thus assures a fairly uniform level of circulating glucose under normal dietary conditions. When the store of liver glycogen becomes too great, the overabundant supply of glucose is converted to fat in certain tissues of the body, prominently in areas immediately beneath the skin. If the store of liver glycogen is in danger of becoming depleted, amino acids can be converted into carbohydrate. Accordingly, during long periods of fast, the liver can synthesize new glucose molecules from amino acid precursors (as well as from glycerol).

The liver has other regulatory functions. Amino acids are not stored in the body. Normally, the intake of protein is greater than the resulting pool of amino acids required for the synthesis of body proteins. Excess amino acids enter into complex chemical transformations in the liver whereby they are converted into carbohydrate or fat. The transformations involve removal of the amino portion (NH_2) of the amino acid molecules. Such *deaminations* lead to the formation of highly toxic ammonia, but the ammonia is rapidly converted by the liver to nontoxic *urea*, which is excreted by the kidney. It bears emphasizing that the ingestion of excessive amounts of protein-rich foods by an adult does not result in a significant accretion of body proteins; the extra amino acids are simply converted into carbohydrate or fat.

LARGE INTESTINE
After the diffusible food materials have been absorbed in the small intestine, the unabsorbed residue passes into the *large intestine*, the last five feet of the alimentary tract. It consists of the *cecum, vermiform appendix, colon* (ascending, transverse, and descending portions), and finally the *rectum*, terminating at the anal opening (fig. 8.1). The cecum in man is scarcely more than a slight enlargement. In rabbits, the cecum is an enormously enlarged pouch where cellulose, the principal component of plant cell walls, is subjected to prolonged digestion by a large population of bacteria. The vermiform (literally, "wormlike") appendix in man is an

ill-fated vestige of a cecum that can no longer fulfill its ancestral role. Although useless, the appendix is often a focal point for serious infection (*appendicitis*).

The residue in the large intestine consists partly of the indigestible plant cellulose. Bacteria in the colon digest much of the cellulose and use the glucose released for their own growth and reproduction. The bacterial population is generally so large that considerable quantities of carbon dioxide are produced; this gas (along with other fermentative gases) accounts for our intestinal gas (*flatus*). Not all bacterial cells survive or thrive; approximately 50 percent of the dry weight of the feces is represented by living or dead bacteria.

Other materials eliminated consist of dead cells from the lining of the intestine, small amounts of salts, mucus, and bile pigments. The main bile pigment is *bilirubin,* a decomposition product derived from the hemoglobin of disrupted red cells. It is the bile pigments that impart the characteristic brown color to feces. In the absence of bile pigments, the feces are clay-colored (grayish white). Feces are normally compact, since much of the water has been reabsorbed across the walls of the large intestine. The longer fecal material remains in the large intestine, the more water is reabsorbed, and a constipated condition may arise.

MINERALS AND VITAMINS

Although there are 90 naturally occurring elements in the universe, about 25 elements are essential to living organisms. These elements (commonly called *minerals*) are listed in table 8.2 in their order of abundance in organisms. Four elements—oxygen, carbon, hydrogen, and nitrogen—compose 96 percent of the tissues of the human body. When the seven next most abundant minerals (specifically, numbers 5 through 11 in table 8.2) are added to the aforementioned four, the eleven account for 99.5 percent of the elements in the human body. Interestingly, these eleven elements in living tissues are also among the most abundant elements in sea water. The remaining fourteen minerals in table 8.2 are known to be required in organisms only in trace amounts. Humans rarely suffer from mineral difficiencies; most foods contain adequate amounts of minerals to replace those lost from the body.

Vitamins are organic substances that are required in minute quantities by the body but which the body itself is unable to synthesize. Vitamin requirements are usually met by a well-balanced diet. The fat-soluble vitamins (A, D, E, and K) are stored in the body for such lengthy periods that liberal or excessive intakes are unnecessary and may even be harmful. In particular, enormous concentrations of vitamins A and D are held to be toxic to the human body. On the other hand, the water-soluble vitamins (members of the B complex and C) tend to be destroyed by prolonged cooking in water and, accordingly, may fail to gain entry into the body in sufficient amounts.

The water-soluble vitamins perform the same functions in all organisms —they are vital components of enzyme systems. As table 8.3 reveals, water-soluble vitamins serve as coenzymes for a variety of enzymes. In contrast, the fat-soluble vitamins are involved in special activities in particular tissues. Vitamin A is concerned with the formation of visual purple, vitamin K is essential for blood coagulation, and vitamin D is required for the utilization of calcium and phosphorus in bone development. The role of vitamin E in the human body has yet to be precisely defined. This vitamin, isolated first from wheat germ oil, has a profound

Table 8.2
Chemical Elements and their
Biological Importance

Element (Symbol)	Percentage in Human Body	Primary Function
1. Oxygen (O)	65%	Component of water and organic compounds; electron acceptor
2. Carbon (C)	18	Major constituent of organic compounds
3. Hydrogen (H)	10	Component of water and organic compounds; electron donor
4. Nitrogen (N)	3	Constituent of amino acids and nucleic acids
5. Calcium (Ca)	1.5	Important component of bones and teeth; required by each cell
6. Phosphorus (P)	1.0	Essential for energy transfer (in ATP); component of phospholipids and nucleoproteins
7. Potassium (K)	0.35	Major inorganic constituent within cells; essential for nerve impulses and muscular contractions
8. Sulfur (S)	0.25	Component of certain amino acids and vitamins
9. Sodium (Na)	0.15	Chief inorganic constituent of extracellular fluids; important for nerve and muscle function
10. Chlorine (Cl)	0.15	Maintain proper osmotic concentration of cells and tissue fluids
11. Magnesium (Mg)	0.05	Cofactor in a variety of enzymes and chlorophyll
12. Iron (Fe)	0.004	Essential component of hemoglobin and myoglobin
13. Manganese (Mn)	<0.001	Cofactor for several enzymes
14. Copper (Cu)	<0.001	Proper utilization of iron in hemoglobin
15. Iodine (I)	<0.001	Constituent of thyroid hormone (thyroxin)
16. Cobalt (Co)	<0.001	Constituent of Vitamin B_{12}
17. Zinc (Zn)	<0.001	Cofactor for several enzymes
18. Selenium (Se)	<0.001	Contributes to liver function
19. Molybdenum (Mo)	<0.001	Cofactor for certain enzymes
20. Boron (B)	<0.001	Important for RNA metabolism in plants
21. Silicon (Si)	<0.001	Structural unit of diatoms (single-celled plants)
22. Fluorine (F)	<0.001	Found in teeth and bones
23. Chromium (Cr)	<0.001	Insulin-like activity
24. Vanadium (V)	<0.001	Aids mineralization of bones and teeth
25. Tin (Sn)	<0.001	Important for metabolism in laboratory animals

effect on the reproductive system of certain laboratory animals. Laboratory male rats deficient in vitamin E exhibit degenerative changes in the testes that result in sterility, and the eggs of experimental hens deficient in vitamin E fail to hatch. There is suggestive evidence that vitamin E in humans may play a role in maintenance of the lipid configuration of cell membranes. More recently, several medical sources have claimed that vitamin E provides partial or total relief for the problems or symptoms of menopause.

Table 8.3
Vitamins and their Biological Importance

Name	Function	Deficiency
Vitamin A	Normal functioning of epithelial tissue; synthesize visual purple	Dry skin; night blindness (inability to perceive objects in dim light)
Vitamin B complex		
Thiamine (B_1)	Coenzyme in sugar metabolism (component of NAD)	Beriberi (nerve degeneration and weakening of heart muscles)
Riboflavin (B_2)	Coenzyme in cellular respiration (component of FAD)	Dermatitis (skin disorder)
Pyridoxine (B_6)	Coenzyme in amino acid metabolism	Severe gastrointestinal disturbances
Cyanocobalamin (B_{12})	Maturation of red blood cells	Anemia
Niacin (nicotinic acid, nicotinamide)	Coenzyme in cellular respiration	Pellagra (skin irritation and muscle weakness)
Pantothenic acid	Coenzyme in cellular respiration (component of coenzyme A)	Neurologic disorders
Folic acid (folacin)	Maturation of red blood cells	Anemia
Biotin	Coenzyme in amino acid and lipid metabolism	Gastrointestinal disturbances
Vitamin C (ascorbic acid)	Formation of intracellular materials in connective tissues (cartilage and bone)	Scurvy (breakdown of blood vessels and impaired wound healing)
Vitamin D (cholecalciferol)	Utilization of calcium and phosphorus in bone development	Rickets in children
Vitamin E (tocopherol)	Essential to reproduction in rats	Sterility in male rats; maintenance of cell membranes (?)
Vitamin K (naphthoquinone)	Anti-hemorrhagic factor (manufactured by bacteria of colon)	Impaired blood coagulation

SUMMARY

The human digestive system is concerned with breaking down complex molecules (starches and proteins, for example) into simpler molecules that can pass through cell membranes. Digestion is accomplished by the action of a series of hydrolytic enzymes, aided by hydrochloric acid and bile. Three accessory organs—the salivary glands, liver, and pancreas—assist the tubular gastrointestinal tract in the processes of digestion and absorption. Almost all absorption of the final products of digestion occurs in the small intestine, the absorptive surface of which is greatly increased by fingerlike projections (villi). No digestion occurs in the large intestine, which serves to reabsorb water back into the body and prepare the indigestible food residue for elimination. Minerals and vitamins are indispensable for the maintenance of normal bodily activities.

Ethical Probe 6
Controversy Over Vitamin C

The U. S. Food and Nutrition Board issues bulletins on the daily minimum allowance for nutrients, including vitamins. The minimum dietary daily dose of a vitamin is that estimated to saturate the human tissues for that vitamin. Over the past 30 years, the recommended daily allowance of certain vitamins has been revised downward. In 1943, the value of vitamin C was set at 75 milligrams a day, and subsequently reduced to 60 milligrams daily. In 1975, the Food and Nutrition Board decreased the daily allowance of vitamin C to 45 milligrams.

The most recent reduction has been termed irresponsible by Linus Pauling, who is a staunch advocate of large daily doses of vitamin C. Pauling argues that the recommended amount is only adequate to prevent the deficiency disease, scurvy. He contends that 45 milligrams is grossly insufficient to promote optimum health. Pauling suggests a range of 250 milligrams to 4 grams daily of vitamin C to protect against common diseases, particularly the common cold. Pauling's opponents have argued that excessive amounts of vitamin C are useless, and more importantly, most of the excess vitamin C is converted to a product, oxalic acid, that is toxic to the body.

Is the intake of a vitamin, or any other substance, solely a matter of individual responsibility or do federal agencies have the right to formulate policies to protect individuals from indiscriminate use or self-indulgence? What is the right of an individual to jeopardize his or her own health?

9 Blood and Circulation

All higher organisms depend on the continuous flow of blood to distribute dissolved nutrients and oxygen to the cells of the body. Blood also transports water, inorganic salts, hormones, vitamins, antibodies, and enzymes. All cells are profoundly influenced by the diverse materials carried in the bloodstream. In turn, the blood is affected by the secretions and waste products of the cells. Although the concentrations of substances fluctuate in the blood, the fluctuations are minimal and kept within remarkably narrow limits. This steady state is achieved through the operation of carefully coordinated stabilizing (homeostatic) processes.

The blood of man circulates continuously in a closed circuit of tubes. The blood is propelled to all parts of the body by the action of a pistonlike pump, the heart. In one part of the circuit, blood passes through the lungs, where it acquires oxygen and releases carbon dioxide. In another part of the circuit, blood courses through the small intestine, where it receives energy-rich glucose. In still other parts of the circuit, it disposes its waste products, such as urea, in the kidney. In the neighborhood of each cell, the walls of the blood vessels become sufficiently thin to permit dissolved substances to diffuse through the walls to reach the cell. The vitally important thin-walled blood vessels are called *capillaries*.

Most of the cells of the body lie outside the capillaries. In other words, the cells are not bathed by blood, but are immediately surrounded by a milieu known as *tissue fluid*. This extracellular fluid acts as the medium of exchange for dissolved nutrients, gases, and waste products between the capillaries and the cells. The efficient functioning of the organism requires the integrative action of cells, blood, and tissue fluid. The intricate human circulatory system is essentially an accomplished apparatus to bring blood in close contact with all cells of the body via the tissue fluid.

PROPERTIES OF BLOOD

Blood constitutes about one-twelfth of the total weight of an adult human body and has an average volume of 5 liters. When blood is centrifuged, it separates into a dense mass of cells and a clear, upper layer of amber fluid. The fluid, or *plasma*, makes up about 55 percent of the total blood volume; the remaining solid mass consists of red blood cells, or *erythrocytes*, capped by a thin layer of white blood cells, or *leucocytes*.

The ratio of the red cell mass to the total blood volume is expressed as the *hematocrit* (fig. 9.1). Normal hematocrit values range from 40 to 45 percent in adult males and 36 to 45 percent in adult females. Thus, about 45 percent of the blood volume in the adult is composed of red blood cells. When the number of erythrocytes is drastically reduced, as in severe

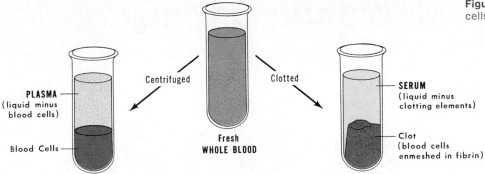

Figure 9.1 The relation of blood cells to plasma and serum.

PLASMA
(liquid minus
blood cells)

Blood Cells

Centrifuged

Fresh
WHOLE BLOOD

Clotted

SERUM
(liquid minus
clotting elements)

Clot
(blood cells
enmeshed in fibrin)

anemia, the hematocrit value may drop as low as 15 percent. In disorders characterized by an overabundance of red blood cells, as in *polycythemia*, the hematocrit value may be as high as 75 percent.

The plasma, although largely water, contains several inorganic minerals (such as sodium and potassium) and several organic compounds such as albumins and globulins). The plasma proteins serve a number of important functions; the immunoglobulins, for example, are antibodies that protect the body against infectious agents. When blood coagulates, the yellowish clear fluid that separates from the clot is called *serum* (fig. 9.1).

BLOOD CELLS

There are three structurally and functionally distinct types of cells in human blood: the *erythrocytes* (*erythros*, "red" and *kytos*, "cell"), the *leucocytes* (*leukos*, "white"), and the platelets (or thrombocytes). The characteristic reddish color of the erythrocyte is due to the presence of *hemoglobin*. The leucocyte lacks a colored pigment and appears translucent (rather than white) in an unstained microscopic preparation. The platelet is not a whole cell, but merely an anucleate cytoplasmic fragment that has split off from a larger nucleated cell (fig. 9.2).

A cubic millimeter (mm³) of blood contains about 5 million erythrocytes. The normal shape of the human red blood cell is that of a biconcave disc. This unusual shape is ideally suited for absorbing and releasing gases quickly. The transport of oxygen and carbon dioxide by the erythrocyte is facilitated by hemoglobin. Although hemoglobin is spoken of as a pigment, it is a complex protein (*globin*) to which is attached iron-containing *heme*. The hemoglobin molecule enters into a loose chemical combination with oxygen molecules and has the capacity to bind and release oxygen readily. Blood has a bright red tint when the hemoglobin is saturated with oxygen; the color changes to a bluish purple when oxygen is released. These color changes account for the familiar commentary that "arterial blood" is bright red whereas "venous blood" is dark blue.

Hemoglobin displays an affinity for gases other than oxygen, notably carbon monoxide. This colorless, odorless gas attaches firmly to hemoglobin and is not released in the bloodstream. Hemoglobin becomes unserviceable for the transport of oxygen as progressively more carbon monoxide molecules attach to hemoglobin molecules. Accordingly, the cells of a person victimized by carbon monoxide are actually starved for oxygen.

In man and other mammals, the nuclei of all erythrocytes are extruded

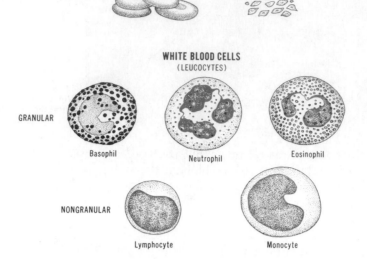

RED BLOOD CELL
(ERYTHROCYTES)

BLOOD PLATELETS

WHITE BLOOD CELLS
(LEUCOCYTES)

GRANULAR

Basophil　　　Neutrophil　　　Eosinophil

NONGRANULAR

Lymphocyte　　　Monocyte

just before they are placed into circulation. All other vertebrates have nucleated red cells. The life span of the mammalian blood cells is curtailed by the lack of a nucleus. The red blood cell survives only four months. Nevertheless, the loss of the nucleus is an adaptation that allows the cell to harbor additional quantities of hemoglobin. Hemoglobin in the mammalian red cells can bind 70 times as much oxygen as an equal volume of plasma, which can carry oxygen only in solution.

The red marrow of bone is the primary source of new erythrocytes. If the oxygen tension of the blood becomes lowered, such as may occur in hemorrhage or from prolonged exposure to high altitudes, the bone marrow responds by producing large numbers of erythrocytes. This homeostatic response elevates the oxygen-carrying capacity of the blood. People residing in mountainous regions have relatively more red blood cells than do individuals living at sea level. The production of new red blood cells (technically called *erythropoiesis*) requires adequate supplies of iron and many of the vitamins of the B complex, especially folic acid and B_{12}.

The leucocytes, or white blood cells, are the body's dominant agents in destroying or inactivating foreign material, including disease-causing bacteria and viruses. Although there are five kinds of leucocytes, they fall into two large classes—the *granulocytes* and the *agranulocytes* (fig. 9.2). The cytoplasm of a granulocyte contains large granules (mostly lysosomes), whereas the cytoplasm of the agranular leucocyte is relatively homogeneous. The leucocyte count is generally given as 10,000 cells per cubic millimeter of blood. This is not the total body count, inasmuch as not all leucocytes are confined to the blood. In fact, greater numbers of leucocytes are found in the connective tissues of various organs (spleen, kidney, and thymus) than in the circulating blood. Leucocytes generally have a short life span (2 to 14 days), although certain ones (antibody-producing lymphocytes) tend to survive longer (100 days or more).

Leucocytes are exceptionally versatile cells. Some leucocytes, particularly the highly motile *neutrophils* and *monocytes,* migrate in a manner similar to that of an ameba (*ameboid movement*) and ingest bacteria and other infectious microorganisms in ameba-like fashion (*phagocytosis*). Both neutrophils and monocytes appear in large numbers in the early

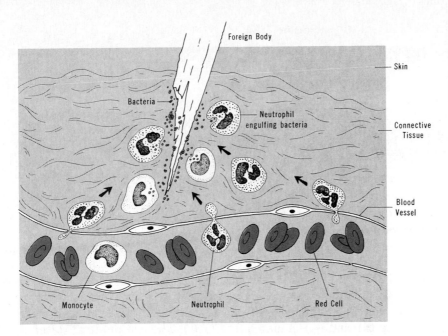

Figure 9.3 The phagocytotic action of neutrophils and monocytes on infectious microorganisms (such as bacteria). These motile leucocytes actually push through the thin walls of capillaries to reach the site of infection.

stages of bacterial infection; both have the remarkable capacity of squeezing through the walls of capillaries (fig. 9.3). Lymphocytes are also mobilized rapidly at points of invasion by foreign substances and invariably may be seen surrounding areas of inflammation. The lymphocytes are highly specialized cells that synthesize and release antibody molecules (*immunoglobulins*). Antibodies are elicited by any foreign protein, for which the general term *antigen* is applied. As will be explained later (chapter 14), the interaction between antigen and antibody is called an *immune reaction*.

Platelets (*platum,* meaning plate or dish) are flat, fragile fragments of cytoplasm that are split off from precursor cells in the bone marrow. Large numbers of platelets (300,000 per mm³) circulate in the bloodstream. Platelets mesh together, in cobblestone fashion, at the site of injured blood vessels to seal off the vessel and minimize blood loss. Simultaneously, the platelets release a blood-clotting factor (*thromboplastin*) that initiates a complicated series of chemical steps leading to the coagulation of blood. As yellow fluid (serum) escapes from the ruptured vessel, the blood solidifies into a gel-like mass, a *clot.* The clot consists of a tangled mass of fibrin threads in which blood cells are trapped. The fibrin strands are actually the insoluble form of the plasma protein, *fibrinogen.* Clots normally form at wound surfaces, but occasionally may occur within an intact blood vessel (*thrombosis*) and may even be transported in the bloodstream to block another vessel (*embolism*). The consequence tends to be serious, since the tissues normally supplied by the blocked vessel no longer can receive the nutrients necessary for survival.

BLOOD VESSELS AND FLOW

Highly elastic, sturdy *arteries* carry the blood from the heart to the various parts of the body. Arteries are constructed to receive blood under great pressure; their thick walls contain both elastic and muscle tissues (fig. 9.4). The elastic tissue cushions the force of impact of blood being delivered vigorously into the lumen of the vessel. When the heart contracts (technically called *systole*), the hydrostatic pressure (generated by the pumping action of the heart) measures 120 mm Hg in the major

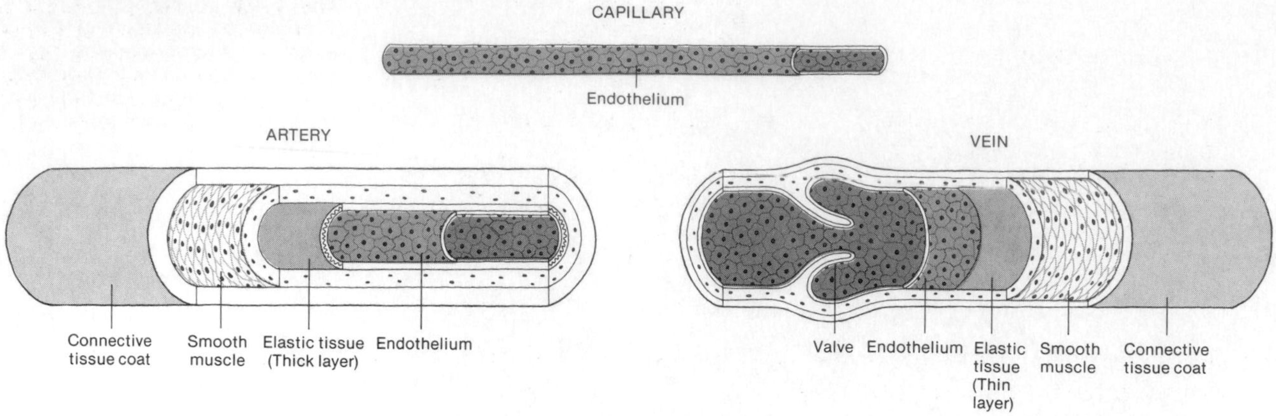

CAPILLARY

Endothelium

ARTERY

VEIN

Connective | Smooth | Elastic tissue | Endothelium
tissue coat | muscle | (Thick layer)

Valve | Endothelium | Elastic tissue (Thin layer) | Smooth muscle | Connective tissue coat

Figure 9.4 Contrasting features of a thick-walled, muscular artery, the relatively flaccid vein, and the thin-walled capillary.

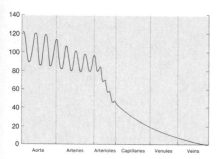

Figure 9.5 Blood pressures in different vessels of the human circulatory system. Note the oscillations (or pulsations) in the major arteries as the heart contracts (systole) and relaxes (diastole). A pulse pressure is negligible or absent in the capillaries and veins.

arteries (such as the brachial artery of the arm). This means that the blood pressure at systole (or *systolic pressure*) can push a column of mercury to a level of 120 mm in a glass manometer tube that is connected to the large artery. When the heart relaxes (*diastole*), the hydrostatic pressure (*diastolic pressure*) declines to 80 mm Hg (fig. 9.5). The systole/diastole relationship is usually designated as 120/80. The arithmetical difference between systolic and diastolic pressure (40 mm Hg) is the *pulse pressure*. Essentially, pulse pressure describes the amplitude of the oscillations, or pulsations, in arterial pressure. The pulsating nature of arterial flow is evident when a large artery is severed—the blood flows out in spurts rather than evenly.

The blood pressure falls as the arteries become progressively smaller branches, termed *arterioles,* which ultimately subdivide in the body tissues as minute, thin-walled vessels, the *capillaries.* The arterioles are important in regulating the flow of blood through the capillary network. The walls of arterioles contain smooth muscle fibers, which effect changes in the diameter of the vessel by relaxing or contracting. Small changes in diameter result in relatively large changes in resistance to the flow of blood, because tube diameter and flow resistance are inversely related. The terminal ends of arterioles are guarded by rings of smooth muscles, known as *precapillary sphincters,* which control the delivery of blood into the capillaries.

Capillaries perform the vital function of bringing the blood in the immediate vicinity of the cells. No cell is far removed from capillaries; accordingly, the exchange of nutrients and metabolic end products is highly efficient (fig. 9.6). In the capillary bed, the cells gain oxygen and dissolved nutrients and lose carbon dioxide and soluble wastes. There is ample time for the exchange of materials as the flow of blood through a capillary is very slow (0.07 cm/sec). A typical capillary is composed of a single layer of flattened cells without elastic tissue or smooth muscle. A capillary is so narrow that the blood cells are conveyed in single file.

The branched capillaries join to form relatively small vessels (*venules*), which in turn unite to form the larger *veins.* Veins have relatively thin walls that are not liberally supplied with elastic or muscle tissue. Veins act as low-resistance channels for the flow of blood from the tissues back to the heart. The venous blood pressure is low because of the large diameter of the vein. The flaccid veins depend largely on the pressure exerted on them by the surrounding tissues to return the blood to the heart.

Most veins, particularly in the limbs, have one-way valves that prevent

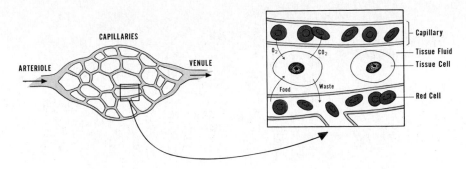

Figure 9.6 Capillary network *(left)* and the diffusion of materials between capillaries and cells, by way of the tissue fluid that bathes the cells *(right)*. (From C. A. Villee, *Biology*, 6th ed., 1972, W. B. Saunders Co.)

the backflow of blood into the capillaries. While standing, a person unconsciously contracts muscles in his legs to force blood through the limb veins. On prolonged standing in one position, the muscular contractions may cease temporarily and blood may pool in the vessels of the feet. Under such an adverse circumstance, a person may faint, as do soldiers standing at attention for exceptionally long periods. An individual can avoid situations not favorable for venous return from the limbs by consciously contracting the limb muscles occasionally, thereby compressing the veins. If the one-way valves of the limb veins become defective, the veins may become greatly swollen (*varicose veins*).

CAPILLARY EXCHANGE OF WATER

The plasma proteins are large molecules that do not normally pass through the capillary membranes. The nonpenetrating proteins are the agents responsible for establishing an osmotic gradient between the plasma in the capillaries and the tissue fluid bathing the cells. Since the high-molecular weight proteins are more concentrated in the blood plasma than in the tissue fluid, water passes by osmosis from the tissue fluid into the capillary (fig. 9.7). However, the hydrostatic pressure within the capillary (generated by the pumping action of the heart) acts in an opposite direction to draw water back into the capillary. Water filters out of the blood capillary when the hydrostatic pressure forcing water out is greater than the retaining action of the plasma proteins.

The hydrostatic pressure at the arterial end of the capillary is 35 mm Hg, and it decreases to 15 mm Hg at the venous end of the capillary. At the arterial end, water flows out of the capillary into the tissue spaces because the hydrostatic pressure is greater than the osmotic pressure. At the venous end, the hydrostatic pressure has become so low that the osmotic pressure draws water back into the capillary. Excess water does *not* normally accumulate in the tissue fluid. The overflow is drained by special vessels that permeate the tissues between the blood capillaries. These special channels are the *lymph capillaries,* thin-walled tubes that resemble veins (fig. 9.7).

Lymph is moved along by pressure applied against the lymph vessels by the contractions of adjacent muscles and the pulsations of neighboring arteries. The lymph capillaries are unique in that they end blindly in the tissues. That is to say, they simply terminate in the tissues without connecting with other lymphatic vessels (fig. 9.8). Lymph itself is essentially the fluid that has drained into the lymph capillaries from the tissue spaces. The lymph capillaries empty into larger lymph ducts, which ultimately return the water to the blood circulation. If there is more water in the tissue fluid than can be drained off by the lymph vessels, the tissue swells. This very common clinical condition is called *edema*. The swelling

Figure 9.7 Flow of fluid across the capillary. At the arterial end of the capillary, hydrostatic pressure drives fluid out of the capillary into the tissue spaces. At the venous end of the capillary, osmotic pressure draws fluid back into the capillary. Excess tissue fluid is drained by lymph vessels.

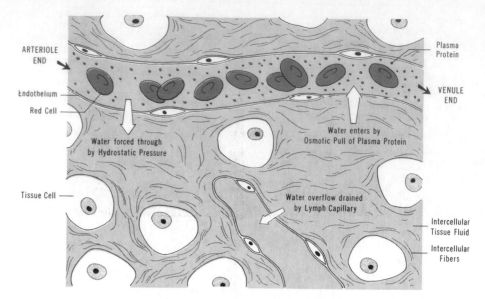

Figure 9.8 Lymph vessels permeating the cells of the body. The lymph vessels end blindly in the tissues. Arrows indicate direction of flow of materials. (From C. A. Villee, *Biology,* 6th ed, 1972, W. B. Saunders Co.)

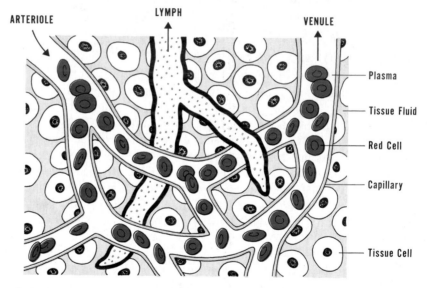

of tissue may occur if the blood pressure rises markedly (with a concomitant elevation in hydrostatic pressure) or if the lymph vessels are blocked by disease.

Normally, nearly all the water that flows out into the tissue fluid at the arterial end of the capillary re-enters the capillary at the venous end. There is thus little net loss or gain of water in the tissue spaces. The mechanism for capillary water exchange assumes great importance when bleeding (hemorrhage) causes not only a drop in blood pressure but also a decrease in blood volume. The loss in blood volume is compensated by the flow of water from the tissue spaces into the capillaries. This compensatory movement of water into the circulatory system may restore the blood volume almost to normal in cases of moderate hemorrhage.

THE HEART

The adult human heart is a muscular organ, about the size of a closed fist, located in the chest (thoracic) cavity (fig. 9.9). The walls of the chambers of the heart contain a meshwork of contractile cardiac muscle cells

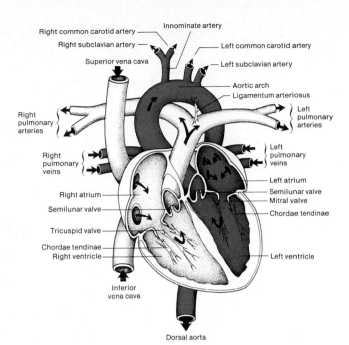

Right common carotid artery — Innominate artery

Right subclavian artery

Left common carotid artery

Superior vena cava

Left subclavian artery

Aortic arch

Ligamentum arteriosus

Right pulmonary arteries

Left pulmonary arteries

Right pulmonary veins

Left pulmonary veins

Right atrium

Left atrium

Semilunar valve

Semilunar valve

Mitral valve

Tricuspid valve

Chordae tendinae

Chordae tendinae

Right ventricle

Left ventricle

Inferior vena cava

Dorsal aorta

Figure 9.9 The four-chambered human heart.

(fibers). The contractions, or "beats," occur 72 times a minute, which amounts to about 100,000 beats a day. The human heart receives blood through veins that empty into two thin-walled chambers, the *atria* (or *auricles*), and distributes blood into arteries through two thick-walled chambers, the *ventricles*. The muscle fibers of the atria act in a coordinated manner and cause both atria to contract simultaneously, forcing blood into the ventricles. The ventricular muscle layers also act in unison; both ventricles contract together to pump blood out of the heart (fig. 9.10). As previously mentioned, the contraction of a heart chamber is called systole, whereas relaxation of the chamber is diastole. The terms are most often used to refer only to the contraction and relaxation of the heavy-walled ventricles.

Individual cardiac muscle cells can contract spontaneously in a rhythmical manner. In a culture medium, isolated muscle cells contract at different rates. When, however, the individual muscle cells are fused together, they contract together at a rate established by the cell with the fastest spontaneous rhythm. The same phenomenon is witnessed in the intact heart. The beat of the heart is initiated by a mass of cells with the fastest inherent rhythm. The dominant pacemaker of the heart is the *sinoatrial* (SA) *node,* which is positioned in the back wall of the upper-right side of the right atrium (fig. 9.11). The impulse from the SA node is transmitted rapidly along specialized bundles of fibers to the left atrium, thereby assuring that all muscle cells in both atria are stimulated simultaneously. The impulse from the SA node also excites a second group of specialized cells, the *atrioventricular* (AV) *node,* located in the wall between the right atrium and right ventricle. The transmission of impulse from the SA node to the AV node is precisely timed to allow the atria to contract and empty their contents into the ventricles before the ventricular muscle cells are stimulated. The impulse from the SA node to the AV node is delayed 0.1 second; thereafter all ventricular muscle cells are stimulated by the AV node to ensure the coordinated contraction of both ventricles.

The inherent beat of the heart is monitored by hormones and nerves.

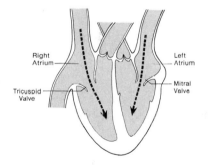

Right Atrium

Left Atrium

Tricuspid Valve

Mitral Valve

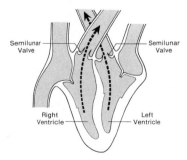

Semilunar Valve

Semilunar Valve

Right Ventricle

Left Ventricle

Figure 9.10 The simultaneous filling of the two ventricles (*left*), followed by the simultaneous emptying (contraction) of the two ventricles (*right*).

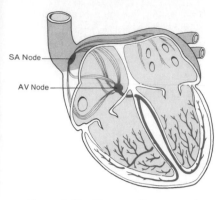

Figure 9.11 Two small masses of specialized cells ("pacemakers") initiate the heartbeat: the sino-atrial node (SA node) and the atrioventricular node (AV node). The excitatory impulse travels from the SA to the AV node. The impulse leaves the AV node and travels rapidly along special bundles of fibers to all parts of the ventricle.

For example, epinephrine, the hormone liberated from the adrenal medulla under conditions of stress, increases the heartbeat. The vagus nerve from the medulla of the brain has an inhibitory effect on the rate of contraction of the heart, whereas sympathetic nerves from the spinal cord accelerate the heartbeat.

VALVES AND HEART SOUNDS

There are two kinds of specialized valves in the heart, the *atrioventricular* (AV) *valves* and the *semilunar valves.* The AV valves permit the flow of blood only from the atrium to the ventricle and not in the reverse direction. The AV valve that separates the right atrium from the right ventricle is the *tricuspid* valve, which derives its name from the presence of three flaps, or cusps (fig. 9.10). The corresponding AV valve on the left side has two cusps, and accordingly was formerly called the *bicuspid* valve. It is now better known as the *mitral* valve. The valves are fastened by fibrous strands to the ventricular walls so as to prevent the valves themselves from being everted into the atria.

Each of the two great arteries—the systemic aorta and the pulmonary trunk—are guarded by semilunar valves (fig. 9.10). These one-way valves occur at the base of the systemic aorta where it emerges from the left ventricle and at the point of entry at the pulmonary aorta as it leaves the right ventricle. The tightly fitting semilunar valves are forced open only when the pressure within the contracting ventricles is higher than within the arteries themselves. The semilunar valves close securely the instant the pressure in the engorged arteries builds up to a level higher than that in the emptying ventricles.

Sound vibrations caused by closure of the heart valves are transmitted to the chest walls. The sounds may be amplified by the use of a stetho-scope or recorded with an oscilloscope. There are basically two promi-nent sounds, commonly denoted as *lub* and *dup.* The first sound, *lub,* is low-pitched and associated primarily with the closure of the AV valves. The AV valves close when the pressure in the ventricles becomes higher than in the atria, and remain closed when the ventricles are contracting. The second sound, *dup,* is higher in pitch and results principally from the closure of the semilunar valves. These valves remain closed through-out the period of relaxation of the ventricles.

Differently pitched, or abnormal, heart sounds are known as *murmurs.* Some heart murmurs are caused by damaged valves that no longer can prevent the backflow of blood into the atria. Murmurs may also be associ-ated with fusions of the valve leaflets, so that only a very narrow opening is left for the passage of blood. Surgical techniques are available today by which damaged valves can be repaired or even replaced.

TWO GREAT BLOOD CIRCUITS

In the human circulatory system, there are two prominent blood circuits —the *pulmonary* and the *systemic* (fig. 9.12). The pulmonary circuit is concerned with the passage of blood from the heart through the lungs and back to the heart. The flow of blood to and from the heart and all organs of the body, except the lungs, constitutes the systemic circuit. One complete cycle of the flow of blood through the systemic circuit can be completed within 90 seconds. The two-circuit arrangement is an efficient circulatory pattern wherein the mixing of oxygenated and deoxygenated blood is avoided.

Deoxygenated (venous) blood from the lower part of the body empties

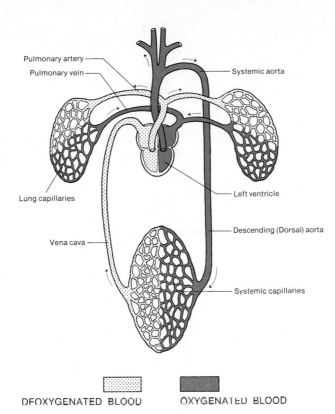

Figure 9.12 The two great blood circuits in the adult circulatory system—the pulmonary and the systemic.

Pulmonary artery

Pulmonary vein

Systemic aorta

Lung capillaries

Left ventricle

Vena cava

Descending (Dorsal) aorta

Systemic capillaries

DEOXYGENATED BLOOD   OXYGENATED BLOOD

eventually into the large *inferior vena cava;* impure blood leaving the head, neck, and arms pours into the *superior vena cava* (fig. 9.9). The deoxygenated blood enters the right atrium, from which it flows into the right ventricle when the heart relaxes. The contraction of the heart forces the blood from the right ventricle into the *pulmonary trunk,* which bifurcates into two *pulmonary arteries* leading to the lungs. In the capillary network of the lungs, the blood loses its supply of carbon dioxide and acquires large quantities of oxygen. The oxygenated (arterial) blood is collected in four *pulmonary veins,* two on each side, which open into the left atrium. Thus, in the pulmonary circuit, blood is pumped from the right half of the heart through the lungs and back to the left half of the heart. From the left *atrium,* the oxygen-rich blood enters the left ventricle and then is delivered into the *systemic aorta.* For convenience, several parts of the systemic aorta are recognized—namely, the *ascending aorta, aortic arch,* and the *descending aorta* (often called the *dorsal aorta*). The dorsal aorta is the largest artery of the body, distributing branches to various tissues and organs. The heart, like other organs, receives its blood supply via branches (*coronary arteries*) that arise from the ascending aorta. Insufficient blood flow through the coronary vessels, most often due to an abnormal thickening of the arterial lining, may lead to damage of the muscular wall of the heart—technically, an *infarction,* or the so-called *heart attack.*

As seen in figure 9.13, some of the representative branches of the dorsal aorta are the *carotid* arteries that supply the neck and head regions; the *subclavian* to the shoulders and arms; the *celiac* with branches to the stomach, liver, pancreas, and spleen; the *mesenterics* to the intestines; the *renal* to the kidneys; the *spermatic* or *ovarian* to the gonads; and the *iliacs* to the pelvic region and lower limbs. Veins with more or less corresponding names return blood to the heart. It is of interest to note that

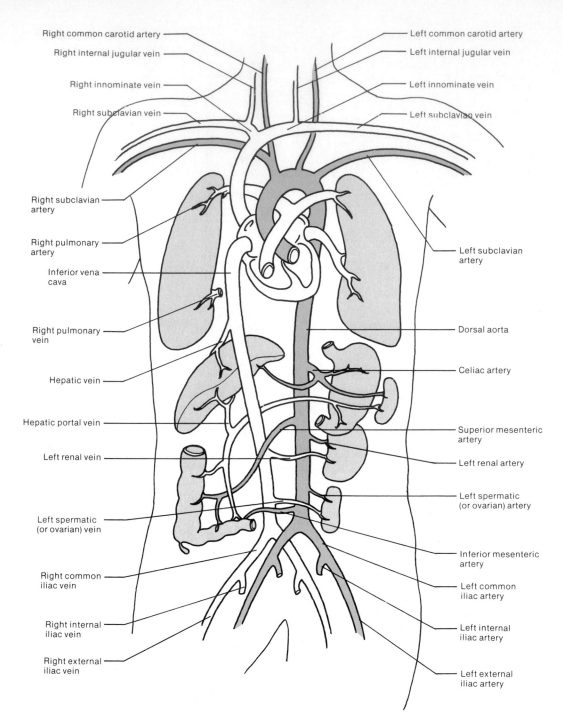

Right common carotid artery — Left common carotid artery

Right internal jugular vein — Left internal jugular vein

Right innominate vein — Left innominate vein

Right subclavian vein — Left subclavian vein

Right subclavian artery — Left subclavian artery

Right pulmonary artery

Inferior vena cava

Right pulmonary vein — Dorsal aorta

Hepatic vein — Celiac artery

Hepatic portal vein — Superior mesenteric artery

Left renal vein — Left renal artery

Left spermatic (or ovarian) vein — Left spermatic (or ovarian) artery

Right common iliac vein — Inferior mesenteric artery

Right internal iliac vein — Left common iliac artery

Right external iliac vein — Left internal iliac artery

Left external iliac artery

Figure 9.13 Adult human circulatory system, showing main arterial and venous routes.

blood from the digestive organs is conveyed into the liver by the *hepatic portal vein*. Blood ramifies in capillaries through the liver and is then collected by the *hepatic vein*, which enters the inferior vena cava.

FETAL CIRCULATION

In the human fetus, the lungs are not functional; the placenta substitutes for the lungs as the organ of gas exchange. *Placental breathing* is an admirable adaptation for the fetus in the uterine environment, but the price of this adaptation is an imperfect separation of "pure" (oxygenated) and "impure" (deoxygenated) blood in the fetal channels. This problem, however, is partially solved by the fetus in a unique way.

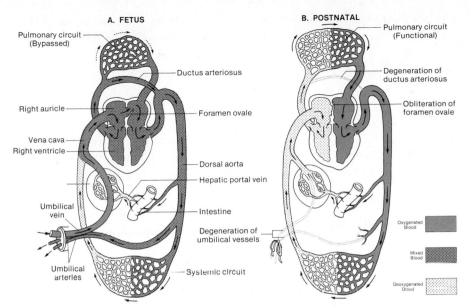

Figure 9.14 Plan of fetal circulation just before birth (A) and changes occurring in circulation at the time of birth (B). Oxygenated and deoxygenated blood are mixed in the fetus, as indicated by the shading of colors. (From B. M. Patten, *Human embryology*, 2d ed., 1953, The Blakiston Co.)

As seen in figure 9.14, oxygenated blood is delivered to the fetus from the placenta by way of the large *umbilical vein*. This highly oxygenated blood mainly bypasses the liver and flows into the inferior vena cava, which enters the right atrium. However, deoxygenated blood being returned from the internal organs (such as that carried by the hepatic portal vein to the liver) contaminates the pure placental blood flowing in the inferior vena cava. Fortunately, the volume of placental blood is large, so that the mixture entering the right atrium is relatively well oxygenated. Ordinarily blood would flow directly from the right atrium into the right ventricle, and in turn, would leave the heart through the pulmonary trunk to the lungs. This would be a useless course in the fetus since the lungs are inactive. To a large extent this course is circumvented. The main volume of the relatively pure blood in the right atrium crosses through a special opening—the *foramen ovale*—into the left atrium. From the latter, the blood reaches the left ventricle, which pumps the blood into the systemic aorta. The branches of the aorta distribute the relatively pure blood through the systemic circuit to the various tissues of the body, including the brain. Thus, the foramen ovale is an important functional device to ensure that a considerable portion of the oxygenated blood passes directly from the right atrium into the left atrium. It is not, however, the sole adaptive shunt, or shortcut. Whatever blood passes from the right auricle to the right ventricle will be directed mainly through a second shunt—the *ductus arteriosus*—that leads to the aorta. Some of the blood will reach the lungs through the pulmonary trunk, but a greater part arising from the right ventricle will continue through the ductus arteriosus to the systemic aorta.

Placental circulation ceases at birth. When the lungs of the newborn expand with air, pulmonary circulation begins so that there will be an adequate supply of oxygen to the body. Constriction of the ductus arteriosus occurs shortly after birth with the result that the blood leaving the right ventricle no longer bypasses the lungs (fig. 9.14). Additionally, the foramen ovale is gradually obliterated by a valve. The ductus arteriosus eventually becomes constricted to a rudimentary cord (ligamentum arteriosum), and the umbilical vessels also become reduced to fibrous cords. As seen in figure 9.14, the normal, postnatal circulation is characterized by the complete separation of "pure" and "impure" blood.

SUMMARY

The formidable task of the circulatory system is to bring blood in the immediate vicinity of all body cells, which are bathed in tissue fluid. Blood furnishes the cells with nutrients, oxygen, and chemical messengers (hormones), and removes from the cells the products of cellular metabolism. Blood has several cellular components with different functions. Erythrocytes (red cells) are involved in gas transport, leucocytes (white cells) protect the body against infectious and foreign agents, and platelets participate in the coagulation of blood.

The blood is continuously circulated by the pistonlike action of the heart to all parts of the body. The heart is essentially a double pump. The right side receives blood from the body and propels it to the lungs, whereas the left side receives blood from the lungs and propels it to all organs of the body (except the lungs). This arrangement establishes two prominent blood circuits—the pulmonary and the systemic, respectively. The two-circuit pattern is effective in preventing the mixing of oxygenated (pure) and deoxygenated (impure) blood.

The actual exchange of materials between the blood and the tissue cells occurs in the meshwork of thin-walled capillaries. The direction of flow of fluid (water) across the capillary depends upon two opposing forces: the hydrostatic pressure generated by the pumping action of the heart and the osmotic force established by nonpenetrating plasma proteins. At the arterial end of the capillary, the hydrostatic pressure drives water out of the capillary into the tissue spaces. At the venous end of the capillary, the plasma protein concentration favors the osmotic flow of water from the tissue spaces into the capillary. Excess water in the tissue spaces is drained by lymph capillaries, thin-walled tubes that permeate the tissues between the blood capillaries.

Gas Exchange and Excretion 10

Life cannot be sustained without oxygen, an indispensable ingredient for the metabolic reactions of the body. All cells are perilously sensitive to the lack of oxygen (anoxia). A person will succumb quickly when deprived of oxygen, even if only for a few minutes. Oxygen from the external atmosphere passes through a branching network of tubes to the final unit of the lungs—the innumerable thin-walled air pockets (*alveoli*) that lie in intimate contact with a rich capillary bed. The oxygen is then conveyed by the bloodstream to the most distant cells of the body. Carbon dioxide is released by the cells and carried by the blood to the lung capillaries, where it diffuses into the respiratory passages and is exhaled.

Large quantities of ammonia are produced when amino acids are degraded. Ammonia, like carbon dioxide, is harmful and must be removed from the organism. Many animals package the ammonia in a chemical form that is less toxic, either soluble *urea* or relatively insoluble *uric acid*. Birds and land reptiles excrete uric acid as crystals with only a modest loss of body fluid (water). Terrestrial mammals are confronted with the problem of flushing out the urea with water without incurring a fluid deficit in the body. The solution in land mammals has been the emergence of an incredibly efficient kidney, which is capable of conserving great quantities of water while discharging large amounts of urea.

BREATHING MECHANICS

The main features of the human respiratory system are shown in figure 10.1. The incoming air is moistened, warmed, and cleansed as it is drawn through the moist, warm membranes of the nasal chamber. The conditioned air enters the pharynx and passes down an unbranched passageway consisting of the *larynx*, or voice box, and the *trachea*, or windpipe. Aside from serving as the organ producing sound, the larynx blocks solids or liquids from entering the air passageway during swallowing. The walls of the trachea are fashioned by rings of firm cartilage, which preclude the collapse of the one-inch-wide tracheal tube throughout its five-inch length. The trachea forks into right and left *bronchi* (air tubes), one leading to each lung. Each brochus, in treelike manner, branches into smaller tubes, the *bronchioles,* which divide repeatedly into *alveolar ducts*. These ducts terminate in numerous grapelike clusters, the *alveolar sacs*, each of which contains several pockets, the *alveoli* (fig. 10.1). The hemispherical alveolus is the ultimate subdivision of the respiratory tree. In each lung, there are an estimated 350 million alveoli. If the innumerable alveoli were to be opened up, they could form a flat surface some 40 times the surface area of the entire skin of an adult—about 70 square meters (the size of a tennis court).

Each thin-walled alveolus is surrounded by equally thin-walled lung capillaries through which the exchange of oxygen and carbon dioxide is

Figure 10.1 Organization of the respiratory system of man.

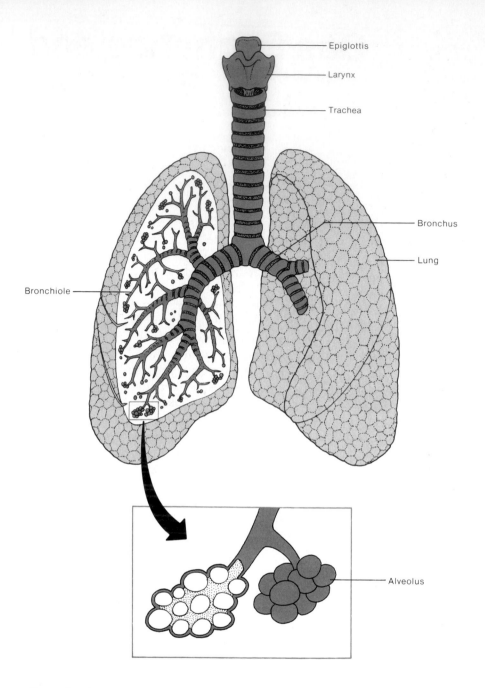

Epiglottis

Larynx

Trachea

Bronchus

Lung

Bronchiole

Alveolus

effected. The exchange is a matter of simple diffusion. Carbon dioxide diffuses from the blood in the lung capillaries into the alveolar pouches and oxygen from the air pockets diffuses into the blood of the lung capillaries. The air in the alveolar pockets is continually refreshed by the breathing movements: *inspiration*, by which fresh air containing more oxygen and less carbon dioxide is drawn into the lungs, and *expiration*, by which the carbon dioxide-laden air is expelled from the lungs. In rhythmically expanding and deflating, the lungs merely respond passively to changes in the volume of the thoracic (chest) cavity.

The breathing movements are more a physical than a biological phenomenon. The thoracic cavity housing the lungs is essentially a closed chamber or cage with a tubelike passageway (trachea) to the exterior. The lungs may be compared to two elastic balloons enclosed in an airtight cage (fig. 10.2). Elliptical-shaped ribs form the sides of the thoracic cage and the dome-shaped *diaphragm* forms the base of the cage. As figure 10.2 shows, the lungs at rest are partly inflated because the pressure in the thoracic cavity is generally slightly negative—that is, less than the pressure of the external atmosphere. If the chest wall were to be punctured, permitting atmospheric air to enter, the negative pressure would be lost and the lungs would collapse.

Inspiration is accomplished by the contraction of the muscles of the cuplike diaphragm, which flattens or lowers the diaphragm and elongates the thoracic cavity (fig. 10.2). Simultaneously, contractions of the rib muscles causes upward and outward movement of the ribs, thereby broadening the thoracic cavity. The lungs themselves expand in response to the decreased pressure within the enlarged thoracic cavity. Air automatically rushes into the lungs because of the greater pressure of the external atmosphere.

Expiration involves a simple reversal of the movements of inspiration. Relaxation of the muscles of the diaphragm and ribs allows the tightened diaphragm and the raised ribs to return to their resting positions. With increased pressure within a thoracic cavity that has become reduced in size, air is forced from the lungs. At each breath, only a relatively small amount of air in the lungs is exchanged. The volume of each breath is about one-sixth the volume of the total air in the lungs.

TRANSPORT OF GASES

Most of the oxygen diffusing into the bloodstream becomes chemically bound to iron-containing hemoglobin molecules within the red blood cells. Only a small fraction (less than three percent) of the total oxygen remains freely dissolved in the plasma. The combination of oxygen with hemoglobin allows for the transportation of 60 times as much oxygen as could be carried if oxygen were solely in simple solution. Each molecule of hemoglobin is capable of carrying four molecules of oxygen. An average human red blood cell contains 280 million molecules of hemoglobin. Accordingly, a single red blood cell, with fully saturated hemoglobin molecules, can transport about one billion oxygen molecules.

The chemical combination of hemoglobin and oxygen is loose and reversible. Hemoglobin associates with oxygen in the capillaries of the lungs to form the bright scarlet *oxyhemoglobin* and dissociates from the union with oxygen in the capillaries of the body tissues to form the dark purplish reduced hemoglobin (*deoxyhemoglobin*). The amount of oxygen carried by hemoglobin depends upon the oxygen pressure (or concentration of oxygen). At normal arterial pressure, nearly all of the hemoglobin (97 percent) is combined with oxygen. At the low pressures of tissue capillaries, hemoglobin readily releases oxygen. At an altitude of 18,000 feet (as in the Andes), where the concentration of atmospheric oxygen is one-half that at sea level, the hemoglobin is only 80 percent saturated. Individuals living at high altitudes compensate for the reduced oxygen pressure by an increased production of red blood cells.

Carbon dioxide is carried in the blood in several forms (fig. 10.3). A small fraction (about 8 percent) remains in solution in the plasma. Another portion of the carbon dioxide (CO_2) combines with the water (H_2O) in the plasma to form carbonic acid (H_2CO_3). The actual amount of carbon dioxide in the blood is negligible because this acid almost completely dissociates into bicarbonate ions (HCO_3^-) and hydrogen ions (H^+). A still larger fraction of the carbon dioxide enters the red blood cells, where the formation and dissociation of carbonic acid also occur. The bicarbonate ions formed in the red blood cells diffuse into the plasma. Thus, about

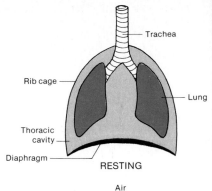

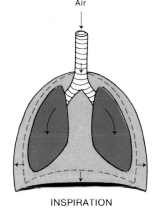

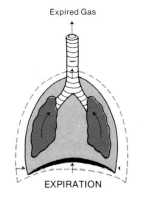

Figure 10.2 The mechanics of breathing in a mammal.

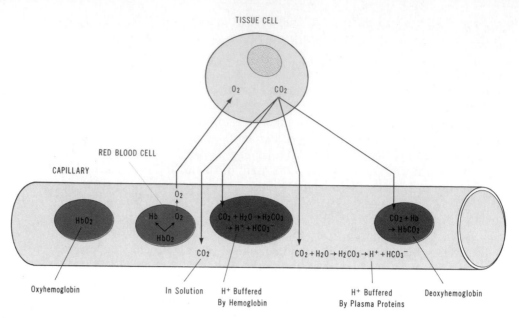

TISSUE CELL

RED BLOOD CELL

CAPILLARY

O_2

HbO_2

$Hb \quad O_2$

HbO_2

$CO_2 + H_2O \rightarrow H_2CO_3$
$\rightarrow H^+ + HCO_3^-$

$CO_2 + Hb$
$\rightarrow HbCO_2$

CO_2

$CO_2 + H_2O \rightarrow H_2CO_3 \rightarrow H^+ + HCO_3^-$

Oxyhemoglobin

In Solution

H^+ Buffered
By Hemoglobin

H^+ Buffered
By Plasma Proteins

Deoxyhemoglobin

Figure 10.3 The transport of carbon dioxide (CO_2) involves several reactions as the blood passes through the tissue capillaries.

67 percent of the carbon dioxide appears in the form of soluble bicarbonate ions in the plasma.

The remaining fraction of the carbon dioxide (about 25 percent) reacts directly with hemoglobin (Hb) to displace oxygen from the molecule and form reduced hemoglobin ($HbCO_2$). The continual release of hydrogen ions would alter the acid-base (pH) balance if it were not for the presence of *buffers* (see Appendix I) that bind the hydrogen ions. In this situation, it is noteworthy that proteins act as the principal buffer molecules. In the plasma, the plasma proteins react with the hydrogen ions; in the red blood cells, the hemoglobin functions to bind the hydrogen ions.

In the lung region, the aforementioned processes are reversed. As carbon dioxide diffuses into the respiratory channels, the amount of dissolved carbon dioxide in the plasma is reduced. The bicarbonate ions are reconverted into carbon dioxide molecules, which diffuse into the alveolar pockets. The high oxygen levels in the alveolar region result in the displacement of carbon dioxide from the hemoglobin and the concomitant formation of oxyhemoglobin. Finally, the hemoglobin and the plasma proteins relinquish their hydrogen ions. These proteins are now made available to serve again as buffers for hydrogen ions in the capillaries supplying the body tissues.

CONTROL OF BREATHING

We do not adjust the rate of breathing to the oxygen content of the blood. The muscles of the diaphragm and ribs are controlled by messages from a specific area of the brain, known as the *respiratory center,* located in the medulla oblongata (see chapter 11). The respiratory center is acutely sensitive to the amount of carbon dioxide in the blood. When the level of carbon dioxide rises, the cells of the respiratory center are stimulated, and breathing becomes faster and deeper. The increased rate of breathing movements causes more carbon dioxide to be released from the lungs, which effectively lowers the carbon dioxide concentration in the blood. The rate of breathing slows down when the carbon dioxide level returns to normal. Thus, the regulation of breathing depends not on a lack of oxygen but rather on the accumulation of carbon dioxide.

The rate of breathing is under automatic control, although one can voluntarily, but only briefly, increase or decrease the breathing movements. Any voluntary action is quickly overridden by the respiratory center. A person can "hold his breath" only until the accumulated carbon dioxide in the blood reflexly stimulates the respiratory center. Accordingly, a child in rage cannot voluntarily asphyxiate himself by simply holding his breath.

HUMAN KIDNEY

Every 24 hours, the human kidneys filter 180 liters of fluid (about 40 gallons) and return to the bloodstream all but 1 to 2 liters of fluid, which are excreted as urine. Approximately 99 percent of the filtered water is retained. Accordingly, the kidney is a highly effective apparatus for clearing useless or harmful substances (particularly urea) from the blood while simultaneously extracting most of the water.

Figure 10.4 Human excretory system, showing the basic structure of a nephron.

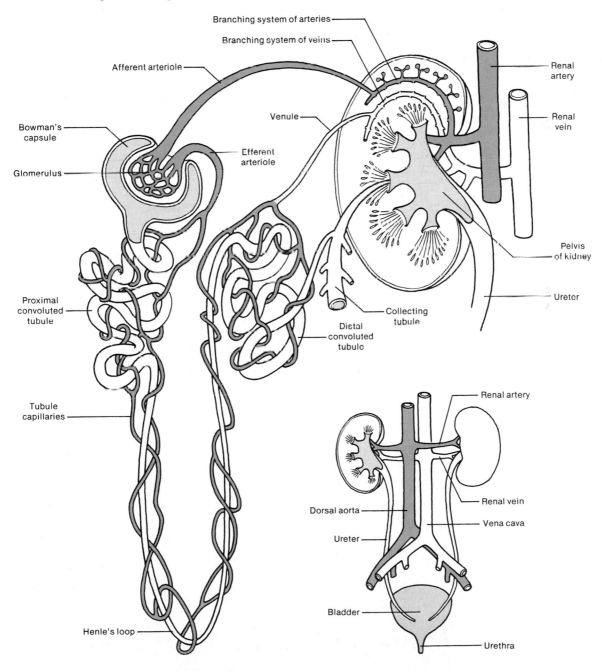

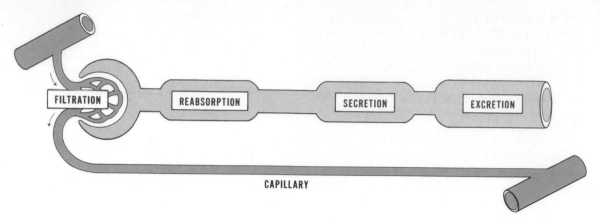

CAPILLARY

Figure 10.5 The principle processes involved in the formation of urine by the mammalian kidney.

The two bean-shaped kidneys are located dorsally in the lower abdominal cavity, one on each side of the backbone. A considerable amount of fatty (adipose) tissue surrounds each kidney, which protects the organ from mechanical blows. As seen in figure 10.4, the *ureters* act as passageways for the urine flowing from the kidney to the *urinary bladder,* a storage chamber. Urine continuously flows into the bladder, where it is stored until voluntarily voided through the *urethra,* the final canal to the exterior. In the human male, the urethra courses through the penis and is about eight inches long. In contrast, the urethra is only an inch and one-half in length in the female; the short length is a contributory factor to the ease with which bacterial infections in this region occur in the female.

The important tasks of the kidney are accomplished by approximately one million microscopic units, termed *nephrons,* in each kidney. A nephron consists of a tuft of capillaries, the *glomerulus,* enclosed in a cap-shaped blind sac, known as *Bowman's capsule,* which opens into a *renal tubule.* As figure 10.5 shows, there are three basic renal processes —*filtration, tubular reabsorption,* and *tubular secretion.* Filtration is the passage of protein-free substances through the glomerular capillaries into Bowman's capsule. The volume and composition of the glomerular filtrate is altered by the other two processes. Tubular reabsorption accounts for the removal of water and useful solutes from the filtrate, and tubular secretion accounts for the addition of certain substances to the filtrate. As the result of these basic processes, a concentrated, low-volume urine is excreted.

BASIC RENAL PROCESSES

Urine formation begins with the process of filtration through the glomerular capillaries. Blood enters the kidney through the renal artery, which fans out into successively smaller arteries into the glomeruli (fig. 10.4). Pressure forces the blood plasma in large quantities through the thin walls of the capillaries into the cavity of Bowman's capsule. Only blood cells, large protein molecules, and fat globules fail to pass into the capsule. The capillaries are freely permeable to water and substances of small molecular dimensions (for example, glucose, chloride, potassium, sodium, and urea). Thus, the glomerular filtrate is very much like the fluid portion (plasma) of the blood in composition without the proteins. The presence of red blood cells or protein in the urine indicates that the filtration process is defective, which most often results when the membranes of the glomerular capillaries are destroyed by disease.

The protein-free fluid (glomerular) filtrate passes into the tubular por-

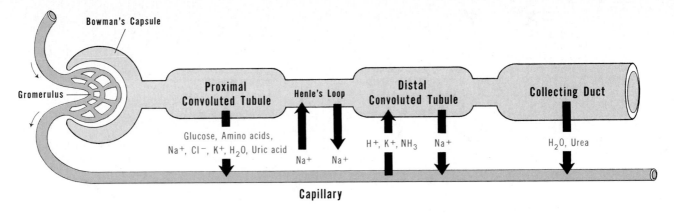

Figure 10.6 The reabsorption and secretion of organic molecules, salts, and water along the tubules of the nephron.

tion of the nephron, which describes a tortuous course. The highly coiled first part of the renal tubule is known as the *proximal convoluted tubule,* the hairpin-like second as the *loop of Henle,* and the twisting last part as the *distal convoluted tubule* (fig. 10.4). The last-mentioned tubule runs into the *collecting duct.* The numerous collecting ducts empty into a large central cavity, the *renal pelvis,* at the base of each kidney.

The winding renal tubule is surrounded by a rich capillary network. The fluid filtrate, in its circuitous passage through the tubule, returns almost all of its nonwaste solutes to the surrounding network of capillaries. Hence, useful substances do not escape from the body but are conserved by the mechanism of tubular reabsorption. Useful substances actually move back into the blood via the capillaries entwining the tubules. For example, glucose is transferred back to the bloodstream, although some may be retained in the urine if the concentration of blood sugar is abnormally high (as in diabetes). The proximal convoluted tubule is responsible for the reabsorption of glucose, amino acids, potassium, phosphate, bicarbonate, and sodium (fig. 10.6). The reabsorption of glucose, amino acids, and sodium requires the expenditure of energy by the tubular cells (active transport). Passively reabsorbed substances (involving no expenditure of energy) include water and urea. Ironically, not all the urea produced is excreted; almost 35 percent is reabsorbed back into the blood.

Some solutes actually leave the blood of the capillaries surrounding the tubules and pass into the tubular urine. This is the phenomenon of tubular secretion (fig. 10.6). Many compounds of medical importance pass into the urine by tubular secretion, including penicillin, salicylate (the active constituent of aspirin), and atabrine (antimalarial drug). The rapid excretion of medical compounds necessitates continual administration during treatment. Other substances that are normally secreted are potassium, ammonia, and hydrogen ions. The secretion of hydrogen ions is carefully regulated to maintain the acidity (pH) of the blood at a reasonably constant level.

THE COUNTERCURRENT PRINCIPLE

Only one percent of the volume of the glomerular filtrate is excreted as urine. The immense quantities of conserved water could not possibly be reabsorbed by active transport (as in glucose reabsorption), since the amount of ATP required would far surpass the energy-producing capabilities of the body. As an economical measure, water reabsorption to yield a concentrated urine is based on the mechanism of osmosis, which

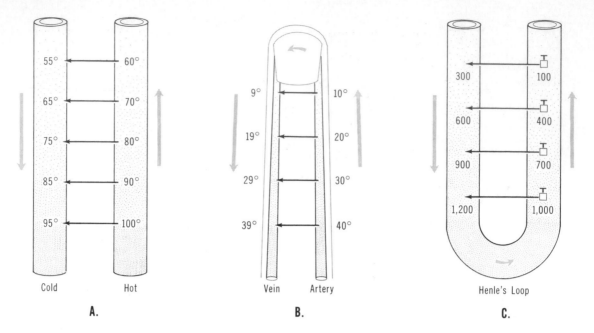

Cold	Hot
55°	60°
65°	70°
75°	80°
85°	90°
95°	100°

A.

Vein	Artery
9°	10°
19°	20°
29°	30°
39°	40°

B.

Henle's Loop

300	100
600	400
900	700
1,200	1,000

C.

Figure 10.7 The principle of countercurrent exchange as exemplified by the flow of water in parallel cold and hot pipes (A), the flow of blood in the fingertips (B), and flow of fluid in the two parallel limbs of Henle's loop (C).

does not require any expenditure of cellular energy. Water reabsorption also depends in an interesting way on a process known as *countercurrent exchange*.

Models for the principle of countercurrent exchange are represented in figure 10.7. The simplest system for countercurrent exchange consists of two parallel pipes in close contact, one carrying hot water and the other carrying cold water in the opposite ("countercurrent") direction (fig. 10.7A). The hot water becomes progressively cooler as heat is transferred to the adjacent pipe. If the two pipes were not closely juxtaposed but far distant from each other, heat would be merely dissipated into the atmosphere and not conserved within the pipes. As a consequence of the transfer of heat, a graded decrease occurs in the temperature of the hot pipe accompanied by a graded increase in the temperature of the cold pipe.

A comparable exchange of heat is witnessed between arterial and venous blood in the fingertips (fig. 10.7B). The cold venous blood returning from the extremity acquires heat from the outgoing warm arterial blood. The transfer of heat from the artery to the vein along the entire length of the vessels serves to keep heat from the extremities as well as to conserve heat at the body end of the system.

In the kidney, the two parallel limbs of Henle's loop satisfy the arrangement required for countercurrent exchange. The glomerular filtrate flows in opposite directions in the ascending and descending limbs of Henle's loop (fig. 10.7C). The two limbs are not in direct contact but are separated by tissue fluid (called *interstitial fluid*). In this instance, sodium ions, rather than heat, are transferred from one parallel tube to the other.

The essential component in establishing countercurrent flow in the kidney is the passage by active transport of sodium ions from the lumen of the ascending limb into the interstitial fluid. The sodium ions then diffuse into the highly permeable, closely adjacent descending limb. Owing to the diffusion of sodium, the glomerular filtrate in the descending limb becomes progressively concentrated as it approaches the hairpin bend. The filtrate shortly becomes progressively diluted as it travels up

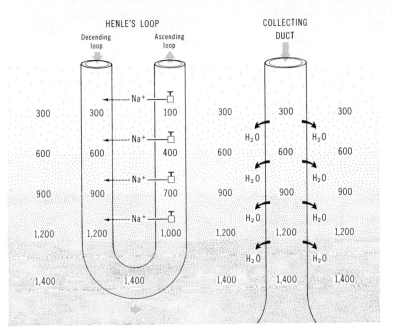

HENLE'S LOOP

Decending loop | Ascending loop

COLLECTING DUCT

| 300 | 300 | Na+ | 100 | 300 | 300 | 300 |

H_2O ... H_2O

| 600 | 600 | Na+ | 400 | 600 | 600 | 600 |

H_2O ... H_2O

| 900 | 900 | Na+ | 700 | 900 | 900 | 900 |

H_2O ... H_2O

| 1,200 | 1,200 | Na+ | 1,000 | 1,200 | 1,200 | 1,200 |

H_2O ... H_2O

| 1,400 | 1,400 | | 1,400 | 1,400 | 1,400 |

Figure 10.8 Operation of the countercurrent principle in the formation of osmotically concentrated urine in the human kidney.

the ascending limb, since sodium ions are transported out of the ascending limb. At first glance, it would seem that little has been achieved other than to concentrate the filtrate in one limb, only to redilute the filtrate almost immediately in the other limb. However, a close examination of figure 10.7C reveals an impressive accomplishment—namely, the establishment of a concentration gradient of sodium from top to bottom of Henle's loop, with the highest concentration of sodium at the hairpin bend. This gradient is necessary to the final step that concentrates the urine.

The transport of sodium ions from one limb to another limb also creates an increasing gradient of sodium in the interstitial fluid adjacent to the limbs. That is to say, the countercurrent mechanism establishes a high osmotic pressure in the interstitial fluid. As figure 10.8 shows, the collecting duct parallels the descending limb of Henle's loop. The site of concentration of urine is the collecting duct, which is highly permeable to water. As the filtrate passes into the collecting duct, water flows passively out of the collecting duct into the interstitial fluid because of the osmotic pressure differential. It bears repeating that water is osmotically drawn out because the interstitial fluid surrounding the collecting duct has become progressively concentrated as a result of the active transport of sodium from the ascending limb of Henle's loop to the interstitial fluid. The ascending limb is impermeable to water so that as sodium is transported from this limb, water does not follow.

The greater the concentration of the filtrate in the hairpin bend of Henle's loop, the more effective the retrieval of water from the collecting duct. The concentration gradient in Henle's loop is established by the active transport of sodium. The mere act of pumping sodium out of the ascending limb would lead only to a modest concentration of the glomerular filtrate at the bottom portion of Henle's loop. If this were the case, there would be merely a weak osmotic differential and limited water retrieval. In reality, the glomerular filtrate becomes very concentrated at the bottom portion of Henle's loop because of countercurrent exchange. The outcome of the operation of the countercurrent principle is that 99

Substance	CONCENTRATION		RATIO
	Filtrate	Urine	Urine:Filtrate
Creatinine	0.001	0.075	75.0
Urea	0.030	2.000	66.7
Ammonia	0.001	0.040	40.0
Uric acid	0.004	0.050	12.5
Potassium	0.020	0.150	7.5
Chloride	0.370	0.600	1.6
Sodium	0.300	0.350	1.2
Bicarbonate	0.300	0.150	0.5
Glucose	0.100	0	0

percent of the water filters out of the collecting duct. The relatively small gradient that could be established by active transport alone is actually *multiplied* because of countercurrent flow within Henle's loop. Because of this enhancing action, the system in the kidney is often referred to as the *countercurrent multiplier system*.

THE URINE

As vast quantities of water are reabsorbed back into the blood, the urine in the collecting duct becomes increasingly concentrated. As the concentration of urea in the collecting duct comes to exceed its concentration in the blood of neighboring capillaries, part of the urea diffuses passively out of the duct into the surrounding capillaries. This accounts for the curious circumstance that only 65 percent of the urea entering the kidney each day is actually eliminated.

The concentrating and reabsorptive capacity of the kidney is revealed in Table 10.1 by the urine:filtrate ratio of the major substances. Almost all of the filtered sodium (99.5 percent) is reabsorbed. As we have seen, sodium ions are the main driving force for the reabsorption of water. Increases in sodium reabsorption lead to increases in water reabsorption. The reabsorption of both salt and water by the renal tubules is enhanced by increasing concentrations of estrogen in the bloodstream. The increased estrogen secretion prior to menstruation accounts for the retention of salt and water (*premenstrual edema*). Diuretics, such as caffeine and thiazides, increase the discharge of urine by inhibiting tubular reabsorption of sodium.

Small quantities of uric acid, an end product of purine metabolism, are eliminated by the kidneys. Normally, almost 90 percent of the uric acid is returned to the bloodstream. Occasionally, some of the circulating uric acid molecules precipitate as crystals in the joints, a condition called *gout*. This disorder may be treated or alleviated by the intake of aspirin or drugs (such as probenecid or sulfinpyrazone), which inhibit tubular reabsorption of uric acid.

THE ARTIFICIAL KIDNEY

Kidney malfunctioning or disease occurs with the progressive loss of functional nephrons and the accumulation of urea in toxic concentrations in the blood. In recent years, an artificial kidney has been devised, which is based on the principle that a substance in the blood will diffuse across a permeable artificial membrane if a concentration gradient is established. In the kidney machine, the selectively permeable membrane consists of thin cellophane, arranged in several layers or coils (fig. 10.9). The cellophane coils are immersed in a large bath of fluid, which has a composition similar to blood with the exception of nitrogenous wastes (urea, uric

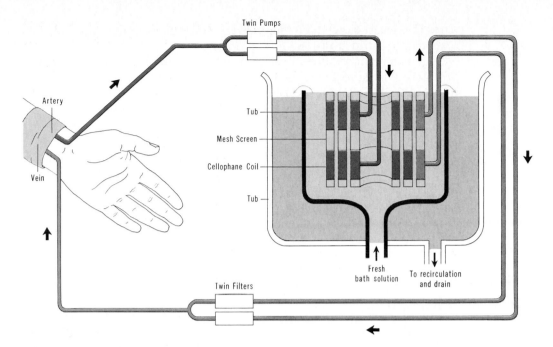

Twin Pumps

Artery

Vein

Tub
Mesh Screen
Cellophane Coil
Tub

Fresh
bath solution

To recirculation
and drain

Twin Filters

acid, and creatinine). Arterial blood is mechanically pumped through the cellophane coils, and the nitrogenous waste metabolites in the blood diffuse across the cellophane membrane into the bath. The passage of solutes across a permeable membrane that separates two solutions of unequal concentrations is called *dialysis,* and the bathing fluid is called a *dialysate.*

The artificial kidney does not provide for the selective reabsorption of useful substances, such as glucose. However, the concentration of glucose is the same in both the blood and the dialysate, so that glucose is prevented from entering the dialysate. In general, the dialysate contains the same concentration of all normal blood constituents, thereby obviating the need for selective reabsorption. Arrangements can be made to add helpful substances to the blood. For example, the concentration of bicarbonate ions can be raised in the dialysate; the bicarbonate ions accordingly move across their concentration gradient into the blood. The elevated blood bicarbonate would serve to correct excessive acidity in the patient's blood. At any given time, the kidney machine contains about 500 milliliters (1 pint) of the patient's blood. A patient is typically hooked up to the machine for 8–12 hours every three or four days.

Figure 10.9 Simplified diagram of the flow of blood through a kidney machine to extract by dialysis the nitrogenous waste metabolites in the blood. Arterial blood is pumped through coils of thin, selectively permeable cellophane. The dialyzed ("cleansed") blood is returned to the vein.

SUMMARY

All cells require continual supplies of oxygen to support their metabolic activities. When organic molecules are degraded, large amounts of carbon dioxide are produced that must be eliminated from the body. The complex respiratory system of man provides a large surface area through which gas diffusion occurs. The lungs contain innumerable thin-walled air pockets (alveoli), through which the exchanges of oxygen and carbon dioxide are effected. Most of the oxygen diffusing into the bloodstream becomes chemically bound to iron-containing hemoglobin molecules within the red blood cells. Carbon dioxide is carried in the blood in several forms, with the bulk appearing in the form of soluble bicarbonate ions in the plasma. The level of carbon dioxide in the blood is an important factor in regulating the breathing movements. The ribs and diaphragm work in concert to produce the pressure differences in the thoracic cavity responsible for inspiration and expiration.

The mammalian kidney is efficient at removing the nitrogenous waste products of metabolism while simultaneously conserving water. The functional unit of the kidney is the nephron, which consists of a capillary tuft (the glomerulus), a cup-shaped Bowman's capsule, and a network of tubules. The formation of urine involves three prominent processes: filtration, tubular reabsorption, and tubular secretion. The ability of the kidney to produce concentrated urine depends on an unusual phenomenon known as countercurrent exchange. Countercurrent flow is established within Henle's loop by the active transport of sodium ions, which creates the conditions for the retrieval of large quantities of water from the collecting duct.

Ethical Probe 7
Scarce Medical Resources

One of the major health problems in the United States is malfunctioning of the kidneys. Each year, there are about 8,000 patients with kidney failure who require dialysis with an artificial kidney machine or, even better, a transplanted organ from a healthy donor. There is, however, an acute shortage of transplantable kidneys from suitable donors. If life-saving transplantable kidneys are at a premium, how are the candidates for treatment to be selected: Some hospitals act solely on a "first-come, first-serve" basis. Accordingly, there are no preferences nor any criteria. A person is simply chosen by purely random procedures. Other hospitals have a committee of physicians and informed citizens that rank the patients in order of priority. In some localities, preference is given to those patients who have the highest anticipated number of years of survival. In other localities, the most consideration is invariably given to older patients over younger ones.

Which of the two procedures is most judicious, in your opinion? Should a person simply "get at the end of the line and wait his turn"? Or, should priority be given to a 65-year-old prominent executive, a five-year-old child, or a mother in a large family? How do you decide? If a committee is to design the criteria, what would be the composition of the committee?

Coordination by Nerves 11

One characteristic property of protoplasm is *irritability;* that is, the protoplasm of a living cell is sensitive to stimuli. In advanced animals, a highly specialized cell that is very irritable is the *nerve cell,* or *neuron.* The cytoplasm of the neuron is drawn out into a long process called the *nerve fiber.* A stimulus applied to a nerve cell results in a wave of excitation along the nerve fiber that is designated a *nerve impulse.* This impulse is associated with a changing electrical potential along the fiber. The electrical potential is generated by charged ions, not by electrons as in an electric current. The neurons in the nervous system of man vary greatly in size, number, and branching of the processes. Within the human brain, for example, there are an estimated 10 billion nerve cells, and each nerve cell can make 10,000 contacts with its neighboring cells by way of *synapses*—the functional junctions between nerve cells.

Only one other type of specialized excitable cell in the human body is as capable as the nerve cell in generating an electrical potential across the cell membrane. This is the muscle cell, known also as a *muscle fiber.* The muscle fibers react to information conveyed by the nerve cells. Essentially, then, nerve cells collect, process, and interpret signals from the external and internal environment, and muscle cells respond with special contractile proteins.

NERVE CELL

The generalized nerve cell depicted in figure 11.1 has a central *cell body* (containing the nucleus) and cytoplasmic processes of two basic kinds. Branching outgrowths, or *dendrites* (Greek, *dendron,* meaning "tree"), convey impulses toward the cell body, whereas the relatively long and straight fiber, or *axon,* carries impulses away from the cell body. Thus, nerve impulses ordinarily travel in only one direction. Axons are typically covered with a fatty insulating material known as *myelin.* The myelin sheath has been shown by electron microscopy to consist of nucleated cells (Schwann cells) that extend their cytoplasm tightly around the surface of the axon. The naked gaps in the insulating myelin sheath are the *nodes of Ranvier.* These nodes are important since they permit the nerve impulse to be transmitted rapidly in a saltatory fashion; that is, the impulse jumps from one gap to another along the axon.

There are three functional classes of neurons: *afferent* neurons, *efferent* neurons, and *interneurons.* Afferent neurons (*affere,* meaning "to carry to") bring information to the brain or spinal cord from sensory receptors (such as the eyes, ears, and skin). Since these neurons are found in sensory receptors and are concerned with detecting environ-

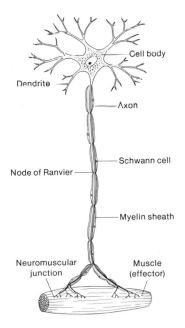

Figure 11.1 Typical motor neuron. The axon is a long, myelinated fiber that courses from the central nervous system to an effector (muscle).

mental stimuli, such as light, sound, and contact, afferent neurons are also termed *sensory* neurons. Efferent neurons (*effere,* "to carry away") transmit impulses away from the brain or spinal cord to effector organs, the principal ones being glands and muscles. Efferent neurons that transmit information to skeletal muscles are termed *motor* neurons. The third class of nerve cells, the interneurons, are contained wholly within the central nervous system, that is, the spinal cord and brain. Interneurons connect afferent neurons to efferent neurons, and also link the neurons from one level of the central nervous system to another. Some interneurons cover only short distances; others may extend for 3 or 4 feet.

The *spinal* cord and *brain* are essentially thickened and expanded collections of interneurons; almost 97 percent of all human nerve cells are interneurons. Throughout animal evolution, the interneurons have become bundled together in the long axis of animals to make up the spinal cord; the expansion of the anterior end of the spinal cord into a brain was associated with increasing accumulations of interneurons. The interlocking network of numerous interneurons in the spinal cord and brain accounts in large part for our ability to experience, or be conscious of, different kinds of sensation.

The number of interneurons in the pathway between afferent and efferent neurons varies according to the complexity of the behavioral action. One of the simplest pathways is the *flexion,* or *withdrawal, reflex,* in which a painful stimulus, such as a pinprick, leads to the withdrawal of the hand (fig. 11.2). Afferent (sensory) neurons transmit impulses to the interneurons, which in turn stimulate the appropriate efferent (motor) neurons. The spinal nerves that carry both sensory and motor fibers divide into two components as they enter the spinal cord. Sensory fibers pass into the spinal cord through the *dorsal roots,* and motor fibers leave the cord by way of the *ventral roots* (fig. 11.2). The cell bodies of the sensory neurons are clustered together in distended areas called *dorsal root ganglia* at the periphery of the cord, whereas the cell bodies of the motor neurons lie within the *gray matter* of the

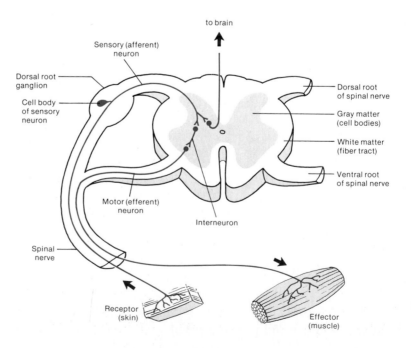

Figure 11.2 Pathway of a simple reflex arc. See text for details.

to brain

Sensory (afferent) neuron

Dorsal root ganglion

Cell body of sensory neuron

Dorsal root of spinal nerve

Gray matter (cell bodies)

White matter (fiber tract)

Ventral root of spinal nerve

Motor (efferent) neuron

Interneuron

Spinal nerve

Receptor (skin)

Effector (muscle)

spinal cord. The butterfly-shaped gray matter is composed principally of countless cell bodies. The *white matter* consists predominantly of myelinated fibers, which collectively impart a whitish appearance.

The chain of neurons leading from the skin receptor to the muscle effector constitutes a *reflex arc,* and the withdrawal response is referred to as *reflex action.* Some of the afferent fibers make synaptic connections with interneurons that convey the sensory stimulus to higher centers of the brain. However, the withdrawal of the hand occurs before the sensation of pain is experienced. In other words, a reflex response is independent of conscious awareness of the stimulus. In a decapitated frog, for example, a reflex response (such as the lifting of a limb) can still be elicited even though the spinal cord pathways, which would normally transmit the afferent information to the brain, have been severed. This is adaptively advantageous to an organism since a prompt, clear-cut avoiding reaction to an injurious stimulus can occur without the delay of interpretation by the brain.

Other bodily readjustments typically occur during or following the withdrawal of the hand from a pinprick, such as movements of the shoulders or the turning of the head. Afferent fibers convey information to several interneurons at different levels of the spinal cord and brain, and these interneurons make associations with several motor neurons that innervate different muscles. Still other branches of afferent neurons activate interneurons that inhibit the motor neurons of antagonistic muscles whose activity would oppose the reflex flexion. Thus, rarely does an incoming signal activate solely a single motor neuron and occasion a single isolated response. The spinal cord and brain provide for a great number and variety of neural connections. In essence, the components of the nervous system work as an integral unit rather than in innumerable separate parts.

NATURE OF THE NERVE IMPULSE

In the 1780s, the Italian scientist Luigi Galvani hypothesized that nerves can generate an electric current. More than a century later, the German physiologist Julius Bernstein in 1902 proposed that the nerve impulse arises when there is no longer a difference in voltage on either side of the membrane of the axon—when the voltage difference, or *resting potential,* is suddenly and rapidly eliminated. A voltage difference across a cell membrane is the consequence of an unequal distribution of charged particles (ions). Bernstein made the observation that the principal ion outside the cell membrane, in the tissue fluid, is the positively charged sodium ion (along with negatively charged chloride ions), whereas the main ion inside the membrane is the positively charged potassium ion (along with negatively charged organic particles). Although negatively charged particles such as chloride ions are involved, the resting membrane potential depends largely on the concentration gradients and membrane permeabilities of the two positively charged particles, the sodium ions (Na^+) and the potassium ions (K^+). The concentration of Na^+ is about 14 times higher outside the axon than inside; the concentration of K^+ is 28 times higher inside than outside (fig. 11.3).

Theoretically, small charged particles, or ions, diffuse readily through a semipermeable membrane from a region of high concentration of ions to a region of lower concentration. However, the unstimulated resting membrane is highly impermeable to sodium ions and moderately per-

Figure 11.3 Nerve impulse. The resting membrane potential (−70 mV) results principally from the diffusion of potassium ions across the axon membrane to the outside surface. The outward flow of potassium ions by diffusion is not counteracted to any appreciable extent by the inward flow of sodium ions. When the axon membrane is stimulated, sodium ions filter through in a fraction of a millisecond and reverse the polarity of the membrane (from −70 mV to +30 mV). The nerve impulse is terminated by an outflow of potassium ions, which tends to restore the original negative charge of the interior of the membrane. (From W. R. Klemm, *Science, the brain, and our future*, 1972, The Bobbs-Merrill Co.)

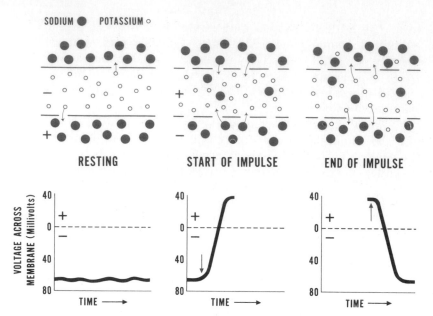

SODIUM ● POTASSIUM ○

RESTING   START OF IMPULSE   END OF IMPULSE

meable to potassium ions. Because the axon membrane is more permeable to potassium than to sodium, the less restricted potassium ions diffuse outwardly. The impermeable sodium ions do not flow inwardly to correct the internal deficit of positive charges created by the outflow of potassium ions. Accordingly, the interior of the axon becomes electrically negative with respect to the exterior. The membrane is said to be *polarized*.

The conduction of a nerve impulse, Bernstein reasoned, involves *depolarization;* that is, the membrane potential falls to zero. Bernstein viewed the propagation of a nerve impulse as a wave of successive depolarizations that sweeps along the axon. After depolarization at a given point, the membrane recovers its resting potential and its excitability. Presumably the establishment of the impulse involves a change in the permeability of the axon membrane to sodium and potassium ions. The mechanism became clarified in the 1940s by the painstaking studies of the English physiologists Allen L. Hodgkin and Andrew F. Huxley of Cambridge University, both later the recipients of the Nobel prize.

GENERATION OF THE NERVE IMPULSE

Today we know that the resting (inactive) potential across an axon membrane has a magnitude of 70 millivolts (mV), the inside of the axon being negative. By convention, the voltage drop is designated relative to the outside of the membrane; hence, the resting potential is said to be −70 mV. The voltage is about one-twentieth of that generated by a common flashlight battery.

Much of our modern knowledge of the nerve impulse has been obtained from studies on the giant axon of the squid. This remarkable axon has a diameter of $1,000\mu$ (1 mm), which is approximately 100 times wider than an axon of a human nerve cell (about 10μ, or 0.01 mm). The inside of a single nerve fiber of the squid can be probed with microelectrodes, and the fate of radioactively labeled substances in and out of the fiber can be followed with relative ease.

Taking advantage of the giant squid axon, the English physiologists Hodgkin and Huxley were able to show that the membrane potential of a stimulated fiber undergoes an abrupt alteration, changing in a fraction of a millisecond from -70 mV to $+30$ mV and then rapidly returning to its original value (fig. 11.3). This almost instantaneous change in the membrane potential is termed the *action potential*, the basis of the nerve impulse. The duration of a single action potential is only one-thousandth of a second, and several hundred action potentials can sweep along a nerve fiber in a single second. It should be noted (fig. 11.3) that not only does the membrane potential fall to zero (that is, the membrane becomes depolarized) as proposed by Bernstein, but it actually becomes reversed momentarily in sign, the outside becoming negative with respect to the inside.

By radioactively tagging ions Hodgkin and Huxley demonstrated that the action potential is the result of changes in the permeability of the axon membrane to sodium and potassium ions. When the axon is stimulated, the permeability barrier to sodium that normally exists across the membrane suddenly breaks down and sodium ions rush into the interior of the axon. The rapid influx of sodium ions decreases the membrane potential by canceling locally the excess negative charge inside the axon. In fact, so many sodium ions filter through that they reverse the polarity of the membrane. This reversal of polarity creates the nerve impulse, or action potential. Immediately after the peak of the action potential, the membrane barrier to sodium is reestablished and the membrane permeability to potassium increases. The outflow of potassium ions tends to restore the original negative charge of the interior of the axon (fig. 11.3). In fact, in the terminal phase of the action potential, the permeability of the membrane to potassium is greater than normal, and the outward diffusion of potassium causes the membrane potential to become briefly more negative than the resting level (fig. 11.4). When the electrical potential falls below the resting value, the membrane is *hyperpolarized*.

Each time an action potential is generated, there is a momentary gain of sodium ions within the axon and a transitory loss of potassium ions to the exterior. After the impulse has passed, the excess sodium ions are extruded out of the axon by active transport. Similarly, potassium ions are actively transported inwardly to replenish the potassium ions that had earlier been lost from the interior. The ATP-dependent mechanisms that drive sodium out of the fiber and restore potassium in the fiber have been graphically referred to as the *sodium pump* and the *potassium pump*, respectively. These energy pumps are responsible for maintaining the original steep concentration gradients of sodium and potassium ions, without which the polarized state of the resting membrane of the axon cannot be established.

The rapid rising and equally rapid falling phases of the action potential appear as a spike on an oscilloscope. The spike may be observed to travel the length of an axon as if it were a burning fuse igniting each area just ahead. The action potential of one specific region changes the permeability of the region immediately ahead of it, and the localized inward rushing of sodium ions initiates another action potential in the adjacent area (fig. 11.5). Most nerve fibers can produce several hundred action potentials per second. Following one action potential, a brief period of time (about one millisecond) is required to return the membrane potential to its original state. This recovery period before another action potential can commence is called the *refractory phase*. The new action potential, once initiated, is virtually identical to the previous one. This precise self-regenerative process enables the impulse to be propagated progressively along the axon. Equally important, the self-regenerative feature

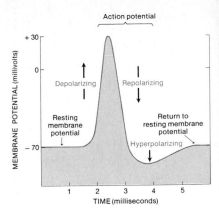

Figure 11.4 Changes in membrane potential during an action potential.

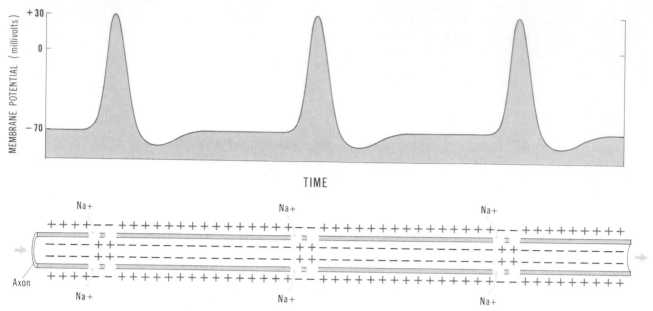

Figure 11.5 The propagation of a nerve impulse progressively along the axon by a series of self-regenerated action potentials.

enables the impulse to reach its destination, no matter how distant, without any distortion or fading of the message.

A stimulus must reach a certain critical level, or *threshold,* to trigger an action potential or, as imaginatively stated, to "fire" a nerve cell. A weak (subthreshold) stimulus evokes only a partial membrane depolarization that is quickly aborted, and a stimulus above the necessary threshold elicits only the same customary action potential as a threshold response. Accordingly, a nerve cell either fires with a single consistent amplitude or does not fire at all (fig. 11.5). This state of affairs is tersely summarized as *"all or none."* Although the all-or-none principle is unfailing, a nerve cell can convey information about the strength of a stimulus or message. It does so by altering its frequency of firing. A whisper, for example, elicits a slow procession of action potentials, whereas a loud noise evokes a rapid succession of action potentials, so that more impulses arrive per unit time at the final destination. Thus, the intensity of a stimulus can change the frequency of a nerve impulse, but not its amplitude (size).

THE SYNAPSE

As recently as 15 years ago, it was thought that the transmission of a nerve impulse from the axon of one neuron to the dendrite of another neuron involved the establishment of an electric field across the synapse. A wealth of evidence now indicates that the axon terminal releases a specific chemical substance, appropriately called a *transmitter,* that diffuses across the synaptic gap and stimulates the postsynaptic neuron, or the nerve cell that receives the impulse at the junction. The anatomical and functional nature of the synaptic junction was clarified by electron microscopy studies. As seen in figure 11.6, the axon terminal of the presynaptic neuron ends in a swollen knob, termed the *synaptic knob.* Within the knob may be seen several energy-producing mitochondria and numerous spherical droplets, or *synaptic vesicles,* the source of the chemical transmitters. All terminal endings of a single presynaptic neuron liberate the same chemical transmitter. There are, however, several kinds of transmitters. The first to be identified was acetylcholine;

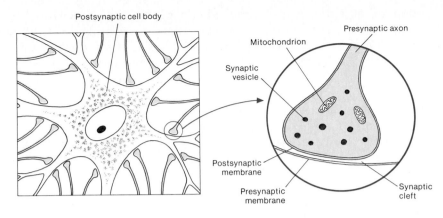

Postsynaptic cell body

Mitochondrion

Presynaptic axon

Synaptic vesicle

Postsynaptic membrane

Presynaptic membrane

Synaptic cleft

Figure 11.6 A synapse. The axon terminal of the presynaptic neuron ends in a swelling, the synaptic knob. Numerous synaptic vesicles within the synaptic knob release transmitter substances (such as acetylcholine). The transmitter diffuses across the synaptic gap and alters the polarization of the postsynaptic membrane of the dendrite or cell body of the contiguous neuron. Each neuron is acted upon by several hundred synapses from numerous presynaptic neurons.

others known or suspected include norepinephrine, γ-aminobutyric acid, serotonin, glycine, and dopamine.

Once the chemical transmitter is released from the synaptic vesicles, it combines with reactive sites in the dendrites of postsynaptic neurons in the same way, and with the same degree of specificity, that an enzyme fits into substrate molecules. Sir John Eccles (Nobel laureate 1963), physiologist at the Australian National University, demonstrated that acetylcholine alters the membrane potential of the dendrite of the postsynaptic neuron in much the same way that an axon's interior is depolarized to generate a nerve impulse. The permeability of the postsynaptic membrane increases and permits an abrupt inflow of sodium ions, which triggers an excitatory action potential, or nerve impulse, in the postsynaptic neuron. The postsynaptic membrane returns to its resting potential through the action of an enzyme (acetylcholinesterase) that destroys the acetylcholine almost as quickly as it is produced (within 5 milliseconds or less).

An important finding by Eccles was that not all chemical transmitters are excitatory. Some transmitters, like glycine and γ-aminobutyric acid, inhibit the firing of the postsynaptic neuron. Under the influence of the inhibitory chemical transmitter, the postsynaptic membrane becomes permeable to potassium ions and not to sodium ions. The outflow of potassium ions makes the inside potential of the dendrite membrane even more negative than the resting membrane potential (-90 mV instead of -70 mV). Since the membrane potential actually moves farther away from the impulse-discharging threshold, the inhibitory transmitters produce hyperpolarization of the postsynaptic membrane.

A curious mode of nervous activity, poorly understood at present, is the phenomenon of inhibition of the nerve impulse before it crosses the synaptic gap (so-called *presynaptic inhibition*). The importance of presynaptic inhibition resides in the fact that the sensory stimulus can be selectively altered; that is, some of the information to the central nervous system can be depressed or perhaps not transmitted at all. On the whole, the synaptic junctions throughout the nervous system assume paramount importance. Each synaptic junction is a decisive point at which the flow of information can be inhibited, modified, or transmitted unchanged. For this reason, one current mode of experimental attack on the brain focuses on drugs that affect the chemical machinery of the synapse.

Attention has focused on drugs that produce changes in mood or emotional responsiveness by affecting the production, storage, or deactivation of norepinephrine. Amphetamines produce an elevated, alert mood by inhibiting the postfiring deactivation or breakdown of norepinephrine, thereby causing additional stimulation of postsynaptic receptor sites. The successively diminished response with repeated administration of amphetamines results from a depletion of norepinephrine from the axon terminals more rapidly than it can be replenished. Tranquilizers, such as reserpine, have a calming effect by suppressing the capacity of the synaptic vesicles to properly bind and concentrate norepinephrine. At present, reserpine is used in the treatment of mild hypertension.

EXCITABILITY OF MUSCLE CELLS

The axon of an efferent (motor) neuron terminates on the membrane of a single muscle fiber. The point of contact of the axon's terminal end and the muscle membrane is known as the *neuromuscular junction*. At this junction, events occur that are basically similar to actions across a synapse. Acetylcholine diffuses from the axon terminals and increases the permeability of the muscle membrane to sodium ions. This generates an action potential in the muscle membrane that triggers the internal machinery of the muscle. The rapid repolarization of the muscle membrane in preparation for the next depolarization (action potential) is associated with the deactivation or destruction of the acetylcholine from the previous impulse.

Several chemical agents can block the events at the neuromuscular junction and cause paralysis of all the skeletal muscles. The odorless, colorless nerve gases (organophosphates) attach firmly to acetylcholinesterase, inhibiting the deactivating enzyme irreversibly. The neurons continue to fire and the muscles become paralyzed because of the strong contractions. The organophosphates are effective in very low concentrations and can cause death within minutes after exposure. Botulism, the deadly food poisoning, is the result of a bacterial toxin that inhibits the release of acetylcholine from the axon terminals. The drug curare, first used by South American Indians as an arrow poison, prevents acetylcholine from activating the receptor sites on the muscle membrane.

From a chemical point of view, the contractile components of muscle are two proteins, the high-molecular-weight *myosin* (500,000) and the low-molecular-weight *actin* (60,000). A single fiber of skeletal muscle consists of numerous parallel elements called *myofibrils,* each of which is composed of alternating thick and thin filaments. Myosin constitutes the thick filaments and actin constitutes the thin filaments. The levels of fibrillar organization within a skeletal muscle are shown in figure 11.7. The conspicuous bands, or transverse striations, are regularly repeated along the length of the myofibril. The functional unit of the contractile system is the *sacromere,* bounded by Z lines. Each sacromere has the same pattern of bands.

The action potential created at the muscle membrane stimulates a reaction between actin and myosin; they combine to form a complex known as *actomyosin*. In the 1930s, the Hungarian biochemist Albert Szent-Gyorgi prepared artificial fibers from precipitated actomyosin, and demonstrated that the artificial fibers can contract when they are immersed in a solution of ATP. The energy released by the splitting of ATP by actomyosin produces the force leading to movement.

Prior to the advent of the electron microscope, it was assumed that

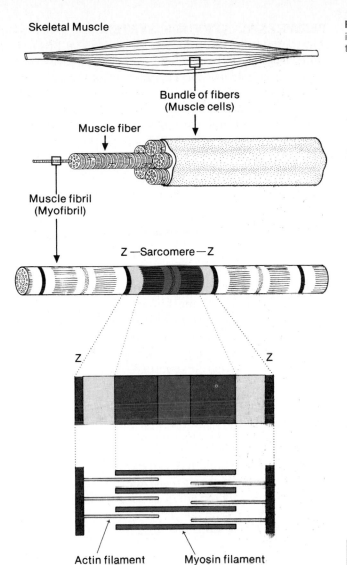

Skeletal Muscle

Bundle of fibers
(Muscle cells)

Muscle fiber

Muscle fibril
(Myofibril)

Z —Sarcomere— Z

Z   Z

Actin filament   Myosin filament

Figure 11.7 Skeletal muscle showing the various levels of organization. See text for details.

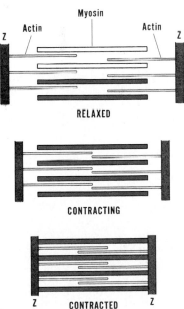

RELAXED

CONTRACTING

Z   CONTRACTED   Z

Figure 11.8 Muscle contractions involve changes in the relative positions of the thick and thin filaments that comprise the myofibril.

contraction of the muscle resulted from a coiling or folding of the actin and myosin molecules. Electron micrographs prepared by H. E. Huxley in the 1950s suggested an even simpler mechanism. As seen in figure 11.8, muscle shortening is due to the relative movements of thick and thin filaments past each other and not to any alteration in the configuration of the protein molecules. The hypothesis, now widely accepted, is termed the *sliding-filament* theory of muscle contraction. Although elucidation of the precise manner by which thick and thin filaments slide along each other requires further study, it is now clear that calcium ions are instrumental in triggering the contractile process. Apparently, calcium ions enable the actin to interact with myosin to initiate the cross-bridge movement.

During relaxation of the muscle, the actin and myosin filaments return to their initial states. The dissociation of actin and myosin requires the presence of ATP. The necessity of ATP in breaking the linkage between actin and myosin is vividly illustrated by the phenomenon of *rigor mortis* (death rigor). The rigid condition of muscles is the direct consequence of the loss of ATP in the dead muscle cells.

PERIPHERAL NERVOUS SYSTEM

Anatomists conventionally categorize the brain and spinal cord as the *central nervous system*. The numerous nerves that extend from the central area constitute the *peripheral nervous system* (fig. 11.9). The word *nerve* is a specific anatomical term that refers to a bundle of fibers in the peripheral nervous system. The peripheral nerves may be classified as *somatic* or *voluntary* (under conscious control) and *autonomic* or *involuntary* (outside the influence of the conscious mind). The familiar voluntary nerves are the sensory and motor fibers associated with the control of skeletal muscles that produce body movement. The pathway of these voluntary nerves has already been presented in the discussion of the reflex arc (fig. 11.2). The contractions of skeletal muscles can be perceived and controlled by the conscious mind.

The situation becomes complicated with respect to autonomic nerves that innervate internal smooth muscles, cardiac (heart) muscles, and internal glands. The contraction of the smooth muscles of the small intestine, the beating of the heart, and the secretions of the pancreas are beyond the reach of conscious control. The nerves involved in such involuntary processes represent the *autonomic nervous system*.

Each internal organ under automatic control receives a dual innervation. The double supply of nerves is accomplished by a division of the autonomic nervous system into two complementary components, the *sympathetic* and the *parasympathetic*. The former emanates from the thoracic (chest) and lumbar (low back) portions of the spinal cord, whereas the latter has its origin from two widely separated parts of the central nervous system, namely, the cranial (skull) and the sacral (pelvic) portion of the spinal cord (fig. 11.10). The two components have opposing effects on the organs they innervate. The parasympathetic reactions tend to conserve the energies of the body, while the sympathetic responses mobilize the body for heightened activities, especially during emergencies or stress. Nerves of the parasympathetic component, for example, slow down the heart rate and accelerate the churning movements of the stomach. Conversely, nerves of the sympathetic component accelerate the heartbeat, reduce the peristaltic activities of the stomach, and increase blood pressure. The dual control of the two systems is roughly analogous to the dual mechanism of an accelerator and a brake in an automobile. A car can be slowed down, even brought to a stop, by merely releasing the pressure on the accelerator. The application of the brake in conjunction with deceleration assures a finer, more faultless level of control.

The autonomic nervous system is unique in that the innervation of involuntary organs involves a relay of two motor neurons. The motor neurons of the autonomic system leaving the spinal cord typically establish synaptic contact with another neuron either in ganglia (for example, sympathetic ganglia) outside the spinal cord or in terminal ganglia in the effector glands or muscles themselves (fig. 11.10). There are thus two kinds of autonomic fibers: *preganglionic* fibers and *postganglionic* fibers. The preganglionic fibers of the parasympathetic division are generally longer than the fibers in the sympathetic division, and proceed great distances to innervate the gland or muscle. These end in small ganglia closely associated with the effector organ. The postganglionic parasympathetic fiber is accordingly short (fig. 11.10).

The terminal end of the parasympathetic postganglionic fiber secretes the familiar acetylcholine to trigger the effector organ. On the other hand,

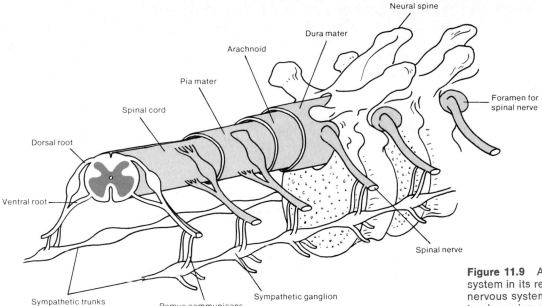

Figure 11.9 Autonomic nervous system in its relation to the central nervous system. The sympathetic trunk carries efferent neurons that innervate many of the internal organs.

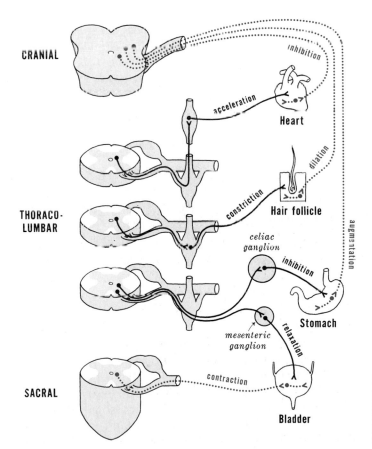

—— SYMPATHETIC (THORACO-LUMBAR)

PARASYMPATHETIC (CRANIO-SACRAL)

Figure 11.10 Sympathetic and parasympathetic components of the autonomic nervous system. The internal organs are innervated by both sympathetic nerves (from the thoraco-lumbar region of the spinal cord) and parasympathetic nerves (from the cranial and sacral regions). The sympathetic and parasympathetic nerves to a given organ function in opposition to each other.

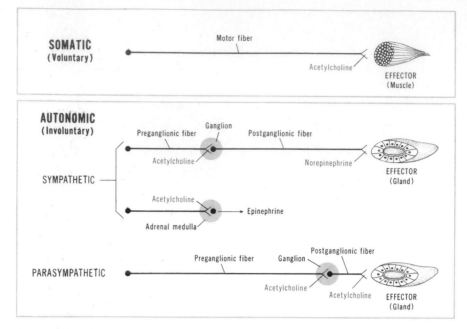

the chemical transmitter at the junction between the sympathetic postganglionic fiber and the effector organ is *norepinephrine*, a substance chemically allied to the hormone *epinephrine* secreted by the adrenal medulla (the core of the adrenal gland). The innervation and action of the adrenal medulla reveal the close interrelation of nervous and endocrine (hormonal) mechanisms. The adrenal medulla is stimulated by a sympathetic preganglionic fiber that uniquely courses directly to the adrenal medulla without making synaptic contact with a postganglionic fiber in a ganglion. Many neuroendocrinologists regard the adrenal medulla as an overgrown sympathetic ganglion devoid of nerve fibers but with the capacity to secrete its chemical transmitters directly into the bloodstream. Epinephrine dilates blood vessels, producing such actions as increased heartbeat and increased pulse. Figure 11.11 summarizes the important differences between the sympathetic and parasympathetic components of the autonomic nervous system.

THE HUMAN BRAIN

In the wave of the rapid advances of cellular and molecular biology, it has been said that the greatest intellectual challenge facing man today is the analytical understanding of the functional integration of neurons in the brain. The application of sophisticated techniques now available may soon permit an accurate description of the functioning of the brain in molecular and submolecular language. One of the current approaches being used, for example, is the recording of membrane potentials in individual brain cells following a variety of induced changes in the input of sensory messages. Such a study extends or supplements the purely anatomical approach that involves primarily the dissection, or extirpation, of specific areas of the mammalian brain and an examination of the subsequent behavior of the organism. At the moment, our level of understanding of the brain remains inadequate.

In simplest terms, the human brain consists of three divisions: the prominent *cerebrum* (cerebral hemispheres), the *cerebellum,* and the *brain stem* (fig. 11.12). The brain stem may be viewed as the stalk of the brain, containing thick bundles of nerve fibers conveying information to

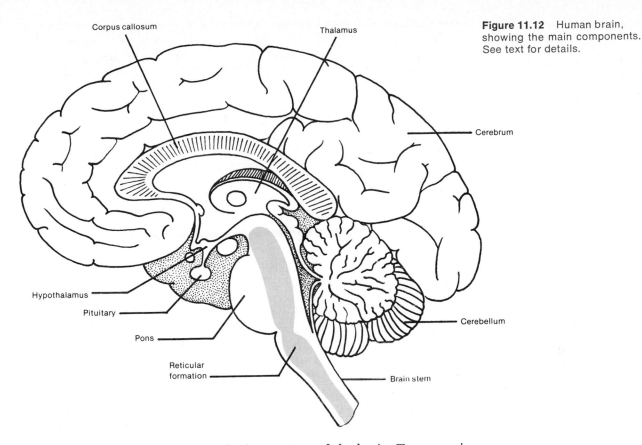

Figure 11.12 Human brain, showing the main components. See text for details.

Corpus callosum

Thalamus

Cerebrum

Hypothalamus

Pituitary

Pons

Reticular formation

Cerebellum

Brain stem

and from the spinal cord and the higher regions of the brain. Two prominent regions of the brain stem are the *medulla oblongata* (or simply, medulla) and the *pons*. The medulla plays an important role in the control of breathing, heart rate, digestion, and other internal functions. The pons contains a large number of fibers that connect the cerebellum with the spinal cord. The last decade has seen the identification of an interlocking network of nerve cells, termed the *reticular formation*, that ramifies throughout the brain stem. It is currently thought that the reticular formation serves as an elaborate integrating center, scrutinizing and censoring messages that surge from the spinal cord to the higher brain centers. A relay of neurons known as the *reticular activating system, or RAS*, is crucial for the dual aspects of sleep and wakefulness. During sleep, the RAS restricts the passage of sensory information of one's environment to the cerebral cortex. Stimuli such as noise and light are not consciously perceived or registered because of the inhibitory actions of RAS neurons. In the awake or conscious state, the cerebral cortex is aroused and alerted by external stimuli freely transmitted by the RAS. The activity of the RAS is very susceptible to drugs. Barbiturates decrease alertness and induce sleep by depressing the reticular activating system. In contrast, hallucinogens (mescaline, psilocybin, and LSD) greatly increase the sensitivity of the RAS to sensory stimuli.

The cerebellum is an elaborately folded area at the rear of the brain stem. The cerebellum processes numerous motor impulses and assures that the muscles of the body respond in an orderly, balanced fashion. It can be demonstrated experimentally in mammals that the coordinated control of muscular activities is lost if the cerebellum is removed or damaged.

The largest and most familiar part of the brain is the cerebrum, divided into right and left hemispheres. The two cerebral hemispheres are connected by a thin strip of nervous tissue called the *corpus callosum*. Most of the higher nervous functions are performed by the thin outer contorted sheet, the *cerebral cortex*, popularly termed the "gray matter." The gray matter is only one-tenth of an inch (2 mm) thick and densely packed with about 14 billion neurons. The cortex is divided into several parts, or *lobes*, each having specific functions (fig. 11.13). Ascending pathways carry information about different sensations (touch, temperature, taste, and so forth) to different areas of the cortex. Similarly, many different areas of the cerebral cortex give rise to nerve fibers that affect a variety of muscular activities. The relay center for the majority of sensory impulses to the cerebrum is the *thalamus*, the thick walls of a cavity deep within the brain, below the cerebrum. To cite an example, consciousness depends on the excitation of cortical neurons by impulses conducted to them from the reticular activating system via the thalamus. Situated just under the thalamus is the *hypothalamus*, the aforementioned mass of nervous tissue that controls the pituitary gland. The hypothalamus exerts a control over human behavior far out of proportion to its size. The hypothalamus is involved in a wide range of behavioral patterns, including the regulation of temperature, the expressions of anger and fear, sexual behavior, and the appetite for food. Amphetamines act as appetite depressants through their effects on the hypothalamus.

One of the enigmas of brain function is that the brain can be bisected, or completely separated, into right and left halves with very little impairment of ordinary behavior detectable by neurological and psychological testing. As reported in 1961 by the psychobiologist Roger W. Sperry of the California Institute of Technology, a split-brain monkey or cat behaves as if it had two separate brains. A split-brain subject can process twice as much visual information as can a normal animal. Moreover, each brain simultaneously can learn tasks that are contradictory to each other. It is as if each of the separated hemispheres is unaware of the other's experience or memories. Any theory of memory must take into account the apparent lack of necessity for intercommunication of the cerebral hemispheres.

Figure 11.13 Somatic and motor areas of the cerebral cortex of the human brain. Specific regions are involved with specific sensory or motor activities. (After W. Penfield and T. Rasmussen, *The cerebral cortex of man,* 1964, Macmillan Publishing Co., Inc. Copyright © 1964 Macmillan Publishing Co., Inc.)

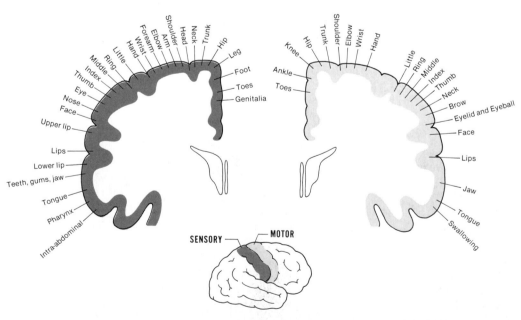

LEARNING AND MEMORY

Defining learning is almost as formidable as defining intelligence. The concept of learning can be ineptly generalized or hopelessly restricted. For ease of discussion, we may view learning simply as the process by which memories are formed. This would require that neurons have the capacity to store information gathered through the senses. As a working hypothesis, then, we can presume that particular neurons become structurally or functionally modified as a consequence of a particular stimulus, and that the alteration persists in these neurons so as to increase the likelihood that a repeat stimulus will engender the same response, or at least, that the particular response will be remembered. We may even conjecture that memory of an event fades or decays as the neuron, although durable in its altered state, eventually returns to its original state, if it does not first disintegrate with age.

Several investigators have suggested that the synaptic knobs at the terminal ends of axons may be the sites for the storage of information. In the quest for "memory molecules," attention has been focused on two large, relatively stable molecules—ribonucleic acid (RNA) and protein—within the neuron. In particular, acquired information might be stored in the specific configuration of the RNA molecules or the proteins that are synthesized. Holger Hydén of the University of Göteborg in Sweden developed a microtechnique for dissecting individual nerve fivers of the brain of a rat and analyzing them by biochemical techniques. In experimental rats that were taught a difficult balancing task, the proportion of RNA bases in the brain neurons was changed significantly. Thus, Hydén proposes that each neuron develops a unique RNA pattern as a result of the past activity of the cell. This new pattern subsequently determines the kind and extent of response of the neuron in a given situation.

Other investigators have proposed that the acquired, or learned, information might be stored in the nucleotide sequences of chromosomal DNA or messenger RNA, just as genetic information is coded by the nucleotide sequences (see chapter 16). Accordingly, DNA or messenger RNA extracts from the brain of one animal might convey coded memory information to another animal. A number of positive reports of such transfers of memory have appeared in the literature, involving subjects such as the flatworm (planaria), goldfish, and rats.

Some investigators argue that the experiments linking memory with RNA or protein have yet to show that a specific learning experience caused a specific change in a specific molecule. Regional changes in amount of RNA may simply be incidental to increased activity of the neurons of the brain. That is to say, the neurons may be synthesizing large quantities or even varied kinds of transmitter substances because of a generally heavier load on the protein-making machinery of the brain cells. Others concede that RNA molecules or protein synthesis may be involved in at least some aspect of the memory problem.

SUMMARY

The nerve impulse and the contraction of muscle can now be expressed in physiochemical terms. The membranes of nerve and muscle cells are polarized—a difference in electrical potential (voltage) exists on either side of the membrane as a consequence of an unequal distribution of charged particles (ions), particularly sodium and potassium. The magnitude of the resting (inactive) potential across the membrane of a nerve axon is 70 mV, the inside of the membrane being negative. When a nerve cell is stimulated, the membrane permeabilities to sodium and potassium ions become altered, causing the membrane potential to change in a fraction of a millisecond from -70 mV to $+30$ mV and then return rapidly to its original value. The almost instantaneous reversal in the membrane potential, known as the *action potential,* creates the nerve impulse. The generation of an action potential in the muscle membrane also triggers the contractile processes of a muscle. The essential chemical ingredients of muscle contractility are special protein molecules, actin and myosin, and the energy source ATP.

When a nerve impulse arrives at the axon terminal, a chemical transmitter (acetylcholine) is released across the synaptic junction, altering the electrical potential of the recipient nerve cell (postsynaptic neuron). Each synaptic junction is a decisive point at which the flow of information can be inhibited, modified, or transmitted unchanged. The brain receives information, analyzes it, and then directs the appropriate response in accord with the analysis. It is likely that memory has a neurochemical basis.

Ethical Probe 8
The Hyperkinetic Child

There is a disorder in children known as *hyperkinesis,* which produces hyperactivity beyond the conscious control of the child. The hyperkinetic child has poor attention span, behaves disorderly in school, and is scholastically weak out of proportion to his or her actual intelligence. Although no organic lesion has been identified, the condition is presumed to have an organic basis and is often referred to as "minimal brain dysfunction." This condition has been observed in 3 percent of American elementary-school-age children.

Amphetamines, popularly called "speed" because they produce alertness and an elevated mood in adults, have a paradoxical effect on hyperkinetic youngsters. Unlike the effects seen in adults, amphetamines have a restraining influence on the hyperkinetic child, increasing the child's willingness to work and reducing distractability. Related stimulants, such as methylphenidate (manufactured under the trade name of Ritalin) and caffeine (administered as two cups of coffee per day) have also been found to produce beneficial effects in hyperkinetic children.

If your child is hyperactive with behavioral problems and poor academic performance in school, would you subscribe to the use of amphetamines or related stimulants in an effort to solve the child's problem? Is there a danger of misuse or drug-induced dependence? Do you suspect a causal relationship between the medical use of amphetamines in the youngster and subsequent drug abuse in the adult?

Coordination by Hormones

12

Humans, like all vertebrates, have an elaborate internal communications system that makes use of chemical messengers. These chemical messengers, called *hormones* (Greek, *hormaein,* meaning "to excite") are secreted into the bloodstream by specialized *endocrine glands.* Since these glands have no ducts and liberate the hormones directly into the circulation, they are also known as *ductless glands.* The hormones are transported by the blood to various parts of the body where they regulate the activities of specific organs. The specific site of action is spoken of as the *target organ* of the hormone concerned. Hormones govern a wide range of chemical processes in their target cells. They may affect the activity of enzymes in crucial metabolic pathways, influence the rate at which proteins are synthesized, and alter the rate of membrane transport of a substance.

The endocrine system supplements the nervous system in coordinating the mechanisms of the body (fig. 12.1). The two great systems are intimately linked in their functions. The focal point of the endocrine system is the pituitary gland, which regulates a number of target glands (thyroid, adrenal cortex, gonads). In turn, the pituitary gland is controlled by an important center in the brain, the hypothalamus. As previously described, the hypothalamus resides at the base of the brain immediately above the pituitary gland. The hypothalamus may be thought of as the managing director of the endocrine system.

NEGATIVE FEEDBACK

The pituitary gland, or *hypophysis,* is a small organ, roughly the size of a pea, weighing about 0.5 gram. The gland is slightly larger in the female than in the male and may increase during pregnancy to a weight of one gram. The pituitary is composed of two distinct parts, or lobes, which have different embryonic origins. The posterior lobe, called the *neurohypophysis,* is formed as a downgrowth from the floor of the developing brain. The neurohypophysis is thus constituted of nervous tissue (Greek, *neuro,* meaning "nerve") and lies under the brain (Greek, *hypophysis,* denoting "undergrowth"). The anterior lobe, called the *adenohypophysis,* is formed as an outgrowth of the roof of the embryonic mouth. As the name implies (Greek, *adenos,* meaning "gland") the adenohypophysis has a more glandular appearance than the neurohypophysis and behaves like a true gland. It is the source of several prominent hormones.

The hormones secreted by the adenohypophysis are called *tropic* hormones, since they, in the main, serve to stimulate other endocrine glands to secrete their hormones. The major tropic hormones are thyrotropin (or thyroid-stimulating hormone, TSH), adrenocorticotropin (or adrenocorticotropic hormone, ACTH), the gonadotropins (FSH and LH),

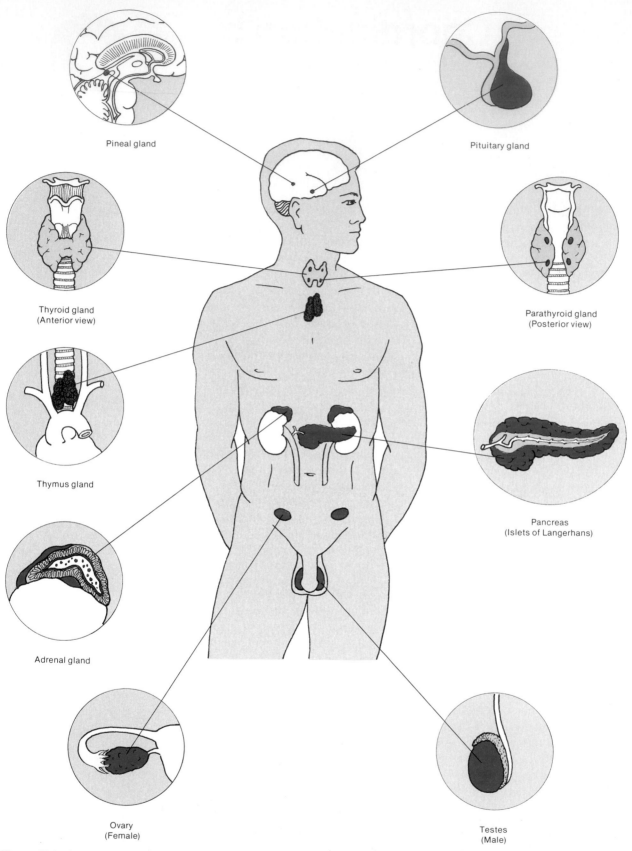

Pineal gland

Pituitary gland

Thyroid gland
(Anterior view)

Parathyroid gland
(Posterior view)

Thymus gland

Pancreas
(Islets of Langerhans)

Adrenal gland

Ovary
(Female)

Testes
(Male)

Figure 12.1 Location of the principal endocrine glands in the human body.

luteotropin (prolactin or luteotropic hormone, LTH), and somatotropin (or growth hormone, GH). All, save somatotropin, influence the activity of some target gland (table 12.1). Somatotropin acts directly on the cells of the body to promote the synthesis of proteins.

The activity of thyroxine reveals the general pattern of *negative feedback* on tropic hormones (fig. 12.2). The thyroid gland produces thyroxine, an iron-containing hormone, in response to stimulation by thyrotropin from the pituitary gland (adenohypophysis). As thyroxine reaches normal levels in the body, it inhibits the release of thyrotropin. Thyroxine does not act directly on the pituitary gland, but rather acts on the hypothalamus to inhibit the release of yet another set of hormonal agents, called *releasing factors*. These agents are produced by the hypothalamus, and are liberated from nerve endings into capillaries that pass into the pituitary gland. The releasing factors regulate the output of specific hormones of the adenohypophysis. Most of the hypothalamic releasing factors (TSH-releasing factor and ACTH-releasing factor, for example) stimulate the release of their relevant hormones. As an apparent exception, the releasing factor that governs the production of prolactin inhibits rather than stimulates prolactin release.

The negative-feedback relationship is continuously at play in the body. A high concentration of hormone from a target gland generally inhibits the production of the relevant releasing factor, and therefore the production of the appropriate stimulating tropic hormone by the adenohypophysis. As the level of tropic hormone declines, the secretion of the target gland is reduced. Such a system is highly effective in maintaining a fairly constant level of a given target hormone in the body. Many factors are now known to affect the hypothalamic neurons that secrete the releasing factors. Since the production of a releasing factor is a neural activity, it can be influenced by stress, age, sex, and anxiety.

Not all target hormones are controlled by the interplay of the pituitary and hypothalamus. No tropic hormone, for example, triggers the secretion of insulin by the pancreas. As will be described in detail in a subsequent section (chapter 13), the major function of insulin is the regulation of the concentration of glucose in the bloodstream. The insulin-secreting cells of the pancreas respond simply and directly to the relative levels of blood glucose.

THE NEUROHYPOPHYSIS

Although the neurohypophysis has few secretory cells, it was believed, until recently, that this lobe synthesized two hormones, oxytocin and vasopressin (or antidiuretic hormone, ADH). Current studies show that these two hormones are actually produced in the hypothalamus, transmitted through nerve fibers into the neurohypophysis, and merely stored in the neurohypophysis until their release. Modern anatomists view the neurohypophysis, which is true neural tissue, as merely an extension of the hypothalamus.

The action of oxytocin has been discussed earlier (chapter 3). Vasopressin was first described by its capacity to stimulate the contraction of smooth muscles in the arterioles. As the arterioles contract, more resistance is offered to the flow of blood and the blood pressure rises. Today, it is generally acknowledged that the role played by vasopressin in maintaining blood pressure is minor. Vasopressin is of prime importance in promoting the reabsorption of water from the glomerular filtrate so as to produce a concentrated urine. Vasopressin is preferably called the anti-

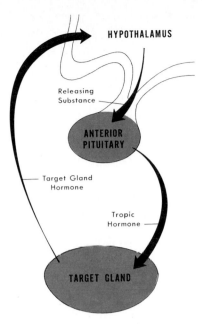

Figure 12.2 The general pattern of negative feedback on tropic hormones.

Table 12.1

Hormones, their Targets, and their Actions

Gland and Hormone	Target	Action
A. Adenohypophysis (Anterior Pituitary)		
1. Growth hormone (GH) or Somatotropin (STH)	All body cells	Promotes synthesis of proteins, particularly in muscles and bone
2. Adrenocorticotropin or Adrenocorticotropic hormone (ACTH)	Adrenal cortex	Stimulates synthesis and release of glucocorticoids
3. Thyrotropin or Thyroid-stimulating hormone (TSH)	Thyroid gland	Controls secretion of thyroxine
4. Follicle-stimulating hormone (FSH)	Gonads	Stimulates maturation of eggs in females and production of sperm in males
5. Luteinizing hormone (LH) or Interstitial cell-stimulating hormone (ICSH)	Gonads	Triggers release of eggs in females and stimulates synthesis of androgens in males
6. Prolactin, Lactogenic hormone, Luteotropin, or Luteotropic hormone (LTH)	Mammary glands	Stimulates milk production after childbirth
B. Neurohypophysis (Posterior Pituitary)	—	No synthesis of hormones; stores and secretes oxytocin and vasopressin
C. Hypothalamus		
1. Releasing factors	Adenohypophysis	Controls release of pituitary tropic hormones
2. Oxytocin	Uterus, Mammary gland	Facilitates contraction of uterus during delivery; promotes flow of milk ("milk letdown")
3. Vasopressin or Antidiuretic hormone (ADH)	Kidney, Arteries	Control of water reabsorption; contraction of smooth muscles
D. Adrenal cortex		
1. Glucocorticoids (predominately cortisol)	Most body cells	Regulates carbohydrate, protein, and fat metabolism; confers resistance to stress

Gland and Hormone	Target	Action
2. Mineralocorticoids (predominately aldosterone)	Kidney	Regulates mineral balance, particularly sodium and potassium
E. Adrenal medulla		
1. Epinephrine (Adrenalin)	Most body cells	"Emergency" hormone; alerts body for "fight or flight."
2. Norepinephrine (Noradrenalin)	Small arteries	"Emergency" hormone
F. Thyroid		
1. Thyroxine	Most body cells	Increases metabolic rate
2. Calcitonin	Blood	Lowers blood calcium level
G. Parathyroid		
Parathyroid hormone (PTH)	Bones and kidneys	Regulates calcium and potassium metabolism
H. Pancreas		
1. Insulin	All body cells	Lowers blood glucose; permits passage of glucose into cells
2. Glucagon	Liver	Stimulates release of glucose from liver
I. Ovary		
1. Estrogens (predominately estradiol)	Most body cells	Development of female secondary sex characteristics
2. Progesterone	Uterus	Thickens uterine endometrium
J. Testis		
Androgens (predominately testosterone)	Most body cells	Development of male secondary sex characteristics
K. Pineal gland		
1. Pineal antigonadotropin (PAG)	Reproductive system	Suppression of ovulation
2. Melatonin	Brain cells (?)	Cue for sleep-wakefulness cycle
L. Prostate, seminal vesicles, brain, and nerves		
Prostaglandins	Uterus	Contraction of smooth muscles

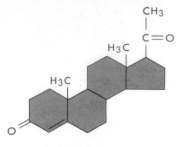

PROGESTERONE

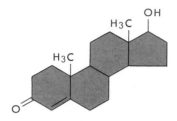

TESTOSTERONE

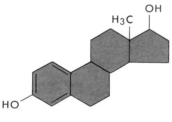

ESTRADIOL

Figure 12.3 The close chemical resemblances of the female sex hormones (progesterone and estradiol) and the male sex hormone (testosterone).

diuretic hormone (ADH). The secretion of ADH, like other hypothalamic activities, is sensitive to factors of an emotional nature. In experimental animals, anxiety and fear increase the output of ADH, with the consequence that more than the usual amounts of water are conserved. In humans, an anxious state is often accompanied by the retention of water in the body tissues.

CHEMICAL STRUCTURES

Although of diverse chemical compositions, hormones fall into two general categories: derivatives of amino acids (peptides, proteins, or glycoproteins) and steroids. The releasing factors of the hypothalamus are small peptides, ranging from 3 to 12 amino acids. Oxytocin and the antidiuretic hormone (ADH) each contains 8 amino acids, and 6 of the 8 are exactly alike. Hence, the different hormonal actions hinge solely on the 2 dissimilar amino acids. All of the hormones of the adenohypophysis and several of those of peripheral origin are amino acid derivatives. In some cases, the whole molecule is not vital for biological activity. For example, adrenocorticotropic hormone (ACTH) can function, without loss of full activity, with peptide fragments consisting only of 19 of the original 39 amino acids.

The hormones of the adrenal cortex and the sex hormones are steroids, which are small molecules with molecular weights of about 300. Figure 12.3 shows the close chemical configurations of the female sex hormones (estradiol and progesterone) and the male sex hormone (testosterone). The chemical differences between estradiol and testosterone are exceedingly slight in comparison to their markedly feminizing and masculinizing actions. The steroids are derived from cholesterol and are only slightly soluble in water.

MODES OF ACTION

There are probably several mechanisms by which hormones act on a cell. At least two modes of action are known, which relate to the structural chemistry of the hormones. The small, fat-soluble steroid hormone can readily pass through the cell membrane of a target cell and directly affect internal processes. On the other hand, the large-sized polypeptide hormone cannot penetrate the cell membrane, and it must exert its effect on the internal machinery from the outside of the cell.

Since the polypeptide hormone itself does not gain entry into the cell, it was reasonably surmised that the hormone stimulates the formation of a hormonal mediator to bring about the observed effect. Evidence supporting the concept of a mediator was provided by the late Earl W. Sutherland of Vanderbilt University, who was awarded the Nobel Prize for physiology and medicine in 1971 for his intensive studies in the 1950s. The hormone at the cell surface activates an enzyme called *adenyl cyclase* in the cell membrane of the target cell (fig. 12.4). The activated adenyl cyclase then catalyzes the conversion of ATP on the inner side of the membrane to the molecule *cyclic 3', 5'-adenosine monophosphate,* better known as cyclic AMP or cAMP. The cyclic AMP then acts within the cell as the mediator to bring about the activity associated with that hormone. As an example, epinephrine (secreted by the adrenal medulla) is responsible, during periods of stress, for the formation of glucose from the glycogen held in reserve in the liver. At the surface membrane of the liver cell, epinephrine stimulates adenyl cyclase, which then catalyzes the synthesis of cyclic AMP from ATP. In turn, cyclic AMP activates the particular enzyme (a phosphorylase) involved in the breakdown of glycogen to glucose. The conversion of the inactive phosphorylase enzyme to an active, functional form is the crucial role of epinephrine in augmenting blood glucose during stress, which is achieved through the mediator, cyclic AMP.

The hormone (epinephrine, in this case) may be thought of as a "first-messenger," since its primary action is to interact with a receptor site on the cell membrane so as to activate adenyl cyclase. The cyclic AMP that is generated within the cell is said to be the "second messenger," since it produces the modification of cell function associated with that hormone. This "two-messenger" pattern has been implicated in the action of many of the amino acid-derived hormones, including ACTH, TSH, ADH, PTH, insulin, and glucagon. Cyclic AMP has come to be recognized as the universal mediator of hormonal stimulation at the cell surface. The receptor sites of the responding cells are highly specific for given hormones, since a particular hormone activates cyclic AMP only in its target cell and not in other cells.

Steroid hormones typically act by promoting the synthesis of proteins (structural proteins and enzymes) in their specific target cells. The steroid hormone passes through the cell membrane into the cytoplasm, where it binds to a cytoplasmic soluble protein. The hormone-specific soluble protein in the cytoplasm has been termed a *cytosol receptor*. The hormone-receptor complex then enters the cell's nucleus and activates ("turns on") specific genes that lead to the production of particular enzymes. We will examine the manner in which genes are activated or expressed in a subsequent chapter.

ADRENAL HORMONES AND STRESS

Like the pituitary gland, the adrenal gland is composed of two distinct kinds of tissues, each of a different embryological origin. The outer portion of the gland, the *cortex*, is derived from mesodermal elements and secretes a variety of steroid hormones. The inner *medulla* is functionally an entirely separate organ. The medulla arises from embryonic neural tissue, as do the ganglion cells of the sympathetic nervous system, and releases hormones whose effects are similar to those resulting from stimulation of the sympathetic nervous system. Unlike the hormones of the adrenal cortex, the medullary hormones are not steroids but are peptides of low molecular weight derived from the amino acid tyrosine.

The hormones of the medulla—epinephrine (or adrenalin) and norepinephrine (or noradrenaline)—are often called "emergency hormones," since they trigger responses that alert and prepare the body for "fight or flight" situations. Actually, the liberation of epinephrine and norepinephrine occurs coincidently with the activation of the sympathetic nervous system. Accordingly, the hormones share and reinforce the responses of the sympathetic system. The overall effect of the various actions is to increase the rate and strength of heart activity, mobilize glucose and fatty acids from storage areas, increase the contractility of skeletal muscles, increase the coagulability of blood, and shunt blood from the viscera to the skeletal muscles.

The hormones of the adrenal cortex are prominently involved in conferring resistance to stressful situations—infection, physical injury, shock, prolonged exposure to cold or heat, pain, fright, and emotional stresses. The adrenal cortical responses to stress are mediated principally by the glucocorticoid hormones, of which cortisol is the most

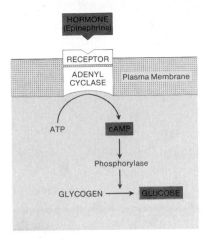

Figure 12.4 The important roles of cyclic AMP (cAMP) and adenyl cyclase in initiating the cellular activity appropriate to the given hormone.

active. One of the main activities of cortisol is to raise the level of glucose in the blood for a sustained period. Cortisol promotes the breakdown of protein and the conversion of the amino acids in the liver into glucose (see chapter 13). Such metabolic reactions are essential for survival during times of prolonged fasting or sustained stress. If cortisol secretion is deficient, the level of sugar in the blood may fall dangerously low. Cortisol also has remarkable anti-inflammatory properties. Synthetic cortisol has been used to alleviate the swelling and related inflammatory symptoms associated with rheumatoid arthritis. In addition, cortisol is effective in relieving the symptoms of asthma and other allergic reactions.

PINEAL GLAND

The pineal gland is a small seedlike organ located opposite the pituitary on the underside of the thalamus. In recent years the pineal gland has attracted attention in view of its inhibitory effects on reproductive activity, particularly in mammals that breed seasonally. A peptide hormone, pineal antigonadotropin (PAG), has been isolated that is capable of suppressing ovulation in experimental rats and hamsters, presumably by restricting the postovulatory surge of LH below the critical level required for ovulation. Knowledge of the effects of PAG in humans is still incomplete.

The pineal gland also secretes melatonin, a hormone derived from the amino acid tryptophan. The blood levels of melatonin vary regularly in a rhythmic manner, with the lowest levels occurring during the day (or in a light environment) and the highest amounts during night (or in a dark environment). The blood levels of melatonin in the dark may be an astonishing 30 times higher than the levels in the light. The rhythmic rate of production of melatonin is consistent in a given animal from day to day. In man, the highest levels of melatonin are found during sleep between 11 p.m. and 7 a.m. The pronounced rhythmic secretions of melatonin suggest that this hormone serves to alert the higher centers of the brain to such recurring events as sunsets and sunrises, or sleep and wakefulness.

PROSTAGLANDINS

In the 1930s, lipid-soluble substances, called *prostaglandins,* were discovered in extracts of human semen and of prostate glands of sheep. The prostaglandins were shown to be potent stimulators of smooth muscle as well as strong vasodilators, capable of lowering blood pressure by dilating peripheral blood vessels. These lipids have been clinically useful in increasing blood flow in the legs of patients suffering from peripheral arteriosclerosis. The prostaglandins have now been isolated from most tissues of the body, and they appear to influence numerous metabolic reactions. The prostaglandins may well be hormonal in nature and, in some instances, may function as hormonal mediators comparable to cyclic AMP. The precise physiological significance of these very active lipids remains to be resolved.

SUMMARY

Hormones are chemical messengers that are produced by specialized endocrine (ductless) glands. A hormone is transported by the blood to a specific site of action (target organ), where it regulates responses appropriate to the organ. One impressive aspect of hormone activity is the phenomenon of negative feedback, wherein the hormone, when it reaches appropriate levels, tends to shut off further secretion of that hormone. The negative-feedback mechanism operates via the hypothalamus, which is responsible for producing hormonal agents called releasing factors. The releasing factors control the output of specific hormones of the pituitary gland, which places the pituitary under the direction of the hypothalamus.

The hormones of the adrenal cortex and the sex hormones are steroids; the remaining hormones are derivatives of amino acids. The small-sized steroid hormone gains entry into the target cell and effects an increased synthesis of proteins by influencing the nuclear constituents. The large-sized polypeptide hormone cannot pass through the cell membrane of the target cell, and exerts its effect at the border of the cell. The polypeptide hormone activates the membrane-bound enzyme adenyl cyclase, which catalyzes the formation of cyclic AMP and ATP. The cyclic AMP then acts within the cell as a mediator to promote the activity associated with the hormone. Cyclic AMP may be viewed as a "second messenger."

Stress (trauma, cold, pain, intense emotion) results in an increased secretion of cortisol by the adrenal cortex. Elevated amounts of cortisol are important in maintaining the proper level of glucose in the blood, particularly during periods of fasting. Epinephrine and norepinephrine, the "emergency hormones" of the adrenal medulla, are also released during many kinds of stress.

13 Homeostasis

The cells of the body function at optimum levels under stable internal conditions. Any disturbing change in the body triggers internal reactions that minimize or neutralize the disturbance and return the body to normal activities. The self-regulated stability that results from precise compensatory responses is called *homeostasis* (Greek, *homoio*, meaning like or same; *stasis*, meaning standing still). Examples of processes that are carefully controlled within narrow limits are the sugar concentration of the blood, the volume and composition of tissue fluids, urinary water loss, and internal body temperature.

Each organ of the body—the liver, lungs, kidney, heart, among others—contributes its share to maintaining the constancy of internal conditions. The compensatory processes occur with such precision and smoothness that the bodily adjustments to disturbing forces are almost unnoticeable. In previous chapters, emphasis was placed on the structure and function of the individual organ systems. Now, we will consider how the various organs interact in a coordinated manner to offset unsettling changes imposed on the body. The refined control mechanisms are strikingly witnessed in the regulation of the sugar level of the blood, the control of body temperature, and the maintenance of the water content of the body.

REGULATION OF BLOOD GLUCOSE

The body's major energy source is glucose, the concentration of which is held at constant levels in the blood despite the great variation in the intake of carbohydrates. During the *absorptive state,* the period when the digestive products are absorbed, glucose enters the bloodstream from the intestinal tract. The quantity of glucose absorbed from the intestine is typically in excess of that required by the body tissues for energy. A large portion of the absorbed glucose is taken up by the liver and converted to glycogen. Some of the absorbed glucose enters adipose tissue to be transformed into fat, and still other portions are stored as glycogen in skeletal muscle. After the excess glucose is withdrawn from the blood, the level of glucose in circulation attains a concentration of about 70 to 100 mg per 100 ml of blood. This quantity is known as the *normal fasting level* of blood sugar. At this concentration, the total amount of sugar in the blood is approximately 5 grams, equivalent to one teaspoonful. This level of blood glucose must be maintained because the cells of the central nervous system, particularly the brain cells, rely largely (although not exclusively) on glucose as an energy source. When the blood sugar level falls to a concentration of 50 mg per 100 ml of blood or less convulsions, coma, and death can occur within minutes.

During periods of fasting between meals (the *postabsorptive state*), the tissues usually utilize glucose at a rapid rate and the blood sugar level declines. The stored glycogen in the liver is then reconverted into glucose and released into the bloodstream. This conversion process is known as *glycogenolysis*. The reservoir of glycogen in the liver is limited and is mobilized quickly. There are about 100 grams of glycogen in the adult liver, which is sufficient to maintain normal blood sugar levels for about 8 to 12 hours. After a fast of 12 hours or longer and in the absence of carbohydrate intake, certain metabolic reactions occur to furnish the required glucose. The liver has the capacity to produce glucose from non-carbohydrate sources or precursors, a process called *gluconeogenesis*. As figure 13.1 shows, the principal substrates for gluconeogenesis are amino acids (resulting from the degradation of muscle proteins) and glycerol (resulting from the breakdown of fats).

The glucose generated by gluconeogenesis in the liver during prolonged fasting is used primarily by cells of the central nervous system, especially the brain. In fact, the demand for glucose by brain cells is so great that virtually all other tissues of the body depend on fat as their energy source. During an extended fast period, the fatty acids from the hydrolysis of fat are liberated into the bloodstream and delivered to the liver. The liver converts the fatty acids into a group of compounds called *ketone bodies* (fig. 13.1). When the requirement for glucose cannot be met by other means, the tissues of the body rely increasingly on ketone bodies as an energy source. Persons undergoing prolonged fasting tend to have a distinctive breath, the consequence of the exhalation of ketone bodies (particularly acetone).

If fasting were to be continued for a long period of time, a significant loss of body proteins might be expected as an outcome of increased gluconeogenesis. The continual utilization of protein for the production of glucose could have very serious consequences if brain cells were unable to utilize any other nutrient for energy except glucose. However, the brain cells are not slavishly dependent on glucose; the cells can, if necessary, utilize ketone bodies as energy sources. By using ketones instead of

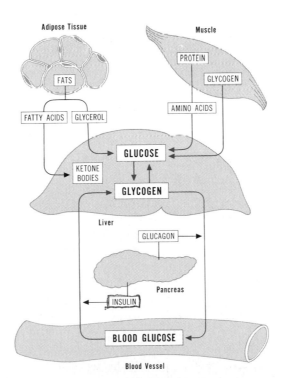

Figure 13.1 The varied pathways involved in the regulation of the concentration of glucose in the blood.

glucose, the brain cells can reduce their glucose requirement based on the degradation of protein. In other words, during a long fast, the synthesis of glucose at the expense of protein does not occur at a sufficient rate to damage the integrity of the body proteins.

INSULIN AND OTHER HORMONES

Several hormones are involved directly or indirectly in the regulation of the level of blood glucose. One of the more important hormones is *insulin,* secreted by the beta (or B) cells of the islets of Langerhans of the pancreas. Insulin acts to facilitate the entry of glucose through the membranes of certain cells. Although the exact mechanism is still unclear, the cell membranes of many tissues are impervious to glucose unless insulin is simultaneously present at the surface of the cell. All muscle cells require insulin for efficient sugar transport, as do the cells of adipose tissue and other kinds of connective tissues. The cells of the liver and brain permit the transport of glucose without the aid of insulin. In the liver, insulin acts to prevent the excessive breakdown of glycogen and inhibits the release of glucose into the blood. In brief, insulin serves to reduce the concentration of glucose in the blood.

The action of insulin is counteracted by *glucagon,* a hormone produced by the alpha (or A) cells of the pancreatic islets of Langerhans. Glucagon stimulates the breakdown of liver glycogen to glucose and promotes gluconeogenesis, both of which result in an elevation in blood glucose levels. The release of insulin as well as glucagon is directly controlled by the concentration of glucose in the blood. Insulin is secreted by the beta cells in response to a rise in blood sugar, whereas the secretion of glucagon is inhibited by elevated blood glucose. The converse is true for low blood sugar levels.

At least three other hormones are involved in controlling the concentration of blood glucose. A decrease in blood sugar promotes the production of growth hormone (GH) by the pituitary, which in turn stimulates the alpha cells of the pancreas to secrete glucagon (fig. 13.2). When the blood glucose levels are very low, the pituitary gland increases the production of adrenocorticotropin (ACTH), which stimulates the release of glucocorticoids (especially cortisol). These steroid hormones promote

Figure 13.2 The varied hormones involved directly or indirectly in the regulation of the level of blood glucose.

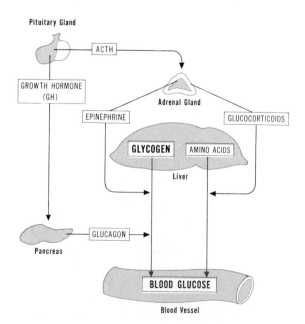

gluconeogenesis, particularly the conversion in the liver of glucose from amino acids (fig. 13.2). Under conditions of stress (pain, fright, excitement), the adrenal medulla secretes epinephrine (adrenalin), which promotes the rate of glycogen breakdown in the liver. The elevation in blood sugar during emergency situations as a result of epinephrine may be as much as 20 mg per 100 ml of blood per minute.

DIABETES

The cause of diabetes is insulin deficiency. The level of glucose in the blood remains high because glucose cannot enter cells (fig. 13.3). In diabetics, we observe an unpleasant incongruity: many cells are starved for glucose because of insulin insufficiency, yet the blood typically has high levels of glucose. Fortunately, the brain is exempt from glucose deprivation since its uptake of glucose is not insulin-dependent. The inability of many body cells to utilize glucose leads to a progressive loss of weight despite the consumption of large amounts of food. The ingested carbohydrates and proteins are converted to glucose, and this only increases, without profit, the level of glucose circulating in the blood. The excess blood glucose is eliminated in the urine.

The two major diagnostic features of diabetes are *hyperglycemia* (elevated blood sugar) and *glycosuria* (spillage of glucose in the urine). Additionally, most diabetics produce unusually large amounts of ketone bodies, such as acetone and acetoacidic acid. To meet the cell requirements for an energy source, fatty acids are substituted for glucose (fig. 13.3). The excessive breakdown of fatty acids results in their increased conversion to ketone bodies. The prolonged accumulation of ketone bodies in the blood may result in an imbalance of salts that, if severe, can lead to coma and eventually, if untreated, to death.

REGULATION OF BODY TEMPERATURE

In the older scientific literature, a sharp distinction was drawn between *homeothermic* animals, such as birds and mammals, which maintain constant body temperatures independent of environmental temperature, and *poikilothermic* animals (fish, amphibians, and reptiles), whose body temperatures fluctuate with changes of the external environment. Poikilothermic animals, however, are not necessarily thermally unstable. In nature, several species of frogs and reptiles can regulate their body temperatures within fairly narrow limits. This regulation is accomplished by

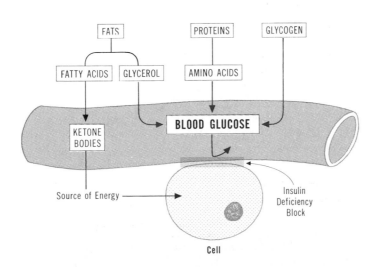

Figure 13.3 The elevation of the concentration of blood glucose as a consequence of insulin deficiency.

behavioral activities. A lizard, for example, basks in the sun to elevate its body temperature to a certain level, and retreats to shady areas when its body temperature rises too high. Such behavioral measures enable the lizard to maintain a moderately stable body temperature between 30°C. and 40°C. Given their capacity for behavioral thermal adjustments, poikilotherms have been more aptly designated by modern investigators as *ectothermic*. This means that such animals are dependent on external sources of heat. Thus, the body temperatures of ectotherms are determined largely by exchanges of heat with the exterior surroundings. In contrast, homeothermic animals produce and control their own sources of heat, and are now said to be *endothermic*. In endotherms, the total heat content of the body is determined by the net difference between the amount of heat produced by the tissues and the amount lost from the body.

HEAT PRODUCTION AND LOSS

In humans, the usual range of resting temperatures when measured orally is between 97°F and 99.5°F, with normalcy considered to be 96.6°F (37°C). The rectal temperature is slightly higher—99.6°F or 37.6°C. In women, there are monthly variations; the temperature in the second half of the menstrual cycle is higher than during the first half. Body temperature tends to be less stable in children than in adults; a child may develop a high fever quickly only to return to normal within a few hours. Newborns have lower body temperatures since their thermoregulatory systems at birth are not well established.

Heat is continually being produced internally through the metabolic activities of cells. Other heat-generating mechanisms supplement the heat normally produced by the cellular oxidation of nutrients. *Shivering,* or the rhythmic involuntary contractions of muscles, is a characteristic compensatory response of the body to augment heat production in a sustained cold environment. These rhythmic contractions may occur at a rate of 10–20 per second, increasing body heat production severalfold within a few minutes. Additionally, active voluntary exercise, if only stamping of the feet or clapping of the hands, will further increase heat production. Moreover, through the addition of clothing, man supplies a warm insulating blanket to trap the heat radiating from the skin.

The exchange of heat between the skin and external environment occurs by a variety of mechanisms. The skin of the body acts as a large *radiating* surface, releasing heat by radiation (like a heat lamp) from a warmer body to the cooler surroundings. A prominent factor in radiative heat loss is the flow of blood through the capillaries of the skin. As more blood is routed through the peripheral vessels (*vasodilatation*), more heat is radiated from the surface. With low peripheral blood flow (*vasoconstriction*), heat is retained by the internal tissues and relatively less heat is lost to the external environment.

As the body loses heat, the air in its immediate vicinity becomes warm. The warm air, being less dense, rises and is replaced by cooler air in a continuous process. These air movements or currents, called *convection,* contribute to the loss of heat by the body. At normal room temperature, convective heat loss is minimal. Forced convective currents, such as produced by artificial air-conditioning, dissipate considerable amounts of heat from the body surface.

Heat is lost from the body through the continual evaporation of water from the skin surface. The small, almost unnoticeable, amounts of water lost by evaporation (called *insensible perspiration*) may be augmented by the increased production of sweat (*sweating*). Technically, sweat is a true secretion—the product of the sweat glands in the skin. Sweat has the same composition as tissue fluid, including carefully regulated amounts of sodium chloride (salt). Persons who sweat profusely often consume salt tablets to compensate for the loss of sodium chloride.

An individual has about 2.5 million sweat glands in the skin. Understandably, sweating is a highly efficient cooling mechanism. The effectiveness of sweating as a cooling agent is greater in hot, dry climates than in hot, humid climates. When the humidity of the air is very high, the sweat droplets do not evaporate but simply roll off the skin. The evaporation of sweat in a hot, moist environment is generally encouraged by artificial air-conditioning (forced convection).

There are mammals that lack sweat glands, such as dogs, cats, and rabbits. These animals resort to evaporation from the upper portions of the respiratory tract to dissipate excessive body heat. In particular, evaporation takes place from the moist surfaces of the nasal cavity, mouth cavity, and tongue. A panting dog evaporates proportionally more fluid during a given interval of time than a sweating human.

THE THERMOSENSITIVE HYPOTHALAMUS

The center of temperature regulation in the human body is the hypothalamus in the floor of the brain. A network of neurons functions as a thermostat, operating to prevent both excessive heating and excessive cooling. The hypothalamus is remarkably sensitive to thermal change; the thermostatic mechanism responds to a change as small as 0.01°C in the temperature of the blood circulating through the hypothalamus. When a person is exposed to cold, the hypothalamus initiates the appropriate reactions to conserve body heat and, at the same time, increase internal heat production. The capillaries of the skin constrict and the secretion of sweat is inhibited, thereby decreasing heat loss from the body. The constriction of peripheral circulation is regarded as an effect of norepinephrine, released by the adrenal medulla in response to a stimulus from the hypothalamus. Heat is produced by an increase in muscular activity and by the initiation of shivering. In a process analogous to burning additional fuel in a furnace, the rate of oxidation of glucose in all cells is increased. The general enhancement of oxidative reactions appears to be associated with increases in the amounts of circulating thyroxine. When the body is exposed to excessive heating, cooling is achieved by the converse actions of vasodilatation of the skin capillaries, increased sweating, decreased muscular activity, and decreased oxidative reactions.

The set-point (98.6°F) of the hypothalamic thermostat can be altered by *pyrogens*, chemical agents that give rise to fever. A notable pyrogen is the toxic secretion (toxin) of infectious bacteria. Bacterial toxins shift the set-point of the hypothalamic thermostat to a higher level, and the hypothalamus proceeds to regulate temperature around the newly established higher reference point (101°F, for example). The hypothalamus is thus victimized in registering that the body temperature is too low, and it responds by promoting measures to heat the body. Fever occurs as the temperature rises until it reaches the new reference point. Extremely high body temperatures are dangerous because the metabolic oxidations in cells increase beyond the level that can be sustained by the usual supply of oxygen. The cells can become asphyxiated and degenerate. When the febrile-causing agent is no longer present, the temperature set-point returns to its normal lower value (98.6°F) and the customary heat loss responses are activated. The febrile episode can be reduced by aspirin (salicylic acid), which seems to act directly on the hypothalamic thermostat. In a manner as yet not known, aspirin is particularly effective in activating evaporative heat-loss responses. The body cools down by copious sweating, even if the external environment is cool.

WATER BALANCE

Organisms control the fluid content in their tissues by balancing their intake and output of water. The intake of water is from food, drink, and metabolic reactions (the oxidation of carbohydrates, for example). Water may be lost through the body surface (by evaporation), through respiratory passages, and by excretion. A variety of mechanisms operate in different forms of life to achieve a favorable water balance.

The frog, inhabiting freshwater ponds, is subjected to considerable water stress. The moist, permeable skin gains water readily and simultaneously loses salt. The heavy water load is counteracted by the production of a copious, dilute urine, and the salt deficit is overcome by the active absorption of salts by skin cells throughout the surface. Freshwater fish also produce a watery urine, with much of the body salts reabsorbed in the kidneys. Additionally, special cells in the gills of freshwater fish actively absorb sodium chloride from the surrounding medium (fig. 13.4).

The problem is different for fish that live in the sea. Threatened with dehydration, marine bony fishes gain water by drinking large quantities of sea water. The water is conserved by excreting a scanty, concentrated urine (fig. 13.4). Both the kidneys and gills are highly specialized to offset the large salt content of sea water. The kidneys secrete salt into the urine,

Figure 13.4 Mechanisms for the maintenance of water balance in the frog, a freshwater fish, and a marine fish.

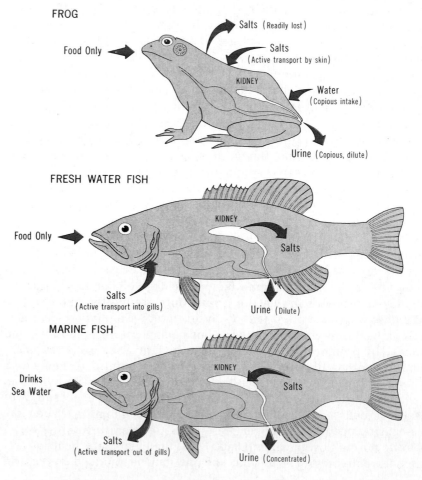

FROG

Food Only ➤

Salts (Readily lost)

Salts (Active transport by skin)

KIDNEY

Water (Copious intake)

Urine (Copious, dilute)

FRESH WATER FISH

Food Only ➤

KIDNEY

Salts

Salts (Active transport into gills)

Urine (Dilute)

MARINE FISH

Drinks Sea Water ➤

KIDNEY

Salts

Salts (Active transport out of gills)

Urine (Concentrated)

and special cells of the gills withdraw salt from the blood and secrete the salt into the sea water. Marine sharks provide yet another solution to the problem of water balance. Sharks have an unusually high tolerance to urea, and retain a large portion of the urea that is normally excreted by most other organisms as a toxic waste product. The urea in the blood of a marine shark is 100 times more concentrated than the urea in the blood of man. The high urea level in the shark's blood raises the osmotic pressure of the blood to a value that closely approximates the osmotic pressure of the surrounding sea water. Accordingly, the shark is in an isosmotic state of equilibrium with its surrounding medium.

Animals in dry habitats conserve water by producing a highly concentrated urine and very dry feces. The small kangaroo rat of the desert survives without drinking; it obtains sufficient water from the metabolism of its food. The kangaroo rat restricts its water loss to a level equal to, or less than, that obtained as metabolic water. The ability of the kangaroo rat to concentrate its urine is so great that it can excrete salt in a concentration twice that in sea water. In fact, the capacity of water conservation is so well developed that the kangaroo rat can even drink sea water without harm. In marked contrast, sea water is intolerable to man because the human kidney cannot eliminate the excessive amounts of salts.

BIOLOGICAL RHYTHMS AND CLOCKS

Many plants and animals, including man, exhibit daily rhythms of behavior and physiology that are controlled or regulated, at least in part, by internal timing devices. So reliable are the internal control mechanisms that they have been termed *biological clocks*. The clocks of some organisms such as butterflies, lizards, and sparrows are set for maximal activity during daylight hours, whereas those of fireflies, mice, and owls are set for nocturnal undertakings. Persistent biological rhythms represent important adaptations of organisms to the normal periodic fluctuations of the physical environment. The clocks are set to enable organisms to adjust their feeding, reproduction, and other activities precisely to recurring rhythmic changes in light, barometric pressure, humidity in the atmosphere, and other factors in their natural surroundings.

Man has a built-in capacity to measure time accurately, although this uncanny sense generally is unnoticed. It is evident in those individuals who can awaken at a specific time without the necessity of an alarm clock, or can strictly observe an appointed time without wearing a watch. Man's biological rhythms are labile, as evidenced by his sensitivity to abrupt switches of time when he travels by air across time zones. The symptoms of jet fatigue are the consequences of time-zone changes rather than duration of the flight. Most travelers adjust to a new behavioral cycle, or schedule of activity, at the rate of one hour a day.

Man shows a persistent daily rhythm of internal temperature in the systematic rise and fall of 2°F every 24 hours. As figure 13.5 shows, body temperature rises in the morning, remains high until late evening, and then declines. Pulse rate and also blood pressure exhibit cyclical patterns that parallel the temperature rhythm. These rhythms do not depend on exercise or eating, since they persist unmodified in persons who are confined to bed, or eat irregularly, throughout the day.

Man's mental keenness and physical skills apparently decrease as the body temperature drops. Hormones of the adrenal cortex fall to their lowest levels in the late evening and reach peak levels shortly before a person arises in the morning. The early morning secretion of adrenocortical hormone is thought to promote the state of wakefulness or alert-

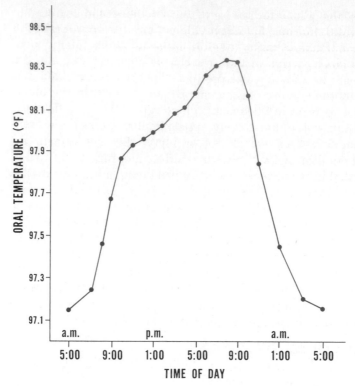

Figure 13.5 Rhythm of oral temperature in a group of 70 males studied by W. P. Colquhoun, laboratory of Experimental Psychology, University of Sussex, England. (From *Biological rhythms and human performance,* 1971, ed. W. P. Colquhoun, Academic Press.)

ness. It has been suggested that low levels of adrenocortical hormone, in association with low body temperature, contribute to fatigue at the end of the day. Dr. Franz Halberg and his associates at the University of Minnesota School of Medicine have found that the dual rhythms of adrenal hormones and body temperature differ from one strain of inbred mice to another. Comparable genetic variation in humans may account for the distinction between alleged "morning" types and "night" types. In morning people, the rise in temperature apparently occurs earlier (and declines earlier) than in night people.

In mice and humans, the levels of glucose and amino acids in the blood follow a 24-hour rhythm. The rate at which a given protein is used appears to depend on the time of day. The amino acid levels in the blood become conspicuously elevated when certain proteins are ingested at 8:00 a.m., but remain unchanged when the same proteins are taken in at 8:00 p.m. This has led some investigators to suggest that foods may be used more efficiently early in the day, the implication being that a hearty breakfast could profitably serve as the main meal of the day. Man's proclivity for a large evening meal, however, may be causally related to his circulating levels of adrenocortical hormone. There is a curious inverse relationship between adrenocortical secretion and taste and smell acuity. Taste and smell sensitivity increases as the blood levels of adrenocortical hormone decrease. Accordingly, in the evening, food tends to taste and smell better.

THEORIES OF THE MECHANISM
The search continues for the stimulus that triggers the rhythmic behavior patterns. One group of scientists contends that the biological clocks are wholly self-contained and independent timepieces that operate even in the absence of external signals. This view holds that the

organism is internally programmed to respond in a specific way at a specific time regardless of any environmental cues. This tenet has been referred to as the *endogenous-clock* hypothesis. Other investigators claim that the biological clocks are governed by forces external to the organism, just as a man-made electric clock cannot function unless it is plugged into an electrical circuit. The organism thus must continually receive information from rhythmical environmental synchronizers such as the changing positions of the sun or moon, or even the recurring fluctuations in the gravitational or magnetic fields of the earth. This view has been called the *exogenous-clock* hypothesis. The conflicting hypotheses, or the difficulties of interpretation, should not obscure the fact that biological rhythms do exist.

The 24-hour biological rhythms persist even when the organism is brought to the laboratory and isolated from the usual natural environmental cues. However, under constant laboratory conditions, the rhythmic activities do not adhere to a *precise* 24-hour cycle. Flying squirrels, for example, under experimental conditions of constant darkness exhibit activity rhythms that range from 23.0 to 24.5 hours. Since biological rhythms only approximate a daily period, Franz Halberg of the University of Minnesota in 1959 designated the rhythm as *circadian*, from the Latin *circa* ("about") and *dies* ("day"). The word *about* is crucial —the rhythm is slightly shorter or longer than 24 hours. Colin S. Pittendrigh of Stanford University, a leading advocate of the endogenous theory, has argued that a rhythm that only approximates a day's length can best be ascribed to an independent, internal timer in the organism. Stated another way, if periodic environmental forces were responsible for the rhythms of an organism, then the precise geophysical cues would be expected to synchronize the activities of the living organism into an exact tempo. Moreover, the phases of a circadian rhythm can be altered or reset by shifting the period of illumination. In essence, the biological clock may be reset by external stimuli, but it is not dependent for its operation on the external cues. It may be compared to a self-winding calendar wristwatch with a built-in timer.

Frank A. Brown, Jr. of Northwestern University has challenged the concept of autonomous timers within the organism. Brown transported oysters, collected in Long Island Sound, westward to his laboratory at Northwestern University in Evanston, Illinois, some 850 miles inland. Initially, the oysters opened and shut their shells in tempo with the tides of the Atlantic seaboard. After about two weeks, however, the oysters lost their original tidal rhythmicity and synchronized the opening and closing of their shells to the time of upper and lower transits of the moon in Evanston. In a sense, the oysters had responded to a different inflow of timing information, "atmospheric" tides rather than ocean tides. Presumably the environment is always generating some sort of rhythmic signal to which the organism is sensitive. Brown and his associates placed young potato plants in a hermetically sealed system, shielding the growing potatoes from such factors as changes in light, temperature, pressure, and humidity. Yet the sprouting potatoes exhibited a characteristic, highly reproducible, 24-hour pattern of variation in oxygen consumption. The growing potatoes may have responded to one or more geophysical periodicities, including variations in electrostatic fields, terrestrial magnetism, and background radiation.

F. A. Brown, Jr. thus contends that organisms are continuously receiving information from natural, subtle geophysical forces that synchronize the organism's behavior. The organism is held to be capable of receiving or counting the oscillations that come from the external pacemakers. However, it would be difficult to pinpoint a particular external force as being responsible for a specific biological rhythm. Since the geophysical environment includes a wide variety of electrostatic, electromagnetic, and magnetic fields, the correctness—or incorrectness—of Brown's concept can scarcely be established.

MEDICAL ASPECTS

Circadian variations in physiological processes in humans are attracting increasing attention among medical scientists and clinicians. Halberg and his associates demonstrated a persistent daily rhythm in the level of certain blood cells (eosinophils) in the circulation of healthy individuals. They could not find, however, a similar rhythm in the blood of patients with Addison's disease, hypopituitarism, or inflammation of the adrenal glands. Patients with diabetes mellitus show periodic variations in the excretion of β-hydroxybutyric acid. It has been suggested that insulin injections in diabetic patients should be timed in accordance with the daily rhythm of β-hydroxybutyric acid. Accordingly, the determination of circadian rhythms in bodily functions could prove useful both in the diagnosis and treatment of a disease.

There are specific rhythms of susceptibility or tolerance to disease-causing bacteria, drugs of various kinds, and alcohol. Laboratory mice, for example, show varied susceptibility to pneumonia depending on the time of day when the mice are exposed to the bacterial *pneumococci*. Experimental rats suffer the greatest mortality from the barbiturate *Nembutal* when this drug is administered during the early part of their activity cycle, which corresponds to the very early morning hours in humans. Mice are especially vulnerable to large doses of alcohol during the early hours of activity, but are tolerant of the same doses at the end of a day's activity. This rhythm of varied tolerance to alcohol seems also to prevail in humans.

Records of birth in various hospitals reveal the presence of a periodicity in human births. As figure 13.6 shows, the highest incidence of deliveries occurs in the small hours of the morning. The peak in birth frequency has been found between 3 a.m. and 4 a.m., with a trough in the

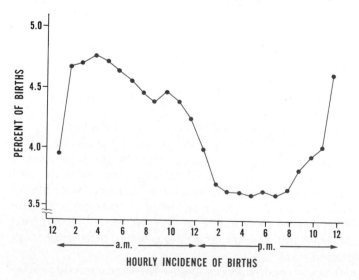

Figure 13.6 Hourly incidence of human births, based on 601,222 deliveries. (Data from studies of I. H. Kaiser and F. Halberg, *Annals of the New York Academy of Sciences* 98 (1962): 1056–58.)

late afternoon between 2 p.m. and 6 p.m. The highest incidences of still-births and births associated with neonatal mortality occur among the late-afternoon deliveries. Although there are many difficulties in analyzing such data, a better understanding of rhythms in birth might enable medical scientists to detect and treat certain malformations before they become serious or crippling.

SUMMARY

Homeostasis denotes the stable internal conditions of living organisms that are maintained by self-regulating processes. The regulatory reactions offset or minimize any disturbing changes imposed upon the body. The constancy of the internal environment is achieved by the coordinated activities of the varied tissues and organs. The careful integration of various systems of the body is evident in the regulation of the sugar level of the blood, the control of internal temperature, and the maintenance of a water balance.

Many organisms have regular cycles of activity that are keyed to one or more rhythmic changes in their natural surroundings. Man behaves in harmony with natural cycles, although most physiological rhythms are generally unnoticed. Body temperature, blood pressure, urinary excretion, blood sugar, and levels of amino acids, among others, vary in a rhythmic manner. It is not yet clear whether the persistent rhythms are generated by independent, internal timing devices in the organism (biological clocks), or whether they are dependent upon a continual input by some outside periodic timekeeper.

Ethical Probe 9
Limitations of Human Behavior

The attainment of good health is a goal that rarely conflicts with personal and social objectives. Nevertheless, there are several personal behaviors, prominent among them excessive cigarette smoking and alcohol intake beyond moderation, that individuals in modern society seem unwilling or unable to recognize as important deterrents to good health. The hazards associated with heavy smoking and chronic drinking are clear and measurable. Beyond doubt, the statistical association between cigarette smoking and lung cancer strongly indicates a cause-and-effect relation. Likewise, degeneration of the liver (cirrhosis) is an inevitable consequence of chronic alcoholism. Yet the remedies to prevent smoking or to curb excessive consumption of alcoholic beverages have not been effective or they have been elusive.

Both smoking and alcohol intake are more than simple personal habits; each behavior is woven into the daily social interactions of people. Despite unrelenting medical warnings and vigorous health campaigns, heavy smokers and problem drinkers have shown a strong disinclination to change. The failure to effect a positive change underlines the strength of the social and psychological factors that contribute to the persistence of each habit.

Whether the problem is cigarette smoking, alcoholism, drug abuse, or any other behavior that society abhors, should it be left solely to the individual to decide if he or she wants to overcome the maladjustment? Are the attitudes of the physician or society regarding the so-called adverse behavior irrelevant? Would you condone treating patients against their wishes, particularly with the knowledge that the treatment is medically correct or appropriate?

14 Transplants and Immunity

The 1960s will go down in medical history as the decade of the heart transplant. The world's first heart transplant patient was Louis Washkansky of Cape Town, South Africa. In 1967, Washkansky's frail heart was replaced with the sound heart of another person by the surgeon Christiaan N. Barnard at the Groote Schuur Hospital, Cape Town. Barnard used the surgical procedures that had been developed by the pioneering efforts of Norman Shumway and Richard Lower at Stanford University in California. The successful operative technique attests to the skill and intrepidity of the surgeon. However, although surgical competence is no longer a limiting factor, it is clear that a more important problem revolves around successfully suppressing or circumventing the patient's immune response.

The principal barrier to successful transplantation of tissues is rejection of the graft by the recipient. A transplanted tissue or organ contains proteins that are foreign to the recipient; such alien proteins are called *antigens*. The antigens elicit in the recipient a specific antagonistic reaction, known as an *immune response*, which involves the formation of *antibodies*. The antibodies destroy the cells of the transplant and remain in the host's system to afford future protection against antigens of the same kind. When a given antibody has been produced and is present in the body, the person is said to possess an *immunity* against the specific antigen that evoked the antibody. Each antigen has its own unique characteristics and the antibody produced is specifically directed against that antigen.

The successful "take" of a transplant depends on damping the host's immune response. Thus far, methods that have been used to depress the patient's immune system have also diminished his capacity to combat infectious bacteria and viruses. The outcome is that the patient often succumbs to infectious microorganisms that he normally would ward off. Since Barnard's initial trial, several hundred human heart transplants have been performed in various parts of the world. Most of the patients failed to survive beyond one month, and few lived for a year. Many medical scientists have urged cautious progress, and in particular, a limit on heart transplantations, if not their discontinuation, until the immune problems are solved. The search continues for the means to mitigate or abolish the recipient's immune mechanism. At the same time, studies on the fundamental nature of the immune response have been intensified.

HISTORICAL ASPECTS

The science of immunology was born with the discovery of the smallpox vaccine by the 18th century English physician Edward Jenner. It was common knowledge among country people that milkmaids, continually exposed to cowpox, rarely contracted the similar but much more serious

184

human disease, smallpox. Jenner reasoned that the milder cowpox protected the milkmaids against the more severe smallpox. In 1796, Jenner deliberately inoculated an eight-year-old boy with matter from cowpox pustules on a milker's hands. Six weeks later he inoculated the boy with the smallpox germ. The boy did not succumb to smallpox; he had built up antibodies against the cowpox antigen that subsequently sheltered him from the smallpox antigen. From these observations, Jenner developed the concept that an induced mild form of a disease would protect the individual against a more virulent form of the disease. Jenner employed the term *vaccine* (Latin *vacca*, meaning "cow") for the inoculant taken from the cowpox sores. Later, Louis Pasteur extended Jenner's findings to other infectious diseases (anthrax, rabies, and chicken cholera) and advocated the expression *vaccination* for protective inoculation in general as homage to Jenner.

Perhaps the most intriguing of Pasteur's many investigations were his experiments on chicken cholera, a bacterial disease that decimated populations of fowls in France in the 1800s. Pasteur isolated the cholera bacteria, and in the late spring of 1879, he grew laboratory cultures of the germ. His research work on cholera was interrupted by other endeavors during the summer months and it was not until the early fall that he managed to reexamine his cultures. Although the bacterial cultures had been left unattended for several months, Pasteur decided to inoculate healthy chickens with these cultures of long standing. The old cultures did not produce cholera in the fowls, or they induced only a mild attack at best. When these same fowls were then inoculated with newly grown, fully virulent bacterial cultures, they showed no signs of cholera. Apparently the old bacterial cultures had immunized the fowls against a culture of full strength. Thus, by the fortunate happenstance of neglecting his cultures, Pasteur arrived at a new principle. Although this reveals how chance discovery can operate in scientific research, we may be reminded of Pasteur's cryptic but penetrating remark: "*Chance favors the prepared mind.*"

Pasteur established the general principle that a host animal could be rendered immune by microorganisms that had been so weakened (attenuated) that they were no longer capable of causing disease. This doctrine is still in force today. Many modern vaccines consist of attenuated or even dead microorganisms that cause the body to produce antibodies that can later stave off any natural infection by the fully virulent microorganism. For example, the Salk polio vaccine consists of inactivated viruses. On the other hand, the Sabin polio vaccine consists of living viruses; although they are infectious, they do not invade the central nervous system but do incite antibody formation.

After a single injection of a vaccine or foreign antigen, a specific antibody appears in amounts that vary with the quantity of antigen administered. The production of antibody after a single initial injection is known as the *primary response*. In the absence of additional injections of antigen, the concentration of antibody declines gradually, although many weeks or even years may elapse before the specific antibody is completely lost from the bloodstream.

When a second injection of antigen is given, new antibody is rapidly synthesized to a point where its concentration is much greater than its original level. This phenomenon of heightened antibody response is known as the *secondary response*. Thus, the antibody level may be maintained at high levels by periodic (booster) injections of antigen.

From the rapid and vigorous nature of the secondary response, it seems that the cells that synthesize the antibodies not only recognize the specific antigen but also "recall" their previous experience with that antigen. Indeed, antibody-synthesizing cells are said to have an *immunological memory*. How the cells possess a memory for producing a specific antibody is one of the searching questions in modern immunology.

MEDAWAR'S SKIN-GRAFTING EXPERIMENTS

That the rejection of a tissue graft, such as a skin transplant, involves an immune response on the part of the recipient was first clearly demonstrated by the English biologist Peter Medawar in the early 1940s. A piece of skin transplanted from one adult mouse to another initially "heals in" well but then shows signs of inflammation by the 4th or 5th day. By the 10th day, the entire graft is completely destroyed (fig. 14.1). The destruction of the skin graft takes place under a massive infiltration of certain white blood cells, specifically the *small lymphocytes*. There is no doubt that the rejection process is set in motion and directed by immunological mechanisms. This is evidenced by the secondary (or second-set) response, in which a second skin graft from the same donor mouse is rejected in an accelerated and much more violent fashion. The inflammatory reaction begins earlier and large numbers of small lymphocytes invade the area of the rejected graft. Survival of the second-set skin transplant extends to no more than 6 days. Evidently antibodies persist in the recipient to protect and mount a rapid attack against a second invasion of the same antigens. It should be mentioned that the same antigens occur in a wide variety of cells of the donor. Thus, a slice of liver or a suspension of spleen cells is capable of sensitizing a recipient against a later graft from the same donor of liver, spleen, or skin.

When skin is transplanted from one region of the body to another within the same person, antibodies are *not* produced. Such a transplant, technically known as an *autograft*, takes successfully and survives indefinitely. Rejection occurs when transplants are made between two individuals of the same species (*allografts*) or between individuals of different species (*heterografts*). In essence, unless the individuals are

Figure 14.1 The immune response. A transplant of skin from one mouse (A) to another (B) is rejected in 10 days (first-set response). A subsequent skin graft from the same donor animal (A) transplanted 10 days later is rejected in a vigorous and accelerated fashion (within 6 days).

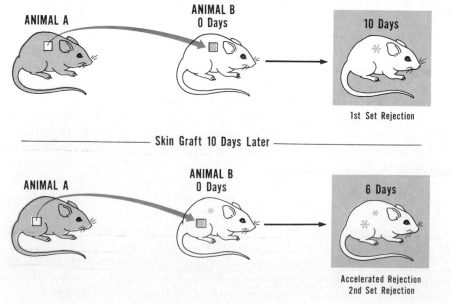

ANIMAL A

ANIMAL B
0 Days

10 Days

1st Set Rejection

——————— Skin Graft 10 Days Later ———————

ANIMAL A

ANIMAL B
0 Days

6 Days

Accelerated Rejection
2nd Set Rejection

genetically identical, it can be expected that the transplantation of tissue between two persons will not be permanently successful.

Whereas antibodies are classically thought of as circulating freely in the bloodstream, the presence of large numbers of small lymphocytes in the rejection site suggests that lymphocytes, rather than soluble (or *humoral*) antibodies, are the more important factors in the rejection of the skin transplant. In 1955, Avrion Mitchison of the National Institute for Medical Research in London showed that the sensitivity to grafts could be readily transferred by lymphocyte-producing tissue (such as the spleen) but not by means of blood serum (fig. 14.2). This finding supports the notion that the rejection of a solid tissue graft is mediated by antibodies bound to the surface of lymphocytes (cell-bound antibodies) rather than by soluble agents in the serum.

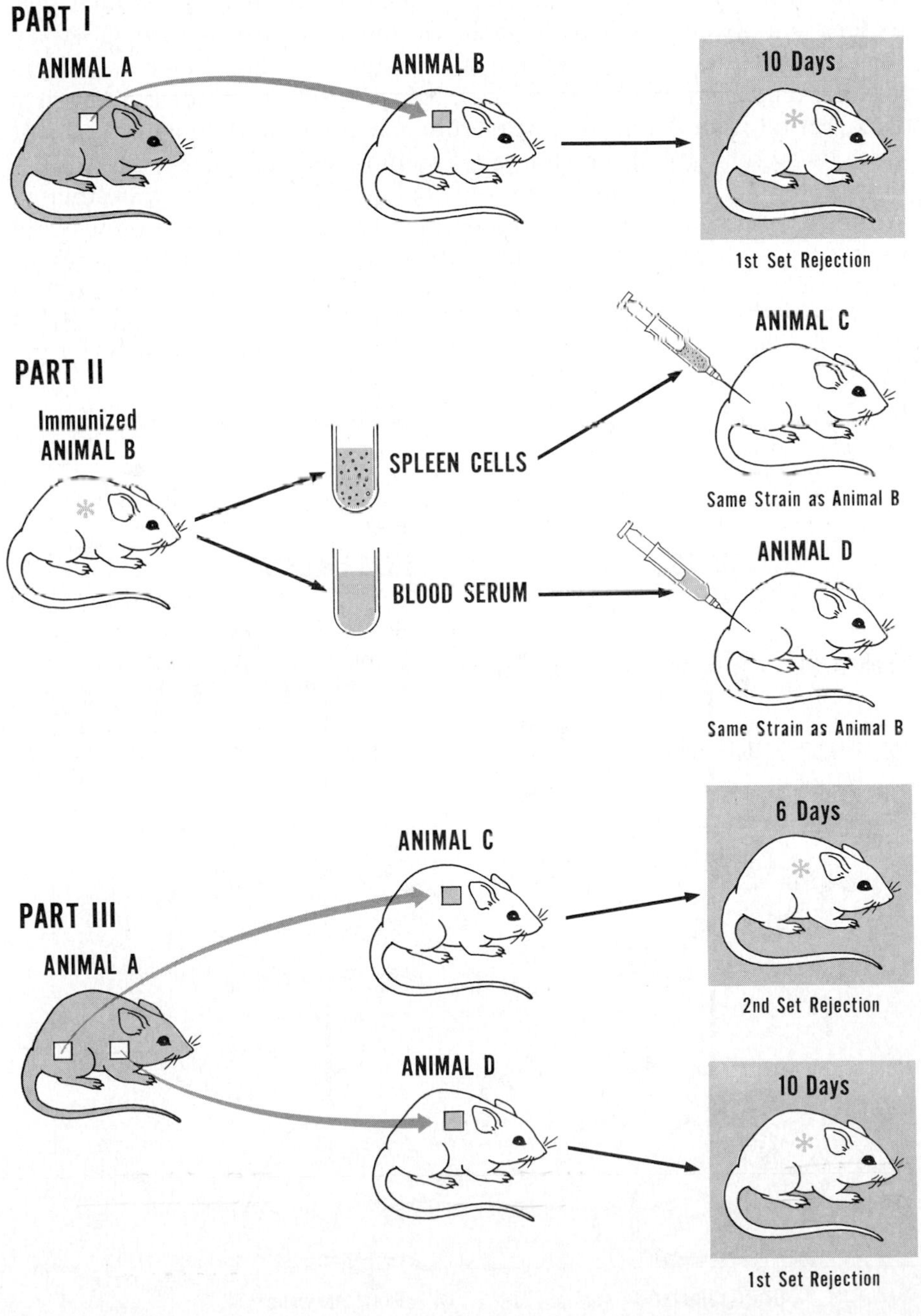

Figure 14.2 Transfer of immunity. In the first phase of the experiment (Part I), skin is transplanted from a strain-A mouse to a strain-B mouse. This graft is rejected in 10 days (first-set response). In Part II, the immunized strain-B host mouse is bled and the spleen is removed. Spleen cells are then injected into a normal mouse (labeled *C* but of the same strain as animal B) and the blood serum is injected into another normal strain-B mouse (labeled *D*). Several days later (Part III), both animals (*C* and *D*) receive a skin transplant from the same strain-A mouse that contributed the initial skin transplant in the first phase (Part I) of the experiment. The skin graft in the animal (*C*) that received the spleen cells is rejected in 6 days (second-set response) whereas the skin graft in the serum-treated animal (*D*) is rejected in 10 days (first-set response). This series of experiments shows that immunity to skin grafts can be transferred by cells (lymphocytes) but not by serum. In other words, the rejection of a solid-tissue graft is a cell-mediated type of immunity rather than one dependent on humoral (circulating) antibodies.

PHENOMENON OF TOLERANCE

In 1949, Sir MacFarlane Burnet and F. Fenner proposed, in an enthralling book entitled *The Production of Antibodies,* that an organism acquires the capacity to distinguish self from nonself antigens during embryonic or early postnatal life. They suggested that foreign, or nonself, antigens introduced into the embryonic period of the host would be treated as self in the later life of the host. In other words, an organism will fail to react against antigens with which it comes into contact in embryonic life. It is as if the host organism has been deceived by the artificial introduction of the foreign antigen and has learned to recognize and accept the antigen as self. In the parlance of transplantation immunity, we say that *tolerance* has been induced in, or acquired by, the host animal.

The concept of tolerance was given a definite status by the experimental work of Medawar and his colleagues in 1953. Tolerance was experimentally induced in a specific strain of mouse (called CBA) by injecting the fetus *in utero* with a suspension of living spleen cells from another mouse strain (A-line mouse). When the CBA recipient after birth was grafted with A-line skin, it readily accepted the A-line graft as if it were its own (fig. 14.3). The tolerance so induced was specific since CBA mice tolerant of A-strain skin rejected grafts from other, unrelated strains. It was subsequently demonstrated that *in utero* injection was not necessary and that mice injected intravenously within a few days of birth could be rendered tolerant. Injections made thereafter were found to be ineffectual in inducing tolerance. Thus, an organism exposed to a foreign antigen in the early developmental stages fails to develop the capacity to respond immunologically to that antigen if introduced again in adult life. For developing the concept of tolerance, Burnet and Medawar shared the 1960 Nobel prize in physiology and medicine.

Figure 14.3 Induction of tolerance. A suspension of spleen cells, prepared from an adult A-strain donor, is injected into a newborn CBA-strain host. When the CBA-strain host becomes an adult, it readily accepts (tolerates) a skin graft from an adult A-strain animal. In contrast, the control CBA-strain animal (one that had not in early life received A-strain spleen cells) rejects in typical first-set fashion a skin graft from an A-strain animal.

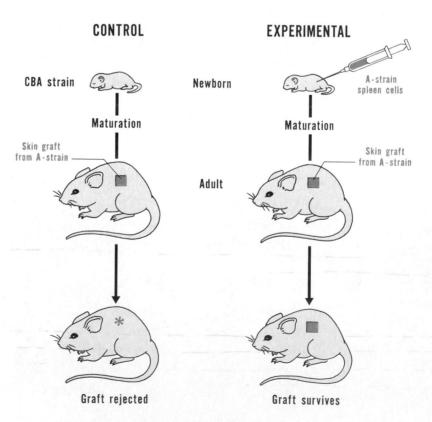

Tolerance depends for its persistence on the continued presence of the tolerance-inducing antigen. In host animals made tolerant by injection at birth of donor spleen cells, the spleen cells actually settle down and form a permanent population in the host. One might surmise that the donor antigenic cells become modified or altered during their residence in the tolerant host. This, however, is not the case. When the donor spleen cells are removed from the tolerant animal and transferred to another host, they elicit an immune response in the secondary host. Accordingly, the donor spleen cells retain their antigenic capacity. How the alien spleen cells inhibit the tolerant host's reactive system is still an open question. We may now turn to a consideration of some experiments that have been directed at elucidating the mechanism of tolerance.

MECHANISM OF TOLERANCE

In 1945, Ray Owen, then a young assistant professor at the University of Wisconsin, observed that dizygotic, or two-egg, cattle twins contain mixtures of two genetically distinct types of blood cells. Each twin possesses not only its own unique erythrocytes (red blood cells) but also erythrocytes proper to the other twin. The presence of a mixed blood cell population—known technically as *blood cell chimerism*—is traceable back to events in fetal life. The union of placental vessels permits the reciprocal exchange of primordial blood cells, and the translocated red cell precursors become established and perpetuate themselves in the blood-forming tissues of the respective hosts. The chimeric twin calves are incapable of reacting to each other's blood antigens. Blood cell chimerism was only one way in which dizygotic cattle twins, with their background of admixture of placental circulations, showed tolerance. Medawar and his colleagues demonstrated that dizygotic cattle twins freely accept skin grafts from each other, even when the twin pairs are of unlike sex. This mutual tolerance is specific since pieces of skin transplanted from other unrelated individuals are quickly rejected.

Tolerance conferred in twin cattle may be viewed as a providential natural experiment. The establishment of blood cell chimerism, accompanied by tolerance, depends on the fortuitous interconnection of fetal vessels. This state of affairs can be experimentally duplicated in the laboratory. In the 1960s, E. Peter Volpe and Bryan M. Gebhardt, both at Tulane University, joined two frog embryos in parabiosis at an early stage of development (fig. 14.4). The embryos were united side-to-side

Figure 14.4 Induction of tolerance by parabiosis. Two frog embryos are joined side-by-side in the region of the gills to ensure the free interchange of blood cells. The united embryos are seen from dorsal, or top, view (a) and ventral, or bottom, view (b). In adult life (c), each partner contains a mixed population of blood cells and each readily accepts a skin graft from the other.

A

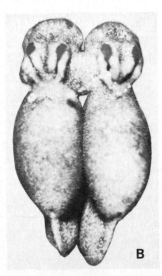
B

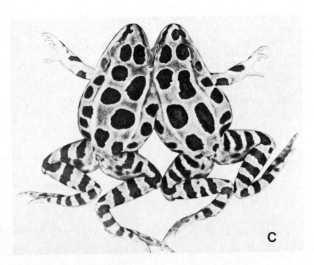
C

in the gill region to ensure mingling of blood. In later life, each member of a pair was found to have blood-forming tissue that could produce two kinds of blood cells, its own kind and that of its partner. Skin grafts exchanged between the parabiotic frogs were fully tolerated. The state of tolerance was characterized by a high degree of individual specificity. That is to say, parabiotic frogs accepted skin grafts only from their partners, and not from any other individual. Maintenance of tolerance in the parabiotic frogs appears to be assured by the persistence of blood cell chimerism. Nevertheless, the mechanism by which tolerance is initially induced still eludes us. Burnet's ingenious theory, described in the following section, may furnish at least a partial answer.

BURNET'S CLONAL SELECTION THEORY

Both immunity and tolerance are responses to antigenic stimulation. In what way do antigen and antibody-synthesizing cells interact to produce one response or the other? In 1956, Sir MacFarlane Burnet proposed that the antibody is made in accordance with genetic instructions contained in the nucleus of the cell synthesizing the antibody. Thus, antibodies are made essentially the same way that other cell proteins are synthesized.

According to Burnet, the antigen does not instruct a previously indifferent cell how to produce an antibody. Stated another way, the antigen molecule does not direct the antibody-producing cell to shape the antibody molecule to fit it. Rather, the necessary information for the synthesis of antibody is already contained, or incorporated, in the genetic mechanism of the cell. The role of the antigen is simply to *select* the cell that is endowed genetically with the capacity for producing the suitable antibody to react against that particular antigen (fig. 14.5).

Burnet's hypothesis demands a prodigious variety of potential antibody-forming cells to account for the wide repertoire of possible antibody responses. The repertoire would include responses against antigens like artificial laboratory-produced proteins, which the animal would scarcely expect to encounter in nature. The view is that the repertoire is like a dictionary that lists only foreign words, and that the dictionary contains all the foreign words even though the cell may never have heard or seen them. Thus, among the cells that produce antibodies, we would find a large, but not infinite, number of patterns (foreign words). A given cell would be able to furnish a complementary specific antibody molecule to correspond with a particular antigenic determinant.

If Burnet's comparison with a foreign dictionary is not easily perceptible, perhaps the analogy furnished by Gerald Edelman of Rockefeller University will be clearer. Edelman likens the antibodies to ready-

Figure 14.5 Two theories of immunity. The *instructive* hypothesis (A) holds that the antigen serves as a template from which a complementary antibody is produced. The *selection* hypothesis (B) holds that a given antigen selects the appropriate antibody-producing cell, and by mere contact with that cell signals the cell to produce the corresponding antibody.

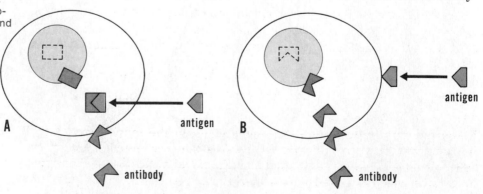

made suits. The antigen is a buyer who selects a suit that has already been manufactured (synthesized) rather than one who informs (instructs) a tailor to make a suit (antibody) to fit him to order. A discriminating buyer shops at a store with a very large stock of suits in a great variety of sizes and styles. The immune system is comparable to a shop with a sufficiently large stock of suits that virtually any customer (antigen) can be accommodated. Since the antigen normally stimulates the antibody-producing cell to make large quantities of the antibody, Edelman's analogy can be extended to include the provision that after a given suit is selected, the manufacturer proceeds to make thousands of exact copies of the suit.

Burnet submits that it is not difficult to visualize how the organism might create its large store of foreign words (or suits). Lymphocytes are the most likely carriers of the words or antibody patterns. In the early stages of embryonic life, the primordial lymphocytes are assumed to be highly susceptible to genetic change. The specificity for all possible antibody patterns could be created by spontaneous, random changes of the genes. Each changed, or *mutated*, cell could divide repeatedly to form a group of identical cells, a *clone*, each of which would possess a pattern for one specific antibody. The process calls for, admittedly, a very high rate of mutation. Evidence for this high mutability in primordial lymphocytes is lacking. Conceivably, the number of specific antibody patterns may not be exceptionally large. Antigen molecules may not be very discriminating or highly selective, in the same way that several buyers (antigens) can fit into one suit (antibody) more or less well.

Burnet's theory provides for the destruction or suppression of forbidden clones—that is, clones of cells potentially able to react against self components. By contact with self antigens at an early stage of development, clones of antibody-producing cells that match the self antigens would be eliminated. Accordingly, at the end of fetal life, the only immunologically competent cells remaining are those capable of synthesizing antibodies to foreign, or nonself, antigens. In a sense, the body has purged itself of all words of its own language.

Burnet's theory also accounts for immunological memory, which is responsible for the observed rapidity and vigor of the secondary immune response. The initial antigenic stimulation selectively causes formation of the appropriate clone by repeated cell division and thus the production of antibody. The animal is then equipped with a large population of specifically sensitized cells, which would be available to react to a fresh antigenic stimulus at a later date.

Finally, the theory can explain the phenomenon of tolerance. When foreign cells are introduced into a host organism during embryonic life (as in chimeric cattle twins or experimentally produced parabiotic frogs), the alien donor cells actually destroy all the antibody-producing cells capable of reacting to the particular donor antigens. The donor antigens thus come to be accepted as self.

Burnet's resourceful clonal selection theory has stimulated a very large amount of fruitful experimental work.

ROLE OF THE THYMUS

Definitive data implicating the thymus gland in the maturation of the immune system were provided by the Australian scientist J. Miller. In 1961, he demonstrated that thymectomy (removal of the thymus) of newborn mice was associated with a marked deficiency in the lymphocyte population of the body and an impairment of the capacity to reject foreign skin grafts. In other words, foreign skin grafts that ordinarily would be quickly rejected exhibited prolonged, if not indefinite, survival in mice thymectomized early in life. However, the removal of the thymus in later, or adult, life did not weaken the immune mechanism. Apparently then, the thymus in early life is an indispensable organ that ensures the normal development of the body's pool of lymphocytes. The lymphocytes, we may recall, are the agents responsible for the destruction of alien skin grafts. One way that the thymus appears to exert its influence is by contributing lymphocytic cells, or their precursors, to the spleen, lymph nodes, and other lymphoid tissues. In support of this seeding function of the thymus is the observation that immunological responsiveness can be restored in young, thymectomized mice by implanting in them suspensions of spleen or lymph nodes.

Whereas the thymus is apparently the principal contributor of lymphocytic cells in early life, the bone marrow appears to gain prominence in later life as the main source of lymphocytes. Current evidence indicates that precursor, or stem, cells from the bone marrow can develop into two distinctly different types of lymphocytes, called *T-lymphocytes* and *B-lymphocytes* (fig. 14.6). On appropriate stimulation by antigen, each type can proliferate and undergo further morphological changes. The B-lymphocyte differentiates into a *plasma cell*. Under the electron microscope, a mature plasma cell is seen to have an extensive rough-surfaced endoplasmic reticulum, which is characteristic of a cell producing protein for export. Indeed, the plasma cell actively synthesizes and secretes the classical humoral antibodies, or soluble agents in the blood that confer immunity against viruses.

Figure 14.6 Two populations of lymphocytes: T-cells and B-cells. Precursor cells from the bone marrow are processed by the thymus gland and gut-associated lymphoid tissues (the bursa of Fabricius in the chicken) to become immunologically competent T-lymphocytes and B-lymphocytes, respectively. T-lymphocytes are involved in cell-mediated immunity; B-lymphocytes are concerned in the synthesis of circulating antibody. (From I. M. Roitt, *Essential immunology,* 1971, Blackwell Scientific Publications.)

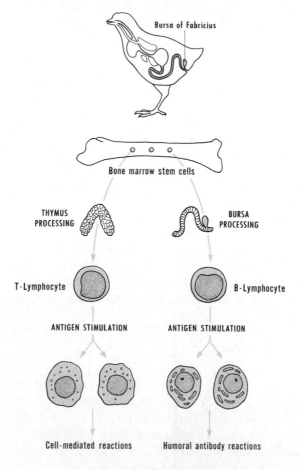

Bursa of Fabricius

Bone marrow stem cells

THYMUS PROCESSING

BURSA PROCESSING

T-Lymphocyte

B-Lymphocyte

ANTIGEN STIMULATION

ANTIGEN STIMULATION

Cell-mediated reactions

Humoral antibody reactions

On the other hand, the T-lymphocyte transforms into a cell, a *lymphoblast*, that has virtually no rough-surfaced endoplasmic reticulum. The lymphoblast has abundant free ribosomes, which are concerned with the synthesis of antibodies built into the plasma membrane but not secreted (at least, not in appreciable amounts) as free antibodies. These lymphoblasts are responsible for cell-mediated immunity, that is, the destruction of solid-tissue grafts, such as skin transplants.

It should be noted (fig. 14.6) that the two types of lymphocytes are under the control of, or processed by, two different organs. The T-lymphocytes are processed by the thymus, or in some way depend on the thymus for their expression. The B-lymphocytes, in the case of chickens at least, depend on the *bursa of Fabricius*, a saclike outgrowth of the wall of the fowl's cloaca (fig. 14.6). That the bursa is significant in maturation of the antibody-synthesizing plasma cells was revealed in an elaborate series of studies in the 1960s by Robert Good, then at the University of Minnnesota and now at Sloan-Kettering Institute for Cancer Research in New York. Good's investigations on the bursa furnished strong evidence for the existence, structurally and functionally, of two separate immunity systems—cell-mediated and humoral. (The implications of the two-immunity system concept for cancer are considered in the next chapter.) No precise equivalent of the chicken's bursa has yet been found in man or other mammals. Several possible candidates have been nominated, which include such gut-associated lymphoid tissues as the tonsils, adenoids, Peyer's patch, and even the vermiform appendix.

Only brief consideration can be given to the voluminous recent work on the chemical nature of the soluble, or humoral, antibodies. The modern era of research on the antibody molecule began in 1959 with investigations conducted at the Rockefeller University by Gerald Edelman and his colleagues. The activity of soluble antibodies had long been associated with the gamma globulin fraction of blood serum. With the recognition of the heterogeneity of globulin molecules, those that can function as antibodies have been collectively called *immunoglobulins*. In man, five principal structural types or classes have been distinguished: immunoglobulin G (abbreviated IgG), IgM, IgA, IgD, and IgE. One of the significant findings is that the immunoglobulin molecule is made up of multiple polypeptide chains instead of a single chain. The chains have been separated from one another by chemical means and have been analyzed. Figure 14.7 shows the symmetrical four-peptide model of IgG

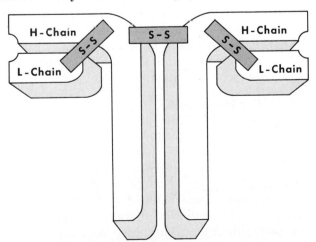

Figure 14.7 Basic structure of an antibody molecule (immunoglobulin), showing the symmetrical four-polypeptide configuration. The two heavy and two light polypeptide chains are linked together by interchain disulfide bonds.

consisting of two heavy and two light chains linked together by interchain disulfide bonds. It is the amino acid sequences of the polypeptide chains that determine the immunological specificity of particular antibodies.

IMMUNOSUPPRESSION

In transplant surgery, the overriding requirement is to create a condition in which the recipient develops a tolerance to the foreign antigens. We have seen that there are experimental means of inducing tolerance in organisms. One involves the introduction of the foreign antigen into the newborn. Another involves the parabiotic union of two embryos. There are still other methods, but all offer little hope of human application since they would not be practicable.

Endeavors in recent years have centered on means of suppressing the host's immune mechanism without rendering the host vulnerable to bacterial infection. In the early days of transplant surgery, the host's immune defenses were assaulted with massive doses of X-irradiation, which often had distressingly severe side effects. More sophisticated methods have recently been developed, which involve the use of immunity-suppression drugs, or *immunosuppressants,* such as azathioprine (Imuran), 6-mercaptopurine, azaserine, and cortisone. Of these, azathioprine is the most widely used by transplant researchers, and is routinely administered to kidney transplant recipients. These agents are antimetabolites that interfere with the synthesis of antibody proteins. Unfortunately, these drugs tend to be toxic to the living system and the results have been far from ideal.

The ideal immunosuppressant would be one that would delete the cell-mediated immune response while leaving intact the humoral immune mechanism to combat disease organisms. In the late 1960s, attention became directed to a type of immunosuppressive drug that held promise of being selective in its action. This is *antilymphocyte serum,* or ALS. The rationale of ALS is as follows. By provoking a specific antiserum against the human lymphocyte in an animal that is an effective antibody producer—the horse, for example—one should be able to direct an immunologic attack against those cells known to participate in the rejection of organ transplants. Antilymphocyte serum acts mainly on lymphocytes and consequently should damage only part of the total immune machinery. Theoretically, the part that is damaged involves those components responsible for the cellular type of immunity that work against solid grafts, while the part that is spared involves those cells that manufacture soluble or circulating antibodies that deal preferentially with bacteria and viruses. Regrettably, it is now clear that cellular immunity is also important for effective humoral defense against viruses, and ALS does inhibit the host's humoral defense against these infective agents. This has tended to encourage conservatism in the use of ALS.

DONOR SELECTION

Just as there are special antigens that distinguish the red blood cells into the classical blood groups (A, B, AB, and O), there are surface antigens in the white blood cells that determine which tissues a host will consider foreign or nonforeign. White blood cell typing is more intricate than red cell typing, but already at least 30 different so-called *histocompatibility antigens* have been isolated and identified. A complete inventory of these antigens will permit the successful matching of donors and recipients. Donor selection based on antigen matching is one of the main hopes of minimizing graft rejection. Antigen matching has proved very useful in kidney transplantation. Part of the success, however, stems from the fact that the donor can spare one of his two kidneys. Accordingly, there can be a larger choice among potential donors with matching antigens from siblings or close relatives.

Transplantation surgery is not likely to become the principal treatment for heart disorders, particularly since it depends on the availability of properly matched hearts from cadavers. Aside from the circumstance that the supply of organs is limited, heart transplantation raises philosophical and ethical questions. Is the donor actually dead if his heart can be resuscitated in another individual?

ARTIFICIAL ORGANS

Many medical scientists are convinced that the ultimate answer will come from the use of artificial, or mechanical, organs. A mechanical kidney was developed in 1966 for clinical use, and a model has now been devised for home use. Few chronic kidney patients can personally afford the costs of an artificial kidney; a massive social program would be exceedingly costly and put a strain on qualified medical manpower. The same may be said for the artificial heart-lung system, which can be operated only by a highly skilled team of technicians. Only the largest hospitals have the elaborate heart-lung apparatus, which has been prominently used in open-heart surgery.

Finally, perhaps the most difficult problem is whether the elderly—those likely to be the candidates for living transplants or mechanical organs—really want them. It has been said that life is judged by its meaning and not merely by its duration. The transplant of a new heart or new lung does not alter the processes of aging and senility. The degenerative aspects of senescence have been graphically described by Aldous Huxley in *After Many a Summer Dies the Swan*, to which the reader is referred.

SUMMARY

In an age that brings technical competence in replacing diseased organs with transplants from donors, rejection of the transplant (graft) by the host body remains a problem. Antibodies are produced in response to an initial contact with foreign proteins (antigens), and the body thereafter possesses an immunity against the same antigens. The thymus gland and bone marrow are important contributors of antibody-producing cells. Antibodies either may be bound to the surface of small lymphocytes (cell-bound antibodies) or may be soluble agents circulating in the blood (humoral antibodies). The cell-mediated antibodies are responsible for the destruction, or rejection, of solid-tissue grafts, such as skin transplants.

An animal will not react against its own antigens (self antigens). It also will not react against a foreign antigen that is introduced in embryonic life. In later life, the animal will recognize, or tolerate, that foreign antigen as self. Much remains to be learned about the mechanism by which an animal recognizes and accepts an otherwise alien antigen as self.

When a person's body is prepared to receive a solid-tissue graft, efforts are made to dampen, or suppress, his immune mechanism without rendering him vulnerable to bacterial or viral infection. However, suppressing the cell-mediated immune response also affects the soluble, or circulating, antibodies that deal with bacteria and viruses, and the infective organisms may flourish, to the detriment of the individual being treated.

Ethical Probe 10
Laetrile Controversy

Laetrile (the chemical amygdalin) is found in the kernels of many fruits, notably apricots, peaches, plums, and bitter almonds. The use of Laetrile as a cancer drug got its first major impetus in the United States in 1920 when Ernst Krebs, a California physician, tried apricot pits in treating cancer patients. In recent years, many American patients have been clamoring for Laetrile, hopeful that the U.S. Food and Drug Administration would approve its use. The FDA has resisted on the grounds that Laetrile is worthless against cancer.

Most cancer researchers oppose the legalization of Laetrile since this chemical has not been demonstrated unequivocally to be effective against cancer. The FDA requires that any drug must be shown to be both safe and effective before the drug can be marketed. If an exception is made for Laetrile, then it would erode FDA's jurisdiction over other drugs. Moreover, If Laetrile were made available to cancer patients, the patients would probably forego life-saving cancer treatments and take Laetrile instead. Supporters of Laetrile believe that cancer patients should have access to any drug they choose irrespective of the edicts of the FDA.

Does a person have the right to choose whatever form of health maintenance or health care he or she wishes?

Cancer, Degenerative Diseases, and Aging 15

There are two great classes of fatal diseases in the later decades of the life of man—*cancer* and *cardiovascular disease*. The former, in large measure, is the antithesis of the latter. Cancer cells grow and proliferate vigorously, are fairly normal in appearance, and are functional, although serving no useful function. In contrast, cardiovascular disease is associated with cell deterioration; the cells are notably disordered and lack structural organization.

The cancer cell stands convicted of dividing repeatedly when it should not. There are many known cancer-inducing agents (*carcinogens*), notably organic chemicals, irradiation, and viruses. For decades, scientists were discouragingly thwarted in their determination to explain the cause of cancer in terms of a single mechanism. The outlook today is dramatically different. Armed with increasing understanding of the machinery of the cell, cell biologists are now convinced that there is a common pathway of action, which resides in the genetic apparatus. Mounting evidence suggests that carcinogens release cells from the state of suppression of their genetic information that normally inhibits cell division.

Cardiovascular disease is the most widespread human ailment, and a principal consequence of aging in man. *Hypertension* (high blood pressure) and *atherosclerosis* (hardening of the arteries) are two prominent forms of cardiovascular degeneration. Although generally thought of as distinct disorders, both hypertension and atherosclerosis (particularly the latter) are so common among the aged that they may be merely inescapable manifestations of growing old. Aging is characterized by the gradual impairment of the structure and function of cells and tissues. Little is known of the causes and mechanisms underlying such deterioration. It has been said that an individual begins to age following conception.

CANCER

Cancer, or malignant neoplasm, may be defined as the uncontrolled multiplication of abnormal cells. It is not a single disease entity; it appears in many forms and in many different tissues and organs of the body. It may exist as a localized solid mass (a *tumor*) or circulate freely in the bloodstream (*leukemia*). Typically the cancerous cells do not remain confined to their original tissues but invade other parts of the body, where they proliferate and form multiple tumor sites. The spread of the abnormal cells to other, distant sites has been termed *metastasis*. Cancer cells exert their deleterious effects by disrupting the vital activities of the organs in which they happen to be proliferating. It is the overgrowth of cancer cells that leads to death of the organ, and if they are unchecked, to eventual death of the organism.

In all industrialized countries (England, the United States, the Netherlands, and Japan, for example), the incidence of cancer among males is increasing. This may reflect, in part, better diagnostic procedures for the detection of cases of cancer of the lungs, prostate gland, and colon. The two prominent areas of cancerous attack in males are the lungs and the skin (fig. 15.1). Women are far less prone to cancer in these two regions, but are highly susceptible to neoplasms of the breast and uterus. The significant decline in recent years in cervical cancer emphasizes the

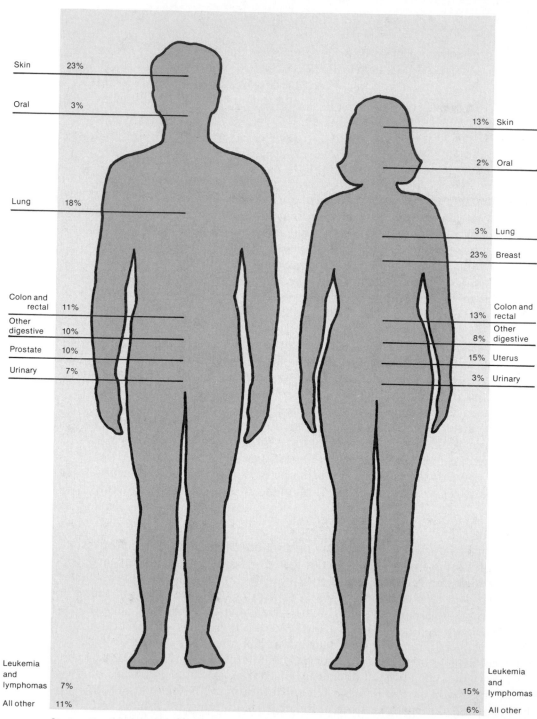

Courtesy, American Cancer Society

importance of mass programs for the cytological (*Papanicolaou*) detection of this type of cancer in its early, curable stage. The incidence of lung cancer among females has shown an upward trend in the last decade, which is the price, some claim, the woman pays for her emancipation as a smoker.

Many factors may contribute to the onset of malignancy. Cancer has been causally linked to cigarette smoking (with air pollution as a superimposed factor), to many organic chemicals, to irradiation, to viruses, and to hormonal imbalance. Heredity undoubtedly plays a role, since certain kinds of cancer occur more frequently in some families than in others.

It is not an easy task to demonstrate unequivocally that a given environmental factor is cancer-inducing, or carcinogenic, in man. An illustrative case is the induction of lung cancer by tobacco smoke. An experimental animal in the laboratory, such as the mouse, is incapable of inhaling smoke voluntarily, as man does, and special apparatuses have been constructed to introduce specified doses of smoke passively into the lungs of the laboratory mouse. Thus, such factors as the mode of administration of smoke or the extent of exposure are not strictly comparable between man and mouse. Notwithstanding the absence of faithful comparability, neoplasms of the lungs have been induced in mice by prolonged exposure to cigarette smoke. Most informed persons no longer challenge the monumental data that have linked cigarette smoking and lung cancer. Cigarette smokers run a significantly greater risk of lung cancer than nonsmokers. One of the deleterious ingredients in tobacco smoke has been identified as N-nitrosodimethylamine.

Carcinogens in polluted air are thought to contribute to the high incidence of lung cancer. Automotive and industrial soot contains benzopyrene, a potent cancer-inducing agent, at least in experimental animals. The list of suspected or known chemical carcinogens is now almost endless. To cite a few more, individuals continually exposed to soot have a high incidence of skin cancer, coal miners and asbestos workers often develop lung cancer, individuals working extensively with benzol tend to develop leukemia, and habitual users of cyclamates are prone to cancer of the bladder.

In certain types of cancer, the relationship between carcinogenic agents and malignancy has been very elusive. For example, the human male may be responsible for creating the conditions for inducing cancer of the cervix in the female. Epidemiologists, who examine the prevalence of diseases, have wryly observed that nuns rarely develop cervical cancer. Equally striking is the finding that the incidence of cervical cancer is exceedingly low among Jewish women whose husbands are circumcised. Moreover, uncircumcised men are treated more often for penial cancer than are circumcised men. The suspicion, then, is that the carcinogenic agent occurs in the smegma, the thick cheesy secretion found under the foreskin. However, the carcinogen in smegma has yet to be identified, although a particular strain of virus has been implicated.

Some interesting parallels have been found between mammary gland cancer in mice and breast cancer in humans. A virus, called *Bittner* virus (after the discoverer), has been shown to induce mammary tumors in mice. The virus is transmitted from the mother to the suckling young through her milk, and all female offspring develop mammary cancer when they reach maturity. Critical proof of the mode of transmission of the milk virus was obtained when newborn females from an unaffected mother were nursed by a foster mother afflicted with cancer. These females later developed mammary cancer. Alternatively, female offspring born of an affected mother fail to develop mammary tumors in later life if they are suckled by a healthy foster mother. Such flawless, decisive experiments are scarcely admissible in humans. Interestingly, many women with breast cancer harbor a viruslike particle in their milk that bears a strong resemblance to the mouse cancer virus. Moreover, the human milk virus occurs predominantly in families with a history of breast cancer, just as certain strains of mice are highly susceptible to mammary cancer whereas others are not vulnerable. It remains to be seen whether the similarities in human and mouse breast cancers are merely fortuitous or valid. One of the complicating, and still puzzling, features of certain viruses is that they may occur in the human with inconsequential effects and yet be powerful carcinogens in experimental animals such as the mouse and hamster.

In man, a particular virus, the so-called *herpes virus,* has been traditionally associated with cold sores, shingles, and chicken pox. This type of virus has been definitely linked to infectious mononucleosis and to Burkitt's lymphoma, a childhood disease related to leukemia that occurs primarily in Africa. A herpes-type virus consistently appears in cultured cells established from patients with various kinds of malignancy, including leukemia of children, chronic leukemia of adults, American Burkitt-like lymphoma, and Hodgkin's disease. Unfortunately, the same type of virus has also been found in the normal cell lines being maintained as controls. Thus, a virus may be detected, or even isolated, in human cancerous conditions, but this by itself does not demonstrate that the virus is the inducer of the cancer.

An unresolved enigma of cancerous growth is the long interval of time that separates the initial exposure to an inductive agent and the manifestation of the detectable cancer. Female mice do not develop mammary cancer until long after they have been weaned. Lung cancer reaches the visible stage many years after the initial encounter with the causative agent. A chemical, *diethylstilbestrol* (DES), widely used to correct estrogen deficiency disorders in women, has been recently incriminated as a carcinogen. Pregnant women have been advised to avoid the use of this compound lest their infant daughters might later develop vaginal cancer.

LUNG CANCER

The process by which a tissue undergoes progressive changes towards malignancy is well illustrated by lung cancer. Microscopic observations of autopsied lungs have revealed that lung cancer typically is initiated in the walls of the bronchi, or air tubes. For this reason, lung cancer is technically designated *bronchogenic carcinoma,* the former word meaning "originating in the bronchus." A carcinoma is a malignant growth consisting of *epithelial cells* that infiltrate surrounding tissues and give rise to multiple tumors. Epithelial cells form the linings, or coverings, of internal surfaces. The pathological changes in lung cancer thus begin in the cells that line the surface of the bronchus.

There are essentially three kinds of cells that contribute to the formation of the epithelial lining of the bronchial wall (fig. 15.2). The cells projecting into the lumen are tall, columnlike (hence, *columnar*) cells that contain hairlike projections, or *cilia*. Interspersed are cuplike *goblet* cells, in which the free ends are distended with mucus for secretion. At the bottom of the epithelium are *basal* cells, which normally form one or two rows above the connective tissue layer of the wall. Epithelial

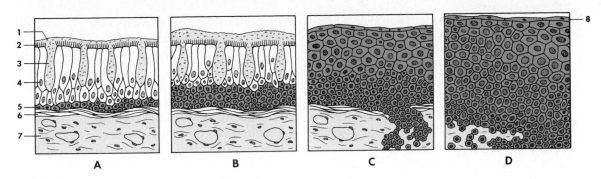

A   B   C   D

cells are protective in function. Cilia sweep inhaled particles (dust and bacteria) back toward the pharynx, and the particles are carried in that direction in the mucus secreted by the goblet cells.

Airborne pollutants, including inhaled smoke, have an irritating effect on the epithelial cells. Some carcinogenic agent acts as a trigger for the wanton process of cell division. The basal cells multiply unchecked and uncontained, and migrate into areas normally occupied by the goblet and columnar cells (fig. 15.2). The goblet cells secrete excessive mucus, with the consequence that the heavy secretions cannot be moved efficiently by the cilia. The cilia then deteriorate. Certain cellular changes thus signal a *precancerous* condition, the most important of which are the multiplication of basal cells and the disappearance of cilia. The nucleus of a cancerous cell tends to be larger than normal, takes a darker stain, and is more irregularly shaped. For the most part, however, the internal structural changes in malignant cells are not striking nor very specific. Thus, a cancerous cell is not particularly sickly in appearance. A precancerous condition is reversible. If the source of irritation is removed, the premalignant cells become replaced with normal cells.

Presumably a cellular mass, or colony, of critical size develops before the tissue becomes irreversibly malignant. With the continued multiplication of basal cells, the columnar cells become displaced. As a result of the loss of cilia, mucus remains stationary within the bronchi. The lung itself now becomes affected since, as mucus accumulates, air becomes trapped in the alveoli, or air sacs. When the walls of the thin air sacs rupture under pressure, the condition called *emphysema* arises. There is no cure for emphysema inasmuch as alveolar tissue cannot be repaired. Its progression, however, can be arrested.

In the absence of arrest of the progression, the outer surface of the lungs becomes marred by *blebs* (pockets of air). In the bronchi, the cancerous basal cells invade the deeper tissues of the wall. Moreover, the malignant flattened (or *squamous*) cells of the internal surface, now in great abundance, block the passageway. At this time, the only hope for survival—although a slim one—is the removal of the patient's lung. More often than not, as is characteristic of carcinomas, the cancerous epithelial cells spread by means of the circulatory system to other parts of the body. Malignant growths in lung cancer patients have been found in such widely scattered areas as the adrenal glands, the liver, and the brain.

FAILURE IN REPRESSION
In an earlier chapter, we learned that different cells become specialized both structurally and functionally, even though each cell has the genetic machinery for performing all the functions of every cell in the body. The manifold potentialities of a cell become restricted during development.

Figure 15.2 Lung cancer. Lung cancer usually starts in the lining (epithelium) of the bronchus (air tube). The normal lining (A) shows columnar cells (4) with hairlike cilia (2), goblet cells (3) that secrete mucus (1), and basal cells (5) from which new columnar cells arise. A basement membrane (6) separates the epithelial cells from the underlying connective tissue (7). In the first stage of lung cancer (B), the basal cells divide repeatedly, and crowd the columnar and goblet cells. The goblet cells secrete excessive mucus, and the cilia function less efficiently in moving the heavy mucus secretion. With the continued multiplication of basal cells (C), the columnar and goblet cells are displaced. The wanton basal cells penetrate the basement membrane, and invade the deeper connective tissue. In the terminal stage of cancer (D), the bronchial lining contains only flattened, or squamous, cancer cells (8), which are so abundant that they block the passageway of the bronchus. The cancer cells may spread throughout the adjacent lung tissue and to other parts of the body.

This restriction in potentialities applies also to the capacity of the cell to divide. Thus, cell differentiation is typically accompanied by the establishment of a control, or regulatory, mechanism that places a premium on cell division. In some differentiated cells, such as adult nerve cells and muscle cells of the heart, the division process is permanently arrested. Other cells, like those that line the intestinal tract and blood cells, multiply at a rate just sufficient to replace damaged or dead cells. Every cell in the body, then, has the information necessary to enable it to divide, but some factor arises during differentiation that acts to restrain cell division. This factor is presumed to be a chemical substance, termed a *repressor,* which attaches to a particular segment of the chromosome and inhibits or limits the flow of information from the gene, a *regulator* gene, that controls cell division. (The concept of repressors and regulator genes will be developed in detail in subsequent chapters.)

Viewed in light of this attractive hypothesis, cancer is a disruption or failure of the genetic mechanism regulating normal cell division. Specifically, the carcinogen—whether it is an organic chemical, irradiation, or a virus—somehow frees the repressor so that the formerly suppressed genetic information may instruct the cell to begin dividing rapidly. If this is a correct interpretation, the genetic machinery must become modified to account for a self-perpetuating change in dividing cells. In support of this view, abnormalities of chromosome structure and numbers are frequently found in cancerous cells. However, many investigators now believe that the abnormal shapes and numbers of chromosomes are not the initial or primary event in carcinogenesis but rather the consequence of malignancy. This is an important change in view, since the implication is that the regulator gene itself is not damaged; rather, the expression of the gene is modified. If the fault resides in the flow of genetic information or gene expression, then cancerous growth becomes more amenable to reversibility to normal if suitable controls can be restored.

Cancer cells are less differentiated than are the normal cells from which they were derived. They apparently revert to their undifferentiated, or totipotent, state. As a striking example, it has been shown that certain carcinomas of the bronchus secrete the hormone ACTH (adrenocorticotrophic hormone), which is normally only the prerogative of pituitary gland cells to produce. Similarly, leiomyomas (tumors of smooth muscles) in females have been found to contain both forms, or types A and B, of the enzyme glucose-6-phosphatase dehydrogenase, whereas normally the individual cells of the female contain type A or type B, but not both. It is difficult to explain these phenomena except as a derepression of the cancerous cells. That is to say, the genetic controls have been removed and the cells become reendowed with embryonic potentialities.

ROLE OF VIRUSES

Several investigators have hypothesized that viral infection is a necessary condition for carcinogenesis. Certain findings suggest the manner in which virus particles can be triggering agents for malignant growth. Most neoplasms, possibly all, are associated with the appearance of new proteins. Interestingly, cells that undergo malignant transformation after experimental infection with a virus also show the appearance of new proteins. Accordingly, it has been suggested that the synthesis of new proteins is directed by the virus. This view is strengthened by our knowledge of viral activity. Isolated virus particles are inert, exhibiting none of the properties attributed to living systems. Virus particles are able to reproduce, or produce copies of themselves, only after they have invaded a living cell. Viruses are slavishly parasitic; they depend completely on the living cell to provide the biochemical machinery and energy for their own duplication. Specifically, when a virus infects a cell, it takes over control of the protein-synthesizing apparatus of the cell and directs it towards synthesis of its own peculiar proteins.

In essence, under the direction of the virus, the cell proceeds to produce proteins that the cell has not previously synthesized. Since the chemical makeup of the cell has been transformed, the new, or virus-directed, proteins may be termed *transforming* proteins. These transforming proteins may be the crucial agents that derepress the cell to cause it to divide in an uncontrolled manner.

A disconcerting aspect is that investigators are often unable to find intact virus particles in experimental animals afflicted with a cancer that was indisputably induced by the virus. It is as if the virus implants instructions for cancer production in the cell nucleus, and then disappears. By the time cancer develops, the infective agent is no longer present, or rather it is undetectable. The solution to the problem of the disappearing virus resides in the finding that a viral particle can become incorporated into the genetic apparatus of the host cell. A virus can actually become integrated into one of the chromosomes of the cell's nucleus, thus bringing in new hereditable information that can be passed on to many cell generations.

We can carry the scheme one step further by suggesting that we harbor, from the moment of conception, the potential cancer-inducing virus in our chromosomes. Indeed, in 1969, Robert Huebner and George Todaro of the National Cancer Institute proposed that the genetic information for cancer is transmitted from parent to child and is present in all normal cells from the beginning of life. The supposition is that infection of cells by certain types of viruses occurred millions of years ago during the course of evolution. Viral particles presumably became incorporated as a result of viral infection in our early ancestors and have been passed down through succeeding generations. At the present time, each cell contains a cancer-associated gene, or *oncogene*, which is normally repressed. The oncogene can be derepressed by a number of carcinogenic agents, including hormonal changes in the body. Some investigators now believe that hormonal imbalances are significant in activating the tumor-producing oncogenes. When the oncogene is derepressed, it expresses itself by producing transforming proteins, and consequently, cancerous growth.

IMMUNITY AND CANCER

Cancer patients often exhibit a marked depression of their immune system. They cannot reject foreign skin grafts or do so only slowly. This had led to the speculation that one important function of the immune system is to destroy precancerous cells before they have a chance to multiply wantonly. It is only when the immune surveillance breaks down that the precancerous cell has the opportunity to proliferate in an unchecked manner. We have seen that the transformation of a normal cell into a malignant cell involves the production of new proteins. These new proteins should be recognized as foreign antigens by the host organism. It has even been suggested that carcinogenesis is a common, recurring event in the human body and that the numerous silent cancers are destroyed by antibodies as soon as they arise.

We are already familiar with the two basic immune responses, *cell-mediated* and *humoral*. The humoral component most likely evolved in higher organisms as protection against the ubiquitous microorganisms. It is difficult to envision the origin of the cell-mediated component, since it could scarcely have emerged in nature as an adaptive response against man-devised skin grafts and organ transplants. Robert Good has proposed that cell-mediated immunity arose as an elaborate defense against antigenic, precancerous cells in the body.

CARDIOVASCULAR DISEASE AND DIABETES

Hypertension and *atherosclerosis* are two complex cardiovascular diseases for which all the causative factors remain obscure. Hypertension, or high arterial pressure, stems from structural changes in the small arteries, or arterioles, which result in a narrowing of the lumen of the vessels. Abnormally high blood pressure may exist for years in early life without producing symptoms, but then take an acute, stormy course in late adult life. The consequences of prolonged hypertension may be heart failure (resulting from constriction of heart vessels), cerebral hemorrhage (rupture of an arteriole in the brain), or kidney damage (occlusion of the renal arteries).

Atherosclerosis is a degenerative condition associated with thickening and hardening of the arteries. The condition is characterized by an excessive accumulation of lipids and deposits of cholesterol in the inner walls of arteries (plate 8). Lipids apparently infiltrate from the blood although some are probably synthesized in the wall itself. Progressive thickening of the wall leads ultimately to complete occlusion of the lumen. The narrowing of one or more coronary arteries may lead to heart attack; the occlusion of cerebral arteries may produce a stroke. The arterial wall may become so weakened that a portion of the wall balloons out, forming an *aneurysm*. The rupture of an aneurysm produces massive hemorrhage and generally death.

The atherosclerotic process progresses steadily with age, as denoted popularly by the pithy aphorism that a person is "as old as his arteries." Some medical authorities contend that atherosclerosis is a disease of young people as well as the old; fatty deposits have been observed to accumulate in infants under five years of age. Atherosclerosis is more prevalent in affluent societies than in countries with low economic standards. In the United States and England, it is the single most common cause of death, an estimated 500,000 deaths per year. Diet and stress apparently are prominent causative or contributory factors. The profile of a high-risk atherosclerotic individual is very clear: a middle-aged male who is obese, physically inactive, experiences anxiety about his responsibilities, and has high blood pressure and high blood cholesterol. Heart attacks from coronary atherosclerosis are 10 times more common among men than among women. The protective agent in women is estrogen, which tends to depress the blood levels of cholesterol as well as forestall the deposition of lipids in the arterial walls.

Because cholesterol is a constituent of the thickened arterial wall widespread attention has been given to reducing cholesterol and saturated fats in the dietary intake. Cholesterol, we may recall, is a component of bile; it is also an important precursor of certain hormones. Our main source of cholesterol is animal fats, including egg yolks. To forestall or arrest the atherosclerotic process, many nutritionists have urged diets containing primarily unsaturated fatty acids, found in vegetable fat. Diets containing unsaturated fats, particularly linoleic acid (present in appreciable amounts in corn, cotton, and safflower oils), apparently cause, in a manner not completely understood, a significant depression of blood cholesterol and other lipids.

Many persons with cardiovascular disease are mild or latent diabetics in whom atherosclerosis overshadows the carbohydrate abnormality. Although hardening of the arteries has a high incidence among nondiabetic subjects, it occurs even more frequently and at an earlier age in diabetic patients. This has suggested to some investigators that a common metabolic disturbance may underlie both diabetes and cardiovascular disease. The immediate cause of diabetes is insulin deficiency and a concomitant disturbance in the way the body uses glucose (see chapter 13).

In the United States, there were 2 million diabetics in 1960; 4 million currently have the disorder; and estimates indicate that 6 million will become clinically diabetic by 1985. There are two general types of diabetes—*juvenile-onset* and *maturity-onset*. The former type, as the name implies, is typically found in children and is the more serious of the two types. Maturity-type diabetes covers about 90 percent of the diabetics, usually overweight individuals between the ages of 35 and 60. Untreated, the diabetic is susceptible to visual disorders (cataracts, glaucoma, and detached retinas), heart attacks, strokes, and kidney ailments. After age 25, women (especially married women) are more likely to develop diabetes than men. In fact, about 67 percent of all diabetics are women.

Heredity has long been recognized as an important factor in the occurrence of diabetes. The scheme in table 15.1 has been used by medical counselors in estimating the risk of diabetes in members of families of diabetics. Viruses have recently been implicated in the pathogenesis of diabetes. The hereditary predisposition to diabetes may be unmasked by particular viruses. In childhood, certain viruses may damage permanently the insulin-producing (beta) cells of the pancreas to cause juvenile-type diabetes. The pancreatic cells may be only affected mildly by the viruses but, in later life, maturity-type diabetes may arise when an extra physiological burden (added weight in middle age, for example) exacerbates the early virus-induced pancreatic weakness. It is also possible that maturity type diabetes is the outcome of the cumulative effects of several viral infections during different periods of life.

Relative with Diabetes		Diabetic Relative on Other Side of Family	Maximum Risk (in Percentages)
Parent	plus	Grandparent, and aunt or uncle	85%
Parent	plus	Grandparent, or aunt, or uncle	60
Parent	plus	First cousin	40
Parent			22
Grandparent			14
First cousin			9

Table 15.1
Probabilities of Diabetes

AGING

The aging process in man is gradual, inexorable, and cumulative. The process cannot be reversed or avoided. Gerontologists (specialists in the study of aging) are hopeful of finding the means of slowing down the aging process. Inevitable changes that occur with age are the graying of hair (the failure to synthesize melanin), wrinkling of the skin (loss of elasticity), loss of teeth, decreased muscular strength and coordination, decline in mental capacity and visual acuity, and decreased sensory perception, among others.

We remarked earlier that cells normally divide at a minimal rate sufficient to replace damaged or dead cells. With the passing of time, cells progressively lose the power to replace themselves. The genetic apparatus becomes increasingly defective, presumably as a result of changes, or mutations, in the genes themselves. Failure in the capacity to divide leads to the loss of cells from tissues and organs, such as the heart, skeletal muscle, brain, and kidney. Evidence that cell loss does occur has been brought forward by Nathan Shock of Stanford University. The human brain, for example, weighs considerably less in old age than it does in the middle years. At the age of 35, a person begins to lose an estimated 100,000 brain cells each day. There is a gradual impairment of virtually all bodily functions (table 15.2). The rate of breathing declines with advancing age, the heart pumps less blood in a given time, the extent of glucose reabsorption in the kidney decreases, and several endocrine glands secrete smaller quantities of hormones. Quite simply, then, aging may be inevitable "wear and tear"—a progressive deterioration in structure and function.

Part of the inability of aging cells to function properly is attributable to changes in the fibrous elements of cells, particularly *collagen* and *elastin*. Collagen becomes more rigid with age, and elastin loses its characteristic resiliency. Wrinkling of the skin and loss of elasticity of the tendons are two examples of changes in these fibrous materials. Ex-

Table 15.2
Functional Losses Accompanying Aging

Type of Decline or Loss	Remaining Functions or Tissues* (In Percent)
Weight of brain	56
Number of spinal nerve fibers	63
Velocity of nerve impulse	90
Flow of blood to brain	80
Adjustment to normal blood pH after displacement	17
Output of heart at rest	70
Number of glomeruli in kidney	56
Glomerular filtration rate	69
Number of taste buds	36
Maximum oxygen uptake during exercise	40
Maximum breathing capacity	43
Hand grip	55
Basal metabolic rate	84
Water content of body	82
Maximum work rate for short burst	40

* Figures are the approximate percentages of functions or tissues remaining in the average 75-year-old male, taking the value found in the average 30-year-old male as 100 percent (based on studies by Nathan W. Shock).

cess collagen is believed to be deposited as a result of stress. Once deposited, the hardened collagen fibers interfere mechanically with the supply of nutrients to the tissue. The importance of collagen cannot be overstated; it constitutes approximately a third of all of the body proteins and serves as a general binding substance of the skin, muscular, and vascular systems.

Some investigators assert that aging is a genetically programmed event. Leonard Hayflick of Stanford University has suggested that the death of cells resulting in the malfunctioning or demise of tissues is a normal, programmed event in the development of the organism. The finite lifetime of normal cells constitutes a programmed mechanism that sets an overall limit on the length of life of the organism. Accordingly, even if we could overcome all of the degenerative diseases, the individual would inevitably succumb to the ultimate failure of normal cells to divide or function. If the life span is genetically programmed, it is not inconceivable that the program can be manipulated or altered to extend life by many years. There is some element of truth to the quixotic comment that the best way to achieve a long life is to choose long-lived parents (table 15.3).

One of the more widely discussed theories is that aging reflects progressive inefficiency of the endocrine system. A dramatic example of profound disturbances in hormonal balance is the curtailment of ovarian estrogens after menopause. The decline of ovarian steroids leads to an enhanced production of gonadotropins by the pituitary. In turn, the elevated secretion of gonadotropin in postmenopausal women is associated with an increased output of gonadotropin-releasing factors by the hypothalamus. The secretion of growth hormone (GH) is also adversely affected by the estrogen decline; the reduced output of GH impairs the normal functioning of the liver, pancreas, and other internal glands. The changing hormonal levels may also depress immunological functions. There is, inescapably, hormonal imbalances in advancing age.

Earlier we noticed that the immune apparatus may be inextricably involved in cancer; it may also be intimately associated with aging. The decline in immune capacity may be related to alterations in thymus-dependent cell-mediated responses, the failure to hold self-reactive cells in check, or the emergence of incompatible cells from formerly normal cells. If the immunological characteristics of a cell were to change, the cell would become a foreign cell in that individual and would be rejected in the same way as a foreign graft. The most likely mechanism by which formerly normal cells become alien is through gene mutation. Thus, changes in the genetic apparatus may be a strong contributing factor to aging. Aging may be due primarily to the deterioration of the genetic program that orchestrates the development of cells. As time goes on, the performance becomes disharmonious with the accumulation of copying errors, or mutations.

Father's Age at Death (In Years)	MOTHER'S AGE AT DEATH (IN YEARS)		
	Under 60	60–80	Over 80
Under 60	32.8*	33.4	36.3
60–80	35.8	38.0	45.0
Over 80	42.3	45.5	52.7

Table 15.3
Influence of Longevity of Both Parents on the Expectation of Life of the Offspring

* Figure represents the average duration of the offspring (in years).

SUMMARY

Cancer cells destroy the tissues in which they are multiplying, and tend to spread to other, distant sites of the body. A variety of agents (carcinogens) have been suspected of causing cancer, including many organic chemicals, irradiation, and viruses. The mechanism by which carcinogens induce cancer is still not established. A unifying hypothesis holds that cancer is a failure in the genetic machinery regulating cell division. There normally exists a control, or regulatory, mechanism that restricts or limits cell division. Carcinogens apparently disrupt the repressor mechanism that ordinarily restrains cell division, and the cells divide in uncontrolled fashion.

Cancer may be triggered by viral particles. Some investigators contend that potential cancer-inducing viruses are present in all normal cells of the body from the moment of conception. The cancer-inducing viruses are normally repressed, but some factor, including hormonal changes in the body, may cause the viruses to express themselves. Many cancer patients exhibit a marked depression of their immune system. The immune system may act to destroy precancerous cells before they have a chance to proliferate wantonly.

Cardiovascular disease is associated with cell deterioration. Cardiovascular disease and diabetes appear to be linked, suggesting a common metabolic disturbance underlying both diseases. Even though the body may manage to stay free of debilitating diseases, aging persists. Normal cells apparently have a finite lifetime. Aging appears to be a normal, programmed event in the history of the individual.

Ethical Probe 11
Formulating Responsible Policy for Health Care

The discovery of polio vaccine was hailed as a significant medical advance. In recent years, however, there has been a sharp drop in the proportions of children receiving polio vaccinations. At present, probably one-third of the children between one and four years are not adequately protected. The problem is particularly acute in poverty areas of major cities, where as many as half the children are without full protection against polio. There are undoubtedly many difficulties facing poor families that make it difficult for them to bring their children to be vaccinated, but the service itself is available in most cities.

The utilization of medical care is voluntary, but evidently the mere availability of a free service does not guarantee its use. Nevertheless, people insist that medical care is, or should be, a "right." If people claim to have a *right* to medical care, do they also have an *obligation* to use it? Are you prepared to accept the obligation that is almost always associated with the granting of a right?

Plate 12 Life in time. (From *Science year, the world book science annual.* © 1973 Field Enterprises Educational Corporation.)

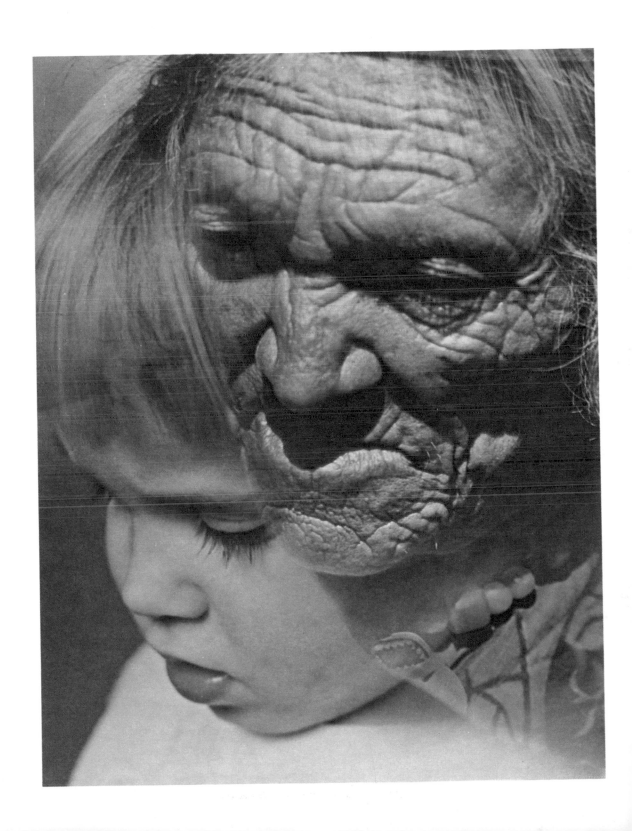

Plate 13 A microscopic view of a normal human artery in cross section (top). In the diseased artery (bottom), the channel is partially occluded by arteriosclerosis. Fatty deposits and other materials have thickened the arterial wall, reducing the blood-carrying capacity. (Alfred T. Lamme for Camera M.D. Studios, Inc.)

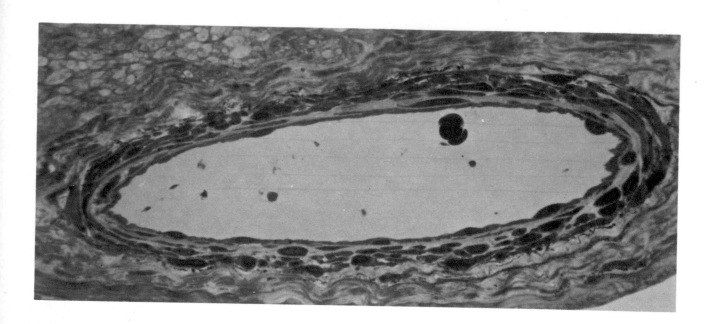

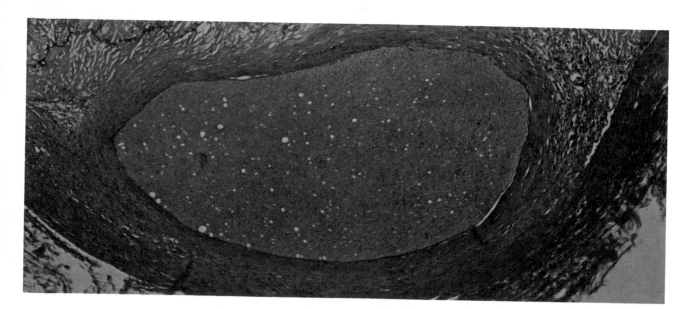

2

Man
Patterns
of Heredity

16 Chemical Basis of Inheritance

More than a century ago, in 1866, the humble Austrian monk Gregor Mendel solved the basic riddle of heredity with his astute observations on the crossbreeding of pea plants in his small monastery garden. Mendel's profound inference was that traits are passed on from parents to offspring, through the gametes, in specific and discrete factors, or units. The individual units do not blend, and do not contaminate one another. The hereditary units of the parents can therefore be reassorted in varied combinations in different individuals at each generation. In the early 1900s, at the suggestion of the Danish botanist Wilhelm Johannsen, the postulated hereditary units became known as genes. Notwithstanding its new name, the existence of the gene remained inferential, being based exclusively on indirect evidence.

In 1902, Walter S. Sutton, then a 26-year-old graduate student at Columbia University, proposed that the genes were located in the microscopically visible, threadlike chromosomes of the nucleus. Extensive studies on the small fruit fly by the American geneticist Thomas Hunt Morgan from 1910 to 1915 provided strong confirmation that the chromosomes do carry the genes. Moreover, the observations made on the fruit fly warranted the interpretation that the genes bear a definite spatial relationship to one another. The genes must be, as Morgan asserted, arranged in a linear fashion in the chromosome.

During the early decades of this century, the picture of genes that had emerged was that of discrete entities, strung together along the chromosome, like individual beads on a string (fig. 16.1). This portrayal carried

Figure 16.1 Changing concept of the gene. The gene is now known to be a segment of a complex molecule (deoxyribonucleic acid, or DNA) rather than an obscure "bead on a string."

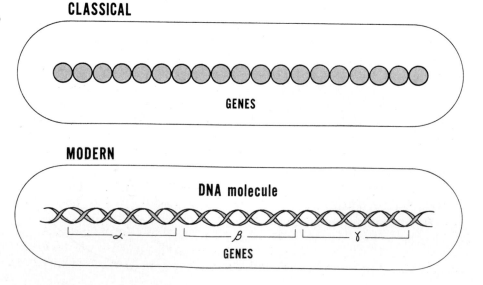

CLASSICAL

GENES

MODERN

DNA molecule

α β γ

GENES

with it the implication that genes were not pure abstractions but actual particles of living matter. Yet until the 1950s the chemical nature of the gene remained enigmatic, and no one knew precisely how genes made additional copies of themselves or how they controlled development of the rest of the cell.

One of the finest triumphs of modern science has been the elucidation of the chemical nature of the gene. The transmission of traits from parents to offspring depends on the transfer of a specific giant molecule that carries a coded blueprint in its molecular structure. This complex molecule, the basic chemical component of the chromosome, is *deoxyribonucleic acid*, or in abbreviated form, DNA. The information carried in the DNA molecule can be divided into a number of separable units, which we now recognize as the genes (fig. 16.1). Stated simply, chromosomes are primarily long strands of DNA and genes are coded sequences of the DNA molecule. The amount of DNA present in a single unfertilized human egg has been estimated to carry information corresponding to 2 million genes. The once theoretical gene has finally been placed on a material (chemical) level.

The trail leading to the unveiling of the architecture of the DNA molecule was a long one. It had its origin in 1869 in a test-tube study by the Swiss pathologist Friedrich Miescher, a contemporary of Mendel.

DISCOVERY OF NUCLEIN

Friedrich Miescher chemically analyzed pus washed from discarded surgical dressings from soldiers wounded in the Franco-Prussian war. Although it was seemingly a strange choice, pus is interesting in that it contains numerous white blood cells with exceptionally large nuclei. Miescher's chemical analysis revealed a substance in the nucleus that did not fall into any known classification; it was not carbohydrate, or protein, or fat. The nuclear substance contained a very high proportion of phosphorus, and appeared to represent a new class of organic compounds. Miescher designated the compound "nuclein," but in later years it was renamed *nucleic acid* when its acidic properties were recognized.

Following the demonstration that the nucleus contains nucleic acid, curiosity as to the structure of the nucleic acid molecule was aroused. Three component submolecules were identified: a 5-carbon sugar, phosphoric acid, and a nitrogen-containing ring compound, or nitrogenous base. The 5-carbon sugar is always the same sugar, known as *deoxyribose*. Because of the invariable presence of the deoxyribose sugar, the name of the nucleic acid of the nucleus was extended to deoxyribonucleic acid, or DNA. The large amounts of phosphorus found by Miescher are accountable by the presence of phosphoric acid, which also explains why DNA is an acid. The sugar molecules are always joined to the phosphoric acid molecules, so as to form a long chain that endlessly repeats the sugar-phosphate sequence (fig. 16.2). The DNA molecule is chemically an example of a high polymer. The characteristic feature of a high polymer is that some chemical unit is linked together repeatedly to form a giant molecule.

To each sugar molecule in the chain is attached a nitrogenous base, a molecule containing rings of carbon and nitrogen atoms. The base is not always the same; it may be one or another of four different types. Two of them are adenine and guanine, both of which belong to a class of nitrogen-containing molecules known as two-ring *purines*, and the other two are thymine and cytosine, both of which are single-ring *pyrimidines* (fig. 16.2). The order in which the bases follow one another along the chain varies from one strand of DNA to another. As we shall see later, the specificity of a given DNA molecule depends on the arrangement of its bases. <u>The DNA molecule is essentially a long chain composed of repeating units called nucleotides. Each nucleotide is a unit composed of one sugar, one phosphoric acid residue, and one nitrogenous base.</u>

Once its chemical structure was determined, the DNA molecule attracted the attention of cytochemists. In 1924, the German cytologist Robert Feulgen devised a dye that specifically stained DNA. With this dye, the DNA assumes a fuchsia color, which is reddish purple in hue. When Feulgen's specific color reaction was applied to the intact cell, the DNA was found to be located almost exclusively in the nucleus. Moreover, the fuchsia-colored stain was localized in the chromosomes of the nucleus. When subsequently the quantity of DNA in different cells was ascertained, it was found that a sperm cell has only half the amount of DNA found in a body cell. This information was of immense interest since a gamete has only half the genetic content of a body cell.

From these early observations, it would seem that DNA should have received serious consideration as the most likely candidate for the genetic material. Yet, as late as 1940, most geneticists persisted in their

Figure 16.2 Portion of a single DNA polynucleotide chain. Each nucleotide is composed of one 5-carbon sugar (deoxyribose), one phosphoric acid residue, and one nitrogenous base (adenine, cytosine, guanine, or thymine). The backbone of the chain consists of alternating phosphate and sugar residues.

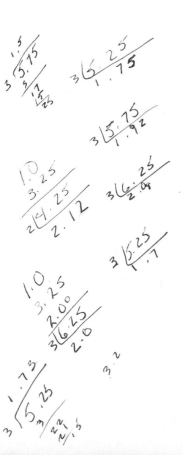

belief that the gene was protein in nature. Since enzymes, antibodies, and several hormones were proteins, it was simple to infer that this adaptable substance also made up the genes. The results of certain experiments in the 1940s were to show that the scientific community was incorrect in this view.

TRANSFORMATION

Modern studies with bacteria provided experimental evidence that forced consideration of DNA as the genetic material. In 1944, Oswald T. Avery, Colin M. MacLeod, and Maclyn McCarty at the Rockefeller Institute established that the genetic character of pneumococcus (the pneumonia-causing bacterium) could be altered, or transformed, by exposing one strain of bacterium to the DNA of another bacterium. Harmless (avirulent) bacterial cells could be changed to virulent forms by mixing the former with a purified DNA extract from the latter. Moreover, the newly acquired virulent trait was heritable, the cells retaining their virulence through subsequent generations. Purified DNA was shown therefore to be the means of transmitting a genetic trait (the character of virulence) that persisted through repeated cell divisions. This phenomenon was termed *transformation*.

The inherited change could only be brought about by a solution of active DNA. When the DNA was destroyed by a specific enzyme (DNase), the extract could no longer convert the avirulent to a virulent strain. It was also observed that protein extracts were ineffectual in inducing transformation.

Since 1944, inheritable transformation of other characters have been demonstrated in bacteria with essentially the same technique. Figure 16.3 shows in simplified form the experiments by Rollin D. Hotchkiss on the induction of streptomycin resistance in formerly sensitive bacteria. The cells of streptomycin-resistant bacterial colonies are disrupted (by treatment with sodium deoxycholate) and the DNA of these cells is precipitated as threads (by the addition of ethanol) and then purified. When the purified DNA of streptomycin-resistant cells is placed in a medium containing streptomycin-sensitive cells, the initially sensitive cells gain the capacity to resist streptomycin and to transmit this ability to their descendants. The bare molecule of DNA has accordingly transferred the capacity to resist streptomycin as an inherited characteristic.

At the time of these investigations, there were several scientists, particularly those who were still committed to the idea that protein was the genetic material, who suggested that the DNA served solely as a mutagenic agent. That is to say, the donor DNA caused the genes of the host bacteria to undergo mutation. However, the frequency of transformations was many orders of magnitude higher than the rare occurrence of mutations. In recent years, the mechanism by which DNA accomplishes transformation has been clarified. The genetic apparatus of the recipient cell actually incorporates a segment of the donor DNA. When the segment includes the sequence of DNA units that is concerned with streptomycin resistance, the recipient cell can then survive and multiply in the presence of streptomycin. Equally important, the DNA blueprint for streptomycin resistance becomes a permanent, heritable property of the recipient cell, which can be passed on to its progeny. It should be clear that <u>no new traits are created by transformation; only those traits already present in the donor bacteria are transferred</u>.

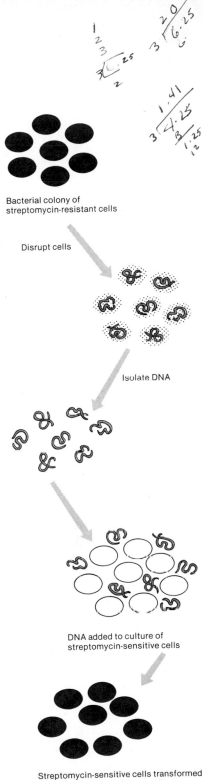

Bacterial colony of streptomycin-resistant cells

Disrupt cells

Isolate DNA

DNA added to culture of streptomycin-sensitive cells

Streptomycin-sensitive cells transformed into streptomycin-resistant cells

Figure 16.3 Transformation of streptomycin-sensitive bacteria to streptomycin-resistant bacteria by the use of purified DNA from streptomycin-resistant bacterial cells.

BACTERIAL VIRUSES

Convincing, or confirmatory, evidence that DNA is the essential component of the hereditary material came from chemical studies on virulent bacteriophages, which are viruses that attack bacterial cells and reproduce only within the bacterial cell. In 1952, A. D. Hershey and Martha Chase, at the Carnegie Laboratory of Genetics at Cold Spring Harbor, studied bacteriophages, known as *T* phages, which infect a common bacteria of the intestinal tract, *Escherichia coli*. This phage, tadpole-shaped as viewed with the electron microscope, has essentially an outer protective coat made of protein, which surrounds a central core composed of DNA (fig. 16.4). The viruses attach to the cell wall of the bacterium by their tail pieces. After penetrating the bacterium, the viruses multiply and produce a large number of progeny. The new viruses ultimately burst out of the host cell and infect other bacteria.

In one of their experiments, Hershey and Chase labeled the protein coat of the viruses with radioactive sulfur (^{35}S). Since sulfur is a com-

Figure 16.4 Experiments by Hershey and Chase revealing that only the DNA component of the bacteriophage (T phage) carries genetic information. Experiment 1: Protein coat of T-phage viruses labeled with radioactive sulfur (^{35}S). Experiment 2: DNA of viruses selectively labeled with radioactive phosphorus (^{32}P).

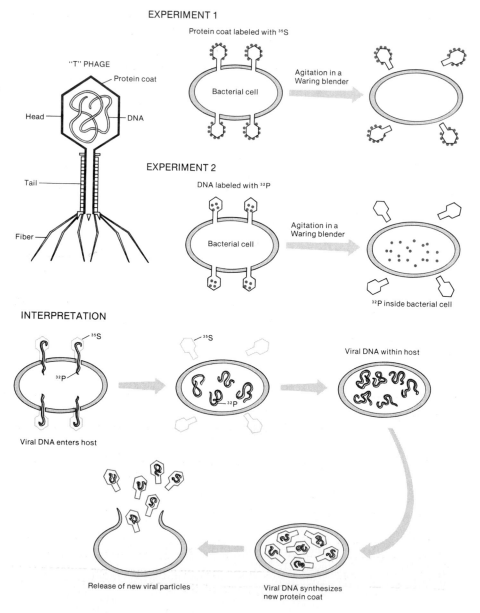

ponent of proteins but not of DNA, only the coat and not the interior core of the phage was radioactive. The labeled viruses were mixed with a suspension of bacterial cells. Shortly after the viruses had attached themselves, a portion of the bacterial suspension was agitated in a Waring blender. This caused the viruses to become separated from the bacteria. When the quantities of radioactive sulfur were then measured, the radioactivity was found to be confined outside the bacterial cells. There was no radioactivity inside the cells; the protein coat of the virus evidently did not enter the bacterial cell. Nevertheless, when the remaining portion of the bacterial suspension was incubated, the bacteria eventually burst, liberating the usual large quantities of new viruses. Hence, some material must have passed from the viruses into the bacteria during the few minutes of attachment.

The second experiment (fig. 16.4) revealed that the material that entered the bacterial cell was the phage DNA. This experiment was similar in design and execution to the first, except that the phage DNA was selectively labeled with radioactive phosphorus (^{32}P). The radioactive phosphorus was later detected in the interior of the bacterial cell, indicating that only DNA enters the bacterial cell. Moreover, since new viral particles, complete with their protein coats, are formed within the bacterial cell, the conclusion is inescapable that the genetic information necessary for the production of new progeny (including the new protein coats!) must reside in the DNA molecule. The DNA molecule was thus firmly established as the chemical substance that passes genetic information from parent to offspring.

NITROGENOUS BASES IN DNA

Recognition of the special significance of the DNA stimulated an array of studies in the 1950s on the chemical and physical properties of the molecule. One active area of investigation concerned the relative proportions of the nitrogenous bases in DNA. In 1950, the American biochemist Erwin Chargaff and his colleagues extracted DNA from a variety of organisms. The remarkable finding was that in the DNA of all species, the ratio of adenine to thymine is 1 to 1; likewise, guanine and cytosine exist in equal concentrations. This suggests that adenine is linked to thymine and that guanine is linked to cytosine. The significance of this finding was not fully appreciated until Watson and Crick in 1953 unveiled the architecture of the DNA molecule.

WATSON-CRICK MODEL OF DNA

The two scientists who worked together in the early 1950s to propose a configuration for the DNA molecule were Francis H. C. Crick, the biophysicist at Cambridge University, and James D. Watson, an American student of virology who was then in attendance at Cambridge on a postdoctoral fellowship to study chemistry. With the invaluable aid of X-ray pictures of DNA crystals prepared by Maurice H. F. Wilkins, the biophysicist at King's College in London, Watson and Crick built an inspired model in metal of the configuration of DNA. This achievement won Watson, Crick, and Wilkins the coveted Nobel prize for medicine and physiology in 1962.

The remarkable feature of DNA is its simplicity of design. The DNA molecule is composed of two long chains of nucleotides arranged in the form of a double helix. Its shape may be compared to a twisted ladder (fig. 16.5). The two parallel supports of the ladder are made up of alternating sugar (deoxyribose) and phosphate molecules. Each rung of the ladder is composed of one pair of nitrogenous bases, held together by specific hydrogen bonds. In making up the model, the investigators found that the nitrogenous bases could be accommodated best if the larger, two-ring purines lay opposite the smaller, one-ring pyrimidines. This is compatible with Chargaff's analytical determination that in molar amount, adenine equals thymine, and guanine equals cytosine. Thus, the arrangement of the bases is not haphazard: adenine in one chain is normally joined with thymine in the other chain, and guanine is typically linked with cytosine. Along any one chain, any sequence of the bases is possible, but if the sequence along one chain is given, then the sequence along the other is automatically determined, because of the precise pairing rule (A = T and G = C). The combination of one purine and one pyrimidine to make up each cross connection is conveniently called a *base pair*.

Now, if DNA is the genetic material, it should have a structure sufficiently versatile to account for the great variety of different genes. The four bases (A, C, G, and T) may be thought of as a four-letter alphabet or code. The uniqueness of a given gene would then relate to the specific order or arrangement of the bases, just as words in our language differ according to the sequence of letters of the alphabet or as a telegraphic message becomes comprehensible by the varied combinations of dots and dashes. The number of ways in which the nitrogenous bases can be arranged in the DNA molecule is exceedingly large. It has been stated that a single unfertilized human egg contains 3 billion base pairs arranged in specific ways in the DNA molecules of the chromosomes. Current estimates indicate that a single gene is a linear sequence of approximately 1,500 base pairs.

Figure 16.5 Watson-Crick double-stranded helix configuration of deoxyribonucleic acid (DNA). The backbone of each twisted strand consists of alternating sugar (S) and phosphorus (P) residues. Enlarged view on right shows that the larger, two-ring purines (adenine or guanine) lay opposite the smaller, one-ring pyrimidines (cytosine or thymine). The nitrogenous bases are held together by hydrogen bonds, three between cytosine (C) and guanine (G), and two between adenine (A) and thymine (T).

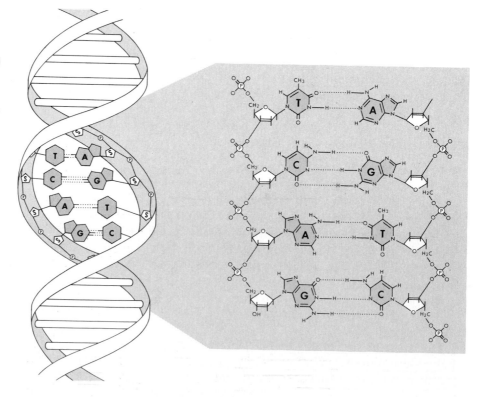

SELF-COPYING OF THE DNA MOLECULE

One fundamental property that has long been ascribed to the gene is its ability to make an exact copy of itself. If the gene is really a linear sequence of base pairs, then the Watson-Crick model of DNA must be able to account for the precise reproduction of the sequences of the bases. The exact replication of the double helix can be visualized with little difficulty. The DNA molecule consists of two parts, each of which is the complement of the other. Accordingly, each single chain can serve as a template to guide the formation of a new companion chain (fig. 16.6). The two nucleotide chains separate, breaking the hydrogen bonds that hold together the paired bases. Each chain then attracts new base units from among the supply of free nucleotides always present in the cell. As separation takes place, each separated lengthwise portion of the chain can begin to form a portion of the new chain. Eventually, the original double helix has produced two exact replicas of itself. If the original two chains are designated A and B, then A will direct the formation of a new B and the old B will guide the production of a new A. Where one AB molecule existed previously, two AB molecules, exactly like the original, exist afterward.

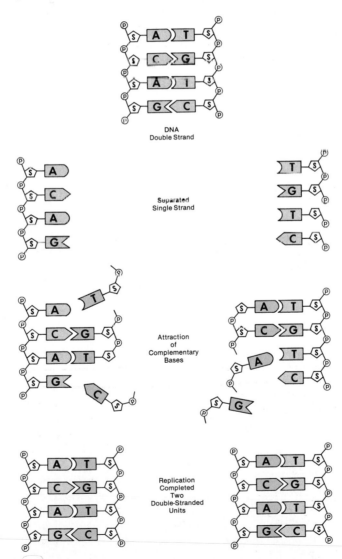

Figure 16.6 Replication of DNA. The parental strands separate, each serving as a guide or template for the synthesis of a new daughter strand. Each new DNA molecule contains one parental and one daughter strand.

DNA
Double Strand

Separated
Single Strand

Attraction
of
Complementary
Bases

Replication
Completed
Two
Double-Stranded
Units

Several lines of evidence support the Watson-Crick scheme of DNA replication. One of these involves labeling DNA molecules, so that the new and old molecules can be distinguished. In 1958, Matthew S. Meselson and Frank W. Stahl, then both at the California Institute of Technology, labeled DNA using an isotope of nitrogen, ^{15}N, which has a mass greater than that of ordinary nitrogen, ^{14}N. The DNA molecules consisting solely of heavy nitrogen (^{15}N) can be distinguished from ^{14}N-containing DNA by their relative densities in a cesium chloride solution, as the following method shows. When a solution of a heavy salt, such as cesium chloride, is spun in an ultracentrifuge, its molecules tend to sediment but they do not separate completely. Rather, a density gradient is established with the greater concentrations of cesium chloride towards the bottom of the tube. When DNA is centrifuged in a cesium chloride gradient, it comes to rest in a band in a region of the tube where its density is the same as the density of the surrounding salt solution. DNA containing only heavy nitrogen forms a band lower down the tube of cesium chloride than does DNA containing only normal nitrogen (fig. 16.7).

Meselson and Stahl first grew bacteria (*Escherichia coli*) in a culture medium containing the heavy isotope of nitrogen (^{15}N). The DNA from these "heavy" bacteria formed a single band in the lower part of the tube, showing that the DNA is more dense than normal. These heavy bacteria were then transferred to an ordinary medium containing normal nitrogen (^{14}N). After the bacteria had doubled their numbers, and hence had undergone one cell division, it was found that the DNA molecules were exactly intermediate in density between heavy and light DNA—as though they were each made up of one heavy nitrogen and one light nitrogen chain. This is exactly what we would expect from the Watson-

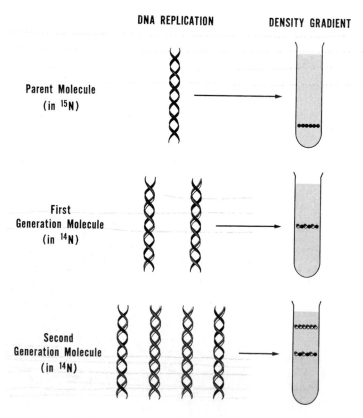

Figure 16.7 Experimental demonstration by Meselson and Stahl that DNA replication is in accord with the self-copying scheme postulated by Watson and Crick.

DNA REPLICATION   DENSITY GRADIENT

Parent Molecule
(in ^{15}N)

First
Generation Molecule
(in ^{14}N)

Second
Generation Molecule
(in ^{14}N)

Crick replication scheme. When the DNA companion chains were formed during cell division, the complementary bases were derived from the lighter nitrogen molecules. The DNA molecule was thus a hybrid—one strand containing ^{14}N and the other, ^{15}N. After two generations of growth in normal medium, when the bacteria had quadrupled in numbers, their DNA contained particles of two densities. One half had the intermediate (hybrid) density, while the remainder had the density of DNA containing only normal nitrogen (fig. 16.7). The results, once again, are completely in accord with the proposed method of DNA replication. When the two strands separate during cell division, each strand serves as a template for the formation of a new partner strand.

DNA SYNTHESIS IN THE TEST TUBE

Even more dramatic evidence in favor of the Watson-Crick hypothesis of DNA replication came from the laboratory of Nobel Laureate Arthur Kornberg and his colleagues, then at Washington University and now at Stanford University. They produced in a test tube the DNA molecule of a bacterial virus. Kornberg had first isolated an enzyme called *DNA polymerase,* which is necessary for directing the synthesis of DNA from nucleotides, that is, linking the nucleotides into a chain. The polymerase was placed in a test tube along with the four different kinds of precursor nucleotides and a preformed DNA strand that served as a template or primer. The enzyme triggered the formation of a new complementary DNA chain, which had the same ratio of A–T pairs to G–C pairs as the primer DNA. In other words, the synthetic DNA was produced by replication of the DNA used as a template. Unlike natural DNA, however, the synthetic DNA was biologically inactive. That is, it could not duplicate itself when introduced into a bacterial cell.

In 1967, Kornberg and his associates succeeded in producing a biologically active, or infective, copy of a viral DNA. They experimented with one of the simplest viruses known, Phi X 174, which is unique in several ways. It has only a single, unpaired chain of DNA, only five or six genes amounting to some 6,000 nitrogenous bases, and is joined at its ends so that it forms a circle (fig. 16.8). With the use of the single-

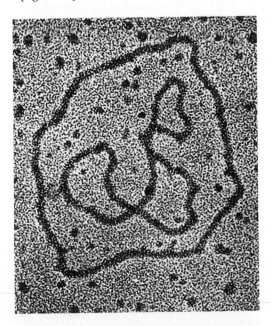

Figure 16.8 Electron micrograph of two duplex circles of artificially synthesized viral (Phi X 174) DNA. Each duplex consists of a template of natural virus associated with a complete synthetic complementary circle. (Courtesy of Arthur Kornberg, Stanford University.)

stranded DNA of this phage as a template upon which the nucleotides could assemble, a complementary DNA chain was artificially synthesized that was capable of infecting a bacterial cell. With admirable scientific thoroughness, Kornberg then repeated the procedure, copying the artificial DNA to make an exact duplicate of the original DNA. The laboratory product was indistinguishable from the viral original and was equally infective.

ISOLATION OF A SINGLE GENE AND ITS SYNTHESIS

The last decade has witnessed two momentous technical achievements: one team of molecular biologists isolated a single gene and another team synthesized a gene. In November of 1969, Jonathan Beckwith and his co-workers at Harvard University isolated the gene that allows the bacterium *Escherichia coli* to metabolize the sugar lactose. Using sophisticated techniques involving the transfer of genes by viruses from one bacterium to another, the "lactose" gene was isolated and its double helical configuration was verified with the electron microscope. In June 1970, the biochemist Har Gobind Khorana, then at the University of Wisconsin, painstakingly assembled a single gene from relatively simple laboratory chemicals containing carbon, hydrogen, oxygen, and phosphorus. The gene specifies the production of a large molecule in the cytoplasm of yeast cells. The artificially synthesized gene is relatively simple, containing only 77 pairs of bases. In 1976, Khorana, now at the Massachusetts Institute of Technology, reported the synthesis of an artificial gene that is capable of functioning in a living cell. The synthetic gene, when inserted into a mutant strain of a bacteriophage, was able to replace the defective gene in that strain. These studies close that chapter in biology in which the existence of the gene was based largely on inference.

LANGUAGE OF LIFE

Cellular proteins are key components of living matter. As we learned earlier, proteins are composed of 20 basic building blocks, the amino acids, arranged in long chains, called *polypeptides*. Each polypeptide chain may be several hundred amino acid units in length. The number of possible arrangements of the different amino acids in a given protein is unbelievably large. In a polypeptide chain made up of 500 amino acid units, the number of possible patterns (given 20 different amino acids) can be expressed by the number 1 followed by 1,100 zeros. How, then, does a cell form the particular amino acid patterns it requires out of the colossal number of patterns that are possible?

We may presume that the sequence of bases of the DNA molecule is in some way the master pattern, or code, for the sequence of the amino acids in the polypeptide chains of the cellular proteins. In 1954, the British physicist George Gamow suggested that each amino acid is dictated by one sequence of three bases in the DNA molecule. As an example, the sequence cytosine-thymine-thymine (CTT) in the DNA molecule might designate that the amino acid glutamic acid is to be incorporated in the formation of the protein molecule, such as hemoglobin (fig. 16.9). Thus, the DNA code is to be found in triplets—that is, three bases taken together code one amino acid. It should be noted that only one of the two strands of the DNA molecule serves as the genetic code. Biochemical chaos would result if both complementary strands of DNA were to encode information.

The importance of the genetic code cannot be overstated. Let us assume the following sequence of bases in one of the strands of the

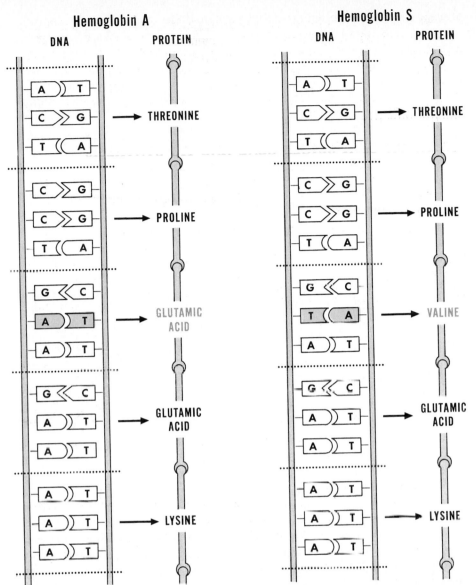

Hemoglobin A

DNA   PROTEIN

| A | T |
| C | G | → THREONINE
| T | A |

| C | G |
| C | G | → PROLINE
| T | A |

| G | C |
| A | T | → GLUTAMIC ACID
| A | T |

| G | C |
| A | T | → GLUTAMIC ACID
| A | T |

| A | T |
| A | T | → LYSINE
| A | T |

Hemoglobin S

DNA   PROTEIN

| A | T |
| C | G | → THREONINE
| T | A |

| C | G |
| C | G | → PROLINE
| T | A |

| G | C |
| T | A | → VALINE
| A | T |

| G | C |
| A | T | → GLUTAMIC ACID
| A | T |

| A | T |
| A | T | → LYSINE
| A | T |

Figure 16.9 The abnormal hemoglobin that occurs in sickle-cell anemia—hemoglobin S—is the consequence of an alteration of a single base of the triplet of DNA that specifies a particular amino acid (glutamic acid) in normal hemoglobin (hemoglobin A). A simple base-pair switch, or mutation, in the DNA molecule results in the replacement of glutamic acid in hemoglobin A by another amino acid, valine, in hemoglobin S. (Based on studies by Vernon M. Ingram.)

DNA molecule: ... CGT ATC GTA AGC ..., and that the triplets in this sequence specify four amino acids, designated R, I, P, and E. In other words, the following code exists: CGT = R, ATC = I, CTA = P, and AGC = E. This section of the DNA molecule thus specifies RIPE, and the message to make RIPE is passed on by this particular sequence from the nucleus to the cytoplasm of the cell. The message continues to flow out in the living cell, and RIPE will be made, copy after copy.

But what if a chance mishap occurs in one of the triplets? Let us say that T in the second triplet is substituted for A, so that the triplet reads TTC instead of ATC, and would specify an A instead of I. The word would now be RAPE instead of RIPE. This makes quite a difference, especially if the word is continually printed incorrectly throughout a novel. And just as a misprinted word can alter or destroy the meaning of a sentence, so an altered protein in the body fails to express its intended purpose. Sometimes the error is not tragic, but often the organism is debilitated by the misprint.

As a striking example, we may consider the case of individuals afflicted with sickle-cell anemia. The hemoglobin molecule in sickle-cell anemic patients is biochemically abnormal. In 1956, Vernon Ingram, then at Cambridge University, succeeded in breaking down hemoglobin, a large protein molecule, into several peptide fragments containing short sequences of identifiable amino acids. Normal hemoglobin and sickle-cell hemoglobin yielded the same array of peptide fragments, with a single exception. In one of the peptide fragments of sickle-cell hemoglobin, the amino acid *glutamic acid* had been replaced at one point in the chain by *valine* (fig. 16.9). The sole difference in chemical composition between normal and sickle-cell hemoglobin is the substitution in a single amino acid unit among several hundred. The detrimental effect of sickle-cell anemia is thus traceable to an exceedingly slight alteration in the structure of the protein molecule. This, in turn, is associated with a highly localized genetic change, or *mutation,* in one of the nucleotide pairs in the DNA molecule in the chromosome (fig. 16.9). Many mutations, as we shall later see, are simply base-pair switches in the DNA molecule.

FUNCTIONAL DEFINITION OF A GENE

The DNA molecule, like a tape recording, carries specific messages for the synthesis of a wide variety of proteins. We shall see presently that DNA does not directly form protein but works in a complex way through a secondary form of nucleic acid, *ribonucleic acid,* or *RNA.* At this point, it is important to recognize that a gene is a coded sequence in the DNA molecule. From a functional point of view, we may say that the gene is *a section of the DNA molecule (about 1,500 base pairs) involved in the determination of the amino acid sequence of a single polypeptide chain of a protein.*

SUMMARY

Modern breakthroughs in genetics and biochemistry have significantly changed our concept of the gene. The evidence is overwhelming that the substance of the genes is deoxyribonucleic acid (DNA). The DNA molecule, according to the widely accepted Watson-Crick model, is composed of two chains of nucleotides arranged in a double helix, like a twisted ladder. The backbone of each chain is formed of alternating sugar (deoxyribose) and phosphate groups. Each rung of the ladderlike molecule is made up of one pair of nitrogen-containing ring compounds, or nitrogenous bases (purines and pyrimidines). Each rung consists of one purine (adenine or guanine) coupled by hydrogen bonds to one pyrimidine (thymine or cytosine). The base pairing is specific: adenine (A) in one chain always pairs with thymine (T) in the other chain, and guanine (G) always pairs with cytosine (C). These two types of paired bases (A–T and G–C) are arranged in certain sequences in different chromosomes, and each gene owes its unique character to a specific arrangement of the base-pair rungs.

The DNA molecule holds the key to the manufacture of protein in the cells. A given DNA molecule has its nitrogenous bases arranged in a particular order, and this order determines the order in which amino acids fall into place in a specific protein molecule. The four kinds of nitrogenous bases (A, T, G, and C) constitute a sort of four-letter alphabet, or genetic code. A sequence of three bases specifies, or codes for, a particular amino acid. Functionally, a gene is defined as a section of the DNA molecule (about 1,500 base pairs) involved in the determination of the amino acid sequence of a single polypeptide chain of a protein.

Ethical Probe 12
Recombinant DNA

One of the most controversial techniques in modern genetical research is the manipulation of the hereditary apparatus of the bacterium, *Escherichia coli,* in such a fashion that it can carry genes from very distantly related organisms, including viruses, frogs, and rabbits. *E. coli* is a normal inhabitant of the human intestinal tract and is usually harmless. This bacterium contains a circular strand of DNA and smaller circles of DNA known as *plasmids.* The plasmids can be isolated in pure form from the bacterial cell and experimentally fragmented into several pieces. Then, the DNA molecule from one of many organisms—insects, mammals, plants, and even tumor viruses—can be isolated and portions of this DNA molecule can be attached to, or "spliced" into, the fragments of plasmids. This newly formed recombinant-DNA molecule, when reintroduced into a bacterium, can replicate precisely and be passed to daughter bacterial cells for many generations. The ability to introduce foreign genes into the plasmids of *E. coli* provides a new and powerful tool for the transmission of genes that code for indispensable molecules. For example, the insertion of the insulin-producing gene of a rat into *E. coli* could lead to the mass production of the invaluable insulin as the bacteria multiply rapidly.

There are undeniable potential risks associated with transferring foreign genes into a bacterium, particularly a strain of bacterium that is normally a resident of the human digestive tract. It is not unimaginable that a laboratory-engineered strain of *E. coli* with transplanted foreign genes that confer resistance to a medically important drug, or even promote the formation of tumors, could escape from the laboratory. Although the strains of *E. coli* commonly used in laboratory studies do not survive well under natural conditions, the fact remains that *E. coli* is intimately associated with humans and is capable of inhabiting humans. Thus, a drug-resistant strain, or a tumor-producing strain, of *E. coli* could establish itself and become widespread in human populations.

Under the auspices of the National Institutes of Health, guidelines have been established under which recombinant-DNA research can be "safely" conducted. But the risks of recombinant-DNA experiments are largely unknown. Since the risks of biological disaster remain undetermined, are you willing to sanction such studies particularly in the face of uncertain prospects for beneficial application? Should scientists declare a moratorium on recombinant-DNA experiments?

17 Physical Basis of Inheritance

The egg and sperm cells are often referred to as *germ cells* because they are the beginnings, or germs, of new individuals. The germ cells represent the only connecting thread between successive generations. Accordingly, the mechanism of hereditary transmission must operate across this slender connecting bridge. In 1868, Charles Darwin proposed an ingenious theory to account for the transmission of traits by the germ cells. Darwin thought that all organs of the body sent contributions to the germ cells in the form of particles, or *gemmules*. These gemmules, or minute delegates of bodily parts, were supposedly discharged into the bloodstream and became ultimately concentrated in the gametes. In the next generation, each gemmule reproduced its particular bodily component. The theory was called *pangenesis*, or "origin from all," since all parental bodily cells were supposed to take part in the formation of the new individual.

Darwin's fanciful explanation of inheritance, however, has no foundation of factual evidence. Indeed, many observations argue against it. In 1909 W. E. Castle of Harvard University provided one of the earliest convincing observations refuting the theory of pangenesis. Castle successfully removed the ovaries of an albino guinea pig and grafted in their place the ovaries of a black guinea pig. The albino foster mother was then mated to an albino male. This pair produced several litters of young, and all the offspring were black. Ordinarily when albinos are crossed only albino offspring are produced. It is obvious, then, that the eggs produced by the transplanted ovaries (from the black guinea pig) were not changed, or instructed otherwise, by their new residence in the albino foster mother guinea pig.

Notwithstanding Darwin's simplistic view, the mechanism of inheritance does reside in the gametes. Although the relatively large egg cell and the comparatively small sperm cell are as strikingly unlike in appearance as any two cells can be, they are equivalent in certain important components—their nuclei and, more particularly, their *chromosomes*. The chromosomes are, in fact, the vehicles for transmitting the blueprints of traits from parents to offspring. Deoxyribonucleic acid (DNA) already has become familiar to us as the *chemical carrier* of the hereditary information. The questions now are: How do the chromosomes serve as the *physical carriers* of heredity? Equally important, how does our model of DNA relate to the larger picture of chromosomes?

THE CHROMOSOMES

Each organism has a definite number of chromosomes, ranging in various species from 2 to more than 200. Man, for example, has 46 chromosomes in the nucleus of every body cell. Not only are the numbers of chromosomes constant for a given species, but the shapes and sizes of the chromosomes in a given species differ to such an extent that it is possible to recognize particular chromosomes and to distinguish one kind from the other. An important consideration is that each kind of chromosome in a zygote is present in duplicate. Stated another way, the chromosomes occur in pairs; hence, man has 23 pairs. The significance of the double, or paired, set of chromosomes, cannot be overstated: *Each parent contributes one member of each pair of chromosomes to the offspring.*

During the division of the fertilized egg into many daughter cells, the chromosomes regularly produce copies of themselves with each cell division. As a result, each of the millions of cells of the developing embryo carries faithful copies of the chromosomes of the fertilized egg (fig. 17.1). The process by which new cells in the body arise from preexisting cells was termed *mitosis* (Greek, *mitos,* "a thread") by the German anatomist Walther Flemming in 1882. Mitosis ensures that the new cells receive identical copies of the chromosome complement of the original cell.

The formation of new cells by mitosis is a continual process in the human body, although certain cells divide more often than others, and some not at all. Cells in the skin, intestine, and blood-forming tissues divide often to replace cells that are continually worn out. Kidney and liver cells are renewed less often, and certain highly specialized cells, such as nerve cells, are not replaced when damaged.

If the gametes were to be produced by the usual mitotic process, and accordingly, if they had the same number of chromosomes as the body cells, then the union of sperm and egg would necessarily double the number of chromosomes at each generation. Such progressive increase is prevented, however, by a special kind of division that guarantees that the gametes contain *half* the number of chromosomes characteristic of the body cells. This special kind of division is referred to as *meiosis.* The term *meiosis* is derived from the Greek word *meioo,* "to make less," combined with *osis,* "a condition or process." Meiosis is a lessening or

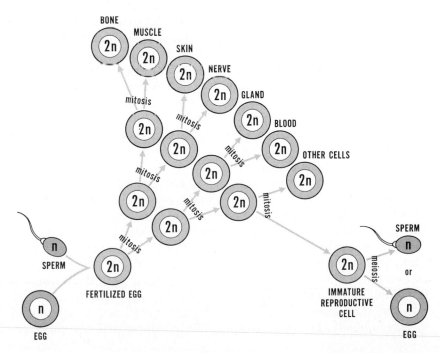

Figure 17.1 Mitosis ensures that each new cell of the developing organism has a complete set of chromosomes (diploid, or 2n) that is a duplicate of the set in the original cell. Through the process of meiosis, the gametes (egg and sperm) come to possess only half of the number of chromosomes (haploid, or 1n).

reducing process, referring specifically to a reduction in the number of chromosomes. In man, for example, during formation of the gametes, the number of chromosomes is reduced from 46 to 23.

The somatic (or body) cells, possessing twice the number of chromosomes as the gametes, are said to be *diploid* (Greek, *diploos*, "twofold" or "double"). In contrast, the gametic number of chromosomes is *haploid* (Greek, *haploos*, "single") or, as some investigators prefer, *monoploid* (Greek, *monos*, "alone"). This can be expressed in abbreviated form by saying that the body cells contain 2n chromosomes and the germ cells contain 1n chromosomes, where n stands for a definite number (fig. 17.1).

With this general orientation we can now examine in detail the mechanisms of mitosis and meiosis. Since the genes (segments of DNA) reside in the chromosome, the problem of the transmission of genes becomes a problem of the transmission of chromosomes. Understanding how the chromosomes behave is thus prerequisite to a genuine appreciation of how inheritance proceeds.

MITOSIS

The nucleus of a cell ordinarily has a netted appearance (fig. 17.2). Early investigators found that the fine network of the material in the nucleus stains deeply with certain dyes, such as the purple coloring matter known as *hematoxylin*. Because of its affinity for dyes, the substance making up the net was termed *chromatin*, from *chroma*, Greek for "color." The chromatin net is actually a tangled mass of thin threads, the chromosomes. The chromosomes are packed like a ball of yarn and hence are not individually recognizable at this time. A cell at this stage is described as "resting." This is a misnomer, as the "resting" cell is actually involved in intense physiological activity to maintain the life of the cell. The cell at this time is more properly said to be in the *interphase* stage.

When a cell begins to divide, the chromosomes become discernible as separate threadlike strands. This early stage of division is known as the *prophase*. In our simple illustrative example (fig. 17.2), only four chromosomes are represented. As the chromosomes become shorter and thicker, it becomes apparent that each chromosome consists of two duplicate, or daughter, threads. The longitudinal duplication of each chromosome actually occurred during the interphase stage. Each daughter thread of a chromosome is known as a *chromatid*. The two daughter chromatids remain joined together only at a small region termed the *centromere*. Thus, a distinctive feature of the chromosomes in early prophase is that they are double rather than single strands. It bears emphasizing that each chromosome consists of two identical chromatid threads attached at the centromere.

By the time the chromosomes are distinguishable as longitudinally doubled, rodlike structures, other changes have taken place. The delicate membrane that surrounds the nucleus has disappeared. Two small bodies lying outside the nucleus, known as *centrioles*, migrate to opposite poles of the cell and give rise to a series of thin fibers, the *spindle fibers*. The chromosomes now collect in the center of the spindle, and are attached to the spindle fibers by their centromeres with their arms extending outward. This stage is referred to as the *metaphase*. It is at this time that the chromosomes are maximally contracted and most conspicuous microscopically. The thick, deeply staining metaphase chromosomes fre-

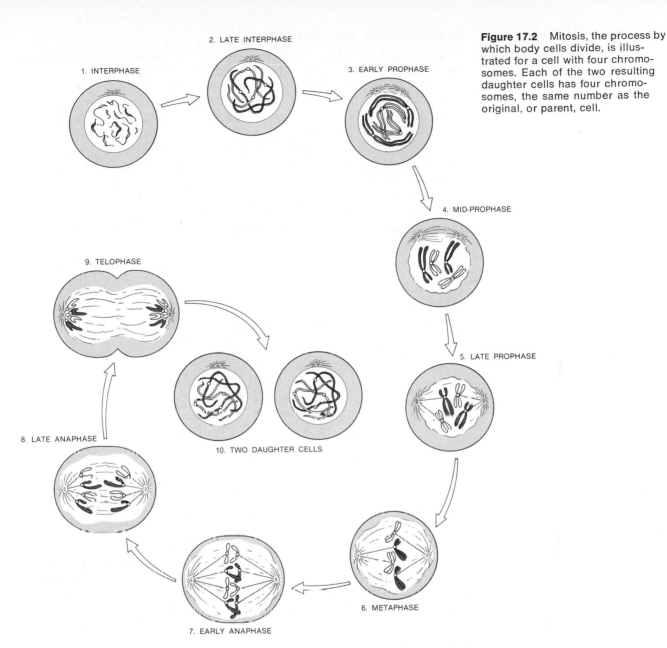

Figure 17.2 Mitosis, the process by which body cells divide, is illustrated for a cell with four chromosomes. Each of the two resulting daughter cells has four chromosomes, the same number as the original, or parent, cell.

1. INTERPHASE

2. LATE INTERPHASE

3. EARLY PROPHASE

4. MID-PROPHASE

5. LATE PROPHASE

6. METAPHASE

7. EARLY ANAPHASE

8. LATE ANAPHASE

9. TELOPHASE

10. TWO DAUGHTER CELLS

quently appear as rod-shaped, V-shaped, or J-shaped bodies. The particular appearance depends on the location of the centromere. The chromosome will appear V-shaped when the centromere is centrally located; it will assume the shape of a J when the centromere is situated near the end of the chromosome.

The centromere of each chromosome then divides, and the spindle fibers pull the chromatids, now called *daughter chromosomes,* to the opposite poles of the cell (the *anaphase* stage). At the same moment, the cell pinches in two. Around each cluster of daughter chromosomes, a new nuclear membrane forms. The protoplasm of the cell completes its separation into two new, or daughter, cells during the *telophase* stage. The spindle fibers vanish, the chromosomes lose their distinct outlines, and the two new cells assume the appearance of "resting" cells.

SIGNIFICANCE OF MITOSIS

Mitosis is the means by which two daughter cells receive identical copies of the chromosome complement of the parent cell. It is also the mechanism for distributing equal amounts of deoxyribonucleic acid (DNA) from the parent cell to the daughter cells. The model of duplication of mitotic DNA in the chromosomes shown in figure 17.3 exactly parallels the mode of replication of DNA molecules postulated by Watson and Crick (chapter 16). The longitudinal duplication of the chromosome necessarily involves the replication of DNA. During DNA replication, the two parallel strands of DNA separate, and the exposed bases in each strand can act as a template to form a complementary strand. The end result is two identical molecules of DNA, each containing one strand of nucleotides present in the DNA molecule before duplication and one strand newly synthesized using the old strand as a template. When two identical molecules of DNA have been formed, one copy is passed on to

Figure 17.3 Longitudinal duplication of the chromosome during mitosis involves the replication of DNA. Each daughter chromosome, or chromatid, contains a double-helix DNA molecule.

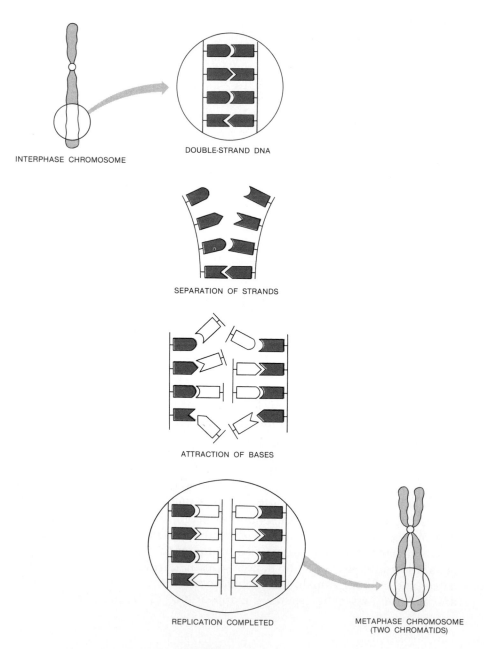

INTERPHASE CHROMOSOME

DOUBLE-STRAND DNA

SEPARATION OF STRANDS

ATTRACTION OF BASES

REPLICATION COMPLETED

METAPHASE CHROMOSOME
(TWO CHROMATIDS)

each of the two daughter cells during cell division. Thus, each daughter cell receives the same set of genetic instructions as was originally present in the parent cell. It should be evident that each chromatid, or daughter chromosome, contains a complete double-helix DNA molecule.

The essential correctness of the model in figure 17.3 was revealed by experimental studies in 1957 by J. Herbert Taylor, then at Columbia University, on dividing cells of seedlings of the bean *Vicia faba*. The seedlings were grown in solutions of radioactive thymidine, a molecule that constitutes one of the nitrogenous bases of DNA. The thymidine was taken up by the chromosomes and all the chromosomes were labeled. After the chromosomes had duplicated in the radioactive thymidine, it was found that the two chromatids of each chromosome at metaphase were radioactive (fig. 17.4). The most reasonable interpretation is that each chain of the double-helix DNA molecule in the parental chromosome built itself a radioactive partner when the parental chromosome duplicated to form two chromatids. Hence, all new daughter chromosomes were labeled.

The cells were then followed through a second mitosis, but the second mitotic division occurred in the *absence* of radioactive thymidine (fig. 17.4). In this case, it was observed that one chromatid arm of the metaphase chromosome was labeled and the other chromatid arm was not labeled. Thus, the DNA of the daughter chromosome, in the presence of nonradioactive thymidine, could build only unlabeled partners during replication. As a result, half of the newly formed chromatids were radioactive and half were not radioactive. The results are in accord with the structure of DNA and its mode of duplication as proposed originally by Watson and Crick.

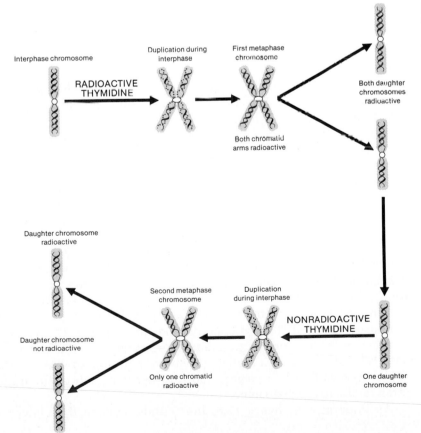

Figure 17.4 DNA molecule in a chromosome consists of two complementary strands wound around each other in a double helix. When a chromosome duplicates in the presence of radioactive thymidine, each daughter chromosome displays radioactivity, each containing a radioactive new DNA strand. When this daughter chromosome duplicates itself again in a *nonradioactive* solution, only one of its descendants contains a labeled strand since DNA in the presence of nonradioactive thymidine can build only unlabeled partners during replication.

Interphase chromosome

RADIOACTIVE THYMIDINE

Duplication during interphase

First metaphase chromosome

Both chromatid arms radioactive

Both daughter chromosomes radioactive

Daughter chromosome radioactive

Second metaphase chromosome

Only one chromatid radioactive

Duplication during interphase

NONRADIOACTIVE THYMIDINE

One daughter chromosome

Daughter chromosome not radioactive

The simplest view of chromosome structure is that each chromosome is composed of a single, highly coiled double-helix DNA molecule. This at first sight may appear to be an oversimplification. The width of a chromosome is very much greater than the diameter of a DNA helix, and the total amount of DNA found in a single human cell during interphase could form an elongated thread about 70 inches long, a distance which is about 100,000 times the diameter of a typical cell. However, the chromosome does not consist solely of a single linear chain of DNA; the nuclear DNA is associated, or complexed, with an appreciable amount of protein (particularly a protein called *histone*). This combination of DNA and protein constitutes the chromatin of the nucleus. The single DNA molecule is complexed with protein along its length and repeatedly folded back on itself to make up the body of the chromosome. Admittedly the helices of DNA would have to be extremely tightly coiled. Unanswered as yet is how this phenomenal amount of tight coiling is undone each time a chromosome replicates. There is thus still a gap between the biochemist's and the microscopist's view of the chromosome.

Another important aspect is revealed by the appearance of the metaphase chromosomes. It is at the metaphase stage that the shapes of the individual chromosomes are most readily discernible. An examination of metaphase plates shows that a given chromosome has a mate that is identical in size and shape. In other words, there are usually two of each type of chromosome. Two identical members are called *homologous chromosomes*, or simply *homologues*. This is comprehensible since one chromosome member has been received from the male parent and the other homologous chromosome has been received from the female parent. Accordingly, the body cell contains two sets of chromosomes, one maternal and the other paternal. This also indicates, as we shall stress later, that a body cell contains two sets of genes, one maternal and the other paternal.

MEIOSIS

In meiosis, the daughter cells receive one member of like pairs of chromosomes. This is unlike mitosis, in which the daughter cells receive an exact duplication of each member of a pair. That the chromosomes unite in pairs before division is one of the distinctive peculiarities of meiosis. The mutual attraction of chromosomes that are alike in size and shape (homologues) is known as *synapsis*. As seen in figure 17.5, homologous chromosomes actually come to lie alongside one another in pairs. Moreover, each chromosome consists of two distinct daughter strands. In other words, each chromosome has duplicated itself longitudinally (as in mitosis) to form two chromatids.

Since two homologous chromosomes pair, and since each chromosome of a homologous pair has duplicated itself, the result is a quadruple chromatid structure known as a *tetrad* (Greek, *tetras*, "a collection of four"). That is to say, a tetrad is a group of four chromatids. For the four chromatids to be distributed individually into four cells, *two* divisions would be required. This is exactly what takes place. Meiosis involves two separate divisions rather than the one that characterizes mitosis. The two divisions accomplish (1) the separation of the homologous chromosomes that had paired, and (2) the separation of the duplicated strands of each chromosome.

As illustrated in figure 17.5, the tetrads arrange themselves in the

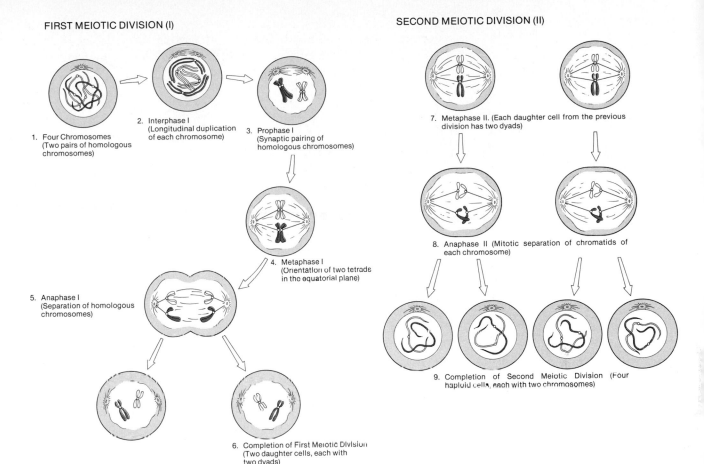

FIRST MEIOTIC DIVISION (I)

1. Four Chromosomes (Two pairs of homologous chromosomes)

2. Interphase I (Longitudinal duplication of each chromosome)

3. Prophase I (Synaptic pairing of homologous chromosomes)

4. Metaphase I (Orientation of two tetrads in the equatorial plane)

5. Anaphase I (Separation of homologous chromosomes)

6. Completion of First Meiotic Division (Two daughter cells, each with two dyads)

SECOND MEIOTIC DIVISION (II)

7. Metaphase II. (Each daughter cell from the previous division has two dyads)

8. Anaphase II (Mitotic separation of chromatids of each chromosome)

9. Completion of Second Meiotic Division (Four haploid cells, each with two chromosomes)

equatorial plane of the spindle and the first meiotic division ensues. Each tetrad is separated into two *dyads* (Greek, *dyas*, "a couple"). One dyad from each tetrad moves to each of the resulting daughter cells. The first meiotic division is said to be *reductional* because it involves the separation of the original synaptic mates, or the original homologous members of chromosomal pairs.

The second meiotic division consists of the separation of the daughter chromatids produced by duplication. Hence, the second division is comparable to mitosis, since it involves separation of the two daughter chromatids of each chromosome. It is said to be *equational*. The overall outcome of meiosis is the formation, from one diploid cell, of four *haploid* cells. Each of the four daughter cells thus has half as many chromosomes as the original parent cell.

MEIOSIS IN HUMANS

Since meiosis occurs during the differentiation, or maturation, of the gametes, the two meiotic divisions are often referred to as the *maturation divisions*. The maturation divisions in the human male are shown in figure 17.6. The germinal cells of the male are termed *spermatogonia* (*gone*, "generation") because they generate the sperm. The spermatogonia, which are diploid, enter into a period of growth and become known as *primary spermatocytes*. In the first maturation division, the primary spermatocyte divides into two *secondary spermatocytes*, each containing halves of the tetrads, or dyads. The secondary spermatocytes

Figure 17.5 Meiosis results in the formation of haploid gametes, each with one member of each pair of chromosomes. Two successive divisions are involved, the first meiotic division (numbers *1* through *6*) and the second meiotic division (numbers *7* through *9*). The outcome of meiosis is the formation from one diploid parent cell (four chromosomes, in this case) of four haploid cells (each with two chromosomes).

Figure 17.6 Meiosis in the human female (oogenesis) and human male (spermatogenesis). For simplicity, only 6 chromosomes are depicted instead of 46 (diploid number). Each diploid spermatogonial cell in the testes of the male produces four haploid sperm cells. Meiosis is essentially the same in the female, except that the division of the cytoplasm is unequal and only one functional haploid egg cell is produced from each diploid oogonium

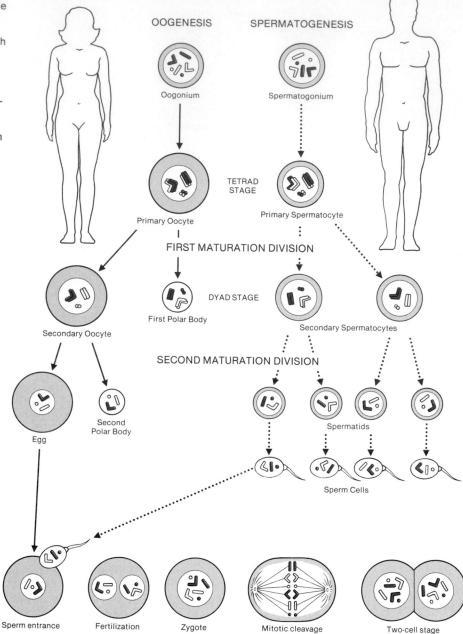

OOGENESIS   SPERMATOGENESIS

Oogonium   Spermatogonium

TETRAD STAGE

Primary Oocyte   Primary Spermatocyte

FIRST MATURATION DIVISION

DYAD STAGE

First Polar Body   Secondary Spermatocytes

Secondary Oocyte

SECOND MATURATION DIVISION

Egg   Second Polar Body   Spermatids

Sperm Cells

Sperm entrance   Fertilization   Zygote   Mitotic cleavage   Two-cell stage

undergo the second maturation division in which the dyads are separated into their individual chromosomal components. The resulting four *spermatids,* which transform into functional spermatozoa, each contain only one set of chromosomes, the haploid number.

The nuclear aspects of meiosis are similar in males and females. There is, however, a marked difference in the cytoplasmic aspects, as shown in figure 17.6. The two meiotic divisions of the *primary oocyte* do not result in four equally mature gametes as in the male, but in only one mature *ovum.* The first meiotic division is vastly unequal with respect to the distribution of cytoplasm. The daughter cell that retains the bulk of the cytoplasm is designated the *secondary oocyte;* the minute cell that is constricted off is the *first polar body.* The first polar body, with its limited cytoplasm, typically degenerates without dividing. The second meiotic division involves another unequal division of the cytoplasm, resulting in the formation of the ovum, with virtually all the original cytoplasm, and a minute, nonfunctional *second polar body*. The ovum, like the sperm, contains the haploid number of chromosomes.

In the illustration (fig. 17.6), the maturation of the primary oocyte is shown parallel to the maturation of the primary spermatocyte. The secondary oocyte and the first polar body have counterparts in the two secondary spermatocytes. The mature ovum and the second polar body are comparable to the four spermatids (or spermatozoa).

SIGNIFICANCE OF MEIOSIS

It should be recalled that each homologous pair of chromosomes consists of one paternal and one maternal chromosome, which were brought together at the antecedent fertilization. The meiotic process leading to the production of gametes results in a segregation of the paternal and maternal chromosome contributions. Accordingly, when gametes are produced, no gamete can have both paternal and maternal chromosomes of a given pair, but can have only one or the other. (This statement ignores the complications of *crossing over*, in which segments of the maternal and paternal chromosomes may exchange with each other.)

Each of the paired chromosomes behaves as though it is entirely independent of all the others so that an individual gamete has an equal chance of obtaining the maternal or the paternal component of each homologous pair of chromosomes. In other words, it is entirely a chance phenomenon as to which member of any chromosome pair moves to a particular gamete. The number of different assortments of maternal and paternal chromosomes is exceedingly large. Suppose a species has only four chromosomes, represented by two paternal chromosomes (labeled A and B) and two maternal chromosomes (labeled a and b). The homologous chromosomes A and a will pair in synapsis; likewise, B and b are synaptic mates. As a result of meiosis, there will be four different assortments of paternal and maternal chromosomes in the gametes—namely, AB, Ab, aB, and ab. These four different kinds of gametes will be produced in equal numbers (25 percent each).

In another example, if the diploid number is six—3 paternal (A, B, C) and 3 maternal (a, b, c)—then 8 (2^3) possible different assortments of maternal and paternal chromosomes are possible. At fertilization, the chances are equal that each of the 8 kinds of sperm will unite with each of the 8 kinds of egg. There will therefore be 64 (8 $\times$ 8) different kinds of fertilized eggs, or zygotes, produced, each of which will have again the double (diploid) set of 6 chromosomes. We need only reflect momentarily on the fact that the diploid chromosome number in man is 46. The amount of diversity in the human gametes is potentially so great as to be scarcely imaginable. Theoretically, over 8 million (2^{23}) different combinations of maternal and paternal chromosomes can result from the distribution of the chromosomes during meiosis. A fertilized egg can have any 1 of over 70 trillion ($2^{23} \times 2^{23}$) possible combinations of maternal and paternal chromosomes. There should be little wonder, then, that no two members of a given family of children are alike, for there is only 1 chance in 70 trillion of their being identical in their heredity—unless, like identical twins, they are products of the division of a single zygote.

In essence, in the production of gametes, the maternal and paternal chromosomes are free to assort themselves, with the limitation that normally one member of every pair of like chromosomes is always represented in each gamete.

THE TRANSMISSION OF TRAITS

When the mature ovum, with its haploid number of chromosomes, is successfully fertilized by a sperm cell, with its haploid number of chromosomes, the diploid number of chromosomes is restored in the nucleus of the ovum—one member of each pair has been obtained from the mother and one from the father. This provides the basis of inheritance from the two parents. The chromosomes are the essential physical agencies in the transmission of hereditary traits between generations. Now that we have some acquaintance with gametes and chromosomes, we shall examine the Mendelian laws of heredity that depend on the behavior of the chromosomes. We shall see that separation of the two members of a pair of homologous chromosomes during meiosis also effects a separation of the members of each pair of genes.

SUMMARY

New cells arise from preexisting cells in the body by cell division, or mitosis. Mitosis is the means by which two daughter cells receive identical copies of the chromosome complement of the parent cell. It is also the mechanism for distributing equal amounts of deoxyribonucleic acid (DNA) from the parent cell to the daughter cells. In the mitotic process, there is a longitudinal duplication of each chromosome followed by a single division of the cell. Only one division is required to separate the duplicated chromosome strands. The outcome of mitosis is the production of two cells with no change in the number of chromosomes.

Meiosis is a special type of cell division by which the gametes (eggs and sperm) are produced. In meiosis, each chromosome duplicates itself as in mitosis. However, unlike mitosis, the homologous chromosomes (one of paternal origin and one of maternal origin) are attracted to each other and come to lie alongside one another in pairs. The result is a quadripartite complex, a tetrad, consisting of four daughter strands. Two divisions are required to effect the separation of the four daughter chromatids. The eventual products are four daughter cells each with one-half the original number of chromosomes. In the meiotic divisions, maternal and paternal chromosomes become freely assorted, and the possibilities for different combinations of maternal and paternal chromosomes in the gametes are numerous. Meiosis thus plays a prominent role in reassorting genes in new combinations.

Mendel's Work and the Principles of Inheritance 18

Our understanding of the principles of inheritance traces largely to the unpretentious studies of the Austrian monk Gregor Johann Mendel (fig. 18.1), who was a contemporary of Charles Darwin, although probably unknown by him. For eight years, Mendel carried out carefully controlled breeding experiments on the common pea plant in his small garden of the monastery of Saint Thomas at Brünn in Moravia (now Brno, Czechoslovakia). He worked with large numbers of plants so that statistical accuracy could be assured. He sent the results of his work to the celebrated botanist Karl von Nägeli of the University of Vienna. Nägeli was one of the outstanding scientists of Europe, and the chief authority of his time on plant hybridization. Nägeli, however, failed to grasp the import of Mendel's efforts.

In 1866, Mendel's results appeared in a publication of the Brünn Society of Natural History. In the small compass of 44 printed pages, one of the most important laws of nature ever discovered by man is clearly revealed. Yet, his paper elicited little interest or comment. No one praised or disputed Mendel's findings. It is likely that the 19th century biologists were baffled by Mendel's mathematical, or statistical, approach to the study of hybridization. Botany and mathematics were strange bedfellows for that period.

Mendel's important contribution lay ignored or unappreciated until 1900, which was 16 years after his death and 34 years after his work was published. His findings were independently rediscovered and verified, almost simultaneously, by three botanists—Hugo de Vries in Holland, Carl Correns in Germany, and Erich von Tschermak in Vienna. Their contributions were published only a few months apart in 1900, and this remarkable triple discovery immediately caught the attention of the scientific world. The science of heredity is recorded as having been born in 1900, and Mendel has since received the scientific acclaim that was denied him in his lifetime. Mendel's principles are sufficiently precise to entitle them to be called *laws*.

Figure 18.1 Gregor Mendel, 1822–1884. (Courtesy of Vítězslav Oriel, Moravian Museum in Brno, Czechoslovakia.)

MENDEL'S LAW OF SEGREGATION

Mendel carried out his breeding experiments in a garden plot measuring only 20 feet by 120 feet alongside the monastery (fig. 18.2). One of the reasons for choosing peas for experimentation was that they were available in many pure breeding varieties. Mendel initially obtained from several seedsmen 34 purebred varieties, which differed in such characteristics as vine height, position of flower, shape and color of seed, and configuration of pod. Each variety was painstakingly grown for two years to establish beyond doubt that each bred true to type. Mendel eventually selected for his experiments those varieties that showed

Figure 18.2 Experimental garden of Gregor Mendel at the monastery in Brno. (From L. C. Dunn, The study of genetics in man—retrospect and prospect. In *Birth Defects: Original Article Series,* ed. D. Bergsma, vol. 1 (2):6, 1965. *New Directions in Human Genetics: A Symposium.* The National Foundation—March of Dimes.)

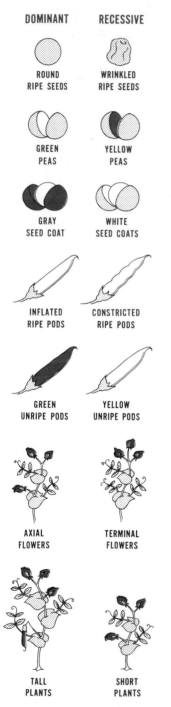

Figure 18.3 Seven pairs of contrasting traits in the pea plant studied by Mendel.

sharp contrasts in certain characters. In particular, he selected seven pairs of sharply recognizable contrasting characters (fig. 18.3), as follows:

1. Shape of ripe seed: round vs. wrinkled
2. Color of pea: yellow vs. green
3. Color of seed coat: gray vs. white
4. Form of ripe pod: inflated vs. constricted between the seeds
5. Color of unripe pod: green vs. yellow
6. Position of flower: axial (distributed along main stem) vs. terminal (bunched at top of stem)
7. Length of stem: tall (from 6 to 7 feet) vs. short (from ¾ to 1½ feet)

Varieties differing in each of these contrasted pairs were crossed and the characteristics of the hybrid offspring were classified. Pea plants are normally self-fertilizing. However, artificial cross-fertilizations can be readily accomplished by removing the pollen-producing organs (stamens) of the flower bud, and subsequently transferring pollen (containing the male gamete, or sperm) from another flower to the egg-producing organ (pistil).

One of Mendel's experiments is illustrated in figure 18.4. A purebred variety of tall plants (about 6 feet in height) was artificially crossed with a purebred short form (about 1 foot high). When seeds of this cross were grown, the plants that emerged were not intermediate in height but all resembled one of the parents. The whole of this first filial (F₁) generation consisted solely of tall plants. Likewise, in crosses involving the other six contrasted pairs, the offspring resembled only one of the parents. When plants with wrinkled seeds were crossed with those with round seeds, all the offspring had round seeds. When yellow peas were crossed with green, the offspring were all green. In each cross, one character and only one prevailed in the F₁ generation. The character that appeared in the F₁ generation was called *dominant.*

When the F₁ plants were allowed to self-fertilize, the second filial, or F₂, generation was found to contain plants of both contrasting types. In our illustrative example (fig. 18.4), the F₂ generation was found to con-

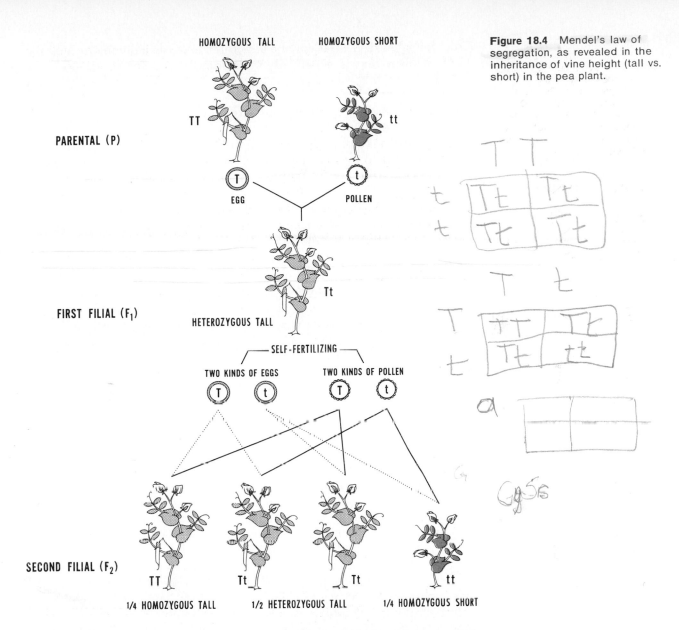

Figure 18.4 Mendel's law of segregation, as revealed in the inheritance of vine height (tall vs. short) in the pea plant.

HOMOZYGOUS TALL   HOMOZYGOUS SHORT

PARENTAL (P)

TT   tt

T   EGG   t   POLLEN

FIRST FILIAL (F₁)

Tt

HETEROZYGOUS TALL

SELF-FERTILIZING

TWO KINDS OF EGGS   TWO KINDS OF POLLEN

T   t   T   t

SECOND FILIAL (F₂)

TT   Tt   Tt   tt

1/4 HOMOZYGOUS TALL   1/2 HETEROZYGOUS TALL   1/4 HOMOZYGOUS SHORT

tain both tall and short plants. Actual counts showed that 75 percent of the F₂ offspring were tall and 25 percent were short. In comparable crosses involving other pairs of traits, Mendel observed that the characteristic that seemingly disappeared in the first generation invariably reappeared to make up one-quarter of the second generation. The character that receded from view in the F₁ generation was called *recessive*. In essence, then, the F₁ hybrids for the seven contrasted pairs each produced offspring consisting of dominants and recessives, always in the proportion of three-fourths dominant and one-fourth recessive.

Mendel concluded that there must be discrete material units, or *factors*, that are transmitted to the offspring from the parents through the gametes. Mendel's factors are now known as *genes*. The genes comprising a given pair may be alike or may be different. If the members are contrasting, one (the dominant gene) typically masks the expression of its partner (the recessive gene). The dominant gene is customarily symbolized by a capital letter (for example, *T*); the recessive gene, by a corresponding small letter *(t)*. A purebred tall plant is said to be *homozy-*

gous for tallness *(TT)*. It may be also referred to as a *dominant homozygote*. A plant that is genetically *tt* is homozygous for shortness, or as we often say, is a recessive homozygote. The F₁ offspring illustrated in the cross in figure 18.4 is a heterozygote; in other words, it is *heterozygous* for tallness, carrying two unlike genes *(Tt)*.

If the genes occur in pairs in an individual, then evidently some process must take place to ensure that each gamete (egg or sperm) contains one, and only one, member of a pair of genes. Mendel had no knowledge of the special kind of nuclear division (meiosis) that occurs during the production of the gametes. However, he correctly inferred that the members of a pair of genes must separate, or segregate, from each other during gamete formation. Thus, a given gamete can carry *T* or *t*, but not both. This fundamental concept that only one member of any pair of genes in a parent is transmitted to each offspring is Mendel's first law, known as the *law of segregation*.

Figure 18.4 shows that the F₁ heterozygote *(Tt)* produces two kinds of pollen cells (sperm); half the pollen carry the *T* gene and the other half carry the *t* gene. The same two kinds occur in equal proportions among the egg cells. Each kind of pollen has an equal chance of meeting each kind of egg. Pollen carrying *T* may fertilize *T* eggs, forming *TT* plants; *T* pollen may fertilize *t* eggs, forming *Tt* plants; *t* pollen may fertilize *T* eggs, also forming *Tt* plants; and *t* pollen may fertilize *t* eggs, forming *tt* plants. Each of these combinations, on the basis of pure chance, is equally likely to occur. The probabilities of occurrence are the same as those illustrated by the tossing of a coin. If two coins are repeatedly tossed at the same time, the result to be expected from the laws of chance is that the combination "head and head" will fall in one-fourth of the cases, the combination "head and tail" in one-half of them, and the combination "tail and tail" in the remaining one-fourth. This is the ratio that occurs in the F₂ generation. The ratio of genetic constitutions in the F₂ generation may be expressed as ¼*TT*:½*Tt*:¼*tt*, or 0.25*TT*:0.50*Tt*:0.25*tt*, or simply 1*TT*:2*Tt*:1*tt*.

Geneticists constantly have to make a distinction between the external, or observable, appearance of the organism and its internal hereditary constitution. They call the former the phenotype (visible type) and the latter the genotype (hereditary type). In our illustrative example, there are three different genotypes: *TT*, *Tt*, and *tt*. The dominant homozygote *(TT)* cannot be distinguished by inspection from the heterozygote *(Tt)*. Thus, *TT* and *Tt* genotypes have the same phenotype, namely, tall. Accordingly, on the basis of phenotype alone, the F₂ ratio is ¾ tall: ¼ short, or 0.75 tall:0.25 short, or finally, 3 tall:1 short.

MENDEL AND THE CHROMOSOME THEORY OF HEREDITY

The lengthy discussion in chapter 17 should permit us to understand the relation of Mendel's work to chromosomes. Mendel, of course, was unaware that his hereditary units were carried in the chromosomes. It was Walter S. Sutton in 1902 who first called attention to the parallelism in the behavior of genes and chromosomes. We have learned that chromosomes occur in pairs and that the members of a pair separate, or segregate, from each other during meiosis. Mendel's experiments reveal that the genes occur in pairs, and that the members of each pair of genes separate from each other in the production of the gametes.

Evidently then, the most reasonable inference is that the genes are located in the chromosomes.

Figure 18.5 shows the separation of the pair of homologous chromosomes during meiosis of the heterozygote carrying the T and t genes. The gene T occupies a particular site, or *locus*, in one of the chromosomes. The alternative gene, t, occurs at the identical locus in the other homologous chromosome. The alternative forms of a given gene, occupying a given locus, are termed *alleles*. Thus, T is an allele of t, or we may also say that T is allelic to t. Now, we have already seen that the heterozygote (Tt) produces two types of gametes, T and t, in equal numbers. It should be evident from figure 18.5 that the gametic ratio $1T{:}1t$ is the consequence of the separation of the two homologous chromosomes during meiosis, one chromosome containing the T gene and its homologue carrying one t allele. The chromosome theory also explains another feature of Mendel's results—the independent assortment of traits.

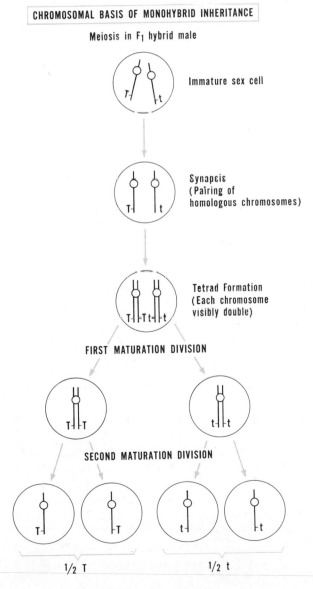

CHROMOSOMAL BASIS OF MONOHYBRID INHERITANCE

Meiosis in F_1 hybrid male

Immature sex cell

Synapsis
(Pairing of homologous chromosomes)

Tetrad Formation
(Each chromosome visibly double)

FIRST MATURATION DIVISION

SECOND MATURATION DIVISION

½ T   ½ t

Figure 18.5 Chromosomal basis of monohybrid inheritance. When one chromosome of a pair carries a given gene (T, in this case), and its homologue carries the alternative form of the gene *(t)*, then meiosis results in the production of two distinct kinds of gametes in equal proportions, T and t.

MENDEL'S LAW OF INDEPENDENT ASSORTMENT

Mendel also established the *law of independent assortment, which states that one trait (one gene pair) segregates independently of another trait (another gene pair).* This principle stemmed from the outcome of crosses of two pea plants that differed from each other in two characteristics. As seen in figure 18.6, a variety characterized by yellow and round seeds *(YYRR)* was crossed with a variety in which the seeds were green and wrinkled *(yyrr).* Only the dominant characteristics (yellow, round) were displayed by the F_1 plants *(YyRr).* In contrast to the uniformity in the F_1 generation, four different phenotypes arose in the F_2 generation, two like the original parents and two new combinations (yellow, wrinkled and green, round). The four F_2 phenotypes appeared in a ratio 9:3:3:1. For such a ratio to be obtained, the F_1 plants *(YyRr)* must have produced four kinds of gametes in equal proportions: YR, Yr, yR, and yr. Stated an-

Figure 18.6 Mendel's law of independent assortment, as revealed in the inheritance of two pairs of characters (color and shape of the seed) in the pea plant.

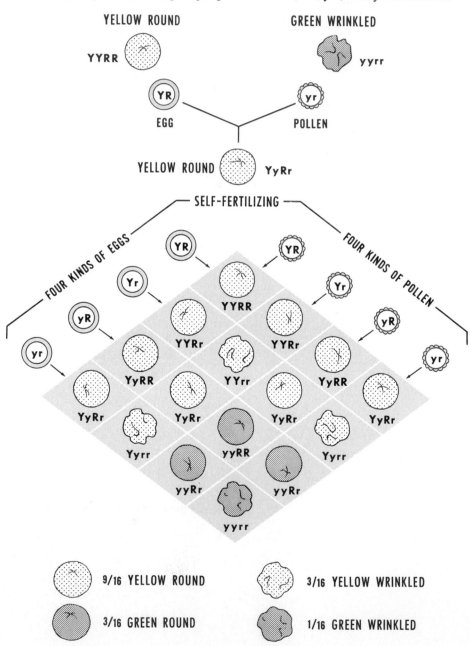

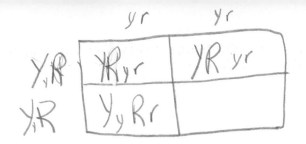

Plate 14 Pelger's nuclear anomaly, a dominant trait that affects the shape of the nuclei of white blood cells. The dominant homozygous state is apparently lethal in man.

MAN   RABBIT

Normal

 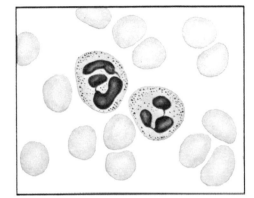

Pelger

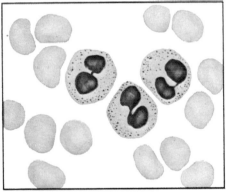 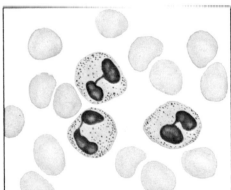

Super-Pelger

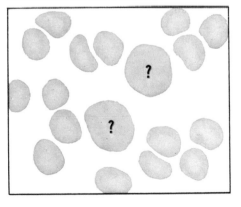 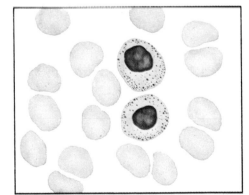

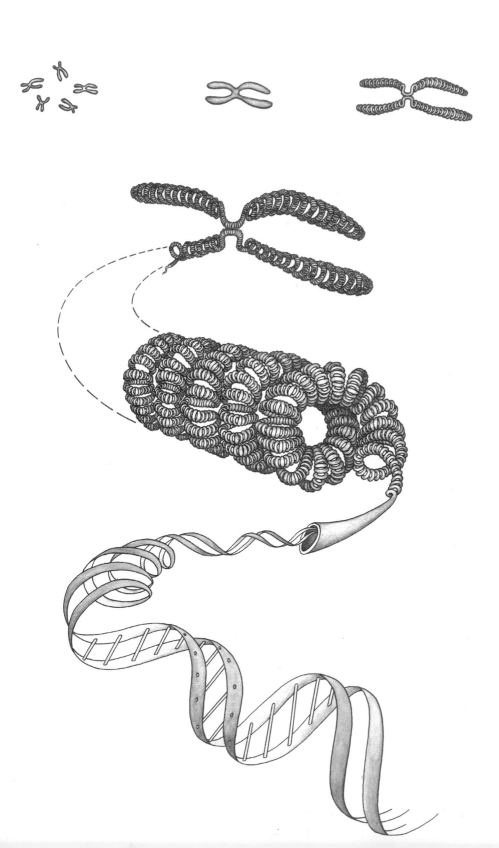

other way, the segregation of the members of one pair of genes must have occurred independently of the segregation of the members of the other gene pair during gamete formation. Thus, 50 percent of the gametes received Y, and of these same gametes, half obtained R and the other half r. Accordingly, 25 percent of the gametes were YR and 25 percent were Yr. Likewise, 50 percent of the gametes carried y, of which half contained as well R and half r (or 25 percent yR and 25 percent yr). The four kinds of egg cells and the four kinds of pollen (sperm) can unite in 16 possible ways, as shown graphically in the F₂ "checkerboard" in figure 18.6.

The convenient checkerboard method of analysis was devised by the British geneticist R. C. Punnett. The eggs and sperm are listed separately on two different sides of the checkerboard, and each square represents an offspring that arises from the union of a given egg cell and a given sperm cell. The reading of the squares discloses the classical Mendelian phenotypic ratio of 9:3:3:1 for two pairs of independently assorting genes.

Figure 18.7 shows how the four types of gametes are produced with equal frequency in terms of the behavior of two pairs of chromosomes during meiosis. Recall from chapter 15 that the homologous chromosomes of one pair were labeled A and a and those of the other pair B and b. The outcome of meiosis was the production of equal numbers of the combinations AB, Ab, aB, and ab. When, as in figure 18.7, the two pairs of alleles R, r and Y, y are inserted at appropriate loci in the two pairs of chromosomes, it becomes apparent that four types of gametes, YR, Yr, yR, and yr, are produced in equal numbers. Once again, the parallelism in the behavior of genes and chromosomes is striking.

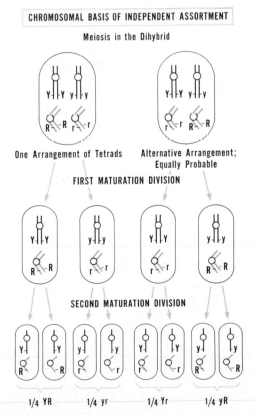

CHROMOSOMAL BASIS OF INDEPENDENT ASSORTMENT

Meiosis in the Dihybrid

One Arrangement of Tetrads   Alternative Arrangement; Equally Probable

FIRST MATURATION DIVISION

SECOND MATURATION DIVISION

1/4 YR   1/4 yr   1/4 Yr   1/4 yR

Figure 18.7 Chromosomal basis of dihybrid inheritance. The two pairs of genes, Y, y and R, r are located in two different pairs of chromosomes. When a dihybrid (YyRr) undergoes meiosis, there are two equally likely ways in which the tetrads may line up. The outcome is the formation of four kinds of gametes, in equal numbers (YR, Yr, yR, and yr).

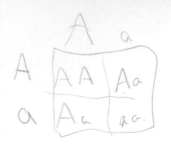

THREE OR MORE GENE PAIRS

When individuals differing in three characteristics are crossed, the situation is naturally more complex, but the principle of independent assortment still obtains. An individual heterozygous for three independently assorting pairs of alleles (for example, *Aa, Bb* and *Cc*) produces eight types of gametes in equal numbers, as illustrated in figure 18.8. Random union among these eight kinds of gametes yields 64 equally possible combinations. Stated another way, Punnett's checkerboard method of analysis would have 64 (8 × 8) squares. An analysis of the offspring reveals that, among the 64 possible combinations, there are only eight visibly different phenotypes. You may wish to verify that the phenotypic ratio is 27:9:9:9:3:3:3:1.

The use of the Punnett square for three or more independently assorting genes is cumbersome. Here we will introduce one of the cardinal rules of probability: *The chance that two or more independent events will occur together is the product of their chances of occurring separately* (see Appendix C). As an example, what proportion of the offspring of the cross *AaBbCc* × *AaBbCc* would be expected to have the genotype *AaBBcc*? The individual computations are as follows, treating each character (or event) independently:

1. The chance that an individual will be $Aa = \frac{1}{2}$
2. The chance that an individual will be $BB = \frac{1}{4}$
3. The chance that an individual will be $cc = \frac{1}{4}$

Figure 18.8 Gamete formation in a trihybrid. The members of the three different pairs of genes assort independently of each other when gametes are formed. The separation of the *Aa* pair, *Bb* pair, and *Cc* pair, respectively, can be treated as independent events. The outcome is eight genetically different gametes.

Trihybrid

Products of meiosis

Gametes

Assuming independence among these three pairs of alternatives, the chance of the three combining together (AaBBcc) is the product of their separate probabilities, as follows:

$$\frac{1}{2} \times \frac{1}{4} \times \frac{1}{4} = \frac{1}{32}.$$

SIGNIFICANCE OF GENETIC RECOMBINATION

An impressively large array of different kinds of individuals can arise from the simple processes of segregation and recombination of independently assorting genes. Figure 18.9 considers a few of the independently assorting traits in the fruit fly *Drosophila melanogaster*. It is seen that the number of visibly different classes (phenotypes) of offspring is doubled by each additional heterozygous pair of independently assorting genes. Each additional heterozygous gene pair multiplies the number of visibly different combinations by a factor of 2. Thus, if the parents are each heterozygous for 10 pairs of genes (when dominance is complete), the number of different phenotypes among the progeny becomes 2^{10}, or 1,024.

Other mathematical regularities are evident as we increase the number of heterozygous pairs (table 18.1). As the number of heterozygous characteristics increases, the chance of recovering one of the parental types becomes progressively less. Thus, when a single heterozygous pair (Aa) is involved, 1 in 4 will resemble one of the original parents in both appearance and genotype (AA or aa). When four heterozygous traits are involved, only 1 in 256 will be genotypically like either of the original parents. Evidently, no single genetic constitution is ever likely to be exactly duplicated in a person (save in identical twins). Each individual is genetically unique.

Figure 18.9 Inheritance of traits in the fruit fly, when the parents are each heterozygous for one (Aa), two (AaBb), and three (AaBbCc) independently assorting traits. The gene for long wings (A) is dominant over the gene for vestigial wings (a); gray body (B) is dominant over ebony (b); and normal eyes (C) is dominant over the eyeless condition (c). The number of visibly different classes (phenotypes) of offspring increases progressively with each additional pair of traits. The generalized formula for determining the number of different phenotypes among the offspring (when dominance is complete) is 2^n, where n stands for the number of different heterozygous pairs of genes.

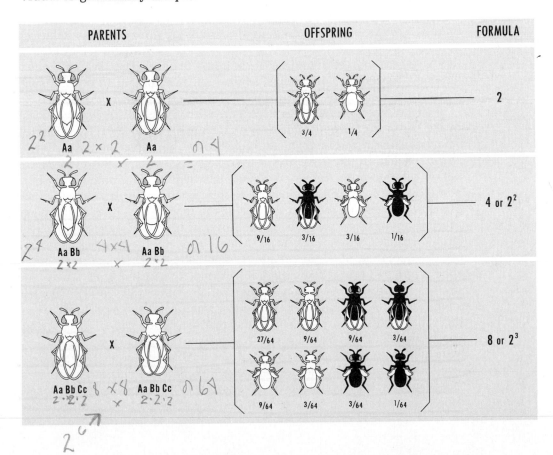

PARENTS	OFFSPRING	FORMULA
Aa × Aa	3/4 1/4	2
Aa Bb × Aa Bb	9/16 3/16 3/16 1/16	4 or 2^2
Aa Bb Cc × Aa Bb Cc	27/64 9/64 9/64 3/64 9/64 3/64 3/64 1/64	8 or 2^3

Number of heterozygous pairs involved in the cross	Number of different types of gametes produced by the F_1 hybrid	Number of visibly different F_2 classes (that is, F_2 phenotypes)*	Number of genotypically different F_2 combinations (that is, F_2 genotypes)	Chance of recovering genotype of either one of the original parents
1	2	2	3	1 in 4
2	4	4	9	1 in 16
3	8	8	27	1 in 64
4	16	16	81	1 in 256
5	32	32	405	1 in 1,024
n	2^n	2^n	3^n	1 in 4^n

* Assumes complete dominance in each pair.

Table 18.1
Characteristics of Crosses Involving Various Pairs of Independently Assorting Genes

LINKAGE

Mendel's principle of independent assortment is based on the assumption that each gene for a trait is carried in a different pair of chromosomes. However, the number of pairs of chromosomes is considerably less than the number of pairs of contrasting genes. Accordingly, many genes must be carried in a single chromosome. Genes located together in any one chromosome are said to be *linked*, and the linked genes tend to stay together during their hereditary transmission. The principle of linkage ranks with segregation and independent assortment as the third major law of inheritance.

The principle of linkage was firmly established by T. H. Morgan and his students by studies on the fruit fly. The fruit fly *Drosophila melanogaster* has only four pairs of chromosomes. Several hundred different genes have been identified in the fruit fly, and all fall into four linkage groups corresponding to the four pairs of chromosomes (fig. 18.10). Corn has 10 chromosome pairs, and the number of groups of linked genes has been found experimentally to be 10. The correspondence between the number of linkage groups and the number of chromosome pairs further substantiates the chromosome theory of inheritance.

T. H. Morgan was able to ascertain with a high degree of accuracy the point on the chromosome that a given gene in the fruit fly occupies. The evidence brought to bear on locating the genes in the different chromosomes of the fruit fly is involved. Essentially, the evidence is based on the interchange of genes between the chromosomes of a homologous pair during meiosis, a phenomenon known as *crossing over* (fig. 18.11). Crossing over occurs during the tetrad stage of meiosis, when four chromatids are present for each pair of homologous chromosomes. Only two of the four chromatid strands are involved in the exchange of corresponding parts, or segments. Typically, two strands twist about each other, and the two members then break and fuse in such a way that each chromatid comes to have a part of the other (fig. 18.11). The frequency of interchange of chromatid segments furnishes a measure of the relative distance between two pairs of linked genes. The farther apart the loci of two linked genes, the greater the likelihood that a crossover will occur between the two loci. The chance of a crossover becomes less likely as the distance between the linked genes decreases.

Because of the phenomenon of crossing over, only two very closely linked genes will tend to be transmitted intact in their passage from one

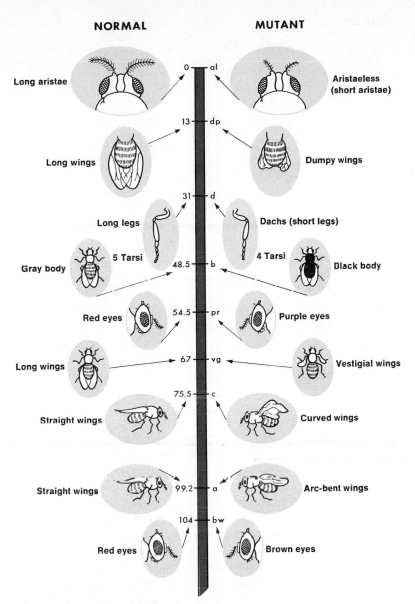

NORMAL   **MUTANT**

Long aristae — 0 — al — Aristaeless (short aristae)

Long wings — 13 — dp — Dumpy wings

Long legs — 31 — d — Dachs (short legs)

Gray body — 5 Tarsi — 48.5 — b — 4 Tarsi — Black body

Red eyes — 54.5 — pr — Purple eyes

Long wings — 67 — vg — Vestigial wings

Straight wings — 75.5 — c — Curved wings

Straight wings — 99.2 — a — Arc-bent wings

Red eyes — 104 — bw — Brown eyes

Figure 18.10 Linked genes in a portion of the second chromosome of the fruit fly *Drosophila melanogaster.* (From James D. Watson, *Molecular biology of the gene,* 3rd ed. Copyright © 1976 by J. D. Watson; W. A. Benjamin, Inc., Menlo Park, California).

generation to the next. In the illustrative example (fig. 18.11), if the two pairs of genes had been so closely linked as to preclude any crossing over between them, only two classes of gametes would have been formed: one gamete containing *AB,* and the other, *ab.* However, as a consequence of crossing over, four genetically different types of gametes are produced. Thus, whereas the effect of linkage is to decrease variability, crossing over provides a mechanism for increasing variability—that is, reshuffling genes in new combinations. Indeed, most of the varied combinations theoretically possible among linked pairs of genes eventually occur as a result of crossing over.

The process of crossing over produces new combinations of linked genes, or *recombinations.* The recombination types (*Ab* and *aB* in fig. 18.11) do not exceed in frequency the original, or old, combination types (*AB* and *ab*). The recombination types are always less than 50 percent

Figure 18.11 Crossing over of chromosomal material during the tetrad stage of meiosis. If the two pairs of genes were *not* linked, the hybrid individual *(AaBb)* would produce four genetically different gametes in equal proportions *(AB, Ab, aB,* and *ab)*. A hybrid containing the two pairs of *linked* genes also produces four genetically different gametes as a consequence of crossing over, but the new combinations of linked genes, or recombination types *(Ab* and *aB)*, arise less frequently than the original combination types *(AB* and *ab)*. The magnitude of deviation from a 1:1:1:1 ratio depends on the frequency with which crossing over occurs between the linked genes.

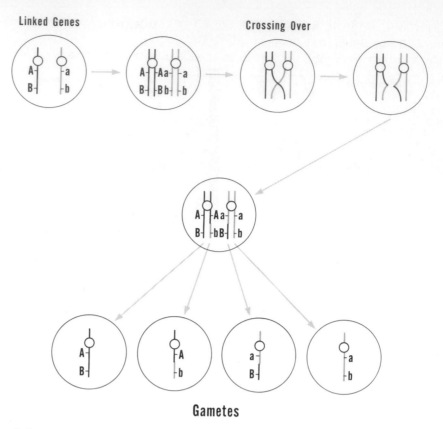

Gametes

of the total gametes produced; most of the gametes carry the old combinations of linked genes. This is because a crossover that might involve the two linked loci does *not* happen in every tetrad. Four kinds of gametes *(AB, Ab, aB,* and *ab)* result from a given tetrad only when a crossover event involving these loci occurs in that tetrad. However, if a crossover fails to occur between the two linked genes in a particular tetrad, only the old combinations are produced *(AB* and *ab)*. The old combination types thus constitute more than 50 percent of the total gametes, the exact percentage depending on the extent to which crossing over occurs between the two loci in the entire population of tetrads.

Mendel's discoveries were striking and far-reaching. It is even more remarkable that the genes for the seven characters studied by Mendel are located in separate chromosomes. It was a most fortuitous circumstance that Mendel selected exactly the same number of contrasting characters as there are chromosome pairs (seven) in the pea plant. If Mendel had happened to work on two linked traits, he certainly would have encountered some puzzling ratios among the offspring, and the discovery of the great principle of independent assortment would in all probability have been long delayed.

SUMMARY

Gregor Mendel's painstaking studies on inheritance in garden peas represent the cornerstone of the science of genetics. Mendel postulated that a given character, or trait, is governed by discrete factors (now called *genes*), which occur in pairs. Mendel formulated two important principles: the first, known as the *law of segregation*, states that only one member of any pair of genes in a parent is transmitted to the offspring; the second, known as the *law of independent assortment*, states that the

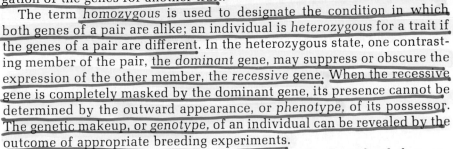

segregation of the genes for one trait is entirely independent of the segregation of the genes for another trait.

The term *homozygous* is used to designate the condition in which both genes of a pair are alike; an individual is *heterozygous* for a trait if the genes of a pair are different. In the heterozygous state, one contrasting member of the pair, the *dominant* gene, may suppress or obscure the expression of the other member, the *recessive* gene. When the recessive gene is completely masked by the dominant gene, its presence cannot be determined by the outward appearance, or *phenotype*, of its possessor. The genetic makeup, or *genotype*, of an individual can be revealed by the outcome of appropriate breeding experiments.

It is now evident that genes assort independently only if they are located in separate chromosomes. Genes are arranged in a linear sequence in the chromosome, and each chromosome provides loci for many genes. Closely adjacent, or *linked*, genes in a chromosome tend to remain together during their hereditary transmission. However, as a result of crossing over—the exchange of chromatid segments during meiosis—the original combination of genes in a particular chromosome can be broken up. The reshuffling of genes by crossing over increases greatly the number of genetically different kinds of gametes that one individual can potentially form.

19 Mendelian Inheritance in Man

The organisms that geneticists favor for study are ones that can be grown experimentally in large numbers and that have short intervals between generations. The fruit fly, the mouse, bacteria, and corn admirably meet these qualifications. The fruit fly can produce a new generation in less than two weeks, and a single mated pair can yield more than 100 offspring. Bacteria have a generation time of only 20 minutes. Humans obviously are not ideal subjects for genetical investigation. The accepted social institution of monogamy, the comparatively long life of the individual, the one child at birth, and the relatively few children born to parents are all limiting factors in the study of human inheritance. With direct experimentation on humans disallowed, the geneticist must content himself with marriages that have already taken place. The analysis of family histories is understandably less precise than controlled breeding experiments in the laboratory. Nevertheless, substantial and invaluable information has accumulated through careful analysis of a very large number of human pedigrees.

FAMILY LAWS

The simplest inheritance pattern is one in which the trait is governed by a single pair of genes—*A* and its alternative allele, *a*. The three different genotypes, *AA*, *Aa*, and *aa*, in a population can give rise to six types of marriages. The six possible marriages and their offspring are listed in table 19.1. The trait used for illustrative purposes in the table is *albinism* (absence of pigment), which in humans is a recessive condition (fig. 19.1). The outcome of each type of marriage follows the Mendelian principles

Table 19.1
Simple Recessive Mendelian Inheritance, Involving a Single Pair of Genes (Normal Pigmentation vs. Albinism)

| MATING TYPES | | GAMETES | | | | OFFSPRING | |
| | | First Parent | | Second Parent | | | |
Genotypes	Phenotypes	50%	50%	50%	50%	Genotypes	Phenotypes
$AA \times AA$	Normal × Normal	A	A	A	A	100% AA	100% Normal
$AA \times Aa$	Normal × Normal	A	A	A	a	50% AA 50% Aa	100% Normal
$Aa \times Aa$	Normal × Normal	A	a	A	a	25% AA 50% Aa 25% aa	75% Normal 25% Albino
$AA \times aa$	Normal × Albino	A	A	a	a	100% Aa	100% Normal
$Aa \times aa$	Normal × Albino	A	a	a	a	50% AA 50% aa	50% Normal 50% Albino
$aa \times aa$	Albino × Albino	a	a	a	a	100% aa	100% Albino

of segregation and recombination. Since the various possibilities pertain to specified types of families, the probabilities of the offspring from the given marriages are often termed the *family laws*.

In table 19.1, the gene for normal pigmentation is designated *A*; the recessive allele for absence of pigment, *a*. The marriage *AA* × *AA* gives rise solely to normal homozygous offspring, *AA*. Two kinds of progeny, *AA* and *Aa* in equal proportions, result from the cross of a homozygous normal parent *(AA)* and a heterozygous parent *(Aa)*. The marriage of two heterozygotes *(Aa* × *Aa)* produces *AA, Aa,* and *aa* offspring in the classical Mendelian ratio of 1:2:1. Only heterozygous offspring *(Aa)* emerge from the marriage *AA* × *aa*. Both heterozygous *(Aa)* and recessive *(aa)* progeny, in equal numbers, arise from the cross of a heterozygous parent *(Aa)* and a recessive parent *(aa)*. Lastly, two recessive parents *(aa* × *aa)* produce only recessive offspring *(aa)*.

It should be understood that the 3:1 phenotypic ratio resulting from the marriage of two heterozygotes, or the 1:1 ratio from the marriage of a heterozygote and a recessive person, are expectations based on probability, and not invariable outcomes. The production of large numbers of offspring increases the probability of obtaining, for example, the 1:1 progeny ratio, just as many tosses of a coin improve the chances of approximating the 1 head:1 tail ratio. If a coin is tossed only two times, a head on the first toss is not invariably followed by a tail on a second toss. In like manner, if only two offspring are produced from a marriage of heterozygous and recessive parents, it should not be thought that one normal offspring is always accompanied by one recessive offspring. With small numbers of progeny, as is characteristic of man, any ratio might arise in a given family.

Stated another way, the 3:1 and 1:1 ratios reveal the risk or odds of a given child having the particular trait involved. If the first child of two

Figure 19.1 Albino person showing the complete absence of pigment in the eyes, hair, and skin. Natives of the Archipelago Coral Islands (100 miles east of the New Guinea mainland) are said to take care of their "pure white" relatives who can hardly see in the glare of the tropical sun. (Courtesy of Wide World Photos.)

heterozygous parents is an albino, the odds that the second child will be an albino remain 1 out of 4. These odds hold for each subsequent child, irrespective of the number of previously affected children. Each conception is an entirely independent event. If this still appears puzzling, consider once again the tossing of a coin. The first time a coin is tossed, the chance of obtaining either a head or a tail is 1 in 2. Whether the toss is repeated immediately or nine months later, the chance of the coin falling head or tail is still 1 in 2, or 50 percent. (See Appendix C.)

FAMILY PEDIGREE CHARTS

The human geneticist uses certain symbols in the construction of pedigree charts (fig. 19.2). A square indicates a male, whereas a circle denotes a female. The male may also be identified by the symbol of Mars, ♂, and the female may be represented by Venus' sign, ♀. The hollow or unshaded symbol denotes a normal person, and the shaded or solid symbol represents a person affected with a disorder. The affected person in the immediate family who has come to the attention of the genetic counselor is referred to as the *propositus*, if a male, and *proposita*, if a female. In the pedigree chart, the position of the propositus (or proposita) is indicated by an arrow.

A marriage between two individuals is indicated by a horizontal line connecting their symbols; the usual practice is to place the male first. Marriages involving close relatives (consanguineous marriages) are represented by two horizontal lines. Successive generations are designated by Roman numerals, while the various individuals within a generation are numbered consecutively from left to right, with Arabic figures. Brothers and sisters (sibs) are indicated in chronological order of birth. Thus, each individual in the pedigree is identified by both a Roman and an Arabic number (for example, II–3).

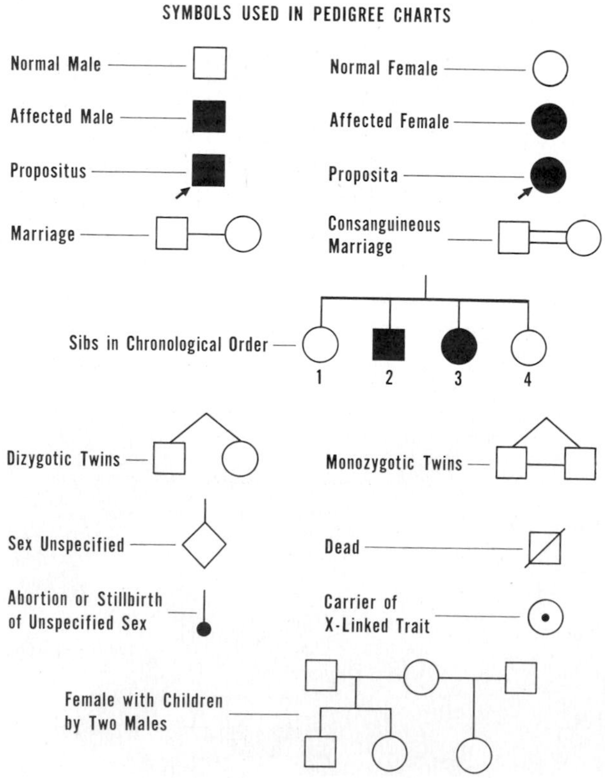

Figure 19.2 Symbols used in the construction of pedigree charts.

SYMBOLS USED IN PEDIGREE CHARTS

Special symbols are used for monozygotic (identical) twins, dizygotic (fraternal) twins, abortions or stillbirths, and deaths (fig. 19.2). The traits under consideration in this chapter are autosomal traits, in which the males and females are equally likely to have or to transmit the trait. In a later chapter, we shall learn of traits in which transmission is influenced by the sex of the parents, the so-called sex-linked traits. Heterozygous carriers of autosomal and sex-linked traits are often symbolized in a special way, as shown in figure 19.2.

RECESSIVELY INHERITED DISORDERS

In the vast majority of cases of recessive inheritance, affected persons are derived from marriages of two heterozygous carriers. In other words, recessive disorders in family histories tend to appear only among siblings, not in their parents. This is exemplified by the family chart in figure 19.3. This pedigree states, in symbolic form, that a normal man married a normal woman. Apparently, both were heterozygous carriers since one of the four children (the first child, designated II–1) exhibited the recessive trait. This son, although affected, had two normal offspring (III–1 and III–2). These two children must be carriers (Aa), having received the a gene from their father (II–1), and the A gene from the unaffected mother (II–2). The genetic constitution of the mother (II–2) cannot be ascertained; she may be either homozygous dominant (AA) or a heterozygous carrier (Aa).

We can also deduce that the daughter (II–6) of the first marriage was a carrier (Aa). Her two children were normal, but it is to be noted that her first child (III–4) married a first cousin (III–3), from which marriage affected children (IV–1 and IV–2) were born. Accordingly, the daughter of the third generation (III–4) must have been heterozygous, and in turn, her mother (II–6) was most likely heterozygous (or else she married a heterozygous man). Similarly, the male involved in the cousin marriage (III–3) must have been heterozygous.

Pedigrees of the above kind typify the inheritance of such recessively determined traits in man as albinism, afibrinogenaemia (an extremely rare blood disease), anophthalmia (complete absence of the eyes), and the Laurence-Moon-Biedl syndrome. The last-mentioned involves a series of disabilities including underdevelopment of the genitalia, eye defects, obesity, mental deficiency, and polydactyly (extra digits).

Special significance is attached to the heterozygous carrier—the individual who unknowingly carries the recessive gene. It is usually difficult to tell, prior to the marriage, whether the individual bears a detrimental recessive gene. Thus, a recessive gene may be transmitted

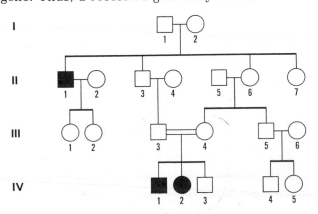

Figure 19.3 Pedigree of a recessively inherited disorder involving a marriage of first cousins. The marriage of close relatives increases the risk that both partners have received the same detrimental recessive gene through a common ancestor. Solid symbol represents a person afflicted with the recessive condition; unshaded symbol denotes an unaffected person.

without any outward manifestation for several generations, continually being sheltered by the dominant normal gene. The recessive gene, however, does become exposed when two carrier parents happen to mate, as we have seen from figure 19.3. This explains cases in which a trait absent for many generations can suddenly appear without warning. Often only one member in a family is afflicted. In such an event, it would be an error to jump to the conclusion that the abnormality is not hereditary solely because there are no other cases in the family.

CONSANGUINITY AND RECESSIVE INHERITANCE

Offspring afflicted with a recessive disorder tend to arise more often from consanguineous unions than from marriages of unrelated persons. Close relatives share more of the same genes than persons from the population at large. If a recessive trait is extremely rare, the chance is very small that unrelated marriage partners will both harbor the same defective gene. The marriage of close relatives, however, increases the risk that both partners have received the same defective gene through some common ancestor.

With increasing rarity of a recessive gene, it becomes more and more unlikely that unrelated parents will carry the same recessive gene. With an exceedingly rare recessive disorder, the expectation is that most affected children will come from cousin marriages. Human geneticists often infer that a rare disorder is transmitted by a recessive gene when they find a high incidence of consanguineous marriages. Thus, the finding that Toulouse-Lautrec's parents were first cousins is the basis for the current view that the French painter was afflicted with *pycnodysostosis* (short stature, narrow lower jaw), which is governed by a rare recessive gene, rather than as had been formerly thought, with dwarfism (*achondroplasia*), which is determined by a dominant gene.

One of the first indications that *phenylketonuria* (PKU) in humans is controlled by a recessive gene was the relatively high percentage of first-cousin marriages among parents of affected children. Data from the United States, England, and Norway indicate that, for this trait, the parents are very often close relatives. Individuals suffering from phenylketonuria have peculiarities of posture and jerky, or convulsive, movements. Phenylketonuric patients are mentally retarded, usually so severely that they are institutionalized. The number of heterozygous carriers of this detrimental recessive gene is about 1 in 80. Thus, the probability that two carriers from the general population will marry is 1 in 6,400 (80 × 80). If both marriage partners are carriers, then theoretically 1 of every 4 children will be afflicted with PKU. The first probability figure (1 in 6,400) multiplied by the second probability figure (1 in 4) gives the total chance of 1 in 25,600 for affected children from two normal persons who marry "at random" from the general population. This probability is increased enormously if two normal individuals marry, both of whom had heterozygous carrier parents. The marital partners would each have a two-thirds chance of being carriers themselves, and the risk of affected children from such a marriage would be 1 in 9! Calculations of the risk of PKU in offspring from different types of marriages are shown in table 19.2.

The aforementioned considerations have led geneticists to establish certain criteria for recognizing recessive inheritance in human families. They may be summarized as follows:

Table 19.2
Risk of Phenylketonuric
(PKU) Offspring in
Various Marriages

| MARITAL PARTNERS | | | | Theoretic frequency of affected children | Chances of affected children from such a mating |
| A | | B | | Chances of affected children if both partners were carriers | |
Carrier status	Chances of carrying gene	Carrier status	Chances of carrying gene		
Unknown	1 in 80	Unknown	1 in 80	1 in 4	1 in 25,600
Unknown	1 in 80	Normal sibling of phenylketonuric	2 in 3	1 in 4	1 in 480
Unknown	1 in 80	Parent of phenylketonuric	1	1 in 4	1 in 320
Unknown	1 in 80	Phenylketonuric	1	1 in 2	1 in 160
Normal sibling of phenylketonuric	2 in 3	Normal sibling of phenylketonuric	2 in 3	1 in 4	1 in 9
Normal sibling of phenylketonuric	2 in 3	Parent of phenylketonuric	1	1 in 4	1 in 6
Normal sibling of phenylketonuric	2 in 3	Phenylketonuric	1	1 in 2	1 in 3
Parent of phenylketonuric	1	Parent of phenylketonuric	1	1 in 4	1 in 4
Parent of phenylketonuric	1	Phenylketonuric	1	1 in 2	1 in 2
Phenylketonuric	1	Phenylketonuric	1	1	1

Note: Data are calculated on prevalence rate of disease as approximately 1 in 25,000.

1. Most affected individuals are children of phenotypically normal parents.
2. Often more than one child in a sibship is affected. On the average, one-fourth of the sibs are affected. Males and females are equally likely to be affected.
3. Affected persons who marry normal persons tend to have phenotypically normal children. (The probability is greater of marrying a normal homozygote than a heterozygote.)
4. When a trait is exceedingly rare, the responsible gene is most likely recessive if there is an undue proportion of marriages of close relatives among the parents of the affected offspring.

GENERAL ASPECTS OF CONSANGUINITY

In a numerically large study of Japanese births, James V. Neel and William J. Shull of the University of Michigan found that the proportion of abnormal progeny was about 2 percent for random marriages and about 3 percent for consanguineous marriages. This increase is not inconsequential, since from the standpoint of the individual family, the risk of a defective child is increased by half with related parents.

One way to show the effects of consanguinity is to consider a situation where a widow marries her late husband's brother. We may suppose, as figure 19.4 shows, that a child with phenylketonuria (III-1) was born in the first marriage of the man (II-1) and the woman (II-2). The man dies, and his brother (II-3) feels obliged (as commanded by certain religious laws) to marry the widow and assume responsibility for the family. We

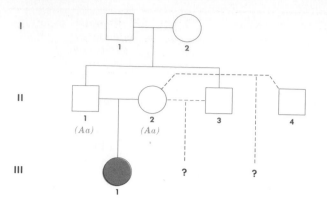

Figure 19.4 There are few prohibitions against a late husband's brother marrying the widow. The pedigree asks symbolically: What are the chances of an affected child if the widow (II–2) marries her late husband's brother (II–3) as compared to a man (II–4) randomly chosen from the general population.

may ask: What are the chances that the second marriage will produce a PKU child? Alternatively, what would be the chances of a PKU offspring if the widow were to marry instead an unrelated man (II-4) with no evidence of phenylketonuria in his immediate or past family?

As figure 19.4 reveals, the widow (II-2) and the late husband (II-1) are each heterozygous. The late husband's brother (II-3) is phenotypically normal, but the probability is ½ that he harbors the recessive gene for phenylketonuria. This recessive gene was transmitted by one of his parents, either I-1 or I-2. (Both parents might have been heterozygous, but since the trait is rare it is more probable that only one parent was a carrier). We may categorize the individual events (probabilities) as follows:
1. Chance that the widow (II-2) is a carrier = 1
2. Chance that the brother (II-3) is a carrier = ½
3. Chance for a homozygous recessive child = ¼

Thus, the total chance that a child of this marriage will be afflicted with PKU is:

$$1 \times \tfrac{1}{2} \times \tfrac{1}{4} = \tfrac{1}{8}$$

Let us assume, now, that the widow marries an outsider rather than her late husband's brother. The probability that the unrelated man (II-4) is a carrier is equal to the frequency with which carriers occur in the general population. As noted earlier, 1 in 80 persons is a carrier of the recessive gene for phenylketonuria. Hence, the chance that a man picked at random from the general population happens to be heterozygous for PKU is 1 in 80. In this circumstance, the individual events are as follows:
1. Chance that the widow (II-2) is a carrier = 1
2. Chance that the unrelated man (II-4) is a carrier = $\tfrac{1}{80}$
3. Chance for a homozygous recessive child = ¼

Therefore, the total chance that the child will be afflicted with PKU is:

$$1 \times \tfrac{1}{80} \times \tfrac{1}{4} = \tfrac{1}{320}$$

It should be evident that if the widow marries her late husband's brother, the likelihood of having a homozygous recessive child is increased fortyfold (⅛ as opposed to $\tfrac{1}{320}$). Clearly, two siblings (in this case, two brothers) have a greater chance of inheriting the same recessive gene from a common ancestor (in this case, one of their parents) than do any two individuals selected at random in a general population. Stated another way, the farther removed two individuals are from a common ancestor, the smaller the likelihood that both individuals will receive the same genes from that ancestor.

Table 19.3
Probabilities of Affected Offspring
of Recessive Genotypes

Parents	First Child	SECOND CHILD IF FIRST IS:	
		Nonaffected	Affected
Both nonaffected; no affected relative	$\frac{1}{4}c^2$	$\frac{1}{4}c^2$	$\frac{1}{4}$
One affected	$\frac{1}{2}c$	$\frac{1}{2}c$	$\frac{1}{2}$
Both nonaffected; one has affected sib	$(\frac{2}{3})(\frac{1}{4})c$	$(\frac{2}{3})(\frac{1}{4})c$	$\frac{1}{4}$
Both affected	1	. . .	1

Note: The probability that an individual in the general population is a carrier is designated c. For example, the value of c for albinism is $\frac{1}{70}$.

Given knowledge of the frequency of heterozygous carriers of recessive disorders, one can calculate the chance of affected offspring in a given marriage. In table 19.3, the probability that an individual is a carrier is designated c. The values of c for representative recessive disorders are as follows: cystic fibrosis, $\frac{1}{16}$; albinism, $\frac{1}{70}$; phenylketonuria, $\frac{1}{80}$; and alkaptonuria, $\frac{1}{500}$.

LETHAL RECESSIVE INHERITANCE

Sometimes a recessive gene is so drastic in its effect that nothing can be done to save the life of the infant or prolong his life to maturity. There are several examples in man of fatal, or lethal, recessive genes. One lethal inherited condition is _infantile amaurotic idiocy_. It is also known as _Tay-Sachs disease_, after its codiscoverers, the British ophthalmologist Warren Tay and the American neurologist Bernard P. Sachs. Affected children appear normal and healthy at birth, but within six months the nerves of the brain and spinal cord exhibit marked signs of deterioration. At first listless and irritable, the infant finds it increasingly difficult to sit up or stand. By the age of one year, the child lies helplessly in his crib. He becomes mentally retarded, progressively blind, and finally paralyzed. The disease takes its lethal toll by the age of three to four years. There are no known survivors and no cure.

A feature of special interest is that 9 out of 10 affected children are of Jewish heritage. It is especially common in Jews of northeastern European origin, particularly from provinces in Lithuania and Poland. In the United States, Tay-Sachs disease is about 100 times more prevalent in the Jewish population than among non-Jews. The frequency of heterozygous carriers has been estimated at 1 in 45 for Jews and 1 in 350 for non-Jews. The factors responsible for the exceptionally elevated incidence of the disease in the Jewish population remain puzzling.

One of the most devastating recessive disorders among children is _cystic fibrosis_ of the pancreas. About 6,000 infants are born with the disease each year in the United States. There are at least 5 million heterozygous carriers, and 1 child in every 1,000 is born with the disease. Virtually all infants with cystic fibrosis are Caucasians; Negroes and Orientals are rarely afflicted.

Less than 35 years ago, cystic fibrosis was not even recognized as a distinct medical entity. Today it has the unenviable reputation of being one of the most important disorders of childhood. Intestinal obstruction is the first symptom of the disease; the infant's stools are frequent, large, and foul. The pancreas secretes a mucous material that is abnormally thick or viscid, with the consequence that digestion is blocked in the intestinal tract. All mucus-secreting tissues are abnormal in this disease. The sticky mucus produced by the lungs is particularly serious; the lungs become clogged and the child has repeated bouts of pneumonia. A characteristic finding, by which cystic fibrosis is most readily diagnosed, is the increased amounts of salt in the sweat.

Before the introduction of antibiotics, affected children invariably died in infancy of constant infection. New drugs, inhaled as vapor, soften the thick mucus of the lungs and have enabled some children to weather the difficult first years. The widespread application of antibiotics has led to a considerable reduction in early mortality. In fact, several women patients with cystic fibrosis responded so well to the special treatment that they now have children of their own. All these children are phenotypically normal. But these normal children born of affected mothers harbor the recessive gene for cystic fibrosis and can pass on the defective gene to their offspring.

DISORDERS OF DOMINANT INHERITANCE

The family pedigree shown in figure 19.5 has certain intriguing features. It may be noted that each affected person has at least one affected parent. Moreover, the normal children of an affected parent, when they in turn marry normal persons, have only normal offspring. In this particular instance, the harmful gene is dominant and the normal gene is recessive. In nearly all instances of dominant inheritance, as exemplified by the pedigree, one parent carries the detrimental gene and shows the anomaly, whereas the other parent is normal. The affected parent will pass on the defective dominant gene, on the average, to 50 percent of the children. The normal children do not carry the harmful dominant gene, and hence their offspring and further descendants are not burdened with the dominant trait.

There are numerous examples in man of defective genes that are transmitted in a dominant pattern. Achondroplasia, a form of dwarfism, is a dominant condition in man. Affected individuals are small and disproportionate, with abnormally short arms and legs (fig. 19.6). The defect is evident at birth, and most achondroplastic dwarfs fail to survive beyond the first year. Only about 20 percent of the affected individuals reach adulthood.

Other examples of dominant traits are tylosis, a condition in which the skin of the palms and soles is excessively thickened; anonychia, a condition in which some or all of the nails of the fingers and toes are absent; and dentinogenesis imperfecta, a disorder in which the crowns of teeth wear down readily. Two relatively common dominant defects are polydactyly (extra fingers or toes) and brachydactyly, a condition

Figure 19.5 Pedigree of dominant inheritance, showing that the dominant disorder is transmitted only by those individuals who display the disorder and not by unaffected individuals. Solid symbol represents a person afflicted with the disorder; unshaded symbol denotes an unaffected person.

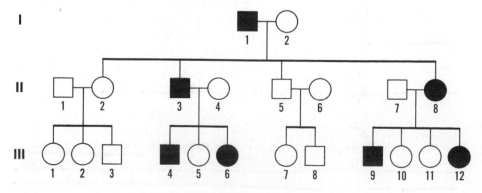

in which the hands of the affected person are short, stocky, and thick. There is a shortening of both the fingers and palms. In sharp contrast, persons afflicted with *Marfan's syndrome* have unusually long, tapering fingers (fig. 19.7). Patients with Marfan's syndrome have poor musculature and long, thin extremities. An individual with Marfan's syndrome "often suggests the subject of an El Greco painting," as stated by Victor McKusick of Johns Hopkins University. Some medical authorities believe that Abraham Lincoln, who was exceptionally long-limbed, suffered from this dominant disorder.

The pedigree of the House of Hapsburg, which reigned over central Europe for several centuries, reveals an extraordinary dominant deformity of the jaw that marked members down to the decline of the monarchies. In most members of this dynasty, the lower jaw is excessively angular and protruding, and the upper jaw is poorly devel-

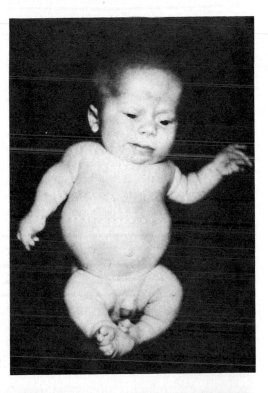

Figure 19.6 Achondroplastic dwarfism, a dominant genetic disorder in which the affected infant has inherited abnormally short arms and legs. (Courtesy of Dr. Norman Woody, Tulane University School of Medicine.)

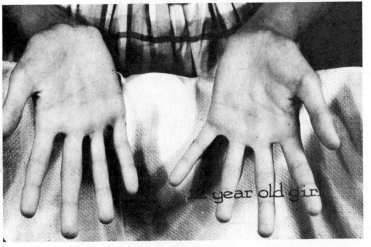

Figure 19.7 Marfan's syndrome in a 12-year-old girl, a dominant trait characterized by unusually long, tapering fingers. (Courtesy of Dr. Norman Woody, Tulane University School of Medicine.)

Figure 19.8 The Hapsburg jaw, a dominant trait found in many members of the Hapsburg dynasty. The angular jaw and protruding lower lip characterized Charles V (1500–1558), Emperor of Germany. (Courtesy of The Bettmann Archive, Inc.)

oped. Charles V, Emperor of Germany in the 16th century, shows the famous jutting jaw in its most exaggerated form (fig. 19.8). It has been written that Charles V learned to regard his unprepossessing angular face with wry humor. Charles V married a cousin afflicted with the same jutting chin, and an exceptional number of cousin marriages perpetuated the anomaly until recent times.

Guidelines for recognizing autosomal dominant inheritance in humans may be summarized as follows:

1. The affected offspring has one affected parent, unless the gene for the abnormal effect was the result of a new mutation.
2. Either parent of the affected offspring is heterozygous or both may be; detrimental dominant traits have rarely been observed in the homozygous state.
3. Unaffected persons do not transmit the trait to their children.
4. Males and females are equally likely to have or to transmit the trait.

LATE-ACTING DOMINANT GENES

Dominant defects that are not very serious may be transmitted through many generations. The more severe dominant anomalies are incompatible with reproduction and accordingly are not transmitted at all. There is, however, one way in which a very serious dominant disorder can be handed on through many generations. Transmission can take place if the anomaly does not manifest itself until comparatively late in life, after the affected person has already had children.

An unfortunate example of such a late-appearing dominant defect is *Huntington's chorea*, characterized by disorganized muscular movements and progressive mental deterioration. The condition is difficult to diagnose, there is no cure, and the progress of the disease is relentless, leading to a terminal state of helplessness. The symptoms that make diagnosis possible do not generally appear until middle life, between the ages of 25 and 55. Death supervenes usually 12 to 15 years after the onset of the involuntary, jerky movements.

A clear and comprehensive clinical description of the disease was first presented in 1872 by Dr. George Huntington, based on his experiences with choreic patients on Long Island in New York. The disease is most prevalent in the New England area of the United States, where it can be traced back to colonists in Massachusetts who left England in 1630 on the famous John Winthrop fleet. In fact, only three men and their wives of these early colonists are held to be responsible for transmitting the disorder to descendants. Today it is estimated that there may be as many as 25,000 persons in the United States afflicted with the disorder. In colonial New England, from 1647 to 1697, choreic women were denounced as witches and were persecuted. Huntington's chorea was then termed *magrums*, meaning "fidgets" or "mad staggers." The involuntary jerking of the arms and legs was considered a curse inherited by the choreics from their forefathers for having blasphemously imitated the Saviour.

Huntington's chorea is sufficiently common to provide two or three cases at any one time at the average large mental hospital. The marriage rate and fertility of choreic persons are both high. The average choreic family has about five children. Unfortunately there is no reliable method of identifying the heterozygotes until the symptoms develop.

LETHALITY OF THE DOMINANT HOMOZYGOTE

Among children whose parents are both heterozygous for a detrimental dominant trait, the expectation according to Mendelian principles is that one-fourth of the offspring will be homozygous dominant and hence afflicted with the trait. However, few detrimental dominant traits have ever been observed in the homozygous dominant state. Apparently the presence of two harmful dominant genes is incompatible with life; that is, the double dose results in the death of the organism while it is still an embryo or fetus.

This circumstance may be illustrated by the case of the "pelger" dominant gene in rabbits (plate 11). In rabbits, as in man, the nuclei of certain white blood cells, known as *polymorphonuclear leucocytes,* typically have at least three segments, or lobes, separated by delicate filaments. The surface of the polymorphic nucleus is accordingly enlarged compared with the usual round nucleus.

In 1938, the Swiss hematologist E. Undritz discovered a peculiarity in the leucocytes of rabbits. The nuclei of the polymorphonuclear leucocytes had two segments only, rather than the normal three (plate 11). Such rabbits were called "Pelger rabbits," named after the Dutch physician K. Pelger, who first described this odd configuration in leucocyte nuclei of human patients. When Undritz crossed two heterozygous Pelger rabbits, he obtained an unexpected result. Instead of the expected ratio of 3 Pelgers to 1 normal among the progeny, the progeny ratio was 2 Pelger:1 normal. Apparently, a double dose of the dominant gene has a lethal effect and homozygous Pelgers perish as fetuses. Thus, all Pelger rabbits are heterozygous. Fortunately, the lethal effect is not absolute. Some homozygous Pelgers have survived beyond parturition. Their leucocyte nuclei are entirely round; there is no stretching nor the slightest segmentation (plate 11).

The same dominant blood deformity has been found in man. The detrimental dominant "pelger" gene is more frequent than was previously supposed. The German geneticist Hans Nachtsheim reported in 1950 an incidence of 1 Pelger person per 1,000 in Berlin. Cases have been described in Holland, Germany, Switzerland, Czechoslovakia, France, United States, and Malaysia. The heterozygous Pelgers are at no obvious disadvantage to normal individuals, and the expectation of a full life is as high for Pelgers as for non-Pelgers. The full viability of the heterozygotes is in marked contrast to the lethality of the dominant homozygotes. Up to now human homozygous Pelgers have not been observed (plate 10). The parallelism of the symptoms of the heterozygous Pelgers in man and rabbits, however, leaves little doubt that the dominant homozygotes are lethal also in man.

SUMMARY

As revealed by analyses of family pedigrees, certain disorders in man follow simple Mendelian rules. Recessive defects in family histories tend to appear among siblings (brothers and sisters), not in their parents. In recessive inheritance, both parents generally are normal but are heterozygous carriers. The recessive gene may be transmitted without any outward manifestation for several generations, continually being sheltered in the heterozygous state by the dominant normal gene. When two heterozygous carrier parents happen to mate, the chance that the first child will be afflicted with the recessive disorder is 1 in 4. These odds hold for each subsequent child, irrespective of the number of previously affected children. With rare recessive conditions, the parents are often related (such as first cousins). The marriage of close relatives increases the probability that both marriage partners have received the same recessive gene through common ancestors.

In dominant inheritance, usually only one parent is affected and the other parent is normal. Persons afflicted with a dominant disorder are almost always heterozygous. The affected parent transmits the defective dominant gene, on the average, to 50 percent of the children. Normal children of an affected parent, when they in turn marry normal persons, have only normal offspring. Certain dominant genes, as in the case of Huntington's chorea, do not manifest their harmful effects until comparatively late in life, after the affected person has already had children.

Ethical Probe 13
Rights of Society

At a recent symposium on the ethical and social implications of medical genetics, a participant presented the following hypothetical circumstance followed by several rhetorical questions. Suppose that a person were to stand on a bridge over traffic and drop bricks on the passing cars below. Let us further assume that the probability of causing serious damage to a car and its occupants is empirically established as one in four. Given this likelihood that a tragic mishap will occur, it can be safely stated that the person will be arrested for his misconduct and that society will ask him to pay for damages.

We may now ask if comparable conditions pertain to parents who have been identified as heterozygous carriers of a serious genetic disorder, such as Tay-Sachs disease or phenylketonuria. Is the risk of danger to their children just as great as the liability of injury to drivers on that particular road? If two carrier parents insist on having children, is such action just as unjustifiable as a person dropping bricks in traffic? If the issue is one of personal freedom to reproduce, who should pay for the great cost of treating the defective child? We may take notice that it costs $25,000 a year to keep a Tay-Sachs child alive, for the few hapless years of its existence.

How far does individual freedom extend? What about the rights of society. Do you have an obligation not to knowingly produce offspring who will be a drain on the resources of society?

Man's Hemoglobins and Gene Action 20

It is now widely accepted that genes provide the information to direct the synthesis of proteins in the cell. The gene—a linear sequence of bases in the DNA—codes for the precise sequence of amino acids that compose a protein. The properties of any protein are determined by the number, identity, and arrangement of the amino acid residues. In a large sense, the molecular basis of the genotype is DNA; the molecular basis of the phenotype is protein. Ultimately all inherited differences in individuals are expressed in their bodily structure through changes in specific proteins.

When a normal gene is transmitted from one generation to the next, it specifies a normal protein each generation. If, however, the gene were to become altered, or undergo a mutational change, we should then expect to find a change in the kind or amount of the protein. Modifications in the *hemoglobin* molecule, an important protein of man, have attracted considerable attention. It was the hemoglobin molecule that provided the first direct proof of the gene-protein relationship. It has been said that hemoglobin served as the Rosetta stone in revealing the hereditary language.

SICKLE-CELL ANEMIA

Hemoglobin, the main component of red blood cells, is responsible for transporting oxygen to all parts of the body. It is a curious fact that there are well over 100 abnormal states of the hemoglobin molecule, each of which results from some defect in the genetic machinery. One of the most serious hemoglobin abnormalities is *sickle-cell anemia*.

This disease was discovered by the American physician James B. Herrick, who in 1904 made an office examination of an anemic West Indian Negro student residing in Chicago. The patient's blood examined under the microscope showed the presence of numerous crescent-shaped erythrocytes. The peculiarly twisted appearance of the red blood cell is shown in figure 20.1. The Negro patient was kept under observation for six years, during which time he displayed many of the distressing symptoms we now recognize as typical of the disease sickle-cell anemia. The bizarre-shaped red cells in the form of a sickle blade are fragile and clog small blood vessels. The obstruction of circulation leads to the necrosis (death) of various tissues. The clogging of small blood vessels is responsible for the localized painful crises of sickle-cell anemia. The victim may suffer from pneumonia as a result of lung damage, rheumatism from muscle and joint deterioration, heart damage, and kidney failure.

Affected persons rarely reach adult life; most die in the first decade and very few survive the third. Physicians can provide care for the patient, but there is no cure. In other words, there is little that can be done for patients in sickle-cell crisis beyond treatment of the symptoms. In

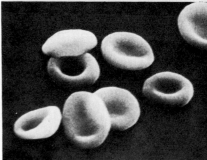

Figure 20.1 Peculiarly twisted shape of red blood cells of an individual suffering from sickle-cell anemia *(top)*, contrasted with spherical appearance of normal red blood cells *(bottom)*. (Courtesy of Wide World Photos.)

1970, Robert Nalbandian, a pathologist in Grand Rapids, Michigan, reported success in de-sickling afflicted blood cells by injecting patients with large amounts of *urea*. The effect of urea is transient, and the efficacy of urea therapy awaits clarification. Anthony Cerami and James Manning at the Rockefeller University in New York have proposed that the agent that relieves sickle-cell crisis in the capillaries is not the urea itself, but an impurity, *cyanate*, present in small amounts in most urea solutions. The anti-sickling effect of cyanate appears to be more enduring, and only small doses of cyanate are required to alleviate the sickle-cell crisis.

Sickle-cell anemia occurs predominantly in Negroes. It is about 6 times more common than the next most common long-term illness of Negro children (diabetes). The incidence at birth of the disabling sickle-cell anemia in the United States is estimated at 2 per 1,000 infants. In recent years, sickle-cell anemia has become the target of a broad-ranging health campaign that rivals the polio drives of the 1950s. Enactment of mass screening laws for the sickle-cell condition has met with vocal opposition, however.

Not until after World War II was the hereditary basis of sickle-cell anemia elucidated. The irregularity was shown in the late 1940s by

Figure 20.2 Types of children that can result from a marriage of two heterozygous carriers of sickle-cell anemia. Individuals homozygous for the variant gene suffer from sickle-cell anemia; the benign heterozygous state is referred to as the *sickle-cell trait*.

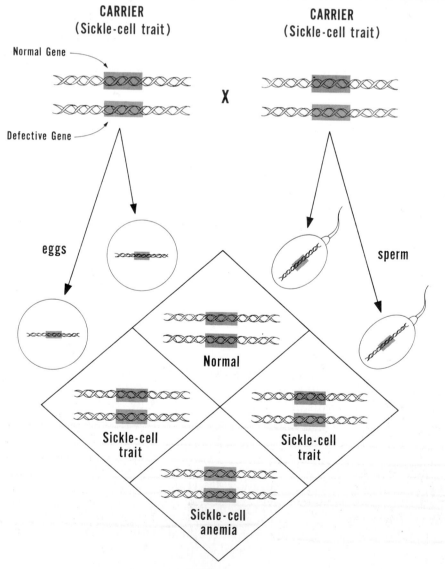

James V. Neel of the University of Michigan to be inherited as a simple Mendelian character. The sickle-cell anemic patient inherits two defective genes, one from each parent (fig. 20.2). Individuals with one normal and one defective (sickling) gene are generally healthy but are carriers —they are said to have *sickle-cell trait*. If two heterozygous carriers marry, the chances are 1 in 4 that a child will have sickle-cell anemia, and 1 in 2 that a child will be a carrier (fig. 20.2).

Since the homozygous state of the detrimental gene is required for the overt expression of the disease, sickle-cell anemia may be considered to be recessively determined. However, although heterozygous individuals are, on the whole, normal, even the red cells of the heterozygotes can undergo sickling under certain circumstances, producing clinical manifestations. As an instance, heterozygous carriers have been known to experience acute abdominal pains at high altitudes in unpressurized planes. The lowering of the oxygen tension, with an increased amount of oxygen released from chemical combination, is sufficient to induce sickling. The abdominal pains can be traced to the packing of sickled erythrocytes in the small capillaries of the spleen.

According to some authors, since the detrimental gene can express itself in the heterozygous state (by producing a positive sickling test under certain circumstances), the gene should be considered dominant. This reveals that dominance and recessiveness are somewhat arbitrary concepts that depend on one's point of view. Indeed, from a molecular standpoint, the relation between the normal and defective gene in this instance may best be described as *codominant*, since, as we shall see, the heterozygote produces both normal and abnormal hemoglobin. There is no blending of inheritance at the molecular level.

SICKLE-CELL HEMOGLOBIN

In 1949, the distinguished chemist and Nobel laureate Linus Pauling and his co-workers made the important discovery that the defective sickling gene alters the configuration of the hemoglobin molecule. Pauling used the then relatively new technique of electrophoresis, which characterizes proteins according to the manner in which they move in an electric field. The hemoglobin molecule travels toward the positive pole. The sickle cell's hemoglobin differs in speed of migration from normal hemoglobin; it moves more slowly than the normal molecule (fig. 20.3). The defective gene thus functions differently from the normal gene, and, in fact, acts independently of its normal partner allele. As a result, the heterozygote, while not producing an intermediate product, elaborates both kinds of hemoglobin in nearly equal quantities—the normal type (designated *hemoglobin A*, or *Hb A*) and the sickle-cell anemic

HEMOGLOBIN ELECTROPHORETIC PATTERN

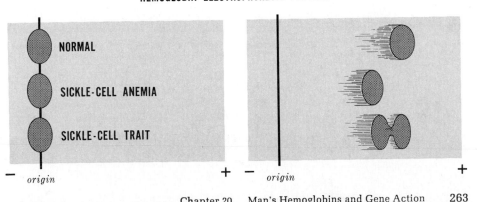

NORMAL

SICKLE-CELL ANEMIA

SICKLE-CELL TRAIT

–   *origin*   +   –   *origin*   +

Figure 20.3 Electrophoretic patterns of hemoglobins. The hemoglobin of the heterozygous person with sickle-cell trait is not intermediate in character, but is composed instead of approximately equal proportions of the normal hemoglobin and the sickle-cell anemia variety. (Based on studies by Linus Pauling.)

Figure 20.4 Chromatographic "fingerprints" of normal hemoglobin A and sickle-cell hemoglobin S. One peptide spot in the sickle-cell hemoglobin differs in position from the corresponding normal peptide. (Based on studies by Vernon Ingram.)

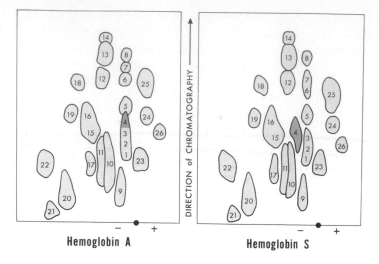

Hemoglobin A   Hemoglobin S

DIRECTION of CHROMATOGRAPHY

variety *(Hb S)*. The dual electrophoretic pattern of hemoglobin from a heterozygous individual can actually be duplicated experimentally by mechanically mixing the hemoglobins taken from blood cells of a normal person and a sickle-cell anemic patient. The mixed solution separates in an electric field into the same two hemoglobin components as those characteristic of a heterozygous person with sickle-cell trait.

It remained for the chemist Vernon Ingram, then at the Medical Research Unit in Cambridge, England, and now at the Massachusetts Institute of Technology in Cambridge, Massachusetts, to ascertain how the hemoglobin molecule is altered by the aberrant gene. In 1956, Ingram pioneered an analytical technique called *peptide fingerprinting*. The hemoglobin molecule was fragmented by a proteolytic enzyme (trypsin) into short peptide chains. To separate the peptides, Ingram used a combination of chromatography and paper electrophoresis. The separated peptide fragments—or "fingerprints"—showed up on the chromatographic paper in the patterns shown in figure 20.4. The two hemoglobin molecules—normal and sickle-cell—were separable into 26 different peptide fingerprints, identical at every location except one. In other words, there was one particular peptide spot in the sickle-cell hemoglobin that differed in position from the corresponding normal peptide.

Further chemical analysis of this one particular peptide revealed that sickle-cell hemoglobin differed only slightly in its chemical constitution from normal hemoglobin. It lacked one amino acid called *glutamic acid*, and in its place was another amino acid called *valine* (fig. 20.5). Thus, the

Figure 20.5 Amino acid sequences in a small section of the normal hemoglobin molecule and of the sickle-cell hemoglobin. The substitution of a single amino acid, glutamic acid by valine, is responsible for the abnormal sickling of human red blood cells. (Based on studies by Vernon Ingram.)

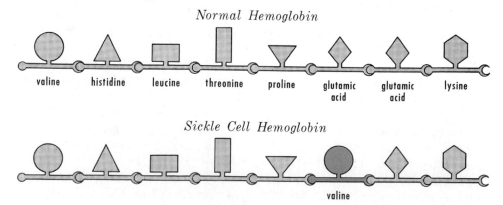

Normal Hemoglobin

valine   histidine   leucine   threonine   proline   glutamic acid   glutamic acid   lysine

Sickle Cell Hemoglobin

valine

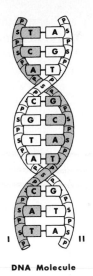

DNA Molecule

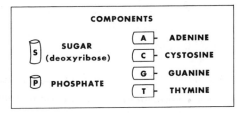

COMPONENTS

S SUGAR (deoxyribose)	A ├ ADENINE
	C ├ CYSTOSINE
P PHOSPHATE	G ├ GUANINE
	T ├ THYMINE

Figure 20.6 Molecular events leading to a mutation. When cell division occurs, the two twisted strands separate and each strand attracts unbound nucleotides (containing nitrogenous bases) to rebuild the DNA molecule. The nitrogenous bases are adenine (A), thymine (T), cytosine (C), and guanine (G). The illustration shows events through two successive cell divisions, commencing with strand I in the original DNA molecule. During the first division, an adenine radical (A) undergoes a chemical change to A′, which misattracts cytosine (C) instead of thymine (T). At the next division, cytosine (C) attracts its customary partner, guanine (G). The net result is that the grand-daughter DNA molecule contains a C–G pair where a T–A pair was formerly located. This highly local-ized change in one of the pairs of nitrogenous bases qualifies as a gene mutation.

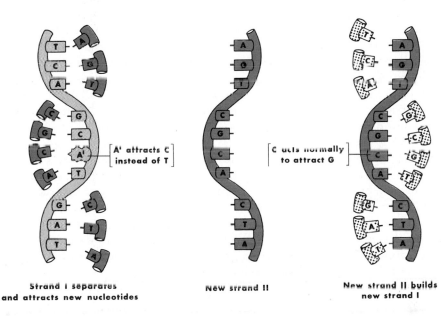

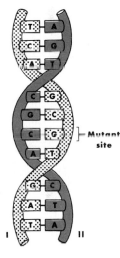

Strand I separates and attracts new nucleotides	New strand II	New strand II builds new strand I	DNA Molecule with mutation
[A′ attracts C instead of T]	[C acts normally to attract G]		—Mutant site

sole difference in chemical composition between normal and sickle-cell hemoglobin is the incredibly minute substitution of a single amino acid unit among several hundred. In turn, the abnormality can be ac-counted for by a change in a single nucleotide of the DNA molecule. Let us now examine a possible way in which an inheritable change—or mutation—in the DNA molecule might occur.

It has been established that each of the bases in DNA can exist in several rare alternative forms known as *tautomers*. The tautomeric al-ternatives differ in the positions at which certain atoms are attached in the molecule. The significance of the tautomeric alternatives lies in the changed pairing qualities they impart. Whereas, for example, the nor-mal form of adenine pairs with thymine, one of its rare tautomeric forms actually attracts and couples with cytosine. Such a tautomeric shift in the adenine molecule may thus make possible a new purine-pyrimidine base pair arrangement in the DNA molecule. As seen in figure 20.6, an adenine (labeled A¹) has undergone a tautomeric shift and attracts the wrong partner (cytosine instead of thymine). At the next replication of the strand, the misattracted cytosine acts normally to join with guanine. Hence, a C–G pair is established where a T–A pair was formerly located. At this point in the DNA molecule, the gene is modified and may be expected to produce a mutant effect, that is, to alter the structure of one protein. Indeed, only one amino acid may be expected to be altered in the protein.

It is generally conceded that most viable mutations are base pair replacements. More radical alterations of the DNA molecule are likely to be lethal to the organism. Single base pair replacements are expected to cause the substitution of only one amino acid in a protein. This statement will become comprehensible when we consider the relation between DNA and protein synthesis.

TRANSCRIPTION OF DNA

Since the DNA molecule is in the chromosome of the nucleus, and whereas proteins are assembled within the part of the cell outside the nucleus, we are confronted with determining how genetic information is transmitted from the nucleus to the cytoplasm. In the 1960s, it became evident that DNA does not directly form proteins but works in a complex way through a secondary form of nucleic acid, *ribonucleic acid,* or RNA. The RNA molecule resembles the DNA molecule in structure except in three important respects. The pyrimidine base, *uracil,* is found in RNA, which replaces the thymine that is characteristic of DNA (fig. 20.7). Secondly, the sugar in RNA is *ribose,* which contains one more oxygen atom than does the deoxyribose sugar. Thirdly, RNA has only a *single* strand instead of two.

As seen in figure 20.8, one of the two strands of DNA (always the same one, apparently) forms a complementary strand of RNA. The same rules of pairing hold as in replicating a copy of DNA, except that adenine attracts uracil instead of thymine. This RNA strand, which is responsible for carrying DNA's instructions out into the cytoplasm, is appropriately termed *messenger RNA,* or *mRNA.* The amino acids of a polypeptide chain are specified by the messenger RNA. In a large sense then, the genetic code applies to RNA rather than to DNA itself.

Scientists have broken the genetic code into its main elements. Each three-letter unit of the messenger RNA is called a *codon.* Each of the 20 main amino acids, ranging from alanine to valine, has been shown to be specified by at least one codon. In fact, most amino acids have more than one codon. The amino acid serine, for example, has 6 codons, glycine has 4, and lysine has 2. Only methionine and tryptophan have 1 each. Because most amino acids are specified by more than one codon, the code is claimed to be degenerate. However, this kind of degeneracy is welcome since it ensures that the code works. Details of the code are shown in table 20.1. This table of the genetic code represents for the biologist what the periodic table of the elements represents for the chemist. It may be noted that three of the codons (UAA, UAG, and UGA) do not code for any of the 20 amino acids. They were originally, perhaps facetiously, described as "nonsense codons," but they are now known to function as *terminating codons.* They serve to signal the termination of the formation of a polypeptide chain.

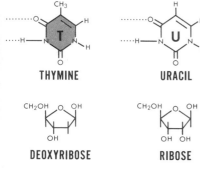

Figure 20.7 Chemical differences between DNA and RNA. Ribonucleic acid contains uracil in place of thymine and the sugar component is ribose instead of deoxyribose. *Deoxy* means "minus one oxygen," which constitutes the only difference between deoxyribose sugar and ribose sugar.

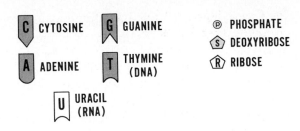

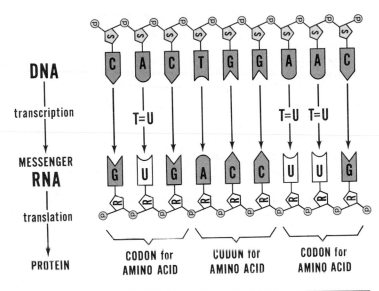

Figure 20.8 The language of life. The DNA molecule forms a single strand of messenger RNA that carries DNA's instructions out into the cell. The four bases of DNA (A, T, C, and G) are responsible for the three-letter code words, or codons, of messenger RNA. Each of the 20 amino acids that make up the variety of body proteins is specified by at least one codon.

Table 20.1

The Three-Letter Codons of Messenger RNA, and the Amino Acids Specified by the Codons

AAU AAC } Asparagine	CAU CAC } Histidine	GAU GAC } Aspartic acid	UAU UAC } Tyrosine
AAA AAG } Lysine	CAA CAG } Glutamine	GAA GAG } Glutamic acid	UAA UAG } (Terminator)*
ACU ACC ACA ACG } Threonine	CCU CCC CCA CCG } Proline	GCU GCC GCA GCG } Alanine	UCU UCC UCA UCG } Serine
AGU AGC } Serine AGA AGG } Arginine	CGU CGC CGA CGG } Arginine	GGU GGC GGA GGG } Glycine	UGU UGC } Cysteine UGA (Terminator)* UGG Tryptophan
AUU AUC } Isoleucine AUA AUG Methionine	CUU CUC CUA CUG } Leucine	GUU GUC GUA GUG } Valine	UUU UUC } Phenylalanine UUA UUG } Leucine

* Terminating codons signal the end of the formation of a polypeptide chain.

The answer as to which codon signifies which amino acid emerged in 1961 from the laboratory of Marshall W. Nirenberg and J. H. Matthaei at the National Institutes of Health in Bethesda, Maryland. By using known sequences of RNA bases, they succeeded in matching certain base sequences with certain amino acids. They first synthesized an artificial messenger RNA from a single base, uracil. This synthetic RNA was called "poly U" since all the codons were UUU. They then prepared a cell-free system, from fractionated bacterial cells, that contained the necessary ingredients (enzymes and ribosomes) to combine the amino acids into proteins. To the cell-free system were added the synthetic "poly U" and a variety of amino acids. Polypeptides were formed that when analyzed were found to consist solely of one amino acid—phenylalanine. Hence, the mRNA codon for phenylalanine must be UUU. In like manner, the coding properties of other messenger RNAs were established (table 20.1). For his role in deciphering the genetic code, Marshall Nirenberg was one of the recipients of the 1968 Nobel prize in physiology and medicine.

One of the most intriguing findings is that the genetic code is essentially universal. The same codon calls forth the same amino acid in organisms as widely separated phylogenetically as a bacterium (E. coli), a flowering plant (wheat), an amphibian (the South African clawed toad), and mammals (guinea pig, mouse, and man). The essential universality of the genetic code supports the view that the code had its origin at least by the time bacteria evolved, 3 billion years ago. The genetic code may be said to be the oldest of languages.

The transfer of information from DNA to messenger RNA has been called transcription. For many years, molecular geneticists maintained that RNA is transcribed from DNA, and that RNA could not make DNA. In 1970 the University of Wisconsin virologist Howard Temin established the existence of an enzyme (now called either RNA-directed DNA polymerase or reverse transcriptase) that enables an RNA blueprint to make DNA. Temin's discovery is particularly important to the thesis that viruses cause cancer because most viruses known to induce cancer contain only RNA. Prior to Temin's impressive finding, no known mechanism could account for the hypothesis that DNA could be transcribed from viral RNA.

TRANSLATION INTO PROTEINS

The transfer of information from messenger RNA to proteins is termed translation. The sites of active protein synthesis are the globular ribosomes in the cytoplasm. These ribosomes, which contain a high-molecular-weight ribosomal RNA, have been thought of as the workbenches on which the coded message is read and the amino acids are assembled into chains. The important task of transporting free amino acids in the cytoplasm to the ribosomes is performed by another variety of RNA, called transfer RNA, or tRNA. The structure of tRNA has been compared to a hairpin twisted into a spiral (fig. 20.9). At one open end of the hairpin, a particular amino acid is attached. At the central bend of the hairpin are a sequence of three bases (called the anticodon) that fits only the corresponding codon in the messenger RNA. At least one type of transfer RNA exists for each amino acid.

The building of a specific protein is illustrated in simplified fashion in figure 20.9. Messenger RNA threads itself through a ribosome as a ribbon runs through a typewriter. As the ribosome "reads" a particular codon of messenger RNA, an appropriate type of transfer RNA is attracted to the ribosome. The transfer RNA anticodon fits itself onto the messenger RNA codon, thus placing the transfer RNA molecule in position to transfer its amino acid to the forming protein chain. For example, the transfer RNA molecule carrying threonine (anticodon UGG) recog-

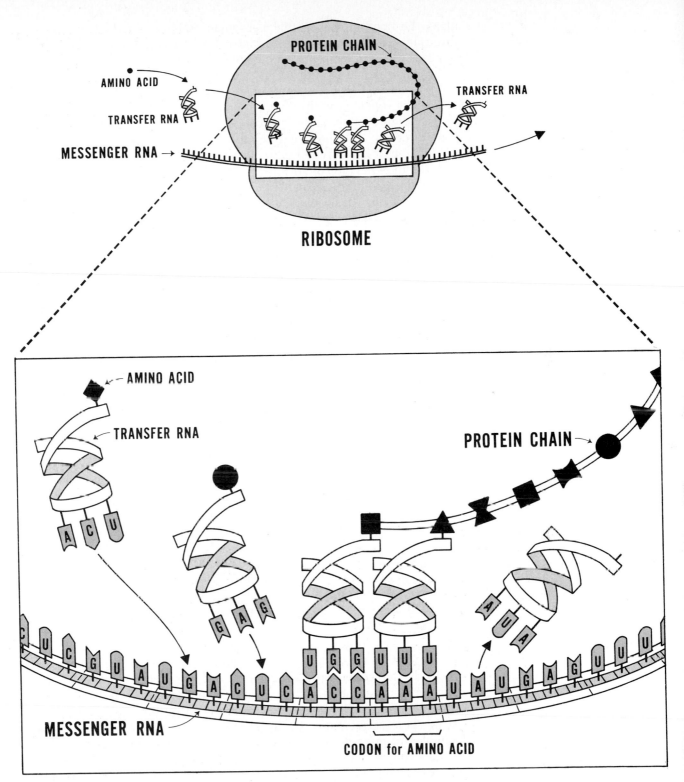

Figure 20.9 Protein synthesis in a living cell. See text for details.

nizes the codon ACC in the messenger RNA molecule and brings its threonine into position. The transfer RNA, having served its purpose, releases the threonine, which becomes attached to the immediately preceding amino acid (lysine in fig. 20.9) of the growing polypeptide chain. As the messenger RNA continues to pass through the ribosome, the process is repeated with other molecules of transfer RNA, each adding its particular amino acids to those already attached in sequence to the protein chain. A terminating codon, such as UAA, triggers the release of the completed polypeptide chain from the ribosome. A polypeptide chain is thus begun, constructed, and released in the cytoplasm according to the genetic message that was encoded on the messenger RNA as it was formed from the DNA in the nucleus.

ABNORMAL HEMOGLOBINS REVISITED

We may now take a closer look at sickle-cell hemoglobin (hemoglobin S). This abnormal hemoglobin is caused by a mutation in one gene that codes a polypeptide chain 146 amino acid units in length. As we learned earlier, the mutation alters only one amino acid unit in the entire chain, changing a glutamic acid present in normal hemoglobin into another amino acid, valine. The result is an alteration of the net electrical charge of the molecule. Since a protein's solubility depends on the distribution of positive and negative charges on its exterior surface, the replacement of glutamic acid by valine reduces the solubility of the hemoglobin molecule and promotes its precipitation out of solution. When oxygen is released from its combination with hemoglobin, the precipitated hemoglobin S molecules tend to cling together or stack up in long, semirigid rods. As these hemoglobin rods form, they attain sufficient length to push against the cell membrane and distort the red cell into the odd, crescent shape.

The substitution of valine for glutamic acid can be accounted for by an alteration of a single base of the triplet of DNA that specifies the amino acid, as depicted in figure 20.10. A single base replacement constitutes the simplest—and presumably the most probable—type of inheritable mutation and accounts for most of the inherited abnormalities of hemoglobin. This is demonstrated by another abnormal hemoglobin molecule, *hemoglobin C*. The same glutamic acid residue that is replaced by valine in hemoglobin S is replaced by *lysine* in hemoglobin C. The mutant genes for hemoglobin S and hemoglobin C are said to be *allelic*. That is to say, *two* independent mutations occurred in the same sequence of bases in the DNA that make up a *single* gene. It bears emphasizing that there may be more than one site of mutation within a single gene locus, and that mutations at different sites within this gene locus lead to different alterations in the function that the gene normally performs. This should be comprehensible since a single gene is a linear sequence of many bases, and a mutational change can occur in any one of the bases of the particular gene. Figure 20.10 shows the derivation of mutant hemoglobins S and C from hemoglobin A by two different nucleotide changes within the same gene.

In the preceding chapter, we observed that a gene may exist in two contrasting forms, for example, the gene for tallness and its allele for shortness in the pea plant. Now we learn that the gene for hemoglobin can exist in three contrasting forms—the normal gene for hemoglobin A and its two abnormal alleles responsible for hemoglobin S and hemo-

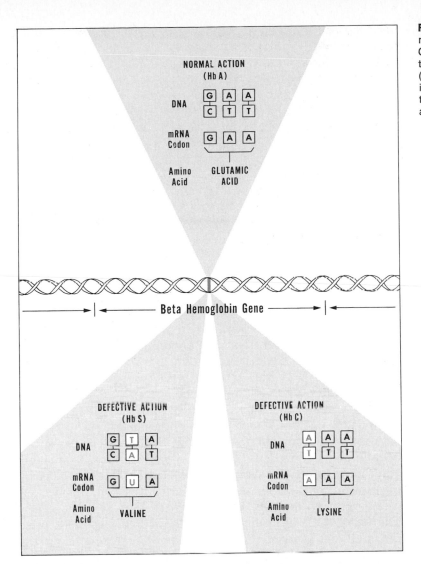

Figure 20.10 Derivation of abnormal hemoglobin S and hemoglobin C from normal hemoglobin A by two different nucleotide changes (that is, two independent mutations) in the same sequence of DNA bases that normally codes for glutamic acid.

globin C respectively. Several contrasting forms of a given gene are referred to as *multiple alleles*. The concept of multiple allelism will be treated in detail in the next chapter.

THE POLYPEPTIDE CHAINS OF HEMOGLOBIN

There are additional facts concerning the hemoglobin molecule that warrant our attention. Normal hemoglobin (Hb A) is made up of four polypeptide chains: two *alpha* (α) chains and two *beta* (β) chains (fig. 20.11). The two chains of each kind are linear chains of amino acids; the alpha chain consists of 141 amino acid units, or residues, and the beta, 146 residues. Many hemoglobins with abnormal alpha chains as well as abnormal beta chains have been found. Hemoglobin S and hemoglobin C represent alterations in the beta chain (specifically, modifications of the 6th amino acid of the 146-amino-acid chain). Thus far, all amino acid substitutions in human hemoglobin can be attributed to single mutations, and a single mutation affects only one polypeptide chain. This is striking confirmation of the theory that each polypeptide chain is under the control of a separate gene.

The synthesis of the alpha and beta chains of hemoglobin A are

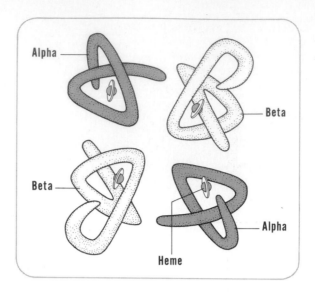

Figure 20.11 Schematic representation of the two *alpha* and *beta* chains of the hemoglobin molecule. Each globin chain has *heme,* a complex iron-containing ring structure.

Alpha

Beta

Beta

Alpha

Heme

specified by two pairs of genes at different loci. This state of affairs is shown in figure 20.12, where α and β denote the respective genes that control the synthesis of normal polypeptide chains. The illustration also reveals that normal *adult* hemoglobin is made up of two fractions: hemoglobin A (Hb A), which is the largest component, and hemoglobin A_2 (Hb A_2), which constitutes about 2.5 percent. Hemoglobin A_2 consists of two alpha chains, which are identical to those in hemoglobin A, and two delta (δ) chains. The δ locus is closely adjacent to the β locus.

A different hemoglobin is present during fetal life. The alpha chain of fetal hemoglobin (Hb F) is chemically identical to the alpha chain of adult hemoglobin (Hb A) and under control by the same gene. However, in place of the beta chain, fetal hemoglobin contains a chemically different gamma (γ) chain that is governed by a separate gene (fig. 20.12). The level of Hb F is high during the last trimester of pregnancy, but then falls off gradually until there is virtually none six months postnatally. As the synthesis of the gamma chain decreases, the synthesis of the beta chain takes over. How this switch in synthesis might occur is the subject of another section (chapter 23).

CISTRON AND MUTON

We have seen that a gene is a specific linear sequence of nucleotide bases. A given gene functions by specifying the number and linear sequence of amino acids in a polypeptide chain of a protein. The gene operates in the nucleus, like an original blueprint kept in the foreman's office. From its headquarters, the DNA transfers its genetic information to ribonucleic acid (RNA), which constitutes the "working drawings" used in the cytoplasmic factory.

The gene may consist of 1,000 or more base pairs. Functionally, then, it is a large unit, and any one of its bases may change or mutate. The functional unit is often referred to as the *cistron.* Each cistron is separable into *mutons,* which may be defined as the smallest number of bases independently capable of producing a mutant phenotype. Typically a mutation represents an alteration of a single base. Since innumerable mutations can occur within a single gene, a given gene can exist in several alternative forms. This, we have noted, is referred to as *multiple allelism.*

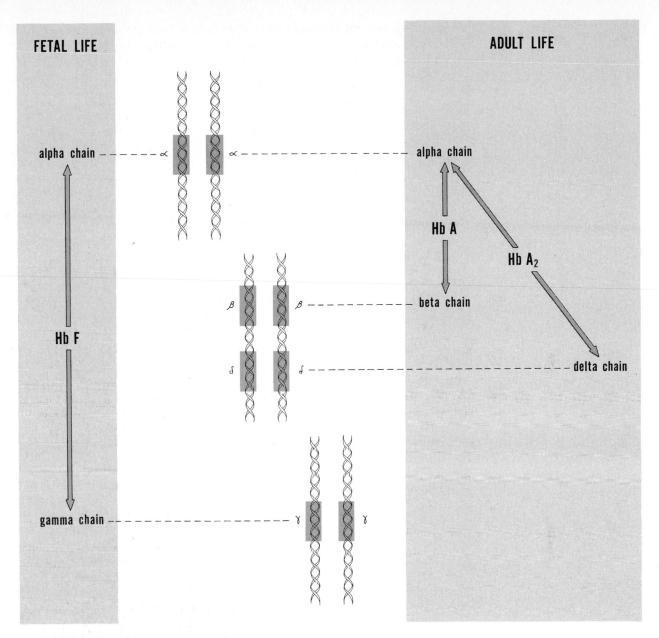

FETAL LIFE

ADULT LIFE

alpha chain — — — — ∝ — — ∝ — — — — — — — — — — alpha chain

Hb A

Hb A₂

β — — — β — — — — — — — beta chain

δ — — — δ — — — — — — — — — — — — — — — delta chain

Hb F

gamma chain — — — — — — — — — — — γ — — γ

In the next chapter, we will consider the multiple allelic series involved in the determination of the ABO blood groups of man.

Figure 20.12 Genetic control of hemoglobin synthesis by four loci. The *beta* and *delta* loci are closely linked in the same chromosome.

SUMMARY

The gene functions by specifying the linear sequence of amino acids in a polypeptide chain of a protein. A mutation in a gene—an inheritable change in a single nucleotide base of the gene—results in a single specific amino acid replacement in the polypeptide chain. This is clearly shown by studies of normal and abnormal human hemoglobins. Normal hemoglobin consists of two different kinds of polypeptide chains, alpha and beta, each of which is controlled by a separate gene. A single mutational change, such as that responsible for sickle-cell hemoglobin, affects only one kind of polypeptide chain. The sole difference in chemical composition between normal and sickle-cell hemoglobin is the substitution of one amino acid unit in the beta chain: the glutamic acid residue at a specific site in normal hemoglobin is replaced by valine in sickle-cell hemoglobin. Since a gene consists of approximately 1,500 nucleotide pairs, and mutations can occur at different sites (base pairs) within a single gene locus, a given gene can exist in several alternative forms. All known amino acid substitutions in human hemoglobin can be accounted for by alterations of single nucleotide bases.

Proteins are not synthesized directly on the DNA template. The genetic information (genetic code) of DNA is first transcribed to single-stranded messenger RNA. Messenger RNA carries the code for a specific polypeptide from the nucleus to ribosomes in the cytoplasm, the sites of protein synthesis. Messenger RNA directs the assembly of various amino acids at the ribosome surface. The translation of the information of messenger RNA is performed by scores of different transfer RNAs, which transport appropriate free amino acids to the ribosomes.

Human Blood Groups and Hemolytic Disease

21

In the early 1900s the Austrian pathologist Karl Landsteiner discovered that when the red blood cells of one person were mixed with the blood serum of another person, the serum frequently caused the cells to form clumps, or agglutinate (fig. 21.1). The agglutination reaction did not occur in every combination of serum and cells. Landsteiner hypothesized that the serum of certain persons reacts to the cells of others as if the cells were a foreign substance, or *antigen*. The serum contains a chemically active substance, or *antibody*, that binds specifically to the antigen, much in the same manner that antibodies attack and destroy infectious microorganisms and foreign grafts.

Further investigation of this phenomenon revealed that there may be two distinct types of protein molecules, or *antigens* A and B, on the surface of the human blood cells. From what we have learned of the synthesis of proteins, we should predict that the two antigens are controlled by two different alleles. Moreover, the allele responsible for antigen A and the allele governing antigen B would act independently of each other when present together, so that a person with both alleles would have both antigens. This is precisely the situation.

The human blood groups not only illustrate clearly and simply the basic mechanism of the inheritance of multiple alleles, but also permit an appreciation of a uniquely human disorder known as *hemolytic disease of the newborn*.

Figure 21.1 Agglutination reaction of red blood cells when they are mixed with antibodies (anti-A) specific to the antigens (A) in the cell membranes. The antibodies, being bivalent, can attach to two different cells and bind them together. Anti-B antibodies do not fit the A antigens; hence, agglutination, or clumping, of cells carrying antigen A does not occur in the presence of anti-B antibodies.

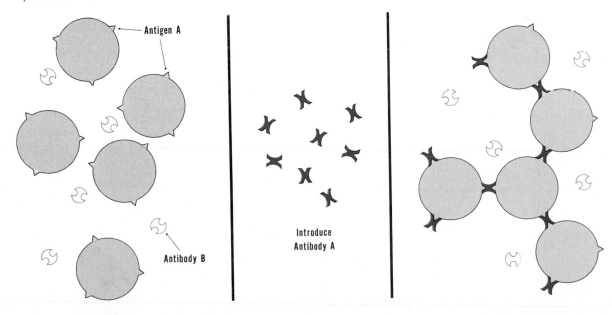

RED BLOOD CELLS (Type A)

Introduce Antibody A

Cells Agglutinate

Antigen A

Antibody B

ABO BLOOD GROUPS

A person may have one or the other of the two antigens (A or B) in his blood cells, or he may have both or neither. A person possessing antigen A is said to belong to blood group A; a person having antigen B belongs to group B; a person having both antigens is in group AB; and a person having neither belongs to group O. Landsteiner showed that there are two antibodies in the serum of blood, which he designated as anti-A and anti-B. If serum containing anti-A is mixed with a suspension of blood cells bearing antigen A, the cells will clump together in large granular masses (fig. 21.2). On the other hand, if anti-A is mixed with B blood cells, or anti-B with A blood cells, there is no reaction; the cells remain suspended without clumping. This simple principle is the basis for blood-group tests.

Whatever antigen a person has in his cells, the corresponding antibody is lacking in the serum (table 21.1). A person obviously does not have the antibody that is capable of destroying his own red cells. He may, however, have the antibody that reacts against the antigen possessed by another person. For example, type A individuals lack anti-A but contain the antibody against B. This knowledge provides the basis for the successful transfusion of blood between individuals. The cardinal rule is to avoid introducing antigens that can be destroyed (or agglutinated) by antibodies in the serum of the recipient. Antibodies in the donor are inconsequential because the amount of blood transfused is small relative to the total blood volume of the recipient and the antibodies are quickly diluted out by the recipient's blood. Type O persons are the acknowledged "universal donors" since they contain no antigens that could be acted upon by the recipient's antibodies. Type AB persons lack both antibodies and accordingly can receive blood from persons of all types without fear of destroying the cells contributed by the donor.

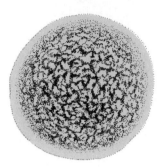

Figure 21.2 Blood typing. Two drops of blood have been mixed with serum from type B (*top*) and from type A (*bottom*), respectively. Only the red cells on the bottom have clumped; hence, the blood of the person being tested is type A.

Table 21.1
ABO Blood Groups in Man

Group	Genotype	Antigens in Cells	Antibodies in Serum	Can Donate Blood to:	Can Receive Blood from:
A	$I^A I^A$ or $I^A i$	A	anti-B	A, AB	A, O
B	$I^B I^B$ or $I^B i$	B	anti-A	B, AB	B, O
AB	$I^A I^B$	A and B	none	AB	A, B, AB, O
O	ii	none	anti-A and anti-B	A, B, AB, O	O

INHERITANCE OF THE ABO BLOOD GROUPS

In humans, the hereditary basis of a trait is sought by observing the numbers and distributions of the phenotypic variants in families. The blood groups are an excellent example of how the mode of inheritance has been deduced from an analysis of large numbers of family pedigrees. Representative marriages are shown in figure 21.3.

When both parents are AB, only three types appear among the offspring: A, B, and AB (cross 1 in fig. 21.3). Type O children do not arise from such marriages, and the AB offspring arise twice as often as either the A or B sib. The ¼ A : ½ AB : ¼ B phenotypic ratio is clearly the result to be expected from the mating of two heterozygous parents. Each heterozygous parent can be said to carry an allele (designated I^A) responsible for the production of antigen A as well as an allele (I^B) responsible for antigen B. Both alleles are denoted by capital letters, since neither one is dominant to the other and both express themselves in the heterozygote, who has both A and B antigens.

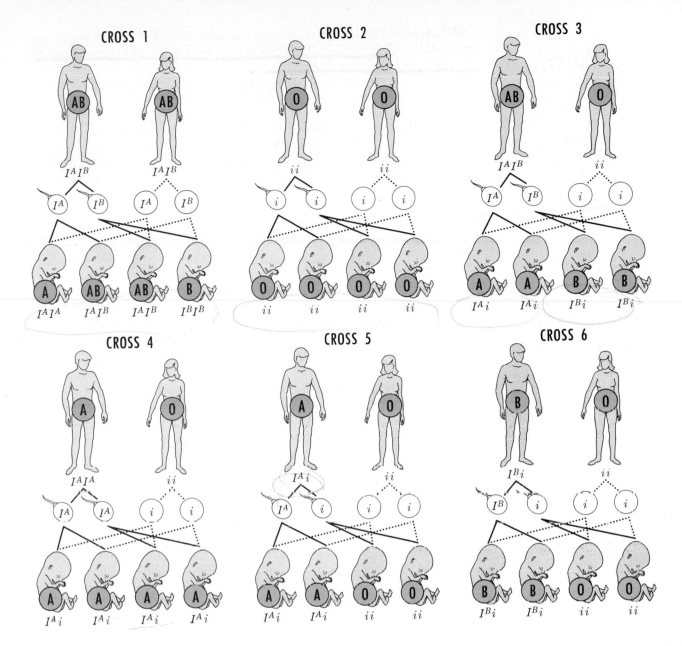

Figure 21.3 Inheritance pattern of ABO blood groups in man. Three different genes are involved (I^A, I^B, and i), but a given person can possess only two of the three genes.

Cross 2 in figure 21.3 reveals that type O parents have only O children. This suggests that the parents and their offspring are homozygous for a recessive gene (designated i). The relation among the three alleles (I^A, I^B, and i) becomes clear from the analysis of AB × O marriages (cross 3, fig. 21.3). Children from such marriages are either A or B, in equal proportions, and never O. Thus, genes I^A and I^B, although exhibiting no dominance over each other, are each dominant to allele i.

The outcome of an A × O marriage depends on whether the A parent is homozygous or heterozygous (crosses 4 and 5, fig. 21.3). If the A parent is homozygous ($I^A I^A$), only A children are possible; if heterozygous ($I^A i$), both A and O children can be produced. Likewise, as seen in cross 6 (fig. 21.3), type O children can arise from a B × O marriage only when the B parent is heterozygous ($I^B i$).

We are thus able to recognize that there are three alternative forms, or three alleles, of one gene: (1) I^A for production of the A antigen; (2) I^B for production of the B antigen; and (3) i, which results in neither A nor B antigen. The *i* allele is recessive to both I^A and I^B, but I^A and I^B are codominant. <u>*Only two of the three alleles may normally occur in an individual, and only one in the gamete*</u>.

We assume that, at some time in the past, mutations occurred at this one gene locus. We do not know which of the three is the original allele, and which two are the mutant alleles. Further analysis has revealed two chief subdivisions of group A, based on the presence on the red cells of two separate antigenic factors, A_1 and A_2. There are accordingly more than three alleles at this one locus. Since a given gene contains many sites at which mutations can occur, it is not surprising that different alleles with dissimilar functions have arisen.

PARENTAGE AND ABO BLOOD GROUPS

Cases of disputed parentage may sometimes be resolved by blood-group tests. The tests can be used only as negative tests; that is, they can disprove paternity or maternity, but they cannot prove them. Suppose that the mother has blood of type O; the child, type A; and the alleged (or putative) father, type O. The man in question cannot be the father. because the child has antigen A, which is lacking in both the mother and putative father. On the other hand, if the man had belonged to A or AB, he would not have been excluded. Nor could he have been proven the father, since any other man with either A or AB could have been involved. Thus, it is not possible to state that the putative father is, in fact, the real father. It can only be stated that he may be, or cannot be, the father. Table 21.2 shows the ABO blood groups of offspring that can, or cannot, arise from the varied combinations of parents.

Similar tables can be prepared for the MN, Rh, and other red blood cell systems (Kell, Lewis, Duffy, Kidd, and so forth). The chances that an accused man will be exonerated by the ABO blood-group test alone are

Table 21.2
Blood Groups of Offspring from Different Combinations of Parents

Alleged Father	Known Mother	Possible Children	Children Not Possible (Decisive for Nonpaternity)*
O	O	O	A, B, (AB)*
O	A	O, A	B, AB
O	B	O, B	A, AB
O	AB	A, B	AB, (O)
A	O	O, A	B, (AB)
A	A	O, A	B, AB
A	B	O, A, B, AB	
A	AB	A, B, AB	(O)
B	O	O, B	A, (AB)
B	A	O, A, B, AB	
B	B	O, B	A, AB
B	AB	A, B, AB	(O)
AB	O	A, B	O, (AB)
AB	A	A, B, AB	O
AB	B	A, B, AB	O
AB	AB	A, B, AB	(O)

* Blood groups in parentheses represent individuals who could not be under any circumstance (save a mutational event) children of the corresponding mothers.

about 1 in 6. Addition of the MN and Rh systems increase his chances of establishing nonpaternity to about 1 in 2.

ABO INCOMPATIBILITY

It may happen that the fetus contains an A or B antigen (inherited from the father) that is not present in the mother herself. The mother, for example, may be type O and her baby may be type A. The mother in this case would carry the naturally occurring antibodies in her serum, anti-A and anti-B. The anti-A of the mother may enter the fetal circulation through the placenta and destroy the fetal red cells, which are carrying the A antigen. This may result in a blood disorder known as *hemolytic disease of the newborn,* in which the infant is delivered with anemia and jaundice. Hemolytic disease due to anti-A (or anti-B) is much milder than such disease caused by the familiar anti-Rh; it rarely requires an exchange transfusion of blood. Hemolytic disease due to ABO incompatibility, however, often occurs in the firstborn.

The principal clinical manifestation of ABO hemolytic disease is jaundice. When the fetus' red cells hemolyze (break down), the hemoglobin liberated from the ruptured cells is transformed into a yellow pigment called *bilirubin.* The liver ordinarily would convert the bilirubin into harmless bile. But the amount of yellow bilirubin in the infant is unmanageable and accumulates in the blood, turning the plasma into an almost yellow-orange liquid. The infant is consequently deeply jaundiced—that is, the skin assumes a deep yellow-orange tint.

Theoretically, 20 percent of all babies have ABO blood types that are potentially incompatible with the mother's type. The actual number of affected infants is below expectation; about 1 in 150 of all births. Evidently, many newborn of ABO incompatible pregnancies are protected in some way. An examination of table 21.3 reveals that type AB women do not have "incompatible" babies and type O babies are always "compatible." Clinically, it has been observed that if a baby has hemolytic disease due to anti-A or anti-B, the mother is usually type O, and very seldom type A or B. Type O women produce antibodies of low molecular weight (the so-named 7S gamma globulin fraction), which readily cross the placental barrier.

A disquieting finding in recent years is that anti-A and anti-B manifest their harmful effects primarily in early pregnancy. There is a significantly greater rate of spontaneous abortion among type O women married to men of type A or B than among A or B women married to O men. In terms of large numbers of pregnancies terminating prematurely, ABO incompatibility looms as more frightening than Rh incompatibility. Ironically, as we shall see, ABO incompatibility between mother and fetus may have beneficial consequences under certain circumstances.

Mother's Type	Antibodies in Mother's Serum	Types of Incompatible Babies	Types of Compatible Babies
A	anti-B	B, AB	O, A
B	anti-A	A, AB	O, B
AB	none	none	A, B, AB
O	anti-A and anti-B	A, B	O

Table 21.3
ABO Groups of Mothers and Their Babies

RH INCOMPATIBILITY

A relation between the Rh factor (antigen) and hemolytic disease was first postulated by Dr. Philip Levine and his colleague Dr. B. E. Stetson in 1939, when they discovered a then unknown antibody in the serum of a woman who had recently delivered a stillborn infant. The antibody was subsequently identified as *anti-Rh*, which is produced by the mother in response to, and directed against, the Rh antigen of the blood cells of her own fetus. Clinical records reveal that the mothers of affected newborn lack the Rh antigen (that is, are *Rh-negative*) whereas their husbands and affected infants possess the Rh antigen (that is, are *Rh-positive*).

The Rh antigen in the blood cell is controlled by a dominant gene, designated *R*. An Rh-positive person has the dominant gene, either in the homozygous *(RR)* or heterozygous *(Rr)* state. All Rh-negative individuals carry two recessive genes *(rr)* and are incapable of producing the Rh antigen. The inheritance of the Rh antigen follows simple Mendelian laws (fig. 21.4). A mother who is Rh-negative *(rr)* need not fear having Rh-diseased offspring if her husband is likewise Rh-negative *(rr)*. If the husband is heterozygous *(Rr)*, half of the offspring will be Rh-negative *(rr)* and none of these will be afflicted. The other half will be Rh-positive *(Rr)*, just like the father, and are potential victims of hemolytic disease. If the Rh-positive father is homozygous *(RR)*, then all the children will be Rh-positive *(Rr)* and potential victims. In essence, an Rh-positive child carried by an Rh-negative mother is the setting for possible, though not inevitable, trouble.

The chain of events leading to hemolytic disease begins with the inheritance by the fetus of the dominant *R* gene of the father. The Rh antigens are produced in the red blood cells of the fetus. The fetal red cells bearing the Rh antigens escape through the placental barrier into the mother's circulation, and stimulate the production of antibodies (anti-R) against the Rh antigens on the fetal red cells (fig. 21.5). The mother, having produced antibodies, is said to be immunized (or sensitized) against

Figure 21.4 Offspring that may arise from a marriage of an Rh-negative woman and an Rh-negative man (in this case, heterozygous). The mother must be sensitized to the Rh antigen before delivering a child affected with Rh disease.

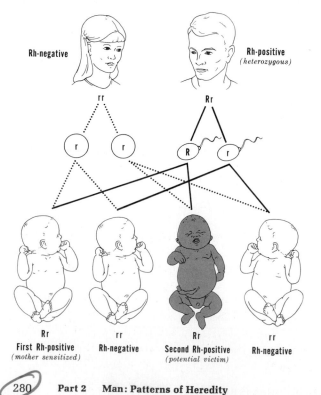

Rh-negative   Rh-positive *(heterozygous)*

rr   Rr

r   r   R   r

Rr — **First Rh-positive** *(mother sensitized)*

rr — Rh-negative

Rr — **Second Rh-positive** *(potential victim)*

rr — Rh-negative

her baby's blood cells. The maternal antibodies almost never attain a sufficient concentration during the first pregnancy to harm the fetus. In fact, although fetal cells cross the placenta throughout pregnancy, they enter the maternal circulation in much larger numbers during delivery, when the placental vessels rupture. It is now generally conceded that sensitization of the mother takes place shortly *after* the delivery of the first Rh-positive child. Accordingly, the firstborn is rarely affected, unless the mother had previously developed antibodies from having been transfused with Rh-positive blood or has had a prior pregnancy terminating in an abortion.

The antibodies remain in the mother's system, and may linger for many months or years (fig. 21.5). If the second baby is also Rh-positive, the mother may send sufficient antibodies into the fetus' bloodstream to destroy its red cells. The majority of affected fetuses survive for the usual gestation period but are born in critical condition from anemia. Severely anemic individuals are likely to be jaundiced and develop heart failure. A grave threat to the newborn infant is bilirubin, which, as described earlier, is a product of red cell destruction. During pregnancy fetal bilirubin is transported across the placenta and eliminated by the mother. From the time of birth, however, bilirubin accumulates as the affected infant fails to dispose of it. Bilirubin has been shown to be highly toxic to the soft brain tissues; the brain may be permanently damaged.

Another aspect of the hemolytic condition, which has given it its original name *(erythroblastosis fetalis)*, is the presence of immature red cells (the erythroblasts) in the circulating blood. It is as if the liver and the spleen in an attempt to combat the severe anemic condition produce vast numbers of "unfinished" red blood cells. Unattended, erythroblastosis fetalis leads to stillborn or neonatal death. Many of the erythroblastotic babies are saved by exchange transfusion of Rh-negative blood; others, however, die despite treatment. Exchange transfusion is essentially a flushing-out process, whereby the infant's blood is gradually diluted with Rh-negative donated blood until at the end of the procedure most of the infant's circulating blood is problem-free. In severe cases, where it has been predicted that the fetus would die before it was mature enough for premature delivery, intrauterine transfusions have been used successfully.

As might have been anticipated, the Rh gene has turned out to be more complex than initially envisioned. There are several variant alleles, and a corresponding diversity of antigenic constitutions. This diversity need not concern us here. The most common antigen is the one that was first recognized, known more specifically now as Rh_0 or D. It is the presence of Rh_0 that is tested in ordinary clinical work.

INCIDENCE OF RH DISEASE

Among Caucasians in the United States, the incidence of Rh-negative persons is approximately 16 percent. In certain European groups, such as the Basques in Spain, the frequency of Rh-negative individuals rises as high as 34 percent. Non-Caucasian populations are relatively free of Rh hemolytic disease. The incidence of Rh-negative persons among the full-blooded American Indians, Eskimos, African Negroes, Japanese, and Chinese is 1 percent or less. In contrast, the frequency of Rh-negative American Negroes is high (9 percent), which reflects the historical consequences of intermarriages.

● Rh ANTIGEN
ᶜ Rh ANTIBODY

DURING PREGNANCY

AT DELIVERY

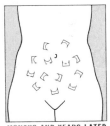

MONTHS AND YEARS LATER

SUBSEQUENT PREGNANCY

Figure 21.5 Rh disease in the newborn. The fetus inherits the Rh-positive gene from the father and produces Rh-positive red blood cells. Fetal Rh-positive blood cells enter the Rh-negative mother's bloodstream through placental hemorrhage at delivery, sensitizing her to the Rh-positive antigen and causing her to produce anti-Rh antibody. The anti-Rh antibodies remain in the mother's bloodstream for many months or years. In a subsequent pregnancy, anti-Rh antibodies in the mother's circulation cross the placenta to react with and destroy fetal red blood cells containing the Rh antigen (if the second infant is Rh-positive). The fetus then is afflicted with Rh disease.

Table 21.4
Frequencies of Marriages by
Chance of Rh-positive and
Rh-negative Individuals in
Caucasian Populations

Female (♀)	Male (♂)		
	36% RR	48% Rr	16% rr
36% RR	12.96% RR × RR	17.28% RR × Rr	5.76% RR × rr
48% Rr	17.28% Rr × RR	23.04% Rr × Rr	7.68% Rr × rr
16% rr	5.76% rr × RR	7.68% rr × Rr	2.56% rr × rr

Note: Rh-negative persons make up 16% of the population; among Rh-positive persons, 36% are homozygous dominant and 48% are heterozygous.

It is instructive to calculate the frequencies of marriages that are at a risk with respect to Rh hemolytic disease. Table 21.4 shows the different types of marriages that can occur when individuals choose their mates by sheer chance—that is, without regard to each other's Rh makeup. Of the two kinds of marriages that can result in Rh-positive pregnancies, 5.76 percent would be rr (females) × RR (males) and 7.68 percent would be rr (females) × Rr (males). Thus approximately 13 percent of all marriages, or 1 out of every 8, are risky with regard to erythroblastosis fetalis.

From these data, we can ascertain the frequency of potentially dangerous pregnancies. All pregnancies from the rr (females) × RR (males) would yield an Rh-positive fetus, but only one half of the infants from the rr (females) × Rr (males) would be Rh-positive. Thus, the frequency of all potentially troublesome pregnancies is 5.76 + 3.84 = 9.60 percent, or slightly less than one-tenth of all pregnancies.

Theoretically, then, 1 out of 9 or 10 pregnancies should result in an erythroblastotic child. However, in actuality, only 1 in 200 pregnancies results in an afflicted baby. The reasons for the low observed incidence are not entirely clear. Apparently, differences in the ease of sensitization exist among Rh-negative women. The Rh antigen of the fetus may fail to get through the placenta, or some Rh-negative mothers are incapable of responding to the antigen. The low occurrence may also reflect a peculiar protective role of the ABO blood groups in reducing the risk of Rh incompatibility. In 1943, Dr. Philip Levine called attention to the fact that infants of Rh-negative, type O mothers develop Rh disease less often than those of type A or B, Rh-negative mothers. If the infant's red cells are type A or type B, the maternal anti-A and anti-B antibodies in type O women destroy the infant's Rh-positive red cells when they enter the Rh-negative mother's bloodstream. Thus, the invading fetal cells are eliminated before they have the opportunity to sensitize the mother. Strange as it may seem, then, the ABO incompatibility protects the mother and child against a simultaneous Rh incompatibility. A double incompatibility clearly affords a lower risk of fetal loss than Rh incompatibility alone.

THE CONTROL OF RH DISEASE

In the 1960s Drs. Vincent Freda and John Gorman at the Columbia-Presbyterian Medical Center in New York and Dr. William Pollack at the Ortho Research Foundation in New Jersey sought the means of suppressing the production of antibodies in Rh-negative mothers who had recently delivered an Rh-positive infant. Experiments performed 50 years earlier by the distinguished American bacteriologist, Dr. Theobald Smith, furnished an important clue to the solution. In 1909, Smith arrived at the general principle that passive immunity can prevent active immunity. That is, an antibody given passively by injection can inhibit the recipient from producing its own active antibody. After five years of experimentation and testing, Drs. Freda, Gorman, and Pollack successfully developed an immunosuppressant consisting of a blood fraction (gamma globulin) rich in Rh antibodies. Injected into the bloodstream of the Rh-negative mother no later than three days after the birth of her first Rh-positive child, the globulin-Rh antibody preparation (known as RhoGAM) suppresses the mother's antibody-making activity. Several hundred mothers have already received the preparation; none have formed active antibodies. More impressive, some of them have now delivered a second Rh-positive baby and none of the babies were afflicted with Rh disease. The evidence is overwhelming that the immunosuppressant is effective.

The immunosuppressant does not prevent hemolytic disease if maternal antibody is already present by earlier pregnancies or by previous transfusion of Rh-positive blood. For this reason the preparation is administered only to Rh-negative women who do not have anti-Rh in their sera at the time of delivery. With each delivery opportunity for exposure to Rh-positive fetal cells is repeated. The protection given at the delivery of the first infant does not protect the mother from exposure to antigen received at a subsequent pregnancy. Hence, the immunosuppressant must be given immediately following each pregnancy.

SUMMARY

The four human blood groups in the classical ABO system—A, B, AB, and O—are determined by three alternative forms of one gene, or multiple alleles. Only two of the three alleles may normally occur in an individual, and only one in the gamete. The alleles affect the surface proteins (antigens) of red blood cells by which they respond to specific components (antibodies) in the blood serum. The allele (I^A) responsible for antigen A and the allele (I^B) governing antigen B act independently of each other when present together, so that a person with both alleles $(I^A I^B)$ possesses both antigens (type AB). Whatever antigen a person has in his red blood cells, the corresponding antibody is lacking in the blood serum. The third allele (i) is essentially an inactive gene; type O persons (ii) produce neither antigen A nor antigen B (but contain anti-A and anti-B antibodies).

It is possible for the fetus by inheritance from the father to have an antigen in the ABO group for which the mother has the corresponding antibody, and this situation may result in *hemolytic disease of the newborn*. Hemolytic disease due to ABO incompatibility tends to be mild and is rarely severe enough to threaten the life of the newborn. However, there is suggestive evidence that ABO incompatibility may be responsible for spontaneous abortion in early pregnancy. Fetal-maternal incompatibility involving the Rh antigen is the more common cause of hemolytic disease of the newborn. An Rh-positive fetus carried by an Rh-negative mother is the setting for possible, though not inevitable, Rh incompatibility. The recent measure of giving Rh-negative mothers of Rh-positive newborns an immunosuppressant (anti-Rh gamma globulin) shortly after delivery has already reduced the incidence of hemolytic disease and promises to make this disease a clinical rarity in the near future.

22 Inborn Errors of Metabolism

The currently accepted tenet is that an inheritable change of a gene reveals itself as a modification in the composition and function of a specific protein molecule. The modification of the protein may be a simple substitution of one amino acid for another in the polypeptide chain or a more complex change affecting the rate of synthesis of the polypeptide chain. We have already noted the consequences of changes in the amino acid sequence for the important blood protein of man, hemoglobin. Not all proteins, of course, are structural proteins like hemoglobin. Many proteins have only enzymatic functions, and enzymes are just as subject to alteration as the structural proteins are. Indeed, many of the inherited biochemical anomalies in man, or *inborn errors of metabolism,* have been shown to be due to enzymatic deficiencies.

It should be pointed out that little is known about the specific manner that a given enzyme is altered. In contrast to our understanding of the hemoglobin molecule, the precise nature of an enzyme alteration has rarely been elucidated. However, the consequences of an enzyme deficiency—direct impairment of specific metabolic pathways—have been well characterized, and the metabolic impairment is generally responsible for the appearance of a disease.

HISTORICAL ASPECTS

In 1897, the British physician Archibald Garrod studied several cases of a peculiar disorder in which his patients excreted black urine. From an analysis of family histories, Garrod concluded that this anomaly, known as *alkaptonuria,* was recessively inherited. The condition manifests itself when the child inherits one defective recessive gene from each of his parents. Garrod emphasized that alkaptonuria was a "chemical sport," or as he later called it, an "inborn error of metabolism." Alkaptonuria was the first example of recessive inheritance to be recognized in man. Although the disease is rare and sporadic, about 200 cases of alkaptonuria have been reported in the world literature. Most of the reported cases have been in Caucasians.

In 1908, Garrod expanded his ideas. He theorized that the defective gene prevents formation of a particular enzyme. In other words, a single enzyme is missing in the alkaptonuric patient. As seen in figure 22.1, the normal gene specifies the synthesis of the enzyme that transforms homogentisic acid to another product, acetoacetic acid. In an alkaptonuric patient, the enzyme is absent or deficient and homogentisic acid accumulates since its conversion to acetoacetic acid is blocked or hindered. The abnormal amounts of homogentisic acid are then eliminated in the urine. Urine containing homogentisic acid, on exposure to air, gradually turns dark. A half century later, in 1958, Garrod's hypothesis

284

NORMAL PERSON

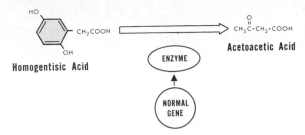

Homogentisic Acid   Acetoacetic Acid

ENZYME

NORMAL GENE

ALKAPTONURIC PERSON

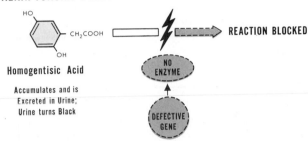

Homogentisic Acid   REACTION BLOCKED

Accumulates and is
Excreted in Urine;
Urine turns Black

NO ENZYME

DEFECTIVE GENE

Figure 22.1 Alkaptonuria, an inherited biochemical disease resulting from the absence or deficiency of a specific enzyme. The enzyme cannot be produced because of a defective, or mutant, gene.

was substantiated by the biochemical demonstration of the absence of the enzyme in the liver of a patient with alkaptonuria.

Important as Garrod's ideas have proved to modern science, they were not recognized as such by his colleagues of the day. His theory that an inborn error of metabolism resulted from the absence of an enzyme fell on deaf ears. Verification came, however, in the 1940s from experiments performed on the pink bread mold (*Neurospora crassa*) by Nobel Laureates G. W. Beadle and Edward L. Tatum, then at the California Institute of Technology. They found that mutation of a particular gene blocks a specific metabolic reaction so that a vital amino acid is not produced, with the consequence that the mold is unable to survive unless furnished the essential amino acid. Beadle and Tatum set forth with special clarity and thoroughness the *one gene–one enzyme* concept, which states that each gene controls the formation of a single enzyme and thereby a single metabolic reaction. With increasing knowledge of the nature of genes in recent years, the one gene–one enzyme thesis has been greatly reinforced and expanded. It has been extended to include all cellular proteins, not necessarily those that are enzymes, and has been more precisely defined as the *one gene–one polypeptide* principle.

MODEL OF BLOCKED METABOLIC REACTIONS

The consequences of an alteration of a single enzyme are shown in figure 22.2, which depicts the model reaction sequence A ⟶ D and the relevant genes for each step. It is assumed that each gene acts independently and each is responsible for formation of a specific enzyme. The substance A is converted to the end product D through a series of metabolic steps, each of which is catalyzed by a separate enzyme. As illustrated, a number of consequences may arise if the "gamma" enzyme is not formed because transcription of the "gamma" gene is faulty as a result of a mutational change. One effect would be the lack of formation of product D, the absence of which could lead to a clinical disorder. In addition, the immediate precursor of the blocked reaction, C, could

Figure 22.2 Metabolic block stemming from a mutation (single base change) that leads to a single amino acid substitution in the enzyme. The absence of a functional enzyme results in abnormally high levels of substrate C, an absence of the substance D distant to the metabolic block, and the increased use of other pathways (X to Z), resulting in greater production of alternative products (Z).

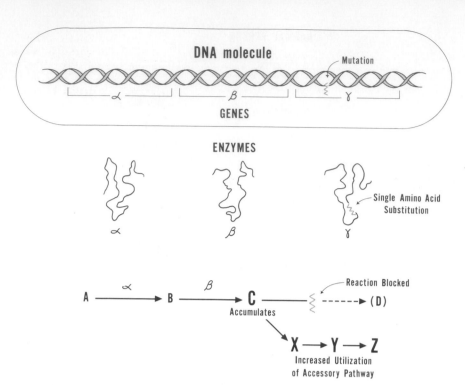

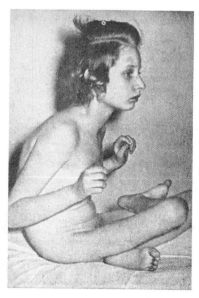

Figure 22.3 Peculiar characteristic sitting position of severely defective phenylketonuric patients. (Courtesy of Dr. Konrad Lang, Die phenyl-pyruvische oligophrenie, *Ergebnisse der Inneren Medizin und Kinder-neilkunde* 6:78.)

accumulate in abnormal amounts. We have already seen that in alkaptonuria homogentisic acid accumulates, since its conversion to aceto-acetic acid is blocked. This leads to a notable increase in urinary excretion together with other pathological conditions (deposition of pigment in various tissues of the body). The block between C and D may also cause increased use of other pathways, resulting in greater production of alternative products. For example, in phenylketonuria a single enzymatic block results not only in the accumulation of phenylalanine (product D) but also in gross overproduction of phenylpyruvic acid (product Z). With this general orientation, we may consider some of the inborn errors of metabolism in man.

PHENYLKETONURIA

One of the best known of the inherited metabolic diseases is *phenylketonuria*, abbreviated PKU. The first case of PKU was described by the Norwegian physician-chemist Asbjörn Fölling in 1934. Persons suffering from PKU are mentally retarded, usually so severely that they are institutionalized. The majority of untreated PKU patients have IQs below 30 and fewer than 1 percent have IQs above 70. Affected persons frequently have a light complexion (blondish hair and bluish eyes) because the production of brown-black pigment (melanin) is impaired. Most affected individuals also have postural peculiarities (fig. 22.3), convulsive or jerky movements, and a diagnostic body odor, described as "musty" or "barny." Phenylketonuric individuals have a short life expectancy; fewer than 1 out of 4 live beyond 30 years of age. The incidence of PKU has been estimated at 1 in 25,000 live births, or about 250 cases per year in the United States. The disability occurs most often among northern Europeans and least frequently among Jews, Negroes, and Orientals.

Shortly after birth, the affected infant has an unusually high concentration of phenylalanine in the blood. Phenylalanine is one of the

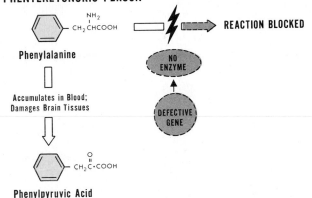

NORMAL PERSON

Phenylalanine

ENZYME

NORMAL GENE

Tyrosine

PHENYLKETONURIC PERSON

Phenylalanine

Accumulates in Blood;
Damages Brain Tissues

NO ENZYME

DEFECTIVE GENE

REACTION BLOCKED

Phenylpyruvic Acid

Excreted in Urine

Figure 22.4 Phenylketonuria (PKU), an inherited biochemical disease resulting from the enzymatic failure of phenylalanine to be converted to tyrosine.

essential dietary amino acids; that is, it cannot be synthesized in the body. Some of the phenylalanine is incorporated into various body proteins. Most of it, however, is normally converted to a slightly different amino acid, *tyrosine*, which is involved in several metabolic pathways, including the formation of pigment. In 1953, the New York physician Dr. George Jervis found that PKU infants are deficient in a liver enzyme *(phenylalanine hydroxylase)* that converts phenylalanine into tyrosine. Phenylalanine thus accumulates in the body fluids and tissues in large quantities, up to 20 times normal in many patients. The increased concentration of phenylalanine leads, in turn, to an increased rate of formation of *phenylpyruvic acid*, which is excreted in the urine (fig. 22.4). Excess phenylpyruvic acid in sweat accounts for the strange body odor of PKU patients.

It is not the lack of tyrosine that produces the abnormal consequences, but rather the excessive amounts of phenylalanine. High levels of phenylalanine are damaging to the rapidly developing brain tissues of the infant in early life. Brain damage in the untreated patient develops after birth and not before. Within six months, the afflicted infant shows definite signs of mental retardation.

In 1961, Dr. Robert Guthrie of the Buffalo Medical School Children's Hospital devised a sensitive and reliable blood test to detect abnormal levels of phenylalanine in the infant during the first few days of life (fig. 22.5). Only a few drops of blood from the infant's heel are required to detect PKU. Called a *bacterial inhibition assay*, the Guthrie test depends on the growth of the bacterium *Bacillus subtilis*. Normally, a particular chemical substance, β-2-thienylalanine, will inhibit the growth of these bacteria on an agar plate. However, certain concentrations of phenylalanine in the blood will override the effects of the inhibitor, and allow *Bacillus subtilis* to grow normally. The rate of growth

Figure 22.5 Guthrie test, based on the ability of phenylalanine to prevent the inhibition of growth of *Bacillus subtilis* in a medium that contains β-2-thienylalanine. Blood obtained by a puncture is applied to thick filter paper; after autoclaving, a disc is punched out of the paper and placed, with other test samples, on agar prepared with β-2-thienylalanine and *B. subtilis* inoculum. Control discs *(top row of bottom photograph)* are prepared by spotting blood with known, increasing concentrations of phenylalanine on filter paper. In test samples containing phenylalanine, a bacterial growth zone (halo) appears after the plate has been incubated at 37°C for 8 to 16 hours. Sample from infant in this instance *(arrow)* contains a large concentration of phenylalanine. (From D. Hsia, "A critical evaluation of PKU screening," *Hospital Practice* 6 (4):109, 1971.)

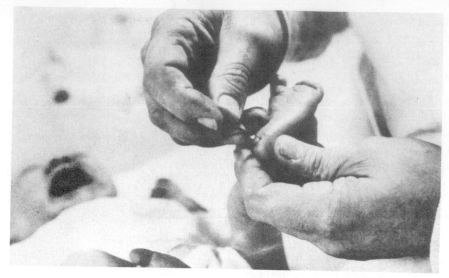

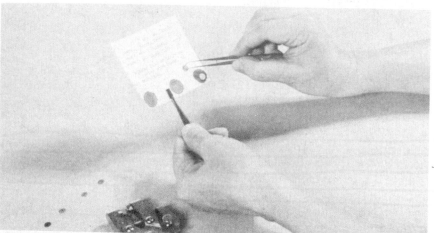

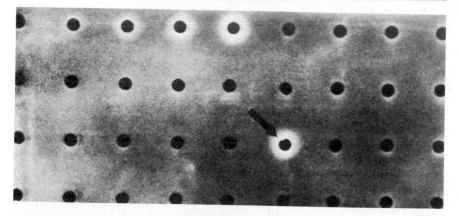

is a measure of the amount of phenylalanine added. A phenylalanine level of more than 4 mg per 100 ml in the infant's blood is grounds for suspecting PKU. The Guthrie blood test or some modification of it has become mandatory in many hospitals in the United States. There are now indications that although PKU is rare, its incidence may be much greater than had been previously estimated. Approximately 1 in 10,000 newborn infants tested nationally in the early 1960s was found to be phenylketonuric.

Many of the newborn infants afflicted with PKU, if treated, have a chance to develop normally. Treatment of PKU has been directed toward reducing the intake of phenylalanine in the diet. In 1954, Drs. H. Bickel, J. Gerrard, and E. M. Hickmans devised a synthetic diet rich in the necessary proteins but low in content of phenylalanine. Although additional investigations are needed, the results have thus far been encouraging. Many phenylketonuric children who received the special diet early in life (from three to six weeks of age onward) have shown marked improvement in both physical and mental development. When the diet is temporarily discontinued, patients typically suffer a relapse. Because the PKU diet has seen widespread use only since the late 1950s, it is still not known whether patients must remain on it for a lifetime or whether it can be discontinued after several years.

The administration of a low phenylalanine diet early in the infant's life is especially important. The earlier the special diet is introduced, the more beneficial the effect. The crucial enzyme (phenylalanine hydroxylase) develops after birth, or at least is not normally active before birth. Thus, the phenylketonuric infant at birth has not sustained any damage to the brain. The key to successful treatment is to curtail the potentially harmful substrate (phenylalanine) before it has an opportunity to accumulate in the infant.

Phenylketonuria is an autosomal recessive condition. Heterozygous parents are phenotypically (clinically) normal, but since they harbor a recessive gene that is functionless, the expectation is that they would produce less than the normal amount of the enzyme phenylalanine hydroxylase. A phenylalanine tolerance test does reveal that phenylalanine hydroxylase activity is partially deficient in heterozygotes. By stressing the enzyme system (that is, administering individuals a load of phenylalanine by mouth), the partial deficiency is aggravated and the heterozygote can be distinguished from the normal homozygote. Heterozygotes are not able to handle the large dose of phenylalanine as well as the normal homozygotes do.

THE PHENYLALANINE DEFICIENCIES

Phenylalanine is the starting point for a chain of chemical reactions essential in the metabolism of man. Connected with this chain of chemical reactions are four inherited defects: alkaptonuria, phenylketonuria, albinism, and tyrosinosis. Each of the four metabolic disorders results from a block at a different point in the same chain of chemical reactions beginning with phenylalanine. The locations of the enzymatic blocks in the overall scheme of metabolism of phenylalanine are shown in figure 22.6.

In patients with *albinism*, the body is incapable of synthesizing the pigment melanin, which, as seen in figure 22.6, is a metabolite of tyrosine. The exact mechanism is still uncertain; one possibility is the inactivation of tyrosinase, the enzyme that mediates one of the metabolic steps between tyrosine and melanin.

Tyrosinosis is exceptionally rare, and is probably an autosomal recessive trait. The primary biochemical abnormality is a decrease in activity of p-hydroxyphenylpyruvic oxidase, which leads to a block between p-hydroxyphenylpyruvic acid and homogentisic acid, resulting in the excretion of p-hydroxyphenylpyruvic acid in the urine.

Newborns, especially those of low birthweight, tend to have unusually high values of tyrosine in their blood. This neonatal tyrosinemia is a

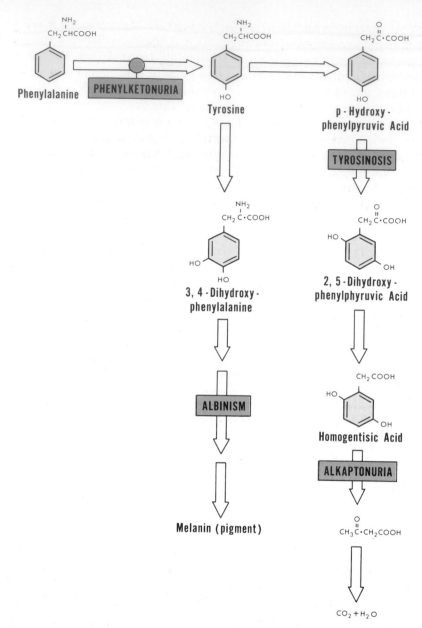

Figure 22.6 Four inherited metabolic disorders, each resulting from an enzymatic block at a different point in the chain of chemical reactions beginning with phenylalanine.

benign, transient defect in tyrosine metabolism. The blood tyrosine usually becomes normal (less than 4 mg per 100 ml) within a few weeks. Infants with neonatal tyrosinemia show a positive Guthrie test; hence, care must be exercised in diagnosing a newborn for PKU.

GALACTOSEMIA

One of the most extraordinary inborn errors of metabolism is *galactosemia*, a condition in which the breast-fed infant is "poisoned" by the mother's milk. Afflicted infants are unable to use the particular kind of sugar, *galactose*, that is found in milk. Galactose ordinarily is converted to glucose, and oxidation thereafter provides energy. In affected infants, galactose is not transformed and accumulates in various tissues. The infant suffers from malnutrition, becomes severely retarded mentally, and develops cataracts. Characteristically the liver becomes grossly enlarged. Unattended, the infant usually dies.

In 1956, Vernon Schwartz and his co-workers made the important observation that galactosemia resulted from a block in the conversion of the phosphate compound of galactose (galactose-1-phosphate) to glucose-1-phosphate. A year later Herman Kalckar and his collaborators at the National Institutes of Health in Bethesda demonstrated that the enzyme (a *transferase*) for this particular reaction was deficient. In turn, the absence of the enzyme is the consequence of a single defective recessive gene. In all cases of affected infants, both parents have proved to be heterozygous carriers. The heterozygous state can now be detected by simple chemical tests; the level of transferase activity is intermediate between levels of patients and normal persons.

If the diagnosis of galactosemia is made before the disease is too far advanced, nearly all the symptoms of the disease disappear if galactose is excluded from the diet of the infant. The liver returns to normal size, nausea and vomiting cease, and nutrition and growth improve markedly. Unfortunately, unless therapy of a galactose-free diet is instituted promptly at birth, there is usually no recovery from the mentally retarded state. The damage to the liver, brain, and eyes occurs in the very first few days of life. Accordingly, if the newborn infant is a member of a high-risk group (for example, the sib of a child with galactosemia), the diagnosis should be made by testing the blood of the umbilical cord for the presence or absence of the necessary enzyme before any milk is given to the infant. Estimates for the prevalence of galactosemia vary widely—from 1 in 18,000 to 1 in 70,000 babies.

GLUCOSE-6-PHOSPHATE DEFICIENCY

Galactosemia is an inherited response to a substance that is universally present in the diet. Inherited conditions are known that manifest themselves in the presence of environmental agents that are not normally present in the diet. Striking examples are the sensitivity reactions of certain individuals to primaquine (an antimalarial drug), the broad, or fava, bean (commonly eaten in Mediterranean countries), sulfanilamide, and acetanilid (a painkiller). Sensitive individuals develop anemia and jaundice. The destruction of blood cells has been linked to the finding that the erythrocytes are unable to oxidize glucose normally because of a deficiency, or lack, of the enzyme *glucose-6-phosphate dehydrogenase* (G-6-PD). This is thus another case of an inborn error of metabolism involving a single deficient enzyme.

The condition is more common among males than among females because it is a sex-linked recessive characteristic (see chapter 26). It occurs in about 10 percent of American Negroes as a rather mild clinical condition, and death is uncommon. In contrast, in non-Negro subjects, this enzyme deficiency may result in a more severe reaction, particularly following exposure to fava beans. Fava-induced hemolysis occurs within a few hours of eating fava beans, tends to be more damaging than primaquine sensitivity, and may require a blood transfusion to compensate for the massive destruction of red blood cells that may occur. The various types or manifestations of glucose-6-phosphate deficiency are thought to represent a series of slightly different mutations at the same gene locus.

Some of the inborn errors of metabolism that are known today are listed in table 22.1. The selection illustrates the wide variety of metabolic disorders and the clinical findings associated with them.

Condition	Enzyme	Main Clinical Features	Treatment
Acatalasia	Catalase	Mild oral lesions	None required
Adrenogenital syndrome	21-hydroxylase	Virilization in males; pseudohermaphrodism in females	Cortisone
Albinism	Tyrosinase	Lack of melanin pigment	None available
Atypical pseudocholinesterase	Pseudocholinesterase	Prolonged apnea (breathing difficulties) from succinylcholine	Avoid drug
Cystic fibrosis	Unclear	Chronic bronchiolar obstruction with infection	Antibiotics
Galactosemia	Galactose-1-phosphate uridyl transferase	Mental retardation, cataracts, cirrhosis	Dietary (omit galactose)
Glycogen deposition disease (von Gierke's)	Glucose-6-phosphatase	Enlarged liver, hypoglycemia (abnormally diminished content of blood sugar)	Prevent hypoglycemia by diet (frequent feedings)
Histidinemia	Histidase	Mental retardation, speech defects	None reported
Homocystinuria	Cystathionine synthetase	Mental deficiency, epileptic seizures, dislocated lenses	None reported

Table 22.1
Inborn Errors of Metabolism, Clinical Features, and Known Treatment, If Any

CELL CULTURES AND GENETIC DISORDERS

The diagnosis of several inborn errors has been immeasurably enhanced by the study of cell cultures established from blood cells or biopsies of tissues, particularly skin. More recently, the techniques of cell culture have been applied to cells obtained from the amniotic fluid that surrounds the developing fetus. This procedure permits the prenatal diagnosis of genetic disorders (see chapter 27).

Although the cells are grown in an artificial nutrient medium, they do not lose their enzymatic machinery when cultured. Thus, biochemical analyses can reveal the presence or absence of specific enzymes. The disorders that can be detected by assay of enzyme activity in cultured cells include many of those listed in table 22.1 and also Tay-Sachs disease (the degenerative cerebral condition), Hurler's syndrome (inflammatory changes in the connective tissue), and the Lesch-Nyhan syndrome (characterized by spasticity, mental retardation, and self-mutilation). Of special interest is that genetic carriers can be distinguished from otherwise indistinguishable noncarriers. Heterozygous carriers of several of the inherited metabolic disorders have demonstrably decreased levels of enzyme activity. Thus, if both parents can be shown to be carriers for a particular metabolic defect, provisions can be made for the careful monitoring of pregnancies and the immediate neonatal care of treatable disorders.

Certain rare inborn errors of metabolism (such as Hurler's and Hunter's syndromes) are associated with an accumulation of mucopolysaccharides in various tissues of the body. The cells of these patients contain cytoplasmic bodies, or inclusions, that harbor the excessive mucopolysaccharides. In the late 1960s, Alexander Bearn and Shannon

Condition	Enzyme	Main Clinical Features	Treatment
Hypophosphatasia	Alkaline phosphatase	Generalized bone disease; rickets in childhood	No specific treatment
Maple syrup urine disease	Branched-chain keto acid decarboxylase	Mental retardation; feeding problems; persistent vomiting	Dietary (low in branched-chain amino acids, such as leucine, isoleucine, and valine)
Methemoglobinemia	Erythrocyte diaphorase	Methemoglobin formation	Avoid methemoglobin-producing drugs
Phenylketonuria	Phenylalanine hydroxylase	Mental retardation; muscular hypertonicity; agitated behavior; seizures	Dietary (low in phenylalanine)
Porphyria	δ-aminolevulinic acid synthetase	Abdominal colic, varied neurologic manifestations, including psychosis	None adequate
Primaquine sensitivity	Glucose-6-phosphate dehydrogenase	Hemolysis from primaquine (antimalarial drug)	Avoid offending drug
Wilson's disease	Disturbance of copper (ceruloplasmin) metabolism	Degenerative changes in brain; cirrhosis of liver; violent tremors and convulsions	Use of effective cupric agent (penicillamine)
Xanthinuria	Xanthine oxidase	Renal dysfunction; renal stones	Prevent stones by appreciable fluid intake and alkali

Danes at the Rockefeller University demonstrated that these cytoplasmic inclusions exhibit a bright pink color when stained with toluidine blue O. This metachromasia ("change in color") not only manifests itself in affected individuals but also in unaffected carriers of the defective gene.

The technique of staining abnormal cells with a metachromatic dye held great promise for the detection of another important clinical condition, cystic fibrosis. However, the phenomenon of metachromasia lacks specificity, and several investigators have found that the prenatal test of metachromasia is not reliable, particularly for prenatal diagnosis of cystic fibrosis.

GENE SURGERY

Galactosemia and glucose-6-phosphate deficiency vividly illustrate the interplay of genetic factors and environmental factors. The defective recessive gene, when homozygous, is expressed only under certain environmental conditions. In galactosemia, the particular environment happens to be the usual or normal one, since galactose is a main component of milk. Thus, under ordinary circumstances, all homozygous recessive offspring are vulnerable to galactosemia. However, if the environment is modified—that is, if galactose is eliminated from the diet—the disorder is curtailed or prevented. Postnatal brain damage, for example, can be prevented by dietary treatment. The individual will continue to lack the ability to manufacture the appropriate enzyme, and remain always intolerant of galactose. In essence, since the underlying enzyme problem is not corrected by the therapeutic measures, the disease is not cured.

The essential principles underlying treatment of inherited metabolic disorders at present are the avoidance of the harmful environmental factors and the restoration of a normal internal metabolism by modifications of the diet. Attempts to alleviate the metabolic disorder by directly supplying the deficient enzyme are wrought with considerable difficulties since the body tends to inactivate the administered enzyme or form antibodies against it.

Biochemical geneticists are now looking at the possibility of a more fundamental approach, namely, replacing the defective gene itself or transplanting cells capable of synthesizing the missing enzyme. The practical barriers to the artificial synthesis of a normal human gene for a metabolic disorder are at present insurmountable. The incorporation of an already functional gene into the human living cell appears to be a less formidable task. Indeed, in October of 1971, in an investigation that has been hailed as revolutionary, Dr. Carl Merril and his associates at the National Institutes of Health transplanted the genes of a virus into living human cells in culture. Human fibroblast cells taken from a patient suffering from galactosemia were infected with a nonvirulent virus. The virus had one interesting attribute: it had previously acquired from a bacterial cell (the common intestinal bacteria, *Escherichia coli*) a cluster of genes that directs the synthesis of the same galactose-metabolizing enzyme produced by normal human cells. The remarkable finding was that the virus instructed the galactosemic human cells to manufacture the galactose-metabolizing enzyme that was formerly missing in the defective cells. Moreover, the newly endowed cells passed on the capacity to synthesize the enzyme when they divided to produce daughter cells. The transmission of genes from a virus to a human cell, at least *in vitro*, can no longer be relegated to the realm of science fiction.

SUMMARY

Enzymes, being proteins, are regulated by genes and are subject, like structural proteins, to alteration. A single gene controls the formation of a single enzyme; more specifically, one gene controls one polypeptide chain, whether of a structural or an enzymatic protein. The consequence of a genetic alteration of an enzyme is an impairment of metabolism—an *inborn error of metabolism*. The model for the study of inborn errors of metabolism is phenylketonuria (PKU), the first metabolic disease for which newborns were screened on a massive scale. Phenylketonuria results from a genetically determined deficiency of a liver enzyme (phenylalanine hydroxylase), as a result of which phenylalanine accumulates in the blood and spinal fluids. An excess of phenylalanine usually leads to severe mental retardation. Considerable success has attended the treatment of phenylketonuric infants with diets low in phenylalanine. In like manner, infants afflicted with galactosemia have improved greatly when therapy of a galactose-free diet has been instituted promptly at birth.

Several methods are now available for identifying the heterozygous carriers of certain recessively determined inborn errors of metabolism. If both parents can be shown to be carriers for a particular metabolic defect, provisions can be made for the careful monitoring of pregnancies and the immediate neonatal care of treatable disorders. Precautionary and dietary measures are probably more practical than what is not, however, beyond the realm of possibility—transplanting into patients cells capable of synthesizing the missing enzyme, or even replacing the defective gene itself with the normal gene.

Ethical Probe 14
Tragic Choices

Since the early 1950s, many phenylketonuric patients have been spared mental retardation by having received in early life a synthetic diet low in content of phenylalanine. Substantial numbers of women with phenylketonuria are now known to have reproduced. Phenylketonuric women have tended to marry normal men, and the expectation is that their offspring would be genetically normal heterozygotes. However, the offspring of phenylketonuric mothers have *not* been normal—all have IQ's of under 50. The intrauterine environment of a homozygous pregnant woman contains high levels of phenylalanine. Large amounts of phenylalanine pass through the placenta and adversely affect the developing fetal brain.

Phenylalanine acts as a teratogenic agent—inducing an environmental rather than a genetical malformation—since the fetus is genetically heterozygous and theoretically should be normal.

Phenylalanine has proved to be more harmful to the developing fetus of a phenylketonuric woman than did phenylalanine to the woman herself. For each case of mental retardation spared in the first generation several severely retarded offspring have been gained in the second generation! Should phenylketonuric women be urged to adopt highly effective birth control measures? Should female offspring of phenylketonuric women be counseled to refrain from reproduction?

23 Regulation of Gene Action

The fertilized egg divides into two cells, the two into four, the four into eight, and so on until ultimately the number of cells has multiplied literally into billions. During embryonic development, the cells become specialized into many different kinds—muscle, bone, blood, nervous, and a horde of others. All the differentiated cells owe their origin to the zygote, which contains a single nucleus. One of the basic tenets of biology is that the successive divisions of the zygote provide all the resulting cells with the same nuclear constitution. If the genes in the nuclei of all cells of the body are truly equivalent or identical, how can the genes be responsible for controlling or directing the differentiation of the vastly different kinds of cells? The critical question may be posed as follows: Do the nuclei remain genetically unaltered during embryonic development or do the nuclei become changed as the various parts of the embryo develop? Stated another way, do the genes become irreversibly altered as a given cell undergoes specialization?

NUCLEAR TRANSPLANTATION

In the 1950s, Robert Briggs and Tom King, then at the Institute for Cancer Research in Philadelphia, performed experiments directed at determining exactly how the nucleus functions in embryonic development. Briggs and King were successful in their attempts to replace the nucleus of an unfertilized egg of a frog with a nucleus from a cell of a developing embryo of a frog. Their plan was to transplant nuclei from a variety of developmental stages to determine whether nuclei from different stages would or would not promote normal development.

The experimental design is shown in figure 23.1. The recipient unfertilized egg is first stimulated, or activated, with a sharp fine needle. This activation causes the egg to rotate so that the nucleus is uppermost (fig. 23.1A). The egg nucleus, which now lies just under the surface of the animal pole, is removed by placing a glass needle directly beneath the nucleus and then pulling the needle up through the egg surface (fig. 23.1B). The small mass of cytoplasm lifted out contains the egg nucleus, and is trapped in the jelly coat surrounding the egg, as illustrated in figure 23.1C. A prospective donor cell is taken from a blastula that has been dissociated (that is, separated into individual cells) in a special solution (fig. 23.1D). The donor cell is carefully drawn up into a micropipette that has a bore smaller than the diameter of the cell (fig. 23.1E). The cell membrane is broken by this treatment, but the donor nucleus is surrounded and protected by its own cytoplasm. The broken donor cell is injected into the previously enucleated recipient egg, thus liberating the nucleus into the egg cytoplasm (fig. 23.1F).

It was found that many of the enucleated eggs injected with nuclei from a blastula developed into normal embryos. The successful transfers

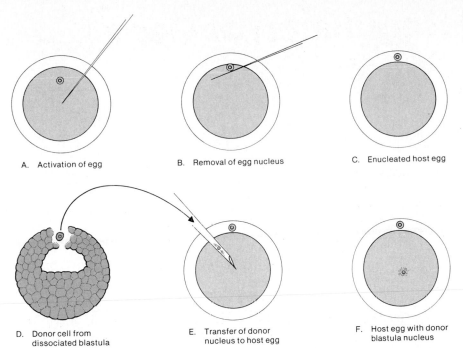

A. Activation of egg

B. Removal of egg nucleus

C. Enucleated host egg

D. Donor cell from dissociated blastula

E. Transfer of donor nucleus to host egg

F. Host egg with donor blastula nucleus

of nuclei from the early gastrula also led to normal development of recipient embryos. A typical experiment is shown in figure 23.2A, in which the enucleated host egg received a nucleus from the animal hemisphere region of an early gastrula. Of such recipient eggs, 77 percent developed into complete, normal embryos. The results indicate that the nuclei of cells of the blastula and early gastrula are not differentiated, since when they are transferred into enucleated eggs, they act much like zygotic nuclei. In other words, there are no irreversible genetic changes in the nuclei during pregastrula development. These results were not unexpected, since the prospective fates of the various regions of the blastula and early gastrula are not irrevocably determined.

However, after gastrulation has been completed, the various presumptive regions are no longer plastic, and accordingly, they develop by self-differentiation. To ascertain whether the determination of the germ layers in late gastrulation involved changes in the nuclei as well, Briggs and King initially chose donor cells from the chordamesoderm and the presumptive neural plate ectoderm. The animal hemisphere cells of the late gastrula are very small and admittedly technically difficult to handle. The recipient eggs cleaved normally, but many of them later became abnormal by the late neurula stage. The vast majority—as high as 80 percent—failed to develop into normal embryos. Two interpretations of the failure of the recipient eggs to develop normally were advanced. One was that the nuclei of the determined areas of the late gastrula had undergone a change restricting their capacity to promote normal development of the enucleated test eggs. The second possibility was that the donor nuclei might have been damaged during transplantation in such a way as to lead to the same result. Briggs and King were justifiably cautious in not discounting the second possibility that the small, fragile donor nuclei suffered damage during the transfer.

To obtain more decisive evidence of nuclear changes during development, Briggs and King performed experiments using the nuclei of endodermal cells from the floor of the archenteron of the late gastrula (fig.

Figure 23.2 Progressive restriction in the capacity of the nucleus to promote normal development, as revealed in experiments by Briggs and King in which the donor nuclei are derived from an animal hemisphere cell of an early gastrula *(A),* an endodermal cell of a late gastrula *(B),* and an endodermal cell from the neural fold stage of development *(C).*

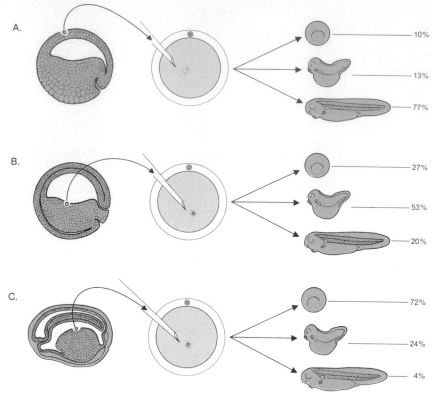

23.2*B).* These endodermal cells are large and are easily handled; the transplantation operation could therefore be carried out with a minimal risk of damage to the nuclei. The endodermal nuclei elicited normal cleavage and blastula formation; however, subsequent development of these embryos was greatly impaired. As figure 23.2*B* shows, 27 percent of the endodermal nuclei were totally incapable of promoting gastrulation and the formation of mesoderm. Fifty-three percent produced embryos that were deficient in ectodermal derivatives such as the nervous system and sense organs. Twenty percent of the endoderm nuclei were apparently still unchanged and competent to promote normal development of the recipient eggs. The ability of endoderm nuclei to promote differentiation was found to be even more restricted when the nuclei were derived from the neural fold stage of development (fig. 23.2*C).* With such advanced donor nuclei, most of the test eggs (72 percent) became arrested at gastrulation and only 4 percent developed normally to a late embryonic stage.

From these experiments, it appears that the nucleus undergoes a progressive restriction in its capacity for promoting normal development. The transplantation experiments with endoderm nuclei from the late gastrula and neurula tend to show that the nucleus changes in the course of development. Even here, however, not all nuclei are restricted in their developmental capacities. Some, although very few, of the nuclei from the late gastrula and neurula are still able to support relatively normal development. This raises the question as to the nature of the change that the nuclei presumably undergo during development.

IRREVERSIBILITY OF NUCLEAR CHANGES

In 1956, Briggs and King tested whether the restricted capacity of the endoderm nuclei was stable or irreversible. Figure 23.3 illustrates their

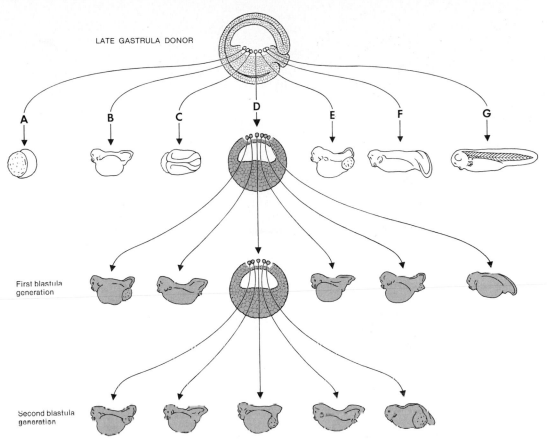

LATE GASTRULA DONOR

A   B   C   D   E   F   G

First blastula
generation

Second blastula
generation

procedure, known as *serial transplantation*. Several endoderm nuclei of a late gastrula were transplanted individually into enucleated eggs. The development of the recipient eggs ranged from early abnormalities (embryo A) to normal differentiation (embryo G). One of the original recipient eggs (D) was sacrificed in the blastula stage to provide nuclei for a new series of transfers. In contrast to the varied types of development previously seen, the first-generation test embryos were uniformly arrested in postgastrula development with the same kind of abnormalities. The second-generation embryos derived from nuclei of one member of the first generation were again uniform in their developmental defects. There were no indications of reversal of the nuclei to an undifferentiated state. Evidently, then, the alterations in the functional properties of endoderm nuclei are not only stabilized but also transmissible from one generation to the next.

THE NUCLEAR-CYTOPLASMIC FEEDBACK

In 1960, John A. Moore, then at Columbia University, demonstrated in an interesting way that irrevocable changes apparently do occur in the embryonic nuclei. When a female leopard frog (*Rana pipiens*) is crossed with a male of another species, the wood frog (*Rana sylvatica*), the hybrid embryos are inviable. Development of the hybrid embryo is arrested at the late blastula or early gastrula stage. As seen in figure 23.4, John Moore transplanted a nucleus from the blastocoel roof of a normal *R. pipiens* blastula into the enucleated, unfertilized egg of the *R. sylvatica* frog. The outcome was an abnormal embryo that deteriorated, or cytolyzed, in the blastula stage. This is in sharp contrast to the normal development of the embryo when a *R. pipiens* donor nucleus is transplanted into cytoplasm of its own species.

Figure 23.3 Serial transplantation experiments by Briggs and King. Donor nuclei, all taken from a single late gastrula, promote varied types of development when injected into enucleated eggs (*A* through *G*). One of the original recipients (*D*), sacrificed at the blastula stage, provides nuclei for a new group of enucleated eggs. These first generation embryos were uniform with respect to their developmental defects. The procedure is repeated to produce a second generation. The second generation embryos are again rather similar in the abnormalities displayed. The interpretation is that the nuclear changes or restrictions are stable, irreversible, and transmissible. (Based on experiments performed by Briggs and King.)

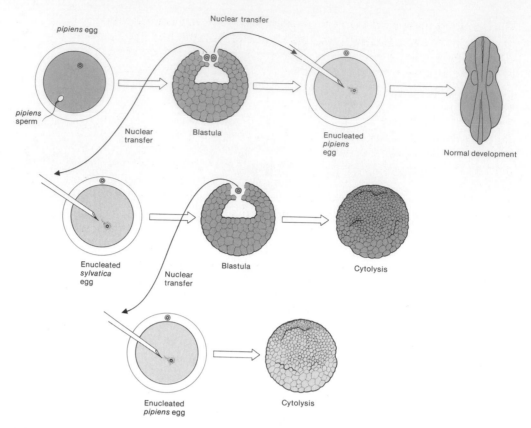

Figure 23.4 Alteration of a *pipiens* nucleus when placed in a foreign *(sylvatica)* cytoplasm. When the *pipiens* nucleus is reintroduced into its own *(pipiens)* cytoplasm, it can no longer support normal development. (Based on experiments performed by John A. Moore.)

In early development, the zygote divides many times. Each cleavage stage is associated with a duplication of the chromosome complement, so that each of the two daughter cells will have the same number of chromosomes as the parent cell. The *R. pipiens* chromosomes form replicas of themselves from precursor substances found in the *R. sylvatica* cytoplasm. After several divisions, are the chromosomes still characteristically *R. pipiens,* or have they been altered by their residence in the *R. sylvatica* cytoplasm? The question can be answered by reimplanting nuclei from the recipient *R. sylvatica* blastula into a *R. pipiens* egg. If the *R. pipiens* chromosomes have been unaltered, the resulting test embryos should be normal. If the *R. pipiens* chromosomes have been changed, abnormal development would be expected.

When this experiment was performed, the embryos died in the early gastrula stage (fig. 23.4). Hence, when a *R. pipiens* nucleus is placed in a *R. sylvatica* cytoplasm, the *R. pipiens* chromosomes do become altered. The altered *R. pipiens* nucleus can no longer act as a genetically intact *R. pipiens* nucleus since it cannot support normal development when reintroduced into cytoplasm of its own species.

DIFFERENTIAL GENE ACTION

The serial transplantation studies by Briggs and King, and the hybrid studies by Moore, seem to indicate that the nucleus becomes irreversibly altered. The implication is that the differentiation of a cell involves a true modification of the genetic material itself, or stated another way, a permanent inactivation of the genes themselves. The change would be a lasting one; the genes for hemoglobin synthesis, for example, would be irreversibly modified in an intestinal cell.

Experiments in the 1960s by the Oxford University embryologist J. B.

Gurdon have cast doubt on the permanence, or even semipermanence, of nuclear changes. Gurdon used donor nuclei from highly differentiated ciliated epithelial cells of the intestine of a feeding tadpole. The transplantation studies were performed on a different amphibian species, the African clawed frog, *Xenopus laevis*. The remarkable finding was that some of the enucleated eggs that received transplanted intestinal nuclei developed into entirely normal tadpoles, possessing both blood and muscle cells. Some of these tadpoles became sexually mature male and female frogs. Thus, since the nuclei in these frogs were derived mitotically from a single nucleus that was once part of an intestinal cell, the genes for a variety of syntheses had not been permanently lost or inactivated, but only temporarily inactivated. As an example, since blood cells were present in the nuclear-transplant tadpoles, the genes for hemoglobin synthesis in the intestinal cell must have been activated again. The genes that would normally remain inactive in the specialized cell were made to become active again by transplanting the nucleus to an egg cytoplasm.

The proportion of transplanted intestinal nuclei that supported normal development was small—rarely more than 35 percent and often only 1–2 percent. This, however, does not invalidate the basic contention by Gurdon that the genetic material is *not* irreversibly altered. To account for the results of Briggs and King, Gurdon suggests that the failure of endoderm nuclei to support normal development is the result of damage inflicted on the nuclei during the transfer, and that the degree of damage is propagated in the serial transfer.

CHEMICAL EVIDENCE OF NUCLEAR REVERSIBILITY

In the late 1960s, Gurdon collaborated with Donald Brown of the Carnegie Institution of Washington in a study designed to test the tenet that nuclear changes are reversible. They took advantage of an earlier finding that a particular type of ribonucleic acid, *ribosomal RNA* (see chapter 20), is synthesized at different rates during development of the embryo of the African clawed frog. Ribosomal RNA is not synthesized during the early cleavage stages; synthesis begins at gastrulation and continues subsequently at an accelerated rate. Gurdon and Brown transplanted to an enucleated egg a nucleus from an embryo that was actively synthesizing ribosomal RNA. Specifically, the donor nucleus was taken from an endoderm cell of an embryo at the neural fold stage. The question was whether the host egg would retain the pattern of RNA synthesis characteristic of the more differentiated donor embryo or whether the synthetic pattern would revert to that found in a fertilized egg. If the RNA-synthesizing genes that are active in the neural fold stage of development are repressed, or turned off, by the new and different cytoplasmic environment of the host egg, then no ribosomal RNA would be synthesized by the host embryo during cleavage. On the other hand, if the genes that are once active always remain active, then ribosomal RNA would be synthesized at a great rate during the cleavage of the host egg. It was found that RNA synthesis abruptly ceased in the host egg. Evidently, the egg cytoplasm had turned off the RNA-synthesizing genes that had been functional in the advanced embryo.

In another experiment, the host embryo, having received the donor nucleus, was allowed to grow to the advanced neural-fold stage of development. The host embryo then commenced to synthesize ribosomal RNA, just as normal advanced embryos do that are reared directly from fertilized eggs. These experiments demonstrate a very precise control of gene activity by the cytoplasm, since not only were previously active genes repressed, but the same genes were made active again at a later stage of development when the cytoplasm of the embryo had changed. This is strong evidence for a reversible change in the activity of a nucleus. Apparently, the same nucleus can provide different kinds of information at different stages of development.

CONCEPT OF DIFFERENTIAL GENE ACTION

The results obtained with Xenopus suggest that the nuclei of all specialized cells contain the whole range of genetic information needed for promoting the development of all other cell types. In normal development, certain parts of the genetic material of cell nuclei become specifically activated so as to restrict the range of information that these nuclei can provide. However, the information provided by the nuclei is entirely dependent on the cytoplasmic environment in which their chromosomes lie, and any restrictive nuclear changes that take place are entirely reversible. It remains to be seen whether the nuclei of all kinds of highly differentiated cells possess an unrestricted range of genetic information. Nevertheless, the preponderance of evidence favors *differential gene action,* which means that specialized cells differ only according to which genes are expressed or activated. Certain sets of genes may be active in one specialized cell and quiescent in another.

CONTROL MECHANISM

There must be a control mechanism that determines which genes are to be expressed, or activated, in a given type of cell. Unless some genes are activated while others are dormant or repressed, a liver cell would not have a different protein and enzymatic machinery than has a brain cell. Stated another way, all cells have the genetic apparatus to synthesize the hemoglobin molecule, for example, yet only the erythrocytes do so. It is likely that in all cells except the red cells the genes governing hemoglobin synthesis are permanently "shut off." Each type of cell manufactures only the kinds of proteins for its specific needs. The control mechanism becomes even more apparent when one considers that the erythrocyte of the fetus makes a particular hemoglobin that differs from adult hemoglobin. Obviously some kind of information is signaled during late gestation to effect a switch from the production of the fetal type to the adult type of hemoglobin.

It was only during the 1960s that experiments began to reveal how the control of gene action is achieved. An ingenious theory was proposed in 1961 by the geneticist Francois Jacob and the biochemist Jacques Monod of the Pasteur Institute in Paris. For this and other work, they shared the Nobel prize for physiology and medicine in 1965.

THE OPERON HYPOTHESIS

Jacob and Monod focused their attention on three closely adjacent genes in the bacterium *Escherichia coli* that code for the production of three enzymes involved in the breakdown, or hydrolysis, of a sugar called *lactose.* The three enzymes, known as β-galactosidase, β-galactoside permease, and thiogalactoside transacetylase, are synthesized only when lactose is present in the medium. Enzymes that are produced only when their substrates are available in the growth medium are termed *inducible enzymes.* Since the three genes are inactive in the absence of the substrate, Jacob and Monod speculated that a fourth gene, which they named the *regulator,* codes for a protein, called a *repressor,* that blocks the expression of the three genes (fig. 23.5). They further proposed that the repressor acts by binding to a short DNA region very close to the beginning of the set of the three enzyme-producing genes. This short DNA section is called an *operator*. The operator is held to be an "on-off" switch for the three genes: it is "on" only when lactose is present in the cell; it is "off" when the repressor protein is bound to it. The three enzyme-producing genes together with the operator gene constitute the *operon* (in this case, the lactose operon).

The operation of the system may be seen in figure 23.5. The three genes produce their enzymes only when lactose is present in the cell. When lactose is present, it combines with the repressor so that the operator switch is "on," or *derepressed*. This permits the three genes to transcribe messenger RNA and cause enzyme synthesis. Since lactose, by binding with the repressor, frees the operator and consequently turns on the genes, it has been called an *inducer*. In the absence of lactose, the repressor becomes bound to the operator region so that the operator turns off the three genes. The three genes involved in the synthesis of the enzymes may be termed *structural* genes to distinguish their action from the regulator gene.

In essence, an operon is a group of adjacent structural genes that are activated or deactivated by an operator locus situated at one end of this set of genes. The operator responds to a repressor substance that a regulator gene produces; in the presence of the repressor the operon cannot function. The function of the inducer (in our example, lactose) is to inactivate the repressor.

The studies of Jacob and Monod have led to new concepts of gene

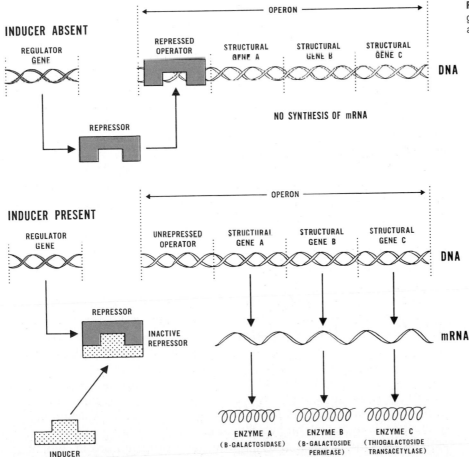

Figure 23.5 Operon model of gene action, postulated by Jacob and Monod. See text for details.

action. An essential feature is that two classes of genes have been defined: (1) *structural* genes, which are responsible for the actual synthesis of specific enzymatic and structural cellular proteins, and (2) *control* genes, whose main function is regulating other genes, the structural genes. The control genes have been divided into two categories—operator genes and regulator genes. The operator gene is located next to the structural gene, along the chromosome. The regulator gene, by furnishing a repressor, holds back the synthesis-initiating function of the operator gene.

As complicated as the Jacob-Monod scheme appears, there is experimental evidence in bacteria for the existence of regulator genes and the repressor proteins produced by them. Whether all organisms have the operon type of gene regulation remains to be seen. Some aspects of gene regulation in multicellular organisms, particularly man, appear to support the operon model.

HORMONES AND GENE ACTION

It is now clear that one of the important functions of hormones is to influence the activity of genes. By acting as gene depressors, steroid hormones stimulate the synthesis of messenger RNA, and in turn, increased amounts of protein. When estrogen is administered to an experimental animal after its ovaries have been removed, the synthesis of protein in the cells of the uterus increases enormously. The stimulating effects of estrogen can be blocked by puromycin, which is a known inhibitor of protein synthesis. Similarly, the rate of RNA synthesis in a variety of cells increases markedly in a male after the injection of testosterone. Dramatic increases in RNA synthesis and enzyme levels are also observed in the rat liver after the administration of cortisone. There is accordingly a growing body of data that indicates that steroid hormones have their effect at the level of gene transcription.

SUMMARY

Not all genes can express their potential in each cell of the organism. The preponderance of evidence favors differential gene action, a term indicating that specialized cells differ only according to which genes are expressed ("turned on") or not expressed ("turned off"). Certain genes are normally turned off in a differentiated cell, but these genes probably can be activated again under special conditions.

Since each kind of specialized cell has a unique protein content, a control mechanism must exist that determines which genes are to be expressed, or activated, in a given type of cell. A provocative model of genetic regulation of protein synthesis, based on microorganisms (bacteria), was formulated by Jacob and Monod. Certain genes, called *structural* genes, determine the amino acid sequence of specific polypeptides of cellular proteins. Other genes, called *control* genes, regulate the expression of the structural genes. Control genes are of two types: *operator* and *regulator* genes. The operator gene is located next to the structural genes and initiates transcription of messenger RNA by the adjacent structural genes. The coordinated unit of operator and structural genes is termed an *operon*. The regulator gene controls the activity of the operator gene by producing a specific substance, a *repressor*, that can associate reversibly with the operator locus. The repressor blocks the action of the operator gene, thereby preventing, or turning off, synthesis of proteins by the structural genes composing the operon. Certain specific inducer substances in the cytoplasm may bind to the repressor and inactivate it. This releases the operator gene from inhibition, which can then activate, or turn on, the adjacent structural genes. The inducer substances may be substrates of the proteins to be produced, as demonstrated in bacteria, or hormones, as indicated by certain findings in higher organisms.

Whether the Jacob-Monod operon model of gene regulation is universal among organisms remains to be seen. Supplementary or alternative mechanisms for regulating the activities of genes may have evolved in complex multicellular organisms. Nevertheless, the evidence is clear that, in multicellular organisms, genes are selectively activated at different developmental periods and by different chemical states of the cytoplasm.

Figure 23.6 Disquieting consequence of the possible propagation of a person by nuclear transplantation, or cloning. (Drawing by Lorenz; © 1973 The New Yorker Magazine, Inc.)

"I'm afraid, Son, this will never be yours. I'm having myself cloned."

Ethical Probe 15
Prospect of Cloning of Humans

Experiments on nuclear transplantation demonstrate that a nucleus from a somatic cell (for example, an intestinal cell) can promote normal development of an enucleated egg, thereby bypassing the usual process of fertilization of egg by sperm. This raises the startling possibility of producing several exact copies, or genetic replicas, of a human being from a single parent. An individual may be able to confer immortality on himself by giving up a few of his body cells. Thus, as seen in figure 23.6, an individual in one generation can prepare additional copies of himself for another trial in the next generation. This would involve the implantation of somatic nuclei—even from long-stored frozen cells—into several freshly obtained, enucleated eggs. Such unlimited numbers of similar offspring—technically, a *clone*—would be as identical genetically as monozygotic twins. The cloned individual is, in reality, *not* an offspring; he is his own parent reincarnated in new cytoplasm.

Some scientists dismiss the possible application of the nuclear transplant technique to man as the blue-sky ramblings of imaginative scientists and flamboyant journalists. There are technical difficulties in manipulating the human egg, which is about one-twelfth the size of the frog's egg. Moreover, even if the enucleation of the human egg were to become a reality, such technical mastery would not be sufficient reason to attempt to clone a human. Even under the most optimum conditions an appreciable number of the nuclear-transplant frog embryos are grossly abnormal. There is no basis for being more optimistic about the outcome in human clones.

If the experimental procedure of cloning were to be undertaken in humans, what would you do with the malformed embryos that might unavoidably arise? Do the issues of the production and disposition of deformed cloned embryos provide sufficient ethical grounds for resisting or rejecting any endeavor to produce human clones?

24 Human Chromosomes and Autosomal Abnormalities

Up until 1956, it was confidently thought that the number of chromosomes in the body cells of man was 48. In 1923, Theophilus Painter, the late eminent geneticist at the University of Texas, examined microscopic preparations of human testicular tissue and concluded that man has 48 chromosomes. Two years earlier, in 1921, Painter had observed 46 chromosomes in several clear metaphase figures, but he apparently decided that 48 was the more characteristic number. Other investigators of his day supported the value 48, and this number was then viewed as definitive.

With the perfection of techniques in the 1950s that allowed the growth of human cells *in vitro*, new avenues of approach to the study of human cells were realized. In 1956, the cytologists J. H. Tjio and Albert Levan, of the Institute of Genetics at Lund in Sweden, cultured the cells of the lungs from four therapeutically aborted human embryos. Tjio and Levan "were surprised to find that the chromosome number 46 predominated in the tissue cultures from all four embryos." The pictures of the chromosomes they presented were of a degree of clarity previously unrivaled for human cells. Their unexpected finding was quickly substantiated by C. E. Ford and J. L. Hamerton in England and subsequently by many others. The correct number of chromosomes in man is thus 46, and not 48, as believed for decades. Beginning in the late 1950s and continuing to date, the study of the human chromosome complement has been actively pursued, particularly in terms of the relation of chromosomal aberrations to certain congenital disorders.

NORMAL HUMAN CHROMOSOME COMPLEMENT

Until very recently the study of human chromosomes had been hampered by technical difficulties. The mitotic chromosomes are most readily visible during the metaphase stage, when the chromosomes are short and thick. The metaphase stage is but a brief period in the division of the cell. Moreover, in ordinary microscopic preparations of dividing cells, the numerous human chromosomes are crowded in a small nuclear area and typically lie helter-skelter on top of one another.

The last two decades have witnessed an explosive surge of new techniques. The first significant advance was the perfection of procedures for culturing cells *in vitro*. The second innovation was the application to human cell cultures of *colchicine*, a chemical substance obtained from the roots of the autumn crocus plant (fig. 24.1). Botanists had known for years that colchicine has a unique action in arresting cell division at the metaphase stage. When colchicine was applied to cultures of dividing human cells, it was observed that the spindle fibers did not

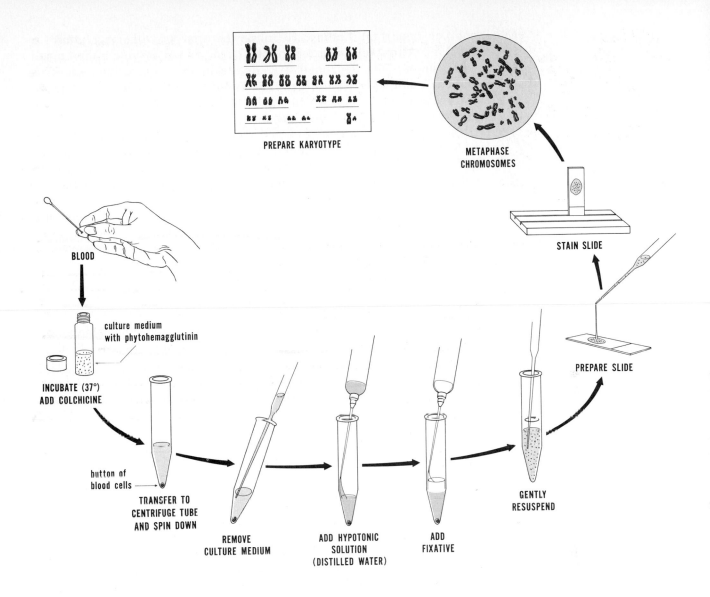

PREPARE KARYOTYPE

METAPHASE
CHROMOSOMES

STAIN SLIDE

PREPARE SLIDE

BLOOD

culture medium
with phytohemagglutinin

INCUBATE (37°)
ADD COLCHICINE

button of
blood cells

TRANSFER TO
CENTRIFUGE TUBE
AND SPIN DOWN

REMOVE
CULTURE MEDIUM

ADD HYPOTONIC
SOLUTION
(DISTILLED WATER)

ADD
FIXATIVE

GENTLY
RESUSPEND

form and the chromosomes, unable to move into an equatorial plane, remained stationary in the nucleus.

But even given large numbers of cells in permanent metaphase, there remained the problem of spreading apart the clustered metaphase chromosomes. Human cells are normally grown in a balanced salt medium, one that contains concentrations of salts that approximate the salt content of the blood. In 1952, the cytogeneticist T. C. Hsu of the University of Texas introduced an unbalanced, or *hypotonic,* salt solution to his preparation of dividing cells. The hypotonic solution (of low salt concentration) forced the cells to absorb water and swell. In dramatic fashion, the metaphase chromosomes scattered, spreading out individually over a large area.

It remained for Tjio and Levan in 1956 to employ the new techniques to discover that man had 46 chromosomes. But the technical advances did not stop there. From the research laboratory of Peter Nowell of the University of Pennsylvania School of Medicine there emerged in 1960

Figure 24.1 Modern technique of preparing human chromosomes for analysis. See text for details.

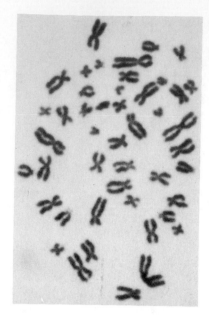

Figure 24.2 Normal chromosome set prepared from a culture of blood cells of a human male. Each chromosome consists of two strands (chromatids) joined at the centromere. (Prepared by Dr. Elizabeth M. Earley, Tulane University.)

another important finding. He observed that *phytohemagglutinin*, a substance extracted from red kidney beans, could stimulate the human white blood cells (leucocytes) to divide in the culture medium. This made possible the preparation of metaphase chromosomes from peripheral (circulating) blood, which can be obtained much more readily from the body than internal solid tissues.

A chromosome spread prepared from a culture of peripheral blood cells of a human male is shown in figure 24.2. As expected from our knowledge of metaphase chromosomes, each chromosome is longitudinally doubled, and the two strands (or chromatids) are held together by a centromere. It should also be recalled that the chromosomes occur in pairs, one member of each chromosome pair coming from the mother and the other from the father. Thus, each chromosome has a homologous mate in the metaphase spread.

The chromosomes can be systematically arranged in a sequence known as a *karyotype* (fig. 24.3). In the karyotype, the chromosomes are paired and classified into groups according to their length and to the location of the centromere. A centromere situated in the middle divides the chromosomes into two arms of equal length. A chromosome with a medially located centromere is technically called *metacentric*. When the centromere is located away from the midline, one arm of the chromosome appears longer than the other. Such a chromosome is termed *submetacentric*. In some chromosomes (*acrocentric*), the centromere is nearly terminal in position, imparting a wishbone appearance to the chromosome.

There are 22 matching pairs of chromosomes that are called *autosomes*. The autosome pairs are numbered 1 to 22 in descending order of length, and further classified into seven groups, designated by capital

Figure 24.3 Karyotype of the 23 pairs of chromosomes of a normal male arranged from the chromosomes of the cell shown in figure 24.2. (Prepared by Dr. Elizabeth M. Earley, Tulane University.)

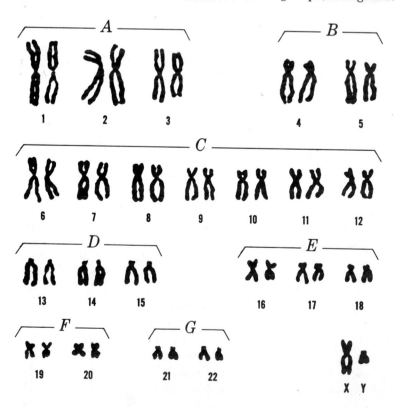

letters, A through G. In addition, there are two *sex chromosomes*, which are unnumbered. As seen in figure 24.3, the male has one X chromosome and one unequal-sized Y chromosome. The X is of medium size, and the Y is one of the smallest chromosomes of the complement. The female has two X chromosomes of equal size and no Y chromosome. Thus, the complement of 46 human chromosomes comprises 22 pairs of autosomes plus the sex chromosome pair, XX in normal females and XY in normal males. In current nomenclature, the female is described as "46,XX" and the male, "46,XY." It is of peculiar interest that the long arm of the Y chromosome varies in length in normal individuals. About 3 percent of normal males exhibit variation in the length of the long arms of the Y with no apparent influence on fertility or virility.

IDENTIFICATION OF INDIVIDUAL CHROMOSOMES

The individual chromosomes cannot be identified unequivocally on the basis of appearance alone. The X chromosome, for example, resembles morphologically members of the C group of chromosomes (fig. 24.3). Radioactive labeling has been used to reveal subtle differences among the chromosomes. It has been found that the chromosomes manifest consistent differences in the timing of their DNA replication. In other words, not all chromosomes duplicate themselves (replicate their DNA) at the same time. Even the various regions of a given chromosome have different patterns of DNA replication. This has been demonstrated by exposing cell cultures to thymidine containing radioactive tritium (an isotope of hydrogen). The radioactive thymidine is incorporated in newly forming DNA. If the chromosomes are labeled with tritiated thymidine shortly before they have completed DNA synthesis, one can determine which chromosomes (or even regions) have ceased incorporating tritiated thymidine and which are still in the process of DNA synthesis. Early-replicating chromosomes, which have already completed DNA synthesis when the labeled material is added, can easily be distinguished from late-replicating chromosomes, which incorporate significant amounts of the radioactive label.

The three group D chromosomes have been separated on this basis. The first of these (no. 13) is late-replicating throughout its length, whereas the third (no. 15) is an early-replicating chromosome. Chromosome 14 can be distinguished from the other two because it is late-replicating only in the region near the centromere. Similarly pairs 4 and 5 of the B group and members 17 and 18 of the E group have unique patterns of chromosome replication. More than half of the chromosomes of the human complement can be clearly identified by radioactive labeling.

Greater precision in identification of individual chromosomes has been attained in recent years through newer techniques. Each human chromosome can be identified unambiguously by treating cell preparations with a fluorescent dye, *quinacrine mustard* (QM). The fluorescence of QM can be detected with a microscope equipped with ultraviolet light. The QM-treatment produces a pattern of bands, called *Q-bands*, along the metaphase chromosomes (fig. 24.4). Fluorescence analysis shows, for example, that the long arm of the Y is brightly fluorescent. It is the fluorescent region of the Y that varies in length in different males, which suggests that the testis-differentiating factors reside in the constant, nonfluorescent short arm. Differential staining of human chromosomes can also be obtained by pretreating a cell preparation with trypsin or sodium hydroxide (NaOH) and then treating it with a *Giemsa* stain. Such staining permits precise identification of distinct regions of the arms of the chromosomes. The precision achieved with fluorescent-stained and Giemsa-stained preparations enables the medical scientist to pinpoint certain defects to specific chromosomes and their regions.

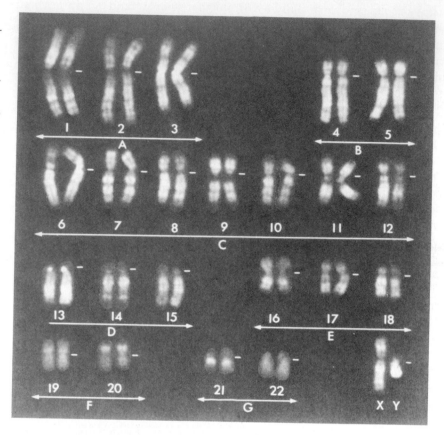

Figure 24.4 Fluorescent staining pattern of the chromosome complement of a normal male arranged in a karyotype. The pattern of bands (Q-bands) permits the unequivocal identification of each chromosome. Note that the long arm of the Y chromosome is brightly fluorescent. (From *Birth Defects: Original Article Series,* ed. D. Bergsma, Paris Conference, 1971. Standardization in Human Cytogenetics 8 (7):7, 1972. The National Foundation—March of Dimes.)

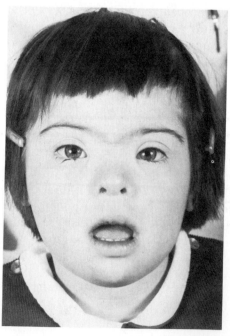

Figure 24.5 Facial features of a 3½-year-old girl afflicted with Down's syndrome. (From M. Bartalos and T. A. Baramski, *Medical cytogenetics,* 1967, The Williams & Wilkins Co.)

DOWN'S SYNDROME

Down's syndrome was the first developmental disorder to be traced to an alteration in the human chromosome complement. This congenital disability is unmistakably stamped on the afflicted child's face: a prominent forehead, a flattened nasal bridge, a habitually open mouth, a projecting lower lip, a large protruding tongue, and a skin fold (epicanthic fold) at the inner corners of the eye (fig. 24.5). The first comprehensive description of this disorder was provided in 1866 by the English physician John Langdon Down. Down unjustifiably seized upon the Oriental-like cast of the eye to designate the condition as "mongolism" or "mongoloid idiocy." Down's theory was that the condition represented regression to an earlier and more primitive human form analogous to Mongolian peoples. Down's peculiar ethnic viewpoint is, of course, untenable and the labels "mongoloid idiot" and "mongol" are currently being discarded in the literature. Medical scientists today have proposed to call the disorder *Down's syndrome,* a term that has gained acceptance and use.

Down's syndrome affects 1 infant in 600. The incidence of this disorder is known to rise markedly according to the age of the mother—from about 1 in 2,000 births at maternal age 20 to 1 in 100 at age 40 (table 24.1). Among women over 45, 1 in 40 infants may be expected to be afflicted with Down's syndrome. The age of the father appears to be of little or no significance. The true cause of the disorder was discovered only in the last two decades. At one time or another, syphilis, tuberculosis, malnutrition, thyroid deficiency, emotional shock during pregnancy, and even alcoholism were incriminated as causes of the disorder. In 1959, the long quest for the cause ended when a French team headed by the pediatrician Jérôme Lejeune demonstrated the existence of an extra chromosome in the cells of infants with Down's syndrome. Affected individuals do not contain the normal chromosome number of 46, but rather 47. The extra chromosome turns out to be an additional chromosome in the G group. This group contains the two smallest chromosome pairs (Nos. 21 and 22) of the human complement. Affected individuals are said to display trisomy (three rather than two) of chromosome G, or simply, *trisomy G.* Clinically, the condition is often referred to as *trisomy 21* since the 21st chromosome is generally involved.

Mother's Age (Years)	Risk of Occurrence
20–29	1 in 2,000
30–34	1 in 750
35–39	1 in 500
40–44	1 in 100
45–49	1 in 40

Table 24.1
Relation of Maternal Age to Down's Syndrome (Trisomy G)

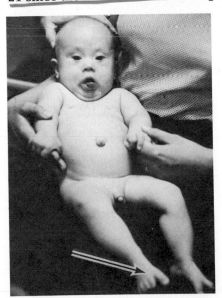
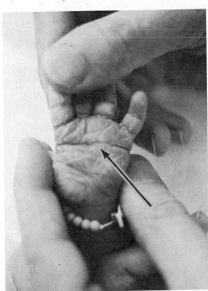

Figure 24.6 Infant with Down's syndrome, showing the short, incurved fifth finger; the wide gap between the first and second toes; and the strong crease in the palm, the so-called simian line. (From C. B. Jacobson, "Cytogenetic techniques and their clinical uses," in *Genetics in medical practice,* ed. M. Bartalos, 1965, J. B. Lippincott Co.)

An extra chromosome means that numerous genes are represented three times rather than twice. Since a given chromosome carries a variety of genes with different functions, an additional complement of the various genes would be expected to disturb several different bodily processes. This explains what was once considered an unexplicably strange assortment of defects in patients with Down's syndrome. The neck is short and broad, the skin is rosy but rough and dry, the teeth are abnormally shaped and irregularly aligned, the heart is malformed, and the gonads and genitalia are underdeveloped. The palm of the hand has a prominent single transverse fold or crease, the so-called simian line. The feet, often short and clumsy, have a characteristic well-marked gap between the first and second toe (fig. 24.6). Affected individuals also have an increased risk of developing leukemia. Sixty percent of the patients die by the age of 10 years with congenital heart disease as the leading cause of death.

Figure 24.7 Nondisjunction during the first meiotic division produces two types of gametes: one kind possessing two of a given chromosome instead of the usual one, and a second kind that lacks the particular chromosome.

ORIGIN OF TRISOMY G

The process of meiosis (described in chapter 17) is complex and subject to error. It does not always proceed normally. Occasional accidents do occur that affect the normal functioning of the spindle fibers and impede the proper migration of one or more chromosomes. During the first meiotic division, the members of a given pair of homologous chromosomes

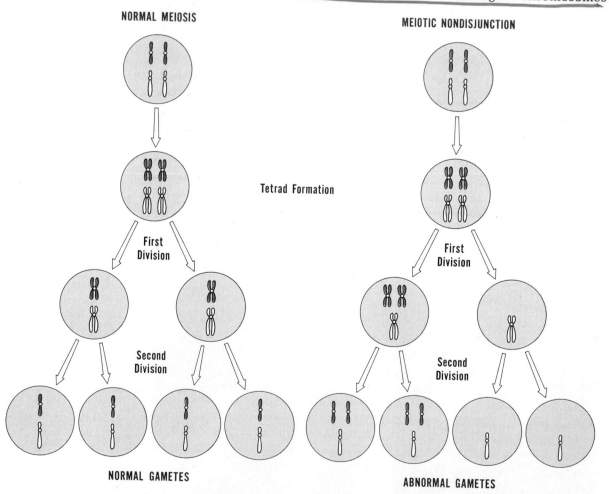

NORMAL MEIOSIS   MEIOTIC NONDISJUNCTION

Tetrad Formation

First Division

Second Division

NORMAL GAMETES   ABNORMAL GAMETES

may fail to separate from each other (fig. 24.7). Such failure of separation, known as *nondisjunction*, can result in an egg containing both members of a given pair of chromosomes. The nondisjunction of the 21st pair of chromosomes, for example, would result in an egg cell that possesses two 21st chromosomes instead of the usual one. Such an egg cell, when fertilized by a normal sperm, would give rise to an individual that is trisomic for the 21st chromosome.

It should be noted in figure 24.7 that meiotic nondisjunction of one chromosome pair results in two types of egg cells, in equal proportions: one kind contains the two chromosomes and the other lacks the particular chromosome. If the latter egg cell is fertilized by a normal sperm, the outcome is a *monosomy*. Monosomy, when it occurs in the autosomes, appears to be incompatible with implantation, perhaps even with fertilization. There is no unequivocal case of an autosomal monosomy in humans, even among abortuses. Theoretically, however, autosomal monosomies should be as equally common as autosomal trisomies.

It has been found that 20 percent of early abortuses examined are trisomic for one of the autosomes. Since many more genes are carried in the larger chromosomes than in the smaller chromosomes, trisomies involving the large autosomes (such as those of the A and B groups) are likely to have lethal consequences. Trisomies involving the smaller chromosomes might permit increased chances of survival. There are two autosomal trisomies, in addition to trisomy G, that enable the infant to survive through birth—one of these occurs in the D group of chromosomes (13–15) and the other in the E group (16–18).

Among newborns, about 1 in 1,500 has a group D chromosome in triplicate; about 1 in 1,000 is trisomic for the E chromosome (typically 18). Both trisomic conditions, resulting in an abnormal count of 47 chromosomes, are usually fatal within the first year of life. Common anomalies in trisomy D include cleft palate (often with harelip), sloping forehead with relatively small braincase, defective eye development, and polydactyly (fig. 24.8). Developmental disorders of the heart and kidney contribute to an early death of the infant. Common clinical features of trisomy E infants are a recessed chin, malformed ears, spasticity due to a defective nervous system, and peculiarly pliable fingers.

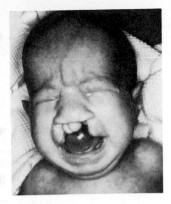

Figure 24.8 Deformed infant (4½ months) possessing an extra D chromosome (trisomy D). Cleft palate and harelip are common anomalies in trisomy D. (Courtesy of Dr. S. Schneider, Loma Linda University Medical School.)

ETIOLOGY OF NONDISJUNCTION

Meiotic nondisjunction is thought to occur primarily in the maternal oocyte. This supposition is based on the fact that the incidence of Down's syndrome (as well as trisomies D and E) is strongly correlated with the age of the mother, and not with the age of the father. A number of hypotheses have been advanced to explain the higher incidence of nondisjunction in the oocytes of older women. None of the theses has been substantiated. In 1968, James German, a geneticist at Cornell University, proposed delayed fertilization as the basic cause of nondisjunction. He suggested that the high risk of Down's syndrome may be related to the decreasing frequency of coitus in marriages of long duration. Since sexual relations tend to become sporadic or less frequent after the early years of marriage, the chances are greater in older women that sperm may not be present to fertilize the egg as soon as it is released from the ovary. Thus, German contends that infrequent sexual relations and the consequent danger of delayed fertilization are important factors

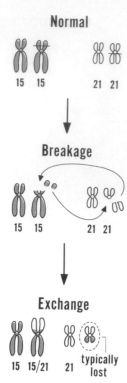

Normal

15 15   21 21

Breakage

15 15   21 21

Exchange

15   15/21   21   typically lost

Figure 24.9 Phenomenon of translocation produces a single large chromosome (designated *15/21*) and a small fragment that is usually lost without affecting the person adversely.

Figure 24.10 Translocation-type Down's syndrome carries a great risk of producing children afflicted with Down's syndrome. From a marriage of a woman carrying the 15/21 translocation chromosome and a normal male, 1 viable offspring in 3 will be affected. Of the two other viable offspring, one will be a carrier of Down's syndrome for future generations. *Note:* Chromosomes are depicted as they appear in the metaphase stage (each with two chromatids joined at the centromere).

in the etiology of nondisjunction. The English geneticist L. S. Penrose, however, was unable to find a correlation between duration of marriage and Down's syndrome.

The meiotic cells are known to be peculiarly sensitive to a variety of external agents—viruses, X rays, and cytotoxic chemicals. Any of these agents can interfere with division by damaging the spindle mechanism. Alan Stoller of the Mental Health Research Institute in Victoria, Australia, has proposed that meiotic nondisjunction is triggered by a virus, affecting older women to a greater degree. Stoller supports his claim by showing that the peak of incidence of infectious hepatitis (caused by a virus) in Melbourne, Australia, is correlated with a high incidence of Down's syndrome *nine months later*. Moreover, infectious hepatitis has now been shown to produce chromosome breaks *in vivo*. Further investigations are needed of the interactions of viruses and chromosomes.

TRANSLOCATION

Not all chromosomal errors involve nondisjunction of a pair of chromosomes. Another chromosomal aberration is *translocation*—the transfer of a part of one chromosome to another, nonhomologous chromosome. This occurs when two chromosomes break and then rejoin in another combination. As figure 24.9 shows, the exchange of broken parts is often reciprocal, and may involve loss of chromosomal material. The first translocation error in humans was found by a British team of investigators headed by C. E. Ford. They analyzed the chromosomes in the bone marrow cells of an infant with Down's syndrome born to a mother only 21 years old. They found 46 chromosomes in the affected child instead of the expected 47. However, detailed examination of the chromosomes revealed that one of the chromosomes had an unusual configuration. It

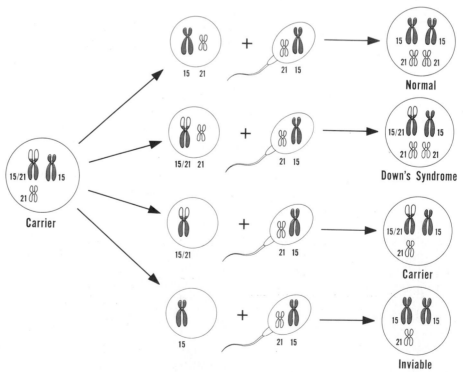

appeared to consist of two chromosomes fused together. The interpretation advanced was that the affected child had inherited an extra chromosome and that this extra chromosome had become integrally joined to another chromosome. Stated another way, one chromosome was in fact represented three times, but the third was almost concealed on another chromosome.

Ford's interpretation is shown in figure 24.10. A translocation had occurred in the mother's cells between a normal D chromosome and a normal G chromosome. In the original analysis, the culpable chromosomes were thought to be number 15 and number 21, respectively. It is still not clear whether the responsible G chromosome is number 21 or number 22. Clarification has been attained, however, for the D member: it is not number 13, usually number 14, and rarely number 15. For the sake of convenience, we may use the original designations. The exchange of unequal pieces between the two chromosomes results in a single large chromosome that incorporates the greater part of both chromosomes 15 and 21. This newly formed large chromosome is referred to as the 15/21 translocation chromosome. The small fragment containing relatively few genes is lost, but this is without clinical consequence. The consequences, however, of the mother bearing the 15/21 translocation chromosome are vast for her children.

The woman carrying the 15/21 translocation chromosome is normal in appearance (fig. 24.10). When she produces eggs, some will contain two number 21 chromosomes (one of them fused to chromosome 15) and others will have none. Specifically, she can produce four kinds of eggs, which when fertilized by normal sperm would result in four possible outcomes: (1) a completely normal child with an entirely normal chromosome set; (2) a normal child that has the 15/21 translocation chromosome like the mother, and has the potential to inflict her children with translocation-type Down's syndrome; (3) an afflicted child with three number 21 chromosomes, one of which is fused to chromosome 15; and (4) an embryo that lacks completely one of the pairs of chromosome 21 and dies before term.

Unlike Down's syndrome associated with advancing maternal age (nondisjunction trisomy G), the translocation type runs in families. In other words, more than one child in a family may be affected. As we have seen, the risk of an affected child among those developing to term is 1 chance in 3. This is the theoretical expectation. Empirically, from studies of actual family pedigrees, the chance is nearer 1 in 5—the difference probably being due to the lessened viability of the trisomic embryo. Nevertheless, this contrasts sharply with nondisjunction trisomy, where the risk of giving birth to an affected child is about 1 in 600.

The 15/21 translocation event is not necessarily confined to the mother. The consequences to the child are the same if the translocation occurs in the father. Cases are known in which the father has been implicated as the carrier. Curiously, when the father carries the translocation, the empirical chance of having a Down's child is only about 1 in 20. The reason for this unexpected drop in chance is not known. The deficiency of affected children may be due to the inviability of chromosomally unbalanced sperm cells.

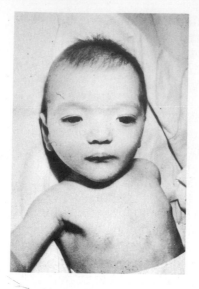

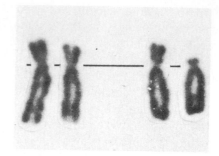

DELETION

Sometimes a piece of chromosome breaks off, resulting in a deletion of genetic material. The effects of the loss of a portion of a chromosome depend on the particular genes lost. A large deletion, with the loss of many genes, is incompatible with life.

Dr. Jérôme Lejeune and his colleagues at the University of Paris described in 1963 the peculiar effects in an infant of the loss of a portion of the number 5 chromosome (group B). Affected infants have a rounded, moonlike face and utter feeble, plaintive cries described as similar to the mewing of a cat (fig. 24.11). In fact, the disorder has been named the *cri du chat* ("cat cry") syndrome. Such unfortunate infants are mentally and physically retarded. Although originally thought to be exceedingly rare, at least 70 cases of the cri du chat disorder have been reported since the initial discovery.

THE PHILADELPHIA CHROMOSOME AND LEUKEMIA

Leukemia is a cancerous malignancy arising in the blood-forming tissues. Like cancer in general, leukemia is a clinically heterogeneous entity, appearing in many forms. In 1960, Peter Nowell and D. A. Hungerford noted the presence of an exceptionally minute chromosome in dividing cells from the bone marrow of patients with chronic myeloid leukemia. This particular form of leukemia is characterized by abnormal numbers of immature granulocytes (one of the white blood cells) in bone marrow and blood. The unusually small chromosome, evidently with a piece missing, proved to be one of the 22nd pair (fig. 24.12). The patient with chronic myeloid leukemia thus has 46 chromosomes, but chromosome number 22 is marred by a deletion. Because the finding was made in Philadelphia, the abnormal chromosome has been called the *Philadelphia chromosome*. The deleted piece of the Philadelphia chromosome is not lost, but becomes translocated onto, or joined to, another chromosome (generally number 9, occasionally number 8).

The association between leukemia and the chromosome aberration suggests that the hereditary material of the 22nd chromosome is concerned with the maturation of blood cells. This supposition is given

22

Philadelphia chromosome
with deletion

Figure 24.12 Philadelphia chromosome, a no. 22 chromosome marred by a deletion. This abnormal chromosome is often found in patients with chronic myeloid leukemia.

added weight by the finding that the incidence of leukemia in patients with Down's syndrome is nearly 6 times that in normal persons. It will be recalled that Down's syndrome is a disorder involving the G chromosome. The suggested relationship limps a little since the Philadelphia deletion occurs in the non-Down's number 22 chromosome rather than the Down's number 21 chromosome.

SUMMARY

Extraordinary technical developments in recent years have permitted an accurate and detailed study of the individual chromosomes of man. Beginning in 1956 with the demonstration that the normal human chromosome number is 46 instead of 48, a large body of information has amassed that links aberrations in the chromosome set to several previously known developmental disorders. Individuals affected with Down's syndrome (mongolism) have 47 chromosomes, the extra member being one of the small chromosomes of the G group. This trisomy condition is the consequence of meiotic nondisjunction, or failure of proper separation of a pair of homologous chromosomes during the maturation divisions of the egg. Down's syndrome (trisomy G) appears with increasingly higher frequencies among children of mothers of advancing age; the oocytes of older women are apparently prone to the abnormal process of nondisjunction. In rare instances, Down's syndrome is not caused by nondisjunction, but by another chromosomal aberration, translocation. Whereas the birth of a trisomy G child is a sporadic event, the translocation type of Down's syndrome recurs in successive generations (runs in families).

Other human disorders, such as the cri du chat syndrome, are traceable to a loss, or deletion, of a portion of a chromosome. A type of cancer (chronic myeloid leukemia) has been associated with a specific aberrant chromosome (Philadelphia chromosome). A large proportion, as many as 25 percent, of early aborted human fetuses have been found to possess abnormal chromosome complements.

Ethical Probe 16
Quality of Life

A baby boy born to a couple in a hospital was diagnosed as having the characteristics of Down's syndrome. Chromosomal analysis substantiated the medical diagnosis with the finding of trisomy 21. The physicians also identified the condition of duodenal atresia, an intestinal obstruction that would prevent the infant from taking food by mouth. The intestinal defect could be corrected readily by an operation of little risk.

The hospital physicians kept the infant alive intravenously and made plans for corrective intestinal surgery. The parents, however, refused to grant operative permission to the physicians. The parents had decided that the quality of life of a child with Down's syndrome is so poor that it would be kinder to let the child die. Moreover, the parents felt that it would be unfair to inflict the burden of a retarded child on their other children. The medical staff at the hospital was powerless to operate without the parents' consent. In the absence of surgery to correct the intestinal obstruction, the infant died after 11 days.

Who has the responsibility for acting on behalf of the newborn—the parents, the physician, or the state? If a lifesaving treatment is undertaken on the infant against the parents' wishes, would the parents then tend to neglect or reject the child? Was the decision by these parents morally acceptable to you? If you were one of the parents, would you favor corrective surgery to unblock the intestinal obstruction, or would you allow your child to die?

Sex Chromosome Abnormalities 25

Most of the gross aberrations of human autosomes are incompatible with life. Autosomal monosomic zygotes are inviable, and most of the autosomal trisomies, with the exception of the G trisomies, perish before birth or in the neonatal period. In marked contrast, many of the abnormalities of the human X and Y chromosomes are compatible with a long life, even though they are typically associated with infertility and mental retardation. Thus, a monosomic X individual and a trisomic XXY individual can survive to adulthood, although more often than not the monosomic X embryo fails to survive the gestational period. Moreover, certain types of trisomic individuals, such as XXX, have no apparent physical abnormalities and can be fertile. Some aberrations of the sex chromosomes occur with surprisingly high frequency.

MEIOTIC NONDISJUNCTION

It is well known that the normal female differs from the normal male in carrying two X chromosomes; the male is XY. Sex is determined at the moment of conception. A female arises from the union of an X-bearing egg with an X-bearing sperm, whereas a male results from fertilization of the X-bearing egg by a Y-bearing sperm. The Y chromosome establishes maleness.

Through maternal nondisjunction, two kinds of eggs are possible: one with an extra X chromosome and the other with no X chromosome at all. The consequences of such eggs being fertilized by normal sperm are shown in figure 25.1.

Figure 25.1 Meiotic nondisjunction results in an egg cell containing two X chromosomes instead of one, and an egg cell lacking an X chromosome. Only chromosomally abnormal offspring (generally clinically abnormal) arise from such eggs when fertilized by normal sperm.

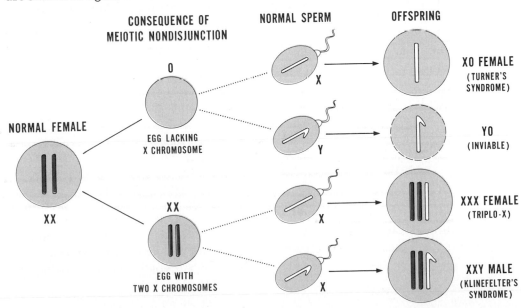

CONSEQUENCE OF MEIOTIC NONDISJUNCTION   NORMAL SPERM   OFFSPRING

NORMAL FEMALE
XX

0
EGG LACKING X CHROMOSOME

XX
EGG WITH TWO X CHROMOSOMES

X — XO FEMALE (TURNER'S SYNDROME)

Y — YO (INVIABLE)

X — XXX FEMALE (TRIPLO-X)

X — XXY MALE (KLINEFELTER'S SYNDROME)

Figure 25.2 Klinefelter's syndrome occurs in males whose Y chromosome is accompanied by two X chromosomes instead of one. One symptom is enlarged breasts, as seen in these three patients. The patient in photograph *A* was one of the original cases described by Dr. Henry Klinefelter in 1942. (From M. Bartalos and T. A. Baramski, *Medical cytogenetics*, 1967, The Williams & Wilkins Co.)

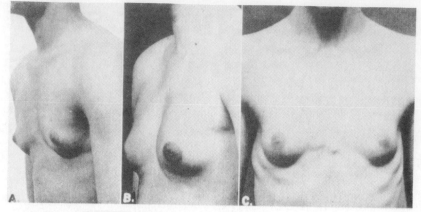

One-fourth of the offspring may be expected to have the XXY constitution, which results in a sex anomaly known as *Klinefelter's syndrome*, named after Harry F. Klinefelter, an American physician who first described the condition in 1942. Although individuals with this syndrome are male in general appearance, their testes are underdeveloped and their breasts are enlarged (fig. 25.2). Most patients are sterile; the extra X chromosome impairs the normal development of the testes. The limbs of affected patients are longer than average and body hair is sparse. Many affected individuals are mentally defective. The XXY disorder occurs once in every 800 liveborn phenotypic males. As in Down's syndrome, affected males are born more often to older women.

Individuals with higher polysomies have been found, such as XXXY, XXXXY, and XXXXXY constitutions. Such individuals are invariably severely retarded. As a general rule, the greater the excess of X chromosomes, the greater the degree of mental abnormality. Despite numerous X chromosomes, however, the presence of the Y chromosome enables the patient to have masculine characteristics.

As previously mentioned, an egg can be produced through nondisjunction that has no X chromosome at all. When such an egg is fertilized by an X-bearing sperm, the offspring will be XO, O signifying the absence of a sex chromosome (fig. 25.1). Women with the XO constitution suffer from *Turner's syndrome*, an anomaly first noticed in 1938 by Dr. Henry H. Turner of the University of Oklahoma School of Medicine. At that time, however, the true cause of the anomaly was unknown. Women with Turner's syndrome have rudimentary ovaries, if any at all, and undeveloped breasts. Anatomically and psychologically they are females, although unable to menstruate or ovulate. Instead of normal ovaries, only ridges of whitish tissue occur, a finding that has caused the term *streak gonads* to be applied. In addition, many authors use the term *gonadal dysgenesis* in place of "Turner's syndrome." Affected women are also unusually short, have a peculiar webbing of the skin of the neck, and are of subnormal intelligence (fig. 25.3).

The XO woman is not a case of sex reversal, since testes and other male components are absent. Rather, she is an undeveloped female who would have developed as a normal female had she not been denied the other X chromosome. The XO embryo obtained from spontaneous abortion possesses a normal complement of germ cells and the primitive gonad does differentiate in the direction of an ovary. However, the ovary begins to lose its oocytes during fetal development. By birth the number

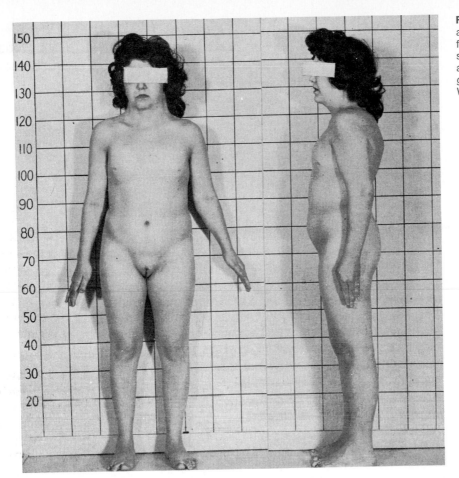

Figure 25.3 Turner's syndrome in a 22-year-old female. Conspicuous features are the short stature and sexual infantilism. (From M. Bartalos and T. A. Baramski, *Medical cytogenetics,* 1967, The Williams & Wilkins Co.)

of oocytes is severely diminished and by adolescence the ovarian tissue has regressed to ridges of white streaks devoid of oocytes. The degeneration of the ovary has secondary consequences such as inhibition of breast development.

The incidence of Turner's syndrome is surprisingly low, 1 in 3,500 newborns, in comparison with the incidence of Klinefelter's syndrome (1 in 800). It is now generally conceded that there is high intrauterine mortality of the XO embryo; that is, the XO constitution almost approaches a lethal condition. In support of this view, the XO chromosomal constitution has been found to be one of the common causes of spontaneous abortion—nearly 1 in 10!

As seen in figure 25.1, a third type of offspring is possible—the *triplo-X* (XXX) female. The XXX constitution occurs once in every 1,000 newborn females. The condition predisposes the female to mental retardation. However, most triplo-X females have no apparent physical abnormalities and many are fertile. Apparently, the presence of an additional X chromosome does not impair fertility; its presence is far less hazardous to the developing oocyte than the absence of an X (as in XO females). There are indications that the developing oocytes of the XXX female actually discard the additional Xs by a mechanism known as *selective disjunction*. Thus, no XXY or XXX offspring can be born to XXX females and, indeed, no such offspring are known. Children born to triplo-X females have been either normal males or normal females.

Finally, from figure 25.1, it is seen that a fourth type of offspring is theoretically possible. This is the YO zygote, resulting from the union of an egg lacking an X chromosome with a Y-bearing sperm. The YO constitution is incompatible with fertilization; no embryo or fetus with this constitution has been observed.

SEX DETERMINATION

For many years, the genetic sex-determining mechanism in the fruit fly (*Drosophila*) has served as a model for other organisms, including man. In *Drosophila*, sex is governed largely by the X chromosome—an XXY fly is a fertile female and an XO fly is a sterile male. The Y chromosome is essentially inert in relation to sex determination, although necessary for male fertility.

It seems clear that in humans the Y chromosome, far from having a passive role in sex determination, contains potent male-determining genes. An individual who carries a Y chromosome is a male, even if he has one, two, or three X chromosomes associated with the Y. An individual lacking the Y chromosome is a female, whether she is XO, XX, or XXX.

The statement that maleness in humans is a function of the Y chromosome requires qualification. Most true hermaphrodites—individuals in which both ovarian and testicular tissues are present—have 46 chromosomes with an XX constitution. None of the hermaphrodites are fertile, although egg and sperm may be formed. The presence of testicular tissue in hermaphrodites tends to negate the view that the Y chromosome is necessary for the formation of a testis. However, a few hermaphrodites have been found to be *mosaics*, that is, containing cells of two kinds, XX and XY. The mosaic state would make possible the development of both testicular and ovarian tissue. The possibility thus exists that hermaphrodites with an apparent XX constitution originate as XX/XY mosaics, but the XY cells have been either lost or undetected.

Another explanation has been advanced to account for the apparently normal XX karyotype of the true hermaphrodite. An exchange of material might have occurred between the father's X and Y chromosomes, possibly as a result of accidental crossing over at the first meiotic division. In this manner, a portion of the Y chromosome containing male determinants would become an integral part of the X chromosome in the sperm cell. Fertilization of a normal ovum by such a sperm cell would produce an individual with two apparently normal XXs, which would in reality be a normal X plus an X with Y-bearing male determinants. Thus, once again, we notice how necessary at least a portion of the Y chromosome is for differentiation of a testis.

MITOTIC NONDISJUNCTION

In 1961, Dr. Raymond Turpin and his colleagues in France encountered an unusual circumstance in a pair of monozygotic (identical) twins. One member of the pair was a male with an XY constitution and the other a sterile female with an XO constitution. Clearly, the XO constitution originated by the loss of one of the second chromosomes when the zygote divided into two. Thus, one of the sex chromosomes can be lost either by *mitotic nondisjunction* or by a process known as *anaphase lag*, both of which are illustrated in figure 25.4. Mitotic nondisjunction can result in a mosaic individual with one cell line that is trisomic and the other cell line that is monosomic. In anaphase lag, one chromosome becomes ac-

Zygote

FIRST CLEAVAGE DIVISION

Figure 25.4 Origin of mosaicism following fertilization. Normal division of the fertilized egg is contrasted with mitotic nondisjunction and anaphase lag. In mitotic nondisjunction, the two duplicated chromatids (daughter chromosomes) fail to separate during anaphase movements. In anaphase lag, one daughter chromosome is accidentally lost in the process of cell division.

NORMAL

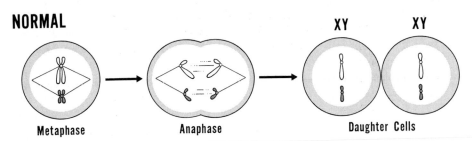

Metaphase → Anaphase → Daughter Cells

MITOTIC NONDISJUNCTION

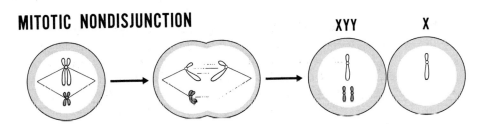

ANAPHASE LAG

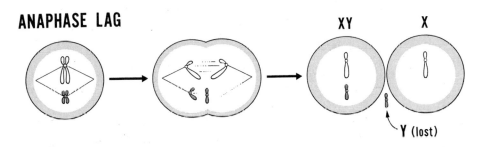

Y (lost)

cidentally lost during cell division. In this circumstance, one cell line would have the normal chromosome complement and the other cell line would be monosomic for the lost chromosome.

It often happens that one of the cell lines does not survive. When both cell lines do become established, however, the result is clearly a mosaic individual, with the two types of cells. The clinical record includes a large listing of mosaic individuals—XX/XO, XY/XO, XX/XXY, XY/XXY, and many others. The actual phenotypic manifestation of mosaicism depends on the relative proportion and distribution of the two types of cells in the body. As a consequence of the many bizarre mosaic combinations, a graded series of clinical patients have been found ranging from Turner's or Klinefelter's syndrome to a near physically normal female or male with lowered (or even approaching normal) fertility.

The phenomenon of mitotic nondisjunction may explain the following self-contradictory finding. Individuals affected with Klinefelter's syndrome are born more often to older women, yet a maternal-age effect cannot be demonstrated for Turner's syndrome. If both disorders were to stem from a meiotic nondisjunction event—during the formation of the mother's gametes—as originally depicted (fig. 25.1), then both should be subject to the same potent influence of the mother's age. This has led certain investigators, prominently James German, to conclude that the vast majority of Turner's cases arise from chromosomal errors that occur in a cell of the early embryo by mitotic nondisjunction rather than a cell of the maternal (or paternal) gonad by meiotic nondisjunction.

THE XYY MALE

The evidence indicates that the Y chromosome is strongly male-determining. Conceivably an extra Y chromosome might cause overaggressiveness through an overproduction of male hormones. There is suggestive evidence that men of XYY constitutions are prone to violence and antisocial behavior.

The occurrence of an XYY chromosome abnormality was first reported in 1962 by T. S. Hauschka and his co-workers at the Roswell Park Memorial Institute in Buffalo, New York. Subsequently, a possible link between the abnormal karyotype and aberrant behavior was suggested in 1965 when the XYY complement was detected in nearly 4 percent of the inmates at a maximum-security prison in Lanarkshire, Scotland. Additional surveys in Britain and North America lent support to the possibility that the additional Y chromosome increases predisposition to criminality. The afflicted males are usually taller than average (more than 6 feet tall), tend to have barely normal IQs, and suffer persistent acne.

The XYY constitution remains a controversial issue. It is premature to conclude that all XYY men exhibit violent behavior. Indeed, there are reports of apparently well-adjusted XYY males, and even reports denying the strong association between this chromosomal condition and deviant behavior. It is not known whether the XYY male has inherently subnormal intelligence or whether the aberrant behavioral attributes hinder the attainment of normal intelligence. The XYY constitution is by no means uncommon; it is suspected to arise once in every 700 liveborn males. With 1.4 million males born in the United States each year, 2,000 of them could be automatically stigmatized at birth with excessive impulsiveness!

BARR BODY

In 1949, Murray L. Barr and E. G. Bertram of the Medical School of the University of Western Ontario noted, in a routine examination of nerve cells of cats, an unusually dark spot at the periphery of the nucleus of some of the cells (fig. 25.5). The darkly stained body appeared only in the nuclei of cells from female cats. It was absent in the nerve cells of males. This small nuclear body that distinguishes the sexes is called *sex chromatin,* or after its discoverer, a *Barr body.* The Barr body was then shown to be present in other female cells besides the nerve cells, including the inner-cheek cells in humans.

Barr bodies are seen in resting cells, in which the individual chromosomes are not distinguishable. Yet it appeared likely that these round bodies were related in some manner to the X chromosome of the female. That a relationship does exist became apparent from studies of individuals suffering from chromosomal sex anomalies. When the sex chromatin test was applied to patients with Klinefelter's syndrome (XXY), most of them were found to have a Barr body in the nucleus of the cheek

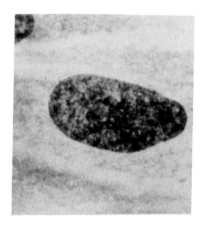

Male

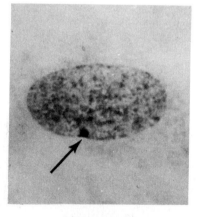

Female

Figure 25.5 Barr body, a small, darkly stained spot at the periphery of the nucleus that distinguishes the sex: absent in the normal male and present in the normal female. (Courtesy of Dr. Elizabeth M. Earley, Tulane University.)

cell. In other words, these patients, male in general appearance, have the chromatin-positive pattern of the normal female (XX). On the other hand, the majority of females with Turner's syndrome (XO) were shown to be chromatin-negative. They lack Barr bodies, as does the normal male (XY). It is thus evident that the presence of a Barr body is associated with the presence of two X chromosomes, while the absence of sex chromatin is associated with the presence of a single X chromosome.

Further studies in the 1950s revealed a striking relation between the number of Barr bodies and the number of X chromosomes. The cells of triplo-X females (XXX) contain two Barr bodies instead of one. Individuals with four X chromosomes—males (XXXXY) as well as females (XXXX)—have three Barr bodies. The maximum number of Barr bodies is therefore always one less than the number of X chromosomes present.

It has now been convincingly shown that one of the two X chromosomes (the late-replicating X) in each somatic cell of the normal female takes up a position against the nuclear membrane and condenses to form the Barr body. The condensation of the X chromosome is associated with genetic inactivation. That is to say, only one X chromosome is genetically active in the female; the other (or condensed) X is inactive. Inactivation of one of the X chromosomes occurs very early in embryonic life. Investigators have been able to demonstrate the Barr body (the condensed X) in human female embryos immediately before the blastocyst becomes implanted in the uterine wall. The time of inactivation is probably about the sixth day of embryonic life, if not earlier.

The question then arose as to which one of the two Xs of the embryo —the X contributed by the mother or the father's X—is relegated to the status of the dark Barr body. The evidence indicates that neither of the two is selected for the role. It is solely a matter of chance; the paternal X may become condensed in some cells, theoretically half the cells, and the maternal X in the remaining cells of the embryo. The outcome, as seen in figure 25.6, is that the female is a genetic mosaic of paternal Xs and maternal Xs. The interesting consequences of this mosaicism are discussed in the next chapter.

SUMMARY

Meiotic nondisjunction of the sex chromosomes in the female can result in eggs that, when fertilized by normal sperm, produce zygotes with either one or three of the sex chromosomes: XXY, XXX, XO, and YO (O signifying absence of a sex chromosome). The XXY zygote develops into a male whose testes are underdeveloped (Klinefelter's syndrome); the XO constitution produces a sexually infantile female (Turner's syndrome); the XXX zygote gives rise to a triplo-X female with few, if any, abnormal clinical signs; and the YO constitution has not been observed. The Y chromosome in humans has a decisive role in sex determination; the Y chromosome is strongly male-determining. Observations of a controversial nature suggest that men of XYY constitution are prone to violence and antisocial behavior.

Cells of normal females have a small, darkly stained mass—the Barr body—present at the nuclear periphery. The Barr body is an X chromosome that has become condensed and remains genetically inactive in the cell. The number of Barr bodies in a nucleus is always one less than the number of X chromosomes present in the individual. The Barr body is not seen in cell smears from normal males.

The clinical and cytological picture of chromosomal disorders is com-

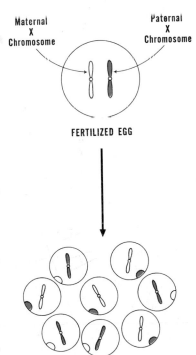

Figure 25.6 One of the two X chromosomes in each cell of the early female embryo takes up a position against the nuclear membrane and condenses to form the Barr body. Either the maternal X or the paternal X may form the Barr body in a given female cell.

plicated by the occurrence of <u>mosaicism—the presence of chromo-</u><u>somally dissimilar cells in the same individual</u>. The chromosomal com-position of a mosaic depends on the type of divisional error (mitotic nondisjunction or anaphase lag), the stage of development at which the aberration occurs, and the viabilities of the different cell lines. As a consequence of many bizarre mosaic combinations, a graded series of clinical patients have been found ranging from classical Turner's or Klinefelter's syndrome to near physically normal females or males.

Ethical Probe 17
Situation of Doubt

A 42-year-old woman became unexpectedly pregnant. She was considered at high risk for the birth of a child with a chromosomal aberration. Amniocentesis was performed at the appropriate time, and the fetal cells were analyzed chromosomally. The karyotype was not free of complications. Instead of the usual XX chromosome of the female or the XY of the male, the fetus' sex chromosomes were of the XYY composition.

Her physician is aware that the findings on XYY males are inconclusive. Some studies suggest that XYY males are prone to violence and antisocial behavior. Contrarily, other studies indicate that XYY individuals do not inherently have aberrant behavioral attributes. The physician is faced with a dilemma, since he cannot at present make any definitive statements about the outcome of the XYY constitution. Scientific information in the future might clarify the nature of the XYY condition, but the woman's situation demands a decision today.

If you were the physician, what would you tell (or advise) the woman? How would you convey the information in comprehensible terms so that the woman can make an informed decision? If you were the woman, what would you do?

Sex-Linked Inheritance and Dosage Compensation

26

The sex chromosomes were discovered long before their role in sex determination was suspected. Henking in 1891 accurately described the female sex chromosome, but in the absence of a clear notion of its function, he labeled it "X." For the same abstruse reason, the other partner chromosome was later symbolized "Y." Today it is clear that the X and Y not only carry sex-determining factors but are associated with several traits that have no relation to sexual development.

The X chromosome is the principal carrier of *sex-linked*, or more properly, *X-linked* genes. Among the X-linked genes are those responsible for hemophilia, red-green color blindness, glucose-6-phosphate dehydrogenase deficiency, and a particular form of muscular dystrophy. The X-linked detrimental genes are recognized by their transmission from mother to son; they are not transmitted directly from father to son. The direct father-to-son transmission of a *Y-linked* trait has not been witnessed or documented, save possibly for the expression of "hairy ear," a profuse growth of hair on the edge of the lobes, found principally in Asiatic Indians. Nevertheless, the importance of the Y chromosome cannot be understated. The Y chromosome is instrumental in assuring testicular differentiation. It may also be important in controlling stature or height.

TRANSMISSION OF HEMOPHILIA

The special features of X-linked inheritance are seen in the transmission of *hemophilia*. This condition, often called *bleeder's disease*, is a disorder of the blood in which a vital clotting factor is lacking, causing abnormally delayed clotting. Hemophilia exists almost exclusively in males, who receive the defective gene from their mothers. The transmission of hemophilia is exemplified in the cross illustrated in figure 26.1. Since the male has only one X chromosome, he carries only a single, unpaired X-linked gene. He is said to be *hemizygous* for the X-linked gene; there is no corresponding gene on the Y chromosome. Thus, if the male carries a single defective X-borne gene, he is abnormal. If the given single gene is normal, he is normal. In essence, the effects of X-linked recessive genes are never obscured in the male.

In figure 26.1, the normal X-borne gene for proper clotting is indicated by a plus symbol, $+$. The abnormal allele is designated h. It can be seen that there are four possibilities among the offspring when a normal man marries a carrier woman. Each son has a 50–50 chance of being victimized by hemophilia, and each daughter has a 50–50 chance of being a carrier. Hemophilic females are exceedingly rare since they can only be derived from an extremely remote marriage—that of a hemophilic man marrying a carrier woman. A few hemophilic women have been

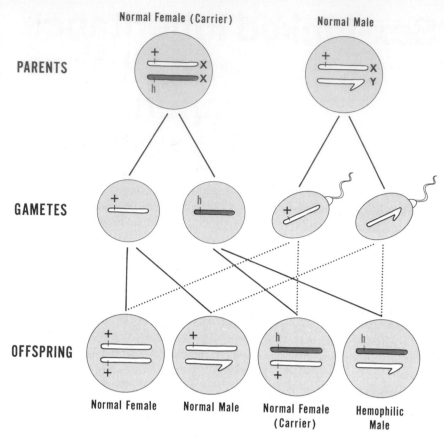

recorded in the medical literature; some have married and given birth to hemophilic sons.

There is no known cure for hemophilia. The victim of hemophilia lives in constant danger of severe bleeding from the most minor wounds, such as a facial scratch or a tooth extraction. Hemorrhages can only be checked with transfusions of fresh whole blood (or plasma) or concentrates of the clotting protein, known as *antihemophilic globulin* (AHG). The vast majority of hemophilics (about 80 percent) lack AHG: the other victims have been found to lack another clotting component, called *plasma thromboplastin* (PTC). This has led to the recognition of two forms of hemophilia, the classical type (hemophilia A, or deficiency of AHG) and the newly discovered type (hemophilia B, or deficiency of PTC). Hemophilia B is also called *Christmas disease,* after the surname of the first hemophilic B patient identified. The average life expectancy in both conditions is approximately 18 years. The National Hemophilic Foundation estimates that hemophilia affects about 100,000 Americans. About 80 percent of the known cases have a family history of "bleeders." The other 20 percent are "new" cases which have arisen from newly mutated genes in the X chromosome of the egg.

The males afflicted with hemophilia in the royal families of Europe trace their ancestry to Queen Victoria of England (fig. 26.2). Queen Victoria was the original carrier of the fateful gene. Since none of her forebears or relatives was afflicted, the gene for hemophilia apparently originated by mutation in Victoria herself or in a gamete contributed by one of her parents. One of Victoria's four sons suffered from hemophilia and two of her five daughters proved to be carriers of the gene. Through her two carrier daughters, Alice and Beatrice, hemophilia was carried into the Russian and Spanish ruling families. The last czarevitch

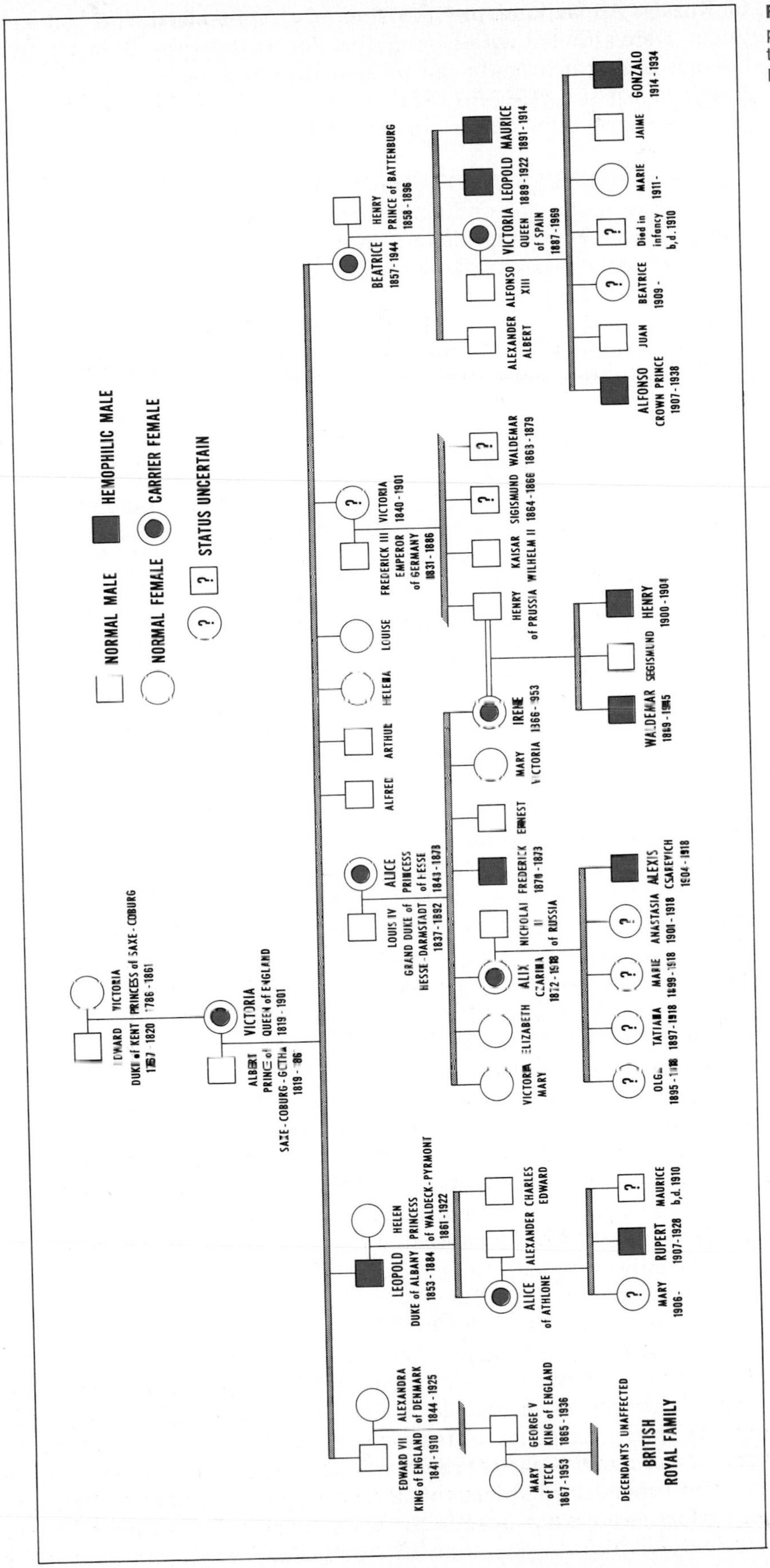

Figure 26.2 Pedigree of hemophilia in the royal families of Europe, traceable to Queen Victoria of England.

of Russia, Alexis, and the two sons of Alfonso XIII, the last king of Spain, were afflicted with hemophilia. Fortunately, the devastating gene has not been carried into the present British royal family. Queen Victoria's eldest son, King Edward VII, was not hemophilic and could not have transmitted the disease to any of his descendants.

COLOR BLINDNESS AND MUSCULAR DYSTROPHY

We have seen that hemophilia, once considered a single entity, consists rather of two genetically distinct entities: hemophilia A and hemophilia B (Christmas disease). Likewise, it was originally thought that only one X-linked locus was involved in red-green color blindness. It has recently been demonstrated that there are two distinct loci, one for the so-called *deuton* type and the other for the *proton* type. In both cases, there is a confusion of red and green. However, the two genes affect different cones of the retina; the deuton mutant gene affects the cones involved in green perception whereas the proton mutant gene alters the red-sensitive cone. About 6 percent of the men in the United States suffer from the deuton type; 2 percent are afflicted with the proton type. As expected from sex-linked inheritance, relatively few women are affected with red-green color blindness, about 1 in 250 color-blind individuals.

In some primitive societies, such as the Australian aborigines, the incidence of color blindness is very low. It has been suggested that a color-blind male would be at a considerable disadvantage in a society of hunters, and hence would be less likely to transmit his genes to the next generation. As societies evolved to a more civilized state, the apparent disadvantage of the color-blind trait waned and the trait became more widespread.

Probably the most severe and tragic of the sex-linked disorders is the type of muscular dystrophy known as *Duchenne muscular dystrophy*, named after its discoverer, Benjamin Duchenne, in 1868. It occurs in about 1 in every 25,000 male births. The muscles of the affected male gradually deteriorate during early childhood. At about the third year of life, the afflicted child experiences difficulty in climbing stairs or rising from the floor. Subsequently the muscles atrophy, leading to invalidism between the ages of 9 and 12 and then death in the early twenties. There is no known cure. Heterozygous females are normal, although some show slight signs of the disorder.

Since affected boys do not survive and cannot perpetuate the deleterious gene, the incidence of heterozygous female carriers does not reach high levels (contrary to the case for color blindness). The proportion of women who are carriers is about 1 in 20,000. It can be shown that one-third of all affected males are the result of new mutations, occurring either in the mother's or father's gametes. Accordingly, in several family pedigrees, the affected boy is the solitary member of the family to be afflicted.

DOSAGE COMPENSATION

Since the X chromosome carries genes that control the production of proteins, a female with a double dose of the X chromosome should produce twice as much of a given protein as does the male with one X. But she actually does not. Some mechanism of *dosage compensation* must be operative whereby two doses of the genes of the female produce the same effect as does one dose in the male.

In the early 1960s, the British geneticist Mary F. Lyon formulated the intriguing concept that one X chromosome of the female becomes genetically inactive early in embryonic development and remains a muted or silent partner of the functional X throughout life. The inactive X hypothesis, so brilliantly set forth, has become known as the *Lyon hypothesis*. There is a wealth of evidence in support of the hypothesis. Indeed, it is now quite evident that the inactivated X becomes condensed to form the *Barr body*. The inactive X can be either the maternal X or the paternal X in different cells of the same female. Inactivation is thus random and independent in each cell. On the average then, 50 percent of the paternal X chromosomes and 50 percent of the maternal X chromosomes become inactivated. There is one apparent exception to this rule: if one of the X chromosomes is abnormal in shape, then the abnormal X is always inactivated.

If one of the two X chromosomes is inactive, then we should be able to find two types of somatic cells in the female: one with the active maternal X and one with the active paternal X. Some women are heterozygous for an X-linked condition called *anhidrotic ectodermal dysplasia*. The abnormal mutant gene produces an agent that inhibits, or checks, the secretion of sweat. Heterozygous females have patches of normal, perspirable skin alternating with patches of affected skin incapable of perspiring. Most female heterozygotes are unaware of this peculiar condition and remain continually perplexed over their uneven bodily perspiration. Since inactivation of the X chromosome occurs early in embryonic life, it follows that the heterozygote woman will be a mosaic of two populations of cells—normal and affected.

Convincing confirmation of the Lyon hypothesis was provided in 1962 by the studies of Ernest Beutler and his co-workers at the City of Hope Medical Center at Duarte, California. They examined the red blood cells of females heterozygous for a recessive X-linked gene that affects the production of a certain enzyme important in sugar metabolism, namely, glucose-6-phosphate dehydrogenase. Either the male carries the normal gene on his sole X chromosome, in which case he produces the normal amount of the enzyme, or he carries the mutant gene and is accordingly unable to produce the enzyme at all. As we learned earlier (chapter 20), the male carrying the defective X-linked gene is vulnerable to hemolysis of his blood cells if he eats fava (or broad) beans or takes one of the modern antimalarial drugs, especially primaquine. The heterozygous female is not victimized since she bears both the normal and mutant gene. But Dr. Beutler found that the cells of the heterozygous female do not all uniformly produce the important enzyme. She contains rather a mixture of normal enzyme-producing cells and mutant enzyme-deficient cells, as if the normal X chromosome were inactivated in some cells and the mutant X chromosome in others (fig. 26.3).

Further substantiation of the inactive X hypothesis came from the laboratory of Dr. M. M. Grumbach, who found that the level of glucose-6-phosphate dehydrogenase activity is substantially the same in persons who have from one to four X chromosomes. This would follow from the Lyon hypothesis, since whatever the number of X chromosomes present in any individual, only a single one remains active. The Lyon hypothesis would also explain the curious finding that triplo-X females (XXX) are relatively free of defects. In these females only one X is functional; two of the three X chromosomes became Barr bodies at about the time of implantation of the embryo.

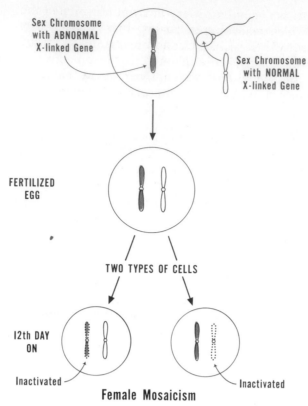

Figure 26.3 Lyon hypothesis. One of the X chromosomes is genetically inactivated in some cells and the other X is inactivated in the other cells. The female has only one functional X in each somatic cell throughout life.

Sex Chromosome with **ABNORMAL** X-linked Gene

Sex Chromosome with **NORMAL** X-linked Gene

FERTILIZED EGG

TWO TYPES OF CELLS

12th DAY ON

Inactivated

Inactivated

Female Mosaicism

There are, however, certain findings that are difficult to reconcile with the inactivation of all but one X chromosome. Presumably both the XO female and the XX female have but one active X, yet there is a considerable difference between the two. The former female suffers from Turner's syndrome whereas the latter is normal. Moreover, the gain of one X chromosome as in the XXY Klinefelter's syndrome also makes an appreciable difference. The apparent inconsistencies may be resolved by assuming that inactivation does not involve the entire X chromosome but spares part of the chromosome so that at least a portion remains genetically active. It is thought that X inactivation affects primarily the long arm, the loss of which produces no somatic damage. The short arm of the X would remain active, since its absence, as we shall see, produces marked somatic abnormalities.

SEX CHROMOSOMES AND STATURE

Two cardinal signs of the XO condition, or Turner's syndrome, are infertility and short stature. Apparently two complete Xs are required for normal development of the oocytes, since the loss of only one arm of the X chromosome results in the usual streak gonad of Turner's syndrome. The loss, or deletion, of the *short* arm produces the typical Turner's syndrome including short stature. However, the loss of the *long* arm of the X chromosome produces infertility but *not* short stature. This suggests that there are determinants on the *short* arm of the X chromosome that regulate normal height.

For proper development of stature in males, the determinants on the short arm of the X chromosome are most likely matched by genes on the Y chromosome. A characteristic feature of XYY males is that they are tall. The tall stature of the XYY syndrome may be due to trisomy of the height-determining segments. As there is no abnormality of height in women with the XXX syndrome, we must assume that X inactivation prevents the growth effect of the trisomy condition from manifesting itself. The current hypothesis, then, is that at least part of the short arm of the X chromosome is homologous with part of the Y chromosome, and that these segments carry factors that regulate a person's height.

SEX-LIMITED INHERITANCE

A sex-limited trait is one that, for all practical purposes, is confined to males although the responsible genes do *not* exist on the sex chromosomes. The responsible gene is found on the autosome, and manifests itself primarily, if not almost exclusively, in the male. An example is a common form of premature frontal baldness (fig. 26.4). The gene for baldness may be considered dominant in the male and recessive in the female. The male becomes prematurely bald (before 30 years of age) if he inherits either one gene or both for baldness. Thus, unlike sex-linked traits, men can transmit the condition to their sons. Women must have both genes in order to manifest the condition, and then only when adequate levels of male (androgenic) hormones are present. The gene apparently expresses itself when the output of androgenic hormone is high, as in males. Males who have been hormonally deficient and receive androgen therapy tend to enhance their masculinity but also lose their hair. In this case, the gene expresses itself when the level of androgen increases. It is estimated that approximately 26 percent of the males over 30 in the United States are bald.

SEX DIFFERENTIATION

The ovary and the testis have a similar embryonic origin, and until late in the sixth week of embryonic life they are indistinguishable. Both the ovary and the testis are said to be in an "indifferent" stage of development. Along with these indifferent gonads, a double set of genital ducts is present (fig. 26.5). One set, destined to become the male ducts, is not newly formed but is claimed from the regressing primitive urinary ducts known as *mesonephric ducts*. These ducts represent the persistence of ancestral developmental structures. In the frog, for example, the mesonephric system is the functional urinary apparatus. In the human, the mesonephric ducts are transitory urinary tubes. When the permanent human kidney emerges, the mesonephric ducts (also called *Wolffian ducts*) become appropriated into the reproductive system of the male, but not of the female (fig. 26.5). Specifically, the mesonephric ducts are converted into the main sperm ducts, the vasa deferentia.

The other set of ducts, known as the *Müllerian ducts,* arises independently and adjacent to the mesonephric ducts. The Müllerian ducts give rise to the genital canal of the female. The two duct systems occur together for a period of time in both males and females. Thus, just as there are indifferent gonads, there is an indifferent stage of the genital ducts. If the embryo develops into a male, the potentially female ducts (Müllerian ducts) degenerate and the mesonephric ducts transform into the main sperm ducts. On the other hand, in female embryos, the Müllerian ducts form the oviducts, uterus (through a fusion of ducts), and upper segment of the vagina; the potentially male ducts (mesonephric ducts) fail to persist.

The differentiation of a neuter gonad into a testis or an ovary depends on the nature of the sex chromosomes. During the seventh week in the

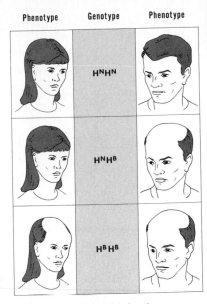

Phenotype	Genotype	Phenotype
	$H^N H^N$	
	$H^N H^B$	
	$H^B H^B$	

H^N - Normal Hair Growth
H^B - Pattern Baldness

Figure 26.4 Pattern baldness, a sex-limited trait. The presence of only one gene for baldness causes the condition in the male, whereas the condition does not occur in the female unless she possesses both genes for baldness.

Figure 26.5 Indifferent, primitive genital system, and its differentiation into the definitive female and male types. The Müllerian ducts are the forerunners of the oviducts, uterus, and vagina of the mammalian female. The Müllerian ducts in the male and the mesonephric ducts in the female both become rudimentary.

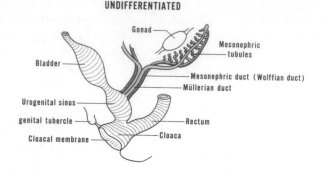

UNDIFFERENTIATED

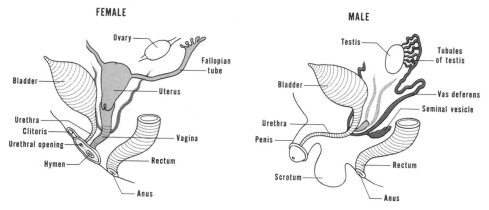

FEMALE

MALE

genetic male (XY), the gonad differentiates into a testis. In the genetic female (XX), the indifferent gonad persists until the 10th or 11th week before characteristics appear that mark the organ positively as an ovary. The chromosomal constitution (XX or XY) determines only whether ovaries or testes develop. Once the gonads are differentiated, then the individual's subsequent sexual development is controlled, or regulated, by the testes or ovaries. In other words, the differentiated gonads themselves determine the fate of the two sets of indifferent genital ducts and also the external genitalia. This control has certain intriguing aspects.

In experimentation on the rabbit and rhesus monkey, the developing gonad can be removed without affecting the viability of the fetus. The removal of the indifferent gonad from a female embryo does *not* interfere with the normal differentiation of the female genital ducts and external genitalia. On the other hand, the removal of the indifferent gonad from a male embryo results in the degeneration of the Wolffian ducts, the complete feminine differentiation of the Müllerian ducts, and the development of female external genitalia. Thus, in the absence of gonads, the genital ducts and external genitalia undergo female development, *regardless of the genetic sex (XX or XY).*

These results have been interpreted to indicate that the male genital system cannot differentiate without some stimulus from the testes. The testicular stimulus has been identified as testosterone, which masculinizes the primitive Wolffian ducts. The testicular secretion of testosterone accounts also for the development of the external genitalia (fig. 26.6). In the presence of testosterone, the indifferent genital tubercle differentiates into a penis rather than a clitoris. The urethral folds of skin on both sides of the genital groove wrap around the penis to cover the organ and form the foreskin; in the absence of testosterone, the urethral folds remain as bilateral labia minora and the clitoral hood. Testosterone also induces

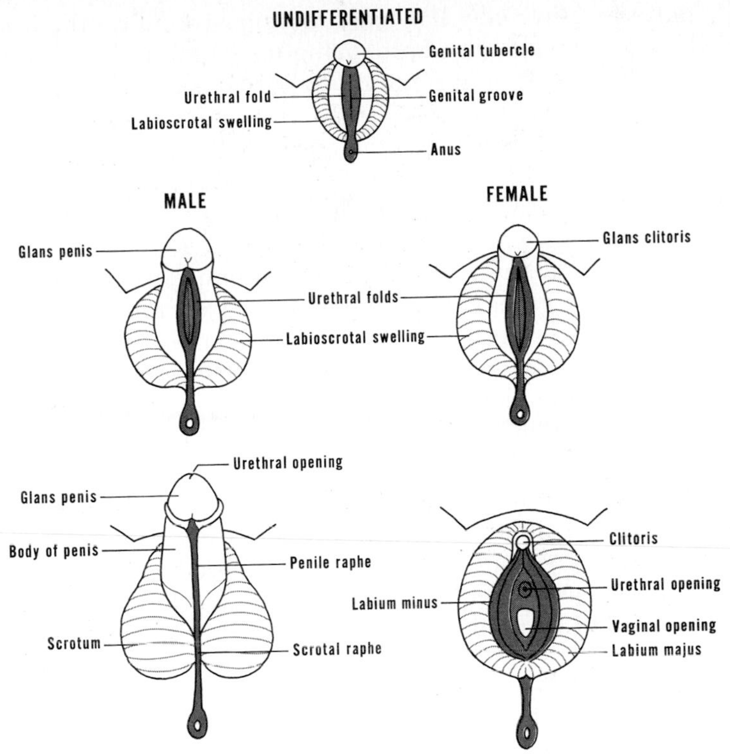

UNDIFFERENTIATED

Genital tubercle
Urethral fold
Labioscrotal swelling
Genital groove
Anus

MALE
Glans penis
Urethral folds
Labioscrotal swelling

FEMALE
Glans clitoris

Glans penis
Body of penis
Urethral opening
Penile raphe
Scrotum
Scrotal raphe

Clitoris
Labium minus
Urethral opening
Vaginal opening
Labium majus

Figure 26.6 Differentiation of the external genitalia of the male and the female from the same rudimentary components.

the outer labioscrotal swellings to fuse in the midline to form the scrotum. In the female, the labioscrotal swellings remain in place as the bilateral labia majora (fig. 26.6).

The importance of testicular testosterone is revealed in experiments in which the pituitary gland is severed in male rabbit fetuses. The pituitary gland (through the hypothalamus) regulates the production of testosterone by the testes. As a result of removal of the pituitary gland, the internal reproductive ducts become feminine in form as in castrated fetuses. Thus, once again, the presence or absence of testicular testosterone decisively determines the fate of the primitive Müllerian and Wolffian ducts. Female development is not dependent on any ovarian secretion, since in the absence of any gonads at all, the Fallopian tubes, uterus, and vagina develop routinely.

SEXUAL DIFFERENTIATION IN THE BRAIN

Recent research indicates that fetal sex hormones affect the nervous circuits in the hypothalamus, which is the part of the brain that controls the release of the pituitary hormones (see chapter 12). We have seen that the differentiation of female genital ducts requires only the absence of testicular secretion. It now appears that a female hypothalamus—one that can cause the cyclical release of LH-releasing factor and hence cyclical ovulation—is established, or imprinted, shortly after birth unless a functional testis (or its secretion, testosterone) is present at the critical time (within one week from birth). Thus, testosterone present in the newborn determines the future reproductive pattern—the cyclicity of the female (cyclical secretion of LH-releasing factor) or the acyclicity of the male (fixed, continuous release of LH-releasing factor.)

If a newborn female rat is given a single dose of testosterone, she will fail to ovulate at maturity and will exhibit the sexual behavior patterns of a male. If a male rat is castrated on the first day of life, he becomes incapable of producing testosterone and will display a female receptive pattern in response to doses of estrogen. If this rat is given an ovary transplanted from an adult female, it will ovulate cyclically and develop corpora lutea in the normal female cyclic pattern. Clearly then, the presence of testosterone in the critical first days of birth influences, or even shapes, the hypothalamus and dictates that the animal will behave as a male at maturity. In the absence of an early stimulus of testosterone, the animal will manifest feminine sex behavior as an adult.

These experiments were performed on rabbits, rats, and the rhesus monkey; whether the same principles apply to man remains to be seen. The results do reveal that testosterone acts in an inductive way on the undifferentiated brain to organize it into a male-type brain. The absence of testosterone signifies a female-type brain. In a sense, all mammals at birth are *physiologically* female but capable of masculine transformation if functional testes are present. If the hypothalamus of the brain can be imprinted or typed according to sex, it may be that other nervous tissues in the brain are similarly sex-typed. One may then ask how, and to what extent, our capacity to perceive in general and to respond to stimuli in general is influenced or controlled by the sex-type of the brain.

SEX RATIO

Despite a 12 percent higher mortality rate of males *in utero*, approximately 106 boys are born for every 100 girls. The mortality rate among males is higher at all ages, and is evidenced in the first days of life. Females enjoy a 32 percent lower mortality rate in the first week of life and are less subject to sudden infant death. The male-to-female ratio drops to 100:100 at age 20, and progressively declines thereafter to reach the staggering figure of 62 males for every 100 females at age 85. There are no satisfactory explanations for the higher male mortality. Part of the higher male mortality may be attributable to X-linked detrimental genes. It has been mockingly stated that being a male became hazardous ever since Adam lost a rib.

The reasons for the greater number of male conceptions are largely unknown. It seems likely that equal numbers of X-bearing and Y-bearing sperm are produced, although the possibility of unequal production in favor of Y-bearing sperm cannot be discounted. The Y-bearing sperm is probably more viable than the X-bearing sperm, or more proficient in fertilization. It has been suggested that the Y-bearing sperm has a greater chance of reaching and penetrating the egg. The X chromosome is larger than the Y, and accordingly has a greater mass. Since velocity is influenced by mass, the sperm carrying the Y chromosome should be able to travel in the female reproductive canal at a greater speed with the same amount of energy than the sperm bearing the X chromosome. This explanation may be regarded as reasonable, although not proved.

ALTERING THE SEX RATIO

Several studies have shown that the sex of the first two children has a significant effect on the ultimate family size. More families have limited family size to two children when the first two children were of different sexes than when they were of the same sex. These findings suggest that the scientists' attempts to predetermine the sex of the unborn child are more than of academic interest.

One theory advanced in the 1940s was that the sex of the offspring could be controlled by adjusting the pH of the fluids in the vagina. An alkaline condition, such as that brought about by the introduction of sodium bicarbonate into the vagina, was judged to increase the rate of travel of Y-bearing sperm, and accordingly, to increase the proportion of male conceptions. Although some publicity-gaining claims were made, careful investigations have failed to provide supporting evidence.

In a microscopic study of sperm specimens from hundreds of normal males, Dr. Landrum B. Shettles of Columbia University detected two distinct types of sperm cells. One kind, believed to be the X-bearing sperm, has an elongated, oval-shaped head, while the other, presumably the Y-bearing sperm, has a more compact, round head (fig. 26.7). Eventually, it may be possible to separate the two varieties in a test tube (before insemination), either on the basis of their differing electric charge or their difference in weight. Some positive results have already been reported in separating X-bearing and Y-bearing sperm of rabbits and cattle by passing an electric current through the semen. The X-bearing sperm are apparently attracted to the anode, and Y-bearing sperm are attracted to the cathode. It remains to be seen whether a consistent difference of some sort can be found in human sperm.

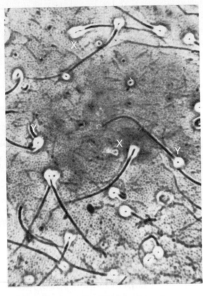

Figure 26.7 Two distinctive shapes of human sperm, as seen by phase contrast microscopy. Sperm with round heads apparently carry the Y chromosome; sperm heads that are oval in shape are thought to carry the X chromosome. (Courtesy of Dr. Landrum B. Shettles, Columbia Presbyterian Medical Center.)

SUMMARY

The X chromosome carries genes for traits that are unrelated to sexual development. These X-linked genes are recognized by their transmission from mother to son. Hemophilia, for example, exists almost exclusively in males, who receive the detrimental X-linked gene from the mother. Since the male has only one X chromosome, the effects of X-linked detrimental genes are not obscured in the male. Although the Y chromosome has relatively few genes, there is circumstantial evidence that genes concerned with body height are located in the Y (as well as in the homologous portion of the X chromosome). The tall stature of XYY individuals may be due to trisomy of the height-determining genes of the sex chromosomes.

The normal female has two X chromosomes, but only one X chromosome is functional in a given cell. Early in embryonic life, one X chromosome becomes genetically inactivated and remains a silent partner of the functional X throughout life. The functional X can be either the maternal X or the paternal X in different cells of the same female. Accordingly, the female is a genetic mosaic—some cells express one set of X-linked genes whereas other cells express the other set.

The XX or XY chromosomal constitution determines whether the embryonic gonads become ovaries or testes. Subsequent sexual differentiation is regulated by the gonads themselves. The presence of functional testes (or testicular testosterone) stimulates development of the reproductive structures of the male. In contrast, ovaries need not be present for the female genital ducts and external genitalia to develop; female differentiation requires only the absence of testicular secretion. The presence or absence of testicular testosterone also affects the pattern of nervous pathways of the brain.

As yet unexplained, more eggs are fertilized by Y-bearing sperm than by X-bearing sperm. Nevertheless, the human sex ratio (male to female) declines progressively with advancing age levels, for unknown cause. Limited progress has been achieved in experimental attempts to distinguish and separate unequivocally, either morphologically or chemically, the X-bearing and Y-bearing sperm.

Ethical Probe 18
Parental Sex Preferences

It is of interest to speculate on the societal changes that might arise if an effective and practical method is devised of predetermining, prior to conception, the sex of the unborn child. Couples would be able to realize their ideal family, with respect to number, spacing, and sex composition of the children. In light of the current acceptance in economically advanced countries of small families (particularly, the two-child family), demographers have expressed concern over the persistent widespread parental preference for sons. Surveys continue to show that men and women overwhelmingly would like their first child to be a boy. In a recent study in the United States concerning the firstborn child, 80 percent of the men desired a boy, while only 4 percent wanted a girl, and 16 percent listed no preference. The women chose similarly: 79 percent wanted a male child first, 12 percent wanted a female, and 9 percent listed no preference.

If many parents were to satisfy their strong preference for firstborn sons, the impact on females might be unfavorable. A consistent finding is that firstborns are more likely to achieve academic and professional success. Females could then be at a competitive disadvantage if daughters were to become more often secondborns in a society characterized by two-child families. On the other hand, sex control would ensure that fewer children of the "wrong" sex would be born. This might be viewed as favorable for females, inasmuch as every female born would be a wanted child since she would have been specifically chosen.

If sex-predetermination techniques become feasible, do we want or need it? Is the strong preference for sons a serious problem? If every daughter is truly a wanted child, would females then be more appreciated?

Genetic Engineering and Genetic Counseling

27

The success of scientists in deciphering the genetic code, synthesizing biologically active DNA, and isolating pure genes has opened the door to the possibility of correcting, or mitigating, the hereditary defects of man. Conceivably a normal gene can be artificially synthesized and then introduced into a patient possessing the defective allele. Or methods may be devised to repair or eliminate, by chemicals or radiation, the base sequence of the defective piece of DNA in sufferers of genetic disorders. However, the direct manipulation of individual genes presents formidable problems. We cannot easily add a piece of DNA to the human chromosome, nor can we change a particular base at a precise point in the sequence. There are possibly insuperable technical difficulties concerned with confining the action of a chemical or physical agent to a particular or restricted region of the DNA molecule. Moreover, if only the body cells of the patient are altered, only the phenotype of the individual is affected and the change does not carry over to future generations.

If the objective is to alleviate needless human anguish, then attention might be more profitably focused on reducing the occurrence of a given defect, rather than on repairing the defective gene itself. Despite the many advances, the prevention of a disorder remains as the key tool in relieving the acute suffering that accompanies many of the abnormalities. This aspect falls within the province of genetic counseling, which is emerging today as a significant human endeavor. New techniques have enabled the genetic counselor to predict the risks of occurrence and recurrence of inherited disorders with far greater accuracy than in the past.

TRANSDUCTION
Ordinarily when a virus enters a bacterial cell, it multiplies within that cell and the bacterial cell becomes lysed when the new viral progeny emerge. Occasionally, however, the virus may become incorporated into the bacterial chromosome. When the viral genes reproduce themselves, a portion of the bacteria's hereditary material may become incorporated in the new viral particles. Then, when these viral particles subsequently invade a new bacterial cell, that bacterial cell may exhibit some of the traits of the previous bacterial cell. This process by which a virus mediates the transfer of bacterial genes from one bacterial cell to the next bacterial cell it invades is termed *transduction* (fig. 27.1). This phenomenon was first described in 1951 by Norton D. Zinder and Joshua Lederberg for bacteria of the *Salmonella* group.

The full extension of transduction to human cells awaits new technical developments and additional knowledge. Several of the pilot

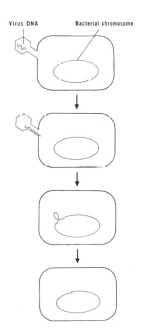

Figure 27.1 Basis of the phenomenon of transduction. Viral DNA can become incorporated in the chromosome of the bacterial host.

studies have attracted widespread interest. For example, when human cells in tissue culture are infected with the SV40 virus of monkeys, specific DNA sequences of the virus become integrated into the chromosomal DNA of the human cell without apparently harming the cell. This suggests the possibility of engineering the viral DNA—that is, artificially modifying the virus so that it may carry a DNA sequence that codes for a particular protein. Thus, it may be possible to attach to the DNA molecule of an innocuous virus a sequence of bases that specifies the production of the enzyme phenylalanine hydroxylase. The carrier virus can then be introduced into an infant afflicted with phenylketonuria, with the expectation that the tailor-made virus would promote production of the enzyme that has been errant in the patient. Ideally, the virus should be inserted only in liver cells, which are the only cells in the body that normally exhibit phenylalanine hydroxylase activity. Uncertainty exists about how the carrier virus would express itself in other cells. A disquieting aspect is that the newly integrated virus might inaccurately express itself even in the liver cell and direct the synthesis of "transforming" proteins that are associated with cancerous growth (see chapter 15).

In the study by Carl Merril and his associates, mentioned in chapter 22, the investigators took advantage of a particular virus whose DNA contained a cluster of genes, previously obtained from a bacterial cell, that specified the production of a galactose-metabolizing enzyme. Transduction of the galactose genes to human fibroblast cells in culture was achieved. The human cells, formerly deficient in their ability to synthesize galactose, not only acquired this ability but passed on the enzyme-making ability when they reproduced themselves. It should be stressed that the experiments have been performed in the artificial *in vitro* environment of a tissue culture system; the techniques have yet to be successfully applied to *in vivo* systems.

Viruses are not the only means of introducing new genes into mammalian cells. The cell biologist Henry Harris at Oxford University in England has used the technique of *cell fusion* to insert functional genes of chick red blood cells into mouse fibroblast cells grown in tissue culture. When the two disparate types of cells are fused, the nuclear membrane of each disappears and the resulting hybrid nucleus contains both complements of chromosomes. However, the chromosomes of the chick red blood cell quickly fragment. Prior to or during fragmentation, the chick chromosomes leave some of their DNA sequences in the mouse chromosomes. Although only mouse nuclei appear in the daughter cells after mitosis, some of the daughter cells gained the ability to synthesize enzymes that are unique to the chick red blood cells.

In recent years, researchers have become attracted to bacterial *plasmids, which are small circles of cytoplasmic DNA* in addition to the main, large circular strand of DNA. Plasmids do not have the same sequences of nucleic acid bases as the main DNA and replicate independently of the main DNA. A single bacterial cell can harbor as many as 25 plasmids, and each plasmid can carry from 2 to 250 genes, depending on the size of the ring. A plasmid can be detached from a bacterial cell and experimentally broken at specific points. Then, the DNA molecule from another organism—an insect, a frog, or a rat, for example—can be isolated and portions of this DNA molecule can be attached to the fragments of the plasmid to form a new circle, or a *recombinant-DNA molecule*. This newly formed recombinant-DNA molecule, when reintroduced into a bacterium, can replicate precisely and be passed on to daughter bacterial cells for many generations. This technique permits the large-scale transmission of genes that code for indispensable molecules. Thus, the insertion of the insulin-producing gene of a rat could lead to the mass production of invaluable insulin as the bacteria multiply rapidly.

TISSUE AND ORGAN TRANSPLANTATIONS

Another approach to alleviation of inherited disorders is the transplantation of tissues and organs from one individual to another. When bone marrow is transplanted, the transplanted blood cells colonize the host's marrow in the long bones, multiply in these sites, and produce blood cells that are characteristic of the donor. Moderate success has been attained in injecting immunologically sound bone marrow cells into human patients suffering from *agammaglobulinemia*, a disorder characterized by a deficiency or lack of antibodies. Transplantation of bone marrow has been attempted in humans as therapy for leukemia, but the results have been thus far unrewarding. Ultimately, the transplantation of healthy donor tissues may prove to be the most important way of controlling or curing many genetic diseases of blood cells such as sickle-cell anemia, thalassemia, and hemophilia.

Kidney transplantation has been used in attempts to treat hereditary disorders affecting the kidney, notably a condition known as cystinosis. This is a congenital metabolic disturbance in the kidney cells characterized by crystalline cystine deposits, which impair renal functioning. Transplantation, in effect, replaces enzymatically normal cells for the abnormal ones. The effect is immediate relief to the patient but the long-term consequences have yet to be demonstrated. The use of transplantation has been extended to other hereditary anomalies affecting the kidney and other organs, especially the liver. Many genetic diseases affect enzymes specific to the liver. So far, liver transplantation has met with only limited success, mainly for technical reasons, although synthesis of donor-specific proteins following liver transplants has been reported.

The greatest obstacle in organ transplantation is graft rejection based on genetic incompatibilities between donor and host. There is also the portentous issue of obtaining a sufficient supply of viable organs as transplants. It is not inconceivable that when more is known about the immune mechanism, it will become possible to use the organs of our primate relatives for transplant purposes.

COMPLEXITIES OF GENETIC SURGERY

In spite of the significant advances cited, it should be emphasized that the externally supplied genetic material benefits only those defective cells that have incorporated the externally supplied gene. Improving the body cells in this manner without altering the germ cells does not prevent transmission of the hereditary defect. A positive genetic effect will occur only if the correction of the gene can be made in the germ cells—the egg cell and the sperm cell. The means of genetically manipulating the gametes are not in sight.

It should also be clear that the traits we have thus far considered are sharply differentiated and are governed essentially by single gene determiners. There are, however, many characteristics in man that cannot be classified into two discrete, alternative classes but show a great range of variation and many gradations between the extremes. These are the measurable or *quantitative* characters, such as certain physical attributes, like height and weight, and mental capacities, expressed as intelligence. Quantitative characters result from the action and interaction of many genes, or *polygenes*. Polygenic inheritance, particularly as it concerns intelligence, will be discussed in another section of this book. Here we may prophetically comment that the improvement of a quantitative trait would certainly necessitate the transfer of large, if not many, sequences of the DNA molecule. The replacement of large sections of DNA, particularly in a controlled manner, is difficult to imagine in the immediate, or even foreseeable, future.

GENETIC COUNSELING

A socially acceptable and completely voluntary approach is currently available for reducing the occurrence of genetic disorders and alleviating the associated human anguish. This approach embraces counseling individuals and families so that they can avoid the disastrous occurrence of genetic disorders. Centers for genetic counseling in hospitals, clinics, and medical schools have grown in the United States from 20 in 1955 to well over 200 today.

We earlier learned that the majority of detrimental genes are carried by heterozygotes. Moreover, heterozygous individuals are not as rare as might be supposed. As shown in table 27.1, the frequency of heterozygous carriers is many times greater than the frequency of homozygous individuals afflicted with a trait. Thus, an extremely rare disorder, like alkaptonuria, occurs in one in 1 million persons. This detrimental gene, however, is carried in the hidden state by 1 out of 500 persons. There are 2,000 as many genetic carriers of alkaptonuria as there are individuals afflicted with this defect. For another recessive trait, cystic fibrosis, 1 out

Table 27.1
Frequencies of Recessive Homozygotes and Heterozygous Carriers

Frequency of Homozygotes (aa)	Frequency of Heterozygous Carriers (Aa)	Ratio of Carriers to Homozygotes
1 in 500 (sickle-cell anemia)[a]	1 in 10	50:1
1 in 1,000 (cystic fibrosis)	1 in 16	60:1
1 in 6,000 (Tay-Sachs disease)[b]	1 in 40	150:1
1 in 20,000 (albinism)	1 in 70	285:1
1 in 25,000 (phenylketonuria)	1 in 80	310:1
1 in 50,000 (acatalasia)[c]	1 in 110	460:1
1 in 1,000,000 (alkaptonuria)	1 in 500	2,000:1

[a] Based on incidence among American Negroes (see chapter 31).

[b] In the United States, the disease occurs once in 6,000 Jewish births and once in 500,000 non-Jewish births.

[c] Based on prevalence rate among the Japanese (see chapter 28).

of 1,000 individuals is afflicted with this homozygous trait. It may be thought that most affected children come from marriages of two affected individuals. This is not true. The majority of affected children—more than 99 percent—come from marriages of two normal parents, both of whom are heterozygous carriers. One of 16 persons is a carrier of cystic fibrosis.

The implications are clear. A successful genetic counseling program requires two important ingredients. First, there must be a simple, inexpensive means of detecting heterozygous carriers of inherited disorders. Secondly, there must be a means of diagnosing the disorder in the fetus of the expectant mother. Both these conditions have already been satisfied for certain genetic disorders. We may consider the recessively inherited condition of *Tay-Sachs disease*, a fatal, untreatable cerebral degenerative disorder. The basic defect is the accumulation in the brain cells of a fatty substance (specifically, ganglioside GM$_2$) resulting from the absence of a particular enzyme, β-D-N-acetylhexosaminidase A (or in short form, hexosaminidase A). The storage of massive amounts of the lipid leads to profound mental and motor deterioration, and death between the ages of two and four years. The disorder is found largely in the Ashkenazic Jews who live or have lived in eastern and central Europe. It is estimated that Tay-Sachs disease occurs 100 times more frequently in Ashkenazic Jews than in other Jewish groups and in non-Jewish populations.

Differentiation of the heterozygous carriers from the normal homozygote is now possible with a serum assay developed by John S. O'Brien and his colleagues at the University of California School of Medicine in San Diego. Heterozygous carriers have markedly decreased levels of hexosaminidase A activity in their blood. If both parents are identified as carriers, they can be informed that the risk of a defective child is 1 in 4. Moreover, fetal deficiency of hexosaminidase A is detectable early in gestation, as evidenced by enzyme studies on cultured cells of fetuses of mothers heterozygous for Tay-Sachs disease. This detection, made possible by *transabdominal amniocentesis*, offers parents the opportunity of having children without the risk of producing defective infants. Many of the genetic disorders that at present can be detected prenatally by studies of cultured fetal cells are listed in table 27.2.

Table 27.2
Genetic Disorders Detectable Prenatally by Amniocentesis

Adrenogenital syndrome	Hunter's disease
Arginosuccinic aciduria	Hurler's disease
Chromosomal abnormalities	Hypervalinemia
(Down's syndrome,	I-Cell disease
XXX, XYY, etc.)	Isovaleric acidemia
Citrullinemia	Lesch-Nyhan's syndrome
Cystathioninuria	Maple syrup urine disease
Cystinosis	Metachromatic leucodystrophy
Fabry's disease	Methylmalonic acidemia
Fucosidosis	Niemann-Pick disease
Galactosemia	Refsum's disease
Gangliosidosis	Sandhoff's disease
Gaucher's disease	Sanfilippo disease
Glycogen storage disease	Tay-Sachs disease
(Type 2)	Wolman's disease
Homocystinuria	

TRANSABDOMINAL AMNIOCENTESIS

The technique of transabdominal amniocentesis has become an important tool in the prenatal detection of certain hereditary disorders. As seen in figure 27.2, the technique consists of inserting a hypodermic needle into the uterus of the expectant mother, and withdrawing a small sample of amniotic fluid. Most reports of the application of the technique indicate no, or minimal, maternal or fetal complications. The procedure is typically performed at 16 weeks' gestation, but can be successfully at 14 weeks' gestation. The procedure is precarious earlier than 14 weeks' gestation because of the small amount of amniotic fluid in relation to the size of the fetus.

The cells in the amniotic fluid are then examined both biochemically and chromosomally. The amniotic-fluid cells are of fetal origin, derived mainly from the fetal skin. In the case of Tay-Sachs disease, the amniotic cells can be cultured and analyzed for the presence—or absence—of the essential enzyme. If the biochemical analysis indicates that the fetus has Tay-Sachs disease, the parents can consider a therapeutic abortion. Analysis of the fetal chromosome complement can also detect chromosomal abnormalities. When either parent is a known translocation carrier of Down's syndrome, or where the woman is over 40 years of age, the high risk of bearing a chromosomally abnormal child makes amniocentesis undeniably advisable.

A special problem arises for pregnant women who are carriers of X-linked disorders. Prenatal sex identification has become possible by looking for the presence or absence of the Barr body in amniotic-fluid cells (chapter 25). The presence of a dark spot implies a female fetus; its absence signifies a male, except in the case of an XO chromosomal anomaly (Turner's syndrome). Recent studies suggest the possibility of an accurate means of distinguishing normal and hemophilic cultured amniotic cells. If confirmed, the prenatal diagnosis of hemophilia may become a reality. Since hemophilia is treatable, but presently incurable, many thoughtful critics have pondered whether we are socially and morally prepared to cope with therapeutic abortion of the male fetus diagnosed unequivocally as hemophilic.

Techniques are currently being developed and refined for the visualization of the developing fetus. An instrument, called a *fetoscope*, can be

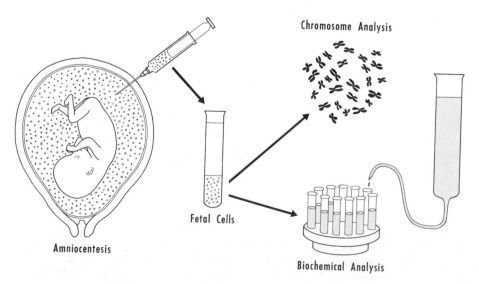

Figure 27.2 Technique of transabdominal amniocentesis. Small samples of amniotic fluid are withdrawn by inserting a needle through the abdomen into the uterine cavity at 14–16 weeks of pregnancy. The amniotic fluid contains fetal cells, which can be grown in tissue culture and analyzed biochemically. Approximately 30 familial biochemical disorders can be detected. Additionally, chromosome analysis of the cultured cells permits the prenatal detection of chromosomal aberrations (Down's syndrome, for example).

Chromosome Analysis

Fetal Cells

Biochemical Analysis

Amniocentesis

inserted into the uterus and the various parts of the fetus can be viewed with an optical system attached to the fetoscope. This technique of *fetoscopy* permits the detection of gross physical abnormalities, such as deformities of the limbs and spina bifida, which are not expressed in the amniotic fluid or amniotic cells. Additionally, the perfection of procedures for withdrawing a sample of fetal blood (from placental blood vessels or directly from the fetus) would allow for the diagnosis of abnormalities of the blood, including sickle-cell anemia and thalassemia.

THERAPEUTIC ABORTION

Different views and attitudes may be expected concerning the early interruption of pregnancy. Human life is sacred, yet the human suffering associated with an unmanageable genetic disorder is so great that the avoidance of the birth of an incurably afflicted infant may be the most acceptable and humane solution. As expressed by Joseph Dancis of New York University, the right to be born is becoming qualified by another right: *the right of the infant to have a reasonable chance of a happy and useful life.* In the years to come, many couples may be able to plan children only on the condition that the expectant mother will be offered screening of the embryo and the termination of pregnancy if the unborn infant is demonstrably abnormal. In essence, the decision to abort a defective fetus may ultimately become the private judgment of the parents. This point of view is disconcerting to those persons who believe that parents should not have the final or sole responsibility of choice for the quality of their offspring.

The fervent hope is that continued research will result in the discovery of an effective treatment or cure for the fatal genetic disorders. However, in the absence of a cure for debilitating disorders, the tragedy of the birth of a hopelessly defective child can be averted by the management of pregnancies: carrier identification, prenatal diagnosis, and abortion of demonstrably affected fetuses.

CASE AGAINST COMPULSORY SCREENING

Any program designed to curtail birth deformities must, if it is to be in accord with human values, be based on the voluntary cooperation of each couple. Genetic counselors act solely in an advisory capacity to those who voluntarily seek counsel. It is generally held that no person should be required to submit himself to a screening test, nor should identification as a carrier be used to influence unduly the carrier's decision concerning procreation. When sickle-cell anemia became acknowledged as a major genetic disease of Negroes in the United States, many states in 1971 enacted sickle-cell screening laws. Since compulsory testing in large programs goes beyond the counselor-couple relation, neither legal nor ethical protection of privacy and confidentiality apply.

Many couples do wish to know whether they are carriers of specific genetic disorders, and to learn what options are open to them. They can then freely choose the path to take. Voluntary learning and individual choice are profoundly more effective than coercive measures.

SUMMARY

Although the phenomenal advances in molecular genetics have erased many of the conceptual barriers to correcting hereditary defects at the gene level, there are still formidable problems involved in the direct manipulation of human genes. A programmed sequence of synthetic DNA cannot easily be inserted in the human chromosome, nor can defective nucleotides of human DNA readily be removed or eliminated in a controlled manner. Only additional research can lead to the development of refined techniques that can make the prospect of gene therapy a reality and a reasonably safe procedure. There are both limitations and hazards associated with present manipulative techniques; we are largely ignorant of the consequences of introducing, for example, viruslike particles with modified DNA sequences into the human cell.

Though at present we cannot favorably and safely program human cells with synthetic genetic information, the occurrences of severe inherited disorders can be reduced by genetic counseling. Genetic counselors act solely in an advisory capacity to those who voluntarily seek counsel. New techniques have enabled the genetic counselor to predict the risks of occurrence and recurrence of inherited disorders with far greater accuracy than in the past. For several recessively determined disorders, there are available sensitive methods of detecting heterozygous carriers. The technique of transabdominal amniocentesis has become an important tool in the prenatal detection of certain hereditary disorders. In the absence of a cure for severe debilitating disorders, the tragedy of the birth of a hopelessly defective child can be averted by the management of pregnancies: carrier identification, prenatal diagnosis, and abortion of demonstrably affected fetuses.

Ethical Probe 19
Right to a Normal Life

Some assert that the right to be born is being qualified by another right: the right of the infant to have a reasonable chance of a happy and useful life. A New Jersey Supreme Court recently declared that "justice requires that the principle be recognized that a child has a legal right to begin life with a sound mind and body."

If this legal principle becomes generally acknowledged or accepted, do children then have the right to sue their parents for knowingly delivering them in a defective state? Can the child logically or legally complain that he or she should never have been born? If the child had not been born, he or she could not possibly be in a position to complain!

Part 3

Man
Origin
and Evolution

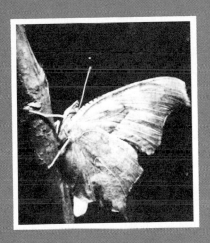

28 Darwinian Scheme of Evolution

Figure 28.1 Charles Darwin at the age of 31 (1840), four years after his famous voyage around the world as an unpaid naturalist aboard H. M. S. *Beagle.* (From a watercolor by George Richmond; courtesy of the American Museum of Natural History.)

The word *evolution* is derived from the Latin *evolutio,* meaning "an unraveling" or "an unfolding." The term suggests gradual change. Broadly speaking, evolution conveys the idea of a continually changing universe as opposed to a universe at a standstill. Organisms throughout life's history have not remained constant but have gradually and endlessly changed. Change is the rule of living things.

The occurrence of organic evolution does not in itself reveal *how* evolution is brought about. An event or phenomenon may be known to us and accepted as true, even though the forces that determine its existence may not be fully understood. Scientists no longer debate that evolution, as an event, has occurred. It is in the *explanation* of evolution that differences of opinion have arisen. One may challenge an interpretation, but to contest the interpretation is not to deny the existence of the event itself. A widespread fallacy is to discredit the truth of evolution by seizing on points of disagreement concerning the mechanism of evolution.

It bears emphasizing that there is a great difference between the *fact* —not theory—that evolution, or organic change, has occurred and the *theories* that have been devised to account for the exact processes involved in evolutionary change. Stated another way, we may be certain that change occurs without knowing very much about how it occurs. For example, we have discussed at length the manifold changes in the development of a fertilized egg through the embryonic stages to a definitive adult state. No scientist today claims to understand the whole formidable mechanism by which development is effected, but no one would argue that development (or change!) does *not* take place.

Charles Robert Darwin (fig. 28.1) was the first person to reach a meaningful understanding of the mechanism of evolution. The concept of *natural selection* that he masterfully put forward in *Origin of Species,* in 1859, remains the keystone of the evolutionary process. The principle of natural selection is now firmly established as the main driving force of evolution. However, the Darwinian thesis has been enriched and refined by recent advances in systematics, ecology, cytology, and paleontology, and above all, in genetics. The modern extension of the great work of Gregor Mendel in heredity has profoundly influenced current thoughts about evolution.

We shall begin our study of evolution by examining the events that compelled Darwin to perceive that evolution was a fact and also permitted him to arrive at a most plausible mechanism.

DARWIN'S FIVE-YEAR VOYAGE
In 1831, Charles Darwin, then 22 years old and fresh from Cambridge University, accepted the post of naturalist, without pay, on board H.M.S.

Beagle, a ship commissioned by the British Admiralty for a surveying voyage around the world. Although Darwin was an indifferent student at Cambridge, he did show an interest in the natural sciences. He was an earnest collector of beetles, enjoyed bird-watching and hunting, and was an amateur geologist.

It took the *Beagle* nearly five years to circle the globe, from 1831 to 1836 (fig. 28.2). When Darwin first embarked on the voyage, he did not dispute the dogma that every species of organism had come into being at the same time and had remained permanently unaltered. He shared the views of his contemporaries that all organisms had been created about 4000 B.C.—more precisely, at 9:00 a.m. on Sunday, October 23, in 4004 B.C., according to the extraordinary pronouncement of Archbishop James Ussher in the 17th century. Darwin had, in fact, studied for the clergy at Cambridge University. But he was to make observations on the *Beagle's* voyage that he could not reconcile with accepted beliefs.

Darwin's quarters on the *Beagle* were cramped, and he took only a few books on board. One of them was the newly published first volume of Charles Lyell's *Principles of Geology,* a parting gift from his Cambridge mentor, John Henslow, professor of botany. Lyell rejected the prevailing belief that the earth's history has been characterized by successive episodes of creation and catastrophic destruction. He argued that the earth's mountains, valleys, rivers, and coastlines were shaped not by Noah's Flood, but by the ordinary action of the rains, the winds, earthquakes, volcanoes, and other natural forces. Darwin was impressed by Lyell's emphasis on the great antiquity of the earth's rocks, and gradually came to perceive that the characteristics of organisms, as well as the face of the earth, could change over a vast span of time.

The living and extinct organisms that Darwin observed in the flat plains of the Argentine pampas and the Galápagos Islands sowed the seeds of Darwin's views on evolution. From old river beds in the Argentine pampas, he dug up bony remains of extinct mammals of large size.

Figure 28.2 Five-year world voyage of H. M. S. *Beagle.* Darwin's observations on this voyage convinced him of the reality of evolution. Particularly impressive to him were the fossil remains of mammals unearthed in the Argentine pampas (see fig. 28.3) and the variety of tortoises and birds in the small group of volcanic islands, the Galápagos Islands (see plates 10 and 18 and fig. 37.3).

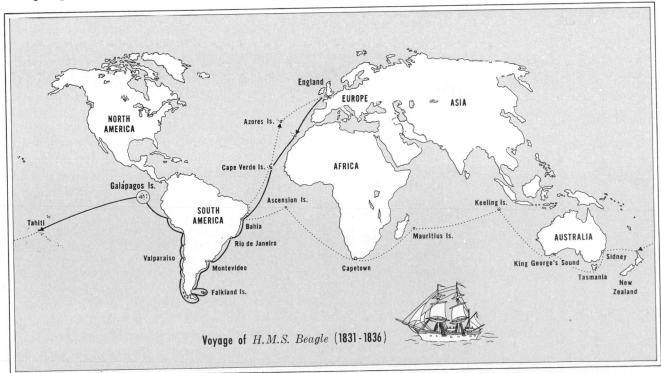

Voyage of *H.M.S. Beagle* (1831-1836)

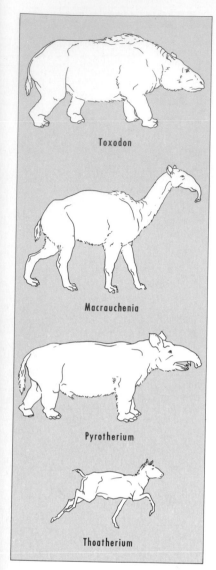

Figure 28.3 Curious hoofed mammals (ungulates) that flourished on the continent of South America some 60 to 70 million years ago, and have long since vanished from the scene. Bones of these great mammals were found by Darwin on the flat treeless plains of Argentina.

Toxodon

Macrauchenia

Pyrotherium

Thoatherium

One fossil finding was the massive *Toxodon*, whose appearance was likened to a hornless rhinoceros or a hippopotamus (fig. 28.3). Another fossil that attracted Darwin's attention was the skeleton of *Macrauchenia*, which he erroneously thought was clearly related to the camel because of the structure of the bones of its long neck. Other remarkable creatures were the huge *Pyrotherium*, resembling an elephant, and the light and graceful single-toed *Thoatherium*, rivaling the horse. The presence of *Thoatherium* testified that a horse had been among the ancient inhabitants of the continent. It was the Spanish settlers who reintroduced the modern horse, *Equus*, to the continent of South America in the 16th century. Darwin marveled that a native horse should have lived and disappeared in South America. This was one of the first indications that species gradually became modified with time, and that not all species survived through the ages.

When Darwin collected the remains of giant armadillolike and slothlike animals on an Argentine pampa, he pondered deeply on the fact that, although they clearly belonged to extinct forms, they were constructed on the same basic plan as the small living armadillos and sloths of the same region. This experience started him thinking of the fossil sequence of a given animal species through the ages and the causes of extinction. He wrote: "This wonderful relationship in the same continent between the dead and the living will, I do not doubt, hereafter throw more light on the appearance of organic beings on our earth, and their disappearance from it, than any other class of facts."

What Darwin had realized was that living species have ancestors. This fact is commonplace now but it was a revelation then. On traveling from the north to the south of South America, Darwin observed that one species was replaced by similar, but slightly different, species. In the southern part of Argentina, Darwin caught a rare species of ostrich that was smaller and differently colored from the more northerly, common American ostrich, *Rhea americanus*. This rare species of bird was later named after him, *Rhea darwini*. It was scarcely imaginable to Darwin that several minor versions of a species would be created separately, one for each locality. It appeared to Darwin that species change not only in time but also with geographical distance. He later wrote: "It was evident that such facts could only be explained on the supposition that species gradually became modified; and the subject haunted me."

In the Galápagos Islands, Darwin's scientific curiosity was sharply prodded by the many distinctive forms of life. The Galápagos consist of an isolated cluster of islands of volcanic origin in the eastern Pacific, on the equator about 600 miles west of Ecuador. One of the most unusual animals is the giant land-dwelling tortoise, which may weigh as much as 500 pounds and attain an age of 200 to 250 years (plate 15). The Spanish word for tortoise, *galápago*, gives the islands their name. Darwin noticed that the tortoises were clearly different from island to island, although the islands were but a few miles apart. In isolation, Darwin reasoned, each population had evolved its own distinctive features. Yet all the island tortoises showed basic resemblances not only to each other but to relatively large tortoises on the adjacent mainland of South America. All this revealed to Darwin that the island tortoises shared a common ancestor with the mainland forms. The same was true of a group of small black birds, known today as *Darwin's finches*. Darwin observed that the finches were different on the various islands, yet they were obviously closely related to each other. Darwin reasoned that the finches were derived from an ancestral stock that originally populated the islands from the mainland.

The principle of divergence, or the origin of several varieties or species from a single ancestral group, was portrayed by Darwin in the form of a *phylogenetic tree*. The tree shown in figure 28.4 was actually drawn by Darwin and appears in his book, *Origin of Species*. The main trunks represent different groups of organisms that have evolved from the common ancestor at the base. The branches represent additional arrays of organisms that have emerged from the main trunks. The diagram might well serve to illustrate the evolution of the higher primates, although it was originally not designed to do so. The base *A* might be the insectivorelike common ancestor, *m* might be the line of evolution of monkeys, *a* might be the line of evolution of the great apes, and *f* might be the line of evolution of man.

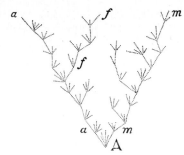

Figure 28.4 Phylogenetic tree drawn by Darwin to show the plan of evolution of a group of organisms. See text for explanation of letters

MECHANISM OF EVOLUTION

When Darwin left England in 1831, he had accepted the established theory that different species had arisen all at once and remained unchanged. On his return, however, in October 1836, he was convinced of the truth of the idea of descent—that all organisms, including man, are modified descendants of previously existing forms of life. Darwin's observations on the nature and distribution of animals during his voyage assured him that evolution, or change, was a fact. We can discern two stages in the development of Darwin's thoughts: the first was the realization of the fact of evolution; the second was an explanation of the process of evolution.

At home, Darwin began to assemble data relevant to the mechanism of evolution. He became intrigued by the extensive domestication of animals and plants brought about by man's conscious efforts. Throughout the ages, man has been a powerful agent in modifying wild species of animals and plants to suit his needs and whims. Through careful breeding programs, man determines which characteristics are to be incorporated or discarded in his domesticated stocks. By conscious *selection*, man has perfected the toylike Shetland pony, the Great Dane, the sleek Arabian race horse, and vast numbers of cultivated crops and ornamental plants.

Many clearly different domestic varieties have evolved from a single species through man's efforts. As an example, we may consider the many varieties of domestic chickens (fig. 28.5), all of which have been derived from a single wild species of red jungle fowl (*Gallus gallus*) present at one time in northern India. The red jungle fowl dates back to 2000 B.C. and has been so modified as to be nonexistent today. The variety of fowls perpetuated by fowl fanciers ranges from the flamboyant ceremonial cocks (the Japanese *Onaga-dori*) to the leghorns, bred especially to deposit spotless eggs. In the plant world, horticulturists have evolved the astonishing range of begonias shown in figure 28.6. The wild begonia, from which most of the modern varieties have been bred, was found in 1865 and still exists today in the Andes.

In the late 1830s, Darwin attended the meetings of animal breeders and intently read their publications. Animal breeders were conversant with the variability in their pet animals, and dwelled on the technique of *artificial selection*. That is to say, the breeders selected and perpetuated those variant types that interested them or seemed useful to them.

Figure 28.5 Evolution under domestication. A variety of domestic chickens have evolved from a single wild species (now extinct) as a result of man's continual practice of artificial selection.

BLACK-TAILED JAPANESE BANTAM

FULL-SIZED AND BANTAM WHITE LEGHORN

SEBASTOPOL GOOSE

CRESTED WHITE DUCK

ONAGA-DORI COCK

FRIZZLED SULTAN ROOSTER

BIRCHEN GAME BANTAM

ARAUCANA

Figure 28.6 Selection in the hands of skilled horticulturists has led to several varieties of the begonia.

WILD BEGONIA

CAMELLIA

CARNATION

MARMORATA

SUNSET

PICOTEE

ROSEBUD

The breeders, however, had only vague notions as to the origin, or inheritance, of the variable traits.

Darwin acknowledged the unlimited variability in organisms, but was never able to explain satisfactorily how a variant trait was inherited. He was unaware of Gregor Mendel's contemporaneous discovery. Rather, Darwin was influenced in his views of inheritance by Jean Baptiste de Lamarck, the French naturalist of the late 1700s and early 1800s. Lamarck had proposed the now famous theory of the *inheritance of acquired characteristics,* wherein bodily changes acquired or developed during one's lifetime are transmitted to the offspring. The concept of Lamarckism has no foundation of factual evidence. We know, for example, that a woman who has enriched her feminine form by injections of silicone does not automatically endow her daughter with a bounteous figure. Circumcision is still necessary in the newborn male despite a rite that has been practiced for well over 4,000 years. It is sufficient to state that the results of countless laboratory experiments testing the possibility of the inheritance of acquired, or environmentally induced, bodily traits have been negative.

Darwin followed Lamarck in assuming that biological variation is chiefly conditioned by direct influences of the environment on the organism. He believed that the changes induced by the environment became inherited. The bodily changes in the parents leave an impression or mark on their germ cells. This view formed the basis of Darwin's *pangenesis* theory (see chapter 17).

Having explained the origin of variation (although incorrectly), Darwin wondered how artificial selection (a term familiar then only to animal breeders) could be carried on in nature. There was no breeder in nature to pick and choose. In 1837, Darwin wrote: "How selection could be applied to organisms living in a state of nature remained a mystery to me." Slightly more than a year later, Darwin found the solution. In his autobiography, Darwin explained: "In October 1838, that is fifteen months after I had begun my systematic enquiry, I happened to read for amusement *Malthus on Population* . . . at once it struck me that under these circumstances favourable variations would tend to be preserved and unfavourable ones destroyed. The result of this would be the formation of new species." The circumstances mentioned by Darwin were those associated with Malthus' thesis that population is necessarily limited by the means of subsistence.

MALTHUS' POPULATION THEORY

The book by the English clergyman Thomas Robert Malthus is recognized as the beginning of modern population theory. His book entitled *Essay on the Principle of Population* was first published anonymously in 1798, when the author was 32 years old. The second edition, published five years later, carried his authorship. There were seven editions of the essay, the last of which was published posthumously in 1872.

Malthus' essay was prepared as a reaction against the doctrine of *mercantilism,* an economic and political school of thought that prevailed in Europe during the 17th and 18th centuries. This was a period characterized by the fanatical desire of national states, particularly England and France, to enhance their wealth and power by encouraging large population growth, both at home and abroad. A large labor force at home was deemed necessary to augment national income, and a large overseas population was considered imperative to aggrandize the power of the state in another quarter of the globe.

The axiom was that a large population is good and a larger one better. Nevertheless, many writers of the day continually noted the mass poverty that was engendered by the accelerated population growth, and the high incidence of vagrancy and crime associated with overcrowding. In his book, Malthus asserted that all plant and animal populations, including human populations, tend to increase at such a rate that their numbers outstrip their resources. Population, when unchecked, doubles once every generation. Each species has the potential to increase at a geometric rate, while its subsistence increases only in arithmetical progression. Thus, the human species increases as the numbers 1, 2, 4, 8, 16, 32, 64, 128, 256, whereas its subsistence increases as the numbers 1, 2, 3, 4, 5, 6, 7, 8, 9.

Among plants and "irrational animals," according to Malthus, the potential increase is actual, and its "superabundant effects are repressed afterwards by want of room or nourishment." Rational man, with his higher faculties, can consider the effects of his potential fertility and curb his natural instinct. The human population can be contained within the limit set by subsistence by the operation of *preventive* and *positive checks*. The principal preventive check is moral restraint, or the deferment of marriage by prospective spouses until they are in a position to support a family. Positive checks include war, pestilence, and famine.

Malthus concluded that the preventive aspect that reduced fertility has on population growth is less influential, or less important, than the positive aspect that heavy mortality brings about. Malthus did not foresee the widespread adoption of the variety of contraceptive methods for family limitation, nor did he envision the great advances that were to be made in agriculture and manufacturing. Although present-day population theories (see chapter 40) have shifted away from Malthusian thinking, the long-established mercantilist idea that unlimited population growth is advantageous and should be actively encouraged still plagues many nations of the world.

DARWIN'S CONCEPT OF NATURAL SELECTION

Malthus' writings provided the germ for Darwin's thesis of natural selection. In essence, Malthus expressed the realistic view that the reproductive capacity of mankind far exceeds the food supply available to nourish an expanding human population. Men compete among themselves for the necessities of life. This unrelenting competition engenders vice, misery, war, and famine. It thus occurred to Darwin that competition exists among all living things. Darwin then envisioned that the "struggle for existence" might be the means by which the well-adapted individuals survive and the ill-adjusted are eliminated. Darwin was the first to realize that perpetual selection existed in nature in the form of *natural selection*. In natural selection, as contrasted to artificial selection, the animal breeder or horticulturist is replaced by the conditions of the environment that prevent the survival and reproduction of certain individuals. The process of natural selection occurs without a conscious plan or purpose. Natural selection was an entirely new concept, and Darwin was its proponent.

It was not until 1844 that Darwin developed his idea of natural selection in an essay, but not for publication. He showed the manuscript to the geologist Charles Lyell, who encouraged him to prepare a book. Darwin still took no steps towards publishing his views. It appears that Darwin might not have prepared his famous volume had not a fellow naturalist in the Dutch East Indies, Alfred Russel Wallace, independently conceived of the idea of natural selection. Wallace had spent many years exploring and collecting in South America and the East Indies. Wallace was also inspired by reading Malthus' essay, and the idea of natural selection came to him in a flash of insight during a sudden fit of malarial fever. In June of 1858, Wallace sent Darwin a brief essay on his views. The essay was entitled *On the Tendencies of Varieties to Depart Indefinitely from the Original Type*. With the receipt of this essay, Darwin was then induced to make a statement of his own with the statement of Wallace.

Wallace's essay and a portion of Darwin's manuscript, each containing remarkably similar views, were read simultaneously before the Linnaean Society in London on July 1, 1858. The joint reading of the papers stirred little interest. Darwin then labored for eight months to compress his voluminous notes into a single book, which he modestly called "only an Abstract." Wallace shares with Darwin the honor of establishing the mechanism by which evolution is brought about, but it was the monumental *Origin of Species*, with its impressive weight of evidence and argument, that left its mark on mankind. The full title of Darwin's treatise was *On the Origin of Species by Means of Natural Selection, or the Preservation of Favoured Races in the Struggle for Life*. The first edition, some 1,500 copies, was sold out on the very day it appeared, November 24, 1859. The book was immediately both acidly attacked and effusively praised. In showing *how* evolution occurs, Darwin convinced skeptics that evolution *does* occur. Today, the *Origin of Species* remains the one book to be read by all serious students of nature.

As a whole, the principle of natural selection stems from three important observations and two deductions that logically follow from them. The first observation is that all living things tend to increase their numbers at a prolific rate. A single oyster may produce as many as 100 million eggs at one spawning; one tropical orchid may form well over 1 million seeds; and a single salmon can deposit 28 million eggs in one season. It is equally apparent (the second observation) that no one group of organisms swarms uncontrollably over the surface of the earth. In fact, the actual size of a given population of any particular organism remains relatively constant over long periods of time. If we accept these readily confirmable observations, the conclusion necessarily follows that not all individuals that are produced in any generation can survive. There is inescapably in nature an intense "struggle for existence."

Darwin's third observation was that individuals in a population are not alike but differ from one another in various features. That all living things vary is indisputable. Those individuals endowed with the most favorable variations, concluded Darwin, would have the best chance of surviving and passing their favorable characteristics on to their progeny. This differential survival, or "survival of the fittest," was termed *natural selection*. It was the British philosopher Herbert Spencer who proposed the expression "survival of the fittest," which Darwin accepted as equivalent to natural selection. Spencer was a fervent supporter of Darwin's views. Spencer suggested that Darwin had discovered not merely the laws of biological evolution but also those governing human societies.

Darwin presents the essence of his concept of natural selection in the introduction to *Origin of Species*, as follows:

As many more individuals of each species are born than can possibly survive; and as, consequently, there is a frequently recurring struggle for existence, it follows that any being, if it vary however slightly in any manner profitable to itself, under the complex and sometimes varying conditions of life, will have a better chance of surviving, and thus be *naturally selected*. From the strong principle of inheritance, any selected variety will tend to propagate its new and modified form.

SURVIVAL OF THE FITTEST

The survival of favorable variants is one facet of the Darwinian concept of natural selection. Equally important is the corollary that unfavorable variants do not survive and multiply. Nature selects against those individuals who are not suited for given conditions of existence. Consequently, natural selection necessarily embraces two aspects, as inseparable as the two faces of the same coin: the negative (elimination of the unfit) and the positive (perpetuation of the fit). In its negative role, natural selection serves as a conservative or stabilizing force, pruning out the aberrant forms from a population.

The superior, or fit, individuals are popularly extolled as those that emerge victoriously in brutal combat. Fitness has often been naively confused with physical, or even athletic, prowess. This glorification is traceable to such seductive catch phrases as the "struggle for existence" and the "survival of the fittest." What does fitness actually signify?

The true gauge of fitness is not merely survival, but the organism's capacity to leave offspring. An individual must survive in order to reproduce, but not all individuals that survive do, or are able to, leave descendants. An individual is biologically unfit if he fails to make a contribution to the next or succeeding generations. He is unfit if he leaves no progeny. He is also unfit if he does produce progeny, none of whom survives to maturity. Fitness of an individual can mean only the extent to which the organism is represented by descendants in succeeding generations. Fitness, therefore, is measured in terms of reproductive effectiveness. Natural selection can thus be thought of as *differential reproduction,* rather than differential survival.

EVOLUTION DEFINED

Any given generation is descended from only a small fraction of the previous generation. It should be evident that the genes transmitted by those individuals who are most successful in reproduction will predominate in the next generation. Because of unequal reproductive capacities of individuals with different hereditary constitutions, the genetic characteristics of a population become altered each successive generation. This is a dynamic process that has occurred in the past, occurs today, and will continue to occur as long as inheritable variation and differing reproductive abilities exist. Under these circumstances, the composition of a population can never remain constant. This, then, is evolution— *changes in the genetic composition of a population with the passage of each generation.*

The outcome of the evolutionary process is adaptation of the organism to its environment. Many of the structural features of organisms are marvels of construction. It is, however, not at all remarkable that organisms possess particular characteristics that appear to be precisely and peculiarly suited to their needs. This is comprehensible because the individuals that leave the most descendants are most often those that are best equipped to cope with the special environmental conditions to which they are exposed. In other words, the more reproductively fit individuals tend to be those that are better adapted to the environment.

Throughout the ages, appropriate adaptive structures have arisen as the result of gradual changes in the hereditary endowment of a population. Admittedly, events that occurred in the past are not amenable to direct observation or experimental verification. There are no living eyewitnesses of very distant events. So, the process of evolution in the past has to be inferred. Nevertheless, we may be confident that the same evolutionary forces we witness in operation today have guided evolution in the past. We shall now direct our attention to an outstanding example in which man has actually observed evolution in progress.

INDUSTRIAL MELANISM

Populations of organisms are continuously subject to natural selection, even though the genetic changes in the population may not be immediately obvious to an observer. Of particular interest, then, would be a situation in nature in which the evolutionary change is not only conspicuous but rapid as well. A striking example of a rapid evolutionary change witnessed by man has been the emergence and predominance in modern times of dark, or *melanic,* varieties of moths in the industrial areas of England and continental Europe. Slightly more than a century ago dark-colored moths were exceptional. The typical moth in the early 1800s had a light color pattern, which blended with the light coloration of tree trunks on which the moths alighted. But then the industrial revolution intervened to alter materially the character of the countryside. As soot and other industrial wastes poured over rural areas, the vegetation became increasingly coated and darkened by black smoke particles. In areas heavily contaminated with soot, the formerly abundant light-colored moths have been supplanted by the darker varieties. This dramatic change in the coloration of moths has been termed *industrial melanism.* At least 70 species of moths in England have been so affected by man's disturbance of the environment.

During the past two decades, several scientists, particularly E. B. Ford and H. B. D. Kettlewell at the University of Oxford, have analyzed the phenomenon of industrial melanism. Kettlewell photographed the light and dark forms of the peppered moth, *Biston betularia,* against two different backgrounds (fig. 28.7). The light variety is concealed and the dark form is clearly visible when the moths rest on a light lichen-coated trunk of an oak tree in an unpolluted rural district. Against a sooty black oak trunk, the light form is conspicuous and the dark form is well camouflaged. Records of the dark form of the peppered moth date back to 1848, when its occurrence was reported at Manchester in England. At that time, the dark form composed less than 1 percent of the population. By 1898, only 50 years later, the dark form had come to dominate the Manchester locale, having attained a remarkably high frequency of occurrence estimated at 95 percent. In fact, the incidence of the melanic type has reached 90 percent or more in most British industrial areas.

The rapid spread of the dark variety of moth is explicitly intelligible. The dark variants are protectively colored in the smoke-polluted industrial regions. They more easily escape detection by predators, namely, insect-eating birds. Actual films taken by Kettlewell and Niko Tinbergen revealed that birds prey on the moths in a selective manner. That is to

Figure 28.7 Dark and light forms of the peppered moth *(Biston betularia)* clinging to a soot blackened oak tree in Birmingham, England *(top)* and to a light, lichen-coated oak tree in an unpolluted region *(bottom).* (Courtesy of Dr. H. B. D. Kettlewell.)

say, predatory birds more often capture the conspicuous light-colored moths in polluted woodlands. In a single day, the numbers of light forms in an industrial area may be pared by as much as one-half by bird predation.

Experimental breeding tests have demonstrated that the two varieties differ principally by a single gene, with the dark variant dominant to the light one. The dominant mutant gene was initially disadvantageous. However, as an indirect consequence of industrialization, the mutant gene became favored by natural selection and spread rapidly in populations in a comparatively short period of time. In unpolluted or nonindustrial areas in western England and northern Scotland, the dominant mutant gene does not confer an advantage on its bearers and the light recessive moth remains the prevalent type.

One of the many impressive features of Kettlewell's studies lies in the unequivocal identification of the selecting agent. Selection, we may recall, has been defined as differential reproduction. The act of selection in itself does not reveal the factors or agencies that enable one genotype to leave more offspring than another. We may demonstrate the existence of selection, yet remain baffled as to the precise causative agent of selection. We might have reasonably suspected that predatory birds were directly responsible for the differential success of the melanic forms in survival and reproduction, but Kettlewell's laboriously accumulated data provided that all-important, often elusive ingredient: *proof*.

If the environment of the peppered moth were to become altered again, then natural selection would be expected to favor the light variety again. In the 1950s, the British Parliament passed the Clean Air Act, which decreed, among other things, that factories must switch from soft high-sulfur (sooty) coal to less smoky fuels (see chapter 46). The enforcement of this enlightened smoke-abatement law has led to a marked reduction in the amount of soot in the atmosphere. In the 1970s, the University of Manchester biologist L. M. Cook and his colleagues reported a small, but significant, increase in the frequency of the light-colored peppered moth in the Manchester area. This is further substantiation of the action and efficacy of natural selection.

SUMMARY

The appearance of Charles Darwin's monumental *Origin of Species* in 1859 ushered in a new understanding of evolution. Darwin's extensive studies resulted in the establishment of the fact of evolution and its explanation by natural selection. The world of life, including man, is a product of continual change. Existing living organisms show affinity with extinct organisms, and have originated by descent with modification from ancestral organisms. Darwin formulated a rational explanation of the causes of evolution. The capacity for reproduction of a given population of organisms far exceeds the numbers than can actually survive. Individuals in a population are not all identical, but show variations in various traits. Natural selection is the executive agency of the environment. Those individuals that possess variant traits in the direction of more effective adaptation to the conditions of the environment survive and become the parents of the next generation. The less fit variants are reduced in frequency or eliminated. The elimination of unfavorable variants can be best described as occurring through failure to leave descendants rather than through sheer extermination. The keystone of natural selection is *differential reproduction*. As a result of unequal reproductive capacities of individuals having different hereditary constitutions, the genetic characteristics of a population become altered each successive generation. Evolution can thus be defined as changes that occur in the genetic composition of a population through time. The outcome of the evolutionary process is increasing adaptation of organisms to their environment.

Ethical Probe 20
Equal Time to Creationism

The legislative body of the State of Tennessee enacted a law, on April 30, 1973, which states in part:

> Any biology textbook used for teaching in the public schools, which expresses an opinion of, or relates to a theory about, origins or creation of man and his world shall be prohibited from being used as a textbook in such a system unless it specifically states that it is a theory as to the origin and creation of man and his world and is not represented to be scientific fact. Any textbook so used in the public education system which expresses an opinion or relates to a theory or theories shall give in the same textbook and under the same subject commensurate attention to, and an equal amount of emphasis on, the origins and creation of man and his world as the same is recorded in other theories, including, but not limited to, the Genesis account in the Bible. . . .

The Tennessee law was subsequently declared unconstitutional, but the State has appealed the ruling. Comparable bills have been considered by the legislatures of other states, but none has thus far been passed.

Do you believe that an "equal amount of emphasis" should be given in college texts or courses to the accounts of creation found in Genesis? Should the account of creation be the King James Version, or the views expressed in Shintoism, Buddhism, Hinduism, and Islam? Should every bible to be used henceforth in all schools also give equal weight, in parallel columns, to an explanation of Darwinism? Can the two conflicting views (evolutionism *vs.* creationism) be reconciled?

29 Genetic Variation and Mutation

Darwin recognized that the process of evolution is inseparably linked to the mechanism of inheritance. But he could not satisfactorily explain how a given trait is transmitted from parent to offspring, nor could he adequately account for the sudden appearance of new traits. Unfortunately, Darwin was unaware of the great discovery in heredity made by a contemporary, the humble Austrian monk Gregor Mendel.

As we have already learned (chapter 18), the mechanism of inheritance in sexually reproducing organisms permits an endless variety of combinations of genes generation after generation. The number of gene combinations that can arise is so immense that no single genetic constitution is ever likely to be exactly duplicated in a person (save in identical twins). Another important feature is that previously concealed recessive genes are brought to light through the mechanism of heredity. A variant trait absent for many generations can suddenly appear without warning. Once a variant character expresses itself, its fate will be determined by the ability of the individual displaying the trait to survive and reproduce in a given environment. In other words, its fate will be determined by natural selection.

The recombination of genes may be compared, on a very modest scale, to the shuffling and dealing of playing cards. One pack of 52 cards can yield a large variety of hands. And, just as in poker a full house is far superior to three of a kind, so in organisms certain combinations of genes confer a greater reproductive advantage to its bearer than other combinations. Natural selection favors the more reproductive genotypes.

The ultimate source of genetic variation is *mutation*. A mutation, an inheritable change in the structure of the gene, is typically a simple alteration in one of the nitrogenous bases of the DNA molecule. The variant traits earlier considered—short vine height in the pea plant, vestigial wings in the fruit fly, and albinism in man—all stem from the action of altered, or mutant, genes. *All differences in the genes of organisms have their origin in mutation.*

CAUSES OF MUTATION

New mutations arise from time to time, and the same mutation may occur repeatedly. It is often quite difficult to distinguish between new mutations and old ones that occurred previously and were carried concealed in ancestors. A recessive mutant gene may remain masked by its normal dominant allele for many generations, and reveal itself for the first time only when two heterozygous carriers of the same mutant gene happen to mate.

Each gene runs the risk of becoming changed to an alternative form. The causes of naturally occurring, or *spontaneous*, mutations are largely unknown. The environment contains a background of inescapable radiation from radioactive elements, cosmic rays, and gamma rays. It is generally conceded that the amount of background radiation is too low to account for all spontaneous mutations. In other words, only a small fraction of spontaneous mutations can be attributed to background radiation.

In 1927, the late Nobel laureate Hermann J. Muller of Indiana University discovered that genes are highly susceptible to the action of X rays. By irradiating fruit flies with X rays, he demonstrated that the process of mutation is enormously speeded up. The production of mutations depends on the total dosage of X rays, measured in units called *roentgens* (R units). The yield of mutations is related to the magnitude of radiation exposure. It has long been held that the mutagenic effect is the same whether the dose is given in a short time or spread over a long period. In other words, low intensities of X rays over long periods of time produce as many mutations as the same dose administered in high intensities in a short period of time. Recent experiments on mice have cast some doubt on this view, for it has been shown that, at least in mice, the mutagenic effect of a single exposure to the germ cells is greater than the effect of the same exposure administered as several smaller doses separated by intervals of time. Nevertheless, there does not appear to be a critical, or *threshold,* dose of roentgens below which there is no effect. In essence, no dose is so low (or safe) that it carries no risk of inducing a mutation. Modern workers stress that any amount of radiation, no matter how little, can cause a mutation. Aside from *point mutations* (alterations of single DNA bases), chromosome breakage and gross chromosomal rearrangements have been observed repeatedly in cells following their exposure to X rays.

At the time of Muller's discovery, no one conceived that within a generation the entire population of man would be exposed to a significant increase of high-energy radiation as a consequence of the creation of the atomic bomb. The additional amount of high-energy radiation already produced by fallout from atomic explosions has undoubtedly increased the mutation rate. Most of the radiation-induced mutations are recessive and most of them are deleterious.

In discussing the hazards of X rays and other ionizing radiations, we must be careful to distinguish between *somatic damage* and *genetic damage.* Injury to the body cells of the exposed individual himself constitutes somatic damage. On the other hand, impairment of the genetic apparatus of the sex cells represents genetic damage. Typically the genetic alterations do not manifest themselves in the individual himself but present a risk for his descendants in the immediate or succeeding generations.

There are documented records of the *somatic* consequences of exposure to the 1945 atomic blasts in Hiroshima and Nagasaki. Among 161 children born of women who were exposed to the atomic bomb while pregnant, 29 were microcephalic (head size considerably below normal) and 11 of these 29 were mentally retarded. As might have been expected, the detrimental effects were most pronounced among the infants of women who were in an early stage of pregnancy (less than 15 weeks' gestation) at the time of exposure. Moreover, most of the women who gave birth to deformed infants were less than 1.3 miles from the center (hypocenter) of the explosion. The adverse effects on the fetus diminished in frequency and severity as the distance from the hypocenter increased. Analyses have also revealed that 15 percent more people died per year in the decade 1950 to 1960 from a sample of 99,393 atomic blast survivors of all ages compared with unexposed control groups. Many of the increased deaths were due to acute leukemia, which substantiates the association found in other studies between whole-body exposure to radiation at high dose levels and the incidence of leukemia.

Estimates of the magnitude of possible *genetic* damages have been of uncertain significance. The statistical methods used are too insensitive to detec' the occurrence of radiation-induced point mutations. There was no greater amount of gene-determined defects in infants born to women who were pregnant at the time of the atomic blasts at Hiroshima and Nagasaki compared with populations that were not exposed. However, it must be stressed that most of the recessive mutations that may have been induced would not be expressed for several generations.

In an effort to measure immediate damaging genetic effects, a possible shift in the sex ratios among children of exposed parents was sought. Theoretically, if fatal, or lethal, mutations are induced on the X chromosome, they will be immediately expressed in the sons of the woman (fig. 29.1). Deaths of male fetuses prior to birth can be indirectly gauged by a decrease in the number of males born to irradiated mothers. An early, limited study on the offspring of Japanese mothers who received a heavy dose of radiation revealed a slight significant reduction of male births, but a later study, based on a larger sample, showed no alteration of the sex ratio.

Although the actual data available have failed to reveal unequivocal genetic effects of radiation, it would be patently fallacious to conclude that atomic radiation has had no mutagenic effect. American and British geneticists estimate that each person currently receives a total dose of 7.8 roentgens to the reproductive cells during the first 30 years of life (table 29.1). Of this amount, 3.1 roentgens are derived from natural background radiation, 4.6 roentgens from various medical uses of ionizing radiation, and an additional 0.1 roentgen from the testing of nuclear weapons. The additional amount of radiation (0.1 roentgen) received

Figure 29.1 Death of male fetuses resulting from radiation-induced lethal mutations in one of the X chromosomes of the mother. Theoretically, the sex ratio (the proportion of males to females) among children conceived after exposure of the expectant mother to radiation should be diminished.

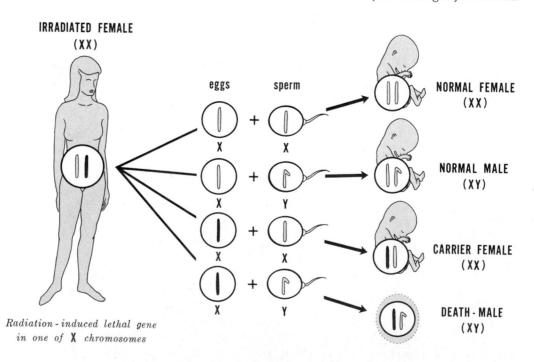

IRRADIATED FEMALE
(XX)

eggs   sperm

NORMAL FEMALE
(XX)

NORMAL MALE
(XY)

CARRIER FEMALE
(XX)

DEATH - MALE
(XY)

*Radiation - induced lethal gene
in one of* **X** *chromosomes*

Table 29.1
Average Exposure to Radiation of
the Gonads (in Roentgen Units, R)

Sources of radiation	
1. Background ————————— 3.1 R per 30 years	
External	
Cosmic rays —0.84	
Terrestrial —1.41	
Atmospheric—0.16	
Internal	
Natural radioactive atoms	
(^{40}K, ^{14}C, etc.)—0.69	
2. Medical uses of radiation ————— 4.6 R	
3. Fallout from exposures ————— 0.1 R	
7.8 R per 30 years	

from nuclear fallout may seem trivial. However, the exposure of our population to 0.1 roentgen is calculated to induce sufficient mutations to result in 3,750 defective offspring among 100 million births.

SPONTANEOUS ORIGIN OF MUTATIONS

Penicillin, sulfonamides (sulfa drugs), streptomycin, and other modern antibiotic agents made front-page headlines when first introduced. These wonder drugs were exceptionally effective against certain disease-producing bacteria, and contributed immeasurably to the saving of human lives in World War II. However, the effectiveness of these drugs has been reduced by the emergence of resistant strains of bacteria. Medical authorities regard the rise of resistant bacteria as the most serious development in the field of infectious diseases over the past decade. Bacteria now pass on their resistance to antibiotics faster than people spread the infectious bacteria.

Mutations have occurred in bacterial populations that enable the mutant bacterial cells to survive in the presence of the drug. Here again we notice that mutations furnish the source of evolutionary changes and that the fate of the mutant gene is governed by selection. In a normal environment, mutations that confer resistance to a drug are rare or undetected. In an environment changed by the addition of a drug, the drug-resistant mutants are favored and supplant the previously normal bacterial strains.

It might be thought that the mutations conferring resistance are actually caused or induced by the drug. This is not the case. Drug-resistant mutations arise in bacterial cells irrespective of the presence or absence of the drug. An experiment devised by the Stanford University geneticist Joshua Lederberg provides evidence that the drug acts as a selecting agent, permitting preexisting mutations to express themselves. As seen in figure 29.2, colonies of bacteria were grown on a streptomycin-free agar medium in a petri plate. When the agar surface of this plate was pressed gently on a piece of sterile velvet, some cells from each bacterial colony clung to the fine fibers of the velvet. The imprinted velvet could now be used to transfer the bacterial colonies onto a second agar plate. More than one replica of the original bacterial growth can be made by pressing several agar plates on the same area of velvet. This ingenious technique has been appropriately called *replica plating.*

In preparing the replicas, Lederberg used agar plates containing streptomycin. On these agar plates, only bacterial colonies resistant to streptomycin grew. In the case depicted in figure 29.2, one colony was resist-

SPONTANEOUS ORIGIN OF MUTATION

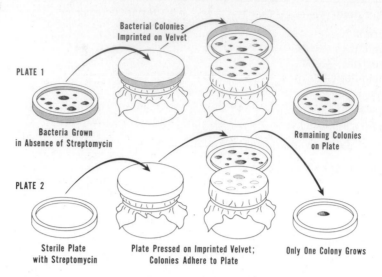

PLATE 1

Bacterial Colonies
Imprinted on Velvet

Bacteria Grown
in Absence of Streptomycin

Remaining Colonies
on Plate

PLATE 2

Sterile Plate
with Streptomycin

Plate Pressed on Imprinted Velvet;
Colonies Adhere to Plate

Only One Colony Grows

ISOLATION AND TEST OF COLONIES

ORIGINAL PLATE 1

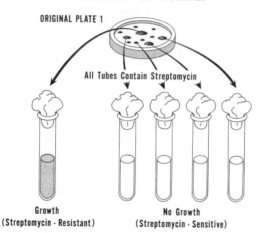

All Tubes Contain Streptomycin

Growth
(Streptomycin - Resistant)

No Growth
(Streptomycin - Sensitive)

ant. Significantly, this one type of resistant colony was found in exactly the same position in all replica plates. If mutations arose in response to exposure to a drug, it is hardly to be expected that mutant bacterial colonies would arise in precisely the same site on each occasion. In other words, a haphazard or random distribution of resistant bacterial colonies, without restraint or attention to location in the agar plate, would be expected if the mutations did not already exist in the original bacterial colonies.

Now, we can return to the original plate with the streptomycin-free medium, as Lederberg did, and test samples of the original bacterial colonies in a test tube for sensitivity or resistance to streptomycin (bottom part of fig. 29.2). It is noteworthy that the bacterial colonies on the original plate had not been previously in contact with the drug. When these original colonies were isolated and tested for resistance to streptomycin, only one colony proved to be resistant. This one colony occupied a position on the original plate identical with the site of the resistant colony on the replica plates. The experiment demonstrated conclusively that the mutation had not been induced by streptomycin but had already been present before exposure to the drug.

FREQUENCY OF MUTATIONS

The rate at which any single gene mutates is generally low, but constant. The average rate of mutation per gene in the fruit fly *Drosophila melanogaster* is thought to be about 1 in 100,000 gametes. In other words, any given gene, on the average, mutates approximately once in every 100,000 sperm cells or egg cells produced. Some genes change more often than others. Some indication of the rate of mutation can be obtained from how often a genetic disorder occurs in the population. In humans, the dominant condition *achondroplasia* (see chapter 19) occurs in 1 child in nearly 12,000 born to *normal* parents. Since the parents are normal, each new case of this dominant disorder must result from a newly mutated gene that originated in either the sperm or the egg cell. Twelve thousand births represent a total contribution of 24,000 gametes. Accordingly, a new mutation for this particular type of dwarfism arises at a rate of 1 in 24,000 gametes, or roughly 4 in 100,000 gametes (4×10^{-5}).

We hasten to point out that the foregoing calculated rate of mutation is undoubtedly too high for a single gene. At the outset, the estimate is unreliable because it is not based on a sufficiently large population sample of the incidence of achondroplasia. In addition, there is evidence that this deformity may result from mutations at two or more different gene loci. Hence, the rate of 4×10^{-5} may actually be the product of two or three separate rates of as many loci. Other methods of gauging mutation rates are also not free of noteworthy complications. In our present state of knowledge, the mutation rate in man for any single gene locus must be considered a very rough estimate. Estimates for mutation rates for certain genetically determined abnormalities in man are shown in table 29.2. It may be noted that the mutation rates are of the order of magnitude of 1 per 100,000 gametes (1×10^{-5}).

OVERALL MUTATION RATE

Although the mutation rate of a single gene may be low, the mutability of the organism as a whole is obviously much higher when we take into account the total complement of genes within an individual. A single unfertilized human egg has been estimated to contain 3 million (3×10^6) nucleotide pairs in its nuclear DNA. This incredible number of nucleotide pairs can carry information corresponding to 2 million genes. This number of genes is overwhelming when one considers the comparatively small number of genetic defects in man with a simple mode of inheritance. We may presume that not all single base changes (point mutations) are detrimental, just as the majority of base substitutions in the hemoglobin genes do not have adverse effects on the hemoglobin molecule (see chapter 20).

Let us suppose that there are 25,000 genes in man in which a point mutation (simple base substitution) can lead to a phenotypically noticeable deviation. The average rate of mutation per gene in man is generally held to be about 1 per 100,000 gametes. If the value of $\frac{1}{100,000}$ mutation per gene (1×10^{-5}) is multiplied by the conservative figure of 25,000 genes (2.5×10^4), then the average number of new mutations per gamete is 0.25. Thus, 1 of every 4 gametes produced by a person would bear a new mutant gene capable of having an adverse effect.

Each offspring is the product of two gametes. Let us envision the random union of sperm cells and egg cells to form zygotes and adopt the aforementioned estimate that 25 percent of all gametes bear one newly mutated detrimental gene. The chance that an egg cell containing a newly

Table 29.2
Estimated Mutation Rates in Man

Disease (Mode of Inheritance)	Brief Description	Mutations per 100,000 Gametes per Generation
Achondroplasia (Dominant)	Short-limbed dwarfism	1.0–4.0*
Albinism (Recessive)	Absence of pigment	2.8
Anhidrotic ectodermal dysplasia (Sex-linked)	Absence of sweat glands	0.1–0.5
Aniridia (Dominant)	Absence of iris	0.3–0.5
Duchenne type of muscular dystrophy (Sex-linked)	Infantile atrophy of muscles	4.3–9.5*
Dystrophia myotonica (Dominant)	Degeneration of muscles, particularly of neck and face	0.8–1.6
Epiloia (Dominant)	Tumors on surface of brain	0.8
Hemophilia A (Sex-linked)	Lack of blood clotting factor	1.3–3.2
Hemophilia B (Christmas disease) (Sex-linked)	Lack of blood clotting factor	0.2–0.3
Huntington's chorea (Dominant)	Progressive deterioration of nervous system	0.2–0.5
Ichthyosis congenita (Recessive)	Dry, scaly skin	1.1
Marfan's syndrome (Dominant)	Long, slender digits; heart anomalies	0.4–0.6
Microphthalmia (Dominant)	Abnormally small eyes	0.5
Osteogenesis imperfecta (Dominant)	Brittle bones	0.7–1.3
Pelger's anomaly (Dominant)	Abnormally shaped nuclei of leucocytes	0.9
Polyposis intestinalis (Dominant)	Multiple intestinal polyps	1.0–3.0
Retinoblastoma (Dominant)	Malignant tumor of eye	0.4–2.3**
Tay-Sachs disease (amaurotic infantile idiocy) (Recessive)	Blindness, paralysis, mental retardation	1.1

* Most likely more than one genetic locus involved.

** Several cases of retinoblastoma are environmentally induced rather than inherited genetically.

Table 29.3
Newly Mutated Genes in Man

1. Average rate of spontaneous mutation per gene: 1 in 100,000 gametes, or 1×10^{-5} (Given gene mutates once in every 100,000 sperm or egg cells)
2. Estimated total number of human genes: 25,000, or 2.5×10^4
3. Average number of new spontaneous mutations per gamete:
    $(1 \times 10^{-5})(2.5 \times 10^4) = 0.25$
    (25% of all gametes produced bear a new mutant gene)
4. Newly mutated gene in egg cell: M'
    Newly mutated gene in sperm cell: M''
    Gamete free of new mutation: N

		Egg	
		0.25 M'	0.75 N
Sperm	0.25 M''	0.0625 $M'M''$	0.1875 $M''N$
	0.75 N	0.1875 $M'N$	0.5625 NN

43.75% $\begin{cases} \text{6.25\% carry two new mutant genes} \\ \text{37.50\% carry one new mutant gene} \end{cases}$
56.25% do not carry any new mutant genes

mutated gene will be fertilized by a sperm cell carrying a new mutant gene is 1 in 16, or 6.25 percent. (Recall that the probability that both coins will show heads when tossed together is the product of the individual probabilities.) Other pertinent calculations are shown in table 29.3. The chance that a zygote will be free of a new mutant gene is 56.25 percent. Finally, the chance that a zygote will carry one newly mutated gene contributed by either the sperm cell or the egg cell is 37.5 percent. It should be apparent that slightly more than 40 percent of all human offspring will contain at least one newly mutated detrimental gene. This assertion, based on crude computations, is in accord with currently accepted notions. As expressed by the English geneticist Harry Harris, every newborn infant, on the average, may be "expected, as a result of a new mutation in either of its parents, to synthesize at least one structurally variant enzyme or protein." Viewed in this manner, the phenomenon of mutation should become very real to us.

It is of interest that of all human pregnancies that continue longer than four or five weeks, 12 to 15 percent end as abortions before the end of the 27th week of pregnancy, and 2 percent terminate as stillbirths. Moreover, the proportion of zygotes lost earlier than the fourth week of pregnancy has been estimated at 10 to 15 percent. Taken all together, 30 percent of all human embryos fail to survive *in utero*. Not all failures are due to detrimental mutations, but the mutation phenomenon undoubtedly is an important contributing factor.

DOUBLING DOSE

It is generally agreed that a doubling of the existing mutation rate would be harmful, though opinions differ on the extent of the damage. The increase in radiation necessary to double the mutation rate is known as the *doubling dose*. There are many uncertainties in the calculation of this doubling dose and estimates of it differ widely. The amount of radiation that would cause the appearance of a number of mutations twice that occurring spontaneously has been placed between 30 and 80 roentgens per generation. We may consider in an elementary way some of the factors that have entered into this estimate. Experiments have shown

Table 29.4
Medical Sources of Radiation

Type of X ray	Dosage to Surface of Body (R Units)
Chest, posterior-anterior, 14 × 17-inch film	0.1
Chest, posterior-anterior, photofluoroscopic X ray	1.0
Lumbar spine, anterior-posterior	1.5*
Lumbar spine, lateral	5.7*
Pelvis	1.1*
Pregnancy, anterior-posterior	3.6*
Pregnancy, lateral	9.0*
Abdomen	1.3*
Cardiac fluoroscopy and catheterization	10–140
Gastrointestinal series (6 films)	4.0*
Gastrointestinal fluoroscopy	10–20/minute*
Gallbladder	0.6*
Extremities (lower)	0.3*
Skull, posterior-anterior	1.3
Full-mouth dental films	5.0

* Only the procedures indicated with an asterisk may result in direct irradiation of the gonads.

that in mice, 1 roentgen of acute exposure produces 25 new mutations in 100,000,000 genes, or 2.5×10^{-7}. If we accept this value for man and work once again with a mere 25,000 genes, then the average number of induced new mutations per gamete in man, after exposure to 1 roentgen, would be $(2.5 \times 10^4) (2.5 \times 10^{-7}) = 0.00625$, or 6.25×10^{-3}. Exposure of the gametes to 40 roentgens would mean that the number of new mutations induced per gamete would be $(6.25 \times 10^{-3}) (40) = 0.25$, or 25 percent. Thus, 1 of every 4 gametes produced by a person irradiated with 40 roentgens would bear a new mutant gene induced solely by irradiation. It should be noted that this value is the same as the value that arises from spontaneous mutations (table 29.3). Taking all factors into account, the National Academy of Sciences has recommended that the total accumulated dose of ionizing radiation to the reproductive cells from conception to age 30 should not be more than 10 roentgens. The amounts of roentgen units delivered to the surface of the body during medical diagnoses and therapy are shown in table 29.4.

HARMFUL NATURE OF MUTATIONS
Most by far of the gene mutations observable today in organisms are changes for the worse. This is not unexpected. Existing populations of organisms are products of a long evolutionary past. The genes that are now normal to the members of a population represent the most favorable mutations selectively accumulated over eons of time. The chance that a new mutant gene will be more advantageous than an already established favorable gene is slim. Nonetheless, if the environment were to change, the previously adverse mutant gene might prove to be beneficial in the new environmental situation. The microscopic water flea, *Daphnia*, thrives at a temperature of 20 °C and cannot survive when the temperature rises to 27 °C. A mutant strain of this water flea is known that requires temperatures between 25 °C and 30 °C and cannot live at 20 °C. Thus, at high temperatures, the mutant gene is essential to the survival of the water fleas. This little episode reveals an important point: *A muta-*

tion that is inferior in the environment in which it arose may be superior in another environment.

Ideally, mutations should arise only when advantageous, and only when needed. This is fanciful thinking. Mutations occur irrespective of their potential usefulness. The mutations responsible for achondroplasia and retinoblastoma in man are certainly not beneficial. But novel inheritable characters repeatedly arise as a consequence of mutation. Only one mutation in several thousands might be advantageous, but this one mutation might be important, if not necessary, to the continued success of a population. The harsh price of evolutionary progress is the continual occurrence and elimination of mutant genes with detrimental effects. Thus, in evolutionary terms, a population, if it is to continue to evolve, depends on the occasional errors that occur in the copying process of its genetic material.

SUMMARY

The ultimate source of genetic variation is mutation—an inheritable change in the structure of the gene. Mutations are the building blocks of evolution. Although the quality or direction of a mutational change is unpredictable, newly mutated genes are usually recessive and deleterious. The chance that a new mutant gene will be more advantageous than an already established favorable gene is slim. Nevertheless, if environmental conditions change, as they inevitably do, the adverse mutant gene (either newly arisen or previously concealed as a recessive in the gene complex) may produce a phenotype that is better adapted to the new environmental situation.

Any given gene in the fruit fly or man mutates spontaneously, on the average, approximately once in every 100,000 sperm cells or egg cells produced. Mutagenic agents, such as X rays and other ionizing radiations, accelerate the frequency with which mutations occur. In considering the hazards of high-energy radiation (such as that produced by fallout from atomic explosion), somatic damage must be distinguished from genetic damage. Whereas somatic, or bodily, damage can be readily demonstrated, the genetic effects are less demonstrable since recessively induced mutations are not immediately expressed in the next generation. The National Academy of Sciences has recommended that the total accumulated dose of ionizing radiation to the human reproductive cells from conception to age 30 should not exceed 10 roentgens.

It can be estimated that 4 out of 10 newborn human infants contain at least one newly mutated harmful recessive gene, as a result of a new mutation in either of its parents. Approximately 30 percent of all human embryos fail to survive in utero. Not all failures are due to detrimental mutations, but the mutation phenomenon is an important contributing factor.

30 Concept of Genetic Equilibrium

One important factor that influences the genetic composition of a population is the system of mating among individuals. The simplest scheme of breeding activity in a population is referred to as *random mating*, wherein any one individual has an equal chance of pairing with any other individual. Random mating does not mean promiscuity; it simply means that those who choose each other as partners in marriage do not do so on the basis of similarity or dissimilarity in a given trait or gene. The absence of preferential mating in a population has interesting consequences. We shall examine how random mating in humans affects the incidence of a certain disorder known as *acatalasia*.

Acatalasia is a rare condition first recognized among the Japanese and inherited as an autosomal recessive trait. The disorder was discovered in patients with ulcerating lesions of the oral cavity, where the addition of hydrogen peroxide caused the tissues to turn black. Normally, individuals contain the enzyme catalase, which degrades hydrogen peroxide. Individuals suffering from this condition, however, lack catalase and accordingly hydrogen peroxide is free to exert its destructive effects.

In Japan, the frequency of individuals homozygous for the recessive gene is 2 per 100,000, or 0.00002. With a population of 88 million persons, the expectation would be 1,760 cases of acatalasia. Since people are usually unaware of their reaction to hydrogen peroxide, probably no one selects his mate according to whether he or she experiences a reaction to hydrogen peroxide. Now, if marriages in Japan occur at random, will the incidence of acatalasia decrease, increase, or remain the same in the next or subsequent generations?

It is the purpose of this chapter to show that the same proportion of acatalasia sufferers will persist indefinitely, as long as persons marry without regard to their ability or inability to degrade hydrogen peroxide. Moreover, we can predict that the frequency of heterozygous carriers is 0.009; hence, there are 792,000 carriers in a population of 88 million. We shall learn how the population geneticist arrives at this value.

MENDELIAN INHERITANCE

We may designate the normal gene as *A,* and the recessive gene for acatalasia as *a*. Thus, the three possible genotypes would be *AA* (normal), *Aa* (normal but a carrier), and *aa* (acatalasia). The kinds and proportions of offspring that can arise from matings involving the three genotypes are shown in table 30.1. Six different types of matings are possible. The mating *AA* × *AA* gives rise solely to normal homozygous offspring, *AA*. Two kinds of progeny, *AA* and *Aa* in equal proportions, result from the cross of a homozygous normal parent *(AA)* and a heterozygous parent *(Aa)*. The mating of two heterozygotes *(Aa* × *Aa)* produces *AA*, *Aa*, and

Table 30.1
Mendelian Laws for a Pair of Autosomal Genes

Parents (Mating Types)	Probability of Offspring		
	AA	*Aa*	*aa*
AA × *AA*	1.00	—	—
AA × *Aa*	0.50	0.50	—
AA × *aa*	—	1.00	—
Aa × *Aa*	0.25	0.50	0.25
Aa × *aa*	—	0.50	0.50
aa × *aa*	—	—	1.00

aa offspring in the classical Mendelian ratio of 1:2:1. Only heterozygous offspring (*Aa*) emerge from the mating *AA* × *aa*. Both heterozygous (*Aa*) and recessive (*aa*) progeny, in equal numbers, arise from the cross of a heterozygous parent (*Aa*) and a recessive parent (*aa*). Lastly, two recessive parents (*aa* × *aa*) produce only recessive offspring (*aa*).

These principles of Mendelian inheritance merely inform us that certain kinds of offspring can be expected from certain types of matings. If we are interested in following a population from one generation to the next, then additional factors enter the scene.

RANDOM MATING

We know that a certain percentage of the individuals in Japan are afflicted with acatalasia. Let us suppose that random mating prevails. For ease of presentation, the size of the population is reduced to 48 males and 48 females. Moreover, for each sex, we may simplify the mathematical computations by assuming that 36 are normal (12 *AA* and 24 *Aa*) and 12 have acatalasia (*aa*). Accordingly, one-quarter of the individuals of each sex are homozygous dominant, one-half are heterozygous, and one-quarter are recessive. Now, if mating occurs at random, will the incidence of acatalasia (now 25 percent) decrease, increase, or remain the same in the next generation?

The problem may be approached by determining how often a given type of mating occurs. Here we will bring into play, once again, a cardinal rule of probability: *The chance that two independent events will occur together is the product of their chances of occurring separately.* The proportion of *AA* males in our arbitrary population is ¼. We may also say that the chance that a male is *AA* is ¼. Likewise the probability that a female is *AA* is ¼. Consequently, the chance that an *AA* male will occur together, or mate, with an *AA* female is 1/16 (¼ × ¼). The computations for all types of matings can be facilitated by coupling the males and females in a multiplication table, as shown in table 30.2.

Table 30.2 shows that there are nine combinations of marriages, and that some types occur more frequently than others. It may be helpful to express the frequencies in terms of actual numbers. Thus, for a total of 48 marriages, 3 (= 1/16 × 48) would be *AA* ♀ × *AA* ♂, 6 (= 2/16 × 48) would be *AA* ♀ × *Aa* ♂, 12 (= 4/16 × 48) would be *Aa* ♀ × *Aa* ♂, and so forth. The numbers of each type of marriage are listed in table 30.3.

Our next step is to ascertain the kinds and proportions of offspring from each marriage. We shall assume that each mated pair yields the same number of offspring—for simplicity, four offspring. We also take for granted that the genotypes of the four progeny from each mating are those that are theoretically possible in Mendelian inheritance (see table 28.1). For example, if the parents are *Aa* × *Aa*, their offspring will be 1 *AA*, 2 *Aa*, and 1 *aa*. In another instance, if the parents are *AA* × *Aa*, then the offspring will be 2 *AA* and 2 *Aa*. The outcome of all crosses is shown in table 30.3. It is important to note that the actual numbers of

Table 30.2

Female (♀)	Male (♂)		
	¼ *AA*	2/4 *Aa*	¼ *aa*
¼ *AA*	1/16 *AA* × *AA*	2/16 *AA* × *Aa*	1/16 *AA* × *aa*
2/4 *Aa*	2/16 *Aa* × *AA*	4/16 *Aa* × *Aa*	2/16 *Aa* × *aa*
¼ *aa*	1/16 *aa* × *AA*	2/16 *aa* × *Aa*	1/16 *aa* × *aa*

Table 30.3

Type of Mating (Female × Male)	Number of Each Type of Mating*	Number of Offspring		
		AA	Aa	aa
AA × AA	3	12		
AA × Aa	6	12	12	
AA × aa	3		12	
Aa × AA	6	12	12	
Aa × Aa	12	12	24	12
Aa × aa	6		12	12
aa × AA	3		12	
aa × Aa	6		12	12
aa × aa	3			12
		48 (25%)	96 (50%)	48 (25%)

* Based on a total of 48 matings.

offspring recorded in table 30.3 are related to the frequencies of the different types of matings. For example, the mating of an AA female with an Aa male occurs six times; hence, the numbers of offspring are increased sixfold (from 2 each of AA and Aa to 12 each of the two genotypes).

An examination of table 30.3 reveals that the kinds and proportions of individuals in the new generation of offspring are exactly the same as in the parental generation. There has been no change in the ratio of normal individuals (75 percent AA and Aa) to persons with acatalasia (25 percent aa). The proportions of phenotypes (and genotypes) will remain the same in all successive generations, provided that the system of random mating is continued.

GENE FREQUENCIES

There is a less tedious method of arriving at the same conclusion. Rather than figure out all the matings that can possibly occur, we need only to consider the genes that are transmitted by the eggs and sperm of the parents. Let us assume that each parent produces only 10 gametes. The 12 homozygous dominant males (AA) of our arbitrary initial population can contribute 120 sperm cells to the next generation, each sperm containing one A. The 24 heterozygous males (Aa) can transmit 240 gametes, 120 of them with A and 120 with a. The remaining 12 recessive males (aa) can furnish 120 gametes, each with a. The total pool of genes provided by all males will be 240 A and 240 a, or 50 percent of each kind. Expressed as a decimal fraction, the frequency of gene A is 0.5; of a, 0.5.

Since the females in our population have the same genetic constitutions as the males, their gametic contribution to the next generation will also be 0.5 A and 0.5 a. The eggs and sperm can now be united at random in a genetical checkerboard (fig. 30.1).

It should be evident from figure 30.1 that the distribution of genotypes among the offspring is 0.25 AA : 0.50 Aa : 0.25 aa. The random union of eggs and sperm yields the same result as the random mating of parents (refer to table 30.3). Thus, using two different approaches, we have answered the question posed in the introductory remarks to this chapter. *If persons afflicted with acatalasia are equally as fertile as the normal individuals and leave equal numbers of offspring each generation, then*

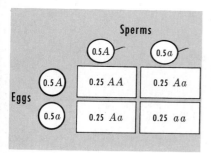

Figure 30.1 Random union of eggs and sperm yields the same outcome as the random mating of parents (refer to table 30.3).

the anomalous condition of acatalasia will persist in the population with the same frequency from one generation to the next.

HARDY-WEINBERG LAW

A population in which the proportions of genotypes remain unchanged from generation to generation is said to be in *equilibrium*. The fact that a system of random mating leads to a condition of equilibrium was brought to light independently by Godfrey H. Hardy and Wilhelm Weinberg, and has come to be widely known as the *Hardy-Weinberg law*. This law states that the proportions of *AA, Aa,* and *aa* genotypes, as well as the proportions of *A* and *a* genes, will remain constant from generation to generation provided that the bearers of the three genotypes have equal opportunities of producing offspring in a large, randomly mating population.

The preceding statement can be translated into a simple mathematical expression. If we let p be the frequency of the gene *A* in the population, and q equal the frequency of its allele, *a*, then the distribution of the genotypes in the next generation will be p^2 *AA*:2pq *Aa*:q^2 *aa*. This relationship may be verified by the use, once again, of a genetical checkerboard (fig. 30.2). Mathematically inclined readers will recognize that p^2:2pq:q^2 is the algebraic expansion of the binomial $(p + q)^2$. The frequencies of the three genotypes (0.25 *AA*:0.50 *Aa*:0.25 *aa*) under the system of random mating is the expanded binomial $(0.5 + 0.5)^2$.

We may consider another arbitrary population in the equilibrium state. Suppose that the population consists of 16 *AA*, 48 *Aa*, and 36 *aa* individuals. We may assume, as before, that 10 gametes are contributed by each individual to the next generation. All the gametes (numerically, 160) transmitted by the 16 *AA* parents will contain the *A* gene, and half the gametes (240) provided by the *Aa* parents will bear the *A* gene. Thus, of the total of 1,000 gametes, 400 will carry the *A* gene. Accordingly, the frequency of gene *A* is 0.4 (designated p). In like manner, it can be shown that the frequency of gene *a* is 0.6 (q). Substituting the numerical values for p and q in the Hardy-Weinberg formula, we have:

$$p^2 \, AA : pq \, Aa : q^2 \, aa$$
$$(0.4)^2 \, AA : 2(0.4)\,(0.6) \, Aa : (0.6)^2 \, aa$$
$$0.16 \, AA : 0.48 \, Aa : 0.36 \, aa$$

Hence, the proportions of the three genotypes are the same as those of the preceding generation.

IMPLICATIONS

The Hardy-Weinberg law is entirely theoretical. The set of underlying assumptions that are made can scarcely be fulfilled in any natural population. We implicitly assume the absence of recurring mutations, the absence of any degree of preferential matings, the absence of differential mortality or fertility, the absence of immigration or emigration of individuals, and the absence of fluctuations in gene frequencies due to sheer chance. But therein lies the significance of the Hardy-Weinberg law. In revealing the conditions under which evolutionary change cannot occur, it brings to light the forces that could operate to cause a change in the genetic composition of a population. The Hardy-Weinberg law thus depicts a static situation. There are several factors or forces that pro-

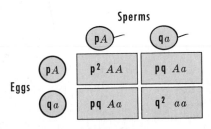

Figure 30.2 The distribution of genotypes in the next generation is p^2AA:2pq *Aa*:q^2aa (Hardy-Weinberg formula).

foundly modify the gene frequencies in natural populations. In the next chapter, we shall consider how one of the forces, natural selection, or differential reproduction, can lead to dynamic evolutionary changes.

In the introductory remarks, we made certain assumptions concerning the condition of acatalasia. We assumed that all cases of acatalasia are due to a gene change at the same locus, that there is an essentially uniform distribution of the gene throughout Japan, and that there is random mating. We can now point out that these assumptions are invalid. Although initially thought to be a discrete clinical and genetic entity, acatalasia appears to exist in several variant forms. There are grounds for suspecting three different mutant alleles of acatalasia among the Japanese. Moreover, the distribution of acatalasia in Japan is not uniform but varies widely in different regions. Finally, the marriages have not been consummated at random. In 17 pedigrees of acatalasia, consanguinity of some degree has been recorded; 10 of the 17 marriages involved first cousins.

In essence, the Hardy-Weinberg equilibrium is not applicable to acatalasia. Yet, when a genetic entity is first uncovered, the use of the Hardy-Weinberg equilibrium permits first approximations of the gene frequency of the disorder itself as well as of the frequency of the heterozygous carriers. We shall now examine how the frequency of heterozygous carriers can be estimated.

ESTIMATING THE FREQUENCY OF HETEROZYGOTES

It comes as a surprise to many to discover that the heterozygotes of a rare recessive abnormality are not comparatively rare but rather common. Recessive albinism may be used as an illustration. The frequency of albinos is about $\frac{1}{20,000}$ in human populations. When the frequency of the homozygous recessive (q^2) is known, the frequency of the recessive gene (q) can be calculated, as follows:

$$q^2 = \frac{1}{20,000} = 0.00005$$
$$q = \sqrt{0.00005} = 0.007$$
$$= \text{about } \frac{1}{140} \text{ (frequency of recessive gene)}$$

The heterozygotes are represented by $2pq$ in the Hardy-Weinberg formula. Accordingly, the frequency of heterozygous carriers of albinism can be calculated as follows:

$$q = 0.007$$
$$p = 1 - 0.007 = 0.993$$
$$\therefore 2pq = 2 \, (0.993 \times 0.007) = 0.014$$
$$= \text{about } \frac{1}{70} \text{ (frequency of heterozygote)}$$

Thus, although 1 person in 20,000 is an albino (recessive homozygote), about 1 person in 70 is a heterozygous carrier. There are 280 times as many carriers as affected individuals! It may be further noted from these calculations that the proportion of heterozygous individuals is approximately twice the frequency of the recessive gene.

Let us return to the consideration of acatalasia, the genetic disorder mentioned in the introductory remarks of this chapter. The frequency of heterozygous carriers of acatalasia can be determined readily. Since $q^2 = 0.00002$, q equals approximately 0.0045. It is sufficiently accurate to double the value of q to obtain the frequency of the heterozygotes, or 0.009 (1 person in 110). Once again, a rare disorder such as acatalasia is accompanied by a high incidence of carriers. In fact, when the frequency of the recessive gene is extremely low, nearly all the recessive genes are in the heterozygous state. This, you may recall, was an important consideration in our discussion of genetic counseling in chapter 27. The reader may now comprehend how we arrived at the frequencies of heterozygous carriers listed in table 27.1 of that chapter. It bears emphasizing that the rarity of a recessive disorder does not signify a comparable rarity of heterozygous carriers.

SUMMARY

A recessive trait is not destined to become rare simply because it happens to be governed by a recessive gene. A recessive trait will persist in the population with the same frequency indefinitely in successive generations if random mating prevails provided that the individuals affected with the recessive trait are equally as fertile as normal individuals and leave equal numbers of offspring. The mathematical theorem describing this stable state was formulated independently in 1908 by Hardy and Weinberg. The Hardy-Weinberg law states that the proportions of AA, Aa, and aa genotypes, and also the proportions of A and a genes, will remain constant from generation to generation provided that the bearers of the three genotypes have equal opportunities of producing offspring in a large, randomly mating population.

The population assumed under the Hardy-Weinberg law is a static population in that it does not change genetically. Ideal assumptions are made that can scarcely be fulfilled in a real, or natural, population. Nonetheless, the Hardy-Weinberg law represents the cornerstone of population genetic studies, since deviations from the Hardy-Weinberg expectations direct attention to the evolutionary forces that upset the theoretical expectations. Evolution can be plausibly defined as a disturbance of, or shift in, the Hardy-Weinberg equilibrium.

The Hardy-Weinberg formula may be applied to large populations to obtain an estimate of the proportion of heterozygous carriers in relation to the frequency of affected recessive individuals. When the frequency of a recessive gene is extremely low, nearly all the recessive genes are in the heterozygous state. The rarity of a recessive disorder does not signify a comparable rarity of heterozygous carriers.

Concept of Selection

We have already emphasized that detrimental recessive genes are harbored mostly in the heterozygous state. Moreover, the heterozygous carriers *(Aa)* generally cannot be distinguished from the normal homozygotes, or noncarriers *(AA)*. These facts militate against any scheme aimed at completely eradicating an undesirable genetic trait in a population.

Some of us might presume that a deleterious mutant gene can be completely eliminated in the face of the severest form of selection. Yet our knowledge of the properties of mutation and selection informs us that this is *not* the case. We shall direct our attention to this statement and its implications.

SELECTION AGAINST RECESSIVE DEFECTS

In our consideration of the Hardy-Weinberg law in the preceding chapter, we assumed that the recessive homozygotes *(aa)* were as reproductively fit as their normal kin *(AA* and *Aa)* and left equal numbers of living offspring each generation. Now, however, let us presume that all homozygous recessive individuals fail to reach sexual maturity generation after generation. Will the incidence of the recessive trait decline to a vanishing point?

We may start with the same distribution of individuals in the initial generation previously postulated in chapter 30, namely, 24 *AA*, 48 *Aa*, and 24 *aa*, with the sexes equally represented. Since the recessive homozygotes *(aa)* are now unable to participate in breeding, the parents of the next generation comprise only the 24 *AA* and 48 *Aa* individuals. The heterozygous types are twice as numerous as the homozygous dominants; accordingly, two-thirds of the total breeding members of the population are *Aa* and one-third are *AA*. We may once again employ a genetical checkerboard (table 31.1) to ascertain the different types of matings and their relative frequencies.

The frequencies of the different matings shown in table 31.1 may be expressed as whole numbers rather than fractions. In a total of 36 matings, 4 (= ⅑ × 36) would be *AA* ♀ × *AA* ♂, 8 (= ²⁄₉ × 36) would be *AA* ♀ × *Aa* ♂, 8 (= ²⁄₉ × 36) would be *Aa* ♀ × *AA* ♂, and 16 (= ⁴⁄₉

Table 31.1

Female	Male (♂)	
(♀)	⅓ *AA*	⅔ *Aa*
⅓ *AA*	⅑ *AA* × *AA*	²⁄₉ *AA* × *Aa*
⅔ *Aa*	²⁄₉ *Aa* × *AA*	⁴⁄₉ *Aa* × *Aa*

$\times$ 36) would be Aa ♀ $\times$ Aa ♂. These numbers are recorded in table 31.2.

Our next task is to determine the outcome of each type of cross. We shall assume that each mated pair contributes an equal number of progeny to the next generation (say, four offspring). As revealed in table 31.2, the offspring are distributed according to Mendelian ratios, and the actual numbers of offspring reflect the frequencies of the different kinds of matings. For example, a single AA ♀ $\times$ Aa ♂ mating yields 4 off-spring in the Mendelian ratio of 2 AA:2 Aa. There are, however, 8 matings of this kind; the numbers of offspring are correspondingly increased to 16 AA and 16 Aa.

Even though all the recessive individuals fail to reproduce, the detrimental recessive genes are still transmitted to the first generation. The emergence of recessive homozygotes in the first generation stems from the matings of two heterozygous persons. However, as seen from table 31.2, the frequency of the recessive homozygotes (aa) decreases from 25 percent to 11.11 percent in a single generation.

The effects of complete selection against the recessive individuals in subsequent generations can be determined by the foregoing method of calculation, but the lengthy tabulations tend to become wearisome. At this point we may apply a formula that will enable us to establish in a few steps the frequency of the recessive gene after any number of generations of complete selection. This formula is:

$$q_n = \frac{q_0}{1 + nq_0}$$

In this expression, q_0 represents the initial or original frequency of the recessive gene, and q_n is the frequency after n generations. Thus, with the initial value $q_0 = 0.5$, the frequency of the recessive gene after two generations $(n - 2)$ will be:

$$q_2 = \frac{q_0}{1 + 2q_0} = \frac{0.5}{1 + 2(0.5)} = \frac{0.5}{2.0} = 0.25$$

If the frequency of the recessive gene itself (a) is q, then the frequency of the recessive individual (aa) is q^2. Accordingly, the frequency of the recessive homozygote is $(0.25)^2$, or 0.0625 (6.25 percent). In the second generation, therefore, the incidence of the recessive trait drops to 6.25 percent.

Table 31.2

Type of Mating (Female $\times$ Male)	Number of Each Type of Mating*	Number of Offspring		
		AA	Aa	aa
$AA \times AA$	4	16		
$AA \times Aa$	8	16	16	
$Aa \times AA$	8	16	16	
$Aa \times Aa$	16	16	32	16
		64	64	16
		(44.44%)	(44.44%)	(11.11%)

* Based on a total of 36 matings.

Generations	Gene Frequency	Recessive Homozygotes %	Heterozygotes %	Dominant Homozygotes %
0	0.500	25.00	50.00	25.00
1	0.333	11.11	44.44	44.44
2	0.250	6.25	37.50	56.25
3	0.200	4.00	32.00	64.00
4	0.167	2.78	27.78	69.44
8	0.100	1.00	18.00	81.00
10	0.083	0.69	15.28	84.03
20	0.045	0.20	8.68	91.12
30	0.031	0.10	6.05	93.85
40	0.024	0.06	4.64	95.30
50	0.020	0.04	3.77	96.19
100	0.010	0.01	1.94	98.05

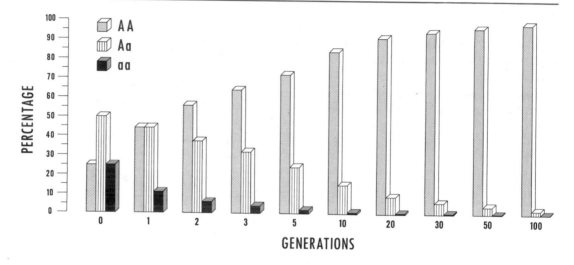

Figure 31.1 Effects of complete selection against recessive homozygotes (aa) occurring initially (0 generation) at a frequency of 25 percent. The effectiveness of selection in reducing the incidence of the recessive trait decreases with successive generations. The frequency of recessive homozygotes drops markedly from 25 percent to 6.25 percent in 2 generations. However, 8 generations are required to reduce the incidence of the recessive trait to 1.0 percent, 30 generations are needed to achieve a reduction of 0.1 percent, and approximately 100 generations to depress the frequency to 0.01 percent (see table 31.3).

If we perform comparable calculations through several generations, we emerge with a comprehensive picture that is tabulated in table 31.3 and portrayed in figure 31.1. In the third generation, the frequency of the recessive homozygote declines to 4.0 percent. Progress in terms of the elimination of the recessive trait is initially rapid, but becomes slower as selection is continued over many successive generations. About 20 generations are required to depress the incidence of the recessive trait to 2 in 1,000 individuals (0.20 percent). Ten additional generations are necessary to effect a reduction to 1 in 1,000 individuals (0.10 percent). Thus, as a recessive trait becomes rarer, selection against it becomes less effective. The reason is quite simple: Only very few recessive homozygotes are exposed to the action of selection. The now rare recessive gene (a) is carried mainly by heterozygous individuals (Aa) where it is sheltered from selection by its normal dominant partner (A).

When the frequency of an abnormal recessive gene becomes very low, most affected offspring (aa) will come from matings of two heterozygous carriers (Aa). For example, in the human population, the vast majority of newly arising albino individuals (aa) in a given generation (more than 99 percent of them) will come from normally pigmented heterozygous parents. There is no question that detrimental recessive genes in a population are harbored mostly in the heterozygous state.

INTERPLAY OF MUTATION AND SELECTION

Theoretically, if complete selection against the recessive homozygote were to continue for several hundred more generations, then the abnormal recessive gene would be completely eliminated and the population would consist uniformly of normal homozygotes (*AA*). But, *in reality,* the steadily diminishing supply of abnormal recessive genes is continually being replenished by recurrent mutations from normal (*A*) to abnormal (*a*). Mutations from *A* to *a*, which inevitably occur from time to time, were not taken into account in our determinations. Mutations, of course, cannot be ignored.

All genes undergo mutation at some definable rate. If a certain proportion of *A* genes are converted into *a* alleles in each generation, then the population will at all times carry a certain amount of the recessive mutant gene (*a*) despite selection against it. Without any sophisticated calculations, it can be shown that a point will be reached at which the number of the abnormal recessive genes eliminated by selection just balances the number of the same recessive gene produced by mutation. An analogy shown in figure 31.2A will help in visualizing this circumstance. The water level in the beaker remains constant when the rate at which water enters the opening of the beaker equals the rate at which it leaves the hole in the side of the beaker. In other words, a state of equilibrium is reached when the rate at which the recessive gene is replenished by mutation equals the rate at which it is lost by selection. It should be clear that it is not mutation alone that governs the incidence of deleterious recessives in a population. The generally low frequency of harmful recessive genes stems from the dual action of mutation and selection. The mutation process tends to increase the number of detrimental recessives; the selection mechanism is the counteracting agent. Mathematically, the frequency of the deleterious recessive gene at equilibrium can be calculated by the following formula, where q represents the frequency of the recessive gene and u represents the mutation of that gene:

$$q = \sqrt{u}$$

What would be the consequences of an increase in the mutation rate? Man today lives in an environment in which high-energy radiation promotes a higher incidence of mutations. We may return to our analogy (fig. 31.2B). The increased rate of mutation may be envisioned as an increased input of water. The water level in the beaker will rise and water will escape more rapidly through the hole in the side of the beaker. Similarly, mutant genes will be found more frequently in a population, and they will be eliminated at a faster rate from the population. As before, a balance will be restored eventually between mutation and selection, but now the population has a larger store of deleterious genes and a larger number of defective individuals arising each generation.

The supply of defective genes in the human population has already increased through the greater medical control of recessive disorders. The outstanding advances in modern medicine have served to prolong the lives of genetically defective individuals who might otherwise not have survived to reproductive age. This may be compared with partially plugging the hole in the side of the beaker (fig. 31.2C). The water level in the beaker will obviously rise, as will the amount of deleterious genes in a population. Evidently, the price of our humanitarian principles is the enlargement of our pool of defective genes.

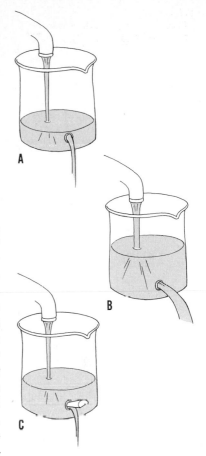

Figure 31.2 Interplay of detrimental mutant genes (water from faucet) and their elimination by selection (water escaping through hole) in a population (beaker) containing a pool of the harmful genes (water in beaker). *(A)* State of genetic equilibrium (constant water level in beaker) when the rates at which water enters and leaves the beaker are equal. *(B)* Effect of an increase in mutation rate (increased flow of faucet water) as might be expected from the continued widespread use of ionizing radiation. A new equilibrium (new constant water level) is established, but the frequency of the detrimental gene in the population is higher (higher water level in beaker). *(C)* Effect of reducing selection pressure (decreased exit of water) as a consequence of improving the reproductive fitness of genetically defective individuals by modern medical practices. Mutation rate (inflow of water) is the same as in *A*. The inevitable result is a greater incidence of the harmful mutant gene in the population (higher level of water in the beaker).

PARTIAL SELECTION

We have treated in discussion the severest form of selection against recessive individuals. Complete, or 100 percent, selection against a recessive homozygote is often termed *lethal* selection, and the mutant gene is designated as a *lethal* gene. A lethal gene does not necessarily result in the death of the individual, but does effectively prevent him from reproducing or leaving offspring. Not all mutant genes are lethal; in fact, the majority of them have less drastic effects on viability or fertility. A mildly handicapped recessive homozygote may reproduce but may be inferior in fertility to the normal individual. When the reproductive capacity of the recessive homozygote is only half as great as the normal type, he is said to be semisterile and the mutant gene is classified as *semilethal*. A *subvital* recessive gene is one which, in double dose, impairs an individual to the extent that his reproductive fitness is less than 100 percent but more than 50 percent of normal proficiency.

The action of selection varies correspondingly with the degree of detrimental effect of the recessive gene. Figure 31.3 shows the results of different intensities of selection in a population that initially contains 1.0 percent recessive homozygotes. With complete (lethal) selection, a reduction in the incidence of the recessive trait from 1.0 percent to 0.25 percent is accomplished in 10 generations. Twenty generations of complete selection reduces the incidence to 0.11 percent. When the recessive gene is semilethal (50 percent selection), 20 generations, or twice as many generations as under complete selection, are required to depress the frequency of the recessive homozygote to about 0.25 percent. Selection against a subvital gene (for example, 10 percent selection) results in a considerably slower rate of elimination of the recessive homozygotes. When the homozygote is at a very slight reproductive disadvantage (1.0 percent selection), only a small decline of 0.03 percent (from 1.0 percent to 0.97 percent) occurs after 20 generations. It is evident that mildly harmful recessive genes may remain in a population for a long time.

These considerations are shown in table 31.4 also. Here, the results are expressed in terms of the value *s*, or the *selection coefficient*. The selec-

Figure 31.3 Different intensities of selection against recessive homozygotes occurring initially (0 generation) at a frequency of 1.0 percent. The elimination of recessive individuals per generation proceeds at a slower pace as the strength of selection decreases.

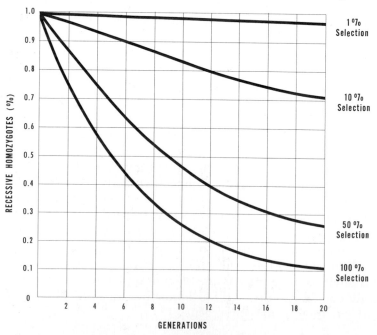

Generations	s = 1.0	s = 0.50	s = 0.10	s = 0.01
0	1.00*	1.00	1.00	1.00
10	0.25	0.46	0.84	0.98
20	0.11	0.26	0.71	0.97

Table 31.4
Effects of Selection against a
Recessive Trait on the Frequency in
Percentage of Individuals
Homozygous for the Recessive
Gene

* The initial frequency of the recessive homozygote in all cases is 1 percent, as in figure 29.3.

tion coefficient is a measure of the contribution of one genotype relative to the contributions of the other genotypes. Thus, an s value of 1 means that the individual leaves no offspring; the recessive homozygote is lethal. An s value of 0.10 signifies that the *aa* homozygote contributes only 90 offspring to the next generation as compared with *AA* and *Aa* individuals, each of which contributes 100 offspring. It may be noticed, once again, that the rate of decline of the recessive homozygotes becomes slower as the selection coefficient decreases in value.

SELECTION AGAINST DOMINANT DEFECTS

If complete selection acts against an abnormal trait caused by a dominant gene *(A)*, so that none of the *AA* or *Aa* individuals leave any progeny, then all the *A* genes are at once eliminated. In the absence of recurrent mutation, all subsequent generations will consist exclusively of homozygous recessives *(aa)*.

However, we must contend again with ever-occurring mutations and the effects of partial selection. The geneticist Curt Stern, of the University of California, provides us with a simple, clear model of this situation. Imagine a population of 500,000 individuals, all of whom initially are homozygous recessive *(aa)*. Thus, no detrimental dominant genes *(A)* are present and the population as a whole contains 1,000,000 recessive *a* genes. In the first generation, 10 dominant mutant genes arise, as a result of the recessive gene's mutating to the dominant state at a rate of 1 in 100,000 genes. We shall now assume that the dominant mutant gene is semilethal; in other words, only 5 of the newly arisen dominant genes are transmitted to the next, or second, generation. For ease of discussion, this is pictorially shown in figure 31.4 and represented also in table 31.5. It can be seen that the second generation would contain a total of 15 dominant genes—5 brought forth from the first generation and 10 new ones added by mutation. In the third generation, the 5 dominant genes carried over from the first generation would be reduced to 2.5, the 10

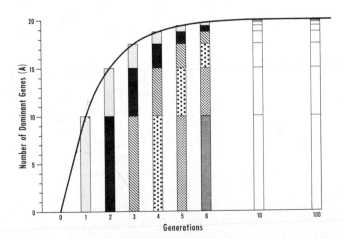

Figure 31.4 Establishment of a constant level of a semilethal dominant gene *(A)* in a population over the course of several generations. The fixed number of new dominant genes introduced each generation through mutations from a to *A* eventually exactly balances the number of dominant genes selectively eliminated each generation. In this particular case, an equilibrium is reached (after about 12 generations) when the total number of dominant genes is approximately 20 (see table 31.5).

Table 31.5
Equilibrium Frequency of a
Dominant Gene

Conditions: 1. Size of Population: 500,000 individuals
2. Mutation Rate $(a \longrightarrow A)$: 1 in 100,000 (1×10^{-5})
3. Selection Coefficient (s): 0.5 (semilethal)

| Generation | Recessive Gene a | Dominant Gene A | | |
		Left Over from Former Generations	Newly Mutated	Total
0	1,000,000	—	—	—
1	1,000,000*	—	10	10
2	1,000,000	5	10	15
3	1,000,000	5 + 2.5	10	17.5
4	1,000,000	5 + 2.5 + 1.25	10	18.75
5	1,000,000	5 + 2.5 + 1.25 + 0.625	10	19.375
∝	1,000,000	5 + 2.5 + 1.25 + 0.625 + 0.3125 + . . .	10	20.00

* The total number of recessive genes should be reduced by the total number of dominant genes each generation, but this minor correction would be inconsequential.

dominant alleles of the second generation would be depressed to 5, and 10 new abnormal alleles would arise anew by mutation. The total number of dominant genes would increase slightly each subsequent generation, until a point is reached (about 12 generations) where the rate of elimination of the abnormal dominant gene balances the rate of mutation. In other words, the inflow of new dominant alleles by mutation each generation is balanced by the outflow or elimination of the dominant genes each generation by selection.

The equilibrium frequency of the detrimental dominant gene in a population can be altered by changing the rate of loss of the gene in question. In man, retinoblastoma, or cancer of the eye in newborn babies, has until recently been a fatal condition caused by a dominant mutant gene. With modern medical treatment, approximately 70 percent of the afflicted individuals can be saved. The effect of increasing the reproductive fitness of the survivors is to raise the frequency of the abnormal dominant gene in the human population. The accumulation of detrimental genes in the human gene pool is a matter of growing awareness and concern.

CONCEALED VARIABILITY IN NATURAL POPULATIONS

From what we have already learned, we should expect to find in natural populations a large number of deleterious recessive genes concealed in the heterozygous state. It may seem that this expectation is based more on theoretical deduction than on actual demonstration. This is not entirely the case. Penetrating studies by a number of investigators of several species of the fruit fly Drosophila have unmistakably indicated an enormous store of recessive mutant genes harbored by individuals in nature. We may take as an illustrative example the kinds and incidence of recessive genes detected in Drosophila pseudoobscura from California populations. The following data are derived from the studies of the noted geneticist Theodosius Dobzhansky, then at Columbia University but later at the University of California in Davis.

Flies were collected from nature, and a series of elaborate crosses were performed in the laboratory to yield offspring in which one pair of chromosomes carried an identical set of genes. The formerly hidden recessive genes in a given pair of chromosomes were thus all exposed in the homozygous state. All kinds of recessive genes were uncovered in different chromosomes, as exemplified by those unmasked in one particular chromosome, known simply as "the second." About 33 percent of the second chromosomes harbored one or more recessive genes that proved to be lethal or semilethal to flies carrying the second chromosome in duplicate. An astonishing number of second chromosomes—93 percent of them—contained genes that produced subvital or mildly incapacitating effects when present in the homozygous condition. Other unmasked recessive genes resulted in sterility of the flies or severely retarded the developmental rates of the flies. All these flies were normal in appearance when originally taken from nature. It is apparent that very few, if any, outwardly normal flies in natural populations are free of hidden detrimental recessive genes.

GENETIC LOAD IN HUMAN POPULATIONS

The study of the concealed variability, or genetic load, in man cannot be approached, for obvious reasons, by the experimental breeding techniques used with fruit flies. Estimates of the genetic load in the human population have been based principally on the incidence of defective offspring from marriages of close relatives (consanguineous marriages). It can be safely stated that every human individual contains at least one newly mutated gene. It can also be accepted that any crop of gametes contains, in addition to one or more mutations of recent origin, at least 10 mutant genes that arose in the individuals of preceding generations and that have accumulated in the population. The average person is said to harbor four concealed lethal genes, each of which, if homozygous is capable of causing death between birth and maturity. The most conservative estimates place the incidence of deformities to detrimental mutant genes in the vicinity of 2 per 1,000 births. *It is evident that man is not uniquely exempt from his share of defective genes.*

MULLER'S AID PLAN

Modern medicine, by finding ways to keep alive individuals who carry deleterious genes, encourages the survival of those who more than likely will pass on their defects to future generations. The conventional ethics of medicine is shaken when, with increasing knowledge, it becomes clear that to save the life of a child with a hereditary disorder is to ensure the retention and increase of detrimental genes that ordinarily would be kept at very low frequencies by natural selection. Can we continue indefinitely to load our population with hereditary disabilities?

Some geneticists have looked on this situation with grave concern. In particular, the late Nobel Laureate Hermann J. Muller was most distressed about the continual pollution of the human gene pool. Muller had been predicting genetic disaster since 1935, and throughout his career he was a persuasive and articulate prophet of doom. Muller presented the most vivid portrayal of the impending genetic disintegration of the human species. In the not too distant future, according to Muller, the task of taking care of genetically defective individuals will consume all the energy that society can mobilize. Most everyone will be an invalid. Muller's gloomy forecast was that the human species would end up with two types of individuals: one kind would be so genetically incapacitated as to be wheelchair patients, and the other kind would be somewhat less disabled but would spend all their time taking care of the first kind. It is unreasonable, Muller contended, to expect medicine to keep up with the problem, especially because medical men themselves

Table 31.6
Selection Relaxation for a Formerly Lethal Recessive Whose Fitness Is Restored to 100 Percent by Medical Therapy

Conditions:

1. Initial Frequency of Recessive Defect at Birth: 1 in 100,000 (1×10^{-5})
2. Mutation Rate $(A \longrightarrow a)$: 1 in 100,000 (1×10^{-5})

Generation	Frequency of Recessive Defect at Birth
0	1×10^{-5}
1	1.01×10^{-5}
3	1.02×10^{-5}
10	1.06×10^{-5}
30	1.20×10^{-5}
100	1.73×10^{-5}

in that near or distant future will be subject to the same genetic decomposition. Eventually even the most sophisticated techniques available could no longer suffice to save men from their genetic deterioration. According to Muller, then, mankind is doomed unless positive steps are taken to regulate its genetic endowment.

Muller was convinced that man would be unable to reduce the load of unfavorable genes. He suggested as a countermeasure, therefore, a program designed to increase significantly the number of favorable genes in the human population. Muller proposed a plan called *AID*, or Artificial Insemination from Donors. He recommended the establishment of sperm banks, which would make available the sperm of highly qualified donors whose family histories showed the least possible likelihood of defects or abnormalities. To make sure of the eminence of the donors, the sperm would be frozen and made available only after 20 years or more, when the donor would no longer be alive, and posterity could judge dispassionately of his value. When a woman decided to have children, she would need only to choose sperm from the donor whose qualities she most admired. "How many women," Muller cried when he enunciated his plan, "would be eager and proud to bear and rear a child of Aldous Huxley or Charles Darwin!"

A number of serious questions must be answered before encouraging artificial insemination on the grand scale that Muller proposed. In the present state of knowledge even the best of geneticists would disagree on who should be the donors. There is no guarantee that even the most distinguished donor would be free of hidden detrimental genes. As one scientist stated, "The trouble with Muller's sperm bank is that he's always having to take people out of it." One of his rejects, for example, is Abraham Lincoln, who is now suspected of having suffered from a genetic disorder called Marfan's syndrome. Patients with Marfan's syndrome have poor musculature, long, thin extremities, and heart defects.

More important, people would be asked to surrender their pride in generating their own biological children and substitute for this pride the greater satisfaction to be gained from the knowledge that the child has the best possible set of genes. Muller confidently expected the gradual emergence of a new superior form of self-esteem and gratification in contributing to the genetic improvement of the human species. It seems more likely, however, that people would be rather uneasy at giving up their claim to having their own biological descendants.

Other geneticists do not share Muller's pessimism that the human species is deteriorating genetically. Calculations indicate that the increase in the frequency of detrimental recessive genes due to the relaxation of selection by medical therapy would be *extremely slow*. For example, given the conditions presented in table 31.6, it would take well over 100 generations (or 3,000 years) for a recessive trait to double in frequency from 1 in 100,000 to 2 in 100,000. If the recessive defect occurred initially with a frequency of 1 in 10,000, then slightly more than 30 generations would be required to double the incidence. In essence, although relaxation of selection tends to engender an increase in the incidence of genetic defects in future generations, the increase occurs very slowly.

SUMMARY

Natural selection, or differential reproductive success of genetically different individuals, determines the fate of mutant genes in a population. A detrimental recessive gene can be reduced by selection to a very low frequency in a population, but cannot be completely eradicated. As a deleterious recessive gene becomes rare, it exists almost entirely in the heterozygous state. Most affected offspring (aa) will come from matings of two heterozygous carriers (Aa). The reproductive incapacity of the recessive homozygote (aa) removes two recessive genes from the population. But the steadily diminishing supply of the abnormal recessive gene is continually replenished by recurrent mutations from normal (A) to abnormal (a). A point of genetic equilibrium is reached in the population when the number of abnormal recessive genes eliminated by selection is balanced by the number of the same recessive genes produced by mutation. Detrimental dominant genes are also maintained at low frequency in a population by a comparable interplay of recurrent mutation and natural selection.

As man is continually modifying his environment, he changes the selective forces operating on his gene pool. Modern medical treatment, in easing the harmful effects of deleterious genes, increases the reproductive fitness of sufferers, so that the net effect is to enlarge the human pool of defective genes. However, the increase in the frequency of detrimental recessive genes due to the relaxation of selection by medical therapy can be calculated to be very slow, extending over many generations.

Ethical Probe 21
The Dysgenic Effect of Therapeutic Abortion

A highly successful screening program for the detection of Tay-Sachs disease was undertaken, under the direction of Johns Hopkins University, among the Ashkenazic Jewish community in Baltimore and Washington. Tay-Sachs disease, a recessive lethal disorder, can be detected in the fetus during early pregnancy by the technique of amniocentesis. The use of amniocentesis in conjunction with therapeutic abortion of affected fetuses affords carrier parents the opportunity to have only normal children. From an evolutionary viewpoint, we may now inquire: To what extent does prenatal diagnosis coupled with therapeutic abortion modify the frequency of the detrimental Tay-Sachs gene in the population?

Prior to prenatal diagnosis, carrier parents tended to avoid additional conceptions after the birth of an afflicted child—for fear of having a second abnormal child. With the advent of amniocentesis, there has been a marked tendency for parents to replace the aborted fetuses with normal children. Although normal, each replacement child has a two-thirds chance of

being a heterozygote. In other words, healthy children born to carrier parents are more often heterozygous carriers than normal homozygotes. Thus, the spread of the harmful Tay-Sachs gene is not at all arrested. Indeed, therapeutic abortion followed by reproductive compensation results in an increase in the frequency of this lethal gene in future generations.

Calculations show that with mass screening and the selective elimination of the affected homozygotes *in utero,* there would be a 0.02 percent increase in heterozygotes per generation. In 350 generations (or 10,500 years), the number of heterozygotes would double (from 1 in 40 to 1 in 20). Admittedly, the projected increase in the detrimental gene occurs very slowly over many generations. Nevertheless, should carrier parents show concern for the future genetic welfare of the human species by refraining from having additional children? Stated another way, should carrier parents of a lethal recessive gene consciously avoid reproductive compensation?

32 Selection and Infectious Diseases

In 1859, a small colony of 24 wild rabbits (*Oryctolagus cuniculus*) was brought from Europe to an estate in Victoria in the southeastern corner of Australia. From such modest beginnings, the rabbits multiplied enormously and by 1928 had spread over the greater part of the Australian continent. They became an economic pest of unmanageable proportions. Estimates placed the number of adult rabbits at over 500 million in an area of about 1 million square miles. In overrunning the open grassy plains, the rabbits caused extensive deterioration to sheep grazing pastures and to wheat fields.

For many years, the Australian government spent large sums of money on various measures to control the population explosion of these prolific rabbits. Trapping, rabbit-proof fencing, poisoning of water holes, and fumigation all proved to be largely ineffectual. Then, beginning in 1950, outstanding success in reducing the rabbit population was achieved by inoculating rabbits with a virus that causes the fatal disease *myxomatosis*. The deadly virus was implanted into the tissues of rabbits in the southern area of Australia. In a remarkably short period of time, the virus had made its way, aided by insect carriers (mosquitoes), into most of the rabbit-infested areas of the continent. The initial outbreaks of myxomatosis were characterized by a high mortality rate. By 1953, more than 95 percent of the rabbit population of Australia had been annihilated.

However, after their drastic decline in the early 1950s, the rabbit populations began to build up again almost as dramatically as they had been eliminated. Evolutionary changes have occurred in both the pathogen (virus) and the host (rabbit). Mutations conferring resistance to the myxomatosis virus have selectively accumulated in the rabbit populations. At the same time, the viruses themselves have undergone genetic changes; less virulent strains of the virus have evolved.

There are several other interesting examples of evolutionary interplay between pathogen and host, including some in which man has been the host.

THE EVOLUTIONARY RESPONSE

Selection would favor the emergence of less virulent strains of a pathogen leading to less severe expressions of the disease. The advantage to the pathogen is comprehensible, since a pathogen that would cause the instantaneous death of the host also would cause its own prompt demise from lack of an immediate host. Experiments by the Australian scientist F. Fenner in the 1950s showed that new strains of the myxomatosis virus had arisen. Highly susceptible standard laboratory rabbits were infected with different preparations that had been isolated in successive epidemics in Australia. The early, or original, virus strains caused greater mortality in the laboratory rabbits than strains taken from the later epidemics. Wth each successive epidemic, a less virulent strain had evolved. In nature, the original, highly virulent strain of virus had killed the rabbits within a few days, which limited the virus' chances of being transmitted to a new host through the mosquito vector. However, when a virus of lower virulence appeared, the duration of the disease in the rabbit was extended, with the consequence that the less virulent mutant strain improved its chances of being transmitted to unaffected rabbits through the bite of a mosquito. Accordingly, attenuated, or weakened, strains of the virus progressively displaced in nature the original highly virulent strain.

Experiments by Fenner and his collaborators also demonstrated that the rabbits had become genetically resistant to the virus. Uniform doses of a standard virus preparation were injected into laboratory offspring of rabbits that had been trapped in successive epidemics. Significantly greater numbers of experimental offspring of parents from the first drastic epidemic succumbed to the inoculated virus compared with offspring of parents from the later, relatively mild epidemics. Thus, successive epidemics fostered the accumulation of genes protecting the rabbits against death from the myxomatosis virus. Stated another way, genetically susceptible rabbits had died, leaving the more genetically resistant rabbits to contribute more offspring each generation.

In essence, natural selection had favored a mutual accommodation between the virus and the Australian rabbit. The dual emergence of host resistance and pathogen nonvirulence serves as an instructive model of how genetically determined resistance to infectious disease evolves.

GENETIC EXPERIMENTS ON RESISTANCE TO DISEASE
Populations of organisms contain a large store of concealed genetic variability. It would not be surprising if this store included heritable factors for resistance to disease. In fact, this can be demonstrated experimentally. In the laboratory, experiments on guinea pigs, rabbits, and mice have shown that it is possible to select individuals in successive generations that have genetic determinants conferring on them a higher resistance to a pathogen. As an example, the typhoid pathogen, *Salmonella typhimurium,* was introduced intraperitoneally into laboratory mice in each of 12 generations of offspring. The dose of pathogen was held constant in each generation. The initial mouse population was highly susceptible to the pathogen. In the first generation, the population had 35 percent survivors. The resistance of the host population, however, increased with each successive generation of selection. By the 12th generation, 85 percent of the mice were resistant to the typhoid pathogen.

The data indicate that selection over a number of generations results in a decrease in mortality of the experimental animals. The problem that arises is whether the decrease in mortality is due primarily to the transfer of passive immunity or to an accumulation of heritable factors for resistance. Passive (or acquired) immunity involves the placental transfer of protective antibodies from the mother to the developing fetus. One can test for the possible influence of acquired immunity by crosses involving the survivors of the later generations of selection, particularly the 12th generation (designated S_{12} in table 32.1), and members of the initial, highly susceptible generation (designated S_0). As seen in table 32.1, the percentage of offspring of S_{12} females that succumbed to the

Table 32.1

Test for Possible Influence of Acquired Immunity to Typhoid Pathogen in Laboratory Mice

Matings of Laboratory Mice	Number of Progeny Injected with Pathogen	Number Dead	Percent Mortality
S_{12} ♂ × S_0 ♀	133	28	21%
S_0 ♂ × S_{12} ♀	138	33	24%

Note: S_0 are unselected mice (original generation).
S_{12} are mice after 12 generations of selection.

typhoid pathogen was comparable to the percentage of offspring of S_0 females that failed to survive. This is adequate proof against the transmission of passive immunity through surviving females.

INFECTIOUS DISEASES IN MAN

The British geneticist J. B. S. Haldane has suggested that infectious diseases were one of the most potent agents of natural selection of man in the past. It is difficult to prove unequivocally that genetic changes have occurred in the resistance of man to his pathogens during widespread epidemics in the past. Nevertheless, it is a reasonable supposition that major epidemics eliminated a large percentage of genetically susceptible individuals, and permitted the selective survival and multiplication of individuals endowed with greater genetic resistance.

Up until 10,000 years ago, man subsisted by food gathering and hunting alone. Widely dispersed groups of nomadic peoples lived at low population densities. Contact between groups was limited, and contagious diseases occurred infrequently. With the development of agriculture and the establishment of village settlements, human populations became dense and concentrated in relatively small regions. This set the stage for infectious community diseases, spread by contact, such as tuberculosis and bubonic plague, both caused by bacteria. Viral diseases such as measles, mumps, chickenpox, and smallpox posed serious threats to the health of preindustrial man. With the advent of the industrial revolution, the densely populated urban areas witnessed repeated outbreaks of typhus, typhoid, smallpox, diphtheria, and cholera. In industrial times, many diseases—in particular, tuberculosis—flared up to ravage entire populations.

An infectious disease tends to reach epidemic proportions in populations that have had no previous exposure to the disease. As the medical geneticist Arno Motulsky of the University of Washington has stressed, when populations are first exposed to a contagious disease, the mortality is high and the infecton is acute. On evolutionary principles, repeated exposure over many generations should lead to a genetic reconstruction of the population, with a raised frequency of genetically resistant individuals. Thus, in subsequent episodes of the disease, the expectations are lowered mortality and less severe manifestations of the disease. Certain specific disorders in man seem to bear out these views.

TUBERCULOSIS

Strong presumptive evidence that heritable resistance can arise through selection is furnished by the change, with time, in the incidence and character of tuberculosis among the Plains Indians of the Qu'Appelle Valley Reservation in Saskatchewan, Canada. In 1881, the Plains Indians, shortly after arriving at the reservation, became exposed to the tuberculosis germ for the first time. By 1886, almost everyone in the reservation had contracted the infection. The annual death rate from tuberculosis in 1886 reached the incredible figure of 900 per 10,000, or approximately 10 percent of the total population. The disease was not only widespread but also highly virulent, causing damage to bone, meninges, kidney, and other parts of the body. Such multiple disorders reflect the inability of the host to localize the infection. In 1921, however, the disease showed a pronounced tendency to localize in the lungs and to pursue the chronic course characteristic of pulmonary tuberculosis. Mortality dropped to 7 percent among Indian school children in 1921, and in 1950, mortality declined to 0.2 percent. Accordingly, in but a few generations, less than 1 percent of the Indian children died of tuberculosis. It should be stressed that this dramatic decline occurred in absence of specific chemotherapy and modern public health measures.

Other communities of the world have shown the same pattern of evolutionary change. Europeans typically exhibit a mild form of tuberculosis. René Dubos, a renowned microbiologist at the Rockefeller Institute, has carefully analyzed the available data, and concludes that Europeans today are the beneficiaries of an exacting selective process brought about by repeated outbreaks of tuberculosis a few generations ago. During the 18th and 19th centuries, tuberculosis spread with the growth of cities, and created havoc throughout the industrialized world. It became known as the "Great White Plague." Annual mortality rates during the industrial era were as high as 500 per 100,000.

Tuberculosis is a highly contagious disease. Minute droplets of sputum, discharged by cough or sneeze of an affected person, contain literally thousands of tubercle bacteria, which can survive in the air for several hours. Even thoroughly dried sputum, when it is inhaled, can be infective. Tuberculosis flared in crowded London in 1750, and then swept uncontrollably through the large cities of continental Europe. Immigrants from Europe brought the devastating disease to the United States in the early 1800s. The death toll was highest in cities with large immigrant populations—New York, Philadelphia, and Boston. As tuberculosis advanced across the nation, it became the chief cause of death in the United States in the 19th century. Tuberculosis then declined steadily in the 20th century in all industrialized countries. From a high value of 500 deaths per 100,000 in the 19th century, the mortality rate dropped in Europe and the United States to approximately 190 per 100,000 in 1900. By 1945, the rate fell to about 40 per 100,000.

The decline in mortality cannot be attributable, in any large measure, to general advances in living conditions, or to therapy. The decline was in full force before effective medical steps were taken, and indeed, even before the discovery of the tubercle bacteria. The causative agent was discovered only in 1882 by Robert Koch in Germany. The available information suggests strongly that the reduction in mortality has been primarily the result of an evolutionary attenuation of the virulence of the pathogen coupled with a heightened, genetically conditioned resistance level of the host. In other words, the severity of infection has most likely been diminished by genetic selection and has been essentially independent of medical or public health intervention.

It is only since the 1940s that the benefits of chemotherapy have become detectable in the Western world. Today, cases of tuberculosis occur at an annual rate of 20 per 100,000, and most cases are permanently arrested by treatment with drugs such as isonicotinic acid hydrazide

(INH) and para-amino salicylic acid (PAS). The effectiveness of modern drugs seems to indicate that populations of parts of the world in which tuberculosis still prevails can avoid the remorseless selective process in which death eliminates the susceptible genotypes. Yet some 3 million persons each year succumb to tuberculosis in Latin America, Africa, and Asia. Although effective drugs to combat tuberculosis are available for worldwide distribution, most of the poorly developed nations have inadequate medical and health services, and large proportions of their populations have only remote contact with medical facilities of any kind.

BUBONIC PLAGUE

Bubonic plague is a bacterial disease that infected rats spread, passing it on to man through the bite of their fleas. The plague bacteria cause the inflammation and swelling of lymph nodes. An acutely inflamed node is technically called a *bubo*, which gives the plague its name. Numerous authors have dramatized the repeated epidemics that riddled Europe for many centuries (plate 16). Europe first experienced local outbreaks of plague in the 6th century, had several severe outbursts in the 11th century, and then witnessed the most ravaging epidemic in the 14th century, when it became known as the "Black Death." It has been conservatively estimated that Black Death carried off one-fourth of the population of Europe, or 25 million people, during the 14th century. Plague periodically attacked large sections of Europe for an additional 300 years. The Great Plague of London broke out in 1665. The number of deaths recorded in London that year was approximately 70,000 in a population estimated at 460,000. After the epidemic of 1665, plague disappeared from England and gradually retreated from western Europe. It smoldered in eastern Europe until the first half of the 19th century. The long reign of plague on the continent ended with an isolated outbreak in Constantinople in 1841.

The cessation of plague in Europe has been ascribed to effective quarantine measures and gradual improvements in housing. Of some importance also was the decline of the black rat in the face of competition with the hardier brown rat. The latter, known as the "sewer rat," comes less frequently in contact with human beings. Additionally, it would be difficult to deny that natural selection also had an effect. Present-day Europeans probably have relatively high genetic resistance to the plague bacteria. Europeans are less susceptible to pneumonic plague than are Negroes and Orientals. Pneumonic plague is caused by the same bacteria that cause bubonic plague, but it is transmitted directly from man to man in sputum.

Although genetic resistance factors in man have not been demonstrated, it can be shown that wild rats themselves have developed some degree of genetic immunity to the plague germ they harbor. Marked differences in susceptibility to infection exist among black rats from different parts of India, where these rats are still the principal reservoir of human plague bacteria. Wild rats captured from Bombay, a city that has experienced severe epidemics of human plague, were inoculated with a standard dose of plague bacteria. This same treatment was also given to wild rats trapped in Madras, a region relatively free of plague. Many of the rats of Bombay survived the experimental dose of plague bacteria whereas most of those from Madras perished. These findings suggest that the Bombay rats, descendants of populations that harbored the plague germ for many generations, are genetically conditioned to plague as a consequence of natural selection.

MALARIA

Malaria, an ancient scourge of mankind, is still a serious menace to health in many parts of the world. Paul F. Russell of the International Health Division of the Rockefeller Foundation estimates that there are at least 350 million cases of malarial fever each year throughout the world, of which 1 in 200 is fatal. Part of the difficulty in malarial control programs has been the tendency of mosquitoes to develop genetically resistant strains against insecticides (for example, DDT) and antimalarial drugs (for example, quinine).

Malaria in man is caused by a protozoan parasite, which feeds on the liver and red blood cells of an infected person and multiplies in these cells. When the French scientist Alphonse Laveran in 1880 identified the protozoan parasite (technically *Plasmodium*) as the causative agent of malaria, he dispelled the time-honored belief that *mal aria* (Italian, meaning "bad air") was the cause of the disease. Shortly thereafter, the female of certain species of mosquitoes *(Anopheles)* was incriminated in the transmission of the parasite from one human being to another. After the female anopheline mosquito has fed on the blood of an infected person, the ingested parasites undergo a complex series of developmental changes within the mosquito before being passed on, by further feeding, to infect another person.

Figure 32.1 shows the life cycle of a typical *Plasmodium*. Since the

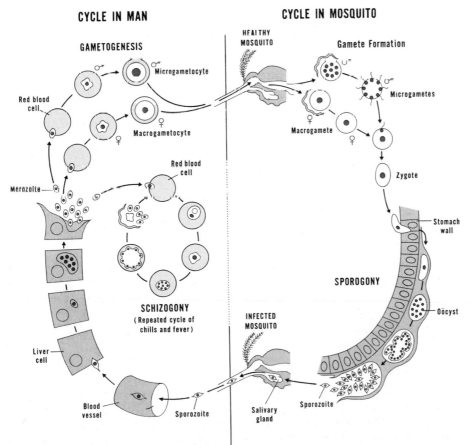

CYCLE IN MAN

GAMETOGENESIS

Micrngametocyte

Red blood cell

Macrogametocyte

Merozoite

Red blood cell

SCHIZOGONY
(Repeated cycle of chills and fever)

Liver cell

Blood vessel

Sporozoite

Salivary gland

INFECTED MOSQUITO

CYCLE IN MOSQUITO

HEALTHY MOSQUITO

Gamete Formation

Microgametes

Macrogamete

Zygote

Stomach wall

SPOROGONY

Oöcyst

Sporozoite

Figure 32.1 The life cycle of the malarial parasite, *Plasmodium*. When the female mosquito feeds on a person, it introduces an anticoagulant (to prevent coagulation of the host's blood) and a stage of the parasite called a *sporozoite*. These elongate cells leave the bloodstream to infect tissue cells, particularly liver cells. The sporozoites divide repeatedly (asexually) to produce numerous *merozoites*, which invade red blood cells (erythrocytes). The merozoites produce a whole brood of offspring by multiple divisions (technically, a process termed *schizogony*). One complete cycle of schizogony takes 48 hours; the liberation of many new merozoites is accompanied by the release of toxins that cause the cyclic bouts of fever (every 48 hours). Some of the merozoites have a different destiny; these develop into large *macrogametocytes* (forerunners of female gametes) or *microgametocytes* (forerunners of male gametes). The gametocytes, after being sucked up by a mosquito, transform into female gametes (*macrogametes*) or male gametes (*microgametes*). Fertilization occurs in the stomach wall of the mosquito. The *zygote* develops into a wartlike oöcyst on the outer surface of the stomach. Numerous divisions of the oöcyst yield large numbers of sporozoites. A single oöcyst may produce 10,000 sporozoites, and there may be as many as 50 oöcysts in the stomach wall of one mosquito. The sporozoites are released into the body cavity of the mosquito, and then migrate to the salivary glands. The life cycle is renewed when the sporozoites are discharged into the saliva with the bite of the mosquito.

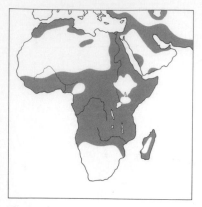

Figure 32.2 Distribution of falciparum malaria in Africa.

malarial parasite is introduced into man when the female mosquito feeds, malaria is said to be vector-borne (Latin, *vehere*, meaning "to carry"). The malarial protozoan undergoes sexual development and multiplication within the female mosquito, and asexual multiplication (repeated divisions) in the liver cells and red blood cells of man. The periodic release of asexual daughter cells from the disrupted blood cells causes the characteristic recurrent attacks of chills and fever. An attack begins with a shivering chill, which may be accompanied by severe convulsions. The chill state is followed by a burning fever, in which the temperature may rise to 106°F. A period of profuse sweating then occurs. The attack subsides as sweating gradually diminishes and the temperature drops. The sequence of chills, fever, and sweating may last 12 hours and occur every other day, in declining severity, for 2 to 6 weeks. In the absence of reinfections, some strains of the malarial parasite may perish within 6 to 8 months whereas other strains may persist for several years.

Although malaria is a worldwide disease, it occurs predominantly in the tropics and subtropics, where climatic conditions are favorable for the *Anopheles* mosquito to breed throughout the year. In fact, in tropical Africa, individuals are continually reinfected. A common type of malaria in Africa is *falciparum malaria,* the most devastating of the malarial varieties. Red blood cells infected with *Plasmodium falciparum* tend to cling together and clog capillaries. Sudden death by a "stroke" often occurs when blood flow is impeded in the parasite-clogged vessels of the brain.

In many regions of Africa (fig. 32.2), malarial infection in the earliest years of life is commonplace. Nearly all babies are infected before they are five months old. For children up to the age of four years, the disease may be fatal. Children who survive the early acute attacks acquire a low-grade immunity. They still remain heavily infected with parasites and are subject to periodic attacks that, though not incapacitating, are debilitating. The low-grade immunity depends on the action of phagocytic macrophages. The macrophages actually engulf and destroy the entire parasitized red blood cells and not merely the parasites themselves. The immunized individuals also develop a marked capacity for the rapid production and mobilization of macrophages. Thus, the body reacts quickly to renewed infections, and the intermittent attacks of chills and fever are relatively mild.

From an evolutionary standpoint, the protozoan parasite is well adapted to coexist with the anopheline mosquito. Although the parasite invades several internal tissues of the mosquito, the normal functioning or life span of the mosquito is not impaired in any way. This suggests a finely balanced evolutionary accommodation of parasite and mosquito. Such a harmonious interaction between the parasite and man apparently has not evolved, inasmuch as human malaria is often severe and sometimes fatal. The failure of a genetic strain of parasite better adapted to living in harmony with man is inexplicable. On the other hand, as we shall see presently, mutations that confer increased resistance to the malarial parasite have selectively accumulated in man.

SUMMARY

In the pathological relation of infecting agent and host, both organisms tend to undergo evolutionary changes. This has been clearly shown to be the case for rabbits in Australia infected with a virus that causes the disease myxomatosis. Whereas the rabbits initially succumbed in large numbers to the viral disease, genes for disease resistance gradually accumulated in the rabbit populations during successive epidemics so that present-day rabbits show less severe manifestations of the disease. Simultaneously, the viruses themselves have undergone genetic changes; less virulent strains of the virus have evolved. This is understandable since a highly virulent pathogen that causes the instantaneous death of the host also causes its own prompt demise from lack of an immediate host.

The relative incidence and severity of several infectious diseases affecting man have changed in the course of time. Genetic changes most likely occurred in the resistance of man to his pathogens during repeated epidemics of infectious diseases. It is reasonable to suppose that widespread epidemics in the past have eliminated a large percentage of genetically susceptible individuals, so that the ones that have survived and multiplied can be credited with having highly specific genetic resistance to particular diseases. There have been epidemics, as of tuberculosis and bubonic plague, that destroyed large segments of the human population on first contact; subsequent similar epidemics among the same populations have been considerably less severe. The decline in mortality to tuberculosis among Europeans, for example, was in full force before the advent of specific chemotherapeutic treatment and effective public health measures. It is interesting to speculate whether the modern use of chemotherapeutic agents has arrested the spread or selective accumulation of genetic factors that confer inheritable resistance to tuberculosis.

33 Balanced Polymorphism

The concepts presented in the preceding chapters have led us to believe that selection operates at all times to reduce the frequency of an abnormal gene to a low equilibrium level. This view is not entirely accurate. We are aware of genes with deleterious effects that occur at fairly high frequencies in natural populations. A striking instance is the high incidence in certain human populations of a mutant gene that causes a curious and usually fatal form of blood cell destruction, *sickle-cell anemia*. It might be presumed that this detrimental gene is maintained at a high frequency by an exceptionally high mutation rate. There is, however, no evidence to indicate that the sickle-cell gene is unusually mutable. We now know that the maintenance of deleterious genes at unexpectedly high frequencies involves a unique, but not uncommon, selective mechanism, which results in a type of population structure known as *balanced polymorphism*.

SICKLE-CELL ANEMIA

As stated in chapter 20, individuals homozygous for a particular abnormal hemoglobin gene, $Hb^S Hb^S$, are severely afflicted with a sickle-cell anemia and usually die in childhood. The heterozygote, said to possess the sickle-cell trait, has one normal allele (Hb^A) and one sickling allele (Hb^S). Sickle-cell anemic individuals are usually derived from the marriage of two sickle-cell trait carriers.

Since persons with sickle-cell anemia ordinarily do not survive to reproductive age, it might be expected that the abnormal gene would pass rapidly from existence. Each failure of the homozygous anemic individual ($Hb^S Hb^S$) to transmit his genes would result each time in the loss of two aberrant genes from the population. And yet, the sickle-cell gene reaches remarkably high frequencies in the tropical zone of Africa (fig. 33.1). In several African populations, 20 percent or more of the individuals have the sickle-cell trait, and frequencies as high as 40 percent have been reported for some African tribes. The sickle-cell trait is not confined to the African continent. It has been found in Sicily and Greece, and in parts of the Near East. What can account for the high incidence of the sickle-cell gene, particularly in light of its detrimental action?

THEORY OF BALANCED POLYMORPHISM

For simplicity in the presentation of population dynamics, we will consider the sickling gene to be recessive. Accordingly, we can symbolize the normal gene as *A* and its allele for sickling as *a*. Now, the explanation for the high level of the deleterious sickle-cell gene is to be found in the possibility that the heterozygote (*Aa*) is superior in fitness to *both* homozygotes (*AA* and *aa*). In other words, selection favors the heterozy-

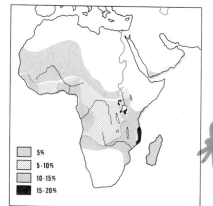

Figure 33.1 Distribution and frequency of the sickle-cell gene in Africa.

5%
5-10%
10-15%
15-20%

gote and both types of homozygotes are relatively at a disadvantage. Let us examine the theory behind this form of selection.

Figure 33.2 illustrates the theory. The classical case of selection discussed in preceding chapters is portrayed in the first part of the figure. In this case, when *AA* and *Aa* individuals are equal in reproductive fitness, and the *aa* genotype is completely selected against, the recessive gene will be eliminated. Barring recurring mutations, only *A* genes will ultimately be present in the population.

Now let us assume (case II in fig. 33.2) that both homozygotes (*AA* as well as *aa*) are incapable of leaving surviving progeny. The only effective members in the population are the heterozygotes (*Aa*). Obviously, the frequency of each gene, *A* and *a*, will remain at a constant level of 50 percent. The inviability of both homozygous types probably never exists in nature, but the scheme does reveal how a stable relation of two alleles at high frequencies is possible. If, as in case III, the *AA* genotype leaves only half as many progeny as the heterozygote, and the recessive homozygote is once again inviable, then it is apparent that more *A* alleles are transmitted each generation than *a* alleles. Eventually, however, the *A* gene will reach an equilibrium point at 0.67. Here, it may be noted that although the recessive homozygote is lethal, the frequency of the recessive allele (*a*) is maintained at 0.33. In the last illustrative example (case IV), the recessive homozygote is not as disadvantageous as the dominant homozygote, but both are less reproductively fit than the heterozygote. Here also, both genes remain at relatively high frequencies in the population. Indeed, the recessive allele (*a*) will constitute 67 percent of the gene pool.

We have thus illustrated in simplified form the selective forces that serve to maintain two alleles at appreciable frequencies in a population. This phenomenon is known as *balanced polymorphism*. The loss of a deleterious recessive gene through deaths of the homozygotes is balanced by the gain resulting from the larger numbers of offspring produced by the favored heterozygotes.

Figure 33.2 Equilibrium frequencies of two alleles (*A* and *a*) under different conditions of selection (ignoring mutation). In contrast to Case I (complete selection and total elimination of *a*), the recessive gene can be retained at appreciable frequencies in a population when the heterozygote (*Aa*) is superior in reproductive fitness to *both* homozygotes (Cases II, III, and IV, showing different relative fitnesses of the two homozygotes, *AA* and *aa*).

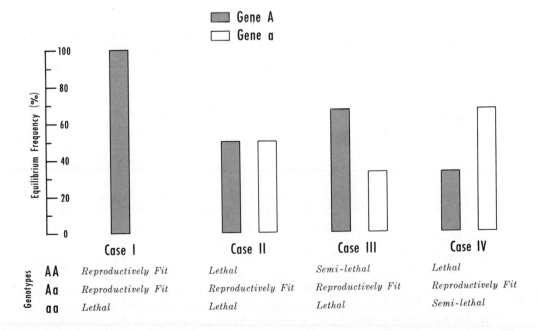

| Gene A | Gene a |

Genotypes	Case I	Case II	Case III	Case IV
AA	*Reproductively Fit*	*Lethal*	*Semi-lethal*	*Lethal*
Aa	*Reproductively Fit*	*Reproductively Fit*	*Reproductively Fit*	*Reproductively Fit*
aa	*Lethal*	*Lethal*	*Lethal*	*Semi-lethal*

Table 33.1
Calculation of Equilibrium
Frequency of Recessive Gene in a
Balanced Polymorphic State

1. Heterozygote (Aa) is superior in fitness to both homozygotes $(AA$ and $aa)$ and is assigned a value of 1.

	AA	Aa	aa
Fitness (f)*	$1 - s_1$	1	$1 - s_2$

2. Equilibrium value of recessive gene a:

$$q_a = \frac{s_1}{s_1 + s_2}$$

3. Example: If fitness (f) of $AA = 0.85$, then selection
coefficient $(s_1) = 0.15$
If fitness (f) of $aa = 0.10$, then selection
coefficient $(s_2) = 0.90$.

$$q_a = \frac{0.15}{0.15 + 0.90} = \frac{0.15}{1.05} = 0.14$$

* Fitness (f), another measure of the reproductive efficiency of a particular genotype, is the converse of the selection coefficient (s).

Balanced polymorphism results in a stable equilibrium of the two alleles; their equilibrium frequencies are determined by the relative fitness of the two homozygotes. If the fitness of Aa is set equal to 1, of AA equal to $(1 - s_1)$, and of aa equal to $(1 - s_2)$, where s denotes the selection coefficient, then the frequency of the recessive gene q_a at equilibrium can be calculated by the following formula:

$$q_a = \frac{s_1}{s_1 + s_2}$$

An example of the use of the formula is shown in table 33.1. When the relative fitness of the recessive homozygote is only 0.10 and that of the dominant homozygote is 0.85, the obviously harmful recessive gene still reaches a high stable frequency of about 14 percent.

EXPERIMENTAL VERIFICATION OF BALANCED POLYMORPHISM
A simple experiment, using the fruit fly *Drosophila melanogaster,* can be performed to demonstrate that an obviously lethal gene can be maintained at a stable, relatively high frequency in a population. The geneticist P. M. Sheppard of the University of Liverpool in England introduced into a breeding cage a population of flies of which 86 percent were normal and 14 percent carried the mutant gene *stubble,* which affects the bristles of the fly. The stubble gene is lethal when homozygous; hence all stubble individuals are heterozygous. Ordinarily the heterozygous fly does not have any reproductive advantage over the normal homozygote. Sheppard, however, created a situation whereby the heterozygote would be favored by removing 60 percent of the normal flies from the population each generation. Consequently, the heterozygote was rendered superior in fitness to either homozygote by virtue of the natural lethality of the stubble homozygote and the enforced reproductive incapacity of many of the normal homozygotes. The results of the experiment are recorded in table 33.2.

It should be noted that the frequency of the stubble gene increased in the early generations, but then became stabilized at a level of about 0.365. The equilibrium level is reached when as many stubble genes are lost from the population, through death of the stubble homozygotes, as are gained as a result of the reproductive advantage of the heterozygote.

Table 33.2
Equilibrium State under Balanced
Polymorphism

Generation	Percentage of Stubble Flies	Frequency of Stubble Gene
1	14.3	0.0715
2	33.7	0.1685
3	57.6	0.2880
4	63.2	0.3160
5	69.1	0.3455
6	73.5	0.3675
7	72.9	0.3645
8	73.4	0.3670
9	72.9	0.3645

Source: From P. M. Sheppard, *Natural selection and heredity,* 1959.

Although the stubble gene is lethal, the population, under the constant conditions of the experiment, remained at a stable state with a high number of heterozygotes.

The frequency of the stubble gene will fall rapidly when the usual reproductive potential of the normal homozygote is restored. When the normal homozygotes and heterozygotes are equal in reproductive fitness (refer to case I, fig. 33.2), the normal gene will supplant the abnormal stubble gene in the population. With these considerations in mind, we shall return to our discussion of sickle-cell anemia.

SUPERIORITY OF THE HETEROZYGOTES

The high frequency of the sickle-cell gene in certain African populations can be explained by assuming that the heterozygotes (individuals with sickle-cell trait) have a selective advantage over the normal homozygotes. What might be the nature of the advantage? Field work undortaken in Africa in 1949 by the British geneticist Anthony Allison revealed that the incidence of the sickle-cell trait is high in regions where malignant falciparum malaria is hyperendemic—that is, transmission of the infection occurs throughout most of the year. Thus, the population is almost constantly reinfected with malaria, and susceptible individuals suffer from severe and prolonged attacks. Under such circumstances, relative immunity to falciparum malaria would be most beneficial.

Allison examined blood from African children and found that carriers of the sickle-cell trait were relatively resistant to infection by the parasite *Plasmodium falciparum,* the causative agent of falciparum malaria. The heterozygous carriers were infected less often with the parasite than the homozygous dominant nonsicklers. Moreover, among those heterozygotes that were infected, the incidence of severe, or fatal, attacks of malaria was strikingly low. The evidence is strong that the sickle-cell gene affords some degree of protection for young children against malarial infection. Hence, in areas where malaria is common, children possessing the sickle-cell trait will tend to survive more often than those without the trait and are more likely to pass on their genes to the next generation. The heterozygotes ($Hb^A Hb^S$) are thus superior in fitness to both homozygotes, which are likely to succumb either from anemia on the one hand ($Hb^S Hb^S$) or malaria on the other ($Hb^A Hb^A$).

A state of balanced polymorphism is established by the relative superiority of the heterozygote. The mortality from malaria among nonsicklers ($Hb^A Hb^A$) has been estimated at 15 percent. If the fitness of the dominant homozygote is 0.85 relative to the fitness of 1 for the heterozygote $(Hb^A Hb^S)$, and if the fitness of the recessive homozygote afflicted with sickle-cell anemia is placed at 0.10, then the equilibrium frequency of the sickling gene (Hb^S) would be 0.14 (see table 31.1). With this value of q, the frequency of the heterozygous carrier, or $2pq$, can be calculated $(p$, you will recall, equals $1 - q)$. Under these conditions, the expectation is that the carriers of sickle-cell trait would compose 24 percent of the population $(2pq = 2 \times 0.86 \times 0.14 = 0.24)$. This frequency of the heterozygote occurs in several populations in Africa.

Frank B. Livingstone of the University of Michigan has impressively revealed the relationship among the spread of agriculture, malaria, and sickle-cell anemia. The spread of the sickling gene was greatly enhanced by the development of agriculture. The clearing of the forest in the preparation of ground for cultivation provided new breeding areas for the mosquito *Anopheles gambiae,* the vector, or carrier, of the malaria plasmodium. The spread of malaria has been responsible for the spread of the selective advantage of the sickle-cell gene, which in the heterozygous state imparts resistance to malaria. In essence, the selective advantage of the heterozygote tends to increase in direct proportion to the amount of malaria present in a given area. Hunting populations in Africa show a very low incidence of malaria and an equally low frequency of the sickling gene. The Pygmies of the Ituri Forest constitute a good example.

Communities in Africa with the greatest reliance on agriculture (rather than on hunting or animal husbandry), then, tend to have the highest frequencies of the sickle-cell trait. A high incidence of the sickle-cell trait in an intensely malarious environment has the consequence of reducing the number of individuals who can be infected by the malarial parasite, and accordingly, lowering the mortality from such infections. More human energy, or greater manpower, is thus made available for raising and harvesting crops. Coincidentally, the sickle-cell trait carries with it the beneficial effect of enabling tribes to develop and maintain an agricultural culture rather than adhere to a hunting or pastoral existence. This is a curious, but striking, instance of the interplay of biological change and socioeconomic adaptation.

In a similar finding, evidence exists that persons whose red blood cells are deficient in the enzyme G6PD (glucose-6-phosphate-dehydrogenase) are also less likely to be affected by malaria. Data also show a strong correlation between the incidence of malaria and the frequency of thalassemia in the Italian peninsula and in Sardinia. Malaria apparently has had a profound influence on human events.

RELAXED SELECTION

We should expect the frequency of the sickle-cell gene to be low in malaria-free areas, where the selective advantage of the heterozygote would be removed. It has been found that the lowest frequencies of the sickle-cell gene occur consistently in regions relatively free of malaria. The frequency of the sickle-cell gene has fallen to low levels in the Negro population of the United States. The frequency of the sickle-cell trait among American Negroes is about 9 percent, corresponding to a gene frequency of approximately 0.05. The incidence at birth of the disabling sickle-cell anemia is estimated at 2 per 1,000 individuals.

The relaxation of selection in this case is eugenic; that is, the changes occur in the desired direction. The disappearance of malaria disrupts the

Conditions: Initial fitness of recessive homozygote: 0.33
Initial gene frequency of sickling gene: 0.10
Initial frequency of heterozygote: 0.18

Table 33.3
Selection Relaxation against
Sickle-Cell Anemia (in
Nonmalarial Areas)

Generation	% Heterozygote (Sickle-Cell Trait)	% Recessive Homozygote (Sickle-Cell Anemia)
0	18.0	1.0
1	17.0	0.88
3	15.3	0.70
10	11.4	0.37
30	6.5	0.11
100	2.6	0.02

balanced polymorphic state, and the elimination of sickle-cell anemia then begins and proceeds to completion. Table 32.3 presents computations of the gene frequencies of the heterozygotes and the recessive homozygotes, starting with the frequency of the carrier at 18 percent. It may be noted that 30 generations are required for the incidence of the heterozygous carrier to be depressed from 18.0 to 6.5 percent. At present, medical researchers are attempting to find a cure for sickle-cell anemia. If sickle-cell anemic individuals could be completely cured, then obviously selection would be thwarted and the sickle-cell gene would no longer decline in frequency.

TAY-SACHS DISEASE AND CYSTIC FIBROSIS

As previously discussed (chapter 19), Tay-Sachs disease is a recessively inherited condition that is untreatable and fatal. This disease is especially common in Jews of northeastern European origin. It has been suggested that the Ashkenazi Jews, who have lived for several millennia in the urban ghettos in Poland and the Baltic states, have been exposed to different selective pressures than other Jewish groups who have lived in countries around the Mediterranean and Near East. The densely populated urban ghettos may have experienced repeated outbreaks of infectious diseases. In 1972, the geneticist Ntinos Myrianthopoulos of the National Institutes of Health in Bethesda, Maryland, presented data that show that pulmonary tuberculosis is virtually absent among grandparents of children afflicted with Tay-Sachs disease, although the incidence of Jewish tuberculosis patients from eastern Europe is relatively high. The findings indicate that the heterozygous carrier of Tay-Sachs disease is resistant to pulmonary tuberculosis in regions where this contagious disease is prevalent.

A reproductive advantage for the heterozygote would account also for the high frequency of the recessive gene for cystic fibrosis in Caucasian populations. The magnitude of the selective advantage of the heterozygous carrier over the normal homozygote need only be 2 percent to maintain an incidence of the disorder at 1 in 2,500 births. To ascertain the reproductive advantage, one could obtain information on the fertility of heterozygous parents. However, the overall reproductive performance of heterozygous parents tends to be biased by the birth of a child with cystic fibrosis and by the knowledge that this lethal hereditary disorder can arise in subsequent pregnancies.

An unbiased estimate of the fertility of unsuspecting heterozygotes, who unknowingly perpetuate the gene, can be obtained by assessing the fertility of the *grandparents* of the affected children. It may be assumed that at least one of the grandparents (maternal or paternal) of an affected child is a heterozygote. Thus, the size of the sibship from grandparental matings of the type $AA \times Aa$ (where a is the allele for cystic fibrosis) can be compared with the sibship size of grandparental matings of the type $AA \times AA$. It should be noted that family size cannot be attributed to knowledge of the disorder since by the time a grandchild with cystic fibrosis has been identified, the fertility of the grandparents has been completed. Such a study was undertaken in 1967 by Alfred Knudson and his co-workers at the City of Hope Medical Center at Duarte, California. The grandparents of patients with cystic fibrosis were found to have an average of 4.34 offspring compared with 3.43 offspring for the appropriate control group. Thus, on the average, matings of type $AA \times Aa$ have one additional child compared with $AA \times AA$ matings. The greater reproductive fitness of the heterozygous carrier suggests that the detrimental gene for cystic fibrosis is being maintained at exceptionally high frequencies by balanced polymorphism.

SELECTION AGAINST THE HETEROZYGOTE

The mother-child blood incompatibility in humans, *erythroblastosis fetalis*, represents an interesting case of selection *against* the heterozygote. The erythroblastotic infant is always the heterozygote (Rr). Each death of an erythroblastotic infant (Rr) results in the elimination of one R and one r gene. In such a situation, where selection continually operates against the heterozygote, the rarer of the two genes should ultimately become lost (or decline to a low level to be maintained solely by mutation). In populations where the R gene is much more common than the r allele, we should be witnessing a gradual dwindling of the r gene.

No decline, however, in the frequency of the r gene is evident. One counterbalancing factor is the tendency of parents who have lost infants from erythroblastosis to compensate for their losses by having relatively large numbers of children. Thus, if a father is heterozygous (Rr) and the mother is homozygous (rr), there is an even chance that the infant will be rr and unaffected. Each unaffected child born restores two r genes lost by the death of two Rr erythroblastotic sibs. Accordingly, an excess of homozygous children (rr) counterbalances the r genes lost through erythroblastosis. This consideration alone overrides the selective force against the heterozygote.

In recent years, the management and prevention of Rh disease have advanced considerably. We may foresee the end of Rh disease as a troublesome clinical problem. We can also anticipate that the recessive r allele will not disappear from the human gene pool, but rather endure.

IMPLICATIONS OF BALANCED POLYMORPHISM

According to the classical concept of selection (discussed in chapter 31), a deleterious gene has a harmful effect when homozygous and virtually no expression in the heterozygous state. Deleterious genes will be reduced in frequency by selection to very low levels and will be maintained in the population by recurrent mutation. The fittest individuals are homozygous for the normal, or "wild-type," allele at most loci. Stated another way, the fittest individuals carry relatively few deleterious genes in the heterozygous state.

In this chapter, we have considered examples of genes that impair fitness when homozygous and actually improve fitness in the heterozygous state. To what extent are individuals heterozygous at their gene loci? Geneticists estimate that 20 to 50 percent of the loci in an individual exist in two or more allelic forms. If the alternative alleles at these polymorphic loci are maintained by selection that favors the heterozygote, then low fitness would have to be assigned to an unusually large number of homozygous loci. In other words, an unreasonably high level of unfitness would prevail in the population because of the selective disadvantage of many alleles in the homozygous state.

The possibility exists that most of the alternative alleles at polymorphic loci are *selectively neutral*—that is, the different alleles at one locus confer neither selective advantage or disadvantage on the individual. Much of the observed variation, then, would represent merely the accumulation of neutral mutations. The notion of selectively neutral alleles has been much debated. Are there mutant alleles whose effects on fitness are not at all different from the more frequent alleles that lead to a normal phenotype? And, can some of these neutral mutant alleles reach frequencies purely by chance as high as the frequencies that characterize the state of balanced polymorphism? These vexing questions have yet to be resolved satisfactorily.

SUMMARY

When a deleterious gene continues to be present at an unexpectedly high frequency in a population, we can suspect that the deleterious gene is being maintained by the selective advantage of the heterozygote. A stable equilibrium called *balanced polymorphism* results when the heterozygote (Aa) is superior in fitness to both homozygotes (AA and aa). In areas where subtertian (falciparum) malaria is prevalent, the heterozygous carriers of the sickle cell gene (that is, individuals with the sickle-cell trait) are relatively resistant to infection by the malarial parasite. The heterozygote has a reproductive advantage over both homozygotes—the sickle-cell anemia patient, who succumbs to anemia, and the normal homozygote, who is apt to succumb to malaria. The larger numbers of offspring produced by the favored heterozygotes serve to maintain the deleterious sickle-cell gene at high frequencies in malarial regions. The frequency of the sickle-cell gene declines to low levels in malaria-free areas (as in the United States), where the selective advantage of the heterozygote is removed.

In the case of the Rh blood-group genes, selection operates against the heterozygote since the Rh-diseased infant is always heterozygous (Rr). However, the expected decline in the recessive allele (r) has not been witnessed, probably because parents who have lost infants due to Rh incompatibility tend to compensate for their losses by having relatively large numbers of children.

At least 20 percent of the loci in an individual exist in two or more allelic forms. It is not known whether most of the alternative alleles at polymorphic loci are selectively neutral or are maintained by selection that favors the heterozygote.

Ethical Probe 22
Sacrificing the Truth

Dr. Robert Murray, Chief of the Medical Genetics Unit of Howard University, relates the following story. A couple was interviewed to discuss the psychological effects of sickle-cell anemia on their four-year-old child. The husband and wife appeared to be genuinely compatible with each other and their actions and attitude with their child were notably wholesome. The mother volunteered that only she had the sickle-cell trait. The absence of the carrier status (sickle-cell trait) in the husband would, of course, make it highly improbable that their child could have sickle-cell anemia. The couple did not fully comprehend the mode of inheritance.

An entirely lucid and candid explanation of the genetics of sickle-cell anemia would certainly raise the question of nonpaternity and perhaps lead to the disruption of what appeared to be a commendable marital relationship. The genetic counselor simply stated that an egg from the mother containing the sickle-cell gene was fertilized by a sperm in which a new or "fresh" mutation producing a sickle-cell gene had occurred. This explanation was sufficient for the couple. The counselor did not volunteer the information that such mutations are extremely rare and that the probability of his explanation was extremely remote.

In a situation like this where there is a conflict between human relations and total scientific truth, would you have also withheld the full information? How would you respond if the couple sought your opinion as to the advisability of their having additional children?

Genetic Drift and Gene Flow

34

We have seen that harmful recessive genes in a population tend to be carried mostly in the heterozygous state. The probability that two or more heterozygous carriers will actually meet is obviously greater in a small population than in a large breeding assemblage. In fact, the number of matings of carriers of a particular recessive gene in a population is mainly a function of the size of the population. Most populations are not infinitely large, and many fluctuate in size from time to time.

During a period when a population is small, chance matings and segregations could lead to an uncommonly high frequency of a given recessive gene. For example, a large population in which the albino gene is ordinarily held at low frequency could become sharply reduced in size by an acute epidemic. By sheer chance, an unusually large proportion of heterozygous carriers of albinism might have survived the epidemic and prevailed as parents. In this manner, the albino gene, although not at all advantageous, would occur with an extraordinarily high incidence in the new generation of offspring. Such a fortuitous change in the genetic makeup of a population that may arise when the population becomes restricted in size is known as *genetic drift*.

ROLE OF GENETIC DRIFT

Examination of a situation in nature that may be illustrative of genetic drift will lead us into a simplified mathematical consideration of the concept. Coleman Goin, a naturalist at the University of Florida, studied the distribution of pigment variants of a terrestrial frog, known impressively as *Eleutherodactylus ricordi planirostris*. We shall refer to the frog simply by its vernacular name, the greenhouse frog. This frog may possess either of two pigmentary patterns, mottled or striped (fig. 34.1). A unique feature of the greenhouse frog is the terrestrial development of its eggs. That is to say, the eggs need not be submerged completely in water, but can develop in moist earth. This important quality may have considerable bearing on the dispersal of the frogs. Goin reared eggs successfully in a flowerpot two-thirds filled with beach sand and placed in a finger bowl of water. Examination of a large number of progeny hatched from many different clutches of eggs revealed that the striped pattern is dominant to the mottled pattern.

The greenhouse frog is widespread in Cuba and the Bahama Islands, and has only recently become established in Florida. Cuba apparently has been the center of dispersal from which the Florida populations have been derived. The present distribution of the greenhouse frog in Florida consists of a series of small, isolated colonies. As shown in figure 34.1, the proportions of the two patterns vary in different colonies in Florida.

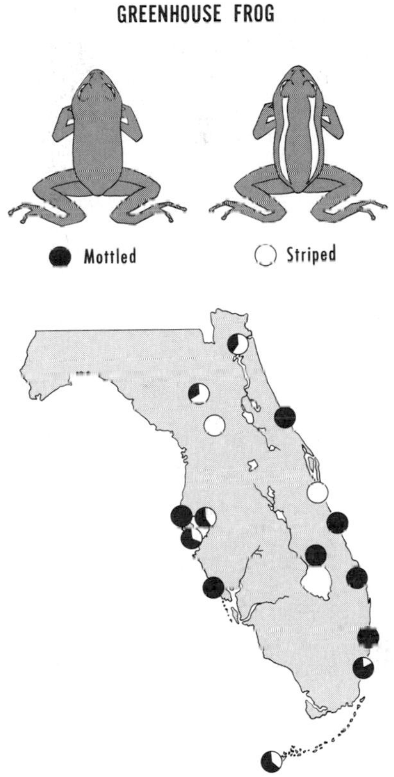

GREENHOUSE FROG

● Mottled   ○ Striped

Figure 34.1 Distribution of the greenhouse frog in Florida, and the relative frequencies of the two pattern variants, mottled and striped. The populations are small and isolated, and differ appreciably in the incidences of mottled and striped forms. The varied frequencies may not be due to natural selection, but may represent the outcome of chance fluctuations of genes, or genetic drift. (Based on studies by Coleman Goin.)

403

In several colonies, only the mottled type occurs. What can account for the local preponderance of one or the other pattern, or even the absence of one of the contrasting patterns?

Goin conjectures that the greenhouse frog was introduced into Florida by means of clutches of eggs accidentally included in shipments of plants from Cuba, a distinct possibility in view of the terrestrial development of the eggs. Thus, a single clutch of introduced eggs could initiate a small colony that in turn would establish at the outset a given pattern or proportion of patterns. The presence of only mottled forms in a population may be due to the chance circumstance that only mottled eggs were introduced. Or, perhaps both striped and mottled eggs were included in the shipment, but by sheer accident one type was lost in succeeding generations.

It should be understood that Goin has not proved that the unusual distribution and frequency of the two pigment patterns are due solely to chance. The demonstration of genetic drift in any natural population is an extremely difficult task. Genetic drift of the variant pigment patterns is, however, a reasonable explanation.

THEORY OF GENETIC DRIFT

The theory of genetic drift was systematically developed in the 1930s by the geneticist Sewall Wright, then at the University of Chicago and later at the University of Wisconsin. Indeed, the phenomenon of drift is frequently called the *Sewall Wright effect*. The Sewall Wright effect refers specifically to the random fluctuations (or drift) of gene frequencies from generation to generation in a population of small size. Because of the limited size of the breeding population, the gene pool of the new generation may not be at all representative of the parental gene pool from which it was drawn.

The essential features of drift may be seen in the following modest mathematical treatment. Let us assume that the numerous isolated colonies in Florida were each settled by only two frogs, a male and a female, both of constitutions *Aa*. Let us further suppose that each mated pair produces only two offspring. The possible genotypes of the progeny, and the chance associations of the genotypes, are shown in table 34.1.

Several meaningful considerations emerge from table 34.1. For example, the chance that the first offspring from a cross of two heterozygous parents will be *AA* is ¼. The second event is independent of the first; hence, the chance that the second offspring will be *AA* is also ¼.

Table 34.1
Chance Distribution of Offspring of Two Heterozygous Parents (Aa × Aa)

Genotype of First Offspring	Probability of First Event	Genotype of Second Offspring	Probability of Second Event	Total Probability
AA	¼	*AA*	¼	Both offspring *AA*, ¹⁄₁₆
AA	¼	*Aa*	²⁄₄	*AA* followed by *Aa*, ²⁄₁₆
AA	¼	*aa*	¼	*AA* followed by *aa*, ¹⁄₁₆
Aa	²⁄₄	*AA*	¼	*Aa* followed by *AA*, ²⁄₁₆
Aa	²⁄₄	*Aa*	²⁄₄	Both offspring *Aa*, ⁴⁄₁₆
Aa	²⁄₄	*aa*	¼	*Aa* followed by *aa*, ²⁄₁₆
aa	¼	*AA*	¼	*aa* followed by *AA*, ¹⁄₁₆
aa	¼	*Aa*	²⁄₄	*aa* followed by *Aa*, ²⁄₁₆
aa	¼	*aa*	¼	Both offspring *aa*, ¹⁄₁₆

The chance that *both* offspring will be *AA* is the product of the separate probabilities of the two independent events, $\frac{1}{4} \times \frac{1}{4}$, or $\frac{1}{16}$.

We may now ask: What is the probability of producing two offspring, one *AA* and the other *Aa, in no particular order?* From table 34.1, it may be seen that the chance of obtaining an *AA* individual followed by an *Aa* individual is $\frac{2}{16}$. Now, the wording of our question requires that we consider a second possibility, that of an *Aa* offspring followed by an *AA* offspring (also $\frac{2}{16}$). These two probabilities must be added together to arrive at the chance of producing the two genotypes irrespective of the order of birth. Hence, in the case in question, the chance is $\frac{2}{16} + \frac{2}{16}$, or $\frac{4}{16}$. In like manner, it may be ascertained that the expectation of obtaining one *AA* and one *aa* offspring (in no given order) is $\frac{2}{16}$, and that the expectation of producing one *Aa* and one *aa* (in any sequence) is $\frac{4}{16}$.

The essential point is that any one of the above circumstances may occur in a given colony. We may concentrate on one situation. The probability that a colony will have only two *AA* offspring is 1 in 16. Thus, by the simple play of chance, the parents initiating the colony might not leave an *aa* offspring. The *a* gene would be immediately lost in the population. Subsequent generations descended from the first-generation *AA* individuals would contain, barring mutation, only *AA* types. Chance alone can therefore lead to an irreversible situation. A gene once lost could not readily establish itself again in the population. The decisive factor is the size of the population. When populations are small, striking changes can occur from one generation to the next. Some genes may be lost or reduced in frequency by sheer chance; others may be accidentally increased in frequency. Thus, the genetic architecture of a small population may change irrespective of the selective advantage or disadvantage of a trait. Indeed, a beneficial gene may be lost in a small population before natural selection has had the opportunity to act on it favorably.

FOUNDER EFFECT

When a few individuals or a small group migrate from a main population, only a limited portion of the parental gene pool is carried away. In the small migrant group, some genes may be absent or occur in such low frequency that they may be easily lost. The unique frequencies of genes that arise in populations derived from small bands of colonizers, or "founders," has been called the *founder effect*. This expression essentially emphasizes the conditions or circumstances that foster genetic drift.

The American Indians afford a possible example of the loss of genes by the founder principle. North American Indian tribes, for the most part, surprisingly have no I^B genes that govern type B blood. However, in Asia, the ancestral home of the American Indian, the I^B gene is widespread. The ancestral population of Mongoloids that migrated across the Bering Strait to North America might well have been very small. Accordingly, the possibility exists that none of the prehistoric immigrants happened to be of blood group B. It is also conceivable that a few individuals of the migrant band did carry the I^B gene but failed to leave descendants.

The interpretation based on genetic drift should not be considered definitive. Natural selection cannot be flatly dismissed. Most of the North American Indians possess only blood group O, or stated another way, they contain only the blood group allele *i*. With few exceptions, the North American Indian tribes have lost not only blood group allele I^B but gene I^A as well. The loss of both alleles, I^A and I^B, by sheer chance perhaps defies credibility. Indeed, many modern students of evolution are convinced that some strong selective force led to the rapid elimination of the I^A and I^B genes in the American Indian populations. If this is true, it would offer an impressive example of the action of natural selection in modifying the frequencies of genes in a population.

North American Indians are also known to have a high frequency of albinism. The incidence of albinism among the Cuna Indians of the San Blas Province in Panama is about 1 in 200, which contrasts sharply with the 1 in 20,000 figure for European Caucasians. The Hopi Indians of Arizona and the Zuni Indians of New Mexico, like the Cuna Indians, are also remarkable for the high numbers of albino individuals.

Since these American Indian populations are small, one might suspect genetic drift, notwithstanding the deleterious effects of the albino gene. It is difficult to imagine, however, that by chance alone this detrimental gene could reach a high frequency independently in several American Indian populations. Charles M. Woolf, the geneticist at Arizona State University, has suggested that the high incidence of albinism among the Hopi Indians of Arizona reflects an inimitable form of selection that he terms *cultural selection*. Albinos have been highly regarded in traditional Hopi society, and actually have enjoyed appreciable success in sexual activity. The albino male has been admired, and some have become legendary for leaving large numbers of offspring. Woolf further notes that the fading of old customs among the Hopi Indians is beginning to nullify any reproductive advantage held by albino males in past generations. The frequency of albinism may be expected to decline with the dissolution of the traditional Hopi way of life.

RELIGIOUS ISOLATES

The most likely situation to witness genetic drift is one in which the population is virtually a small, self-contained breeding unit, or *isolate*, in the midst of a larger population. This typifies the Dunkers, a very small religious sect in eastern Pennsylvania. The Dunkers are descendants of the Old German Baptist Brethren, who came to the United States in the early 18th century. Bentley Glass of Johns Hopkins University has studied the community of Dunkers in Franklin County, Pennsylvania, which numbers about 300 individuals. In each generation, the number of parents has remained stable at about 90. The Dunkers live on farms intermingled with the general population, but are genetically isolated by rigid marriage customs. The choice of mates is restricted to members within the religious group.

Glass, with his colleagues, compared the frequencies of certain traits for the Dunker community, the surrounding heterogeneous American population, and the population in western Germany from which the Dunker sect had emigrated two centuries ago. Such a comparison of a small isolate with its large host and parent populations should reveal the effectiveness, if any, of genetic drift. In other words, if the small isolated population shows aberrant gene frequencies in comparison with the large parent population, and if the other forces of evolution can be excluded, then the genetic differences can be ascribed to drift.

Analyses were made of the patterns of inheritance of three blood group systems—the ABO blood groups, the MN blood types, and the Rh blood types. In addition, data were accumulated on the incidences of four external traits—namely, the configuration of the ear lobes (which either may be attached to the side of the head or hang free), right- or left-handedness, the presence or absence of hair on the middle segments of the fingers (mid-digital hair), and "hitchhiker's thumb," technically termed "distal hyperextensibility" (fig. 34.2).

The frequencies of many of these traits are strikingly different in the Dunker community from those of the general United States and west Germany populations. Blood group A is much more frequent among the Dunkers; the O group is somewhat rarer in the Dunkers; and the frequencies of groups B and AB have dropped to exceptionally low levels in the Dunker community. In fact, the I^B gene had almost been lost in the isolate. Most of the carriers of the I^B gene were not born in the community, but were converts who entered the isolate by marriage.

A noticeable change has also occurred in the incidences of the M and N blood types in the Dunker community. Type M has increased in frequency, and type N has dwindled in frequency as compared with the incidences of these blood types in either the general United States population or the west Germany population. Only in the Rh blood groups do the Dunkers conform closely to their surrounding large population.

In physical traits, equally striking differences were found. Briefly, the frequencies of mid-digital hair patterns, distal hyperextensibility of the thumb, and attached ear lobes are significantly lower in the Dunker isolate than in the surrounding American populations. The Dunkers do, however, agree well with other large populations in the incidence of left-handedness. It would thus appear that the peculiar constellation of gene frequencies in the Dunker community—some uncommonly high, others uniquely low, and still others, unchanged from the general large population—can be best attributed to chance fluctuations, or genetic drift.

There is no concurrence of opinion among evolutionists concerning the operation of genetic drift in natural populations, but few would deny that small religious isolates have felt the effect of random sampling. It should be clear, however, that genetic drift becomes ineffectual when a small community increases in size. Fluctuations or shifts in gene frequencies in large populations are determined almost exclusively by selection.

AMISH OF PENNSYLVANIA

We have seen that gene frequencies in small religious isolates may differ significantly from the original large populations from which the isolates were derived. Another feature of small isolates is the occurrence of rare recessive traits in greater numbers than would be expected from random mating in a large population. This is witnessed among the Old Order Amish societies in eastern United States.

The Amish sect is an offshoot of the Mennonite Church; both religious groups settled in the United States to escape persecution in Europe in past centuries. The Amish are old-fashioned, rural-living people who cultivate the religious life apart from the world. Present-day communities were founded by waves of Amish immigration that began about 1720 and continued until about 1850. The great majority of Amish live in relatively isolated colonies in Pennsylvania, Ohio, and Indiana. Each community is descended from a small immigrant stock, as attested by the relatively few family names in a given community. Analyses by the geneticist Victor A. McKusick of Johns Hopkins University have shown that eight names account for 80 percent of the Amish families in Lancaster County, Pennsylvania. Other Amish communities also are char-

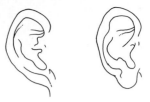

Attached Lobe   Free Lobe

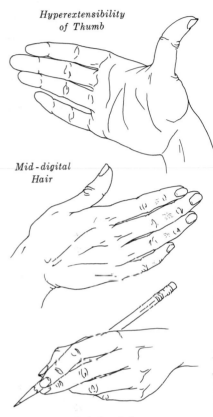

Hyperextensibility of Thumb

Mid-digital Hair

Left-handedness

Figure 34.2 Inheritable physical traits—nature of ear lobes, "hitch-hiker's thumb," mid-digital hair, and handedness—studied by Bentley Glass and his co-workers in members of the small religious community of Dunkers in Pennsylvania. The distinctive frequencies of most of these traits in the Dunker population suggest the operation of genetic drift.

acterized by a high frequency of certain family names, as table 34.2 shows.

Marriages have been largely confined to members of the Amish sect, with a resulting high degree of consanguinity. Marriages of close relatives have tended to promote the meeting of two normal, but carrier, parents. Four recessive disorders manifest themselves with uncommonly high frequencies, each in a different Amish group: the Ellis–van Creveld syndrome, pyruvate-kinase-deficient hemolytic anemia, hemophilia B (Christmas disease), and a form of limb-girdle muscular dystrophy (Troyer syndrome).

In the Ellis–van Creveld syndrome, which occurs in the Lancaster County population, affected individuals are disproportionately dwarfed (short-limbed), have malformed hearts, and possess six fingers on each hand (fig. 34.3). Fifty-two affected persons have been identified in 30 sibships, most of which have unaffected parents. Pedigree analysis has revealed that Samuel King and his wife, who immigrated in 1744, are ancestral to all parents of the sibships. Either Samuel King or his wife carried the recessive gene. None of their children were affected, but subsequent generations were. Evidently, previously concealed detrimental recessive genes are brought to light by the increased chances of two heterozygotes meeting in a small population.

Table 34.2
Older Order Amish Family Names in Three American Communities

Lancaster Co., Pa.		Holmes Co., Ohio		Mifflin Co., Pa.	
Stolzfus*	23%	Miller	26%	Yoder	28%
King	12%	Yoder	17%	Peachey	19%
Fisher	12%	Troyer	11%	Hostetler	13%
Beiler	12%	Hershberger	5%	Byler	6%
Lapp	7%	Raber	5%	Zook	6%
Zook	6%	Schlabach	5%	Speicher	5%
Esh**	6%	Weaver	4%	Kanagy	4%
Glick	3%	Mast	4%	Swarey	4%
	81%		77%		85%

Totals:
1,106 families, 1957   1,611 families, 1960   238 families, 1951

Source: From data compiled by Victor A. McKusick of Johns Hopkins University.
  * Including Stolzfoos.
** Including Esch.

Figure 34.3 Six-digited hands, one of the manifestations of the Ellis–van Creveld syndrome in humans, a rare recessive deformity. Affected offspring generally come from two normal, but carrier, parents, each of which harbors the abnormal recessive gene. (Courtesy of Dr. Victor A. McKusick.)

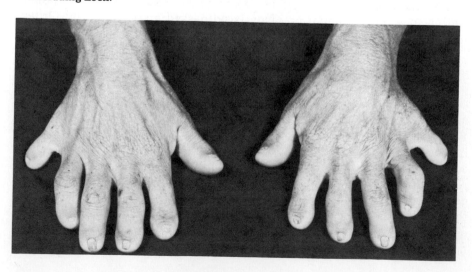

PROTEIN EVOLUTION

We had earlier learned (chapter 20) that a gene (a linear array of bases in the DNA) codes for the precise sequence of amino acids that compose a protein. The substitution of one amino acid for another is traceable typically to a single point mutation—that is, an alteration of a single base of the triplet of DNA that specifies the amino acid. Single amino acid substitutions that interfere with the function of the protein, or decrease drastically the rate of synthesis of the protein, are likely to be discarded by natural selection.

We now have substantial knowledge of the amino acid sequence of cytochrome c, a respiratory enzyme containing about 100 amino acids. This protein has been analyzed in more than 30 species of organisms, and the same amino acids have been found at 20 positions in all organisms tested from mold to man. Apparently, the 20 amino acids at specific positions are irreplaceable, and any substitutions at these sites are likely to interfere with the function of the enzyme. In the remaining portion of the chain, however, several different amino acids appear at a given position. The variable nature of these remaining amino acids could be interpreted as indicating that amino acid replacements at some positions are irrelevant for the function of the protein. That is, amino acid substitutions at certain positions are not likely to provide either an evolutionary advantage or disadvantage, and can be preserved by chance. In essence, it may be that certain amino acid replacements result from neutral mutations that are fixed by genetic drift.

The notion that amino acid substitutions may be fixed by the random drift of neutral mutations remains controversial. Advocates point to the analysis of fibrinopeptide A, a polypeptide concerned with the blood-clotting mechanism. Among several mammalian species, there is an extraordinarily high level of amino acid substitutions in fibrinopeptide A. This polypeptide presumably functions equally well with numerous different amino acid sequences. It has been argued that the mutations responsible for the many different amino acids must be neutral. In other cases, however, it is difficult to deny the role of natural selection. Certain histones (which form complexes with DNA) are highly conserved in their amino acid sequences. For example, histone IV from such divergent organisms as the pea plant and the calf differ in only two of 102 amino acid residues. All other amino acid substitutions apparently would disrupt the activity of histone IV, and such substitutions that may have appeared in the evolutionary past were probably eliminated by natural selection.

GENE FLOW

A rich archaeological record reveals considerable movement on the part of early human populations. Some migrations were sporadic, in small groups; others were more or less continual streams, involving large numbers of peoples. Large-scale immigrations followed by interbreeding have the effect of introducing new genes to the host populations. The diffusion of genes into populations through migrations is referred to as gene flow.

The graded distribution of the I^B blood-group gene in Europe represents the historical consequence of invasions by Mongolians who pushed westward repeatedly between the 6th and 16th centuries (fig. 34.4). There is a high frequency of the I^B gene in central Asia. In Europe, the frequency of the I^B gene diminishes steadily from the borders of Asia to a low level of 5 percent or less in parts of Holland, France, Spain, and Portugal. The Basque peoples, who inhabit the region of the Pyrenees in

Spain and France, have the lowest frequency of the I^B gene in Europe—below 3 percent. From a biological standpoint, the Basque community of long standing is a cohesive, endogamous mating unit. The exceptionally low incidence of the I^B gene among the Basques may be taken to indicate that there has been little intermarriage with surrounding populations. It is possible that a few centuries ago the I^B gene was completely absent from the self-contained Basque community.

The exchange of genes between populations may have dramatic consequences. Until recently, hemolytic disease of the newborn, or Rh disease, was virtually unknown in China. All Chinese women are Rh-positive (RR). However, intermarriage of immigrant Americans and the native Chinese has led to the introduction of the Rh-negative gene (r) in the Chinese population. No Rh disease would be witnessed in the immediate offspring of American men and Chinese women. By contrast, all marriages of Rh-negative American women (rr) and Chinese Rh-positive men (RR) would be of the incompatible type. All children by Chinese fathers (RR) would be Rh-positive (Rr) and potential victims of hemolytic disease.

Whereas American immigrants introduce the Rh-negative gene (r) into Chinese populations, where it formerly was not present, Chinese immigrants (all of whom are RR) introduce more Rh-positive genes (R) into the American populations, thus diluting the Rh-negative gene pool in the United States. Initially the Rh-positive Chinese men (RR) married to Rh-negative American women (rr) would result in an increased incidence of Rh-diseased infants. In later generations, however, the frequency of Rh-negative women in the United States would be lower, inasmuch as women of mixed Chinese-American origin would be either RR or Rr, predominantly the former. Thus, in the United States, the long-range effect of Chinese-American intermarriage is a reduction in the incidence of hemolytic disease of the newborn.

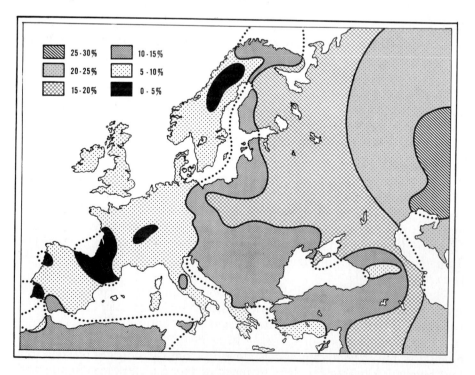

Figure 34.4 Gradient of frequencies of the I^B blood-group gene from central Asia to western Europe. (Based on studies by A. E. Mourant.)

Legend:
- 25-30%
- 20-25%
- 15-20%
- 10-15%
- 5-10%
- 0-5%

CAUCASIAN GENES IN AMERICAN NEGROES

In the United States, from a beginning more than 250 years ago, there has occurred an admixture of Caucasians with Negroes who were brought from Africa to the New World as slaves. The overall Caucasian contribution to the American Negro gene pool has been estimated at approximately 25 percent. This percentage must be considered as a gross estimate, inasmuch as different Negro populations in the United States have undergone varied degrees of admixture.

The geneticist T. Edward Reed of the University of Minnesota has measured the frequency with which a particular blood-group gene appears in Caucasians, African Negroes, and American Negroes. The particular gene is the Fy^a gene of the Duffy blood group system, and may be referred to simply as "the Duffy factor." As seen in table 34.3, the Duffy factor is virtually absent in the African Negro populations from which most of the original immigrant slaves were derived. The highest frequency of the Duffy factor in the stem populations in Africa is an exceedingly low 0.04, whereas the value for representative Caucasian populations in the United States is 0.4, or 10 times as great (table 34.3). Among Negroes living in New York City, Detroit, and Oakland, the gene reaches a frequency of about 0.10. This signifies that the magnitude of Caucasian ancestry in Negroes in these localities may be as high as 26 percent. In contrast, the frequency of the Duffy factor among Negroes in Charleston, South Carolina is 0.02, which indicates that the Negro population in Charleston has only a small amount of Caucasian ancestry. Thus, although the extent of Caucasian-Negro hybridization has been variable, it is clear that various American Negro populations derive between 4 percent and 26 percent of their genes from Caucasian ancestors, and that these Caucasian genes have been introduced through hybridization since 1700.

Table 34.3
Duffy Blood Factor (Fy^a Gene) In Caucasian, African, Negro, and American Negro Populations

Region	Frequency of Duffy Factor	Percentage of Caucasian Contribution
African Negro		
Liberia	0.00	—
Ivory Coast	0.04	—
Upper Volta	0.00	—
Dahomey	0.00	—
Ghana (Accra)	0.00	—
Nigeria (Lagos)	0.00	—
Caucasian		
Oakland, California	0.43	
Evans and Bullock counties, Georgia	0.42	
American Negro		
A. Nonsouthern		
New York, New York	0.08	18.9
Detroit, Michigan	0.11	26.0
Oakland, California	0.09	22.0
B. Southern		
Charleston, South Carolina	0.02	3.7
Evans and Bullock counties, Georgia	0.05	10.6

Source: Based on data compiled by T. Edward Reed of the University of Minnesota.

SUMMARY

In small, relatively isolated populations, gene frequencies tend to fluctuate purely by chance. This random fluctuation of gene frequencies, called *genetic drift,* may explain certain unusual distributions of traits in populations. Genetic drift may be the cause of the absence of type B blood in most North American Indian tribes. The sample of the gene pool contained in the original small migrant tribe may have included only a small fraction of the genetic variability present in the original large parent population in Asia, the ancestral home of the American Indians. Thus, the possibility exists that none of the prehistoric immigrants happened to be of blood type B. Or, perhaps a few individuals of the migrant band did possess the gene governing this particular blood type, but by sheer chance the gene was lost in succeeding generations. Isolated religious communities in the United States, such as the Dunkers and the Amish, also show unique gene frequencies as compared to the parental populations in Europe from which they were originally derived.

Gene flow, or the influx of genes from one population to another through migrations, can result in the admixture of genetically diverse populations. The American Negro population is an admixture of Caucasians with the African Negroes who were brought to the New World as slaves. Although the extent of Caucasian-Negro hybridization has been variable, various American Negro populations derive between 4 percent and 26 percent of their genes from Caucasian ancestors, introduced through hybridization since 1700.

Polygenic Inheritance and Intelligence

35

In simple Mendelian inheritance, each character is sharply divided into two clearly distinguishable classes. Individuals either have the trait in question, or they do not have the trait. Thus, the dominant trait achondroplasia with its resultant dwarfism is distinctly different from the normal condition; similarly, the recessive condition albinism is clearly differentiated from the normal. Such easily recognized traits are each due to the effects of a single pair of genes and have sharply contrasting alternative forms.

Actually, many differences between individuals show *continuous variation*. Characters such as height, weight, skin color, and intelligence have all degrees of intermediate conditions between one extreme and the other. Such traits are often called *quantitative* in distinction to the simpler, or qualitative, traits. Inheritance of quantitative traits is said to be *polygenic*, since it involves many genes, each of which makes a small contribution to the total effect. Polygenic inheritance is not a special type of inheritance, but rather a special case of gene action. The numerous genes, or polygenes, are inherited as independent units, but they are not independent in their expression. Indeed, they interact with each other in an interesting way.

THEORY OF POLYGENIC INHERITANCE

A polygenic system is constructed of several pairs of genes. The gene pairs may be treated as pairs of coins. If we toss two coins simultaneously, the outcome is a 1:2:1 ratio, as indicated in table 35.1. When four

Table 35.1
Model for Quantitative Traits

Tossing of Coins	Result	Frequency	Trait Value
2 Coins	2 Heads (HH)	1	2
	1 Head, 1 tail (Ht)	2	1
	2 tails (tt)	1	0
4 Coins	4 Heads (HHHH)	1	4
	3 Heads, 1 tail (HHHt)	4	3
	2 Heads, 2 tails (HHtt)	6	2
	1 Head, 3 tails (Httt)	4	1
	4 tails (tttt)	1	0
6 Coins	6 Heads (HHHHHH)	1	6
	5 Heads, 1 tail (HHHHHt)	6	5
	4 Heads, 2 tails (HHHHtt)	15	4
	3 Heads, 3 tails (HHHttt)	20	3
	2 Heads, 4 tails (HHtttt)	15	2
	1 Head, 5 tails (Httttt)	6	1
	6 tails (tttttt)	1	0

coins are tossed simultaneously, then the distribution becomes 1:4:6:4:1. This distribution tends to approach what mathematicians call the *normal curve*, a pattern in which the classes reach a peak at the mean and fall away in frequency on either side. The bell-shaped curve of distribution becomes better approximated when six coins are tossed simultaneously, the outcome being 1:6:15:20:15:6:1.

To evaluate the effects of the individual genes on the trait in our coin-tossing analogy, let us assign a value of 1 to each of the "Heads" and a value of 0 to each "tail." Thus, each H contributes 1 unit—height, weight, or color, say—to the quantitative trait in question. Only the dominant H makes a contribution; the recessive t has no expression. The effect of each H is cumulative; that is, the effect of 1 H is added to the effect of another H. With six coins (or three pairs of genes), the maximum effect on the trait results when 6 Hs are present. We may now consider a concrete example.

One of the simplest instances of polygenic inheritance is witnessed in the inheritance of kernel color in wheat, as reported by Nilsson-Ehle. Individual kernels show a range of intensity, or shades, of red color. Nilsson-Ehle postulated the existence of 3 independent pairs of genes for color inheritance, each dominant gene having a cumulative, or additive, effect. When an intensely red strain of wheat (represented by the genotype *AABBCC*) is crossed with a colorless, or white, strain *(aabbcc)*, the F₁ products are uniform and intermediate between the parents in color, essentially pink *(AaBbCc)*. When these intermediate hybrids are self-pollinated, the F₂ generation shows a marked increase in the range of color types. One in 64 has all 6 dominant genes for the deep red color *(AABBCC)*; at the other extreme, 1 in 64 possesses white kernels, or lacks any of the pigment-producing dominant genes *(aabbcc)*. Relatively large numbers of the F₂ generation ($^{20}\!/_{64}$) are pink, possessing 3 dominant alleles in varied combinations (*AABbcc*, or *AaBbCc*, or *aaBBCc*, and so on). Any 3 of the 6 genes in the dominant state suffice to produce the pink color, since the effect of each dominant gene is to add 1 unit of color. Aside from pink, other intermediate grades have 5 dominant genes ($^{6}\!/_{64}$), 4 dominant genes ($^{15}\!/_{64}$), 2 dominant genes ($^{15}\!/_{64}$), and 1 dominant gene ($^{6}\!/_{64}$), in accordance with the distribution shown in table 33.2. Thus, the F₂ generation shows many gradations from one extreme to the other. In essence, the gradations of color in

Table 35.2
Variability in Red Kernal Color Resulting from Cross of Two Intermediate (Pink) Wheat Plants (AaBbCc × AaBbCc)

	Number of Dominant (Red) Genes						
	Six	*Five*	*Four*	*Three*	*Two*	*One*	*None*
Genotypes and Frequencies	1 *AABBCC*	2 *AABBCc* 2 *AABbCC* 2 *AaBBCC*	4 *AABbCc* 4 *AaBbCC* 4 *AaBBCc* 1 *AABBcc* 1 *AAbbCC* 1 *aaBBCC*	8 *AaBbCc* 2 *AABbcc* 2 *AaBBcc* 2 *AabbCC* 2 *AAbbCc* 2 *aaBbCC* 2 *aaBBCc*	4 *AaBbcc* 4 *AabbCc* 4 *aaBbCc* 1 *AAbbcc* 1 *aaBBcc* 1 *aabbCC*	2 *Aabbcc* 2 *aaBbcc* 2 *aabbCc*	1 *aabbcc*
Phenotypes and Distribution	1 Deep red	6 Dark red	15 Medium red	20 Pink	15 Moderately pink	6 Light pink	1 Colorless

wheat kernels are best explained by the existence of 3 pairs of genes, A and a, B and b, and C and c, with the dominant alleles representing the color-producing genes.

It should be clear that the principle of independent assortment (discussed in chapter 18) still holds. The intermediate pink F_1 hybrid is heterozygous for 3 independently assorting pairs of alleles: Aa, Bb, and Cc. Such a trihybrid, you may recall, produces 8 kinds of gametes. If we use Punnett's checkerboard method of analysis, it will be obvious that there are 64 (8 × 8) squares and that the classes of offspring are expressed in 64ths. Random fertilization of the gametes yields 27 different genotypes among the progeny, which can be grouped, as shown in table 35.2, according to the numbers of dominant, color-producing (red) genes. In contrast to classical Mendelian inheritance, the individual genes in polygenic inheritance are cumulative in their effects. Polygenes, thus, are members of several sets of alleles that produce more or less equal additive effects on the same character.

NEGRO-CAUCASIAN CROSS

In the early 1900s, the American geneticist C. B. Davenport made extensive observations on the outcome of Negro-Caucasian marriages in Jamaica and the descendants of the mulattoes resulting from such crosses. Davenport's data indicate that the difference in the amount of black pigment between the Negroes native to West Africa and Caucasians rests upon two major pairs of genes. The polygenes for skin color in the Negro may be represented by AABB; in the Caucasian, by aabb. Each pair of genes segregates independently, but the pigment-producing alleles (A and B) act in a cumulative fashion. Davenport's hypothesis is presented in the accompanying chart.

All offspring of the cross of a Negro (AABB) and a Caucasian (aabb) are medium brown, or mulatto (AaBb). The offspring of two mulatto parents are variable in skin color, with the majority ($^6/_{16}$) being mulatto (fig. 35.1). The extreme classes, however, can be recovered, black (AABB) or white (aabb), each with a probability of 1 in 16.

Davenport's scheme is a reasonable explanation of the inheritance of skin color, although the English geneticist R. Ruggle Gates has suggested that three pairs of polygenes, rather than two pairs, fit the observed facts

Genotype	Phenotype
AABB	Black skin
AABb AaBB	Dark-brown skin
AaBb AAbb aaBB	Medium-brown skin (Mulatto)
Aabb aaBb	Light-brown skin
aabb	White skin

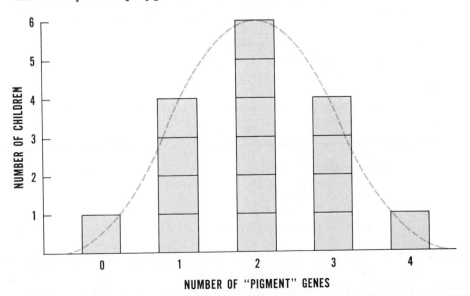

Figure 35.1 Outcome of cross between two mulatto parents (AaBb × AaBb), based on the assumption that two pairs of genes are involved, with the dominant alleles representing the pigment-producing genes. The offspring are variable in skin color, with the majority (6/16) being mulatto.

better. Whether two pairs or three pairs are involved, it is not possible, contrary to popular belief, for a Caucasian and a light-skinned Negro to produce a black-skinned child. Genetically, in the marriage of a Caucasian woman and a man of Negro ancestry, children of the union cannot be darker than the husband.

HEIGHT IN MAN

The normal curve of distribution of heights of fully grown males is shown in figure 35.2. The average, or *mean,* is 68 inches, with a *standard deviation* of 2.6 inches. Standard deviation is a measure of the variability of a population. Briefly, if a given population is normally distributed, then approximately two-thirds of the population lies within 1 standard deviation on either side of the mean—in this case, 68 plus 2.6 and 68 minus 2.6, or between 65.4 inches and 70.6 inches. Ninety-five percent of the individuals, or 19 in 20, may be expected to fall within the limits set by 2 standard deviations on either side of the mean. Thus, 1 in 40 is exceptionally tall (more than 73.2 inches) and 1 in 40 exceptionally short (less than 62.8 inches).

The distribution of height is what we should expect where there is polygenic inheritance—that is, several genes each contributing additively to the trait. The number of pairs of polygenes is not known, but for simplicity, we may assume that two pairs affect height, with each dominant gene (*A* or *B*) contributing 3 inches. The recessive genes make no contribution to the trait; the minimum height with all recessive genes (*aabb*) would be 62 inches. With this model, the heights for the nine possible genotypes are as in the accompanying chart.

			Genotypes		
	aabb	*Aabb* *aaBb*	*AAbb* *aaBB* *AaBb*	*AABb* *AaBB*	*AABB*
Height (in inches)	62	65	68	71	74
Frequency	1	4	6	4	1

Figure 35.2 Bell-shaped curve showing the distribution of heights of adult human males.

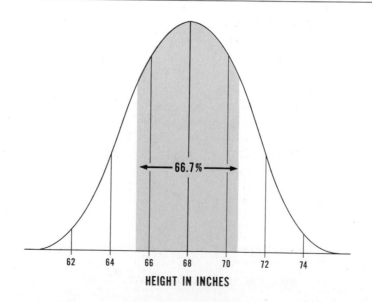

HEIGHT IN INCHES

One of the first scientists to study systematically the inheritance of height in humans was Sir Francis Galton. This British geneticist, working at the turn of the century, noticed that sons of the tallest men tend to be tall, but not as tall as their fathers. Alternatively, the sons of the shortest men tend to be short, but taller than their fathers. Although the sons show variation in height, the mean values fall halfway between the height of the father and the average height of the general population. Thus, tall fathers 74 inches in height have sons who average 71 inches; similarly, short fathers 62 inches in height have sons who average 65 inches. Galton termed this phenomenon the *law of filial regression;* it holds that progeny of extreme variants tend to return towards the average of the population. Specifically, when there are no complicating factors, a son's height regresses from the height of the father halfway towards the mean population height. This is depicted in figure 35.3.

Assuming polygenic inheritance, we can expect filial regression towards the mean under the following conditions—the actions of the genes must be strictly cumulative, and random mating must prevail. An uncommonly tall father, one 74 inches in height, can transmit only half of his dominant genes. In a randomly breeding population, the son's height will have a higher probability of being halfway between the exceptional height of his father and the average height of the population. A tall father *(AABB)* produces a gamete that has only one composition for height *(AB)*; this gamete can unite with any of four kinds of gametes produced at random by the women in the population, according to the accompanying chart.

	♀ Gametes			
	(AB)	*(Ab)*	*(aB)*	*(ab)*
♂ gamete *(AB)*	AABB 74 inches	AABb 71	AaBB 71	AaBb 68

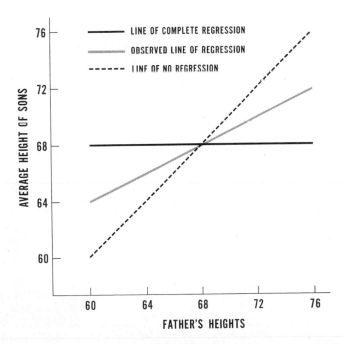

Figure 35.3 Galton's law of filial regression. The line of *no* regression signifies that the heights of the fathers and sons would be the same. The line of *complete* regression indicates that all sons would tend toward the mean of the population, irrespective of the heights of the fathers. The line of *Galtonian,* or *observed,* regression reveals that a given son's height regresses halfway towards the mean of the population from the height of the father.

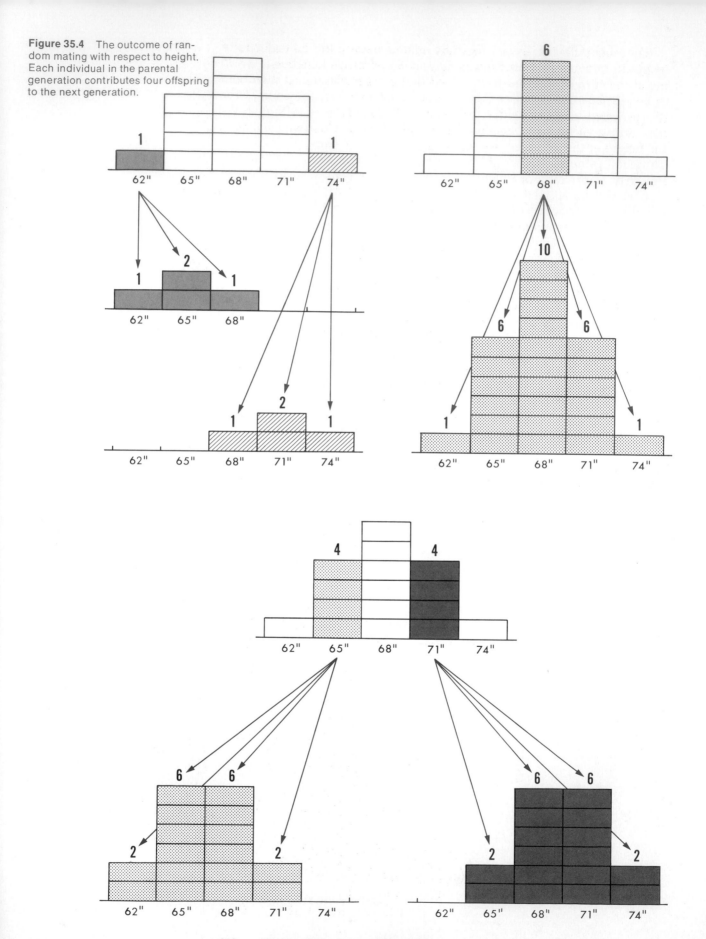

Figure 35.4 The outcome of random mating with respect to height. Each individual in the parental generation contributes four offspring to the next generation.

The numerical data in the foregoing chart are presented in visual form in figure 35.4. It may be readily seen that 50 percent of the sons are 71 inches tall, 25 percent are as tall as the father (74 inches), and 25 percent correspond to the average height of the general population (68 inches). In like manner, short men (62 inches), who produce only one kind of gamete (ab), tend to have taller children in a randomly breeding population, as seen in the chart below and in figure 35.4.

	♀ Gametes			
	(AB)	(Ab)	(aB)	(ab)
♂ gamete (ab)	AaBb 68 inches	Aabb 65	aaBb 65	aabb 62

A comparable situation exists for males of genotype Aabb, or those who are 65 inches tall. They yield offspring in the frequency 1 (71 inches):3 (68):3 (65):1 (62), with an average value of 66.5 inches. The outcome of all possible marriages is shown in figure 35.4.

We now arrive at a very simple generalization that can be easily overlooked. The tendency for regression does not imply any reduction in height variation for the next generation. With random mating, the resulting distribution in the offspring generation is exactly the same (1:4:6:4:1) as in the parental generation. This state of affairs is depicted in figure 35.5. Even if the extreme classes do not mate, they can be represented among the progeny through the mating of two persons of average height (68 inches × 68 inches). This is an important consideration. In

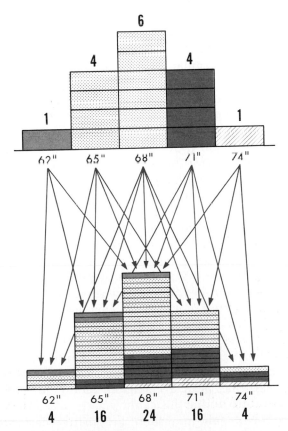

Figure 35.5 Constancy of the distribution of height from one generation to the next despite filial regression. The assumption is made that each individual in the parental generation contributes four offspring to the next generation.

order to keep the entire gamut of genetic repertoires intact in a population, all that is required is for the average heterozygous classes to be represented. Another important feature is that for any given class of parents, the offspring can be scattered into several classes; for any given class of offspring, the parents can come from several classes. Thus, a son of average height (68 inches) can be derived from any one of five fathers: *aabb* (62 inches) *Aabb* (65 inches), *AaBb* (68 inches), *AABb* (71 inches), and *AABB* (74 inches). Like does beget like; it also begets unlike. And heredity is equally responsible for both.

COMPLICATING INFLUENCES ON HEIGHT

It may have surprised you to find that the distribution of a quantitative trait, such as height, in the offspring generation remains the same as in the parental generation under a certain set of conditions. What suppositions have we used? One of the assumptions is that the effects of the polygenes are simply additive, and furthermore, there are no interactions between the alternative forms of the genes. Other assumptions are that marriages occur entirely at random with respect to height, and that all kinds of marriages are equally fertile. In addition, we assumed that there is no selection for or against an increase in height. We also ignored environmental influences on height.

Any one of those factors could change the outcome that the distribution of heights is stationary from one generation to the next. If we do find that stature in man has increased between generations, then we are confronted with the task of deciding which of the medley of different factors is primarily responsible for the increase in height. As a matter of fact, human stature has increased steadily during the past century in most industrial societies. This is particularly striking in Japan, where the average height of the population has increased 2 inches in only the last 30 years. In an extensive study of Italian males, the geneticist Cavalli-Sforza of Stanford University estimates a mean increase of stature of 1.25 inches per generation during this century. As another dramatic example, Frederick Hulse, of the University of Arizona, investigated in 1968 the heights of Italian Swiss in Switzerland and their descendants born in California. He found a difference of about 1.5 inches in height at maturity in favor of the offspring of migrants to California as compared with the sedentary population in Switzerland—those who had not emigrated.

One factor that might account, at least in part, for a change in human stature is *positive assortative mating,* or *homogamy,* in which like individuals preferentially mate with each other. (Negative assortative mating, or disassortative mating, occurs when unlike individuals preferentially mate with each other.) The available data indicate that marriages are far from random in respect to stature. There is a tendency for like to marry like—that is, for tall people to marry tall people and short to marry short. The degree of positive assortative mating is considerably lower for the intermediate statures. The effect of continual or prolonged homogamy would be to increase the proportions of the two extreme classes—the tall and the short—and to decrease the proportion of the intermediate classes. However, there is no evidence in human populations of the expected polarization of height nor of any marked loss of intermediate heterozygotes. In essence, positive assortative mating probably has been a negligible factor in the observed rate of increase in stature during this century.

Not only may there be positive assortative mating, but differential selection may occur among the classes. If tall marital partners were to consistently leave more offspring, in contrast with partners of short stature, then the level of height would rise in the population from one generation to the next. Cavalli-Sforza was able to show that stature was related to socioeconomic groups, with tall people occupying the high professional levels and shorter persons being more often found among the lowest income groups. This led to the suggestion that tall persons might have a higher reproductive fitness. If they do, selection would be operating for increased stature. It is difficult, however, to evaluate to what extent tall persons have increased viability or fertility. If there is selection for tallness, agreement seems to be general that the impact of selection is minimal or inconsequential.

The assumption that the effects of the polygenes are additive and that there are no interactions between the alternative forms of the genes are probably oversimplifications. Several geneticists have argued that the heterozygote, with two kinds of alleles, is physiologically superior to either homozygote, in which only a single allele is represented. Under this concept, the greater the number of heterozygous loci, the greater the *hybrid vigor* in quantitative traits. Thus, intermingling of parental populations that were largely homozygous would lead to a generation of offspring that would be largely heterozygous. The effects of heterozygosity are represented in the chart below.

	Homozygous Parent	Homozygous Parent
Genotype	A A b b	a a B B
Gene effect (unit of increment)	3 3 0 0	0 0 3 3
Height	68 inches	68 inches

	Progeny
Genotype	Aa Bb
Gene effect (unit of increment)	6 6
Height	74 inches

In the example of the chart, the interaction of two different alleles (such as A and a, when together) intensifies the height. This implies that divergent alleles at the same locus influence each other's action. Although the exact nature of the complementary effect is still not fully understood, hybrid vigor, the action we have been describing, has long been observed by both plant and animal breeders. In corn, for example, the F_1 hybrids from inbred homozygous strains show a marked increase in height over the parental strains. The mule is perhaps the most familiar example of a vigorous hybrid animal.

Several authors have suggested that the extensive commingling of formerly isolated human populations has favored increased heterozygosity and therefore an increase in stature. For example, hybrid vigor may account in part for the greater height of the California-born Italian Swiss previously discussed. Not all geneticists, however, support the notion of distinct effects of heterozygosity on height.

The possibility of selective migration raises but another complicating factor. It would be surprising if the migrant population were to be genetically a perfect random sample of the parent population from which they were derived. Some studies suggest that migrants are slightly taller than the sedentary individuals; this has been claimed to be the case for the Japanese that migrated to Hawaii.

It is evident that it is difficult to draw dependable conclusions from the available information. We cannot as yet completely assess the relative importance of the various factors that influence the inheritance of height in man. Most geneticists are inclined to believe, however, that the increase in height is largely the outcome of improved environmental conditions, particularly of nutrition. Thus, better living conditions are invoked as the main contributory cause, notwithstanding the high degree to which the genetic component (so-called *heritability*) contributes to stature. There is no doubt that height is a trait that is largely determined by inherited polygenic factors. Additional supporting evidence for the high heritability stems from the degree of resemblance between identical twins. When identical twins have been brought up together, differences of more than 1 inch in height between them are most unusual. Even when the identical twins have been brought up apart and thus experience differing environments, the differences between them are exceedingly slight. The adult differences in height are often less than 0.5 inch.

Even though there is a large genetic component to height, this does not mean that major environmental changes cannot affect the trait. Phenylketonuria has a very high heritability value, for instance, yet special modifications of the diet can offset this metabolic disorder. Although the environmental component to height has been judged to be small, the period of the last 100 years has seen the average human stature change by more than 1 inch per generation.

Our lingering, if not measured, treatment of height should prove instructive for analyzing another quantitative trait—the expression of mental ability (intelligence).

INTELLIGENCE IN HUMANS

In 1905, Alfred Binet, director of the Laboratory of Experimental Psychology at the Sorbonne, devised a test to identify those children of less-than-average ability who would benefit more from special education than from regular public school education. Accordingly, the test was devised for educational guidance. The test proved to be effective in predicting scholastic success of the child, and gained wide acceptance in Western countries. Unfortunately, the test also became widely known as an "intelligence" test. The test is little more than a general measure of academic readiness—that is, it serves to evaluate the ability of the child to adapt or adjust to the educational standards and values that the society in which he lives imposes on him. The more knowledge already demonstrated by the child in the examination, the greater his readiness to assimilate additional knowledge in the future. In some circles, scores on these "intelligence" tests are still interpreted as measures of inborn, or native, mental potential. No matter how sophisticated the present-day standard intelligence tests have become, they still mainly measure achieved ability and not native endowment. Whether we can draw valid inferences about inherent mental ability from the performance on the test is a matter of continuing debate. It appears difficult to draw firm conclusions, since from the moment of birth, the expression of a person's innate mental capacity is continually affected by learning experiences, motivation for learning, and cultural patterns.

In Caucasian samples, IQ scores have a mean of 100 and a standard deviation of about 15 (fig. 35.6). Since the array of scores approximates a normal distribution, IQ has been treated as if it were a quantitatively measurable character like height or weight. Yet, IQ is not an absolute measurement; it is, rather, a relative measurement. The conventional method of scoring is to assign a mental age to a child, which is the age at which average children achieve the same results on the test as the child in question. The intelligence quotient (IQ) is then derived by dividing the child's mental age by his chronological age and multiplying by 100. For example, a 6-year-old child who scores as high as the average 9-year-old would have an IQ of 150; if he scored as low as an average child of 3 years of age, his IQ would be 50. In essence, IQ scores indicate relative standings of individuals in a given population. The assumption is made, however, that such rank order is an indirect measure of intelligence. In other words, if intelligence could be measured directly and plotted in absolute terms, the values within each age group would be normally distributed. This aspect cannot be resolved because, unlike height, there is no known unit of intelligence, such as an inch or a foot, by which to make an absolutely reliable measurement.

Perhaps more disconcerting is that the IQ scores are virtually forced into a normal distribution by the very design of the examination. The examination is so constructed or tailored as to ensure that the scores conform closely to a normal distribution. Thus, the familiar bell-shaped curve does not happen by chance, but is a foregone conclusion. Nevertheless, it has been argued that continuous variation in intelligence, approaching a normal distribution, would still be observed if it were possible to measure this intangible quality directly like a metrical character. If intelligence is normally distributed, polygenic inheritance suggests itself for this attribute. Indeed, some investigators have estimated that as many as 11 pairs of polygenes may be involved. In our consideration, we shall assume that intelligence is governed by several genetic loci, each contributing additively to the trait. Additionally, whenever the term *intelligence* is henceforth used, it refers only to that quality as **measured by IQ tests.**

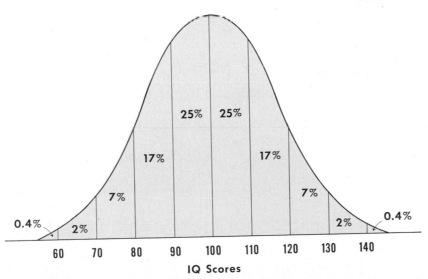

Figure 35.6 Normal curve of distribution of IQ scores, showing the expected percentages of the population in each IQ range. Except at the extremes, the percentages shown are close to those recorded in actual Caucasian samples. The IQ scores of roughly 95 percent of the Caucasian population are within the range of $100 \pm 2 \times 15$ (standard deviation), or between 70 and 130.

Several lines of inquiry suggest that heredity is an important factor in determining intelligence (as measured by standard tests). The first comes from the degree of relation of the IQs of two groups of individuals or relatives—that is, the correlation between such IQs. We direct our attention first to studies on pairs of identical (monozygotic) twins. A *correlation coefficient* expresses numerically the degree of association or resemblance of the twin members to each other. A hypothetical correlation coefficient of 1 between the IQ scores of identical twins would signify such a strong influence of heredity as to preclude any environmental effects. The extent to which the coefficient departs from unity (the amount of 1) indicates the disturbing effects of the environment, or stated differently, the importance of the environment. Figure 35.7 shows graphically the extensive data that L. Erlenmeyer-Kimling and Lissy F. Jarvik of the New York State Psychiatric Institute compiled in 1963. The mean correlation coefficient for IQ scores of monozygotic twins raised together in the same home is about 0.9; for monozygotic twins reared apart in different homes, approximately 0.8. These values would seem to indicate the predominant role of inherited factors in intelligence. Caution, however, must be exercised in interpreting the results. Monozygotic twins raised apart have likely been placed in families with similar socioeconomic and educational levels. The environments of each separated member of the pair thus may not have been substantially different and may even have been equally stimulating for learning opportunities. In essence, such twins would be correlated not only in their heredities, but also in the environments in which they have been reared.

Specifically, investigators have found that the average difference between the IQs of identical twins who have lived together is 5 points and between separated twins, 8 points. A difference of 5 points is not likely to be significant, since the accuracy of the tests themselves is only 5 or 6 points. *Accuracy* here means that the same individual on a repeat test, on the average, might score 5 points higher or lower. The greater difference (8 points) between separated twins suggests that IQ is somewhat modified by differences of experience. One could contend that the difference would have been even greater than 8 points if the twins had been placed in homes offering vastly different educational opportunities and markedly different expectations of achievement.

Concerning other sets or groups of related individuals, figure 35.7 **shows that the correlation coefficients of the following paired groups**

Figure 35.7 Correlation coefficients compiled from the published literature by L. Erlenmeyer-Kimling and L. F. Jarvik of the New York State Psychiatric Institute. Horizontal lines show the range of correlation coefficients in IQ scores between individuals of varied degrees of relationship. For example, the correlation coefficients of samples of parents and children from various studies (*top* horizontal line) range from about 0.20 to 0.80. The vertical line intersecting each horizontal line represents the mean value.

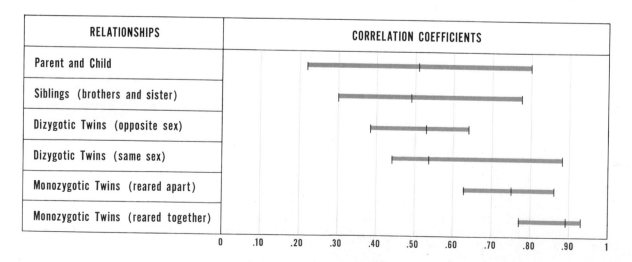

are very nearly 0.5—between parent and child, between siblings, between fraternal (dizygotic) twins of the same sex, and between fraternal twins of the opposite sex. The value of 0.5 is what would be expected if we assume the polygenic inheritance model, and discount environmental influences or complications of any kind. Specifically, the average variation between siblings (brothers and sisters) is 12.5 IQ points. In this case, it has been concluded that the difference of 12.5 points is too great to be ascribed to variations in educational stimulation or other conditions in the home environment.

Studies on adopted children have been interpreted as indicating that intelligence (as measured by IQ tests) is strongly heritable. The IQ of an adopted child correlates closely with the IQs of its real, or biological, parents even though the child is reared by adoptive parents. This, however, may not be too surprising since adoption agencies usually place a child in a matching home.

DIFFERENTIAL FERTILITY AND INTELLIGENCE

In an earlier era, Sir Francis Galton predicted that the average level of intelligence in the general population should decline. His concern was based on the negative correlation between IQ and fertility. Since IQ exhibits a descending gradient with educational status, and since the lower educational groups produce more children than the higher groups (table 35.3), Galton expected the mean intelligence in the population to decline with time. Raymond Cattell reiterated the same concern in 1940—that a differential birth rate with respect to intelligence would gradually result in a lower IQ in the general population. However, no evidence exists for any such decline in IQ over time. Data from Scotland, Sweden, Honolulu, and other sources do not support the pessimistic prognoses of Galton and Cattell.

The most extensive study was on Scottish children, conducted by the Scottish Council for Research in Education. In 1932, some 87,000 11-year-old school children in Edinburgh (constituting about 90 percent of all 11-year-olds) were given a verbal intelligence test. In 1947, this same test was administered to a similar population of children totaling more than 70,000. The average performance did not decline, but rather im-

Table 35.3
Relation of Fertility and Educational Status

Schooling Completed by Mothers (in Years)	Mean Number of Children per Woman	Mean Number of Children per Married Woman
None	3.95	4.97
Grade school		
1–4	4.33	4.54
5–6	3.74	3.97
7–8	2.78	3.04
High school		
1–3	2.37	2.61
4	1.75	2.03
College		
1–3	1.71	2.07
4 or more	1.23	1.83

Source: U.S. Bureau of the Census 1940 Report. Figures based on numbers of children born to American women aged 45–49 years (that is, those who had completed their childbearing).

proved, with a gain of 2 points on the IQ scale. The interpretation of the increase is not obvious. It is unlikely that the observed rise resulted from genetic improvement of the population. It would be difficult to invoke positive assortative mating or hybrid vigor. It appears reasonable to suppose that some nongenetic factor accounted for the rise in IQ. Some possible factors may have been the difference in sibship size of the 1932 and 1947 groups, greater familiarity with testing procedures (test sophistication), better educational facilities, and improved quality of instruction.

Sibship size, or number of brothers and sisters in a family, is intriguing, particularly when one considers the reported findings in the 1930s and 1940s of a significant negative correlation between IQ and family size. These data showed that the bright children came from small families, and alternatively, the less gifted children came from large families. Crowded living conditions in large families appear to be responsible, in part, for the negative relation between IQ and family size. An indication of the importance of the environmental component is shown by data on twins. It has been found that the mean IQ of identical twins is 5 points lower than the mean IQ of nontwins (those siblings singly born). The most likely explanation is the inevitable reduction in the attention parents can give to each of two children born at the same time, although we cannot overlook the possibility of differential effects of the *in utero* maternal environment on identical twins.

Given the negative relation between IQ and family size, we should again be inclined to predict a decline in IQ from one generation to another. In the 1960s, investigators at the Dight Institute of Human Genetics at the University of Minnesota, led by J. V. Higgins and S. Reed, reconsidered the problem. Their important finding was that the negative correlation between family size and intelligence was counterbalanced by the poor reproductive capacity of those persons with very low IQs. The intensive study revealed that almost a third of the persons whose IQs are 70 or lower have no children. Considerably fewer individuals with higher IQs were childless—only one-tenth of persons in the IQ range of 101–110 and about one twenty-fifth of those of IQs higher than 131. Previous analyses did not take sufficient account of those individuals in the low IQ groups who never marry or who fail to reproduce when married. Because of the large numbers of childless members of the low IQ group, this group as a whole does *not* produce more children than groups with higher intelligence do.

In essence, the intelligence level in the general population is not eroding. In fact, C. J. Bajema's study in 1963 of a population in Kalamazoo County, Michigan, suggests a reversal in the reproductive pattern—that is, a positive relation between intelligence and fertility rate is arising. Bajema reports that individuals with high IQs are now producing more children, at least in the population studied, than individuals of average or low IQ.

NEGROES AND INTELLIGENCE

The educational psychologist Arthur R. Jensen, in his controversial article in the *Harvard Educational Review* in 1969, stressed the importance of inherited factors in the determination of individual differences in intelligence. He hypothesized that the average genetic potential for intelligence is substantially less in Negroes (blacks) than in Caucasians (whites). In other words, Jensen claims that American blacks have an intrinsically lower mean genetic endowment. Other investigators have ascribed the lower average performance of blacks on IQ tests to a complex of environmental factors associated with social and economic deprivation. In view of the sharply different socioeconomic experiences of black groups and white groups in the United States, most investigators consider the *environmental disadvantage* hypothesis the more plausible.

Many studies have revealed that appreciable differences exist in the performance on IQ tests of blacks and whites in the United States. Black children score, on the average, about 15 points lower than whites on standard IQ tests. Much has also been made of the finding that blacks from northern states tend to have higher IQ scores than the average southern black. This finding has been the subject of varied interpretations. Some claim that the northern blacks are not as socially and economically disadvantaged as their counterparts in the South. Others suggest that the blacks that migrated to seek economic opportunities in the North were genetically more intelligent than those that remained in the South. Some recent studies support the former notion that a change to better environmental circumstances, combined with appropriate motivation, has enabled blacks to raise their test scores after settling in the North. These studies show that migrant blacks have a clear pattern of improvement in IQ scores associated with their increasing length of residence in the North. Apparently, then, the better performance of northern blacks is primarily related to increasing exposure to educational and economic opportunities, and an enhanced motivation to make use of the opportunities offered.

The hypothesis of differences in the gene pool for migrant populations as compared with the parent population has been invoked on more than one occasion. The American blacks are descendants of involuntary immigrants from Africa. Conceivably, the American blacks may be descendants of a highly selected sample of African blacks who were less intelligent than the total group. In other words, slavery may have tended to select for less intelligence rather than more, even though unselected blacks and whites are not genetically different in ability. To most geneticists, this possibility appears unlikely. In our earlier discussion of polygenic inheritance, we noted that any fair-sized genotypically variable population can in time produce individuals who have widely varied genetic makeups. If there are a certain number of heterozygotes in the middle range, the mean of the population can reproduce a wide genetic spectrum in one or two generations.

Although the possibility of a genetic difference in IQ between black Americans and white Americans cannot be excluded, it appears more likely that environmental factors can account for most, if not all, of the differences in performance on IQ tests. Even within a single racial group (whites), there exists appreciable variation in IQ scores. As previously stated, the mean IQ difference between identical twins reared apart is 8 points, and identical twins differ as much as 5 points from their nontwin sibs, with the twins having the lower IQs. However, the average score differences between blacks and whites are of a greater order of magnitude than the twin differences. The IQ tests are not free of cultural bias. The IQ tests have been designed for Caucasian populations and standardized thereon. In particular, the content of the IQ test is based largely on the attitudes, values, and expectations of whites in a Western industrial society. Since the IQ test has been tailored to the requirements of the European-American culture, it appears to be culturally inappropriate, or of dubious value, for Afro-Americans (and for that matter, Mexican-Americans, Puerto Ricans, and American Indians). Indeed, it is scarcely imaginable that the IQ scores could be at all comparable between cultures that have disparate educational opportunities, different expectations of achievement, and different degrees of motivation for learning. One may reasonably conclude that the IQ tests serve almost exclusively to illuminate cultural differences.

SUMMARY

Quantitative traits, like height, show continuous variation, or gradations from one extreme to the other. Inheritance of a quantitative trait involves numerous genes, or polygenes, each of which makes a small contribution to the total effect. Offspring of extreme variants tend to return, or regress, towards the average of the population. Specifically, a son's height regresses from the height of the father halfway towards the mean population height. However, the tendency for regression does not affect the total frequency distribution for the next generation. In the absence of complicating factors, the offspring generation shows the same distribution in height variation as the parental generation. There are, however, a host of complicating influences that can alter the frequency distribution in height from one generation to the next. These include: nonadditive effects of the polygenes, interactions between the alternative forms of the gene pairs (heterosis, or hybrid vigor), nonrandom mating (assortative mating), differential selection, selective migration, and environmental changes.

When we find that stature in man has increased between generations, it is difficult to arrive at firm conclusions concerning which of the medley of different modifying factors is primarily responsible for the increase in height (although improved environmental conditions, particularly nutrition, appear to be important contributory factors). In like manner, when we find that two groups of populations differ in the expression of mental ability (intelligence), we cannot completely assess the relative importance of the various factors that could cause the difference. Moreover, unlike height, there is no known unit of intelligence, such as an inch or a foot, by which to make an absolutely reliable measurement. Conventional IQ tests evaluate principally the ability of the child to adapt or adjust to the educational standards and values imposed upon him by the society in which he lives.

Races and Species

36

Any large assemblage representing a particular organism is generally not distributed equally or uniformly throughout its territory or range in nature. A widespread group of plants or animals is typically subdivided into numerous local populations, each physically separated from the others to some extent. The environmental conditions in different parts of the range of an organism are not likely to be identical. We may thus expect that each local population will consist of genetic types that are adapted to a specific set of prevailing environmental conditions. The degree to which each population maintains its genetic distinctness is governed by the extent to which interbreeding of the populations occurs. A free interchange of genes between populations tends to blur the differences between the populations. But what are the consequences when gene exchange between populations is greatly restricted or prevented?

VARIATION BETWEEN POPULATIONS

To answer the question, our first consideration is to demonstrate that inheritable variations do exist among the various breeding populations in different geographical localities of an organism. Jens Clausen, David Keck, and William Hiesey of the Carnegie Institution of Washington at Stanford, California, have shown that each of the populations of the yarrow plant *Achillea lanulosa* from different parts of California is adapted to its respective habitat. As figure 36.1 shows, the variations in height of the plant are correlated with altitudinal differences. The shortest plants are from the highest altitudes, and the plants increase in height in a gradient fashion with decreasing altitude. The term *cline*, or character gradient, has been applied to such situations for which a character varies more or less continuously with a gradual change in the environmental terrain.

The observation by itself that the yarrow plants are phenotypically dissimilar at different elevations does not indicate that they are genetically different. If the claim is to be made that the observed variations represent local adaptations resulting from natural selection, then a hereditary basis for the differences in height should be demonstrated. It is often difficult to obtain data that disclose the hereditary nature of population differences. In this respect, the studies of Clausen and his co-workers are commendable. The plants shown in figure 36.1 had actually been grown together in a uniform experimental garden at Stanford, California. The plants, transplanted from various localities, developed differently from one another in the same experimental garden, revealing that each population had evolved its own distinctive complex of genes.

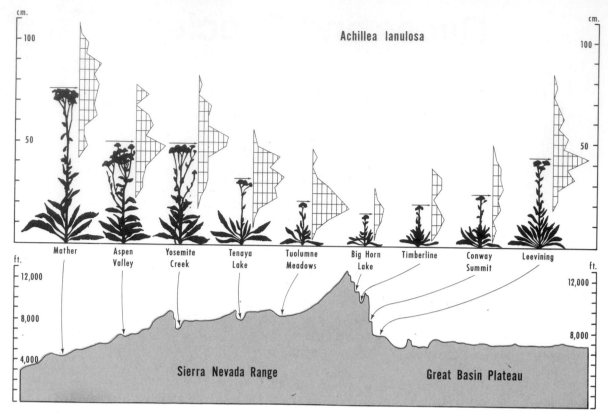

Achillea lanulosa

Mather Aspen Valley Yosemite Creek Tenaya Lake Tuolumne Meadows Big Horn Lake Timberline Conway Summit Leevining

Sierra Nevada Range   Great Basin Plateau

Figure 36.1 Clinal variation in the yarrow plant, *Achillea lanulosa*. The increase in height of the plant is more or less continuous with decreasing altitude. The plants shown here are representatives from different populations in the Sierra Nevada Mountains of California that were grown in a uniform garden at Stanford, California. Each plant illustrated is one of average height for the given population; the graph adjacent to the plant reveals the distribution of heights within the population. (From Clausen, Keck, and Hiesey, *Carnegie Institution of Washington Publication 581*, 1948.)

RACES

The variation pattern in organisms may be discrete, or discontinuous, particularly when the populations are separated from each other by pronounced physical barriers. This is exemplified by the varieties of the carpenter bee *(Xylocopa nobilis)* in the Celebes and neighboring islands of Indonesia (fig. 36.2). As shown by the studies of J. van der Vecht of the Museum of Natural History at Leiden in the Netherlands, there are three different varieties on the mainland of Celebes, and at least three kinds on the adjacent small islands. These geographical variants differ conspicuously in the coloration of the small, soft hairs that cover the surface of the body. The first abdominal segment is invariably clothed with bright yellow hairs. However, each variety has evolved a unique constellation of colors on the other abdominal segments and also on the thorax.

The variations in the carpenter bees within and between islands are well defined and easily distinguishable. One may refer to populations with well-marked discontinuities as *races*. Races are simply geographical aggregates of populations that differ in the incidence of genetic traits. How genetically different two assemblages of populations must be to be called different races is an open question.

Some of the problems inherent in delimiting races are exemplified by the different temperature-adapted populations of the North American leopard frog, *Rana pipiens*. John A. Moore, then at Columbia University and later at the University of California, has tested the effects of temperature on the development of the embryos of frogs from widely different localities. He wished to ascertain the limits of temperatures that the embryos could endure or tolerate. The findings on four different geographic populations in the eastern states are shown in figure 36.3.

Embryos of northern *Rana pipiens* populations are more resistant to

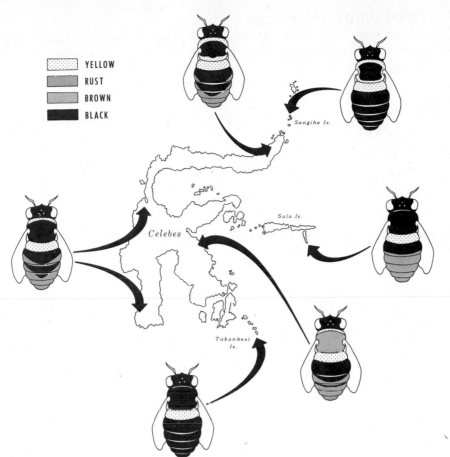

Figure 36.2 Geographic variation of color pattern in females of the carpenter bee, *Xylocopa nobilis,* in the Celebes and neighboring islands in Indonesia. Each geographic race has evolved a distinctive constellation of colors. (Based on studies by J. van der Vecht.)

YELLOW
RUST
BROWN
BLACK

Sangihe Is.

Sula Is.

Celebes

Tukanbesi Is.

low temperatures and less tolerant of high temperatures than are embryos from southern populations. Embryos of populations from Vermont and New Jersey have comparable ranges of temperature tolerances. These northern embryos can resist temperature as low as 5°C. Embryos from Florida differ markedly from those of northern populations. Embryos from southern Florida (latitude 27°N) can tolerate temperatures as high as 35°C, but are very susceptible to low temperatures. Hence, northern and southern populations have become adapted to different environments in their respective territories.

We may refer to the northern populations as the cold-adapted race of the leopard frog, and designate the southern populations as the warm-adapted race. It is evident that we are being arbitrary in drawing a fine line of demarcation between northern and southern races. Data are presently lacking for the geographically intermediate populations, but further studies will probably reveal that the temperature adaptations of the frog embryos change gradually from north to south. Even with the present information, one may wish to recognize more than two temperature-adapted races, or perhaps, as some investigators firmly argue, refrain completely from making racial designations.

Races may be best thought of as units of organization below the species level. In other words, races may be considered as stages in the transformation of populations into species. But what constitutes a species? Up to this point we have assiduously avoided the term *species.* A discussion of the process leading to the formation of species will facilitate understanding of the term itself.

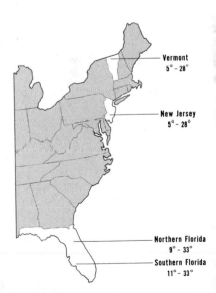

Vermont
5° - 28°

New Jersey
5° - 28°

Northern Florida
9° - 33°

Southern Florida
11° - 33°

Figure 36.3 Limits of temperature tolerance of embryos of the leopard frog *(Rana pipiens)* from different geographical populations. Embryos of northern populations are more resistant to low temperatures and less tolerant of high temperatures than are embryos from southern populations. (Based on studies by John A. Moore.)

FORMATION OF SPECIES

Let us imagine a large assemblage of land snails subdivided in three geographical aggregations or races, *A*, *B*, and *C*, each adapted to local environmental conditions (fig. 36.4). There are initially no gross barriers separating the populations from each other, and where *A* meets *B* and *B* meets *C*, interbreeding occurs. Zones of intermediate individuals are thus established between the races, and the width of these zones **depends on the extent to which the respective populations intermingle.**

Geographical Variation

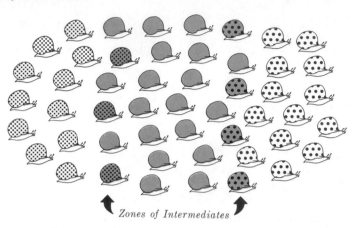

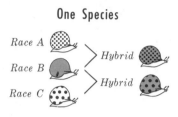

One Species

Race A ⟩ *Hybrid*
Race B ⟩
Race C ⟩ *Hybrid*

Zones of Intermediates

Isolating Action of Geographic Barrier

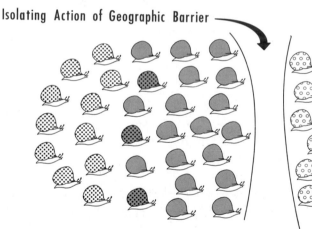

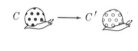

$C \longrightarrow C'$

Removal of Geographic Barrier

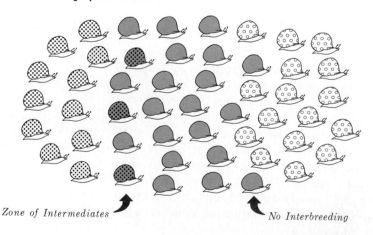

Zone of Intermediates   *No Interbreeding*

Original Species

Race A ⟩ *Hybrid*
Race B ⟩

New Species

C'

It is important to realize that races are fully capable of exchanging genes with one another.

We may now visualize (fig. 36.4) some striking physical feature, such as a great river, forging its way through the territory and effectively isolating the land snails of race C from those of B. These two assemblages may be spatially separated from each other for an indefinitely long period, affording an opportunity for race C to pursue an independent evolutionary course. Two populations that are geographically separated, like B and C in our model, are said to be *allopatric*. (Technically speaking, A and B are also allopatric, since they, for the most part, occupy different geographical areas.)

After eons of time, the river may dry up and the hollow bed may eventually become filled in with land. Now, if the members of populations B and C were to extend their ranges and meet again, one of two things might happen. The snails of the two populations might freely interbreed and establish once again a zone of intermediate individuals. On the other hand, the two populations might no longer be able to interchange genes because they have become so different genetically that they cannot. If the two assemblages can exist side by side without interbreeding, then the two groups have reached the evolutionary status of separate species. *A species is a breeding community that preserves its genetic identity by its inability to exchange genes with other such breeding communities.* In our model (fig. 36.4), race C has become transformed into a new species, C'. Two species (A-B and C') have now arisen where formerly only one existed. It should be noted that races A and B are treated as members of a single species since no barriers to gene exchange exist between them.

NOMENCLATURE

The scientific names that the taxonomist would apply to our populations of land snails deserve special comment. The technical name of a species consists of two words, in Latin or in latinized form. An acceptable designation of the original species of land snails depicted in figure 36.4 would be *Helix typicus*. The first word is the name of a comprehensive group, the genus, to which land snails belong; the second word is a name unique to the species. The taxonomist would be obliged to create a different latinized second name for the newly derived species of land snail, the C' population in figure 36.4. This new species might well be called *Helix varians*. The name of the genus remains the same since the two species are closely related. The genus, therefore, denotes a group of interrelated species. Taxonomists choose a given latinized species name for a variety of reasons, and more often than not, the latinized name does not connote much information about the organism itself. Thus, the student should not imagine that the key features of each species are encoded in the name, any more than a person's given name is particularly revealing of his or her attributes. The names are important, however, in revealing relationships.

The binomial (two-named) system of nomenclature, universally accepted, was devised by the Swedish naturalist Carolus Linnaeus (born Karl von Linné) in his monumental work, *Systema Naturae*, first published in 1735. Convention dictates that the first letter of the generic name be capitalized and that the specific name begin with a small letter. It is also customary to print the scientific name of a species in italics, or in a type that is different from that of the accompanying text. A modern refinement of the Linnaean system is the introduction of a third italicized name, which signifies the subspecies. Geographical races are recognized taxonomically as subspecies. Thus, it would be appropriate to designate races A and B (fig. 36.4) as *Helix typicus elegans* and *Helix typicus eminens*, respectively. Such a species composed of two (or more) subspecies is said to be *polytypic*. A monotypic species is one that is not differentiated into two or more geographical races or subspecies; *Helix varians* would be a monotypic species.

REPRODUCTIVE ISOLATING MECHANISMS

We have seen that two populations (or races), while spatially separated from each other, may accumulate sufficient genetic differences in isolation that they would no longer be able to interchange genes if they came into contact with one another. When the geographical barrier persists, it is difficult to judge the extent to which the two allopatric populations have diverged genetically from each other. Only when the two populations come together again does it become apparent whether or not they have changed in ways that would make them reproductively incompatible. Two populations that come to occupy the same territory are called *sympatric*. The ways or agencies that prevent interbreeding of sympatric species are known as *reproductive isolating mechanisms*.

Reproductive isolating mechanisms take varied forms, and one or more of the different types may be found separating two species. The various types may be grouped into two broad categories. One category includes the prezygotic (or premating) mechanisms, which serve to prevent the formation of hybrid zygotes. The other category encompasses the postzygotic (or postmating) mechanisms, which act to reduce the viability or fertility of hybrid zygotes. The specific types of isolating mechanisms under these two groupings can be listed as follows:

A. Prezygotic (premating) mechanisms
   1. Habitat (ecological) isolation
   2. Seasonal (temporal) isolation
   3. Sexual (ethological) isolation
   4. Mechanical isolation
   5. Gametic isolation
B. Postzygotic (postmating) mechanisms
   1. Hybrid inviability
   2. Hybrid sterility
   3. Hybrid breakdown

Two related species may live in the same general area, but differ in their ecological requirements. The scarlet oak (*Quercus coccinea*) of eastern North America grows in moist or swampy soils, whereas the black oak (*Quercus velutina*) is adapted to drier soils (fig. 36.5). The two kinds of oaks are thus effectively separated by different *ecological* or *habitat* preferences. Two sympatric species may also retain their distinctness by breeding at different times of the year (*seasonal isolation*). Evidently, cross-fertilization is not feasible between two species of frogs that release their gametes on different months even in the same pond, or between two species of pine that shed their pollen in different periods. The breeding seasons of two species may overlap, but interbreeding may not occur because of the lack of mutual attraction between the sexes of the two

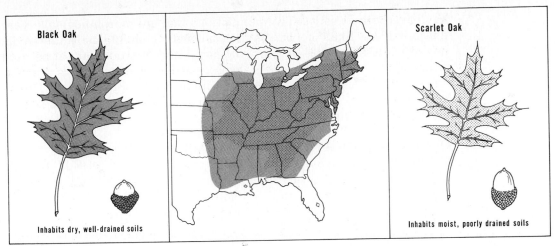

Within the figure:

Black Oak — Inhabits dry, well-drained soils

Scarlet Oak — Inhabits moist, poorly drained soils

species *(sexual isolation)*. Among birds, for example, elaborate courtship rituals play important roles in species recognition and the avoidance of interspecific matings.

In many insects, interbreeding of species is hindered by differences in the structure of the reproductive apparatus *(mechanical isolation)*. Copulation is not possible because the genitalia of one species is physically incompatible with the genitalia of the other species. In fact, several closely related species of insects can often be accurately classified by their distinctive genitalia. In some instances, the male of one species may inseminate the female of the other species, but the sperm cells may be inviable in the reproductive tract of the female. This form of *gametic isolation* is not unique to animals; in plants, such as the Jimson weed *(Datura)*, the sperm-bearing pollen tube of one species encounters a hostile environment in the flower tissue of the other species and is unable to reach the egg.

Cross-fertilizations between two species may be successful, but the hybrid embryos may be abnormal or fail to reach sexual maturity *(hybrid inviability)*. For example, two species of the chicory plant, *Crepis tectorum* and *Crepis capillaris*, can be crossed, but the hybrid seedlings die in early development. Crosses between the bullfrog, *Rana catesbeiana*, and the green frog, *Rana clamitans*, result in inviable embryos. In certain hybrid crosses, such as between females of the toad species *Bufo fowleri* and males of *Bufo valliceps*, the hybrids may survive but are completely sterile *(hybrid sterility)*. The familiar example of hybrid sterility is the mule, the offspring of a male ass and a female horse. In some situations, the F_1 hybrids appear to be vigorous and fertile, but the viability of a subsequent generation is very reduced. Such a case of *hybrid breakdown* has been described in several species of cotton—*Gossypium hirsutum* and *Gossypium barbadense*. They produce normal, fertile F_1 hybrids, but the majority of the F_2 hybrid cotton seedlings fail to germinate.

In essence, two populations can remain genetically distinct, and be designated as species, when gene exchange between them is prevented or limited by one or more reproductive isolating mechanisms. We are often unable to obtain direct evidence for the presence or absence of interbreeding in nature between two groups. The degree of reproductive isolation is then indirectly gauged by the extent to which the members of two populations differ in morphological, physiological, and behavioral characteristics. Two populations that are morphologically very dissimilar are likely to be distinct species. It should be understood, however, that the level of morphological differentiation cannot be used with implicit confidence as an absolute criterion of a species. For example, two species of fruit flies, *Drosophila pseudoobscura* and *Drosophila persimilis*, are reproductively isolated, but are almost indistinguishable on morphological grounds.

ORIGIN OF ISOLATING MECHANISMS

How do reproductive isolating mechanisms arise? In the 1940s, John A. Moore undertook a series of instructive evolutionary studies on the leopard frog, *Rana pipiens*. The leopard frog is widely distributed in North America, ranging from northern Canada through the United States and Mexico into the lower reaches of Central America. Moore obtained leopard frogs from different geographical populations and crossed them in the laboratory. When frogs from northeastern United States (Vermont) were crossed with their southerly distributed lowland relatives in eastern Mexico (Axtla in San Luis Potosi), the hybrid embryos failed to develop normally. Thus, the geographically extreme members of this species have diverged genetically to the extent that they are incapable of producing viable hybrids in the laboratory.

It must be admitted that the possibility of a Vermont frog crossing with a Mexican frog in nature is extremely remote. It took a biologist to bring these two frogs together. Yet it is just this point that emphasizes that an isolating mechanism, such as hybrid inviability, does not develop for the effect itself; it is simply the natural consequence of sufficient genetic differences accumulated in two populations during a long geographical separation. The late Hermann J. Muller of Indiana University was among the first to advance the concept that isolating mechanisms originate as a by-product of genetic divergence of allopatric populations. The genetic changes that arise to adapt one population to particular environmental conditions may also be instrumental in reproductively isolating that population from other populations that are themselves developing adaptive gene complexes. Indeed, the embryos of Vermont leopard frogs differ considerably in their range of temperature tolerance from embryos of eastern Mexican frogs. It might well be, then, that the embryonic defects in hybrids between these northern and southern frogs are associated with the different temperature adaptations of the parental eggs.

If the Vermont and Mexican leopard frogs were ever to meet in nature, then any intercrosses between them would lead to the formation of inviable hybrids. This would represent a wastage of reproductive energy of the parental frogs. Theodosius Dobzhansky has advanced the interesting hypothesis that under such conditions, natural selection would promote the establishment of isolating mechanisms that would guard against the production of abnormal hybrids. In frogs, a normal mating or a mismating in a mixed population depends principally on the discrimination of the female. The reproductive potential is obviously lower for an undiscriminating female than for a female who leaves normal offspring. If the tendency to mismate is inheritable, then the genes responsible for this tendency will eventually be lost or sharply reduced in frequency by elimination of the indiscriminate females, an elimination effectively accomplished by the inviability of their offspring. Thus, the continual propagation of females that most resist the attentions of "foreign" males will lead eventually to a situation in which mismatings do not occur and abnormal hybrids are not produced at all.

Karl Koopman, an able student of Theodosius Dobzhansky, has tested the hypothesis that natural selection tends to strengthen, or make complete, the reproductive isolation between two species coexisting in the same territory. Koopman used for experimentation two species of fruit flies, *Drosophila pseudoobscura* and *Drosophila persimilis*. In nature, sexual selection between these two sympatric species is strong, and interspecific matings do not occur. However, in a mixed population in the laboratory, particularly at low temperatures, mismatings do take place. Koopman accordingly brought together members of both species in an experimental cage and purposely kept the cage at a low temperature (16 °C). Hybrid flies were produced and were viable, but Koopman in effect made them inviable by painstakingly removing them from the breeding cage when each new generation emerged. Over a period of several generations the production of hybrid flies dwindled markedly and mismatings in the population cage were substantially curtailed. This is a dramatic demonstration of the efficacy of selection in strengthening reproductive isolation between two sympatric species.

MAN: A SINGLE VARIABLE SPECIES

There is only one present-day species of man, *Homo sapiens*. Different populations of man can interbreed successfully, and, in fact, do. The extensive commingling of populations renders it difficult, if not impossible, to establish discrete racial categories in man. Races are geographically defined aggregates of local populations. The populations of mankind are no longer sharply separated geographically from one another. Multiple migrations of peoples and innumerable intermarriages have tended to blur the genetical contrasts between populations. The boundaries of human races, if they can be delimited at all, are at best fuzzy, ever shifting with time.

The term *race* is regrettably one of the most abused words in the English vocabulary. The biologist views a race as synonymous with a geographical subspecies; a race or subspecies is a genetically distinguishable subgrouping of a species. It is exceedingly important to recognize that a *race* is not a community based on language, literature, religion, nationality, or customs. There are Aryan languages, but there is not an Aryan race. Aryans are peoples of diverse genetical makeups who speak a common tongue (Indo-European). *Aryan* is therefore nothing more than a linguistic designation. In like manner, there is a Jewish religion, but not a Jewish race. And there is an Italian nation, but not an Italian race. A race is a reproductive community of individuals occupying a definite region, and in one and the same geographical region may be found Aryans, Jews, and Italians. Every human population today consists of a multitude of diverse genotypes. A pure population, or race, in which all members are genetically alike, is a myth and a blatant absurdity.

SUMMARY

The maintenance of a given species as a discrete breeding community is possible only if the members are unable to exchange genes with other distinct breeding communities of species. Unless two species are isolated geographically, they preserve their genetic identities by reproductive isolating mechanisms that take a variety of forms. Reproductive isolating mechanisms may be ecological, seasonal, ethological, or mechanical barriers to interbreeding; if cross-fertilizations do occur, the extent of gene exchange is typically restricted by hybrid inviability or hybrid sterility. The development of isolating barriers, at least initially, is the consequence of the accumulation of genetic differences in the incipient species while they are spatially separated from each other. Natural selection can strengthen, or make complete, the reproductive isolation between the two incipient species when they come together in the same territory. Any gene that raises the barrier to hybridization of coexisting species would have a positive selective value and would become incorporated in the gene complex.

Races are geographical populations of a species. Races are fully capable of exchanging genes with one another. The boundaries of races are often difficult to delimit, particularly in human populations. Multiple migrations of peoples and innumerable intermarriages have tended to blur the genetical contrasts between human populations. The concept of race, especially in man, is of limited usefulness.

Adaptive Radiation 37

The capacity of a population of organisms to increase its numbers is governed to a large extent by the availability of resources—food, shelter, and space. The available supply of resources in a given environment is limited, whereas the organism's innate ability to multiply is unlimited. A particular environment will soon prove to be inadequate for the number of individuals present. It might thus be expected that some individuals would explore new environments where competition for resources is low. The tendency of individuals to exploit new opportunities is a factor of major significance in the emergence of several new species from an ancestral stock. The successful colonization of previously unoccupied habitats can lead to a rich multitude of diverse species, each better fitted to survive and reproduce under the new conditions than in the ancestral habitat. The spreading of populations into different environments accompanied by divergent adaptive changes of the emigrant populations is referred to as *adaptive radiation*.

GALÁPAGOS ISLANDS

One of the biologically strangest, yet fascinating, areas of the world is an isolated cluster of islands of volcanic origin in the eastern Pacific, the Galápagos Islands. These islands, which Darwin visited for five weeks in 1835, lie on the equator, 600 miles west of Ecuador (fig. 37.1). The islands are composed wholly of volcanic rock; they were never connected with the mainland of South America. The rugged shoreline cliffs are of gray lava and the coastal lowlands are parched, covered with cacti and thorn bushes. In the humid uplands, tall trees flourish in rich black soil.

Giant land dwelling tortoises still inhabit these islands (plate 16). After many years of being needlessly slain by pirates and whalers, these remarkable animals now live protected in a sanctuary created in 1959. Still prevalent on the islands are the world's only marine iguana and its inland variety, the land iguana (fig. 37.2). These two species of prehistoric-looking lizards are ancient arrivals from the mainland. The marine forms occur in colonies on the lava shores, and swim offshore to feed on seaweed. The land iguana lives on leaves and cactus plants. Cactus fills most of the water needs of the land iguana.

At least 85 different kinds of birds have been recorded on the islands. These include rare cormorants that cannot fly, found only on Narborough Island, and flamingos, which breed on James Island. Of particular interest are the small black finches. These black birds exhibit remarkable variations in the structure of the beak and in feeding habits. The finches afford an outstanding example of adaptive radiation. It was the marked diversity within this small group of birds that gave impetus to Darwin's

Figure 37.1 Galápagos Islands ("Enchanted Isles") in the Pacific Ocean, 600 miles west of Ecuador. Darwin had explored this cluster of isolated islands, and found a strange animal life, a "little world within itself." The four stamps shown were issued by Ecuador to commemorate the centenary of Darwin's visit of 1835.

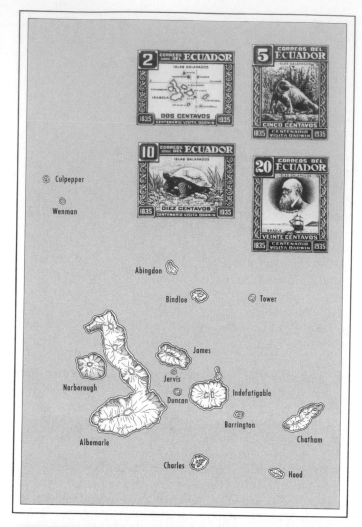

Figure 37.2 Land iguana on one of the Galápagos Islands. Despite their horrendous appearance, these bizarre inland lizards are mild, torpid, and vegetarians. They feed on leaves and cactus plants. (Courtesy of the American Museum of Natural History.)

evolutionary views. Darwin had correctly surmised that the diverse finches were modified descendants of the early, rather homogeneous, colonists of the Galápagos. Our present knowledge of these birds, now appropriately called "Darwin's finches," derives largely from the accomplished work of David Lack at Oxford, who visited the Enchanted Isles in 1938.

DARWIN'S FINCHES

Darwin's finches descended from seed-eating birds that inhabited the mainland of South America. The ancestors of Darwin's finches were early migrants to the Galápagos Islands, and probably the first land birds to reach the islands. These early colonists have given rise to 14 distinct species, each well adapted to a specific niche (fig. 37.3). Thirteen of these species occur in the Galápagos; one is found in the small isolated Cocos Island, northeast of the Galápagos.

The most striking differences among the species are in the sizes and shapes of the beak, which are correlated with marked differences in feeding habits. Six of the species are ground finches, with heavy beaks specialized for crushing seeds. Some of the ground finches live mainly on a diet of seeds found on the ground; others feed primarily on the flowers of prickly pear cacti. The cactus eaters possess decurved, flower-probing beaks. Their beaks are thicker than the beaks of typical flower-eating birds.

Figure 37.3 Representatives of Darwin's finches. There are 14 species of Darwin's finches, confined to the Galápagos with the exception of one species that inhabits Cocos Island. Closest to the ancestral stock are the six species of ground finches, primarily seed-eaters. The others evolved into eight species of tree finches, the majority of which feed on insects.

Small Insectivorous Tree Finch

Large Insectivorous Tree Finch

Warbler Finch

Medium Insectivorous Tree Finch

Woodpecker Finch

Large Ground Finch (seed-eater)

Medium Ground Finch (seed-eater)

Small Ground Finch (seed-eater)

Large Cactus Ground Finch

All the other species are tree finches, the majority of which feed on insects in the moist forests. One of the most remarkable of these tree dwellers is the woodpecker finch. It possesses a stout, straight beak, but lacks the long tongue characteristic of the true woodpecker. Like a woodpecker, it bores into wood in search of insect larvae, but then it uses a cactus spine or twig to probe out its insect prey from the excavated crevice (plate 18). Equally extraordinary is the warbler finch, which resembles in form and habit the true warbler. Its slender, warbler-like beak is adapted for picking small insects off bushes. Occasionally, like a warbler, it can capture an insect in flight.

FACTORS IN DIVERSIFICATION

No such great diversity of finches can be found on the South American mainland. In the absence of vacant habitats on the continent, the occasion was lacking for the mainland birds to exploit new situations. However, given the unoccupied habitats on the Galápagos Islands, the opportunity presented itself for the invading birds to evolve in new directions. In the absence of competition, the colonists occupied several ecological habitats, the dry lowlands as well as the humid uplands. The finches adopted modes of life that ordinarily would not have been opened to them. If the true warblers and true woodpeckers had already occupied the islands, it is doubtful that the finches could have evolved into warblerlike and woodpeckerlike forms. Thus, *a prime factor promoting adaptive radiation is the absence of competition.*

The emigration of the ancestral finches from the mainland was assuredly not conscious or self-directed. The dispersal of birds from their original home was at random, resulting from the pressure of increasing numbers on the means of subsistence. By chance, some of the birds reached the Galápagos Islands. The original flock of birds that fortuitously arrived at the islands was but a small sample of the parental population, containing at best a limited portion of the parental gene pool. It may be that only a small amount of genetic variation was initially available for selection to work on. What evolutionary changes occurred at the outset were mainly due to random survival (genetic drift). However, the chance element would become less important as the population increased in size. Selection unquestionably became the main evolutionary agent, molding the individual populations into new shapes by the preservation of new favorable mutant or recombination types. More than one island was colonized, and the complete separation of the islands from each other promoted the genetic differentiation of each new local population.

Today we observe that each island is occupied by more than one species of finch. Different species ultimately spread to various islands. It is axiomatic that two species with identical ecological requirements —using similar resources—cannot coexist indefinitely in the same locality (see chapter 42). This is a highly theoretical concept, since it is very unlikely that any two related species can have exactly the same needs. But if it were at all possible for them to be alike in needs, one species would eventually supplant the other. Accordingly, on islands where several species of finches exist together, we should expect to find that each species is adapted to a different ecological niche. This is precisely what we find. The three common species of ground finches—small (*Geospiza fuliginosa*), medium (*Geospiza fortis*), and large (*Geospiza magnirostris*)—occur together in the coastal lowlands of several islands.

Each species, however, is specialized in feeding on a seed of a certain size. The small-beaked *Geospiza fuliginosa,* for example, feeds on small grass seeds, whereas the large-beaked *Geospiza magnirostris* eats large hard fruits. Different species, with different food requirements, can thus exist together in an environment with varied food resources.

MAJOR ADAPTIVE RADIATIONS

The diversity of Darwin's finches had its beginning when migrants from the mainland successfully invaded the variety of vacant habitats on the Galápagos Islands. The pattern of adaptive radiation manifested by Darwin's finches has been imitated repeatedly by different forms of life. Organisms throughout the ages have seized new opportunities open to them by the absence of competitors and have diverged in new environments. The habitats available to Darwin's finches were certainly few in comparison with the enormous range of ecological habitats in the world. The larger the region and the more diverse the environmental conditions, the greater the variety of life.

Approximately 400 million years ago, during a period of history that geologists call the *Devonian,* the vast areas of land were monotonously barren of animal life. Save for rare creatures like scorpions and millipedes, animal life of those distant years was confined to the water. The seas were crowded with invertebrate animals of varied kinds. The fresh and salt waters contained a highly diversified and abundant assemblage of cartilaginous and bony fishes. The vacant terrestrial regions were not to remain long unoccupied. From one of the many groups of fishes inhabiting the pools and swamps in the Devonian period emerged the first land vertebrate. The initial modest step onto land started the vertebrates on their conquest of all available terrestrial habitats. The story of the origin and diversification of the backboned land dwellers began then and has continued.

INVASION OF LAND

Prominent among the numerous Devonian aquatic forms were the lobe-finned fishes, the Crossopterygii, which possessed the ability to gulp air when they rose to the surface. These ancient air-breathing fishes represent the stock from which the first land vertebrates, the amphibians, were derived (fig. 37.4). The factors that led these ancestral lobe-finned fishes to venture onto land are unknown. The impelling force might have been population pressure or simply the inherent tendency of individuals, particularly the young, to disperse. A. S. Romer of Harvard University has advanced the irresistible conjecture that the crossopterygians were forced to crawl on dry land on those occasions when the pools they inhabited became foul, stagnant, or completely dry. There is convincing geological evidence that the Devonian years were marked by excessive seasonal droughts. It is not unimaginable that the water in some pools periodically evaporated. The suggestion, then, is that the crossopterygians wriggled out of stagnant and shrinking water holes onto land to seek pools elsewhere in which water still remained. Thus, paradoxically, the first actual movements on land might not have been associated at all with an attempt to abandon aquatic existence, but rather to retain it.

The foregoing hypothesis is admittedly speculative. However, the fact remains that those crossopterygians that emerged on land, though crudely adapted for terrestrial existence, did not encounter any competi-

Figure 37.4 Evolution of land vertebrates in the geologic past. From air-breathing, lobe-finned fishes (crossopterygians) emerged the first four-footed land inhabitants, the amphibians. Primitive amphibians (labyrinthodonts) gave rise to the reptiles, the first vertebrates to become firmly established on land. The birds and mammals owe their origin to an early reptilian stock (cotylosaurs). An important biological principle reveals itself: each new vertebrate group did not arise from highly developed or advanced members of the ancestral group, but rather from early primitive forms near the base of the ancestral stock. The thickness of the various branches provides a rough measure of the comparative abundance of the five vertebrate groups during geologic history. The Devonian period is often called the *Age of Fishes;* the Mississippian and Pennsylvanian periods (frequently lumped together as the Carboniferous period) are referred to as the *Age of Amphibians;* the Mesozoic era is the grand *Age of Reptiles;* and the Cenozoic era is the *Age of Mammals.*

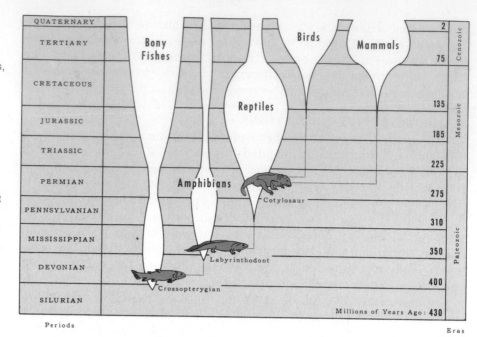

tors that could immediately spell doom to their awkward initial trial on land. It is also instructive to note that the lobe-finned fishes did possess certain capacities that would prove to be important under the new conditions of life. Evolutionists speak of such potential adaptive characters as *preadaptations.*

The preadaptations of the lobe-finned fishes included primitive membranous lungs and internal nostrils, both of which are important for atmospheric breathing. It should be understood that such preadapted characters were not favorably selected with a view to their possible utility in some future mode of life. There is no foresight or design in the selection process. Nor do mutational changes occur in anticipation of some new environmental condition. A trait is selected only when it imparts an advantage to the organism in its immediate environment. Accordingly, lungs in the crossopterygians did not evolve with conscious reference toward a possible future land life, but only because such a structure was important, if not essential, to the survival of these air-breathing fishes in their immediate surroundings.

The crossopterygians did not possess typical amphibian limbs. However, their lateral fins contained fleshy lobes, within which were bony elements that were basically comparable to those of a limb of a terrestrial vertebrate. Figure 37.5 shows a restoration of a widespread Devonian form, *Eusthenopteron,* in which the lateral fins had developed into stout muscular paddles.

Before the close of the Devonian period, the transition from fish to amphibian had been completed. The early land-living amphibians were slim-bodied with fishlike tails, but having limbs capable of locomotion on land. The four-footed amphibians flourished in the humid coal swamps of Mississippian and Pennsylvanian times, but never did become completely adapted for existence on land. All the ancient amphibians, such as *Diplovertebron* (fig. 37.5), spent much of their lives in water, and their modern descendants—the salamanders, newts, frogs, and toads—must return to water to deposit their eggs. Thus, the am-

phibians were the first vertebrates to colonize land, but were, and still are, only partially adapted for terrestrial life.

CONQUEST OF LAND

From the amphibians emerged the reptiles, true terrestrial forms. The appearance of a shell-covered egg, which can be laid on land, freed the reptile from dependence on water. The elimination of a water-dwelling stage was a significant evolutionary advance. The first primitive reptile most likely arose during Carboniferous times, but the fossil beds of this period have yet to reveal the appropriate reptilian ancestor. The ancestral reptile probably possessed the body proportions and well-developed limbs of the more advanced terrestrial forms of amphibians, such as *Seymouria* (fig. 37.6). *Seymouria* is not a reptile, but its skeletal features suggest terrestrial habits. This advanced amphibian may have been a descendant of an earlier amphibian group in the lower Carboniferous that was ancestral to the reptiles.

The terrestrial egg-laying habit evolved very early in reptilian evolution. A key feature of reptiles (and higher vertebrates) is the *amniotic egg* (see chapter 3). The egg of a reptile (or bird) contains a large amount of nourishing yolk. Moreover, development of the embryo takes place entirely within a thick shell. These circumstances call for a special provision whereby food derived from the yolk and oxygen obtained from an external source can be made accessible to all parts of the developing embryo. The embryo itself constructs a complex system of membranes, known as *extraembryonic membranes*, which serve for protection, nutrition, and respiration. As discussed in detail earlier (chapter 3), these extraembryonic membranes are the amnion, chorion, yolk sac, and allantois.

With the perfection of the amniotic egg, the reptiles exploited the wide expanse of land areas. The ancestral reptilian stock initiated one of the most spectacular adaptive radiations in life's history. The reptiles endured as dominant land animals of the earth for well over 100 million years. The Mesozoic era, during which the reptiles thrived, is often referred to as the "Age of Reptiles."

Figure 37.7 reveals the variety of reptiles that blossomed from the basal stock, the cotylosaurs. The dinosaurs were by far the most awe-

Figure 37.5 Stages in the transition of the lobe-finned fishes into amphibians, as reconstructed by W. K. Gregory and painted by Francis Lee Jaques. *Left*, the primitive Devonian air-breathing crossopterygian, *Eusthenopteron*, floundering on a stream bank with its muscular, paddlelike fins. *Right*, the Pennsylvanian tailed amphibian, *Diplovertebron*, with limbs capable of true locomotion on land. Much of the life of this early tetrapod was spent in water. (Courtesy of the American Museum of Natural History.)

Figure 37.6 *Seymouria*, an advanced amphibian with reptilianlike body proportions (short trunk region and well-developed limbs). *Seymouria* is known only from Permian rocks (275 million years ago), long after the reptiles had appeared. It may represent a relict of an earlier amphibian group that was ancestral to the reptiles.

Figure 37.7 Adaptive radiation of reptiles. A vast horde of reptiles came into existence from the basal stock, the cotylosaurs, at the beginning of the Mesozoic era, roughly 225 million years ago. This matchless assemblage of reptiles was triumphant for a duration well over 100 million years. Then, before the close of the Mesozoic era, the great majority of reptiles passed into oblivion.

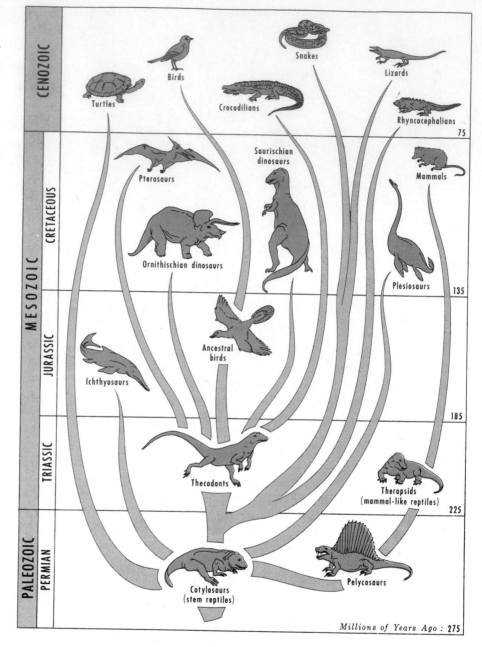

inspiring and famous. They reigned over the lands until the close of the Mesozoic era before suffering extinction. The dinosaurs were remarkably diverse; they varied in size, bodily form, and habits. Some of the dinosaurs were carnivorous, such as the brutish *Tyrannosaurus,* whereas others were vegetarians, such as the feeble-toothed but ponderous *Brontosaurus.* The exceedingly long necks of certain dinosaurs were adaptations for feeding on the foliage of tall coniferous trees. Not all dinosaurs were immense; some were no bigger than chickens. The dinosaurs were descended from the thecodonts—slender, fast-running, lizardlike creatures. In fact, there were two great groups of dinosaurs, the Saurischia and the Ornithischia (fig. 37.7), which evolved independently from two different lines of the thecodonts.

The thecodonts gave rise also to bizarre reptiles that took to the air, the pterosaurs. These "dragons of the air" possessed highly expansive

Figure 37.8 *Dimetrodon,* one of the pelycosaurs that flourished during Permian times. The gaudy "sail" may have served as a heat-regulating device. (From a restoration by Charles R. Knight; courtesy of the American Museum of Natural History.)

wings and disproportionately short bodies. It seems as though the huge membranous wings developed at the sacrificial expense of the body. The winged pterosaurs succumbed before the end of the Mesozoic era. Another independent branch of the thecodonts led to eminently more successful flyers, the birds. The origin of birds from reptiles is revealed by the celebrated *Archaeopteryx,* a Jurassic form that was essentially an airborne lizard (fig. 37.7). This feathered creature possessed a slender, lizardlike tail and a scaly head equipped with reptilian teeth. Some authors contend that birds descended from reptiles that were already warm-blooded (endothermic) rather than, as often assumed, cold-blooded (ectothermic). Under this view, the endothermic birds are merely aerial extensions of a terrestrial endothermic stock.

Certain reptiles returned to water. The streamlined, dolphinlike ichthyosaurs and the long-necked, short-bodied plesiosaurs were marine, fish-eating reptiles. These aquatic reptiles breathed by means of lungs; they certainly did not redevelop the gills of their very distant fish ancestors. Indeed, it is axiomatic that a structure once lost in the long course of evolution cannot be regained. This is the doctrine of irreversibility of evolution, or *Dollo's law,* after Louis Dollo, the eminent Belgian paleontologist to whom the principle is ascribed.

Among the early reptiles present at the beginning of Mesozoic days were the pelycosaurs, notable for their peculiar saillike extensions of the back (fig. 37.8). The function of the gaudy sail is unknown, but it should not be thought that this structural feature was merely ornamental or useless. As we have emphasized, traits of organisms are selected for their adaptive utility. Means of maintaining a stable body temperature are poorly developed in reptiles. It is not inconceivable that the pelycosauran sail was a functional device to achieve some degree of heat regulation. Be that as it may, the pelycosaurs gave rise to an important group of reptiles, the therapsids. These mammallike forms bridged the structural gap between the reptiles and the mammals (fig. 37.7).

EXTINCTION AND REPLACEMENT

The history of the reptiles attests to the ultimate fate of many groups of organisms—*extinction*. The reptilian dynasty collapsed before the close of the Mesozoic era. Of the vast host of Mesozoic reptiles, relatively few have survived to modern times; the ones that have include lizards, snakes, crocodiles, and turtles. The famed land dinosaurs, the great marine plesiosaurs and ichthyosaurs, and the flying pterosaurs all became extinct. The cause of the decline and death of the tremendous array of reptiles is obscure. The demise of the giant reptiles is generally attributed to their inability to adapt to some radical change in environmental conditions. In general, most species of organisms do become highly specialized. Perhaps many species pass unavoidably into oblivion when they cannot genetically adapt to radical environmental changes.

Whatever may be the cause of mass extinctions, the fact remains that as one group of organisms recedes and dies out completely, another group spreads and evolves. The decline of the reptiles provided evolutionary opportunities for the birds and the mammals. The vacancies in the habitats could then be occupied by these warm-blooded vertebrates. Small and inconspicuous during the Mesozoic era, the mammals arose to unquestionable dominance during the Cenozoic era, which began approximately 75 million years ago. The mammals diversified into marine forms (for example, the whale, dolphin, seal, and walrus), fossorial forms living underground (for example, the mole), flying and gliding animals (for example, the bat and flying squirrel), and cursorial types well adapted for running (for example, the horse).

The various mammalian groups are adapted to their different modes

Figure 37.9 Varied forelimbs of vertebrates, all of which are built on the same structural plan. The best explanation for the fundamentally similar framework of bones is that man and all other vertebrates share a common ancestry. Homologous bones are indicated as follows: humerus (upper arm)—crosshatching; radius (forearm)—light strippling; ulna (forearm)—color; carpals (wrist)—white; metacarpals (palm) and phalanges (digits)—heavy strippling. The number of phalanges in each digit is indicated by a numeral, beginning with the first digit (thumb).

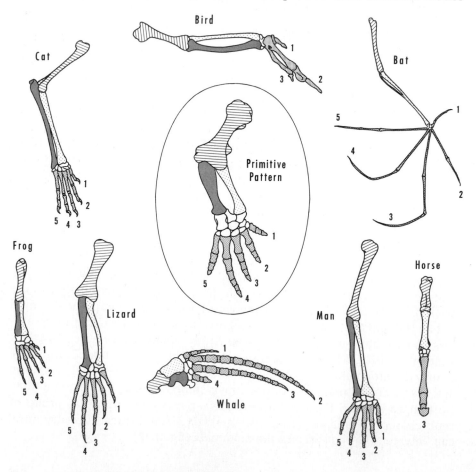

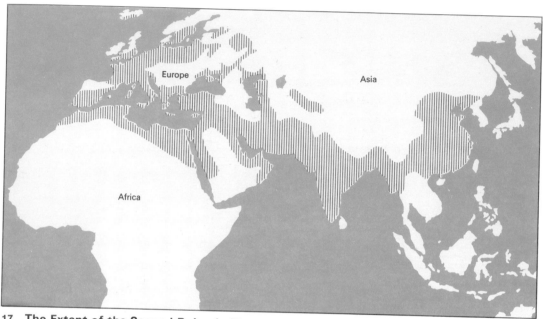

Europe

Asia

Africa

17   The Extent of the Second Bubonic Plague Epidemic, 1200 to 1450

18

of life. The appendages, in particular, are specialized for flight, swimming, or movement on land. An important lesson may be drawn from the variety of specialized appendages. Superficially there is scant resemblance between the arm of a man, the flipper of a whale, and the wing of a bat. And yet, a close comparison of the skeletal elements (fig. 37.9) shows that the structural design, bone for bone, is basically the same. The differences are mainly in the relative lengths of the component bones. In the forelimb of the bat, for instance, the metacarpals and phalanges (except those of the thumb) are greatly elongated. Although the bones of the bat's wing are highly modified, they are not fundamentally different from the bones of other mammals. The conclusion is inescapable that the limb bones of man, the bat, and the whale are modifications of a common ancestral pattern. The facts admit no other logical interpretation. As seen in figure 37.9, the forelimbs of all tetrapod vertebrates exhibit a unity of anatomical pattern intelligible only on the basis of common inheritance. The corresponding limb bones of tetrapod vertebrates are said to be *homologous,* since they are structurally identical with those in the common ancestor. In contrast, the wing of a bird and the wing of a butterfly are *analogous;* both are used for flight, but they are built on an entirely different structural plan.

EVOLUTION OF HORSES

The cardinal feature of adaptive radiation is the emergence from a central, generalized stock of a large number of divergent branches or lineages. Not all branches persist; indeed, the general rule is that all but a few perish. The disappearance of many branches in the distant past may lead the observer today to the mistaken impression that the evolution of a particular group was not at all intricately forked. Thus, the evolution of horses is commonly, but erroneously, depicted as an undeviating, straight-line progression from the small, terrier-sized *Hyracotherium* (better known as *Eohippus,* the "dawn horse") to the large modern horse, *Equus.* On the contrary, the detailed work of modern paleontologists, prominent among them being George Gaylord Simpson, has revealed convincingly a pattern of many divergent lineages. The major lineages directly or indirectly involved in the emergence of the modern horse are shown in figure 37.10.

The ancestry of horses can be traced back to the beginning of the Eocene epoch, some 60 million years ago. The diminutive *Hyracotherium* was about 10 inches high and had four functional toes on the front foot and three on the hind. It was not adapted for speed and browsed on the soft leaves and fruits of bushes. This dawn horse could scarcely have grazed on harsh grass, as its molar teeth had low crowns and very weak grinding surfaces. *Hyracotherium* spread over North America and Europe, but the European assemblage left no descendants. The derivatives of the North American dawn horse in the Eocene were *Orohippus* and *Epihippus,* and these gradually gave way to more progressive kinds of horses in the Oligocene, *Mesohippus* and *Miohippus.* Both of these Oligocene horses were about 24 inches high with only three toes on each foot, but they remained browsers with low-crowned teeth. The *Miohippus* stock subsequently radiated out into a variety of types that lived in the Miocene epoch. Most of the Miocene offshoots (for example, *Anchitherium* and *Hypohippus*) continued the browsing habits of their ancestors. However, one stock—*Merychippus*—had successfully exploited a new mode of life associated with the expansion of grasslands

Figure 37.10 Phylogenetic tree of horses through time, with its many divergent branches. All branches died out, save one which eventually culminated in the modern group of horses, *Equus*. The history of horses dates back to early Cenozoic times, some 60 million years ago. (The Cenozoic *era* is divided into *periods*, which in turn are subdivided into *epochs*.)

in Miocene times. *Merychippus* was the first true grazing form, well equipped with high-crowned, complexly ridged teeth effective in grinding stout grass.

From the slow-footed, three-toed *Merychippus* emerged the fleet-footed, one-toed *Pliohippus* during the Pliocene epoch. The appearance of the one-toed condition was a landmark in horse history, an event doubtlessly fostered by natural selection. Grazing horses in the open, grassy plains were subject to appreciable predation from carnivores. Natural selection favored reduction of the toes, lightening the legs for speed. However, not all descendants of *Merychippus* evolved the

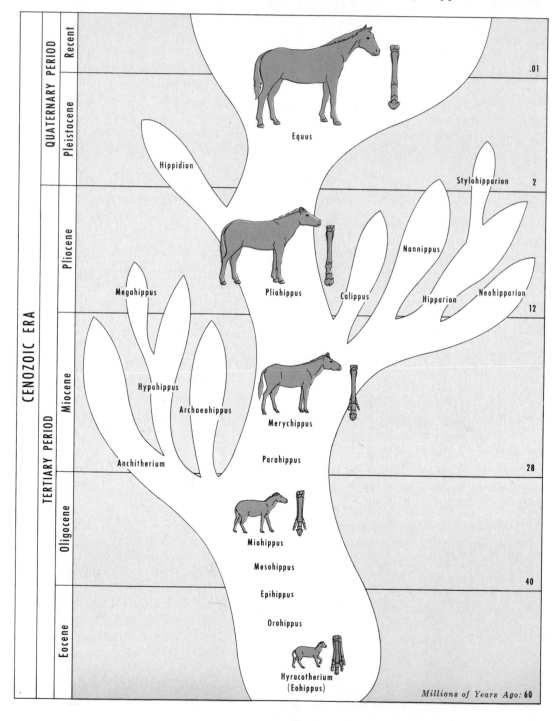

progressive single-toed condition. Several lines of Pliocene horses, such as *Hipparion* and *Nannippus*, retained the conservative three-toed pattern. These conservative Pliocene horses represent evolutionary blind alleys, removed from the main line of ancestry of the modern horse (fig. 37.10). Only *Pliohippus*, the first one-toed horse, remained to become the progenitor of the modern form, *Equus*. The modern horse arose in North America at the close of the Pliocene epoch, and spread rapidly over most of the world. *Equus* inexplicably vanished in North America a few thousand years ago, before the arrival of the first white colonist. The modern horse was reintroduced from Europe in the early 1500s by the Spaniards. All present-day horses are domestic; it is doubtful whether there are any existing stocks of truly wild horses that are not descendants of populations at one time domesticated.

SUMMARY

A phenomenon of immense importance in the evolutionary histories of organisms is *adaptive radiation*. It occurs when one ancestral group colonizes previously unoccupied territories and diverges, or radiates, into several diverse species, each adapted to a specific ecological habitat. The process is exemplified by Darwin's finches—14 different species of birds presently inhabiting the Galápagos Islands that were derived in the distant past from one common ancestral stock from the South American mainland. All the ecological habitats were vacant and available when the first colonizers arrived from the mainland. More than one island was colonized, and the geographical separation of the cluster of islands promoted the adaptive differentiation of each new local population. In the absence of competition, the colonists occupied several ecological habitats. In addition, the spatial separation of the islands enabled the separate populations to evolve reproductive isolating mechanisms—that is, to differentiate into species.

The pattern of adaptive radiation on a large scale is seen in the emergence of amphibians from fishes, of reptiles from amphibians, and of birds and mammals from reptiles. Each major transition involved breakthroughs into new territories with unoccupied habitats. On each level the adaptive divergence was pronounced, leading to the reign of amphibians in the Carboniferous period, the spectacular dynasty of reptiles during the Mesozoic era, and the unquestionable dominance of mammals during the Cenozoic era.

The final phase of the evolution of a group or lineage is apparently extinction. Although the causes of extinction are complex, the fact remains that the ultimate fate of many groups of organisms has been extinction.

38 Origin and History of Life

We have been unceasingly taught not to believe in spontaneous generation, the view that living things can originate from lifeless matter. The classical experiments of Francesco Redi in 1688, Lazzaro Spallanzani in 1765, and Louis Pasteur in 1862 provided proof that new life can come only from existing life. However, these experiments revealed only that life cannot arise spontaneously under conditions that exist on earth today. Conditions on the primeval earth billions of years ago were assuredly different from present conditions, and the first form of life, or self-duplicating particle, can only have arisen spontaneously from chemical inanimate substances. It should be clear that the conditions under which life originated were unique; the reorigin of life on present-day earth is scarcely possible.

PRIMITIVE EARTH

The view that life emerged by a long and gradual process of chemical evolution was first convincingly set forth by the Russian biochemist Alexander I. Oparin, in 1924, in an enthralling book entitled *The Origin of Life*. The transformation of lifeless chemicals into living matter extended over some 2 billion years. Such a transformation, as Oparin points out, is no longer possible today. If by pure chance a living particle approaching that of the first form of life should now appear, it would be rapidly decomposed by the oxygen of the air or quickly destroyed by the countless microorganisms now populating the earth.

Our earth is estimated to be 5 billion years old. It was formerly thought that the earth originated as a fiery mass that was torn away from the sun. Astronomers now generally accept that the earth (like other planets in the solar system) condensed out of a whirling cloud of gas surrounding the primitive sun. The atmosphere of the pristine earth was quite unlike our present atmosphere. Oxygen in the free gaseous state was virtually absent; it was bound in water and metallic oxides. Accordingly, it is important to note that any complex organic compound that might arise during this early time would not be subject to degradation by free oxygen.

The early gas cloud was especially rich in hydrogen. The hydrogen (H_2) of the primordial earth chemically united with carbon to form methane (CH_4), with nitrogen to form ammonia (NH_3), and with oxygen to form water vapor (H_2O). Thus, the early atmosphere was strongly reducing (nonoxygenic), containing primarily hydrogen, methane, ammonia, and water. The atmospheric water vapor condensed into drops and fell as rain; the rains eroded the rocks and washed minerals (such as chlorides and phosphates) into the seas. The stage was set for the combination of the varied chemical elements. Chemicals from the atmosphere mixed and reacted with those in the waters to form a wealth of hydrocarbons, that is, compounds of hydrogen and carbon. Water, hydrocarbons, and ammonia are the raw materials of amino acids, which, in turn, are the building blocks for the larger protein molecules. Thus, in the primitive sea, amino acids accumulated in considerable quantities and were joined to form proteins.

Complex carbon compounds such as amino acids and proteins are termed *organic* because they are made by living organisms. Our present-day green plants use the energy of sunlight to synthesize organic compounds from simple molecules. What, then, was the energy source in the primitive earth, and how was synthesis of organic compounds effected in the absence of living things? It is generally held that ultraviolet rays from the sun, electrical discharges such as lightning, and dry heat from volcanic activity furnished the means to join the simple carbon compounds and nitrogenous substances into amino acids. Is there a valid basis for such a widely accepted view?

EXPERIMENTAL SYNTHESIS OF ORGANIC COMPOUNDS

In the early days of chemistry, it was believed that organic compounds could be produced only by living organisms. But in 1828, Friedrich Wöhler succeeded in manufacturing the organic compound *urea* under artificial conditions in the laboratory. Since Wöhler's discovery, a large variety of organic chemicals (amino acids, monosaccharides, purines, and vitamins) formerly produced only in organisms have been artificially synthesized.

In 1953, Stanley Miller, then at the University of Chicago and a student of Nobel laureate Harold Urey, synthesized organic compounds under conditions that were made to be like the primitive atmosphere of the earth. He passed electrical sparks through a mixture of hydrogen, water, ammonia, and methane. The electrical discharges duplicated the effects of violent electrical storms in the primitive universe. In the laboratory, the four simple inorganic molecules interacted, after a mere week, to form several kinds of amino acids, among them being alanine, glycine, aspartic acid, and glutamic acid. Miller's instructive experiment has been successfully repeated by a number of investigators; amino acids can also be obtained by irradiating a similar mixture of gases with ultraviolet light.

The synthesis of amino acids is only a small step towards the synthesis of a living cell. In 1964, Sidney W. Fox, then at Florida State University and later at the University of Miami, reasoned that proteins were synthesized from amino acids in the primitive earth by thermal energy, or heat. He accordingly heated a mixture of 18 amino acids to temperatures of 160–200 °C for varying periods of time. He obtained stable, proteinlike macromolecules, which he termed *proteinoids*. These thermally produced proteinoids are similar to natural proteins in many ways. As a striking instance, bacteria can actually use the proteinoids in a culture medium, degrading them enzymatically into individual amino acids. Equally important, when the proteinoid material was cooled and examined under a microscope, Fox observed small, spherical, cell-like units that had arisen from aggregations of the proteinoids. These molecular aggregates, called *microspheres*, exhibited a general resemblance to spherical bacteria. Such microspherelike aggregates could have been the forerunners of the first living organism. However, there remains a large hiatus between the formation of organic microspheres and the appearance of the first living cell, capable in its organization of specific catalytic functions, reproduction, and mutation.

LIFE'S BEGINNINGS

It is evident that organic compounds can be formed without the intervention of living organisms. Thus, it appears likely that the sea of the primitive earth spontaneously accumulated a great variety of organic molecules. The sea became a sort of dilute organic soup (an aquatic Garden of Eden), in which the molecules collided and reacted to form new molecules of increasing levels of complexity. Proteins capable of catalysis, or enzymatic activity, had to evolve, and nucleic acid molecules capable of self-replication must also have developed. However, the incisive question has yet to be settled—whether the initial process involved first the appearance of the machinery for self-replication (that is, self-duplicating nucleic acids) followed by the development of the cytoplasm and membrane, or whether a cytoplasm with internal organization and metabolic capacities preceded the nuclear mechanism. Those who advocate a naked gene (DNA) as the first living unit must reconcile their view with the fact that a gene, like a virus, requires a well-coordinated metabolic system in order to function. We may recall that a virus depends on living cells for its existence; hence, parasitic viruses could not have arisen before cells had evolved.

We may assume that the first living systems drew on the wealth of organic materials in the sea broth. Organisms that are nutritionally dependent on their environment for ready-made organic substances are called *heterotrophs* (Greek, *hetero*, "other," and *trophos*, "one that feeds"). The primitive one-celled heterotroph probably had little more than a few genes, a few proteins, and a selectively permeable cell membrane. The heterotrophs multiplied rapidly in an environment with a plentiful supply of dissolved organic substances. However, the primitive heterotrophs could survive only as long as the existing store of organic molecules lasted. Eventually, living systems had to evolve the ability to synthesize their own organic requirements from simple inorganic substances. In the course of time, *autotrophs* (*auto*, meaning "self") arose, which could manufacture organic nutrients from simpler molecules.

The first simple autotroph arose in an anaerobic world, one in which little, if any, free oxygen was available. The primitive autotrophs obtained their energy from the relatively inefficient process of fermentation (the breakdown of organic compounds in the absence of oxygen). Thus, the early fermentative autotrophs were much like our present-day anaerobic bacteria and yeast. The metabolic processes of the anaerobic autotrophs resulted in the liberation of large amounts of carbon dioxide into the atmosphere. Once this occurred, the way was paved for the evolution of organisms that could use carbon dioxide as the sole source of carbon in synthesizing organic compounds and could use sunlight as the sole source of energy. Such organisms would be the photosynthetic cells.

Early photosynthetic cells probably split hydrogen-containing compounds such as hydrogen sulfide. In other words, as is still performed today by sulfur bacteria, hydrogen sulfide is cleaved into hydrogen and sulfur. The hydrogen is used by the cell to synthesize organic compounds, and the sulfur is released as a waste product (as evidenced by the earth's great sulfur deposits). In time, the process of photosynthesis was refined so that water served as the source of hydrogen. The result was the release

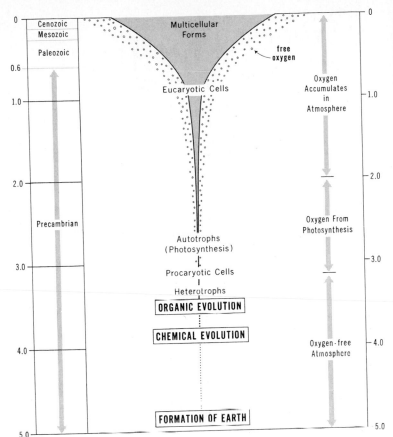

Figure 38.1 Major events in the history of life. Chemical evolution preceded biological evolution. The first self-duplicating life forms were heterotrophs. Oxygen began to accumulate in the atmosphere with the appearance of photosynthetic autotrophs. Rising levels of atmospheric oxygen were associated with the emergence of eucaryotes. The last 600 million years has witnessed a great diversity of life in an oxygen-rich atmosphere.

of oxygen as a waste product. At this stage, free oxygen became established for the first time in the atmosphere.

The first organisms to use water as the hydrogen source in photosynthesis were the blue-green algae. Since blue-green algae were active photosynthesizers, atmospheric oxygen accumulated in increasing amounts. Many primitive anaerobic bacteria, incapable of adapting to free oxygen, remained in portions of the environment that were anaerobic, such as sulfur springs and oxygen-free muds. New kinds of bacteria, however, arose that were capable of utilizing the free oxygen. Today, there are bacterial types that are anaerobic as well as aerobic.

The earth's atmosphere gradually changed from a reducing, or hydrogen-rich, atmosphere to an oxidizing, or oxygen-rich, atmosphere. The rising levels of atmospheric oxygen set the stage for the appearance of one-celled eucaryotic organisms, between 600 million and 1 billion years ago (fig. 38.1). Then, within the comparatively short span of 600 million years, the one-celled eucaryotes evolved in various directions to give rise to a wealth of multicellular life forms inhabiting the earth.

EVOLUTION OF EUCARYOTES

Present-day organisms can be classified into two groups according to two quite different types of cells they possess—the relatively small and simple *procaryotic* cells and the larger, more complex *eucaryotic* cells. The former, which lack nuclear organization and have only poorly developed membranous organelles, include only the bacteria and blue-green algae. Not all bacteria are anaerobic; many species are aerobic, using oxygen to obtain energy through respiration.

Figure 38.2 Evolution of eucaryotes through symbiosis. The eucaryotic animal cell may have arisen through a symbiotic relationship between a procaryotic cell and an aerobic bacterium. The eucaryotic plant cell may have originated by a comparable symbiotic relationship between a blue-green alga and a eucaryotic animal cell.

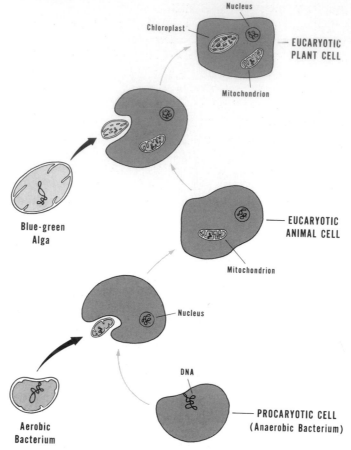

ORIGIN OF A EUCARYOTIC CELL

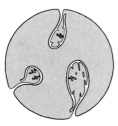

DNA

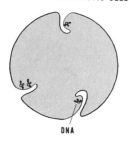

Mitochondrion

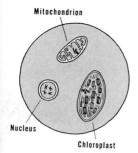

Nucleus

Chloroplast

Figure 38.3 Hypothetical scheme of the origin of a eucaryotic cell by the invagination, or drawing inward, of the surface membrane in several places.

Modern eucaryotic cells contain either mitochondria alone or mitochondria and chloroplasts. Some venturesome biologists have suggested that a blue-green algal cell is basically equivalent to the chlorophyll-containing chloroplast of higher plant cells and that an aerobic bacterial cell can be equated with mitochondria. We can now speculate that the first eucaryotic cells arose about a billion years ago by engulfing or "enslaving" aerobic bacteria and blue-green algae (fig. 38.2). Those predatory cells that engulfed but did not digest the aerobic bacterial cells became the eucaryotic animal cells. Those predators that captured both the photosynthetic blue-green algal cells and aerobic bacteria evolved into eucaryotic plant cells. In essence, the engulfed prey became permanent residents within the predator cell either as mitochondria or as chloroplasts. This account of the origin of the earliest eucaryotic organisms is highly speculative, but provocative.

Some authors regard the relatively abrupt origin of the organelles of eucaryotes by a process of symbiosis (fig. 38.2) as improbable. The evolution of living organisms normally proceeds through a series of gradual changes. Continual modification of the surface membrane may have been the basic evolutionary mechanism in the differentiation of eucaryotic cells from procaryotic cells. The organelles of eucaryotic cells may have evolved by the invagination, or drawing inward, of the surface membrane of a primitive cell. Figure 38.3 shows the postulated mechanism for the origin of the mitochondrion, the membrane enclosed nucleus, and the chloroplast—all from invaginated cell surfaces. This hypothesis is simpler than the origin of eucaryotic organelles by an "engulfing" process, and is considered more plausible by several investigators.

FOSSILS AND THE HISTORICAL RECORD

An organism becomes preserved as a fossil when it is trapped in soft sediment that settles at the bottom of a lake or ocean. The deposits of mud and sand harden into the sedimentary, or stratified, rocks of the earth's crust. Fossils, then, are the remains of past organisms preserved or imprinted in sedimentary rocks. Not all fossils are mere impressions of buried parts. In the case of petrified wood, for example, the wood had become infiltrated with mineral substances that crystallized and hardened. Some components of organisms are resistant to decay, such as the silica walls of diatoms, which accumulate to form diatomaceous earth.

The sample of past life is incomplete and uneven. In many places of the earth, the sedimentary rocks have been so subjected to pressure and heat after their deposition that the fossils in them have been destroyed. Moreover, organisms with soft tissues (jellyfishes and insects, for example) are not favorable for preservation. In contrast, the woody parts of plants, the shells of mollusks, and the bones of vertebrates are relatively common as fossils. Despite the imperfections of the fossil record, the available fossil assemblage contains an extraordinary amount of information. The older strata of rock, those deposited first, bear only relatively simple kinds of life, whereas the newer or younger beds contain progressively more and more complex types of life. Each species of organism now living on the earth has developed from an earlier and simpler ancestral form.

Geologists and paleontologists have divided the earth's past history into five main divisions, or eras, associated with five major rock strata. The eras embrace a number of subdivisions, or periods, and the periods are further subdivided into epochs. The most ancient era is the Archeozoic, followed by the Proterozoic, Paleozoic, Mesozoic, and lastly, the Cenozoic, the era of recent types of life. Fossils appear in abundance at the beginning of the Paleozoic era, technically the Cambrian period, 600 million years ago. However, as noted earlier, at least 3 billion years of slow organic evolution preceded the diversity of life of the Cambrian period. In recent years, explorations of Precambrian rocks have uncovered the remains of procaryotic bacteria and blue-green algae.

One of the most remarkable discoveries of Precambrian life was reported in 1965 by the micropaleontologists Elso S. Barghoorn and J. William Schopf of Harvard University. Electron microscopic examinations of samples of deep sedimentary rock from South Africa (the so-called Fig Tree sediments) revealed remnants of rod-shaped, bacterialike organisms that existed 3.2 billion years ago. In addition, minute traces of two chemical substances, phytane and pristane, have been found in the Fig Tree rocks. These chemicals are the relatively stable breakdown products of chlorophyll. Thus, photosynthesis by algae, in which oxygen is released, may have begun about 3 billion years ago. Other ancient rocks —such as the 2-billion-year-old Gunflint rock formation in Ontario, Canada—contain an assemblage of fossil microorganisms that appear to be blue-green algae, possibly red algae, and even some fungi. Eucaryote organization is clearly in evidence in deposits that are approximately 1 billion years old. The Bitter Springs formation of Australia contains eucaryote fossils that represent higher algae and fungi. The transition from procaryote to eucaryote organization apparently occurred during the late Precambrian.

The general character of plant life from the dawn of the Cambrian period to recent times is depicted in figure 38.4. Only the broader aspects of plant evolution are portrayed. It is evident that the flora has changed in composition over geologic time. New types of plants have continually

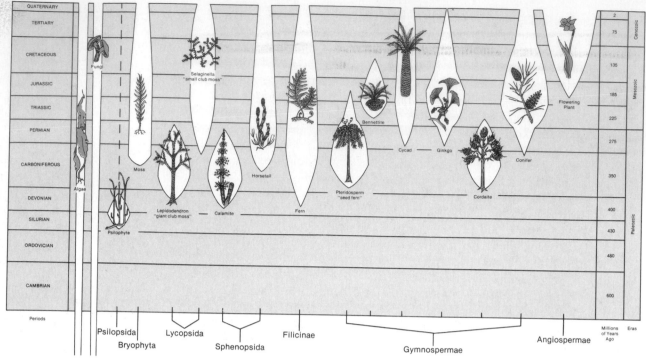

Figure 38.4 Historical record of plant life. Plant life during the Cambrian and Ordovician, the first two periods of the Paleozoic era, was confined to the water; seaweeds (algae) of immense size, often several hundred feet in length, dominated the seas. Land plants came into existence in Silurian time, in the form of strange little vascular plants, the psilophytes. In the Carboniferous period, imposing spore-bearing trees (Lepidodendrids and Calamites) and primitive naked-seeded plants (Pteridosperms and Cordaites) reached their peak of development. The end of the Paleozoic era marked the extinction of the majority of the luxuriant trees of the Carboniferous coal swamps. The Mesozoic era was the *Age of Gymnosperms,* as evidenced by the abundance of cycads, ginkgoes, and conifers. Flowering plants (Angiosperms) rose to ascendency toward the close of the Mesozoic era and established themselves as the dominant plant group of the earth. The illustration does not reveal the evolutionary relationships between the different plant groups, but each new group that appeared is related to one in the past.

appeared. Some types thrived for a certain time and then disappeared. Others arose and continued to flourish. Still others have survived until the present only in much reduced numbers.

The Cambrian and Silurian periods were characterized by a diverse group of algae in the oceans and the seas. One of the most significant advances, which occurred during the Silurian period, was the transition from aquatic existence to life on land. The first plants that established themselves on land were diminutive herbaceous forms, the *psilophytes,* literally "naked plants," in allusion to their bare, leafless stems. Their existence made possible the subsequent emergence of an infinite variety of tree-sized plants that flourished in the swamps of Carboniferous times. Carboniferous forests included the giant club moss, *Lepidodendron,* the tall *Calamites,* the coarse-leaved *Cordaites,* and the "seed ferns," *Pteridosperms,* which were the first seed-bearing plants and not true ferns at all. These ancient groups dwindled toward the close of the Paleozoic era and shortly became extinct. Their decomposed remains furnished the substance of extensive coal beds throughout the world. Figure 38.5 shows the appearance of a Carboniferous swamp as reconstructed from fossils.

By far the greater number of Paleozoic species of plants failed to survive. The Paleozoic flora was largely replaced by the seed-forming gymnosperms, which became prominent in the early Mesozoic era. A diverse assemblage of cycads, ginkgoes (maidenhair trees), and conifers formed elaborate forests. During the closing years of the Mesozoic, the flowering plants (angiosperms), which began very modestly in the Jurassic period, underwent a phenomenal development and constitute today the dominant plants of the earth. The angiosperms have radiated into a variety of habitats, from sea level to mountain summits and from the humid tropics to the dry deserts. Associated with this diversity of habitat is great variety in general form and manner of growth. Many angiosperms have reverted to an aquatic existence. The familiar duck-weed, which covers the surface of a pond, is a striking example.

Figure 38.5 Luxuriant forests of giant trees with dense undergrowth flourished in the Great Coal Age (Carboniferous period), between 350 million and 275 million years ago. The massive trunks at the left are the Lepidodendrids, an extinct group whose modern relatives include the small, undistinguished club mosses (Selaginella) and the ground pines (Lycopodium) The tall, slender tree with whorled leaves at the right is a Calamite, represented today by a less prominent descendant, the horsetail Equisetum. The fernlike plants bearing seeds (at the left) are seed ferns (Pteridosperms), which resembled ferns but were actually the first true seed-bearing plants (Gymnosperms). (Courtesy of the Chicago Natural History Museum.)

In the animal kingdom, we witness a comparable picture of endless change. The deep Cambrian rocks contain the remains of varied marine invertebrate animals —sponges, jellyfishes, worms, shellfishes, starfishes, and crustaceans (fig. 38.6). These invertebrates were already so well developed that their differentiation must have taken place during the long period preceding the Cambrian. That this is actually the case has been revealed by the important finding, by the Australian geologists R. C. Sprigg and Martin F. Glaessner, of a rich deposit of Precambrian fossils in the Ediacara Hills of South Australia. The fossil-bearing rocks lie well below the oldest Cambrian strata, and contain imprints of jellyfishes, tracks of worms, traces of soft corals, and other animals of uncertain nature. Additionally, the Dartmouth University geologist Andrew McNair uncovered Precambrian remains of invertebrate animals (worms and brachiopods) in rocks 700 million years old, on Victoria Island in the Canadian Arctic.

Dominating the scene in early Paleozoic waters were bizarre arthropods, the trilobites and the large scorpionlike eurypterids. Common in all Paleozoic periods were the nautiloids, related to the modern nautilus, and the brachiopods, or lampshells, relatively inconspicuous today. The odd graptolites, colonial animals whose carbonaceous remains resemble pencil marks, attained the peak of their development in the Ordovician period and then abruptly declined. No land animals are known for Cambrian and Ordovician times. Seascapes of the early Paleozoic are shown in figure 38.7

Many of the prominent Paleozoic marine invertebrate groups became extinct or declined sharply in numbers before the Mesozoic era. During the Mesozoic, shelled ammonoids flourished in the seas, and insects and reptiles were the predominant land forms. At the close of the Mesozoic, the once successful marine ammonoids perished and the reptilian dynasty collapsed, giving way to the birds and mammals. Insects have continued to thrive and have differentiated into a staggering variety of

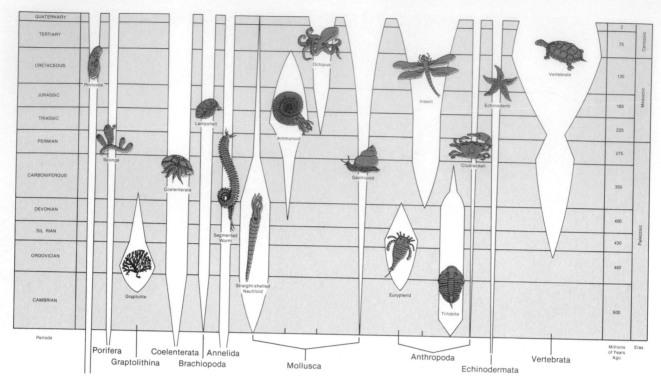

Periods									Millions of Years Ago	Eras

Figure 38.6 Historical record of animal life. Many of the invertebrate groups were already highly diversified and abundant in the Cambrian, the first period of the Paleozoic era, approximately 600 million years ago. The Paleozoic era is often called the *Age of Invertebrates*, with its multitude of nautiloids, eurypterids, and trilobites. Brachiopods with hinged valves were the commonest shellfish of the Paleozoic seas. In the Mesozoic era, air-breathing insects and vertebrates, notably the widely distributed reptiles (see fig. 38.4), held the center of the stage. The Mesozoic seas were populated with large, shelled ammonoids, now extinct. Warm-blooded vertebrates (birds and mammals) became prominent in the Cenozoic era, and man himself arrived on the scene in the closing stages of this era (see chapter 38).

species. Well over 600,000 different species of insects have been described, and conservative estimates place the total number of living species today at 3 million.

During the course of evolution, plant and animal groups interacted to each other's advantage. There is little doubt, for example, that the rise and spread of flowering plants fostered the diversification and dispersal of insects. As flowering plants became less and less dependent on wind for pollination, a great variety of insects emerged as specialists in transporting pollen. The colors and fragrances of flowers evolved as adaptations to attract insects. Flowering plants also exerted an important influence on the evolution of birds and mammals. Birds, which feed on seeds, fruits, and buds, evolved rapidly in intimate association with the flowering plants. The emergence of herbivorous mammals coincided with the widespread distribution of nutritious grasses over the plains during the Cenozoic era. In turn, the herbivorous mammals furnished the setting for the evolution of carnivorous mammals. The interdependence of plants and animals continues to exist in nature today.

EVOLUTIONARY STABILITY

The multitude of different kinds of present-day organisms is impressive. Yet the inhabitants of the world today are only a small percentage of the tremendous array of organisms of earlier periods. As we have seen, the fate of most lineages of organisms throughout time is extinction. Apparently, only those populations that can continue to adapt to changing environmental conditions avoid extinction. Yet some types of organisms have not changed appreciably in untold millions of years. Long-standing stability of organization seems antithetical to the concept of evolution. The opossum has survived almost unchanged since late Cretaceous, some 75 or more million years ago. The horseshoe crab, *Limulus*, is not very different from fossils uncovered some 500 million years ago. The maidenhair, or ginkgo, tree of the Chinese temple gardens differs little from its

Figure 38.7 Highly diversified assemblage of invertebrates of early Paleozoic seas. *Top:* Ordovician period. Large organism in foreground is a straight-shelled nautiloid. Other prominent forms are trilobites, massive corals, smaller nautiloids, and a snail. *Bottom:* Cambrian period. Conspicuous animals are the trilobite *(center foreground),* eurypterid *(center background),* and the jellyfish *(left).* Other animals include brachiopods, annelid worms, sea cucumbers, and varied shelled forms. (*Top,* courtesy of Chicago Natural History Museum; *bottom,* courtesy of the American Museum of Natural History.)

ancestors 200 million years back. The treasured ginkgo has probably existed on earth longer than any other tree that is now living. Darwin called the ginkgo "a living fossil." We have no adequate explanation for such unexpected stability of organization. Perhaps some organisms have reached an almost perfect adjustment to a relatively unchanging environment. One thing, however, is certain: such stable forms are not at all dominant in our present-day world. One of the dominant forms today is man, a mammal that has evolved rapidly in a relatively short span of years.

SUMMARY

Chemical evolution preceded biological evolution. The atmosphere of the pristine earth contained no free oxygen, but was rich in hydrogen, methane, ammonia, and water vapor. Organic compounds essential for life were most likely synthesized by energy from the sun in the form of ultraviolet light, aided by heat from volcanic activity and electrical discharges such as lightning. This view accords with ongoing experimental studies, intensified by advances in molecular biophysics. In 1953, Stanley Miller passed electrical discharges through gas mixtures resembling the earth's primitive atmosphere, and recovered a variety of amino acids. Subsequently, Sidney Fox experimentally obtained proteinlike macromolecules (proteinoids) from a mixture of amino acids, and spherical, bacterialike molecular aggregates (microspheres). Although there remains a hiatus between the formation of organic microspheres and the first living cell, it is probable that the first organisms were heterotrophic, maintaining themselves on ready-made organic substances in the primitive sea broth. Autotrophic organisms later evolved, which were able to manufacture organic nutrients from simpler molecules. The evolution of photosynthetic autotrophs (green plants) was of great significance, since the process of photosynthesis resulted in the liberation of free gaseous oxygen in the atmosphere. Life could then become aerobic, with unlimited chemical energy. The twin processes of photosynthesis and aerobic respiration made possible a rich diversity of life, ever changing. The fossilized remains of plants and animals in the strata of the earth's crust attest to the constantly changing character of life. New types of plants and animals have continually appeared. Some types thrived for a period and then became extinct. Others arose and have continued to flourish.

Emergence of Man 39

Man has unique attributes; he is nonetheless an animal and the product of the same natural evolutionary forces that have shaped all animal life. There is almost universal unanimity that the closest relatives of man are the apes. The line leading ultimately to man diverged from the ape branch during Tertiary times. There are several candidates among Tertiary fossil manlike apes that qualify for the position ancestral to man. One often hears stated, hesitatingly and perhaps in the form of an apology, that man is not really a descendant of the apes but merely shares a very distant ancestry with the apes. By indirection, the evasive idea is conveyed that our remote generalized ancestor would not be at all apelike. This is sheer deception. There is simply no blinking the question that modern man's ancestors and modern ape's ancestors were close relatives, and not distant relatives.

PRIMATE RADIATION

Primates, the order to which man belongs, underwent adaptive radiation when it first arose in Cenozoic times, approximately 70 million years ago. The primates are primarily tree dwellers; only man is fully adapted for life on the ground. Many of the noteworthy characteristics of the primates evolved as specializations for an arboreal mode of life. Depth perception is important to a tree-living animal; the majority of the primates are unique in possessing binocular, or stereoscopic, vision, wherein the visual fields of the two eyes overlap. The hands evolved as prehensile organs for grasping objects, an adaptation later useful to man for manipulating tools. The use of the hands to bring objects to the nose (for smelling) and to the mouth (for tasting) was associated with a reduction of the snout, or muzzle, and a reduction of the olfactory area of the brain. Primates generally have a poor sense of smell. Closely associated with enhanced visual acuity and increased dexterity of the hands was the marked expansion of the brain, particularly the visual and memory areas of the brain. Progressive enlargement of the brain culminated, in man, in the development of higher mental faculties.

The primate stock arose and differentiated from small, chisel-toothed, insectivorous ancestors (fig. 39.1). The Asiatic tree shrew, *Tupaia,* an agile tree climber that feeds on insects and fruits in tropical forests, survives as a model for the ancestor of the primates. Most authorities place the tree shrew in the mammalian order Insectivora, while a few hold the view that the tree shrew is a primitive, generalized member of the primates. The order Primates is generally divided into two groups or suborders, the *Prosimii* and the *Anthropoidea.* The prosimians are aboreal and largely nocturnal predators; they include such tropical forms as the lemurs, the lorises, and the tarsiers. As adaptations to an aboreal-noc-

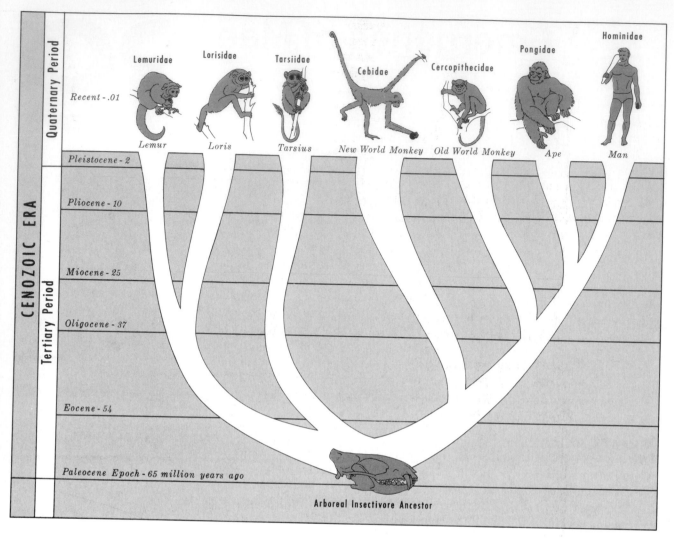

Figure 39.1 Adaptive radiation of the primates from a basic stock of small, insect-eating placental mammals, the Insectivora (whose living kin include the shrews, moles, and hedgehogs). Based on paleontological and anatomical evidence, the pongid (ape) and hominid (man) lineages diverged during the Miocene epoch, about 20 million years ago. Estimates based on biochemical data (*e.g.*, comparative immunology of serum albumin) are presently at variance with the fossil data. The biochemical evidence suggests that the lineage leading to man split off from the ape line only about 4 million years ago.

turnal niche, these prosimians evolved large, forwardly placed eyes and strong, grasping hands and feet. The lemurs are largely confined to Madagascar, the lorises are found principally in eastern Asia, and the tarsiers are limited to southeastern Asia. The tarsiers represent the most advanced group of prosimians and may be said to foreshadow the higher primate trends of the Anthropoidea.

The more advanced primates, the anthropoids, are composed of the New World monkeys, the Old World monkeys, the apes, and man. All are able to sit in an upright position, and thus the hands are free to investigate and manipulate the environment. The monkeys are normally quadrupedal, running along branches of trees on all fours. Among the apes, gibbons habitually use their arms for hand-over-hand swinging in a motion known as brachiation. The great apes (orangutan, chimpanzee, and gorilla) can maintain prolonged semierect postures. When on the ground, the chimpanzee and gorilla are "knuckle-walkers," the weight being placed on the knuckles of the hands rather than on the extended fingers. Man alone is specialized for erect bipedal locomotion.

The anatomical and physiological features that distinguish modern man from the living great apes are comparatively few. The resemblances in skeletal structures, muscular anatomy, physiological processes, serological reactions, and chromosome patterns are all strikingly close. The close relation of man and the apes shows up clearly in molecular comparisons of the alpha chain of the hemoglobin molecule. In the sequence of 146 amino acids of the alpha chain, there is only one difference in the composition of the amino acid residues between man and the gorilla. This contrasts sharply with differences, for example, of 19 amino acid residues in the alpha chain between man and the pig, or differences of 26 amino acid residues between man and the rabbit.

The pronounced differences between man and the apes relate mainly to locomotory habits and brain growth. Man has a fully upright posture and gait, and an enlarged brain. The cranial capacity of a modern ape rarely exceeds 600 cubic centimeters, while the average human cranial capacity is 1,350 cubic centimeters. Much of man's mastery of varied environments has been the result of his superior intelligence, gradually acquired throughout evolution.

When we speak of man, we inevitably think of him as he exists today. Present-day man is certainly different from his predecessors, in much the same manner that the modern horse is different from his forerunners. Thus, when a Pleistocene fossil specimen is designated an "ape-man" or a "near-man," it should not be imagined that such an extinct form possessed the qualities of man as we know him today. It is important to recognize that there have been different kinds of men. The evolutionary process of adaptive radiation led to a family of men, recognized formally as the Hominidae, of which modern man—*Homo sapiens,* or "man the wise"—is only one member and the sole survivor.

FOSSIL PRE-MAN

Fragmentary remains have been uncovered of apelike primates that inhabited the Old World during Miocene and early Pliocene times, spanning roughly the period from 25 million to 10 million years ago (fig. 39.2). Most are clearly members of the ape family (Pongidae), such as *Pliopithecus,* a Miocene gibbonlike creature that is generally regarded as ancestral to today's gibbons. A fossil form that once aroused lively debate is *Oreopithecus,* unearthed in Italian coal beds that date back to the early Pliocene, approximately 10 million years ago. In the 1950s, the Swiss scholar Johannes Hürzler championed the view that *Oreopithecus* is a primitive hominid in the direct line of man's ancestry. The current consensus is that *Oreopithecus* is an aberrant offshoot of the pongid stock and disappeared without issue (fig. 39.2).

Miocene sediments of Europe, Africa, and Asia (especially of India) have yielded remains of *Dryopithecus,* the oak-ape, so called because of the presence of oak leaves in the fossil deposits. Known collectively as the dryopithecines, these primitive oak-apes were the early forerunners of the modern orangutan, chimpanzee, and gorilla. The African variety, *Dryopithecus africanus*—first named *Proconsul,* after a famous chimpanzee at the London Zoo—may not be far removed from the common stock from which apes and men arose (fig. 39.2). Although primarily a tree dweller, *Dryopithecus africanus* apparently wandered on the ground and may have availed himself of vegetable foods in the open grasslands (fig. 39.3). The transition from tree dwelling to ground living might well have first appeared at this time. In the Miocene epoch, the great expanse of tropical rain forest in eastern Africa dwindled, leaving patches of dry wooded areas separated by open bushy grasslands. The capacity for

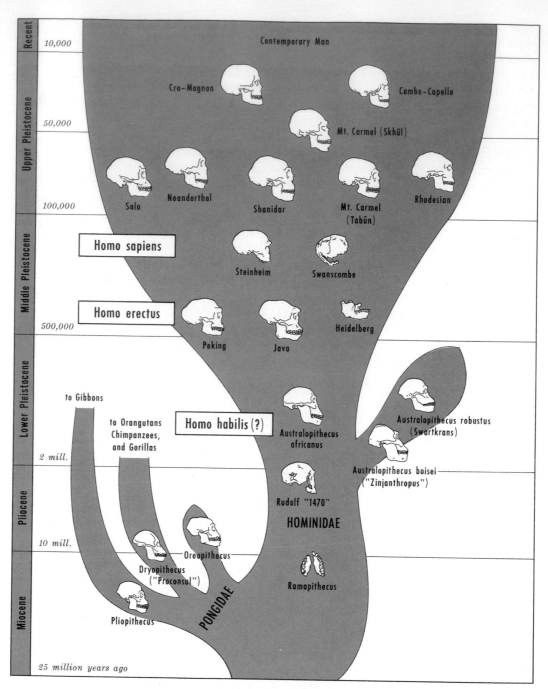

Figure 39.2 Geologic past of man. The late Miocene epoch witnessed the separation of the pongid (ape) and hominid (man) assemblages. The evolution of man was not limited to a single lineage. Several branches forked off from the main stem and were not directly ancestral to modern man, *Homo sapiens*.

ground walking may have evolved as an adaptation enabling arboreal forms to cross the open plains in passing from one patch of woodland to another. Thus, *Dryopithecus africanus* may have become a ground dweller in order to continue to live successfully in the trees. This is a seeming paradox, parallel to the intriguing conjecture that water-living vertebrates evolved terrestrial habits so that they could retain, and not abandon, their aquatic mode of life.

An impressive series of Miocene fossils has been placed in the genus *Ramapithecus*. An upper jaw, with unmistakable hominid dentition, was first found by G. Edward Lewis in 1935 in the Silawik Hills of northern India. This fragmentary specimen was named after the Indian god, Rama. In the 1960s, Louis S. B. Leakey uncovered jaw fragments of *Ramapithe-*

cus in eastern Africa (Kenya) in deposits of a geological age of 14 million years ago. These important fossil jaws show reduced canine teeth, relatively small incisors, and hominidlike, low-crowned molars. *Ramapithecus* evidently ranged widely throughout Africa and Asia in late Miocene and early Pliocene times. This fossil specimen may be close to the base of the stem of the hominid family. That is, this fossil form may mark the point where the hominid lineage separated from the pongid assemblage (fig. 39.2). The roots of man's family tree apparently date back 20 to 25 million years.

Several authors accept *Ramapithecus* as the earliest member of the family of men (Hominidae). The hominid status implies that this ancestral form was bipedal and ventured into open country to forage for food. There is no evidence that *Ramapithecus* was a hunter or tool user, or that he was a habitual ground-dwelling biped. It would seem that the distinctive dental adaptations of hominids evolved before the bipedal mode of locomotion became habitual or methodical. The evolutionary development of the capacity for efficient bipedalism probably required millions of years.

APE-MEN OR NEAR-MEN

In 1924, an epochal discovery in South Africa was announced by Raymond Dart, an Australian anatomist at the University of Witwatersrand in Johannesburg. In a Pleistocene limestone quarry near the small village of Taung in Bechuanaland was found the fossilized skull of a juvenile, corresponding to the skull of a child of about six years. The little Taung skull bears some resemblance to the skull of a young chimpanzee, but many of its components, notably the teeth, show pronounced affinities to man. Dart named the remarkable skull *Australopithecus africanus* (*austral*, for "south," and *pithekos*, for "ape"). Dart asserted that the southern ape-man was related to the ancestral stock of man rather than to the great apes (fig. 39.2). In other words, the Taung fossil represented an early member of the Hominidae, the family of man, rather than of the Pongidae, the family of apes.

Dart's declaration, which several scientists initially vigorously disputed, was fortified by findings in the 1930s by the late Robert Broom, a Scottish paleontologist. Adult skulls of *Australopithecus* were dug out from caves in Sterkfontein, Kromdraai, and Swartkrans in South Africa. The adult skulls confirmed the hominid anatomical pattern seen in the juvenile Taung cranium. The several new fossil forms were originally given different names. However, in recent years, it has become customary to refer to the South African ape-men collectively as the australopithecines. They were short, 4 to 5 feet in height, with a small, ape sized brain (cranial capacity range of 450 to 600 cubic centimeters). Nonetheless, the australopithecines stood upright, walked bipedally, and dwelt in open country (fig. 39.4). These circumstances nullify the popular view that man was an intelligent animal when he first came down out of the trees. It seems clear that erect bipedal locomotion on the ground preceded the development of a large complex brain.

The australopithecines are decidedly early representatives of the hominid lineage. However, spirited debate exists over which of the australopithecines occupy a prominent place in the direct ancestry of man. Current evidence favors the idea that there were two distinct species of australopithecines—the light-jawed, lightly built *Australopithecus africanus* and the heavy-jawed, larger *Australopithecus robustus* (fig.

Figure 39.3 *Dryopithecus*, an apelike type that prowled East Africa 20 to 25 million years ago. *Dryopithecus africanus* apparently led an agile life both on and off the ground. [Painting by Maurice Wilson; courtesy of the British Museum (Natural History).]

Figure 39.4 *Australopithecus*, an apeman of about 1 million years ago who stood upright, walked bipedally, and dwelt in open country. [Painting by Maurice Wilson; courtesy of the British Museum (Natural History).]

39.2). The former species was not over four feet tall and weighed no more than 60 pounds, whereas the latter species was a foot taller and at least 30 pounds heavier. When two contemporaneous species occupy the same habitat, ecologists have observed that the potential competitors become differentially specialized to exploit different components of the local environment. Thus, direct competition for food resources is minimized and the two species are able to coexist. It is thought that *Australopithecus robustus* became or remained exclusively vegetarian, whereas *Australopithecus africanus* increasingly supplemented its diet with animal food. The dietary difference is supported by the finding that *A. africanus* had smaller molars than *A. robustus*.

If, as it appears likely, the two *Australopithecus* species did coexist at the same time in the same region, then only one of the two could have been the progenitor of a more modern species of man. It has been suggested that the vegetarian *A. robustus* perished without leaving any descendants and that *A. africanus* was the forebear of a more advanced hominid. The dietary change to carnivorism may have represented one of the most important steps in transforming a bipedal ape into a tool-making and tool-using man.

The South African finds have been supplemented and extended by fossil discoveries in eastern Africa since 1959 by Louis and Mary Leakey at the 25-mile-long Olduvai Gorge in Tanzania, and in more recent years by Richard Leakey at the eastern shore of Kenya's Lake Rudolf. In 1959 at Olduvai Gorge, Louis and Mary Leakey uncovered bony fragments of a robust australopithecine, characterized by extremely massive jaws. This heavy-jawed fossil form was called *Zinjanthropus*, or the Nutcracker Man. Fossil remains of *Zinjanthropus* were found in strata judged by a new potassium-argon dating method (instead of the conventional uranium-lead technique) to be about 1.8 million years old. Most scientists today agree that *Zinjanthropus* is essentially an eastern African variety of *Australopithecus robustus*. Others contend that *Zinjanthropus* has more exaggerated, or coarser, features than *A. robustus* and warrants recognition as a separate species, *Australopithecus boisei*. It would thus represent a third species in the australopithecine complex.

In the 1960s, Louis and Mary Leakey found remains of a light-jawed hominid that they claimed was more advanced than *Australopithecus africanus*. Estimates of the brain capacities of the skulls averaged 637 cubic centimeters. This light-jawed type of Olduvai Gorge was said to be the first civilized or humanized man deserving of the rank of *Homo*, namely *Homo habilis* (fig. 39.2). The specific name *habilis* means "able, handy, mentally skillful, vigorous," from the inferred ability of this man to make stone tools. The recognition of *Homo habilis* indicates that this primitive human being was evolving alongside the less hominized australopithecines and lived side-by-side with them. The coexistence of *Homo habilis* and the australopithecines has been the subject of much concern among evolutionists. Some writers argue that *Homo habilis* did not cross the threshold between the pre-human and human grades and represented only an advanced member of *Australopithecus africanus*.

In 1972, Richard Leakey unearthed from the dessicated fossil beds of Lake Rudolf a nearly complete skull that has been placed at 2.8 million years. The specimen has been cautiously designated only by its museum identification number—"1470." The cranial capacity of the "1470" skull measures 780 cubic centimeters, which is significantly larger than any australopithecine specimen. Skull "1470" clearly belongs to the genus

Homo, although no species name has yet been designated. It may represent *Homo habilis,* and it may be the linear ancestor of *Homo erectus.*

In 1975, Mary Leakey and her co-workers discovered fossil jaws and teeth in sediments at a site 25 miles south of Olduvai Gorge called Laetolil. These hominid jaw fragments bear a strong resemblance to the mandible and teeth of skull "1470." The Laetolil specimens are impressive in that they have been dated at 3.35 to 3.75 million years. Mary Leakey has classified the jaw fragments as the remains of the eastern African *Homo habilis.* If this is the case, the existence of *Homo habilis* has been extended back to at least 3.5 million years ago; accordingly, this human species is older than any known australopithecine. This would indicate that *Homo habilis* is not the direct descendant of the australopithecines. It may be, however, that an older, as yet undiscovered *Australopithecus* (from Pliocene sediments) gave rise to *Homo habilis.*

EVOLUTION OF HUNTING

The lower Pleistocene hominids (*Australopithecus africanus* or *Homo habilis,* depending on one's views) fabricated crude tools out of pebbles. The ability to fashion and wield tools followed, or accompanied, the emancipation of the hands that bipedal locomotion made possible. The open African savanna offered to the early plains-dwelling hominids a new food resource; namely, herbivorous animals of all sizes adapted to the grassland habitat. A meat-eating hominid, however, cannot tear the thick hide of an antelope or a deer with his fingernails and teeth. A strong selective premium was placed on the acquisition of new manipulative skills for more efficient tool or weapon construction. To shape a stone into a sharp-pointed blade or to fashion a stick into a spear depends on improved mental capacities. Increased and more efficient tool use brought about selective pressures favoring increased brain size and complexity. Although these views lean heavily on speculation, it appears likely that adoption of the hunting habit shaped the behavior pattern of the human species. Human hunting became more than a mere technique; it became a way of life. As discussed in a subsequent section, the hunting habit led to a division of labor between the sexes, the introduction of food sharing, and the eventual establishment of a unique family organization.

EARLY TRUE MAN

The famous Java man, first described as *Pithecanthropus erectus,* undoubtedly had crossed the threshold between prehuman and human grades (fig. 39.2). This primitive human being was discovered at Trinil, Java, in 1894 by Eugene Dubois, a young Dutch army surgeon. Dubois had been profoundly influenced by the writings of Charles Darwin, and had become imbued with the idea that he could find the origins of man in the Far East. He surprised the world with the discovery of the earliest human. Curiously, Dubois, in his later years, inexplicably doubted his own finding and contended that *Pithecanthropus erectus* was merely a giant manlike ape. In the 1930s, additional fossil finds of *Pithecanthropus* were unearthed in central Java by the Dutch anthropologist G. H. R. von Koenigswald. The new findings confirmed the human status of *Pithecanthropus.*

Java man lived during middle Pleistocene times, between 500,000 and 300,000 years ago (fig. 39.2). This low-browed man was a toolmaker and a hunter who had learned to use fire. He probably had some powers of speech. Java man's ability to exploit his environment is reflected in the expanded size of his brain. The brain cavity had a capacity of 770 to 1,000 cubic centimeters.

In the 1920s, elaborate excavations undertaken by the Canadian anatomist Davidson Black of caves in the limestone hills near Peking, China, led to the discovery of another primitive man, *Sinanthropus pekinensis,* or Peking man (fig. 39.5). The cranial capacity in Peking man varied from 900 to 1,200 cubic centimeters. He fashioned tools and weapons of stone and bone, and he kindled fire. There is a strong suspicion that Peking man was cannibalistic and savored human brains, for many of the fossil braincases show signs of having been cracked open from below.

Java man and Peking man were originally each christened with a distinctive Latin name, *Pithecanthropus erectus* and *Sinanthropus pekinensis,* respectively. There is, however, no justification for recognizing more than the single genus of humans, *Homo.* Accordingly, modern taxonomists have properly assigned both Java man and Peking man to the genus *Homo.* Moreover, the morphological differences between these two fossil men are readily within the range of variation that we observe in living populations today. These forms therefore represent two closely related geographic races (subspecies) of the same species. Lastly, both Java and Peking men are distinct enough from modern man (*Homo sapiens*) to warrant being placed together in a different species, *Homo erectus.*

These nomenclatural changes may appear to be trivial, but the implications are great. One important implication is that human populations at any one time level were differentiated into geographical races of one species—not into distinct species or even genera. We can envision, for example, that approximately 500,000 years ago, there existed a single widespread species of man, with Eastern populations represented by the Java and Peking variants and the Western populations constituted by types resembling Heidelberg man (found in an early Pleistocene sand deposit near Heidelberg, Germany). The suspected wide distribution of *Homo erectus* has been confirmed by the recent discoveries of this early type of man in North Africa (Ternifine, Algeria) and East Africa (Oldu-

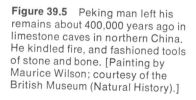

Figure 39.5 Peking man left his remains about 400,000 years ago in limestone caves in northern China. He kindled fire, and fashioned tools of stone and bone. [Painting by Maurice Wilson; courtesy of the British Museum (Natural History).]

vai Gorge, Tanzania). Evidently then, populations of *Homo erectus* spread successfully through the continents, from the tropical regions of Africa to southeast Asia.

EVOLUTION OF HUMAN SOCIETY

The hunting-gathering economy of *Homo erectus* necessitated or permitted collaborative, or cooperative, interactions of individuals. Adult males became increasingly interdependent in their hunting efforts. *Homo erectus* hunted in small groups in open country, using wooden spears, clubs, and stones. Dismembering and sharing the animal prey or kill became a fundamental disposition of the group or band. The sharing of food regularly is a social achievement unique to man; only rarely do apes share food. To this day, humans express sentiments of comradeship and trust by coming together in common meals.

There is no evidence that the early hominid female participated in the hunting of large game; the adult female was increasingly encumbered with a fetus or by the care of the young, or by both. The long period of dependency of the young strengthened mother-child bonds but also restricted the mobility and activity of the woman. It appears likely the female remained at home as a food-gatherer and domestic while the male engaged in hunting. The immobility of the female and the prolonged immaturity of the young, coupled with the limitations imposed on the male in the number of females he could possibly support, radically transformed a basically polygamous society into a monogamous structure.

A primary human innovation was thus relatively permanent pair-bonding, or monogamy. Sustained pair-bonding proved to be advantageous in several respects. It served to reduce sexual competition and the prolonged sexual contact increased the probability of leaving descendants. The heterosexual pair-bonding relationship became fortified as the estrus cycle of the female became modified into a condition of continuous sexual receptivity. The sustained sex interests of the partners made possible by the obliteration of estrus in the female increased the stability of the family unit, and facilitated the development of permanent family-sized shelters for rest, protection, and play. In essence, strong interpersonal bonds between a male, a female, and their children became the basis of the uniquely human family organization. The human male had become incorporated into the mother-young social group of the monkeys and apes.

Human language was fostered as the hunters recorded experiences with each other and transmitted information to their mates and children. In turn, the women conveyed events on the domestic scene to the returned hunters. Speech favored cooperation between local groups, and the fusion of small groups into larger communities. Speech also fostered the successful occupation of one geographical area after another. The exchange of ideas over wide areas permitted human cultures of great complexity to develop. Evidently then, early man's assumption of the hunting habit was preeminent in shaping the social organization of early (and later) human society.

EMERGENCE OF MODERN MAN

The classic Neanderthal man was first unearthed in 1856 in a limestone cave in the Neander ravine near Dusseldorf, Germany (fig. 39.6). It is one of the best known of fossil men, having been subsequently found at numerous widely separate sites in Europe, particularly in France. Neanderthal man was a cave dweller, short (about 5 feet) but powerfully

built, with prominent facial brow ridges, and a large brain with an average capacity of 1,450 cubic centimeters (as opposed to 1,350 cubic centimeters in modern man). Neanderthal man first arose some 100,000 years ago (fig. 39.2). He roamed over Europe up to about 40,000 years ago (Upper Pleistocene), and then he dramatically disappeared. He was replaced by men of a modern type, much like ourselves, which have been grouped under the common name of Cro-Magnon.

The transition from Neanderthal man to Cro-Magnon man is problematical. Prior to the time of the Neanderthalers themselves, about 200,000 to 100,000 years ago, there emerged types of men, such as Swanscombe from England, Steinheim from Germany, and Fontéchevade from France, that did not conform to the classic Neanderthal type. Indeed, the Swanscombe and Steinheim skulls (fig. 39.2) are not markedly different from the skull of modern man. Is it possible that a modern type of man arose before Neanderthal? We have grown accustomed to the idea that Neanderthal man was our direct ancestor, but now it appears that we may be closer to the truth by considering him a sterile offshoot. The picture is far from clear. In the Middle East about 100,000 to 30,000 years ago there existed an exceptionally heterogeneous group of men. These are represented by the Palestinian Mount Carmel man, dug out of caves at Tabūn and Skhūl, and the Shanidar man, excavated from caves in the mountains of northern Iraq (fig. 39.2). These men ranged from individuals with almost typically western European Neanderthal features to individuals that are barely distinguishable from modern man.

Another element of uncertainty is the relation of the European Neanderthal man to other Upper Pleistocene men in widely scattered parts of the world—Rhodesian man of Central Africa and Solo man of Java (fig. 39.2). Some authorities have considered Rhodesian and Solo men to be the geographical equivalents of Neanderthal man of Europe. This would lead us to believe that the classic Neanderthal man was widely distributed in the Old World. These findings present knotty problems.

STATUS OF NEANDERTHAL MAN

Authorities do not all agree on the status of Neanderthal man. The populations of Neanderthal man in Europe disappeared rather abruptly and were replaced by a modern group (Cro-Magnon) that definitely belongs to *Homo sapiens*. Does this indicate that two separate species, *Homo neanderthalensis* and *Homo sapiens*, actually existed together in Europe, and that the latter species displaced the former without hybridization occurring between the two? The evolutionist Theodosius Dobzhansky has expressed perceptive views on this question. Dobzhansky calls attention to the Mount Carmel fossil populations in Palestine, particularly the one found at Skhūl. This extraordinary fossil assemblage consists of individuals ranging from classical European Neanderthal types to forms closely resembling *Homo sapiens*. This suggests a racial mixture of the two groups. It appears, then, that the European Neanderthal man and Middle Eastern modern men were not reproductively incompatible, as would be two species, but rather were races of the same species *(Homo sapiens)*. In other words, the Mount Carmel locality represented a zone of integradation of a kind usually found at the boundaries of geographic races. The emergence of Cro-Magnon man may have resulted, at least to some extent, from the amalgamation of the European Neanderthal race and the Middle Eastern modern-type race invading Europe.

Although this interpretation seems reasonable, some authorities claim that the classic Neanderthalers were not directly involved in the ancestry of modern man. Clark Howell, professor of anthropology at Chicago University, suggests that little, if any, opportunity existed for the exchange of genes between the Neanderthal populations of western Europe and populations in the Middle East or elsewhere. During the Pleistocene epoch, glacial ice sheets covered many parts of Europe. It may be that the Neanderthalers of western Europe were geographically isolated by the Ice Age of 100,000 years ago. Neanderthal man may have perished in isolation before modern man arrived, or may have been overrun by more progressive Middle Eastern contemporaries who had spread into western Europe. Under this viewpoint, Neanderthal man represented an evolutionary dead end in man's ancestry. Modern man evolved independently of Neanderthal man, and arose by separate origin via the middle Pleistocene *sapiens*-like stock—Steinheim man and Swanscombe man (fig. 39.7)—and the more advanced Mount Carmel men in Upper Pleistocene.

Cro-Magnon man, a representative of our own species, *Homo sapiens*, can be traced back about 35,000 years. His remains have been found in many sites in western and central Europe. The Cro-Magnon men showed individual differences, just as man today exhibits individual variation. One of the notable variants is Combe-Capelle man from France (fig. 39.8). Little is known of modern man in other continents during the time that Cro-Magnon flourished in Europe. Modern man may have been cradled in Asia or Africa.

PLEISTOCENE OVERKILL

Cro-Magnon man was an accomplished hunter, so much so that he has been held responsible for the high rate of destruction and extinction of the mammalian fauna—such as the giant sloth, mammoths, saber-toothed cat, and giant ox—in the upper Pleistocene. The large-scale annihilation

of many game mammals by man has been called *Pleistocene overkill* by the evolutionist Paul S. Martin. Martin has noted that more than a third of the genera of large mammals met extinction in Africa about 50,000 years ago, and that nearly all of the larger game genera in North America perished 12,000 to 15,000 years ago. The latter event coincided with the migrations of early Mongoloid bands into North America via the Bering Strait. So devastating were the hunting activities of man in North America that only a few forms of larger mammals survived, notably the bison and pronghorn antelopes. Such drastic reductions in game animals throughout the world may have been one of the precipitating factors in man's transition some 10,000 years ago from a hunting economy to an agricultural economy.

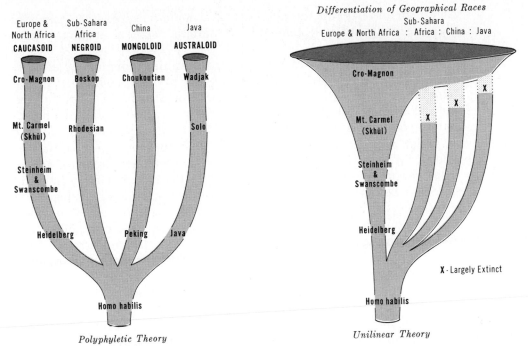

Differentiation of Geographical Races

Europe & North Africa
CAUCASOID

Sub-Sahara Africa
NEGROID

China
MONGOLOID

Java
AUSTRALOID

Cro-Magnon — Boskop — Choukoutien — Wadjak

Mt. Carmel (Skhül) — Rhodesian — Solo

Steinheim & Swanscombe

Heidelberg — Peking — Java

Homo habilis

Polyphyletic Theory

Differentiation of Geographical Races

Sub-Sahara
Europe & North Africa : Africa : China : Java

Cro-Magnon

Mt. Carmel (Skhül) X X X

Steinheim & Swanscombe

Heidelberg

X - Largely Extinct

Homo habilis

Unilinear Theory

ORIGIN OF RACES OF MAN

We do not know the birthplace of modern man. Nevertheless, we do *not* believe that Cro-Magnon man originated simultaneously in widely different parts of the world. Rather, he arose in one place, then migrated to various regions of the globe and became differentiated into geographical races. This is the orthodox and established pattern of geographical origin of races. There is, however, a school of thought, chiefly identified with Franz Weidenreich and Carleton Coon, that conceives of the modern races of man as descending from different ancient hominid lineages evolving independently of one another. Thus, as seen in figure 39.9, Java man was the early progenitor of the Australoid race; Peking man was the forerunner of the Mongoloid race; Rhodesian man gave rise ultimately to the Negroid race; and a Middle Eastern type, perhaps Mount Carmel, led to the Caucasoid race. According to this theory, the races of man would need to be considered older than the species *Homo sapiens* itself.

At this point, we may digress to consider the phenomenon of parallel evolution, or *parallelism*, whereby two organisms acquire similar characteristics independently of one another although they have stemmed from related ancestral stocks. An illustrative case would be the structural resemblances of New World and Old World porcupines, the familiar spine-bearing rodents. The New World porcupines are native to South America; their counterparts in North America are relatively recent immigrants from the South American forests. The Old World porcupines are common in Africa and have spread into southern parts of Eurasia. Some students of the subject believe that the South American porcupines are direct descendants of the African forms. It has been suggested that the African porcupines crossed the South Atlantic on raftlike floating objects. A transoceanic dispersal route, however, seems improbable to several authorities. An alternative explanation, championed by the paleontologist Albert Wood of Amherst College, is that the South American and African porcupines have been derived independently of each other from an ancient generalized (nonporcupine) rodent stock that inhabited both the New World and the Old World. Thus, the South

Figure 39.9 Racial origins of man. The polyphyletic hypothesis envisions a distant separation of the principal races of man. The four major geographical races had evolved independently and in parallel fashion over hundreds of thousands of years. This thesis that the major races of mankind can be traced far back in prehistoric antiquity is scarcely defensible in light of modern evolutionary concepts. The recent origin of the living races of man, as expressed by the unilinear theory, is more tenable. Racial differentiation occured only after modern man (Cro-Magnon) arose and became distributed over a large area of the world. The unilinear theory does not exclude the persistence of some local traits from ancient regional lineages. Certain geographical populations reflect admixture of the immigrant Cro-Magnon group and the older indigenous stocks.

American and African porcupines share a common ancestor (a primitive rodent stock), but independently, in parallel fashion, acquired structural resemblances.

Is it possible that widely separated geographical populations of early Pleistocene men followed independent, but parallel, courses of evolutionary development, much as the New World and Old World porcupines? Let us examine the situation carefully. By no stretch of the imagination could the South American and African porcupines be considered as *racial variants of one species*. These two porcupine groups are certainly reproductively incompatible. The Weidenreich-Coon school would argue that geographic separation of the different early hominid branches did *not* lead to reproductive isolation, as might be expected of populations of long standing that are spatially separated and that differentiate along independent lines. It is, however, exceedingly difficult to imagine how several hominid races, diverging in different parts of the world, can evolve independently and yet repeatedly in the same direction, leading only to one species, *Homo sapiens*. The parallel origin of races is not hopelessly out of the question, but if it occurs, it must be the very rare exception to the normal process. Indeed, modern evolutionists are disposed to relegate the Weidenreich-Coon notion of parallel evolution of races to the category of the highly improbable.

There seems little doubt that *Homo sapiens* originated in a single area, then spread the world over and differentiated into regional populations (fig. 39.9). These ancient geographic groups, once spatially separated to a large extent, have intermingled and intercrossed for untold thousands of years. The distinguishing features of the basic racial groups have become increasingly blurred by the countless migrations and intermixings. The whole world today is a single large neighborhood. Modern man potentially lives in one great reproductive community.

PROBLEMS OF PRESENT-DAY MAN

We have seen that the hunting way of life dominated man's existence for well over 600,000 years. Man discarded the arboreal, defensive, and herbivorous habits of his primate relatives and became a terrestrial, weapon-making, carnivorous predator. Man became endowed with genetic characteristics that enabled him to be successful as a predatory hunter. It is highly probable that many of the inherent adaptive characteristics of the hunting era have continued to persist in present-day man. Today man lives for the most part in an environment of his own making. It is still an open question whether he can govern himself prudently in an environment that he has so drastically altered. Is it possible that contemporary man is unable to cope with himself or with his very recent environmental changes because those unique genetic propensities that were once highly adaptive in the hunting era are no longer adaptive in the modern era?

SUMMARY

Modern man—*Homo sapiens*—is the only living member of the family Hominidae. In the distant past, there were several kinds of man. The fossil evidence indicates that the hominid stock diverged from the pongid (great apes) branch between 10 and 25 million years ago. *Dryopithecus*, a semiterrestrial form, sired two distinct lines: the forest-dwelling, arboreal apes and bipedal, prairie-dwelling prehumans of the *Australopithecus* type. One of the branches of the australopithecines survived to become the progenitor of man *(Homo)*. The assumption of an upright stance by the earliest hominids emancipated the hands for tool-wielding and tool-making. Two characteristics probably developed together, reinforcing each other—the skillful use of the hands and increased complexity of the brain. With improved mental capacities and more efficient tools, the early plains-prowling hominids became aggressive, carnivorous predators. The adoption of the hunting habit apparently shaped the behavior pattern of the human species. Early man hunted in bands, and such group activity fostered cooperation and communication among the hunters. The hunting mode of life promoted the development of speech and language, permanent male-female relationships (pair-bonding), and an integrated family organization. The mass slaughter of mammals by man during the Pleistocene was probably one of the precipitating factors in man's transition some 10,000 years ago from a hunting economy to an agricultural economy. The change to settled agriculture (and later industrialization) is only of recent origin, which renders it likely that many of the inherent adaptive characteristics of the hunting era have continued to persist in present-day man.

Man
Environment
and Behavior

40 Population Dynamics

All species of animals and plants have a great capacity to reproduce, which unrestrained would result in multitudinous swarms of organisms within a few generations. An individual oyster, for example, can spawn 100 million eggs. A blue crab of the Western Atlantic can harbor on her relatively small abdomen well over 1 million eggs. In a period less than three weeks, the ordinary housefly can deposit six clutches of eggs, each containing about 140 eggs. This extravagant reproductive capacity is a potential that is scarcely ever realized in a natural population. The remarkable reproductive potentials of organisms are regulated by disease, predation, limitations of the food supply, territoriality, and a host of other forces that hold the reins on population size. No organism has been able to free itself indefinitely of the stabilizing forces that operate in nature's elaborate system of checks and balances. Man is no exception to this principle.

LOGISTIC THEORY OF POPULATION GROWTH

The word *population* is derived from the Latin *populus,* meaning "people." From a biological standpoint, a population is the total number of individuals of a particular species inhabiting a certain locality at some specific time. A biological population is a *species population*—that is, it is a local breeding unit in which the constituent individuals are capable of exchanging genes with each other. There are ordinarily no barriers to interbreeding within a species population.

Each population exhibits a number of measurable attributes—natality, mortality, age structure, mating system, dispersion (spatial distribution), dispersal (immigration and emigration), and density (degree of crowding), as well as various complex relationships with the environment. *Natality,* or the production of new-generation offspring, is antithetic to *mortality,* or the loss of individuals in unit time through death. Given no immigration or emigration, the population will remain stable when the birth rate balances, or equals, the death rate. An increase in death rate over birth rate yields negative growth, or a population decline.

Under controlled experimental conditions, particularly with simple asexually reproducing organisms, the growth pattern of a population is sigmoidal, or S-shaped. As figure 40.1 shows, a slow increase in numbers is first evident. This initial slow rate of growth is followed by a period of rapid increase in numbers. The accelerated growth is said to be exponential, or geometric; it is caused by a sharp increase in the natality rate in contrast to minimal mortality. The rate of growth becomes progressively lower as the population approaches an upper limit of its growth. The growth curve levels out horizontally, or becomes asymptotic. Such an S-shaped curve (also called a *logistic* curve) is obtained when the conditions are carefully controlled, as in the classic studies on

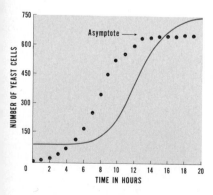

Figure 40.1 Sigmoidal, or S-shaped, growth curve. The initial rapid population growth decelerates to reach an asymptotic limit. (Based on growth of yeast cells in laboratory cultures observed by Raymond Pearl.)

480

small laboratory populations of one-celled protozoa by the Russian biologist G. F. Gause.

In 1934, Gause observed the growth of a population of one protozoan species, *Paramecium aurelia,* under uniform environmental conditions, that is, constant space and a constant supply of food. At the beginning of the experiment, he placed 20 paramecia in a test tube containing a carefully balanced salt solution, appropriate to the growth of the paramecia. Each day, Gause added a constant quantity of bacteria (*Bacillus pyocyaneus*), which served as food for the paramecia. The numbers of paramecia in the tube were estimated daily, and every other day the culture was washed with bacteria-free medium to prevent the accumulation of waste products. The pattern of growth of the paramecia was found to be S-shaped. During the early growth of the population, the number of protozoa in the limited space increased appreciably. The increased density, however, then had a damping effect on the rate of growth: the natality rate decreased and the mortality rate increased. The population leveled off, or reached its asymptote, when the natality and mortality rates became balanced.

The asymptotic limit represents the maximum population that can exist in the stipulated environment under exacting culture conditions. The S-shaped curve implies a smooth and orderly pattern of growth, in which the asymptote is approached gradually and predictably. We may now ask: Does the S-shaped curve characterize, or typify, the pattern of growth of *natural* populations?

NATURAL POPULATIONS

Gause's experiment approaches closely a uniform, if not ideal, set of environmental conditions. The temperature was carefully regulated, the volume and chemical composition of the medium was kept constant, a food of uniform quality was renewed in equal quantities each day, and the waste products were removed at frequent intervals. There was also no immigration or emigration of paramecia to or from adjacent populations. Moreover, other species of organisms were excluded from the experiment.

Such controlled conditions are probably never met by populations in nature. Natural populations rarely, if ever, have an unlimited quantity of food and space, and rarely have no other kinds of organisms with which to contend. The growth of natural populations, at least of animals with complex life cycles, fails to agree with the simple S-shaped pattern, particularly in the later phases of growth. Many natural populations follow a sigmoid course during the first phase, when the density of the population is increasing continuously and the available resources are excessive. But in the later phases of growth, the population usually does not remain steady about an asymptote. Rather, more often than not, natural populations undergo profound oscillations or fluctuations. After an initial rapid rate of growth, a limit to further population growth is imposed by such factors as a decline in the food supply, an exhaustion of space, an increased probability of parasitism and disease, and an increased competition for the available resources. The eventual restraint on the *biotic potential* (the innate capacity of the population to grow) by some force in the environment has been designated by ecologists as *environmental resistance.* We may also say that environmental factors impose an upper limit of growth on a population. The limit at which the environment can support a population is often referred to as the *carrying capacity* of the environment.

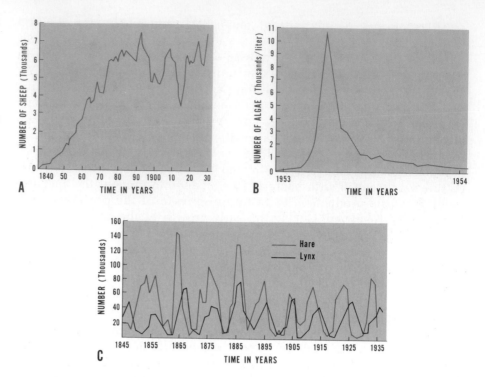

Figure 40.2 Population fluctuations. *(A) Saw-toothed curve,* as exemplified by growth of the sheep population of South Australia. (Based on data by J. Davidson.) *(B) Irruptive,* or *J-shaped, curve,* in which the population increases sharply and then rapidly crashes to a very low level. (Based on growth of golden-brown algae observed by S. Stankovic.) *(C) Cyclic curves,* in which populations increase and decline at regular intervals. The 10-year oscillations in populations of the snowshoe hare and lynx are based on pelt records of the Hudson Bay Company. (Adapted from work of D. A. Maclulich.)

POPULATION FLUCTUATIONS

Natural populations generally do not remain perfectly steady around an asymptote. Rather, many natural populations are characterized by a saw-toothed curve as a result of periodic upward and downward growth swings. As seen in figure 40.2A, the early exponential growth of sheep populations in southern Australia was followed by irregular departures up and down from the so-called equilibrium, or asymptote, level. Although the growth pattern is not smooth or orderly, the population is relatively stable. The population fluctuates mildly within the bounds of the carrying capacity of the environment.

Some populations, particularly those that grow seasonally, undergo such rapid growth initially that they increase sharply and abruptly, or *irrupt.* As seen in figure 40.2B, the population actually overshoots the carrying capacity of the area. It may exhaust an unusually abundant (although temporary) food supply, and then precipitously fall, or crash, to a very low level. In such instances, the growth curve is said to be *J-shaped.* This kind of growth pattern can be observed among many annual plants that grow in an unrestricted fashion during the favorable spring and summer months, but then decline drastically in growth as frost arrives. One of the most dramatic of irruptions is the sudden increase (called a *bloom*) of populations of certain plankton organisms (minute dinoflagellates) in the seas along both the Atlantic and Pacific oceans. The periodic bloom, or plague, of dinoflagellates has long been known as the "red tide," since the large population discolors the waters with a red tinge.

On occasions, the population fluctuations occur at exceedingly regular intervals. Sharp increases in numbers are followed by equally sharp crashes. In populations of snowshoe hares in Canada, there are population peaks and troughs every 9 to 10 years (fig. 40.2C). The 10-year oscillation (cycle) is also characteristic of the Canadian lynx, which preys

Figure 40.3 Lynx and snowshoe hare. The 10-year cycle of the lynx *(top),* the predator, lags just behind that of the hare *(bottom),* the prey (see fig. 40.2). (Courtesy of the Michigan Department of Natural Resources.)

largely on the snowshoe hare (fig. 40.3). The 10-year cycle of the lynx lags just behind the cycle of the hare. The brown lemming of the tundra of North America exhibits a shorter, three- to four-year cycle of sharp increases and crashes. The lemmings are vulnerable to predation by the arctic fox and the snowy owl. When the numbers of lemmings become drastically reduced, these two predators, which have few alternative prey species on which to feed, also experience sharp declines in numbers. Many snowy owls avert starvation by migrating far to the south in search of food, some moving as far south as North Carolina.

The conventional, and perhaps simplest, view of population oscillations is that a set of environmental factors, which act essentially as negative controls, regulates populations. The main external, or extrinsic, forces that keep the density of populations within certain limits are starvation, predators, parasites, and disease. Food supply has been traditionally considered a primary factor in regulating population size. Food shortages may cause a reduction of life expectancy and a decline in reproductive capacity through malnutrition or starvation. Emigration is also associated with acute food shortages. Mortality and emigration decrease the size of a local population to a low level. At such a low level, the food supply may once more become adequate and the population begins to increase again.

The conventional notion that a population is regulated chiefly by food shortage, predators, and disease is now thought to be an oversimplification. For example, in recent studies of the brown lemming in northern Canada, there were no evidences of extensive depletion of the vegetation, nor of any specific disease epidemic, nor of any evident starvation during the entire four-year cycle of the lemming. A wealth of data has accumulated that reveals that factors *within* the population are instrumental in regulating the density. These internal, or intrinsic, factors have been termed *self-regulating* factors. They take the form of behavioral, physiological, and social responses among the constituent members of the population.

SELF-REGULATING FACTORS

Each population apparently has an optimal density. The density of a population may be defined as the total number of individuals inhabiting a given area at a particular time. Predators and parasites are more likely to cause higher mortality in a dense population than in a sparse population. But aside from these external agents, the density of a population also affects the manner in which the constituent individuals interact with each other.

A low density may be almost as detrimental to a population as a high density. A sparse population diminishes the opportunity for the sexes to meet and mate. The average fecundity of the population decreases when many females remain unfertilized. The American ecologist Thomas Park found that female beetles produced eggs at a reduced rate in a population of low density, primarily because of infrequent contacts between the males and females. There was also some indication of a reduction in life expectancy associated with a sparse population. W. C. Allee has estimated that a herd of 25 elephants is the smallest number that can persist and maintain a surviving population in South Africa. Reindeer inhabiting the tundra areas of northern Eurasia must maintain herds of 300 to 400 individuals if the population is to preserve its stability. Smaller herds are particularly vulnerable to attack by large predators. In Louisiana, muskrat populations do not thrive when the density falls below a threshold of about 1 pair per 15 acres of marshland. The period of estrus in female muskrats is very limited, and in thinly distributed populations, the males too often fail to find the females.

High population densities have adverse effects on the longevity and fecundity of the individuals. When the density of adult flour beetles in a culture increases to a relatively high level, the chances of survival for the eggs and young are markedly decreased. The adult females become cannibalistic and prey on their own eggs. Figure 40.4 shows the relation between the density of a population and fecundity in insects. Egg deposition is appreciably reduced as the population increases beyond an optimum point. Apparently, the increased frequencies of contacts between individuals in a population tend to disturb the egg-laying capacity of the female. With crowding, the frequency of copulation declines and fewer eggs are deposited.

Experimental studies on density-induced stress have been extended to mammalian species. In the 1960s, John B. Calhoun of the National Institute of Mental Health in Bethesda, Maryland investigated the effects of crowding on the social behavior of populations of rats and mice (fig. 40.5). In one of his studies, Calhoun confined a small population of Nor-

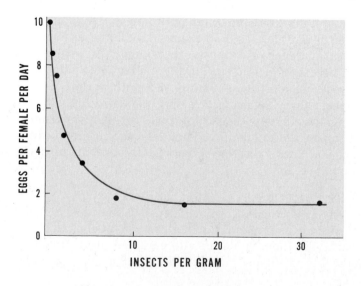

Figure 40.4 Relationship between the density of a population of adults of the grain borer *(Rhizopertha dominica)* and the fecundity of the females. At relatively high densities, fewer eggs are laid. (Based on data by A. C. Crombie.)

Figure 40.5 John B. Calhoun, behaviorist at the National Institute of Mental Health, stands amid the mousery he designed for the study of the effects of overcrowding. The 10-foot-square enclosure provided for all the physical needs of the mice, but allowed for no escape when the mouse population began to exceed tolerable limits. From an initial 8 colonizers (4 male and 4 female mice), the population soared to 2,200 individuals. As the density of the population increased, many abnormal behaviors and disturbances of reproduction appeared. The population eventually collapsed when nest-building behavior became completely disrupted and females failed to carry fetuses to term. (Courtesy of J. B. Calhoun.)

way rats in a one-quarter-acre enclosure. Many of the factors that ordinarily curtail population growth were carefully avoided. No predation existed and diseases were excluded or minimized. Food, water, and shelter were provided in excess of what was required to sustain a population of 5,000 individuals. The rate of growth of the population was initially high, resulting in approximately 2,000 individuals. However, stress from enforced social interactions became accentuated as the density of the population increased. The behavioral pathologies became so strong as to reduce the size of the population to a mere 150 adults by the end of 27 months.

The social structure in the community of rats became increasingly disrupted with rising population densities. Basic biological needs such as feeding, nest building, and care of the young became aberrant. Infant mortality became extremely high through nest desertion and cannibalism. Many females were unable to carry pregnancy to term; there were stillbirths and failures of lactation. Males displayed erratic sexual behavior patterns—they mounted other rats regardless of their age, sex, or receptivity. In essence, notwithstanding the abundance of food and the absence of predation and disease, the community of rats became disrupted with increasing density because of pathological social interactions. Needless to say, the theory underlying the simple, smooth S-shaped population curve did not effectively take account of the behavioral consequences of rising population density.

Whether these observations on caged rats have more than marginal relevance to human behavior in dense aggregations cannot yet be answered with precision or confidence. There is a widespread feeling that high population density in humans increases the probability of aggressive behavior, conflict, and violence. This generalized negative feeling may not be defensible. It is important to recognize that Calhoun had created a highly artificial, if not bizarre, environment. No animal in nature would be confined in a repressive enclosure. If stress were to occur in a natural population, it would be relieved most likely by the adaptation of dispersal.

SOCIAL STRESS

The Canadian ecologist Dennis Chitty was one of the first to advocate that fluctuations in populations are related to social interactions within the population. He studied the cyclic oscillations in populations of voles (*Microtus agrestis*) in a certain district in Wales. According to Chitty, the decline, or crash, of the vole population could not have been caused by weather, moisture, shortage of food, migration, predators, or disease. Rather, the decline was associated with strife during the breeding season. Chitty has argued that a high population density leads to "physiological derangement" among the adults, resulting in high fetal mortality, decreased litter size, and decreased infant survival.

John Christian of the State University of New York (Binghamton) has suggested that social stresses act on the individual through a physiological feedback involving the pituitary and adrenal glands. Decreased production of the pituitary gonadotrophic hormones is responsible for the decline in fecundity. Another important consequence of density-induced stress is the enlargement of the adrenal glands and concomitant overproduction of cortical steroid hormones. Oversecretion of cortisone leads to severe physiological stress and eventually death. Christian believes that social stress and its accompanying hormonal imbalance is the single factor common to all populations; that is, stress is the fundamental or basic factor underlying population fluctuations.

Other ecologists, notably Frank Pitelka of the University of California and Norman Negus of the University of Utah, caution us that we cannot overlook nutritional and climatic factors, which are basic to all animal populations. Pitelka associates the cyclic fluctuations in lemming populations with changes in the nutrient levels or quality of plant foods. An increase in lemming population size leads to overgrazing and deterioration of the soil, particularly loss of essential nutrients. The subsequent food shortage results in higher death rates among the lemmings. The decomposition of lemmings restores essential nutrients to the soil, which leads in turn to an improved quality of plant growth. The more nutritive plants set the stage for another population burst among the lemmings.

The studies by Norman Negus on populations of the rice rat on Cape Breton Island (off the shore of Louisiana) failed to show the changes in the adrenal glands and the gonadal regression that Christian postulated. The reproductive behavior of the rice rat remained normal even at high population densities, which suggests that pathological behavior may develop only under abnormally dense conditions not usually met in nature. In other words, abnormal physiological responses associated with social stress do not arise in most natural populations, or if they do, they are of secondary importance in the regulation of natural populations.

STRESS AND NATURAL SELECTION

The concept of social stress as a population-regulating mechanism has attracted considerable attention and debate. The student of evolution finds it difficult to reconcile this concept with the well-established mode of action of natural selection. As we have repeatedly emphasized, selection operates to increase or maximize the reproductive fitness of individuals. Inasmuch as curtailment of reproductive activity even under enforced social interactions is certainly not adaptively advantageous, selection would tend to eliminate from the population those individuals who exercise reproductive restraint or are reproductively impaired. Thus, through the action of selection, the population would become adjusted over time to include primarily sexually active individuals rather than nonreproducing individuals. Stated another way, if environmental circumstances were such as to allow an extremely dense population to build up, natural selection would promote those individuals whose behavioral and physiological response to high population density did *not* entail any abridgment of reproduction.

As a result of the foregoing arguments, investigators now acknowledge that insufficient attention has been paid to the genetic aspects, or genetic quality, of a population. Charles Krebs, at the University of British Columbia, has proposed that *differential dispersal* is the critical factor for population regulation. The individuals who migrate are genetically superior to the sedentary individuals; that is, they have the innate capacity to exploit successfully new environments and have the highest reproductive potential. Hence, the more reproductively inferior members remain as residents in the parent population. Not only are the residential individuals less prolific, but they are apparently more susceptible to environmental factors that cause mortality. When environmental conditions become rigorous, the mortality rate of the reproductively inferior sedentary individuals increases and the parent population declines, often abruptly.

In essence, naturalists still argue over whether population fluctuations can be ascribed solely to intrinsic, self-regulating mechanisms or are determined primarily by such external environmental variables as food supply. It would be safe to say that both extrinsic variables and intrinsic mechanisms are involved in the complex fluctuations observed in populations.

It would be ideal if a population could limit its growth long before starvation would otherwise occur or before the individuals would otherwise suffer stress or physiological derangement. An approach to this ideal is the behavioral system of *territoriality*, whereby the individual, generally the male, gains possession of a certain area, or territory, and excludes all other males of his species, and often all other females but his mate. Territoriality is well known in birds, but the practice is not exclusive to this group. Many mammals, from bears to deer mice, also exhibit territorial behavior, as do fishes, amphibians, and lizards (see chapter 48).

HUMAN POPULATION GROWTH

The logistic, or S-shaped, curve may be viewed as the outcome of a search for a simple, natural law of population growth. However, this simple, smooth curve does not take into account the social behavior of individuals in a population, particularly in dense populations. It is of interest that early investigators had hoped that human populations would ultimately reveal a logistic pattern. Raymond Pearl, for example, in the early 1920s, forecast that the human population would gradually and asymptotically approach an upper limit. He predicted that the world population would stabilize at 2.6 billion by the year 2100. This population level was exceeded more than 15 years ago; Pearl's figure is 1.4 billion below the 4 billion recorded in 1970. Evidently, population forecasts by means of the logistic model are attended with considerable hazard.

The modern focus of population research has shifted away from the logistic theory. Scientists and demographers are still eagerly seeking guidelines for population growth in humans to provide a concrete basis for population planning. It now appears that human population growth is not subject to an immutable natural law; it is the resultant of many variables, including a complex interplay of ecology and social behavior. Population growth and movements in humans are related to social and cultural changes and to a host of economic factors. The weight of evidence suggests that a decline in birth rate is almost wholly due to *human volition;* that is, it is the result of conscious and deliberate efforts by married couples to limit the size of their families.

AGE STRUCTURE IN POPULATIONS

One of the most fundamental features of any population is that fertility and mortality vary greatly with age. Accordingly, it can be expected that the growth of a population will be influenced by its age composition, or the proportion of individuals in different age groups. A. S. Bodenheimer has classified populations into three main categories according to age distribution. As seen in figure 40.6A, a rapidly expanding population contains a large proportion of individuals in the younger age groups. Fertility is high and each successive generation is more numerous than the preceding generation. In a declining population, characterized by a large proportion of old individuals, the pyramid becomes urn-shaped (fig. 40.6C). A stationary bell-shaped population (fig. 40.6B) has a rather even distribution of age classes.

Demographers draw population pyramids to reveal the age and sex structure of human populations in different areas of the world. It is customary to segregate the sexes, and to group the ages by five-year or ten-year periods. The percentage in the different age classes is shown by the relative lengths of successive horizontal bars. Population pyramids differ appreciably from one country to another. Figure 40.7 compares the declining population of Sweden with the rapidly growing wide-based population of Algeria. The pyramid of Algeria is representative of most of the countries of Africa, Latin America, and South Asia. Forty-four percent of the population of Algeria is below 15 years of age; in marked contrast, only 24 percent in Sweden is represented by a similar

Figure 40.6 Age structure of populations: *(A)* an expanding population, with a very large proportion of young individuals; *(B)* a *stable* population, with relatively equal prereproductive and reproductive age groups; and *(C)* a *diminishing* population, with a low percentage of young individuals. (From E. J. Kormondy, *Concepts of ecology,* 1969, Prentice-Hall, Inc.)

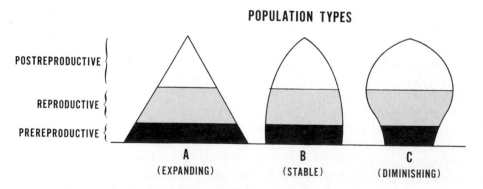

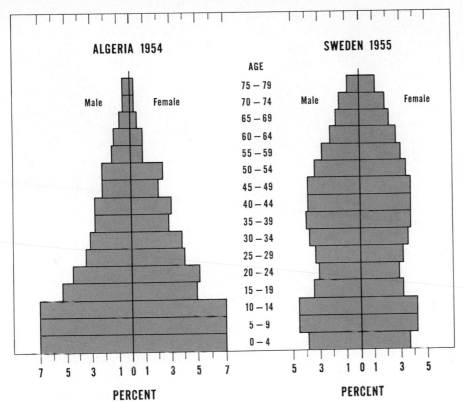

ALGERIA 1954

SWEDEN 1955

Male   Female

AGE

75 — 79
70 — 74
65 — 69
60 — 64
55 — 59
50 — 54
45 — 49
40 — 44
35 — 39
30 — 34
25 — 29
20 — 24
15 — 19
10 — 14
5 — 9
0 — 4

Male   Female

PERCENT

PERCENT

Figure 40.7 Age composition of populations of Algeria (1954) and Sweden (1955). The Algerian population is expanding greatly, with a large proportion of young dependents (under 15 years of age). In contrast, the ratio of young dependents to the productive, or working, age group (15–64) is much lower in economically advanced Sweden. (From H. F. Dorn, *Science* 135:288, 1962. Copyright 1962 by the American Association for the Advancement of Science.)

young age group. In Sweden, the comparatively low birth rate is accompanied by a low death rate. Rapid declines in infant mortality, together with the traditionally high birth rate, account for the extremely wide-based pyramid of Algeria. It bears emphasizing that the reductions in mortality rates have been concentrated heavily at the young ages. This high proportion of young persons constitutes a large fertility potential for future years. Indeed, in rapidly expanding populations, it is primarily the sharply declining death rate instead of an increasing birth rate that brings about a population explosion.

AGE COMPOSITION

The age composition of a population is not static, but continually changing. The nature and extent of change are illustrated vividly by comparing the age pyramids for the United States for the years 1900, 1940, and 1958 (fig. 40.8). As indicated in figure 40.8A, the population profile for the white population of the United States in 1900 was virtually a perfect pyramid. With advancing five-year age groups, there were successively smaller proportions of people. The base of the pyramid is broad, reflecting high birth rates, and the top of the pyramid tapers off sharply and consistently.

The 1940 pyramid, depicted in figure 40.8B, shows marked erosion of the base, owing to the sharp decline in fertility that had been under way during the twenties and early thirties. In 1940, because of almost two decades of sharp declines in birth rates, there were fewer persons in the 10–14 age group than in the 15–19 age group, fewer 5–9 than 10–14, and fewer under 5 than 5–9. The base might have eroded even more if infant mortality had remained at a relatively high level; however, infant mortality in 1940 had been reduced to about half its 1900 level. In addi-

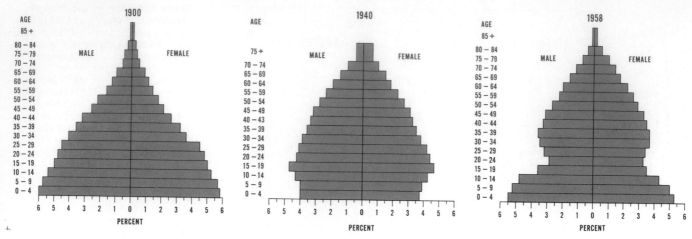

Figure 40.8 Changing age pyramids through the years (1900, 1940, and 1958) for the population of the United States. The eroded base of the 1940 pyramid reflects the decline in fertility during the Depression; the expanded base of the 1958 pyramid reflects the restorative effect of the post–World War II baby boom. (Based on data from the U.S. Bureau of the Census.)

tion, between 1900 and 1940, some 15 years had been added to the average life expectancy of a person.

The 1958 age profile (fig. 40.8C) reflects the restorative effect of the post–World War II baby boom on the base of the pyramid. Demographers did not foresee this baby boom. Birth rates were relatively high for at least a decade following the end of the war in 1945. The postwar increases in fertility in the United States increased the proportions of people in the young age groups and lowered the median age of the population. In addition, the proportion of people 65 years of age and over has continued to increase. Reflecting the differing rates of growth among age groups, the United States population has increased most at the two extremes—the young and the old. Thus, during 1950–58, the estimated increase was 15 percent for the total population. It was 29 percent for those under 20, 1 percent for those 20–44, 15 percent for those 45–64, and 23 percent for 65 and over.

BIRTH AND FERTILITY RATES

Figure 40.9 shows the fluctuations in birth rates in the United States. The birth rate is expressed as births per 1,000 individuals of a population. Demographers aptly refer to the calculation of the birth rate as "crude," since it is based on total population and not on proportion of women in the childbearing years. The crude birth rate was higher in 1947 than in any recent year, but a new record for the largest annual number of births was scored in 1957 (a peak of 4.3 million births). The comparatively low birth rate in 1957 was offset by the high *fertility rate* in 1957. The fertility rate is the annual number of live births per 1,000 women of childbearing age (between 15 and 44 years of age). In 1947, the year with the very high birth rate, the fertility rate was only 113 births per 1,000 women (fig. 40.10). In 1957, the fertility rate was about 120 per 1,000. Thus, although fewer babies were born in proportion to the total population in 1957, more babies were born in relation to the population of women in the childbearing years.

As a consequence of differing fertility rates, the number of live births in any two years may be quite different even if the birth rates are the same. For example, in 1932 and 1965, the birth rate was about the same, 19.5 per 1,000 and 19.4 per 1,000, respectively. Yet, in 1932, the

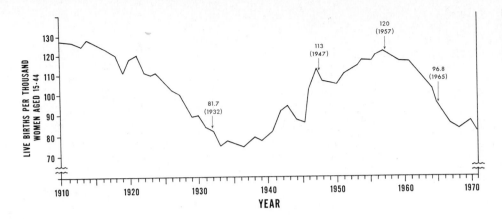

Figure 40.9 Trend in crude birth rates in the United States, 1910–1972. (After *Population Profile*, Population Reference Bureau, March, 1967).

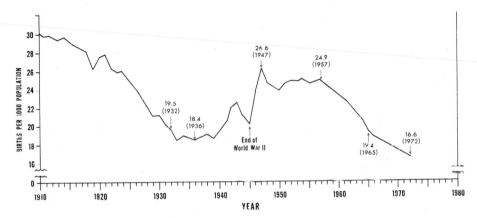

Figure 40.10 Fertility rate: The number of births per year per 1,000 women 15 to 44 years of age. The fertility rate has been declining in the United States since 1957 (except for a short-term increase in 1970). Since 1970, the fertility rate has dropped below 80, apparently in response to various socioeconomic pressures. (After *Population Profile*, Population Reference Bureau, March, 1967.)

number of births was a mere 2.4 million compared with 3.8 million in 1965. In 1932, the fertile female group (between 15 and 44 years of age) constituted 23.9 percent of the population and their fertility rate was 81.7. In contrast, in 1965, women of comparable age composed only 20 percent of the population, but their fertility rate was 96.8. Accordingly, the fertility rate is a better indicator of birth trends than the crude birth rate. It concentrates on the relevant factors and is not distorted by extraneous trends in the population at large.

As an additional refinement, we can confine our attention to the number of women in the prime reproductive years (20–29 years of age) —the so-called highly fertile females. There were 11 million of these highly fertile females in the United States in 1960. In 1970, this group increased to 15.5 million. By 1980, the projection for women 20–29 years of age is 20 million. The bulge of highly fertile females in the 1980s provides a great potential for population growth. Even if the women of the 1980s average 2 children, the population of the United States would continue to grow for many years. As figure 40.11 shows, the population in the United States would reach 300 million by the year 2025. This projection assumes the continuation of immigration at its present level (an annual immigration of 400,000 persons). To arrive at a state of "no growth" (or "zero population growth"), women would have to limit fertility to an all-time low of 1.7 children. In this event, the population would reach 252 million by the year 2020 and level off to 250 million shortly thereafter. If the average American woman has 2.7 children, the popula-

Figure 40.11 Projections of the population of the United States into the next century, assuming 1.7 children, 2.1 children, and 2.7 children per woman. (Based on estimates of the U.S. Bureau of the Census.)

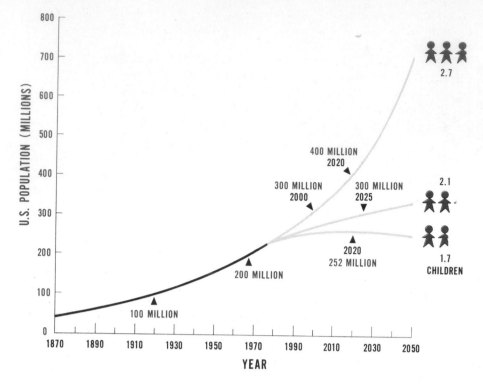

tion would climb to 300 million by the year 2000 and keep rising with each subsequent year.

It should be clear that the United States will not attain "no growth" before the end of the century. A "zero population growth" can be attained by the middle of the 21st century if women limit themselves to 1.7 children. Evidently, the fertility rate holds the key to future population trends. What the fertility behavior of young couples will be in future years cannot be predicted. In essence, the amount and rate of population growth depend in large measure on the attitudes and intentions of today's and tomorrow's young couples.

SUMMARY

Populations of organisms grown experimentally under ideal conditions exhibit an S-shaped course of growth—first a slow increase in numbers, followed by a rapid acceleration in exponential form, and then a deceleration to a constant (asymptotic) level. In natural populations, the asymptote of the sigmoid curve is neither smooth nor orderly. Natural populations may fluctuate mildly (saw-toothed curve), drastically (irruptive, or J-shaped, curve), and even cyclically (oscillatory, or cyclic, curve). The conventional, simplest view of population swings is that an array of environmental factors, such as climate, food availability, disease, and predators, regulates population growth. There may also be internal self-regulating factors. Their existence has been observed in experimental populations of high density, in which effects of stress on the longevity and fecundity of the species are markedly adverse. The social stresses associated with overcrowding in mammalian populations, at least in laboratory situations, are held to be mediated by hormonal disturbances. Population cycles may also be the consequence of the changing genetic composition of the population. The migration of reproductively superior animals from the parent population during periods of high density could alter significantly the character of the resident population.

Man has overexploited the available resources, and is subject to the ultimate check of limited resources. Restraints in human population growth are to be found also in sociological and behavioral factors. Immediate population limitation depends largely on man's willingness to curb his reproductive potential.

Ethical Probe 23
Lifeboat Ethics

Dr. Garrett Hardin, Professor of Human Ecology at the University of California in Santa Barbara, has prepared numerous provocative manuscripts on issues concerned with the human population explosion. Perhaps the most controversial article is "Living on a Lifeboat," which appeared in *BioScience* (vol. 24, no. 10, October 1974). Garrett Hardin presents the metaphor that the United States and other economically advanced nations constitute a lifeboat that contains comparatively affluent individuals. The peoples of the impoverished countries of the world are struggling in the water outside, hoping to be admitted to the prosperous lifeboat. Hardin concludes that, to preserve the safety (prosperity) of the lifeboat that is already limited in capacity, the affluent passengers must prevent others from boarding. In essence, the economically advanced countries should take an isolationist attitude and repel boarders, primarily by curtailing immigration and restricting the export of foods.

The relative differences in the living standards of the rich nations and the poor nations are likely to become greater. The struggling peoples of the poorer countries are doubling in numbers every 35 years, on the average, whereas members of affluent societies are doubling every 87 years. What should the occupants of the fortunate lifeboat do? Can the passengers afford to provide a helpful hand? Should the passengers be guided by humanitarian principles and take all the needy into the boat—only to suffer the likely possibility that the boat will sink? Should the passengers admit only a few boarders and exclude the majority? How do you discriminate, and how do you answer to those who are excluded? Should the passengers admit no outsiders at all and thus preserve the safety of the boat—that is, preserve their relative high standard of living? Is the lifeboat truly self-sufficient or is it highly dependent on, if not exploitive of, the resources of other countries to sustain its own high living standards?

41 Prevalence of People

A singular important aspect of human population change has been the element of death, or mortality. Man has uniquely used his intellectual capability to reduce dramatically his mortality rate. Reasons for the extraordinary and sustained drop in mortality are numerous—conquest of infectious diseases, widespread use of vaccines and antibiotics, advances in public health measures, better personal hygiene, and improved nutrition. Our success in controlling, or lowering, the death rate throughout the world has been the most significant single factor contributing to the unprecedented increase in world population.

Our ability to increase life expectancy has created a precarious imbalance between birth rates and death rates. In 1970, about 120 million children were born, whereas only 50 million persons died. The net gain in world population was therefore 70 million people in one year alone. About 85 percent of this gain occurred in the poorly developed nations of Asia, Africa, and Latin America. The world population is now growing by 2 percent a year, which means that *every day* there are 180,000 more persons on the earth. If this growth rate is maintained, the world population will double in 35 years. Logic alone dictates that the present rate of world population growth cannot continue indefinitely.

The prophetic forecast is wholesale famine and malnutrition, depleted resources, and economic and social disaster if the world's population growth is not curtailed. Population growth can be controlled by lowering the birth rate or raising the death rate, or both. Since it is unlikely that we shall choose to reverse the downward trend in mortality, stabilization of the world's population level must come about through a decline in fertility. Even if man were wondrously to engineer his way around the scarcities of food supply and limited natural resources, the control of the birth rate remains a necessity if only to alleviate, or halt, the deterioration in the overall level and quality of human life.

POPULATION CHANGES THROUGH TIME

World population size was relatively stable over a long period of history. A precipitous increase in population size has occurred only during the last few centuries. As figure 41.1 shows, the world population at the birth of the Christian era has been estimated at 250 million people. About 11 generations ago, in 1650, the world population was only 0.5 billion. The total population reached the 1 billion mark in 1850. Within 80 years, from 1850 to 1930, the population had doubled to 2 billion. By 1970, the population had reached 3.6 billion—an increase of more than 1.5 billion in the short duration of 40 years. If present fertility and mortality trends persist, 7 billion persons will be contending for a place on earth by the year 2000.

So rapid has been the acceleration in growth that half the population now living on the earth was born since 1945. As previously discussed (chapter 40), an increasing number of young people are moving into the reproductive ages. The number of women in the high-fertility age group (20–29 years old) will increase by approximately a half in the next 20 years. This enlarging fertility potential adds dramatically to the gravity of the population crisis.

In 1963, the United Nations issued population projections for the world to the end of the century. These estimates are published as high, low, and medium variant projections. The low estimate gives a world population in the year 2000 of 5.4 billion; the medium projection is 6.1 billion (fig. 41.2). On the basis of the high projection, presented in table 41.1, the population as a whole will increase to 7 billion by the year 2000.

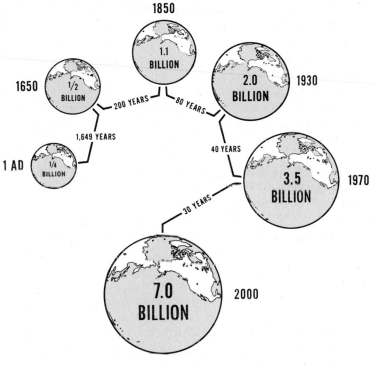

Figure 41.1 A rapidly swelling population threatens the existence of mankind. Population increase is a luxury that man can no longer afford.

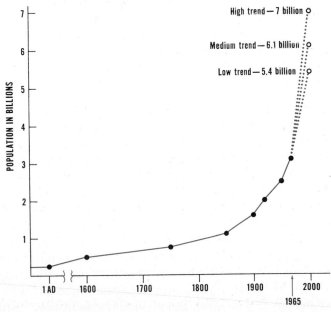

Figure 41.2 Population projections of the United Nations. Forecasts for the growth of world population to the end of the century are estimated as low, medium, and high. (From E. J. Kormondy, *Concepts of ecology,* 1969, Prentice-Hall, Inc.)

Table 41.1

World Population by Major Areas, 1960 to 2000, According to the High Variant Projection of the United Nations (in Millions)

Area	1960	1970	1980	1990	2000
World total	2,998	3,659	4,551	5,690	6,994
More developed areas	976	1,102	1,245	1,402	1,574
Europe	425	458	492	526	563
Soviet Union	214	254	296	346	403
Northern America	199	233	275	323	376
Oceania	16	19	23	29	35
Less developed areas	2,022	2,557	3,306	4,288	5,420
East Asia	794	956	1,171	1,405	1,623
South Asia	865	1,108	1,448	1,910	2,443
Africa	273	348	463	629	864
Latin America	212	283	383	522	686
Northern areas	1,632	1,901	2,234	2,600	2,966
Southern areas	1,366	1,758	2,317	3,090	4,028

Today, approximately two-thirds of the world's people inhabit Asia, Africa, and Latin America—the less developed or emerging areas of the world. Between now and the century's end, the less developed nations will experience higher growth rates than the economically advanced nations (table 41.1). By the year 2000, the less developed areas may well number some 5.4 billion persons; the economically advanced nations, some 1.6 billion. Thus, while the modernized nations will increase by some 600 million during the next 30 years, the less developed nations could increase by about 3 billion, or 5 times as much. By 2000, it is possible that the population in the currently less developed areas will have increased to 77 percent of the world's total, and that the population in the developed areas will have dwindled to 23 percent.

POPULATION EXPLOSION

The population explosion is, in essence, the outcome of the fact that man has effected great reductions in the death rate well in advance of any corresponding declines in the birth rate. Greatly accelerated growth—the excess of births over deaths in any given period—has been witnessed twice on a grand scale: the first, in European populations during the 18th and 19th centuries, and the second, in the less developed areas of the world since World War II.

It is not surprising that the massive reductions in infant mortality coincided with the industrial revolution in the Western world. The conquest of infectious diseases and the improvement in public health measures during the industrial revolution reduced death rates precipitously without having an immediate effect on the birth rates. As a result of dramatic decreases in death rates, the 100 million Europeans of 1650 had, three centuries later, about 940 million descendants.

The areas that are today classed as "developed" or "economically advanced"—primarily western Europe and northern America—have witnessed reductions in mortality since 1800. Initially, birth rates remained at relatively high levels, but then, as the standards of living increased, birth rates declined. Although the causes of declining birth rates have not been fully elucidated, it is clear that the voluntary regulation of family size is associated with improved standards of living. A rise in the social, economic, and educational level of the people tends to foster a low birth rate. In populations of Europe, North America, and more recently Japan, birth rates have declined from highs of 30 to 40 births per 1,000 to below 20 per 1,000. Since death rates in these populations have now dropped to the level of 10 per 1,000, annual growth rates are 1 percent or less. Specifically, as of 1968, annual growth rates averaged 0.8 percent in Europe and in the United States, 1.0 percent in the Soviet Union and in Canada, and somewhat higher in Japan, Australia, and New Zealand.

The economically advanced nations can ill afford to become complacent concerning their now relatively slow growth rate. The sociologist Lincoln Day of Yale University reminds us that whereas the main portent of population growth in the less developed countries is to *life itself*, the main threat in the more affluent countries is, instead, to the very *quality of life*. Should the population in the United States, for example, continue to grow about 0.8 percent per year, the population will increase by nearly 100 million people by the close of this century. The great majority will be concentrated, or crowded, in urban areas with all the attendant environmental and resource problems.

Since World War II, a second population explosion has occurred in Asia, Africa, and Latin America. Western medicine has administered its sophisticated techniques in these developing areas. With the infusion of modern drugs, sanitation techniques, and extensive medical aid, death control became rapid and widespread in the less developed nations. In Latin America, for example, the death rate decreased between 1945 and 1965 from over 30 per 1,000 people per year to 17 per 1,000. The emerging Asian, African, and Latin American countries have been experiencing what Europe experienced a century or two ago—a period of falling death rates coupled with relatively high birth rates, resulting inevitably in rapid growth. However, the time scale of this change is different in the less developed areas from the timing in industrial Europe. Death rates have been halved in a matter of years, not centuries. This spectacular change in death rates is seen in figure 41.3. Hence, the population growth in the emerging nations has been truly explosive. Twentieth-century death rates have been imposed on populations that are still burdened by medieval birth rates. Most of the developing nations have birth rates above 40 per 1,000 annually. Annual growth rates in the developing nations are above 2 percent—many above 3 percent. Many countries in Latin America are growing at a rate that will double the population in 20–25 years —which represents less than a single generation. The growth rate of the

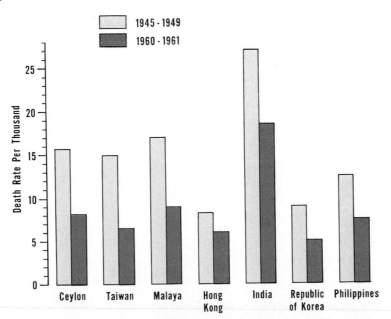

Figure 41.3 Dramatic changes in death rates in selected Asian nations during the course of but a few years. (After *Population Bulletin*, vol. 20, no. 2.)

world population as a whole is thus accelerating despite the historical fertility decline in the economically advanced nations.

Control over birth rates must ultimately be achieved in the less developed nations. There is inevitably a time lag between the decline in the death rate and the fall in the birth rate. At the moment, the critical question is whether the less developed nations can successfully make the demographic transition to a low birth rate–low death rate society without widespread famine and unmerciful disaster.

DEMOGRAPHIC TRANSITION

The change from wastefully high birth and high death rates to a more efficient and humane reproductive pattern of low birth and low death rates has been termed the *demographic transition*. A model of this transition is shown in figure 41.4. The agrarian, low-income economy is characterized by high birth and high death rates of approximately the same magnitude (stage I). High fertility is counterbalanced by severe mortality associated with malnutrition and endemic disease. Little, if any, population increase occurs. In the next stage (II), the death rate declines under the impact of improving medical knowledge and greater industrialization. Since the birth rate continues high in stage II, the success of death control is manifested in a rapid population increase, or a population explosion. The next stage (III) is characterized by a strong downward trend in natality, while the death rate continues to fall. At this time, the birth rate becomes responsive to voluntary decisions, or individual choice. An increasing voluntary or deliberate parctice of birth control appears to be associated with improving standards of living. In an agrarian society, numerous children are viewed as assets in that they serve as extra hands on a farm. In a highly industrialized society, parents are inclined to curb the family size so as to provide better educational and economic opportunities for their children. In the final stage (IV), the demographic transition is completed when birth and death rates reach a near-equilibrium condition (fig. 41.4). Levels of living are high, life expectancy is long, and birth rates are very sensitive to economic forces. The Western world achieved this demographic transition around the turn of the 20th century.

According to the theory of demographic transition, one would expect the emerging nations to follow the experience of the Western world in reduction of the birth rate. This must occur if there is to be a humane solution to the problems of overpopulation. The birth rates are expected

Figure 41.4 The demographic transition from a society with high birth and high death rates to a more efficient and humane reproductive pattern of low birth and low death rates.

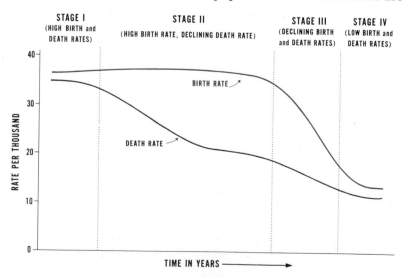

to drop when the emerging countries achieve major socioeconomic advances. However, we are dealing with populations in less developed nations that are increasing by the billions, not the millions as in the industrial revolution in Europe. The emerging nations will be unable to industrialize until they reduce their current phenomenal rate of population growth. But, the demographic concept informs us that the population growth will not slow down without industrialization. It would thus appear that the pattern of the past demographic transition must somehow be violated. The reduction in the birth rate must accompany the socioeconomic changes, and not lag behind.

It is quite clear that conditions that existed in Western societies during the past demographic transition are no longer present. The pressure of the growing population in Europe during the demographic transition was immediately relieved by the emigration of large numbers of Europeans to America and to other parts of the world that were then sparsely populated. The safety valve provided by emigration is no longer available. The human population has essentially become imprisoned. Man has found himself increasingly circumscribed on the earth. There are few, if any, uncolonized frontier areas.

FOOD AND MALNUTRITION

A problem of paramount importance is the global shortage of high-protein foods necessary for proper nutrition (fig. 41.5). In the underdeveloped nations of the world, grains of poor protein quality furnish the bulk of the daily diet. It is estimated that malnutrition, particularly protein insufficiency, afflicts 60 percent of the world's children, half of whom are likely to die before reaching adulthood. In protein-poor India alone, severe nutritional deficiencies, worsened by the effects of infectious diseases, result in the death of 1 of 5 children under six years of age.

The most widespread and serious nutritional disease is *kwashiorkor*. The term is a combination of two West African words meaning "first" and "second." Among Africans, it is said to be a sickness that attacks the first child when he is displaced at his mother's breast by the second infant. Kwashiorkor is a morbid condition of acute protein starvation that appears shortly after weaning, when the child is fed predominantly cereal grains—rice, wheat, and corn—that are the staple fare in less developed countries. The disease is characterized by apathy, impaired growth, skin ulcers, swollen hands and feet, and a grossly enlarged liver (fig. 41.6). If the condition is left unattended, the child usually dies.

If the child's diet is deficient in both calories and protein, he falls victim to *marasmus*, another disorder. Such victims of oppressive calorie-protein starvation usually succumb to stunted growth and extreme wasting of the muscles. In both kwashiorkor and marasmus, brain growth and development are impaired, often irreversibly.

All of the essential amino acids are typically furnished by animal products—meat, fish, poultry, eggs, and dairy derivatives. In impoverished countries, meats and other animal products are expensive and in short supply. Several of the less-developed nations have now embarked on the production of low-cost, protein-rich food mixtures for infants. Most of the new protein supplements are extracted from soybean, cottonseed, peanut, sesame, sunflower, and other oil-rich and protein-laden seeds. Only a very small fraction of the world's production of oil-rich seeds has been used in the past for human consumption.

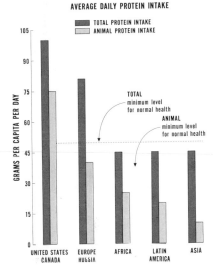

Figure 41.5 Human diets are deficient in animal protein (and total protein) in the less developed countries of the world. Only in North America, Western Europe, Russia, and certain isolated countries are proteins consumed in sufficient quantities for proper body maintenance and growth. (Based on data from the United States Department of Agriculture, Foreign Agricultural Service.)

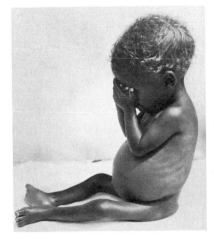

Figure 41.6 Kwashiorkor, a morbid condition resulting from acute protein starvation. A distended abdomen and thin legs are common symptoms. (Courtesy of UNICEF.)

Until recently, vast amounts of oilseeds were used almost exclusively as fertilizer.

The solution to the problem of malnutrition and starvation apparently is not to be found in an increase or surge in agricultural production. In the early 1960s, the so-called *green revolution* was ushered in with a fanfare of promises that new miracle varieties of wheat and rice would vastly increase yields of Asian crop plants. The dramatic green revolution was confidently expected to make India self-sufficient in food production by 1970–71. The high-yield seeds have not, however, brought any significant respite from hunger and malnutrition in Asia. Grain production did increase, at least for a few years, but so did the population. In India, grain production increased from 68 million metric tons in 1960–61 to a high of 92 million metric tons in 1970–71. At the same time, however, India's population had grown from 440 million to 590 million. Thus, about 25 percent more people now live on 25 percent more food at the same bare subsistence level. Moreover, grain production with the new seeds is now showing signs of dwindling. The high-yield varieties require optimum or near-perfect conditions for growth as well as an enormous input of fertilizers and modern irrigation. Less than one-third of India's wheatlands can be planted with the new seeds. In 1972–73, adverse weather conditions created a critical shortage of wheat. Once again, population threatens to overtake the food supply. In 1972–73, India was obliged to import 2 million tons of grain. It has been said that India is losing the battle between production and reproduction.

The urgent need, then, is a regulation of the birth rate. The economically advanced countries are offsetting the consequences of death control by the planned control of birth. The Western world may be regarded as a contraceptive-using society. It may be that the pattern of the past demographic transition can only be broken, or shortened, by a *contraceptive revolution* rather than an industrial revolution. Only through the ready availability of contraceptive measures and the widespread acceptance of family planning can the growth of the more populous regions of the world be brought under control. To persuade hundreds of millions of men and women to abandon their tradition-hallowed views of fertility is not an easy endeavor, for it represents a huge effort in educating masses of poor, hungry people. Efforts to lower the birth rate in the less developed areas are now judged as having come too late, and achieving too little.

Given the myth of the green revolution and the formidable difficulties of implementing birth control in an effective way, several biologists conclude that only inexorable tragedy awaits the less developed countries. Paul Ehrlich in his book *The Population Bomb* and William Paddock and Paul Paddock in their book *Famine—1975!* predict that massive numbers of people will succumb to calamitous and outright starvation. The population explosion will thus end, or be appreciably slowed down, by a devastating rise in the death rate. The demographer Michael Sligh has proposed that this catastrophic phenomenon be termed *demographic transposition,* wherein the relative positions of the death rates and birth rates become transposed.

THE AFFLUENT NATIONS

The complaint has been voiced that the economically advanced countries, most prominently the United States, account for only a small share of the world's population but consume the major share of the natural resources of the world. With only 6 percent of the earth's population, the United States uses about 33 percent of the world's annual production of fossil fuels, 25 percent of the newly mined minerals, and 17 percent of the timber. Each American has an average of 3,000 calories of food energy available daily, which is twice the minimum required to sustain life. In stark contrast, literally millions of children in the less developed nations are undernourished.

The affluent nations are confronted with the urgency of shifting from national to global priorities. The economically advanced nations do profess to the goal of bringing the less developed nations up to acceptable standards of living. Yet an acceptable standard of living by Western criteria entails excessive depletion of the resources and continued despoliation of the environment. Long-term planning for the world population seems to demand a redefinition of the word *acceptable*.

Peoples of affluent nations have become increasingly aware of the global poverty problem, but the affluent peoples give primarily moralistic lectures to the peoples of the poor nations. In turn, the poor peoples have become aware of how the affluent peoples live, and they resent the preachings and their severe deprivations. The rising aspirations of the poor peoples of the world cannot conceivably be met unless the affluent nations shift their priorities and commit their wealth and power to the survival of mankind.

SUMMARY

The explosive expansion of the world population is the most urgent problem now confronting the human species. The acceleration in population growth has been especially pronounced in the last few decades. The progress of medical science has radically reduced the death rate, particularly of children in the less developed nations, without any comparable reduction in the birth rate. The precipitous decline in mortality in the less developed countries is occurring simultaneously with the spectacle of malnutrition and starvation. It is unlikely that the less developed, or emerging, nations can follow the experience of the industrialized Western world in making the demographic transition from wastefully high birth and high death rates to a more efficient and humane reproductive pattern of low birth and low death rates. According to the theory of demographic transition, birth rates are expected to decline when the emerging nations achieve major socioeconomic advances. However, the emerging nations will be unable to industrialize until they reduce their current phenomenal rate of population growth.

There must be a realization throughout the world of the necessity for constructive thinking about, and implementation of, birth control. The economically advanced countries are offsetting the consequences of death control by the planned control of birth. The pattern of the past demographic transition can only be broken, or shortened, by a contraceptive revolution rather than an industrial revolution. Additionally, the affluent nations are faced with the necessity of shifting from national to global priorities. The rising aspirations of the poor peoples of the world cannot conceivably be met unless the affluent nations shift their priorities and commit their wealth and power to the survival of mankind.

Ethical Probe 24
Sacrificing Affluence

An inadequate supply of protein of high quality is a pressing problem in the developing nations of the world. The industrialized countries persist in relying on livestock for their main source of protein. The economically advanced nations continue to feed domestic animals with grains that are highly suitable for human consumption. For each 20 grams of plant (grain) protein fed to a cow, only one gram is returned to man in the form of beef. Other livestock are more efficient in the usage of grain; only 8 grams of plant protein are required to produce one gram of pig protein and only 5 grams of grain protein are needed to produce a pound of chicken protein. Nonetheless, the greater efficiency of certain livestock does not obviate the basic problem: the use of rich agricultural resources to feed domestic animals instead of humans. If the agricultural products were consumed in a more direct and efficient way, the surplus grain could be used to alleviate the protein-deficiency diseases that plague the developing countries of the world.

Traditionalists contend that adequate protein cannot be obtained from plant sources alone. It is true that most plant proteins are deficient in one or more essential amino acids. However, the amino acid requirements of man can be fulfilled by the judicious selection of varied plants. For example, although rice is deficient in lysine, beans are exceptionally high in this essential amino acid. When eaten together, rice and a legume (such as, kidney beans) provide protein of comparable quality to that of beef. In fact, one cup of legume and two cups of rice provide the equivalent of seven ounces of high-quality beef protein. In this manner, it is possible to have a diet of high-quality protein without relying solely on animal products.

If combinations of plant proteins were to replace, largely or in part, beef protein in economically advanced nations, then sufficient protein-rich plant foods could become part of the daily diet in the developing countries. As a member of a prosperous nation, are you willing to sacrifice the extravagance of having meat as the center of every meal? Can economically advanced countries morally afford the luxury of fattening cattle with protein-rich grain when malnutrition, particularly protein insufficiency, afflicts 60 percent of the world's children?

Interactions of Populations

42

A population of a particular species does not exist in isolation, but interacts with populations belonging to other species in a given locality. When two populations of different species are obliged (under experimental conditions) to use a common nutrient, the two will compete with each other for the common resource. Under competition for the identical needs, only one of the two species populations will survive; the other will be eliminated or excluded by competition. This is the principle of *competitive exclusion*. It is also known as *Gause's principle*, after the Russian biologist G. F. Gause, who first demonstrated experimentally that under controlled laboratory conditions, one of the two competing species perishes.

A fundamental principle has been enunciated based primarily on observations of bottle populations in the laboratory. The competition experiments reveal that two species populations cannot exist together if they are competing for precisely the same limited resource. Alternatively, if two species in nature were to occupy the same habitat, the expectation is that each would have different ecological requirements, even though the degree of difference is slight. Ecologists have demonstrated the validity of this view. In virtually every natural situation carefully examined, two co-inhabiting species have been found to differ in some requirement. The heterogeneous resources of the environment in a given locality are typically partitioned among the co-inhabiting species so as to minimize direct competition and enable the two (or more) species to coexist.

Besides the twin phenomena of competition and coexistence, there are other interactions of species populations such as predator-prey relationships and symbiosis.

COMPETITIVE EXCLUSION

Competition may be defined as the interaction of species populations that utilize a limited resource (for example, food) in an environment common to them. In 1934, Gause studied the interactions of two protozoan species, *Paramecium caudatum* and *Paramecium aurelia*, under carefully controlled culture conditions. When each species was grown separately in a standard medium in a test tube containing a fixed amount of bacterial food *(Bacillus pyocyaneus)*, each population showed the typical sigmoidal growth pattern (fig. 42.1A). When the two species were placed together in the same culture vessel, however, the growth of *P. caudatum* gradually diminished until the population became eliminated (fig. 42.1B). In enforced competition for the same limited food supply, *P. aurelia* was the more successful species.

The competitive exclusion of one species by another has also been shown in mixed laboratory cultures of two species of flour beetles,

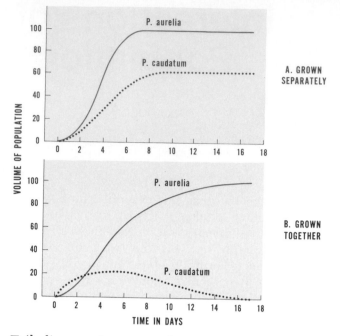

Figure 42.1 Experimental demonstration of competitive exclusion. Comparison of the growth of two closely related protozoans, *Paramecium aurelia* and *Paramecium caudatum,* when grown separately (*A*) and in mixed culture (*B*). In competition, *P. caudatum* is eliminated by *P. aurelia.* (After G. F. Gause, *The struggle for existence,* 1934, The Williams & Wilkins Co., Baltimore. Copyright © 1934 The Williams & Wilkins Co., Baltimore.)

Tribolium castaneum and *Tribolium confusum.* As Thomas Park demonstrated in 1948, one or the other species eventually was eliminated. The final outcome, in terms of which species survived, was governed in large measure by the conditions of temperature and humidity. The more successful species was *T. castaneum* at 34 °C and 70 percent relative humidity. When the temperature was lowered to 24 °C and the humidity lowered to 30 percent, *T. confusum* was the survivor. Thus, Park demonstrated that changing the environmental conditions could alter or reverse the competitive advantage of one or the other species. In any given locality in nature, there is a great diversity of environmental conditions. Park's experiment could be interpreted to indicate that in nature two or more related species could continue to exist together in the same general area if the members of each species could live or establish themselves under different environmental variables congenial to each.

In 1945, the English biologist A. C. Crombie showed that, even in laboratory cultures, two species can live together indefinitely if they differed ever so slightly in their food requirements. Crombie reared populations of the two beetles *Rhizopertha dominica* and *Oryzaephilus surinamensis* in regulated quantities of wheat grain. Each of the two species has a unique feeding habit. The larvae of *Rhizopertha* thrive on nutrients in the interior of the grain, whereas the larvae of *Oryzaephilus* confine their feeding to the external covering of the grain. This trifling difference is enough to permit each species of beetle to exist together in the same culture vessel. Thus, the slightest amount of heterogeneity in the ecological requirements of two species promotes coexistence in a seemingly homogeneous medium.

In another instructive study, Crombie in 1946 placed small segments of fine-glass tubing in a container of flour in which two species of beetles lived. Inside the tubes, the larvae of the smaller species of beetle (*Oryzaephilus*) could find refuge and were protected from attack by the larger species (*Tribolium*). Both species were able to flourish in the same general environment (fig. 42.2). Accordingly, if the environment is not completely uniform, two species can successfully coexist.

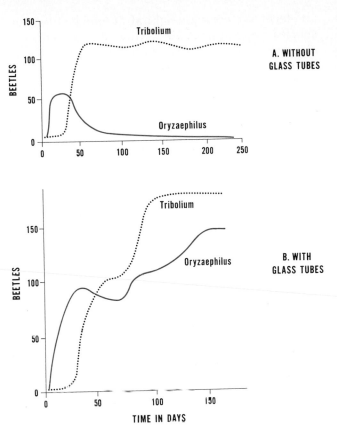

Figure 42.2 Experimental demonstration of coexistence. When populations of two different flour beetles, *Tribolium* and *Oryzaephilus,* were confined together in the same jar of flour, the large-sized *Tribolium* eliminated the smaller *Oryzaephilus* (as shown in *A*). When, however, small pieces of glass tubing were added to the flour, in which the small-sized *Oryzaephilus* sought refuge, both populations of beetles flourished in the same jar of flour (as shown in *B*). (Based on data by A. C. Crombie.)

COEXISTENCE

Gause's principle may be stated in the following form: No two species with identical requirements can continue to exist together. However, it is exceedingly unlikely that two species in nature would have *exactly* the same requirements for food and habitat. The sum total of environmental requirements for a species to thrive and reproduce has been termed the *niche* of that species population. The term *niche,* as ecologists use it, is more than simply the physical space that the species population occupies. It is essentially the way of life peculiar to a given species: its structural adaptations, physiological responses, and behavior within its habitat. Experience has shown that the likelihood of two species having identical niches is almost nil.

Direct evidence of the process of competition between species in nature is difficult to obtain. Observable competitive interaction is a relatively fleeting stage in the relation of two species populations. What the ecologist observes is the end result of competitive contact, when the actual or potential competitors have become differentially specialized to exploit different components of a local environment and accordingly live side by side. The outcome, then, of incipient competitive interaction is the *avoidance* of competition through differential specialization, or in the terminology of ecologists, through *niche diversification.*

Indirect arguments have been used to support the view that two closely related species populations come to exploit different ecological niches in the same locality after a beginning of competitive interaction. We may envision a situation in which two closely related species, with almost similar ecological requirements, expand their geographic ranges

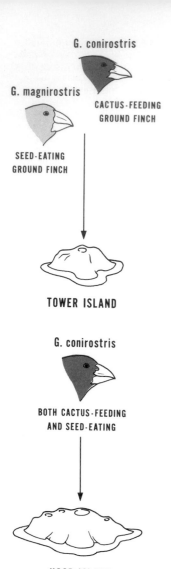

G. conirostris

G. magnirostris

CACTUS-FEEDING
GROUND FINCH

SEED-EATING
GROUND FINCH

TOWER ISLAND

G. conirostris

BOTH CACTUS-FEEDING
AND SEED-EATING

HOOD ISLAND

Figure 42.3 Niche diversification. In the absence of competition, the ground finch *Geospiza conirostris* on Hood Island has evolved a large beak that enables it to exploit a variety of food items (seed and cacti). On the island of Tower, the same ground finch *Geospiza conirostris* has evolved a specialized beak adapted solely for cactus feeding, thus reducing or avoiding competition for food resources with the seed-eating ground finch *Geospiza magnirostris*. The latter species does not exist on Hood Island.

and meet in a common habitat. It may be presumed that each of the two species populations has appreciable genetic variability, and that the resources in the common habitat are varied. The two species populations would initially compete for suitable ecological niches in the new common habitat. However, we can expect that the members of the two species will ultimately become so different in structure and behavior that each species will become specialized to use different components of the environment. In other words, if genetic differences in morphological and behavioral characteristics tend at first to reduce competition between the two species, then subsequently natural selection will act to augment the differences between the two competing species. It is especially noteworthy that the differences between the two species become more pronounced as a consequence of selection *reducing* competition rather than *intensifying* competition.

A striking case of niche diversification has been described by David Lack for certain species of *Geospiza* in the Galápagos. Where two species occur together on an island, there is a conspicuous difference in the size of the beaks and food habits. Where either species exists alone on other islands, the beak is adapted to exploit more than one food resource. Thus, on the island of Tower (fig 42.3), the cactus-feeding *Geospiza conirostris* and the large seed-eating ground finch *Geospiza magnirostris* live side by side. The former species occurs also on the island of Hood, but the latter species is absent, presumably having failed to invade or reach the island. In the absence of competition, *G. conirostris* on Hood Island has evolved a larger beak that is adapted to feeding on both cactus and seeds. The sharp separation in beak size of the two species on Tower Island is understandable if we assume that competition initially fostered the differentiation of the beaks to permit each of the two species to adapt to a limited or restricted range of the available food resources. Each species is now genetically specialized in food habits, and competition between the two is now avoided.

There are many examples to illustrate how two or more species avoid competition. Among warblers that inhabit the spruce forests of Maine, each species confines its feeding to a particular region of the spruce tree. As Robert MacArthur demonstrated, the myrtle warbler preys on insects in and below the spruce tree, whereas the Blackburnian warbler prefers those insects on the exterior leaves of the top of the tree (fig. 42.4). The warblers can exist together because they use different resources of the same tree.

We may conclude by stating that competition between two species populations achieves, paradoxically, the avoidance or reduction of further competition, and not an intensification. In natural populations, coexistence of two species, rather than competitive exclusion, is the general rule. The end result is that each species is part of a highly organized community (see chapter 44) in which each plays a constructive, or stabilizing, role. Nevertheless, there is one species—*Homo sapiens*—that seems unable to live in harmony with other species. Man's destruction of natural habitats has led to the extinction of several species of wildlife (for example, the passenger pigeon) and the reduction in rank of many others (for example, the bison). The survival of numerous species continues to be threatened, among them the grizzly bear, the ivory-billed woodpecker, and the whooping crane (fig. 42.5). In the United States alone, approximately 100 species of wildlife were listed in 1971 as being in danger of becoming extinct.

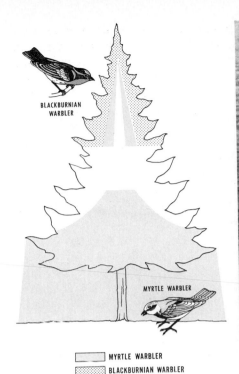

MYRTLE WARBLER
BLACKBURNIAN WARBLER

Figure 42.4 Coexistence of natural populations of two species of North American warblers. The myrtle warbler and the Blackburnian warbler have comparable food requirements, but each forages in a particular part of the spruce tree with a minimum of overlap. (Based on studies by R. MacArthur.)

Figure 42.5 Whooping cranes on the wintering grounds in Texas at the Arkansas National Wildlife Refuge. Man's disturbance of the specialized habitat requirements of this species has contributed to its endangered status. (Courtesy of the United States Department of the Interior, Bureau of Sport Fisheries and Wildlife. Photographer Luther C. Goldman.)

PREDATOR-PREY RELATIONSHIPS

The complex interaction of predator and prey populations involves a dynamic and delicate balance between the two populations. When the prey population increases, the numbers of predators also increase. An increase in predators tends, in turn, to depress the prey population. The predator-prey interaction generally results in an oscillatory, or a cyclic, pattern. However, the cyclic relation is so precariously balanced that extinction of the prey (and hence the predator) can occur, at least in experimental situations.

Gause in 1934 studied the interaction of two protozoans, *Paramecium caudatum*, which feeds on bacteria, and *Didinium nasutum*, which is a predator of *P. caudatum*. As seen in figure 42.6A, the prey *P. caudatum* was first introduced in a small test tube, followed two days later by the predator *D. nasutum*. Several days later both predator and prey populations became extinct. Increasing predation by *D. nasutum* eliminated the prey population, after which the predator *D. nasutum* also became extinct, dying of starvation.

In another experiment, shown in figure 42.6B, Gause periodically added both predator and prey to the experimental population so that the populations were not allowed to die out. The addition at regular intervals of both species enabled the two populations to live together indefinitely, and equally important, the two coexisted in the expected oscillatory pattern. The prey population, under periodic reprieve by immigrations, did not become extinct, and it continued to grow. Thus, a self-sustained predator-prey relationship cannot occur without immigration (or abundance) of the prey.

In nature, there is a very subtle, or sensitive, balance between predator and prey. The predator consumes as many of the prey as keeps the prey population at or below the limit of the environmental capacity. Two countervailing selective forces apparently operate in nature: highly efficient predators are selectively favored, while simultaneously,

Figure 42.6 Predator-prey interactions. *Top:* The predator, *Didinium*, thrives until it exhausts its prey, *Paramecium. Bottom:* The prey population, under periodic reprieve by additional individuals (immigrants), does not decline to extinction. As a result of repeated immigrations, both populations persist in an oscillatory state. (After G. F. Gause, *The struggle for existence*, 1934, The Williams & Wilkins Co., Baltimore. Copyright © 1934 The Williams & Wilkins Co., Baltimore.)

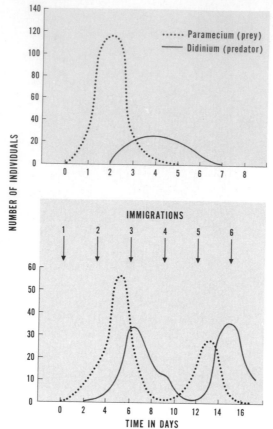

selection favors that prey most adept at avoiding the predator. Viewed in this manner, the predators primarily remove the surplus individuals of the prey species. Moreover, predation tends to eliminate the weak and disease-ridden prey individuals. Accordingly, predation is actually beneficial to the prey species, since its population size is regulated both qualitatively and quantitatively.

Caution must be exercised in the disruption of a stably balanced predator-prey relation. It appears that any factor that is detrimental to both predator and prey will have a more adverse effect on the predator. The population growth of the scale insect *Icerya purchasi,* a parasite of citrus trees, at one time was constrained by a natural predator, the ladybird beetle, *Novius cardinales.* The insecticide DDT was then introduced as an additional measure of control of the scale insect. However, the populations of scale insects began to increase, rather than decline, because DDT had a more negative effect on the predator.

Another aspect of predation is that many predators have alternative sources of prey, particularly in times of relative scarcity of the regular source. The horned owl and buteo hawk can pursue a variety of species of small rodents. The coyote devours livestock (cattle, sheep, and goat) as well as rodents and rabbits. Sheep ranchers still express consternation over the notion that coyotes may perform a beneficial population-control function. A study of the feeding habits of coyotes has revealed that livestock constitutes only 14 percent (by volume) of the coyote's diet in marked contrast to the 50 percent represented by grass-consuming rabbits and rodents. When a rancher has the craving to shoot a coyote on sight, he might well weigh the relative merits or value of losing a few sheep compared with the heavy loss of forage on his ranch from rodents and rabbits that the coyote would otherwise have eliminated.

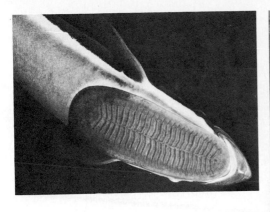

Figure 42.7 Commensal relation of the remora and the shark. The dorsal fin of the remora has been modified into a sucking disc. The remora eats "table scraps" that the shark leaves. (© Photo Researchers, Inc.)

SYMBIOSIS

Special and close associations of individuals of different species populations have been given a particular name: *symbiosis*. Symbiosis signifies the living together of members of two different species. There are at least three different kinds of symbiotic relationships between organisms— *commensalism, mutualism,* and *parasitism.* The types of associations differ according to the degree of dependence shown by both members of the association.

Commensalism literally means "being at table together." This type of association is exemplified by the remora fish and the shark (fig. 42.7). The dorsal fin of the remora fish (also known as the "shark sucker") has been modified into an ovoid sucking disc that can attach firmly to the outer surface of the shark. The remora feeds on scraps of food the shark leaves. The remora benefits from the association, but the shark is neither benefited nor adversely affected. This type of relation may be viewed as unilateral dependency. Among plant commensals are the *epiphytes,* or air plants, such as the orchid and Spanish moss. The Spanish moss, which adorns southern live oaks, is not a true moss but a flowering plant (a member of the pineapple family). Epiphytes grow upon the branches of trees but are not parasitic upon them, contrary to popular opinion. They derive support from the tree but draw their water from moisture in the humid air.

A close relationship in which both organisms benefit is termed *mutualism.* The classic example of mutualism in the plant kingdom is the *lichen,* an intimate composite of certain species of green algae and colorless fungi. The nonphotosynthetic fungus derives its organic nutrients from the alga; the fungus, in turn, provides the alga with water and minerals. Another mutually beneficial association is the relation between flagellated protozoans that swarm in the digestive tract of wood-eating termites. The termites themselves cannot digest the cellulose of wood, and depend wholly on the internal protozoans, who possess the cellulose-digesting enzymes. The wood chips that the termites ingest furnish virtually the entire diet of the protozoans. Under certain experimental conditions, the protozoans can be removed from the intestinal tract of the termite. Although such defaunated termites continue to ingest large quantities of wood, they soon die of starvation.

Assuredly the most complex kind of symbiotic relation is *parasitism,* which means "eating at the expense of another." The parasite lives in or

Figure 42.8 Dutch elm disease, caused by a parasitic fungus that has victimized the American elm tree. *Top:* Elm-lined Gillet Avenue in Waukegan, Illinois, as it appeared in 1962. *Bottom:* Gillet Avenue in 1969, after the elms were destroyed by the parasitic fungus. (Courtesy of Elm Research Institute.)

on the body of another organism for a considerable period of its life cycle, and derives nutrient directly from the host. The relationship may be permanent, as in the case of flukes residing in the liver of vertebrates, or temporary, as in the case of external blood-sucking ticks and mites. The diversity of parasites is truly astonishing; no living organism is devoid of parasites. Some parasites debilitate and eventually destroy the host; other parasites—the evolutionarily more advanced ones—cause relatively little harm to the host.

The scientific literature on symbiosis provides examples of parasites that grade imperceptibly into mutualistic organisms. Indeed, it has been suggested that long-standing parasitism evolves eventually into mutualism. The parasite may ultimately produce a metabolic by-product that it does not require itself, but which the host can use. A parasite that has no pathogenic effect on the host is certainly biologically superior to a harmful parasite, since a parasite that kills the host perishes along with the host.

Parasite-host interactions are often as sensitively balanced as predator-prey interactions. The European elm tree is relatively resistant to a particular parasitic fungus *(Ceratostomella),* having evolved specific defense mechanisms against the potentially destructive parasite. A few decades ago, this parasitic fungus spread to North America and victimized the American elm tree, which lacked a long-standing resistance to the parasite. In many areas of eastern United States, the American elm has been eliminated by the Dutch elm disease that the parasitic fungus causes (fig. 42.8). There has been insufficient time for the emergence of a stable interaction of the fungus and the American elm.

It is generally the case that a parasite inflicts greater damage during its initial encounter with a host than after a long evolutionary association with the host. The havoc wrought on the lake trout population by parasitic lamprey that invaded the Great Lakes in recent times attests to the destructive effects of a parasite when originally introduced to a host. The lamprey, a primitive cartilaginous fish, has a sucking disc lined with teeth by which it rasps an opening through the skin and feeds on the blood and body fluids of its host (fig. 42.9). A trout that manages to survive the direct attack of the lamprey usually succumbs subsequently to bacterial and fungal infections in the open-wound area. Uncontrolled parasitism for well over a decade virtually threatened the existence of the commercially important lake trout. In the late 1950s, a specific poison

Figure 42.9 Lake trout showing scars where parasitic lamprey had attached. (Courtesy of the Michigan Department of Natural Resources.)

was finally developed (3, 4, 6-trichlo-2-nitrophenol) that selectively destroys the larvae of the lamprey without harming the trout or other fish. As a result of persistent chemical treatment of lamprey-spawning streams, the lamprey population in the Great Lakes exists today only in relatively small numbers. Aided by repeated stockings of lake trout, the gradual process of restoration of Great Lakes fisheries has begun.

COMPLEXITY OF PARASITES

The life patterns of parasites are often exceedingly complicated. Many parasites dwell in several hosts during various stages of their life cycle. Parasites have great reproductive capabilities, reproducing both asexually and sexually. The parasitic protozoan that causes malaria, for example, has both asexual and sexual phases in its life cycle (see chapter 32). Malaria has been claimed to be a man-made disease. The clearing of the forests for agriculture provided marshy breeding grounds for increased population growth of the mosquitoes. Moreover, severe increases in human malaria occurred in agricultural communities where tractors replaced the buffalo. Apparently, buffaloes were in the past the preferred prey of mosquitoes, but with the demise of these herds, man became the new victim.

Another serious vector-borne disease in vast areas of Africa is *trypanosomiasis*, or African sleeping sickness. It is caused by the flagellated protozoan *Trypanosoma*, which is introduced into man by the bite of the tsetse fly (*Glossina*), a relative of the common housefly (fig. 42.10). There are at least 20 different species of tsetse fly that transmit trypanosomiasis to both humans and animals. Unlike malaria, the parasite can be transmitted to man from domestic mammals (pigs, goats, sheep, and cattle). The occurrence of animal reservoir hosts complicates endeavors to eradicate, or control, the disease.

A number of species of tapeworms, and also flatworms, are known to parasitize man. The familiar tapeworm (*Echinococcus*) tends to infect dogs, wolves, and foxes more often than man. Among the disease-causing flatworms are the liver fluke (*Fasciola*), the oriental lung fluke (*Paragonimiasis*), and the blood fluke (*Schistosoma*). Infections caused by the

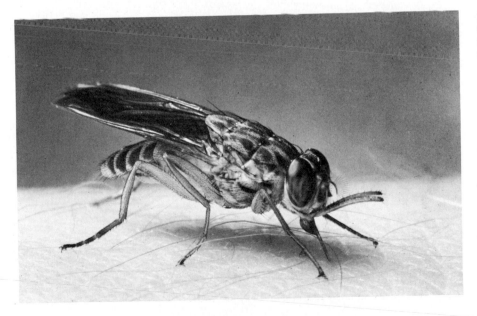

Figure 42.10 Tsetse fly, the insect vector of African sleeping sickness. (Courtesy of the American Museum of Natural History.)

blood fluke are presently incurable. Human schistosomiasis is a serious, energy-sapping disease, in which the essential intermediate host is the freshwater snail (fig. 42.11). Adult blood flukes inhabit the intestinal veins of man. Eggs, released in the blood, are ultimately passed out in the feces. If the feces are deposited in water, an egg hatches into a larva (the so-called miracidium) that requires a suitable snail for its continued existence. After a sequence of developmental changes, infective larvae (cercariae) leave the snail and, on contact with a human, penetrate the skin. In many underdeveloped countries with poor sanitation, irrigation ditches have become a favorite haunt of the snail hosts. One of the drastic consequences of expansion of irrigation in modern times has been an increase in the incidence of schistosomiasis.

Among many of the dire problems that have arisen from the ill-conceived construction in the 1960s of the much publicized Aswan High Dam on the Nile in Egypt has been the widespread exposure of people to schistosomiasis. Although the construction of the dam was intended to provide year-round irrigation of the lower Nile basin, it was not foreseen (or it was ignored) that the slow-flowing, silt-free waters in the irrigation ditches would provide a favorable habitat for the snail hosts of schistosomiasis. As a matter of record, the clear, regular flow of water has proved to be ideal for the growth of the host snails. Prior to the construction of the Aswan High Dam, the Egyptian Ministry of Health estimated that approximately 47 percent of their people were afflicted with schistosomiasis. Today, as a consequence of the conversion of the Nile basin above Cairo to perennial irrigation, approximately 80 percent are affected; the majority of these (90 percent) are agricultural workers. With 3 million new cases of schistosomiasis since the completion of the dam in 1964, it seems that the cost in human lives outweighs the increased agricultural productivity (which has been only moderately realized). Like malaria, schistosomiasis is truly a man-made disease, which man seems intent on perpetuating.

Figure 42.11 Simplified life cycle of *Schistosoma*. Blood fluke adults live in the human intestinal blood vessels. Fertilized eggs are voided in the feces, and the encapsulated eggs deposited in water hatch into larvae, the miracidiae, which penetrate a snail. After several developmental events within the snail, infective larvae (cercariae) emerge to reinfect man. (After R. D. Barnes, *Invertebrate zoology,* 3rd ed., 1974, W. B. Saunders Co.)

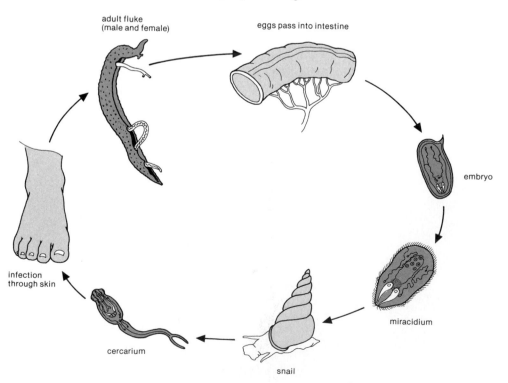

adult fluke
(male and female)

eggs pass into intestine

embryo

miracidium

snail

cercarium

infection
through skin

SUMMARY

Competition is the interaction of two or more populations of species sharing a limited resource in a common environment. Under controlled laboratory conditions, it can be demonstrated that two species competing for precisely the same limited resource cannot continue to exist together (Gause's principle). In nature, the outcome of incipient competitive interaction of two closely related species is the reduction or avoidance of competition through differential specialization (niche diversification). In exploiting different ecological niches in the same locality, the co-inhabiting species are able to exist side by side. Coexistence is the general rule among natural species populations. In manipulating and controlling other species, man seems intent on breaking this rule.

The delicate balance of organisms in nature is vividly revealed in predator-prey relations. Natural selection operates to favor the efficient predator, and also the efficient prey that can avoid the predator. Predation culls the surplus and ill-adapted members of the prey species, and is thereby important in the biological control of that species. By indiscriminant destruction of predators alleged to be pests, man adversely affects the sensitive balance of nature.

Symbiosis involves interspecific associations (commensalism, mutualism, and parasitism) of varying degrees of benefit to the different species who live together. Of these, parasitism is the most complicated. Parasites cause several serious, energy-sapping diseases in man, prominent among them malaria, trypanosomiasis, and schistosomiasis.

43 Biotic Communities: Plants As Producers

The student of evolution classifies and groups different species according to their evolutionary relationships or affinities to one another. The ecologist, on the other hand, arranges different species according to their functional association with each other. A natural assemblage or aggregation of different species in a given habitat is defined by the ecologist as a *biotic community*. Each community has its own characteristic size, structure, and composition of species. There are obvious differences between such large communities as a tropical rain forest and a desert. The differences are equally great for such small communities like a rotting log or a drop of pond water. Each community, large or small, embraces an assemblage of species that, of necessity, are mutually dependent. Each species must contribute in some way to maintain the stability of the community.

Photosynthetic green plants are the producers in a community. These chlorophyll-containing plants are the primary source of chemical energy for animals (the consumers). The photosynthetic green plants can capture and convert solar energy into the chemical energy of organic compounds. Stated another way, green plants furnish chemical energy in a form (glucose) that the consumers can use. This should not be construed as indicating that a plant exists solely to accommodate the consumer. The plant itself assimilates a considerable portion of the synthesized carbohydrate to provide energy for its own maintenance, growth and reproduction. Animals consume the organic compounds that are stored in the plant. It is estimated that the green plants on earth today synthesize yearly 87 billion tons of organic molecules beyond that which they use for their own metabolism. The process of photosynthesis also releases untold quantities of oxygen into the atmosphere for use by both plants and animals.

PHOTOSYNTHESIS

The two fundamental energy-extracting processes in living organisms are *respiration* and *photosynthesis*. During respiration in both plants and animals, glucose is broken down by stepwise enzyme-mediated reactions and the energy extracted from the carbon-hydrogen bonds of glucose is conserved in adenosine triphosphate (ATP)—the cell's immediate source of energy for its manifold activities (see chapter 6). By the process of photosynthesis, plant cells extract, or harness, solar energy and translate the light energy into chemical energy, which is ultimately locked in the synthesized glucose molecule. The catalyst for the reaction is the green pigment *chlorophyll*. The function of chlorophyll is to absorb light energy so that it can be used to effect chemical changes. In simplified form, the overall equation for photosynthesis is:

$$6CO_2 + 6H_2O + \text{absorbed light energy}$$
$$\longrightarrow C_6H_{12}O_6 + 6O_2 + \text{chemical energy}.$$

The preceding equation is a gross oversimplification, particularly since it implies that carbon dioxide combines directly with water to produce sugar. In reality, there is an intricate series of chemical reactions, which can be grouped into two main stages—the *light* reaction and the *dark* reaction. The primary feature of the light reaction is the conversion of light energy into chemical energy in the form of ATP. This process is called *photophosphorylation*. Additionally, the light reaction provides for the production of an appropriate hydrogen carrier in the form of the reduced coenzyme, $NADPH_2$. (This coenzyme is essentially the same as nicotinamide adenine dinucleotide, NAD, except that it contains an additional phosphate group. The coenzyme NADP is also known as *triphosphopyridine nucleotide*, TPN.) During the dark reaction, which does not require light, the plant cell uses ATP as an energy source and $NADPH_2$ as a reducing agent to transform carbon dioxide into carbohydrate. Water molecules donate the hydrogen to NADP when they are split into their component parts, hydrogen and oxygen. Thus gaseous oxygen is released by the cleavage of water, *not* of carbon dioxide (as plant physiologists had thought for decades).

The second main stage occurs independently of light (hence, the dark reaction) and is concerned with the conversion of carbon dioxide into glucose. Basically, the synthesis of glucose involves the transfer of hydrogen (from the first stage) to carbon dioxide, using the energy of ATP. By the use of radioactive ^{14}C, Melvin Calvin and his associates at the University of California were able to identify and trace many of the intermediate steps through which the carbon passes from carbon dioxide to carbohydrates. Calvin received the Nobel prize in chemistry in 1961 for elucidating the main features of the complex path of carbon in photosynthesis. A highly simplified scheme of the reactions of photosynthesis is shown in figure 43.1. Below we will explore some of the intricacies of photosynthesis.

Figure 43.1 Simplified scheme of dark and light reactions of photosynthesis.

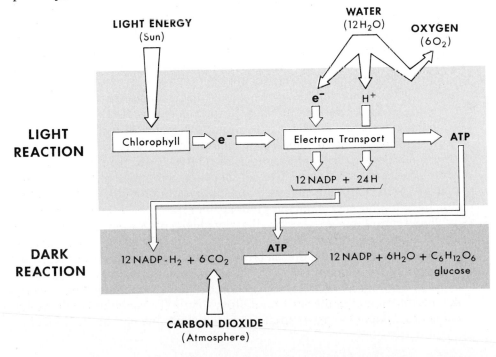

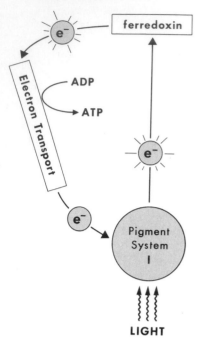

ferredoxin

ADP

ATP

Electron Transport

e⁻

Pigment System I

LIGHT

Figure 43.2 The process of cyclic photophosphorylation in photosystem I.

LIGHT REACTION

When light energy is absorbed by chlorophyll, the absorbed energy activates or raises an electron of the chlorophyll molecule to an orbital of a higher energy level. By virtue of the newly energized electron, the chlorophyll molecule is brought from its normal ground state to a chemically more reactive, or *excited*, state. Chlorophyll molecules with activated electrons are unstable, and release their high-energy electrons to other carrier molecules. The beneficiaries of the excess energy of excited electrons are ATP and $NADPH_2$. The transfer of energized electrons to ATP and $NADPH_2$ is not direct or immediate, but involves a chain of reactions in which the excited electrons slowly release their energy. After the excited electrons give up their excess energy, they settle back to their normal and stable level.

Several types of chlorophyll molecules have been distinguished, of which chlorophyll *a* and chlorophyll *b* are the best known and most abundant. A variety of *accessory pigments* (carotenoids and phycobilins) also play a role in absorbing light energy. In aerobic plants, two light-reaction systems, called *photosystem I* and *photosystem II,* are involved in trapping the radiant energy of sunlight. Each photosystem contains a specific assortment of accessory pigments and different molecular forms of chlorophyll, which are arranged in orderly structures within the chloroplasts.

In photosystem I (fig. 43.2), activated electrons flow from excited chlorophyll molecules to an iron-containing protein, *ferredoxin.* The electrons then pass from ferredoxin through a chain of electron-carrier molecules, some of which are the familiar *cytochromes.* As the electrons move along the electron-transport system, sufficient energy is tapped off to generate high-energy phosphate bonds in ATP. The electrons emerging from the electron-transport chain, having now lost their excess energy, return to the chlorophyll molecules from which they originated, thereby reestablishing the ground state of these chlorophyll molecules. The electron pathway is said to be *cyclic* since an electron that is ejected from a chlorophyll molecule ultimately returns to its original position in the chlorophyll molecule. The synthesis of ATP as a result of this cyclic transport is called *cyclic photophosphorylation.* This process of cyclic photophosphorylation in photosystem I accounts for the production of some ATP that is necessary for the dark reaction, but does not account for the $NADPH_2$ that is also indispensable to the dark reaction.

The production of $NADPH_2$ occurs by a pathway of electron flow that is *not* cyclic. Activated electrons are used to reduce—that is, add electrons to—NADP, which in its reduced form becomes $NADPH_2$. Since the added electrons in $NADPH_2$ are eventually drained off by the dark reaction of photosynthesis, these electrons do not return to their original chlorophyll molecules. The synthesis of ATP resulting from a noncircular route of electrons is referred to as *noncyclic photophosphorylation.* As figure 43.3 shows, noncyclic photophosphorylation requires the participation of both photosystem I and photosystem II.

The illumination of chlorophyll molecules in photosystem II results in a flow of energized electrons to *plastoquinone* molecules, which in turn donate the electrons to the electron-transport chain. As the electrons move along the chain of carriers, energy is contributed for the synthesis of ATP. The energy-depleted electrons are then accepted by electron-deficient chlorophyll molecules in photosystem I. These chlorophyll molecules are deficient because their activated electrons end up in $NADPH_2$.

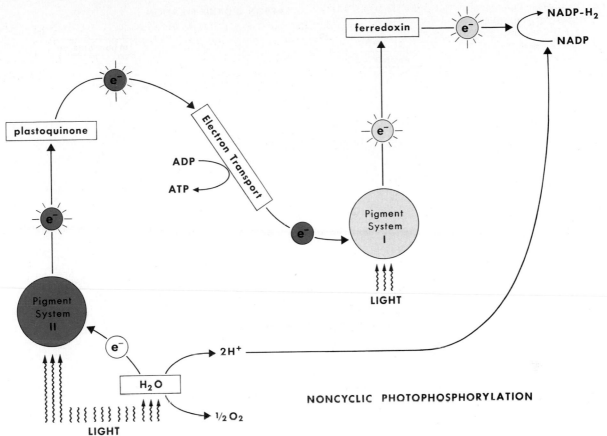

NONCYCLIC PHOTOPHOSPHORYLATION

Figure 43.3 The process of non-cyclic photophosphorylation, involving both photosystem I and photosystem II.

Specifically, as figure 43.3 shows, excited electrons from chlorophyll molecules in photosystem I pass to ferredoxin molecules, which transfer the electrons to NADP molecules. Since these electrons do not return to the original chlorophyll molecules, electrons from photosystem II make up for the electrons lost by the chlorophyll molecules of photosystem I.

The chlorophyll molecules in photosystem II are now themselves deficient of electrons. These chlorophyll molecules reestablish their ground-state condition by accepting electrons from an external source, namely, *water*. The splitting of water molecules provides electrons to replace the electrons ejected from the chlorophyll molecules in photosystem II, and also furnishes hydrogen ions for the conversion of NADP and $NADPH_2$. Thus, water serves as a donor of electrons and hydrogen ions. A by-product of the cleavage of water is free oxygen (fig. 43.3).

DARK REACTION

In the dark reaction, $NADPH_2$ is instrumental in reducing carbon dioxide to carbohydrate, with ATP supplying the energy. The assimilation of carbon dioxide in the organic structure of glucose by a series of enzyme-mediated reactions is referred to as *carbon dioxide fixation*. As figure 43.4 shows, carbon dioxide combines with a 5-carbon compound, ribulose diphosphate, to form an unstable 6-carbon intermediate. This intermediate compound breaks up into two molecules of 3-phosphoglyceric acid, which in turn is converted to 1, 3-diphosphoglyceric acid. In this conversion, ATP serves as the phosphate donor. The 1, 3-diphosphoglyceric acid is then converted to 3-phosphoglyceraldehyde, a reaction in which $NADPH_2$ acts as the hydrogen donor. The 3-phosphoglyceraldehyde is

Figure 43.4 Pathways of the dark reaction of photosynthesis, which are concerned with the conversion of carbon dioxide into glucose.

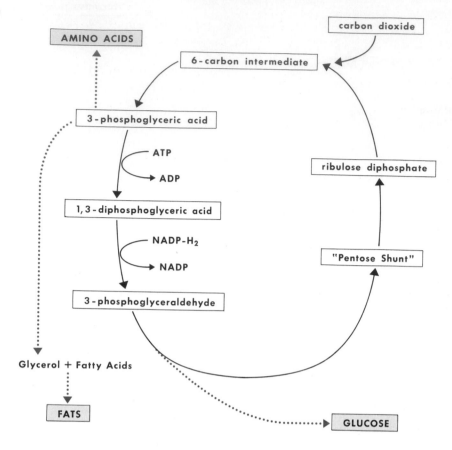

rearranged in a series of steps, ultimately to become glucose. Additionally, ribulose diphosphate is regenerated in a series of reactions abbreviated in figure 43.4 as "pentose shunt."

Many of the intermediate products are identical with those formed when glucose is oxidized during respiration. As in animals, the intermediate compounds can be used for the synthesis of amino acids and fats. Accordingly, the process of photosynthesis is not limited to the production of carbohydrate. The pathways of the dark reaction permit the interconversion of carbohydrate, fat, and protein.

PHOTOSYNTHESIS AND EVOLUTION

The open-ended route of noncyclic photophosphorylation yields oxygen and also ATP and NADPH$_2$, whereas the closed path of cyclic photophosphorylation produces only ATP. It is likely that cyclic photophosphorylation is the primitive process and the first to have appeared in the earliest organisms, when the earth's atmosphere contained little free oxygen. The cyclic path would permit primitive organisms to make ATP anaerobically, in the presence of light.

Certain present-day pigmented bacteria synthesize organic compounds by a noncyclic pathway but, unlike green plants, oxygen is not a product of the reaction. These bacteria use hydrogen sulfide as electron donors instead of water and liberate elemental sulfur instead of gaseous oxygen. It would seem, then, that the noncyclic pathway first evolved in bacterialike organisms that made use of electron donors other than water.

A major evolutionary advance, achieved by the green plants, was the capacity to use water as the electron donor in noncyclic photophosphorylation. This step not only enabled green plants to generate additional quantities of ATP but also established free oxygen in the atmosphere. Aerobic respiration thus became possible as oxygen accumulated in the atmosphere. It is noteworthy, from an evolutionary standpoint, that modern green plants have retained the ancestral capacity for cyclic photophosphorylation even though they have a more efficient system for generating ATP.

LAND PLANTS

In a typical land plant, the major site of photosynthesis is the leaf. The broad, flat surface of the leaf is an adaptive feature that facilitates the absorption of sunlight. As a barrier to excessive water loss, a waxy lining, called the *cuticle,* coats the upper and lower surfaces of the leaf (fig. 43.5). The waterproof cuticle is secreted by the *epidermis,* a layer of cells that surrounds the internal chloroplast-containing cells. Gas exchanges (O_2 and CO_2) occur through microscopic pores, or *stomata,* in the epidermis. The size of the stomatal aperture is regulated by changes in the shapes of two specialized epidermal cells, the *guard* cells.

The stomatal pore opens when the guard cells swell, or become turgid. The wall of a guard cell is uneven in thickness; the wall is thicker on the surface facing the stomatal pore. When water flows into the guard cell, the thin walls, which are more easily stretched than the thick ones, curve outward. Accordingly, the stomatal opening enlarges automatically as the paired guard cells change from relatively straight to curved configurations (fig. 43.6).

The factors responsible for the flow of water into a guard cell continue to be debated. For many years the cherished theory centered on osmotic changes resulting from the enzymatic breakdown of granular starch into soluble sugar molecules. The increase in sugar concentration in the guard cell leads to an increase in osmotic water uptake. Since the stomata are generally open during the day and usually closed during the night, it appeared likely that the lowered carbon dioxide concentrations (due to photosynthesis) and the associated decreased acidity in the cytoplasm promote the activity of enzymes that convert starch into sugar. The process is reversed at the close of the day. With elevated carbon dioxide

Figure 43.5 Component parts of a leaf.

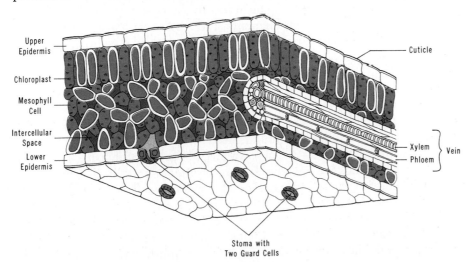

Upper Epidermis

Chloroplast

Mesophyll Cell

Intercellular Space

Lower Epidermis

Cuticle

Xylem
Phloem } Vein

Stoma with Two Guard Cells

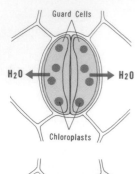

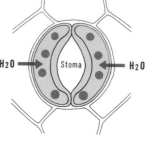

Figure 43.6 Changes in the shape of the paired guard cells are related to the opening of a stoma.

in the dark and a concomitant increase in acidity, the enzymatic conditions are favored for the conversion of sugar into starch. In recent years interest has focused on the accumulation of potassium ions in the guard cells as a stoma opens. Some investigators now contend that the osmotic effects associated with the opening and closing of a stoma can be accounted for almost exclusively by changes in the relative concentrations of potassium ions.

The loosely packed cells within the leaf (technically, *mesophyll* cells) contain numerous chloroplasts. The air spaces between the mesophyll cells *(intercellular spaces)* are saturated with water vapor. Since a leaf of a land plant is surrounded by air that is rarely saturated with water vapor, the leaf loses water by diffusion through the stomata. The evaporation of water from wet surfaces of the leaf cells is referred to as *transpiration.* In most plants, the stomata close at night, retarding transpirational loss. However, during the day, large quantities of water are lost through the open stomata. The amounts lost are replaced rapidly by the uptake of water from the stem to the leaf. There is a highly efficient water-transport system in the *veins* of the leaf, which is continuous with the conducting tissues of the stem and root.

TRANSPORT SYSTEM

The transport system of the land plant, often called a *vascular system,* is made up of two major tissue components. One, the *xylem,* functions in the movement of water and dissolved salts from the roots to the upper parts of the plant (fig. 43.7). The other component, the *phloem,* is involved in the transport of sugar manufactured in the leaves to all parts of the plant. The constituent cells of xylem tissue form a continuous water-filled system throughout the plant. Two prominent types of water-conducting xylem cells are the *tracheids* and *vessels.* A tracheid is a slender cell with a closed tapering end wall; pits occur in the wall that permit the lateral diffusion of water from one tracheid to another. A vessel cell is wider than a tracheid and its end walls have been broken through. The end walls of adjacent vessels fuse to form long, continuous tubes. Both tracheids and vessels are devoid of any living cellular contents—they are essentially inert pipes. These pipelike elements are prevented from collapsing by various patterns of thickened areas containing lignin. In woody plants, the stem thickens and forms a cylinder of xylem in which the innermost xylem rings cease to be active in the transport of water. These older, nonconducting xylem elements, referred to as *heartwood,* tend to accumulate substances (such as tannins) that impart a reddish hue. The active, functional xylem tissue of a woody plant is called *sapwood.*

The specialized conducting cell in the phloem tissue is known as a *sieve tube.* Sieve tubes are connected end to end, with the interconnections taking the form of sievelike perforations in the cell wall (fig. 43.7). Strands of protoplasm pass through the pores from one sieve cell to the next, resulting in a continuous network of protoplasm. Thus, unlike a tracheid or vessel, a sieve tube contains living protoplasm. The sieve tube, however, lacks a nucleus. It may be that the activity of the sieve tube is regulated by the nucleus of an adjacent cell, almost invariably present and appropriately called a *companion cell.*

There are continuous columns of water from the roots to the leaves. Water moves into the roots as a consequence of a concentration differential. Numerous outgrowths, the *root hairs,* facilitate water uptake by in-

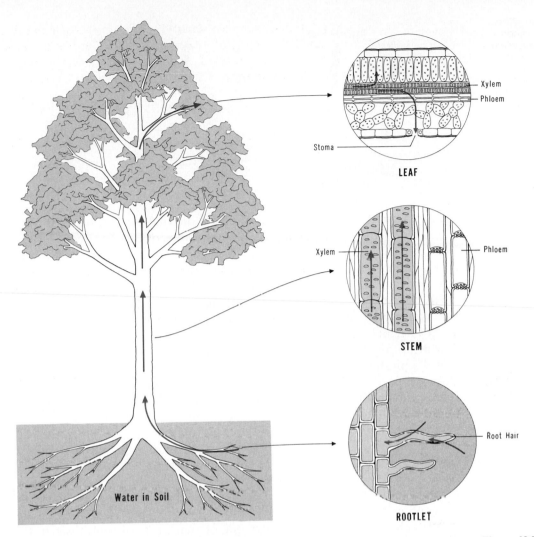

Xylem
Phloem

Stoma

LEAF

Xylem

Phloem

STEM

Root Hair

ROOTLET

Water in Soil

creasing the surface area of the roots (fig. 43.7). The columns of water in the xylem are held together by the cohesion of the water molecules, or the attraction of like molecules to each other. As previously mentioned, the intercellular spaces of the leaf are saturated with water vapor. The water that is lost when the stomata are open is replaced by water that evaporates from cells bordering the air spaces. In turn, these cells remove water from neighboring cells. Ultimately, water is withdrawn from xylem cells in the leaf veins. Thus, the continual diffusion and evaporation of water from the leaf apparently provides most of the "pull" on the upward rise of water.

Figure 43.7 The flow of water and nutrients through the tissues of the root, stem, and leaf of a tree.

GREENHOUSE EFFECT

Plants carry on photosynthesis at a rate that varies almost directly with the concentration of carbon dioxide in the atmosphere. In other words, plants increase their photosynthetic activity as the concentration of atmospheric carbon increases, and decrease their rate of photosynthesis as the level of carbon dioxide falls. Thus, in the absence of disturbing factors, the level of carbon dioxide in the atmosphere should remain relatively constant at all times. There are, however, indications that man's extensive combustion of fossil fuels (coal, natural gas, and oil) has increased atmospheric CO_2 concentration beyond the ability of

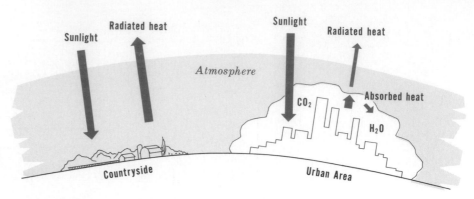

Figure 43.8 Greenhouse effect. Most of the sun's energy is converted to heat. In the countryside, the surface temperature tends to remain constant as the heat is largely dissipated into space. In urban areas, where man's extensive combustion of fossil fuels greatly increases atmospheric carbon dioxide, the accumulated carbon dioxide absorbs some of the reflected heat. The atmosphere is accordingly warmer and the surface temperature becomes elevated. (From M. E. Clark, *Contemporary biology,* 1973, W. B. Saunders Co.)

plants to use it. A century ago, the carbon dioxide content was 283 parts per million (that is, an average of 283 molecules of CO_2 for every million total molecules in the air); today the level is estimated to be 330 ppm (parts per million). The most immediate impact of increasing amounts of atmospheric carbon dioxide is the so-called greenhouse effect on the earth's temperature, wherein the average temperature of the earth becomes elevated (fig. 43.8). The implications of a warming trend on the earth's surface will be discussed in chapter 45.

Marine algae (phytoplankton) account for 40 to 60 percent of the world's photosynthetic activity. The ecologist Lamont Cole, of Cornell University, has voiced concern that the continued contamination of the seas with pesticides and industrial wastes will ultimately impair the photosynthetic activity of the marine algae. We cannot conclude, however, that the poisoning of the seas will have a dire effect on the oxygen supply to man himself or other terrestrial organisms. As John McClendon, of the University of Nebraska, has stated, the marine organisms themselves use almost all the oxygen liberated in marine photosynthesis in their own respiration. In essence, marine algae produce oxygen for their own survival, and do not yield oxygen for man's welfare. The paramount threat of impairment of marine photosynthesis is the irreparable depletion of food resources for a wide array of organisms.

SUMMARY

A biotic community is an organized association of different, interacting species. There is a flow of nutrients through a succession of different organisms in the community. The photosynthetic green plants are the producers in a community, since they are the organisms that can capture and convert solar energy into the chemical energy of organic compounds. The process of photosynthesis involves an intricate series of chemical reactions, which can be grouped into two main stages—the *light* reaction and the *dark* reaction. The catalyst for photosynthesis is the green pigment *chlorophyll*. The tissues of land plants are so organized as to ensure that the chlorophyll-containing cells receive adequate quantities of light, carbon dioxide, and water. Light energy is absorbed by the leaves, carbon dioxide enters the leaves through specialized pores *(stomata),* and water is absorbed by the roots. The water-conducting system in the land plant provides for unbroken columns of water from the roots to the leaves. The cohesion of the water molecules keeps the columns intact, and the major force drawing water upward is the evaporation of water from the leaf.

Biotic Communities: Energy Flow

44

A biotic community is an organized assemblage of different, mutually dependent species. There is a flow of nutrients (energy) through the succession of diverse organisms in the community. The flow of energy within a community is *not* cyclical; it is a *one-way* sequence in which usable energy becomes progressively less available to the higher levels of organisms. Energy flow in a community would cease in the absence of a continuous inflow of energy. Communities do not readily fade away, so there must be an uninterrupted energy input from an outside source. There is such an ultimate source—the radiant energy from the sun. All organisms ultimately rely on solar energy. More immediately, organisms rely on the primary producers, the green plants, to capture and convert the solar energy into the chemical energy of organic compounds.

FOOD CHAINS

The sequence of organisms through which energy is channeled is called a *food chain.* The green plant constitutes the *producer* at the base of the food chain, since it furnishes chemical energy in a form (glucose) that the consumers can use. Those animals that feed directly on plants are the *primary consumers,* or herbivores, such as the snowshoe hare, deer, and seed-eating birds. Carnivores that prey on the herbivores are the *secondary consumers;* the frog that consumes the grasshopper is a secondary consumer. Higher categories of carnivorous animals may exist in a community, in which case we may speak of them as tertiary and quarternary consumers. An example of different categories of consumers would be the hawk feeding on a snake that, in turn, preys on a frog. We may thus envision a food chain in a meadow community as follows: clover ⟶ grasshopper ⟶ frog ⟶ snake ⟶ hawk. The hawk would represent the final consumer, or the top carnivore.

The foregoing food chain is artificial in the sense that it depicts a linear series of species, one living wholly on the other. Actually, a given resource is typically shared by several species. Plants are eaten by a variety of insects, birds, and mammals, and a given animal may be consumed by several kinds of predators. The feeding interrelations of organisms are better depicted in terms of more or less discrete functional *trophic levels* (fig. 44.1). Thus all organisms that share the same general source of nutrition belong to the same trophic level. We may consider a community as having four or five trophic levels, each level containing a variable number of species. The first trophic level is represented by the *producers,* or the variety of green plant species. *Herbivores,* the plant feeders, compose the second trophic level (and, as earlier stated, may be called primary consumers). *Carnivores* that feed on the herbivorous animals constitute the third trophic level (and may be called secondary

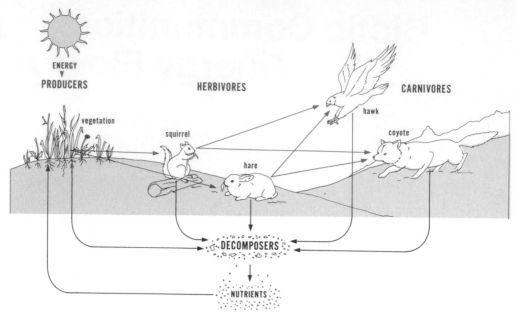

ENERGY

PRODUCERS

HERBIVORES

CARNIVORES

vegetation

squirrel

hawk

coyote

hare

DECOMPOSERS

NUTRIENTS

Figure 44.1 Trophic levels in a simple community. The first trophic level consists of photosynthetic plants, the *producers*. The plants are utilized by *herbivores* (second trophic level), which, in turn, are the energy source for *carnivores* (third trophic level). *Decomposers*, chiefly microorganisms (bacteria, and fungi), degrade the remains and wastes of plants and animals.

consumers). Still higher categories of carnivores that prey on the secondary consumers would occupy the fourth and even the fifth trophic levels.

As a general rule, the further removed an organism is from the initial source of nutrients (the producer), the less likely it is to depend solely on the preceding trophic level for subsistence. Indeed, many consumers do not restrict their feeding activities to one trophic level alone. As examples, the red fox, bear, and man occupy herbivorous and carnivorous levels. They are *omnivorous*, eating everything, as the term implies (Latin, *omnis*, "all," plus *vorare*, "to eat greedily").

As figure 44.1 shows, the food chain is associated within another essential link, the *decomposer*. The decomposers are organisms of decay —the bacteria and fungi—that break down the organic molecules of dead plants and animals to simpler inorganic components. These simpler substances are cycled back to the community as vital nutrients (nitrates, phosphates, and sulfates) for the development and growth of new plant producers. The decomposers are typically microscopic and occur in countless numbers. They exhibit a high degree of specialization; specific types of bacteria and specific kinds of fungi are involved in particular reactions in the total process of organic decomposition.

FOOD WEBS

In a biotic community, numerous food chains are interwoven in a complex *food web*. A food web may be defined as a network of interlocking food chains. A simple food web is shown in figure 44.2; many more species must be added even to approximate the complexity of food webs found in nature. It is axiomatic that the greater the diversity of species in a food web, the greater the stability of the food web.

A highly diversified biotic community is less vulnerable to disruptive influences. It may be compared roughly to an industrial organization that has diversified its products; depressed sales of one product can be offset by augmented sales of another product. If one herbivorous species in a heterogeneous biotic community should decline because of some adverse factor, another herbivorous species with comparable nutritional require-

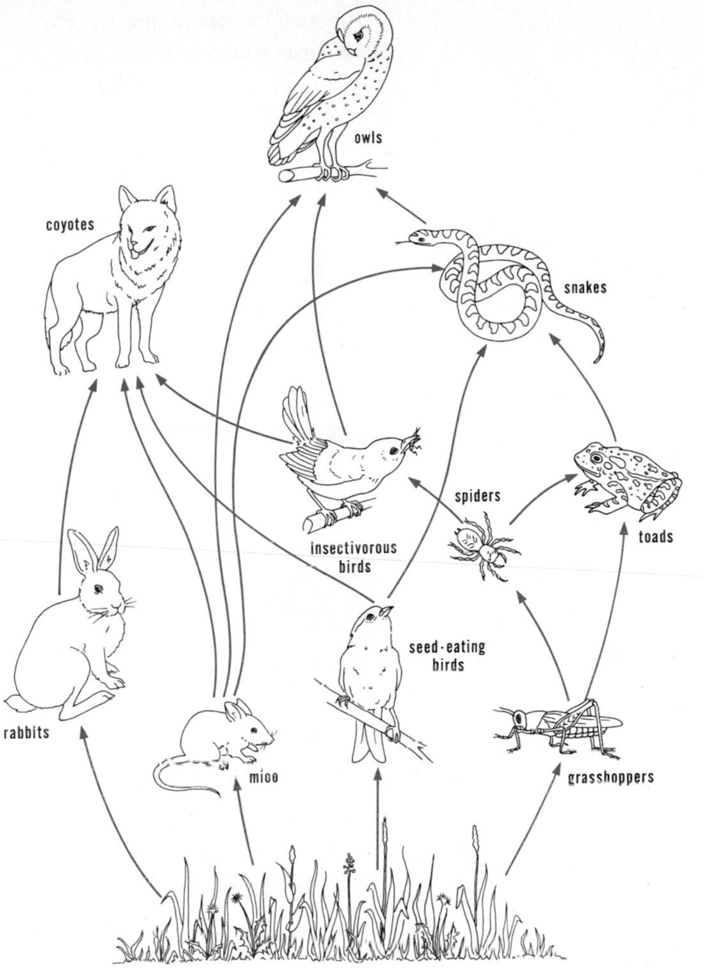

Figure 44.2 A simplified food web: an interlocking network of food chains. The greater the diversity of species in a food web, the greater the stability of the food web.

owls

coyotes

snakes

insectivorous birds

spiders

toads

rabbits

seed-eating birds

mice

grasshoppers

ments would most likely, in the resulting absence of direct competition, consume more of the common food sources. Accordingly, it can be expected that the same amount of harvest of the producers would be utilized. Moreover, the lowered numbers of the decimated herbivorous species would be augmented by the increased numbers of the flourishing herbivorous species. Carnivores (secondary consumers), which ordinarily would prey on limited numbers of both of these herbivores, would now devour greater numbers of the flourishing herbivorous species and thus have approximately the same level of nutrients available to them as before. Evidently, many interlocking food chains in a community permit compensatory adjustments and the maintenance of overall stability.

ENERGY FLOW

Organisms at successively higher trophic levels pass on to others less energy than they received (fig. 44.3). In other words, the organisms at one trophic level have available to them less energy for growth, reproduction, and self-maintenance than the organisms at the preceding level. This follows from the two basic laws of thermodynamics (see chapter 6). The *first law of thermodynamics* relates to the conservation of energy: energy on earth is neither created nor destroyed. Energy can be transformed from one form to another—from light energy to chemical energy to heat energy—and there is no net gain or loss in the total energy. As

Figure 44.3 Energy flow. At each step, an appreciable portion of the energy originally trapped by the producer is lost as heat. Accordingly, organisms in each trophic level pass on less energy than received.

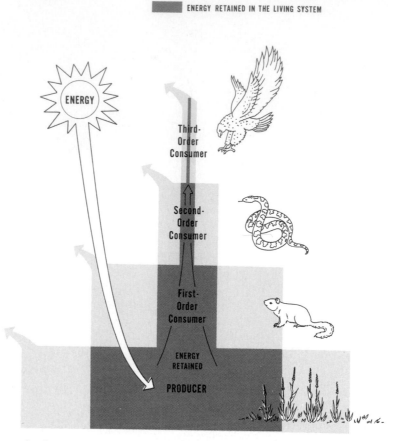

□ ENERGY LOST FROM THE LIVING SYSTEM

■ ENERGY RETAINED IN THE LIVING SYSTEM

ENERGY

Third-Order Consumer

Second-Order Consumer

First-Order Consumer

ENERGY RETAINED

PRODUCER

applied to living organisms, the *second law of thermodynamics* informs us that at each energy transformation, a certain proportion of the available energy is inevitably dissipated as heat. Although the total amount of energy for the earth remains constant, there is a progressive loss of useful, or usable, energy from lower to higher trophic levels. Thus, as previously mentioned, the flow of energy within a community is not cyclical but unidirectional.

Most of the solar radiation reaching the surface of the earth is absorbed or reflected into space. The plant physiologist E. I. Rabinowitch estimates that only 2 percent of the incoming solar energy is trapped by the leaves of green plants. Moreover, plants are less than 1 percent efficient in converting solar energy into chemical energy. With subsequent energy transformations in the community, only about 10 percent of the energy absorbed by one trophic level can be transmitted to the next trophic level. About 90 percent of the energy at a given level is lost through respiration or is not assimilated at all. Although carnivores tend to be more efficient than herbivores in using energy, it is generally conceded that the energy available to one trophic level averages one-tenth of the energy available to the preceding level. About 0.02 percent of the original energy fixed by the producers manages to reach the top carnivore at the highest trophic level.

Given these considerations, we find that the *biomass*, the total amount of living matter (in terms of total dry weight, or caloric value, or other measure), tends to decrease from lower to higher trophic levels (fig. 44.4). The top carnivores generally are individually larger but their numbers

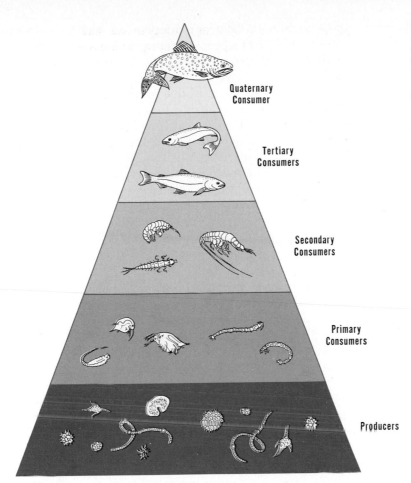

Quaternary Consumer

Tertiary Consumers

Secondary Consumers

Primary Consumers

Producers

Figure 44.4 Ecological pyramid in a lake. Plankton, the producers at the base of the pyramid, compose the greatest numbers of organisms. They support a smaller number of primary consumers. Successively higher levels of consumers decrease in numbers; the top consumer (lake trout, in this case), is least abundant. The total weight, or biomass, of a given organism is limited by the amount of energy received from the preceding level. The shorter the links in the food chain, the greater the total mass that the terminal species can attain.

are less abundant than organisms at preceding levels. It should be evident that the shorter the food chain, the greater the total mass that the terminal species can attain. A three-linked food chain, such as algae ⟶ minnow ⟶ bass, provides more energy for growth and reproduction to the bass population than the five-link chain, algae ⟶ crustacean ⟶ insect ⟶ minnow ⟶ bass. Stated another way, a given lake can support a larger bass population (more biomass) if it contains algae-eating minnows in the absence of insect-eating minnows.

HUMAN COMMUNITIES

The loss of energy at successive levels in a food chain has obvious implications for human population growth. We have seen that the most terminal member of an extensive food chain is least abundant in a population. One important factor contributing to the small population size of Eskimos is that they exist as top carnivores of a relatively elaborate food chain, as follows: marine algae ⟶ zooplankton ⟶ fish ⟶ seals ⟶ whales ⟶ man. In densely populated countries such as those in the Far East, man has intentionally eliminated the intermediate consumers and has reduced the food chain to its simplest terms: rice ⟶ man. Replacement of the herbivores (cow, sheep, or pig) circumvents the energy loss that ordinarily would occur between trophic levels.

Figure 44.5 illustrates an energy pyramid of a simple chain of food in a lake. If man were the only link in the plankton-man food chain, over a hundred times more energy would be available to him than he now receives as the terminal member of the more elaborate chain: plankton

Increasing Efficiency

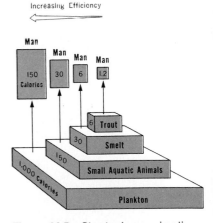

Figure 44.5 Shortening or simplifying the food chain would increase the amount of energy available to man, but at a risk of disturbing the natural stability of the food chain.

$\longrightarrow$ small aquatic animal (for example, copepods) $\longrightarrow$ smelt $\longrightarrow$ trout $\longrightarrow$ man. For this reason, research has been directed in recent years to cultivating the single-celled alga *Chlorella* in a controlled manner in the laboratory. However, practical algal culture on a large scale for food purposes is still a vague hope rather than a present reality.

In shortening or simplifying the food chains in nature, man has increased the efficiency of energy utilization for himself. However, this has been done at the risk of disturbing the natural stability of the food chain. A short food chain is especially susceptible to an ecologic catastrophe. With a food chain oversimplified to its barest components (rice $\longrightarrow$ man), any interruption (such as the destruction of the rice crop by disease and erratic monsoons) would abruptly decimate the *whole* chain. We have already commented on the continual battle against hunger and malnutrition in the underdeveloped countries because of their dependence on primarily one crop. The world would like to forget the food famines of recent times in India, and also the starvation and malnutrition in Ireland in the 1840s, when blight (a plant disease caused by a fungus) destroyed the main staple, the potato. Yet, even today in economically advanced countries such as the United States, farmers in the central Midwest have been encouraged to plant but one or two crops over vast areas.

The potential for increasing the world's food supply by cultivating the open oceans is limited. Just as high-yield varieties of rice and wheat have required enormous amounts of industrial fertilizers, greater growth of plankton and fish would entail a tremendous investment of nutrient salts. Moreover, the marine fishes of economic importance to man occupy the higher trophic levels, which are subject to the reduction in energy that the second law of thermodynamics upholds. To obtain more food from the sea would require an oversimplification of the food chain—the removal of zooplankton and small fish. Then man would be placed in more direct competition with the birds, whales, and seals. Most likely, gross instability of the marine community would ensue; man has already demonstrated his capabilities in causing the demise, or near-extinction, of one of the higher members of the marine pyramid, the blue whale. As a result of commercial exploitation, the blue whale population is but a small remnant—now less than 600—of a once great assemblage. Moreover, when the population density becomes too low, the chance meeting and mating of a bull and cow becomes increasingly unlikely. Several years ago, the International Whaling Commission, represented by many nations, voted into effect a worldwide ban on the killing of blue whales. Despite our highest resolve and best collective efforts, nations have persisted in the hunting of the blue whale.

SUMMARY

A biotic community is an organized assemblage of different, mutually dependent species. Nutrients (energy) flow through a succession of different organisms (food chain) in the community. The producers are green plants that convert the energy of the sun into stored chemical energy. Functionally, producers occupy the first trophic level of the community. Plant components are consumed by herbivores (second trophic level), herbivores by carnivores (third trophic level), and carnivores by other carnivores (fourth and higher trophic levels). Decomposer organisms (bacteria and fungi) degrade the organic wastes and the remains of plants and animals in the food chain, converting them to chemical elements in the soil that can again be utilized by green plants.

The stored chemical energy of green plants is gradually consumed by metabolism through the food chain and dissipated as heat. As a result, there is less energy and less biomass in the higher trophic levels than in the lower ones. The longer the food chain, the less energy there is available for the terminal members.

A biotic community with a great diversity of interacting species is more stable than a community with relatively few species. When man intentionally eliminates intermediate consumers, thereby maximizing the energy flow passing to him, he does so at the risk of disturbing the natural stability of communities. Biotic communities with shortened or simplified food chains are especially vulnerable to ecologic catastrophes.

Ethical Probe 25
Do Whales Have a Future?

Many species of whales are being overexploited. Marine conservationists estimate that one whale is killed every 12 minutes. Most "great" whales—such as the 100-foot blue and the fin whales—have been reduced drastically in numbers. The smaller "great" whales—the sei and the 30-foot minke—are also declining markedly as a result of indiscriminate hunting. At the United Nations Conference on Human Environment at Stockholm in 1972, the conferees voted in favor of a 10-year moratorium on the killing of all "great" whales. The 10-year period would enable the populations of most whale species to recover.

No conservation measure has been acceptable to Russia and Japan. These two marine-oriented countries are economically dependent on pelagic whaling, and presently harvest more than two million tons of protein per year for their own immediate gain. Does the extermination of the most intelligent of marine mammals justify the economy these mammals feed? Aside from the purely biological misgivings of witnessing the extermination of a graceful animal and the disruption of a marine ecosystem, is it acceptable that only two countries monopolize a resource that should be the common heritage of all nations? Is it reasonable to continue to use these valuable mammals for lipsticks and lubricating engine oils?

45 The Ecosystem

We have seen that plants and animals form highly organized and remarkably efficient communities. We generally think of communities in terms of their living, or biotic, components. However, organisms do not exist apart from their chemical and physical environment. Trees cannot be separated from the air that surrounds them or from the water and minerals in the soil. To express the fact that the living (biotic) and the nonliving (chemicophysical) components make up a natural entity or ecological system, the British ecologist Sir Arthur George Tansley in 1935 proposed the useful term *ecosystem*. The ecosystem brings together the community of animals and plants and also the chemical and physical components of the immediate environment in which the community exists. The ecosystem is a self-contained unit characterized by an orderly flow of energy and materials between the organisms and their environment.

Not only is man part of the various ecosystems of the world, but he has come to exert a dominant influence on all of them. His attitude and actions are oriented toward monopolizing and manipulating other species of organisms and exploiting the environment as well. He views nature as existing for no other reason than to serve his wants and needs. He has managed to disturb or stress many of the components of various ecosystems. The disturbance of one component of an ecosystem almost invariably results in changes, often unwelcome, in other aspects of the system.

COMPONENTS OF THE ECOSYSTEM

Figure 45.1 portrays the essential features of a pine forest ecosystem. Despite its apparent complexity, four basic components may be recognized in the ecosystem: producer organisms, consumer organisms, decomposer organisms, and abiotic substances. Although we have previously considered the biotic components, we may reexamine briefly the functional roles of the varied kinds of organisms. The producers are the green plants that convert the flow of solar energy into stored chemical energy. Since the producers can trap light energy and manufacture carbohydrates from simple inorganic substances, they are said to be *autotrophic* (self-nourishing). The organic materials synthesized by the plants are utilized, directly or indirectly, by the consumers. The consumers are *heterotrophic* (other-nourishing), lacking the ability to manufacture their own organic nutrients.

The organisms of decay are the decomposers, the bacteria and fungi that break down the complex compounds of dead plants and animals. Their nutrition is termed *saprophytic* (*sapros,* "rotten") since they live

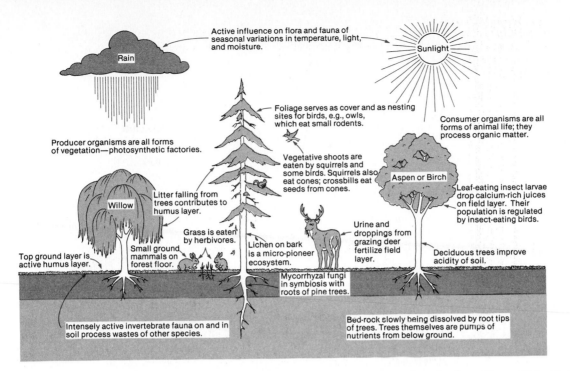

Within the illustration:

Active influence on flora and fauna of seasonal variations in temperature, light, and moisture.

Rain

Sunlight

Foliage serves as cover and as nesting sites for birds, e.g., owls, which eat small rodents.

Consumer organisms are all forms of animal life; they process organic matter.

Producer organisms are all forms of vegetation—photosynthetic factories.

Vegetative shoots are eaten by squirrels and some birds. Squirrels also eat cones; crossbills eat seeds from cones.

Aspen or Birch

Leaf-eating insect larvae drop calcium-rich juices on field layer. Their population is regulated by insect-eating birds.

Willow

Litter falling from trees contributes to humus layer.

Grass is eaten by herbivores.

Lichen on bark is a micro-pioneer ecosystem.

Urine and droppings from grazing deer fertilize field layer.

Deciduous trees improve acidity of soil.

Top ground layer is active humus layer.

Small ground mammals on forest floor.

Mycorrhyzal fungi in symbiosis with roots of pine trees.

Intensely active invertebrate fauna on and in soil process wastes of other species.

Bed-rock slowly being dissolved by root tips of trees. Trees themselves are pumps of nutrients from below ground.

on dead or decaying organic matter. These organisms return chemicals to the soil, water, or air, from which these chemicals become available again as vital nutrients for the green plants. These chemicals are the *abiotic substances,* which include a wide array of basic elements such as carbon, nitrogen, hydrogen, oxygen, sulfur, and phosphorus. Chemicals in an ecosystem flow continually between the organisms and the environment in circular pathways that are known as *biogeochemical cycles* (bio for "life," geo signifying "earth, ground, soil," and *chemical,* pertaining to the composition of substances). Chemicals pass back and forth in an ecosystem, whereas energy follows a one-way route into and out of the system. It may be recalled that energy cannot be transferred from one organism to another without some of the energy at each transfer being dispersed into unavailable heat energy.

BIOGEOCHEMICAL CYCLES

Approximately 92 elements of the chemist's periodic table occur in nature. About 40 elements are known to be required by living organisms, of which the following are of paramount importance: carbon, hydrogen, oxygen, nitrogen, sulfur, phosphorus, sodium, potassium, calcium, magnesium, iron, manganese, cobalt, copper, and zinc. Our attention here will be restricted to the cyclic passage of carbon, nitrogen, sulfur, and phosphorus.

The main features of the carbon cycle are shown in figure 45.2. Carbon exists in the atmosphere primarily as gaseous carbon dioxide (CO_2), in which form it is used by land plants as an essential raw material in the synthesis of carbohydrates. Carbon dioxide reenters the atmosphere through the respiratory activities of both plants and animals and by the decomposition of waste materials and dead organic matter in the soil. Carbon dioxide is also assimilated by aquatic plants (phytoplankton) in the oceans, and the decomposition of organic material releases carbon dioxide back into solution. Carbon dioxide is dissolved in the ocean

Figure 45.1 Highly simplified illustration of integration within the comparatively simple pine forest ecosystem. (From F. F. Darling and R. F. Dasmann, in *Impact of science on society,* vol. 19, No. 2, 1969. By permission of UNESCO; © UNESCO 1969.)

Figure 45.2 The carbon cycle in the ecosystem. (From R. L. Smith, *Ecology and field biology*, 2d ed, 1974. Copyright © 1974 by R. L. Smith. Reprinted by permission of Harper & Row, Publishers.)

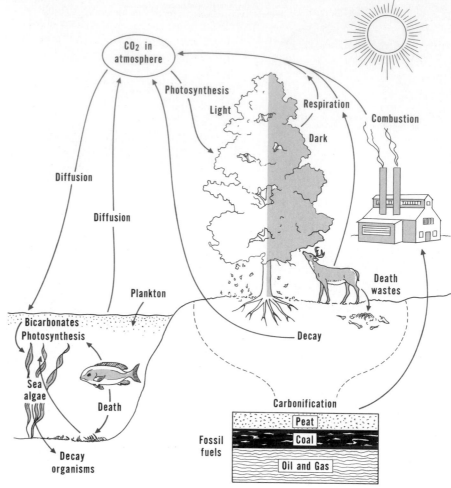

waters in the form of the bicarbonate ion (HCO_3^-). The total world ocean contains approximately 60 times as much CO_2 as the atmosphere.

Only a small percentage of the earth's carbon actually circulates in the atmosphere. Most of the carbon is locked in the earth's crust as organic fossil deposits—chiefly oil shale, coal, and petroleum—that have accumulated over millions of years. Beginning with the industrial revolution, man has increasingly burned large amounts of these fossil fuels. In the United States alone, the equivalent of 1.9 billion tons of fossil fuels is now combusted each year (representing 30 percent of the world's consumption). The worldwide demand for energy is growing at such a rate—an estimated doubling every 15 years—that many regard this situation as the world's most basic economic problem. From a biological standpoint, the accelerated combustion of fossil fuels implies continued increases in the amount of carbon dioxide in the atmosphere. The atmosphere CO_2 concentration has been steadily increasing since 1958 at an average rate of 0.2 percent per year. The prediction is that the amount of CO_2 in the atmosphere will rise from its present value of 330 ppm to 400 ppm by the year 2000.

The long-term consequences of anticipated increases in atmospheric CO_2 continue to be debated. One possible effect is the warming of the earth's surface. Since carbon dioxide molecules have the property of absorbing or trapping the infrared (heat) radiation of the sun, the temperature on the earth's surface rises from the trapped radiation. A potentially serious consequence of increased warming of the earth's surface would be the melting of the polar ice caps. This would drastically raise the sea levels, with the outcome that vast coastal areas of the world would be inundated or flooded. However, through human activities, a variety of extraneous particulate matter has been added to the atmosphere. Ironically, man's pollution of the atmosphere tends to counteract the effect of carbon dioxide. Smoke, dust, and particulate matter in the atmosphere increases the atmosphere's reflectivity of solar radiation. In other words, smoke and particulates scatter heat radiation and thereby reduce the amount of heat energy absorbed by the earth's surface. The outcome thus is a cooling of the earth's surface.

Human activities have also affected the cyclic pathways of nitrogen through the ecosystem (fig. 45.3). Nitrogen is essential to the life processes of organisms, occurring in such compounds as chlorophyll, hemoglobin, insulin, and DNA. Although the atmosphere consists of 78 percent nitrogen gas (N_2), green plants in their syntheses cannot make direct use of the free atmospheric nitrogen. Nitrogen is taken up by plants in the form of the ammonium ion (NH_4^+) or nitrate (NO_3^-), the latter being derived from the oxidation of ammonium. Specialized microorganisms, the *nitrogen-fixing bacteria*, accomplish the conversion, or fixation, of atmospheric nitrogen into nitrates. *Fixation* means that nitrogen is incorporated, or combined, in a chemical compound that can be used by plants. Some nitrogen-fixing bacteria are free-living in the soil; others live symbiotically in nodules in the roots of leguminous plants (such as the pea plant). When nitrates are released into the soil, the green plants absorb these salts through their roots. The fixed nitrogen is incorporated in the protein molecules distinctive to the green plants. When animals consume the plants, the plant proteins are converted into amino acids and the latter are built up into proteins characteristic of the particular animal. It should be noted (fig. 45.3) that nitrogen fixation is a two-way street, since certain types of soil bacteria (*denitrifying bacteria*) return nitrogen to its atmospheric form by breaking down nitrates.

Through death and bacterial action, the nitrogenous compounds of plants and animals (chiefly amino acids) are decomposed, or converted, to ammonium ions. The process is called *ammonification*, and is accomplished by the action of a wide variety of *ammonifying bacteria*. The ammonium ion is oxidized to nitrite (NO_2^-) by *nitrite bacteria*, and the nitrite further oxidized to nitrate (NO_3^-) by *nitrate bacteria*. The series of reactions by which the ammonium ion is transformed to nitrate has been termed *nitrification*. Soluble nitrates, such as potassium nitrate and calcium nitrate, are absorbed directly by plants and involved once again in protein synthesis.

The nitrogen cycle exemplifies most biogeochemical cycles in revealing the necessity for a variety of highly specialized species of bacteria. It has been said that the removal of merely a dozen species of bacteria involved in the nitrogen cycle could lead to the extinction of all life on earth. Nitrogen is fixed into nitrates by man's industrial processes as well as by bacteria. A discouraging problem is that industrially fixed nitrate fertilizers are carried by groundwater into lakes, where the increased nitrate concentrations may contribute to an undesirable increase in algal growth. The industrial activities of man also affect the nitrogen

Figure 45.3 The nitrogen cycle in the ecosystem. (From R. L. Smith, *Ecology and field biology*, 2d ed, 1974. Copyright © 1974 by R. L. Smith. Reprinted by permission of Harper & Row, Publishers.)

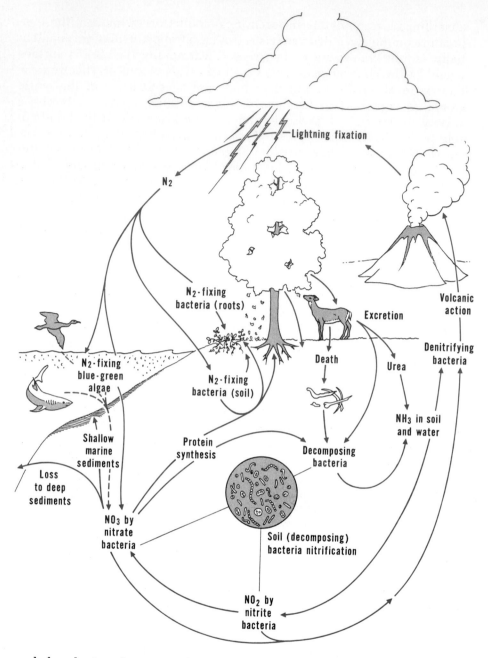

cycle by placing about 20 million tons of nitrogen dioxide (NO_2) annually in the atmosphere. Nitrogen dioxide, as an air pollutant, is a key substance in the photochemical production of smog (see chapter 46).

Sulfur (S) is an important constituent of certain amino acids, such as methionine, cystine, and cysteine. Sulfur atoms also contribute to the three-dimensional integrity of a protein molecule by bonding, or linking, one segment of the protein molecule to another. Sulfur is taken up by plants in the form of sulfate ions (SO_4^-); if such ions are deficient in the soil, plant growth is conspicuously stunted. The sulfur-containing proteins in plants and animals are degraded to hydrogen sulfide (H_2S) by a variety of soil bacteria, and the highly toxic H_2S is then converted to sulfates by sulfur-oxidizing bacteria. Sulfate-reducing bacteria transform sulfates to hydrogen sulfide. Sulfur exists as an impurity in fossil fuels, and sulfur dioxide (SO_2) is one of the unwelcome by-products of the combustion of coal and oil. Some 6 million tons of sulfur are released annually to the atmosphere by the industrial burning of fossil fuels in the United States alone. High atmospheric concentrations of SO_2 have been held responsible for the 3,000 to 4,000 deaths during the great London smog of December 1952 (see chapter 46).

Like nitrogen and sulfur, organic phosphorus is made available to plants through the action of soil bacteria, which transform some of the organic phosphorus into soluble phosphate compounds (for example, $CaHPO_4$). However, it is of especial interest that much of the phosphorus in the soil occurs largely as *insoluble* phosphate salts of calcium, aluminum, and iron, which cannot be used as such by plants. Thus, most of the earth's phosphorus is immobilized or locked up in the form of insoluble phosphate rocks. Through erosion of the rocks, phosphorus finds its way into lakes and the ocean, where it becomes precipitated to the bottom sediment and becomes largely unavailable and unrecoverable. Thus, phosphorus, unlike most elements, is essentially a nonrenewable resource and is often a limiting factor in the productivity of many ecosystems.

Man has artificially recovered phosphorus and has returned it to the soil for plant use by mining phosphatic rock and preparing phosphate fertilizers. However, the amounts of phosphorus that are lost to the ocean sediments are much greater than the phosphorus inputs to the soil as a result of man's activities. Additionally, the major part of phosphorus added as fertilizer is not efficiently used since, once again, most of the added phosphorus is rapidly bound and immobilized as rocks by calcium, aluminum, and iron. Concern has been voiced that if the world population grows at an annual rate of 2 percent and if the use of phosphate fertilizers continues to increase at a rate of 5 percent annually, then the known supply and reserves of phosphorus will be used up in 90 years. A workshop of scientists on "Global Ecological Problems" in 1971 recommended, among other things, that nations should reduce the ratio of phosphates to nitrates in fertilizers so as to conserve phosphorus and that the uses of phosphorus for purposes other than fertilizers (in the preparation of phosphate detergents, for example) should be sharply curtailed. The high phosphate content of detergents has been a contributing factor in the pollution of lakes.

ECOSYSTEM HOMEOSTASIS

The functioning of a pine forest, or any other natural ecosystem, depends on the breakdown of the organic remains and the turnover of chemical materials so that they can reenter the system. There is no waste in a natural ecosystem. The organic products of any one species are the raw materials of other species. Each constituent organism is important. There is a balanced interplay among the producers, consumers, and decomposers. The ecosystem as a whole tends to be balanced and self-contained. A *homeostatic* condition exists in an ecosystem. Faced with disturbing conditions, the ecosystem can self-regulate. However, there are limits in its capacity to adjust and to endure.

The capacity of an ecosystem to adapt to an environmental catastrophe (such as fire or drought) or to a sudden increase in numbers of one species is largely a function of its diversity. The greater the diversity of species, the greater the stability of the ecosystem. When, for example, a given species (a particular insect, for example) begins to multiply excessively and assume pest proportions, the outbreak of that species will tend to be controlled by a natural predator of that species—if, and only if, the ecosystem is diverse enough to contain the suitable predator species in the food chain or web. In the absence of species diversity, the ecosystem is vulnerable to a disturbing change and may be unable to adjust to the change. As a striking example, Australia became drastically and massively colonized by rabbits primarily because there were no effective predators. The Australian ecosystem remained markedly unstable for many years until man intervened by inoculating rabbits with a deadly virus (see chapter 32). In this case, man's action was beneficent; more often than not, however, man adversely disturbs the internal self-regulation of ecosystems.

In his agricultural practices, man has impaired the natural regulatory capacities of several ecosystems. He has replaced stable natural communities of several thousand species with monocultures of a single crop plant. He has deliberately eliminated all competitors and predatory species from his chosen plants. He eliminates rabbits in his carrot patch, birds in his cornfield, and rodents in his wheat fields. Weed plants, which are part of the balance of nature, are destroyed by chemical herbicides, and insect pests are controlled by insecticides. In an ecological sense, man as a cultivator of nature has represented a catastrophe in that he has created instability by decreasing the complexity of the ecosystem. The more he has reduced the number of species in his managed ecosystem, the more unstable the system has become. As a consequence of limited species diversity, greater opportunity is provided for certain species to multiply rapidly and reach pest and disease proportions. Now, in the absence of natural enemies to check the uncontrolled growth of the pests, man's only alternative is to employ still more and stronger chemicals to control the pest. And certain pesticides, such as DDT, have been found to be extremely toxic to most forms of life, including man (see chapter 46).

Man has conspicuously reduced the productive potential of the land by removing the topsoil faster than it can be formed by the natural erosion of rocks. To open areas for grazing by his domestic herds, he has drastically reduced the populations of bisons, wolves, and coyotes. He has also permitted his domestic cattle to overgraze the land, so much so that several annual plants in many localities have been unable to reseed themselves.

Additional problems in ecological management also become evident whenever man congregates into villages, towns, and cities. In these centers, there develop great accumulations of organic debris—the body wastes and food scraps of human activities. The heavy load of waste products is generally beyond the capabilities of a natural ecosystem. In particular, domestic and industrial wastes are flushed into a river or lake, and the added vast quantities of nutrient material serve only to overtax the aquatic ecosystem. The consequences of such an overload are vividly exemplified by the deterioration of Lake Erie.

DETERIORATION OF A GREAT LAKE
More than one-third of America's 100,000 lakes now show signs of unnatural stress as direct or indirect consequences of man's activities (fig. 45.4). One of these, Lake Erie, has deteriorated so severely that many valued fishes—lake herring, blue pike, whitefish, and sturgeon, among others—that once thrived in the cool bottom waters have declined pre-

cipitously. All lakes tend to become filled with sediments and become affected with overgrowth of bloom-forming algae with the passage of time. The natural process of the accumulation of nutrients and aging of a lake has been termed *eutrophication*. The term (Greek, *eutrophia*, "well nourished") was intended to suggest that a lake matures or ages with excessive nourishment. A pristine lake is said to be *oligotrophic* (underfed) and a lake in its prime of life is *mesotrophic* (moderately fed). The terms are important if only to impress on us that a lake (like any ecosystem) does alter its character with time. But Lake Erie has aged prematurely by many thousands of years in only the past few decades. Man, the world's greatest waste producer, has enormously accelerated the normal process of eutrophication; today, the unsightly lake is at a stage it should have not reached before A.D. 95,000.

Lake Erie became threatened when the human population mushroomed in its immediate vicinity. In the late 1700s, 10,000 persons had settled on the shores of Lake Erie. At that time, the lake water was clear throughout the year and free of blooms of algae, and it supported a large population of cold-water fishes. At present, approximately 13 million people, about one-twentieth of the whole United States population, are concentrated in its watershed. As people congregated and industry grew, the problems of waste disposal intensified. The extensive dumping of domestic sewage and household detergents, combined with the discharge of agricultural and industrial wastes, has given the lake the unenviable reputation of being the most polluted large body of water in the world. The lake essentially became precociously overproductive; the once clear water became murky green as algae thrived and fishes perished.

When large quantities of untreated sewage are added to an aquatic ecosystem, the biogeochemical cycle is disturbed or stressed. Raw, untreated sewage represents a massive input of degradable organic substances. The organic substances are transformed into inorganic salts by decomposers, the bacteria of decay. Several bacterial species utilize the available dissolved oxygen for degrading (oxidizing) the organic matter. The expression *biochemical oxygen demand*, or BOD, is used by microbiologists to designate the oxygen-consuming property of samples of waste water or, indirectly, the amount of organic matter in the water. The BOD serves as a measure of organic pollution; a high BOD value indicates large amounts of degradable organic materials.

Oxygen in lake water normally comes from two sources: the photosynthesis by plants in the water and the exchange of atmospheric gases at the surface of the water. However, oxygen, because of its low solubility in water, often becomes a limiting factor within the lake. When large amounts of organic matter are dumped into a lake, the aerobic metabolism of the bacterial decomposers can lead to a depletion of oxygen. The lake, particularly during warm weather, then becomes stratified into upper, aerobic, and lower, anaerobic, layers. Colder, dense water sinks to the bottom, and cold-water fishes that seek the bottom water die from lack of oxygen. It is thus no accident that many valued cold-water fishes in Lake Erie—lake trout, herring, whitefish, and blue pike—have succumbed. Only hardy fishes such as the blueheads and bluegills can live in the warm surface waters.

Oxygen loss in Lake Erie continued to persist despite man's endeavor to reduce the BOD by treating the sewage. Most waste treatment systems involve two phases: *primary* treatment, designed to remove large objects (wooden and metallic trash), and *secondary* treatment, designed

Figure 45.4 Dead fish decomposing along the shore of one of the Great Lakes. (From P. K. Anderson, *Omega: murder of the ecosystem and suicide of man*, 1971, Wm. C. Brown Company Publishers.)

to degrade organic materials. Secondary treatment simulates the action of bacteria in an aquatic ecosystem; varied populations of aerobic bacteria acclimated to grow in the disposal plant convert the organic materials to inorganic substances. After secondary treatment, the residue is discharged into the lake, and theoretically, the outflow material should not tax the oxygen supply in the lake water. However, the effluent from the treatment systems contains two important minerals, nitrate and phosphate, which result from the bacterial degradation of the secondary treatment. The effluent is richer in phosphates than in nitrates, since a major portion of the nitrate in the waste water has been denitrified in the process of secondary treatment. The phosphates and nitrates serve as nutrients for the growth of algae, particularly blue-green algae. The enhanced growth of algae contributes to an even greater demand for oxygen, with disastrous consequences.

The microscopic, one-celled blue-green algae require the same nutrients—nitrates and phosphates—as grass in lawns. When the algae are enriched, or fertilized, they flourish. The result is the appearance, typically during the summer, of massive algal blooms, or scums, floating on the surface. Thick, soggy mats of algae wash up on the beach to choke the shoreline (plate 21). The lake has become overnourished, or eutrophic. Since man has been the agent for adding the excess nutrients, the process has been appropriately termed *cultural eutrophication*. In recent years, sewage has become an even more effective fertilizer for the blue-green algae because of the large quantities of phosphate-containing detergents in waste water.

Literally billions of algae die and rot because the microscopic animals (zooplankton) that feed on algae cannot keep the algal growth in check. The decaying algal organic matter sinks to the bottom, where it becomes so abundant that it exhausts the dissolved oxygen from the bottom water. Scarcely any bottom fish can survive under these extreme conditions. In the absence of oxygen, anaerobic bacteria degrade the bottom organic slime, producing hydrogen sulfide and other noxious compounds as a result. Uncontrolled, the lake ultimately deteriorates into a marsh, dense with weeds.

Evidently, to save a lake, ways must be developed to eliminate or drastically reduce the nutrient compounds from the waste products. The paramount consideration is the management of phosphate, since this nutrient is the principal limiting factor for the growth of algae in oligotrophic lakes. Stated another way, algal productivity is low in an unenriched lake primarily because the water is relatively deficient in phosphorous. Concerted efforts have been made to reverse the process of cultural eutrophication in several regions of the United States. An additional third-stage, or *tertiary*, treatment of sewage has mitigated the problem in some areas.

Wise management policies call for greater cooperative international, or across-the-boundary, attitudes and actions. In recent years, both the United States and Canada have promoted programs to abate nutrient loading in Lake Erie from municipal sewerage and detergents. In April 1972, the United States and Canada signed a water quality agreement; if this program is adequately funded, the important animal life in Lake Erie may be restored. Full restoration of the historical fish communities, however, is most unlikely, if only for the reason that the currently established large populations of freshwater fish (carp, drumfish, and goldfish) probably would constrain the ascendancy of reintroduced species such as the blue pike, lake herring, and lake whitefish.

SUMMARY

When we add the chemical and physical components of the environment to the biotic community, we have an *ecosystem*, a self-regulating unit in which there is an orderly exchange of materials between the living and nonliving components. Key elements, such as carbon, hydrogen, oxygen, nitrogen, phosphorus, and sulfur, flow continuously between organisms and the nonliving environment in circular pathways known as *biogeochemical cycles*. Whereas energy follows a one-way route into and out of an ecosystem, chemicals are conserved and recycled in the system.

Ecosystems tend to be self-contained and balanced, but there are limits in their capacity to self-regulate when disturbed. Many natural ecosystems have been significantly modified by man's activities. In manipulating agricultural ecosystems for food production, man has replaced stable natural communities of many interacting species with a few strains of crops. He maintains his managed agricultural ecosystems in a productive state only by loading them with the products of chemical technology—fertilizers, pesticides, and weedicides.

Man extracts materials from the environment, processes them, and returns them as waste. He has overtaxed aquatic ecosystems by adding vast quantities of domestic and industrial wastes to rivers and lakes. The organic wastes cause an overload on the bacterial decomposers, resulting in the depletion of oxygen and the death of many valued cold-water fishes. Excessive nutrients (particularly phosphates) released from sewage treatment plants overnourish the lake, leading to a devastating cycle of increased algal growth, death and decomposition of the profuse algae, oxygen demand, and the accumulation of bottom organic slime.

Ethical Probe 26
Organic Chemicals in the Environment

The immense growth of the chemical industry during the past two decades has led to a massive increase in the production of organic chemicals, both in terms of volume and range of synthetic compounds. The variety of organic chemicals include methanol, ethanol, glycol ethers, chlorofluorocarbons, organic pesticides, and detergents. It is estimated that 20 million tons of manufactured organic chemicals pour into the environment annually. The potential danger of these man-made chemicals depends on the extent and rapidity with which they are biodegraded by microorganisms. Bacterial species are able to degrade a wide range of chemicals, and can decompose most manufactured organic molecules that occur as well in nature. Many of the organic compounds are broken down so rapidly that there is little risk of toxic concentrations. The cause for concern are those new synthetic compounds that are not known in nature, and for which the microorganisms have yet to successfully utilize as nutrients.

Examples of compounds that do not occur in nature are the chlorofluorocarbons (once widely used in aerosol propellants) and polybrominated biphenyl, or PBB (once widely used as an industrial fire retardant for plastics). These organic compounds are exceedingly stable, and there is no evidence that they can be metabolized by microorganisms. The degradation-resistant synthetic chemicals may enter food chains and produce unforseen adverse effects. In fact, traces of PBB are still being found in cattle, milk, and humans in certain localities.

Should the manufacture of all degradation-resistant chemicals be banned? Should their manufacture be continued, with careful monitoring of the quantities that enter the environment? Should their manufacture be continued unabated, with the knowledge that species in the microbial community have the ability to adapt eventually to the new organic nutrients?

46 Man's Modification of the Environment

Figure 46.1 Wastes of consumption of a growing human population. (From P. K. Anderson, *Omega: murder of the ecosystem and suicide of man,* 1971, Wm. C. Brown Company Publishers.)

In natural ecosystems, organic and mineral nutrients are reused, or recycled, by the coordinated actions of living organisms. This is in sharp contrast to the actions of man in his modern technological world. He draws on the natural resources and shapes them into consumer goods with great facility. With equal facility and abandon, however, he consigns the wastes of manufacture and consumption to the air, rivers, dumps, and junkyards (fig. 46.1). Man plays the role of a spoiled disposer —he takes the raw materials, reshapes and uses them, and then releases the toxic wastes into the environment (plate 18). The outcome has been massive contamination of the air, water, and soils with his waste products, by-products, and spillovers. As the population increases, the accompanying increases in consumption of resources and production of wastes only intensify the pollution problem.

Man can ultimately preserve his environment by ensuring the recycling of resources. All materials—paper, aluminum, plastics, liquids, solid wastes—should be processed through the human economic production system in the same way that basic elements in nature are conserved and recycled through the natural ecosystem. The flow of materials must be a complete cycle, not the one-way dumping process that characterizes man's present actions and behavior. Man's future existence is not threatened by any species except his own.

AIR POLLUTION

The thin envelope of air that surrounds the earth is roughly 78 percent nitrogen, 21 percent oxygen, 1 percent of other gases—inert gases (mostly argon), carbon dioxide, methane, and hydrogen—and small, but variable amounts of water vapor (moisture). For centuries man has discharged other gases as well as extraneous particulate matter into the atmosphere. A steel mill releases sulfur-containing compounds, particularly sulfur dioxide (SO_2), to the atmosphere; a paint factory discharges hydrocarbons; and the exhaust of an automobile pours toxic carbon monoxide, nitrogen oxides, and lead particles into the air (plate 19). Man rarely has considered the consequences of his actions. Paul K. Anderson of the University of Calgary in Canada has aptly stated:

> We indulge in a surprising degree of idealism with respect to release of substances of all sorts into the biosphere. Any chemical thus released is considered innocent of all ill effects until proven guilty. Along the same lines, the courts of law often refuse to consider claims for pollution damage unless *economic loss* can be demonstrated.

On many mornings in Los Angeles and other metropolises in the world, a veil of hazy air overhangs the city (fig. 46.2). The air is heavily laden with carbon monoxide, hydrocarbons, oxides of nitrogen (NO and NO_2),

540

and such particulate matter as soot (tiny particles of carbon), pollen, and dust. These pollutants, spewed largely by automobiles, interact with sunlight to produce smog. In particular, hydrocarbons react with nitric oxides in the presence of sunlight to yield photochemical smog. One of the end products of this reaction, produced in the atmosphere, is ozone (O_3). In a city like Los Angeles, which is flanked by mountains, smog is trapped in the basin by a *temperature inversion*. Normally, warm air at ground level rises and is dispersed upward; the atmosphere becomes cooler with increasing altitude. During a temperature inversion, a layer of warm air settles above the city, overlies the ascending cooler air below, and effectively prevents the ground-level air from rising.

Most, if not all, of the ingredients of smog are health hazards. The colorless, odorless carbon monoxide (CO) competes with oxygen for bonding sites on the hemoglobin molecule in the blood. In fact, carbon monoxide binds to hemoglobin more efficiently than does oxygen. Nitric oxide (NO) also reduces the oxygen-carrying capacity of the blood. Ozone, singly or in combination with other pollutants, may contribute to, or precipitate, such diseases as bronchitis, pulmonary emphysema, asthma, and hardening of the arteries. It also causes extensive damage to trees, fruits, vegetables, and ornamental flowers.

The great London smog of December 1952 awakened interest in the dangers of air pollution. In this case, the source of smog was the excessive burning of soft coal with a high sulfur content. In the winter of 1952, severe cold weather brought on the increased consumption of coal. The worst of the smogs blanketed London on December 5. For five consecutive days, the city's normal daily death rate of 300 tripled. That winter, some 4,000 deaths in excess of the numbers considered normal for the period were ascribed to smog. Subsequent smogs in the following winters also took their toll. In 1956, Parliament passed a Clean Air Act, which prohibited the burning of soft, high-sulfur coal in factories and homes in critical areas of the city. The use of less smoky fuels—hard coal, low-sulfur oil, gas, or electricity—was prescribed. Although there have been economic repercussions since low-sulfur fuels are costly, London's air has become clearer and healthier.

Soft coal combustion results in the discharge of large quantities of sulfur into the atmosphere, largely in the form of sulfur dioxide (SO_2). This gas reacts with moisture in the air to form droplets of sulfuric acid (H_2SO_4), which are strongly corrosive. Mists of sulfuric acid droplets damage many materials, including metals, building stones, marble monuments, and clothing (fig. 46.3). Both SO_2 and H_2SO_4 are harshly irritating to the tissues of the respiratory tract.

Figure 46.2 Air pollution. *Top:* Aerial view of Los Angeles on a clear day in 1956. *Middle:* a dramatic example of a temperature inversion; a layer of warm air settles over the city, preventing the ground-level air from rising. *Bottom:* The trapped smoggy air accumulates rapidly, blanketing the city. (Courtesy of the Air Pollution Control District of the County of Los Angeles.)

Figure 46.3 Monument to pollution. Wind-driven chemicals have eaten away the statue of Alexander Hamilton in Washington, D.C. (Photographed in 1966. Courtesy of the United States Environmental Protection Agency.)

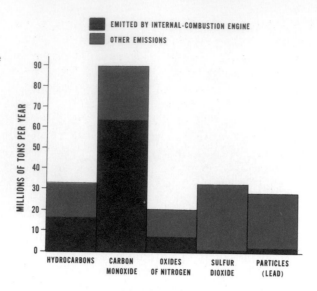

Comparatively little sulfur dioxide originates from the operation of gasoline-burning internal combustion engines. Gasoline-driven automobiles, however, contribute the major portions of atmospheric carbon monoxide, unburned hydrocarbons, and oxides of nitrogen (fig. 46.4). More than 60 percent of the air pollution in the United States is derived from the exhaust pipes of automobiles. Possible replacements for the internal combustion engine include the steam (external combustion) engine, the diesel engine, and the exhaust-free electric engine. Each of these engines would produce appreciably less air pollution than does the internal combustion engine. However, widespread adoption of a non-polluting engine would necessitate a radical shift in economic philosophy. The use of the electric vehicle, for example, would occasion a large increase in electric power requirements and the building of many more generating plants. It has been said that the conversion of the world's several million petroleum-powered automobiles to electricity would be a severe economic trauma, inasmuch as the economy of many nations is geared to the internal combustion engine. The disruption of the complex human economy for the sake of clean air does not appear to be defensible or acceptable to industry, government, or even many segments of the public.

It has been suggested that some atmospheric pollutants are mutagenic hazards—that is, they cause mutations. Laboratory experiments have shown that chemicals such as mustard gas and nitrous acid (HNO_2) can alter single bases in the DNA molecule. Nitrous acid in the atmosphere is readily derived from nitrogen dioxide (NO_2), a common pollutant in the air. Hence, nitrous acid could be a potent mutagen in nature. We considered earlier the possibility that degenerative diseases, and aging in general, may be the consequences of the deterioration of DNA in the body cells. Some investigators assert that environmental pollutants, acting as mutagens, contribute to an increased incidence of degenerative diseases.

RADIOACTIVE WASTES
Nuclear energy used for industrial and medical purposes is on the whole cleaner than the energy derived from burning fossil fuels (coal and oil) and is therefore more desirable. However, nuclear energy has one serious drawback: it produces large quantities of radioactive wastes. Present-

day nuclear power plants produce extremely hazardous and long-lived radioisotopes such as strontium 90, iodine 131, and cesium 137. Just as DDT and other pesticides accumulate in the living tissues of organisms, so radioisotopes become concentrated many times greater than their concentrations in the air and water surrounding the living organisms. Strontium 90 tends to accumulate in the bones of vertebrates; iodine 131 lodges in the thyroid gland; and cesium 137 concentrates in the muscles. The principal hazard to man from strontium 90 is the internal radiation of the red bone marrow, which may lead to the development of leukemia.

Especially high concentrations of cesium 137 have been found in certain plants, such as the Arctic lichen, which derives its mineral nutrients directly from dust particles that settle on it. This has subjected the Eskimos of the Arctic to a unique radioactivity hazard. The lichens efficiently collect cesium 137 from fallout, and lichen-eating caribou further concentrate the toxic substance. In turn, Eskimos eat the caribou, and incorporate cesium 137 in various parts of their body. It has been found that Eskimos have absorbed more radioactive cesium than most people in other parts of the world that have been more directly exposed to this radioisotope.

The development of nuclear power as fuel could be a boon to man's technological society. The risks from nuclear fuel must be balanced against the risks of continued air pollution resulting from the burning of gas, oil, or coal. Atomic experts claim that the risk of radioisotope damage to the body is many times less than the risk of driving a car on a public highway or of living in a smog-filled city such as Los Angeles. However, risks that are imposed are not as acceptable to people as risks that are voluntarily assumed.

There is no absolutely safe level of a given radioactive waste, although certain permissible concentrations have been established. For example, the maximum permissible concentration of strontium 90 has been set at 1 microcurie per 1,000 grams of calcium. At present, the level of strontium 90 is well below the level of the permissible concentration. Strontium 90 cannot now be regarded as a significant hazard to the human population. However, an interesting question is: What would happen if population pressure forced man to shorten his food chain and rely more heavily on direct consumption of field crops that efficiently intercept and retain radioactive wastes?

WATER POLLUTION

We have seen (chapter 45) that excessive nutrients, particularly nitrates and phosphates, pollute lakes by nourishing the lavish growth of algae. Man has hastened the aging of lakes through the use of agricultural fertilizers (in which the nutrients are carried away by flowing water to the lakes) and the use of modern detergents that contain phosphates. He has also channeled into flowing waters a variety of domestic and industrial waste organic compounds that bacteria can degrade, but only very slowly. Industry has poured into the waters heavy toxic metals such as lead, arsenic, and mercury. Each of these metals has the property of becoming concentrated in organisms. In the 1950s, in a coastal area of Japan known as Minamata Bay, fishermen and their families were stricken with a disease that was eventually diagnosed as mercury poisoning. Both vision and muscular coordination were impaired, sometimes accompanied by paralysis and death. The affliction was traceable to high concentrations of mercury in the fish the individuals ate. The Minamata

Bay received the mercury-containing effluent from a local plastics factory. Lead enters the environment from a variety of sources. It is liberated not only by industries, but in the exhaust of automobiles and boats that use leaded gasoline. Symptoms of lead poisoning in man include depression and impaired mental function.

The vast oceans have not escaped pollution by man's activities. It has been estimated that 10 million tons of oil are poured into the oceans each year. Oil reaches the ocean through routine shipping losses, leaks from offshore deposits, tanker wrecks, harbor spills, and tanker bilge washings. When the tanker *Torrey Canyon* ran aground off the southern coast of England, it was loaded with 110,000 tons of crude oil. The most visible victims of the massive oil spill were the sea birds; heavy casualties were suffered by diving birds—guillemots, razorbills, cormorants, and shags. However, we must acknowledge that the highest mortality of marine life —fish, limpets, barnacles, and seaweeds—resulted from the toxic detergents used to emulsify and disperse the oil. Some 2 million gallons of detergents were used to treat the oil. Unfortunately, the detergent cure proved much more damaging than the oil itself.

Off the coast of Santa Barbara, a blowout in a channel spilled from 1 to 3 million gallons of oil into the coastal waters. In this case, detergents were used sparingly in the vicinity of the leak area; straw was the main agent used to treat the slick. Nevertheless, the immediate biological effect of this spill was massive bird mortality, principally in diving birds.

The *Torrey Canyon*, Santa Barbara, Louisiana, Cape Cod, and a host of other oil spills attest to the inadequate technology available for transporting petroleum by sea and for producing it from offshore oil deposits. With the recent discovery of oil in Alaska, the arctic tundra may be in danger of pollution. Construction has been authorized of immense pipelines that would extend nearly 800 miles across Alaska. Just one break in the pipelines could flood thousands of acres of tundra and woodlands and miles of pristine streams and lakes.

PESTICIDES (DDT)

An incredibly potent insecticide is the chlorinated hydrocarbon compound dichloro-diphenyl-trichloroethane, known simply as DDT. During World War II, this pesticide was used extensively with great success against mosquitoes and body lice. Then DDT became an important agent in protecting the world's food harvest. Malaria was brought under control through the use of DDT in many regions of the world.

As a pesticide, DDT has the attractive quality of remaining effective long after its initial application. This feature, however, has unfortunate aspects; DDT is an extremely stable compound and is not readily broken down (biodegraded) by microorganisms. Moreover, DDT is fat-soluble and tends to accumulate in the fatty tissues of organisms. As DDT is transferred from one organism to another, it becomes increasingly concentrated at each higher trophic level (fig. 46.5). Thus, the highest concentrations occur in the top carnivores. Concentrations of DDT in carnivorous birds such as the osprey have been found to be at least 50 times greater than the levels in the fish on which they prey.

The long-lasting DDT residues have spread within two decades throughout the world by wind and water in much the same way as radioactive fallout. The DDT compound has been found in areas of the globe where this insecticide has never been used. Penguins and crab-eating seals in the Antarctic, far removed from any actual spraying, have ac-

Figure 46.5 Concentrations of DDT increase as DDT residues pass along the food chain. High concentrations occur in birds of prey, such as the peregrine falcon and osprey.

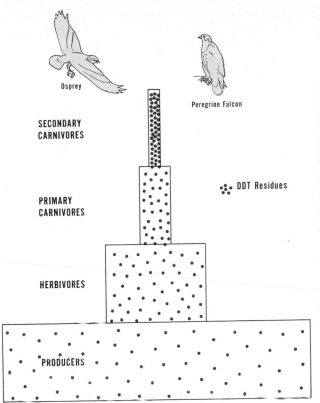

Osprey

Peregrine Falcon

SECONDARY CARNIVORES

•.• DDT Residues

PRIMARY CARNIVORES

HERBIVORES

PRODUCERS

Figure 46.6 Crushed egg in the nest of a brown pelican off the California coast. The shell was so thin that the weight of the nesting parent's body destroyed it. (Courtesy of Dr. Joseph R. Jehl, Jr., Natural History Museum, San Diego, California.)

cumulated traces of the compound. It has been estimated that there are approximately 1 billion pounds of DDT currently circulating in the biosphere.

The DDT levels in the gonads and eggs of several species of birds have seriously impaired the reproductive potential of these organisms. Since DDT interferes with the mobilization of calcium in the oviduct, the eggs are laid with exceedingly thin shells, subject to hairline cracks, or with no shell at all (fig. 46.6). Consequently birds of prey, such as the bald eagle and osprey, are now on the brink of extinction (fig. 46.7). Whereas ospreys formerly averaged 2.5 young a year, today they are barely able to produce 1 young a year. As William Mudoch of the University of California (Santa Barbara) stated, "No amount of technological ingenuity can reconstruct a species of osprey once it is extinct." As another example, the formerly large colony of California brown pelicans on Anacapa Island raised 5 young in 1969 and only 1 in 1970. None of the thin-shelled eggs of the double-crested cormorant hatched in California in 1969. The data indicate a direct correlation between the amount of DDT and the hatchability of eggs—the more DDT present in the eggs, the fewer young hatched.

The potent DDT has proven to be toxic to a wide variety of species. Because of the high levels of DDT, fish (for example, the coho salmon) from several inland lakes have been condemned as unfit for human consumption. Several commercial shipments of pacific mackerel from the Pacific ocean have also been condemned. In Hanover, New Hampshire, 70 percent of the robin population was eliminated in the early 1960s when Dutch elms were sprayed with DDT. Man retains DDT in his fatty tissues, and presently harbors relatively low levels. Although not immediately toxic to man, DDT may have detrimental long-term effects. It was Rachel

Figure 46.7 Osprey, a species endangered by DDT and other pesticides. As a carnivore high in the food chain, this bird accumulates unusual amounts of DDT. (Courtesy of the Michigan Department of Natural Resources.)

Figure 46.8 Rachel Carson (1907–1964). Through her book, *Silent Spring*, published in 1962, she exposed the danger of the indiscriminate use of long-lived chemical pesticides. She had also authored *The Sea Around Us, Under the Sea Wind,* and *The Edge of the Sea*, in each of which she portrayed the interrelations of all forms of life. (© Magnum Photos, Inc.)

Carson's impressive book, *Silent Spring*, set forth in dramatic form in 1962, that first awakened people to the deleterious effects of pesticides (fig. 46.8). But it has only been in recent years that the United States has banned the use of DDT and other chlorinated hydrocarbons (chlordane, dieldrin, endrin, and heptachlor) in the spraying of lands and tidal marshes.

Indiscriminate spraying of pesticides and insecticides has been fatal to crops and wildlife populations over large areas of land. In an endeavor to eradicate the fire ant in the southern part of the United States, dieldrin and heptachlor were aerially sprayed over 2.5 million acres in 1957. The outcome was widespread damage to crops and the decimation of various wildlife vertebrates. The lack of selectivity of the pesticides and the extensive ecological damage prompted the Georgia Academy of Science to evaluate the pest control program and, in particular, to seek facts concerning the biological activities of the fire ant. The findings of the academy were startling: there was scant justification for the federal expenditure of $2.4 million for the fire ant eradication program inasmuch as the fire ant is *not* a significant economic pest that threatens the survival of man's crops. The fire ant, although it does damage crops, represents more a nuisance or a source of annoyance to people.

ECOLOGICAL GUIDELINES

Natural resources are not inexhaustible and the environment is not limitless in its capacity to accumulate toxic metabolites. The environment is not a stockroom, and toxic substances are not transient or diluted to a harmless state. Man can scarcely afford to continue to view the environment as a resource to be manipulated and overtaxed for short-term personal, regional, or national gain.

It is illusory to assume complacently that the solution to an environmental crisis is more sophisticated technology. The failure of more technology is dramatically revealed in the building of the Aswan High Dam on the upper Nile (see chapter 42), the indiscriminate use of DDT throughout the world, and the ill-fated endeavor to solve the world's food problem by the green revolution (see chapter 41). Each of these technological solutions only exacerbated the original environmental problem or had disturbing side effects.

An equilibrium must be restored between man's needs and the capacities of the environment. The primary objectives should be to ensure that organic and mineral nutrients are conserved and recycled, and that natural ecosystems are not further endangered or continually simplified by the actual or potential elimination of valuable species of organisms. The problem of living in harmony with the biotic and abiotic environment is heightened and highlighted by man's growing numbers. The increase in population automatically places increased pressure on natural resources. A constructive and conservative attitude toward environmental resources cannot be achieved if man fails to regulate his numbers.

SUMMARY

Man has exploited the environment for his own ends, and has drastically altered, in some cases irreversibly, relatively stable ecosystems that existed formerly. He has ravaged the land and slaughtered its wildlife. He has poured vast quantities of domestic and industrial wastes into lakes and rivers. He has defiled the atmosphere with smoke and exhaust gases.

And he has contaminated the land with pesticides. He has essentially viewed the natural resources as adversaries to be conquered and squandered.

It is no longer possible to relax in an easy reliance that more sophisticated technology is the solution to the environmental crisis. Man must adopt a new ethic, replacing the view of unlimited exploitation with one of enlightened conservation. An equilibrium must be restored between man's needs and the capacities of the environment. Corollary to success in this direction is regulating man's numbers. Man will exceed the carrying capacity of the environment if he fails to control his numbers.

Ethical Probe 27
Food Additives

In industrialized countries, foods in their natural states have been supplemented, modified, and even disguised by the use of innumerable chemicals. The average American consumes about three pounds per year of chemical food additives. Although most of the chemical food additives appear to have little, or no, short-term biological effects, the possible long-term hazards are difficult to assess. Some of the chemicals we ingest are now suspected of having deleterious effects. In particular, several classes of artificial sweeteners—the cyclamates and the ingredients in commercial "sweet-and-low"—have been implicated in the induction of cancer of the bladder, at least in laboratory animals. With chemical food additives, insecticides, antibiotics, and hormones increasingly finding their way into the human diet, industrialized societies may be creating a paramount problem in public health unheard of even a decade ago.

Some additives could be eliminated if the housewife were willing to grow her own food, harvest and grind it, and spend long hours cooking and canning. Others could be eliminated if she were willing to accept bland, uncolored, substances of short shelf-life. Do you favor limiting the use of food additives? If so, which ones?

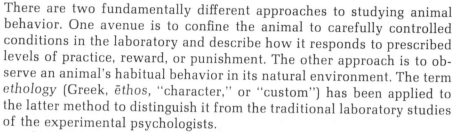

47 Ethology: The Comparative Study of Behavior

There are two fundamentally different approaches to studying animal behavior. One avenue is to confine the animal to carefully controlled conditions in the laboratory and describe how it responds to prescribed levels of practice, reward, or punishment. The other approach is to observe an animal's habitual behavior in its natural environment. The term *ethology* (Greek, *ēthos,* "character," or "custom") has been applied to the latter method to distinguish it from the traditional laboratory studies of the experimental psychologists.

Ethology may be defined simply as the comparative study of the behavioral characteristics of species. Ethology is essentially an evolutionary approach to the study of behavior. The ethologist is interested in tracing behavior patterns among related species, examining the component parts of a behavioral act in much the same way that a comparative anatomist examines the detailed morphology of a physical structure. The ethologist is concerned more with modifications of behavior fostered by natural selection than with an animal's behavioral changes produced by learning. The ethological viewpoint is best represented by the Austrian zoologist Konrad Lorenz and his colleagues Niko Tinbergen and Irenäus Eibl-Eibesfeldt, all of whom were reared in the Darwinian tradition.

The outlook of the ethologist is refreshing in that it views behavior as part of the organism's adaptation to its total environment. The ethologist typically examines complex sequences of behavior that are more than manifestations of the well-known simple reflex actions. He continually inquires into the selective advantage that the sequence of activities confers on the animal. If a complex behavior has selective value, it increases the likelihood that the behavioral pattern is *innate;* that is, the propensity for the act is inherited. Thus, the establishment and defense of a territory by birds, or the schooling orientation of fishes, are complex behavior patterns that contribute to the perpetuation of the species and do not appear to require specific learning influences for expression.

FIXED, OR PROGRAMMED, PATTERNS

Konrad Lorenz speaks of innate behavioral acts as *fixed action patterns,* or simply, *fixed patterns.* These fixed, or genetically programmed, activities can be performed by an organism without any previous experience or conditioning. A bird will automatically open its beak wide at the moment of hatching, a newly hatched chick will peck at particles on the ground, and a duckling will spontaneously oil its feathers. In humans, the newborn infant exhibits spontaneously a rhythmic searching movement of its head (fig. 47.1). The songs of birds are genetically programmed; the whitethroat bird *(Sylvia communis),* for example, can develop the complete repertoire of species-specific calls when raised in isolation from its

Figure 47.1 Rhythmic searching for the breast. The searching movements of the head of the newborn infant are performed without any previous experience or conditioning.

parents in soundproof chambers. The domestic chicken raised in an incubator vocalizes normally. Even if one were to admit of learning influences in the manifestation of the foregoing activities, the important consideration is that these behavioral patterns are constant, inherent characteristics of a species, just as certain morphological and physiological attributes characterize a species. Even when the learning process does enter into the development of the behavioral pattern, it still can be demonstrated that the basic pattern is inborn. When a male European chaffinch (*Fringilla coelebs*) is raised in acoustical isolation, it develops a song that is deficient in several respects (fig. 47.2). The production of the species-characteristic song entails learning from other singing males of its species. Interestingly, when a newly hatched chaffinch in a soundproof room is exposed to tape recordings of several bird songs of different species, it imitates only those notes that have certain characteristics in common with the normal chaffinch song. Accordingly, although a learning input is required, the chaffinch inherits a tendency to produce only species-characteristic notes. The unique gene complex of the chaffinch predisposes it to generate the song of its species.

The ethologist's views are valuable in that they refrain from interpreting an animal's behavior in terms of purposeful intentions. The goal of executing an act is the discharge of the act itself, rather than the gratification of a specific physiological need such as hunger or rest. All animals, whether in their natural or strange environment, show a marked tendency to explore their surroundings. The general restlessness or exploratory behavior of an animal has been called *appetitive behavior*. Appetitive behavior is considered an expression of an internal readiness to act, that is, an expression of an inner *motivational drive*. A frog, for example, shows appetitive behavior by turning his body to follow a small crawling organism or any moving object of small size. The frog then flicks his tongue at the moving organism or object, an action that constitutes the *consummatory act*. The physiological satisfaction of obtaining food is *secondary* to the satisfaction of terminating the restless, seeking behavior with a flick of the tongue. The exploratory behavior thus ends in the performance of a drive-reducing specific act. This consummatory act is terminal and is followed by a relative state of rest.

Evidently, an organism does not wait passively for an appropriate

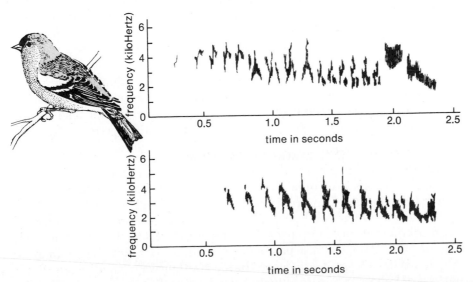

Figure 47.2 Sound spectrograms of songs of the adult male chaffinch. Top: Customary song of the chaffinch. *Bottom:* Song of a chaffinch raised in isolation. Although the song pattern of the acoustically isolated chaffinch is deficient, it does approximate the loudness and duration of the normal species. (Reprinted by permission of the publisher from R. A. Suthers and R. A. Gallant, *Biology—the behavioral view*, 1973, Xerox College Publishing. © 1973 by Xerox Corporation.)

external stimulus but is motivated from within to search restlessly. The generalized, unoriented seeking persists until the appropriate stimulus permits the discharge of the consummatory act. The organism need not be satiated to complete the act. It has been repeatedly observed that a thirsty dog will drink water for only a certain period of time. The same discontinuance of drinking after a prescribed period of time will also occur in a dog provided with an esophageal fistula, that is, a pipe inserted in the esophagus so that the water drains outside. Mothers have also observed that the bare performance of an infant sucking on an empty bottle will often satisfy the infant as if the sucking movements abate the motivational drive. In each situation, the experimental dog's thirst or the infant's hunger was certainly not satisfied physiologically, yet the behavioral sequence had been consummated. In essence, an innate behavior is not guided by a conscious purpose or design.

SIGN STIMULI

A given behavioral act is triggered or elicited by a specific stimulus, referred to as a *sign stimulus*. In 1909, the European naturalist von Uexküll showed that an animal, such as the common tick, selects certain sign stimuli and ignores others. The tick is unresponsive to the mere sight of a passing mammalian host. Only the specific odor of butyric acid generated by mammalian skin glands causes the tick to respond by dropping from the twig of a tree onto the host. The tick then inserts its feeding mouthparts and sucks blood. That the tick responds only to the chemical stimulus can be demonstrated by smearing butyric acid on a rock. The rock emanates the specific odor that is attractive to the tick; the tick is actually deceived into attacking the rock and usually breaks its mouthparts in the process.

The large carnivorous water beetle, *Dytiscus marginalis,* reacts in the same automatic way as the tick. This beetle preys on fish, tadpoles, grasshoppers, and worms. The feeding activities of a foraging beetle are uninfluenced by what it sees; the beetle reacts to dissolved odors emanating from the prey. The beetle will disregard a tadpole if the latter is enclosed in a test tube. When the tadpole is placed in a bag of cheesecloth, however, the beetle engages in vigorous, thrashing movements to clasp the object (tadpole). The same frantic reaction can be evoked by simply placing tadpole-conditioned water into the beetle's tank.

The fixed action pattern thus appears to be an internally coordinated sequence whose expression requires a specific releasing stimulus. The behavioral act is performed without any indication of insight on the part of the organism. The absence of insight is underscored by a hen's failure to respond to a chick in distress under a glass bell within her sight (fig. 47.3). She will, however, engage in a searching behavior if she can hear the distressing cries even if she cannot see the chick. In this case, sound is the specific releasing signal for the hen's maternal behavior.

INNATE RELEASING MECHANISM (IRM)

Lorenz and Tinbergen have advanced the notion that an inhibitory mechanism exists in an organism's nervous system that prevents the continuous discharge of internal motivating drives. They postulated that inhibitions are removed by an *innate releasing mechanism* (IRM) when appropriate sensory impulses are received. Each innate releasing mechanism responds to a particular stimulus, or a key sign stimulus, which has been termed a *releaser*. Stated another way, each specific fixed pattern of behavior remains blocked until a specific releaser activates the

Figure 47.3 Differential response of a hen to the distress signals of her chicks. The distress call evokes a searching behavior from the hen even when she cannot see the chick. No response is elicited from the hen when the call is muted although the chick under the glass bell is within the hen's sight. (From N. Tinbergen, *The study of instinct,* 1951, The Clarendon Press, Oxford.)

innate releasing mechanism, which causes the particular consummatory act to be performed. Innate releasing mechanisms are said to possess a capacity for increased selectivity through individual experience or conditioning. That conditioning can restrict or limit a response is clear from the feeding behavior of a toad. The toad will at first snap indiscriminately or unselectively at any small moving object, but learns, with each successive exposure, to avoid inedible or noxious insects. This kind of negative conditioning or learning is called *habituation*.

The innate releasing mechanism has been defined solely in functional terms. There is no known neurophysiological basis or mechanism for the IRM. It should be clear that the ethologist largely observes external events, and draws inferences concerning the externally observable events. The mechanisms by which sensory impulses are evaluated by the central nervous system and by which the responses are selected remains one of the cardinal problems of both ethology and neurophysiology.

Releasers assume a variety of forms. A given releaser may be a call, a scent, a visual cue, or a behavioral activity of another animal. The intriguing responses of organisms to each other's behavior were vividly shown by Tinbergen in his studies in the 1940s of the courtship behavior of the three-spined stickleback (*Gasterosteus aculeatus*), a small fish common to European waters. Sticklebacks live in the sea or in brackish water for most of the year, but in the spring they migrate up the rivers and into the shallow, freshwater streams. When the males arrive in the streams, their bellies are colored bright red. Each male takes up a position in the stream and stakes out a territory that he defends against intruding males.

The male can recognize the red reproductive markings of another male and the swollen abdomen of the female. The sight of a red belly elicits threatening or fighting behavior, whereas the sight of a swollen abdomen evokes courting behavior. The red belly may be considered the releaser for territorial defense, the swollen abdomen the releaser for courtship. Tinbergen constructed a dummy model of a female that was faithful in every structural detail except for the swollen abdomen and a very crude model not particularly femalelike but possessing a swollen abdomen (fig. 47.4). Tinbergen maneuvered the two models like submerged puppets into the territory of a male. The male stickleback was attracted to the crude model on the basis of the swollen abdomen and rejected the exact replica of the female without the swollen abdomen.

In another simple, but instructive, experiment (fig. 47.5), Tinbergen

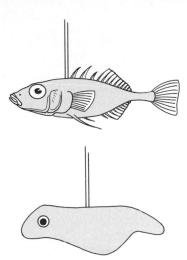

Figure 47.4 Significance of the swollen abdomen of the female stickleback. A male will court a crude model of a female on the basis of the swollen abdomen *(bottom)*, but will not be attracted to an exact replica of the female without the swollen abdomen *(top)*. (From N. Tinbergen, *The study of instinct*, 1951, The Clarendon Press, Oxford.)

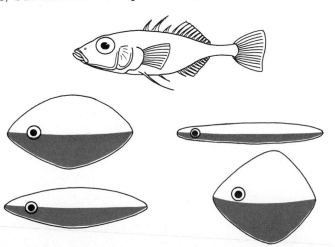

Figure 47.5 Models of male sticklebacks used by Niko Tinbergen. The realistically shaped model of a male *(top)*, in lacking a red belly, hardly evokes any aggressive reactions from male sticklebacks compared with oddly shaped models *(bottom)* with red bellies, which are vigorously attacked by male sticklebacks. (From N. Tinbergen, *The study of instinct*, 1951, The Clarendon Press, Oxford.)

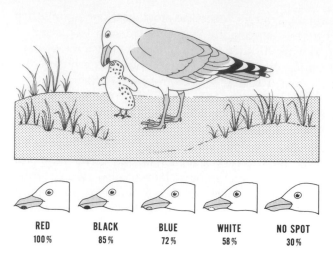

Figure 47.6 Behavioral sign stimulus in the herring gull. Five cardboard models were used to test the function of the patch of color on the parent's bill in releasing the feeding response of the newly hatched chick. As judged by the relative frequencies (shown in percentages) of the pecking responses of the chicks, the red patch (the natural color) is the most effective signal. (Based on studies by N. Tinbergen.)

confronted a territorial male with a series of male models, only one of which was an exact replica but lacking the red coloration of the belly. The accurate model of the male fish, devoid of the red color, was allowed in the territory without protest. But the other models—with shapes ranging from cigars to plates—elicited territorial defense since they featured an eye and a red belly (fig. 47.5). Moreover, the red color must be on the rival's belly, for if the red color is on the back, the territorial male will not attack. These studies show not only that the sign signals or releasers are specific for certain actions, but also how these behavioral releasers form the basis for social interactions.

The feeding behavior of nestlings of the herring gull also emphasizes the importance of appropriate sign stimuli or releasers. The young gull pecks food from its parent's bill, which has a red spot on the lower mandible. When incubator-hatched gulls are presented with different models of the parent's bill, they respond more vigorously and more often to the model bearing a red patch—the natural color of the adult's spot—than to models with any other color (fig. 47.6). Since an incubator-hatched chick had not previously seen an adult gull, its programming with respect to pecking the appropriately colored bill must have been done internally (plate 22).

The human infant reacts in a specific, stereotyped way to selected stimuli. The newborn infant, up to two months, will smile at a flat facial mask as long as the mask has two properly spaced eyelike dots (fig. 47.7). The smile is elicited automatically even if a variety of other facial features are twisted out of shape, such as a grotesquely placed nose or mouth.

Figure 47.7 Only one model—the *topmost*—is ineffective in eliciting a smile when each of the models is presented face-on to a human infant (between one-month and two-months of age).

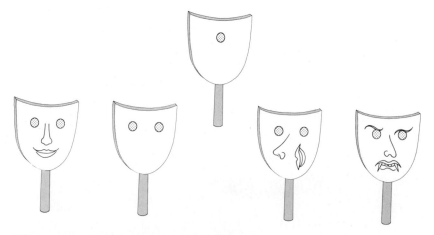

The only feature that cannot be distorted is the pair of eyes—a mask with only one dot cannot trigger a smile from the baby.

REACTION CHAINS

A complicated sequence of behavior can be elicited by a *chain* of releaser-response interactions between two animals. In the courtship behavior of two sticklebacks, each animal's action serves as a releaser for the other animal's subsequent response (fig. 47.8). The courtship pattern is a series or hierarchy of well-coordinated behavior patterns; incorporated in each level are one or more innate releasing mechanisms.

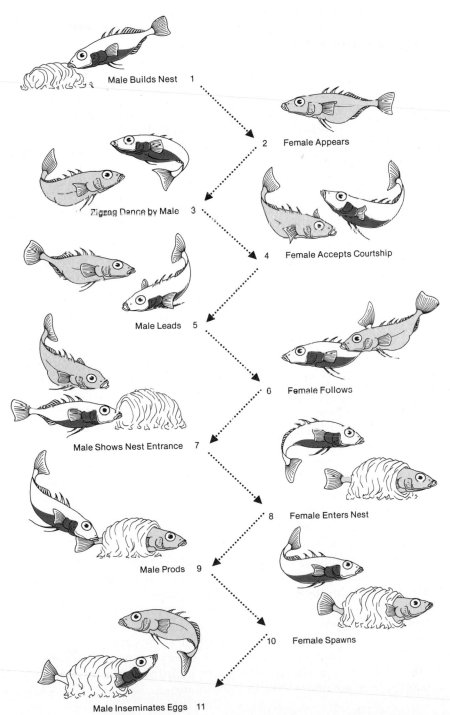

Figure 47.8 Chain of releaser-response interactions in the mating behavior of sticklebacks. See text for details. (Based on studies by N. Tinbergen.)

Male Builds Nest 1

2   Female Appears

Zigzag Dance by Male 3

4   Female Accepts Courtship

Male Leads 5

6   Female Follows

Male Shows Nest Entrance 7

8   Female Enters Nest

Male Prods 9

10   Female Spawns

Male Inseminates Eggs 11

Figure 47.9 The prod that induces spawning. The female stickleback normally releases her eggs after being prodded by the male. The prodding that induces spawning can be duplicated with a glass rod manipulated by a human investigator. (Based on studies by N. Tinbergen.)

Once a male stickleback has secured a breeding site, he constructs a nest with strands of algae (step 1 in fig. 47.8). When a female stickleback, swollen with unfertilized eggs, appears in his territory (2), the male reacts in a series of swift, vaulting movements known as a "zigzag" dance (3). She acknowledges his courtship dance by swimming directly toward him with a head-up sign of acceptance (4). Her action incites the male to lead (5), or swim rapidly toward the nest. She follows (6), an action that prompts the male to show her the nest entrance by pointing inside with his snout (7). She reacts by entering the nest (8). The male then prods (9) the base of the female's tail with his snout, which induces her to spawn (10). She swims out after the eggs are deposited and he enters the nest to inseminate the clutch of eggs (11). The male then protects the developing young.

In such reaction chains, each reaction depends on specific releasers or sign stimuli, mostly visual, which are different for each of the links and are essential to the next action in the series. Several of the releasers can be simulated by experimental stimuli. The male's prodding of the female to induce spawning can be duplicated with a glass rod manipulated by an investigator (fig. 47.9). Hence, in this instance, it is not the presence of the male that is important, but simply the stimulus that the prodding itself provides.

IMPRINTING

Although we have emphasized that the capacity for recognizing appropriate sign stimuli is inborn, it should be understood that the inherited potential can be influenced or modified by experience or learning. This is dramatically witnessed in the phenomenon of *imprinting*, wherein an extensive and permanent modification of behavior can result by exposure to a relevant stimulus during a specific and brief period in early life. Thus, if the first moving object that a newly hatched gosling follows is a human being rather than its parents, it will thereafter faithfully remain attached to the human and deny any association with its parents (plate 22). A gosling can become imprinted on a variety of objects, including a moving wooden decoy, and in later life, the gosling will exhibit courting behavior to the model in preference to live members of its own species. Apparently, early social contacts with the parents are indispensable to the establishment of normal adult social relations.

Imprinting is viewed as a special, distinctive form of learning. It is distinctive in that the capacity for imprinting is limited to a fixed and relatively brief period in the life of the organism. In chicks, for example, the formation of the primary social attachment with the hen through contact or visual cues occurs within the first 72 hours after hatching. If exposure to the hen does not occur during this critical period, the chick will later remain independent of the rest of the flock and show no concern for any member.

Although imprinting is usually associated with birds, similar effects have been seen in rats, sheep, and monkeys. In primates, the primary social bond to the mother tends to be established almost immediately after birth through the extensive visual explorations of the newborn. When rhesus monkeys are isolated at birth and raised on dummy mothers, they generally exhibit disturbed adult reproductive and parental behaviors. In particular, female monkeys deprived of early social contact tend to vigorously attack the courting male, and if they do conceive, they are inattentive to their offspring.

APPEASEMENT POSTURES

Many species of animals have evolved methods of reducing the frequency of aggressive combat among the constituent members. One strategy that has been employed is submissive, or *appeasement*, behavior. The appeasement behavior of an animal is the antithesis of aggressive display. For example, in many fish, birds, and mammals, a direct frontal gaze at the rival or opponent is a threatening sign. In appeasement behavior the eyes gaze in any direction other than that of the opponent. This facing away is in a sense a symbolic fleeing, yet the appeaser does not actually flee. Appeasement behavior not only reduces the incidence of aggression but also provides a positive incentive for the maintenance of proximity or contact. This type of behavior thus plays an important role in promoting peace and cohesion in groups of animals.

Tinbergen has stated that appeasement behavior is motivated by a mixture of the tendency to attack and the tendency to escape. In fact, appeasement behavior is part of the courtship sequence in several species of animals. Despite the sexual attraction between the male and female, their close proximity to each other also evokes aggressiveness and fear. In the black-headed herring gull, the two sexes are alike in appearance as well as in display— aggressiveness is not an exclusively male attribute. The male attracts the female with a loud utterance, termed the "long call." When the female gull alights near the male, both assume a threatening position known as the "forward" posture (fig. 47.10). After a few seconds, the two sexes simultaneously adopt a "face-away" posture, turning their heads away from each other. Facing away is an act of appeasement.

The two sexes initiate their courtship by threatening each other and then moderate their hostility by appeasement behavior. But the female

Figure 47.10 Motivational conflicts (attack, escape, sex) in the black-headed herring gull. The male and female are alike in appearance. The male's response to another bird's approach, whether male *(top),* or female *(bottom),* at the boundary of his territory is a long call uttered in the oblique posture. In a boundary dispute, the two males are in a motivational conflict; both the tendency to attack and to flee are aroused. The two males may intimidate one another by adopting a forward posture, in which they face each other in a threatening manner. One and then the other may assume an upright posture, another hostile posture. Typically the upright posture passes over to a retreat on the part of the invading male. Similar tendencies to attack and escape are seen in the courtship behavior of a male and female *(bottom* illustrations). The male greets the female with a long call. Both male and female adopt a hostile posture similar to the forward posture between two males in a territorial encounter. The male and female moderate the hostility by each turning its head away. This face-away posture, in which the gulls avert the menacing beak, is an appeasement act. The courtship behavior thus involves the simultaneous arousal of the tendencies to attack, to escape, and to stay near one another. (Based on studies by N. Tinbergen.)

AGGRESSIVE BEHAVIOR (MALE TO MALE)

Long Call Forward Posturing Upright Posture

COURTSHIP BEHAVIOR (MALE TO FEMALE)

Long Call Forward Posturing Face-Away Posture

still remains ambivalent. She typically flies off, only to return. A pair of black-headed gulls may repeat several times the courtship sequence of threat and appeasement. Gradually, the threat displays decrease in vigor and frequency, aggressiveness and fear lessen, and the purely sexual movements gain prominence. How the transition from hostility to mutual sexual responsiveness occurs is not known in detail. The overriding sexual responses appear to be mediated by endocrine changes.

REDIRECTED AND DISPLACEMENT ACTIVITIES

When a male faces an opponent, unable to decide whether to attack or flee, or approaches a potential mate with strong tendencies both to threaten or to court, he may make neither choice. Instead the conflicting impulses are redirected at a meaningless object, such as a pebble or a blade of grass. Grass pulling in herring gulls is a good example of a *redirected activity* arising from ambivalence. In contests over territorial boundaries, herring gulls often peck violently at the ground, uproot the grass, and toss the blades of grass sideways with the flick of the head. The pecking is indistinguishable from that aimed at rivals in actual attacks, and the pulling movements are identical with those seen when a gull seizes an opponent's wing. These innocuous actions are directed at the ground, rather than at the intruder for whose benefit the actions are undertaken. Among humans similar expressions of inner conflict are common and easily recognized. An angry man may take out his feelings on a substitute target—a table, which he bangs with his fist, or a chair, which he kicks.

Another type of behavior, known as *displacement activity*, may occur when two motivations are in conflict with each other. Given two conflicting drives, the organism may perform a third, seemingly irrelevant act. Stated another way, the behavior pattern has no relevance whatever to the circumstance in which the animal finds himself. The animal may preen, start ineffectual nest-building movements, or pantomime feeding. An angry man, unable to express his feelings directly, scratches his head in frustration.

One of the best examples of displacement activity is the irrelevant nest-building movements of male stickleback fish. When patrolling his territorial borders, the male stickleback frequently may be seen excavating a nest as if he were engaged in true nest building. He displays this behavior when faced with his neighboring male territory holder, a formidable opponent. Interestingly, the displaced nest-building activity has evolved into a sign stimulus that serves to inhibit the aggression of the opponent. The opponent also commences to engage in the same nest-building movements. The outcome is that the mutual display of displacement digging keeps the aggressive tendencies of the territorial males from becoming self-destructive by excess fighting.

GENETICS OF BEHAVIOR

Behavioral patterns are as much a product of the evolutionary process as are adaptive morphological structures. Aside from certain behavioral acts in higher primates that have been culturally transmitted, behavioral activities have arisen by the operation of natural selection on inherited variations. Thus, we might expect that natural populations are as highly variable for genes that affect behavior as they are for variant genes that affect morphological and physiological characters. Indeed, there is evidence that single gene differences can result in behavioral changes often in very striking ways. This has been shown, for example, in the courtship activity of the fruit fly *Drosophila melanogaster*. A normal male fruit fly stimulates the female fly by vibrating his wings. A single mutant gene, designated *y* (yellow body color), has the effect of reducing the duration of vibrating movements in the male during courtship. As a result, the yellow-bodied male has less mating success than the normal (wild-type) male.

As might be expected, wingless male flies are also less successful in courtship than intact males. The point of interest here, however, is the wing-preening movements of the wingless male. He fastidiously arranges his body in the manner typical of a winged male. The wing-preening activity of the wingless male may be viewed as a behavioral remnant, or vestige, just as a functionless morphological structure may persist as a vestige.

Since the genetic structure of a population changes with time under the impact of natural selection, we should expect evolutionary changes in behavioral patterns. One of the intriguing phylogenetic changes that has been deduced by ethologists is the *ritualization* of a behavioral act, which is established when a movement or action that is functional in another context acquires a secondary value as a display signal. Certain courtship displays in birds take their origin from, or are by-products of, a generalized preening behavior associated with the care of the body surface. For example, all species of ducks preen their wings as part of the care of their plumage. In certain species of ducks, preening has become part of the behavior pattern of courtship. The interpretation is that courtship preening has been derived from ordinary preening, in much the same way that a specialized morphological structure, such as a lobster's claw, has been derived from a generalized appendage.

AGGRESSION IN MAN

The ethological view is that aggression in all animals, including man, is part of the organism's overall adaptive response to its environment. The aggressive drive has evolved or been selected as an adaptive characteristic, and is therefore aimed at perpetuating the species rather than destroying it. This is contrary to the older, but still prevalent, view that aggression is nothing more than a destructive and negative impulse. Aggressive behavior does not necessarily lead to violence. If aggression is thought of as behavior directed toward causing harm, serious injury, or death to a member of the same species, then the evolutionary process might have been expected to have exerted a strong selection pressure against destructive aggressive behavior. As a matter of fact, aggression between individuals of the same species almost never ends in death and rarely results in serious injury to the combatants. Fighting in most animal species is highly ritualized and more nearly resembles a tournament than a mortal struggle. Thus ceremonial combat routines and submissive postures have evolved to forestall the death or injury that might result from fighting.

If selective forces have operated in the past in animal populations to prevent or minimize the wastage of reproductive energy that would arise from excessive deaths through combat, then we may inquire why man is still prone to behavior that actually results in the mortal wounding of his own kind. We may assume that, in the very distant past, man's subhuman primate ancestors, like other animal groups, were characterized by aggressive behavior patterns in which little bodily harm resulted from encounters. Some forces or factors brought about a change in aggressive behavior for the worse. It may be, as Sherwood Washburn has stated, that man's propensity for inflicting harm is an evolutionary product of the success of the hunting adaptation of early man. Man evolved as a hunter; indeed, the hunting way of life has sustained the human species for 99 percent of its history on earth. We can only speculate that the innate inhibitory mechanisms for violent behavior that once were in existence became less effective, or even useless, as man became more carnivorous and a predator. It seems, then, that man became genetically programmed for excessive aggressiveness through his hunting behavior. Moreover, since man has only recently freed himself from dependence on the hunting mode of life, there has been insufficient time, from an evolutionary standpoint, for genetically based restraints for aggression to have evolved in present-day man.

The aggressive behavior in man cannot yet be portrayed in neurophysiological terms. Nevertheless, there is no incontrovertible evidence that aggressive behavior is, at the physiological level, any less innate than other fixed behavioral patterns in man. It is not clear whether, in the absence of stimulation, the aggressive motivational drive must find a spontaneous outlet. If key stimuli are required, we are largely ignorant of the specific releasers that trigger or instigate aggressive reactivity, particularly violent behavior. We would like to remove the conditions (if they can be identified) that direct aggressive behavior towards violence, but this is not to suggest that all aggressive behavior be abolished or strongly redirected since certain aspects of aggression may be essential components of sexual behavior associated with the perpetuation of the species.

SUMMARY

The ethologist views behavior as part of the organism's adaptive response to its total environment. The basic repertoire of complex behavior patterns is inborn or innate. A behavior pattern is as inherently characteristic of a species as its morphological attributes. A genetically programmed behavior activity can be altered by learning influences or experience. The modification of behavior by learning can be striking and distinctive, as in the case of imprinting.

A given behavioral act is triggered or elicited by a specific stimulus from the environment, referred to as a *sign stimulus,* or *releaser.* The releaser may be a call, a scent, a visual cue, or the behavioral activity of another animal. A prey, for example, is a strong releasing stimulus for the prey-catching response (or consummatory act) of the predator. The consummatory act is performed when the specific releaser activates the *innate releasing mechanism* (IRM) in the organism's nervous system, a mechanism that normally prevents the release of neurosensory impulses when the stimulus is inappropriate.

Many species of animals have evolved methods of reducing aggressive combat within their memberships. The strategies include appeasement behavior, redirected activity, and displacement activity. Aggression between individuals of the same species almost never ends in death and rarely results in serious injury to the combatants. Man, however, is still prone to behavior that actually results in the mortal wounding of his own kind. One theory holds that man became genetically programmed for excessive aggressiveness during his prolonged existence as a predatory hunter. There is, however, no documented biologically based reason why men cannot live in harmony.

Ethical Probe 28
Single Motherhood

A growing number of women in Western societies are stirring controversy by deliberately choosing single motherhood. The single woman elects a close male friend to sire the child, but does not marry the man. Psychiatrists and sociologists have expressed concern that the single parent-child relationship may nurture unhealthy dependencies. The child to mother relation might be given exaggerated importance and be used to fill emotional needs in the adult to the detriment of the child. The son, for example, may assume the role of a surrogate husband for the mother. Several single mothers have now acknowledged that they failed to foresee the importance of the father for the child, as well as for them.

The advent of artificial insemination with donor sperm (AID) adds another dimension to the delicate situation. How is it to be decided who will "qualify" for donor insemination? Should AID be offered to unmarried women who wish to be inseminated? Is this situation much different from that of a single woman who bears a fatherless child or adopts a child through an agency? Should the option of having children by AID be extended to married, fertile men whose wives are sterile? Who would choose the surrogate mothers needed to bear the children of these men?

48 Social Behavior

Many species of higher organisms, particularly birds and mammals, exhibit social interactions that are highly structured: the individual members of the same species gather together in response to one another. Conspicuous examples of such social groupings are the schooling of fishes, the flocking of birds, and the herding of mammals. Social animals do much more than merely stay together. Group activity facilitates the search for food and offers a measure of protection from predation by other species. The formation of social units enhances reproductive activity by ensuring the presence of both sexes at the appropriate time. In addition, the opportunities for parental care increase the chances for survival of the offspring. On the negative side, it may be argued that group actions increase the intensity of competition for all resources and promote the spread of disease. We may well ask: Has group formation been fostered by natural selection, and to what extent has intergroup competition been minimized or prevented?

DOMINANCE HIERARCHY

A variety of mechanisms have evolved, including the development of submissive postures, which reduce actual combat and limit aggression to a mere exchange of display signals at a distance. A particularly effective manner in which aggression is minimized is the establishment of a *dominance hierarchy.* In 1922, T. Schjelderup-Ebbe, a Norwegian psychologist, discovered this type of organization among chickens, which he termed "peck order." In any flock, one hen dominates all the others: she can peck any without being pecked in return. The rest of the flock is arranged in a descending hierarchy ending in the lowest-ranking hen, which is pecked by all and can peck no one. Cocks do not normally peck hens, but they have their own dominance hierarchy. A breeding flock accordingly has two hierarchies, one for each sex.

When grown birds that are strangers to one another are placed together in a pen, they engage in a series of single combats, each pairing off against one opponent at a time, until a peck order has been established for the whole flock. Once the peck order has been determined, pecking begins to decline in frequency as members of the hierarchy recognize their superiors. Eventually, a mere raising or lowering of the head is sufficient to signify dominance or submission, respectively. Thus, the flock becomes comparatively peaceful and conserves energy. The dominant member has priority of access to food as well as of choice of mates and nest sites.

In social groups characterized by dominance hierarchies, it can be shown that the high-ranking animals have the greatest reproductive success. For example, in breeding colonies of elephant seals, less than one-third of the males in residence during a season copulate, and as few as five active males account for 50 percent of the matings in a given season. The frequency of copulation is directly related to social status—the higher a male's social rank, the more frequently he copulates. Comparable findings have been reported for male rhesus monkeys. Those males at the top of the dominance hierarchy show the most frequent courting behavior and are the most successful in completing copulations. Presumably then, by fostering the reproduction of the fittest individuals (at least those that are behaviorally the fittest), the genetic composition of the species population improves with time.

In some social animals, the dominance hierarchy expresses itself only during the breeding season. The male red deer, for example, seeks dominance status when it comes into reproductive condition (rut). During the rutting season in the fall, the high-ranking buck collects and dominates a harem of does and vigorously defends the harem against intrusion of other males. Rejected or subordinate bucks explore widely and may travel as far as 75 miles from their habitual ranges to establish their own harem. Out of rut, high-ranking bucks do not assert dominance over other males and, in fact, show few intergroup social interactions. The females, formerly subordinate to the males during rut, then assume the primary responsibility of maintaining the herd (mothers and their young) with one or a few of the oldest females standing at the top of the dominance hierarchy. The red deer herd is thus essentially a matriarchal society in which social control is maintained by the oldest females.

DOMINANCE IN BABOONS

An unusual type of dominance hierarchy has been found in several wild species of ground-adapted baboons, particularly the common savanna baboon (Papio ursinus) in Africa, and their close relatives, the Asian macaques. Much of our knowledge of the social behavior of wild baboons derives from the extensive field studies in the early 1960s of the anthropologist Irven DeVore of Harvard University. The African baboons are large monkeys (males may weigh up to 100 pounds) that venture at daybreak into the open savannas in groups, or troops, numbering 30 to 50. When a baboon troop moves to a feeding area or a water hole, the subordinate males (young adult males) take up positions at the front and along the sides of the formation (plate 25). The females and juveniles stay near the old, dominant males in the center of the group. Thus, although the young adults walk in the vanguard, they are not the leaders of the troop. At the first sight of a predator, the older dominant males emerge from the heart of the troop and lead all of the adult males in concerted action against the predator, while the females and young retreat to the safety of the trees.

One of the intriguing aspects of the baboon social life is that the dominant males form a ruling coalition, or clique. Since rule by a single individual can be hazardous, the dominant males maximize their strength by joining forces. Accordingly, peace in the large troop is preserved by a force stronger than any one individual can command. The coalition exerts a restraining influence on the dominance strivings of the maturing young males. Additionally, the male hierarchy is not readily split by threatening adult males that have recently joined from a neighboring troop.

Peace is enforced within the troop by the dominant males by a showy repertoire of threatening gestures and grunts. As seen in figure 48.1,

Staring

Glaring
(mouth open)

Bobbing

Figure 48.1 Repertoire of threats of the macaque. The first gesture is a *stare*, which may intensify to an open-mouthed *glare*, and finally find extreme expression in *bobbing* of the head. (Based on studies by I. DeVore).

the first of three basic gestures is a *stare* at the offender, which is essentially a prolonged, harsh look serving to intimidate. The threat may intensify to the second stage, the *open-mouthed glare*, which serves to expose the daggerlike canines. The facial gestures may then be reinforced by *bobbing*, or the rigorous movement up and down of the head. On being threatened by any one or all of these gestures by a dominant male, the subordinate male is likely to display submission. The subordinate male presents his rump as a gesture of submission.

Young female baboons remain in close and dependent contact with their mother for many years. DeVore observed that young female baboons are never far from the mother's side and help her in the rearing of infants. The experience gained in handling infants is invaluable to the young female baboon when she comes of childbearing age. When maturing female baboons in captivity are denied this experience, they often exhibit awkward and antagonistic behavior toward their firstborn.

DOMINANCE STRIVINGS IN HUMANS

Several investigators have suggested that dominance hierarchies are fundamental to all primate societies, including man. However, a strict dominance hierarchy, representing a central organizing principle, is prevalent only among the ground-living baboons and macaques. Wild chimpanzees, who move in fluid bands, show little signs of overt dominance interactions. They exhibit relatively few patent aggressive or submissive behaviors. Nevertheless, it may be that the aggressive acts of chimpanzees have become so ritualized that their dominance-striving aggressive behaviors appear relatively calm to the human observer. Chimpanzees have a large variety of greeting and reassurance gestures, which may have subtle status connotations. In a given band, certain chimpanzees enjoy a high popularity as measured by the amount of grooming that these individuals receive. The ability of a given male to make friendships with others appears to be a prerequisite for high-ranking status.

A biologically based hierarchy is difficult to ascertain in humans; and it may be that the status structure in humans is one of mutual attraction, as it appears to be in chimpanzees. Desmond Morris suggests that dominance striving based on aggression (as in baboons) was the basic pattern in very early human societies, but the aggressive dominance hierarchy became modified or dampened by the necessity for cooperation and mutual respect when the males banded together in organized hunting endeavors.

Whatever dominance behavior exists in man today may be primarily culturally conditioned. Civilized men show striving for dominance, but they also show the capacity on most occasions to subordinate themselves if they cannot rank highest. Man alone has the intellectual capacity and freedom to choose the most appropriate social action. If man's dominance behavior has a biologically fixed component, this innate force or urge can generally be overruled by persuasion and reason. The difficulty has been that it has not been possible to persuade all men to act for the social good, purely on rational grounds.

TERRITORIALITY

Territoriality is a type of organization that is closely connected with dominance in the control of aggression in animal societies. The significance of this phenomenon was first appreciated in 1920, when the

English ornithologist Eliot Howard published his popular book, *Territory in Bird Life*. In general, the male bird selects a clearly defined area, or territory, in which he will not permit other males of the same species to intrude. Courtship of the female, nest building, raising of the young, and feeding are carried out within the territory. In essence, the constituent individuals of a territory tend to control a given property or tract of habitat, which they actively defend against other members of the same species. We may define a *territory* as an area defended against encroachment by conspecifics.

When rival males venture into each other's territory, displays of threat rather than actual fighting are more likely to ensue. Prancing, posturing, and calling usually suffice to make the intruder avoid a battle. There are a variety of other checks on aggression, such as the *displacement activities,* discussed in the preceding chapter. When rivals meet at the common boundary of their territories, they are motivated both to attack and to flee. The animals resolve the conflict by engaging in totally irrelevant activities. Thus, the herring gull tears out grass by its roots and a duck preens its feathers just at the moment when combat seems inevitable. Very rarely do animals of the same species engage in fatal combat. Territoriality may be viewed as a method of organizing societies for minimal disruption by aggression.

A peculiarly specialized form of territoriality occurs in certain species of birds in which the males congregate at a communal display area, or site, called an *arena* or a *lek*. The male secures a display station and then attempts to mate with as many females as he can attract. Lek formation is shown by some shore birds such as the European ruff, various grassland species of grouse, and prairie chickens of the North American grasslands (fig. 48.2). Typically, large numbers of males stake out miniature, individual territories, often only 30 to 100 square yards, in close proximity. When females appear, the males engage in a frenzy of visual displays, dancing and strutting. The sage grouse also issues forth a resounding loud vocalization, called a "boom." The females are attracted more often to the centrally located displaying males, appropriately termed "master cocks." It has been observed that as few as four master cocks can inseminate 85 percent of the sage grouse females attracted to the display arena. Vast numbers of males, despite the heavy investment of time and energy, fail to be chosen by the females. The females depart after mating and raise their young in isolation. Thus, the arena is solely a display and courtship territory, restricted to mating and does not serve for nesting or the rearing of the young.

Ordinarily territorial defense is the prerogative of the male only. However, in certain song birds, such as the English robin, the female is just as vigorous in the aggressive defense of the territory as her mate. Moreover, as witnessed among lek-oriented birds, a given territory need not serve as the source of food supply for the mated pair and their brood. As another example, the green heron does not gather food on its nesting territory. This heron forages for fish in the saltwater marshes at a considerable distance from the breeding territory.

In some birds, such as the Mexican jays, a given territory is handed down through the generations by the same genetic lineage (or clan). The territory does not exist merely for the lifetime of one set of parents, but becomes the domain of the genetic clan from one generation to the next. The close genetic relationships among members of the clan are maintained by a high degree of inbreeding. Such clan-dominated territories

Figure 48.2 Sexual displays of the greater prairie chicken *(A)*, the sage grouse *(B)*, and the ruffed grouse *(C)*. (From P. A. Johnsgaard, *Animal behavior,* 1970, Wm. C. Brown Company Publishers.)

tend to have many surviving young. Although the breeding season is generally short, the parents have several broods. One factor that promotes a large clan is that the young of one brood actively participate in feeding their siblings of a subsequent brood during the same breeding season. Therefore, the energies of the parents can be largely devoted to reproduction.

Monkeys and apes in the wild are not nomadic—a given group confines its activities to a circumscribed, definable area. The geographic area over which a band of primates normally travels in pursuit of routine activities has been called the *home range*. In many instances, the home ranges of different primate groups overlap to varied degrees. Despite the proximity of the home ranges, contacts between the various groups are relatively infrequent. The groups remain apart not by overt aggression or fighting but by loud vocalizations. The strong, long-distance quality of the calls of monkeys and apes suggests that the vocalizations serve mainly to impart information concerning the relative locations of neighboring groups.

V. C. Wynne-Edwards of Aberdeen University has suggested that the territorial system in animals has evolved by natural selection to distribute the adult breeding pairs and assure each pair adequate food for raising a family. The supposition is that territorial animals control their reproductive output so as not to overexploit the resources in their environment. In particular, the subordinate individuals in a territory refrain from reproducing with the view of promoting the welfare of the whole population. It is doubtful, however, that natural selection can operate to abridge the reproductive fitness of individuals for the long-term benefit of the group. This aspect will be treated in greater detail in the next chapter.

TERRITORIALITY IN MAN

There has been considerable speculation in recent years that human social organization is based on a ritualized territorial instinct. Some writers, such as R. Ardrey in his book *The Territorial Imperative* (1966), argue that territoriality is a fundamental biologic need in man, which accounts for his warlike tendencies. However, not all of man's primate relatives are territorial in the sense of defending a demarcated area and engaging in formal territorial tournaments. The gibbon and the howler monkey are clearly territorial, whereas the rhesus monkey and chimpanzee exhibit little ritualized or formal territorial defense behavior. Chimpanzees do form regional groupings or parties, but the parties are flexible or overlapping. The members tend to split up as the party wanders through the savanna but then the members congregate again to feed. The males may travel alone but more often the strong companionability of the males binds them together into single-sexed clubs. There appears to be a real bond of comradery among chimpanzee males. Jane van Lawick–Goodall concludes that the only basic family unit of chimpanzee society is the mother and her infants.

Like the chimpanzees, the early human communities may have operated as shifting, fluid bands. The human bands may have wandered and hunted over an area of land in which the boundaries were ill-defined and not rigorously defended. However, Desmond Morris in his *Naked Ape* (1967) has asserted that local groups of hunters did defend their hunting domains from aggressive neighbors. He thus suggests that man acquired territoriality when he became a carnivorous hunter. A view that is contrary has been expressed by the Australian anthropologist Frances Barnes. She proposed in 1970 that territoriality became a pronounced feature of human social life only over the last 10,000 years, when man gave up his hunting mode of life and settled into an agricultural and industrial economy. The necessity for protecting herds and crops may have been the impetus for territorial behavior in man. The anthropologist L. Hiatt of the University of Sydney has reinforced Barnes's views by contending that civilized man exhibits territorial behavior more in common with caged apes than with meandering wild ones. Hiatt states that "the period of human captivity began some 10,000 years ago when man shackled himself with crops and herds."

PARENTAL BEHAVIOR

In the familiar placental mammals, the young develop slowly and the prolonged period of caring for the young is almost exclusively restricted to the female. In most mammals, including the nonhuman primates, social life is not organized around a biological family unit but rather around a group or tribe, and is associated chiefly with protection against enemies. Most nonhuman, mammalian males generally do not establish even a semblance of a permanent relationship with the pregnant and nursing female. In its extreme form, such as in cats and bears, the female actually ejects the male from any contact with the young. It is as if the mammalian male is biologically superfluous after insemination. Apart from insemination, most nonhuman, mammalian females have little use for the males —except possibly to protect them from other males. It is only exceptionally, as in wolves and humans, that the male plays an important role in the social interactions of mother and child. In humans, the male is integrated into a closely knit, cooperative family organization.

The prolonged helplessness of the human infant and the burden of several dependent young on the human female were probably contributing factors in incorporating the male in the family unit, if only initially for the economically crucial aspect of the male assuming responsibility for obtaining food for his mate and young. Figure 48.3 shows that the immature phase during which the child is dependent on the parents, particularly the mother, is a relatively long proportion of the total life of the human. The human newborn, compared with its lower-primate counterpart, is much less advanced in terms of percentage of growth. Much of the growth of the human brain takes place after birth, since the development and size of the fetal head must necessarily be constrained by the demands of the mother's pelvis. It should also be noted (fig. 48.3) that the infantile period, during which the child depends physically and emotionally on the mother, is progressively greater as one ascends the primate scale. What is the adaptive significance of the elongation of infancy and childhood in humans? The explanation frequently offered is that an extended period of dependency enhances the opportunities for learning and socialization. Some writers have noted the persistence in the human adult of infantile characteristics—namely, playfulness, curiosity, and inventiveness. It may be that the long period of immaturity enables us to retain throughout life the high level of inquisitiveness and exploration that contributes to the uniqueness of being human.

Studies in the 1960s by Harry F. Harlow at the Wisconsin Regional Primate Center dramatically revealed the importance of mother-infant social interactions in rhesus monkeys. Bodily contact with the mother is necessary for the normal maturation of the infant. The mother is more than a physiological provider of milk; she is also the psychological source of softness and warmth to the infant. The comfort, or reduction of anxiety, derived from bodily contact may even be more important to the

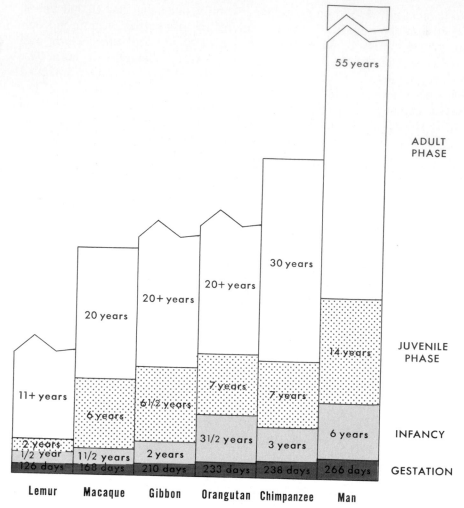

Figure 48.3 Duration of stages of life of various primates. (From A. Jolly, *The evolution of primate behavior*, 1972. Macmillan Publishing Co., Inc. Copyright © 1972 by Alison Jolly.)

ADULT PHASE

JUVENILE PHASE

INFANCY

GESTATION

	Lemur	Macaque	Gibbon	Orangutan	Chimpanzee	Man
Adult	11+ years	20 years	20+ years	20+ years	30 years	55 years
Juvenile	2 years	6 years	6½ years	7 years	7 years	14 years
Infancy	½ year	1½ years	2 years	3½ years	3 years	6 years
Gestation	126 days	168 days	210 days	233 days	238 days	266 days

Figure 48.4 Infant rhesus monkey maintains contact with his soft pseudomother even while reaching for milk from his barbwired pseudomother. (Courtesy of Harry F. Harlow, University of Wisconsin Primate Laboratory.)

infant than the satisfaction of nutritional needs. When given the choice of a dummy mother made solely of barbed wire or one covered with a soft terry cloth, the baby monkey will invariably choose the terry-cloth pseudomother. In fact, an infant monkey will attach itself semipermanently to the cloth-covered surrogate mother (Plate 24). The infant will maintain contact with the soft pseudomother even while reaching for milk from a hard, barb-wired pseudomother (fig. 48.4). Indeed, the sense of security associated with soft objects or bodily contact is retained into adult life.

Harlow studied the effects of social deprivation in infant monkeys by denying the newborn any contact with the biological mother as well as other infants. The deprived baby monkeys, from birth onward, were permitted to associate only with dummy mothers (pseudomothers). When these motherless baby monkeys grew up, they were strikingly abnormal in their social behavior. They were unable to establish social contact with other monkeys. Neither the males nor the females could engage in normal sexual relationships. Several of the females, however, were forcibly mounted by normal, experienced males and did become pregnant and give birth. However, these females mistreated their own newborn, actively rejecting them by pushing them aside.

Additional studies revealed that contact of the motherless monkeys with other juveniles, during the first six months of life, largely ameliorated

Figure 48.5 Together-together monkeys. Constant contact and play of juveniles compensates in part for the lack of mothering. (Courtesy of Harry F. Harlow, University of Wisconsin Regional Primate Center.)

the lack of mothering (fig. 48.5). Visual contact alone, however, was not sufficient; the motherless infants had to have the opportunity for touching, grooming, and rough-and-tumble play with other juveniles. Continual playful interactions with peers can convert the troubled motherless infant into an enthusiastic participant in social interactions. As described below, the unseemly activity of play within a peer group is essential for the full development of social behaviors.

PLAY

Play is now recognized as a highly significant activity during the development of a primate. The successful initiation of interactive play is crucial for the complete physical and social development of the individual. During play, infants establish and maintain social affinities and learn to communicate with each other. Infants also develop a repertoire of play relations that facilitate normal adult sexual behaviors.

The daily life of the rhesus monkey, between four and eight months of age, is dominated by play activity. The interactive patterns are primarily of two types. The first behavior pattern is one of rolling about vigorously and wrestling, which has been designated by Harlow as "rough-and-tumble" play. The second type of play, called "approach-withdrawal," is a milder form of interaction between two individuals. One animal pursues and the other retreats; the subjects alternate roles in quick succession without establishing strong physical contact. Juvenile male monkeys play more often and more vigorously than juvenile female monkeys. Young males show a preference for rough-and-tumble play, which young females generally avoid. Females enjoy approach-withdrawal exchanges and are chased more than they pursue.

As early as four months of age, males and females engage in sexual posturing. During subsequent months, the infants develop a high level of proficiency in mounting and thrusting. Harlow and other investigators have emphasized that adult sexual patterns have their genesis in the play of young monkeys. Rhesus monkeys do not become sexually mature until about the fourth year, yet the foundations of sexual behavior are established very early in life.

At the end of the first year, the play behaviors of the infants display a progressively aggressive quality. Aggressive play is characterized by biting and pulling, but injury is rarely inflicted. When aggressive play develops, sexual separation within the play groups becomes pronounced. The females interact almost exclusively among themselves, while the males struggle for dominance position within the male group. The overt aggression among the males diminishes as the dominance order emerges. The emergent dominant male protects his female friends from any aggressive overtures of subordinate males. In this manner, the female friends of the dominant male enjoy social status.

Severe behavioral maladjustments arise when rhesus monkeys are raised without contact with peers. Infants that are deprived of the opportunity to interact with peers subsequently avoid playful contact with others, are unable to control their aggressions, and are sexually incompetent. In essence, it is primarily through play that young monkeys learn to interact in a social group. The play repertories of infants contain the rudiments of virtually all behaviors that characterize adult social life.

ORIGIN OF THE HUMAN FAMILY

We have already suggested (chapter 39) that the assumption by primitive or protocultural man of the hunting behavior—hunting game in open country—was the determining factor in the development of man's unique social and sexual behavior. The hunting of large game favored cooperative behavior among the males and promoted for the first time the sharing of food within the group. Except for man, primates do not share food; primate mothers do not even give up their food to their infants, or they do so only rarely.

It may be that the primitive humans initially wandered in open, chimpanzeelike fashion and the males did not commit themselves to particular females until economic necessity made it impractical for a given male to maintain a large harem. There is no evidence that the early hominid female participated in the hunting of large game; the adult female was increasingly encumbered with a fetus or by the care of the young, or by both. The long period of dependency of the young strengthened mother-child bonds but also restricted the mobility and activity of the woman. It appears likely that the female remained at home as a food gatherer and domestic while the male alone engaged in hunting. The immobility of the female and the prolonged immaturity of the young, coupled with the limitations imposed upon the male in terms of the number of females he could possibly support, radically transformed a basically polygamous society into a monogamous structure.

A primary human innovation was thus relatively permanent mated pairs, or monogamy. The heterosexual pair-bonding relationship became fortified as the estrus cycle of the female became modified into a condition of continuous sexual receptivity. The sustained sex interests of the partners made possible by the obliteration of estrus in the female increased the stability of the family unit, and facilitated the development of permanent family-sized shelters for rest, protection, and play. In essence, strong interpersonal bonds between a male, a female, and their children became the basis of the uniquely human family organization. The human male had become incorporated into the mother-young social group of the monkeys and apes.

Human language was fostered as the hunters recorded experiences with each other and transmitted information to their mates and children. In turn, the women conveyed events on the domestic scene to the returned hunters. Speech favored cooperation between local groups and the fusion of small groups into larger communities. Speech also fostered the successful occupation of one geographical area after another. The exchange of ideas over wide areas permitted human cultures of great complexity to develop.

SUMMARY

Regular and predictable behavior patterns are witnessed when members of a species interact in a social context. In social aggregations, aggressive behavior is minimized by the establishment of a dominance hierarchy and the closely allied phenomenon of territoriality. Dominant members of a hierarchy secure priority of access to food and choice of mates and territory. A biologically based hierarchy is difficult to ascertain in humans; whatever dominance behavior exists in man today may be primarily culturally conditioned.

Territoriality in organisms is most evident during the reproductive period. It serves to space out the adult breeding pairs and assure each pair adequate food for raising a family. Wynne-Edwards views territoriality as a mechanism that limits population size at a level commensurate with the resources of the area. Under his view, natural selection operates on the population as a whole to establish appropriate group behavior patterns that keep the population from reaching such high densities as to threaten depletion of the resources. This thesis of group selection is unsupported by our present understanding of the operation of natural selection. It is also untenable in its application to man; a balance between population density and consumable resources is clearly not in evidence in human populations.

The social behavior of nonhuman primates differs largely in degree, rather than in kind, from human behavior. Both maternal-infant interactions and peer-play interactions are important for the development of normal social behaviors. One unique characteristic of human social behavior is the integration of the male into the family life. The prolonged immaturity of the human infant and the long dependency period of the juvenile were probably contributing factors in incorporating the male in the family unit. The heterosexual pair-bonding relationship became fortified as the estrus cycle of the female became modified from well-defined mating periods to a condition of continuous sexual receptivity.

Ethical Probe 29
A Subtle Form of Coercion

In France, a law was passed recently that states that, unless requested otherwise, at death all organs in a person's body may be used for transplantation purposes. This ushers in the ready availability of transplantable hearts, lungs, livers, kidneys, and eyes. Prior to the new legislation, a person had to state specifically, in writing, the desire to donate a given part of his or her body. Even then, the written wish could be voided by a grieving spouse or next of kin. Thus, in the past, transplantable organs were rare. In the United States, a voluntary program of organ donation continues to exist. However, there are advocates for a changeover to the system recently adopted by the French government.

Do you feel than an agency or anyone other than you has the right to decide the fate of your body without your expressed consent? If, in future years, you would decline to donate your organs for obviously humanitarian purposes, would your attitude be looked upon as selfish, if not almost criminal?

49 Sociobiology

We may recall that ethology represents an evolutionary approach to the understanding of behavior. An offshoot of ethology is the modern field of *sociobiology*, which is the application of evolutionary thought to the study of the social interactions of all animals, including humans. The view of sociobiology is that the social interplay of animals, no matter how complex, has evolved by natural selection. Accordingly, sociobiologists attempt to place social behavior on sound evolutionary principles.

If the behavioral attributes of animals are the products of the same evolutionary forces that shape morphological and physiological traits, then social behavioral patterns should be adaptive. That is to say, be-havioral dispositions should be optimally designed to confer reproductive success upon the individual. There are, however, behavioral acts that are detrimental to the individual performing the act but which promote the reproductive advantage of other members of the population. A female worker bee, for example, completely forsakes procreation and devotes her entire existence to enhancing the reproductive fitness of the queen. Is it possible to select for behaviors that are individually disadvantageous but beneficial to the species as a whole? This is one of the searching questions in sociobiology today.

GROUP SELECTION

In 1932, the English geneticist J. B. S. Haldane speculated on the possi-bility that a trait may be selected that confers an advantage for the group but is costly to the individual. He used the term *altruism* for such a trait and defined an altruistic act as one that is disadvantageous to the orga-nism performing the act but is beneficial to the population as a whole. Thus, a prairie dog that emits a loud warning call (or alarm) when it spots a coyote improves the chances that his fellow conspecifics will survive. In protecting the group, the prairie dog (alarmer) attracts attention to itself and places itself in immediate danger of being captured by the predator. The act by the alarmer is essentially self-sacrificial; the term *altruism* may be equated with self-sacrificial or selflessness. Haldane acknowledged the difficulty in explaining, in a mathematical model, the establishment of an altruistic trait that apparently is harmful to the individual.

In 1962, the Scottish ecologist V. C. Wynne-Edwards evoked the con-cept of *group selection* to account for altruism as it relates to territorial behavior. Wynne-Edwards views territoriality as a method of population control. When a given population becomes excessive, many individuals cannot find territories and therefore cannot breed. Wynne-Edwards sug-gests that the territorial system has evolved by natural selection as part of a mechanism to stabilize the population density at a level that can be supported by the available food resources of the area. Wynne-Edwards's thesis assumes that natural selection operates for the benefit of the group as a whole. The implication is that many individuals are genetically or internally programmed to refrain from reproducing so as not to endanger the welfare or survival of the stock. In other words, natural selection has fostered both territorial "winners" and "losers" for the good of the species as a whole. Stated another way, a "loser" promotes the reproductive advantage of the "winner" at its own expense.

The curtailment of reproductive activity in "losers" is inconsistent with the notion of individual selection. An abridgment of reproductive behavior certainly does not benefit the individual. Natural selection characteristically operates on individuals (not groups) to augment (not decrease) individual reproductive capability. Since selection presumably operates solely to maximize the reproductive success of each individual, it is difficult to imagine how individuals can be selected for behaviors that are individually disadvantageous albeit beneficial to the species as a whole.

From a theoretical standpoint, can reproductive curtailment or restraint on the part of an individual evolve in a population so as to confer a reproductive advantage upon the group as a whole? Let us suppose that gene a_1 promotes reproductive capability and its allele, a_2, tends to curtail the reproductive capacity of an individual. Can the a_2 allele persist, or even spread, in a population when its effect is to impair the reproductive fitness of its possessor in the present and succeeding generations? The a_2 allele necessarily is selected against since the possessors of the alternative allele, a_1, obviously leave more offspring than the possessors of the a_2 gene. Ultimately, the self-sacrificial a_2 allele will be replaced by the reproductively advantageous a_1 gene.

KIN SELECTION

Altruism apparently cannot evolve without violating the principle of individual selection since the individuals displaying self-sacrificial behavior are less biologically fit than their selfish (or egotistical) colleagues. Yet altruistic behaviors are clearly evident, particularly among birds and mammals. A female bird behaves altruistically when she protects her brood against predation; a male baboon will emerge from the heart of a troop to attack a leopard that threatens the group; and a human will place his or her life in jeopardy to rescue a drowning person. In 1964, W. D. Hamilton of the London School of Economics proposed an alternative route for the evolution of altruism that is not based on the indefensible premise of group selection.

Hamilton explained altruism as the outcome of a selective process called *kin selection*. The concept is based on the fact that close relatives share a high proportion of the same genes. Altruistic behavior can be favorably selected if the probability is high that the beneficiaries of the altruistic act also have the same genes as the self-sacrificial altruist. Under this view, kin selection is a special manifestation of *gene selection*. It is the gene coding for a particular behavior that is optimized or favorably selected. A given allele a_1 will spread if the behavior associated with this gene adds a greater number of a_1 alleles to the next generation than in the preceding generation. This can happen only if the reproductively successful individuals are close relatives of the altruist, thereby increasing the probability that they carry the same a_1 allele.

An instructive phenomenon is the special chirp, or warning call, in bird populations, by which one member alerts the flock to the danger of a predator. We may assume that the warning note is governed by an a_1 allele. A warning call originating as a signal from a parent to its offspring during the breeding season is selectively advantageous, because the degree of relatedness between the caller and recipient is high. Gene a_1 will persist in the population since the alarm call by the parent (bearing gene a_1) increases the fitness of sufficient numbers of offspring also possessing a_1. By protecting the offspring, the parent invests in its own genetic representation in subsequent generations.

Essentially, then, an individual can transmit its genes directly through its own reproduction as well as indirectly through its close relatives who share genes by common descent. An individual is said to maximize an *inclusive fitness*—its own reproductive fitness plus the reproductive fitness of close relatives. The degree of relatedness has a crucial bearing on the likelihood that two individuals will behave altruistically toward one another. In diploid species, the degree of relatedness of an individual to his or her full siblings is $\frac{1}{2}$; to half-siblings, $\frac{1}{4}$; to children, $\frac{1}{2}$; and to cousins, $\frac{1}{8}$. An altruistic gene will be perpetuated if the behavior of the bearer of the altruistic gene adds to the reproductive success of biologically related individuals. Stated in very specific terms with respect to parent and offspring, an altruistic gene will spread if the beneficial effect on the offspring of the parent's altruistic act increases the offspring's biological fitness by at least twice the amount by which the act lowers the parent's fitness. A variety of altruistic behavioral dispositions in the human species—the sharing of food, the sharing of implements, and the caring of the sick—probably evolved by kin selection in the early hominid hunting bands, which consisted largely of close kin.

THE SELFISH GENE

The alarm calls of birds are often cited as an excellent example of kin selection. It is generally the case that a close kin is sufficiently near the caller to benefit from the warning call. However, some authors contend that the habit of warning cries evolved by conventional individual selection rather than by kin selection. A warning call may *not* serve to draw the attention of the predator to the alarmer. Rather the call note is intended to mislead the predator as to the position of the prey.

Under this view, the alarmer utters a call that the predator cannot easily locate. Since the predator cannot readily detect the location of the call, it would appear that the alarmer issues the warning note to protect itself and not its colleagues (conspecifics). Suppose a flock of birds is feeding in a meadow and a hawk flies past in the distance. The hawk has not seen the flock, but there is the danger that he will soon spot the flock. The noisy rummaging activity of members of the flock could attract the hawk's attention. The alarmer who first detects the hawk issues a warning call to its companions, but does so only to curtail the noise of the flock. Accordingly, the caller reduces the chance that the flock will inadvertently summon the hawk into his own vicinity. In large measure, the caller is not acting *altruistically* but rather *selfishly*.

The same situation may be viewed in another selfish vein. Suppose the caller fails to signal, quietly taking flight by itself without warning its unsuspecting conspecifics. In this event, the hawk might be easily attracted to a single bird flying off. The issuance of an alarm would be better than no alarm at all. An alarmer that issues a call curtails his risks by flying up into the tree—and simultaneously arouses the other members to fly with him into the tree. In corralling the conspecifics, the caller ensures protective cover for himself in flight. The conspecifics benefit from the caller's act, but in increasing his own safety, the caller benefits even more!

The portrait of a biological individual that emerges from these examples is one of self-serving opportunism. It seems that an individual is programmed to care about itself. It may be, as several investigators contend, that acts of apparent altruism are actually selfishness in disguise.

RECIPROCAL ALTRUISM

When a self-sacrificial parent saves his own child from some potentially tragic event, the parent acts to protect his share of genes invested in the child. If, however, an individual saves the life of an unrelated party or nonrelative, kin selection is ruled out. In this instance, the individual may have behaved altruistically with the expectation that the beneficent behavior will be reciprocated at some future occasion. This is the concept of *reciprocal altruism,* first proposed in 1971 by Robert L. Trivers of Harvard University. An altruist who places himself in danger for a biologically unrelated person incurs a reduction in fitness because of the energy consumed and the risks involved. However, a future reciprocal act by the recipient is likely to bring returns that are equal to, or greater than, the altruist's original expenditure.

There is definite survival value to both donor and recipient when altruistic acts are mutually exchanged. If, however, a recipient fails to reciprocate when the situation arises, that recipient would no longer have the benefits of future altruistic gestures to him. The nonreciprocator would then be at a selective disadvantage since subsequent adverse effects on his life would not be overcome by altruistic acts that might be lifesaving. The ultimate effect of unreciprocating would be for altruists to restrict their altruism to faithful fellow altruists, with the consequence that genes for reciprocal altruism would be perpetuated through the generations. In fact, the chance of selecting for altruistic genes is improved as more altruistic acts occur in the lifetime of the altruist. By the continual exchange of beneficent acts, altruists accrue more fitness in the long run than the nonreciprocators. Overall, altruists gain fitness, rather than lose fitness, from selfless acts.

IMPLICATIONS FOR SOCIETY

The term *altruism* means different things to different people. When, for example, a male baboon protects members of his troop by attacking a predator, he tends to reduce his own individual fitness but he simultaneously increases his inclusive fitness. Is the baboon's action beneficent or selfish? Some writers declare that any behavioral act that increases biological fitness (individual or inclusive) is selfish and exploitative. In particular, the psychologist Donald Campbell of Northwestern University states that man's basic behavioral tendencies are essentially selfish. Campbell advocates that society must counter the individual selfish tendencies that are promulgated by natural selection and, through learning and socialization, promote positive or beneficent expressions of social interplay. The implication is that our genetically based social tendencies are "bad" and only culturally imposed restraints are "good." Campbell presupposes that a social system works best by placing restraints on individual biological fitness. He also presumes that biological evolution and cultural evolution are sharply separated from one another. He thus revives the old, untenable nature-nurture dichotomy. In reality, the complex social behavior pattern of the human species is the outcome of the complementary interaction of biological evolution and cultural evolution. The coaction of these two processes is stressed below.

CHARACTERISTICS OF CULTURAL EVOLUTION

Some 10,000 years ago, man gave up the precarious hunting and gathering way of life for a more settled and secure existence based on agriculture and the breeding of animals. This initial trial at cultivating the land ushered in the so-called Neolithic revolution. When Neolithic man domesticated plants and animals, he took the first step in controlling nature rather than being at its mercy. Man placed nature at his service with his ideas, discoveries, and inventions. He began to control his own food supplies, to congregate into more stable communities, and to establish a distinctive civilization.

Man has since modified his external surroundings at an ever-increasing rate. The rapidity and efficiency with which man has dominated the environment reflects his capacity for learning and for transmitting his accumulated knowledge. This capacity for *cultural evolution* has had a profound influence on the biology of man himself—on his way of life and on his destiny.

There are important differences between biological and cultural evolution, one of the major differences being in the tempo of change (table 49.1). The brisk pace of cultural evolution contrasts sharply with the gradual progress of biological evolution. The acquisition and transmission of learned ideas occurs through the generations from mind to mind rather than through the germ cells. The generation time for cultural evolution is as rapid as communication methods and man's inventiveness can make it. A given cultural change can be passed on to large groups of unrelated individuals, whereas a given genetic modification can be transmitted only to direct descendants, who are generally few. Biological evolution is necessarily slow since it depends on accidental mutational changes in the DNA molecule, and each chance genetic change may take many generations before it can become established in the population under the force of natural selection.

Man's existence has been extraordinarily influenced by his creative, or cultural, pursuits. It would, however, be inaccurate to assert that cultural evolution has completely replaced biological evolution. For example, human pregnancy wastage remains high, and constitutes a strong selective factor for certain genes. The magnitude of human pregnancy wastage is of the order of 50 percent. Current evidence indicates that 10–15 percent of the fertilized eggs fail to implant properly and 35–40 percent of the

Table 49.1
Comparison of Biological and Cultural Evolution

	Biological Evolution	Cultural Evolution
Agents	Genes	Ideas
Rate of change	Slow	Rapid
Direction of change	Random variations (mutations) and subject to selection	Usually purposeful and directional
Nature of new variant	Often harmful	Often beneficial
Transmission	Parents to offspring	Wide dissemination by many means
Distribution in nature	All forms of life	Unique to man

conceptuses are arrested in development within the first three weeks of gestation. An appreciable portion of the defective embryogenesis has been ascribed to chromosomal anomalies, of which autosomal trisomies, XO monosomy, and triploidy have been found most commonly in early abortuses. Accordingly, natural selection still operates as an evolutionary agency in the human species.

Cultural evolution does not supercede biological evolution; rather it interacts with biological evolution. As a striking example, population geneticists have noted that the incidences of two major congenital malformations, spina bifida and anencephaly, have declined in recent years in certain areas of the world, notably in Britain. Genetic factors are instrumental in the etiology of these two neural tube abnormalities; there are twice as many afflicted offspring in marriages of first cousins as in marriages of unrelated persons. Moreover, both disorders exhibit a familial concentration, in that more than one sibling is often affected. The recent decline in these birth defects in Britain has been attributed to two important social, or cultural, considerations. The first is the increased awareness of the familial nature of the disorders, which has caused many parents of an affected child to avoid subsequent pregnancies. The second is the increased acceptance and effectiveness of contraceptive measures, which have enabled parents to restrict family size more successfully. In terms of biological evolution, the long-term impact of deliberate family limitation practiced in a large scale would be a reduction of the pool of detrimental genes responsible for these neural tube disorders. Evidently, social or cultural considerations, or changes in one's way of life, can influence the course or direction of biological evolution. Cultural evolution can influence, but not replace, biological evolution.

INFANTICIDE AND EUTHANASIA

In ancient Greek and Roman times, malformed babies were either left to perish by exposure in the mountains or cast into the rivers and seas. *Infanticide*, or the taking of life of a sickly infant, was then a common practice. Today, we view with repugnance the primitive procedure of abandonment of the sickly infant. Indeed, we take a jaundiced view of incidents of infanticide in any of the primates. Nevertheless, infanticide is a distinctive feature of the social system of langur monkeys in India. When a male langur is triumphant in a fight for an already established troop, the newly ascendant male destroys the young offspring that were sired by the vanquished male. This behavior is not pathological, but an adaptive strategy by which the victor elicits the appropriate conditions for successful mating. It is generally the case that many females in the newly conquered troop are nursing their infants; such lactating females are not especially receptive to the male. With the infants removed, physiological and behavioral changes associated with estrus occur in the female that prepare her for mating. Thus, the new dominant male has the opportunity to father his own offspring. This might be considered as the ultimate form of kin selection.

Will contemporary human society come to accept or allow, as a regular practice, the termination of life of a severely deformed infant? In the absence of prenatal detection of a severe deformity, it is only at birth that a gross malformation becomes glaringly observable. The birth of a hopelessly deformed child imposes an emotional crisis on the parents to which adjustment is slow and agonizing, and the suffering of the child can be enormous. We may recall the thalidomide disaster (chapter 4) in which a supposedly harmless sleeping pill, when taken by the pregnant woman, caused a grotesque deformity in the newborn: severely shortened and malformed limbs. The thalidomide affair has brought more fully to public awareness the problem of the seriously deformed infant. It has stimulated thought and court action on a most sensitive topic. The clash of opinions and values became dramatically evident in the court trial at Liège, France in 1962. The parents of a thalidomide-affected baby had been charged with murdering their limbless child. In an unprecedented verdict, the parents were acquitted. Although it is still too early to determine the final impact of the court decision, we may have witnessed the emergence of a new ethical and legal outlook.

Will it be considered ethical to end in compassion a life that is destined undeniably to be burdensome, in the expectation that a better new life may be conceived in a subsequent pregnancy? Opinions and consciences are greatly divided on these delicate questions but, in the years to come, the "crime" of infanticide may receive more kindly treatment.

An equally sensitive issue is the prolonging of life of a patient with a lingering or incurable sickness. In extending the existence of a hopelessly incurable patient, we may well ask: Are we prolonging life or merely prolonging the process of dying? Should the terminally ill patient have the freedom to request medical aid to end personal suffering without commission of crime? Over the years, public opinion about euthanasia— the deliberate taking of a person's life in the event of an incurable, painful, and terminal illness—appears to have been changing. To many persons, euthanasia, or "mercy killing," is proper and humane.

There is a reformation of conscience from one generation to another. Each new generation has a different sense of values than the previous generation. The present generation seems to look on life more from the aspect of quality than of quantity. The present generation apparently leans toward the attitude that an individual has the absolute right to control his or her own bodily destiny in regard to reproduction, medical treatment, and the termination of life.

SUMMARY

The evolutionary process is expected to produce individuals who are optimally designed for reproduction. The conventional view is that natural selection operates to maximize the reproductive success of each individual. There are, however, particularly among birds and mammals, social behavioral tendencies—said to be *altruistic*—that appear to be beneficial to the species as a whole but reproductively costly to the individual. Because natural selection is concerned only with the representation of genes in succeeding generations, an altruistic disposition can be selected if it enhances the reproductive effectiveness of close relatives who share genes by common descent. Although an individual by its altruistic behavior reduces the probability of transmitting its genes directly through its own reproduction, the altruist increases the probability of transmitting its genes indirectly through its offspring or other relatives. This indirect pathway to genetic representation in a subsequent generation is known as *kin selection*. Altruism can also be selectively advantageous between individuals who are not biologically related given certain conditions of reciprocity (the phenomenon of *reciprocal altruism*).

20

21

22

23

24

Plate 25 Cuddling up to a cloth-covered surrogate mother. (Nina Leen, Time-LIFE Picture Agency.)

Plate 26 *Top:* subordinate males (young adult males) walk in the vanguard; older, dominant males protect the females with nursing young in the center of the group.

Bottom: When threatened, older dominant males lead the attack. Based on studies of the African savanna baboon, *Papio ursinus,* by I. DeVore. (From *Science year, the world book science annual.* © 1970 Field Enterprises Educational Corporation.)

■ Infant ■ Juvenile ■ Adult female ■ Subadult male ■ Young adult male ■ Dominant male

Strategy on the African Savanna

Acts of altruism are likely to bring returns greater than the expenditure they entail. An altruistic act may be thought of as an investment that brings a later substantial profit. Accordingly, some authors contend that an altruistic individual is opportunistically selfish and exploitative. These same authors suggest that the genetic programming of selfishness in humans can (and should) be modified for positive expressions of social interactions through learning and socialization.

Ethical Probe 30
The Aged in Society

Society has yet to cope effectively with the new reality of a longer life span. The proportion of elderly citizens (over 65 years of age) in the United States is about 20 percent of the total population. Most are living in increasing loneliness, with decreasing financial resources and declining ability to care for themselves. The problems of old age are compounded by ill health; a staggering 86 percent of the aged suffer from one or more chronic diseases.

Although research has been directed at prolonging the life span, little attention has been directed at improving the quality of life of the aged so that the later years are worth living. Many writers have underscored the importance of sociological factors in the problems of the aged. Most of the elderly have a restricted social life. One insistent task of present-day society is to correct the image of the old person as someone who prefers to be alone and idle. Opportunities should be provided for the elderly for useful work in order to maintain self-esteem and promote contacts with others.

As a young person in our overcrowded society, can you fulfill your needs, particularly in terms of gainful employment, without forcing older people out of active society? How can you help to bring the elderly, at least the majority of them, back into society?

Epilogue

The uniqueness of man resides not only in his biological attributes but also in his capacity for cultural adaptation. A cultural heritage is not shared by any other animal on this earth. Other forms of life have evolved, and have spread by adaptive radiation into different available ecological situations. Most species of organisms have become highly specialized, and many have passed unavoidably into oblivion with the onset of radical environmental changes to which the species have been unable to adjust or adapt. Indeed, a cardinal theme of evolution is that most species of organisms eventually decline and pass out of existence. There is accordingly no natural law or force that assures the future survival of any species, including man.

In a large sense, man is averting, or at least forestalling, extinction by cultural adaptation. Man's control over nature arises out of his unique powers to analyze and modify his external surroundings. He can form ideas out of experience and can transform the ideas into fruitful hypotheses and experimental procedures. He has thus been able to insinuate his will into the formidable processes of nature.

Cultural changes provide both potential opportunities and potential disasters. Each innovative cultural change is rooted in new knowledge and is accompanied by new outlooks and responsibilities. However, too often new information is distorted to fit proexisting patterns of attitudes, beliefs, and actions. Despite the onrush of new knowledge, man still remains encumbered by dogmas that trace their roots to early historic times. People are generally more comfortable in adhering to old values. However, many of our old values and prescribed actions are much too inflexible to cope adequately with the profound changes and variety of real-life situations that we are witnessing today. Adjustments in values have to be made when new knowledge in a changing situation does not reinforce past values based on a different set of circumstances.

Faced with the imperative need of establishing new values, how do we decide on new moral standards to guide our actions? The question of new values proceeds from the assumption that we know what we want. Man for the first time has the capacity to engineer himself—to design himself and his future. Man has intervened in nature, and now has the capability of changing his own nature. Engineering the engineer, however, is quite different from engineering other organisms or mechanical objects. A particularly knotty aspect of the problem is that the rapid advances in science and technology are known only in bits by a myriad of specialists in different branches. The plain man in the street must now rely on specialists for information on nearly any problem that he encounters. More often than not, the specialists or authorities do not agree.

One simplistic solution to the thorny problem is to permit each individual to establish his own moral code. Morality becomes simply the dictates of individual conscience. But, can each problem lend itself to personal conviction or individual conscience for resolution? Can each of us pursue his own ends without thwarting other people in the pursuit of their goals?

In the final analysis, there are two radically different ways of looking at morality. Under one view, moral rules are a set of commands to be obeyed as absolute standards. Moral goodness is thought to lie in conformity to rules for their own sake. The rules are in no way dependent for their validity on the good or bad consequences of obedience. In the other way of looking at morality, moral rules are considered to be subordinate to ends. Moral principles exist solely for achieving ends, and are to be judged by their tendency to promote those ends. In the eyes of many, moral rules are to be judged by their tendency to promote human happiness. Some would argue that moral rules are to be judged by their ability to promote the continued survival of human culture. Whatever may be the purpose of moral rules, we must be willing to keep them under review and to discard or modify those that, in the light of new knowledge and experience, we find unnecessary or obstructive.

The last two decades have seen a surge of scientific knowledge and technological advances that few could have foreseen or dared to prophesy. Equally, we can be sure that the next two decades will contain surprises that promise to strain even more existing cultural and moral fabrics. This evinces either a tragic sense of despair that man can become lost in his own machinations, or a sober realization that man has the capabilities to manage constructively his own destiny.

Basic Chemistry

Whereas the fundamental unit of living systems is the cell, the basic constituent of all matter is the *atom*. An atom may be viewed as the smallest particle that can exist as an element. The word *atom* is derived from the Greek *atomos*—*a* meaning "not" and *tomos* meaning "slice," or "cut." The etymology would lead us to believe that the atom cannot be cut or fissioned into smaller particles. Today it is clear that an atom can be split into smaller units. Modern physicists conceive of the atom not as the ultimate particle of matter but as a complex system. In fact, modern wave mechanics discourages the use of mechanical models of the atom, and prefers a mathematical formulation in describing the atom. Nevertheless, mechanical models of the atom, although static and imprecise, remain useful pedagogically.

An atom has a central core, the *nucleus*, in which most of the mass of the atom is concentrated (fig. A.1). Within the nucleus are tightly packed particles of two kinds: *neutrons*, which are electrically uncharged, and *protons*, which possess a positive charge (+). Negatively charged *electrons* (−) spin about at varying distances from the nucleus in spaces called *orbitals*. The orbital path of an electron is not as regular, or as spherically symmetrical, as depicted in a conventional drawing (fig. A.1, bottom). The configuration shown at the right in figure A.1 is a better way of visualizing the atom. The dumbbell-shaped orbitals of the outer electrons are essentially probability curves—the outline of a given curve or shape encloses the probability of finding the electron at any distance from the nucleus 90 percent of the time. (There remains 1 chance in 10, or a 10 percent probability, that an electron will be located outside the boundaries of its orbital shape at any given instant.)

The classical portrayal of spherically symmetrical electrons about the nucleus is still serviceable for the purpose of describing chemical bonds. In the conventional model, the orbital paths are commonly called the *shells* of the atom. The first shell, nearest the nucleus, houses only 2 electrons. The second shell never has more than 8 electrons, and each successive shell also has a limit to the number of electrons it can house. The outermost shell cannot contain more than 8 electrons, and only the electrons in the outermost level participate in chemical reactions. When protons (+) and electrons (−) are present in equal numbers, the atom is electrically neutral. Through the loss of electrons an atom becomes positively charged, since the relative number of protons has increased. Conversely, if electrons are gained so that they outnumber the protons, an atom becomes negatively charged.

Each different kind of atom is called an *element*, and each has a specific name and symbol. An element may de defined as a substance that cannnot be separated or decomposed into substances different from itself by ordinary chemical or electrical means. More than 100 different

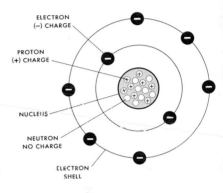

OXYGEN ATOM

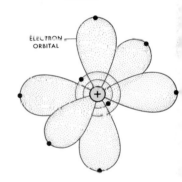

ELECTRON SPACE MODEL
OF OXYGEN

Figure A.1

Element	Symbol	Atomic Number	Atomic Weight	Number of Electrons			
				Shell 1	Shell 2	Shell 3	Shell 4
Hydrogen	H	1	1	1	0	0	0
Carbon	C	6	12	2	4	0	0
Nitrogen	N	7	14	2	5	0	0
Oxygen	O	8	16	2	6	0	0
Sodium	Na	11	23	2	8	0	0
Magnesium	Mg	12	24	2	8	1	0
Phosphorus	P	15	30	2	8	2	0
Sulfur	S	16	32	2	8	5	0
Chlorine	Cl	17	35	2	8	6	0
Potassium	K	19	39	2	8	7	0
Calcium	Ca	20	40	2	8	8	1
Iron	Fe	26	56	2	8	8	2
							8

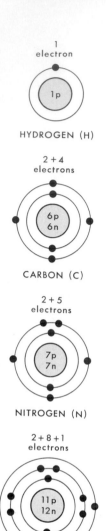

1
electron

HYDROGEN (H)

2 + 4
electrons

CARBON (C)

2 + 5
electrons

NITROGEN (N)

2 + 8 + 1
electrons

SODIUM (Na)

Figure A.2

elements are known, of which about 35 commonly occur in living organisms. The more important elements of living organisms are presented in table A.1.

The simplest element is the hydrogen atom; its nucleus is composed of a single proton and only a single electron occupies the space around the nucleus. Carbon has 6 protons and 6 electrons; nitrogen has 7 protons and 7 electrons; and sodium has 11 protons and 11 electrons (fig. A.2). One of the more complex elements, uranium, has 92 protons and 92 electrons arranged in seven shells. The number of protons in the atomic nucleus of an element is equal to the *atomic number* of the element. The atomic number determines the position of an element in the chemist's periodic table. The sum of the number of protons and neutrons in the nucleus constitutes the *atomic weight* of the element. Oxygen, for example, has an atomic weight of 16 (table A.1). The numbers of protons and neutrons in a given element are not necessarily equal. The atomic weight of uranium is 238, represented by 92 protons and 146 neutrons.

ISOTOPES AND RADIOACTIVITY

Atoms of the same element that possess varying numbers of neutrons but the same number of protons are called *isotopes* (Greek, *isos*, "same," *topos*, "place"). Isotopes may be thought of as atomic "brothers"—they have different weights but have the same chemical properties. The hydrogen atom, for example, exhibits isotopic variation. Light hydrogen, or *protium* (^1H), has one proton in its nucleus and is devoid of neutrons, whereas heavy hydrogen, or *deuterium* (^2H), contains one neutron in association with the proton (atomic weight of 2). The addition of a second neutron to the nucleus (atomic weight of 3) yields a form of hydrogen called *tritium* (^3H). In this case, the imbalance of protons to neutrons disturbs the stability of the nucleus, resulting in the spontaneous emission of rays from the nucleus. An atom such as tritium is said to be *radioactive*. Radioactive atoms eject one or more of three kinds of penetrating rays: *alpha* (α) rays (streams of doubly charged helium ions); *beta* (β) rays (composed of electrons); and *gamma* (γ) rays (shortwave X rays). The emission of these rays leads to a more stable nuclear state.

With the discovery of isotopes, the word *element* can be redefined as a substance of which all the atoms have the same atomic number. About 1,000 isotopes—most of them radioactive—have been discovered. In nature, radioactivity typifies all heavy elements, such as uranium and radium, that have greater numbers of neutrons than protons. Uranium (atomic weight 238) disintegrates spontaneously over a characteristic period of time, producing at one stage radium (atomic weight 218), and ultimately "uranium lead" (atomic weight 206). Although most of the lighter, biologically important elements are not naturally radioactive, radioactive isotopes of many of them—carbon, phosphorus, sulfur, oxygen, and others—can be prepared synthetically today. Synthetic radioactive isotopes have proven valuable in tracing the course of atoms in biochemical reactions. For example, the use of heavy oxygen (^{18}O) led to the demonstration that the oxygen produced by photosynthesis is split off from water (H_2O), not carbon dioxide (CO_2). In another instance, tagged carbon (radioactive ^{14}C instead of stable ^{12}C) was used to reveal that animals, not only plants, are capable of "fixing" CO_2 (converting CO_2 to organic molecules).

CHEMICAL BONDS

Two or more atoms can unite chemically to form a *molecule*. The oxygen we breathe is composed of two atoms of the same element (O_2). When a molecule contains different kinds of atoms (that is, different elements), it is a *compound*. Carbon dioxide (CO_2) and methane (CH_4) are examples of compounds. The properties of a compound are different from the properties of the elements of which it is composed. All compounds are molecules (since compounds consist of two or more atoms), but not all molecules are compounds (since some molecules contain only atoms of the same element).

The atoms of a compound are held together by specific forces called *chemical bonds*. Chemical bonding depends on the behavior of the electrons in the outermost shell of an atom. To achieve chemical stability, an atom tends to complete its outer electron shell by interchanging, or sharing, electrons with another atom. There are two prominent ways in which an originally incomplete outer shell of an atom can become complete. The first way is *ionic bonding*, which involves the transfer of electrons from metal atoms to nonmetal atoms during a chemical reaction. The second method is *covalent bonding*, which involves the sharing of electrons between atoms during a chemical reaction.

IONIC BOND

The formation of sodium chloride (NaCl) illustrates ionic bonding (fig. A.3). The sodium atom (Na) has only 1 electron in its outer shell, whereas the chlorine atom (Cl) has 7 outer electrons, or 1 electron too few to saturate its outer shell. Sodium reacts with chlorine by transferring its single outer electron to the outer shell of the chlorine atom, saturating that shell with the maximum 8 atoms. The sodium atom, having lost the single electron in its outermost shell, is positively charged since there is 1 less electron than protons in the nucleus. The chlorine atom, having completed its outermost shell with an extra electron, is now negatively charged. Both charged particles are called *ions*. Positively charged ions are referred to as *cations*, and negatively charged ions, *anions*. The ionic nature of the components of NaCl is denoted symbolically as Na^+ and Cl^-. The electrical attraction of cations and anions that holds them together is called an *ionic bond*, and the formation of the salt NaCl from the positive metal ion (Na^+) and the negative nonmetal ion (Cl^-) is an *ionic reaction*. In the solid state, the sodium ions and chloride ions are bound in an orderly, rigid structure known as an *ionic crystal lattice*.

Ionic salts, such as sodium chloride, are soluble in water, in which the crystal lattice comes apart and the ions are free to move about. The movement of ions in the liquid state accounts for the electrical conduc-

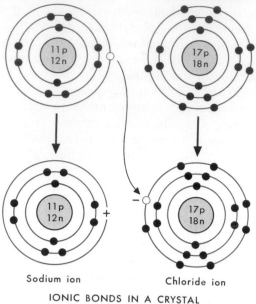

Figure A.3 Sodium (Na) atom   Chlorine (Cl) atom

Sodium ion   Chloride ion

IONIC BONDS IN A CRYSTAL
OF SODIUM CHLORIDE

tivity of water solutions of ionic salts. Ionic compounds are known as *electrolytes* since their solutions conduct electrical currents.

COVALENT BOND

Atoms can achieve completeness by sharing their electrons rather than actively acquiring or releasing electrons to one another. When electrons are mutually shared, *covalent bonds* are formed. The biologically important carbon atom has 6 electrons, 2 in its inner shell and 4 in the outer shell. Accordingly, 4 additional electrons are required to fill the outer shell. A carbon atom can form 4 covalent bonds with 4 hydrogen atoms, sharing an electron with each hydrogen atom (fig. A.4). The resulting compound is CH_4, or *methane,* which is the principal component of natural gas. In CH_4, the pair of electrons of each covalent bond is simultaneously a part of the electron configuration of the carbon atom and of the hydrogen atom. Methane may be depicted as follows:

$$
\begin{array}{ccc}
\text{H} & & \text{H} \\
\text{..} & & | \\
\text{H : C : H} & or & \text{H—C—H} \\
\text{..} & & | \\
\text{H} & & \text{H}
\end{array}
$$

In the configuration at the right, a simple *dash* between atoms represents the bonding electron pair. Each interconnecting dash thus signifies that H is sharing its 1 electron with C and that C is sharing 1 of its outer electrons with H. The number of shareable electrons of an atom is its *valence.* The valence of carbon is 4 and that of hydrogen is 1.

A single covalent bond can occur between two carbon atoms. The three remaining bond sites on each of the two carbon atoms can be occupied by hydrogen atoms. The resulting compound is *ethane,* H_3C—CH_3, or:

$$
\begin{array}{cc}
\text{H} & \text{H} \\
| & | \\
\text{H—C—C—H} \\
| & | \\
\text{H} & \text{H}
\end{array}
$$

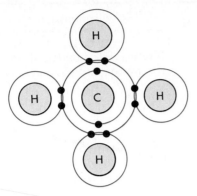

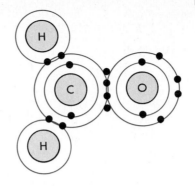

COVALENT BONDS: METHANE
(4 Single Bonds)

FORMALDEHYDE
(Double Bond)

A *double bond* arises when two carbon atoms share 2 of each of their electrons with each other. Each of the carbon atoms still has two bonding sites, and if these are associated with hydrogen, the compound that is formed is *ethylene*, $H_2C{=}CH_2$, or:

$$H{-}C{=}C{-}H$$
$$\phantom{H{-}C{=}}|\phantom{{=}C}|$$
$$\phantom{H{-}C{=}}H\phantom{{=}}H$$

The carbon atom undergoes covalent bonding with a variety of other atoms, such as oxygen, nitrogen, and sulfur. For example, two oxygen atoms may form double bonds with one carbon atom ($O{=}C{=}O$), forming the familiar molecule of carbon dioxide (CO_2). When a single atom of oxygen is double-bonded to a carbon atom, and the remaining bonding sites of the carbon atom are occupied by hydrogen atoms, formaldehyde ($H_2C{=}O$) is formed (fig. A.4).

Since carbon atoms can form covalent bonds with each other and also with other kinds of atoms, relatively large molecules with long carbon chains can result. With notably few exceptions (such as carbon dioxide), almost all carbon-containing compounds are classified as *organic*. The organic compounds that are common in living organisms—carbohydrates, proteins, and lipids (fats)—are discussed in chapter 4; nucleic acids are treated in chapter 14.

Some of the common building blocks that occur in biologically important organic compounds are listed in table A.2. Of particular interest are the two subunits of amino acids, the *carboxyl group* and *amino group* (or *amine*). In the carboxyl group (COOH), a carbon atom shares 2 of its electrons with an oxygen atom in a double covalent bond and, additionally, it shares 1 electron with a second oxygen atom in a single covalent bond. The latter oxygen atom is bonded to a hydrogen atom (hydroxyl group). The remaining bonding site of the carbon atom may be satisfied by a hydrogen atom or an atom of a continuing molecule, designated by the symbol R. The result is as follows:

$$R{-}C{-}O{-}H$$
$$\phantom{R{-}}\|\phantom{{-}O{-}H}$$
$$\phantom{R{-}}O$$

In the formation of the amino group (NH_2), two atoms of hydrogen occupy two of the three available bonding sites of the nitrogen atom. Typically the remaining bonding site of the nitrogen atom is filled by a carbon atom.

Group	Structural Formula	Biological Importance
Aldehyde	$\begin{array}{c} -C-H \\ \parallel \\ O \end{array}$	Intermediate compounds in respiration and photosynthesis
Amino	$\begin{array}{c} H \\ \vert \\ -N-H \end{array}$	Amino acids
Carbonyl	$\begin{array}{c} -C- \\ \parallel \\ O \end{array}$	Intermediate compounds in breakdown and synthesis of amino acids and fats
Carboxyl	$\begin{array}{c} -C-OH \\ \parallel \\ O \end{array}$	Amino acids, fatty acids
Phosphate	$\begin{array}{c} OH \\ \vert \\ -O-P-OH \\ \parallel \\ O \end{array}$	ADP, ATP, intermediate compounds in respiration
Sulfhydryl	$-S-H$	Proteins, especially enzymes

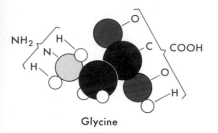

Glycine

Figure A.5

All amino acids consist of a central carbon atom in which the four bonding sites are occupied by a hydrogen atom, an amino group (NH_2), a carboxyl group (COOH), and a fourth group, or side chain (R), which varies appreciably from acid to acid. The general formula for an amino acid is:

$$\begin{array}{c} H \\ \vert \\ R-C-COOH \\ \vert \\ NH_2 \end{array}$$

The simplest amino acid is *glycine;* the side chain (R) is merely a hydrogen atom. A model of a molecule of glycine is shown in figure A.5. Amino acids unite with one another in linear chains as a *protein.* The bond between two amino acids is called the *peptide bond,* and the union is known as a *peptide linkage.* As figure A.6 shows, the formation of a peptide bond involves the release of hydrogen and oxygen atoms, which in the living system form water. In the laboratory, the peptide bonds can be broken down by acid treatment, which is essentially the reacceptance of the hydrogen and oxygen atoms by the individual amino acid units.

All chemical reactions result in an exchange of energy. Energy is required to form a chemical bond, and energy is released when a bond is broken. As a rule, the stronger the bond, the greater the release of energy. Covalent bonds between different kinds of atoms have different amounts of energy, as indicated in table A.3.

HYDROGEN BOND

A unique type of chemical bonding that is of biological importance is *hydrogen bonding.* When a hydrogen atom shares its electron in a covalent bond with another atom (such as oxygen), it becomes virtually a bare proton resting on the surface of the larger, negatively charged

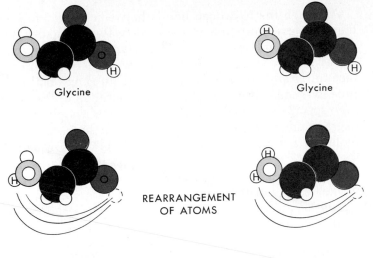

Glycine   Glycine

REARRANGEMENT
OF ATOMS

DISJOINING OF BONDS

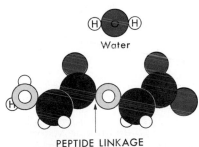

Water

PEPTIDE LINKAGE
GLYCYL-GLYCINE (DIPEPTIDE)

Table A.3
Average Bond Energies

Type of Bond	Energy (kilocalories/mole)
C—S	62
C—N	80
S—H	81
C—C	83
C—O	85
N—H	93
C—H	99
H—H	104
O—H	111
C=C	146
C=O	178

oxygen atom (fig. A.7). Since the hydrogen atom carries a positive charge, it is attracted to parts of molecules having a net negative charge. If several water molecules are near each other, the hydrogen atom of one water molecule is strongly attracted to the oxygen atom of another water molecule. A *hydrogen bond* between molecules is said to occur when a hydrogen atom that is covalently bound to an electronegative atom in one molecule is attracted to a similar atom of a neighboring molecule. In the absence of hydrogen bonding, water would be a gas at ordinary temperatures, and life as we know it could not exist. Hydrogen bonds are also essential to the structure and properties of DNA (see chapter 14).

In a given water molecule, the two hydrogen atoms are attached eccentrically to the oxygen atom—that is, they both occur on one side of the oxygen atom (fig. A.7). The angle between the two hydrogen atoms in a water molecule is 105°. Consequently, the hydrogen side of the water molecule is relatively more positive (or electropositive) as compared with the oxygen side, which is slightly negative (or electronegative). Since the water molecule has an uneven charge distribution, it is said to be a *polar molecule,* or more specifically, a *dipole.* Dipole-dipole attractive forces are weaker than ionic or covalent attractive forces.

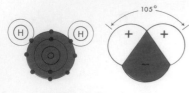

COVALENT BONDING WITHIN
A WATER MOLECULE

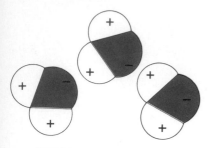

HYDROGEN BONDING AMONG
WATER MOLECULES

Figure A.7

Although the hydrogen bonds between water molecules are weaker than the covalent bonds in the same water molecules, they promote the coherence of the water molecules. Hydrogen bonding is responsible for the high surface tension of water (the tendency for the water-air interface to resist disturbance), the high melting and boiling points of water (due to tendencies to resist greater separation of the molecules), and the high specific heat of water (its capacity to absorb more heat energy per degree than most other substances). The dipole character of the water molecule permits the solubility, or dissolution, of salts (such as NaCl) in water. Certain organic compounds, particularly alcohols, are also soluble in water since they tend to share their hydrogen atoms with the oxygen atoms of the water molecules. Fats are insoluble in water primarily because they are largely devoid of polar regions that can form hydrogen bonds with water molecules.

ACIDS, BASES, AND BUFFERS

When placed in water, inorganic compounds tend to separate into free ions, a process termed *ionic dissociation*. When ordinary table salt (NaCl) is dissolved in water, the molecules dissociate into sodium ions (Na$^+$) and chlorine ions (Cl$^-$). In like manner, an acid molecule like hydrochloric acid (HCl) in a water solution dissociates into H$^+$ ions and Cl$^-$ ions. As the following examples show, these dissociations involve an equilibrium between the associated and dissociated form of the molecule.

$$\text{NaCl} \rightleftharpoons \text{Na}^+ + \text{Cl}^-$$
Sodium chloride — Sodium ion — Chloride ion

$$\text{H}_2\text{CO}_3 \rightleftharpoons \text{H}^+ + \text{HCO}_3^-$$
Carbonic acid — Hydrogen ion — Bicarbonate ion

$$\text{NH}_4\text{OH} \rightleftharpoons \text{NH}_4^+ + \text{OH}^-$$
Ammonium hydroxide — Ammonium ion — Hydroxyl ion

A molecule is said to be an *acid* when its dissociation liberates a hydrogen ion (H$^+$). Since the hydrogen ion is essentially a proton, an acid can also be defined as a *proton donor*. The sour taste of an acid reflects the presence of hydrogen ions. The more readily a molecule places hydrogen ions into solution, the more strongly acid is the molecule. Hydrochloric acid is a *strong* acid since it dissociates completely, whereas carbonic acid is a *weak* acid, dissociating only slightly and remaining in solution mainly in the intact, or associated, state.

A *base* is a molecule that is capable of accepting hydrogen ions furnished by an acid. In other words, a base is a *proton acceptor*. A few examples of molecules (and charged ions) that can accept hydrogen ions are shown below.

$$\text{NH}_3 + \text{H}^+ \rightleftharpoons \text{NH}_4^+$$
Ammonia — Hydrogen ion — Ammonium ion

$$\text{HPO}_4^{--} + \text{H}^+ \rightleftharpoons \text{H}_2\text{PO}_4^-$$
Monohydrogen phosphate — Hydrogen ion — Dihydrogen phosphate

$$\text{NaOH} + \text{H}^+ \rightleftharpoons \text{Na}^+ + \text{H}_2\text{O}$$
Sodium hydroxide — Hydrogen ion — Sodium ion — Water

The familiar bases are those, such as sodium hydroxide, that yield the hydroxyl ion (OH$^-$) upon dissociation in a water solution. The brackish, or alkaline, taste of a basic solution is related to the presence of the OH^- in solution. *Strong* bases, like sodium hydroxide (NaOH) and potassium hydroxide (KOH), undergo almost complete dissociation, whereas *weak* bases, like ammonium hydroxide (NH_4OH), undergo partial dissociation.

Bases neutralize the action of acids. Given equal numbers of molecules of a strong base and a strong acid, a solution is neither acidic nor basic, but *neutral*. As the following reaction shows, the combination of an acid and base characteristically produces a salt and water.

$$NaOH + HCl \leftrightharpoons NaCl + H_2O$$

or

$$Na^+ + OH^- + H^+ + Cl^- \leftrightharpoons Na^+ + Cl^- + H_2O$$

The standard expression for the acidity or alkalinity of a solution is the *pH*. A pH of 7 defines neutrality. Solutions with pH values below 7 are acidic; those above 7 are basic or alkaline. The pH is defined as the negative logarithm of the hydrogen ion concentration, or the logarithm of the reciprocal of the hydrogen ion concentration, as in the following equation.

$$pH = \log \frac{1}{[H^+]}$$

Since the scale is logarithmic, an increase of one pH unit indicates a tenfold decrease in the concentration of hydrogen ions.

Life activities are confined to a narrow, relatively constant pH range, close to neutrality (pH between 6 and 8). For example, the pH of human blood is 7.4, which is slightly alkaline. The constancy of the pH level in fluids of living organisms is maintained through the action of *buffers*. A buffer is a solution that contains a weak acid and a salt of that acid, or a weak base with one of its salts. A common buffer solution that is important in biological systems is the bicarbonate buffer, consisting of a water solution of appropriate proportions of carbonic acid (H_2CO_3) and sodium bicarbonate ($NaHCO_3$). A solution of H_2CO_3 dissociates only slightly into hydrogen ions (H^+) and bicarbonate ions (HCO_3^-), whereas the solution of $NaHCO_3$ dissociates completely into Na^+ and HCO_3^-, as follows:

$$H_2CO_3 \leftrightharpoons H^+ + HCO_3^-$$
$$NaHCO_3 \leftrightharpoons Na^+ + HCO_3^-$$

This buffer system resists changes in pH that might otherwise result from the addition of some other substance, such as the strong acid HCl or the strong base NaOH. If a small amount of HCl is added, the introduced H^+ ions combine with HCO_3^- ions to form H_2CO_3. The excess H^+ ions are thus effectively trapped in the weakly ionized carbonic acid, and the pH of the medium remains virtually unchanged. If a small amount of NaOH is added, the ionization of H_2CO_3 is promoted and the introduced OH^- ions combine with H^+ ions to form neutral H_2O. Buffer systems, such as the bicarbonate buffer and the phosphate buffer ($HPO_4^{--}/H_2PO_4^-$), are the means by which living organisms maintain a relatively constant pH level despite the varying chemical circumstances of their body fluids.

Appendix B
Probability

The theoretical frequencies of kinds of offspring in Mendelian inheritance are comparable to the expected outcomes of tossing a coin or a die. When an ordinary coin is suitably tossed and allowed to come to rest, the likelihood that one particular face of the coin (head) will be uppermost is equal to the likelihood that the other face (tail) will be uppermost. We say that the probability of obtaining a head (or a tail) is 1 out of 2, or $\frac{1}{2}$. In the random tossing of a six-sided die, the probability of obtaining the ace face (or any one specified face) is 1 out of 6, or $\frac{1}{6}$. Thus, the probability of success—that is, the likelihood that a desired event will occur—depends on the number of alternative, or equally likely, events possible. Probability is frequently expressed as a fraction, in which the denominator is the total number of equally likely events (or the sum of all possible events) and the numerator is the numerical figure for the desired, or specified, event.

Consider now a vase that contains eight marbles of identical size and shape. Three of the marbles are red, marked R1, R2, and R3, and the remaining five are blue, marked B1 through B5, respectively. The probability of withdrawing, blindfolded, the red marble marked R2 from the vase is $\frac{1}{8}$. The probability of success, however, of obtaining any red marble is $\frac{3}{8}$. In this instance, the attainment of the desired event (a red marble irrespective of markings) can occur by drawing any one of the three red marbles from the vase.

ADDITION RULE OF PROBABILITY

The chances for success of a desired event may occur in two or more different ways, each way excluding the others. Events are said to be *mutually exclusive* when the occurrence of any one of them excludes the occurrence of the others. In a single toss of a die, the securing of an ace face ("one") is mutually exclusive of securing a "two" face. We may now ask: What is the expectation or probability of obtaining *either* a "one" *or* a "two" in a single toss of a die? The probability is $\frac{1}{6} + \frac{1}{6} = \frac{1}{3}$. In generalized form, the probability that one or the other of any number of mutually exclusive events will occur is the *sum* of the separate probabilities.

We may consider again the vase that contains a mixture of three individually marked red marbles and five individually marked blue marbles. If we are interested only in the probability of obtaining a red marble irrespective of identifying marks, the withdrawal of any one of the three red marbles will satisfy the conditions of the problem. Since the desired event has three alternative (mutually exclusive) possibilities, the probability of success of drawing a red marble is $\frac{1}{8} + \frac{1}{8} + \frac{1}{8} = \frac{3}{8}$, or the sum of the individual probabilities of the three alternative possibilities.

In chapter 34 (see specifically table 34.1), we asked: What is the probability of producing two offspring, one *AA* and the other *Aa*, in no partic-

Table B.1

	Offspring	Probability
First Alternative	*AA* followed by *Aa*	$\frac{1}{8}$
Second Alternative	*Aa* followed by *AA*	$\frac{1}{8}$
	Combined Probability	$\frac{1}{8} + \frac{1}{8} = \frac{1}{4}$

ular order, from a marriage of two heterozygous parents ($Aa \times Aa$)? The addition rule of probability is applicable since there are two alternative ways of having the two kinds of offspring, the *AA* birth first or the *Aa* birth first, as table B.1 shows.

MULTIPLICATION RULE OF PROBABILITY

The chances for success of a desired outcome may depend on two or more events that occur simultaneously or in succession. Two or more events are said to be *independent* when the occurrence (or failure) of any one of them does not effect or influence the occurrence (or failure) of any of the others. What, for example, is the probability of obtaining two aces in the random tossing of a pair of dice? Since the probability of obtaining "one" in the toss of a die is $\frac{1}{6}$ and that of obtaining "one" in the other die is also $\frac{1}{6}$, then the probability of two "ones" arising in a roll of dice is $\frac{1}{6} \times \frac{1}{6} = \frac{1}{36}$. Generalizing, the probability of two or more independent events occurring together (simultaneously or successively) is the *product* of the probabilities of the individual events involved.

Consider again the vase with the three red and five blue marbles, and let us set up a second vase with a similar mixture of marbles. When a single marble is withdrawn from *each* vase, the probability of obtaining two red marbles is $\frac{3}{8} \times \frac{3}{8} = \frac{9}{64}$. The multiplication rule also comes into play in calculating the probability of producing the two specific kinds of offspring from the two heterozygous parents previously mentioned (see table B.1). The chance that the first offspring from the cross of two heterozygous parents ($Aa \times Aa$) will be *AA* is $\frac{1}{4}$. The event of a second child is independent of the first; hence, the chance that the second offspring will be *Aa* is $\frac{1}{2}$. The probability that an *AA* offspring will be followed by an *Aa* offspring is the product of the separate probabilities, or $\frac{1}{4} \times \frac{1}{2} = \frac{1}{8}$. The tabular material earlier presented (table B.1) can be reconstructed to reveal the operation of both the *multiplication* and *addition* rules of probability, as table B.2 shows.

Table B.2

	First Offspring	Second Offspring	Probability
First Alternative	*AA* (Probability of $\frac{1}{4}$)	*Aa* (Probability of $\frac{1}{2}$)	$\frac{1}{4} \times \frac{1}{2} = \frac{1}{8}$
Second Alternative	*Aa* (Probability of $\frac{1}{2}$)	*AA* (Probability of $\frac{1}{4}$)	$\frac{1}{2} \times \frac{1}{4} = \frac{1}{8}$
		Combined Probability	$\frac{1}{8} + \frac{1}{8} = \frac{1}{4}$

MENDELIAN RATIOS AND FAMILY SIZE

A Mendelian ratio of 1:1 or 3:1 describes the probability for a *single birth*. From the mating of heterozygous (*Aa*) and recessive (*aa*) parents, the odds are 1:1 (or a probability of $\frac{1}{2}$) that any given offspring will be recessive (*aa*). When the parents are both heterozygous ($Aa \times Aa$), the classical 3:1 ratio means that for any given birth the probability is $\frac{3}{4}$ that the child will display the dominant phenotype and $\frac{1}{4}$ that the child will exhibit the recessive trait.

In sibships of small size, as in many human families, the expected distribution of traits according to ideal Mendelian ratios may not be observed. The deviations from ideal ratios, however, do *not* mean that the basic principles of hereditary transmission are invalid. Let us consider the marriage $Aa \times aa$, and calculate the expected frequencies of genotypes in sibships of four children. As table B.3 shows, five different sibships may result from an $Aa \times aa$ mating.

The probability rules are used to calculate the expected relative frequencies of the five sibships. The likelihood that all four births will result in Aa progeny is the product of the four separate probabilities, $(\frac{1}{2})^4$ or $\frac{1}{16}$. A sibship of three Aa and one aa may occur in four different ways since the aa offspring could be born first, second, third, or fourth. The probability of *each* of the four birth sequences is $(\frac{1}{2})^4$ or $\frac{1}{16}$, and the total probability of obtaining the four different sequences is the sum of the individual probabilities of the four alternative sequences, or $\frac{4}{16}$. Families of 2 Aa and 2 aa children may be attained by any of six birth sequences. Using the multiplication and addition rules of probabilities, we can calculate that the probability of $Aa \times aa$ parents having two Aa and two aa children is $\frac{6}{16}$. Other computations (table B.3) show that the probability of obtaining one Aa and three aa in a sibship is $\frac{4}{16}$, and the probability of four aa offspring is $\frac{1}{16}$. It should be clear that the probable frequencies of some sibships is greater than others.

The classical or ideal Mendelian ratio for offspring of $Aa \times aa$ parents is two Aa and two aa (or 1:1). Yet, the ideal 1:1 ratio in sibships of five occurs only in 6 out of 16 cases. In families of five children, the classical ratio of two Aa and two aa has less probability of being attained ($\frac{6}{16}$) than of *not* being attained ($\frac{10}{16}$). Nevertheless, the ideal 1:1 ratio has the *highest single probability* ($\frac{6}{16}$) when compared on an individual basis with the remaining four sibship probabilities (namely, $\frac{1}{16}$ or $\frac{4}{16}$ or $\frac{4}{16}$ or $\frac{1}{16}$). Thus, in families of limited size, the sibship predicted by the clas-

Table B.3

Sibship	Sequence of Children	Multiplication Rule	Addition Rule	Probability
4 Aa, 0 aa	Aa, Aa, Aa, Aa	$(\frac{1}{2})^4$	—	$\frac{1}{16}$
3 Aa, 1 aa	Aa, Aa, Aa, aa Aa, Aa, aa, Aa Aa, aa, Aa, Aa aa, Aa, Aa, Aa	$(\frac{1}{2})^4 = \frac{1}{16}$ $(\frac{1}{2})^4 = \frac{1}{16}$ $(\frac{1}{2})^4 = \frac{1}{16}$ $(\frac{1}{2})^4 = \frac{1}{16}$	$\frac{4}{16}$	$\frac{4}{16}$
2 Aa, 2 aa	Aa, Aa, aa, aa Aa, aa, Aa, aa Aa, aa, aa, Aa aa, Aa, Aa, aa aa, Aa, aa, Aa aa, aa, Aa, Aa	$(\frac{1}{2})^4 = \frac{1}{16}$ $(\frac{1}{2})^4 = \frac{1}{16}$ $(\frac{1}{2})^4 = \frac{1}{16}$ $(\frac{1}{2})^4 = \frac{1}{16}$ $(\frac{1}{2})^4 = \frac{1}{16}$ $(\frac{1}{2})^4 = \frac{1}{16}$	$\frac{6}{16}$	$\frac{6}{16}$
1 Aa, 3 aa	Aa, aa, aa, aa aa, Aa, aa, aa aa, aa, Aa, aa aa, aa, aa, Aa	$(\frac{1}{2})^4 = \frac{1}{16}$ $(\frac{1}{2})^4 = \frac{1}{16}$ $(\frac{1}{2})^4 = \frac{1}{16}$ $(\frac{1}{2})^4 = \frac{1}{16}$	$\frac{4}{16}$	$\frac{4}{16}$
0 Aa, 4 aa	aa, aa, aa, aa	$(\frac{1}{2})^4$	—	$\frac{1}{16}$
			Total	$\frac{16}{16}$

sical Mendelian ratio is the one that is *most likely* to be attained. Accordingly, the geneticist's statement that the cross $Aa \times aa$ is "expected" to yield offspring in a 1 Aa:1 aa ratio means that this ratio is the one that is "most often expected" in small sibships.

BINOMIAL EXPRESSION

The binomial expression, $(p + q)^n$, permits a determination of the probabilities of obtaining specific combinations of two alternative independent events. In the binomial expression, p and q represent the probabilities of the two alternative independent events, respectively, and the power n to which the binomial is raised represents the number of trials. In two tosses of a coin (or two coins tossed simultaneously), with $p =$ the chance of head and $q =$ the chance of tail, there are four combinations, as table B.4 shows.

Table B.4

First Toss	*Probability*	*Second Toss*	*Probability*	*Combined Probability*
Head	½ (p)	Head	½ (p)	¼ (p^2)
Head	½ (p)	Head	½ (q)	¼ (pq)
Tail	½ (q)	Tail	½ (p)	¼ (pq)
Tail	½ (q)	Tail	½ (q)	¼ (q^2)
			Total	1

The total "1" in table B.4 is equal to $p^2 + 2pq + q^2$. This expression is the expansion of the binomial $(p + q)^2$. Thus, $(p + q)^2 = p^2 + 2pq + q^2$. Since, in this instance, p and q each equals ½, then the value of the expression becomes $(\frac{1}{2})^2 + 2\,(\frac{1}{2} \times \frac{1}{2}) + (\frac{1}{2})^2$, or $\frac{1}{4} + \frac{2}{4} + \frac{1}{4}$. The combinations of two heads, one head and one tail, and two tails are thus realized in the ratio of 1:2:1.

Table B.5 shows the expansion of the binomial $(p + q)^n$ through the fifth power or up to 5 tosses of a coin, where n corresponds to the number of tosses.

Table B.5

Toss	*Combinations and Frequencies of Occurrence*	*Equivalent Binomial Expression*
1	$1H + 1T$	$(p + q)^1$
2	$1H^2 + 2HT + 1T^2$	$(p + q)^2$
3	$1H^3 + 3H^2T + 3HT^2 + 1T^3$	$(p + q)^3$
4	$1H^4 + 4H^3T + 6H^2T^2 + 4HT^3 + 1T^4$	$(p + q)^4$
5	$1H^5 + 5H^4T + 10H^3T^2 + 10H^2T^3 + 5HT^4 + 1T^5$	$(p + q)^5$

If we were to toss four coins together a large number of times, we could predict the outcome by using the expression $(p + q)^4$. The appropriate term from the binomial expression is selected for any combination of heads and tails and the numerical values for p and q are substituted. Since p represents *head*, then the first term of the expanded binomial, H^4 or $(\frac{1}{2})^4$, constitutes the probability of all four coins coming up heads simultaneously. Stated another way, four heads are expected in 1 toss out of 16. In like manner, we can determine the probability for any other combination of four coins. The expected frequencies for two heads and two tails can be calculated by using the term that contains two Hs and two Ts, namely, the third term, $6H^2T^2$. Substituting the numerical values of H and T, we obtain:

$$6H^2T^2 = 6 \times (\tfrac{1}{2})^2 \times (\tfrac{1}{2})^2 = \tfrac{6}{16}$$

Accordingly, two heads and two tails are expected in 6 tosses out of every 16. The numerical coefficient of each term is of interest in revealing the number of different sequences of heads and tails in a particular combination. Thus, the coefficient in the third term, $6H^2T^2$, means that there are 6 different sequences of two heads and two tails.

With the binomial method, we can ascertain the chance or probability of having, for example, two girls and a boy in a family. The appropriate binomial is $(p + q)^3$, where p equals the chance of a girl, q equals the chance of a boy, and the power 3 represents the total number of children. The second term of the expanded binomial, $3p^2q^1$, represents the condition of two girls and a boy. Substituting the individual numerical probabilities for having a boy or a girl ($\tfrac{1}{2}$ in each case), we obtain:

$$3 \times (\tfrac{1}{2})^2 \times \tfrac{1}{2} = \tfrac{3}{8}$$

Accordingly, the probability of producing two girls and a boy is $\tfrac{3}{8}$. In other words, in 3 out of every 8 families of three children, we should expect two girls and a boy.

The chance of various combinations of any two independent events happening together can be calculated by expanding the appropriate binomial. The lengthy calculations in table C.3 can be appreciably simplified by expanding the binomial $(p + q)^4$. In this case, n (or 4) is the number of children in the sibship. The probability of occurrence of the genotype Aa is p (or $\tfrac{1}{2}$), and the probability of occurrence of the genotype aa is q (or $\tfrac{1}{2}$). For sibships of four children, the expanded binomial $(Aa + aa)^4$ is:

$$1(Aa)^4 + 4(Aa)^3(aa) + 6(Aa)^2(aa)^2 + 4(Aa)(aa)^3 + 1(aa)^4$$

The coefficients 1, 4, 6, 4, 1 indicate the number of different sequences of genotypes in a given sibship. For example, as table C.3 also shows, there are 6 different ways in which two Aa and two aa offspring can be produced or arranged (in terms of birth orders). The five terms of the expanded binomial reveal the probabilities of the five kinds of sibships possible with four children: $\tfrac{1}{16}$ that all four children will be Aa, $\tfrac{4}{16}$ that there will be three Aa children and one aa child, and so forth (see table B.3).

As a final illustrative example, suppose that the first child of two parents is afflicted with the recessive disorder phenylketonuria (PKU), which indicates that each parent is a heterozygous carrier. If the parents plan to have three additional children, we can determine the probability that one of the three proposed children will be affected with PKU. In essence, we calculate the likelihood of occurrence of two normal offspring and one PKU offspring in the three proposed children. The appropriate binomial expression is $(p + q)^3$, where p is the probability of a normal child ($\tfrac{3}{4}$) and q is the probability of a PKU child ($\tfrac{1}{4}$). From the expanded binomial, we select the term $3p^2q$ and with the proper numerical substitutions, we obtain:

$$3p^2q = 3 \times (\tfrac{3}{4})^2 \times (\tfrac{1}{4}) = \frac{27}{64}$$

In terms of percentages, the chance that the parents under consideration will have one additional PKU child if they plan three more children is 42 percent.

Standard Units of Measurement

The metric system of measurement is widely used in scientific work because of its simplicity. The metric system is based entirely on the number 10, and its multiples, rather than the awkward mutiples of 12 of the British-American system. The basic units in the metric system are the *gram* for mass (weight), the *meter* for linear measure (length), and the *liter* for capacity (volume).

LINEAR UNITS OF MEASUREMENT

Quantity	Symbol	Numerical Value
1 meter	m	Basic unit $= 10$ decimeters
1 decimeter	dm	10^{-1} meter $= 10$ centimeters
1 centimeter	cm	10^{-2} meter $= 10$ millimeters
1 millimeter	mm	10^{-3} meter $= 1,000$ microns
1 micron* (or micrometer)	μ (μm)	10^{-6} meter $= 1,000$ millimicrons
1 millimicron* (or nanometer)	mμ (nm)	10^{-9} meter $= 10$ Å
1 Ångstrom* (or decinanometer)	Å (dnm)	10^{-10} meter $= 10^{-1}$ millimicron
1 kilometer	k	10^3 meters

Conversion Factors for Linear Units

1 centimeter = 0.39 inch	1 inch = 2.54 centimeters
1 meter = 39.37 inches	1 foot = 0.31 meter
1 kilometer = 0.62 mile	1 yard = 0.91 meter
	1 mile = 1.61 kilometers
	(1,760 yards)

* Micron, millimicron, and Ångstrom are special names, inconsistent with the system of metric prefixes. These names are gradually being replaced by micrometer, nanometer, and decinanometer, respectively.

VOLUMETRIC UNITS OF MEASUREMENT

Quantity	Symbol	Numerical Value
1 liter	l	Basic unit $= 1,000$ milliliters
1 milliliter*	ml	10^{-3} liter $= 1,000$ microliters
1 microliter**	μl	10^{-6} liter

Conversion Factors for Volumetric Units

1 milliliter = 0.06 cubic inch	1 cubic inch = 16.39 milliliters
1 liter = 1.06 quarts (U.S.)	1 pint (U.S.) = 0.47 liter
	1 quart (U.S.) = 0.95 liter
	1 gallon (U.S.) = 3.79 liters

* 1 milliliter = 1 cubic centimeter (cc or cm^3)
** 1 microliter = 1 cubic millimeter (mm^3)
        = 1,000 lambda (λ)

MASS UNITS OF MEASUREMENT

Quantity	Symbol	Numerical Value
1 gram	g	Basic unit $=$ 10 decigrams
1 decigram	dg	10^{-1} gram $=$ 10 centigrams
1 centigram	cg	10^{-2} gram $=$ 10 milligrams
1 milligram	mg	10^{-3} gram $=$ 1,000 micrograms
1 microgram	μg	10^{-6} gram $=$ 1,000 millimicrograms
1 millimicrogram (or nanogram)	mμg (ng)	10^{-9} gram $=$ 10^{-3} microgram
1 kilogram	kg	10^{3} gram

Conversion Factors for Mass Units

1 gram $=$ 0.04 ounce	1 ounce $=$ 31.10 grams
1 kilogram $=$ 2.21 pounds (35.27 ounces)	1 pound $=$ 453.59 grams

Classification of Organisms

Aristotle (384–322 B.C.), the great philosopher and naturalist, aptly declared that Nature is marvelous in each and all her ways. Although Aristotle did not view different kinds of organisms as being related by descent, he arranged all living things in an ascending ladder with man at the top. A formal scheme of classification was developed by the Swedish naturalist Carl von Linné (1707–1778), whose name generally appears in latinized form, Carolus Linnaeus. Life was divided by Linnaeus into two grand kingdoms, *Animals* and *Vegetables,* broadly defined as follows:

> ANIMALS adorn the exterior parts of the earth, respire, and generate eggs; are impelled to action by hunger, congeneric affections, and pain; and by preying on other animals and vegetables, restrain within proper proportion the numbers of both.
>
> They are bodies *organized,* and have *life, sensation,* and the power of locomotion.
>
> VEGETABLES clothe the surface with verdure, imbibe nourishment through bibulous roots, breathe by quivering leaves, celebrate their nuptials in a genial metamorphosis, and continue their kind by the dispersion of seed within prescribed limits.
>
> They are bodies *organized,* and have *life* and not sensation.

Linnaeus was convinced that all species of animals and plants were fixed, unchanging entities, and that "there are just as many species as there were created in the beginning." Modern taxonomists have departed completely from Linnaeus' stand. Present-day taxonomy is based on the proposition of evolutionary change. The modern classification scheme is an expression of the evolutionary relationships among groups of organisms. Our present system of classification is imperfect to the extent that our knowledge is imperfect. The classification scheme is continually being modified as new information of the evolutionary relations of organisms comes to light. In 1969, R. H. Whittaker suggested a radical departure from the traditional two-kingdom system. He has grouped organisms into five separate kingdoms. Whittaker's system takes into consideration the fundamental difference between procaryotic and eucaryotic levels of organization, and stresses the principal modes of nutrition—photosynthetic, absorptive, and ingestive (fig. D.1). The five kingdoms are the Monera (unicellular, procaryotic organisms), Protista (unicellular, eucaryotic organisms), Plantae (multicellular higher algae and green plants). Fungi (multinucleate plantlike organisms lacking photosynthetic pigments), and Animalia (multicellular animals). Whittaker's scheme has been favorably received, although by no means universally accepted. It is presented here in modified form, and is intended for reference rather than for careful study.

Kingdom MONERA	Unicellular procaryotic organisms lacking distinct nuclei and membrane-bound organelles. Nutrition principally by absorption, but some are photosynthetic or chemosynthetic.

Phylum CYANOPHYTA	Blue-green algae
Phylum SHIZOMYCOPHYTA	Bacteria
Phylum SPIROCHAETAE	Spirochetes

Kingdom PROTISTA	Unicellular or colonial eucaryotic organisms with distinct nuclei and organelles. Nutrition by photosynthesis, absorption, or ingestion.

Phylum EUGLENOPHYTA	Plantlike flagellates (*Euglena*)
Phylum CHRYSOPHYTA	Golden algae and diatoms
Phylum PYRROPHYTA	Dinoflagellates
Phylum XANTHOPHYTA	Yellow-green algae
Phylum ZOOMASTIGINA	Flagellated protozoans (*Trypanosoma*, *Chilomonas*)
Phylum SARCODINA	Ameboid protozoans (*Ameba*, *Foraminifera*)
Phylum CILIOPHORA	Ciliated protozoans (*Paramecium*, *Didinium*)
Phylum SPOROZOA	Parasitic protozoans (*Plasmodium*)

Kingdom PLANTAE	Multicellular eucaryotic organisms with rigid cell walls and chlorophyll. Nutrition principally by photosynthesis.

Phylum CHLOROPHYTA	Green algae (*Spirogyra, Volvox*)
Phylum RHODOPHYTA	Red algae (Predominantly marine; seaweeds)
Phylum PHAEOPHYTA	Brown algae (Almost entirely marine; kelp)
Phylum BRYOPHYTA	Liverworts, hornworts, mosses
Phylum TRACHEOPHYTA	Vascular plants
Subphylum LYCOPSIDA	Club mosses
Subphylum SPHENOPSIDA	Horsetails
Subphylum PTEROPSIDA	Ferns
Subphylum SPERMOPSIDA	Seed plants
Class GYMNOSPERMAE	Conifers, cycads, ginkgoes
Class ANGIOSPERMAE	Flowering plants

Subclass
    DICOTYLEDONEAE   Grasses, lilies,
                             and orchids

Subclass
    MONOCOTYLEDONEAE Shrubs and
                             trees

Kingdom FUNGI   Multinucleate plantlike organisms lacking photosynthetic pigments. Nutrition absorptive.

    Phylum MYXOMYCOPHTYA   Slime molds

    Phylum EUMYCOPHYTA   True fungi
        Class PHYCOMYCETES   Algallike fungi
                          (Bread molds)

        Class ASCOMYCETES   Sac fungi
                          (Yeast and
                            mildews)

        Class BASIDIOMYCETES Club fungi
                          (Mushrooms and
                          rusts)

Kingdom ANIMALIA   Multicellular organisms without cell walls or chlorophyll. Nutrition principally ingestive with digestion in an internal cavity.

    Phylum PORIFERA   Sponges
    Phylum COELENTERATA   Radically symmetrical
                              marine animals

        Class HYDROZOA   *Hydra*, Portuguese
                          man-of-war

        Class SCYPHOZOA   Jellyfish
        Class ANTHOZOA   Sea anemones and corals

    Phylum CTENOPHORA   Comb jellies
    Phylum PLATYHELMINTHES   Flatworms

        Class TURBELLARIA   Free-living flatworms
                          (Planaria)

        Class TREMATODA   Parasitic flukes
        Class CESTODA   Parasitic tapeworms

    Phylum ASCHELMINTHES   Roundworms
                          (*Trichina, Necator*)

    Phylum TROCHELMINTHES   Rotifers
    Phylum BRYOZOA   Moss animals
    Phylum MOLLUSCA   Soft-bodied, unsegmented animals

        Class AMPHINEURA   Chitons
        Class GASTROPODA   Snails and slugs
        Class SCAPHOPODA   Tooth shells
        Class PELECYPODA   Clams and mussels
        Class CEPHALOPODA   Squids and octopuses

    Phylum ANNELIDA   Segmented worms

        Class POLYCHAETA   Sand worms
        Class OLIGOCHAETA   Earthworms
        Class HIRUDINEA   Leeches

    Phylum ARTHROPODA   Joint-legged animals; exoskeleton

Kingdom ANIMALIA
(Continued)

	Class CRUSTACEA	Lobsters, crabs, barnacles
	Class ARACHNIDA	Spiders, scorpions, ticks
	Class CHILOPIDA	Centipedes
	Class DIPLOPODA	Millipedes
	Class INSECTA	Grasshoppers, termites, beetles
Phylum ECHINODERMATA		Marine; spiny radially symmetrical animals
	Class CRINOIDEA	Sea lilies and feather stars
	Class ASTEROIDEA	Starfish
	Class OPHIUROIDEA	Brittle stars
	Class ECHINOIDEA	Sea urchin and sand dollar
	Class HOLOTHUROIDEA	Sea cucumbers
Phylum HEMICHORDATA		Acorn worms
Phylum CHORDATA		Dorsal supporting rod (notochord) at some stage; dorsal hollow nerve cord; pharyngeal gill slits
Subphylum UROCHORDATA		Tunicates
Subphylum CEPHALOCHORDATA		Lancelets
Subphylum VERTEBRATA		Vertebrates
	Class AGNATHA	Jawless fishes (Lampreys, hagfishes)
	Class CHONDRICHTHYES	Cartilaginous fishes (Sharks, rays)
	Class OSTEICHTHYES	Bony fishes
	Class AMPHIBIA	Frogs, toads, salamanders
	Class REPTILIA	Snakes, lizards, turtles
	Class AVES	Birds
	Class MAMMALIA	Mammals
	Order MONOTREMATA	Duckbill platypus, spiny anteater
	Order MARSUPIALIA	Opossums, kangaroos
	Order INSECTIVORA	Shrews, moles
	Order CHIROPTERA	Bats
	Order EDENTATA	Anteaters, armadillos
	Order RODENTIA	Rats, mice, squirrels
	Order LAGOMORPHA	Rabbits and hares

Order CETACEA	Whales, dolphins, porpoises	Kingdom ANIMALIA *(Continued)*
Order CARNIVORA	Dogs, bears, skunks	
Order PROBOSCIDEA	Elephants	
Order SIRENIA	Manatees	
Order PERRISODACTYLA	Horse, hippopotamus, zebra	
Order ARTIODACTYLA	Pigs, deer, cattle	
Order PRIMATES	Monkeys, apes, man	

Full Classification of Man

Kingdom Animalia
Phylum Chordata
Subphylum Vertebrata
Superclass Tetrapoda
Class Mammalia
Subclass Theria
Infraclass Eutheria
Order Primates
Suborder Anthropoidea
Superfamily Hominoidea
Family Hominidae
Subfamily Homininae
Genus *Homo*
Species *Homo sapiens*

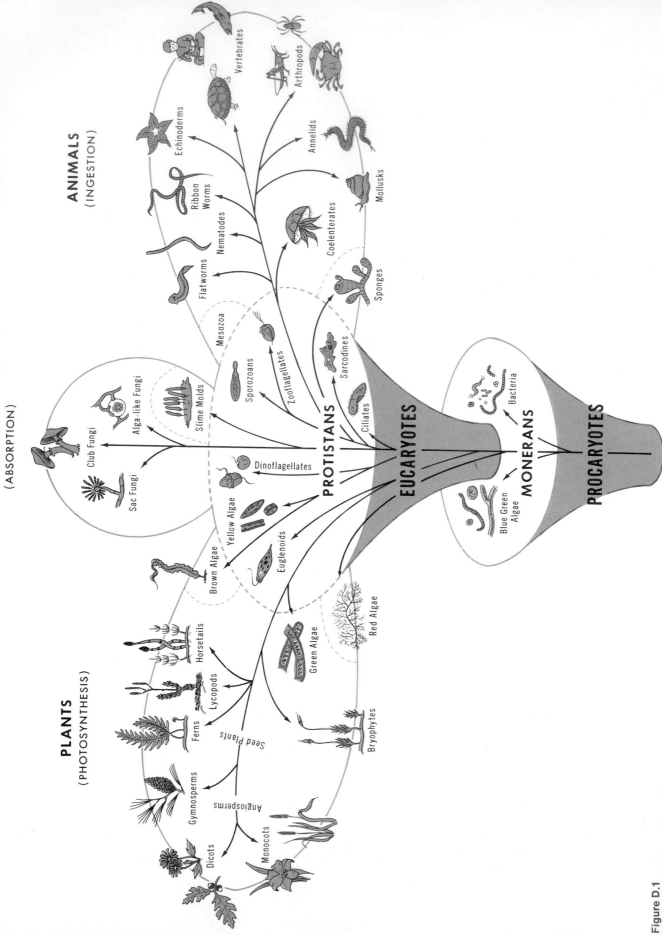

Figure D.1
Original design contributed by Prof. Stuart S. Bamforth, Tulane University.

Glossary

abiotic. Without life; pertains to nonliving components of the environment.

abortion. Premature expulsion (spontaneous or induced) of a fetus before it is capable of sustaining independent life.

absorption. Passage of dissolved substances and fluids through membranes into cells or tissues.

acetylcholine. Chemical substance released by the terminal end of a nerve fiber that stimulates an adjacent cell.

achondroplasia. Deficiency in cartilage formation, resulting in dwarfism.

acquired character. Noninheritable modification of a trait resulting from a response to an environmental condition.

acrosome. Anterior prominence of the sperm that initiates penetration of the egg during fertilization.

actin. One of the two major proteins of muscle; composes the thin filaments of myofibrils.

action potential. A reversal in polarity of a polarized cell membrane that creates the nerve impulse.

activation energy. The amount of energy necessary to initiate the reaction of chemical substances.

active site. Region on the surface of an enzyme to which the substrate binds in an enzyme-catalyzed reaction.

active transport. Transport of materials across cell membranes against a concentration gradient that requires an expenditure of energy by the cell.

adaptation. Morphological, physiological, or behavioral characteristic that enhances the ability of the organism to cope with its prevailing environment.

adaptive radiation. Evolution from a single ancestral species of a variety of types specialized for diverse modes of living.

adenosine triphosphate (ATP). A phosphorylated compound in which energy for biological functions is stored in the high-energy bonds that link the three phosphate groups.

adipose. Of a fatty nature; fat present in the cells of adipose tissue.

adrenal gland. Endocrine (ductless) gland on the anterior surface of the kidney, the source of the hormone epinephrine (adrenalin).

aerobic. Requiring, or occurring in, the presence of molecular oxygen.

afferent. Conveying toward a central point.

afferent neuron. Nerve cell that responds to external or internal stimuli and transmits impulses to the central nervous system; also called sensory neuron.

afterbirth. Placenta and allied membranes expelled from the uterus after delivery of the fetus.

agglutination. Reaction in which particles (such as red blood cells or bacteria) suspended in a liquid collect into clumps; occurs especially as a response to a specific antibody.

alkaptonuria. Metabolic (genetic) disorder characterized by blackening of the urine.

allantois. Saclike organ of respiration and excretion of embryos of reptiles and birds; in mammals, it contributes to the formation of the umbilical cord and placenta.

allele. One of a pair of contrasting genes or one of a series of alternative forms of a gene occupying the same position (locus) in homologous chromosomes.

allograft. Piece of tissue transplanted from one individual to a genetically unrelated individual.

allopatric. Pertains to populations that are spatially isolated from one another.

altruism. Self-sacrificial behavior that is disadvantageous to the individual performing the act but beneficial to the population as a whole.

alveolus. Microscopic, thin-walled air sac in the lungs, the site of gas exchange.

ameboid movement. Mode of locomotion resembling the one-celled organism (ameba) of irregular shape that moves by extending part of its mass into temporary armlike extensions.

amino acid. Organic acid containing carboxyl (—COOH) and amine (—NH$_2$) groups; the basic structural unit of protein.

amniocentesis. Tapping of the amnion of the human fetus for a fluid sample for biochemical and chromosomal analyses of fetal cells.

amnion. Thin membranous sac surrounding the embryos of amniotes (reptiles, birds, and mammals) that contains a watery fluid to protect the embryo against shock or adhesion; popularly, the "bag of waters."

anabolism. Constructive phase of metabolism involving the synthesis of complex molecules from simpler molecules.

anaerobe. Organism that can carry on respiration in the absence of free oxygen.

anaerobic respiration. Breakdown of fuel molecules (glucose) in the absence of oxygen.

analogous. Similar in function but different in structure and origin.

anaphase. Stage of nuclear division (mitosis) characterized by the movement of daughter chromosomes toward opposite poles of the dividing cell.

androgen. Hormone that promotes masculinizing activities, such as testosterone.

anemia. The reduction below normal in the number of red blood cells or the quantity of hemoglobin.

aneurysm. A blood-filled sac formed by the dilatation of the walls of an artery or of a vein.

antibody. A protein that destroys or inactivates cells or substances that are foreign to the organism.

anticodon. A set of three adjacent nucleotides in transfer RNA that is complementary to the codon in messenger RNA.

antigen. A foreign substance, usually a protein, that stimulates the production of agents (antibodies) against it.

appetitive behavior. Innate restless or searching behavior of an organism.

archenteron. Cavity of the early vertebrate embryo that is the forerunner of the adult digestive cavity.

arteriole. A small artery.

artery. Vessel that carries blood away from the heart.

atherosclerosis. Chronic disease characterized by abnormal thickening and hardening of the arterial walls.

autograft. Piece of tissue transplanted from one area of an individual to another location in the same individual.

autonomic nervous system. Portion of the vertebrate nervous system consisting of motor neurons that are not under direct voluntary control and that innervate internal organs.

autosome. Chromosome other than a sex (X or Y) chromosome.

autotroph. Organism that can produce its own organic nutrients from simple inorganic elements (for example, a green plant).

axon. Process, or fiber, of a nerve cell that carries impulses away from the nerve cell body.

backcross. Mating of a progeny with one of its parents.

background radiation. Total of all natural ionizing radiations derived from cosmic radiation and radioactive elements in the earth's crust.

bacteriophage. A virus that infects bacteria; often simply called "phage."

bacterium. Microscopic unicellular organism (procaryote) with a simple DNA molecule not contained in a nuclear membrane; possesses a cell wall and is incapable of carrying out photosynthesis with the release of molecular oxygen.

balanced polymorphism. Maintenance of more than one allele at high levels in a population by the selective superiority of the heterozygote over both types of homozygotes.

Barr body. Small, darkly stained mass at the periphery of the nucleus of cells of normal females; it represents an X chromosome that has become condensed and remains genetically inactive.

base pairing. Pairing of specific purines and pyrimidines in complementary strands of DNA (for example, adenine and thymine).

bilirubin. A bile pigment derived from the decomposition of hemoglobin of red blood cells; occurs in the blood tissues in jaundice.

binomial nomenclature. Taxonomic scheme of designating an organism by two names: a generic (capitalized) name followed by a specific name (such as Homo sapiens).

bioassay. Determination of the character and strength of a substance by studying its effects on a laboratory organism.

biochemical oxygen demand (BOD). Amount of oxygen required to degrade organic matter in a given volume of water; used as an index of water pollution.

biodegradable. Capable of being chemically altered or decomposed by the action of organisms in the environment.

biogenesis. Origin of living organisms from other living organisms.

biogeochemical cycle. The circular passage and transformation of a chemical element (such as nitrogen) from living organisms to and from the physical environment.

biological clock. Postulated internal timer, or control mechanism, in the organism that regulates rhythmic behavior of the organism.

biomass. Total weight of all living matter or some designated species in a particular habitat or area.

biosphere. Part of the earth and its atmosphere that can support life.

biotic. The living components of the environment.

biotic community. Association of varied interacting species existing in a common environment.

biotic potential. Inherent reproductive capabilities of individuals or populations. Essentially, the maximum growth rate that could occur in the absence of limiting environmental factors.

bipedal gait. Walking on hind limbs alone; the upright carriage of man.

blastocyst. Hollow, ball-like stage of the human embryo consisting of an inner cell mass and a trophoblast just before it implants in the uterus.

blastomere. One of many cells produced by divisions of the fertilized egg.

blastula. Early developmental stage consisting of a spherical layer of cells surrounding a hollow, fluid-filled central cavity (blastocoel).

bloom. Explosive population growth of plants (particularly algae) typically generated by nutrient enrichment.

B-lymphocyte. White blood cell capable of differentiating into an antibody-producing cell (plasma cell) that circulates in the blood and confers immunity against viruses and bacteria.

brachiation. Locomotory process of swinging from one place to another by arms; characteristic of gibbons.

Caesarean section. Delivery of the baby through the abdomen by means of a surgical incision through the abdominal and uterine walls. So named from belief that Julius Caesar was delivered in this manner.

calorie. Amount of heat required to raise the temperature of one gram of water one degree Celsius; a *dietary* calorie (kilocalorie) consists of 1,000 of these units.

cancer. Malignant growth of tissue associated with uncontrolled multiplication of cells locally and the tendency to spread to other organs.

capacitation. Final physiological changes by which the sperm cell acquires the capacity to fertilize an egg.

capillary. Any one of the numerous minute vessels that connect arteries and veins; the thin walls of capillaries provide for the interchange of dissolved substances between the blood and tissue fluid.

carcinogen. Substance or agent capable of inducing cancerous growth.

carnivore. A flesh-eater; an animal that preys or feeds on other animals.

carrier molecule. Protein molecule associated with cell membranes to facilitate passage of certain molecules (such as glucose) in and out of cells (a process known as *facilitated diffusion*).

carrying capacity. The limit at which a particular habitat can support a given population of organisms without the resources of the habitat being depleted.

catabolism. Destructive, or energy-yielding, phase of metabolism involving the breakdown of complex organic molecules by living cells into simpler substances.

catalyst. Substance (enzyme) that increases the rate of a chemical reaction without itself being permanently altered.

Celsius. Pertains to a temperature scale in which the interval between two standard points, the freezing point and boiling point of water, is divided into 100 parts, or degrees (0° as freezing point and 100° as boiling point). Commonly called *centigrade,* abbreviated C. Formula for converting Celsius temperature to Fahrenheit is $°C = 5/9 \ (°F - 32)$.

centromere. Special region of the chromosome to which the spindle fiber is attached during mitosis and meiosis; holds daughter chromatids together in prophase.

cervix. Narrow, lower end of the uterus opening into the vagina; popularly called the "neck of the womb."

chimerism. Mixture of cells or tissues of different genetic (or chromosomal) constitution in the same individual; also called *mosaicism.*

chlorophyll. Green pigment that captures light energy for use in the manufacture of carbohydrates from carbon dioxide and water (photosynthesis).

chloroplast. Membrane-bound structure within the cells of green plants that contains the light-absorbing pigments (particularly chlorophyll) and the enzymes necessary for the photosynthetic production of sugar.

cholesterol. White, crystalline alcohol found in bile, gallstones, egg yolk, and animal fats.

chorion. Membrane enveloping the embryo of reptiles, birds, and mammals, external to and enclosing the amnion. In placental mammals, it contributes to the structure of the placenta.

chorionic villus. Fingerlike outgrowth of the outermost fetal membrane that becomes embedded in the uterus and acquires blood vessels to carry on metabolic exchanges between the fetus and mother.

chromatid. Each of two daughter strands resulting from longitudinal duplication of a chromosome during cell division (mitosis).

chromosome. Nucleoprotein rodlike body in the nucleus of the cell that bears the hereditary determiners (genes) in linear order.

chyme. Partially digested liquefied food mass in the stomach.

cilia. Vibratile hairlike protoplasmic projections from the free surface of certain types of cells.

circadian. Pertains to rhythmic activity cycles that recur at approximately (but not precisely) 24-hour intervals, even under constant laboratory conditions.

circumcision. Surgical removal of the foreskin (prepuce) of the penis.

cirrhosis. Disease of the liver characterized by accumulations of hardened fibrous (scar) tissue; occurs in chronic alcoholism.

cistron. The gene as defined functionally—a segment of DNA specifying one polypeptide chain in protein synthesis.

cleavage. Cell (mitotic) division of the fertilized egg, resulting in numerous small cells (blastomeres).

climacteric. Combination of hormonal and psychic changes occurring at the end of the human reproductive period (as, among women, the menopause); popularly called the "change of life."

clitoris. Small body of erectile tissue at the anterior end of the female external genitalia; homologous (similar in origin) to the penis in the male.

cloaca. Chamber at the posterior end of the vertebrate body into which the intestinal, urinary, and reproductive ducts open; in most mammals, it is only a transient structure in embryonic development; from Latin, meaning "sewer."

clone. A group of genetically identical individuals all descended from a single common ancestor.

codominance. Condition in heterozygotes where both members of an allelic pair express their effects, each contributing to the manifestation of the phenotype (as in AB blood type and sickle-cell trait).

codon. Sequence of three adjacent nucleotides in the messenger RNA molecule that codes for a specific amino acid in protein synthesis.

coelom. Body cavity between the digestive tract and body wall that is lined with tissue of mesodermal origin.

coenzyme. Substance, such as a vitamin, that is required before a specific enzyme can function.

coitus. Act of sexual intercourse; copulation.

coitus interruptus. Contraceptive method consisting of the withdrawal of the penis from the vagina before ejaculation.

commensalism. Two different species of organisms living together in which one benefits from the association and the other is neither harmed nor benefited.

competition. Interaction between members of the same or different species for a mutually required resource.

competitive exclusion. Principle that two or more species competing for exactly the same limited resource cannot coexist.

conception. Fertilization of the egg by sperm; act of becoming pregnant; state of being conceived.

conceptus. Products of conception, the fetus and placenta.

congenital. Pertaining to a condition existing at, or dating from, birth. A congenital disorder is generally thought of as a deviation from the normal in fetal development that is not hereditary.

consanguineous. Pertains to persons who are related by descent from a common ancestor.

consummatory act. Specific, stereotyped motor response or action that satisfies a particular motivational drive.

corpus luteum. Progesterone-producing secretory structure formed from the ovarian follicle after the egg has been released.

countercurrent exchange. Exchange of heat or matter (such as, salts) between two fluids flowing past each other in opposite directions.

crista. Shelflike fold of the inner membrane of the mitochondrion projecting into the central matrix of the mitochondrion.

crossing over. Exchange of corresponding genetic material between adjacent chromatids of a homologous pair of chromosomes during the tetrad stage of meiosis.

cryptorchidism. Developmental defect in which the testes fail to descend into the scrotal sac, remaining within the pelvis.

cultural eutrophication. Accelerated aging of a lake through man's action of pouring in the waters excessive amounts of plant nutrients, thereby promoting explosive growth of aquatic plants, especially algae.

cultural evolution. The transmission of ideas and accumulated knowledge through the human generations from mind to mind rather than through the germ cells.

curet. An instrument, usually spoon-shaped, for removing growths from the walls of cavities.

curettage. The removal of growths or other materials from the wall of a cavity or other surface, as with a curet.

curie. Unit used in measuring the radioactivity of materials.

deamination. Removal of an amino group ($-NH_2$) from an amino acid or similar compound.

decidua. Portion of the lining of the uterus that undergoes special modifications in preparation for and during pregnancy; the maternal component of the placenta.

decomposer. Organism, such as a bacterium or fungus, that converts dead organic matter into inorganic substances (plant nutrients).

deletion. Loss of a section of the genetic material from a chromosome; the loss may involve a single nucleotide or a large segment of the chromosome containing many genes.

demographic transition. Change from a high birth rate–high death rate society to a society with a low birth rate and a low death rate.

demography. Study of populations with reference to their size, density, age distribution, birth rate, death rate, geographical distribution, and other statistics.

dendrite. Short, branched extension of a nerve cell that conducts impulses toward the cell body.

density. The number of individuals in a given unit of area.

deoxyribonucleic acid (DNA). The chemical substance in the chromosome whose structural arrangement is the basis of inheritable characteristics.

dialysis. The process of separating substances in solution by the difference in their rates of diffusion through a differentially permeable membrane.

diethylstilbestrol (DES). An estrogenic compound used in treating menopausal symptoms and suppressed lactation; now suspected of being carcinogenic.

differentially permeable. Property of the cell membrane that allows some substances to penetrate, or pass through, and restricts others.

differential reproduction. Reproduction in which different genetic types of individuals do not contribute proportionately to the next generation; the basis of natural selection.

differentiation. Developmental series of structural and biochemical changes that a cell undergoes in becoming specialized for a particular function.

diffusion. Movement of molecules from a region of high concentration to a region of low concentration as a consequence of their random motion.

digestion. Enzymatic breakdown of insoluble organic molecules into simpler, soluble components that can be assimilated by the organism.

dihybrid. Offspring of parents differing in two independently assorting traits.

dilatation. Act of enlarging or stretching; dilatation of the cervix is a measure of the progress of labor during childbirth.

diploid. Bearing two full sets of chromosomes, as in a zygote after the union of egg and sperm (each of which has only one, or the haploid, set of chromosomes).

dispersal. Movement of organisms away from the place of birth, or away from areas of high population density.

dispersion. Pattern of spacing of individuals in a local population.

displacement activity. The performance of an irrelevant act arising from ambivalence, or conflicting motivational drives.

distal. Located away from some reference point (usually the main part of the body); the opposite of proximal.

dizygotic. Developed from two fertilized eggs (zygotes), as fraternal twins; distinguished from monozygotic (developed from a single zygote, as identical twins).

DNA. See deoxyribonucleic acid.

dominance hierarchy. Orderly ranking of individuals in a social group, established and maintained by aggressive encounters.

dominant. Refers to a gene that expresses itself fully in the heterozygous state, masking the expression of its partner (recessive) allele.

dorsal. Pertaining to, or situated near or on, the back of an animal; the opposite of ventral.

dorsal root ganglion. Cluster of the cell bodies of sensory neurons that is located immediately outside the spinal cord.

dosage compensation. Describes the situation whereby two normal X-linked genes of the female produce the same effect as one normal X-linked gene in the male.

Down's syndrome. Preferred medical designation of the human congenital disorder associated with a specific extra chromosome (mongolism).

ductus arteriosis. Short vessel connecting the pulmonary artery and the descending aorta of the fetus, effectively bypassing the pulmonary circulation; also called the ductus Botalli.

duplication. Occurrence of an extra copy of a gene or chromosome segment in the genetic makeup of the cell or individual.

dysgenic. Effect or situation that tends to be harmful to the genetic qualities of present or future generations.

ecological niche. The role played by an organism in the ecology of the community of which it is a part.

ecological pyramid. Graphic portrayal in triangular fashion showing the sequence of diminishing numbers, biomass, or available energy in successively higher trophic levels.

ecology. Study of the interrelations of living organisms and their environment.

ecosystem. A community of organisms interacting with associated chemical and physical factors in the environment.

ectoderm. Outermost of the three embryonic (germ) layers that gives rise to the skin, nervous system, and sense organs.

ectopic pregnancy. Lodging of the fetus elsewhere than in the uterus, as in the Fallopian tube or in the abdominal cavity.

ectotherm. Animal that is dependent upon external sources of heat for its body temperature; characteristic of poikilothermic animals.

edema. Abnormally large amounts of fluid in the tissue (intercellular) spaces of the body.

effector. Muscle or gland that receives the nerve impulses, which evoke muscular contraction and gland secretion.

efferent. Conveying away from a central point.

efferent neuron. Nerve cell within the central nervous system that extends its fiber (axon) to muscles or glands; also called motor neuron.

ejaculum. The semen (sperm and their nutrient fluids) discharged from the penis at ejaculation (act of expulsion).

electron transport system. Series of metabolic reactions in which electrons are passed along a chain of carrier molecules with the concurrent production of ATP; also called the respiratory chain.

embolism. The blocking of a blood vessel by a clot that was carried to the site of obstruction by the blood current.

embryonic induction. Process whereby one group of embryonic cells directs or influences the development (differentiation) of an adjacent group of cells.

emphysema. Disease of the lungs in which breathing is impaired as a result of destruction or rupture of the air sacs (alveoli).

endemic. Confined to, or peculiar to, a particular locality; an endemic disease is one that is constantly present in a region, as distinguished from an epidemic disease, which prevails widely at some one time, or occurs periodically.

endocrine gland. Ductless organ that releases its secretion (hormone) directly into blood vessels, which carry the hormone to the target organ.

endoderm. Innermost of the three embryonic (germ) layers that gives rise to the lining of the digestive and respiratory tracts.

endogenous hypothesis. Tenet that cyclic rhythms of activity are governed by internal timers, or biological clocks, that operate independent of external forces or cues.

endometrium. Glandular lining of the uterus that breaks down during menstruation and is transformed into the decidua (maternal part of the placenta) during pregnancy.

endoplasmic reticulum (ER). Cell organelle in the form of a complex series of tubules enclosed by folded membranous sheets, often coated with ribosomes.

endotherm. Animal that produces and controls its own sources of heat; characteristic of homeothermic animals.

end product. A chemical compound that is the final product of a sequence of metabolic reactions.

energy barrier. Amount of energy that a molecule must gain to become sufficiently "excited" to enter into a chemical reaction.

enteric. Pertaining to the intestine, as in enteric disease (inflammation or disorder of the intestine).

environmental resistance. Sum total of factors in the environment that limit the numerical increase of a population in a particular region.

enzyme. Protein (or polypeptide) produced by the living cell that functions as a catalyst in cellular reactions.

epiboly. Process during gastrulation (as in frog development) in which animal hemisphere cells grow over and enclose the cells of the vegetal hemisphere.

epidemiology. Study of the incidence of disease in a population rather than in a single individual.

epididymis. Elongated, cordlike structure along the posterior border of each testis, in the ducts of which the sperm are stored.

epigenesis. Idea that development starts from a structureless cell, and consists of the successive formation of new structures that do not preexist in the fertilized egg; opposed to preformation.

epinephrine. Hormone secreted by the adrenal medulla that stimulates the heart and constricts blood vessels; better known by its trade name, adrenalin.

epiphyte. Nonparasitic plant that grows on the surface of other plants, usually above the ground (such as arboreal orchid and Spanish moss).

epithelium. One or more sheetlike layers of tightly packed cells that cover the external and internal surfaces of the body.

equipotent. Refers to the ability of a cell to develop into any type of cell; also referred to as totipotent.

erythroblastosis fetalis. Hemolytic anemia of the fetus or newborn resulting from the breakdown of Rh-positive fetal red blood cells by maternally derived anti-Rh antibodies.

erythrocyte. Red blood cell containing hemoglobin, the carrier of oxygen and carbon dioxide.

estrogen. A class of female steroid hormones produced by the ovary (estradiol, for example, is one of several estrogens).

estrus. Period of maximum sexual receptivity, or heat, in the female of many mammalian species; generally coincident with ovulation.

ethology. Study of complex patterns of behavior in animals in their natural environments, with special attention to adaptive and comparative aspects.

eucaryote. Cell or organism that has an organized membrane-enclosed nucleus and other membrane-bound organelles such as mitochondria; distinguished from a procaryote (bacterium and blue-green alga), which lacks membrane-bound organelles.

eugenics. An approach that proposes to improve the hereditary qualities of a population (especially of the human species) by the application of genetic principles and social controls.

euthanasia. Act or practice of painlessly putting to death a person suffering from an incurable disease; mercy death.

eutrophication. Natural process of enrichment of a body of water by the accumulation of nutrients that promote a dense growth of aquatic plants, the decay of which creates an oxygen demand.

evolution. Genetic changes that occur in populations of organisms with the passage of time, resulting in increasing adaptation of organisms to the prevailing environment.

excretion. Elimination of the waste products of metabolic activity.

exogenous hypothesis. Tenet that rhythms of biological activity are set or governed by external geophysical factors that vary cyclically.

exponential growth. Pattern of population growth where the number of individuals increases according to a geometric progression; logarithmic growth.

external fertilization. Union of gametes outside the body of a parent.

extraembryonic membranes. Structures formed of embryonic tissue that are not within the embryo proper and are concerned with protection and nutrition; in vertebrates, the amnion, chorion, allantois, and yolk sac.

facilitated diffusion. Transport of material (such as glucose) across a membrane with the aid of a carrier molecule; also called catalyzed diffusion.

Fallopian tubes. Narrow, paired ducts connecting the ovaries and uterus of mammals; the site of fertilization of the egg; also called *oviducts.*

fallout. Radioactive substances in the form of dust dispersed by thermonuclear explosion.

fauna. Collective term for all the animals in a given geographic region or in a given geologic period.

feces. Excrement discharged from the digestive tract, consisting of bacteria, dead intestinal cells, secretions of the liver, and indigestible food residue.

fecundity. Quality or power of producing offspring, especially rapidly and in large numbers.

feedback control. Control of a particular step induced by the presence or absence of a product of one of the later steps.

fermentation. Enzymatic breakdown of organic compounds, especially of carbohydrates, in the absence of oxygen, usually producing alcohol or lactic acid; also called *anaerobic respiration.*

fertility. The capacity to conceive or induce conception.

fertilization. Union of sperm and egg to form the single cell (zygote) from which the embryo develops.

fetal. Pertaining to the mammalian fetus; in the human, pertaining to the unborn offspring after the second month of gestation.

fetus. Postembryonic period of development in mammals; the developing young in the human uterus from the end of the second month to birth.

filial regression. Tendency for a quantitative trait (such as height) in the son to return to the average of the population (specifically, halfway between the father's characteristic and the population average).

filtration. The passage of a liquid through a filter, accomplished by a pressure differential.

first filial generation (F₁). The first generation of offspring arising from a cross of two parents.

first law of thermodynamics. Fundamental principle that although energy can be transformed from one form to another, it cannot be created or destroyed; also expressed as the *law of conservation of energy* (the sum total of energy in the universe remains constant).

fistula. Abnormal passage or communication, frequently leading from an internal organ to the surface of the body.

fitness (Darwinian). Measure of the degree to which an individual succeeds in contributing offspring to the next generation.

fixed action pattern. Genetically programmed, or innate, behavioral act whose expression requires a specific stimulus.

flagellum. Threadlike, whiplike organelle extending from the surface of some cells; the locomotory organelle of sperm cells, certain bacteria, and certain protozoa.

flatus. Gas or air in the intestinal tract; noisy expulsion of gas from the bowels.

flora. Collective term for all the plants in a given geographic region or in a given geologic period.

fluke. Parasitic flatworm that causes certain diseases (such as the blood fluke, *Schistosoma*).

follicle (ovarian). Cluster of cells in the ovary associated with nourishing the developing egg and secreting the female sex hormone (estrogen).

follicle-stimulating hormone (FSH). Pituitary hormone that stimulates the maturation of egg follicles in the ovaries and regulates the activities of the seminiferous tubules (sperm production) in the testes.

food chain. Sequence of organisms in a biologic community dependent upon one another for nutrients (energy), from the primary producers (green plants) to successive consumers (herbivores and carnivores).

food vacuole. Membrane-bound cavity within a cell in which food is digested.

food web. The complex interconnected chains in a biologic community.

foramen ovale. Natural opening or passage in the fetal heart that provides a communication between the auricles.

foreskin. Covering fold of skin at the end of the penis that is removed by circumcision; technically, the prepuce.

fossil. Preserved remains or traces of an organism that lived in the past.

fossil fuel. Fuel formed by the alteration of the remains of ancient plant and animal life (coal, petroleum, natural gas).

founder effect. Concept that a small band of emigrants (colonizers) contains only a small portion of the genetic variability of the larger parent population.

fungus. Primitive, nonphotosynthetic plant (such as mushroom and mold) that lives chiefly on decaying matter.

gallbladder. A small sac attached to the liver that stores bile produced by the liver.

gamete. Functional haploid reproductive cell (egg or sperm); also called *germ cell* or *sex cell.*

gametogenesis. Specialized series of divisions that results in the production of gametes; termed *oogenesis* in the female and *spermatogenesis* in the male.

gamma globulins. Specific proteins in blood plasma that function as circulating antibodies against bacteria and viruses.

gamma rays. High energy radiation originating in the nucleus of a radioactive atom.

ganglion. Cluster of cell bodies of sensory neurons that are located outside the central nervous system.

gastrula. Three-layered embryonic stage of vertebrates following the blastula stage; consisting of ectoderm, endoderm, and mesoderm, each of which gives rise to certain tissues and organs of the adult animal.

gastrulation. Process of germ layer formation in embryonic development.

Gause's principle. The principle of competitive exclusion, which states that two species cannot occupy exactly the same ecological niche within a community.

gemmules. Hypothetical units assumed to be thrown off by the somatic cells, to be stored in the germ cells, and to determine the development of certain characters.

gene. Basic unit of heredity carried in the chromosome; functionally, a segment of DNA that specifies one polypeptide chain in protein synthesis.

gene flow. Spread of genes between populations by immigrants through interbreeding.

gene frequency. The incidence of a particular gene in a population, relative to its alleles.

gene pool. Total aggregate of all genes in a breeding population at a particular time, regardless of the relative proportions of the existing genes.

genetic code. The three-symboled system of contiguous bases in DNA (and its product, messenger RNA) that specifies the sequence of amino acids in particular proteins.

genetic drift. Fluctuations in the genetic composition of a small population resulting from chance, or sampling error.

genetic equilibrium. Constancy of particular frequencies of allelic members of a gene through successive generations in a population.

genetic isolate. A self-contained breeding population that does not exchange genes with any other group.

genetic load. Store of concealed detrimental (semilethal and lethal) genes in a population; when expressed or exposed, these genes can result in selective death.

genetic map. The arrangement of genes on a chromosome as deduced largely from genetic recombination (linkage) studies.

genitalia. Reproductive organs of animals, both external and internal.

genome. The basic set of genes, as contained in the haploid assortment of chromosomes.

genotype. Hereditary constitution (genetic makeup) of an individual, as distinct from his outward appearance (or phenotype).

genus. Group of structurally related species judged to be closely allied (descended from a common ancestor); the first part of an organism's scientific (Latin) name.

geographical barrier. A geographical feature (such as a mountain or river) that prevents gene flow between populations.

germ cell. The gamete, or even the special cell in the gonad that gives rise to the gamete.

germ layer. One of the three primary embryonic layers of cells (ectoderm, endoderm, and mesoderm), each of which differentiates into certain body parts.

gerontology. Study of the problems of aging in all their aspects—clinical, biological, historical, and sociological.

gestation. Period of intrauterine development from fertilization to birth in mammals; the duration of pregnancy.

gill slit. Opening between the pharynx and the exterior, used for gas exchange in aquatic vertebrates; present at least in rudimentary form during the embryonic development of all vertebrates.

gland. Organ producing one or more secretions that are discharged to the outside of the organ.

glans. Cap-shaped tip of the penis in mammalian males.

glomerulus. A tuft or cluster; often used anatomically to designate the cluster of capillaries within the cup of Bowman's capsule in the vertebrate kidney.

gluconeogenesis. The formation of sugar from molecules that are not themselves carbohydrates, as from protein or fat.

glycogen. Complex carbohydrate (polysaccharide) that serves as the principal storage form of sugar in animals.

glycogenolysis. The conversion of stored glycogen into glucose in the body tissues.

glycolysis. Series of chemical reactions in which glucose (or glycogen) is degraded to pyruvic acid in the absence of oxygen with the release of only a small amount of energy (ATP).

goblet cell. An epithelial cell distended at the free end with mucus for secretion, as in cells lining the stomach and intestines.

Golgi apparatus. Cluster of flattened, parallel membranous sacs in the cytoplasm involved in the packaging, storage, and release of cellular secretory products.

gonad. A gamete-producing gland; an ovary or testis.

gonadotrophins. Class of pituitary hormones that regulates the activity of the ovaries and testes; principally, FSH and LH (or ICSH).

Graafian follicle. A mature ovarian follicle filled with fluid and containing the egg ready to be released.

grana. Chlorophyl-containing granules within the chloroplast, the site of the light reactions of photosynthesis; each granum is a series of stacked thylakoids.

gray crescent. Crescent-shaped area on the surface of the fertilized frog's egg that marks the future location of the primary organizer (dorsal lip of the blastopore).

gray matter. Refers to regions of the brain and spinal cord that consist largely of nerve cell bodies (and fibers lacking myelin sheaths).

greenhouse effect. Heat-trapping action of the atmosphere due to the accumulation of gases (carbon dioxide and water vapor) that block the return passage of solar radiation reflected from the ground.

group selection. The selection of a trait that confers an advantage for the population (group) as a whole but may be costly to an individual member.

guard cells. Specialized cells surrounding leaf pores (stomata) that regulate the size of the stomatal opening.

habitat. Place where a particular organism or species lives.

habituation. Process by which an organism becomes accustomed by repeated exposure to a specific stimulus, and ceases to respond to that stimulus.

haploid. Bearing only a single set of chromosomes, as normally found in a gamete (abbreviated 1n); in contrast to diploid (2n).

Hardy-Weinberg law. In a large, randomly breeding population in the absence of mutation and selection, the frequency of genes does not change from generation to generation.

helix. A coiled structure; in the double helix of DNA, each chain or coil contains information specifying the other chain.

hematocrit. The volume percentage of erythrocytes in whole blood.

hemizygous. Possessing only one of a pair of genes that influence the determination of a particular trait, as in the male with one X-linked gene for a given trait.

hemoglobin. Iron-containing protein in vertebrate blood that binds and transports respiratory gases (oxygen and carbon dioxide).

hemophilia. Inherited sex-linked disease in which the blood clotting mechanism fails to function properly.

herbivore. Animal that consumes living plants or their parts.

heredity. Genetic transmission of traits from parent to offspring.

heritability. Proportion of the phenotypic variability in a population that is attributable to differences in genotype.

hermaphrodite. Individual possessing gonadal tissues of both sexes.

heterosexual. Pertaining to the two sexes, or attraction to persons of the opposite sex; opposed to homosexual.

heterosis. Superior attributes of the heterozygous genotype over corresponding homozygous states; also called *hybrid vigor* or *overdominance.*

heterotroph. Organism that cannot synthesize organic compounds from inorganic substances, and accordingly depends on an external source of organic substances for its food and energy.

heterozygous. Having two dissimilar alleles at a gene locus for a particular character.

histocompatible. Capable of being accepted and remaining functional; applied to tissues that survive when grafted in another organism.

histone. Protein associated with chromosomal DNA that may suppress transcription of genetic information.

homeostasis. Maintenance of a relatively stable, or constant, internal physiological state in the face of varying external conditions.

homeotherm. Animal that maintains a constant body temperature independent of variations in the environmental temperature (e. g., bird, mammal).

hominid. Member of the family of upright, bipedal primates (family Hominidae) that includes modern man and his related ancestors.

Hominidae. Family of living human beings and extinct men; derived from the Latin *homo,* a man.

homogamy. The mating of like with like; also called *assortative mating.*

homogenate. The material obtained after disrupting a cell in a solution.

homologous chromosomes. Two matched, or structurally similar, chromosomes, one from each parent, that have the same sequence of gene loci.

homologous structures. Body parts that are similar in structure owing to common evolutionary or developmental origins; in contrast to *analogous structures* (similar in function but not structure).

homozygous. Having two alleles at a gene locus for a particular character.

homunculus. Name given to preformed, diminutive human figure encased within the head of the sperm cell; imagined by 18th century scientists (preformationists).

hormone. Chemical substance, secreted by a ductless (endocrine) gland, that affects in a specific way the activity of an organ in another part of the body.

host. In parasitology, organism on or in which a parasite lives; in immunology, the recipient of a graft of tissue.

humoral. Pertaining to the fluid materials (humors) of the body (such as blood and lymph).

Huntington's chorea. Inherited nervous disorder characterized by spasmodic twitching that develops in adult life and ends in dementia (after the American physician G. Huntington).

hyaluronidase. An enzyme that catalyzes the breakdown of hyaluronic acid, the cement substance of tissues.

hybridization. Crossing of individuals from genetically different strains, populations, or species.

hybrid vigor. Refers to progeny that are genetically superior (often larger and hardier) than each of the inbred parental strains.

hydrocephaly. Condition characterized by abnormal accumulation of fluid in the brain, accompanied by enlargement of the head, prominence of the forehead, and mental weakness and convulsions.

hydrolysis. Splitting of a molecule (breaking of a chemical bond) by the insertion of water.

hydrophilic. Possessing a strong affinity for water, as chemical substances that are not easily coagulated in water.

hydrophobic. Lacking an affinity for water, as chemical substances that do not mix with water.

hymen. The vascularized, thin membrane that partially or wholly occludes the external opening of the vagina in the human female.

hyperendemic. Pertains to a disease that is continually present to a great degree in a given area.

hyperosmotic. Having a sufficiently high concentration of solutes as to gain water across a selectively permeable membrane from another solution (of lower solute concentration).

hypertension. Abnormally high arterial blood pressure, which may be symptomless or accompanied by nervousness and dizziness.

hyposmotic. Having such a low concentration of solutes as to lose water across a selectively permeable membrane to another solution (of higher solute concentration).

hypothalamus. Portion of the ventral region (floor) of the brain that exerts control over several internal activities (such as visceral functions, water balance, temperature, and sleep).

hypothesis. A tentative supposition provisionally adopted to explain certain facts that can be tested by controlled experiments. A hypothesis that is validated by experimentation and is applicable to related phenomena becomes a theory.

immune response. Production of a specific antibody against a foreign antigen.

immunity. The ability of an organism to resist or overcome an infectious agent or its antigens by the presence or production of antibodies.

immunogenetics. Branch of genetics concerned with the inheritance of antigens and antibodies associated with the immune response.

immunoglobulin. Protein of the blood plasma that functions as an antibody.

implantation. The insertion of an object or tissue in a site of the body; the penetration of the developing mammalian embryo (blastocyst) through the epithelial lining (endometrium) of the uterus.

imprinting. A narrow form of learning occurring during a very short period in the early life of an animal, in which the animal identifies permanently with one other animal or object.

impulse. A physiochemical excitation propagated over the length of a nerve fiber resulting from changes in membrane voltage potentials.

inborn error of metabolism. Inherited defect resulting from the absence or deficiency of an enzyme that catalyzes a metabolic reaction.

inbreeding. The mating of closely related individuals, or of individuals having closely similar genetic constitutions.

independent assortment. The segregation of one pair of genes (distribution into the gametes) occurs independently of the segregation of other pairs of genes located in different chromosomes.

indigenous. Native to a given area; not introduced from outside the particular region.

induction. Process, especially in the developing embryo, whereby one substance or group of cells (inducer or organizer) causes or promotes the differentiation of another group of cells.

industrial melanism. Appearance and spread of dark or melanistic forms of moth species in industrial regions, particularly in Britain.

infancy. The early period of life; generally considered to designate the human young from birth to the assumption of erect posture (12 to 14 months).

infanticide. The taking of the life of an infant.

infertility. Absence of the ability to conceive, or to induce conception; sterility.

ingestion. The act of taking solid material (food) by mouth into the body.

inguinal canal. Internal space in the groin region through which passes the spermatic cord containing the sperm duct (vas deferens).

inner cell mass. Region of the mammalian blastocyst that develops into the embyro proper.

inorganic. Pertains to chemical substances that do not contain a carbon skeleton.

insecticide. Substance designed to kill insects (such as DDT, endrin).

inspiration. The intake of air from the outside owing to an imbalance of air pressure created by an expansion of the thoracic cavity.

instinct. Genetically determined, or innate, complex pattern of behavior that requires no previous experience or conditioning.

insulin. Hormone produced by the pancreas that regulates sugar metabolism (promotes the conversion of glucose to the storage form, glycogen).

interneuron. Nerve cell that connects afferent (sensory) and efferent (motor) nerve cells; forms the bulk of the central nervous system.

interphase. Period in the life of a cell when it is not dividing; although often called the "resting stage," the cell is most active at this time in transcribing and translating genetic information.

interstitial-cell-stimulating hormone (ICSH). Pituitary hormone regulating the activities of testicular interstitial cells (the primary source of the male sex hormone, testosterone); chemically similar to luteinizing hormone (LH).

intra-. Prefix meaning within; for example, intracellular, within the cell, and intrauterine, within the uterus.

intrauterine device (IUD). Semipermanent contraceptive device consisting of inert plastic material of varied shapes inserted into the uterus.

in utero. Inside the uterus.

invagination. The infolding of one part within another; specifically, a process of gastrulation in which one region infolds to form a double-layered embryo.

inversion (temperature). Condition in which a layer of cool air is trapped by a layer of warm air above it; possible pollutants in the cool air accordingly cannot rise and be dispersed.

invertebrate. An animal without a backbone or spinal column.

in vitro. Within a glass; observable in culture or in a test tube.

in vivo. Within the living organism.

involution. A rolling or turning inward over a rim; one of the movements involved in the gastrulation of the frog embryo.

ion. An electrically charged atom resulting from ionization—the loss or gain of one or more electrons from the atom.

irritability. The general property of living protoplasm to react, or be sensitive, to external stimuli.

irruptive. Pertains to the tendency of certain populations to increase suddenly and rapidly in numbers, as in algal blooms.

iso-. Prefix meaning equal; similar to *homo-*.

isolating mechanism. Morphological, behavioral, physiological, or geographical barrier that prevents or limits gene exchange between different species.

isosmotic. Having idential osmotic concentrations (i. e., having the same concentration of solutes as that of the solution on the other side of a selectively permeable membrane).

isotope. Any of several forms of a chemical element differing from one another in the number of neutrons in the atomic nucleus, but not in chemical properties.

jaundice. Yellow appearance of the skin resulting from the deposition of bile pigment.

jelly coat. Soft, translucent substance that coats and protects the frog's egg.

juvenile. Pertaining to youth or childhood; young or immature.

karyotype. Arrangement of the chromosomes of a species in an orderly fashion (usually in order of descending size).

keratin. A tough, fibrous protein found in vertebrate skin, nails, feathers, hair, and scales.

kilocalorie. A large calorie; 1,000 times the standard calorie.

kinetic energy. Energy of motion; energy in the process of doing work.

kin selection. A special form of selection based on the fact that close relatives share a large number of the same genes.

Klinefelter's syndrome. A trisomic condition (XXY) in the male characterized by sexual abnormalities and mental retardation.

Krebs cycle. Series of cellular reactions in aerobic organisms in which pyruvic acid (produced by glycolysis) is converted to carbon dioxide and water, with the release of energy (ATP).

kwashiorkor. A disease of children resulting from protein deficiency.

label (radioactive). A radioactive atom introduced into a molecule to facilitate observation of chemical transformations.

labium. A fleshy border or liplike fold of skin, as in the labia majora and labia minora of the female genitalia.

labor. The act or process of giving birth to a child; also called *parturition*.

lactation. The secretion of milk by mammary glands; act or period of giving milk.

lacteal. A lymph vessel in the villus of the intestinal wall.

lacuna. A small pit or hollow cavity, as in the blood lacuna (blood-filled space) in the trophoblast of the human embryo; also called "lake."

Lamarkism. The theory of the inheritance of acquired characteristics, as proposed by Jean Baptiste de Lamarck.

lamella. A thin leaf or plate, as of bone; a platelike arrangement.

lampbrush chromosomes. Conspicuous chromosomes in the amphibian oocyte characterized by loops that accumulate demonstrably large amounts of messenger RNA.

laparoscopy. Examination of the interior of the abdomen by means of an instrument (laparoscope) inserted through a small abdominal incision.

larva. Immature stage in the life history of the animal that does not resemble the adult form.

learning. Process through which experience modifies behavior patterns.

leiomyoma. A benign tumor derived from smooth muscle.

lek. A communal display ground, where males of certain bird species assert territorial rights to attract and mate with females; also called an *arena*.

lethal. Refers to a gene that, when expressed, is fatal to its bearer.

leucocyte. Colorless (white) blood cell of vertebrates concerned with combating infections; also spelled *leukocyte*.

leukemia. Fatal disease of the blood-forming organs, characterized by a marked increase in the number of leucocytes (white blood cells) and their precursors in the circulating blood.

lichen. Symbiotic association of a fungus and an alga entwined together in a single structure.

limiting factor. Any component of the environment that limits the abundance or distribution of a species in nature.

linkage. Association of genes for different characteristics on the same chromosome; in the absence of crossing over, linked genes do not assort randomly.

lipase. A fat-digesting enzyme.

lipid. Organic substance that is insoluble in water but easily extracted by organic solvents such as alcohol, ether, and chloroform; term embraces fats, oils, waxes, and steroids.

locus. The position of a gene in the chromosome (plural, loci).

logistic curve. Sigmoid, or S-shaped, curve describing the growth of a population under carefully controlled laboratory conditions.

lumen. Cavity or channel within a tubular organ, such as the lumen of the digestive tract.

lunar rhythmicity. Behavioral cycle correlated with the phases or periodicity of the moon; related to the lunar day of 24.8 hours.

luteinizing hormone (LH). Pituitary hormone that promotes development of the corpus luteum in the ovary and stimulates testosterone production in the male (called ICSH in the male).

lymph. Clear, yellowish fluid, rich in white blood cells, that fills tissue spaces, serves as the medium of circulation for fats, and is conveyed to the bloodstream by lymphatic vessels.

lymphatic system. A complex system of thin-walled ducts (lymphatic vessels) that returns protein and other macromolecules in the tissue fluid to the bloodstream.

lymphocyte. A type of white blood cell (leucocyte) involved in the rejection of solid tissue grafts.

Lyon hypothesis. Concept that one X chromosome of the female becomes genetically inactive in embryonic development and becomes a silent partner of the functional X throughout life; formulated by the British geneticist Mary F. Lyon.

lysin. Antibody capable of causing the dissolution (lysis) of cells.

lysosome. Membrane-bound droplet of hydrolytic enzymes that can digest most of the macromolecules found in the cell.

macro-. Prefix meaning large or of abnormal size; for example, macromolecule, macrocephaly.

macromolecule. Molecule of high molecular weight; for example, proteins, polysaccharides, and nucleic acids.

malformation. Defective or abnormal formation; deformity.

malignancy. Tendency to become progressively worse and to result in death.

mammals. Highest class of vertebrate animals that possess hair and suckle their young.

mammary. Pertaining to the breast (mamma), the glandular structure of the female that secretes milk for nourishment of the young.

maramus. Progressive emaciation and malnutrition in infants resulting from deficiencies in the diet of both calories and protein.

marrow. The soft material that fills the cavity of bones; an important site of the formation of blood cells in vertebrates.

marsupial. A mammal, like the opossum and kangaroo, that possesses an abdominal pouch (the marsupium) in which the young are carried and nourished.

matrix. The groundwork on which anything is cast; the material in which a cell is embedded.

mean. The arithmetic average; the sum of all values for a group, divided by the number of individuals.

medulla. A general term to designate the middle, or inmost, portion of an organ or structure, such as the adrenal medulla (inner part of the gland).

meiosis. Special kind of nuclear division, occurring in the maturation of gametes, by means of which each daughter nucleus receives half the number of chromosomes characteristic of the somatic (body) cells of the species.

melanin. Dark brown or black pigment of the skin and hair.

membrane potential. Voltage difference that exists across the surface membrane of a cell.

membranes (fetal). Membranous structures that protect the embryo and provide for its nutrition, respiration, and excretion; includes the yolk sac, allantois, amnion, and chorion.

memory. Mental faculty involving storage and retrieval of sensations, impressions, and ideas.

menopause. Cessation of menstruation in the human female, occurring usually between the age of 46 and 50.

menses. The monthly flow of blood ("period") from the uterus of the human female during her reproductive life.

menstruation. Periodic uterine bleeding that normally recurs, at four-week intervals, in the absence of pregnancy during the reproductive period of the human female.

mesenchyme. Meshwork of loosely connected mesodermal cells; prominent in vertebrate embryos.

mesentery. Membranous fold attaching various organs to the body wall; commonly used with specific reference to the peritoneal fold attaching the small intestine to the dorsal body wall.

meso-. Prefix signifying middle, either situated in the middle or being intermediate in time; for example, mesoderm, mesonephros, Mesozoic.

mesoderm. Middle layer of the three primary germ layers of the embryo, lying between the ectoderm and the endoderm; from it are derived the connective tissue, cartilage and bone, muscles, blood, and most of the urogenital system.

messenger RNA (mRNA). Strand of ribonucleic acid that is synthesized off one of the strands of DNA; carries genetic information for the synthesis of proteins.

meta-. Prefix denoting a change or a transformation to a new form or level; for example, metamorphosis, metanephros.

metabolism. The sum of all chemical processes in the living organism; embraces constructive metabolism (anabolism) in which organic molecules are synthesized and destructive metabolism (catabolism) in which energy is made available by the degradation of organic molecules.

metacentric. Refers to the median location of the centromere of a chromosome.

metachromasia. Condition in which tissues do not stain true with a given colored dye, or the same dye colors different tissues in different tints.

metamorphosis. Change of shape or structure; particularly a transition from one developmental stage to another, as in insects and frogs.

metaphase. Stage of mitosis during which the longitudinally duplicated chromosomes become oriented at the center of the cell.

metastasis. Transfer of a disease-producing agency (pathogenic microorganisms or cancerous cells) from the site of the disease to another part of the body.

methane. Odorless, flammable gas that develops in nature from decomposing organic matter; also called *marsh gas*.

micelle. Tiny droplet of partly digested fats.

micro-. Prefix designating small size; for example, microcephaly, microorganism.

micron. Unit of microscopic measurement; 1/1,000 of a millimeter, or 1/25,000 of an inch; abbreviated μ.

microorganism. Minute, usually microscopic, living organism (such as bacteria, viruses, and yeasts).

microvillus. Fine projection of protoplasm, produced by the folding of the plasma membrane, that increases the cell's surface area for absorption.

miscarriage. Spontaneous abortion; premature expulsion of the fetus.

mitochondrion. Rod-shaped organelle that is the main site of cellular respiration; harbors the enzymes for the Krebs cycle and the respiratory chain.

mitosis. Nuclear division by means of which two daughter nuclei receive identical chromosome complements of the parent nucleus.

molecular weight. Sum of the atomic weights of the constituent atoms in a molecule.

molecule. Association or combination of two or more atoms to form a specific chemical substance.

mongolism. See *Down's syndrome*.

mono-. Prefix meaning one, or single.

monoculture. Practice of cultivating only a single crop or timber in large acreage to the exclusion of other land uses.

monogamy. Formation of single breeding pairs that persist for a long duration.

monohybrid cross. Cross involving only one pair of contrasting traits; for example, tall vs. dwarf, normal wing vs. vestigial wing.

monolayer. A layer of cells that is uniformly one cell thick.

monoploid. Possessing only a single set of chromosomes in a cell; equivalent to haploid.

monosaccharide. A simple sugar; a carbohydrate that cannot be decomposed by hydrolysis.

monosomy. Absence of one chromosome from a diploid complement.

monotreme. The lowest group of mammals, including the duckbill platypus and the spiny anteater, that lay shelled eggs similar to those of reptiles and nourish their young by a rudimentary mammary gland that has no nipple.

monotypic. Refers to a species that is not divided into subspecies, or geographical races.

morphogenesis. Process by which embryonic tissues are shaped into adult organs.

morula. Grapelike mass of cells resulting from cleavage divisions of the fertilized egg.

mosaicism. Genetical term referring to the presence in an individual of two or more cell populations having different chromosome complements; sometimes called *chimerism*.

motivational drive. The internal state of an animal that fosters a behavioral act.

motor neuron. Nerve cell that conducts an impulse from the central nervous system to muscles or glands; also called *efferent neuron*.

mucosa. A mucous layer of epithelial cells that lines internal cavities; secretions of glands produce the viscous slime, or mucus.

mulatto. The first generation offspring of a Negro and a Caucasian; in popular use, any person of mixed Caucasian and Negro ancestry.

multicellular. Consisting of more than one cell; in contrast to *unicellular*.

multiple alleles. A series of more than two alternative forms of a gene at a single locus.

mutagen. Substance or agent (chemicals, radiation) capable of inducing mutations.

mutation. An alteration of the gene that results in a transmissible change in a trait; the deletion, addition, or substitution of one or more nucleotide bases of the DNA strand.

muton. Smallest segment of DNA (subunit of a cistron) that can undergo mutational change.

mutualism. Symbiotic relationship in which both participating species benefit from the association.

myelin. Fatty material surrounding the axon of a vertebrate nerve cell.

myofibril. Thin cylindrical element (about 1 to 2μ in diameter) running through the length of the voluntary muscle cell (fiber).

myofilaments. Thin protein strands (either actin or myosin) that make up the myofibrils in skeletal (voluntary) muscle cells (fibers).

myosin. One of the two major contractile proteins of muscle; composes the thick filaments of myofibrils.

natality. Production of offspring; the birth rate in any community.

natural selection. Differential contribution of offspring to the next generation by individuals of different genotypes in a population.

nausea. An unpleasant sensation, often culminating in vomiting.

navel. Umbilicus, or shriveled remnant of the umbilical connection.

necrosis. Death of tissues, usually as individual cells, groups of cells, or in localized areas.

neonatal. Pertaining to the newborn infant (neonate), usually the first four weeks after birth.

neoplasm. Any new and abnormal growth, such as a tumor.

nephron. Anatomical and functional unit of the kidney, consisting of the glomerulus, Bowman's capsule, and various tubules.

nerve. Cordlike bundle of nerve fibers that convey impulses.

nerve fiber. Extension of a nerve cell that transmits a nerve impulse; an axon.

neural plate. Flat plate of thickened ectodermal cells in the vertebrate embryo that gives rise to the central nervous system.

neural tube. Dorsally located channel in the vertebrate embryo that later becomes the brain and spinal cord.

neuromuscular junction. The point of contact between a nerve cell and a muscle cell.

neuron. A nerve cell; the basic unit of the nervous system.

neurula. Term applied to the vertebrate embryo during the closure of the neural folds to form the neural tube.

niche. The role played by an organism in the ecology of the community of which it is a part; the distinctive manner in which the organism relates to, and interacts with, all the components of its immediate environment; also referred to as *ecological niche.*

niche diversification. Evolutionary process whereby two potentially competing species come to occupy different niches in a biotic community and thus avoid or minimize competition.

nicotinamide adenine dinucleotide (NAD). Organic compound that functions as a hydrogen-carrying coenzyme, or electron acceptor.

nipple. Conic tip of the breast that contains the outlets of the milk ducts.

nitrification. The conversion of ammonia to nitrate by microorganisms (soil bacteria).

nitrogen fixation. Conversion of gaseous nitrogen to nitrate by microorganisms (bacteria).

nondisjunction. Failure of a pair of chromosomes (or a pair of chromatids) to separate at meiosis (or at mitosis), so that one daughter cell has both members of the pair and the other daughter cell lacks that particular chromosome.

nonrenewable resource. A raw material that cannot be used again in its original form and cannot be replaced by natural processes (such as coal and ores).

notochord. Dorsal supporting rod of the vertebrate embryo, later replaced by the vertebral column.

nucleic acid. Long-chain polymer of alternating sugar and phosphate groups, with organic bases (adenine, thymine or uracil, guanine, cytosine) as side chains; for example, deoxyribonucleic acid (DNA) and ribonucleic acid (RNA).

nucleolus. Round body within the cell nucleus; rich in ribonucleic acid and the site of synthesis of ribosomal RNA.

nucleotide. A basic, repeating unit in a nucleic acid, consisting of a five-carbon sugar molecule, a phosphoric acid, and a ring-shaped nitrogenous base.

nucleus. Spheroid body within the cell that is bounded by a double membrane and contains the gene-bearing chromosomes.

nurse cell. One of several cells of the ovarian follicle that nourishes the developing egg cell.

nutrient. Any substance required by an organism for normal growth and maintenance.

oligotrophic. Pertains to a body of water with a low nutrient content and low productivity, as a pristine lake with very clear water.

omnivorous. Refers to an animal (omnivore) that eats both plants and animals.

oncogene. Postulated cancer-associated gene that is present in a repressed state in all normal cells from the beginning of life; cancer presumably occurs when the oncogene is de-repressed by a carcinogenic agent.

ontogeny. The developmental history of the individual organism; in contrast to *phylogeny.*

oocyte. A growing ovarian egg that has not yet completed its maturation process; may be a primary oocyte or a secondary oocyte.

oogenesis. Development of the ovum (egg) from germinal cells in the ovary.

oogonium. Primordial cell from which the ovarian egg arises; a stage in the growth of the egg before it becomes a primary oocyte.

operator. Refers to the site on the DNA molecule (or region of an operon) that can bind with a specific protein repressor and prevent transcription.

operon. A genetic unit of transcription, typically consisting of a control region or site (operator) and a cluster of adjacent structural genes (cistrons).

organ. A group of different tissues that are integrated to perform a specific function for the body (for example, heart, lungs, liver).

organelle. A membrane-bound structure within the cell that is specialized for a particular function (for example, ribosomes, mitochondria, Golgi apparatus).

organic. Pertaining to any aspect of living matter.

organic compound. Carbon-containing chemical compound that is normally synthesized by living organisms.

organism. An organized body of living economy; a living creature, plant or animal.

organizer. A group of cells of an embryo that influences or directs the differentiation of another group of cells.

osmosis. The passage of water from a solution of higher concentration of water (pure water or a hypotonic solution) to one of lower concentration when the two solutions are separated by a membrane that selectively prevents the passage of solute molecules but is permeable to water.

ovary. The sexual gland, or gonad, of the female in which the ova, or eggs, are formed.

overdominance. See heterosis.

oviduct. Passage through which the egg travels from the ovary either to the exterior of the body (as in frogs) or to the uterus (as in placental mammals); called the Fallopian tube in humans.

ovulation. Discharge of the egg from the mature (Graafian) follicle into the oviduct.

ovum. Female gamete or egg; plural, ova.

oxidation. The removal of electrons from an atom or molecule; oxidation in biological systems generally involves the removal of hydrogen electrons.

oxidation-reduction reactions. Chemical reactions involved in the transfer of energy within cells; oxidation (the loss of an electron) takes place simultaneously with reduction (the gain of an electron) as the electron lost by one atom is accepted by another.

oxygen debt. Amount of oxygen required to oxidize excess lactic acid accumulated during periods of relative oxygen deficiency (as during strenuous muscle exercise).

ozone. A highly active form of oxygen gas produced in smog; contains three atoms of oxygen per molecule; toxic to plants and animals in low concentrations.

paleo-. Prefix signifying old.

paleontology. The scientific study of fossils and all aspects of past life.

pancreas. Gland near the stomach that produces several digestive enzymes and insulin.

pangenesis. Erroneous concept that all organs of the body are represented by blood-borne particles (gemmules) that are transmitted to the offspring, thus accounting for the hereditary transmission of traits, particularly acquired bodily changes.

Papanicolaou (Pap) test. Method of staining smears of various body secretions, especially from the genital tract, for the examination of exfoliated cells to detect the presence of a malignant process; after George N. Papanicolaou, physician and cytologist, 1883–1962.

para-. Prefix meaning beside, accessory to, against, or at the side of.

parabiosis. The union of two individuals, usually joined by surgical means.

parasitism. Symbiotic relation in which one organism (the parasite) lives upon or within another organism (the host) at whose expense it obtains some advantage.

parasympathetic division. One of the two divisions of the autonomic nervous system that regulates the internal environment of the body; its effects on internal organs are counter to those of the sympathetic system, generally returning the body to normal after an emergency.

parthenogenesis. Development of an egg without being fertilized by sperm; development can be initiated artificially by chemical or mechanical stimulation.

parturition. Act or process of giving birth to a child.

passive immunity. Protection from communicable diseases or foreign antigens by specific antibodies obtained from other persons or animals.

pathogen. An organism that causes disease.

pathology. Study of the structural and functional changes in diseased tissues and organs.

pecking order. Hierarchy among social animals in which the more dominant members assert control over the less dominant members; also called dominance hierarchy.

pedigree. An ancestral line; lineage; a genealogical tree.

penis. Male copulatory organ through which sperm are deposited in the female genital tract and that functions also as a passage for the excretion of urine.

peptide. Compound of two or more amino acid units linked together; peptides of large numbers of amino acids are called polypeptides.

peristalsis. Waves of muscular contractions passing along tubular organs (such as the alimentary canal) that propel the contents within the tube.

peritoneum. Epithelial membrane of mesodermal origin that lines the body cavity (coelom) and forms the covering of the visceral organs.

Peyer's patches. Oval, elevated areas of lymphoid tissue (closely packed lymphocytes) in the lining of the small intestine; after J. C. Peyer, Swiss anatomist, 1653–1712.

pH. Symbol used in expressing the hydrogen ion concentration of a solution; the measure of acidity and alkalinity. The neutral point is pH 7; below 7 acidity increases and above 7 alkalinity increases.

phagocytosis. Engulfing of solid particles by a cell, such as the intake of food (microorganisms) by the primitive amoeba and the trapping of foreign particles by the amoebalike vertebrate white blood cell.

phalanx. Any bone of a finger or toe; plural, phalanges.

phenotype. Outward (observable) manifestation of an individual's genetic makeup; distinguished from genotype.

phenylketonuria (PKU). Recessively inherited disorder characterized by mental retardation that results from the deficiency of a particular enzyme involved in phenylalanine metabolism.

phloem. Vascular tissue that transports sugar and other organic molecules from the leaves to other parts of the plant.

phosphorylation. The addition of a phosphate group to a molecule, as in the phosphorylation of ADP to ATP.

photosynthesis. Metabolic process of green plants by which the energy of sunlight is trapped by chlorophyll and used to synthesize energy-rich compounds (glucose and ATP) from carbon dioxide and water, with the release of oxygen.

phylogeny. The evolutionary history of a particular group of organisms; distinguished from ontogeny (the development of the individual organism).

pinocytosis. Uptake of droplets of surrounding medium into the interior of the cell by engulfing the material in a pocket of cell membrane.

placenta. Flat, platelike vascular structure in the pregnant uterus that represents the site of exchange of respiratory, nutritive, and excretory products between the fetus and mother; the afterbirth.

plankton. Minute, floating animal and plant life of an aquatic community, such as blue-green algae (phytoplankton) and protozoa (zooplankton).

plasma. The fluid portion of the blood in which the corpuscles are suspended; distinguished from serum, which is plasma from which the clotting protein (fibrinogen) has been separated.

plasma cell. Specialized lymphoid cell rich in ribosomal RNA that produces circulating (humoral) antibodies.

plasma membrane. Semipermeable, lipoprotein membrane that forms the outer limit of a cell and regulates the movement of molecules in and out of the cell.

plasmolysis. Shrinking of a cell as a consequence of the outflow of water into a hypotonic medium.

platelet. Colorless, enucleated cell fragment concerned with the coagulation of blood in mammals.

poikilotherm. Animal whose body temperature fluctuates with changes of the environmental temperature (e. g., fish and amphibians).

polar body. Small, nonviable cell resulting from unequal division of the oocyte during the formation of the ovum (oogenesis).

polarized. Term applied to a cell membrane across which a voltage potential exists, owing to the unequal distribution of chemical ions on the two sides of the membrane.

pollution. The contamination of a medium (air, water, or soil) with impurities to a level that is detrimental to organisms or the balance of nature.

poly-. Prefix meaning many, or much.

polygamy. Custom or practice of a male pairing with several females at one time (polygyny) or a female pairing with several males at one time (polyandry); usually the former.

polygenic inheritance. Determination of a quantitatively varying trait by the additive effects of several independently assorting genes.

polymer. Large molecule made up of many repeating, or like, subunits.

polymorphism. Occurrence in the same breeding population of two or more distinct hereditary types (or allelic genes), the rarest of which occurs with a frequency higher than that possible through recurrent mutation.

polyploid. Having three or more complete sets of chromosomes in a cell (such as triploid, tetraploid, pentaploid).

polysaccharide. Carbohydrate consisting of many repeating sugar (monosaccharide) units, such as starch, cellulose, and glycogen.

polytypic species. Wide-ranging species that is subdivided into two or more subspecies, or geographical races.

pongid. Member of the family (Pongidae) of anthropoid apes (gorillas, chimpanzees, orangutans, and gibbons).

Pongidae. Family of the apes, taken from the generic name of the orangutan, Pongo.

population. Individuals of a species that form a local breeding community in a particular region.

portal vein. Blood vessel that carries blood from one capillary system to another (such as hepatic portal vein).

postnatal. Occurring after birth.

preadaptation. Refers to a trait in an organism that has survival value in an environment to which the organism has not yet been exposed.

predatory. Living by preying upon, or destroying, other organisms; predaceous.

preen. To trim, or arrange, one's feathers or fur fastidiously; said especially of birds.

preformation. Invalid theory that the fully formed individual exists in minute form either in the egg or sperm; opposed to epigenesis.

primordium. Earliest discernible indication during embryonic development of a tissue or organ; also called anlage or rudiment.

pro-. Prefix signifying before, in front of, or a stage coming first; for example, prophase and pronephros.

procaryote. Organism in which the genetic material is not enclosed in a membrane-bound nucleus and that lacks complicated internal membrane systems; essentially bacteria and blue-green algae.

producer. Organism, especially a green plant, that synthesizes organic compounds from inorganic constituents of the environment; the autotroph in an ecosystem.

progesterone. Hormone produced by the corpus luteum of the ovary that prepares the lining of the uterus for the reception of the fertilized egg; often termed the "pregnancy hormone."

prophase. First stage of cell division (mitosis) during which the individual chromosomes thicken and reveal their longitudinally doubled structure (daughter chromatids).

prostaglandin. Chemical substance, first found in the semen of man and sheep, that causes strong contractions of smooth muscles; may induce abortion by causing contractions of uterine muscles.

prostate. A male gland that surrounds the urethra at the level of the bladder and secretes a large portion of the seminal fluid.

protein. Long-chain polymer of amino acids that represents one of the principal constituents of the cell protoplasm.

protozoa. One-celled organisms including the flagellates, amoebas, and ciliates.

proximal. Nearest; situated close to a point of reference; opposed to *distal.*

pseudopregnancy. False pregnancy; physiological state resembling pregnancy that is induced in experimental mammals (rabbits and mice) following sterile copulation with a vasectomized male.

puberty. Period during which sexual maturity is achieved; marked by functional maturation of the reproductive organs, development of secondary sex characters, and onset of menstruation in the female.

pulmonary. Pertaining to the lungs.

Punnett square. Checkerboard diagram used for convenient analysis of the recombination of genes (in gametes) to form individuals (zygotes).

purine. A two-ringed nitrogenous compound, such as adenine and guanine; constituent of DNA and RNA.

pyramid (energy). Triangular representation of the energy relationships among various trophic levels in a particular food chain.

pyrimidine. A one-ringed nitrogenous compound; constituent of DNA (thymine and cytosine) and RNA (uracil and cytosine).

pyrogen. A fever-producing substance or agent (typically bacteria).

q. Symbol for the relative frequency of a gene, especially of the recessive allele when *p* is used for the frequency of the dominant allele.

quadruped. Having four feet; using four limbs in walking, as most mammals.

qualitative. Pertaining to quality; that which cannot be defined in measurable or numerical amount; contrasted with *quantitative.*

quantitative. Pertaining to quantity; that which is measurable or can be defined in numerical amount; contrasted with *qualitative.*

quarantine. To detain or isolate individuals suspected of being carriers of communicable disease; restrictions placed on the transportation of plant and animal pests.

race. A geographical subdivision of a species, recognized formally as a subspecies; a geographically defined breeding population with a constellation of genes different from other geographical populations.

radioactivity. The release of radiant energy (alpha, beta, or gamma rays) as a result of changes (decay) in the nuclei of unstable atoms.

radioautography. Experimental technique in which emissions from radioactive materials are recorded on photographic film.

random mating. Pattern of breeding in which an individual of one genetic makeup has an equal probability of mating with any individual of other genetic constitutions.

recapitulation. Repetition in the individual during its development of the stages of evolution of earlier organisms.

receptor. Sense organ or specialized sensory cells that respond to stimuli of various kinds (light, sound, heat, mechanical pressure).

recessive. Refers to a gene whose expression is masked by a dominant allele and accordingly manifests itself only in the homozygous state.

reciprocal altruism. Concept that an individual will act selflessly (altruistically) with the expectation that the beneficent behavior will be reciprocated at some future occasion.

recombination. New combinations of genes in the progeny resulting from independent assortment of alleles and rearrangement of genes through crossing over during meiosis.

recycling. Process by which mineral nutrients pass continually to and from nonliving and living components of an ecosystem.

redirected activity. Direction of aggressive behavior away from the primary target and toward an innocuous object.

reducing atmosphere. Atmosphere devoid of molecular oxygen.

reduction. Gain of an electron by an atom or molecule in a chemical reaction; occurs simultaneously with oxidation (loss of an electron by another atom or molecule).

reduction division. Separation of the homologous chromosomes that had earlier undergone synaptic pairing during meiosis.

reflex. Rapid and consistent automatic behavior response to a stimulus, involving relatively few neurons.

reflex arc. Simple nerve pathway along which the impulses involved in an involuntary, rapid response (reflex) are transmitted to and from the central nervous system (spinal cord).

regeneration. Replacement or renewal of a substance or part, such as a lost or injured tissue or organ.

regression. A return to an earlier or former state; tendency of offspring of extreme parents to return to the average of the population (Galton's law of regression).

regulator. Site or gene on the DNA molecule that produces the repressor protein, which controls or regulates the operon at the operator site.

releaser. Term used in ethology to signify a key stimulus (sign stimulus) that evokes a specific, or appropriate, response.

releasing factor. Chemical substance produced by neurosecretory cells of the hypothalamus that regulates or stimulates the release of hormones by the pituitary gland.

renal. Pertaining to the kidney.

replication. Repetition; a duplication or exact copying, as in the formation of replicate daughter strands of DNA.

repressor. Protein produced by the regulator gene that can bind to the operator site on the DNA molecule and prevent transcription of the structural genes of the operon.

reproductive isolation. Inherent inability of members of different breeding populations (particularly species) to cross with each other.

reproductive potential. The maximum capacity of an organism to reproduce under optimum, or ideal, conditions.

respiration. The burning or oxidation of organic compounds to release energy.

respiratory chain. Integrated series of complex molecules (including cytochromes) capable of oxidation and reduction; the elaborate transfers of electrons are associated with the production of appreciable ATP.

resting potential. The voltage potential existing across the membrane of a nerve (or muscle) fiber when the fiber is inactive.

reticulum. A weblike structure or network, as in endoplasmic reticulum.

retina. Layer of light-sensitive cells (rods and cones) at the rear of the eyeball upon which falls the image focused by the lens.

Rh factor. Inherited antigen in human red blood cells (first discovered in rhesus monkeys); individuals possessing this antigen are Rh-positive; those lacking it are Rh-negative.

rhizoid. Resembling a root; anchoring structure in primitive plants such as *Acetabularia*.

Rhogam. Commercial name for the specific gamma globulin containing an anti-Rh antibody that counteracts the tendency of an Rh-negative woman to produce Rh antibodies against introduced Rh-positive cells.

rhythm. Recurrence of an action or function at regular intervals.

ribonucleic acid (RNA). A polymer of ribonucleotides, each composed of phosphate, sugar (ribose), and a purine or pyrimidine; involved in protein synthesis.

ribosome. Minute RNA-containing granule, usually attached to the membranes of the endo-plasmic reticulum of the cell; the site of protein synthesis.

ritualization. The evolutionary modification of a behavioral pattern into a specific communicative signal.

RNA. *See* ribonucleic acid.

roentgen (R). A unit of measurement of the number of ionizations caused by radiation in air.

rut. Period or season of heightened sexual desire and activity in certain mammals (deer, cattle) that coincides with the time of ovulation in the females.

saprophyte. Organism, generally a bacterium or fungus, that obtains its nutrients from dead organic matter.

sarcomere. Segment or unit of a muscle fibril that is repeated regularly throughout the length of the fibril (unit between two Z lines).

saturated. Pertaining to a compound that does not form addition products; applied especially to fatty acids that contain no double or triple bonds between carbon atoms.

savanna. A tropical grassland containing scattered trees; also spelled *savannah*.

Schwann cells. Cells that form a sheath around peripheral nerve axons (fibers).

scrotum. Sac in mammals that contains the testes and their associated ducts (particularly epididymides).

seaweed. Marine algae, such as kelp, rockweed, and sea lettuce.

secondary sex characteristics. Physical traits apart from the primary gonads (ovaries and testes) that distinguish male from female, such as distribution and growth of pubic and facial hair, voice level, muscular development, fat deposition, and breasts.

second filial generation (F_2). All of the offspring resulting from the mating of two individuals of the first filial generation.

second law of thermodynamics. Physical principle that states that all energy transformations in a system are less than 100 percent efficient; the restoration of order requires the addition of free energy into the system from the outside.

second-set response. Heightened, or vigorous, antibody response to a second graft containing the same antigens that evoked the original (first-set) response.

secretion. Product of a cell or gland that is released through the cell membrane.

sedimentary rock. Rock formed of sediments (particles) of chemical or organic origin.

segregation (of genes). Separation, during gamete formation, of members of pairs of alleles.

selection coefficient (S). Mathematical expression of the relative reproductive efficiency or fitness of a genotype in a breeding population.

selection (natural). Differential contribution of offspring to the next generation by individuals of different genotypes in a population.

semen. Whitish secretion of the male reproduction organ, composed of sperm in their nutrient fluids (fluids secreted by the prostrate, seminal vesicles, and various other glands).

seminal. Pertaining to the semen, as in seminal fluid.

seminiferous tubules. Highly coiled ducts within the male testes that produce and convey sperm.

semipermeable. Refers to a membrane that permits some substances to pass through while restraining the passage of others; also termed *differentially permeable* or *selectively permeable.*

sensory neuron. Nerve cell that detects environmental stimuli and conveys these stimuli to the central nervous system; also called *afferent neuron.*

serum. Clear liquid that remains after clotting of the blood (that is, after separation of blood cells and fibrinogen).

sessile. Fixed in place or sedentary; said of animals.

sex chromosomes. Chromosomes associated with the determination of sex; designated X and Y in mammals.

sex-limited. Refers to traits, such as frontal baldness, transmitted by autosomal genes that typically affect one sex only.

sex-linked. Refers to traits, such as color blindness, that are transmitted by genes located in the sex-determining chromosomes, particularly the X chromosome.

sexual reproduction. Act or process of reproducing that involves the union of two sex cells, or gametes (egg and sperm).

sibling. Another offspring of the same parents as the person of reference; a brother or sister; also called *sib.*

sickle-cell anemia. Inherited disorder characterized by distorted, crescent-shaped red blood cells caused by an abnormal hemoglobin molecule.

sigmoid growth curve. S-shaped pattern of growth of a population with time, particularly under carefully controlled laboratory conditions.

sign stimulus. An external cue that elicits an appropriate behavior.

smog. Mixture of gaseous and particulate pollutants in the atmosphere that interacts with sunlight to produce a hazy veil of air that is hazardous to health.

smooth muscle. Involuntary muscle tissue composed of short, spindle-shaped fibers (cells) that line the walls of the digestive tract, blood vessels, and various ducts.

sociobiology. The application of evolutionary concepts to the study of the social interactions of animals.

sodium pump. A transport system incorporated in the cell membrane that moves sodium ions out of cells against a concentration gradient.

solute. A substance dissolved in a solution; a solution consists of a solute and a solvent.

solution. A mixture in which the molecules of a dissolved substance (solute) are dispersed among the molecules of a liquid (solvent).

solvent. A liquid that is capable of dissolving another substance (solute).

somatic. Pertaining to the body, such as somatic cell (body cell as distinguished from germ cell).

somite. One of the paired, blocklike masses of mesoderm adjacent to the neural tube of the embryo that contributes to the formation of the vertebral column.

soot. Small particles of carbon emitted during the combustion of fossil fuels.

spawn. To produce or deposit gametes in the water; said of aquatic animals.

species. A breeding community that preserves its genetic identity by its inability to exchange genes with other such breeding communities.

spermatogenesis. Process by which haploid male gametes (sperm) are derived by meiosis from diploid germinal cells.

spermatogonium. Undifferentiated germ cell of the vertebrate male that ultimately develops into a sperm cell.

spermatozoon. Mature male germ cell produced by the testes; plural, *spermatozoa* or *sperm.*

sphincter. A ringlike muscular band that surrounds, and is capable of closing, a natural opening or passage, as in various parts of the digestive tract.

spinal nerves. Nerves that branch off from each segment of the spinal cord in vertebrates.

spindle. Mitotic structure consisting of microtubules that function in the movement of chromosomes to opposite poles of the cell during anaphase.

spontaneous generation. Concept that a living organism develops from nonliving matter.

starch. A complex carbohydrate (polysaccharide); the storage form of sugar in green plants.

stereoscopic vision. Imparting a solid appearance to, or a three-dimensional view of, an object.

stillbirth. Birth of a dead child.

stimulus. A physical or chemical change in the environment that influences the activity of the organism or part of the organism.

stoma. Microscopic pore in the leaf surface through which gas exchange and water loss take place; plural, *stomata.*

striated muscle. Skeletal, voluntary muscle tissue in which the arrangement of the fibers imparts the appearance of striations across the muscle.

structural gene. A gene that encodes a polypeptide chain of a protein; one of the genes of an operon; a cistron.

subcutaneous. Situated or occurring beneath the skin.

subspecies. A geographical race of a species.

substrate. The substance upon which an enzyme acts.

supernatant. The generally clear, lighter material that remains in suspension in the liquid above the precipitate following centrifugation.

symbiosis. An intimate association of two dissimilar species; the association may be beneficial to both (mutualism), beneficial to one without adverse effect on the other (commensalism), or beneficial to one and detrimental to the other (parasitism).

sympathetic division. One of the two divisions of the autonomic nervous system that serves to prepare the body for emergencies.

sympatric. Refers to populations that occur together in the same general geographic region, or whose geographic ranges overlap.

synapse. The junction of processes of two adjacent nerve cells, where the nerve impulse is transmitted from the axon of one nerve cell to the dendrite of the other.

synapsis. The attraction and pairing of homologous chromosomes during meiosis.

syncytium. A multinucleate mass of protoplasm produced by the merging of cells.

synthesis. The formation of a more complex substance from simpler ones.

systematics. Study of the diversity, interrelations, and classification of organisms.

taxonomy. Classification of organisms into appropriate categories (taxa) on the basis of the evolutionary relationships among them.

Tay-Sachs disease. Recessively inherited lethal condition of blindness and mental retardation; also called infantile amaurotic idiocy; after codiscoverers Warren Tay and Bernard Sachs.

template. A pattern or mold; a structure that serves as a mold for the construction of another, complementary copy.

teratogen. An agent that interferes with normal development of the embryo, causing malformations or anomalies.

territory. A defined geographical area defended, usually for breeding purposes, by one animal, or a band of animals, against other members of the same species.

testis. The male sperm-producing gonad.

testosterone. Testes-producing hormone that functions in the induction and maintenance of male secondary sex characteristics.

tetrad. Set of four DNA strands resulting from the duplication and pairing of homologous chromosomes during meiosis.

thalamus. Part of the human brain that serves as the relay center for sensory impulses from the spinal cord to the cerebral cortex.

theory. A hypothesis that is supported by extensive observations and experiments.

thoracic cavity. Chest cavity, containing the heart and lungs, enclosed by the ribs and diaphragm.

threshold. The point or level at which a physiological effect is produced, such as the degree of stimulation of a nerve that just produces a response.

thromboembolism. Obstruction of a blood vessel with a thrombus that has broken loose from its site of formation.

thrombus. Clot in a blood vessel, formed by coagulation of the blood.

thylakoid. A saclike membranous structure in the chloroplast; stacks of thylakoids from the grana.

thymus. Ductless gland at the base of the neck, filled with lymphocytes, that is important in early life for the proper development of the body's immune mechanism.

tissue. Group of similarly specialized cells that perform a particular function, such as muscle tissue and nerve tissue.

totipotency. Ability of a cell to develop into any type of cell; also termed equipotency.

transcription. Synthesis of a complementary strand of messenger RNA from a DNA template.

transduction. The transfer of genetic material (DNA) from one cell (bacterium) to another cell (bacterium) mediated by a virus (bacteriophage) carrier.

transfer RNA (tRNA). Low-molecular-weight cytoplasmic RNA of which there are at least 20 varieties, one specific for each amino acid; involved in protein synthesis.

transformation. Genetic modification induced by the incorporation into a cell (bacterium) of DNA extracted and purified from another cell (bacterium or virus).

translation. Process whereby the base sequences in messenger RNA direct the order of specific amino acids in the formation of polypeptides (proteins).

translocation (genetic). The interchange of chromosome segments between nonhomologous chromosomes.

transmitter substance. A chemical, such as acetylcholine, secreted by the terminal end of the axon that crosses the synaptic gap and affects the membrane permeability of the postsynaptic nerve cell.

transplantation. The grafting of tissues from one organism to another.

trimester. A period of three months; one of the three phases of a nine-month pregnancy.

triplet. Sequence of three consecutive bases in chromosomal DNA that specifies one amino acid residue in protein synthesis.

triploid. Containing three sets of the basic chromosome complement; designated 3n.

trisomic. Having one extra chromosome in a diploid set.

tritium (^3H). Radioactive hydrogen; an isotope of hydrogen that has two neutrons and one proton in its nucleus.

trophic level. Position occupied by a given species in a food chain; one of several successive links in the transfer of energy through an ecosystem.

trophoblast. Layer of extraembryonic ectodermal tissue that attaches the human embryo to the uterine wall and subsequently aids in the formation of the placenta.

tubal ligation. Surgical procedure whereby Fallopian tubes (oviducts) are cut and tied to effect sterilization of the female.

tumor. Mass of new tissue formed by rapidly dividing abnormal cells; a neoplasm.

turbidity. Cloudiness; decrease in visibility resulting from the scattering of light by suspended particles.

ulcer. Disintegration of the mucous surface of the tissue lining a tubular organ.

ultrastructure. Too small to be seen with an ordinary microscope; details visible only by electron microscopy.

umbilical cord. Cord, containing two arteries and one vein, that connects the placenta with the fetus; transmits oxygen and nutrients from mother to fetus.

umbilicus. Site or scar on the abdomen marking the point of attachment of the umbilical cord during fetal development; the navel.

uni-. Prefix meaning one or single, as in a unicellular (one-celled) organism.

unit membrane. Term describing the triple-layered structural configuration of the cell (plasma) membrane, consisting of a layer of phospholipid sandwiched between two layers of protein.

urea. A conversion product of ammonia, formed mainly in the liver, that is the chief nitrogenous constituent of urine.

ureter. Tube that conveys urine from the kidney to the bladder.

urethra. Canal that conveys urine from the bladder to the exterior of the body.

urine. Waste fluid containing urea that is secreted by the kidneys, stored in the bladder, and discharged by the urethra.

uterus. Thick-walled, muscular organ (womb) of the mammalian female in which the fetus develops.

vaccination. The injection of vaccine for the purpose of inducing immunity.

vaccine. Preparation of weakened or dead microorganisms (bacteria, viruses) administered to an individual to induce immunity by stimulating antibody production against the disease-causing microorganisms.

vacuole. Membrane-bound vesicle within a cell filled with water and dissolved substances.

vacuum aspiration. Surgical technique, performed during the first trimester of pregnancy, of drawing off the conceptus by suction (by a device producing a partial vacuum).

vagina. Canal in the female that receives the penis during coitus and through which the child passes during delivery; commonly called birth canal.

vascular. Containing or concerning vessels that conduct fluid.

vas deferens. Duct through which sperm pass from the epididymis to the urethra; plural vasa deferentia.

vasectomy. Surgical procedure of cutting the sperm ducts (vasa deferentia) to effect sterility in the male.

vasoconstriction. Narrowing of the diameter of a blood vessel, especially of small arteries leading to decreased blood flow to a part.

vasodilatation. Enlargement (dilation) of a blood vessel, especially of small arteries leading to increased blood flow to a part.

vector. A carrier, usually an insect, that transfers an infective, disease-causing agent from one host organism to another; the Anopheles mosquito, for example, is the vector of the malarial parasite.

vegetal hemisphere. Part of the fertilized egg (opposite the animal hemisphere) that is heavily laden with yolk.

vein. Blood vessel carrying blood from the tissues and organs to the heart.

venereal. Pertaining to sexual intercourse; arising from sexual intercourse with an infected person, as in venereal disease.

ventral. Pertaining to, or situated near or on, the lower surface of an organism (in man, the abdominal region); the opposite of dorsal.

ventricle. Thick-walled chamber of the heart that receives blood from an auricle (atrium) and pumps blood out of the heart to the lungs or body.

vertebrate. Animal possessing a backbone (vertebral column) of bony segments (vertebrae) that encloses and protects the nerve cord (spinal cord); principal groups are fishes, amphibians, reptiles, birds, and mammals.

vestigial. Refers to a degenerate or imperfectly developed structure or organ that is fully developed and functional in an ancestral species.

viable. Capable of remaining alive; capable of continuing development, as in viable seeds or viable eggs.

villus. Vascular protrusion from the free surface of a cell or lining that increases the surface area of the cell or lining; plural, villi.

virus. Infectious, submicroscopic particle composed of a DNA or RNA core surrounded by a protein coat that replicates only within living host cells.

viscera. Collective term for the internal organs of an animal, especially those within the abdominal cavity (liver, intestines, spleen, pancreas).

vitalism. View that biological activities are expressions of more than chemical and physical interactions of molecules, possibly directed by a supernatural force or vital principle.

vitamin. Organic molecule that an organism cannot synthesize but is required in small or trace quantities; many function as a coenzyme.

vitelline membrane. The plasma (cell) membrane of the egg.

vulva. Region of the external genital organs of the female, including the labia majora, labia minora, clitoris, and vestibule of the vagina.

white matter. Regions of the brain and spinal cord composed of great masses of myelinated nerve fibers (axons), transmitting impulses from one part of the brain or cord to other parts.

wild type. The trait (phenotype) most frequently observed, or the most frequent allele, in a natural population.

Xylem. Complex vascular tissue that conducts water and minerals from the roots to other parts of the plant.

yolk. Protein-rich nutritive material of the egg used by the developing embryo.

yolk sac. Vascular extraembryonic membrane, enclosing the yolk, that is the source of nutrition for the developing embryos of reptiles and birds; small and functionless in the human embryo.

zona pellucida. Transparent, noncellular layer that surrounds the human fertilized egg.

zoo-. Prefix meaning animal, or motile.

zooplankton. Minute, free-floating aquatic animals that together with plant representatives (phytoplankton) make up the plankton of natural waters.

zygote. Diploid cell resulting from the union of two haploid gametes; the fertilized egg.

Supplementary Readings

1 Seeds of Life

Austin, C. R., and Short, R. V., eds. 1972. *Reproduction in mammals.* New York: Cambridge University Press.

Corcos, A. 1972. The little man who wasn't there. *Amer. Biol. Teacher* 34: 503–506.

DeLora, J. S., and Warren, C. A. B. 1977. *Understanding sexual interaction.* Boston: Houghton Mifflin Co.

Gagnon, J. H. 1977. *Human sexualities.* Glenview, Illinois: Scott Foresman and Co.

Goldstein, B. 1976. *Human sexuality.* New York: McGraw-Hill.

Levine, S. 1966. Sex differences in the brain. *Scientific American*, April, pp. 84–90.

Loraine, J. 1972. Hormones and homosexuality. *New Scientist* 53: 270–271.

Masters, W. H., and Johnson, V. E. 1966. *Human sexual response.* Boston: Little, Brown and Co.

Rugh, R., and Shettles, B. 1971. *From conception to birth: the drama of life's beginnings.* New York: Harper & Row, Publishers.

Segal, S. J. 1974. The physiology of human reproduction. *Scientific American*, September, pp. 53–62.

2 Control of Fertility

Chasteen, E. R. 1971. *The case for compulsory birth control.* Englewood Cliffs, N.J.: Prentice-Hall, Inc.

Edwards, R. G. 1966. Mammalian eggs in the laboratory. *Scientific American*, August, pp. 72–81.

Hardin, G. 1970. *Birth control.* Indianapolis: The Bobbs-Merrill Co., Inc.

———, ed. 1969. *Population, evolution, and birth control: a collage of controversial ideas.* San Francisco: W. H. Freeman and Company Publishers.

Jackson, H. 1973. Chemical methods of male contraception. *Amer. Sci.* 61: 188–193.

Kinsey, A. C., Pomeroy, W. B., and Martin, C. E. 1948. *Sexual behavior in the human male.* Philadelphia: W. B. Saunders Co.

Peel, J., and Potts, M. 1969. *Textbook of contraceptive practice.* New York: Cambridge University Press.

Tietze, C., and Lewit, S. 1969. Legal abortion. *Scientific American*, January, pp. 21–27.

3 Development, Implantation, and Placentation

Apgar, V., and Beck, J. 1972. *Is my baby all right?* New York: Trident Press.

Corner, G. W. 1943. *The hormones in human reproduction.* Princeton, N.J.: Princeton University Press.

Edwards, R. G. 1966. Mammalian eggs in the laboratory. *Scientific American*, August, pp. 72–81.

Emmens, C. W., and Blackstraw, A. W. 1956. Artificial insemination. *Physiological Reviews* 36: 277–306.

Farris, E. J. 1959. *Human ovulation and fertility.* Philadelphia: J. B. Lippincott Co.

Folley, S. J. 1957. *The physiology and biochemistry of lactation.* Springfield, Ill.: Charles C Thomas, Publisher.

Francoeur, R. T. 1973. *Utopian motherhood: new trends in human reproduction.* Cranbury, N.J.: A. S. Barnes & Co., Inc.

Michelmore, S. 1965. *Sexual reproduction.* Garden City, N.Y.: Doubleday & Co., Inc., The Natural History Press.

Wood, C. 1969. *Human fertility: threat and promise.* New York: Funk & Wagnalls, Inc.

4 Molecules of Life and Placental Transfer

Arey, L. B. 1965. *Developmental anatomy.* Philadelphia: W. B. Saunders Co.

Berrill, N. J. 1968. *The person in the womb.* New York: Dodd, Mead & Co.

Corner, G. W. 1944. *Ourselves unborn.* New Haven, Conn.: Yale University Press.

Nilsson, L., Ingelman-Sundberg, A., and Wirsén, C. 1965. *A child is born.* New York: Dell Publishing Co., Inc., Delacorte Press.

Patten, B. M. 1968. *Human embryology.* New York: The Blakiston Co.

Rugh, R., and Shettles, L. B. 1971. *From conception to birth: the drama of life's beginnings.* New York: Harper & Row, Publishers.

Saxen, L., and Rapola, J. 1969. *Congenital defects.* New York: Holt, Rinehart and Winston, Inc.

Taussig, H. B. 1962. The thalidomide syndrome. *Scientific American,* August, pp. 29–35.

5 Biological Membranes and the Architecture of Cells

Allfrey, V. G., and Mirsky, A. E. 1961. How cells make molecules. *Scientific American,* September, pp. 74–82.

Brachet, J. 1961. The living cell. *Scientific American,* September, pp. 50–61.

DeDuve, C. 1963. The lysosome. *Scientific American,* May, pp. 64–72.

DeRobertis, E. D. P., Nowinski, W. W., and Saez, F. A. 1975. *Cell biology.* Philadelphia: W. B. Saunders Co.

Fawcett, D. 1966. *The cell: its organelles and inclusions.* Philadelphia: W. B. Saunders Co.

Fox, C. F. 1972. The structure of cell membranes. *Scientific American,* February, pp. 30–38.

Green, D. E. 1964. The mitochondrion. *Scientific American,* January, pp. 63–74.

Holter, H. 1961. How things get into cells. *Scientific American,* September, pp. 167–80.

Loewy, A. G., and Siekevitz, P. 1969. *Cell structure and function.* New York: Holt, Rinehart and Winston, Inc.

Margulis, L. 1971. Symbiosis and evolution. *Scientific American,* August, pp. 48–57.

Moscona, A. A. 1959. Tissues from dissociated cells. *Scientific American,* May, pp. 132–144.

Neutra, M., and LeBlond, C. P. 1969. The golgi apparatus. *Scientific American,* February, pp. 100–107.

Novikoff, A. B., and Holtzman, E. 1976. *Cells and organelles.* New York: Holt, Rinehart and Winston, Inc.

Robertson, J. D. 1962. The membrane of the living cell. *Scientific American,* April, pp. 64–72.

6 Cellular Metabolism

Baker, J. J. W., and Allen, G. E. 1974. *Matter, energy, and life.* Reading, Mass.: Addison-Wesley Publishing Co., Inc.

Chamber, R. W., and Payne, A. 1962. *From cell to test tube.* New York: Charles Scribner's Sons.

Changeux, J.-P. 1965. The control of biochemical reactions. *Scientific American,* April, pp. 36–45.

Frieden, E. 1959. The enzyme-substrate complex. *Scientific American*, August, pp. 119–25.

Gerard, R. W. 1949. *Unresting cells.* New York: Harper & Row, Publishers.

Green, D. E. 1960. The synthesis of fat. *Scientific American*, February, pp. 46–51.

Hayashi, T. 1961. How cells move. *Scientific American*, September, pp. 184–204.

Lehninger, A. L. 1960. Energy transformation in the cell. *Scientific American*, May, pp. 102–14.

———. 1961. How cells transform energy. *Scientific American*, September, pp. 62–73.

Mercer, E. A. 1962. *Cells: their structure and function.* Garden City, N.J.: Doubleday & Co., Inc., The Natural History Press.

Moner, J. G. 1972. *Cells, their structure and function.* Dubuque, Iowa: Wm. C. Brown Company Publishers.

Mott-Smith, M. 1964. *The concept of energy simply defined.* New York: Dover Publications, Inc.

Pfeiffer, J., and the editors of Time-Life Books. 1964. *The cell.* New York: Time-Life Books.

Phillips, D. C. 1966. The three-dimensional structure of an enzyme molecule. *Scientific American*, November, pp. 78–90.

Rosenberg, E. 1971. *Cell and molecular biology.* New York: Holt, Rinehart and Winston, Inc.

Solomon, A. K. 1962. Pumps in the living cell. *Scientific American*, August, pp. 100–108.

Stumpf, P. K. 1953. ATP. *Scientific American*, April, pp. 82–92.

Wagner, A. F., and Folkers, K. 1964. *Vitamins and coenzymes.* New York: Interscience Press.

Wolfe, S. L. 1972. *Biology of the cell.* Belmont, Calif.: Wadsworth Publishers.

Balinsky, B. I. 1970. *An introduction to embryology.* Philadelphia: W. B. Saunders Co.

Barth, L. G. 1953. *Embryology.* New York: The Dryden Press, Inc.

Barth, L. J. 1964. *Development: selected topics.* Reading, Mass.: Addison-Wesley Publishing Co., Inc.

Bloom, W., and Fawcett, D. W. 1968. *A textbook of histology.* Philadelphia: W. B. Saunders Co.

Ebert, J. D., and Sussex, I. M. 1970. *Interacting systems in development.* New York: Holt, Rinehart and Winston, Inc.

Etkin, W. 1966. How a tadpole becomes a frog. *Scientific American*, May, pp. 76–88.

Hamburg, M. 1971. *Theories of differentiation.* New York: American Elsevier Publishing Co., Inc.

Huettner, A. F. 1949. *Fundamentals of comparative embryology of the vertebrates.* New York: Macmillan, Inc.

Kennedy, D., ed. 1967. *From cell to organism.* San Francisco: W. H. Freeman and Company Publishers.

Moore, J. A. 1972. *Heredity and development.* New York: Oxford University Press, Inc.

Spemann, H. 1962. *Embryonic development and induction.* New York: Macmillan, Inc., Hafner Press.

Spratt, N. T., Jr. 1971. *Developmental biology.* Belmont, Calif.: Wadsworth Publishing Co., Inc.

Sussman, M. 1964. *Animal growth and development.* Englewood Cliffs, N.J.: Prentice-Hall, Inc.

Wessells, N. K., and Rutter, W. J. 1969. Phases in cell differentiation. *Scientific American*, March, pp. 36–44.

Willier, B. H., and Oppenheimer, J. M., eds. 1964. *Foundations of experimental embryology.* Englewood Cliffs, N.J.: Prentice-Hall, Inc.

7 Cellular Differentiation

8	Digestion and Absorption	Davenport, H. W. 1972. Why the stomach does not digest itself. *Scientific American,* January, pp. 86–93.

8 Digestion and Absorption

Davenport, H. W. 1972. Why the stomach does not digest itself. *Scientific American,* January, pp. 86–93.

Fried, J. J. 1975. *The vitamin controversy.* New York: E. P. Dutton.

Griffin, D. R., and Novick, A. 1970. *Animal structure and function.* New York: Holt, Rinehart and Winston, Inc.

Guyton, A. C. 1969. *Functions of the human body.* Philadelphia: W. B. Saunders Co.

Kappas, A., and Alvares, A. P. 1975. How the liver metabolizes foreign substances. *Scientific American,* June, pp. 114–121.

Kermode, G. O. 1972. Food additives. *Scientific American,* March, pp. 15–21.

Lieber, C. S. 1976. The metabolism of alcohol. *Scientific American,* March, pp. 35–44.

Schmidt-Nielsen, K. 1972. *How animals work.* New York: Cambridge University Press.

Steincrohn, P. J. 1972. *Low blood sugar.* Chicago: Henry Regnery.

Verret, J., and Carper, J. 1974. *Eating may be hazardous to your health.* New York: Simon and Schuster.

9 Blood and Circulation

Adolph, E. F. 1967. The heart's pacemaker. *Scientific American,* March, pp. 32–37.

Beck, W. S. 1971. *Human design: molecular, cellular, and systematic physiology.* New York: Harcourt Brace Jovanovich, Inc.

Carrier, O., Jr. 1965. The local control of blood flow: an illustration of homeostasis. *Bioscience* 15: 665–68.

Chapman, C. B., and Mitchell, J. H. 1965. The physiology of exercise. *Scientific American,* May, pp. 88–96.

Comroe, J. H., Jr. 1966. The lung. *Scientific American,* February, pp. 56–68.

Mayerson, H. 1963. The lymphatic system. *Scientific American,* June, pp. 80–90.

Perutz, M. F. 1964. The hemoglobin molecule. *Scientific American,* November, pp. 64–76.

Ponder, E. 1957. The red blood cell. *Scientific American,* January, pp. 95–102.

Vander, A. J., Sherman, J. H., and Luciano, D. C. 1975. *Human physiology.* New York: McGraw-Hill.

Wiggers, C. J. 1957. The heart. *Scientific American,* May, pp. 74–87.

Wood, J. E. 1968. The venous system. *Scientific American,* January, pp. 86–96.

Zweifach, B. W. 1959. The microcirculation of the blood. *Scientific American,* January, pp. 33–39.

10 Gas Exchange and Excretion

Barrington, E. J. W. 1968. *The chemical basis of physiological regulation.* Glenview, Illinois: Scott Foresman.

Chapman, C. B., and Mitchell, J. H. 1965. The physiology of exercise. *Scientific American,* May, pp. 88–96.

Comroe, J. H., Jr. 1966. The lung. *Scientific American,* February, pp. 56–68.

Fenn, W. O. 1960. The mechanism of breathing. *Scientific American,* January, pp. 138–48.

Hock, R. J. 1970. The physiology of high altitude. *Scientific American,* February, pp. 52–62.

Moffat, D. B. 1971. The control of water balance by the kidney. *Oxford Biology Reader,* No. 14, pp. 1–16. London: Oxford University Press.

Perutz, M. F. 1964. The hemoglobin molecule. *Scientific American,* November, pp. 64–76.

Ponder, E. 1957. The red blood cell. *Scientific American,* January, pp. 95–102.

Schmidt-Nielsen, K. 1972. *How animals work.* New York: Cambridge University Press.

Schmidt-Nielsen, K. 1971. How birds breathe. *Scientific American,* December, pp. 72–79.

Smith, C. A. 1963. The first breath. *Scientific American,* October, pp. 27–35.

Agranoff, B. W. 1967. Memory and protein synthesis. *Scientific American*, June, pp. 115–22.

Atkinson, R. C., and Shiffrin, R. M. 1971. The control of short-term memory. *Scientific American*, August, pp. 82–90.

Baker, P. F. 1966. The nerve axon. *Scientific American*, June, pp. 74–82.

Corning, W. C., and John, E. R. 1961. Effect of ribonuclease on retention of conditioned response in regenerated planarians. *Science* 134: 1363–65.

Eccles, J. 1965. The synapse. *Scientific American*, January, pp. 56–66.

Griffin, D. R., and Novick, A. 1970. *Animal structure and function.* New York: Holt, Rinehart and Winston, Inc.

Grundfest, H. 1960. Electric fishes. *Scientific American*, October, pp. 115–24.

Hayashi, T. 1961. How cells move. *Scientific American*, September, pp. 184–204.

Heimer, L. 1971. Pathways in the brain. *Scientific American*, July, pp. 48–60.

Hoyle, G. 1970. How is muscle turned on and off? *Scientific American*, April, pp. 84–93.

Huxley, H. E. 1965. The mechanism of muscular contraction. *Scientific American*, December, pp. 18–27.

Hydén, H., and Lange, P. W. 1965. A differentiation in RNA response in neurons early and late during learning. *Proceedings of the National Academy of Sciences* 53: 946–52.

Katz, B. 1961. How cells communicate. *Scientific American*, September, pp. 209–20.

———. 1966. *Nerve, muscle, and synapse.* New York: McGraw-Hill.

Klemm, W. R. 1972. *Science, the brain, and our future.* Indianapolis: The Bobbs-Merrill Co., Inc.

Olds, J. 1956. Pleasure centers in the brain. *Scientific American*, October, pp. 105–16.

Schmidt-Nielsen, K. 1960. *Animal physiology.* Englewood Cliffs, N.J.: Prentice-Hall, Inc.

Smith, D. S. 1965. The flight muscles of insects. *Scientific American*, June, pp. 76–88.

Snider, R. S. 1958. The cerebellum. *Scientific American*, August, pp. 84–90.

Wilson, D. M. 1968. The flight-control system of the locust. *Scientific American*, May, pp. 83–90.

Wilson, V. J. 1966. Inhibition in the central nervous system. *Scientific American*, May, pp. 102–10.

11 Coordination by Nerves

Corner, G. W. 1963. *The hormones in human reproduction.* New York: Atheneum Press.

Csapo, A. 1958. Progesterone. *Scientific American*, April, pp. 40–46.

Davidson, E. H. 1965. Hormones and genes. *Scientific American*, June, pp. 36–45.

Frye, B. E. 1967. *Hormonal control in vertebrates.* New York: Macmillan Co.

Gray, G. W. 1950. Cortisone and ACTH. *Scientific American*, March, pp. 30–37.

LeBaron, R. 1972. *Hormones: A delicate balance.* New York: Pegasus.

Li, C. H. 1963. The ACTH molecule. *Scientific American*, July, pp. 46–54.

Rasmussen, H. 1961. The parathyroid hormone. *Scientific American*, April, pp. 56–63.

Wilkins, L. 1960. The thyroid gland. *Scientific American*, March, pp. 119–129.

Williams, R. H. 1962. *Textbook of endocrinology.* Philadelphia: W. B. Saunders Co.

Wurtman, R. J. and Axelrod, J. 1965. The pineal gland. *Scientific American*, July, pp. 50–60.

Zuckerman, S. 1957. Hormones. *Scientific American*, March, pp. 76–87.

12 Coordination by Hormones

Bakker, R. T. 1975. Dinosaur renaissance. *Scientific American*, April, pp. 58–78.

Brown, F. A., Jr., Hastings, J. W., and Palmer, J. D. 1970. *The biological clocks: two views.* New York: Academic Press, Inc.

13 Homeostasis

Cannon, W. B. 1939. *The wisdom of the body*. New York: W. W. Norton & Co.

Carey, F. G. 1973. Fishes with warm bodies. *Scientific American*, February, pp. 36–44.

Carlson, A. J., and Johnson, V. 1937. *The machinery of the body*. Chicago, Illinois: University of Chicago Press.

Irving, L. 1966. Adaptations to cold. *Scientific American*, January, pp. 94–101.

Langley, L. L. 1965. *Homeostasis*. New York: Reinhold Publ. Corp.

Luce, G. G. 1973. *Body time*. New York: Bantam Books, Inc.

Moore, S. 1967. *Biological clocks and patterns*. New York: Criterion Press.

Morse, R. A. 1972. Environmental control in the beehive. *Scientific American*, April, pp. 92–98.

Palmer, J. D. 1975. Biological clocks of the tidal zone. *Scientific American*, February, pp. 70–79.

Pengelley, E. T., and Asmundson, S. J. 1971. Annual biological clocks. *Scientific American*, April, pp. 72–79.

Schmidt-Nielsen, K. 1959. The physiology of the camel. *Scientific American*, December, pp. 140–151.

Thompson, E. O. P. 1955. The insulin molecule. *Scientific American*, May, pp. 36–41.

Warren, J. V. 1974. The physiology of the giraffe. *Scientific American*, November, pp. 96–105.

14 Transplants and Immunity

Abramoff, P., and La Via, M. F. 1970. *Biology of the immune response*. New York: McGraw-Hill.

Billingham, R., and Silvers, W. 1971. *The immunobiology of transplantation*. Englewood Cliffs, N.J.: Prentice-Hall, Inc.

Burnet, F. M. 1961. The mechanism of immunity. *Scientific American*, January, pp. 58–67.

————. 1969. *Self and non-self*. New York: Cambridge University Press.

Fudenberg, H. H., Pink, J. R. L., Stites, D. P., and Wang, A.-C. 1972. *Basic immunogenetics*. New York: Oxford University Press, Inc.

Good, R. A., and Fisher, D. W. 1971. *Immunobiology*. Stamford, Conn.: Sinauer Associates, Inc.

Hildemann, W. H. 1970. *Immunogenetics*. San Francisco: Holden-Day, Inc.

Holborow, E. J. 1968. *An ABC of modern immunology*. Boston: Little, Brown and Co.

Humphrey, J. H., and White, R. G. 1970. *Immunology for students of medicine*. Oxford, England: Blackwell Scientific Publications.

Levey, R. H. 1964. The thymus hormone. *Scientific American*, July, pp. 66–77.

Medawar, P. B. 1961. Immunological tolerance. *Science* 133: 303–6.

Merrill, J. P. 1961. The artificial kidney. *Scientific American*, July, pp. 56–64.

Miller, J. F. A. P., and Osoba, D. 1967. Current concepts of the immunological function of the thymus. *Physiological Reviews* 47: 437–520.

Nossal, G. J. V. 1964. How cells make antibodies. *Scientific American*, December, pp. 106–15.

————. 1969. *Antibodies and immunity*. New York: Basic Books, Inc., Publishers.

Porter, R. R. 1967. The structure of antibodies. *Scientific American*, October, pp. 81–90.

Rapaport, F. T., and Dausset, J., eds. 1968. *Human transplantation*. New York: Grune & Stratton, Inc.

Roitt, I. M. 1971. *Essential immunology*. Oxford, England: Blackwell Scientific Publications.

Russell, P., and Monaco, A. 1965. *The biology of tissue transplantation*. Boston: Little, Brown and Co.

Volpe, E. P. 1972. Embryonic tissue transplantation incompatibility in an amphibian. *American Scientist* 60: 220–28.

Adler, W. H. 1975. Aging and immune function. *Bioscience* 25:652–57.

Curtis, H. J. 1963. Biological mechanisms underlying the aging process. *Science* 141:686–94.

Dole, V. P. 1959. Body fat. *Scientific American,* December, pp. 70–76.

Dulbecco, R. 1967. The induction of cancer by viruses. *Scientific American,* April, pp. 28–37.

Finch, C. E. 1975. Neuroendocrinology of aging: a view of an emerging area. *Bioscience* 25:645–50.

Hayflick, L. 1968. Human cells and aging. *Scientific American,* March, pp. 44–52.

Isaacs, A. 1961. Interferon. *Scientific American,* May, pp. 51–57.

Johnson, H. A. 1963. Redundancy and biological aging. *Science* 141:910–12.

Lilienfeld, A. M. 1956. The relationship of cancer of the female breast to artificial menopause and marital status. *Cancer* 9:927–34.

Mayer, J., and Thomas, D. W. 1967. Regulation of food intake and obesity. *Science* 156:328–37.

Moment, G. B. 1975. The Ponce de Leon trail today. *Bioscience* 25:623–28.

Olson, R. E. 1957. Dietary fat in human nutrition. *American Journal of Public Health* 47:1537–41.

Prescott, D. M. 1973. *Cancer: the misguided cell.* Indianapolis: The Bobbs-Merrill Co., Inc.

Shock, N. W. 1962. The physiology of aging. *Scientific American,* January, pp. 70–76.

Sinex, F. M. 1961. Biochemistry of aging. *Science* 134:1402–5.

Spain, D. M. 1966. Atherosclerosis. *Scientific American,* August, pp. 48–56.

Surgeon General of the United States. 1972. *The health consequences of smoking.* Washington, D.C.: U.S. Public Health Service.

Waife, S. O., ed. 1970. *Diabetes mellitus.* Indianapolis: Lilly Research Laboratories.

15 Cancer, Degenerative Diseases, and Aging

Asimov, I. 1962. *The genetic code.* New York: Signet Science Library.

Beadle, G. W., and Beadle, M. 1966. *The language of life.* Garden City, N.Y.: Doubleday & Co., Inc.

Benzer, S. 1962. The fine structure of the gene. *Scientific American,* January, pp. 70–84.

Borck, E. 1965. *The code of life.* New York: Columbia University Press.

Cairns, J. 1966. The bacterial chromosome. *Scientific American,* January, pp. 36–44.

Crick, F. H. C. 1954. The structure of the hereditary material. *Scientific American,* October, pp. 54–61.

———. 1962. The genetic code. *Scientific American,* October, pp. 66–74.

———. 1966. The genetic code: III. *Scientific American,* October, pp. 55–62.

Edgar, R. S., and Epstein, R. H. 1965. The genetics of a bacterial virus. *Scientific American,* February, pp. 70–78.

Fraenkel-Conrat, H. 1964. The genetic code of a virus. *Scientific American,* October, pp. 46–54.

Hotchkiss, R. D., and Weiss, E. 1956. Transformed bacteria. *Scientific American,* November, pp. 48–53.

Ingram, V. 1958. How do genes act? *Scientific American,* January, pp. 68–74.

Kornberg, A. 1968. The synthesis of DNA. *Scientific American,* October, pp. 64–78.

Meselson, M., and Stahl, F. W. 1958. The replication of DNA in *Escherichia coli. Proceedings of the National Academy of Science* 44: 671–82.

Mirsky, A. E. 1968. The discovery of DNA. *Scientific American,* June, pp. 78–88.

Nirenberg, M. 1963. The genetic code: II. *Scientific American,* March, pp. 80–94.

Papazian, H. P. 1967. *Modern genetics.* New York: W. W. Norton & Co., Inc.

Sinsheimer, R. 1962. Single-stranded DNA. *Scientific American,* July, pp. 109–16.

16 Chemical Basis of Inheritance

Watson, J. D. 1968. *The double helix.* New York: Atheneum Publishers.
————. 1976. *Molecular biology of the gene.* New York: W. A. Benjamin, Inc.

17 Physical Basis of Inheritance

DeRobertis, E. D. P., Nowinski, W. W., and Saez, F. 1965. *Cell biology.* Philadelphia: W. B. Saunders Co.

Dunn, L. C. 1965. *A short history of genetics.* New York: McGraw-Hill.

DuPraw, E. J. 1970. *DNA and chromosomes.* New York: Holt, Rinehart and Winston, Inc.

Koller, P. C. 1971. *Chromosomes and genes.* New York: W. W. Norton & Co., Inc.

Levine, L. 1969. *Biology of the gene.* St. Louis: The C. V. Mosby Co.

Levine, R. P. 1968. *Genetics.* New York: Holt, Rinehart and Winston, Inc. ic.

Levinson, H. 1963. *Chance, luck, and statistics.* New York: Dover Publications, Inc.

Mazia, D. 1953. Cell division. *Scientific American,* August, pp. 53–63.

————. 1961. How cells divide. *Scientific American,* September, pp. 100–120.

Parker, G., Reynolds, W. A., and Reynolds, R. 1968. *Mitosis and meiosis.* Chicago: Educational Methods, Inc.

Peters, J. A., ed. 1959. *Classic papers in genetics.* Englewood Cliffs, N.J.: Prentice-Hall, Inc.

Sinnott, E. W., Dunn, L. C., and Dobzhansky, T. 1958. *Principles of genetics.* New York: McGraw-Hill.

Snyder, L. H., and David, P. R. 1957. *Principles of heredity.* Lexington, Mass.: D. C. Heath & Co.

Strickberger, M. W. 1968. *Genetics.* New York: Macmillan, Inc.

Swanson, C. P. 1960. *The cell.* Englewood Cliffs, N. J.: Prentice-Hall, Inc.

Taylor, J. H. 1958. The duplication of chromosomes. *Scientific American,* June, pp. 36–42.

Wilson, G. B. 1966. *Cell division and the mitotic cycle.* New York: Reinhold Publishing Corporation.

18 Mendel's Work and the Principles of Inheritance

Bonner, D. M., and Mills, S. E. 1964. *Heredity.* Englewood Cliffs, N.J.: Prentice-Hall, Inc.

Gardner, E. J. 1968. *Principles of genetics.* New York: John Wiley & Sons, Inc.

Herskowitz, I. H. 1965. *Genetics.* Boston: Little, Brown and Co.

Iltis, H. 1932. *Life of Mendel.* New York: W. W. Norton & Co., Inc.

Mendel, G. 1948. *Experiments in plant hybridization.* Cambridge, Mass.: Harvard University Press. (Translation of Gregor Mendel's original paper first published in 1866.)

Moore, J. A. 1972a. *Heredity and development.* New York: Oxford University Press, Inc.

————. 1972b. *Readings in heredity and development.* New York: Oxford University Press, Inc.

Peters, J. A. 1959. *Classic papers in genetics.* Englewood Cliffs, N.J.: Prentice-Hall, Inc.

Srb, A. M., Owen, R. D., and Edgar, R. S. 1965. *General genetics.* San Francisco: W. H. Freeman and Company Publishers.

Stern, C., and Sherwood, E. R. 1966. *The origin of genetics.* San Francisco: W. H. Freeman and Company Publishers.

Sturtevant, A. H. 1965. *A history of genetics.* New York: Harper & Row, Publishers.

Winchester, A. M. 1977. *Genetics.* Boston: Houghton Mifflin Co.

19 Mendelian Inheritance in Man

Carson, H. L. 1963. *Heredity and human life.* New York: Columbia University Press.

Carter, C. O. 1969. *An ABC of medical genetics.* Boston: Little, Brown and Co.

Clarke, C. A. 1964. *Genetics for the clinician.* Philadelphia: F. A. Davis Co.

Emery, A. E. H. 1968. *Heredity, disease, and man.* Berkeley: University of California Press.

Lenz, W. 1963. *Medical genetics.* Chicago: University of Chicago Press.

Levitan, M., and Montagu, A. 1971. *Textbook of human genetics.* New York: Oxford University Press, Inc.

Macalpine, I., and Hunter, R. 1969. Porphyria and King George III. *Scientific American,* July, pp. 38–46.

McKusick, V. A. 1969. *Human genetics.* Englewood Cliffs, N.J.: Prentice-Hall, Inc.

Montagu, A. 1963. *Human heredity.* New York: The New American Library Inc.

Nagle, J. J. 1974. *Heredity and human affairs.* Saint Louis: C. V. Mosby Co.

Neel, J., and Schull, W. 1954. *Human heredity.* Chicago: University of Chicago Press.

Penrose, L. S. 1959. *Outline of human genetics.* New York: John Wiley & Sons, Inc.

Roberts, J. 1967. *An introduction to medical genetics.* New York: Oxford University Press, Inc.

Roderick, G. W. 1968. *Man and heredity.* New York: Macmillan, Inc.

Scheinfeld, A. 1965. *Your heredity and environment.* Philadelphia: J. B. Lippincott Co.

Stern, C. 1973. *Principles of human genetics.* San Francisco: W. H. Freeman and Company Publishers.

Sutton, H. 1965. *An introduction to human genetics.* New York: Holt, Rinehart and Winston, Inc.

Whittinghill, M. 1965. *Human genetics and its foundations.* New York: Reinhold Publishing Corporation.

20 Man's Hemoglobins and Gene Action

Benzer, S. 1962. The fine structure of the gene. *Scientific American,* January, pp. 70–84.

Bryson, V., and Vogel, H. J., eds. 1965. *Evolving genes and proteins.* New York: Academic Press, Inc.

Clark, B. F. C., and Marcker, K. A. 1968. How proteins start. *Scientific American,* January, pp. 36–42.

Dayhoff, M. O. 1969. Computer analysis of protein evolution. *Scientific American,* July, pp. 86–95.

Hurwitz, J., and Furth, J. J. 1962. Messenger RNA. *Scientific American,* February, pp. 41–49.

Ingram, V. M. 1963. *The hemoglobins in genetics and evolution.* New York: Columbia University Press.

———. 1965. *The biosynthesis of macromolecules.* New York: The Benjamin Co., Inc.

Jacob, F., and Wollman, E. L. 1961. Viruses and genes. *Scientific American,* June, pp. 92–107.

Livingstone, F. 1967. *Abnormal hemoglobins in human populations.* Chicago: Aldine Publishing Co.

Nirenberg, M. W., and Leder, P. 1964. RNA codewords and protein synthesis. *Science* 145: 1399–1407.

Nomura, M. 1969. Ribosomes. *Scientific American,* October, pp. 28–35.

Rich, A. 1963. Polyribosomes. *Scientific American,* December, pp. 44–53.

Stent, G. S. 1971. *Molecular genetics.* San Francisco: W. H. Freeman and Company Publishers.

Yanofsky, C. 1967. Gene structure and protein structure. *Scientific American,* May, pp. 80–94.

Zuckerkandl, E. 1965. The evolution of hemoglobin. *Scientific American,* May, pp. 110–18.

21 Human Blood Groups and Hemolytic Disease

Aird, I., Bentall, H. H., and Roberts, J. A. F. 1953. A relationship between cancer of stomach and the ABO blood groups. *British Medical Journal* 1: 799–801.

Clarke, C. A. 1961. Blood groups and disease. In *Progress in medical genetics*, ed. A. G. Steinberg, vol. 1, pp. 81–119. New York: Grune & Stratton, Inc.

———. 1968. The prevention of "rhesus" babies. *Scientific American*, November, pp. 46–52.

Edwards, J. H. 1963. The genetic basis of common disease. *American Journal of Medicine* 34: 627–38.

Lawler, S., and Lawler, L. 1957. *Human blood groups and inheritance*. Cambridge, Mass.: Harvard University Press.

Levene, H., and Rosenfield, R. E. 1961. ABO incompatibility. In *Progress in medical genetics*, ed. A. G. Steinberg, vol. 1, pp. 120–57. New York: Grune & Stratton, Inc.

Race, R., and Sanger, R. 1968. *Blood groups in man*. Philadelphia: F. A. Davis Co.

Roberts, J. A. F. 1963. *An introduction to medical genetics*. New York: Oxford University Press, Inc.

Snyder, L. H., and David, P. R. 1957. *The principles of heredity*. Lexington, Mass.: D. C. Heath & Co.

Stern, C. 1960. *Principles of human genetics*. San Francisco: W. H. Freeman and Company Publishers.

Weiner, A., and Wexler, I. 1958. *Heredity of the blood groups*. New York: Grune & Stratton, Inc.

22 Inborn Errors of Metabolism

Apgar, V., and Beck, J. 1972. *Is my baby all right?* New York: Trident Press.

Beadle, G. W. 1948. The genes of men and molds. *Scientific American*, September, pp. 30–39.

Bearn, A. G. 1956. The chemistry of hereditary disease. *Scientific American*, December, pp. 126–36.

Emery, A. E. H. 1968. *Heredity, disease, and man*. Berkeley: University of California Press.

Harris, H. 1959. *Human biochemical genetics*. New York: Cambridge University Press.

———. 1963. *Garrod's inborn errors of metabolism, 1908 edition*. Oxford, England: Oxford University Press.

———. 1970. *The principles of human biochemical genetics*. Amsterdam, Netherlands: North Holland Publishing Co.

Hsia, I. 1966. *Lectures in medical genetics*. Chicago: Year Book Medical Publishers, Inc.

Knox, W. E. 1969. Inherited enzyme defects. *Hospital Practice*, November, pp. 33–41.

Knudson, A., Jr. 1965. *Genetics and disease*. New York: McGraw-Hill.

Lenz, W. 1963. *Medical genetics*. Chicago: University of Chicago Press.

Lyman, F. L., ed. 1963. *Phenylketonuria*. Springfield, Ill.: Charles C Thomas, Publisher.

Roderick, G. W. 1968. *Man and heredity*. New York: Macmillan, Inc.

Stanbury, J., Wyngaarden, J., and Frederickson, D. 1966. *The metabolic basis of inherited disease*. New York: McGraw-Hill.

Sutton, H. E. 1962. *Genes, enzymes, and inherited diseases*. New York: Holt, Rinehart and Winston, Inc.

23 Regulation of Gene Action

Barth, L. J. 1964. *Development: selected topics*. Reading, Mass.: Addison-Wesley Publishing Co., Inc.

Beermann, W., and Clever, U. 1964. Chromosome puffs. *Scientific American*, April, pp. 50–58.

Changeux, J.-P. 1965. The control of biochemical reactions. *Scientific American*, April, pp. 36–45.

Davidson, E. H. 1965. Hormones and genes. *Scientific American,* June, pp. 36–45.

Ebert, J. D. 1965. *Interacting systems in development.* New York: Holt, Rinehart and Winston, Inc.

Ephrussi, B., and Weiss, M. C. 1969. Hybrid somatic cells. *Scientific American,* April, pp. 26–35.

Fischberg, M., and Blackler, A. W. 1961. How cells specialize. *Scientific American,* September, pp. 124–40.

Gurdon, J. B. 1968. Transplanted nuclei and cell differentiation. *Scientific American,* December, pp. 24–35.

Hamburgh, M. 1971. *Theories of differentiation.* New York: American Elsevier Publishing Co., Inc.

Hartman, P. E., and Suskind, S. R. 1969. *Gene action.* Englewood Cliffs, N.J.: Prentice-Hall, Inc.

Jacob, F., and Monod, J. 1961. Genetic regulatory mechanisms in the synthesis of proteins. *Journal of Molecular Biology* 3: 318–56.

Ptashne, E., and Gilbert, W. 1970. Genetic repressors. *Scientific American,* June, pp. 36–44.

24 Human Chromosomes and Autosomal Abnormalities

Bartalos, M., and Baramki, T. A. 1967. *Medical cytogenetics.* Baltimore: The Williams & Wilkins Company.

Bearn, A. G., and German, J. L., III. 1961. Chromosomes and disease. *Scientific American,* November, pp. 66–76.

Benda, C. E. 1956. Mongolism: a comprehensive review. *Archives of Pediatrics* 73: 391–407.

Ferguson-Smith, M. A. 1964. The techniques of human cytogenetics. *American Journal of Obstetrics & Gynecology* 90: 1035–54.

Lejeune, J. 1964. The 21 trisomy: current stage of chromosomal research. In *Progress in Medical Genetics,* eds. A. G. Steinberg and A. G. Bearn, vol. 3, pp. 144–77. New York: Grune & Stratton, Inc.

McKusick, V. A. 1971. The mapping of human chromosomes. *Scientific American,* April, pp. 104–13.

Penrose, L. S. 1961. Mongolism. *British Medical Bulletin* 17: 184–89.

Redding, A., and Hirschhorn, K. 1968. *Guide to human chromosome defects.* Birth Defects: Original Article Series, The National Foundation—March of Dimes, vol. 4, pp. 1–16.

Smith, D. W., Patau, K., Therman, E., and Inhorn, S. L. 1962. The no. 18 trisomy syndrome. *Journal of Pediatrics* 60: 513–27.

Stern, C. 1959. The chromosomes of man. *Journal of Medical Education* 34: 301–

Thompson, H. 1965. Abnormalities of the autosomal chromosomes associated with human disease: selected topics and catalogue. Part I. *American Journal of the Medical Sciences* 250: 718–34.

———. 1966. Abnormalities of the autosomal chromosomes associated with human disease: selected topics and catalogue. Part II. *American Journal of the Medical Sciences* 251: 706–35.

Thompson, J., and Thompson, M. 1966. *Genetics in medicine.* Philadelphia: W. B. Saunders Co.

25 Sex Chromosome Abnormalities

Carr, D. H. 1971. Chromosome studies in selected spontaneous abortions: polyploidy in man. *Journal of Medical Genetics* 8: 164–74.

Caspersson, T., and Zech, L. 1972. Chromosome identification by fluorescence. *Hospital Practice,* September, pp. 51–62.

Ferguson-Smith, M. A. 1965. Karyotype-phenotype correlations in gonadal dysgenesis and their bearing on the pathogenesis of malformations. *Journal of Medical Genetics* 2: 142–55.

———. 1970. Chromosomal abnormalities II: sex chromosome defects. *Hospital Practice,* April, pp. 88–100.

Gartler, S. M., Waxman, S. H., and Giblett, E. 1962. An XX/XY human hermaphrodite resulting from double fertilization. *Proceedings of the National Academy of Sciences* 48: 332–35.

German, J. 1970. Studying human chromosomes today. *American Scientist* 58: 182–201.

Hook, E. B. 1973. Behavioral implications of the human XYY genotype. *Science* 179: 139–50.

Jacobs, P. A., Price, W. H., Brown, C., Brittain, R. P., and Whatmore, P. B. 1968. Chromosome studies on men in a maximum security hospital. *Annals of Human Genetics* 31: 339–58.

Miller, O. J. 1964. The sex chromosome anomalies. *American Journal of Obstetrics & Gynecology* 90: 1078–1139.

Mittwoch, U. 1973. *Genetics of sex differentiation.* New York: Academic Press, Inc.

Money, J. 1968. *Sex errors of the body.* Baltimore: The Johns Hopkins Press.

Ruddle, F. H., and Kucherlapati, R. S. 1974. Hybrid cells and human genes. *Scientific American,* July, pp. 36–44.

Sohval, A. R. 1961. Recent progress in human chromosome analysis and its relation to the sex chromatin. *American Journal of Medicine* 31: 397–441.

26 Sex-Linked Inheritance and Dosage Compensation

Barr, M. L., and Carr, D. H. 1960. Sex chromatin, sex chromosomes, and sex anomalies. *Canadian Medical Association Journal* 83: 979–86.

Davidson, R. G., Nitowsky, H. M., and Childs, B. 1963. Demonstration of two populations of cells in the human female heterozygous for glucose-6-phosphate dehydrogenase variants. *Proceedings of the National Academy of Sciences* 50: 481–85.

German, J. 1970. Abnormalities of human sex chromosomes: a unifying concept in relation to gonadal dysgeneses. *Clinical Genetics* 1: 15–27.

Grüneberg, H. 1967. Sex-linked genes in man and the Lyon hypothesis. *Annals of Human Genetics* 30: 239–57.

Jacobson, C. B., and Arias-Bernal, L. 1967. Cytogenetic techniques in sexual anomalies. *Journal of the American Medical Woman Association* 22: 875–84.

Lyon, M. F. 1962. Sex chromatin and gene action in the mammalian X-chromosome. *American Journal of Human Genetics* 14: 135–48.

McKusick, V. A. 1964. *On the X chromosome of man.* Washington, D.C.: American Institutes of Biological Sciences.

———. 1965. The royal hemophilia. *Scientific American,* August, pp. 88–95.

Mittwoch, U. 1963. Sex differences in cells. *Scientific American,* July, pp. 54–62.

Moore, K. L., ed. 1966. *The sex chromatin.* Philadelphia: W. B. Saunders Co.

Seegmiller, J. E. 1972. Lesch-Nyhan syndrome and X-linked uric acidurias. *Hospital Practice,* April, pp. 79–90.

Stern, C. 1957. The problem of complete Y-linkage in man. *American Journal of Human Genetics* 9: 147–66.

———. 1963. The genetics of sex determination in man. *American Journal of Medicine* 34: 715–20.

Whissel, D. Y., Hoag, M. S., Aggeler, P. M., Kropatkin, M., and Garner, E. 1965. Hemophilia in a woman. *American Journal of Medicine* 38: 119–29.

27 Genetic Engineering and Genetic Counseling

Augenstein, L. 1969. *Come let us play God.* New York: Harper & Row, Publishers.

Baer, A. S., ed. 1973. *Heredity and society. Readings in social genetics.* New York: Macmillan, Inc.

Bajema, C. J. 1971. The genetic implications of population control. *Bioscience* 21: 71–75.

Bergsma, D., ed. 1970. Genetic counselling. *Birth Defects Original Article Series* 6: 1–85.

Bresler, J. B., ed. 1973. *Genetics and society.* Reading, Mass.: Addison-Wesley Publishing Co., Inc.

Davis, B. D. 1970. Prospects for genetic intervention in man. *Science* 170: 1279–83.

Dobzhansky, T. 1967. Changing man. *Science* 155: 409–15.

Etzioni, A. 1968. Sex control, science, and society. *Science* 161: 1107–12.

Fraser, F. C. 1971. Genetic counseling. *Hospital Practice,* January, pp. 49–56.

Friedmann, T. 1971. Prenatal diagnosis of genetic disease. *Scientific American,* November, pp. 34–42.

Friedmann, T., and Roblin, R. 1972. Gene therapy for human genetic disease? *Science* 175: 949–55.

Guthrie, R. 1972. Mass screening for genetic disease. *Hospital Practice,* June, pp. 93–106.

Hamilton, M., ed. 1972. *The new genetics and the future of man.* Grand Rapids, Mich.: Wm. B. Eerdmans Publishing Co.

Hilton, B., Callahan, D., Harris, M., Condliffe, P., and Berkley, B. 1973. *Ethical issues in human genetics.* New York: Plenum Publishing Corporation.

Ingle, D. J. 1973. *Who should have children? An environmental and genetic approach.* Indianapolis: The Bobbs-Merrill Co., Inc.

Jacobson, C. B., and Barter, R. H. 1967. Intrauterine diagnosis and management of genetic defects. *American Journal of Obstetrics & Gynecology* 99: 796–807.

Lederberg, J. 1970. Genetic engineering and the amelioration of genetic defect. *Bioscience* 20: 1307–10.

Lerner, I. M. 1968. *Heredity, evolution, and society.* San Francisco: W. H. Freeman and Company Publishers.

Motulsky, A. G., and Hecht, F. 1964. Genetic prognosis and counseling. *American Journal of Obstetrics & Gynecology* 90: 1227–41.

Osborn, F. 1968. *The future of human heredity.* New York: David McKay Co., Inc., Weybright & Talley.

Parker, W. C. 1970. Some legal aspects of genetic counseling. In *Progress in medical genetics,* eds. A. G. Steinberg and A. G. Bearn, vol. 7, pp. 217–31. New York: Grune & Stratton, Inc.

Porter, I. H., and Skalko, R. G., eds. 1973. *Heredity and society.* New York: Academic Press, Inc.

Potter, V. R. 1971. *Bioethics: bridge to the future.* Englewood Cliffs, N.J.: Prentice-Hall, Inc.

Pringle, J. W. S., ed. 1972. *Biology and the human sciences.* New York: Oxford University Press, Inc., Clarendon Press.

Reed, S. 1963. *Counseling in medical genetics.* Philadelphia: W. B. Saunders Co.
———. 1944. *Parenthood and heredity.* New York: John Wiley & Sons, Inc.

Sinsheimer, R. L. 1969. The prospect for designed genetic change. *American Scientist* 57: 134–42.

Tips, R. L., and Lynch, H. T. 1963. The impact of genetic counseling upon the family milieu. *Journal of the American Medical Association* 184: 183–86.

Zinder, N. D. 1958. "Transduction" in bacteria. *Scientific American,* November, pp. 38–43.

Carter, G. S. 1957. *A hundred years of evolution.* London: Sidgwick & Jackson, Ltd., Publishers.

Darwin, C. 1958. *The origin of species* (1859). New York: The New American Library Inc.
———. 1960. *The voyage of the Beagle* (1840). New York: Bantam Books, Inc.

Dobzhansky, T. 1956. *The biological basis of human freedom.* New York: Columbia University Press.

Eiseley, L. 1957. *The immense journey.* New York: Random House, Inc.

28 Darwinian Scheme of Evolution

Gastonguay, P. R. 1974. *Evolution for everyone.* Indianapolis: The Bobbs-Merrill Co., Inc.

Grant, V. 1963. *The origin of adaptations.* New York: Columbia University Press.

Greene, J. C. 1961. *The death of Adam.* New York: The New American Library Inc.

Hamilton, T. H. 1967. *Process and pattern in evolution.* New York: Macmillan, Inc.

Huxley, J. 1953. *Evolution in action.* New York: The New American Library Inc.

Kettlewell, H. B. D. 1959. Darwin's missing evidence. *Scientific American,* March, pp. 48–53.

Lerner, I. M. 1968. *Heredity, evolution, and society.* San Francisco: W. H. Freeman and Company Publishers.

Merrell, D. J. 1962. *Evolution and genetics.* New York: Holt, Rinehart and Winston, Inc.

Moody, P. A. 1962. *Introduction to evolution.* New York: Harper & Row, Publishers.

Moore, R., and editors of Time-Life Books. 1964. *Evolution.* New York: Time-Life Books.

Moorehead, A. 1969. *Darwin and the Beagle.* New York: Harper & Row, Publishers.

Ryan, F. J. 1953. Evolution observed. *Scientific American,* October, pp. 78–82.

Simpson, G. G. 1951. *The meaning of evolution.* New York: The New American Library Inc.

Stebbins, G. L. 1971. *Processes of organic evolution.* Englewood Cliffs, N.J.: Prentice-Hall, Inc.

Swanson, C. P. 1973. *The natural history of man.* Englewood Cliffs, N.J.: Prentice-Hall, Inc.

Tax, S., ed. 1960. *Evolution after Darwin.* 3 vols. Chicago: University of Chicago Press.

Volpe, E. P. 1977. *Understanding evolution.* Dubuque, Iowa: Wm. C. Brown Company Publishers.

Wallace, B., and Srb, A. M. 1964. *Adaptation.* Englewood Cliffs, N.J.: Prentice-Hall, Inc.

29 Genetic Variation and Mutation

Crow, J. F. 1959. Ionizing radiation and evolution. *Scientific American,* September, pp. 138–60.

———. 1961. Mutation in man. In *Progress in medical genetics,* ed. A. G. Steinberg, vol. 1, pp. 1–26. New York: Grune & Stratton, Inc.

Dobzhansky, T. 1964. *Heredity and the nature of man.* New York: The New American Library Inc.

Loutit, T. F. 1962. *Irradiation of mice and men.* Chicago: University of Chicago Press.

Miller, R. W. 1969. Delayed radiation effects in atomic-bomb survivors. *Science* 166: 569–74.

Morton, N. E. 1960. The mutational load due to detrimental genes in man. *American Journal of Human Genetics* 12: 348–64.

Muller, H. J. 1950. Our load of mutations. *American Journal of Human Genetics* 2: 111–76.

———. 1955. Radiation and human mutation. *Scientific American,* November, pp. 58–68.

Puck, T. T. 1960. Radiation and the human cell. *Scientific American,* April, 142–53.

Schull, W. J., and Neel, J. V. 1958. Radiation and the sex ratio in man. *Science* 128: 343–48.

Schull, W. J., Neel, J. V., and Hashizume, A. 1966. Some further observations on the sex-ratio among infants born to survivors of the atomic bombings of Hiroshima and Nagasaki. *American Journal of Human Genetics* 18: 328–38.

Stevenson, A. C. 1958. The genetic hazards of radiation. *Practitioner* 181: 559–71.

United Nations Scientific Committee. 1967. *The genetic risk from radiation.* New York: United Nations.

Wallace, B. 1966. *Giant molecules, and evolution.* New York: W. W. Norton & Co., Inc.

———. 1970. *Genetic load.* Englewood Cliffs, N.J.: Prentice-Hall, Inc.

Wallace, B., and Dobzhansky, T. 1959. *Radiation, genes, and man.* New York: Holt, Rinehart and Winston, Inc.

Dobzhansky, T. 1970. *Genetics of the evolutionary process.* New York: Columbia University Press.

Dunn, L. C., and Dobzhansky, T. 1952. *Heredity, race, and society.* New York: The New American Library Inc.

Eckland, B. K. 1968. Theories of mate selection. *Eugenics Quarterly* 15: 71–84.

Hardy, G. H. 1908. Mendelian proportions in a mixed population. *Science* 28: 49–50.

Li, C. C. 1955. *Population genetics.* Chicago: University of Chicago Press.

———. 1961. *Human genetics.* New York: McGraw-Hill.

Mettler, L. E., and Gregg, T. G. 1969. *Population genetics and evolution.* Englewood Cliffs, N.J.: Prentice-Hall, Inc.

Stern, C. 1943. The Hardy-Weinberg law. *Science* 97: 137–38.

———. 1973. *Principles of human genetics.* San Francisco: W. H. Freeman and Company Publishers.

Wallace, B. 1968. *Topics in population genetics.* New York: W. W. Norton & Co., Inc.

30   Concept of Genetic Equilibrium

Bajema, C. J., ed. 1971. *Natural selection in human populations.* New York: John Wiley & Sons, Inc.

Cavalli-Sforza, L. L., and Bodmer, W. F. 1971. *The genetics of human populations.* San Francisco: W. H. Freeman and Company Publishers.

Crow, J. F. 1961. Population genetics. *American Journal of Human Genetics* 13: 137–50.

Dobzhansky, T. 1950. The genetic basis of evolution. *Scientific American,* January, pp. 32–41.

———. 1961. Man and natural selection. *American Scientist* 49: 285–99.

Ford, E. B. 1960. *Mendelism and evolution.* London: Methuen & Co., Ltd.

Hardin, G. 1959. *Nature and man's fate.* New York: The New American Library Inc.

Morris, L. N. 1971. *Human populations, genetic variation, and evolution.* New York: Chandler Publishing Co.

Neel, J. V., and Schull, W. J. 1968. On some trends in understanding the genetics of man. *Perspectives in Biology and Medicine* 11: 565–602.

31   Concept of Selection

Damon, A. 1969. Race, ethnic group, and disease. *Social Biology* 16: 69–80.

Dubos, R. 1959. *Mirage of health.* New York: Harper & Row, Publishers.

———. 1968. *So human an animal.* New York: Charles Scribner's Sons.

Dubos, R., and Dubos, J. 1952. *The white plague: tuberculosis, man and society.* Boston: Little, Brown and Co.

Dubos, R., Pines, M., and the editors of Time-Life books. 1965. *Health and disease.* New York: Time-Life Books.

Fenner, F. 1959. Myxomatosis in Australian wild rabbits—evolutionary changes in an infectious disease. *The Harvey Lectures 1957–58.* New York: Academic Press, Inc.

Haldane, J. B. S. 1961. Natural selection in man. In *Progress in Medical Genetics,* ed. A. G. Steinberg, vol. 1, pp. 27–37. New York: Grune & Stratton, Inc.

32   Selection and Infectious Diseases

Harrison, G., Weiner, J., Tanner, J., and Barnicot, N. 1964. *Human biology: an introduction to human evolution.* New York: Oxford University Press, Inc.

Langer, W. L. 1964. The black death. *Scientific American,* February, pp. 114–21.

Motulsky, A. G. 1960. Metabolic polymorphisms and the role of infectious diseases in human evolution. *Human Biology* 32: 28–62.

Neel, J. V. 1957. Human hemoglobin types. Their epidemiologic implications. *New England Journal of Medicine* 256: 161–71.

————. 1958. The study of natural selection in primitive and civilized human populations. *Human Biology* 30: 43–72.

Williams, R. J. 1956. *Biochemical individuality.* New York: John Wiley & Sons, Inc.

33 Balanced Polymorphism

Allison, A. C. 1956. Sickle cells and evolution. *Scientific American,* August, pp. 87–94.

Anfinsen, C. B. 1963. *The molecular basis of evolution.* New York: John Wiley & Sons, Inc.

Brues, A. M. 1954. Selection and polymorphism in the ABO blood groups. *American Journal of Physical Anthropology* 12: 559–97.

Chernoff, A. 1959. The distribution of the thalassemia gene: a historical review. *Blood* 14: 899–912.

Crow, J. F., and Morton, N. E. 1960. The genetic load due to mother-child incompatibility. *American Naturalist* 94: 413–19.

Harris, H. 1969. Enzyme and protein polymorphism in human populations. *British Medical Bulletin* 25: 5–13.

Ingram, V. 1963. *The hemoglobins in genetics and evolution.* New York: Columbia University Press.

Knudson, A. G., Wayne, L., and Hallett, W. Y. 1967. On the selective advantage of cystic fibrosis heterozygotes. *American Journal of Human Genetics* 19: 388–392.

Livingstone, F. B. 1958. Anthropological implications of sickle cell gene distribution in West Africa. *American Anthropologist* 60: 533–62.

————. 1967. *Abnormal hemoglobins in human populations.* Chicago: Aldine Publishing Co.

Myrianthopoulos, N. C., and Aronson, S. M. 1966. Population dynamics of Tay-Sachs disease. I. Reproductive fitness and selection. *American Journal of Human Genetics* 18: 313–327.

Newcombe, H. B. 1963. Risk of fetal death to mothers of different ABO and Rh blood types. *American Journal of Human Genetics* 15: 499–64.

Price, J. 1967. Human polymorphism. *Journal of Medical Genetics* 4: 44–67.

Sheppard, P. M. 1959. *Natural selection and heredity.* New York: Philosophical Library, Inc.

Wiesenfeld, S. L. 1967. Sickle-cell trait in human biological and cultural evolution. *Science* 157: 1134–40.

34 Genetic Drift and Gene Flow

Boyd, W. C. 1963. Four achievements of the genetical method in physical anthropology. *American Anthropologist* 65: 243–52.

Candela, P. B. 1942. The introduction of blood-group B into Europe. *Human Biology* 14: 413–43.

Cavalli-Sforza, L. L. 1969. "Genetic drift" in an Italian population. *Scientific American,* August, pp. 30–37.

Dunn, L. C. 1966. *Heredity and evolution in human populations.* New York: Atheneum Publishers.

Dunn, L. C., and Dunn, S. P. 1957. The Jewish community of Rome. *Scientific American,* March, pp. 118–28.

Glass, B. 1953. The genetics of the Dunkers. *Scientific American,* August, pp. 76–81.

————. 1954. Genetic changes in human populations, especially those due to gene flow and genetic drift. *Advances in Genetics* 6: 95–139.

————. 1956. On the evidence of random genetic drift in human populations. *American Journal of Physical Anthropology* 14: 541–55.

Glass, B., and Li, C. C. 1953. The dynamics of racial intermixture—an analysis based on the American Negro. *American Journal of Human Genetics* 5: 1–20.

Goldsby, R. A. 1971. *Race and races.* New York: Macmillan, Inc.

McKusick, V. A., Hostetler, J. A., Egeland, J. A., and Eldridge, R. 1964. The distribution of certain genes in the Old Order Amish. *Cold Spring Harbor Symposium on Quantitative Biology* 29: 99–114.

Mourant, A. E. 1954. *The distribution of the human blood groups.* Oxford, England: Blackwell Scientific Publications.

Pollitzer, W. S. 1958. The Negroes of Charleston (S.C.): a study of hemoglobin types, serology and morphology. *American Journal of Physical Anthropology* 16: 241–63.

Reed, T. E. 1969. Caucasian genes in American Negroes. *Science* 165: 762–68.

Woolf, C. M., and Dukepoo, F. C. 1969. Hopi Indians, inbreeding, and albinism. *Science* 164: 30–37.

Workman, P. L. 1968. Gene flow and the search for natural selection in man. *Human Biology* 40: 260–79.

Wright, S. 1951. Fisher and Ford on "The Sewall Wright Effect." *American Scientist* 39: 452–58.

Barnes, R. H. 1971. Nutrition and man's intellect and behavior. *Federation Proceedings* 30: 1429–33.

Bloom, B. 1969. Letter to the editor. *Harvard Educational Review* 39: 419–21.

Bodmer, W. F., and Cavalli-Sforza, L. L. 1970. Intelligence and race. *Scientific American,* October, pp. 19–29.

Cancro, R., ed. 1971. *Intelligence: genetic and environmental influences.* New York: Grune & Stratton, Inc.

Carter, C. O. 1965. *Human heredity.* Baltimore: Penguin Books Inc.

Cavalli-Sforza, L. L., and Bodmer, W. F. 1971. *The genetics of human populations.* San Francisco: W. H. Freeman and Company Publishers.

Coleman, J. E. 1966. *Equality of educational opportunity.* Washington, D. C.: U.S. Government Printing Office.

Dobzhansky, T. 1962. *Mankind evolving.* New Haven, Conn.: Yale University Press.

Erlenmeyer-Kimling, L., and Jarvik, L. F. 1963. Genetics and intelligence: a review. *Science* 142: 1477–79.

Eysenck, H. J. 1971. *The IQ argument.* New York: Library Press.

Falek, A. 1971. Differential fertility and intelligence: current status of the problem. *Social Biology* 18 (supplement): 50–59.

Glass, D. D., ed. 1968. *Genetics.* New York: Rockefeller University Press and Russell Sage Foundation.

Herrnstein, R. 1971. I. Q. *Atlantic,* September, pp. 43–64.

Higgins, J. V., Reed, E. W., and Reed, S. C. 1962. Intelligence and family size: a paradox resolved. *Eugenics Quarterly* 9: 84–90.

Jencks, C. 1969. What color is I. Q.?—Intelligence and race. *The New Republic,* September, pp. 25–29.

Jensen, A. R. 1969. How much can we boost IQ and scholastic achievement? *Harvard Educational Review* 39: 1–123.

Klineberg, O. 1935. *Negro intelligence and selective migration.* New York: Columbia University Press.

Lerner, I. M. 1968. *Heredity, evolution, and society.* San Francisco: W. H. Freeman and Company Publishers.

35 Polygenic Inheritance and Intelligence

Lewontin, R. 1970. Race and intelligence. *Bulletin of the Atomic Scientists,* March, pp. 2–8.

Li, C. C. 1961. *Human genetics: principles and methods.* New York: McGraw-Hill.

Mead, M., Dobzhansky, T., Tobach, E., and Light, R. E., eds. 1968. *Science and the concept of race.* New York: Columbia University Press.

Meade, J. E., and Parkes, A. S., eds. 1966. *Biological aspects of social problems.* Edinburgh, England: Oliver & Boyd.

Montagu, A. 1963. *Human heredity.* New York: The New American Library Inc.

Newman, H. H., Freeman, F. N., and Holzinger, K. J. 1937. *Twins: a study of heredity and environment.* Chicago: University of Chicago Press.

Scarr-Salapatek, S. 1971. Race, social class, and IQ. *Science* 174: 1285–95.

Senna, C., ed. 1973. *The fallacy of IQ.* New York: The Third Press.

Shuey, A. M. 1966. *The testing of Negro intelligence.* New York: Barnes & Noble Books, Social Science Paperbacks.

Spuhler, J. N., and Lindzey, G. 1967. Racial differences in behavior. In *Behavior Genetic Analysis* ed. J. Hirsch. New York: McGraw-Hill.

Stern, C. 1973. *Principles of human genetics.* San Francisco: W. H. Freeman and Company Publishers.

Vandenberg, S. G., ed. 1968. *Progress in human behavior genetics.* Baltimore: The Johns Hopkins Press.

Vernon, P. E. 1969. *Intelligence and cultural environment.* London, England: Methuen, Ltd.

Wiseman, S., ed. 1967. *Intelligence and ability.* Baltimore: Penguin Books Inc.

36 Races and Species

Dobzhansky, T. 1951. *Genetics and the origin of species.* New York: Columbia University Press.

Dowdeswell, W. H. 1960. *The mechanism of evolution.* New York: Harper & Row, Publishers.

Goldsby, R. A. 1971. *Race and races.* New York: Macmillan, Inc.

King, J. C. 1971. *The biology of race.* New York: Harcourt Brace Jovanovich, Inc.

Laughlin, W. S. 1966. Race: a population concept. *Eugenics Quarterly* 13: 326–40.

Mayr, E. 1942. *Systematics and the origin of species.* New York: Columbia University Press.

Mead, M., Dobzhansky, T., Tobach, E., and Light, R. E., eds. 1968. *Science and the concept of race.* New York: Columbia University Press.

Montagu, A. 1964. *The concept of race.* New York: Free Press of Glencoe.

———. 1965. *Man's most dangerous myth: the fallacy of race.* New York: Macmillan, Inc.

Simpson, G. G. 1953. *The major features of evolution.* New York: Columbia University Press.

Stebbins, G. L. 1966. *Processes of organic evolution.* Englewood Cliffs, N.J.: Prentice-Hall, Inc.

Wallace, B., and Srb, A. 1964. *Adaptation.* Englewood Cliffs, N.J.: Prentice-Hall, Inc.

37 Adaptive Radiation

Colbert, E. H. 1955. *Evolution of the vertebrates.* New York: John Wiley & Sons, Inc.

———. 1961. *Dinosaurs, their discovery and their world.* New York: E. P. Dutton & Co., Inc.

Hotton, N. 1968. *The evidence of evolution.* New York: American Heritage Publishing Co., Inc.

Johansen, K. 1968. Air-breathing fishes. *Scientific American,* October, pp. 102–11.

Kurtén, B. 1969. Continental drift and evolution. *Scientific American*, March, pp. 54–64.

Lack, D. 1947. *Darwin's finches*. London, England: Cambridge University Press.

———. 1953. Darwin's finches. *Scientific American*, April, pp. 66–72.

Mayr, E. 1963. *Animal species and evolution*. Cambridge, Mass.: Harvard University Press.

Newell, N. D. 1963. Crises in the history of life. *Scientific American*, February, pp. 76–92.

Romer, A. S. 1959. *The vertebrate story*. Chicago: University of Chicago Press.

Simpson, G. G. 1951. *Horses*. New York: Oxford University Press, Inc.

———. 1953. *Life of the past*. New Haven, Conn.: Yale University Press.

Smith, H. W. 1961. *From fish to philosopher*. Garden City, N.Y.: Doubleday & Company, Inc.

Stirton, R. A. 1959. *Time, life, and man*. New York: John Wiley & Sons, Inc.

Young, J. Z. 1950. *The life of vertebrates*. New York: Oxford University Press, Inc.

Barghoorn, E. S. 1971. The oldest fossils. *Scientific American*, May, pp. 30–42.

Bold, H. C. 1964. *The plant kingdom*. Englewood Cliffs, N.J.: Prentice-Hall, Inc.

Buchsbaum, R. 1948. *Animals without backbones*. Chicago: University of Chicago Press.

Calvin, M. 1969. *Chemical evolution*. New York: Oxford University Press, Inc.

Eglinton, G., and Calvin M. 1967. Chemical fossils. *Scientific American*, January, pp. 32–43.

Fingerman, M. 1969. *Animal diversity*. New York: Holt, Rinehart and Winston, Inc.

Fox, S. W., and Dose, K. 1972. *Molecular evolution and the origin of life*. San Francisco: W. H. Freeman and Company Publishers.

Glaessner, M. F. 1961. Precambrian animals. *Scientific American*, March, pp. 72–78.

Hanson, E. 1964. *Animal diversity*. Englewood Cliffs, N.J.: Prentice-Hall, Inc.

Keosian, J. 1967. *The origin of life*. New York: Reinhold Publishing Corp.

Miller, S. L. 1953. A production of amino acids under possible primitive earth conditions. *Science* 117: 528–29.

Oparin, A. I. 1953. *The origin of life*. New York: Dover Publications, Inc.

Orgel, L. E. 1973. *The origins of life*. New York: John Wiley & Sons, Inc.

Ponnamperuma, C. 1972. *The origins of life*. New York: E. P. Dutton & Co., Inc.

Romer, A. S. 1945. *Vertebrate paleontology*. Chicago: University of Chicago Press.

Smith, K. M. 1962. *Viruses*. Cambridge: Cambridge University Press.

Stirton, R. A. 1959. *Time, life, and man*. New York: John Wiley & Sons, Inc.

Wald, G. 1954. The origin of life. *Scientific American*, August, pp. 44–53.

38 Origin and History of Life

Birdsell, J. B. 1974. *Human evolution*. Chicago: Rand McNally College Publishing Co.

Bleibtreu, H. K., ed. 1969. *Evolutionary anthropology*. Boston: Allyn & Bacon, Inc.

Campbell, B. G. 1966. *Human evolution*. Chicago: Aldine Publishing Co.

Clark, W. E. LeGros. 1964. *The fossil evidence for human evolution*. Chicago: University of Chicago Press.

Eimerl, S., DeVore, I., and editors of Time-Life Books. 1965. *The primates*. New York: Time-Life Books.

Howell, F. C., and editors of Time-Life Books. 1965. *Early man*. New York: Time-Life Books.

Howells, W. W. 1959. *Mankind in the making*. Garden City, N.Y.: Doubleday & Co., Inc.

39 Emergence of Man

————. 1960. The distribution of man. *Scientific American,* **September,** pp. 112–27.

————. 1966. *Homo erectus. Scientific American,* **November,** pp. 46–53.

Leakey, L. S. B. 1960. *Adam's ancestors.* New York: **Harper & Row,** Publishers.

Lee, R. B., and DeVore, I. 1968. *Man the hunter.* **Chicago: Aldine** Publishing Co.

Medawar, P. B. 1961. *The future of man.* New **York: The New** American Library Inc.

Montagu, A. 1961. *Man in process.* New **York: The New** American Library Inc.

————. 1962. *Man: his first million years.* **New York: The** New American Library Inc.

Morris, D. 1968. *The naked ape.* New **York: McGraw-**Hill.

————. 1969. *The human zoo.* New **York: Dell Publishing** Co., Inc.

Napier, J. 1967. The antiquity of human **walking.** *Scientific American,* April, pp. 56–66.

Pearson, R. 1974. *Introduction to anthropology.* New York: Holt, Rinehart and Winston.

Pfeiffer, J. E. 1969. *The emergence of man.* New York: Harper & Row, Publishers.

Pilbeam, D. R. 1972. *The ascent of man.* New York: Macmillan Co.

Shepard, P. 1973. *The tender carnivore and the sacred game.* New York: Charles Scribner's Sons.

Simons, E. L. 1964. The early relatives of man. *Scientific American,* July, pp. 50–62.

Washburn, S. L. 1960. Tools and human evolution. *Scientific American,* September, pp. 62–75.

Young, L. B., ed. 1970. *Evolution of man.* New York: Oxford University Press, Inc.

40   Population Dynamics

Anderson, P. K. 1971. *Omega: murder of the ecosystem and suicide of man.* Dubuque, Iowa: Wm. C. Brown Company Publishers.

Boughey, A. S. 1973. *Ecology of populations.* New York: Macmillan, Inc.

Bresler, J. B., ed. 1966. *Human ecology.* Reading, Mass.: Addison-Wesley Publishing Co., Inc.

Brown, H. 1967. *The challenge of man's future.* New York: The Viking Press, Inc.

Calhoun, J. B. 1962. Population density and social pathology. *Scientific American,* February, pp. 139–48.

Chitty, D. 1960. Population processes in the vole and their relevance to general theory. *Canadian Journal of Zoology* 38: 99–113.

Christian, J. J., and Davis, D. E. 1964. Endocrines, behavior and population. *Science* 146: 1550–60.

Cipolla, C. M. 1970. *The economic history of world population.* Baltimore: Penguin Books, Inc.

Darnell, R. M. 1973. *Ecology and man.* Dubuque, Iowa: Wm. C. Brown Company Publishers.

Deevey, E. S., Jr. 1960. The human population. *Scientific American,* September, pp. 194–204.

Ehrlich, P. R., and Ehrlich, A. H. 1970. *Population, resources, environment: issues in human ecology.* San Francisco: W. H. Freeman and Company Publishers.

Emmel, T. C. 1973. *An introduction to ecology and population biology.* New York: W. W. Norton & Co., Inc.

Hardin, G. J. 1969. *Population, evolution, and birth control: a collage of controversial readings.* San Francisco: W. H. Freeman and Company Publishers.

Heer, D. M. 1968. *Society and population.* Englewood Cliffs, N.J.: Prentice-Hall, Inc.

Kormondy, E. J. 1969. *Concepts of ecology.* Englewood Cliffs, N. J.: Prentice-Hall, Inc.

Moran, J. M., Morgan, M. D., and Wiersma, J. H. 1973. *An introduction to environmental sciences.* Boston: Little, Brown and Co.

Negus, N. C., Gould, E., and Chipman, R. K. 1961. Ecology of the rice rat, Orzyomys palustris (Harlan), on Breton Island, Gulf of Mexico, with a critique of the social stress theory. *Tulane Studies in Zoology* 8: 95–123.

Odum, E. P. 1971. *Fundamentals of ecology.* Philadelphia: W. B. Saunders Co.

Pearl, R. 1930. *The biology of population growth.* New York: Alfred A. Knopf, Inc.

Pitelka, F. 1957. Some aspects of population structure in the short-term cycle of the brown lemming in Northern Alaska. *Cold Spring Harbor Symposium on Quantitative Biology* 22: 237–51.

Ricklefs, R. E. 1973. *Ecology.* Newton, Mass.: Chiron Press.

Shepherd, P., and McKinley, D., eds. 1968. *The subversive science.* Boston: Houghton Mifflin Co.

Southwick, C. H. 1972. *Ecology and the quality of our environment.* New York: Van Nostrand Reinhold Co.

Wagner, R. H. 1971. *Environment and man.* New York: W. W. Norton & Co., Inc.

Wynne-Edwards, V. 1965. Self-regulating systems in populations of animals. *Science* 147: 1543–48.

41 Prevalence of People

Allison, A., ed. 1970. *Population control.* Baltimore: Penguin Books.

Berelson, B. 1969. Beyond family planning. *Science* 163: 533–43.

Blake, J. 1971. Reproductive motivation and population policy. *Bioscience* 21: 215–20.

Boerma, A. H. 1970. A world agricultural plan. *Scientific American,* August, pp. 54–69.

Borgstrom, G. 1967. *The hungry planet.* New York: Macmillan Publishing Co., Inc., Collier Books.

———. 1973. *World food resources.* New York: Intext Press, Inc.

Brown, H., Bonner, J., and Weir, J. 1963. *The next hundred years.* New York: The Viking Press, Inc.

Brown, L. R. 1970. *Seeds of change.* New York: Praeger Publishers, Inc.

Chasteen, E. R. 1971. *The case for compulsory birth control.* Englewood Cliffs, N.J.: Prentice-Hall, Inc.

Commoner, B., 1971. *The closing circle: nature, man, and technology.* New York: Alfred A. Knopf, Inc.

Day, L., and Day, A. 1964. *Too many Americans.* New York: Macmillan, Inc.

Dorn, H. F. 1962. World population growth: an international dilemma. *Science* 135: 283–90.

Draper, E. 1965. *Birth control in the modern world.* Baltimore: Penguin Books.

Ehrlich, P. R. 1968. *The population bomb.* New York: Ballantine Books, Inc.

Ehrlich, P. R., and Harriman, R. L. 1971. *How to be a survivor: a plan to save spaceship earth.* New York: Ballantine Books, Inc.

Francis, R. G., ed. 1958. *The population ahead.* Minneapolis: University of Minnesota Press.

Fraser, D. 1971. *The people problem.* Bloomington: Indiana University Press.

Greep, R. O., ed. 1963. *Human fertility and population problems.* Cambridge, Mass.: Schenkman Publishing Co., Inc.

Hauser, P. M., ed. 1963. *The population dilemma.* Englewood Cliffs, N.J.: Prentice-Hall, Inc.

———. 1971. The census of 1970. *Scientific American,* July, pp. 17–25.

Holdren, J. P., and Ehrlich, P. R., eds. 1971. *Global ecology: readings toward a rational strategy for man.* New York: Harcourt Brace Jovanovich, Inc.

Langer, W. L. 1972. Checks on population growth: 1750–1850. *Scientific American,* February, pp. 92–99.

Meadows, D. H., Meadows, D. L., Randers, J., and Behrens, W. W. 1972. *The limits to growth.* New York: Universe Books.

Osborn, F. 1962. *Our crowded planet.* Garden City, N.Y.: Doubleday & Co., Inc.

Paddock, W., and Paddock, P. 1967. *Famine—1975!* Boston: Little, Brown and Co.

Sax, K. 1960. *Standing room only: the world's exploding population.* Boston: Beacon Press.

Wagner, K. A., Bailey, P. C., and Campbell, G. H. 1973. *Under seige: man, men, and earth.* New York: Intext Press, Inc.

42 Interactions of Populations

Allee, W. C., Emerson, A. E., Park, O., Park, T., and Schmidt, K. P. 1949. *Principles of animal ecology.* Philadelphia: W. B. Saunders Co.

Andrewartha, H. G., and Birch, L. C. 1954. *The distribution and abundance of animals.* Chicago: University of Chicago Press.

Benarde, M. A. 1970. *Our precarious environment.* New York: W. W. Norton & Co., Inc.

Commoner, B. 1966. *Science for survival.* New York: The Viking Press, Inc.

Dansereau, P. 1970. *Challenge for survival.* New York: Columbia University Press.

DeBell, G. 1970. *The environmental handbook.* New York: Ballantine Books, Inc.

Dowdeswell, W. H. 1961. *Animal ecology.* New York: Harper & Row, Publishers.

Ehrlich, P. R., Ehrlich, A. H., and Holdren, J. P. 1973. *Human ecology: problems and solutions.* San Francisco: W. H. Freeman and Company Publishers.

Errington, P. 1967. *Of predation and life.* Ames, Iowa: Iowa State University Press.

Farb, P., and the editors of Time-Life Books. 1970. *Ecology.* New York: Time-Life Books.

Hazen, W. E., ed. 1970. *Readings in population and community ecology.* Philadelphia: W. B. Saunders Co.

Jackson, W. 1973. *Man and the environment.* Dubuque, Iowa: Wm. C. Brown Company Publishers.

Manners, I. R., and Mikesell, M. W., eds. 1974. *Perspectives in environment.* Washington, D. C.: Commission on College Geography.

Mason, W. H., and Folkerts, G. W., eds. 1973. *Environmental problems: principles, readings, and comments.* Dubuque, Iowa: Wm. C. Brown Company Publishers.

Milne, L. 1960. *The balance of nature.* New York: Alfred A. Knopf, Inc.

Murdoch, W. W., ed. 1971. *Environment: resources, pollution, and society.* Stamford, Conn.: Sinauer Associates, Inc.

Quick, H. F. 1974. *Population ecology.* Indianapolis: The Bobbs-Merrill Co., Inc.

Storer, J. H. 1968. *Man in the web of life.* New York: The New American Library Inc., Signet Books.

Sutton, D. B., and Harmon, N. P. 1973. *Ecology: selected concepts.* New York: John Wiley & Sons, Inc.

Thomas, W. L., ed. 1955. *Man's role in changing the face of the earth.* Chicago: University of Chicago Press.

43 Biotic Communities: Plants As Producers

Allen, D. L. 1967. *The life of prairies and plains.* New York: McGraw-Hill.

Bates, M. 1960. *The forest and the sea.* New York: Random House, Inc., Vintage Books.

———. 1964. *Man in nature.* Englewood Cliffs, N. J.: Prentice-Hall, Inc.

Brooks, P. 1971. *The pursuit of wilderness.* Boston: Houghton-Mifflin Co.

Farb, P., and the editors of Time-Life Books. 1969. *The forest.* New York: Time-Life Books.

Fisher, J., Simon, N., and Vincent, J. 1969. *Wildlife in danger.* New York: The Viking Press, Inc.

Laylock, G. 1969. *America's endangered wildlife.* New York: W. W. Norton & Co., Inc.

Leopold, A. S., and the editors of Time-Life Books. 1967. *The desert.* New York: Time-Life Books.

Milne, L., and Milne, M. 1971. *The nature of life: earth, plants, animals, man and their effect on each other.* New York: Crown Publishers, Inc.

Whittaker, R. H. 1970. *Communities and ecosystems.* New York: Macmillan, Inc.

Zobel, B. J. 1971. The genetic improvement of southern pines. *Scientific American,* November, pp. 94–103.

44 Biotic Communities: Energy Flow

Borland, H., ed. 1970. *The crisis of survival.* New York: William Morrow & Co., Inc.

Brock, T. D. 1966. *Principles of microbial ecology.* Englewood Cliffs, N. J.: Prentice-Hall, Inc.

Chapman, V. J. 1970. *Seaweeds and their uses.* London, England: Methuen Ltd.

Commoner, B. 1971. *The closing circle.* New York: Alfred A. Knopf, Inc.

Cox, G. W., ed. 1969. *Readings in conservation ecology.* New York: McGraw-Hill.

Ehrenfeld, D. W. 1970. *Biological conservation.* New York: Holt, Rinehart and Winston, Inc.

Eiseley, L. 1970. *The invisible pyramid.* New York: Charles Scribner's Sons.

Engel, L., and the editors of Time-Life Books. 1968. *The sea.* New York: Time-Life Books.

Fuller, J. 1970. *Whaling world.* Garden City, N. Y.: Doubleday & Co., Inc.

Gates, D. M. 1962. *Energy exchange in the biosphere.* New York: Harper & Row, Publishers.

Grossman, M. L., Grossman, S., and Hamlet, J. H. 1969. *Our vanishing wilderness.* New York: Grosset & Dunlap, Inc.

Holt, S. J. 1969. The food resources of the ocean. *Scientific American,* September, pp. 178–94.

Kuiper, G. B. 1954. *The earth as a planet.* Chicago: University of Chicago Press.

Low, I. 1967. Prospects for sea fish farming. *New Scientist* 35: 31–33.

McCoy, J. J. 1970. *Saving our wilderness.* New York: Macmillan, Inc.

Owen, O. S. 1971. *Natural resource conservation: an ecological approach.* New York: Macmillan, Inc.

Pinchot, G. B. 1970. Marine farming. *Scientific American,* December, pp. 14–21.

Schwartz, W., ed. 1969. *Voices for the wilderness.* New York: Ballantine Books, Inc.

Southwick, C. H. 1972. *Ecology and the quality of our environment.* New York: Van Nostrand Reinhold Co.

Wenk, E., Jr. 1969. The physical resources of the ocean. *Scientific American,* September, pp. 166–76.

45 The Ecosystem

Anderson, E. 1952. *Plants, man, and life.* Boston: Little, Brown and Co.

Bardach, J. E. 1968. Aquaculture. *Science* 161: 1098–1106.

Bigger, J. W., and Corey, R. B. 1969. *Eutrophication: causes, consequences, and correctives.* Washington, D.C.: National Academy of Sciences.

Billings, W. D. 1970. *Plants, man, and the ecosystem.* Belmont, Calif.: Wadsworth Publishing Co. Inc.

Bolin, B. 1970. The carbon cycle. *Scientific American,* September, pp. 124–32.

Bormann, F. H., and Likens, G. E. 1970. The nutrient cycles of an ecosystem. *Scientific American,* October, pp. 92–101.

Carson, R. L. 1951. *The sea around us.* New York: Oxford University Press, Inc.

Claiborne, R. 1970. *Climate, man, and history.* New York: W. W. Norton & Co., Inc.

Cloud, P., and Gibor, A. 1970. The oxygen cycle. *Scientific American,* September, pp. 110–23.

Cox, G. W., ed. 1969. *Readings in conservation ecology.* New York: Appleton-Century-Crofts.

Darling, F. F., and Dasmann, R. F. 1969. The ecosystem view of human society. *Impact* 19: 109–21.

Darling, F. F., and Milton, J. P., eds. 1967. *Future environments of North America.* Garden City, N.J.: Doubleday & Co., Inc., Natural History Press.

Darnell, R. M. 1970. Evolution and the ecosystem. *American Zoologist* 10: 9–15.

Deevey, E. S., Jr. 1970. Mineral cycles. *Scientific American,* September, pp. 148–58.

Delwiche, C. C. 1970. The nitrogen cycle. *Scientific American,* September, pp. 136–46.

Ehrlich, P. R., Holdren, J. P., and Holm, R. W., eds. 1972. *Man and the ecosphere (Readings from Scientific American, 1971).* San Francisco: W. H. Freeman and Company Publishers.

Engel, L., and the editors of Time-Life Books. 1969. *The sea.* New York: Time-Life Books.

Eyre, S. R. 1968. *Vegetation and soils, a world picture.* Chicago: Aldine Publishing Co.

Hammond, A. L. 1972. Ecosystem analysis: biome approach to environmental research. *Science* 175: 46–48.

Helfrich, H. W., Jr. 1970. *The environmental crisis.* New Haven, Conn.: Yale University Press.

Herndon, B. 1971. *The great land.* New York: Weybright and Talley, Inc.

Hynes, H. B. N. 1960. *The biology of polluted water.* Liverpool, England: Liverpool University Press.

Isaacs, J. D. 1969. The nature of oceanic life. *Scientific American,* September, pp. 146–62.

Leopold, A. S., and the editors of Time-Life Books. 1961. *The desert.* New York: Time-Life Books.

Maas, A. 1951. *Muddy waters: the Army engineers and the nation's rivers.* Cambridge, Mass.: Harvard University Press.

McHarg, I. L. 1969. *Design with nature.* Garden City, N.Y.: Doubleday & Co., Inc., Natural History Press.

Odum, E. P. 1969. The strategy of ecosystem development. *Science* 164: 262–70.

Pinchot, G. B. 1970. Marine farming. *Scientific American,* December, pp. 14–21.

Powers, C. F., and Robertson, A. 1966. The aging Great Lakes. *Scientific American,* November, pp. 94–104.

Pratt, C. J. 1970. Sulfur. *Scientific American,* May, pp. 62–72.

Richards, P. W. 1952. *The tropical rain forest.* Cambridge: Cambridge University Press.

Shepard, P. 1967. *Man in the landscape.* New York: Random House, Inc.

Smith, R. L. 1966. *Ecology and field biology.* New York: Harper & Row, Publishers.

Whittaker, R. H. 1970. *Communities and ecosystems.* New York: Macmillan, Inc.

Woodwell, G. M. 1967. Toxic substances and ecological cycles. *Scientific American,* March, pp. 24–31.

46 Man's Modification of the Environment

Aaronson, T. 1971. Mercury in the environment. *Environment* 13: 16–23.

Altshuller, A. P. 1966. Air pollution: photochemical aspects. *Science* 151: 1105–6.

Aron, W. I., and Smith, S. H. 1971. Ship canals and aquatic ecosystems. *Science* 174: 13–20.

Baron, R. A. 1970. *The tyranny of noise.* New York: St. Martin's Press, Inc.

Brady, N. C., ed. 1967. *Agriculture and the quality of our environment.* Washington, D.C.: American Association for the Advancement of Science.

Brown, H. 1970. Human materials production as a process in the biosphere. *Scientific American*, September, pp. 194–208.

Calder, R. 1962. *Living with the atom*. Chicago: University of Chicago Press.

Carson, R. L. 1962. *Silent spring*. Boston: Houghton-Mifflin Co.

Chisolm, J. J., Jr. 1971. Lead poisoning. *Scientific American*, February, pp. 15–23.

Clark, J. R. 1969. Thermal pollution and aquatic life. *Scientific American*, March, pp. 18–27.

Croome, A. 1967. Before and after Torrey Canyon. *New Scientist* 35: 569.

Detwyler, T. R. 1971. *Man's impact on environment*. New York: McGraw-Hill.

Disch, R., ed. 1970. *The ecological conscience: values for survival*. Englewood Cliffs, N.J.: Prentice-Hall, Inc.

Edelson, E. 1966. *Poisons in the air*. New York: Pocket Books.

Edwards, C. A. 1969. Soil pollutants and soil animals. *Scientific American*, April, pp. 88–99.

Fermi, L. 1969. Cars and air pollution. *Bulletin of the Atomic Scientists*, October, pp. 35–37.

Fisher, J. N., Simon, N., and Vincent, J. 1969. *Wildlife in danger*. New York: The Viking Press, Inc.

Galston, A. W. 1971. Some implications of the widespread use of herbicides. *Bioscience* 21: 891–92.

Goldman, M. I. 1970. The convergence of environmental disruption. *Science* 170: 37–42.

Goldwater, L. J. 1971. Mercury in the environment. *Scientific American*, May, pp. 15–21.

Graham, F., Jr. 1970. *Since silent spring*. Boston: Houghton-Mifflin Co.

Hasler, A. D. 1969. Cultural eutrophication is reversible. *Bioscience* 19: 425–31.

Hynes, H. B. N. 1971. *The biology of polluted waters*. Toronto, Canada: University of Toronto Press.

Lewis, H. R. 1965. *With every breath you take*. New York: Crown Publishers, Inc.

Marx, W. 1967. *The frail ocean*. New York: Coward-McCann & Geoghegan, Inc.

McHarg, I. L. 1969. *Design with nature*. Garden City, N. Y.: Doubleday & Co., Inc., Natural History Press.

McKelvey, V. E. 1972. Mineral resource estimates and public policy. *American Scientist* 60: 32–40.

Moats, S., and Moats, W. A. 1970. Toward safer use of pesticides. *Bioscience* 20: 459–64.

Newell, R. E. 1971. The global circulation of atmospheric pollutants. *Scientific American*, January, pp. 32–42.

Nicholson, H. P. 1967. Pesticide pollution control. *Science* 158: 871–76.

Novick, S. 1969. *The careless atom*. Boston: Houghton-Mifflin Co.

Pattison, E. S. 1970. Arsenic and water pollution hazard. *Science* 170: 870.

Peakall, D. B. 1970. Pesticides and the reproduction of birds. *Scientific American*, April, pp. 72–78.

Peakall, D. B., and Lovett, R. J. 1972. Mercury: its occurrence and effects in the ecosystem. *Bioscience* 22: 20–25.

Pimentel, D. 1971. Evolutionary and environmental impact of pesticides. *Bioscience* 21: 109.

Pinney, R. 1963. *Vanishing wildlife*. New York: Dodd, Mead & Co.

Plass, G. N. 1959. Carbon dioxide and climate. *Scientific American*, July, pp. 41–47.

Revelle, R., and Landsberg, H. L., eds. 1950. *America's changing environment*. Boston: Houghton-Mifflin Co.

Rosen, W. G. 1970. The environmental crisis: through a glass darkly. *Bioscience* 20: 1209–11, 1216.

Rudd, R. L. 1964. *Pesticides and the living landscape*. Madison: University of Wisconsin Press.

Smith, F. G. W. 1972. What the ocean means to man. *American Scientist* 60: 16–19.

Smith, J. E., ed. 1968. *Pollution and marine life.* New York: Cambridge University Press.

Strobbe, M. A. 1971. *Understanding environmental pollution.* Saint Louis: C. V. Mosby Co.

Thomas, W. L., ed. 1956. *Man's role in changing the face of the earth.* Chicago: University of Chicago Press.

Turk, A., Turk, J., and Wittes, J. T. 1972. *Ecology, pollution, environment.* Philadelphia: W. B. Saunders Co.

Weinstock, B., and Niki, H. 1972. Carbon monoxide balance in nature. *Science* 176: 290–92.

Williams, C. M. 1967. Third-generation pesticides. *Scientific American,* July, pp. 13–17.

Woodwell, G. M. 1967. Toxic substances and ecological cycles. *Scientific American,* March, 24–31.

Woodwell, G. M., Craig, P. P., and Johnson, H. A. 1971. DDT in the biosphere: where does it go? *Science* 174: 1101–7.

47 Ethology: The Comparative Study of Behavior

Arendt, H. 1970. *On violence.* New York: Harcourt Brace Jovanovich, Inc.

Barnett, S. A. 1967. *Instinct and intelligence: behavior of animals and man.* Englewood Cliffs, N.J.: Prentice-Hall, Inc.

Bennet-Clark, H. C., and Ewing, A. W. 1970. The love song of the fruit fly. *Scientific American,* July, pp. 84–92.

Camhi, J. M. 1971. Flight orientation in locusts. *Scientific American,* August, pp. 74–81.

Dethier, V. G., and Stellar, E. 1961. *Animal behavior.* Englewood Cliffs, N.J.: Prentice-Hall, Inc.

Ehrman, L., Omenn, G. S., and Caspari, E., eds. 1972. *Genetics, environment, and behavior.* New York: Academic Press, Inc.

Eibl-Eibesfeldt, I. 1970. *Ethology: the biology of behavior.* New York: Holt, Rinehart and Winston, Inc.

———. 1972. *Love and hate: the natural history of behavior patterns.* New York: Holt, Rinehart and Winston, Inc.

Fuller, J. L., and Thompson, W. R. 1960. *Behavior genetics.* New York: John Wiley & Sons, Inc.

Gardner, R. A., and Gardner, B. T. 1969. Teaching sign language to a chimpanzee. *Science* 165: 664–72.

Hess, E. H. 1964. Imprinting in birds. *Science* 146: 1128–39.

Johnsgard, P. A. 1972. *Animal behavior.* Dubuque, Iowa: Wm. C. Brown Company Publishers.

Johnson, R. N. 1972. *Aggression in man and animals.* Philadelphia: W. B. Saunders Co.

Klopfer, P. H. 1962. *Behavioral aspects of ecology.* Englewood Cliffs, N.J.: Prentice-Hall, Inc.

Lorenz, K. 1970a. *On aggression.* New York: Bantam Books, Inc.

———. 1970b. On killing members of one's own species. *Bulletin of the Atomic Scientists,* October, pp. 2–5, 51–56.

Marler, P., and Hamilton, W. J. 1968. *Mechanisms of animal behavior.* New York: John Wiley & Sons, Inc.

McGill, T. E., ed. 1965. *Readings in animal behavior.* New York: Holt, Rinehart and Winston, Inc.

Montagu, M. F. A., ed. 1968. *Man and aggression.* New York: Oxford University Press, Inc.

Morris, D., ed. 1969. *Primate ethology.* Garden City, N.Y.: Doubleday & Co., Inc.

Otten, C. M. 1973. *Aggression and evolution.* Lexington, Mass.: Xerox College Publishing.

Scott, J. P. 1963. *Animal behavior.* Garden City, N.Y.: Doubleday & Co., Inc.

Southwick, C. H., ed. 1971. *Animal aggression: selected readings.* New York: Van Nostrand Reinhold Co.

Stokes, A. W., and Cox, L. M. 1970. Aggressive man and aggressive beast. *Bioscience* 20: 1092–95.

Storr, A. 1970. *Human aggression.* New York: Bantam Books, Inc.

Thorpe, W. H. 1963. *Learning and instinct in animals.* New York: McGraw-Hill.

Tinbergen, N. 1959. *Social behaviour in animals.* New York: John Wiley & Sons, Inc.

————. 1960. The evolution of behavior in gulls. *Scientific American,* December, pp. 118–30.

————. 1969. *Curious naturalists.* Garden City, N.Y.: Doubleday & Co., Inc.

Todd, J. H. 1971. The chemical languages of fishes. *Scientific American,* May, pp. 98–108.

48 Social Behavior

Alland, A., Jr. 1967. *Evolution and human behavior.* Garden City, N.Y.: Doubleday & Co., Inc., The Natural History Press.

Allee, W. C. 1958. *The social life of animals.* Boston: Beacon Press.

Ardrey, R. 1960. *African genesis.* New York: Dell Publishing Co., Inc.

————. 1966. *The territorial imperative.* New York: Atheneum Publishers.

Boulding, K. E. 1962. *Conflict and defense.* New York: Harper & Row, Publishers.

Brower, L. P. 1969. Ecological chemistry. *Scientific American,* February, pp. 22–29.

Eimerl, S., and DeVore, I., and the editors of Time-Life Books. 1965. *The primates.* New York: Time-Life Books.

Emlen, J. M. 1966. Natural selection and human behavior. *Journal of Theoretical Biology* 12: 410–18.

Etkin, W., ed. 1964. *Social behavior and organization among vertebrates.* Chicago: University of Chicago Press.

Frisch, K. von. 1965. *Dancing bees.* New York: Harcourt Brace Jovanovich, Inc.

Galle, O. R., Gove, W. R., and McPherson, J. M. 1972. Population density and pathology: what are the relations for man? *Science* 176: 23–30.

Glass, D. C., ed. 1968. *Biology and behavior: environmental influences.* New York: Rockefeller University Press and Russell Sage Foundation.

Guthrie, D. A. 1971. Primitive man's relationship to nature. *Bioscience* 21: 721–23.

Harlow, H. F., and Suomi, S. J. 1970. The nature of love—simplified. *American Psychologist* 25: 161–68.

Harlow, H. F., Harlow, M. K., and Suomi, S. J. 1971. From thought to therapy: lessons from a primate laboratory. *American Scientist* 59: 538–49.

Howard, H. E. 1920. *Territory and bird life.* London: John Murray.

Jolly, A. 1972. *The evolution of primate behavior.* New York: Macmillan, Inc.

Lawick-Goodall, J. van. 1971. *In the shadow of man.* Boston: Houghton-Mifflin Co.

Levine, S. 1971. Stress and behavior. *Scientific American,* January, pp. 26–31.

Mazur, A., and Robertson, L. S. 1972. *Biology and social behavior.* New York: The Free Press.

Mykytowycz, R. 1968. Territorial markings by rabbits. *Scientific American,* May, pp. 116–26.

Roe, A., and Simpson, G. G., eds. 1958. *Behavior and evolution.* New Haven, Conn.: Yale University Press.

Sauer, E. G. F. 1958. Celestial navigation by birds. *Scientific American,* August, pp. 42–47.

Schaller, G. B. 1963. *The mountain gorilla: ecology and behavior.* Chicago: University of Chicago Press.

Schultz, A. H. 1969. *The life of primates.* New York: Universe Books.

Smith, N. G. 1967. Visual isolation in gulls. *Scientific American,* October, pp. 94–102.

Southwick, C. H. 1963. *Primate social behavior.* New York: Van Nostrand Reinhold Co.

Tinbergen, N. 1953. *Social behaviour in animals.* London, England: Methuen Ltd.

Tinbergen, N., and the editors of Time-Life Books. 1956. *Animal behavior.* New York: Time-Life Books.

Watts, C. R., and Stokes, A. W. 1971. The social order of turkeys. *Scientific American,* June, pp. 112–18.

Wilson, E. O. 1965. Chemical communication in the social insects. *Science* 149: 1064–71.

Wynne-Edwards, V. C. 1964. Population control in animals. *Scientific American,* August, pp. 68–74.

―――. 1972. *Animal dispersion in relation to social behaviour.* New York: Macmillan Publishing Co., Inc., Hafner Press.

49   Sociobiology

Alcock, J. 1975. *Animal behavior: an evolutionary approach.* Sunderland: Sinnauer Associates.

Alexander, R. D. 1975. The search for a general theory of behavior. *Behavioral Science* 20: 77–100.

Barish, D. P. 1977. *Sociobiology and behavior.* New York: Elsevier.

Campbell, B., ed. 1972. *Sexual selection and the descent of man 1871–1971.* Chicago: Aldine Publishing Company.

Campbell, D. T. 1975. On the conflicts between biological and social evolution and between psychology and moral tradition. *American Psychologist* 30: 1103–26.

Dawkins, R. 1976. *The selfish gene.* London: Oxford University Press.

Emlen, S. T., and Oring, L. W. 1977. Ecology, sexual selection, and the evolution of mating systems. *Science* 197: 215–23.

Hamilton, W. D. 1964. The genetical theory of social behavior. I and II. *Journal of Theoretical Biology* 7: 1–52.

Hinde, R. A. 1974. *Biological bases of human social behaviour.* New York: McGraw-Hill Book Co.

Hrdy, S. B. 1977. *The langurs of Abu.* Cambridge, Mass.: Harvard University Press.

Maynard-Smith, J. 1964. Group selection and kin selection. *Nature* 201: 1145–47.

Sahlins, M. 1977. *The use and abuse of biology: an anthropological critique of sociobiology.* Ann Arbor: The University of Michigan Press.

Trivers, R. I. 1971. The evolution of reciprocal altruism. *Quarterly Review of Biology* 46: 35–57.

Wilson, E. O. 1975. *Sociobiology: the new synthesis.* Cambridge, Mass.: Harvard University Press.

Index

eggs—*cont.*
  amphibian, 96–98
  development of, 37–50, 96–105, 296–302
    302
    human, 8–15, 24–27, 37
    of vertebrates, 4
ejaculation, 17–18
elastin, 206
electrons, 89, 581–583
electron transport system, 89
electrophoresis, 263
elementary particles, 76
elements, 581–584
elm, Dutch, 510
embolism, 125
embryos
  amphibian, 96–104
  artificially conceived, 48–49
  human, 37–48
  hybrid, 435–436
  implantation, 37–39
  membranes, 39–44
  prenatal environment, 61–62
  sex differentiation, 333–336
  spontaneous twinning, 62–64
  urogenital differentiation, 333–334
emergency hormone, 169
emphysema, 201
endocrine system, 163–171
endoderm, 42, 97
endometrium, 7, 29, 38
endoplasmic reticulum, 72
endothermic, 176
energy
  activation, 83–84
  in biotic communities, 525–528
  flow, 525–527
  kinds of, 80–81
  in photosynthesis, 514–518
  thermodynamic laws, 81, 525
engineering, genetic, 339–342
entropy, 81
environment
  air pollution, 540–542
  carrying capacity of, 481
  cycles in, 531–535
  ecological guidelines, 546
  energy flow, 525–527
  organic chemicals, 539
  pesticides, 544–546
  radioactive wastes, 542–543
  water pollution, 536–538, 543–544
environmental resistance, 481
enzymes, 83–85
  digestive, 113
  inducible, 302
epidermis, leaf, 519–520
epididymis, 17
epiglottis, 111
epinephrine, 158, 167–169, 175
epithelial cells, 105, 200
equilibrium, genetic, 373
equipotent, 63
Equus, 449–450
endoplasmic reticulum (ER), 72–73
erythroblastosis fetalis, 281
erythrocyte (red blood cell), 122–123
esophagus, 112
estrogen, 11
  aging, 207

cancer, 200
chemical structure, 168
menopause, 13
menstrual cycle, 10–13
oral contraceptives, 27–30
sexual mood, 15
ethology, 548–558
ethyl alcohol, 87
eucaryotic cell, 78, 455–456
euthanasia, 575–576
eutrophication, 537
evolution, definition of, 356
  in amphibians, 443–444
  of animals, 459–460
  biochemical, 452–455
  cultural, 574–575
  Darwin's theory of, 354–356
  of eucaryotes, 455–456
  of finches, 439–443
  of horses, 449–451
  human, 463–477
  of invertebrates, 457–458
  Lamarck's theory of, 353
  mechanism of, 351–357
  of plants, 457–458
  of primates, 463–465
  of primitive earth, 452–453
  of reptiles, 444–449
evolutionary stability, 460–461
excretion, 135, 139–145, 178–179
excretory system, human, 135, 139–145
existence, struggle for, 355
expiration, 136–137
explosion, population, 496–498
extinction, 448–449
extraembryonic membranes, 39–44

facilitated diffusion, 58–59
Fallopian tube, 6, 37
fallout, radioactive, 362–363
family, human
  laws, 248–250
  origin of, 471, 568–569
  pedigree charts, 250–251
  size, 34–35, 490–492
fat cells, 107
fats, 51–53, 110
fatty acids, 53, 92, 110
feedback inhibition, 14, 163–164
fermentation, 87, 454
ferns, 458
fertility
  differential, 356
  and intelligence, 425–426
  projections, human, 490–492, 495–496
    496
  rate, 490–492
fertilization, 18
  in vitro, 48–49
  and rhythm method, 24–27
fetal circulation, 42–44, 132–134
fetus, human
  abnormalities, 61–62
  lactation, 48
  parturition, 46–47
  placenta, 42–44
  prenatal environment, 61–62
  spontaneous twinning, 62–64
  stages of development, 45–46
fiber, muscle, 107, 154–155

fibrinogen, 125
filial regression, 417–420
filtration, kidney, 140
finches, Darwin's, 441–443
fish
  behavior of, 550–552
  courtship of, 553–554
  effects of pesticides on, 554
  effects of water pollution on, 536–538, 543, 544
    538, 543, 544
  evolution of, 443–444
  water balance in, 178–179
flatus, 118
flour beetle, 484, 504–505
fluid-mosaic model, 68
flukes, 511–512
fly
  fruit, 243–245, 382, 437, 557
  tsetse, 511
follicle, ovarian, 9
follicle-stimulating hormone (FSH), 11–17, 166
  11–17, 166
food
  chain, 523–524
  and energy, 525–527
  and human communities, 527–528
  and malnutrition, 499–500
  from oceans, 528
  synthesis of, 514–519
  web, 524–525
foramen ovale, 133
foreskin, 18
fossils
  historical record, 457–460
  human, 465–476
founder effect, 405–406
fraternal twins, 62
frog
  behavior of, 549
  development of, 96–105
  egg of, 4
  geographical studies on, 430–431
  hybridization studies on, 436
  nuclear transplantation in, 296–302
  water balance in, 176
fructose, 51
fruit fly, 243–245, 382, 437, 557

galactosemia, 290–293
Galápagos Islands, 349–350, 439–443
gallbladder, 114
gallstones, 114
Galton, Sir Francis, 417, 425
gamete, 19
gamma globulin, 60
ganglion, dorsal root, 148
gas exchange
  in animals, 135–139
  in plants, 519–522
gasoline, 542
gastric juice, 112
gastrulation, 97–98, 297
Gause's principle, 503
gemmule, 224
gene, 19, 210
  action, 220–222, 266–270, 296–305
  and blood groups, 275–283
  chemical nature of, 215
  coding, 220–222, 266–270

immunosuppression, 194, 283
implantation of embryo, 37–39
imprinting, 554
impulse, nerve, 149–152
in vitro fertilization, 48–50
inbreeding, effect of, 252–255
incompatibility
ABO, 276–279
Rh, 280–283
independent assortment, law of, 240–243
induced ovulator, 15
induction, embryonic, 102
industrial melanism, 357–358
infanticide, 575
infectious diseases, 388–391
inheritance, principles of, 235–243
innate releasing mechanism (IRM), 550–553
inner cell mass, 37
insect, evolution of, 460
insecticides, 544–546
insectivores, 463–464
inspiration, 136–137
insulin, 54, 59, 174–175
intelligence, 422–428
interneuron, 147–148
interphase, of mitosis, 226
interstitial cells, 16
interstitial-cell-stimulating hormone (ICSH), 17
intestinal tract, human, 109–118
intrauterine device (IUD), 21, 30–31, 34–35
invertebrates, evolution of, 457–459
iodine, 119
ions, 90, 149, 581–584
ionizing radiation, 361–363
IQ (intelligence quotient), 423–428
IRM. see innate releasing mechanism
iron, 119
irrigation, 512
islets of Langerhans, 174
isolates, religious, 406–408
isolating mechanisms, 434–437
isosmotic, 70
isotopes, 582–583
IUD. see intrauterine device

jaundice, 279
jejunum, 113
Jenner, Edward, 184
jet fatigue, 179

karyotype, 308
keratin, 53
ketone bodies, 173
kidney, 135
artificial, 144–145, 195
development of, 333
as excretory organ, 139–144
transplant of, 194–195
kilocalorie, 82
Klinefelter's syndrome, 320
Koch, Robert, 389
Krebs cycle, 88–99

kwashiorkor, 499

labia
majora, 8, 335
minora, 8, 334
labor, 46
lactase, 114
lactation, 48
lacteal, 116
lactic acid, 87
laetrile, 196
lakes, 526–528, 536–538
Lake Erie, 536–538
Lamarck, Jean Baptiste de, 353
Lamarckian theory, 353
lamprey, 510
land
conquest of, 445–447
invasion of, 443–445
plants, 519–521
land plants. see plants, terrestrial
Landsteiner, Karl, 275
Langerhans, islets of, 174
language, 471, 568–569
laparoscopy, 31, 49
large intestine, 117
larynx, 111, 135
law
of filial regression, 417
Hardy-Weinberg, 373–374
of independent assortment, 240–243
of segregation, 235–238
of thermodynamics, 81, 525–526
leaf, 519–521
learning, 161, 554
lemming, 483
lemurs, 463–464
Lesch-Nyhan syndrome, 292
lethal gene, 255–256, 380
leucocyte, 122–124
leukemia, 197, 316–317
LH. see luteinizing hormone
libido, 34
lichen, 509
life
expectancy, 336, 488–492, 496–499
history of, 457–462
human, definition of, 20
origin of, 452–456
ligation, tubal, 31–32
light energy, 81, 453, 514–519, 523, 525–526
limb buds, 45
linkage, 244–246
Linnaeus, Carolus, 433
lipids, 52–53, 67–68, 92, 114–115
liver, 117, 174
lobe-finned fishes, 443–445
locus, 239
lock-and-key concept, 84
logistic curve, 480
loop of Henle, 141–143
Lorenz, Konrad, 548, 550
lung, 130–133, 135–139
luteinizing hormone (LH), 11–14, 17, 44
lymph, 116, 127–128
lymphocytes, 125, 186–194
lynx, 482–483

Lyon hypothesis, 331
lysis, 18, 74
lysosome, 18, 73–75

macaque, 561–562
malaria, 391–392, 397–398, 511
malnutrition, 499–500
Malthus, Thomas R., 353–354
mammals, 448–449, 460
mammary glands, 29, 48
mammography, 79
Marfan's syndrome, 257
mating
assortative, 420
random, 371–372
maturation divisions, 231–233
measles, German, 61
medulla oblongata, 159
meiosis, 230–234, 244, 312–313
meiotic nondisjunction, 312–313
melanism, industrial, 357–358
melatonin, 170
membranes, biological, 41–42, 57, 66–79, 149–150, 455–456
memory, 161
Mendel, Gregor J., 235
Mendelian genetics, 235–243
menopause, 13, 207
menstrual cycle, 10–13
menstruation, 7, 10–13
mercury pollution, 543–544
mesoderm, 42, 97–100
messenger RNA, 266–271
metabolism
cellular, 80–94
inborn errors of, 284–286
in first living systems, 454–455
metachromasia, 293
metaphase, 226, 306
metastasis, 197
methane, 452–453
microorganisms, 524
microvilli, 115
middle piece, 15
milk letdown, 48
minerals, 109, 118, 531–535
mitochondria, 76–77, 78, 456
mitosis, 226–231
mitotic nondisjunction, 322–324
mitral valve, 130
molecular bonds, 583–588
monkey, rhesus, 561, 565–568
monocyte, 124–125
monosaccharide, 51, 110
monotremes, 5
monotypic species, 434
monozygotic twins, 63–64, 424
morning-after pill, 33–34
morula, 37
mosaicism, 321, 332
mosquito, 391–392, 511
moth, peppered, 357–358
motor neurons, 148, 154
mouse, 186–188, 387
mouth, 110
mucus, 8, 112, 200–201
mule, 435
Müller, Hermann, 361, 383–384, 436
multiple alleles, 272, 276–278